The Expositor's NEW TESTAMENT

KING JAMES VERSION
(Modified by Jimmy Swaggart
for Easier Reading.)

SPECIAL
JIMMY SWAGGART
COUNSELOR'S EDITION

The Expositor's
NEW TESTAMENT

KING JAMES VERSION
(Modified by Jimmy Swaggart
for Easier Reading)

SPECIAL
JIMMY SWAGGART
COUNSELOR'S EDITION

THE
NEW TESTAMENT
OF OUR LORD AND SAVIOUR
JESUS CHRIST

KING JAMES VERSION
(Modified by Jimmy Swaggart
for Easier Reading.)

*TRANSLATED OUT OF THE
ORIGINAL GREEK: AND WITH THE FORMER
TRANSLATIONS DILIGENTLY PREPARED
AND REVISED BY HIS MAJESTY'S
SPECIAL COMMAND*

Expositor's Edition

JIMMY SWAGGART MINISTRIES
P.O. Box 262550
Baton Rouge, Louisiana 70826-2550
(225) 768-7000
Website: www.jsm.org • E-mail: info@jsm.org

ISBN: 978-1-934655-43-6
(Deluxe Black Bonded Leather Edition 08-005)

ISBN: 978-1-934655-40-5
(Economy Black Imitation Leather Edition 08-003)

Published by, and the sole property of,
JIMMY SWAGGART MINISTRIES, BATON ROUGE, LA

12 13 14 15 16 17 18 19 20 21 22 23 24 / RRD / 20 19 18 17 16 15 14 13 12 11 10 9 8

BOOKS OF
THE NEW TESTAMENT

TABLE OF CONTENTS

INTRODUCTION

The Expositor's New Testament, Counselor's Edition, is one of, if not the most, unique of its kind in the world today. It is designed with one thought in mind, and that is to help the Bible student to more properly understand the Word. We have utilized some of the finest Greek Scholars, and yet, the terminology is in layman's language, making it, we think, very easy to understand.

JESUS CHRIST AND HIM CRUCIFIED

The central theme of the Word of God is *"Jesus Christ and Him Crucified"* (I Cor. 1:23; 2:2). In fact, *"The Cross"* is the Foundation Doctrine of the entirety of the Word of God. Peter said:

"Forasmuch as you know that you were not redeemed with corruptible things as silver and gold, from your vain conversation (lifestyle) received by tradition from your fathers;

"But with the Precious Blood of Christ, as of a lamb without blemish and without spot:

"Who verily was foreordained before the foundation of the world, but was manifest in these last times for you" (I Pet. 1:18-20).

So, this means that every single Doctrine in the Word of God must be built upon the Foundation of the Cross, or else it will go into error.

GOD'S PRESCRIBED ORDER OF VICTORY

Being generous, one could probably say that about

10% of the Bible is given over to information regarding Salvation. About 90%, or more, is given over to instruction as it regards living for the Lord. And all of this instruction can be summed up in the extremely abbreviated form of just three phrases: A. The Cross; B. Your Faith; and, C. The Holy Spirit. In overly simplistic form, those three phrases describe God's prescribed order of Victory.

We have done our very best to explain every Scripture in the New Testament according to this illumination.

COUNSELING

As well, we have included the same material on Counseling, as we had in the older Volume, making this Edition an excellent tool. Our prayer is that our efforts will have Glorified Christ, and stayed true to the Word of God, which hopefully, will be a Blessing to you. This effort has been designed to help you to live a victorious, overcoming, Christian Life, and thereby, to be a Blessing to others. If that is the case, we give the Lord all the Praise and Glory.

Jimmy Swaggart

Jimmy Swaggart

For information on *The Expositor's New Testament* – English and Spanish Editions or *The Expositor's Study Bible* – Regular Print, Giant Print, Crossfire, Signature and Spanish Editions, please call 1-800-288-8350.

THE GOSPEL ACCORDING TO
MATTHEW

CHAPTER 1

THE GENEALOGY
OF JESUS CHRIST

THE Book *(account)* of the generation *(lineage)* of Jesus Christ *(Saviour, Messiah)*, the Son of David, the Son of Abraham *(the Incarnation, God becoming man [Isa. 7:14; II Sam. 7:16, 19; Gen. 12:1-3; 17:7; Gal. 3:16])*.

2 Abraham begat *(fathered)* Isaac; and Isaac begat Jacob; and Jacob begat Judas and his brethren;

3 And Judas begat Phares and Zara of Thamar; and Phares begat Esrom; and Esrom begat Aram;

4 And Aram begat Aminadab; and Aminadab begat Naasson; and Naasson begat Salmon;

5 And Salmon begat Boaz of Rahab *(Rahab was not the actual mother of Boaz, but his mother several times removed)*; and Boaz begat Obed of Ruth; and Obed begat Jesse;

6 And Jesse begat David the king; and David the king begat Solomon of her *who had been the wife* of Uriah;

7 And Solomon begat Rehoboam; and Rehoboam begat Abia; and Abia begat Asa;

8 And Asa begat Jehoshaphat; and Jehoshaphat begat Joram; and Joram begat Ozias;

9 And Ozias begat Joatham; and Joatham begat Achaz; and Achaz begat Ezekias;

10 And Ezekias begat Manasses; and Manasses begat Amon; and Amon begat Josias;

11 And Josias begat Jechonias and his brethren, about the time they were carried away to Babylon *(about 593 B.C.)*:

12 And after they were brought to Babylon, Jechonias begat Salathiel; and Salathiel begat Zerubbabel;

13 And Zerubbabel begat Abiud; and Abiud begat Eliakim; and Eliakim begat Azor;

14 And Azor begat Sadoc; and Sadoc begat Achim; and Achim begat Eliud;

15 And Eliud begat Eleazar; and Eleazar begat Matthan; and Matthan begat Jacob;

16 And Jacob begat Joseph the husband of Mary, of whom was born Jesus *(Saviour)*, Who is called Christ *(the Anointed, the Messiah)*.

17 So all the generations from Abraham to David *are* fourteen

generations; and from David until the carrying away into Babylon *are* fourteen generations; and from the carrying away into Babylon unto Christ *are* fourteen generations.

THE BIRTH OF
JESUS CHRIST

18 Now the Birth of Jesus Christ was on this wise: When as His Mother Mary was espoused *(engaged)* to Joseph, before they came together *(before they were married)*, she was found with Child of the Holy Spirit *(by decree of the Holy Spirit)*.

19 Then Joseph her husband, being a just *man*, not willing to make her a public example, was minded to put her away privily *(to quietly break the engagement)*.

20 But while he thought on these things, behold, the Angel of the Lord appeared unto him in a dream, saying, Joseph, thou son of David, fear not to take unto you Mary your wife; for that which is conceived in her is of the Holy Spirit.

21 And she shall bring forth a Son, and you shall call His Name JESUS *(Saviour)*: for He shall save His people from their sins.

22 Now all this was done, that it might be fulfilled which was spoken of the Lord by the Prophet, saying,

23 Behold, a Virgin shall be with Child, and shall bring forth a Son, and they shall call His Name Emmanuel, which being interpreted is, God with us *(Isa. 7:14)*.

24 Then Joseph being raised from sleep did as the Angel of the Lord had bidden him, and took unto him his wife *(immediately went ahead with the wedding ceremony)*:

25 And knew her not *(had no sexual relations with her)* till she had brought forth her Firstborn Son: and he called His Name JESUS *(meaning Saviour; after the Birth of Christ, Joseph did have relations with Mary, with four other boys being born, and several sisters [Mat. 13:55-56])*.

CHAPTER 2

THE VISIT OF THE MAGI
FROM THE EAST

NOW when Jesus was born in Bethlehem of Judaea *(Mic. 5:2)* in the days of Herod the king, behold, there came Wise men from the east to Jerusalem,

2 Saying, Where is He Who is born King of the Jews? for we have seen His Star in the east, and are come to worship Him.

3 When Herod the king had heard *these things*, he was troubled, and all Jerusalem with him.

4 And when he had gathered all the Chief Priests and Scribes of the people together, he demanded of them where Christ should be born.

5 And they said unto him, In Beth-lehem of Judaea: for thus it is written by the Prophet,

6 And thou Beth-lehem, *in* the Land of Judah, are not the least among the princes of Judah: for out of you shall come a Governor, Who shall rule My people Israel *(Mic. 5:2)*.

7 Then Herod, when he had privily *(privately)* called the Wise men, inquired of them diligently what time the star appeared.

8 And he sent them to Beth-lehem, and said, Go and search diligently for the young child; and when you have found *Him*, bring me word again, that I may come and worship Him also.

9 When they had heard the king, they departed; and, lo, the star, which they saw in the east, went before them, till it came and stood over where the young Child was *(not Bethlehem, but some other place, maybe Nazareth)*.

10 When they saw the star *(where the star stopped)*, they rejoiced with exceeding great joy.

11 And when they were come into the house *(not the stable where He was born in Bethlehem)*, they saw the young Child with Mary His Mother, and fell down, and worshipped Him: and when they had opened their treasures, they presented unto Him gifts; gold, and frankincense, and myrrh.

12 And being warned of God in a dream that they should not return to Herod, they departed into their own country another way.

THE FLIGHT INTO EGYPT

13 And when they were departed, behold, the Angel of the Lord appeared to Joseph in a dream, saying, Arise, and take the young Child and His Mother, and flee into Egypt, and stay there until I bring you word: for Herod will seek the young Child to destroy Him.

14 When he arose, he took the young Child and His Mother by night, and departed into Egypt:

15 And was there until the death of Herod: that it might be fulfilled which was spoken of the Lord by the Prophet, saying, Out of Egypt have I called My Son *(Hos. 11:1)*.

SLAUGHTER OF THE CHILDREN IN BETHLEHEM

16 Then Herod, when he saw that he was mocked of the wise men *(they ignored his demand that when they found the Child, they*

were to come back and report to him), was exceeding wroth, and sent forth, and killed all the children who were in Beth-lehem, and in all the coasts thereof, from two years old and under, according to the time which he had diligently inquired of the wise men *(these words decide that two years, or nearly so, had elapsed since Herod had seen the Wise men)*.

17 Then was fulfilled that which was spoken by Jeremiah the Prophet, saying,

18 In Rama was there a voice heard, lamentation, and weeping, and great mourning, Rachel weeping *for* her children, and would not be comforted, because they are not *(Jer. 31:15)*.

THE RETURN FROM EGYPT TO NAZARETH

19 But when Herod was dead, behold, an Angel of the Lord appeared in a dream to Joseph in Egypt *(this is the third of four dreams given to Joseph by the Lord)*,

20 Saying, Arise, and take the young Child and His Mother, and go into the Land of Israel: for they are dead which sought the young Child's life.

21 And he arose, and took the young Child and His Mother, and came into the Land of Israel.

22 But when he heard that Archelaus did reign in Judaea in the room of his father Herod, he was afraid to go thither: notwithstanding, being warned of God in a dream, he turned aside into the parts of Galilee *(the fourth and final dream recorded as given by the Lord to Joseph)*:

23 And he came and dwelt in a city called Nazareth: that it might be fulfilled which was spoken by the Prophets, He shall be called a Nazarene *(the word "Nazarene" is meant to portray the action instead of the location; He would be despised, as Nazareth was despised [Jn. 1:46])*.

CHAPTER 3

THE PREACHING OF JOHN THE BAPTIST

IN those days *(immediately preceding the introduction of Christ)* came John the Baptist, preaching in the wilderness of Judaea *(the area near Jericho)*.

2 And saying, Repent you *(recognize one's wrong direction)*: for the Kingdom of Heaven *(Kingdom from the Heavens, headed up by Jesus Christ)* is at hand *(was being offered to Israel)*.

3 For this is he *(John the Baptist)* who was spoken of by the Prophet Isaiah, saying, The voice of one crying in the wilderness, Prepare you the Way of the Lord,

make His paths straight *(Isa. 40:3)*.

4 And the same John had his raiment of camel's hair, and a leather girdle about his loins; and his meat was locusts and wild honey.

5 Then went out to him Jerusalem, and all Judaea, and all the region round about Jordan *(the Jordan River)*,

6 And were baptized of him in Jordan *(dipped completely under)*, confessing their sins.

7 But when he saw many of the Pharisees and Sadducees *(two sects of self-righteous and zealous Jews)* come to his baptism *(Water Baptism)*, he said unto them, O generation of vipers *(snakes)*, who has warned you to flee from the wrath to come?

8 Bring forth therefore fruits *(evidence)* meet for *(befitting)* Repentance:

9 And think not to say within yourselves, We have Abraham to *our* father *(pride)*: for I say unto you, that God is able of these stones to raise up children unto Abraham *(the Lord has raised up the Gentiles as children unto Abraham [Gal. 3:7, 14])*.

10 And now also the axe is laid unto the root of the trees: therefore every tree which brings not forth good fruit is hewn down, and cast into the fire *(Israel was cut down because of unbelief [Rom. 11:20])*.

11 I indeed baptize you with water unto Repentance *(Water Baptism was an outward act of an inward work already carried out)*: but He *(Christ)* Who comes after me is mightier than I, Whose Shoes I am not worthy to bear: He shall Baptize you with the Holy Spirit, and *with* fire *(to burn out the sinful dross [Acts 2:2-4])*:

12 Whose fan *is* in His Hand *(the ancient method for winnowing grain)*, and He will thoroughly purge His Floor *("purging it, that it may bring forth more fruit" [Jn. 15:2])*, and gather His Wheat into the garner *(the end product as developed by the Spirit)*; but He will burn up the chaff with unquenchable fire *(the wheat is symbolic of the Work of the Spirit, while the chaff is symbolic of the work of the flesh)*.

JOHN'S BAPTISM OF JESUS

13 Then came Jesus from Galilee to Jordan unto John, to be baptized of him *(signifying the greatest moment in human history thus far; the earthly Ministry of Christ would now begin)*.

14 But John forbad Him, saying, I have need to be baptized of You, and come You to me?

15 And Jesus answering said unto him, Suffer *it to be so* now *(permit Me to be baptized)*: for

thus it becomes us to fulfill all Righteousness *(Water Baptism is a type of the death, burial, and Resurrection of Christ [Rom. 6:3-5])*. Then he suffered Him.

16 And Jesus, when He was baptized *(this was the beginning of His earthly Ministry)*, went up straightway *(immediately)* out of the water *(refers to Baptism by immersion and not by sprinkling)*: and, lo, the heavens were opened unto Him *(the only One, the Lord Jesus Christ, to Whom the Heavens would be opened)*, and he saw the Spirit of God *(Holy Spirit)* descending like a dove, and lighting upon Him *(John saw a visible form that reminded him of a dove)*:

17 And lo a Voice from Heaven, saying *(the Voice of God the Father)*, This is My Beloved Son, in Whom I am well pleased *(the Trinity appears here: the Father speaks, the Spirit descends, and the Son prays [Lk. 3:21])*.

CHAPTER 4

THE TEMPTATION OF JESUS IN THE WILDERNESS

THEN *(immediately after the descent of the Holy Spirit upon Him)* was Jesus led up *(urgently led)* of the Spirit *(Holy Spirit)* into the wilderness *(probably close to Jericho)* to be tempted of the Devil *(as the Last Adam, He would* be tempted in all points like as we are [Heb. 4:15; I Cor. 15:21-22, 45, 47])*.

2 And when He had fasted forty days and forty nights, He was afterward hungry *(other than Christ, three men in the Bible fasted forty days and forty nights: Moses [Deut. 9:9, 18, 25; 10:10], Joshua [Ex. 24:13-18; 32:15-17], and Elijah [I Ki. 19:7-8])*.

3 And when the tempter *(Satan)* came to Him, he said, If You be the Son of God *(since You are the Son of God)*, command that these stones be made bread *(Christ was tempted to use His Power for His Own benefit, which He was to never do)*.

4 But He answered and said, It is written, Man shall not live by bread alone, but by every Word that proceeds out of the Mouth of God *([Deut. 8:3]; man is a spiritual being as well as a physical being; therefore, dependent on God)*.

5 Then the Devil took Him up *(a powerful force)* into the Holy city *(Jerusalem)*, and set Him on a pinnacle of the Temple *(its highest point, which Josephus stated, was about 700 feet from the ravine below)*,

6 And said unto Him, If You be the Son of God *(since You are the Son of God)*, cast Yourself down *(literally spoken)*: for it is written, He shall give His Angels

charge concerning You: and in *their* hands they shall bear You up, lest at any time You dash Your foot against a stone *(derived from Psalms 91:11-12)*.

7 Jesus said unto him, It is written again, you shall not tempt the Lord your God *([Deut. 6:16]; to tempt God is to question His Word, which casts doubt on His ability to do what He has promised)*.

8 Again *(the third temptation)*, the Devil took Him up into an exceeding high mountain *(not definitely known, but probably Nebo)*, and showed Him all the kingdoms of the world, and the glory of them *(showed them to Him, not in a physical sense, but rather in a spiritual sense)*;

9 And said unto Him, All these things will I give You, if You will fall down and worship me *(the temptation was that Christ abrogate the Cross, through which He would regain all things)*.

10 Then said Jesus unto him, Get thee hence, Satan *(presents Christ for the first time Personally addressing Satan)*: for it is written, you shall worship the Lord your God, and Him only shall you serve *(Satan desires that mankind worship and serve him; we are to worship and serve the Lord Alone)*.

11 Then the Devil left Him *("departed from Him for a sea-*

son," *meaning that there would be other temptations [Lk. 4:13])*, and, behold, Angels came and ministered unto Him *(in what manner they ministered, we aren't told)*.

JESUS BEGINS HIS MINISTRY; REJECTED IN NAZARETH — MOVES TO CAPERNAUM

12 Now when Jesus had heard that John was cast into prison *(John's Ministry was now finished; he had properly introduced Christ)*, He *(Jesus)* departed into Galilee *(where the central core of His Ministry would be)*;

13 And leaving Nazareth *(refers to His rejection there [Lk. 4:16-30])*, He came and dwelt in Capernaum *(made this city His Headquarters)*, which is upon the sea coast *(refers to the Sea of Galilee)*, in the borders of Zabulon and Nephthalim *(refers to these two Tribes bordering the Sea of Galilee)*:

14 That it might be fulfilled which was spoken by Isaiah the Prophet, saying *(Isaiah prophesied of Christ more than any other Prophet)*,

15 The land of Zabulon, and the land of Nephthalim, *by* the way of the sea *(Sea of Galilee)*, beyond Jordan, Galilee of the Gentiles *(the great Roman Road ran near the Sea of Galilee from Damascus; almost all Gentiles*

traveling in this direction did so on this road; the Headquarters of Christ was within the confines of the Tribe of Naphtali);

16 The people which sat in darkness *(implies a settled acceptance of this darkness; the moral darkness was even greater than the national misery)* saw great Light *(Christ is the Light of the world, and the only true Light)*; and to them which sat in the region and shadow of death *(spiritual death is the result of this spiritual darkness)* light *(spiritual illumination in Christ)* is sprung up.

17 From that time *(the move to Capernaum)* Jesus began to preach *(the major method of the proclamation of the Gospel)*, and to say, Repent *(beginning His Ministry, the first word used by Christ, as recorded by Matthew, was "Repent")*: for the Kingdom of Heaven is at hand *(the Kingdom from Heaven, headed up by Christ, for the purpose of reestablishing the Kingdom of God over the Earth; the Kingdom was rejected by Israel)*.

JESUS CALLS FOUR FISHERMEN

18 And Jesus, walking by the Sea of Galilee, saw two Brethren, Simon called Peter, and Andrew his brother, casting a net into the sea: for they were fishermen.

19 And He said unto them, Follow Me *(the Messiah's advent was signaled by three great words: "Repent," "Follow," and "Blessed" [Mat. 5:3])*, and I will make you fishers of men *(the greatest call of all)*.

20 And they straightway *(immediately)* left *their* nets *(their fishing business)*, and followed Him.

21 And going on from thence, He saw other two Brethren, James the son of Zebedee, and John his brother, in a ship with Zebedee their father, mending their nets; and He called them *(the first three called, Peter, James, and John, were the closest to Christ)*.

22 And they immediately left the ship and their father, and followed Him *(He called them to a higher fishing, as He called David to a higher feeding [Ps. 78:70-72])*.

SECOND TOUR OF GALILEE; JESUS' FAME SPREADS

23 And Jesus went about all Galilee, teaching in their Synagogues, and preaching *(preaching proclaims the Gospel, while Teaching explains it)* the Gospel of the Kingdom *(the good news of the establishment upon Earth of the perfect Government of Heaven; as stated, it was rejected)*, and healing all manner of sickness and

all manner of disease among the people *(Jesus is not only the Saviour; He as well is the Healer)*.

24 And His fame went throughout all Syria *(the account of what He did went beyond the borders of Israel)*: and they brought unto Him all sick people who were taken with divers *(different kinds)* diseases and torments, and those which were possessed with devils *(demons)*, and those which were lunatic *(insane, whether by demon possession, or physical disabilities)*, and those who had the palsy, and He healed them *(He turned no one away)*.

25 And there followed Him great multitudes of people from Galilee, and *from* Decapolis *(the eastern side of the Jordan River)*, and *from* Jerusalem, and *from* Judaea, and *from* beyond Jordan.

CHAPTER 5

SERMON ON THE MOUNT: INTRODUCTION

AND seeing the multitudes, He went up into a mountain *(unknown, but probably was a small mountain near the Sea of Galilee; two sermons, both delivered on mountains, opened and closed the Lord's public Ministry; the last was upon Olivet near Jerusalem [Mat., Chpt. 24])*: and when He was set *(He sat down in order to Teach, which was the custom at that time)*, His Disciples came unto Him *(referring not to the Twelve, but to any and all who closely followed Him at that time)*:

2 And He opened His Mouth *(signifying a carefully thought out Message of purpose and will)*, and taught them, saying *(begins the greatest moment of spiritual and Scriptural instruction that had ever been given in the history of mankind)*,

THE BEATITUDES

3 Blessed *(happy)* are the poor in spirit *(conscious of moral poverty)*: for theirs is the Kingdom of Heaven *(the moral characteristics of the citizens of the Kingdom of the heavens; and so it is apparent that the New Birth is an absolute necessity for entrance into that Kingdom [Jn. 3:3]; this Kingdom is now present spiritually, but not yet physically)*.

4 Blessed *are* they who mourn *(grieved because of personal sinfulness)*: for they shall be comforted *(what the Holy Spirit will do for those who properly evaluate their spiritual poverty)*.

5 Blessed *are* the meek *(the opposite of the self-righteous; the first two Beatitudes guarantee the "meekness")*: for they shall inherit the earth *(speaks of the coming Kingdom Age, when the "King-*

dom of Heaven" will be brought down to Earth, when the Saints will rule, with Christ as its Supreme Lord).

6 Blessed are they which do hunger and thirst (intense desire) after Righteousness (God's Righteousness, imputed by Christ, upon Faith in His Finished Work): for they shall be filled (but first of all must be truly empty of all self-worth).

7 Blessed are the merciful (shows itself in action which goes beyond the thought): for they shall obtain mercy (to obtain mercy from God, we must show mercy to others).

8 Blessed are the pure in heart (those who have received a new moral nature in regeneration): for they shall see God (will see Him manifest Himself in one's life).

9 Blessed are the peacemakers (pertains to peace with God, which comes with Salvation, and all who proclaim such are called "peacemakers"): for they shall be called the Children of God (expresses the "peacemaker" and the one who has received the "peace").

10 Blessed are they which are persecuted for Righteousness' sake (means that those who operate from the realm of self-righteousness will persecute those who trust in God's "Righteousness"): for theirs is the Kingdom of Heaven (having God's Righteous-ness, which is solely in Christ, such have the Kingdom of Heaven).

11 Blessed are you, when men shall revile you, and persecute you, and shall say all manner of evil against you falsely, for My sake (only Christ could say, "For My sake," for He is God; there is an offence to the Cross [Gal. 5:11]).

12 Rejoice (the present inner result of one who is "blessed"), and be exceeding glad (self-righteousness persecuting Righteousness is the guarantee of the possession of Righteousness, and the occasion for great joy): for great is your reward in Heaven (meaning it will not necessarily come while on Earth): for so persecuted they the Prophets which were before you (presents the fact that "God's Way" will bring "persecution," severely so, at times by both the world and the Church).

BELIEVERS ARE AS SALT AND LIGHT

13 You are the salt (preservative) of the Earth: but if the salt have lost his savour, wherewith shall it be salted? it is thenceforth good for nothing, but to be cast out, and to be trodden under foot of men ("Salt" is a type of the Word of God; the professing Believer who no longer holds to the Word is of no use to God or man).

14 You are the Light of the

world (we are a reflector of the Light which comes from Christ). A city that is set on an hill cannot be hid (proper light will not, and in fact, cannot be hid).

15 Neither do men light a candle, and put it under a bushel, but on a candlestick (the light is not to be hid); and it gives light unto all who are in the house (that is the purpose of the light).

16 Let your light so shine before men, that they may see your good works (proper Faith will always produce proper works, but proper works will never produce proper Faith), and glorify your Father which is in Heaven (proper works will glorify our Heavenly Father, while improper works glorify man).

CHRIST AND THE LAW

17 Think not that I am come to destroy the Law (this was the Law of Moses), or the Prophets (the predictions of the Prophets of the Old Testament): I am not come to destroy, but to fulfill (Jesus fulfilled the Law by meeting its just demands with a perfect life, and satisfying its curse by dying on the Cross [Gal. 3:13]).

18 For verily I say unto you (proclaims the ultimate authority!), Till Heaven and earth pass (means to be changed, or pass from one condition to another, which will take place in the coming Perfect Age [Rev., Chpts. 21-22]), one jot (smallest letter in the Hebrew alphabet) or one tittle (a minute ornamental finish to ancient Hebrew letters) shall in no wise pass from the Law, till all be fulfilled (the Law was meant to be fulfilled in Christ, and was in fact, totally fulfilled by Christ, in His Life, Death, and Resurrection, with a New Testament or New Covenant being brought about [Acts 15:5-29; Rom. 10:4; II Cor. 3:6-15; Gal. 3:19-25; 4:21-31; 5:1-5, 18; Eph. 2:15; Col. 2:14-17]).

19 Whosoever therefore shall break one of these least Commandments, and shall teach men so, he shall be called the least in the Kingdom of Heaven (those who are disloyal to the authority of the Word of God shall be judged; "He shall be called the least," means that he will not be in the Kingdom at all): but whosoever shall do and teach them, the same shall be called great in the Kingdom of Heaven (the Lord sets the Bible as the Standard of all Righteousness, and He recognizes no other).

20 For I say unto you, That except your righteousness shall exceed the righteousness of the Scribes and Pharisees (which was self-righteousness), you shall in no case enter into the Kingdom of Heaven (the absolute necessity of the New Birth is declared here as

imperative in every case).

JESUS AND ANGER

21 You have heard that it was said by them of old time *(referring back to the Law of Moses)*, Thou shall not kill *(should have been translated, You shall not murder)*; and whosoever shall kill *(murder)* shall be in danger of the judgment *(Ex. 20:13; Lev. 24:21; Num., Chpt. 35; Deut. 5:17; 19:12)*;

22 But I say unto you *(Christ gives the true interpretation of the Bible, with in fact, the Bible and Christ, in essence, being one and the same)*, That whosoever is angry with his brother without a cause *(places unjust anger in the same category as murder, i.e., "springs from an evil heart")* shall be in danger of the judgment *(certain of judgment)*: and whosoever shall say to his brother, Raca *(the words "Raca" and "thou fool" were Hebrew expressions of murderous anger)*, shall be in danger of the Council *(Sanhedrin)*: but whosoever shall say, Thou fool, shall be in danger of hell fire *(men may beat justice in a human court of law, but will never do such in God's Court of Law)*.

ON RESTITUTION AND PRAYER

23 Therefore if you bring your gift to the Altar *(referring to the Brazen Altar as used in the offering of Sacrifices in the Law of Moses)*, and there remember that your brother has ought against you *(is meant to describe our relationship with our fellow man)*;

24 Leave there your gift before the Altar *(the intimation is that the Lord will not accept our "gift" unless we do all within our power to make things right with the offended party)*, and go your way *(make every effort to bring about reconciliation, if at all possible)*; first be reconciled to your brother, and then come and offer your gift *(worship will not be accepted by the Lord, if we have wronged our brother, and have not done all within our power to make amends)*.

CHRISTIAN RELATIONSHIPS

25 Agree with your adversary quickly, while you are in the way with him *(if we offend our brother and do not make amends, the Lord becomes our adversary, or opponent, which places one in a serious situation indeed)*; lest at any time the adversary deliver you to the judge, and the judge deliver you to the officer, and you be cast into prison *(regarding a Believer who offends a fellow Christian, and will not make am-*

ends, God becomes that person's Adversary, and thereby is Judge instead of his Saviour, and thereby, spiritually speaking, puts such a person in a spiritual prison).

26 Verily I say unto you (the absolute solemnity of this statement), You shall by no means come out thence (come out of this spiritual prison), till you have paid the uttermost farthing (the Lord's method of teaching was symbolic and figurative; if the Believer doesn't make amends with his fellow man who he has wronged, he will suffer one reverse after the other; God will see to it).

JESUS' TEACHING ON ADULTERY

27 You have heard that it was said by them of old time (the Mosaic Law), You shall not commit adultery (the Seventh Commandment [Ex. 20:14]).

28 But I say unto you (the phrase does not deny the Law of Moses, but rather takes it to its conclusion, which could only be done by Christ; the Old Covenant pointed the way to the New Covenant, which came with Christ), That whosoever looks on a woman to lust after her (to look with intense sexual desire) has committed adultery with her already in his heart (the Lord addresses the root of sin, which is an evil heart; the Cross is the only answer).

29 And if your right eye offend you, pluck it out, and cast it from you (as stated, the Lord's method of teaching was symbolic and figurative): for it is profitable for you that one of your members should perish, and not that your whole body should be cast into Hell (the Lord does not intend for His statement to be taken literally, as He has already explained that the offence is not in the "eye" or "hand," but, instead, the heart!; in effect, a blind man can lust).

30 And if your right hand offend you, cut it off, and cast it from you: for it is profitable for you that one of your members should perish, and not that your whole body should be cast into Hell (showing the fact that if such action is not stopped, the person will lose their soul; as stated, the Cross is the only means by which evil passions can be subdued [Rom. 6:3-5, 11, 14]).

ON DIVORCE AND REMARRIAGE

31 It has been said (Deut. 24:1-4), Whosoever shall put away his wife (refers to divorce proceedings), let him give her a writing of divorcement (the Jews had perverted the Law, greatly weakening the sanctity of marriage):

32 But I say unto you *(the Lord now gives the true meaning of the Law)*, That whosoever shall put away his wife *(divorce her)*, saving for the cause of fornication *(cohabiting with others, thereby breaking the marriage vows)*, causes her to commit adultery *(if she marries someone else, but the intimation is that the fault is not hers)*: and whosoever shall marry her who is divorced commits adultery *(the man who marries the woman who is divorced unscripturally, even though it's not her fault, commits adultery as well; we should learn here the sanctity of marriage, with divorce and remarriage allowed only on the grounds of fornication and spiritual desertion [I Cor. 7:10-11])*.

THE SIGNIFICANCE OF WORDS

33 Again, you have heard that it has been said by them of old time *(such phraseology means that the Word of God had been twisted to mean something it did not say)*, You shall not forswear yourself, but shall perform unto the Lord your oaths *(Vss. 33-37 have to do with the Third Commandment, "You shall not take the Name of the Lord your God in vain" [Ex. 20:7])*:

34 But I say unto you *(proclaiming the true meaning of the Law)*, Swear not at all; neither by Heaven; for it is God's Throne *(this has nothing to do with profanity, but rather of flippantly using God's Name)*:

35 Nor by the earth; for it is His footstool: neither by Jerusalem; for it is the city of the great King *(not only must the Name of God not be flippantly used, but as well, His Creation is off limits also)*.

36 Neither shall you swear by your head, because you cannot make one hair white or black *(man is God's highest creation)*.

37 But let your communication be *(verbal communication with others)*, Yes, yes; No, no: for whatsoever is more than these comes of evil *(the followers of Christ must stand out by their truthfulness, honesty, and integrity; subterfuge and doubletalk are out)*.

RETALIATION

38 You have heard that it has been said, An eye for an eye, and a tooth for a tooth *([Ex. 21:24; Lev. 24:20; Deut. 19:21]; the letter of the Law was that which God would carry out in His Own way [Mat. 7:2] man was not to resort to such, even as Jesus will now say)*:

39 But I say unto you, That you resist not evil *(do not reward evil with evil)*: but whosoever shall

smite you on the right cheek, turn to him the other also *(once again, the language is figurative, for the Lord when smitten on the cheek [Jn. 18:22-23] did not turn the other cheek but with dignity rebuked the assailant).*

40 And if any man will sue you at the law, and take away your coat, let him have your cloak also *(this does not refer to righteous action, which is sometimes necessary, but rather to a contentious spirit, which demands one's rights, down to the minute detail).*

41 And whosoever shall compel you to go a mile, go with him two *(the entirety of the idea has to do with the heart of man, not so much his outward actions, but which most surely would guide his actions accordingly).*

42 Give to him who asks of you, and from him who would borrow of you turn not you away *(this pertains to those truly in need, and not those who are lazy and will not work [II Thess. 3:10]).*

THE LAW OF LOVE

43 You have heard that it has been said, You shall love your neighbor, and hate your enemy *(once again, Christ is correcting the perversion of Scripture; the "hating of the enemy" was probably derived from Deut. 7:1-6; but nowhere in that Passage does it say* to hate the enemy; while we are to hate the sin, we are not to hate the sinner [Jn. 3:16]).*

44 But I say unto you, Love your enemies, bless them who curse you, do good to them who hate you, and pray for them which despitefully use you, and persecute you *(the actions of the enemies of goodness and of righteousness are to be "hated" with a holy hatred; but personal hatred is to be met by love);*

45 That you may be the Children of your Father which is in Heaven: for He makes His sun to rise on the evil and on the good, and sends rain on the just and on the unjust *(we are to imitate our Heavenly Father).*

46 For if you love them which love you, what reward have you? do not even the publicans the same? *(Only those who have the true Love of God in their hearts can love those who do not love them.)*

47 And if you salute your Brethren only, what do you more *than others?* do not even the publicans so? *(If our love is of no greater definition than that of the world, then our claims are empty.)*

48 Be you therefore perfect, even as your Father which is in Heaven is perfect *(Jesus is not teaching sinless perfection, for the Bible does not teach such; He is teaching that our imitation of our Heavenly Father must be as per-*

fect as possible; the Holy Spirit Alone can help us do these things, which He does according to our Faith in Christ and the Cross [Rom. 8:1-2, 11]).

CHAPTER 6

JESUS' TEACHING ON GIVING

TAKE heed *(a serious matter)* that you do not your alms *(Righteousness)* before men, to be seen of them *(what is the reason for our giving?)*: otherwise you have no reward of your Father which is in Heaven.

2 Therefore when you do *your* alms *(in this case, giving, and portrays the necessity of giving)*, do not sound a trumpet before you *(do not make a show)*, as the hypocrites do in the Synagogues and in the streets, that they may have glory of men *(be seen of men)*. Verily I say unto you, They have their reward *(God will not reward such, whether on Earth or in Heaven)*.

3 But when you do alms *(Righteousness, and once again, proclaims the necessity of giving)*, let not your left hand know what your right hand does *(not meant to be taken literally, but rather to point to the intent of the heart)*:

4 That your alms may be in secret *(simply means that from the heart it is done as unto the Lord,*

and not for the praise of men): and your Father *(Heavenly Father)* which sees in secret Himself shall reward you openly *(both on Earth and when you get to Heaven)*.

JESUS' TEACHING ON PRAYER

5 And when you pray *(the necessity of prayer)*, you shall not be as the hypocrites *are*: for they love to pray standing in the Synagogues and in the corners of the streets, that they may be seen of men *(they do it for show)*. Verily I say unto you, They have their reward *(meaning that there will be no reward from God in any capacity)*.

6 But you *(sincere Believer)*, when you pray, enter into your closet, and when you have shut your door, pray to your Father which is in secret; and your Father which sees in secret shall reward you openly *(the word "closet" is not to be taken literally, but means that our praying must not be done for show; if we make God's interests our own, we are assured that He will make our interest His Own)*.

7 But when you pray, use not vain repetitions, as the heathen do *(repeating certain phrases over and over, even hundreds of times)*: for they think that they shall be heard for their much speaking

(they will not be heard by God).

8 Be not you therefore like unto them: for your Father *(Heavenly Father)* knows what things you have need of, before you ask Him *(He is omniscient, meaning that He knows all things, past, present, and future).*

THE MODEL PRAYER

9 After this manner therefore pray you *(is meant to be in total contrast to the heathen practice; as well, it is to be prayed in full confidence, that the Heavenly Father will hear and answer according to His Will):* Our Father *(our prayer should be directed toward our Heavenly Father, and not Christ or the Holy Spirit)* Who is in Heaven, Hallowed be Your Name *(we reverence His Name).*

10 Your Kingdom come *(this will definitely happen at the Second Coming),* Your Will be done in earth, as *it is* in Heaven *(the Will of God is all-important; it will be carried out on Earth, beginning with the Kingdom Age).*

11 Give us this day our daily bread *(we are to look to the Lord for sustenance, both natural and spiritual).*

12 And forgive us our debts, as we forgive our debtors *(the word "debts" here refers to "trespasses" and "sins"; His forgiveness on our* part is predicated on our forgiving others).*

13 And lead *(because of self-confidence)* us not into temptation *(help us not to be led into testing — the idea is, in my self-confidence, which stems from the flesh and not the Spirit, please do not allow me to be led into temptation, for I will surely fail!),* but deliver us *(the trap is more powerful than man can handle; only God can deliver; He does so through the Power of the Holy Spirit, according to our Faith in Christ and the Cross [Rom. 8:1-2, 11])* from evil *(the Evil One, Satan himself):* For Yours is the kingdom *(this Earth belongs to the Lord and not Satan; he is an usurper),* and the power *(God has the Power to deliver, which He does, as stated, through the Cross),* and the glory *(the Glory belongs to God, and not Satan),* forever *(none of this will ever change).* Amen *(this Word expresses a solemn ratification; in the Mind of God, the defeat and destruction of Satan and, therefore, all evil in the world, is a foregone conclusion).*

14 For if you forgive men *(it must be the God kind of forgiveness)* their trespasses *(large sins),* your Heavenly Father will also forgive you *(forgiveness rests totally on the Atoning Work of Christ; it is an act of sheer Grace):*

15 But if you forgive not men

their trespasses, neither will your Father forgive your trespasses *(if we want God to forgive us, we must at the same time forgive others; if not, His forgiveness for us is withheld; consequently, such a person is in jeopardy of losing their soul)*.

JESUS' TEACHING ON FASTING

16 Moreover when you fast *(no set time)*, be not, as the hypocrites, of a sad countenance: for they disfigure their faces, that they may appear unto men to fast. Verily I say unto you, They have their reward *(so much in the religious realm falls into this category; it is done for "show" whether it be fasting or giving, etc.; the Lord will never reward such)*.

17 But you *(referring to those who are truly God's Children)*, when you fast, anoint your head, and wash your face *(the "anointing" and the "washing" were actually symbols of joy; this was the opposite of the sad countenance)*;

18 That you appear not unto men to fast *(there is to be no appearance of fasting)*, but unto your Father *(Heavenly Father)* which is in secret: and your Father, which sees in secret, shall reward *(bless)* you openly *(the implication is God was not the "Father" of the Pharisees, and will not be the "Father"*

of any who follow in their train).

TREASURES IN HEAVEN

19 Lay not up for yourselves treasures upon earth *(everything on the Earth is temporal)*, where moth and rust does corrupt, and where thieves break through and steal *(if the eye be set upon treasures on Earth, the life and character of the Believer will be shrouded in moral darkness)*:

20 But lay up for yourselves treasures in Heaven, where neither moth nor rust does corrupt, and where thieves do not break through nor steal:

21 For where your treasure is, there will your heart be also *(a man's aim determines his character; if that aim be not simple and Heavenward but earthward and double, all the faculties and principles of his nature will become a mass of darkness; it is impossible to give a divided allegiance)*.

THE LIGHT

22 The light of the body is the eye *(a figure of speech; He is, in effect, saying that the light of the soul is the spirit)*: if therefore your eye be single *(the spirit of man should have but one purpose, and that is to Glorify God)*, your whole body shall be full of Light *(if the spirit of man is single in its devo-*

tion to God *[meaning not divided]* then all the soul will be full of light).

23 But if your eye be evil, your whole body shall be full of darkness *(if the spirit be evil, the entirety of the soul will be full of darkness).* If therefore the light that is in you be darkness *(the light is not acted upon, but rather perverted)*, how great is that darkness *(the latter state is worse than if there had been no light at all)*!

24 No man can serve two masters: for either he will hate the one, and love the other; or else he will hold to the one, and despise the other. You cannot serve God and mammon *(this is flat out, stated as, an impossibility; it is total devotion to God, or ultimately it will be total devotion to the world; the word, "mammon" is derived from the Babylonian "Mimma," which means "anything at all").*

AGAINST WORRY AND ANXIETY

25 Therefore I say unto you, Take no thought for your life, what you shall eat, or what you shall drink; nor yet for your body, what you shall put on *(don't worry about these things).* Is not the life more than meat, and the body than raiment? *(Life is more than things, and the physical body is* more than the clothes we wear.)

26 Behold the fowls of the air: for they sow not, neither do they reap, nor gather into barns; yet your Heavenly Father feeds them. Are you not much better than they? *(The fowls of the air are a smaller part of God's great Creation. If the Lord has provided for them, most assuredly, He has provided for His Children.)*

27 Which of you by taking thought *(worrying and fretting)* can add one cubit unto his stature? *(Whatever is going to happen cannot be stopped by worry; and if it doesn't happen, there is nothing to worry about. For His Children, the Lord always fills in the bottom line.)*

28 And why do you take thought *(worry)* for *(about)* raiment *(clothes)*? Consider the lilies of the field, how they grow; they toil not, neither do they spin *(the man grows the flax [toil] the woman weaves it [spins]; the statement is meant to proclaim the fact that the beauty of the lily has nothing to do with its effort, but is given completely by the Creator)*:

29 And yet I say unto you, That even Solomon in all his glory was not arrayed like one of these *(it is said that the lilies of Israel had brilliant coloring, and especially the purple and white Huleh Lily found in Nazareth).*

30 Wherefore, if *(since)* God so

clothed the grass of the field *(is meant to portray God's guarantee)*, which today is, and tomorrow is cast into the oven *(portrays how inconsequential is this part of His Creation, and yet, how much care He expends on it)*, shall He not much more *clothe* you, O you of little faith? *(We are told here the reason for our lack; it is "little faith"; because God is Faithful, He can be trusted fully to completely carry out His commitments to us in Christ [I Cor. 1:9; 10:13; II Cor. 1:18; I Thess. 5:24; II Thess. 3:3; etc.].)*

31 Therefore take no thought *(don't worry)*, saying, What shall we eat? or, What shall we drink? or, Wherewithal shall we be clothed? *(The Greek Text actually means that even one anxious thought is forbidden. Such shows a distrust of the Lord.)*

32 (For after all these things do the Gentiles seek:) *(Gentiles had no part in God's Covenant with Israel; consequently, they had no part in God's economy, and, basically, had to fend for themselves)* for your Heavenly Father knows that you have need of all these things *(the phrase is meant to express the contrast between those who do not know the Lord and those who do; if we live for Him, ever seeking His Will, we have the guarantee of His Word, which He will provide for us; is God's Word good*

enough? I think it is!)*.

33 But seek you first the Kingdom of God, and His Righteousness *(this gives the "condition" for God's Blessings; His interests are to be "first")*; and all these things shall be added unto you *(this is the "guarantee" of God's Provision)*.

34 Take therefore no thought for the morrow *(don't worry about the future)*: for the morrow shall take thought for the things of itself *(this is meant to refer back to Verse 27)*. Sufficient unto the day is the evil thereof *(this means that we should handle daily difficulties in Faith, and have Faith for the future that the present difficulties will not grow into larger ones; we have God's assurance that they won't, that is, if we will sufficiently believe Him)*.

CHAPTER 7

JUDGING OTHERS

JUDGE not, that you be not judged *(this statement by Christ harks back to Verses 25 through 34 of the previous Chapter; the idea is, God may permit poverty to test His Child, but fellow Believers are not to err, as Job's friends did, and believe the trial to be a judgment for secret sin; as well, the word, "judging," as used here, covers every aspect of dealing with our fel-*

lowman).

2 For with what judgment *you* judge, *you* shall be judged *(whatever motive we ascribe to others, such motive will ultimately be ascribed to us)*: and with what measure you mete, it shall be measured to you again *(a double emphasis is given here in order to proclaim the seriousness of the Words of our Lord; when we judge others, we are judging ourselves).*

3 And why do you behold the mote that is in your brother's eye *(the Believer is not to be looking for fault or wrongdoing in the lives of fellow Believers),* but consider not the beam that is in your own eye? *(We have plenty in our own lives which need eliminating, without looking for faults in others. The "mote" and "beam" are contrasted! The constant judging of others portrays the fact that we are much worse off than the one we are judging.)*

4 Or how will you say to your brother, Let me pull out the mote out of your eye *(the seriousness of setting ourselves up as Judge, jury, and executioner)*; and, behold, a beam *is* in your own eye? *(Once again draws attention to the fact that the person doing the judging is in far worse spiritual condition than the one being judged.)*

5 You hypocrite *(aptly describes such a person)*, first cast out the beam out of your own eye; and then you shall see clearly to cast out the mote out of your brother's eye *(the very fact that we do not address ourselves, but rather others, portrays the truth that our personal situation is worse; when we properly analyze ourselves, then, and only then, can we "see clearly"; this is speaking of character assassination and not the correction of doctrine).*

6 Give not that which is holy unto the dogs, neither cast you your pearls before swine *(there may be problems in the Church, as Verses 1 through 5 proclaim, but still, the Church is never to reach out into the world, i.e., "dogs," for help in order to solve its internal disputes)*, lest they trample them under their feet, and turn again and rend you *(no help will be coming from the world, but rather destruction.; we are to take our problems to the Lord, obeying His Word, concerning disputes [Mat. 18:15-17]).*

GETTING THINGS FROM GOD

7 Ask, and it shall be given you *(if we ask for wisdom as it regards the settling of disputes, or for anything, it shall be given)*; seek, and you shall find *(the answer may not be forthcoming immediately; therefore, we should "seek" to know the reason why)*;

knock, and it shall be opened unto you *(we must make sure that it is His door on which we are knocking; if it is, it definitely will be opened to us)*:

8 For every one who asks receives; and he who seeks finds; and to him who knocks it shall be opened *(assumes that the person's heart is sincere before the Lord)*.

9 Or what man is there of you, whom if his son ask bread, will he give him a stone? *(Even a human being will not do such, much less God!)*

10 Or if he asks a fish, will he give him a serpent? *(If, in fact, what we are asking for is not God's Will, and would turn out to be a "stone," or "serpent," He will guard us from receiving such, and during the time of waiting and consecration, will show us what we truly need.)*

11 If you then, being evil *(refers to parents sometimes giving their children things which are not good for them, as well as things which are good)*, know how to give good gifts unto your children, how much more shall your Father which is in Heaven give good things to them who ask Him? *(The Lord gives only good things.)*

THE GOLDEN RULE

12 Therefore all things what-soever you would that men should do to you, do you even so to them; for this is the Law and the Prophets *(this rule does not authorize capricious benevolent action, but only what is reasonable and morally helpful, and controlled by Divine imitation [Mat. 5:48]; this principle of action and mode of life is, in fact, the sum of all Bible teaching)*.

THE NARROW WAY AND THE BROAD WAY

13 Enter you in at the strait gate *(this is the Door, Who is Jesus [Jn. 10:1])*: for wide is the gate, and broad is the way, that leads to destruction, and many there be which go in thereat *(proclaims the fact of many and varied religions of the world, which are false, and lead to eternal hellfire)*:

14 Because strait is the gate, and narrow is the way, which leads unto life, and few there be that find it *(every contrite heart earnestly desires to be among the "few"; the requirements are greater than most are willing to accept)*.

FALSE PROPHETS AND DECEPTIONS

15 Beware of false prophets, who come to you in sheep's clothing, but inwardly they are raven-

ing wolves *("beware of false proph- ets" is said in the sternest of mea- sures! there will be and are false prophets, and are some of Satan's greatest weapons).*

16 You shall know them by their fruits *(this is the test as given by Christ as it regards identifica- tion of false prophets and false apostles).* Do men gather grapes of thorns, or figs of thistles? *(It is impossible for false doctrine, gen- erated by false prophets, to bring forth good fruit.)*

17 Even so every good tree brings forth good fruit; but a cor- rupt tree brings forth evil fruit *(the good fruit is Christlikeness, while the evil fruit is self-likeness).*

18 A good tree cannot bring forth evil fruit, neither *can* a cor- rupt tree bring forth good fruit *(the "good tree" is the Cross, while the "corrupt tree" pertains to all of that which is other than the Cross).*

19 Every tree that brings not forth good fruit is hewn down, and cast into the fire *(Judgment will ultimately come on all so- called gospel, other than the Cross [Rom. 1:18]).*

20 Wherefore by their fruits you shall know them *(the acid test).*

AGAINST MERE PROFESSION

21 Not every one who says unto Me, Lord, Lord, shall enter into the Kingdom of Heaven *(the rep- etition of the word "Lord" expresses astonishment, as if to say: "Are we to be disowned?");* but he who does the Will of My Father which is in Heaven *(what is the Will of the Father? Verse 23 tells us).*

22 Many will say to Me in that day, Lord, Lord, have we not Prophesied in Your Name? and in Your Name have cast out devils? and in Your Name done many wonderful works? *(These things are not the criteria, but rather Faith in Christ and what Christ has done for us at the Cross [Eph. 2:8-9, 13- 18]. The Word of God alone is to be the judge of doctrine.)*

23 And then will I profess unto them, I never knew you *(again we say, the criteria alone is Christ and Him Crucified [I Cor. 1:23]):* depart from Me, you who work iniquity *(we have access to God only through Christ, and access to Christ only through the Cross, and access to the Cross only through a denial of self [Lk. 9:23]; any other Message is Judged by God as "in- iquity," and cannot be a part of Christ [I Cor. 1:17]).*

THE TWO BUILDERS: A WISE MAN AND A FOOLISH MAN

24 Therefore whosoever hears these sayings of Mine, and does

them, I will liken him unto a wise man, who built his house upon a rock (the "Rock" is Christ Jesus, and the Foundation is the Cross [Gal. 1:8-9]):

25 And the rain descended, and the floods came, and the winds blew, and beat upon that house; and it fell not: for it was founded upon a rock (the Foundation of our belief system must be Christ and Him Crucified [Gal. 6:14]).

26 And every one who hears these sayings of Mine, and does them not, shall be likened unto a foolish man, who built his house upon the sand (but for the foundation, this house looked the same as the house that was built upon the rock):

27 And the rain descended, and the floods came, and the winds blew, and beat upon that house; and it fell: and great was the fall of it (while the sun shines, both houses look good; but, when adversity comes and come it shall, Faith, which is alone in Christ and Him Crucified will stand [I Cor. 1:18]).

28 And it came to pass, when Jesus had ended these sayings (ended the Sermon on the Mount), the people were astonished at His Doctrine (this Message proclaimed the True intent of the Law of Moses, and, above all, laid the Foundation for the New Cov-enant):

29 For He taught them as one having authority (refers to Divine Authority, which He had by the Power of the Holy Spirit; this Sermon and that of Luke, Chapter 6 are probably one and the same; the Holy Spirit here lays the emphasis on the heart, while in Luke, emphasis is laid on actions produced by the heart; consequently, the distinction between "standing" and "state" is apparent), and not as the Scribes (those who claimed to be expert in the Law of Moses).

CHAPTER 8

JESUS HEALS A LEPER

WHEN He was come down from the mountain (this particular Message is now finished), great multitudes followed Him (this is the result of the "authority" with which He taught).

2 And, behold, there came a leper (leprosy was then considered a symbol of sin) and worshipped Him (did so as Lord, recognizing Him as the Messiah), saying, Lord, if You will, You can make me clean (Christ Alone can cleanse from sin, of which leprosy was a type).

3 And Jesus put forth His Hand, and touched him, saying, I will; be you clean (this statement

forever settles the Will of God as it regards Salvation and Healing; His touch did not cleanse him, but rather His Word; according to the Greek, by the time His Hand touched the man he was already clean; so, Jesus did not break the Law by touching a leper). And immediately his leprosy was cleansed *(immediately upon the word "I will" being spoken).*

4 And Jesus said unto him, See that you tell no man *(the Mission of our Lord in His First Advent was to deal with sin and suffer its judgment at Calvary; He suppressed anything that would hinder that purpose of Grace, and so forbade the man to publish the fact of his healing);* but go your way, show yourself to the Priest, and offer the gift that Moses Commanded, for a Testimony unto them *(the Law of the Cleansing of the leper is found in Leviticus, Chapters 13 and 14).*

HEALING OF THE CAPTAIN'S SERVANT

5 And when Jesus was entered into Capernaum *(His Headquarters),* there came unto Him a Centurion *(a Roman Captain over 100 men),* beseeching Him *(strongly requesting of Him, begging Him; Jesus came not only to cleanse Israel, but to liberate the Gentile as well, and, accordingly, the servant of the Roman officer was set free from his malady),*

6 And saying, Lord *(the leprous Jew had called Jesus, "Lord," and now, the Gentile Centurion calls Him "Lord," proclaiming Him Lord of All),* my servant lies at home sick of the palsy, grievously tormented *(this disease was a paralysis with contraction of the joints, accompanied with intense suffering; the man's life was threatened).*

7 And Jesus said unto him, I will come and heal him *(the emphasis is not on the coming, but, instead, on the One Who is coming, Namely Christ; the "I" is emphatic, meaning, "I can, and I will!" once again, the "I will" settles the question regarding Divine Healing).*

8 The Centurion answered and said, Lord, I am not worthy that You should come under my roof *(probably his referral to being a Gentile)*: but speak the Word only, and my servant shall be healed *(the Word of Christ was all that was needed, and the soldier knew that).*

9 For I am a man under authority, having soldiers under me: and I say to this *man,* Go, and he goes; and to another, Come, and he comes; and to my servant, Do this, and he does *it (the intelligence of this Centurion was remarkable; he argued that the sol-*

diers had to obey him because in his person resided the authority of the Emperor, and, similarly, disease obeyed Jesus because in Him was the Authority of God).

10 When Jesus heard *it*, He marveled *(records one of the only two times He marveled; the "faith" of this Gentile, and the "unbelief" of the Jews [Mk. 6:6]),* and said to them that followed, Verily I say unto you, I have not found so great faith, no, not in Israel *(this is a portrayal of the fact that the Gentiles would accept Christ, while Israel would not).*

11 And I say unto you *(proclaims the acceptance of Christ by the Gentiles, and His rejection by the Jews),* That many *(Gentiles)* shall come from the east and west, and shall sit down with Abraham, and Isaac, and Jacob, in the Kingdom of Heaven *(would come into the Abrahamic Covenant [Gen. 12:1-3; Gal. 3:14]).*

12 But the children of the Kingdom *(Israel)* shall be cast out into outer darkness: there shall be weeping and gnashing of teeth *(would die without God, thereby going to Hell, because of rejecting Christ).*

13 And Jesus said unto the Centurion, Go your way; and as you have believed *(believe, not doing),* so be it done unto you. And his servant was healed in the selfsame hour.

PETER'S MOTHER-IN-LAW HEALED

14 And when Jesus was come into Peter's house *(in Capernaum),* He *(Jesus)* saw his wife's mother laid *(Peter's mother-in-law),* and sick of a fever.

15 And He *(Jesus)* touched her hand, and the fever left her *(immediately):* and she arose, and ministered unto them *(prepared a meal).*

DEMONS CAST OUT; MANY HEALED

16 When the evening was come *(when the Sabbath ended at sunset),* they brought unto Him *(Jesus)* many who were possessed with devils *(demons):* and He cast out the spirits with *His* Word, and healed all who were sick:

17 That it might be fulfilled which was spoken by the Prophet Isaiah *(Isa. 53:4),* saying, Himself took our infirmities, and bear *our* sicknesses *(took our sin penalty and sicknesses).*

TESTS OF DISCIPLESHIP

18 Now when Jesus saw great multitudes about Him, He gave commandment *(instructions)* to depart unto the other side *(the eastern side of the Sea of Galilee).*

19 And a certain Scribe *(expert*

in the Law of Moses) came, and said unto Him, Master, I will follow You wherever You go.

20 And Jesus said unto him, The foxes have holes, and the birds of the air *have* nests; but the Son of Man has nowhere to lay His head *(the Earth had room for foxes and birds, but not Christ; "Son of Man" refers to the fact that He will take back dominion, which was done at the Cross)*.

21 And another of His Disciples *(not one of the Twelve)* said unto Him, Lord, suffer me first to go and bury my father *(take care of my father until he dies)*.

22 But Jesus said unto him *(tone of censure)*, Follow Me *(nothing must stand in the way)*; and let the dead bury their dead *(let the spiritually dead bury their physically dead)*.

JESUS STILLS THE STORM

23 And when He was entered into a ship, His Disciples followed Him,

24 And, behold, there arose a great tempest in the sea *(great storm)*, insomuch that the ship was covered with the waves: but He was asleep.

25 And His Disciples came to *Him*, and awoke Him, saying, Lord, save us: we perish *(He Alone can save us)*.

26 And He said unto them *(the reason for their dilemma)*, Why are you fearful, O you of little faith *(misplaced faith)*? Then He arose, and rebuked the winds and the sea *(great power)*; and there was a great calm *("O you of little faith" occurs four times [care, Mat. 6:30; fear, Mat. 8:26; doubt, Mat. 14:31; reasoning, Mat. 16:8])*.

27 But the men marveled *(were astonished)*, saying, What manner of man is this, that even the winds and the sea obey Him! *(He is man, but as well He is God.)*

THE GERGESENE DEMONIACS

28 And when He was come to the other side *(eastern side of Galilee)* into the country of the Gergesenes, there met Him two possessed with devils *(demons)*, coming out of the tombs *(where they lived)*, exceeding fierce *(maniacs)*, so that no man might pass by that way.

29 And, behold, they cried out *(speaking to Christ)*, saying, What have we to do with You, Jesus, Thou Son of God? *(The demons had more intelligence than do the disciples of modern thought.)* Are You come here to torment us before the time? *(Judgment [Rev. 20:1-3].)*

30 And there was a good way off from them an herd of many swine *(hogs)* feeding.

31 So the devils *(demons)* be-

sought Him, saying, If You cast us out *(since You are casting us out)*, suffer us to go away into the herd of swine *(leave the men and inhabit the hogs)*.

32 And He said unto them, Go *(proclaims His approval)*. And when they were come out, they went into the herd of swine: and, behold, the whole herd of swine ran violently down a steep place into the sea *(the Sea of Galilee)*, and perished in the waters.

33 And they that kept them fled *(quickly)*, and went their ways into the city, and told every thing, and what was befallen to the possessed of the devils *(his complete deliverance)*.

34 And, behold, the whole city came out to meet Jesus: and when they saw Him *(took a little while to find Him)*, they besought *Him* that he would depart out of their coasts *(borders)*.

CHAPTER 9

JESUS HEALS A PARALYZED MAN

AND He entered into a ship, and passed over, and came into His Own city *(Capernaum)*.

2 And, behold, they brought to him a man sick of the palsy *(paralyzed)*, lying on a bed: and Jesus seeing their faith *(the action of faith)* said unto the sick of the palsy; Son, be of good cheer; your sins be forgiven you *(the sickness was caused by sin)*.

3 And, behold, certain of the Scribes *(experts in the Law of Moses)* said within themselves *(murmured among themselves)*, This *man* blasphemes *(they did not recognize Him as Lord)*.

4 And Jesus knowing their thoughts said *(revealed to Him by the Spirit)*, Why do you think evil in your hearts? *(Unbelief!)*

5 For whether is easier, to say, *Your* sins be forgiven you; or to say, Arise, and walk? *(Original sin and its corresponding result, sickness.)*

6 But that you may know that the Son of Man has power on earth to forgive sins *(proclaims His Deity)*, (then said He to the sick of the palsy,) Arise, take up your bed, and go unto your house *(power to forgive sins and heal)*.

7 And he arose *(the physical action of a spiritual result)*, and departed to his house.

8 But when the multitudes saw it *(healing of the man)*, they marvelled, and glorified God, which had given such power unto men *(the multitudes still didn't understand that He was the Messiah)*.

THE CALLING OF MATTHEW

9 And as Jesus passed forth from thence, He saw a man,

named Matthew *(the Spirit directed Him)*, sitting at the receipt of custom *(Matthew was a tax collector — a publican)*: and He *(Jesus)* said unto him *(Matthew)*, Follow Me *(the call to be one of the Twelve)*. And he arose *(immediately)*, and followed Him.

10 And it came to pass *(after a few days)*, as Jesus sat at meat *(a meal)* in the house *(Matthew's house)*, behold, many Publicans *(tax collectors)* and sinners came and sat down with Him and His Disciples *(on His terms, and not on theirs)*.

11 And when the Pharisees saw it *(heard of it a little later)*, they said unto His Disciples, Why does your Master eat with Publicans and sinners *(self-righteousness)*?

12 But when Jesus heard *that (a short time later)*, He said unto them *(His Disciples)*, They who be whole need not a physician, but they who are sick *(He came for sinners, which includes all)*.

13 But go you and learn what *that* means, I will have mercy, and not sacrifice *(the keeping of rituals, i.e., sacrifices, won't save; asking for mercy will)*: for I am not come to call the Righteous *(self-righteous)*, but sinners to Repentance.

FASTING

14 Then came to Him the Disciples of John *(John was now in prison)*, saying, Why do we and the Pharisees fast often, but Your Disciples fast not? *(They fasted twice a week.)*

15 And Jesus said unto them *(introduction of the New Covenant)*, Can the children of the bridechamber mourn, as long as the bridegroom is with them? *(Jesus is the Bridegroom, so it was not the time to fast)* but the days will come, when the Bridegroom shall be taken from them *(Death, Resurrection, and Ascension of Christ)*, and then shall they fast *(fasting pictures something wrong that needs remedying, which the Coming of Christ will address)*.

16 No man puts a piece of new cloth *(New Covenant)* onto an old garment *(Old Covenant)*, for that which is put in to fill it up takes from the garment *(a patch)*, and the rent is made worse *(to revert to Law is to worsen the situation; the Cross is the New Covenant)*.

17 Neither do men put new wine *(New Covenant)* into old bottles *(skins)*: else the bottles break *(new wine splits the wineskin)*, and the wine runs out *(reverting to Law frustrates Grace [Gal. 2:21])*, and the bottles *(skins)* perish *(Law destroys Grace)*: but they put new wine into new bottles *(new skins)*, and both are preserved *(the New Covenant can only function by Faith*

[new skins] and not law).

MIRACLES

18 While He spoke these things unto them *(subject matter of previous Verse)*, behold, there came a certain Ruler *(Jarius)*, and worshipped Him *(as Lord and Messiah)*, saying, My daughter is even now dead *(is dying)*: but come and lay Your hand upon her, and she shall live.

19 And Jesus arose, and followed him *(immediately)*, and *so* did His Disciples.

20 And, behold *(an interruption)*, a woman, which was diseased with an issue of blood *(physically and ceremonially unclean [Lev. 15:25] probably from a female disorder)* twelve years, came behind *Him*, and touched the hem *(border)* of His garment *(a blue and white tassel worn at the four corners of the upper garment [Num. 15:37-41])*:

21 For she said within herself *(inasmuch as she could not get a private audience)*, If I may but touch His garment, I shall be whole *(her faith)*.

22 But Jesus turned Him about *(in response to her touch)*, and when He saw her *(took a moment to find her)*, He said, Daughter *(a change of relationship from "woman" to "daughter")*, be of good comfort *(don't fear)*; your Faith has made you whole *(if He doesn't touch you, you can touch Him)*. And the woman was made whole from that hour *(tradition says her name was Veronica)*.

23 And when Jesus came into the Ruler's house *(Jarius, ruler of the Synagogue)*, and saw the minstrels *(paid mourners, which was the custom then; by now the child had died)* and the people making a noise *(making lamentation over the death of the child)*,

24 He said unto them, Give place *(leave the room where the child was)*: for the maid is not dead, but asleep *(will not remain dead)*. And they laughed Him to scorn *(they knew the child was dead, and surmised that He could do nothing)*.

25 But when the people were put forth *(they didn't go quietly)*, He went in *(He wouldn't go in until the skeptics left)*, and took her by the hand, and the maid arose *(He raised her from the dead; life touched death; no one died or stayed dead in His Presence)*.

26 And the fame hereof went abroad into all that land *(all over Israel and beyond)*.

THE BLIND HEALED

27 And when Jesus departed thence *(left the home of Jarius)*, two blind men followed Him,

crying, and saying, Thou Son of David *(the Messianic title)*, have mercy on us *(a cry to which He always responds)*.

28 And when He was come into the house *(probably the house of Peter)*, the blind men came to Him *(they no doubt heard He had raised the dead)*: and Jesus said unto them, Do you believe that I am able to do this? *(He only required Faith.)* They said unto Him, Yes, Lord.

29 Then touched He their eyes *(light touched darkness)*, saying, According to your Faith be it unto you *(the Law of Faith)*.

30 And their eyes were opened *(instantly)*; and Jesus straitly *(strongly)* charged them, saying, See *that* no man know *it (His fame was already such that Israel would shortly clamor to make Him king, but for all the wrong reasons)*.

31 But they, when they were departed, spread abroad His fame in all that country *(at least they spread His fame and not theirs)*.

DUMB MAN HEALED

32 As they went out *(from the house, probably Peter's)*, behold, they brought to him a dumb man possessed with a devil *(a demon spirit had caused the dumbness)*.

33 And when the devil *(demon)* was cast out, the dumb spoke: and the multitudes marvelled, saying, It was never so seen in Israel *(demon spirits are the cause of many things)*.

34 But the Pharisees said *(strongest religious group in Israel, and were bitterly opposed to Christ)*, He casts out devils *(demons)* through the prince of the devils *(by the power of Satan)*.

35 And Jesus went about all the cities and villages, teaching *(explaining truth)* in their Synagogues, and preaching *(proclaiming truth)* the Gospel of the Kingdom *(good news)*, and healing every sickness and every disease among the people *(preaching, teaching, and healing are the Gospel program)*.

LABOURERS NEEDED

36 But when He saw the multitudes, He was moved with compassion on them *(had great pity and sympathy)*, because they fainted, and were scattered abroad, as sheep having no shepherd *(no spiritual leadership)*.

37 Then said He unto His Disciples, The harvest *(souls to be saved)* truly *is* plenteous, but the labourers *are* few *(not many Preachers of Righteousness)*;

38 Pray you *(intercede)* therefore the Lord of the Harvest *(Christ is the Lord)*, that He will send forth labourers into His

Harvest *(the harvest of souls is His, and must be gathered in His way)*.

CHAPTER 10

THE TWELVE

AND when He had called unto *Him* His Twelve Disciples *(for instruction and a special mission)*, He gave them power *against* unclean spirits, to cast them out, and to heal all manner of sickness and all manner of disease *(all such power comes from God)*.

2 Now the names of the Twelve Apostles are these; The first, Simon, who is called Peter, and Andrew his brother; James *the son* of Zebedee, and John his brother *(none of the twelve were of the aristocracy of Israel)*;

3 Philip, and Bartholomew; Thomas, and Matthew the publican *(tax collector)*; James *the son* of Alphaeus, and Lebbaeus whose surname *(last name)* was Thaddaeus;

4 Simon the Canaanite *(the zealot)*, and Judas Iscariot, who also betrayed him *(eleven were Galileans; one, Judas Iscariot, was a Judaean)*.

THE MISSION

5 These Twelve Jesus sent forth, and Commanded them, saying, Go not into the way of the Gentiles, and into *any* city of the Samaritans enter you not *(Israel must be addressed first; after the Cross, Resurrection, and Ascension, the Command would be to go into all the world [Mk. 16:15])*:

6 But go rather to the lost sheep of the House of Israel *(notice the "lost sheep," which refutes unconditional eternal security)*.

7 And as you go, preach, saying, The Kingdom of Heaven is at hand *(the Kingdom was rejected by Israel)*.

8 Heal the sick, cleanse the lepers, raise the dead, cast out devils *(demons)*: freely you have received, freely give *(a monetary charge is never to be made)*.

9 Provide neither gold, nor silver, nor brass in your purses *(the Lord is to be depended upon for everything)*,

10 Nor scrip for *your* journey, neither two coats, neither shoes, nor yet staves: for the workman is worthy of his meat *(it is criminal to receive the fruit of the labor, without labor)*.

11 And into whatsoever city or town you shall enter, enquire who in it is worthy *(of like faith)*; and there abide till you go thence *(work with them)*.

12 And when you come into an house, salute it *(bestow peace)*.

13 And if the house be worthy *(of like faith)*, let your peace *(bless-*

ing) come upon it: but if it be not worthy *(proves not to be of like faith)*, let your peace return to you *(don't bless it)*.

14 And whosoever shall not receive you, nor hear your words, when you depart out of that house or city, shake off the dust of your feet *(a curse is now upon such)*.

15 Verily I say unto you *(extremely important announcement)*, It shall be more tolerable *(degrees of punishment)* for the land of Sodom and Gomorrha in the Day of Judgment *(Great White Throne Judgment, Rev., Chpt. 20)*, than for that city.

PERSECUTION

16 Behold, I send you forth *(Christ does the sending)* as sheep in the midst of wolves *(most wolves are in the Church)*: be you therefore wise as serpents, and harmless as doves.

17 But beware of men *(religious apostates)*: for they will deliver you up to the Councils, and they will scourge you in their Synagogues *(the religious world is opposed to Christ and the Cross)*;

ENMITY

18 And you shall be brought before Governors and Kings *(persecution by the Church is often fol-lowed by that of the State)* for My sake *(animosity against Christ)*, for a testimony against them *(take the opportunity to witness to them)* and the Gentiles *(a prediction of the soon to come Church)*.

19 But when they deliver you up *(not "if" but "when")*, take no thought how or what you shall speak *(defense is left up to the Lord)*: for it shall be given you in that same hour what you shall speak *(unction of the Spirit)*.

20 For it is not you who speaks, but the Spirit of your Father *(Holy Spirit)* which speaks in you *("in you," Baptism with the Spirit [Acts 2:4])*.

21 And the brother shall deliver up the brother to death, and the father the child: and the children shall rise up against *their* parents, and cause them to be put to death *(animosity against Christ and the Cross is greater than love for loved ones)*.

22 And you shall be hated of all *men* for My Name's sake *(the offense of the Cross)*: but he who endures to the end shall be saved *(persecution will continue until the Second Coming)*.

23 But when they persecute you in this city *(the certainty of opposition)*, flee you into another *(keep evangelizing)*: for verily I say unto you *(remember this)*, You shall not have gone over the cities of Israel *(due to persecution,*

which was the case), till the Son of Man be come *(boldly announcing the Second Coming)*.

INSTRUCTION

24 The disciple is not above *his* master *(as they persecuted Christ, they will persecute His followers)*, nor the servant above his lord *(said in two ways to emphasize certitude of fulfillment)*.

25 It is enough for the disciple that he be as his master, and the servant as his lord *(the Believer must experience the same opposition as his Lord)*. If they have called the master of the house Beelzebub *(of the Devil)*, how much more *shall they call* them of his household?

26 Fear them not therefore *(fear must not guide the Message)*: for there is nothing covered, that shall not be revealed; and hid, that shall not be known *(a reckoning is coming)*.

27 What I tell you in darkness *(in prayer)*, *that* speak you in light *(openly)*: and what you hear in the ear *(what the Spirit reveals)*, *that* preach you upon the housetops *(publicly)*.

28 And fear not them which kill the body, but are not able to kill the soul *(don't fear men)*: but rather fear Him *(God)* which is able to destroy both soul and body in hell.

29 Are not two sparrows sold for a farthing *(cheap)*? and one of them shall not fall on the ground without your Father *(without His knowledge or will)*.

30 But the very hairs of your head are all numbered *(seek to please God Who knows all things, and can do all things)*.

31 Fear you not therefore *(what do we have to fear, serving One Who is all-knowing, and all-powerful?)*, you are of more value than many sparrows *(if God takes care of them, and He does, will He not take care of you?)*.

32 Whosoever therefore shall confess Me before men *(to tie man to God)*, him will I confess also before My Father which is in Heaven *(upon one's confession of Christ, a corresponding confession is made by Christ)*.

33 But whosoever shall deny Me before men *(Christ Alone is the focal point)*, him will I also deny before my Father which is in Heaven.

OPPOSITION

34 Think not that I am come to send peace on earth *(the entrance of Christ into the world manifests the evil of the heart)*: I came not to send peace, but a sword *(the sword against the Righteous will be the response of religious reprobates)*.

35 For I am come to set a man at variance *(odds)* against his father, and the daughter against her mother, and the daughter-in-law against her mother-in-law.

36 And a man's foes *shall be* they of his own household *(speaks not only of immediate family, but at times, of one's Church family)*.

DISCIPLESHIP

37 He who loves father or mother more than Me is not worthy of Me *(Christ must come first in all things)*: and he who loves son or daughter more than Me is not worthy of Me *(worthy to receive what I did for him at the Cross)*.

38 And he who takes not his cross *(total "Faith" in the Cross to the exclusion of everything else)*, and follows after Me *(we can only follow Him by the "Way" of the Cross)*, is not worthy of Me *(not worthy of the blessings afforded by the "victory" of the Cross)*.

39 He who finds his life shall lose it *(he who refuses the Cross loses his life)*: and he who loses his life for My sake shall find it *(places his life into Christ, which is done by the Cross [Rom. 6:3-5])*.

REWARDS

40 He who receives you receives Me *(he who receives My Messenger receives Me)*, and he who receives Me receives Him *(God the Father)* Who sent Me.

41 He who receives a Prophet in the name of a Prophet *(because he is a true Prophet)* shall receive a Prophet's reward; and he who receives a Righteous man in the name of a Righteous man *(because he is a Righteous man)* shall receive a Righteous man's reward *(one on a Righteous Mission)*.

42 And whosoever shall give to drink unto one of these little ones *(newest Believer)* a cup of cold *water* only in the name of a Disciple *(because he is a follower of Christ)*, verily I say unto you, he shall in no wise lose his reward *(a reward is guaranteed)*.

CHAPTER 11

JOHN THE BAPTIST

AND it came to pass, when Jesus had made an end of commanding His Twelve Disciples *(refers to the teaching of the previous Chapter; He commanded, which is different than suggesting)*, He departed thence to teach and to preach *(to explain and to proclaim)* in their cities.

2 Now when John had heard in the prison the works of Christ *(John is now imprisoned, and discouraged)*, he sent two of his disciples *(sent them to Jesus)*,

3 And said unto Him, Are You He Who should come, or do we look for another? *(Doubt is the nemesis of Faith, and plagues every Christian at one time or the other.)*

JESUS' ANSWER TO
JOHN THE BAPTIST

4 Jesus answered and said unto them *(if we ask, we will receive [Mat. 7:8])*, Go and shew John again those things which you do hear and see *(the Divine answer referred him to Isaiah 35:5-6; 61:1-2)*:

5 The blind receive their sight, and the lame walk, the lepers are cleansed, and the deaf hear, the dead are raised up, and the poor have the Gospel preached to them *(Jesus called John's attention away from the political scene — restoring at that time the Kingdom to Israel — to the true purpose of His Mission, the restoration of the individual)*.

6 And blessed is *he*, whosoever shall not be offended in Me *(the Lord adds another Beatitude to those given in Chapter 5)*.

JESUS' TESTIMONY OF
JOHN THE BAPTIST

7 And as they departed *(the two disciples of John the Baptist)*, Jesus began to say unto the multitudes concerning John, What went you out into the wilderness to see? A reed shaken with the wind? *(Despite appearances — John being in prison — Jesus proclaims what John really is.)*

8 But what went you out for to see? A man clothed in soft raiment? behold, they who wear soft *clothing* are in kings' houses *(if Herod's gold could have bought John, he would not now be in prison)*.

9 But what went you out for to see? *(The third time this question is posed.)* A Prophet? yes, I say unto you, and more than a Prophet *(more than all Prophets before him)*.

10 For this is *he*, of whom it is written *(proclaims John as the last of the Old Testament Prophets)*, Behold, I send My messenger before Your face *(John was that messenger)*, which shall prepare Your way before You *(John prepared the way for Christ)*.

11 Verily I say unto you, Among them who are born of women there has not risen a greater than John the Baptist *(places John at the forefront of the Prophets)*: notwithstanding he who is least in the Kingdom of Heaven is greater than he *(speaks of the New Covenant [Heb. 8:6])*.

12 And from the days of John the Baptist *(John introduced "the Kingdom of Heaven")* until now *(speaks of Christ Who would bring in the New Covenant)* the King-

dom of Heaven suffers violence *(the Crucifixion, the price that Christ paid [Gen. 3:15])*, and the violent take it by force *(speaks of Christ taking the dominion away from Satan, who had taken it from Adam [Col. 2:14-15])*.

13 For all the Prophets and the Law prophesied until John *(the Prophets and the Law testified of the coming Christ, and John was the last of those Prophets)*.

14 And if you will receive *it (if you will receive the Kingdom of Heaven)*, this is Elijah, which was for to come *(had the nation received John, he would have represented Elijah to them, and would have been reckoned by God as Elijah [Mal. 4:5-6])*.

15 He who has ears to hear, let him hear *(Israel would not hear)*.

16 But whereunto shall I liken this generation? *(That generation most privileged, rejected Christ.)* It is like unto children sitting in the markets, and calling unto their fellows,

17 And saying, We have piped unto you, and ye have not danced; we have mourned unto you, and ye have not lamented *(Israel refused to mourn with the Baptist when he demanded Repentance, or to rejoice with Christ)*.

18 For John came neither eating nor drinking, and they say, He has a devil *(demon — what the religious said; John had no so-cial life)*.

19 The Son of Man came eating and drinking, and they say, Behold a man gluttonous, and a winebibber, a friend of Publicans and sinners *(this is what Christ's enemies said of Him, and not what was actually true)*. But wisdom is justified of her children *(wisdom justified both courses, that of John and Christ. Israel rejected both)*.

JUDGMENT

20 Then began He to upbraid the cities wherein most of His mighty works were done, because they repented not *(He is speaking mostly of the religious leaders of these places)*:

21 Woe unto you, Chorazin! woe unto thee, Bethsaida! for if the mighty works, which were done in you, had been done in Tyre and Sidon, they would have repented long ago in sackcloth and ashes *(what a condemnation of Israel!)*.

22 But I say unto you, It shall be more tolerable *(different degrees of punishment)* for Tyre and Sidon at the day of judgment *(Great White Throne Judgment)*, than for you *(the pronoun "you" is emphatic; in the Mind of God, the "Judgment" has already been pronounced)*.

23 And you, Capernaum *("you"*

again emphatic, reserving this city for the worst judgment of all), which are exalted unto Heaven *(exalted not because of Christ, but rather because of its economic prosperity)*, shall be brought down to hell *(most of its inhabitants went to Hell)*: for if the mighty works, which had been done in you, had been done in Sodom, it would have remained until this day *(what an indictment on Capernaum!)*.

24 But I say unto you, That it shall be more tolerable for the land of Sodom, in the day of judgment, than for you *(the Christ-rejecter is morally lower than the idolaters of Tyre and Sidon, or the citizens of Sodom, and will be punished accordingly)*.

REJOICING OVER DIVINE REVELATION

25 At that time Jesus answered and said, I thank you, O Father, Lord of Heaven and earth, because You have hid these things from the wise and prudent *(a judicial judgment on the Religious Leaders of Israel)*, and have revealed them unto babes *(to other than the religious leaders)*.

26 Even so, Father *(His Own Personal Father)*: for so it seemed good in Your sight *(the Gospel is hidden to those who reject Christ and the Cross whomever they might*

be, and revealed to those who accept Christ and the Cross; this is "good" in God's sight [Jn. 3:16])*.

27 All things are delivered unto Me of My Father *("All things" mean that Christ is both Saviour and Judge)*: and no man knows the Son, but the Father *(Christ is an eternal Member of the Godhead)*; neither knows any man the Father, save the Son *(the only way to God the Father is through Christ [Jn. 14:6])*, and *he* to whomsoever the Son will reveal *Him (Salvation is never a matter of education but of Revelation)*.

THE GREAT INVITATION

28 Come unto Me *(is meant by Jesus to reveal Himself as the Giver of Salvation)*, all you who labor and are heavy laden *(trying to earn Salvation by works)*, and I will give you rest *(this "rest" can only be found by placing one's Faith in Christ and what He has done for us at the Cross [Gal. 5:1-6])*.

29 Take My yoke upon you *(the "yoke" of the "Cross" [Lk. 9:23])*, and learn of Me *(learn of His Sacrifice [Rom. 6:3-5])*; for I am meek and lowly in heart *(the only thing that our Lord Personally said of Himself)*: and ye shall find rest unto your souls *(the soul can find rest only in the Cross)*.

30 For My yoke *is* easy, and My burden is light *(what He requires*

of us is very little, just to have Faith in Him, and His Sacrificial Atoning work).

CHAPTER 12

JESUS IS LORD OF THE SABBATH

AT that time Jesus went on the Sabbath day through the corn *(either wheat or barley)*; and His Disciples were hungry, and began to pluck the ears of corn, and to eat *(to pluck the sheaf's of wheat or barley).*

2 But when the Pharisees saw it, they said unto Him *(these religious leaders, by now, were watching every move made by Christ and His Disciples; they were trying to find fault)*, Behold, Your Disciples do that which is not lawful to do upon the Sabbath day *(this was a law they had made up themselves; the Law of Moses permitted them to do what they were doing [Deut. 23:25]).*

3 But He said unto *them (His defense was not the Law of Moses, although He could have referred to that, but rather, if David the King when rejected ate the Showbread, the Son of David, when in a similar case might enjoy a similar privilege)*, Have you not read what David did, when he was hungry, and they who were with him;

4 How He entered into the House of God *(the Tabernacle)*, and did eat the shewbread, which was not lawful for him to eat, neither for them which were with him, but only for the Priests *(Sam. 21:6)*?

5 Or have you not read in the Law, how that on the Sabbath days the Priests in the Temple profane the Sabbath, and are blameless? *(The Priests did as much work, if not more, on the Sabbath Day in their preparing the Sacrifices, plus other duties, than possibly any other day! and yet they were not accused of breaking the Law.)*

6 But I say unto you *(meant to portray the Truth of the Word of God)*, That in this place is *One* greater than the Temple *(He was speaking of Himself; He was a greater Prophet than Moses, and a greater King than David).*

7 But if you had known what *this* means, I will have mercy, and not sacrifice *(sacrifice was the means, mercy the end; sacrifice the road, mercy the goal; Israel had lost sight of what the sacrifices actually meant)*, you would not have condemned the guiltless *(He and His Disciples were guiltless, and all who trust Him are likewise guiltless).*

8 For the Son of Man is Lord even of the Sabbath day *(rejected by the nation as Messiah the King, He now presented Himself to them*

as Elohim the Creator of the Sabbath).

HEALING ON THE SABBATH

9 And when He was departed
thence (*refers to the following taking place some days later*), He
went into their Synagogue (*probably happened during the first two
and one-half years of His Ministry, as He was banned from most
Synagogues the last year*):

10 And, behold, there was a
man which had *his* hand withered
(*the "withered hand" was a portrayal of the spiritual condition of
Israel and, as well, of all mankind*).
And they asked Him, saying, Is it
lawful to heal on the Sabbath
days? that they might accuse Him
(*the Pharisees were completely devoid of the understanding and purpose of Christ or the Sabbath*).

11 And He said unto them (*He
always answered their questions*),
What man shall there be among
you, who shall have one sheep,
and if it fall into a pit on the Sabbath Day, will he not lay hold on
it, and lift *it* out? (*The answer to
the question was obvious!*)

12 How much then is a man
better than a sheep? (*The answer
should have shamed them! However, the hardened heart has no
shame.*) Wherefore it is lawful to
do well on the Sabbath Days (*His
question and His answer showed that*

the religious leaders of Israel thought
more of sheep than they did of men;
regrettably, that spirit persists still!*).

13 Then said He to the man (*He
did not ask their permission, and
because they could not control Him,
they hated Him*), Stretch forth
your hand (*spiritually, Christ is
still saying the same thing to all
men*). And He stretched *it* forth;
and it was restored whole, like
as the other.

14 Then the Pharisees went out,
and held a council against Him,
how they might destroy Him (*His
love only excited their hatred*).

MULTITUDES HEALED

15 But when Jesus knew *it* (*refers to the plotting of the Pharisees
and Herodians against Him*), He
withdrew Himself from thence
(*went to another town*): and great
multitudes followed Him, and He
healed them all (*"all" is emphatic,
meaning that not one single person left without healing*);

16 And charged them that they
should not make Him known (*He
would not allow the fame of His
miracles to hinder His purpose of
offering up Himself as a sacrifice
for sin; the latter was His real
mission*):

17 That it might be fulfilled
which was spoken by Isaiah the
Prophet, saying (*Isaiah is quoted
in the Gospels more than any other*

Prophet),

18 Behold My Servant *(He was the Father's Servant)*, Whom I have chosen *(chosen by God and not man, hence rejected by man)*; My Beloved, in Whom My soul is well pleased *(to please God and not man, should be the goal of every Believer)*: I will put My Spirit upon Him *(Holy Spirit)*, and He shall show judgment to the Gentiles *(speaks of the coming Church, which is made up virtually of Gentiles)*.

19 He shall not strive, nor cry *(will not demand His rights)*; neither shall any man hear His voice in the streets *(He never promoted Himself)*.

20 A bruised reed shall He not break, and smoking flax shall He not quench *(even though they rejected Him, He will not give up on Israel)*, till He send forth judgment unto victory *(Israel will accept Him at the Second Coming)*.

21 And in His Name shall the Gentiles trust *(His Name means "Saviour," and even though the Jews rejected Him, the Gentiles accepted Him)*.

BLIND AND DUMB
MAN HEALED

22 Then was brought unto Him one possessed with a devil *(Demon)*, blind, and dumb *(the man represented Israel, and in fact, all*

of mankind): and He healed him, insomuch that the blind and the dumb both spoke and saw *(those who are "born-again" can now spiritually speak and spiritually see)*.

23 And all the people were amazed, and said, Is not this the son of David? *(Had their religious leaders properly led them, the people of Israel would have accepted Christ.)*

BLASPHEMING THE
HOLY SPIRIT

24 But when the Pharisees heard it *(heard what the people were saying about Jesus being the Son of David, which He was)*, they said, This *fellow (the Pharisees never referred to Him even one time by His Name)* does not cast out devils *(demons)*, but by Beelzebub the prince of the devils *(they didn't deny His power, but claimed that it was of Satan)*.

25 And Jesus knew their thoughts *(revealed to Him by the Holy Spirit)*, and said unto them, Every kingdom divided against itself is brought to desolation; and every city or house divided against itself shall not stand *(the idea of the statement is that Satan does not oppose himself! He does not possess one with an evil spirit and then cast out that spirit)*:

26 And if Satan cast out Satan,

he is divided against himself; how shall then his kingdom stand? *(Jesus admits here that Satan has a kingdom, which is the kingdom of darkness.)*

27 And if I by Beelzebub cast out devils *(demons)*, by whom do your children cast *them* out? *(The Pharisees and their disciples claimed to cast out demons, but in reality they didn't; because they were as well of Satan.)* therefore they shall be your judges *(the word "children" refers to the disciples of the Pharisees; Jesus by posing this question did not deny or affirm that they, in fact, actually did cast out demons; He was using the statement only as argument to prove His point).*

28 But if I cast out devils *(demons)* by the Spirit of God *(Jesus did not cast out demons because He was God, but as a man filled with the Spirit)*, then the Kingdom of God is come unto you *(this placed the Pharisees in an untenable position; if the Spirit of God was actually helping Him and He had already made it clear that such could not be done without the Spirit of God, then they must admit that He is the Messiah; their accusation backfired on them!).*

29 Or else how can one enter into a strong man's house *(Satan is pictured here as strong — stronger than men)*, and spoil his goods *(which Jesus did at the Cross)*, ex-cept he first bind the strong man? *(Only Jesus could bind this strong man.)* and then he will spoil his house *(at Calvary Satan was totally defeated [Col. 2:14-15]).*

30 He who is not with Me is against Me *(it is impossible to take a neutral position regarding Christ; the word "against" denotes intense opposition)*; and he who gathers not with Me scatters abroad *(refers to the Truth that one cannot be with "Christ" and "against" His true servants; the presence of Immanuel tests everything and everybody).*

31 Wherefore I say unto you *(addressing the most fearsome statement)*, All manner of sin and blasphemy shall be forgiven unto men *(that is if they properly confess the sin to the Lord [I Jn. 1:9])*: but the blasphemy *against* the Holy Spirit shall not be forgiven unto men *(when they accused Him of casting out demons by the power of Satan, when in reality He was doing so by the Power of the Holy Spirit, they blasphemed the Spirit of God; blaspheming the Holy Spirit can only be committed by someone who professes to know the Lord, as the Pharisees of old, or else has once known Him, and then turned against Him; the unredeemed, who have never known the Lord, cannot blaspheme the Holy Spirit simply because they have no true knowledge of the Spirit).*

32 And whosoever speaks a word against the Son of Man, it shall be forgiven him *(once again, if forgiveness is sought)*: but whosoever speaks against the Holy Spirit, it shall not be forgiven him, neither in this world, neither in the *world* to come *(such a person is doomed! however, the statements do not mean that a backslider cannot come back to the Lord; but they do mean that one who has actually blasphemed the Holy Spirit, will have no desire to come to the Lord, but in fact, will continue to oppose Him; anyone who desires to come to the Lord, which desire is placed there by the Holy Spirit, can do so [Rev. 22:17])*.

GOOD AND CORRUPT FRUIT

33 Either make the tree good, and his fruit good; or else make the tree corrupt, and his fruit corrupt: for the tree is known by *his* fruit *(a single tree cannot bring forth both good fruit and corrupt fruit; either the Pharisees were right, or He was right; both could not be right! His fruit was good, inasmuch as it produced changed lives; their fruit produced nothing but corruption)*.

34 O generation of vipers *(Jesus called the Pharisees snakes, and did so to their face)*, how can you, being evil, speak good things? *(Due to being evil, they could not pro-duce good fruit.)* for out of the abundance of the heart the mouth speaks *(men's words reveal their thoughts and character)*.

35 A good man out of the good treasure of the heart brings forth good things *(the "good man" of this Verse is the same as the "good tree" of Verse 33; as the "good tree" will bring forth good fruit, likewise, the "good man" will bring forth "good treasure" out of his heart)*: and an evil man out of the evil treasure brings forth evil things *(an evil heart cannot do otherwise)*.

36 But I say unto you, That every idle word that men shall speak *(concerns claims of righteousness which did not exist)*, they shall give account thereof in the day of judgment *(the Great White Throne Judgment [Rev. 20:11-15])*.

37 For by your words you shall be justified *(a confession of Christ and the price that He paid on the Cross, justifies any person [Rom. 5:1-2])*, and by your words you shall be condemned *(a confession of anything other than Christ and the Cross will condemn, i.e., "eternally lost")*.

THE SIGN OF JONAH

38 Then certain of the Scribes and of the Pharisees *(the Scribes were a part of the Pharisees, because they shared the same doctrine)* answered, saying, Master

(teacher), we would see a sign from *You (there were signs galore! for instance, they had just seen the man blind, dumb, and demon possessed instantly delivered, and healed; the sign, however, which they actually wanted, was not Deliverance from sin and its effects, but rather from Rome).*

39 But He answered and said unto them, An evil and adulterous generation seeks after a sign *("adulterous" spoke of Israel's spiritual unfaithfulness to God; they were committing spiritual adultery, which means that they were worshiping something other than God; had they been worshiping God, they would have accepted Christ);* and there shall no sign be given to it, but the sign of the Prophet *Jonah (He was speaking of His Death and Resurrection):*

40 For as Jonah was three days and three nights in the whale's belly; so shall the Son of Man be three days and three nights in the heart of the earth *(Christ would be dead three days and three nights; during this time, He would be in Paradise, and would preach to the spirits in prison who were fallen angels [Lk. 23:43; I Pet. 3:19-20] there is no scriptural record that Jesus was in the burning side of Hell, as some teach).*

41 The men of Nineveh shall rise in judgment with this generation, and shall condemn it *(Jesus here proclaims the Gentiles of Nineveh as far more righteous than the Pharisees, for they repented, while the Pharisees wouldn't; this infuriated these religious leaders):* because they repented at the preaching of Jonah; and, behold, a greater than Jonah is here *("this generation" of Israel, was visited by no less than the Son of God, whereas Nineveh was privileged to hear only the Prophet Jonah; as well, Christ performed the greatest miracles ever known, while Jonah performed none; Israel was left with no excuse).*

42 The queen of the south *(Queen of Sheba, another Gentile)* shall rise up in the judgment with this generation, and shall condemn it: for she came from the uttermost parts of the earth to hear the wisdom of Solomon; and, behold, a greater than Solomon is here *(this woman marks a higher stage of inquiry and faith, inasmuch as she traveled a great distance to hear the wisdom of Solomon; by contrast, Jesus came directly to Israel, but still they wouldn't receive Him, even though He was far greater than Solomon in both wisdom and power; what an indictment!).*

THE RETURN OF
UNCLEAN SPIRITS

43 When the unclean spirit is

gone out of a man (regarding Israel, unclean spirits would retreat before Christ), he (the unclean spirit) walks through dry places, seeking rest, and finding none (these spirits of darkness were not actually cast out of Israel, but only retreated before Christ, because He was the stronger Man).

44 Then he (the unclean spirit) says, I will return into my house from whence I came out (which happened when Israel rejected Christ); and when he (the evil spirit) is come, he finds it (Israel) empty, (empty of the Spirit of God) swept (clean of the things of God, meaning there was nothing of God left), and garnished (filled with religious ritual).

45 Then goes he (the evil spirit), and takes with himself seven other spirits more wicked than himself, and they enter in and dwell there (which is what happened when Israel rejected Christ): and the last state of that man is worse than the first. Even so shall it be also unto this wicked generation (having rejected Christ, Israel was now far worse than she was before He came; it is the same with the modern Church, which hears the Message of the Cross, and then rejects it).

JESUS' TRUE FAMILY

46 While He (Christ) yet talked to the people (concerns the terrible Word He has just delivered concerning Israel's present and future state), behold, His mother and His brethren stood without, desiring to speak with Him (Jesus was probably in a particular house, with it being filled with people, with no more room for others to come in, hence His family not able to get to Him; their desire to speak with Him was not in a positive sense).

47 Then one said unto Him, Behold, Your mother and Your brethren stand without, desiring to speak with You (they had things to say to Him, but they little desired to hear what He had to say to them; thankfully, that would change after His Death and Resurrection).

48 But He answered and said unto him who told Him, Who is My mother? and who are My brethren? (This totally refutes the claims later made by the Catholic Church.)

49 And He stretched forth His Hand toward His Disciples (refers to the original Twelve, but is not limited to them, as it refers to any and all who follow Him, as the next Passage proclaims), and said, Behold My mother and My brethren!

50 For whosoever (increases the dimensions of His family to include all who follow Him) shall do the will of My Father which is in Heaven (proclaims the qualifica-

tions for being a part of the Family of God), the same is My brother, and sister, and mother (places no significance on physical birth, but everything on spiritual birth).

CHAPTER 13

THE PARABLE OF THE SOWER

THE same day (the day the teaching was given as recorded in the previous Chapter) went Jesus out of the house (probably Peter's house), and sat by the sea side (Sea of Galilee).

2 And great multitudes were gathered together unto Him (they wanted Him to teach them, which He did), so that He went into a ship, and sat (which was the custom then regarding sitting while one taught); and the whole multitude stood on the shore.

3 And He spoke many things unto them in Parables (a comparison illustration, used in order to explain a truth), saying, Behold, a sower went forth to sow (concerns an illustration with which all would have been familiar);

4 And when he sowed, some seeds (Word of God) fell by the way side, and the fowls (demon spirits) came and devoured them up:

5 Some (seed) fell upon stony places, for they had not much earth: and forthwith they sprung up, because they had no deepness of earth (no depth):

6 And when the sun was up, they were scorched; and because they had no root, they withered away (because of having no depth, persecutions soon caused them to fall by the wayside; all of this pertains to the presentation of the Gospel, and as obvious, completely refutes the unscriptural doctrine of unconditional eternal security).

7 And some (seed) fell among thorns; and the thorns sprung up, and choked them (other things were allowed to come in and hinder the growth of the Word in the heart):

8 But other (seed) fell into good ground (receptive ground), and brought forth fruit, some an hundredfold, some sixtyfold, some thirtyfold (Jn. 15:1-8).

9 Who hath ears to hear, let him hear (whoever hears is responsible to hear, i.e., to obey, and will be so judged; the secret of this first Parable is that only about one-fourth of the expended efforts succeed, and three-fourths fail; subsequent history demonstrates the accuracy of this Prophecy).

JESUS EXPLAINS THE PURPOSE OF SPEAKING IN PARABLES

10 And the Disciples came,

and said unto Him (*seems to pertain to a later time when they were alone*), Why do You speak to them in Parables? (*This portrays consternation on their part!*)

11 He answered and said unto them (*concerns the Lord's method of dealing with two different classes of people, those who really wanted to know God's Ways and those who were merely curious*), Because it is given unto you to know the mysteries of the Kingdom of Heaven, but to them it is not given (*two categories are here presented; in which category are you?*).

12 For whosoever has (*and wants more*), to him shall be given, and he shall have more abundance (*if one wills Righteousness, the Lord wills more Righteousness to them*): but whosoever has not (*no interest for more*), from him shall be taken away even that he has (*he not only loses what he could have had, but even that which he has; to those who accept the Cross, they will have even more, and to those who reject the Cross, they will lose everything, even that which they previously had*).

13 Therefore speak I to them in Parables (*in order to separate those who hunger and thirst for Righteousness from those who don't*): because they seeing see not; and hearing they hear not, neither do they understand (*that is, they do not wish to see or hear or understand; and hence by a just judgment they lose this triple moral ability*).

14 And in them (*those who reject the Cross [I Cor. 1:23]*) is fulfilled the Prophecy of Isaiah, which says, By hearing ye shall hear, and shall not understand; and seeing ye shall see, and shall not perceive (*a willful deafness, a willful blindness, and a willful dullness; this Passage is quoted in one form or the other some seven times in the New Testament [Mat. 13:14-15; Mk. 4:12; Lk. 8:10; Jn. 12:39-40; Acts 28:26-27; Rom. 11:8]*):

15 For this people's heart is waxed gross (*this is the reason for their spiritual dullness and, therefore, rejection of Christ; Spiritual rejection or acceptance begins in the heart*), and their ears are dull of hearing (*they have heard, and heard, and little acted on what they heard, and the Holy Spirit pulls back until they lose even that which they have had*), and their eyes they have closed (*deliberately did so, even in the face of irrefutable proof*); lest at any time they should see with their eyes, and hear with their ears, and should understand with their heart, and should be converted, and I should heal them (*they would not turn to Him; had they done so He would*

most certainly have healed them morally, and spiritually; this speaks of those who have accepted the Lord, but for various reasons will fall by the wayside; as stated, this completely refutes the unscriptural doctrine of unconditional eternal security).

16 But blessed *are* your eyes, for they see: and your ears, for they hear *(this is the group who desires to know the Lord in an even greater way).*

17 For verily I say unto you *(signals a very important statement)*, That many Prophets and righteous *men* have desired to see *those things* which ye see *(that which Christ presented to Israel, but which were rejected)*, and have not seen *them*; and to hear *those things* which you hear, and have not heard *them (contrasted were the many, who "desired" to see, hear, and to understand).*

PARABLE OF THE SOWER EXPLAINED

18 Hear ye therefore the Parable of the sower *(Christ will now explain it).*

19 When any one hears the Word of the Kingdom *(refers to the Word of God; it speaks of God's Way vs. Satan's way)*, and understands *it* not *(does not refer to one who is incapable of understanding, but instead, to one who has* no desire to understand)*, then cometh the wicked *one (Jesus compares Satan to a vulture)*, and catches away that which was sown in his heart *(refers to Satan being allowed to do such a thing by the individual involved; the initiative does not lie with the Lord or with Satan, but with the person).* This is he which receives seed by the way side *(the word "way side" refers to the fact that the individual doesn't give it credence, i.e., "unbelief").*

20 But he who receives the seed *(Word of God)* into stony places *(refers to the second group)*, the same is he who hears the Word, and anon *(immediately)* with joy receives it *(they make a good start, but then fall by the way side);*

21 Yet has he not root in himself *(refers to the "stony places")*, but endures for a while *(he hears the Word of God, believes it, and accepts Christ; it is all done with joy; but then something else happens)*: for when tribulation or persecution arises because of the Word *(which it definitely will)*, by and by *(immediately)* he is offended *(the offense of the Cross [Gal. 5:11]).*

22 He also who received seed *(the Word of God)* among the thorns is he who hears the Word *(he receives the Word; the soil is fertile and good with plenty depth);*

and the care of this world *(ways of this world)*, and the deceitfulness of riches *(deceitful, simply because the acquiring of such makes a person believe erroneous things)*, choke the Word *(stops its growth)*, and he becomes unfruitful *(such a one is ultimately lost [Jn. 15:2, 6])*.

23 But he who receives seed into the good ground *(prepared ground — ground plowed up by the Spirit of conviction because of sin)* is he who hears the Word *(does so with eagerness)*, and understands it *(he wanted to understand, and the Lord rewards such by giving more understanding)*; which also bears fruit *(Christian growth)*, and brings forth, some an hundredfold, some sixty, some thirty *(the idea is one hundred fold; the Holy Spirit strives to bring the thirty fold and the sixty fold up to a hundredfold [Jn. 15:1-8])*.

THE PARABLE OF THE WHEAT AND TARES

24 Another Parable put He forth unto them, saying *(presents the second Parable)*, The Kingdom of Heaven is likened unto a Man *(Christ)* which sowed good seed *(the Word of God)* in his field *(the world)*:

25 But while men slept *(the Church is often asleep)*, His *(Christ's)* enemy came *(Satan)* and sowed tares *(apostates)* among the wheat *(true Christians)*, and went his way *(Satan works mostly through professed Believers)*.

26 But when the blade was sprung up *(refers to the good seed taking root, growing, and having a healthy start)*, and brought forth fruit *(refers to its intended purpose)*, then appeared the tares also *(the Church has both the true and the false)*.

27 So the servants of the householder came and said unto him *(refers to those who had helped sow the "good seed")*, Sir, did not you sow good seed in your field? from whence then has it tares? *(No tares were sowed, so why are they there.)*

28 He said unto them, An enemy has done this *(refers to Satan and his ministers [II Cor. 11:13-15])*. The servants said unto him, Will you then that we go and gather them up? *(Rid the field of the tares?)*

29 But he said, No; lest while you gather up the tares, ye root up also the wheat with them *(while the tares [false doctrine] were to be pointed out, no force was to be used to take them out of the field; to do so, would be to destroy some wheat)*.

30 Let both grow together until the harvest *(refers to the First Resurrection of Life)*: and in the time of the harvest I will say to the

reapers *(refers to the Lord performing this all-important task, because only He has the wisdom and ability to do)*, Gather ye together first the tares, and bind them in bundles to burn them *(the tares will be eternally lost)*: but gather the wheat into my barn *(refers to those who will be in the First Resurrection [I Thess. 4:13-18])*.

THE PARABLE OF THE MUSTARD SEED

31 Another Parable put He forth unto them, saying *(the third Parable)*, The Kingdom of Heaven is like to a grain of mustard seed *(Word of God)*, which a man took *(Christ)*, and sowed in his field *(the world)*:

32 Which indeed is the least of all seeds *(concerns the small beginnings of the Gospel of Jesus Christ)*: but when it is grown *(which it now is)*, it is the greatest among herbs *(Christianity is the largest faith on Earth, with approximately two billion adherents)*, and becomes a tree *(a mustard bush that becomes a tree is abnormal)*, so that the birds of the air *(all kind of birds, representing all kinds of doctrine)* come and lodge in the branches thereof *(thus in conduct and in doctrine the failure of what is called Christianity is here revealed beforehand)*.

THE PARABLE OF THE LEAVEN

33 Another Parable spoke He unto them *(the fourth)*; The Kingdom of Heaven is like unto leaven *(invariably presented in Scripture as a symbol of evil)*, which a woman took *(frequently in Scripture the woman as well is presented as an agent of idolatry)*, and hid in three measures of meal *(the meal is the Word of God)*, till the whole was leavened *(more tares than wheat)*.

JESUS' USE OF PARABLES

34 All these things spoke Jesus unto the multitude in Parables *(relates only to this segment of His Teaching)*; and without a Parable spoke He not unto them:

35 That it might be fulfilled which was spoken by the Prophet *(Asaph [Ps. 78:2])*, saying, I will open My Mouth in Parables; I will utter things which have been kept secret from the foundation of the world *(refers to Truths which have never before been revealed, but are now given, albeit in shadow; as an example, the Gentiles being brought in)*.

THE PARABLE OF THE WHEAT AND THE TARES EXPLAINED

36 Then Jesus sent the multi-

tude away, and went into the house *(He had been teaching by the seaside, and now goes into Peter's home)*: and His Disciples came unto Him, saying, Declare unto us the Parable of the tares of the field *(a private audience)*.

37 He answered and said unto them, He who sows the good seed *(Word of God)* is the Son of Man *(Christ is the Lord of the Harvest)*;

38 The field is the world *(not just the Jews, which in effect, speaks of the coming Church)*; the good seed are the children of the Kingdom *(refers to true Believers of the Word of God)*; but the tares are the children of the wicked one *(they profess to be children of the Kingdom, but in effect, were Satan's ministers in one way or the other [II Cor. 11:13-15])*;

39 The enemy that sowed them *(bad seed)* is the devil; the harvest is the end of the world *(end of the age; the Judgment)*; and the reapers are the Angels *(the Angels which will come back with Christ, and all redeemed Saints, at the Second Coming [Rev., Chpt. 19])*.

40 As therefore the tares *(bad seed)* are gathered and burned in the fire *(Great White Throne Judgment [Rev. 20:11-15])*; so shall it be in the end of this world *(end of this age)*.

41 The Son of Man shall send forth His Angels, and they shall gather out of His Kingdom *(sepa-*rate the tares from the wheat)* all things that offend, and them which do iniquity *(Great White Throne Judgment)*;

42 And shall cast them into a furnace of fire: there shall be wailing and gnashing of teeth *(the Second Resurrection of Damnation, i.e., "the Second Death" [Rev. 20:11-15])*.

43 Then *(the beginning of the Kingdom Age)* shall the Righteous shine forth as the sun in the Kingdom of their Father *(the perfect age to come [Rev., Chpts. 21-22])*. Who has ears to hear, let him hear *(proclaims the certitude of such action)*.

THE PARABLE OF THE HIDDEN TREASURE

44 Again *(the fifth Parable)*, the Kingdom of Heaven is like unto treasure *(the New Covenant)* hid in a field *(the world)*; the which when a man has found *(the treasure is Christ)*, he hides it, and for joy thereof goes and sells all that he has, and buys that field *(the moral is, Christ is worth more than everything else, and by far)*.

THE PARABLE OF THE PEARL OF GREAT PRICE

45 Again *(the sixth Parable)*, the Kingdom of Heaven is like unto a merchant man, seeking goodly

pearls *(this man is rich, but yet not satisfied, and rightly so; "Pearls" are the only substance which cannot be improved by man; this Pearl represents Christ)*:

46 Who, when he had found one pearl of great price *(this one pearl among many pearls, which was greater than all, i.e., "Christ")*, went and sold all that he had, and bought it *(this Pearl is worth everything, and everything is what it will take to obtain it)*.

THE PARABLE OF THE NET

47 Again *(the seventh Parable)*, the Kingdom of Heaven is like unto a net, that was cast into the sea, and gathered of every kind *(all type of Believers come into the Church)*:

48 Which, when it was full *(when the dispensation of the Church runs its course; it is almost over)*, they drew to shore, and sat down, and gathered the good into vessels, but cast the bad away *(the separation of the tares and the wheat)*.

49 So shall it be at the end of the world *(at the end of the age)*: the Angels shall come forth, and sever the wicked from among the just *(the "just" are those who trust in Christ and the Cross)*,

50 And shall cast them *(the wicked)* into the furnace of fire *(Great White Throne Judgment*

[Rev. 20:11-15]): there shall be wailing and gnashing of teeth.

THE HOUSEHOLDER

51 Jesus said unto them, Have you understood all these things? They say unto Him, Yes, Lord.

52 Then said He unto them, Therefore every Scribe *(all Believers are likened here as Scribes, which means they diligently search the Word of God)* which is instructed *(versed in the Word, which should be all Believers)* unto the Kingdom of Heaven is like unto a man *who is* an householder *(possesses the keys to the Kingdom)*, which brings forth out of his treasure *things* new and old *(can enrich others out of his store of Divine Truth; that Truth as to time is old, i.e., eternal, as to experience, power, and character perpetually new)*.

JESUS REJECTED AT NAZARETH

53 And it came to pass, *that* when Jesus had finished these Parables, He departed thence.

54 And when He was come into His own country *(Nazareth)*, He taught them in their Synagogue *(Lk. 4:16-30)*, insomuch that they were astonished *(rendered speechless)*, and said, Whence has this *Man* this wisdom, and *these* mighty works? *(Meant to cast aspersions*

on Christ.)

55 Is not this the carpenter's son? *(This was a denial of His claim regarding Messiahship.)* is not his mother called Mary? and His brethren, James, and Joses, and Simon, and Judas? *(They were denying as well, His Virgin Birth.)*

56 And His sisters, are they not all with us? Whence then has this *Man* all these things? *(If all of these things were so, they were saying, His family, by now, would have mentioned it.)*

57 And they were offended in Him *(Luke said they were "filled with wrath," and would have killed Him had they been able to do so [Lk. 4:28-30]).* But Jesus said unto them, A Prophet is not without honour, save in his own country, and in his own house *(the last phrase "in his own" is revealing; it proclaims the fact that His own family didn't believe in Him [Jn. 7:5]).*

58 And He did not many mighty works there *(in Nazareth)* because of their unbelief *(they would not bring the sick and afflicted to Him; unbelief was the reason).*

CHAPTER 14

JOHN THE BAPTIST BEHEADED

A T that time Herod the Tetrarch *(the son of Herod who slew the infants of Bethlehem)* heard of the fame of Jesus *(it speaks of the miracles Christ performed, even to the raising of the dead)*,

2 And he said unto his servants, This is John the Baptist *(a guilty conscience)*; he is risen from the dead; and therefore mighty works do shew forth themselves in him.

3 For Herod had laid hold on John, and bound him, and put *him* in prison *(the Castle of Machaerus on the shores of the Dead Sea)* for Herodias' sake, his brother Philip's wife *(refers to the reason John had been arrested by Herod and placed in prison)*.

4 For John said unto him, It is not lawful for you to have her *(Herodias was his niece and the wife of his brother Phillip)*.

5 And when he would have put him to death, he feared the multitude, because they counted him as a prophet.

6 But when Herod's birthday was kept, the daughter of Herodias danced before them, and pleased Herod.

7 Whereupon he promised with an oath to give her whatsoever she would ask.

8 And she, being before instructed of her mother, said, Give me here John Baptist's head in a charger *(the mother of Salome, Herodias, was one of the most*

wicked women who ever lived).

9 And the king was sorry: nevertheless for the oath's sake, and them which sat with him at meat *(a meal)*, he commanded *it* to be given *her (to save face).*

10 And he sent, and beheaded John in the prison.

11 And his head was brought in a charger, and given to the damsel: and she brought *it* to her mother.

12 And his disciples came, and took up the body, and buried it, and went and told Jesus *(the mission of John the Baptist was to introduce Jesus; that he did!).*

JESUS FEEDS THE FIVE THOUSAND

13 When Jesus heard *of it*, He departed thence by ship into a desert place apart *(He was grieved over the death of John, His beloved forerunner; He could have stopped the execution; however, it was not the Will of God to do so)*: and when the people had heard *thereof*, they followed Him on foot out of the cities.

14 And Jesus went forth, and saw a great multitude, and was moved with compassion toward them, and He healed their sick.

15 And when it was evening, His Disciples came to Him, saying, This is a desert place, and the time is now past *(the people had been without food all day, and if they were going to find food, they would need to leave now)*; send the multitude away, that they may go into the villages, and buy themselves victuals.

16 But Jesus said unto them, They need not depart; give ye them to eat *(He was speaking then of the physical sense, but His words carried a higher spiritual cogitation; the Body of Christ is to be fed regarding the Word of God).*

17 And they say unto Him, We have here but five loaves, and two fishes *(little is much if God be in it!).*

18 He said, Bring them hither to Me *(the secret is Christ! we are to bring what little we have to Him).*

19 And He commanded the multitude to sit down on the grass *(this presents order and a method by which the distribution was made)*, and took the five loaves, and the two fishes, and looking up to Heaven, He blessed, and brake, and gave the loaves to *His* Disciples, and the Disciples to the multitude *(He took, He Blessed, He did break, and He gave; that is His order with Believers as well).*

20 And they did all eat, and were filled: and they took up of the fragments that remained twelve baskets full *(an astounding miracle!).*

21 And they who had eaten were about five thousand men,

beside women and children *(possibly as many as fifteen thousand people)*.

JESUS WALKS ON
THE WATER

22 And straightway Jesus constrained *(firmly demanded)* His Disciples to get into a ship, and to go before Him unto the other side *(back to Capernaum)*, while He sent the multitudes away *(but He sent them away, filled both physically and spiritually)*.

23 And when He had sent the multitudes away *(implying that they did not want to leave)*, He went up into a mountain apart to pray *(expresses what He often did [Mat. 26:36; Mk. 6:46; 14:32; Lk. 6:12; 9:28; Jn. 17:9-20])*: and when the evening was come, He was there alone.

24 But the ship was now in the midst of the sea *(concerns not only the Sea of Galilee, but as well, the Sea of Life)*, tossed with waves *(turbulence)*: for the wind was contrary *(difficulties, as well, facing mankind as a result of the Fall)*.

25 And in the fourth watch of the night *(between 3 a.m. and 6 a.m.)* Jesus went unto them *(the Holy Spirit revealed to Him, that they were in trouble)*, walking on the sea *(even though the waters were very turbulent, where He walked, it became calm)*.

26 And when the Disciples saw Him walking on the sea, they were troubled *(it was more than they could grasp)*, saying, It is a spirit *(they did not actually think it was Jesus)*; and they cried out for fear *(they thought they were about to die)*.

27 But straightway *(immediately)* Jesus spoke unto them *(once they saw Him)*, saying, Be of good cheer; it is I; be not afraid *(we are to face adverse circumstances with cheer, knowing the Lord will handle the situation)*.

28 And Peter answered Him and said, Lord, if it be You *(better translated, "since it is You")*, bid Me come unto You on the water.

29 And He *(Jesus)* said, Come *(the Master's response to Faith)*. And when Peter was come down out of the ship, he walked on the water, to go to Jesus.

30 But when he saw the wind boisterous, he was afraid *(he now sees the wind instead of Jesus)*; and beginning to sink, he cried, saying, Lord, save me *(a prayer the Lord will always answer)*.

31 And immediately Jesus stretched forth *His* hand, and caught him *(this prevented him from sinking further)*, and said unto him, O you of little faith, wherefore did you doubt? *(We must not allow circumstances to bring about doubt.)*

32 And when they were come into the ship *(every evidence is,

*after Jesus caught him, Peter walk-
ed on the water the second time),*
the wind ceased *(the power of
Christ over the elements).*

33 Then they who were in the
ship came and worshipped Him
(as God), saying, Of a truth You
are the Son of God *(recognized
Him as the Messiah).*

JESUS HEALS THE SICK

34 And when they were gone
over *(came back to Capernaum),*
they came into the land of Gennesaret *(on the western side of the
Sea of Galilee, somewhat inward).*

35 And when the men of that
place had knowledge of Him
*(knowledge of His presence in their
vicinity),* they sent out into all that
country round about, and brought unto Him all who were diseased;

36 And besought Him that
they might only touch the hem
of His garment: and as many as
touched were made perfectly whole
*(if the Hem of His garment is so
rich with Blessing, how rich must
be His Hand and Heart!).*

CHAPTER 15

JESUS REBUKES THE
SCRIBES AND PHARISEES

THEN came to Jesus Scribes
and Pharisees, which were of
Jerusalem, saying *(almost all of
the opposition to Christ came from
religious leaders),*

2 Why do your Disciples
transgress the tradition of the elders? *(Their confidence was in their
man-made rules rather then the
Word of God.)* for they wash not
their hands when they eat bread
*(had no sanitary meaning; this tra-
dition taught that an evil spirit could
sit on the hands of people, and when
the hands were washed, the evil spirit
would be removed).*

3 But He answered and said
unto them *(proclaims Christ drawing them back to the Word of God),*
Why do you also transgress the
Commandment of God by your
tradition? *(He ignored their tradition because it was not Scriptural.
He then tells them that their traditions were causing them to transgress the Commandment of God.)*

4 For God commanded, say-
ing, Honour your father and
mother: and, He who curses father or mother, let him die the
death *(Ex. 20:12; 21:17).*

5 But you say *(in direct contradiction to what God commanded),* Whosoever shall say to *his*
father or *his* mother, It is a gift
*(dedicate their estate to the Temple
so that they wouldn't have to take
care of their aged parents, and a
crooked Priest would then give it
back to them, after taking a percentage),* by whatsoever you

might be profited by Me *(making an illegal profit off of God, which compounded their sin)*;

6 And honour not his father or his mother, *he shall be free (free from responsibility)*. Thus have you made the Commandment of God of none effect by your tradition.

7 You *(was said to their faces)* hypocrites, well did Isaiah prophesy of you, saying,

8 This people draw near unto Me with their mouth, and honor Me with *their* lips; but their heart is far from Me *(this defines the hypocrite)*.

9 But in vain they do worship Me *(worship that was not accepted by God indicative of much of the modern Church as well!)*, teaching *for* doctrines the commandments of men *(anything that adds to or takes away from the Word of God)*.

THE THINGS THAT DEFILE

10 And He called the multitude, and said unto them *(did so in front of the Scribes and Pharisees)*, Hear, and understand *(what He will now say, will be the opposite said by the Scribes and Pharisees)*:

11 Not that which goes into the mouth defiles a man; but that which comes out of the mouth, this defiles a man *(Christ draws the minds of the people away from externals to the true condition of the heart)*.

12 Then came His Disciples, and said unto Him *(concerns a time of private contemplation regarding the things said by Christ)*, Do you not know that the Pharisees were offended *(scandalized)*, after they heard this saying? *(As one divine of old said, "if offence arises from the statement of the Truth, it is more expedient that offence be permitted to arise than that the Truth should be abandoned.")*

13 But He answered and said *(He did not remain silent, but further proclaimed His position)*, Every plant, which My Heavenly Father has not planted, shall be rooted up *(means that the doctrine of the Pharisees was not of divine origin, but of earthly origin; the day is coming when the tares will be removed from among the wheat)*.

14 Let them alone *(does not mean to not address their error, but means that them being offended is not to be a deterrent to preaching the Truth)*: they be blind leaders of the blind *(a designation applied to all who were not following the Word of God)*. And if the blind lead the blind, both shall fall into the ditch *(a guaranteed ultimate conclusion)*.

15 Then answered Peter and said unto him, Declare unto us this parable *(give us more explanation)*.

16 And Jesus said, Are you also yet without understanding? *(The great reason for the need to be filled with the Spirit, and led by the Spirit [Rom. 8:14].)*

17 Do you not yet understand, that whatsoever enters in at the mouth goes into the belly, and is cast out into the draught? *(Proclaims the fact that the eating of food has nothing to do with the spiritual side of man.)*

18 But those things which proceed out of the mouth come forth from the heart; and they defile the man *(not everything that comes out of the mouth of a man is defiling, but only that which proceeds from an evil heart).*

19 For out of the heart proceed evil thoughts, murders, adulteries, fornications, thefts, false witness, blasphemies *(this proclaims the depravity of the unconverted human heart, which was the condition of the Pharisees, despite their religiosity):*

20 These are *the things* which defile a man: but to eat with unwashed hands defile not a man *(Satan is a master at placing the emphasis on the insignificant, instead of the real problem).*

THE HEALING OF THE DAUGHTER OF THE CANAANITE

21 Then Jesus went thence *(left Capernaum)*, and departed into the coasts *(borders)* of Tyre and Sidon.

22 And, behold, a woman of Canaan *(a Gentile)* came out of the same coasts *(borders)*, and cried unto Him *(the woman was desperate)*, saying, Have mercy on me, O Lord, *Thou* Son of David; my daughter is grievously vexed with a devil *(demon).*

23 But He answered her not a word *(being a Gentile, her petition was wrong, addressing Him as "Son of David"; only the Jews were then privileged to use that term).* And His Disciples came and besought Him, saying, Send her away; for she crieth after us *(better translated, "do something for her").*

24 But He answered and said, I am not sent but unto the lost sheep of the house of Israel *(His Mission, at least in His First Advent, was exclusively to the Jews).*

25 Then came she and worshipped Him, saying, Lord, help me *(her position is now beginning to change!).*

26 But He answered and said, It is not meet *(appropriate)* to take the children's bread *(that which belonged to the Jews)*, and to cast it to dogs *(Gentiles were looked at as "dogs," so in effect, He was testing her faith).*

27 And she said, Truth, Lord: yet the dogs eat of the crumbs

which fall from their masters' table *(when she took the place of a "dog," thus admitting that she had no claim, throwing herself on His Grace as Lord, He at once responded, just as He will presently).*

28 Then Jesus answered and said unto her, O woman, great *is* your faith: be it unto you even as you will. And her daughter was made whole from that very hour *(the Lord always responds to faith; only two people are spoken of as having "great Faith"; the first was the Gentile Centurion [Mat. 8:5-10], and now this Gentile woman).*

JESUS HEALS THE SICK

29 And Jesus departed from thence, and came near unto the Sea of Galilee; and went up into a mountain, and sat down there *(probably on the northeast side of the Sea of Galilee).*

30 And great multitudes came unto Him *(could have been several thousands of people),* having with them *those who were* lame, blind, dumb, maimed, and many others, and cast them down at Jesus' feet; and he healed them *(He healed them all)*:

31 Insomuch that the multitude wondered, when they saw the dumb to speak, the maimed to be whole, the lame to walk, and the blind to see: and they glorified the God of Israel.

JESUS FEEDS FOUR THOUSAND

32 Then Jesus called *His Disciples unto Him,* and said, I have compassion on the multitude, because they continue with Me now three days, and have nothing to eat: and I will not send them away fasting, lest they faint in the way *(probably ten thousand or more, had had very little to eat in the last three days and nights).*

33 And His Disciples say unto Him, Where should we get so much bread in the wilderness, as to fill so great a multitude? *(Did they not remember the great miracle He performed a short time before of this same nature? How so quick we are to forget as well!)*

34 And Jesus said unto them, How many loaves have you? And they said, Seven, and a few little fishes.

35 And He commanded the multitude to sit down on the ground.

36 And He took the seven loaves and the fishes, and gave thanks, and broke *them,* and gave to His Disciples, and the Disciples to the multitude *(the Disciples had to keep coming to Jesus for fresh supplies for the need of the multitude; they had no resources of their own; they were dependent totally upon Him; this is what He is teaching us).*

37 And they did all eat, and were filled *(satisfied)*: and they took up of the broken *meat* that was left seven baskets full.

38 And they who did eat were four thousand men, beside women and children *(probably near ten thousand people)*.

39 And He sent away the multitude *(but sent them away filled physically, and spiritually)*, and took ship, and came into the coasts of Magdala *(a small town located about ten miles south of Capernaum)*.

CHAPTER 16

JESUS REBUKES
THE PHARISEES

THE Pharisees also with the Sadducees came *(proclaims the joining of these two groups who were normally antagonistic to each other)*, and tempting desired Him that He would show them a sign from Heaven *(they wanted Him to call fire down from Heaven, as did Elijah; but they would not accept the recent feeding of the thousands with seven loaves and a few fish)*.

2 He answered and said unto them *(His answer to them shows the hostility of the natural heart)*, When it is evening, you say, *It will be* fair weather: for the sky is red.

3 And in the morning, *It will be* foul weather to day: for the sky is red and lowring. O *ye* hypocrites, you can discern the face of the sky; but can you not *discern* the signs of the times?

4 A wicked and adulterous generation seeks after a sign *(regrettably, this characterizes this present generation as well)*; and there shall no sign be given unto it, but the sign of the Prophet Jonah *(Jesus was sent from Heaven, but they would not accept Him; He was the greatest sign of all)*. And He left them, and departed *(He departed both physically and spiritually)*.

5 And when His Disciples were come to the other side *(from the western shore of the Sea of Galilee, to the northeastern shore)*, they had forgotten to take bread.

THE LEAVEN

6 Then Jesus said unto them, Take heed and beware of the leaven *(false doctrine)* of the Pharisees and of the Sadducees.

7 And they reasoned among themselves *(shows an appalling lack of Scriptural and Spiritual knowledge)*, saying, It is because we have taken no bread.

8 *Which* when Jesus perceived, He said unto them *(the Holy Spirit told Him what they were "reasoning")*, O you of little faith *(Faith in Christ and the Cross is the one*

necessary ingredient), why reason you among yourselves, because you have brought no bread?

9 Do you not yet understand *(the insensibility of the Disciples to the Lord's actions and to His teaching, is a humiliating proof of the darkness of man's heart to moral realities)*, neither remember the five loaves of the five thousand, and how many baskets you took up?

10 Neither the seven loaves of the four thousand, and how many baskets you took up?

11 How is it that you do not understand that I spoke *it* not to you concerning bread *(bread that one can eat)*, that you should beware of the leaven of the Pharisees and of the Sadducees? *(Is meant to censure their want of spiritual discernment.)*

12 Then understood they how that He bade *them* not beware of the leaven of bread, but of the doctrine of the Pharisees and of the Sadducees.

PETER'S CONFESSION

13 When Jesus came into the coasts *(borders)* of Caesarea Philippi *(about thirty miles north of the Sea of Galilee)*, He asked His Disciples, saying, Whom do men say that I the Son of Man am? *(The third form of unbelief manifested itself in popular indif-* ference, indolence, or mere curiosity respecting the Messiah Himself. Upon the answer to this all-important question, hinges the Salvation of man.)*

14 And they said, Some *say that you are* John the Baptist: some, Elijah; and others, Jeremiah, or one of the Prophets *(this form of unbelief manifests itself in the frivolity of the natural heart)*.

15 He said unto them, But whom say you that I am? *(Addressed personally to the Twelve.)*

16 And Simon Peter answered and said, You are the Christ, the Son of the Living God *(the Great Confession)*.

17 And Jesus answered and said unto him, Blessed are you, Simon Bar–jona *(Peter is the son of Jonah, as Jesus is the Son of God)*: for flesh and blood have not revealed *it* unto you *(mere human ingenuity)*, but My Father which is in Heaven *(all spiritual knowledge must be by revelation)*.

18 And I say also unto you, That you are Peter *(the Lord changed his name from Simon to Peter, which means "a fragment of a rock")*, and upon this rock *(immovable mass; Jesus is the Living Rock on which the Redeemed as living stones are built; for other foundation can no man lay [I Cor. 3:11])* I will build My Church *(the Church belongs to Christ, and He is the Head [Col. 1:18])*; and the

gates of hell shall not prevail against it *(the power of death caused by sin, shall not prevail against it, which victory was won at the Cross [Vss. 21, 24])*.

19 And I will give unto you *("you" refers to all Believers)* the keys of the Kingdom of Heaven *(refers to symbols of authority, the privilege of preaching or proclaiming the Gospel, which is the privilege of every Believer)*: and whatsoever you shall bind on earth shall be bound in Heaven *(Christ has given the authority and power to every Believer to bind Satan and his minions of darkness, and to do so by using the Name of Jesus [Mk. 16:17-18; Lk. 10:19])*: and whatsoever you shall loose on earth shall be loosed in Heaven *(looses the Power of God according to the usage of the Name of Jesus; this is the authority of the Believer)*.

20 Then charged He *(Commanded)* His Disciples that they should tell no man that He was Jesus the Christ *(the Name as used here, is a proclamation of Messiahship; by this time, it is painfully obvious that Israel has rejected her Messiah, and therefore, any further proclamation is pointless!)*.

JESUS FORETELLS HIS DEATH AND RESURRECTION

21 From that time forth began Jesus to show unto His Disciples, how that He must go unto Jerusalem, and suffer many things of the Elders and Chief Priests and Scribes, and be killed, and be raised again the third day *(His sufferings, and the glories that should follow are always associated in Scripture [I Pet. 1:11; 4:13]; the Cross was ever His destination, the very reason He came; the Resurrection was never in doubt)*.

22 Then Peter took Him, and began to rebuke Him *(Peter chides Jesus for speaking of suffering and death; regrettably, many Preachers continue to do the same, as they reject the Cross)*, saying, Be it far from You, Lord: this shall not be unto You *(at that time Peter, nor any of the Disciples, understood the Cross as it regarded its necessity)*.

23 But He turned, and said unto Peter *(respects strong action; would be the sternest of rebukes)*, Get thee behind Me, Satan *(Jesus used nearly the same words in rebuking Peter, and the other Disciples that He had used to the Devil, and His temptation [4:10]; all denial of the Cross in any form, is of Satan)*: you are an offence unto Me *(speaks directly to Peter, because he is now being used by Satan)*: for you savor not the things that be of God, but those that be of men *(if it's not the Cross, then it's of men, which means it is of Satan)*.

24 Then said Jesus unto His Disciples, If any *man* will come after Me, let him deny himself *(not asceticism, but rather the denial of one's own strength and ability)*, and take up his cross *(the benefits of the Cross, what Jesus did there [Col. 2:14-15])*, and follow Me *(if Christ is not followed by the means of the Cross, He cannot be followed at all)*.

25 For whosoever will save his life shall lose it *(tries to live his life outside of Christ and the Cross; it can only be lived in Christ through the Cross)*: and whosoever will lose his life for My sake shall find it *(lose his life to Christ, which means to give his life to Christ, which can only be done through the Cross; he then finds "newness of life" [Rom. 6:3-5])*.

26 For what is a man profited, if he shall gain the whole world, and lose his own soul? *(Christ refers here to "gain" and "loss.")* or what shall a man give in exchange for his soul? *(Nothing is more important than the soul, because it is eternal.)*

27 For the Son of Man shall come in the Glory of His Father with His Angels *(while the Son must suffer, nevertheless, Glory will follow; He speaks here of the Second Coming)*; and then He shall reward every man according to his works *("every man" refers first of all to the Saints and the Judgment Seat of Christ, where rewards will be handed out, and to the unredeemed at the Great White Throne Judgment, where eternal damnation will be meted out [Rev. 20:11-15])*.

28 Verily I say unto you, There be some standing here, which shall not taste of death, till they see the Son of Man coming in His Kingdom *(refers to the Transfiguration of Christ, which would take place in a few hours, and would be observed by Peter, James, and John)*.

CHAPTER 17

THE TRANSFIGURATION

AND after six days *(is exclusive, meaning, that all the days and time are not included; Luke said, "about eight days," but is inclusive, meaning that everything is included)* Jesus took Peter, James, and John his brother, and brought them up into an high mountain apart *(does not tell us which mountain; "apart" from the other Disciples)*,

2 And was transfigured before them *(means that the Glory did not shine upon Jesus, but instead, shone out from Him through His raiment)*: and His Face did shine as the sun *(Rev. 1:16)*, and His Raiment was white as the light *(the light made it white)*.

3 And, behold, there appeared unto them Moses and Elijah talking with Him (*Moses and Elijah represented the Law and the Prophets, the dead, and raptured Saints; they spoke with Him of His Atoning Death [Lk. 9:31]; this doctrine is the great theme of Heaven [Rev. 1:5; 5:6, 9; 7:14]*).

4 Then answered Peter, and said unto Jesus, Lord, it is good for us to be here: if you will, let us make here three Tabernacles; one for You, and one for Moses, and one for Elijah (*God will not have even the greatest Saints associated with His Beloved Son in worship or teaching*).

5 While He yet spoke, behold, a bright cloud overshadowed them (*this was a demonstration of the Shechinah, a token of the presence of the Most High, which had appeared over the Tabernacle in the wilderness*): and behold a Voice out of the cloud (*the "cloud" overshadowing them was a fore-view of the Work of the Holy Spirit after the Day of Pentecost in glorifying Christ [Jn. 16:14]*), which said, This is My Beloved Son, in Whom I am well pleased (*we have here the Trinity, the Voice out of the cloud, which was the Father, Jesus, standing in a radiant light, and the Holy Spirit present with the overshadowing cloud*); hear ye Him (*Hear Him Alone; everything comes through Christ, and what Christ did at the Cross; the Holy Spirit works accordingly [Rom. 8:2]*).

6 And when the Disciples heard it, they fell on their face, and were sore afraid (*the words, "sore afraid," meant that they were fearful that they would die*).

7 And Jesus came and touched them, and said, Arise, and be not afraid (*ever the Voice of the Saviour to those who are truly sincere, but yet wrong*).

8 And when they had lifted up their eyes (*proclaims them earnestly surveying the locality*), they saw no man, save Jesus only (*everything hinges on Jesus, and what He did at the Cross*).

9 And as they came down from the mountain, Jesus charged them (*Commanded them*), saying, Tell the Vision to no man, until the Son of Man be risen again from the dead (*as stated, due to the Victory of the Cross, the Resurrection was never in doubt*).

JOHN THE BAPTIST AND ELIJAH

10 And His Disciples asked Him, saying, Why then say the Scribes that Elijah must first come? (*They were referring to Malachi 4:5. As well, they were confusing the First and the Second Comings.*)

11 And Jesus answered and said unto them, Elijah truly shall first come, and restore all things

(Christ speaks here of Elijah who will come in the middle of the Great Tribulation, heralding the Second Coming [Rev., Chpt. 11]).

12 But I say unto you, That Elijah is come already, and they knew him not, but have done unto him whatsoever they listed *(had Israel received John the Baptist, they would have received Christ, and John would have been Elijah to Jerusalem at that time, because he came in the spirit and power of Elijah [Lk. 1:17]).* Likewise shall also the Son of Man suffer of them *(Jesus once again predicts the Cross; nine passages in this Gospel foretell the Crucifixion [16:21; 17:12, 22; 20:17-19, 28; 26:20, 28, 31, 45]).*

13 Then the Disciples understood that He spoke unto them of John the Baptist.

THE DISCIPLES' LACK OF POWER

14 And when they were come to the multitude *(to the foot of the mountain)*, there came to Him a *certain* man, kneeling down to Him, and saying,

15 Lord, have mercy on my son: for he is lunatic, and sore vexed: for ofttimes he falls into the fire, and often into the water *(caused by a demon spirit).*

16 And I brought him to Your Disciples, and they could not cure him *(the inadequacy of man, even believing man).*

17 Then Jesus answered and said, O faithless and perverse generation *(wrong direction)*, how long shall I be with you? how long shall I suffer you? *(Perturbed at the lack of faith on the part of His Disciples.)* bring him hither to Me.

18 And Jesus rebuked the devil *(demon)*; and he departed out of him: and the child was cured from that very hour *(the Word of Christ is such that demons must obey).*

PRAYER AND FASTING

19 Then came the Disciples to Jesus apart *(privately)*, and said, Why could not we cast him out?

20 And Jesus said unto them, Because of your unbelief *(improper understanding regarding Christ and the Cross)*: for verily I say unto you, If you have faith as a grain of mustard seed *(symbolism)*, you shall say unto this mountain, Remove hence to yonder place; and it shall remove *(the impossible made possible)*; and nothing shall be impossible unto you *(that which is the Will of God).*

21 Howbeit this kind goes not out but by prayer and fasting *(the fasted life [Lk. 9:23-24]).*

AGAIN FORETELLS DEATH AND RESURRECTION

22 And while they abode in

Galilee, Jesus said unto them *(lends credence to the thought that it was Mount Tabor, which was in Galilee, where the Transfiguration took place)*, The Son of Man shall be betrayed into the hands of men *(draws the Disciples back to the Mission at hand; that Mission was the Redemption of humanity, which would require the offering of the perfect Sacrifice, which was His Body)*:

23 And they shall kill Him *(but only because He allowed such [Jn. 10:17-18])*, and the third day He shall be raised again *(Resurrection)*. And they were exceeding sorry *(but still without understanding)*.

MIRACULOUS PROVISION

24 And when they were come to Capernaum, they that received tribute *money* came to Peter, and said, Does not your master pay tribute? *(Temple tax, of about a half shekel per person, required of every Jew yearly [Ex. 30:13].)*

25 He *(Peter)* said, Yes. And when he was come into the house, Jesus prevented *(confronted)* him, saying, What do you think, Simon? *(Revealed by the Spirit, Jesus questions Peter even before Peter broaches the subject.)* of whom do the kings of the earth take custom or tribute? of their own children, or of strangers? *(Assumes the an-*

swer.)

26 Peter said unto him, Of strangers *(the correct answer)*. Jesus said unto him, Then are the children free *(Jesus was Lord of the Temple, therefore, did not owe the tax, nor His Disciples)*.

27 Notwithstanding, lest we should offend them *(proclaims Him paying the tax, even though not owed, in order that His enemies not have any occasion against Him)*, go thou to the sea *(Galilee)*, and cast an hook, and take up the fish that first comes up; and when you have opened his mouth, you shall find a piece of money: that take, and give unto them from Me and you *(it was a shekel, which was enough to pay the tax for both Peter and Christ)*.

CHAPTER 18

JESUS EXPLAINS GREATNESS

A T the same time came the Disciples unto Jesus *(probably in the home of Peter)*, saying, Who is the greatest in the Kingdom of Heaven? *(Jesus addresses wrong attitudes.)*

2 And Jesus called a little child unto Him, and set him in the midst of them *(the single greatest lesson taught by Christ)*,

3 And He said, Verily I say unto you, Except you be con-

verted *(born-again)*, and become as little children *(a child is totally dependent on its parents, and Believers must be as dependent on Christ)*, you shall not enter into the Kingdom of Heaven *(failure of total dependence on Christ and the Cross, will pull one into unbelief, and, thereby, a lost condition)*.

4 Whosoever *(no exceptions to this rule)* therefore shall humble himself as this little child *(requirement for greatness)*, the same is greatest in the Kingdom of Heaven *(direct opposite of the standard of the world)*.

5 And whoso shall receive one such little child in My Name receives Me *(Believers who depend on self, will not accept the Cross, for this is what this means, and therefore, will not receive such a one who does [Lk. 9:27-28])*.

THE SERIOUSNESS OF OFFENCES

6 But whoso shall offend one of these little ones which believe in Me *(doesn't refer to weak Christians as some believe, but rather to those who trust Christ and the Cross exclusively)*, it were better for him that a millstone were hanged about his neck, and *that* he were drowned in the depth of the sea *(Christ again uses symbolism)*.

7 Woe unto the world because of offences! *(Offences against true Believers.)* for it must needs be that offences come *(due to the Fall)*; but woe to that man by whom the offence cometh! *(All who touch true Believers touch Christ.)*

8 Wherefore if your hand or your foot offend you, cut them off, and cast *them* from you *(symbolism)*: it is better for you to enter into life halt or maimed, rather than having two hands or two feet to be cast into everlasting fire *(while not offending true Believers will not save one, offending them will definitely bring about the most serious degree of punishment in eternity)*.

9 And if your eye offend you, pluck it out, and cast *it* from you: it is better for you to enter into life with one eye, rather than having two eyes to be cast into hell fire *(Christ continues to use symbolism)*.

10 Take heed that you despise not one of these little ones *(one who trusts in Christ and the Cross)*; for I say unto you, That in Heaven their Angels do always behold the Face of My Father which is in Heaven *(every true Believer is assigned an Angel, who reports to the Heavenly Father, any and all things pertaining to that Believer)*.

THE LOST SHEEP

11 For the Son of Man is come

to save that which was lost *(Salvation was paid for at great price; therefore, all who accept that Salvation become the property of God the Father [I Cor. 6:20])*.

12 How do you think? if a man has an hundred sheep, and one of them be gone astray, does he not leave the ninety and nine, and go into the mountains *(proclaims the extensive efforts of the Lord to find the lost one)*, and seeks that which is gone astray? *(Proves that Believers can go astray, and therefore, refutes the unscriptural doctrine of unconditional eternal security.)*

13 And if so be that he find it *(proclaims the fact, that it is possible, that the sheep be not found)*, verily I say unto you, he rejoices more of that *sheep*, than of the ninety and nine which went not astray *(is not meant to place any approval on the straying, but instead, on being found; such proclaims a great victory over Satan)*.

14 Even so it is not the will of your Father which is in Heaven, that one of these little ones should perish *(proclaims the fact that a Believer can cease to believe, and therefore, become an unbeliever; if so, such a one will be lost; this shows the preciousness of the soul)*.

DISPUTES AMONG BELIEVERS

15 Moreover if your brother *(brother in the Lord)* shall trespass against you *(sin against you)*, go and tell him his fault between you and him alone: if he shall hear you, you have gained your brother *(the way to settle disputes)*.

16 But if he will not hear *you*, *then* take with you one or two more, that in the mouth of two or three witnesses every word may be established *(in the hearing of impartial witnesses)*.

17 And if he shall neglect to hear them, tell *it* unto the Church *(Elders of the Church)*: but if he neglect to hear the Church, let him be unto you as an heathen man and a publican *(there can be no fellowship)*.

THE POWER OF BELIEVERS

18 Verily I say unto you, Whatsoever you shall bind on Earth shall be bound in Heaven: and whatsoever you shall loose on Earth shall be loosed in Heaven *(if the Believer conducts himself Scripturally, the decision reached will be honored and ratified in Heaven)*.

THE POWER OF UNITED PRAYER

19 Again I say unto you, That if two of you shall agree on earth as touching any thing that they shall ask, it shall be done for them of My Father which is in

Heaven (*"anything" is conditional on it being the Will of God; God will never allow His Word to be used against Himself*).

20 For where two or three are gathered together in My Name, there am I in the midst of them (*the requirement is to meet in His Name; doing such by even two or three, in the Eyes of God, constitute a "Church"*).

FORGIVENESS

21 Then came Peter to Him, and said, Lord, how often shall my brother sin against me, and I forgive him? till seven times? (*One of the most important questions asked by any Disciple.*)

22 Jesus said unto him, I say not unto you, Until seven times: but, Until seventy times seven (*there must be unlimited forgiveness [Lk. 17:4]*).

23 Therefore is the Kingdom of Heaven likened unto a certain king, which would take account of his servants (*a Parable illustrating the principle of forgiveness*).

24 And when he had begun to reckon (*to check the books*), one was brought unto him, which owed him ten thousand talents (*if in gold, it represented approximately four billion dollars; if silver, it represented approximately eighty million dollars; a tremendous sum to say the least!*).

25 But forasmuch as he couldn't pay, his lord commanded him to be sold, and his wife, and children, and all that he had, and payment to be made (*this represents the sinner who cannot hope to pay such a staggering amount, no matter what he does!*).

26 The servant therefore fell down, and worshipped him, saying, Lord, have patience with me, and I will pay you all (*he couldn't pay such a vast debt, and neither can we, which is meant to illustrate that which we owe to God*).

27 Then the lord of that servant was moved with compassion, and loosed him, and forgave him the debt (*to forgive one, is at the same time, to loose him*).

28 But the same servant went out, and found one of his fellow-servants, which owed him an hundred pence (*represents about three hundred dollars*): and he laid hands on him, and took *him* by the throat, saying, Pay me that you owe (*he did not show the compassion that had been shown him; it becomes more heinous when one considers the difference in the debt*).

29 And his fellow-servant fell down at his feet, and besought him, saying, Have patience with me, and I will pay you all (*basically says the same thing, as the first debtor had said*).

30 And he would not (*would

not forgive him the three hundred dollars): but went and cast him into prison, till he should pay the debt *(which means that him being in prison makes it virtually impossible for him to pay the debt; so he will likely stay there until he dies)*.

31 So when his fellow-servants saw what was done, they were very sorry, and came and told unto their lord all that was done *(to be sure, the Lord always knows what was done)*.

32 Then his lord *(Christ is Lord of all)*, after that he had called him *(the one he had forgiven the ten thousand talents)*, said unto him, O you wicked servant, I forgave you all that debt, because you desired it of me *(unforgiveness of others is wicked, and puts one in the category of a "wicked servant")*:

33 Should not you also have had compassion on your fellow-servant, even as I had pity on you? *(We must never forget how much the Lord has forgiven us, and likewise, show the same spirit toward others, who owe us much less than we owe the Lord.)*

34 And his lord was wroth *(angry)*, and delivered him to the tormentors, till he should pay all that was due unto him *(lack of forgiveness of others revokes the forgiveness of God to us; a sobering thought!)*.

35 So likewise shall My Heavenly Father do also unto you, if you from your hearts forgive not every one his brother their trespasses *(true forgiveness comes from the heart, and God knows when it is true)*.

CHAPTER 19

JESUS SPEAKS CONCERNING DIVORCE

AND it came to pass, *that* when Jesus had finished these sayings, He departed from Galilee, and came into the coasts *(borders)* of Judaea beyond Jordan *(He would not come back; it was His farewell to the scene of most of His Miracles and Ministry)*;

2 And great multitudes followed Him; and He healed them there *(the multitudes trusted Him; the Pharisees tempted Him)*.

3 The Pharisees also came unto Him, tempting Him *(trying to trap Him)*, and saying unto Him, Is it lawful for a man to put away his wife for every cause? *(The question of divorce and re-marriage was the overriding question in Israel of that particular time.)*

4 And He answered and said unto them, Have you not read, that He *(God)* which made *them* at the beginning made them male and female *(destroys the theory of evolution; Jesus was actually the*

Creator *[Jn. 1:1-3])*,

5 And said, For this cause shall a man leave father and mother, and shall cleave to his wife: and they twain shall be one flesh? *(Proclaims God as the founder of marriage, which makes it a Divine institution.)*

6 Wherefore they are no more twain *(two)*, but one flesh *(God looks at a man and his wife not as two, but instead "one")*. What therefore God has joined together, let not man put asunder *(the Will of the Lord is to be sought regarding marriage; however, God recognizes the institution of marriage whether His Will or not)*.

7 They say unto Him, Why did Moses then command to give a writing of divorcement, and to put her away *(Deut. 24:1-2)*?

8 He said unto them, Moses because of the hardness of your hearts suffered you to put away your wives: but from the beginning it was not so *(divorce is not the Will of God; regarding a Christian husband and wife, there are no true grounds for divorce — if both conduct themselves Scripturally, there will never be a need for divorce)*.

9 And I say unto you, Whosoever shall put away his wife, except *it be* for fornication *(an adulterous lifestyle)*, and shall marry another, commits adultery: and whoso marries her which is put away doth commit adultery *(if the marriage is dissolved for Scriptural grounds — fornication or desertion [I Cor. 7:15], remarriage is Scripturally allowed)*.

10 His Disciples say unto Him, If the case of the man be so with *his* wife, it is not good to marry *(their thinking was wrong [Prov. 18:22])*.

11 But He said unto them, All *men* cannot receive this saying, save *they* to whom it is given *(in effect, Christ is saying that all should marry, save the few who are called of God to do otherwise; the next Verse tells us what that is)*.

12 For there are some eunuchs, which were so born from *their* mother's womb *(accident of birth — no sex drive whatsoever)*: and there are some eunuchs, which were made eunuchs of men *(castrated, in order to serve the State, which was a custom then)*: and there be eunuchs, which have made themselves eunuchs for the Kingdom of Heaven's sake *(personal resolve, were not castrated, as the Apostle Paul)*. He who is able to receive *it*, let him receive *it (refers to the last group, and speaks of those called of the Lord for such a task, which would be few)*.

JESUS BLESSES LITTLE CHILDREN

13 Then were there brought

unto Him little children, that He should put *His* hands on them, and pray: and the Disciples rebuked them *(a number of women, hearing the teaching on the sanctity of marriage as given by Christ, brought their children to Jesus for Him to Bless them; their intelligence was higher than that of the Disciples, who tried to prevent this action).*

14 But Jesus said, Suffer little children, and forbid them not, to come unto Me: for of such is the Kingdom of Heaven *(children are dependent on parents; Believers are to be totally dependent on Christ, of which children are an example).*

15 And he laid *His* hands on them, and departed thence.

THE RICH YOUNG RULER

16 And, behold, one came and said unto Him, Good Master *(addressed Him merely as a teacher),* what good thing shall I do, that I may have eternal life? *("Doing" is not the answer, but rather, "believing" [Jn. 3:16].)*

17 And He said unto him, Why do you call Me good? *(You don't recognize Me as God.) there* is none good but one, *that is,* God *(Jesus wasn't saying that He wasn't good; in fact, He definitely was good, because He is God):* but if you will enter into life, keep the Commandments *(is meant to answer the man on the same grounds, which*

he has asked — *the grounds of good works! He will show him that he, in fact, cannot attain to Eternal Life by "keeping Commandments," i.e., "good works").*

18 He said unto him, Which? *(A ridiculous question!)* Jesus said, you shall not commit murder, you shall not commit adultery, you shall not steal, you shall not bear false witness *(Jesus didn't say keep one Commandment, but rather all of them, which the man had not done, nor any other man for that matter — except Christ),*

19 Honour your father and *your* mother: and, you shall love your neighbour as yourself *(this latter Commandment is taken from Leviticus 19:18; it was not a part of the original Ten, but actually summed up all the Commandments, which dealt with one's fellow man).*

20 The young man said unto Him, All these things have I kept from my youth up *(he was mistaken; he had not):* what lack I yet? *(This question proclaims the fact that something was wrong.)*

21 Jesus said unto him, If you will be perfect, go *and* sell that you have, and give to the poor, and you shall have treasure in Heaven: and come *and* follow Me *(Jesus put His finger on the two great Commandments of the Law and said: "If you love your neighbor as yourself, then share your wealth with him; and if you love*

Jehovah your God with all your heart, then follow Me, for one only is good, that is God, and I am He").

22 But when the young man heard that saying, he went away sorrowful: for he had great possessions *(the Gospel makes mad, sad, or glad; Naaman went away in a rage; the rich ruler went away sorrowful; but Zacchaeus received Christ joyfully)*.

A WARNING TO THE RICH

23 Then said Jesus unto His Disciples, Verily I say unto you, That a rich man shall hardly enter into the Kingdom of Heaven *(this was contrary to Jewish doctrine, for they taught that riches signified God's approval)*.

24 And again I say unto you, It is easier for a camel to go through the eye of a needle, than for a rich man to enter into the Kingdom of God *(it is impossible for a camel to go through the eye of a needle, and it is equally impossible for the most deeply religious man to enter Heaven on the principle of merit)*.

25 When His Disciples heard it, they were exceedingly amazed, saying, Who then can be saved? *(Entrance into the Kingdom of God by man as man, however cultivated and moral, is here declared by the Infallible Judge to be impossible.)*

26 But Jesus beheld *them*, and said unto them, With men this is impossible; but with God all things are possible *(so then what cannot be obtained by merit may be received by gift; for the Gift of God is eternal life [Rom. 6:23])*.

REWARDS FOR CONSECRATION

27 Then answered Peter and said unto Him, Behold, we have forsaken all, and followed you; what shall we have therefore? *(This proclaims the fact that it is just as hard for the poor man to leave his little house as it is for the rich noble to forsake his great palace.)*

28 And Jesus said unto them, Verily I say unto you, That you which have followed Me, in the regeneration *(the Millennium)* when the Son of Man shall sit in the throne of His glory *(during the coming Kingdom Age Jesus will reign Personally from Jerusalem and, in effect, govern the entirety of the world)*, you also shall sit upon twelve thrones, judging the twelve tribes of Israel *(this graphically answers the question posed by Peter; they had exchanged a little fishing boat for a Kingdom; it pays to live for God)*.

29 And every one who has forsaken houses, or brethren, or sisters, or father, or mother, or wife, or children, or lands, for My Name's sake, shall receive an hundredfold *(Mark added, "now in*

this time" [Mk. 10:30] Christ meant exactly what He said, but we must take everything into account), and shall inherit everlasting life *(this is freely given on acceptance of Christ [Rom. 6:23]).*

30 But many *who are* first shall be last; and the last *shall be* first *(Israel was "first" and the "Church" is last in relation to time, but in respect to position the last shall be first).*

CHAPTER 20

THE PARABLE OF THE LABORERS

FOR the Kingdom of Heaven is like unto a man *who is* an householder, which went out early in the morning to hire labourers into his vineyard *(a Parable — in effect, Jesus is answering Peter's question, "what shall we have therefore?" the primary lesson that we will learn is that reward of the Kingdom is not of debt, but of Grace).*

2 And when he had agreed with the labourers for a penny a day *(about forty dollars a day in our present money),* he sent them into his vineyard.

3 And he went out about the third hour *(9 a.m. in the morning),* and saw others standing idle in the marketplace,

4 And said unto them; Go ye also into the vineyard, and what-soever is right I will give you. And they went their way *(they left the amount of payment up to the house-holder).*

5 Again he went out about the sixth and ninth hour *(12 o'clock noon and 3 p.m. in the afternoon),* and did likewise.

6 And about the eleventh hour *(5 o'clock in the afternoon)* he went out, and found others standing idle, and said unto them, Why stand you here all the day idle?

7 They say unto him, Because no man has hired us. He said unto them, Go ye also into the vineyard; and whatsoever is right, *that* shall ye receive *(they as well, took him at his word).*

8 So when evening was come *(about 6 p.m.),* the lord of the vineyard said unto his steward, Call the labourers, and give them *their* hire, beginning from the last unto the first *(the ones hired last were to be paid first, with the ones hired first being paid last).*

9 And when they came who *were hired* about the eleventh hour, they received every man a penny *(about forty dollars for the one hour's work).*

10 But when the first came *(the first ones hired),* they supposed that they should have received more; and they likewise received every man a penny *(forty dollars).*

11 And when they had received *it,* they murmured against the

goodman of the house,

12 Saying, These last have wrought *(worked) but* one hour, and you have made them equal unto us, which have borne the burden and heat of the day.

13 But he answered one of them, and said, Friend, I do you no wrong: did not you agree with me for a penny?

14 Take *that* which *is* yours, and go your way: I will give unto this last, even as unto you *(our Lord is teaching Grace here, which means that we do not obtain Salvation from Him by merit, but as well, it speaks of Israel and the Church; the Church although last, will receive just as much as Israel, who was first).*

15 Is it not lawful for me to do what I will with mine own? Is your eye evil, because I am good? *(No man has the right to make a claim on God because of merit. It must all be by Faith in Christ and the Cross [Rom. 3:20-31].)*

16 So the last shall be first, and the first last *(the Church was chosen last, but will be first, because Israel which was chosen first, rejected the Lord)*: for many be called, but few chosen *(many are called, but only a few choose to heed the call).*

JESUS AGAIN FORETELLS HIS DEATH AND RESURRECTION

17 And Jesus going up to Jer-usalem *(when and where He would be Crucified)* took the twelve Disciples apart in the way *(privately)*, and said unto them,

18 Behold, we go up to Jerusalem; and the Son of Man shall be betrayed unto the Chief Priests and unto the Scribes, and they shall condemn Him to death,

19 And shall deliver Him to the Gentiles *(the Romans)* to mock, and to scourge *(to beat Him)*, and to crucify *Him:* and the third day He shall rise again *(both the Jews and the Gentiles condemned Christ).*

THE MOTHER OF JAMES AND JOHN

20 Then came to Him the mother of Zebedee's children *(Salome)* with her sons *(James and John)*, worshipping *Him,* and desiring a certain thing of Him *(the fourth prediction of the Crucifixion failed like that of 17:22-23 to displace in the hearts of the Disciples self-interest and self-importance).*

21 And He said unto her, What do you want? She said unto Him, Grant that these my two sons *(James and John)* may sit, the one on your right hand, and the other on the left, in Your Kingdom *(we see here the first signs of politics in the Church).*

22 But Jesus answered and said, You know not what you ask

(unless the Holy Spirit enlightens the heart, the clearest spiritual teaching has neither meaning nor power; this fact humbles man's pride). Are you able to drink of the cup that I shall drink of *(the cup of suffering)*, and to be baptized with the baptism that I am baptized with? *(This is the baptism that's of suffering. The Cross will illicit opposition from both the Church and the world, but more so from the Church.)* They say unto Him, We are able *(they did not know what they were saying; they were thinking of thrones in glory, and definitely not of suffering)*.

23 And He said unto them, you shall drink indeed of My cup, and be baptized with the baptism that I am baptized with *(every true Christian will suffer the indignities of the Cross; if not, they aren't living and preaching the Cross, which means they are not living and preaching the Gospel)*: but to sit on My right hand, and on My left, is not Mine to give, but *it shall be given to them* for whom it is prepared of My Father *(positions in the Kingdom of the Son were planned by the Father, and the Son, and the Unity of the Godhead, would only give such positions to those to whom the Father had determined to grant them)*.

24 And when the ten *(remaining Disciples)* heard it *(heard what was requested by Salome)*, they were moved with indignation *(they wanted the positions themselves)* against the two brethren *(James and John)*.

25 But Jesus called them *(all twelve)* unto Him, and said, you know that the princes of the Gentiles exercise dominion over them, and they who are great exercise authority upon them *(worldly greatness, which is the opposite of spiritual greatness)*.

26 But it shall not be so among you *(the Believer is not to aspire to worldly greatness)*: but whosoever will be great among you, let him be your minister *(servant)*;

27 And whosoever will be chief among you, let him be your servant *(one giving himself wholly to another's will, at least that which is scriptural)*:

28 Even as the Son of Man came not to be ministered unto *(not to have servants wait on him)*, but to minister *(to serve others)*, and to give His life a ransom for many *(which He did on the Cross)*.

JESUS HEALS TWO BLIND MEN

29 And as they departed from Jericho *(the only time He went to Jericho of which we are aware)*, a great multitude followed Him *(Jesus is on His way to Jerusalem)*.

30 And, behold, two blind men sitting by the way side, when they

heard that Jesus passed by, cried out, saying, Have mercy on us, O Lord, *Thou* Son of David *(Bartimaeus was one of these men; both were healed)*.

31 And the multitude rebuked them, because they should hold their peace *(demanded that they be quiet)*: but they cried the more, saying, Have mercy on us, O Lord, *Thou* Son of David *(this designation recognized Christ as the Messiah)*.

32 And Jesus stood still, and called them, and said, What will you that I shall do unto you?

33 They say unto Him, Lord, that our eyes may be opened.

34 So Jesus had compassion *on them*, and touched their eyes: and immediately their eyes received sight, and they followed Him *(two blind men are mentioned by Matthew in keeping with his Gospel; they represent the Hebrew nation in its two divisions of Israel and Judah; and their receiving sight illustrates and predicts the light that will shine upon the nation in the future day, when the Son of David will make His grand entrance into Jerusalem at the Second Coming)*.

CHAPTER 21

THE TRIUMPHAL ENTRY INTO JERUSALEM

AND when they drew nigh unto Jerusalem *(the last six days of the Lord's earthly life began here)*, and were come to Bethphage *(very near Jerusalem)*, unto the Mount of Olives, then sent Jesus two Disciples *(tradition says that it was Peter and John)*,

2 Saying unto them, Go into the village over against you *(probably refers to Bethphage)*, and straightway *(immediately)* you shall find an ass tied, and a colt with her: loose *them*, and bring *them* unto Me.

3 And if any *man* say ought *(anything)* unto you, you shall say, The Lord has need of them; and straightway *(immediately)* he will send them.

4 All this was done, that it might be fulfilled which was spoken by the prophet, saying,

5 Tell ye the daughter of Sion, Behold, your King comes unto you, meek, and sitting upon an ass, and a colt the foal of an ass *(Zech. 9:9)*.

6 And the Disciples went, and did as Jesus commanded them,

7 And brought the ass, and the colt, and put on them their clothes *(a saddle of sorts)*, and they set *Him* thereon *(He rode the colt, with the other one, its mother, following with its back also prepared for a rider, nevertheless absent, which served as a symbol of Israel which rejected Christ)*.

8 And a very great multitude spread their garments in the way

(concerned the thousands who were coming into Jerusalem to celebrate the three great Feast's, "The Passover, Unleavened Bread, and First-fruits"; Christ would fulfill all three); others cut down branches from the trees, and strawed (scattered) them in the way (probably referred to palm fronds and branches from olive trees).

9 And the multitudes that went before, and that followed (represents Israel before and the Church which followed), cried, saying, Hosanna to the Son of David (this was a Feast of Tabernacles expression, but premature): Blessed is He Who comes in the Name of the Lord; Hosanna in the highest (all of this was terminology by the people recognizing Him as the Messiah; but He was not recognized as such by the religious leaders of Israel).

10 And when He was come into Jerusalem, all the city was moved, saying, Who is this? ("Was moved" refers to "quake" as in an earthquake; thousands before and behind Him, were making the city ring with the great Salutation, "Hosanna in the Highest".)

11 And the multitude said, This is Jesus the Prophet of Nazareth of Galilee (this is the title that was most understandable to the people. On this day, the 69th week [483 years] of Daniel's prediction was completed [Dan. 9:27]).

THE CLEANSING OF THE TEMPLE

12 And Jesus went into the Temple of God, and cast out all them who sold and bought in the Temple, and overthrew the tables of the moneychangers, and the seats of them who sold doves (this was in the Court of the Gentiles; it was a different incident than that narrated in John 2:13; the first commenced the beginning of His Ministry, this last one, its close),

13 And said unto them, It is written, My house shall be called the house of prayer; but you have made it a den of thieves (Isa. 56:7).

14 And the blind and the lame came to Him in the Temple; and He healed them (Heaven condemned the wrong use of the Temple, He now showed them the right use of it).

15 And when the Chief Priests and Scribes saw the wonderful things that He did, and the children crying in the Temple, and saying, Hosanna to the Son of David; they were sore displeased (most of the modern Church world is "sore displeased" as well, at any demonstration of the Holy Spirit),

16 And said unto Him, do You hear what these say? And Jesus said unto them, Yes; have you never read, Out of the mouth of babes and sucklings (little chil-

dren) *You have* perfected praise? *(The strength of the weak is praise, and worship of Christ is strength [Ps. 8:2].)*

THE BARREN FIG
TREE CURSED

17 And He left them *(the religious leaders)*, and went out of the city *(Jerusalem)* into Bethany *(home of Lazarus, Mary, and Martha)*; and He lodged there *(probably out in the open; there was no room for Him when He began His life, and no room for Him at the end of His Life)*.

18 Now in the morning as He returned into the city *(Jerusalem)*, He hungered *(suggests that He did not spend the night with Lazarus, Mary, and Martha, but rather in the open)*.

19 And when He saw a fig tree in the way, He came to it, and found nothing thereon, but leaves only *(symbolic of Israel; all leaves and no fruit)*, and said unto it, Let no fruit grow on you henceforward for ever *(during the whole of time unto Israel's present position)*. And presently the fig tree withered away *(immediately began to wither; Israel, upon her rejection of Christ, immediately began to whither)*.

20 And when the Disciples saw *it*, they marvelled, saying, How soon is the fig tree with-ered away! *(This was the next day. They saw the miracle, but did not know what the miracle was intended to teach.)*

21 Jesus answered and said unto them *(He deals with them on their level, not on the level the miracle was intended to convey)*, Verily I say unto you, If you have faith, and doubt not, you shall not only do this *which is done* to the fig tree, but also if you shall say unto this mountain, Be thou removed, and be thou cast into the sea; it shall be done *(symbolic terminology respecting the power of true Faith; all Faith must rest in Christ and Him Crucified, meaning that its correct object is always the Cross; the Will of God will then be carried out, and mountains of difficulties removed)*.

22 And all things, whatsoever you shall ask in prayer, believing, you shall receive *("all things" according to the Will of God; "Believing" pertains to the correct object of Faith, which must always be the Cross [I Cor. 1:17-18,23; 2:2])*.

JESUS ESTABLISHES
HIS AUTHORITY

23 And when He was come into the Temple *(early in the morning)*, the Chief Priests and the Elders of the people *(religious leaders)* came unto Him as He was

teaching *(interrupted His teaching)*, and said, By what authority do You do these things? and who gave You this authority? *(If He claimed that God gave Him this authority that would have been admittance that He was the Messiah. This they wanted Him to do, in order to accuse Him of blasphemy.)*

24 And Jesus answered and said unto them, I also will ask you one thing, which if you tell Me, I likewise will tell you by what authority I do these things *(in effect, by the question He will pose, will be the answer)*.

25 The Baptism of John *(of repentance)*, from where was it? from Heaven, or of men? And they reasoned with themselves, saying, If we shall say, From Heaven; He will say unto us, Why did you not then believe him? *(John introduced Christ as the Messiah.)*

26 But if we shall say, Of men; we fear the people; for all hold John as a Prophet *(whichever way they answered, put them in a dilemma; if they admitted that John was the predicted forerunner of Christ, then they were bound to receive Jesus as the Messiah)*.

27 And they answered Jesus, and said, We cannot tell *(this was untrue; they were the religious leaders of Israel and were supposed to know right from wrong)*. And He said unto them, Neither tell I you by what authority I do these things *(Jesus showed that they knew and were unwilling to answer.; in effect He said, "If you will not be honest with Me and the people, it is pointless to continue this conversation")*.

THE PARABLE OF THE TWO SONS

28 But what think you? *(This Parable and the next are directed to these religious leaders, as well as the people.)* A certain man had two sons; and he came to the first, and said, Son, go work today in my vineyard *(the "certain Man" represents the Lord; the "two sons" represent the unredeemed, who made no pretense at Salvation, while the second represented the Pharisees and their followers, who made every pretense of religion)*.

29 He answered and said, I will not: but afterward he repented, and went *(this represents the first son, who at the outset made no pretense of Salvation, but later repented)*.

30 And he came to the second, and said likewise. And he answered and said, I *go*, sir: and he went not *(this represents the Pharisees and their followers, who claimed much, but had nothing)*.

31 Which of the two did the will of *his* father? They say unto Him, The first *(this proclaims the only answer that could be given; they*

little realized in their self-righteous piety that the Parable was directed at them; they were the ones who proclaimed their allegiance to God and His Word, but in reality, had no allegiance at all!). Jesus said unto them, Verily I say unto you, That the publicans and the harlots go into the Kingdom of God before you (He said this to their faces, and before the people; He could not have insulted them more, putting them beneath publicans, whom they considered to be traitors, and harlots).

32 For John (John the Baptist) came unto you in the way of righteousness, and you believed him not (speaking to the religious leaders): but the publicans and the harlots believed him: and you, when you had seen it, repented not afterward, that you might believe him (they saw the changed lives as a result of John's Gospel, but still wouldn't believe).

THE WICKED HUSBANDMAN

33 Hear another Parable: There was a certain householder (represents God the Father), which planted a vineyard (the vineyard illustrated the Kingdom of Heaven, which was entrusted to Israel), and hedged it round about (the Lord protected it), and dug a winepress in it (represents Blessings), and built a tower (represents the position of watchmen who were to serve as protectors of the vineyard), and let it out to husbandmen (at the time of Christ, the husbandmen represent the Scribes and the Pharisees), and went into a far country (left the vineyard in their care):

34 And when the time of the fruit drew near (the time when Israel was to extend the Kingdom among other nations), he sent his servants to the husbandmen (the Prophets were sent to Israel), that they might receive the fruits of it.

35 And the husbandmen (religious leaders) took his servants (the Prophets), and beat one, and killed another, and stoned another (Mat. 23:37).

36 Again, he sent other servants (Prophets) more than the first: and they did unto them likewise.

37 But last of all he sent unto them his son (the Lord Jesus Christ), saying, They will reverence my son (this Parable also asserts the Doctrine of the Trinity).

38 But when the husbandmen saw the son, they said among themselves, This is the heir (the religious leaders of Israel knew that Jesus was the Son of God, and therefore, the Messiah of Israel); come, let us kill Him (the religious leaders of Israel were murderers), and let us seize on His inheritance (they imagined that

if they could destroy Christ, they could continue in their position of the inheritance; they killed that they might possess, but killing was the road to their sure destruction).

39 And they caught Him *(that which would take place a few hours later)*, and cast *Him* out of the vineyard *(excommunicated Him, in effect, claiming to Israel that He was an imposter)*, and slew *Him (was done only after they had pronounced their curses upon Him, which in their minds legitimized their hideous action of murder).*

40 When the lord therefore of the vineyard comes, what will he do unto those husbandmen? *(The religious leaders are not quite sure where Jesus is going with this, and consequently, will continue to bite until they hang themselves.)*

41 They say unto Him, He will miserably destroy those wicked men *(they little realized that they were speaking of themselves)*, and will let out *His* vineyard unto other husbandmen *(is exactly what happened! the Lord turned from the Jews to the Gentiles [Acts 18:6])*, which shall render him the fruits in their seasons *(after a fashion, the Church has done that).*

42 Jesus said unto them, Did you never read in the Scriptures *(Jesus directs them to the Word of God)*, The Stone *(Christ)* which the builders rejected *(Israel rejected Christ [Ps. 118:22-23])*, the same is become the Head of the corner *(everything hinged on Christ)*: this is the Lord's doing *(the Plan of God)*, and it is marvellous in our eyes? *(In the eyes of those who accept Christ.)*

43 Therefore I say unto you, The Kingdom of God shall be taken from you *(taken from the religious leaders and the people of Israel, which it was in 70 A.D., when Titus, the Roman General destroyed Jerusalem; in "saving their lives they lost them" [Mat. 16:25])*, and given to a nation bringing forth the fruits thereof *(refers to the Gentiles, of which most of the Church consists, who took the place of the Jews in the Plan of God [Acts 13:46-49; 15:13-18; Rom. 10:19; 11:26]).*

44 And whosoever shall fall on this stone shall be broken *(refers to Judgment and not Blessing, as some claim)*: but on whomsoever it shall fall, it will grind him to powder *(refers to those who put themselves in active opposition to Christ and His Kingdom; they will ultimately be destroyed, and without hope of recovery, which includes every religion of the world).*

45 And when the Chief Priests and Pharisees had heard His Parables, they perceived that He spoke of them *(speaks of the very leading religious leaders, who had conveyed to them that which Jesus had said).*

46 But when they sought to lay hands on Him *(proclaims the wickedness of their evil hearts)*, they feared the multitude *(their only restraint)*, because they took Him for a Prophet *(the last "they" speak of the multitude, and not the Pharisees and Chief Priests, etc.)*.

CHAPTER 22

THE PARABLE OF THE MARRIAGE FEAST

A ND Jesus answered and spoke unto them again by Parables, and said *(Jesus is still in the Temple, and continuing with His Message; "them" refers to the religious leaders of Israel)*,

2 The Kingdom of Heaven is like unto a certain king *(God the Father)*, which made a marriage for his son *(the Lord Jesus Christ)*,

3 And sent forth his servants *(the Prophets)* to call them *(Israel)* who were bidden to the wedding: and they would not come *(they rejected the Prophets and even their Messiah; the phrase proclaims a studied and deliberate rejection)*.

4 Again, he sent forth other servants *(which could well refer to His personal Disciples, and the Apostle Paul, and those in the Early Church, whose Ministry was yet future)*, saying, Tell them which are bidden *(this is an invitation directed personally to the people of Israel; the first few Chapters of the Book of Acts will bear this out)*, Behold, I have prepared my dinner: my oxen and *my* fatlings *are* killed, and all things *are* ready *(a strong sense of urgency, for time is running out)*: come unto the marriage *(respects the last invitation given to the Jews that could well have been given by the Apostle Paul [Acts, Chpt. 23])*.

5 But they made light of *it (Israel's response to the Gospel)*, and went their ways *(their ways instead of God's Ways)*, one to his farm, another to his merchandise *(Israel had no interest in the Gospel; they were more interested in money; how much does this characterize the modern Church!)*:

6 And the remnant *(those of Israel who didn't want the Gospel, which included the religious leaders)* took his servants *(the Apostles)*, and entreated *them* spitefully, and slew *them (the time of the Early Church was glorious, but as well, a time of intense persecution)*.

7 But when the king *(the Heavenly Father)* heard *thereof*, he was wroth *(extremely angry)*: and he sent forth his armies, and destroyed those murderers, and burned up their city *(exactly what happened in A.D. 70, when Titus destroyed Jerusalem)*.

8 Then said he to his servants *(the Plan of God is not halted, only its direction)*, The wedding is

ready *(will go as planned, but with a change of guests)*, but they which were bidden were not worthy *(concerns Israel who would not accept the worthiness of Christ)*.

9 Go ye therefore into the highways *(the balance of the world)*, and as many as you shall find *(love invites "the many")*, bid to the marriage *(give an invitation to the Gentiles, which was the Lord's plan all along, but not in this fashion)*.

10 So those servants *(Apostles and Prophets)* went out into the highways *(world evangelism, actually begun by the Apostle Paul)*, and gathered together all as many as they found *(the Gospel invitation given to everyone; none are excluded)*, both bad and good *(proclaims the fact that the "good" need Salvation, as well as the "bad")*: and the wedding was furnished with guests *(respects the redeemed who will be made up of both Jews and Gentiles)*.

11 And when the king *(God the Father)* came in to see the guests *(it was customary for the host to come and see their guests after they were assembled)*, he saw there a man which had not on a wedding garment *(a wedding garment supplied by the King, which was the custom in those days)*:

12 And he said unto him, Friend *(used in a negative way)*, how did you think you could come in hither not having a wedding garment? *(You have on your own garment, which is self-righteousness, and have refused my garment, which is the Righteousness of Christ.)* And he was speechless *(this man deemed his own garment of self-righteousness good enough for the feast; and it suited him very well until the king came in, and then he was exposed, and cast out)*.

13 Then said the king *(God the Father)* to the servants *(Angels, in this case)*, Bind him hand and foot, and take him away *(also refers to true Preachers who proclaim Salvation to Christ-acceptors, and doom to those who are Christ-rejecters)*, and cast *him* into outer darkness; there shall be weeping and gnashing of teeth *(Hell is the end result of all self-righteousness)*.

14 For many are called *(includes the whole world, which are many — and called by God)*, but few are chosen *(few respond favorably to the call)*.

TRIBUTE MONEY TO CAESAR

15 Then went the Pharisees *(the self-righteous hypocrites to whom Christ was speaking)*, and took counsel *(with the Herodians and Sadducees)* how they might entangle Him in *His* talk *(trap Him so they could arrest Him; how foolish they were!)*.

16 And they sent out unto Him

their Disciples *(Disciples of the Pharisees)* with the Herodians *(those who claimed Herod to be the Messiah)*, saying, Master *(teacher)*, we know that *You are* true, and teach the way of God in truth, neither carest Thou for any *man:* for You regard not the person of men *(flattery, which they did not at all believe, but was a part of their clever trap; they were foolish to try and match wits with Him, but in their stupidity they kept trying).*

17 Tell us therefore, What do you think? Is it lawful *(the Law of Moses)* to give tribute *(pay taxes)* unto Caesar, or not? *(This question raged in Israel at that time. In their thinking, either way He answered would trap Him. If He said it was not lawful, this would have put Him in opposition to the Roman government. Had He said it was lawful, He would have denied His claim as Messiah, the King of Israel.)*

18 But Jesus perceived their wickedness *(pertains to the hypocrisy which prompted their question)*, and said, Why tempt you Me *(He saw through their craftiness)*, you hypocrites? *(He said this to their faces.)*

19 Show Me the tribute money *(the type of coin used to pay the tax)*. And they brought unto Him a penny *(the coin).*

20 And He said unto them, Whose *is* this image and superscription? *(Was probably the image of Tiberius on the coin.)*

21 They say unto Him, Caesar's. Then said He unto them, Render therefore unto Caesar the things which are Caesar's; and unto God the things that are God's *(lawful government is here recognized, and support for government approved; if done correctly, support for government and support for God will not clash).*

22 When they had heard *these words (in this short statement, a new sphere of government was introduced, the two spheres of Church and State to be distinct and not joined)*, they marveled *(were left speechless)*, and left Him, and went their way *(they were silenced, but their evil hearts were not changed).*

THE RESURRECTION

23 The same day came to Him the Sadducees *(the third party in Israel which tried to trap Him)*, which say that there is no Resurrection *(they did not believe in a future life of the soul, or the Resurrection of the body)*, and asked Him,

24 Saying, Master *(teacher)*, Moses said *(they studied the Bible, but not for it to mold their life)*, If a man die, having no children, his brother shall marry his wife, and raise up seed unto his brother *([Deut. 25:5-10] this was only*

under the Old Covenant, and was not carried over into the New Covenant).

25 Now there were with us seven brethren *(a hypothetical case)*: and the first, when he had married a wife, deceased *(died)*, and, having no issue *(no children)*, left his wife unto his brother:

26 Likewise the second also, and the third, unto the seventh.

27 And last of all the woman died also.

28 Therefore in the Resurrection whose wife shall she be of the seven? for they all had her *(they now spring their trap).*

29 Jesus answered and said unto them *(that which seemed to be unanswerable to others, was simple for Him)*, You do err, not knowing the Scriptures *(once again, He takes them to the Word of God)*, nor the power of God *(addresses itself to the denial by the Sadducees of the supernatural).*

30 For in the Resurrection *(this proclaims by Christ the validity of the Doctrine of the Resurrection)* they *(all who are saved)* neither marry, nor are given in marriage, but are as the Angels of God in Heaven *(do not die; as well, Christ proclaims existence of Angels, which the Sadducees also denied).*

31 But as touching the Resurrection of the dead *(guarantees their Resurrection and as well, life after death)*, have you not read that which was spoken unto you by God, saying *(Ex. 3:6, 16),*

32 I am the God of Abraham, and the God of Isaac, and the God of Jacob? God is not the God of the dead, but of the living *(portrays the fallacy of the great Plan of God being built and predicated on that which is non-existent; the Lord is saying that these men of whom He spoke, and all others who had died in the Faith were then alive, and will be ever alive; in this, Christ teaches the immortality of the soul and that God is the God of all departed souls; also, the great investment that Christ would make at the Cross, was definitely not to be made for all the Sainted dead who will have no existence).*

33 And when the multitude heard *this*, they were astonished at His doctrine *(at the simplicity of what He said concerning the Resurrection, by using examples from the Word of God).*

THE GREAT COMMANDMENT

34 But when the Pharisees had heard that He had put the Sadducees to silence, they were gathered together *(they normally hated each other).*

35 Then one of them, *which was* a lawyer *(Scribe)*, asked *Him a question,* tempting Him, and saying,

36 Master *(teacher)*, which *is* the great Commandment of the

law? *(The Law of Moses.)*

37 Jesus said unto him, You shall love the Lord your God with all your heart, and with all your soul, and with all your mind *(this is the foundation of all the Law, and as well, applies to the present Day of Grace).*

38 This is the first and great Commandment *(Love of God must be "first" before anything else can be claimed).*

39 And the second is like unto it, You shall love your neighbour as yourself *(as one loves their neighbor, accordingly, one loves God).*

40 On these two Commandments hang all the Law and the Prophets *(this includes the New Testament, as well!).*

DAVID'S SON

41 While the Pharisees were gathered together *(refers to Jesus speaking to the great crowd in the Temple, which contained many Pharisees)*, Jesus asked them *(concerns the most important question they will ever be asked, because it pertains to the Person of Christ, the Messiah)*,

42 Saying, What do you think of Christ? *(What were their thoughts concerning the Messiah?)* whose Son is He? *(He will now bring them face-to-face with His identity.)* They say unto him, The Son of David *(this is the correct answer as outlined in II Samuel, Chapter 7).*

43 He said unto them, How then does David in spirit call Him Lord, saying *(the Messiah was David's Son — in his lineage — and as well, David's Lord; this was revealed to David by the Holy Spirit, and brings together Christ's Humanity and Deity)*,

44 The LORD said unto My Lord *([Ps. 110:1] this refers to God the Father speaking to God the Son)*, Sit Thou on My Right Hand *(refers to Christ being exalted to the highest position in Heaven, which immediately followed the ascension [Phil. 2:9-11])*, till I make Your enemies Your footstool? *(Refers to all enemies being put down during the Millennium and at its conclusion [I Cor. 15:24-28; Eph. 1:10].)*

45 If David then call Him, Lord, how is He his Son? *(He is David's Lord because He is God; He is David's Son because He became man through Mary of the House of David [Lk. 1:34-35; 3:23-38] this one question presents to them the truth of His Incarnation — God becoming Man.)*

46 And no man was able to answer Him a word *(they could not refute His argument)*, neither does any man from that day forth ask Him any more questions *(portrays the fact that His Spiritual and Scriptural intelligence far exceeded anything they had ever seen or known).*

CHAPTER 23

THE SINS OF THE SCRIBES AND PHARISEES

THEN spoke Jesus to the multitude, and to His Disciples *(this is not the Jesus of the modern Church or fashionable pulpit)*,

2 Saying, The Scribes and the Pharisees sit in Moses' seat *(the "Scribes" proclaimed to be interpreters of the Law of Moses for the people)*:

3 All therefore whatsoever they bid you observe, *that* observe and do *(concerned a correct interpretation of the Scriptures, and not their glosses)*; but do not ye after their works: for they say, and do not *(they do not practice what they preach; remember, Jesus is saying this, in the Temple, before the Pharisees and the people)*.

4 For they bind heavy burdens and grievous to be borne, and lay *them* on men's shoulders *(concerns the glosses and additions that had been made to the law by these hypocrites)*; but they *themselves* will not move them with one of their fingers *(they do not themselves do what they demand of others)*.

5 But all their works they do for to be seen of men *(self-righteousness)*: they make broad their phylacteries *(a small box worn on the arm or forehead, and contain-*

ing Scriptures), and enlarge the borders of their garments *(tassels composed of white and blue threads, intended to remind the wearers of the Commandments of the Lord; they made these overly large to draw attention to themselves)*,

6 And love the uppermost rooms at feasts *(the most honored place at the table)*, and the chief seats in the synagogues *(seats of honor)*,

7 And greetings in the markets *(flowery salutations)*, and to be called of men, Rabbi, Rabbi *("teacher," a favorite title claimed by the Pharisees)*.

8 But you are not to be called Rabbi *(it concerned the greedy ambition which loved the empty title, and took any means to obtain it)*: for One is your Master *(Teacher, Leader, Guide)*, even Christ *(the Lord Jesus Christ)*; and all you are brethren *(no one Believer is higher than another, and neither can have from Christ any authority over other Believers [I Pet. 5:1-8])*.

9 And call no *man* your father upon the earth *(eminent teachers to whom the people were taught to look to rather than God)*: for one is your Father, which is in Heaven *(all true Bible teachers must cause men to look to God, and not to themselves as the source of power and truth)*.

10 Neither be ye called mas-

ters *(means that Preachers are not to be called spiritual leaders)*: for one is your Master, *even* Christ *(actually means that God and Christ are the only One's Who have any right to these titles)*.

11 But he who is greatest among you shall be your servant *(the definition of Christian greatness, i.e., "the servant principle")*.

12 And whosoever shall exalt himself shall be abased *(pride and vanity)*; and he who shall humble himself shall be exalted *(is the universal Law of God's dealings with men)*.

WOES UPON THE SCRIBES AND PHARISEES

13 But woe unto you, Scribes and Pharisees, hypocrites! *(The first of eight woes, and said to their faces. There could be no greater insult to them than being called "hypocrites"!)* for you shut up the Kingdom of Heaven against men *(is the first scheme of Satan, and is carried out through religion)*: for you neither go in *yourselves,* neither suffer ye them who are entering to go in *(they refuse to accept Christ, and stood in the door to bar access to any and all who would attempt to come in)*.

14 Woe unto you, Scribes and Pharisees, hypocrites! for you devour widows' houses, and for a pretence make long prayer *(projects a false piety which deceives people, and the most helpless at that)*: therefore you shall receive the greater damnation *(this tells us that religious wickedness is the greatest wickedness of all)*.

15 Woe unto you, Scribes and Pharisees, hypocrites! for you compass sea and land to make one proselyte *(working zealously to draw people to themselves, instead of the Lord)*, and when he is made, you make him twofold more the child of hell than yourselves *(religious people are the hardest of all to bring to the Lord)*.

16 Woe unto you, you blind guides *(these religious leaders were spiritually blind, but yet they were serving as spiritual guides for the people, which guaranteed the people's spiritual destruction; is it any different presently?)*, which say, Whosoever shall swear by the Temple, it is nothing *(an oath that need not be kept)*; but whosoever shall swear by the gold of the Temple, he is a debtor! *(If one does such, he is bound to hold to his oath.)*

17 You fools and blind *(proclaims Christ adding to the epithets of hypocrites and blind, the word "fools!")*: for whether is greater, the gold, or the Temple that sanctifieth the gold? *(The answer of Christ was not meant to place a seal of approval on swearing oaths, but instead, the foolish-*

ness of such a position. The "gold" didn't sanctify the "Temple" but rather, the opposite!)

18 And, Whosoever shall swear by the Altar, it is nothing *(an oath that doesn't need to be kept)*; but whosoever sweareth by the gift Sacrifice that is upon it, he is guilty *(if one swears an oath by the Sacrifice on the Altar, he's bound to keep such an oath, or so they said)*.

19 You fools and blind: for whether *is* greater, the gift *(Sacrifice)*, or the Altar that sanctifieth the gift? *(The religious leaders of Israel had a wrong conception of the entirety of the Plan of God.)*

20 Whoso therefore shall swear by the Altar, sweareth by it, and by all things thereon *(all were equally important)*.

21 And whoso shall swear by the Temple, sweareth by it, and by Him Who dwells therein *(their sin was the sin of making God a part of their evil; it is the same presently with many modern Preachers)*.

22 And he who shall swear by Heaven swears by the Throne of God, and by Him Who sits thereon *(Christ here says that to swear by "Heaven" includes God and His Throne whether realized or not)*.

23 Woe unto you, Scribes and Pharisees, hypocrites! for you pay tithe of mint and anise and cumin *(small plants used for seasoning)*, and have omitted the weightier *matters* of the Law, Judgment, Mercy, and Faith *(they were meticulous about these insignificant things, but gave little or no heed at all, to those things which really mattered)*: these ought you to have done *(pertaining to Scriptural Judgment, Mercy, and Faith)*, and not to leave the other undone *(make sure, as well, that you pay tithe on all that you have; all of the Word of God is to be obeyed, not just part)*.

24 You blind guides, which strain at a gnat, and swallow a camel *(this is self-righteousness taken to an ultra extreme)*.

25 Woe unto you, Scribes and Pharisees, hypocrites! for you make clean the outside of the cup and of the platter *(outward show)*, but within they are full of extortion and excess *(the heart)*.

26 You blind Pharisee, cleanse first that *which is* within the cup and platter *(the heart)*, that the outside of them may be clean also *(has to do with moral purity which comes from within, and if such is the case, the outside will be clean as well)*.

27 Woe unto you, Scribes and Pharisees, hypocrites! for you are like unto whited sepulchres, which indeed appear beautiful outward *(once a year, the Jews white washed the tombs in order to make them conspicuous that men may not contract ceremonial defilement by touch-*

ing or walking over them [Num. 19:16]), but are within full of dead *men's* bones, and of all uncleanness *(this symbolized the Pharisees).*

28 Even so you also outwardly appear righteous unto men, but within you are full of hypocrisy and iniquity.

29 Woe unto you, Scribes and Pharisees, hypocrites! *(Presents the eighth and final "woe"!),* because you build the tombs of the Prophets, and garnish the sepulchres of the righteous *(speaks of the honors paid to departed Saints, while at the same time, planning to murder living Saints, even Christ!),*

30 And say, If we had been in the days of our fathers, we would not have been partakers with them in the blood of the Prophets *(all the time they were plotting to murder Christ).*

31 Wherefore you be witnesses unto yourselves *(be honest with yourself),* that you are the children of them which killed the Prophets *(you have the same murderous hearts as those you condemn).*

32 Fill ye up then the measure of your fathers *(their wickedness was about to bring judgment, which it did!).*

33 You serpents, you generation of vipers *(He likens them to that old serpent, their father, the Devil [Jn. 8:44; Rev. 12:9; 20:2]),* how can you escape the damnation of hell? *(Eternal destiny of these religious leaders would be hell. What an indictment!)*

34 Wherefore, behold, I send unto you Prophets, and wise men, and Scribes *(pertains to those of the Early Church):* and *some* of them you shall kill and crucify; and *some* of them shall you scourge in your Synagogues, and persecute *them* from city to city *(the Book of Acts records all of this, exactly as stated by Christ):*

35 That upon you may come all the righteous blood shed upon the earth *(speaks of the cup of iniquity being filled; Judgment was about to come, which it did!),* from the blood of righteous Abel *(Gen., Chpt. 4)* unto the blood of Zechariah, son of Barachias, whom you killed between the Temple and the Altar *(more than likely, Zechariah the Prophet [Zech. 1:1]).*

36 Verily I say unto you, All these things shall come upon this generation *(and it did! about thirty-seven years later, in 70 A.D., Jerusalem was totally destroyed by Titus, the Roman General).*

JESUS WEEPS OVER JERUSALEM

37 O Jerusalem, Jerusalem *(presents Jesus standing in the Temple when He gave this sorrowing account), you* who kill the Prophets, and stoned them which are

sent unto you (presents the terrible animosity tendered toward these Messengers of God), how often would I have gathered your children together, even as a hen gathers her chickens under her wings, and you would not! (Proclaims every effort made by the Lord, and made "often," to bring Israel back to her senses.)

38 Behold, your house (the Temple or Jerusalem, are no longer God's habitation) is left unto you desolate (without God, which means they were at the mercy of Satan).

39 For I say unto you, you shall not see Me henceforth, till you shall say, Blessed is He Who comes in the Name of the Lord (the Second Coming).

CHAPTER 24

DESTRUCTION OF THE TEMPLE PREDICTED

AND Jesus went out, and departed from the Temple (when He left, God left): and His Disciples came to Him for to show Him the buildings of the Temple (this structure was one of the most beautiful in the world of that day).

2 And Jesus said unto them, Do you not see all these things? (Is asked by Christ in response to the remarks made by His Disciples concerning the beauty of the Temple.) verily I say unto you, There shall not be left here one stone upon another, that shall not be thrown down (was fulfilled in total exactness; it took place in 70 A.D.).

SIGNS OF THE END TIME

3 And as He sat upon the Mount of Olives (the coming siege of Jerusalem by the Romans some thirty-seven years later, began at this exact spot where Christ was sitting), the Disciples came unto Him privately (out of earshot of the many Pilgrims in the city for the Passover), saying, Tell us, when shall these things be? (Has to do here with the utterance He had just given concerning the destruction of the Temple.) and what shall be the sign of Your coming (refers to the Second Coming), and of the end of the world? (Should have been translated "age.")

4 And Jesus answered and said unto them (will now give the future of Israel, and how it will effect the entirety of the world), Take heed that no man deceive you (places deception as Satan's greatest weapon).

5 For many shall come in My Name (concerns itself primarily with the time immediately before the coming Great Tribulation, and especially its first half), saying, I

am Christ; and shall deceive many *(the greatest of these will be the Antichrist, who will claim to be the Messiah)*.

6 And you shall hear of wars and rumours of wars *(has abounded from the beginning, but will accelerate during the first half of the Great Tribulation)*: see that you be not troubled *(concerns true Believers)*: for all *these* things must come to pass *(we are very near presently to the beginning of fulfillment of what Jesus said)*, but the end is not yet *(the end will be at the Second Coming)*.

7 For nation shall rise against nation, and kingdom against kingdom: and there shall be famines, and pestilences, and earthquakes, in divers places *(few places in the world, if any, will be exempt from these judgments)*.

8 All these *are* the beginning of sorrows *(first half of the Great Tribulation)*.

9 Then shall they deliver you up to be afflicted, and shall kill you *(pertains to the mid-point of the Great Tribulation when the Antichrist, whom Israel thought was the Messiah, will show his true colors)*: and you shall be hated of all nations for My Name's sake *(no nation will come to her rescue; Israel hates Christ, but Christ is the reason that the world hates Israel)*.

10 And then shall many be offended *(some Jews will accept Christ, which will be an offence to others)*, and shall betray one another, and shall hate one another *(the Jews who accept Christ, will be the brunt of this animosity)*.

11 And many false prophets shall rise, and shall deceive many *(they will help the Antichrist)*.

12 And because iniquity shall abound *(the Antichrist called "the man of sin" [II Thess. 2:3])*, the love of many shall wax cold *(some who accept Christ, will turn their backs on Him)*.

13 But he who shall endure unto the end *(refers to the end of the Great Tribulation)*, the same shall be saved *(speaks of survival, and not the Salvation of the Soul)*.

14 And this Gospel of the Kingdom *(refers to the same type of Gospel preached by Christ and Paul)* shall be preached in all the world for a witness unto all nations *(not every person, but to all nations; this is close presently to being fulfilled)*; and then shall the end come *(the Second Coming)*.

THE ABOMINATION OF DESOLATION

15 When you therefore shall see the abomination of desolation, spoken of by Daniel the Prophet, stand in the Holy Place *(speaks of the Antichrist invading Israel, and taking over the Temple)*,

(whoso reads, let him understand:) *(Reads it in the Word of God [Dan. 8:9-14; 9:27; 11:45; 12:1, 7, 11].)*

16 Then let them which be in Judaea flee into the mountains *(when the Antichrist invades Israel at the mid-point of the Great Tribulation)*:

17 Let him which is on the housetop not come down to take any thing out of his house *(houses are flat on top in that part of the world; during the summer, people often sleep on top of the house; speaks of the necessity of haste)*:

18 Neither let him which is in the field return back to take his clothes.

19 And woe unto them who are with child, and to them who give suck in those days! *(The necessity of fleeing will be so urgent, that it will be difficult for pregnant women, and mothers with little babies.)*

20 But pray ye that your flight be not in the winter *(bad weather)*, neither on the Sabbath Day *(concerns the strict religious observance of the Sabbath, doesn't permit travel)*:

GREAT TRIBULATION

21 For then shall be great tribulation *(the last three and one half years)*, such as was not since the beginning of the world to this time, no, nor ever shall be *(the worst the world has ever known, and will be so bad that it will never be repeated)*.

22 And except those days should be shortened, there should no flesh be saved *(refers to Israel coming close to extinction)*: but for the elect's *(Israel's)* sake those days shall be shortened *(by the Second Coming)*.

23 Then if any man shall say unto you, Lo, here is Christ, or there; believe it not *(don't be deceived)*.

24 For there shall arise false Christs, and false prophets *(the Antichrist and the false prophet [Rev., Chpt. 13])*, and shall show great signs and wonders *(which will be offered as proof)*; insomuch that, if it were possible, they shall deceive the very elect *(will attempt to deceive Israel)*.

25 Behold, I have told you before *(is meant to emphasize the seriousness of the matter)*.

26 Wherefore if they shall say unto you, Behold, he is in the desert; go not forth: behold, *he is* in the secret chambers; believe *it* not *(the next Verse will tell the manner of His Coming, which will eclipse all pretenders)*.

THE COMING OF THE SON OF MAN

27 For as the lightning cometh

out of the east, and shineth even unto the west *(is meant to proclaim the most cataclysmic event the world has ever known)*; so shall also the coming of the Son of Man be *(no one will have to ask, is this really Christ; it will be overly obvious!)*.

28 For wheresoever the carcase is *(speaks of the Battle of Armageddon)*, there will the eagles be gathered together *(should have been translated, "there will the vultures be gathered together" [refers to Ezek. 39:17])*.

29 Immediately after the tribulation of those days *(speaks of the time immediately preceding the Second Coming)* shall the sun be darkened, and the moon shall not give her light *(the light of these orbs will be dim by comparison to the light of the Son of God)*, and the stars shall fall from Heaven *(a display of Heavenly fireworks at the Second Coming)*, and the powers of the Heavens shall be shaken *(will work with the Son of God against the Antichrist, at the Second Coming)*:

30 And then shall appear the sign of the Son of Man in Heaven *(pertains to the Second Coming, which will take place in the midst of these Earth and Heaven shaking events)*: and then shall all the tribes of the earth mourn *(concerns all the nations of the world which possibly will see this phenom-*enon by television)*, and they shall see the Son of Man *(denotes Christ and His human, Glorified Body)* coming in the clouds of Heaven with power and great glory *(lends credence to the thought that much of the world will see Him by television as He makes His Descent)*.

31 And He shall send His Angels *(they will be visible)* with a great sound of a trumpet *(announcing the gathering of Israel)*, and they shall gather together His elect *(Israel)* from the four winds, from one end of Heaven to the other *(Jews will be gathered from all over the world, and brought to Israel)*.

THE PARABLE OF THE FIG TREE

32 Now learn a Parable of the fig tree *(the Bible presents three trees, the fig, the olive, and the vine, as representing the nation of Israel, nationally, spiritually, and dispensationally)*; When his branch is yet tender, and putteth forth leaves *(is meant to serve as the illustration of Israel nationally)*, ye know that summer is near *(refers to Israel as the greatest Prophetic Sign of all, telling us that we are now living in the last of the Last Days)*:

33 So likewise ye *(points to the modern Church)*, when you shall see all these things *(which we are

now seeing as it regards Israel), know that it is near, *even* at the doors *(the fulfillment of Endtime Prophecies)*.

34 Verily I say unto you, This generation shall not pass *(the generation of Jews which will be alive at the beginning of the Great Tribulation; as well, it was a prediction by Christ, that irrespective of the problems that Israel would face, even from His day, they would survive)*, till all these things be fulfilled *(there is no doubt, they will be fulfilled)*.

35 Heaven and earth shall pass away *(doesn't refer to annihilation, but rather a change from one condition or state to another)*, but My Words shall not pass away *(what the Word of God says, will be!)*.

36 But of that day and hour knows no *man*, no, not the Angels of Heaven, but My Father only.

DESTRUCTION OF THE WICKED

37 But as the days of Noah *were*, so shall also the coming of the Son of Man be *(the men of Noah's day were insensible to the Prophecies predicting the coming flood, and so will men be blind to these Prophecies announcing the coming of the Son of Man)*.

38 For as in the days that were before the flood they were eating and drinking, marrying and giving in marriage *(refers to an absolute lack of concern respecting Noah's Message of a coming flood)*, until the day that Noah entered into the Ark *(means they watched him build the Ark, and heard him preach Righteousness for many years, but took no heed)*,

39 And knew not until the flood came *(didn't believe the Message until the water began its precipitous rise)*, and took them all away *(they were all drowned, and consequently, eternally lost)*; so shall also the coming of the Son of Man be *(the similarity with Noah's time)*.

40 Then shall two be in the field; the one shall be taken, and the other left *(does not refer to the Rapture as many believe, but rather to the terrible loss of life during the Great Tribulation)*.

41 Two *women* shall be grinding at the mill; the one shall be taken, and the other left.

42 Watch therefore *(a warning to Israel to be prepared)*: for you know not what hour your Lord does come *(present Believers know that the Second Coming will take place during the Battle of Armageddon [Zech., Chpt. 12] but unredeemed Israel will not know)*.

43 But know this, that if the goodman of the house had known in what watch the thief would come, he would have watched,

and would not have suffered his house to be broken up *(as unexpected as this, will likewise be the Coming of the Lord).*

44 Therefore be ye also ready: for in such an hour as you think not the Son of Man cometh *(when Israel, during the Battle of Armageddon, will have given up hope, Jesus will come!).*

PARABLE OF THE FAITHFUL AND UNFAITHFUL SERVANT

45 Who then is a faithful and wise servant *(refers to all Believers for all time)*, whom his Lord has made ruler over His household *(in this case, the Church)*, to give them meat in due season? *(God-called Preachers are responsible for properly feeding the flock.)*

46 Blessed *is* that servant, whom his Lord when He comes shall find so doing *(refers to faithfulness till the Rapture).*

47 Verily I say unto you, That He shall make him ruler over all his goods *(refers to the Resurrected Saints being made "rulers" in the coming Kingdom Age, and the faithful of Israel being placed in the same capacity as the premiere nation in the world).*

48 But and if that evil servant shall say in his heart, My Lord delays His coming *(exactly what many in the modern Church are now saying);*

49 And shall begin to smite *his* fellowservants, and to eat and drink with the drunken *(not only to be in the world, but to be as well, of the world);*

50 The Lord of that servant shall come in a day when he looks not for *Him,* and in an hour that he is not aware of *(not ready for the Rapture; most of the modern Church, sadly, falls into this category),*

51 And shall cut him asunder, and appoint *him* his portion with the hypocrites *(despite his profession)*: there shall be weeping and gnashing of teeth *(will lose his soul, and go to an eternal Hell; most in the modern Church, sadly and regrettably, fall into this category; they are religious but lost!).*

CHAPTER 25

THE PARABLE OF THE TEN VIRGINS

THEN shall the Kingdom of Heaven be likened unto ten *(the number "10" in the Bible speaks of perfection)* virgins *(represents those who belong to the Lord)*, which took their lamps *(represents the Light of Christ in all Believers)*, and went forth to meet the Bridegroom *(Christ).*

2 And five of them were wise, and five *were* foolish *(indicative of modern Christianity).*

3 They who *were* foolish took

their lamps, and took no oil with them *(began to live outside the domain of the Holy Spirit)*:

4 But the wise took oil in their vessels with their lamps *(a constant flow of the Spirit within their hearts and lives, which can only come about and be maintained, by one's Faith in Christ and the Cross [Rom. 8:1-2, 11])*.

5 While the bridegroom tarried, they all slumbered and slept *(does not imply by this that they were doing something wrong)*.

6 And at midnight there was a cry made, Behold, the bridegroom cometh; go ye out to meet him *(the Rapture of the Church)*.

7 Then all those virgins arose, and trimmed their lamps *(but without the oil, the trimming was useless; it is religious activity without the Holy Spirit)*.

8 And the foolish said unto the wise, Give us of your oil; for our lamps are gone out *(it's too late now!)*.

9 But the wise answered, saying, *Not so;* lest there be not enough for us and you: but go you rather to them who sell, and buy for yourselves *(proclaims the truth that spiritual energy cannot be derived from others)*.

10 And while they went to buy, the Bridegroom came; and they who were ready went in with Him to the marriage: and the door was shut *(there will come a time, when it's too late; today is the day . . . [Heb. 3:15])*.

11 Afterward came also the other virgins, saying, Lord, Lord, open to us *(because they were religious, they thought they were saved)*.

12 But He answered and said, Verily I say unto you, I know you not *(millions presently are in the Church, but not in Christ)*.

13 Watch therefore, for you know neither the day nor the hour wherein the Son of Man cometh *(our lives are to be lived as if Jesus would come today)*.

THE PARABLE OF THE TALENTS

14 For *the Kingdom of Heaven is* as a man travelling into a far country, *who* called his own servants, and delivered unto them his goods *(represents Christ at His first Advent)*.

15 And unto one he gave five talents, to another two, and to another one; to every man according to his several abilities; and straightway *(immediately)* took his journey *(every single Believer, none excluded, is given a proper Ministry)*.

16 Then he who had received the five talents went and traded with the same, and made *them* other five talents *(the talents were awarded according to faithfulness)*.

17 And likewise he who *had*

received two, he also gained other two *(he was faithful with what he had)*.

18 But he who had received one went and dug in the earth, and hid his lord's money *(he wasn't faithful)*.

19 After a long time the lord of those servants comes, and reckons with them *(service for the lord ends at death; however, the reckoning is reserved for the Rapture)*.

20 And so he who had received five talents came and brought other five talents, saying, Lord, you delivered unto me five talents: behold, I have gained beside them five talents more *(this will take place at the Judgment Seat of Christ)*.

21 His lord said unto him, Well done, *thou* good and faithful servant: you have been faithful over a few things, I will make you ruler over many things: enter thou into the joy of your lord *(as is obvious, it is faithfulness here that is being rewarded; contrary to popular thought, God hasn't called us to be successful, but rather to be faithful)*.

22 He also who had received two talents came and said, Lord, you delivered unto me two talents: behold, I have gained two other talents beside them *(faithfulness as well!)*.

23 His lord said unto him,

Well done, good and faithful servant; you have been faithful over a few things, I will make you ruler over many things: enter thou into the joy of your lord *(if it is to be noticed, both received equal rewards; as stated, the criterion is faithfulness and not other things)*.

24 Then he who had received the one talent came and said, Lord, I know you and that you are an hard man, reaping where you have not sown, and gathering where you have not planted *(pure and simple, his statements constitute a lie)*:

25 And I was afraid, and went and hid your talent in the earth: lo, *there* you have *that* which *is* yours *(the purpose of the "talent" was not preservation, but rather, multiplication; his action proclaims not only indolence, but, as well, insolence; untold numbers, who claim to be Christians, fall into this category)*.

26 His lord answered and said unto him, *You* wicked and slothful servant, you knew that I reap where I sowed not, and gather where I have not planted *(if you really believed that, you would not have done what you did)*:

27 You ought therefore to have put my money to the exchangers, and *then* at my coming I should have received mine own with usury *(regrettably, the majority of professors of religion, fall into this category)*.

28 Take therefore the talent from him, and give *it* unto him who has ten talents *(this is the law of the faithful; light rejected, is light taken, and given to the one who already has an abundance of light)*.

29 For unto every one who has shall be given, and he shall have abundance: but from him who has not shall be taken away even that which he has *(in fact, this happens unnumbered times, every single day; observe religious denominations, which have rejected light!)*.

30 And cast you the unprofitable servant into outer darkness: there shall be weeping and gnashing of teeth *(these individuals do not merely lose reward, but rather their souls; all of this, as should be overly obvious, completely refutes the unscriptural doctrine of unconditional eternal security)*.

JUDGMENT ON THE NATIONS

31 When the Son of Man shall come in His glory, and all the Holy Angels with Him, then shall He sit upon the Throne of His glory *(the Second Coming)*:

32 And before Him shall be gathered all nations: and He shall separate them one from another, as a shepherd divides *his* sheep from the goats *(this is called the*

"judgment of the nations," which will commence at the outset of the Kingdom Age):

33 And He shall set the sheep on His right hand *(refers to nations which would not cooperate with the Antichrist)*, but the goats on the left *(nations which cooperated with the Antichrist)*.

34 Then shall the King say unto them on His right hand, Come, you blessed of My Father, inherit the Kingdom prepared for you from the foundation of the world *(has nothing to do with Salvation, but rather these particular nations being allowed to enter into the Kingdom Age)*:

35 For I was hungry, and you gave Me meat: I was thirsty, and you gave Me drink: I was a stranger, and you took Me in *(although the adage proves true for all time, Christ is basically here speaking of Israel and her treatment by various nations during the Great Tribulation)*:

36 Naked, and you clothed Me: I was sick, and you visited Me: I was in prison, and you came unto Me.

37 Then shall the righteous answer Him, saying, Lord, when did we see you hungry, and fed *You?* or thirsty, and gave *You* drink? *(The word, "righteous," does not pertain to the righteousness of Christ given to Believers at Salvation, but instead, righteous dealings with*

Israel by these nations.)

38 When saw we You a stranger, and took You in? or naked, and clothed *You?*

39 Or when did we see You sick, or in prison, and came unto You?

40 And the King shall answer and say unto them, Verily I say unto you, Inasmuch as you have done *it* unto one of the least of these My brethren, you have done *it* unto Me *(as stated, the adage holds true for all time, but Christ is primarily speaking here of Israel, and the help given her by certain nations during the Great Tribulation).*

41 Then shall He say also unto them on the left hand *(the goat nations)*, Depart from Me, you cursed, into everlasting fire, prepared for the devil and his angels *(nations that hindered or tried to harm Israel during the Great Tribulation)*:

42 For I was hungry, and you gave Me no meat: I was thirsty, and you gave Me no drink:

43 I was a stranger, and you took Me not in: naked, and you clothed Me not: sick, and in prison, and you visited Me not.

44 Then shall they also answer Him, saying, Lord, when did we see You hungry, or thirsty, or a stranger, or naked, or sick, or in prison, and did not minister unto You?

45 Then shall He answer them, saying, Verily I say unto you, Inasmuch as you did *it* not to one of the least of these, you did *it* not to Me *(to bless one who belongs to God, is to bless God; to harm one who belongs to God, is to harm God; we see here the results of such action).*

46 And these shall go away into everlasting punishment: but the righteous into life eternal *(all of this will happen soon after the Second Coming; the leaders of the nations who tried to help the Antichrist against Israel, during the Great Tribulation, will evidently be executed, and consequently will die eternally lost; conversely, the leaders of the nations who tried to help Israel at that time, will be given an opportunity to accept Christ as Saviour, which they no doubt will, and will thereby be given "life eternal").*

CHAPTER 26

THE PLOT TO KILL JESUS

AND it came to pass, when Jesus had finished all these sayings, He said unto His Disciples *(this concluded His public teaching, even though other discourses were given to the Disciples only [Jn. 13:31; 17:26]),*

2 You know that after two days is *the Feast of* the *Passover,* and the Son of Man is betrayed to be Crucified *(the Holy Spirit re-*

vealed to Christ the fact that Judas would betray Him).

3 Then assembled together the Chief Priests, and the Scribes, and the Elders of the people (possibly other members of the Sanhedrin), unto the palace of the High Priest, who was called Caiaphas (these men plotted to kill Christ, as they would kill a wild beast; Caiaphas committed suicide about two years later),

4 And consulted (the topic of their conversation was the most diabolical crime ever conceived in the hearts of wicked men) that they might take Jesus by subtilty (they couldn't do it openly, so they plotted to do it undercover), and kill Him (their actions would result in the destruction of their nation, and in such a bloody way as to defy description!).

5 But they said, Not on the feast day (should have been translated, "not during the Feast"), lest there be an uproar among the people (many of the people loved Christ).

MARY OF BETHANY ANOINTS JESUS

6 Now when Jesus was in Bethany, in the house of Simon the leper (it is believed by some that Martha was the wife of Simon the leper, Lazarus and Mary being, consequently, brother-in-law and sister-in-law to Simon),

7 There came unto Him a woman (Mary [Jn. 12:3]) having an alabaster box of very precious ointment (worth about twelve thousand dollars in 2003 money), and poured it on His head, as He sat at meat (anointing Him while He was alive, proved that she believed in His Resurrection; seemingly, she was the only one who did; there was only one anointing).

8 But when His Disciples saw it, they had indignation (Judas originated this complaint [Jn. 12:4]), saying, To what purpose is this waste?

9 For this ointment might have been sold for much, and given to the poor (Judas said this [Jn. 12:4] his motives were probably to steal the money [Jn. 12:6]).

10 When Jesus understood it, He said unto them, Why do you trouble the woman? for she has wrought a good work upon Me (it concerned His death at Calvary).

11 For you have the poor always with you; but Me you have not always (He spoke of His human body being removed from the touch and sight of men, and is even now in Heaven).

12 For in that she has poured this ointment on My body, she did it for My burial (this was normally done after death, but Mary believed that He would rise from

the dead).

13 Verily I say unto you, Wheresoever this Gospel shall be preached in the whole world, *there* shall also this, that this woman has done, be told for a memorial of her *(opponents of inspiration deny the fact of prediction; but they cannot deny the fact of this Prophecy; it was made nearly two thousand years ago, and has been fulfilled untold times).*

THE BETRAYAL

14 Then one of the twelve, called Judas Iscariot, went unto the Chief Priests,

15 And said *unto them,* What will you give me, and I will deliver Him unto you? And they covenanted with him for thirty pieces of silver *(this was the price of a slave [Ex. 21:32]; as well, it was prophesied hundreds of years before, that Jesus would be sold for thirty pieces of silver [Zech. 11:13]).*

16 And from that time he sought opportunity to betray Him.

PREPARATION FOR THE PASSOVER

17 Now the first *day* of the *Feast of* Unleavened Bread *(it meant the day was approaching, which was Thursday; the day the following*

question was asked was Tuesday) the Disciples came to Jesus, saying unto Him, Where will You that we prepare for You to eat the Passover? *(Jesus would eat the Passover a day early. In fact, He was the Passover, with His death fulfilling some fifteen hundred years of this ritual.)*

18 And He said, Go into the city *(He went into Jerusalem, for He was presently at Bethany)* to such a man *(who the man was is not known; some think he was the father of John Mark, who wrote the Gospel of Mark),* and say unto him, The Master says, My time is at hand *(the statement that carries with it the meaning of the ages);* I will keep the Passover at your house with My Disciples *(what an honor for that family and that house).*

19 And the Disciples did as Jesus had appointed them; and they made ready the Passover *(speaks of the last Passover that would ever be offered, at least that God would recognize!).*

THE LAST PASSOVER

20 Now when the evening was come, He sat down with the twelve *(it was probably about 6 p.m. Tuesday night; but by Jewish reckoning at that time, it would have been the first hour of the new day of Wednesday; their new day*

always started at sunset, instead of midnight as it now does for us).

21 And as they did eat, He said, Verily I say unto you, that one of you shall betray Me *(presents Christ giving Judas a last chance of repentance before the final act; in fact, Christ made several such like efforts regarding Judas)*.

22 And they *(all the Disciples)* were exceeding sorrowful, and began every one of them to say unto Him, Lord, is it I? *(They realized the import of these words, but it seems that none, at least at this time, suspected Judas.)*

23 And He answered and said, He who dips *his* hand with Me in the dish, the same shall betray Me *(this was spoken to all the Disciples, in as much as all had dipped into the dish; consequently, the information was not too revealing)*.

24 The Son of Man goeth as it is written of Him *(refers to all that the Prophets had said concerning this time)*: but woe unto that man by whom the Son of Man is betrayed! it had been good for that man if he had not been born *(proclaims the eternal consequence of Judas' action, as well as all others who refuse Christ)*.

25 Then Judas, which betrayed Him, answered and said, Master, is it I? He said unto him, You have said *(the Lord's reply was evidently so quiet that the others did not hear)*.

THE LORD'S SUPPER INSTITUTED

26 And as they were eating, Jesus took bread, and blessed *it*, and broke *it*, and gave *it* to the Disciples, and said, Take, eat; this is My body *(this was the symbol of that which He would do, and become; He was the "bread" and consequently, "blessed," likewise, His body was "broken" at Calvary; as well, He "gave" the results of this action at Calvary to the world, for all who would believe [Jn. 3:16])*.

27 And He took the cup, and gave thanks, and gave *it* to them, saying, Drink ye all of it *(the cup is meant to serve as a symbol of His shed Blood at Calvary)*;

28 For this is My Blood of the New Testament *(New Covenant)*, which is shed for many for the remission of sins *(His death at Calvary would settle forever the sin debt, and for all of humanity, at least for all who will believe [Jn. 1:29]; as is obvious, the Lord's Supper ever directs the Believer to the Cross)*.

29 But I say unto you, I will not drink henceforth of this fruit of the vine, until that day when I drink it new with you in my Father's Kingdom *(refers to the coming Kingdom Age)*.

30 And when they had sung an hymn, they went out into the Mount of Olives *(refers to Psalms 115 and 118)*.

JESUS FORETELLS PETER'S DENIAL

31 Then said Jesus unto them, All you shall be offended because of Me this night (all of them would forsake Him, but He would never forsake them): for it is written, I will smite the shepherd, and the sheep of the flock shall be scattered abroad (Zech. 13:7).

32 But after I am risen again, I will go before you into Galilee (it seemed that none believed what He said).

33 Peter answered and said unto Him, Though all men shall be offended because of you, yet will I never be offended (boastful pride!).

34 Jesus said unto him, Verily I say unto you, That this night, before the rooster crows, you shall deny Me thrice.

35 Peter said unto Him, Though I should die with You, yet will I not deny You. Likewise also said all the Disciples (all made boastful claims).

JESUS IN THE GARDEN

36 Then cometh Jesus with them unto a place called Gethsemane (just across the Kidron Valley from Jerusalem, about two hundred yards from the city wall), and said unto the Disciples, Sit you here, while I go and pray yonder.

37 And He took with him Peter and the two sons of Zebedee (James and John), and began to be sorrowful and very heavy (tremendous stress and pressure).

38 Then said He unto them, My soul is exceeding sorrowful, even unto death (means that He, as a Man, could not have endured it but for added Angelic strength [Lk. 22:43-44]): tarry ye here, and watch with Me (He needed their presence, even though it would prove to be of little solace).

39 And He went a little farther (more than physical, the distance He went in agony and prayer at this time, no human being could follow), and fell on His face, and prayed (He did so repeatedly, meaning that He would fall to the ground, struggle to get up, and then fall again), saying, O My Father, if it be possible, let this cup pass from Me (this "cup" was threefold: bearing the sin penalty of humanity, separation from the Father, and death): nevertheless not as I will, but as You will (proclaims the Divine Will as the expression of Divine Righteousness and Love, which limits the exercise of Divine Power, and therefore supplies the necessary check to the expectations which might otherwise arise from the belief in Omnipotence).

40 And He came unto the Disciples, and finding them asleep (portraying the fact that they did

not realize the acute danger for which they were ill-prepared), and said unto Peter (evidently awaking him), What, could you not watch with Me one hour?

41 Watch and pray, that you enter not into temptation (a warning of the temptation that was about to come upon them — the temptation to forsake Him): the spirit (spirit of man) indeed is willing, but the flesh is weak (this battle can be won only by our Faith being placed exclusively in Christ and His Cross, which then gives the Holy Spirit latitude to work within our lives [Rom. 6:3-14; 8:1-2, 11]).

42 He went away again the second time, and prayed, saying, O My Father, if this cup may not pass away from Me, except I drink it, Your will be done (a total acquiescence to God's Will).

43 And He came and found them asleep again: for their eyes were heavy (Love is always ready to excuse weakness, for example, the lateness of the hour, and the fact that they were sleeping for sorrow [Lk. 22:45]).

44 And He left them, and went away again, and prayed the third time, saying the same words (sometimes we must pray the same words again, and again).

45 Then cometh He to His Disciples, and said unto them, Sleep on now, and take your rest (may be translated, "do you sleep on now, continuing to take your rest"?): behold, the hour is at hand, and the Son of Man is betrayed into the hands of sinners (refers to Judas, who is even now entering the Garden with the Temple guard and others in order to arrest Christ).

46 Rise, let us be going: behold, he is at hand who does betray Me (the Holy Spirit had told Him exactly what was happening, and when it would happen).

THE BETRAYAL AND ARREST OF JESUS

47 And while He yet spake, lo, Judas, one of the twelve, came (is given in this fashion by the Holy Spirit in order to enhance his guilt. Never in human history has so perfidious an act been carried out against One Who was so good, kind, and gracious), and with him a great multitude with swords and staves (the Temple guard, and some Roman soldiers), from the Chief Priests and Elders of the people (the Church has ever killed the Lord, in the Name of the Lord).

48 Now he who betrayed Him gave them a sign, saying, Whomsoever I shall kiss, that same is He: hold Him fast (speaks of the most despicable, treacherous moment in human history).

49 And forthwith he came to Jesus, and said, Hail, Master; and kissed Him (Ps. 55:21).

50 And Jesus said unto him, Friend (*said in kindness and not sarcasm*), wherefore are you come? (*Could be translated, "do that for which you are come."*) Then came they, and laid hands on Jesus, and took Him (*presents the beginning of the action of the murderous hearts of the religious leaders of Israel; they hated Christ, and would have done this much sooner, had the opportunity presented itself*).

51 And, behold, one of them which were with Jesus stretched out *his* hand, and drew his sword, and struck a servant of the High Priest's, and smote off his ear (*John said this was Simon Peter; as well, the name of the servant is Malthus; incidentally, Jesus healed the man's ear, which was His last miracle before His death*).

52 Then said Jesus unto him (*unto Peter*), Put up again your sword into his place (*the Magistrate to whom God gives a sword, is responsible to use it against evildoers; that is "his place" [Rom. 13:4]*): for all they who take the sword shall perish with the sword (*the sword has no place in the propagation of the Gospel*).

53 Thinkest thou that I cannot now pray to My Father, and He shall presently give Me more than twelve legions of Angels? (*Seventy-two thousand Angels.*)

54 But how then shall the Scriptures be fulfilled, that thus it must be? (*The word "must" affirms the Divine Inspiration of the Scriptures; for had they been composed by men there would have been no necessity compelling their fulfillment.*)

55 In that same hour said Jesus to the multitudes (*believed to have been approximately six hundred men*), Are you come out as against a thief with swords and staves for to take Me? I sat daily with you teaching in the Temple, and you laid no hold on Me (*Jesus pointing out the fact that they didn't arrest Him in the Temple, because they feared the people*).

56 But all this was done (*could have been translated, "all this has come to pass"*), that the Scriptures of the Prophets might be fulfilled (*through foreknowledge, the Holy Spirit predicted this many centuries in advance [Gen. 3:15; 49:10; Isa. 7:14; Chpt. 53; Zech. 11:12] the Scriptures were ever the foundation of all that was done, and had better be the same presently*). Then all the Disciples forsook Him, and fled (*fulfilled that which was written [Zech. 13:7]*).

THE TRIAL

57 And they that had laid hold on Jesus led *Him* away to Caiaphas the High Priest (*Matthew omits the account of Jesus being led first before Annas, the former*

High Priest, as recorded in Jn. 18:13, 19-24), where the Scribes and the Elders were assembled (pertains to the palace or court of the High Priest).

58 But Peter followed Him afar off (presents the Apostle turning back toward Christ from Whom he had fled at first; no doubt, he is ashamed of his actions, and now in a quandary, timidly follows the route taking Jesus to the Palace) unto the High Priest's palace, and went in, and sat with the servants, to see the end.

59 Now the Chief Priests, and Elders, and all the council, sought false witness (they didn't care if the witness was true or false) against Jesus, to put Him to death (these were the religious leaders of Israel);

60 But found none (found none who would collaborate each other): yes, though many false witnesses came, yet found they none. At the last came two false witnesses (these seized upon a statement made by Christ, and twisted it out of context),

61 And said, This ("fellow" was inserted by the translators, and was not in the original Text; the accuser might have pointed a finger at Christ, referring to Him contemptuously, as "This!") fellow said, I am able to destroy the Temple of God, and to build it in three days (this is a distortion of what He actually said; Jesus had ac-tually said, "destroy this Temple [speaking of His physical body], and in three days I will raise it up" [Jn. 2:19]).

62 And the High Priest (Caiaphas) arose, and said unto Him, Answerest thou nothing? (Presents Christ answering His accusers not at all.) what is it which these witness against You?

63 But Jesus held His peace (fulfilled the Scripture, "He was oppressed, and He was afflicted, yet He opened not His Mouth [Isa. 53:7]). And the High Priest answered and said unto Him, I adjure You by the Living God, that You tell us whether You be the Christ, the Son of God.

64 Jesus said unto him, You have said (presents Christ giving a direct affirmation, with Mark saying it even clearer, "I am" [Mk. 14:62]): nevertheless I say unto you (would have been better translated, "but moreover I say unto you"), Hereafter shall you see the Son of Man (speaking of Himself) sitting on the right hand of power (actually speaks of the Great White Throne Judgment; they are now judging Him; He will then judge them), and coming in the clouds of Heaven (Second Coming).

65 Then the High Priest rent his clothes (ripped the shawl thrown across His shoulder, signifying his supposed horror of Jesus referring to Himself as the Son of God), say-

ing, He hath spoken blasphemy *(meaning He had made Himself One with God)*; what further need have we of witnesses? *(Means they can dispense with all the liars.)* behold, now you have heard His blasphemy *(the entire Sanhedrin had heard His statement; but He did not blaspheme; He spoke the truth)*.

66 What do you think? *(Was spoken by Caiaphas to the Sanhedrin, which was composed of seventy-one members, if all were present.)* They answered and said, He is guilty of death *(when they sentenced Him to death, they sentenced themselves as well!)*.

67 Then *(refers in the modern vernacular to "fair game")* did they spit in His face *(considered to be the greatest insult to a person)*, and buffeted Him *(hit Him with their fist, probably done by the Temple guards, but was undoubtedly done as well by some members of the Sanhedran)*; and others smote Him with the palms of their hands *(should have been translated, "smote Him with rods"; the Prophet had said, "as many as were astonished at You; His visage was so marred more than any man, and His form more than the sons of men" [Isa. 52:14])*,

68 Saying, Prophesy unto us *(Jesus had just done this [Vs. 64])*, Thou Christ *(the words were spoken contemptuously! Christ means* "the Anointed," *and spoke of the Messiah; they were making fun of His claims, and consequently, ridiculing the Anointing of the Holy Spirit upon Him; they were doing what they had accused Him of doing — blaspheming)*, Who is he who smote you? *(Mark and Luke said they blindfolded Him [14:65; 22:64].)*

PETER'S DENIAL

69 Now Peter sat without in the palace *(the way the Court was constructed, Peter could see Christ, and Christ could see Peter [Lk. 22:61])*: and a damsel came unto him *(probably referred to the lady who kept the door, which gave entrance into the court yard)*, saying, You also were with Jesus of Galilee *(with sarcasm)*.

70 But he denied before them all *(first denial, spoken before a number of people standing with the girl)*, saying, I know not what you say.

71 And when he was gone out into the porch *(referred to him seemingly trying to remove himself from those who had just fingered him)*, another maid saw him, and said unto them who were there, This fellow was also with Jesus of Nazareth *(as well, with sarcasm)*.

72 And again he denied with an oath *(what the oath was, we do not

know), I do not know the man (He claims not even to know His Name).

73 And after a while *(represents according to Luke 22:59, about an hour of time)* came unto *him* they that stood by, and said to Peter, Surely you also are *one* of them; for your speech betrays you *(he was a Galilean, as were all the Disciples, with the exception of Judas).*

74 Then began he to curse and to swear *(not profanity, but rather to take a solemn oath such as men do in a Court of Justice, and then to call upon God to curse Him if the oath were false; it was a sin of appalling magnitude and depth),* saying, I know not the man *(meaning that he swore by the name of God that he did not know Christ).* And immediately the cock *(rooster)* crowed.

75 And Peter remembered the word of Jesus, which said unto him, Before the rooster crows, you shall deny Me thrice *(Vs. 34).* And he went out, and wept bitterly *(tradition says that for the rest of his life, Peter could not hear a rooster crow without falling upon his knees and weeping).*

CHAPTER 27

JESUS SENT TO PILATE

WHEN the morning was come *(referred to Wednesday morn-ing; Jesus would be crucified in a matter of hours; He was not crucified on Good Friday as many claim!),* all the Chief Priests and Elders of the people took counsel against Jesus to put him to death *(the morning session was that of the entire Sanhedrin; it followed the unofficial meeting in the High Priest's house [26:57]):*

2 And when they had bound Him, they led *Him* away *(refers to His Hands being tied behind His back with a rope),* and delivered Him to Pontius Pilate the governor *(he held this office for some ten years, at the end of which time he was removed for cruelty and extortion, and banished to Vienne in Gaul, where he committed suicide).*

JUDAS KILLS HIMSELF

3 Then Judas, which had betrayed Him, when he saw that He was condemned *(refers to what the religious leaders had done to Jesus and their brutal treatment of Him; in fact, he probably saw Jesus, and was sickened by what he saw),* and repented himself *(in the Greek, means to have a deep remorse at the consequence of sin, but not deep regret at the cause of it; the word is never used of genuine repentance to God),* and brought again the thirty pieces of silver *(the price he had been given)* to the Chief Priests

and Elders *(concerns the blood money, and the religious leaders with blood on their hands),*

4 Saying, I have sinned *(presents him confessing this sin to man, an evil man at that, but not to God)* in that I have betrayed the innocent blood *("the" emphasizes that the Blood of Christ was the only truly innocent blood that has ever been).* And they said, What is that to us? see thou *to that (they knew that Jesus was innocent, but did not care!).*

5 And he cast down the pieces of silver in the Temple *(presents him flinging the shekels onto the marble floor),* and departed, and went and hanged himself *(he probably hanged himself with his own sash, which was wound around his waist; tradition says that the limb broke from the tree to which the sash was tied, and he fell heavily to the rocks below, where a passing wagon, unable to stop, crushed and disemboweled him).*

6 And the Chief Priests took the silver pieces *(represents the blood money now in their hands where it rightfully belonged all the time!),* and said, It is not lawful for to put them into the treasury, because it is the price of blood *(it is ironic! they were gagging at a gnat and swallowing a camel).*

7 And they *(the Sanhedrin)* took counsel *(institutionalized religion opposed Christ from the* very beginning; it still does!), and bought with them *(the thirty pieces of silver)* the potter's field, to bury strangers in *(Gentiles — a place on the south of Jerusalem, across the valley of Hinnom).*

8 Wherefore that field was called, The field of blood, unto this day *(was not the name given it by the religious leaders of Israel, but others! up to the mid 1800's, it was still being used for this purpose, the burying of the unhonored dead of Jerusalem).*

9 Then was fulfilled that which was spoken by Jeremiah the Prophet *(although the Scriptures do not say, this was probably originally spoken by Jeremiah, and done so by the Holy Spirit, but not written down; it was then repeated and recorded by that same Spirit in Zechariah 11:12-13 or else a copyist made a mistake in copying it from the original text; no original text remains),* saying, And they took the thirty pieces of silver, the price of Him that was valued, Whom they of the Children of Israel did value *(this was the price of a slave; it is given in this manner by the Holy Spirit in order to emphasize the fact that this was the price or worth that Israel placed upon her Messiah);*

10 And gave them *(thirty pieces of silver)* for the potter's field, as the Lord appointed Me *(appointed the Messiah; did not the religious*

leaders of Israel know about this Prophecy?).

JESUS BEFORE PILATE

11 And Jesus stood before the governor *(speaks of Pontius Pilate)*: and the governor asked Him, saying, are You the King of the Jews? *(In reality, Jehoiachin, who reigned some six hundred years before, was the last King recognized by God, to sit on the Throne of Judah [II Chron. 36:9-10].)* And Jesus said unto him, Thou sayest *(in effect, says, "I am the King of the Jews"; as far as is recorded, this is the first time Jesus had made such a claim; John added more of the answer of Christ, with Jesus saying, "My Kingdom is not of this world" [Jn. 18:36]; consequently, Pilate knew that His claims were spiritual, and therefore, not of this world).*

12 And when He was accused of the Chief Priests and Elders, He answered nothing *(He would not defend Himself before people who cared nothing for the truth).*

13 Then said Pilate unto Him, Do You not hear how many things they witness against You? *(Pilate was somewhat confused as to why Jesus did not defend Himself against these accusations.)*

14 And He answered him to never a word *(fulfilling Isaiah 53:7)*; insomuch that the governor marvelled greatly *(Pilate was astonished that Jesus defended Himself not at all against these accusations, seeing that they could lead to His death).*

JESUS CONDEMNED; BARABBAS RELEASED

15 Now at *that feast (the Passover)* the governor was wont *(accustomed)* to release unto the people a prisoner, whom they would *(in other words, the people could choose, and the one chosen would be released; Pilate thought he had found a way out of his dilemma; he knew that Jesus was innocent).*

16 And they had then a notable prisoner *(should have been translated "notorious")*, called Barabbas *(Mark said that Barabbas was a murderer, and had led an insurrection against Roman authority [Mk. 15:7]).*

17 Therefore when they were gathered together *(Pilate and Jesus standing on the porch of the hall, before the people below)*, Pilate said unto them, Whom will you that I release unto you? Barabbas, or Jesus which is called Christ? *(In some manuscripts, Barabbas is referred to as "Jesus Barabbas." So the people were faced with a choice, "Jesus Barabbas, the murderer," or "Jesus Christ, the Giver of Eternal Life.")*

18 For He knew that for envy they had delivered Him *(they envied the respect given Him by the people, and His miracles).*

19 When he was sat down on the judgment seat *(a chair on a raised platform in front of the praetorian),* his wife sent unto him, saying, Have thou nothing to do with that just Man: for I have suffered many things this day in a dream because of Him *(her name was Claudia — another name Procula; tradition says that she ultimately became a Christian; what her dream was, the record does not say; however, in all of the account of the sufferings of Christ this last week before His death, she, a Gentile is the only one, it seems, who gave Him a kind word).*

20 But the Chief Priests and Elders persuaded the multitude that they should ask Barabbas *(asked for the release of Barabbas the murderer; consequently, murderers have ruled them from then until now, even unto this hour, considering the bombings in Israel),* and destroy *(kill)* Jesus.

21 The governor answered and said unto them, Whether of the two will you that I release unto you? *(Presents no alternative but Jesus or Barabbas.)* They said, Barabbas.

22 Pilate saith unto them, What shall I do then with Jesus which is called Christ? *(The great-est question ever asked. The answer to it decides the eternal destiny of the human soul.)* They all say unto him, Let Him be crucified *(they specified "crucifixion," because such a death would cause all the people, they thought, to turn against Him; the Law of Moses condemned anyone hanged upon a tree as being cursed by God [Deut. 21:23]).*

23 And the governor said, Why, what evil has He done? *(He had done no evil. He was perfect! He had never sinned.)* But they cried out the more, saying, Let Him be crucified *(proclaims them offering no answer to the question of Pilate, because they had no answer; as the morning sun begins to break over Olivet, it will dawn on a day of infamy such as the world has never seen before or since).*

24 When Pilate saw that he could prevail nothing, but *that* rather a tumult was made *(he feared that if he did not give in to their demands, a riot might occur, with him then being accused before Rome of refusing to punish a pretender to the Jewish Throne),* he took water, and washed *his* hands before the multitude *(by this act, he attempted to clear himself of guilt, and to cast the guilt upon the people, as if the administration of Justice lay with them and not with him),* saying, I am innocent of the blood of this just

person: see you *to it (him saying it here, did not make it so! he didn't have the courage to do what was right; one cannot take a neutral position as it regards Christ).*

25 Then answered all the people, and said, His Blood *be* on us, and on our children *(the malediction they invoked upon themselves and upon their children rests upon them still, and was, and is, a malediction of appalling horror and suffering).*

26 Then released he Barabbas unto them *(proclaims the choice of the people)*: and when he *(Pilate)* had scourged Jesus *(a punishment so horrible, that sometimes it killed the victim before the act of crucifixion could be employed [Isa. 50:6]),* he delivered Him to be crucified *(Isa., Chpt. 53).*

JESUS CROWNED WITH THORNS

27 Then the soldiers *(Roman soldiers)* of the governor took Jesus into the common hall, and gathered unto Him the whole band *of soldiers (about two hundred men, which was the third part a "cohort").*

28 And they stripped Him *(referred to His robe, not the inner garments),* and put on *Him* a scarlet robe *(either a worn-out officer's cloak or else a cast-off garment from the wardrobe of Herod).*

29 And when they had platted a crown of thorns *(called "victor's thorns" and which grew up to six inches in length),* they put *it* upon His head *(the Greek word for "crown" is "stephanos," and means "a victory crown"; even though they meant it for shame and mockery, by this crown of thorns, the Lord portrayed the Victory of the Cross and its certitude, even before Jesus actually died),* and a reed in His right hand: and they bowed the knee before Him, and mocked Him, saying, Hail, King of the Jews! *(At the coming Great White Throne Judgment, these same soldiers will once again stand before Christ, and once again bow the knee to Him. But this time, it will not be in mocking tone.)*

30 And they spit upon Him, and took the reed, and smote Him on the head *(driving the thorns deeper, which no doubt caused His head to swell).*

31 And after that they had mocked Him, they took the robe off from Him, and put His own raiment on Him, and led Him away to crucify *Him (Crucifixion is supposed to have been invented by Semiramis, Queen of Nimrod, who founded the Babylonian system of mysteries).*

32 And as they came out *(on the way to Calvary),* they found a man of Cyrene, Simon by name *(Alexander and Rufus were the sons of*

Simon [Mk. 15:21; Rom. 16:13]): him they compelled to bear His cross *(it was not the entire Cross, but probably the "patibulum," or the cross bar; it would have weighed not much short of a hundred pounds; in His weakened condition, Jesus could not bear that load).*

THE CRUCIFIXION

33 And when they were come unto a place called Golgotha, that is to say, a place of a skull *(tradition says that Adam was buried here, and that his skull was found here),*

34 They gave Him vinegar to drink mingled with gall: and when He had tasted *thereof,* He would not drink *(this was a stupefying potion, given to help alleviate sufferings; Christ refused it).*

35 And they crucified Him, and parted His garments *(this was their "extra pay" for serving this ghastly duty),* casting lots *(they drew straws, so to speak):* that it might be fulfilled which was spoken by the Prophet, They parted My garments among them, and upon My vesture did they cast lots *(Ps. 22:18).*

36 And sitting down they watched Him there *(made sure that friends didn't come and take the condemned One down, before He died);*

37 And set up over His head His accusation written *(this per-* tained *to the crime for which the accused was condemned),* THIS IS JESUS THE KING OF THE JEWS *(it is said that this was written in three languages, Hebrew, Greek, and Latin; they printed this in mockery, but no words were ever more true).*

38 Then were there two thieves crucified with Him *(Isa. 53:12),* one on the right hand, and another on the left.

39 And they who passed by reviled Him, wagging their heads *(for the most part, these were the religious leaders of Israel [Ps. 109:25]),*

40 And saying, You who will destroy the Temple, and build *it* in three days *(Jesus never said that! He did say, that His physical body would be destroyed, and in three days He would raise it up, which is exactly what happened),* save Yourself *(He didn't come to save Himself, but rather others).* If You be the Son of God, come down from the Cross *(had He come down from the Cross, no one would've ever been saved, and those in the prison of Paradise, would have remained there forever).*

41 Likewise also the Chief Priests mocking *Him,* with the Scribes and Elders, said *(this is religion at work!),*

42 He saved others *(that He did, but the "others" did not include these religious leaders, because they would not accept Him);* Himself

He cannot save (*the actual truth, Himself He will not save*). If He be the King of Israel, let Him now come down from the Cross, and we will believe Him (*blasphemers are also liars!*).

43 He trusted in God (*Ps. 22:8*); let Him deliver Him now, if He will have Him (*they wouldn't have Him, but God would*): for He said, I am the Son of God (*represents exactly what He said!*).

44 The thieves also, which were crucified with Him, cast the same in His teeth (*they both did at first, but a little later, one repented, recorded by Luke 23:42*).

THE DEATH OF JESUS

45 Now from the sixth hour (*12 Noon*) there was darkness over all the land unto the ninth hour (*3 p.m. — for these three hours, God would literally hide His Face from His Son; during this time, Jesus did bear the sin penalty of mankind [II Cor. 5:21] "this darkness" was not the result of an eclipse, for then the moon was full; it was brought on by God in that He could not look upon His Son, as He did bear the sin penalty of the world*).

46 And about the ninth hour Jesus cried with a loud voice (*showing He didn't die from weakness, but rather laid down His Own Life [Jn. 10:17-18]*), saying, Eli, Eli, lama sabachthani? that is to say, My God, my God, why have You forsaken Me? (*The question as to why God had forsaken Him was not asked in a sense of not knowing, but in a sense of acknowledging the act. God didn't deliver Him, even as He always had, because, to have done such, would have forfeited Redemption for mankind. Incidentally, Jesus spoke in Aramaic, which was commonly used by the Lord.*)

47 Some of them who stood there, when they heard *that*, said, This *man* calls for Elijah (*this would have referred to Jews, because Romans would have known nothing about Elijah*).

48 And straightway (*immediately*) one of them ran, and took a sponge, and filled *it* with vinegar, and put *it* on a reed, and gave Him to drink (*the evidence is, it touched His lips, and He died; it had nothing to do with His Life or death*).

49 The rest said, Let be, let us see whether Elijah will come to save Him (*said in mockery!*).

50 Jesus, when He had cried again with a loud voice, yielded up the ghost (*He freely laid down His Life, meaning that He didn't die from His wounds; as well, He didn't die until the Holy Spirit told him to do so [Heb. 9:14]*).

51 And, behold, the Veil of the Temple (*that which hid the Holy of Holies; Josephus said it was sixty feet high from the ceiling to the*

floor, four inches thick, and was so strong, that four yoke of oxen could not pull it apart) was rent in twain from the top to the bottom *(meaning that God alone could have done such a thing; it also signified, that the price was paid completely on the Cross; signified by the rent Veil; regrettably, some say, the Cross — didn't finish the task with other things required; this Verse says differently);* and the earth did quake, and the rocks rent *(represented an earthquake, but had nothing to do with the renting of the Veil, which took place immediately before this phenomenon);*

52 And the graves were opened; and many bodies of the Saints which slept arose *(does not teach "soul sleep" as some claim, but rather that the bodies of the Sainted dead do sleep; not the soul and the spirit, which then went to Paradise, but since the Cross, at death, now go to be with Christ [Phil. 1:23]),*

53 And came out of the graves after His resurrection, and went into the holy city (Jerusalem), and appeared unto many *(while all were delivered out of Paradise, and taken to Heaven, some, even many, stopped over in Jerusalem for a short period of time, "and appeared unto many"; how many there were, we aren't told, and to whom they appeared, we aren't told; Matthew alone gives this account).*

54 Now when the centurion, and they who were with him, watching Jesus, saw the earthquake, and those things that were done, they feared greatly, saying, Truly this was the Son of God *(he was the first Gentile to render this testimony of Faith; tradition affirms that the Centurion's name was Longinus, and that he became a devoted follower of Christ, preached the Faith, and died a martyr's death).*

55 And many women were there beholding afar off, which followed Jesus from Galilee, ministering unto Him *(concerns those who came from Galilee, and were with Him unto the end):*

56 Among which was Mary Magdalene *(Jesus had delivered her [Mk. 16:9; Lk. 8:2]),* and Mary the mother of James and Joseph *(probably the wife of Cleophas [Jn. 19:25]),* and the mother of Zebedee's children *(Salome [Mk. 15:40] the mother of James and John).*

THE BURIAL OF JESUS

57 When the evening was come *(referred to a period of time between 3 p.m. until sunset; was the Passover Sabbath — not the weekly Sabbath),* there came a rich man of Arimathaea, named Joseph *(he was a member of the Sanhedrin, but was no doubt, not present at the so-called trial of Jesus),* who also himself was Jesus' Disciple *(he was a follower*

*of Christ, which means that he had
accepted Him as Lord):*

58 He went to Pilate *(proves
that he had access to the governor),*
and begged the body of Jesus *(it
seems that his devotion to Christ
had previously been "in secret for
fear of the Jews" [Jn. 19:38]).* Then
Pilate commanded the body to
be delivered *(proclaims the Roman Governor as the only one who
could give such an order).*

59 And when Joseph had taken
the body *(had taken it down from
the Cross),* he wrapped it in a clean
linen cloth *(this was the physical
body, prepared by God, to be used
as a Sacrifice, which it was, in order to redeem Adam's fallen race
[Heb. 10:5]),*

60 And laid it in his own new
tomb *(which had never been used),*
which he had hewn out in the
rock *(it was cut out of solid rock):*
and he rolled a great stone to
the door of the sepulchre, and
departed *(this is the same "great
stone" that the Angel rolled away
[28:2]).*

61 And there was Mary Magdalene, and the other Mary *(the
wife of Cleophas, and the sister of
Mary, the Mother of Jesus),* sitting
over against the sepulcher *(all of
this shows that none of them actually had any faith that Jesus would
come from the dead; it seems that
only Mary of Bethany actually believed such [26:6-13]).*

THE TOMB SEALED
AND GUARDED

62 Now the next day, that followed the day of the preparation
*(refers to the High Sabbath and the
Chief Day of the Passover Festival),*
the Chief Priests and Pharisees
came together unto Pilate *(referred
to the day after the Crucifixion),*

63 Saying, Sir, we remember
that that deceiver said, while He
was yet alive, After three days I
will rise again *(their testimony
here confirms that Jesus died and
did not merely swoon as some modern unbelievers claim).*

64 Command therefore that
the sepulchre be made sure until
the third day *(insures three days
and three nights in the Tomb),* lest
His Disciples come by night, and
steal Him away, and say unto the
people, He is risen from the dead
*(by their actions, they will make
the proof of His Resurrection irrefutable):* so the last error shall be
worse than the first *(their claiming that the people's belief in Him
had been an "error," and if they
in any way thought He had risen
from the dead, this would be an
even greater "error").*

65 Pilate said unto them, You
have a watch *(referred to a guard
of four soldiers which was changed
every three hours, meaning that it
was continuous):* go your way,
make it as sure as ye can *(they not*

only had the soldiers at their command, but were free to do whatever else they saw fit to guarantee the security of the Tomb).

66 So they went, and made the sepulchre sure, sealing the stone *(they passed a cord around the stone that closed the mouth of the sepulcher to the two sides of the entrance; this was sealed with wax or prepared clay in the center and at the ends, so that the stone could not be removed without breaking the seals or the cord),* and setting a watch *(the four soldiers took up their position at the mouth of the Tomb and in front of the Stone; His enemies made the proof of His Resurrection incontrovertible).*

CHAPTER 28

THE RESURRECTION OF CHRIST

IN the end of the Sabbath *(the regular weekly Sabbath, which was every Saturday),* as it began to dawn toward the first *day* of the week *(this was just before daylight on Sunday morning; Jesus rose from the dead some time after sunset on Saturday evening; the Jews began the new day at sunset, instead of midnight, as we do presently),* came Mary Magdalene and the other Mary to see the sepulcher *(they wanted to put spices on the body of Christ).*

2 And, behold, there was a great earthquake *(presents the second earthquake, with the first taking place, when Christ died [27:51]):* for the Angel of the Lord descended from Heaven *(was probably observed by the Roman soldiers, who alone witnessed it and gave the account),* and came and rolled back the stone from the door *(Christ had already risen from the dead and had left the Tomb when the stone was rolled away; His glorified body was not restricted by obstacles),* and sat upon it *(this was done as a show of triumph; in other words, death was vanquished!).*

3 His countenance was like lightning, and his raiment white as snow *(there is no evidence that any of the women or Disciples saw this glorious coming of the Angel; however, the next Verse tells us that the Roman guards did see it, and were terrified!):*

4 And for fear of Him *(the Angel)* the keepers *(guards)* did shake, and became as dead *men (inasmuch as this happened at night, the situation was even more frightful).*

5 And the Angel answered and said unto the women *(this was just before dawn, and after the soldiers had run away),* Do not fear: for I know that you seek Jesus, which was crucified *(the Angel now uses this word, "Crucified," in a most glorious manner; it is now "the Power of God and the Wisdom of God"*

[I Cor. 1:23-24]).

6 He is not here (is the beginning of the most glorious statement that could ever fall upon the ears of mere mortals): for he is risen (a dead and risen Saviour is the life and substance of the Gospel [I Cor. 15:1-4]), as He said (the Angel brought to the attention of the women, the fact that Christ had stated several times that He would be crucified and would rise from the dead). Come, see the place where the Lord lay (they were looking for a corpse, but instead, would find a risen Lord; they were looking for a Tomb containing a corpse, but instead, would find it empty).

7 And go quickly, and tell His Disciples that He is risen from the dead (the Disciples should have been the ones telling others, but because of unbelief, the women will tell them; this is the greatest Message that humanity has ever received); and, behold, He goes before you into Galilee; there shall ye see Him (He would reveal Himself to whom and to where He so desired): lo, I have told you (guarantees the certitude of this action).

THE TESTIMONY OF THE WOMEN

8 And they departed quickly from the sepulcher (they had actually gone into the burial chamber, and had seen with their own eyes that Jesus was not there [Lk. 24:3]) with fear and great joy (this was a "healthy fear," which every Believer ought to have; and as is understandable, there was "great joy"); and did run to bring His Disciples word ("they did run" because they had a Message to tell, and what a Message it was! this would be the greatest "word" the Disciples would ever hear).

9 And as they went to tell His Disciples, behold, Jesus met them (this was not the first appearance of Jesus, that being to Mary Magdalene [Mk. 16:9]), saying, All hail (actually meant, "all joy"!). And they came and held Him by the feet, and worshipped Him (they would find that they were touching a human body of flesh and bone, and that it was not an apparition or ghostly figure; they knew He had been raised from the dead; still, they were not at all certain as to what was meant by that; His appearance to them, with them touching Him, removed all doubts as to what the Resurrection meant).

10 Then said Jesus unto them, Be not afraid (it definitely is understandable that they were afraid): go tell My brethren that they go into Galilee, and there shall they see Me (means more than merely an appearance; actually, He would also appear to them in Jerusalem,

even proclaiming great Truths [Jn. 20:19-23]; John in the last Chapter of his Book gives the appearance in Galilee in detail).

THE REPORT OF
THE SOLDIERS

11 Now when they were going (referring to the women after seeing Jesus, going to the Disciples), behold, some of the watch (soldiers) came into the city, and showed unto the Chief Priests all the things that were done (speaks of the four soldiers who had actually seen the coming of the Angel — him rolling the stone away from the mouth of the Tomb).

12 And when they (Chief Priests) were assembled with the Elders (the Sanhedrin), and had taken counsel (how they could counteract what had happened), they gave large money unto the soldiers (all now knew, and beyond the shadow of a doubt that Jesus was Who He had said He was; they knew they had Crucified the Son of God; they knew these Roman soldiers were not making up this story; for them to desert their post was a capital offence; in other words, they could be executed for such an act, but still, they did not repent! such is the hardened heart),

13 Saying, you say, His Disciples came by night, and stole Him away while we slept (what an absurd story, but yet, many Jews believe it unto this hour).

14 And if this come to the Governor's ears, we will persuade him, and secure you (meaning that the Sanhedrin would take full responsibility for this action; no harm ever came to the soldiers; evidently Pilate believed that Jesus had risen from the dead; it is said in one of the Chronicles, of that time, that Pilate sent an account of this matter to Tiberius, who, in consequence, we are told, endeavored to make the Roman Senate pass a decree enrolling Jesus in the list of Roman gods; Tertullian attests this fact).

15 So they took the money, and did as they were taught (means that the matter was rehearsed over, and over again by the Sanhedrin until all had the same story): and this saying is commonly reported among the Jews until this day (it is said that the Jews at that time sent emissaries in all directions to spread this false report).

THE TESTIMONY OF
THE DISCIPLES

16 Then the eleven Disciples went away into Galilee (the sequence seems to indicate that it took place at least a week after the Resurrection [Jn. 20:26; 21:1]; the number "11" is specifically mentioned, in that the Holy Spirit desires that the betrayal not be for-

gotten), into a mountain where Jesus had appointed them *(gives no evidence as to exactly where this mountain was; the word, "appointed," specifies that this was a designated meeting, which would have insured a definite place).*

17 And when they saw Him *(seems to indicate that there were more present than the eleven)*, they worshipped Him *(and rightly so!)*: but some doubted *(not the eleven! who they were, we do not know; why they doubted, we do not know; however, it seems the doubts soon faded).*

THE GREAT COMMISSION

18 And Jesus came and spoke unto them *(the same meeting on the mountain, and constitutes the Great Commission)*, saying, All power is given unto Me in Heaven and in earth *(this is not given to Him as Son of God; for, as God nothing can be added to Him or taken from Him; it is rather a power, which He has merited by His Incarnation and His death at Calvary on the Cross [Phil. 2:8-10]; this authority extends not only over men, so that He governs and* protects the Church, disposes human events, controls hearts and opinions; but the forces of Heaven also are at His Command; the Holy Spirit is bestowed by Him, and the Angels are in His employ as ministering to the members of His Body. When He said, "all power," He meant, "all power!").*

19 Go ye therefore *(applies to any and all who follow Christ, and in all ages)*, and teach all nations *(should have been translated, "and preach to all nations", for the word "teach" here refers to a proclamation of truth)*, baptizing them in the Name of the Father, and of the Son, and of the Holy Spirit *(presents the only formula for Water Baptism given in the Word of God)*:

20 Teaching them *(means to give instruction)* to observe all things *(the whole Gospel for the whole man)* whatsoever I have commanded you *(not a suggestion)*: and, lo, I am with you always *(It is I, Myself, God, and Man, Who am — not "will be" — hence forever present among you, and with you as Companion, Friend, Guide, Saviour, God)*, even unto the end of the world *(should have been translated "age")*. Amen *(it is the guarantee of My Promise).*

THE GOSPEL ACCORDING TO
MARK

CHAPTER 1

THE MINISTRY OF JOHN
THE BAPTIST

THE beginning of the Gospel of Jesus Christ, the Son of God *(could read, "the beginning of the Good News concerning Jesus, the Messiah, the Son of God"; the Holy Spirit begins this Book by testifying to the Kingship and Deity of Christ before setting out His perfection as a Servant; the actual beginning of this Gospel is the Ministry of John the Baptist)*;

2 As it is written in the Prophets *(proclaims the Old Testament as the Word of God)*, Behold, I send My Messenger *(John the Baptist)* before Your Face *(Christ)*, which shall prepare Your Way before You *(preparation for the introduction of the Messiah [Mal. 3:1])*.

3 The voice of one crying *(the preaching of John the Baptist was full of emotion and feeling)* in the wilderness *(typical of Israel's spiritual condition)*, Prepare ye the Way of the Lord *(the sense of a military command)*, make His paths straight *(rightly discern the Word, and obey it)*.

4 John did baptize in the wilderness *(Water Baptism in this fashion was unique)*, and preach the baptism of Repentance *(repentance of the individual)* for the Remission of sins *(should have been translated, "because of the remission of sins"; the people were being baptized because they had already repented in their hearts; there is no Salvation in the ceremony of Water Baptism)*.

5 And there went out unto him all the land of Judaea, and they of Jerusalem, and were all baptized of him in the river of Jordan, confessing their sins *(meaning that the confessing of sins and the act of Water Baptism, were at times, simultaneous)*.

6 And John was clothed with camel's hair *(characteristic of the doctrine which John taught, namely penitence and contempt of the world)*, and with a girdle of a skin about his loins *(a sash)*; and he did eat locusts and wild honey *(the locust were dried to a crispness in the sun and eaten with honey, not uncommon in those days)*;

7 And preached *(deep emotion)*, saying, There comes One *(not merely "one," but rather "The One")* mightier than I *("The Almighty One")* after me *(I will*

prepare the way), the latchet of Whose shoes I am not worthy to stoop down and unloose *(the difference being, the former was a created being, while the Latter is the Creator)*.

8 I indeed have baptized you with water: but He shall baptize you with the Holy Spirit *(due to the Cross, the Holy Spirit can now come into the heart and life of the Believer to abide permanently [Jn. 14:16-17])*.

THE BAPTISM OF JESUS

9 And it came to pass in those days *(the close of the Ministry of John the Baptist)*, that Jesus came from Nazareth of Galilee *(respects the beginning of the Ministry of Christ)*, and was baptized of John in Jordan.

10 And straightway *(immediately)* coming up out of the water *(Water Baptism is by immersion, which alone can satisfy the type, not by sprinkling)*, he *(John)* saw the Heavens opened *(saw the Heavens rent asunder, whatever that might mean)*, and the Spirit like a dove descending upon Him *(Luke said, "in a bodily shape like a dove" [Lk. 3:22] exactly what he saw, we don't know, but he definitely did see something)*:

11 And there came a Voice from Heaven *(The Voice came from the rent or opened Heavens, no form was seen, but a "voice" was heard)*, *saying,* You are My Beloved Son *(in contradistinction to all others)*, in Whom I am well pleased *(this means that God is pleased with us, only as long as we are in Christ; we have here the Trinity, the Voice from Heaven, God the Father, the Holy Spirit being sent, and the Son on Whom He is sent)*.

THE TEMPTATIONS OF JESUS

12 And immediately *(the first act of the Spirit on Christ)* the Spirit *(Holy Spirit)* driveth Him *(strongly moved upon Him)* into the wilderness *(believed to be near Jericho)*.

13 And He was there in the wilderness forty days *(probationary period)*, tempted of Satan *(tempted constantly during the forty days and nights)*; and was with the wild beasts *(the last Adam had an entirely different setting than the first Adam, which was Paradise)*; and the Angels ministered unto Him *(as to exactly how, we aren't told)*.

THE CALL

14 Now after that John was put in prison, Jesus came into Galilee, Preaching the Gospel *(Good News)* of the Kingdom of God *(a realm in which a King, namely Christ exercises His Power to act and control)*,

15 And saying, The time is fulfilled (as predicted by the Prophets, Christ has now come), and the Kingdom of God is at hand (is available): repent ye, and believe the Gospel ("repent and believe" may be regarded as a summary of the method of Salvation. This means that Repentance and Faith are the conditions of admission into this Kingdom, i.e., "the New Covenant").

16 Now as He walked by the sea of Galilee, He saw Simon (Peter) and Andrew his brother casting a net into the sea: for they were fishers.

17 And Jesus said unto them, Come ye after Me, and I will make you to become fishers of men.

18 And straightway (immediately) they forsook their nets, and followed Him.

19 And when He had gone a little farther thence, He saw James the son of Zebedee, and John his brother, who also were in the ship mending their nets.

20 And straightway He called them (the Ministry is a "call" not a career): and they left their father Zebedee in the ship with the hired servants, and went after Him (it seems they had the blessings of their father).

AUTHORITY OVER DEMON SPIRITS

21 And they went into Capernaum (where Jesus made His Headquarters); and straightway (immediately) on the Sabbath Day He entered into the Synagogue, and taught.

22 And they were astonished at His doctrine (what He taught, and the way He taught it; His Doctrine was the Word of God, while the Scribes basically taught tradition): for He taught them as One Who had authority, and not as the Scribes (a group supposed to be expert in the Law of Moses).

23 And there was in their Synagogue a man with an unclean spirit (the word, "unclean" runs the gamut of all the activity of Satan from immorality to deceptive, lying, religious spirits [Rev. 16:13-16]); and he cried out,

24 Saying, Let us alone (the lead demon cried out, but there were more demons than one in this man); what have we to do with You, Thou Jesus of Nazareth? (They resented the intrusion of Christ into their domain.) Are You come to destroy us? (They knew that He had the power to do whatever needed to be done.) I know You Who You are, the Holy One of God (demon spirits knew Who He was, but the religious leaders of Israel didn't know, or rather refused to know).

25 And Jesus rebuked him (the lead demon), saying, Hold your peace, and come out of him (in

effect, He said, "shut up, and come out of him").

26 And when the unclean spirit had torn him *(hastily, trying to come out)*, and cried with a loud voice *(represents a screech of fear — fear of Christ, and fear not to obey Christ immediately)*, he came out of him *(there was no delay)*.

27 And they were all amazed *(speechless)*, insomuch that they questioned among themselves *(the Scribes animated, prolonged discussion)*, saying, What thing is this? *(In effect, "Who is this Man," referring to the possibility, and their thinking, that He might be the Messiah.)* what new doctrine is this? *(Doesn't refer to "new" in respect to time, but instead, in comparison to the dry as dust droning of the Scribes.)* for with authority commands He even the unclean spirits, and they do obey Him *(this is absolute power over Satan and all demon spirits, and with obedience carried out immediately)*.

28 And immediately His fame spread abroad throughout all the region round about Galilee *(when it would spread to Jerusalem, it would infuriate the religious leaders)*.

HEALING

29 And forthwith, when they were come out of the Synagogue, they entered into the house of Simon *(Peter)* and Andrew *(Peter's brother)*, with James and John *(these four were probably the only Disciples He had at that time, which was the early part of His Ministry)*.

30 But Simon's wife's mother lay sick of a fever *(bedridden)*, and anon *(immediately)* they tell Him of her *(there is no mention of the wife of Peter by name in the New Testament; according to the testimony of Clement of Alexandria, and Eusebiu, she suffered martyrdom, and was led away to death in the sight of her husband, whose last words to her were, "remember thou the Lord")*.

31 And He *(Jesus)* came and took her by the hand, and lifted her up; and immediately the fever left her *(healed immediately)*, and she ministered unto them *(probably helped prepare a meal)*.

DEMONS CAST OUT; MANY HEALED

32 And at evening, when the sun did set *(when the Sabbath ended)*, they brought unto Him all who were diseased, and them who were possessed with devils *(demons)*.

33 And all the city was gathered together at the door *(all the sick and afflicted)*.

34 And He healed many who were sick of divers diseases *(many*

and varied types of diseases, and of every kind), and cast out many devils (demons); and suffered not the devils to speak, because they knew Him (means they knew Him to be the Messiah).

A PREACHING TOUR

35 And in the morning, rising up a great while before day (was between 3 a.m. and 6 a.m.), He went out, and departed into a solitary place, and there prayed (the example of a strong prayer life, was a habit with Him, and provides an example for us [Mat. 14: 23; Mk. 1:35; 6:46; Lk. 6:12; 9:28; 11:1]).

36 And Simon and they who were with Him followed after Him (sought to find Him).

37 And when they had found Him, they said unto Him, All men seek for You (the pronoun, "You" is emphatic, meaning that those who sought Jesus would not be satisfied with seeing His Disciples).

38 And He said unto them, Let us go into the next towns (while in prayer, He had heard from Heaven, and had been given direction respecting what to do and where to go), that I may preach there also: for therefore came I forth (He was to cover the majority of the land of Israel).

39 And He preached in their Synagogues throughout all Gali-lee, and cast out devils (healing and deliverance, as important as they were, were secondary to the "preaching" of the Word).

JESUS HEALS A LEPER

40 And there came a leper to Him, beseeching Him (begging Him), and kneeling down to Him (this was not merely a rendering of honor to an earthly being; it was a rendering of reverence to a Divine Being), and saying unto Him, If You will, You can make me clean (leprosy was so loath-some, that the leper didn't know if Jesus would heal him or not, even though he knew, that Jesus had the Power).

41 And Jesus, moved with com-passion (is a portrayal of the Heart of God), put forth His hand, and touched him, and said unto him, I will; be thou clean (according to the Greek, His Word healed the man, and not His touch; when He touched him, the healing had al-ready been effected, and the man was "clean"; the words "I will" for-ever settled the question of the Will of God to heal the sick).

42 And as soon as He had spo-ken, immediately the leprosy departed from him (proclaiming the spoken Word to be enough), and he was cleansed.

43 And He (Jesus) straitly charg-ed him (strongly demanded of him),

and forthwith sent him away *(sent him to the Priest, as the Law demanded [Lev. 14:2])*;

44 And said unto him, See thou say nothing to any man *(not at the present time)*: but go your way *(first)*, show yourself to the Priest, and offer for your cleansing those things which Moses commanded, for a testimony unto them *(this pertained to the Law of the cleansing of the Leper, which was a complicated affair [Lev. 14:1-32])*.

45 But he went out, and began to publish *it* much, and to blaze abroad the matter, insomuch that Jesus could no more openly enter into the city *(was Capernaum)*, but was without in desert places *(because of the press of the great crowds)*: and they came to Him from every quarter *(the man not obeying what Jesus told him to do, gave occasion for the enemies of Christ to accuse Him; in other words, they would say that He had ignored the Law, which of course He hadn't, but the man did, and despite the admonition)*.

CHAPTER 2

JESUS HEALS A PALSIED MAN

AND again He entered into Capernaum after *some* days *(maybe several weeks)*; and it was noised that He was in the house *(Peter's house)*.

2 And straightway *(immediately)* many were gathered together, insomuch that there was no room to receive *them*, no, not so much as about the door: and He preached the Word unto them *(preaching and teaching always came first)*.

3 And they come unto Him, bringing one sick of the palsy *(paralysis)*, which was borne *(carried)* of four.

4 And when they could not come near unto Him for the press *(the great crowd)*, they uncovered the roof where He was *(houses have flat roofs in that part of the world, usually with steps on the outside leading to the top)*: and when they had broken *it* up *(there were usually one or more trap doors in the roof, and it was one of these, which they probably enlarged)*, they let down the bed wherein the sick of the palsy lay.

5 When Jesus saw their faith *(faith without works is dead)*, He said unto the sick of the palsy, Son, your sins be forgiven you *(the wretched physical condition of the sick man was due to his sinful life, therefore, Jesus first of all, addressed the real cause; no condemnation, just forgiveness and healing)*.

6 But there were certain of the Scribes sitting there, and reasoning in their hearts *(represents*

a hostile spirit on their part, which could be felt by Christ),

7 Why does this *man* thus speak blasphemies? *(Would have been correct had Christ been only a man. Inasmuch as He was God manifested in the flesh, they were totally incorrect. They will now come face-to-face with the Deity of Christ.)* who can forgive sins but God only? *(Proclaims a truth, but yet, Jesus was God.)*

8 And immediately when Jesus perceived in His spirit that they so reasoned within themselves *(the Holy Spirit revealed their thinking to Him)*, He said unto them, Why reason ye these things in your hearts? *(This must have been startling to them. They had not spoken these things aloud, had only thought them in their hearts.)*

9 Whether is it easier to say to the sick of the palsy, *Your* sins be forgiven you; or to say, Arise, and take up your bed, and walk? *(God Alone can forgive sins, and God Alone can heal. Therefore, to heal validates the power to forgive sins. As stated, they were now coming face-to-face with His Deity.)*

10 But that you may know that the Son of Man has power on earth to forgive sins, (He said to the sick of the palsy,) *(He did all of this in full view of everyone, even the skeptics, and especially the* skeptics!),

11 I say unto you, Arise, and take up your bed, and go your way into your house *(all there knew, including the skeptics that this man could not take up his bed and carry it, unless he was truly healed; whether they admitted it or not, they also knew that only the Power of God could accomplish this).*

12 And immediately he arose *(the Word of Christ healed him)*, took up the bed, and went forth before them all *(including the skeptics)*; insomuch that they were all amazed *(there was no doubt about the healing)*, and glorified God, saying, We never saw it on this fashion *(whether this included the skeptics or not, we aren't told!).*

JESUS CALLS MATTHEW

13 And He went forth again by the sea side *(Sea of Galilee)*; and all the multitude resorted unto Him, and He taught them.

14 And as He passed by, He saw Levi *(Matthew)* the *son* of Alphaeus sitting at the receipt of custom *(he was a tax collector, an abomination in the eyes of Israel)*, and said unto him, Follow Me *(it was not a request, but a Command)*. And he arose and followed Him *(he did so instantly, responding to the Master's Command).*

JESUS EATS WITH SINNERS

15 And it came to pass, that, as Jesus sat at meat in his house *(the house of Matthew)*, many publicans and sinners sat also together with Jesus and His Disciples *(expresses a gathering called by Matthew, evidently to celebrate him being Called by Christ; he was giving up the tax-collecting business)*: for there were many, and they followed Him *(the indication is, they accepted Him as Lord and Master of their lives)*.

16 And when the Scribes and Pharisees saw Him eat with publicans and sinners, they said unto His Disciples *(it seems that many of the Scribes and Pharisees had heard of the Call of Matthew, and this resulted in their gathering, and had come, although uninvited, to see what was taking place)*, How is it that He eats and drinks with publicans and sinners? *(Poses the idea that they thought that He was committing a great sin by associating with these people. This was their self-righteousness in action.)*

17 When Jesus heard it, He said unto them, They who are whole have no need of the physician, but they who are sick *(explains fully as to the "why" of His Presence)*: I came not to call the Righteous, but sinners to repentance *(Christ was and is the Physician of sinners, not their companion)*.

FASTING

18 And the disciples of John and of the Pharisees used to fast: and they come and say unto Him *(unto Jesus)*, Why do the disciples of John *(John the Baptist, who was now in prison)* and of the Pharisees fast, but Your Disciples fast not? *(Any ordinance or ritual given in the Bible, such as fasting, must never be looked at as holy within itself, but rather as to what it represents.)*

19 And Jesus said unto them, Can the children of the bridechamber fast, while the bridegroom is with them? as long as they have the bridegroom with them, they cannot fast *(Jesus is the Bridegroom)*.

20 But the days will come, when the bridegroom shall be taken away from them *(which took place at the Ascension)*, and then shall they fast in those days *(while fasting helps the Believer in many ways, the greatest way of all is what it symbolizes; in essence, fasting states that things aren't right, and will not be right until Jesus comes back; so fasting, at least in part, is a plea for Him to come quickly)*.

21 No man also sews a piece of new cloth on an old garment: else the new piece that filled it up takes away from the old, and the rent is made worse *(the "new*

cloth" symbolizes the New Covenant which Christ would bring in; it would not be a part of the Old Covenant that being done away, but would be completely new; to try to mix the two, as He states, will not work; regrettably, most modern Christians, whether they realize it or not, are in fact, attempting to mix the two).

22 And no man puts new wine into old bottles: else the new wine does burst the bottles, and the wine is spilled, and the bottles will be marred: but new wine must be put into new bottles (same principle as the "new cloth," given in a different way to emphasize this Truth).

THE SABBATH

23 And it came to pass, that He went through the corn fields (should have been translated barley or wheat fields, because there was not corn in the Middle East, or Europe, as we think of such presently, at that time) on the Sabbath Day; and His Disciples began, as they went, to pluck the ears of corn (stalks of barley or wheat).

24 And the Pharisees said unto Him (means in the Greek that they kept on badgering Him about the matter), Behold, why do they (the Disciples) on the Sabbath Day that which is not lawful? (They claimed the Disciples were breaking the Law of Moses by plucking and eating the grain on the Sabbath; Deuteronomy 23:24-25 said, otherwise.)

25 And He said unto them (He could have taken them to Deuteronomy, but instead, he took them to I Samuel, Chpt. 21; He would take them at their own game), Have you never read what David did, when he had need, and was hungry, he, and they who were with him? (He was showing them the futility of religion and ceremony, when there was no change in the heart.)

26 How he went into the House of God in the days of Abiathar the High Priest, and did eat the shewbread, which is not lawful to eat but for the Priests, and gave also to them which were with him? (David was not a Priest, so by the Law, could not eat one of these special loaves in the Tabernacle; however, he wisely judged that a positive law forbidding the laity to eat this bread, which it did, ought to yield to a Law of necessity and of nature, which it did!)

27 And He said unto them (its original construction contains the idea that He said these things over, and over; it took some talking to get the idea across to their minds, which were warped with a warped theology), The Sabbath was made for man, and not man for the

Sabbath (*the force of the argument is this: the Sabbath was made on account of man, not man on account of the Sabbath; the Sabbath was a day of rest; it was meant to point to the "spiritual rest" which would come in Christ*):

28 Therefore the Son of Man is Lord also of the Sabbath (*in this statement, Christ was saying, "I am the Messiah," and these religious leaders knew what He was saying!*).

CHAPTER 3

JESUS HEALS ON THE SABBATH

AND He entered again into the Synagogue (*on the Sabbath Day, and probably in Capernaum*); and there was a man there which had a withered hand (*a symbol of withered, undone humanity, as a result of the Fall*).

2 And they watched Him, whether He would heal him on the Sabbath Day; that they might accuse Him (*religion really doesn't care for people, only its rules and regulations*).

3 And he said unto the man which had the withered hand, Stand forth (*whatever He did, was done openly; in other words, He threw this challenge to the Pharisees and into their teeth*).

4 And He said unto them (*speaks pointedly to the Pharisees, and in front of everyone present*), Is it lawful to do good on the Sabbath Days, or to do evil? to save life, or to kill? (*He was telling them that living for God was not a question of keeping rules and regulations, but a question of "doing good or evil!" To have the power to set this man free and not do so was "evil".*) But they held their peace (*Wuest says, "theirs was a painful, embarrassing silence"*).

5 And when He had looked round about on them with anger (*proves that "anger" is not necessarily a manifestation of sin and Satan; only its wrong use falls into that category*), being grieved for the hardness of their hearts (*there is no hardness of the heart like religious hardness; He knew that this would lead the Pharisees and Israel to destruction*), He said unto the man, Stretch forth your hand (*once again, being done in full view of all*). And he stretched it out: and his hand was restored whole as the other (*pictures what Christ can do with the human heart*).

6 And the Pharisees went forth (*they were angry; they had no concern for the man who had been miraculously healed*), and straightway (*immediately*) took counsel with the Herodians (*a group who believed that Herod was the Messiah, and whom the Pharisees*

normally hated) against Him, how they might destroy Him (this was the condition of the religions leaders of Israel).

MANY HEALED

7 But Jesus withdrew Himself with His Disciples to the sea: and a great multitude from Galilee followed Him, and from Judaea,

8 And from Jerusalem (the religious leadership of Israel resided in this city), and from Idumaea (this was south of the Dead Sea, and about one hundred miles from the Sea of Galilee, a long way in those days), and from beyond Jordan (east of the Jordan River, which would have included Paneas and the Decapolis); and they about Tyre and Sidon (about fifty miles north of the Sea of Galilee, mostly inhabited by Gentiles), a great multitude, when they had heard what great things He did, came unto Him (this will be repeated in the coming Kingdom Age, but on a far grander scale).

9 And He spoke to His Disciples, that a small ship should wait on Him because of the multitude, lest they should throng Him (this would have been a small boat, pushed out a little distance from the shore, with Him teaching the people from this particular platform).

10 For He had healed many; insomuch that they pressed upon Him for to touch Him, as many as had plagues (all were healed and He never turned one away).

11 And unclean spirits, when they saw Him, fell down before Him, and cried, saying, You are the Son of God (they kept falling down before Him, and kept constantly crying; they knew He was the Son of God, even though the religious leaders of Israel didn't).

12 And He straitly charged them (a military command) that they should not make Him known (He wanted no advertisement from this sort).

THE TWELVE CHOSEN AND ORDAINED

13 And He goeth up into a mountain, and called unto Him whom He would: and they came unto Him (there could have been as many as forty or fifty people personally selected, and maybe even near a hundred).

14 And He ordained (appointed) Twelve (the Biblical number for Government), that they should be with Him (the secret of all power), and that He might send them forth to preach,

15 And to have power (delegated authority, all from Christ) to heal sicknesses, and to cast out devils (demons):

16 And Simon He surnamed Peter *(a stone)*;

17 And James the *son* of Zebedee, and John the brother of James; and He surnamed them Boanerges, which is, The sons of thunder *(the names suggested their impetuosity and zeal, which characterized both the brothers)*:

18 And Andrew, and Philip, and Bartholomew, and Matthew, and Thomas, and James the *son* of Alphaeus, and Thaddaeus, and Simon the Canaanite *(Simon the Zealot)*,

19 And Judas Iscariot, which also betrayed Him *(the only one of the Disciples who was of the Tribe of Judah; Christ was from that Tribe as well!)*: and they went into an house *(probably referred to Peter's house in Capernaum)*.

20 And the multitude came together again *(when they heard He was present)*, so that they could not so much as eat bread.

21 And when His friends heard of it *(His immediate relatives, as Verse 31 proclaims)*, they went out to lay hold on Him *(means they intended to stop Him, even by using force and against His Will, if necessary!)*: for they said, He is beside Himself *(means, they actually believed He was insane; His open opposition to the Pharisees and the religious leaders of Israel, would have occasioned this, with them knowing that it was ultimately going to bring severe trouble; however, His brothers, at that time, did not actually believe that He was the Son of God [Jn. 7:5])*.

THE PHARISEES BLASPHEME THE HOLY SPIRIT

22 And the Scribes which came down from Jerusalem said *(evidently sent by the Sanhedrin in order to find something in which they could undermine His influence)*, He has Beelzebub, and by the prince of the devils casteth He out devils *(they blasphemed the Holy Spirit when they accused Christ of casting out devils by the power of Satan)*.

23 And He called them *unto Him (the Scribes)*, and said unto them in Parables, How can Satan cast out Satan? *(Why would Satan undo what he had done?)*

24 And if a kingdom be divided against itself, that kingdom cannot stand.

25 And if a house be divided against itself, that house cannot stand *(internal fighting respecting a family will ultimately lead to the destruction of that family)*.

26 And if Satan rise up against himself, and be divided, he cannot stand, but has an end *(would wreck his kingdom of darkness)*.

27 No man can enter into a strong man's house *(in this case the house of Satan)*, and spoil his

goods, except he will first bind the strong man *(Jesus overthrew Satan)*; and then he will spoil his house *(Christ defeated Satan at the Cross, by atoning for all sin [Col. 2:14-15])*.

THE UNPARDONABLE SIN

28 Verily I say unto you *(speaking to all, but more directly to the Scribes)*, All sins shall be forgiven unto the sons of men, and blasphemies wherewith soever they shall blaspheme *(providing forgiveness is asked of the Lord; this is a wonderful promise, and has been upheld in the hearts and lives of untold millions)*:

29 But he who shall blaspheme against the Holy Spirit hath never forgiveness *(only a Believer who has ceased to believe, in other words, ceases to evidence Faith in Christ, and a professor of religion, such as these Pharisees, etc., can blaspheme the Holy Spirit; an unsaved person, who has made no profession of faith, cannot blaspheme the Spirit; and when one does blaspheme the Holy Spirit, there will not be any desire to serve Christ, as there was no desire by the Pharisees, etc., to serve Christ)*, but is in danger of eternal damnation *(refers to those who would attribute the Power of God to Satan, as the Pharisees had done; to label anything which is actually of God, as being of Satan is a serious offense indeed!)*:

30 Because they said, He has an unclean spirit *(most serious)*.

JESUS' TRUE KIN

31 There came then His brethren *(He had four brothers [Mat. 13:55], and several sisters)* and his mother, and, standing without *(outside of the house)*, sent unto Him, calling Him *(they sent Him word by way of the crowd that they desired to see Him)*.

32 And the multitude sat about Him, and they said unto Him, Behold, Your mother and Your brethren without seek for You.

33 And He answered them, saying, Who is My mother, or My brethren? *(He meant to place this relationship in its proper setting.)*

34 And He looked round about on them which sat about Him *(presents a look that is serious, but yet not critical)*, and said, Behold My mother and My brethren! *(He gestures toward those who hungrily desired to hear His Words, and answered His Own question.)*

35 For whosoever shall do the Will of God *(proclaims the qualifications for the high and lofty position of being in His family)*, the same is My brother, and My sister, and mother *(places all born-again Believers in a status even greater than flesh-and-blood*

relationships, while never for a moment demeaning those relationships).

CHAPTER 4

THE PARABLE OF THE SOWER

AND He began again to teach by the sea side: and there was gathered unto Him a great multitude, so that He entered into a ship, and sat in the sea (*sat in the ship on the Sea of Galilee*); and the whole multitude was by the sea on the land.

2 And He taught them many things by Parables, and said unto them in His Doctrine (*had He stayed upon the shore the diseased could have touched Him and been healed; but His business as a Servant was to deal with sin rather than with its effects*),

3 Hearken (*be listening*); Behold, there went out a sower to sow (*this Parable is given in Matthew, Chpt. 13, and repeated in Luke, Chpt. 8, but worded somewhat different; these were illustrations taken from everyday life and living, which people understood. But yet, they seldom understood His Parables*):

4 And it came to pass, as He sowed, some fell by the way side, and the fowls of the air came and devoured it up (*the "seed sowed"*

is the Gospel; the "fowls of the air" represent Satan and his demon powers*).

5 And some fell on stony ground, where it had not much earth; and immediately it sprang up, because it had no depth of earth:

6 But when the sun was up, it was scorched; and because it had no root, it withered away (*many start out for Christ, but don't last long; all of this completely refutes the unscriptural doctrine of unconditional eternal security*).

7 And some (*seed*) fell among thorns, and the thorns grew up, and choked it (*cares of this life, etc.*), and it yielded no fruit.

8 And other fell on good ground, and did yield fruit that sprang up and increased; and brought forth, some thirty, and some sixty, and some an hundred (*an hundredfold, etc.*).

9 And He said unto them, He who has ears to hear, let him hear (*those who would properly "hear," would attend to these Words of Christ, pondering them, until somehow the Truth was eventually revealed; the Gospel is designed this way purposely by the Holy Spirit, in order to ferret out the insincere*).

THE PURPOSE OF PARABLES

10 And when He was alone, they who were about Him with

the Twelve *(possibly as many as forty or fifty)* asked of Him the Parable *(what it meant)*.

11 And He said unto them, Unto you it is given to know the mystery of the Kingdom of God *(those who truly want to know)*: but unto them who are without *(who have no desire to know)*, all *these* things are done in Parables *(Parables were used to reject the merely curious, and to pull in the sincerely desirous)*:

12 That seeing they may see, and not perceive; and hearing they may hear, and not understand; lest at any time they should be converted, and *their* sins should be forgiven them *(Judicial blindness and deafness justly befall those who do not wish to see and hear; the emphasis is on the person and not on God. He desires that all see and hear)*.

13 And He said unto them, Know ye not this Parable? *(Contains a gentle reproach. The question as given by the Lord, indicates that they should have known.)* and how then will you know all Parables? *(The Parable of the Sower lays down the principle of all Parables concerning the understanding thereof.)*

PARABLE OF THE SOWER

14 The sower sows the Word *(the Word of God. This "seed" must* be sowed to the entirety of the world *[Mk. 16:15])*.

15 And these *(the ones who merely hear but do not receive)* are they by the way side, where the Word is sown; but when they have heard, Satan comes immediately, and takes away the Word that was sown in their hearts *(the structure of the sentence is these individuals do not have to allow Satan to take away the Word)*.

16 And these *(those who hear and receive, but have no durability)* are they likewise which are sown on stony ground; who, when they have heard the Word, immediately receive it with gladness *(millions fall into this category)*;

17 And have no root in themselves *(once again, it is the fault of the individual)*, and so endure but for a time *(meaning that they truly were born-again)*: afterward, when affliction or persecution ariseth for the Word's sake *(as surely it will)*, immediately they are offended *(can't stand the opposition, because they have no root, meaning that the ground was not sufficiently prepared)*.

18 And these *(make a great start, and even endure for a while, but they allow the world to stop them)* are they which are sown among thorns; such as hear the Word,

19 And the cares of this world, and the deceitfulness of riches,

and the lusts of other things entering in, choke the Word, and it becomes unfruitful *(means that they did bear fruit for a while, but allowed the things of the world to choke it off, until they became totally unfruitful, and lost their way; the Parable of the sower completely refutes the unscriptural doctrine of unconditional eternal security, as should be here obvious)*.

20 And these *(those who hear, receive, bring forth fruit, and continue to bring forth fruit forever; they allow nothing to stop them)* are they which are sown on good ground *(the individual determines whether the ground is good or not)*; such as hear the Word, and receive *it*, and bring forth fruit, some thirtyfold, some sixty, and some an hundred.

THE GOSPEL

21 And He said unto them, Is a candle brought to be put under a bushel, or under a bed? and not to be set on a candlestick? *(The Gospel is not to be merely enjoyed privately, but rather imparted as a lamp imparts its light.)*

22 For there is nothing hid, which shall not be manifested; neither was any thing kept secret, but that it should come abroad *(the Gospel is not meant to be hid, or kept secret, but is to be spread abroad, throughout the world)*.

23 If any man have ears to hear, let him hear *(the Lord will make the Gospel known to all Nations, and all will be held responsible who hear it)*.

24 And He said unto them, Take heed what you hear *(there is no excuse for Believers not hearing correctly)*: with what measure you mete, it shall be measured to you: and unto you who hear shall more be given *(in proportion to the diligence given to Bible Study, so will spiritual intelligence be measured to the student)*.

25 For he who has, to him shall be given: and he who has not, from him shall be taken even that which he has *(spiritual gifts, if exercised, will be developed; if not, they will be lost)*.

THE PARABLE OF THE SEED

26 And He said, So is the Kingdom of God, as if a man should cast seed into the ground *(responsibility of Believers to spread the Gospel)*;

27 And should sleep, and rise night and day, and the seed should spring and grow up, he knows not how *(the Word if properly sown, will without fail, have its proper effect)*.

28 For the earth brings forth fruit of herself; first the blade, then the ear, after that the full corn in the ear *(this is the Law of*

the Gospel in "sowing and reaping").

29 But when the fruit is brought forth, immediately he puts in the sickle, because the harvest is come (has reference to the end of the age, when the Church will be called to account).

THE PARABLE OF THE MUSTARD SEED

30 And He said, Whereunto shall we liken the Kingdom of God? or with what comparison shall we compare it? (Is meant to proclaim the manner in which Satan will endeavor to corrupt the Word of God.)

31 It is like a grain of mustard seed, which, when it is sown in the earth, is less than all the seeds that be in the earth (the Church began very small):

32 But when it is sown, it grows up, and becomes greater than all herbs, and shoots out great branches (Christianity is presently the largest religion on Earth, claiming nearly two billion adherents, in one form or the other); so that the fowls of the air may lodge under the shadow of it (refers to most of Christianity being corrupted by Satanic Powers as explained in Matthew 13:19 and Luke 8:12).

33 And with many such Parables spoke He the Word unto them, as they were able to hear it (able to understand).

34 But without a Parable spoke He not unto them: and when they were alone, He expounded all things to His Disciples (gave them extended instruction).

JESUS STILLS THE STORM

35 And the same day, when the evening was come (refers to the same day that He had been teaching the people through Parables), He said unto them (the Twelve), Let us pass over unto the other side (presents itself as a microcosm of this present life; the storms come, and it is only with Christ, that we can make it to the other shore).

36 And when they had sent away the multitude, they took Him even as He was in the ship (meaning that He was very tired, even to the point of physical exhaustion; as a man, He grew tired, just as we do). And there were also with Him other little ships (referred to those who wanted to be near Him, and understandably so!).

37 And there arose a great storm of wind, and the waves beat into the ship, so that it was now full (represents in the spiritual sense, the storms of life, which come to every person).

38 And He was in the hinder

part of the ship, asleep on a pillow: and they awake Him, and say unto Him, Master, carest Thou not that we perish? *(The Lord had said, "let us pass over unto the other side." This means that despite the storm, or anything else for that matter, they would reach the other shore. The people of God are in the same boat with Christ, and we cannot perish because He cannot perish. But we must expect storms of opposition for they are sure to come [Ps. 93].)*

39 And He arose, and rebuked the wind, and said unto the sea, Peace, be still *(the Greek intimates, "Silence! Hush!").* And the wind ceased, and there was a great calm *(instantly).*

40 And He said unto them, Why are you so fearful? *(This type of fear, shows improper love [I Jn. 4:18].) How is it that ye have no faith? (The Disciples had accepted His Messiahship, but had a most inadequate view of what that office carried with it.)*

41 And they feared exceedingly *(means that their fear of Him, was greater even then their fear had been of the storm),* and said one to another, What manner of man is this, that even the wind and the sea obey Him? *(The Disciples were right! The wind and sea did obey Him, and so does everything else. So why should we fear?)*

CHAPTER 5

THE DEMONIAC DELIVERED

AND they came over unto the other side of the sea *(refers to the eastern shore of Galilee),* into the country of the Gadarenes *(the area of the town of Gadara, which was three miles from the Sea of Galilee).*

2 And when He was come out of the ship, immediately there met Him out of the tombs a man with an unclean spirit *(symbolizes the great mission for which Christ came to the world; He had calmed the storm on the sea, and now He would calm the storm in a man's soul),*

3 Who had *his* dwelling among the tombs *(the wages of sin is death);* and no man could bind him, no, not with chains *(sin and the powers of darkness will yield only to Christ, and what He did at the Cross on our behalf; this rules out humanistic psychology, and anything else instituted by man in order to address this problem):*

4 Because that he had been often bound with fetters and chains, and the chains had been plucked asunder by him, and the fetters broken in pieces *(superhuman strength given to him by the unclean spirit):* neither could any *man* tame him *(once again, reinforces the great Truth that*

Christ and the Cross alone, are the only answer).

5 And always, night and day (there is no peace for those who do not know the Lord), he was in the mountains, and in the tombs, crying, and cutting himself with stones (a symbolic picture, which takes place with all unredeemed in the spiritual).

6 But when he saw Jesus afar off, he ran and worshipped Him (the demon spirit worshiped Him; all demon spirits and Satan himself are made to pay homage to God the Son; Satan and all of his minions were defeated at the Cross [Col. 2:14-15]),

7 And cried with a loud voice, and said, What have I to do with You, Jesus, Thou Son of the Most High God? (Refers to this evil spirit knowing exactly as to who Jesus was!) I adjure Thee by God, that You torment me not (a certain time has been appointed by God to which these spirits will be confined to the pit [Rev. 20:1-3]).

8 For He said unto him, Come out of the man, you unclean spirit (constitutes a direct order, which the unclean spirit must obey).

9 And He (Christ) asked him, What is your name? (Why did Jesus ask this question? He did so, because He knew that other spirits inhabited this man also.) And he answered, saying, My name is Legion: for we are many (the un-clean spirit was the head demon, but many more were there as well).

10 And he besought him (besought Christ) much that He would not send them away out of the country (this area was full of Hellenistic apostate Jews, and evidently was loved by demon spirits; we learn here that demon spirits enjoy places that have little or no mention of Christ).

11 Now there was there near unto the mountains a great herd of swine feeding (they were, no doubt, owned by Jews, even though Jews were forbidden by the Law to eat pork).

12 And all the devils (demons) besought Him, saying, Send us into the swine, that we may enter into them (they could not enter into these hogs without the express permission of Christ, so how much less could they enter into "the sheep of His pasture!").

13 And forthwith Jesus gave them leave (means that He did not command them to do this, but instead, gave them permission). And the unclean spirits went out, and entered into the swine: and the herd ran violently down a steep place into the sea, (they were about two thousand;) and were choked in the sea (many have questioned the right of Christ to do this, which destroyed other people's property; however, even though the Holy Spirit through Mark didn't

explain it, *we know that everything the Lord does is right; it's not merely right because He does it, but because it actually is right)*.

14 And they who fed the swine fled, and told *it* in the city, and in the country. And they went out to see what it was that was done (*a great multitude*).

15 And they come to Jesus (*the loss of the animals would have been nothing in comparison to what they would have received upon their acceptance of Christ, at least, had they done so, which they didn't*), and see him who was possessed with the devil (*had been possessed with demons*), and had the legion, sitting, and clothed (*clothing, no doubt given to him by the Disciples*), and in his right mind (*irrespective as to how much education a person may have, until they come to Christ, they aren't completely in their right mind*): and they were afraid (*regrettably, they did not allow this fear to bring them to Christ*).

16 And they who saw *it* told them how it befell to him who was possessed with the devil, and *also* concerning the swine (*lends credence to the thought that the swine-herders had witnessed the entire episode, concerning the action of Christ in delivering the demoniac, and allowing the demons to go into the hogs*).

17 And they began to pray Him (*Jesus*) to depart out of their coasts (*it is remarkable!; they thought more of the swine than they did of the eternal life that Christ could have given them; and so it is with most of the world*).

18 And when He (*Jesus*) was come into the ship, he who had been possessed with the devil prayed Him that he might be with Him (*he wanted to go with Jesus and the Disciples, and no wonder!*).

19 Howbeit Jesus suffered him not, but said unto him, Go home to your friends, and tell them how great things the Lord has done for you, and has had compassion on you (*A. Go tell, B. Great things which the Lord has done, C. Tell of the compassion*).

20 And he departed, and began to publish in Decapolis (*a region east of the Jordan River, containing a number of towns and cities*) how great things Jesus had done for him (*he became an Evangelist*): and all *men* did marvel (*evidently, many had known him before, and now see what the Lord has done for him; this is the story of untold millions*).

HEALINGS AND MIRACLES

21 And when Jesus was passed over again by ship unto the other side (*back to Capernaum, on the west side*), much people gathered unto Him: and He was near unto

the sea *(means that hundreds, if not thousands, were waiting on the shore for Him to come back to Capernaum)*.

22 And, behold, there cometh one of the rulers of the Synagogue, Jairus by name *(each Synagogue had several rulers)*; and when he saw Him *(Jesus)*, he fell at His feet *(a posture of worship)*,

23 And besought Him greatly *(an impassioned plea)*, saying, My little daughter lies at the point of death *(actually, she probably died about the time that Jarius was importuning Christ)*: I pray You, come and lay Your hands on her, that she may be healed; and she shall live *(the Greek actually says, "to save her from death")*.

24 And *Jesus* went with him; and much people followed Him *(Jesus)*, and thronged Him.

25 And a certain woman *(tradition says her name was Veronica)*, which had an issue of blood twelve years *(speaks of a constant hemorrhage for that period of time. A female disorder)*,

26 And had suffered many things of many physicians *(means that she had suffered extreme pain at the hands of these doctors)*, and had spent all that she had *(many of these physicians had treated her merely for the money, knowing all the time they could not help her)*, and was nothing bettered, but rather grew worse *(had not helped her at all, but had worsened the situation)*,

27 When she had heard of Jesus *(the Greek actually says, "the Jesus" distinguishing Him from all others)*, came in the press behind *(the great crowd of people)*, and touched His garment *(probably referred to the touching of the hem of the shawl thrown over His shoulder, which contained a blue fringe, which the Jews were required to wear, to remind them they were God's people [Num. 15:38-41; Deut. 22:12])*.

28 For she said *(means she kept saying it over and over to herself, or even possibly to others near by)*, If I may touch but His clothes, I shall be whole *(concerns her level of faith)*.

29 And straightway *(immediately)* the fountain of her blood was dried up; and she felt in *her* body that she was healed of that plague *(she knew she was healed)*.

30 And Jesus, immediately knowing in Himself that virtue *(power)* had gone out of Him, turned Him about in the press *(crowd)*, and said, Who touched My clothes? *(The Holy Spirit had not seen fit to reveal to Him who had touched Him.)*

31 And His Disciples said unto Him, You see the multitude thronging You, and You say, Who touched Me?

32 And He looked round about

to see her who had done this thing.

33 But the woman fearing and trembling, knowing what was done in her, came and fell down before Him, and told Him all the truth *(proclaims her now seeking mercy as she had previously sought healing; it would be granted as well!).*

34 And He said unto her, Daughter *(in the 25th Verse, she was addressed merely as "a certain woman," now she is called "daughter," which refers to relationship; He in effect, had made her a member of the Family of God),* your faith has made you whole *(if He doesn't touch us, we can touch Him);* go in peace *(gain Salvation as well as healing),* and be whole of your plague *(meaning that the malady would never return).*

35 While He yet spoke *(was speaking to the woman),* there came from the ruler of the Synagogue's *house certain (a certain one)* which said, Your daughter is dead: why troublest thou the Master any further? *(The faith of this certain one wasn't high enough to believe that Jesus could raise the dead.)*

36 As soon as Jesus heard the word that was spoken *(He overheard what was being said),* He said unto the ruler of the Synagogue, Be not afraid, only believe *(in effect, Jesus said, "stop fearing, and be believing").*

37 And He suffered no man to follow Him, save Peter, and James, and John the brother of James *(He took these three with Him to the home of Jairus).*

38 And He came to the house of the Ruler of the Synagogue, and seeing the tumult, and them who wept and wailed greatly *(hired mourners which was the custom in those days).*

39 And when He was come in *(into the home of Jairus),* He said unto them, Why *do you* make this ado, and weep? *(Jesus was not in sympathy with this custom and practice)* the damsel is not dead, but sleeps *(did not mean that she was actually not dead, but that the child was not dead to stay dead; as well, the word, "sleepeth," brings us to the fact of the Resurrection; in the Scriptures, the dead are constantly referred to as "sleeping"; however, it is only the body which sleeps, with the soul and the spirit at death, instantly going to be with Christ that is, if the person is saved).*

40 And they *(the paid mourners)* laughed Him to scorn *(meaning that they ridiculed Him; what simpletons!).* But when He had put them all out *(demanded that they leave),* He took the father and the mother of the damsel, and them who were with Him *(Peter, James, and John),* and entered in where the damsel was lying *(the word,*

"entereth," actually refers to a person going on a journey; even though only a few feet, at least in this instance, it conveyed the idea of distance; in effect, it pointed forward to the coming Resurrection).

41 And He took the damsel by the hand (refers to a strong grip), and said unto her, Talitha cumi; which is, being interpreted, Damsel, I say unto you, arise (this was spoken in Aramic, the same tongue used concerning our Lord's Words on the Cross, "My God, My God why have You forsaken Me?"; as the original language was reported in these two cases, quite possibly they relate to each other; as Jesus defeated death at the home of Jairus, likewise, and for the whole world, He defeated death at Calvary).

42 And straightway (immediately) the damsel arose, and walked; for she was of the age of twelve years. And they were astonished with a great astonishment (the Scriptures only record three people being raised from the dead by Christ, but Augustine says that He raised many more).

43 And He charged them straitly (commanded them) that no man should know it (they must not relate the account of this miracle; there were reasons for this, the least not being the furor which religious leaders would cause; but it is certain that such news could not be kept); and commanded that something should be given her to eat (due to her illness, which actually killed her, she probably had not eaten for days).

CHAPTER 6

UNBELIEF IN NAZARETH

AND He went out from thence (from Capernaum), and came into His own country (Nazareth); and His Disciples follow Him.

2 And when the Sabbath Day was come, He began to teach in the Synagogue: and many hearing Him were astonished, saying, From whence hath this Man these things? and what wisdom is this which is given unto Him, that even such mighty works are wrought by His Hands? (They did not question the wisdom or the works, but rather His right to do such things. In their thoughts, He wasn't worthy!)

3 Is not this the carpenter (Chrysostom said, that He made ploughs and yokes for oxen; in the minds of His critics, this disqualified Him as a great teacher), the Son of Mary, the brother of James, and Joseph, and of Juda, and Simon? and are not His sisters here with us? (This disproves the claims by the Catholic Church that Jesus had no brothers or sisters.)

And they were offended at Him *(He did not meet their approval)*.

4 But Jesus said unto them *(represents His answer to their unbelief)*, A Prophet is not without honour *(to show deference and reverence)*, but in his own country, and among his own kin, and in his own house *(I don't think that Mary was a part of this unbelief, but it definitely included the balance of the family, with Joseph by now, probably having passed on)*.

5 And He could there do no mighty work *(actually means, not even one; it was not that He couldn't, but they wouldn't bring the sick and the diseased to Him; they would rather see their loved ones sick, than to see Christ heal them!)*, save that He laid His Hands upon a few sick folk *(a few sickly ones)*, and healed *them*.

6 And He marveled because of their unbelief *(expresses the view of His humanity; the Holy Spirit mentions Him marveling twice, once at the faith of a Gentile, and at the unbelief of His Own [Mat. 8:10])*. And He went round about the villages, teaching.

THE TWELVE SENT OUT

7 And He called *unto Him* the Twelve *(speaks of their first Mission where they were sent without Him)*, and began to send them forth by two and two; and gave them power over unclean spirits;

8 And commanded them that they should take nothing for *their* journey *(is not a suggestion, but a Command)*, save a staff only *(a wooden staff for walking)*; no scrip *(a leather pouch for food)*, no bread, no money in *their* purse *(means they were not to store up these things before they went, but were to rather trust the Lord)*;

9 But *be* shod with sandals *(spoke of association with the common people who wore such)*; and not put on two coats *(the most simple of quality and quantity were sufficient)*.

10 And He said unto them, In what place soever you enter into an house, *(they accept you)* there abide till you depart from that place *(don't flit from place to place)*.

11 And whosoever shall not receive you, nor hear you *(basically refers to the area, even the city, and not the house in which they were invited)*, when you depart thence *(meant to express the significance of the visit)*, shake off the dust under your feet for a testimony against them *(a symbolic gesture)*. Verily I say unto you, It shall be more tolerable for Sodom and Gomorrha in the day of judgment, than for that city *(has reference to the fact that Sodom and Gomorrha had no Gospel witness, while these places did)*.

12 And they went out, and

preached that men should repent *(the Message didn't change, and shouldn't change now)*.

13 And they cast out many devils *(demons)*, and anointed with oil many who were sick, and healed *them (oil is symbolic of the Holy Spirit, it has nothing to do with medicine [Ex. 27:20; 30:25; Num. 6:15; I Sam. 16:1,13; Ps. 45:7])*.

JOHN THE BAPTIST BEHEADED

14 And king Herod *(Antipas)* heard of Him *(Jesus)*; (for His name was spread abroad:) and he said, That John the Baptist was risen from the dead, and therefore mighty works do show forth themselves in him *(proclaims a troubled and guilty conscience for putting John the Baptist to death)*.

15 Others said *(refers to the Court of Herod, as well as many in Israel)*, That it is Elijah. And others said, That it is a Prophet, or as one of the Prophets *(it seems that Israel would admit to anything except the Truth that He was the Messiah, the Son of the Living God)*.

16 But when Herod heard thereof, he said, It is John, whom I beheaded: he is risen from the dead *(means he kept saying it over and over, in response to the prediction of others as to Who Christ was!)*.

17 For Herod himself had sent forth and laid hold upon John, and bound him in prison *(the Holy Spirit wanted to make certain that no one misunderstood that it was Herod who had done this dastardly thing)* for Herodias' sake, his brother Philip's wife *(John had been in prison because Herod's wife Herodias, had demanded it)*: for he *(Herod)* had married her.

18 For John had said unto Herod, It is not lawful for you to have your brother's wife *(means that he said it more than once, to both Herod and the people)*.

19 Therefore Herodias had a quarrel against him *(she never let up on her fury toward the Baptist for daring to denounce her private relations with Herod, and waited her time for revenge)*, and would have killed him; but she could not *(means that she did not lack the will, only the way; she would find the way)*:

20 For Herod feared John, knowing that he was a just man and an holy *(means that he was in a continual state of fear respecting the Prophet)*, and observed him *(means he watched over John to keep him safe from the evil plots of Herodias)*; and when he heard him, he did many things, and heard him gladly *(he kept going back to the dank prison cell over, and over*

again to speak with the Prophet; in other words, the Holy Spirit was dealing with Herod's soul).

21 And when a convenient day was come *(refers to a convenient time for Herodias to kill John the Baptist)*, that Herod on his birthday made a supper to his lords, high captains, and chief *estates* of Galilee *(Herodias would find her time for revenge at this gathering)*;

22 And when the daughter of the said Herodias came in, and danced, and pleased Herod and them who sat with him *(she degraded herself in a licentious dance)*, the king said unto the damsel, Ask of me whatsoever you will, and I will give *it* to you *(they were probably drunk, or nearly so. Herodias would now spring her trap)*.

23 And he sware unto her *(puts himself under oath)*, Whatsoever you shall ask of me, I will give *it* to you, unto the half of my kingdom *(he doesn't want to lose face in front of his guests)*.

24 And she went forth, and said unto her mother *(implies her knowledge of at least a part of the plan of revenge)*, What shall I ask? And she said, The head of John the Baptist.

25 And she *(the daughter of Herodias)* came in straightway *(immediately)* with haste unto the king *(presents her immediately making her demand, so the king*

will have no opportunity to renege on his promise), and asked, saying, I will that you give me by and by *(immediately)* in a charger *(on a platter)* the head of John the Baptist.

26 And the king was exceeding sorry; *yet* for his oath's sake, and for their sakes which sat with him *(he would save face)*, he would not reject her *(the life of the greatest Prophet who ever lived, had boiled down to the worth of a lewd dance, at least to these men)*.

27 And immediately the king sent an executioner, and commanded his head to be brought: and he went and beheaded him in the prison *(the prison was actually connected to the palace where the celebration was being held)*,

28 And brought his head in a charger, and gave it to the damsel: and the damsel gave it to her mother *(proclaims Herodias, according to Jerome thrusting the tongue through with a long pen; because she could not bear to hear the truth, therefore, she would puncture the tongue that had spoken the truth; both Herodias and Herod, a short time later, were banished by a decree of the Roman Senate to Lyons where they both perished miserably; Salome, the daughter who danced, died shortly thereafter, by having her head nearly cut off by the sharp edges of broken ice; "Vengeance is Mine; I will repay saith*

the Lord" [Rom. 12:19]).

29 And when his disciples heard *of it* (*the disciples of John the Baptist*), they came and took up his corpse (*Josephus says that after the beheading, the mutilated remains were cast out of the prison and left neglected*), and laid it in a tomb (*and so concludes the life and Ministry of the greatest Prophet who ever lived*).

JESUS FEEDS FIVE THOUSAND

30 And the Apostles gathered themselves together unto Jesus (*relates back to Verse 7 where the Twelve had been sent forth "two and two"; they now come back to report to Christ*), and told Him all things, both what they had done, and what they had taught.

31 And He said unto them, Come ye yourselves apart into a desert place, and rest a while: for there were many coming and going, and they had no leisure so much as to eat.

32 And they departed into a desert place by ship privately (*probably one of the vessels belonging to Zebedee*).

33 And the people saw them departing, and many knew Him, and ran afoot thither out of all cities, and outwent them (*presents them waiting for Him whenever the boat docked in this desert place*), and came together unto Him.

34 And Jesus, when He came out, saw much people, and was moved with compassion toward them, because they were as sheep not having a shepherd (*the nation was more religious than ever before, but with few true shepherds*): and He began to teach them many things (*presents the only true Gospel that many of them had ever heard*).

35 And when the day was now far spent, His Disciples came unto Him, and said, This is a desert place, and now the time *is* far passed (*growing late in the day*):

36 Send them away, that they may go into the country round about, and into the villages, and buy themselves bread: for they have nothing to eat.

37 He answered and said unto them, Give ye them to eat (*He was speaking in both the physical and the spiritual sense*). And they say unto Him, Shall we go and buy two hundred pennyworth of bread, and give them to eat? (*Probably equal to seven or eight thousand dollars presently*).

38 He said unto them, How many loaves have you? (*They were thinking of thousands of loaves.*) go and see. And when they knew, they say, Five, and two fishes (*according to Andrew, this small collection belonged to a boy [Jn. 6:8-9]; little is much if God be in it*).

39 And He Commanded them to make all sit down by companies upon the green grass (considering that the grass was green, it was probably about April).

40 And they sat down in ranks, by hundreds, and by fifties.

41 And when He had taken the five loaves and the two fishes (signifies the beginning of the Miracle, and because it was in His Hands), He looked up to Heaven (it is from God from whence all Blessings come), and blessed (His Blessing guarantees everything), and broke the loaves, and gave them to His Disciples to set before them; and the two fishes divided He among them all (the Miracle took place between the breaking and the giving; each Disciple soon exhausted his supply and so had to return to Jesus for more, and was never disappointed).

42 And they did all eat, and were filled (Jehovah of Psalm 132 here revealed Himself).

43 And they took up twelve baskets full of the fragments, and of the fish.

44 And they who did eat of the loaves were about five thousand men (possibly as many as 10,000 to 15,000 total, including women and children).

JESUS WALKS ON THE SEA

45 And straightway (immediately) He constrained His Disciples to get into the ship (they were reluctant to do so), and to go to the other side before unto Bethsaida, while He sent away the people (but He sent them away healed, fed, and filled).

46 And when He had sent them away, He departed into a mountain to pray (prayer establishes relationship).

47 And when evening was come, the ship was in the midst of the sea, and He alone on the land.

48 And He saw them toiling in rowing; for the wind was contrary unto them (inasmuch as it was night, He could not have seen them physically, so the Holy Spirit must have revealed this to Him): and about the fourth watch of the night He cometh unto them (between 3 a.m. and 6 a.m.), walking upon the sea (the inference is that the sandals of our Lord actually had contact with the water; He walked on the surface of the sea as we walk on a hard pavement), and would have passed by them (should have been translated, "and came near to them").

49 But when they saw Him walking upon the sea (couldn't believe their eyes), they supposed it had been a spirit, and cried out (they thought it was an apparition):

50 For they all saw Him, and were troubled (all Twelve saw

Him). And immediately He talked with them, and said unto them, Be of good cheer: it is I; be not afraid *(He evidently was very near when He said this to them)*.

51 And He went up unto them into the ship *(Mark omits Peter walking on the water, as recorded by Matthew)*; and the wind ceased *(emphasizes the fact that such was done solely because He was now in the ship)*: and they were sore amazed in themselves beyond measure, and wondered *(they had witnessed something beyond the power of their comprehension)*.

52 For they considered not *the miracle* of the loaves: for their heart was hardened *(the desire to make Jesus King as John mentioned, was paramount, in the minds of His Disciples; consequently, the true mission of Christ was lost on them, at least at this time; and deviation from the true Will of God always "hardens the heart"; nothing dulls spiritually like the religious enthusiasm of the carnal nature acting in fellowship with the religious world)*.

JESUS HEALS MANY
SICK PEOPLE

53 And when they had passed over *(the ship had begun without Jesus, but concludes with Him; what a Miracle!)*, they came into the land of Gennesaret, and drew to the shore *(was a fertile plain on the north shore of Galilee and west of the Jordan River)*.

54 And when they were come out of the ship *(insinuates a ship of some size; probably one of the larger fishing vessels of Zebedee)*, straightway *(immediately)* they knew Him,

55 And ran through that whole region round about *(proclaims runners going from village to village announcing that Jesus was in the vicinity)*, and began to carry about in beds those who were sick, where they heard He was *(this was a pathetic, yet understandable sight!)*.

56 And whithersoever He entered, into villages, or cities, or country, they laid the sick in the streets, and besought Him that they might touch if it were but the border of His garment: and as many as touched Him were made whole *(this had to have been a situation astounding to behold!; what a sight it must have been!; it will be this way when He comes back the second time, and even greater)*.

CHAPTER 7

JESUS REBUKES THE SCRIBES
AND PHARISEES

THEN came together unto Him the Pharisees, and certain of the Scribes, which came from Jerusalem (*the religious leaders were becoming alarmed at the tremendous popularity of Jesus*).

2 And when they saw (*means they were earnestly seeking some fault, by which they might accuse Him*) some of His Disciples eat bread with defiled, that is to say, with unwashed, hands, they found fault (*had nothing to do with sanitary cleanliness; the Pharisees taught that demons, unseen, could sit on the hands of anyone, and consequently, if the hands were not washed, the demons could be ingested*).

3 For the Pharisees, and all the Jews, except they wash *their* hands often, eat not (*ceremonial religion*), holding the tradition of the Elders (*this tradition was only of man, and not at all of God, as are many traditions in the modern Church*).

4 And *when they come* from the market, except they wash, they eat not (*spending an inordinate amount of time engaging in this foolishness*). And many other things there be, which they have received to hold, *as* the washing of cups, and pots, brasen vessels, and of tables (*they had a certain religious way to wash these things, all which amounted to nothing*).

5 Then the Pharisees and Scribes asked Him (*means they kept on asking Him, demanding an answer*), Why walk not Your Disciples according to the tradition of the Elders, but eat bread with unwashed hands? (*All of this was outward show only, and brought Christ into direct conflict with these religious leaders.*)

6 He answered and said unto them (*runs through Verse 13, and constitutes a startling answer, which pull no punches and minced no words*), Well has Isaiah prophesied of you hypocrites (*said this to their faces. "You hypocrites" actually says in the Greek, "You, the hypocrites," which means the outstanding ones of all time*), as it is written, This people honor Me with *their* lips, but their heart is far from Me (*hits at the very heart of what true Salvation is and isn't [Isa. 29:13]*).

7 Howbeit in vain (*means empty nothings, no profit*) do they worship Me, teaching *for* doctrines the commandments of men (*the state [Herod] put to death the Preacher of Righteousness [Mat. 14:10], and the Church [the Scribes], corrupted the Word of Righteousness*).

8 For laying aside the Commandment of God, you hold the tradition of men, *as* the washing of pots and cups: and many other such like things you do (*said with sarcasm; they washed cups and pots but not their hearts; the ceremonial washing of their hands could not remove the guilt that stained*

them).

9 And He said unto them, Full well you reject the Commandment of God, that you may keep your own tradition (*it was a studied and deliberate rejection*).

10 For Moses said (*drew their attention back to the Word of God*), Honor your father and your mother; and, Whoso curses father or mother, let him die the death (*is deserving of death*):

11 But you say (*presents a stark contrast to the Word of God*), If a man shall say to his father or mother, *It is* Corban, that is to say, a gift, by whatsoever you might be profited by Me; *he shall be free* (*the Pharisees had made it a practice of claiming they were giving their material possessions to the Temple, which absolved them of responsibility toward their parents, with a crooked Priest then giving it back to them for a small percentage*).

12 And you suffer him no more to do ought for his father or his mother (*to such extremities did these covetous Scribes and Pharisees drive their victims who, were their aged parents, with no way to care for themselves*);

13 Making the Word of God of none effect through your tradition (*Jesus had just nailed them with the Fifth Commandment*), which you have delivered (*meaning that their glosses of the Word had come from men and not from God*): and many such like things do you (*this which Christ had given as an example, was only the tip of the proverbial iceberg*).

JESUS EXPLAINS WHAT DEFILES

14 And when He had called all the people *unto Him* (*He called the people closer so they could hear exactly what He was saying*), He said unto them, Hearken unto Me every one *of you*, and understand (*the people have a choice, they can hear Him or these hypocritical Pharisees and Scribes; it is the same presently*):

15 There is nothing from without a man, that entereth into him can defile him (*refers to food, not intoxicating drinks, narcotics, poisons, or tobacco, etc.*): but the things which come out of him, those are they that defile the man (*it is evident that what comes out of the heart must exist in the heart*).

16 If any man have ears to hear, let him hear (*the Lord is telling the people that they have a choice; they can hear him or the Pharisees, but not both!*).

17 And when He was entered into the house (*probably Peter's house*) from the people (*from teaching the people*), His Disciples asked Him concerning the Par-

able *(regarding that which enters into a man, and that which comes from his heart)*.

18 And He said unto them, Are you so without understanding also? *(Shows some disappointment on the part of Christ respecting His Disciples.)* Do you not perceive, that whatsoever thing from without enters into the man, *it* cannot defile him *(presents the exact opposite of what the Pharisees, and Scribes taught)*;

19 Because it enters not into his heart *(food is not spiritual)*, but into the belly, and goes out into the draught, purging all meats? *(Refers to the digestive and elimination system of the human body.)*

20 And He said, That which comes out of the man, that defiles the man *(an evil heart produces evil actions)*.

21 For from within, out of the heart of men, proceed evil thoughts, adulteries, fornications, murders *(the necessity of the creation of a new heart, i.e., "a new man," is here declared)*,

22 Thefts, covetousness, wickedness, deceit, lasciviousness, an evil eye, blasphemy, pride, foolishness *(this statement by Christ, destroys the belief that the natural heart is good, and makes foolish modern efforts to improve human nature)*:

23 All these evil things come from within, and defile the man *(proclaims the result of the Fall, and the absolute necessity of the new birth)*.

HEALING, THE CHILDREN'S BREAD

24 And from thence He arose, and went into the borders of Tyre and Sidon *(has the idea from the Greek Text that He did not merely cross over the border into Gentile territory, but instead, went deep into the heart of that country)*, and entered into an house, and would have no man know *it*, but He could not be hid.

25 For a *certain* woman *(this is the reason He came)*, whose young daughter had an unclean spirit, heard of Him, and came and fell at His feet:

26 The woman was a Greek, a Syrophenician by nation *(a Gentile)*; and she besought Him that he would cast forth the devil *(demon)* out of her daughter.

27 But Jesus said unto her *(begins the odyssey which will proclaim one of the greatest displays of faith ever!)*, Let the children first be filled *(has reference to Israel)*: for it is not meet *(proper)* to take the children's bread, and to cast *it* unto the dogs *(Jesus used the Word for "little pet dogs")*.

28 And she answered and said unto Him *(proclaims a level of*

faith which should be a lesson to all Believers), Yes, Lord *(the word, "Lord," in the Greek Text, as used by the woman, does not refer to Deity or of Jesus being the Jewish Messiah; she would have had scant knowledge of this; she, instead, uses the word, "Lord," in the sense of Jesus being an important Person, etc.)*: yet the dogs under the table eat of the children's crumbs *(now places her in the position of faith, a position which enables her to receive).*

29 And He said unto her, For this saying *(because you have taken a position of humility)* go your way; the devil *(demon)* is gone out of your daughter *(means that it is out, and will stay out; it is a permanent cure).*

30 And when she was come to her house, she found the devil gone out, and her daughter laid upon the bed *(refers to a restful repose, which indicated that previously she had not been easily restrained).*

JESUS HEALS A DEAF AND DUMB MAN

31 And again, departing from the coasts *(borders)* of Tyre and Sidon, He came unto the Sea of Galilee, through the midst of the coasts *(borders)* of Decapolis *(He was now on the eastern side of the Sea of Galilee).*

32 And they bring unto Him one who was deaf, and had an impediment in his speech *(proclaims the usual difficulties of the deaf)*; and they *(friends of the deaf man)* beseech Him to put His hand upon him.

33 And He took him aside from the multitude *(there was a purpose for this)*, and put His fingers into his ears, and He spit, and touched his tongue *(He probably spat on His finger first, touched the man's tongue, and then put both index fingers in the man's ears; the "spittle" represented His Perfect Life);*

34 And looking up to Heaven *(all help comes from above)*, He sighed *(speaks of the terrible dilemma, due to the Fall, in which man now finds himself)*, and said unto him, Ephphatha, that is, Be opened *(expresses the command).*

35 And straightway *(immediately)* his ears were opened, and the string of his tongue was loosed, and he spoke plain *(symbolizes in the physical that which takes place in the spiritual, as it regards the Salvation of the Soul).*

36 And He charged *(commanded)* them that they should tell no man: but the more He charged them, so much the more a great deal they published *it;*

37 And were beyond measure astonished *(what Jesus had done, was beyond their comprehension),*

saying, He has done all things well *(means in the Greek that they said this, and continued to say it over, and over)*: He makes both the deaf to hear, and the dumb to speak *(His whole life on Earth was one connected, continued manifestation of lovingkindness)*.

CHAPTER 8

JESUS FEEDS FOUR THOUSAND

IN those days the multitude being very great *(numbering thousands)* and having nothing to eat *(outside of Christ, the world "has nothing to eat")*, Jesus called His Disciples *unto Him*, and said unto them,

2 I have compassion on the multitude *(portrays the Love of God; it would be the same as saying, "My heart goes out to them")*, because they have now been with Me three days, and have nothing to eat *(they wanted so much to be in His presence that they slept where they could, and ate what little they had, if anything, with that long since having run out)*:

3 And if I send them away fasting to their own houses, they will faint by the way: for divers *(many)* of them came from far.

4 And His Disciples answered Him, From whence can a man satisfy these *men* with bread here in the wilderness? *(The insensibility of the natural heart appears in this Verse. The Disciples apparently learned nothing from the previous feeding of the multitude [Chpt. 6].)*

5 And He asked them, How many loaves have you? And they said, Seven *(before they had "five" loaves, which is God's number of Grace, while now they have "seven," which is God's perfect number of completion)*.

6 And He commanded the people to sit down on the ground: and He took the seven loaves *(in the Disciples hands they were nothing, in His hands they are everything!; the action is not in the loaves, but rather in Him)*, and gave thanks, and break, and gave to His Disciples to set before *them (proclaims the actual time of the multiplication; the giving was a continual act, until all were filled)*; and they did set *them* before the people.

7 And they had a few small fishes *(did not give the number)*: and He blessed, and commanded to set them also before *them*.

8 So they did eat, and were filled: and they took up of the broken *meat (bread)* that was left seven baskets.

9 And they who had eaten were about four thousand *(probably didn't include women and children, which would have in-*

creased it by several thousands): and He sent them away (but only after they were healed and filled).

THE DEMAND FOR A SIGN

10 And straightway (immediately) He entered into a ship with His Disciples, and came into the parts of Dalmanutha (on the western shore of Galilee).

11 And the Pharisees came forth (Matthew said the Sadducees were present as well [Mat. 16:1]), and began to question with Him (they were standing before the Creator of the Ages, Who had the answer to all things, but yet, they are so spiritually stupid, that they will ply Him only with silly questions), seeking of Him a sign from Heaven, tempting Him (and these were the religious leaders of Israel!).

12 And He sighed deeply in His Spirit (meaning, He groaned in His Spirit), and said, Why does this generation seek after a sign? (It is useless to give evidence to unbelief.) verily I say unto you, There shall no sign be given unto this generation (no more signs then what had already been given, which were astounding to say the least, regarding healings and miracles, etc.).

13 And He left them (spiritually speaking, He left them to their doom), and entering into the ship again departed to the other side (the northeastern shore).

THE LEAVEN

14 Now the Disciples had forgotten to take bread, neither had they in the ship with them more than one loaf (the short trip would take several hours).

15 And He charged them (in the Greek Text, means that He kept on speaking to them, making certain they understood that of which He was speaking), saying, Take heed, beware of the leaven of the Pharisees (false doctrine), and of the leaven of Herod (the claim by some Jews that this despot was the Messiah, which they did for financial prosperity).

16 And they reasoned among themselves, saying, It is because we have no bread (they had not the slightest idea of what He was speaking).

17 And when Jesus knew it, He said unto them (the Holy Spirit revealed to Him their confusion), Why reason you, because you have no bread? (In other words, I'm not talking about physical bread.) perceive ye not yet, neither understand? have ye your heart yet hardened? (They were looking too much in the physical, and not at all in the spiritual.)

18 Having eyes, see ye not? (Pertains to spiritual eyes they were not using.) and having ears,

hear ye not? *(They were not hearing correctly, they were not hearing spiritually.)* and do you not
remember? *(We should remember what the Lord has done for us
in the past, and take a lesson.)*

19 When I broke the five loaves
among five thousand, how many
baskets full of fragments took ye
up? They say unto Him, Twelve.

20 And when the seven among
four thousand, how many baskets
full of fragments took ye up? And
they said, Seven.

21 And He said unto them,
How is it that you do not understand? *(The question would have
been better translated, "do you yet
not understand?"; there is a hint
in the Greek Text that, in fact, they
finally did begin to understand;
actually, Matthew tells us this was
the case [Mat. 16:12].)*

JESUS HEALS A BLIND MAN

22 And He comes to Bethsaida
*(probably refers to Bethsaida Julias
situated on the northeast shore of
the Sea of Galilee)*: and they bring
a blind man unto Him, and besought Him to touch him.

23 And He took the blind man
by the hand, and led him out of
the town *(Jesus had already placed
a curse on this city because of their
refusal to repent; consequently, He
would not perform another miracle in its confines [Mat. 11:21])*;

and when He had spit on his eyes
*(pertains to the second time such
was done [7:33]; He probably put
spittle on His Finger and touched
the man's eyes)*, and put His hands
upon him, He asked him if he
saw ought *(has in the Greek Text
that He kept on asking him)*.

24 And he looked up, and said,
I see men as trees, walking *(the
Greek Text actually says, "I see
men; for I behold them as trees,
walking"; the word, "walking,"
refers to the men and not to the
trees"; there seemed to be a mist
of sorts over his eyes, which disfig-
ured things)*.

25 After that He put *His* hands
again upon his eyes, and made
him look up: and he was restored, and saw every man clearly
*(the only incident in the four Gos-
pels, of Jesus dealing with someone the second time in this fashion; why did Jesus have to lay His
hands on him a second time?; the
next Verse possibly tells us)*.

26 And He sent him away to
his house *(implies that he was not
a native of Bethsaida Julias)*, saying, Neither go into the town, nor
tell it to any in the town *(refers to
the fact, as stated, that Jesus had
placed a curse on this town for
their refusal to repent [Mat. 11:21];
due to this, Christ seemed unwilling to give Bethsaida any more
evidence of the visitation of God;
this could well be the reason why*

Jesus had to lay His hands on the man a second time; the curse had been pronounced and the die cast, consequently, it was as if the door was shut).

PETER'S CONFESSION

27 And Jesus went out, and His Disciples, into the towns of Caesarea Philippi (*places Him about forty miles north of the Sea of Galilee, and about forty miles south of Damascus*): and by the way He asked His Disciples, saying unto them, Whom do men say that I am? (*Constitutes Who He really was, and the drawing out of the Disciples, as to Who they thought He was. The Greek Text says, "He kept on asking," meaning that the question so startled them that at first they did not answer.*)

28 And they answered, John the Baptist: but some *say*, Elijah; and others, One of the Prophets (*their answers were strange, but yet reflected the thinking of much of Israel at that particular time*).

29 And He said unto them, But whom say you that I am? (*Concerns the greatest question that could ever be asked. It is a question that all must ultimately answer.*) And Peter answered and said unto Him, You are the Christ (*Peter actually said, "You are the Messiah," because that's what the Word "Christ" actually means; it*

was the Great Confession).

30 And He charged them (*commanded them*) that they should tell no man of Him (*relates the fact that it was now obvious that Israel had rejected Him, and consequently, there was no further point in projecting the issue*).

JESUS FORETELLS HIS DEATH AND RESURRECTION

31 And He began to teach them (*proclaims an explanation as to what was to happen, despite the fact that He was the Messiah*), that the Son of Man must suffer many things (*proclaimed the fact, that they believed otherwise!*), and be rejected of the Elders, and of the Chief Priests, and Scribes ("*rejected*" *means that the religious leaders of Israel put Jesus to the test; however, He did not meet their specifications; He was not the kind of a Messiah the Jews wanted; they wanted a military leader who would liberate them from the yoke of Rome, not a Saviour who would free them from their bondage of sin*), and be killed (*the crucifixion*), and after three days rise again (*the Resurrection was never in doubt, due to the victorious success of the Cross in atoning for all sin*).

32 And He spoke that saying openly (*means that He kept saying it*). And Peter took Him (*probably put His hands on the shoulders of*

Christ), and began to rebuke Him *(means that He spoke with force, denying what Jesus had said).*

33 But when He had turned about and looked on His Disciples, He rebuked Peter *(He did not at all take lightly what Peter had said; and now, He made sure that His Disciples understood His reaction)*, saying, Get thee behind Me, Satan *(presents Jesus speaking directly to Satan, and not Peter; however, the Words of our Lord, brands Peter's words as Satanic; the words, "behind Me," in effect, say, "get out of my Face!")*: for you *(now speaks to Peter)* savor not the things that be of God, but the things that be of men *(unredeemed man doesn't want what God wants).*

34 And when He had called the people *unto Him* with His Disciples also, He said unto them *(speaks of an interval of some period of time between His rebuke of Peter and this present statement)*, Whosoever will come after Me, let him deny himself *(deny his own strength, ability, talent, power, and carnal intellect)*, and take up his Cross *(not suffering as many suppose, but rather the benefits of the Cross)*, and follow Me *(implying that Jesus cannot be followed, unless it's by the way of the Cross).*

35 For whosoever will save his life shall lose it *(if one refuses to place his life in Christ)*; but whosoever shall lose his life for My sake and the Gospel's, the same shall save it *(to place one's life entirely in Christ, which can only be done by way of the Cross, and in doing so, saves one's life, and does so forever).*

36 For what shall it profit a man, if he shall gain the whole world, and lose his own soul? *(The simple equation of profit and loss, which states that one's soul, is worth more than the whole world.)*

37 Or what shall a man give in exchange for his soul? *(The soul is eternal, therefore, worth more than anything.)*

38 Whosoever therefore shall be ashamed of Me and of My Words *(the present conduct of the individual now determines Christ's future conduct with reference to that person)* in this adulterous and sinful generation *(pertains to the character of Israel at the time of Christ, and as well, to every generation which has followed)*; of him also shall the Son of Man be ashamed *(means that such attitude will be reciprocated in like kind)*, when He comes in the Glory of his Father with the Holy Angels *(the Second Coming).*

CHAPTER 9

THE TRANSFIGURATION

AND He *(Jesus)* said unto them *(the twelve)*, Verily I say unto you, That there be some of them who stand here (in this case, Peter, James, and John), which shall not taste of death (did not mean they would not ultimately die, but that before they died, they would see beyond the veil into the Kingdom), till they have seen the Kingdom of God come with power (this was an anticipatory picture of the coming Millennium).

2 And after six days (Luke says "eight days" [Lk. 9:28]; there is no discrepancy; in Luke the Greek phrase is inclusive, meaning that all the time was addressed, while in Mark it is exclusive, meaning that all the days and time were not included) Jesus took with Him Peter, and James, and John (the second experience in which they were included, but not the other Disciples; the raising of the daughter of Jairus from the dead was the first), and leadeth them up into an high mountain apart by themselves (we aren't told which mountain): and He (Jesus) was transfigured before them (refers to the act of giving outward expression of one's inner character).

3 And His raiment became shining, exceeding white as snow; so as no fuller on earth can white them (the radiance of glory shining from within Him).

4 And there appeared unto them Elijah with Moses (their appearance had to do with the coming Kingdom Age): and they were talking with Jesus (the Greek Text indicates that the conversation was a protracted one).

5 And Peter answered and said to Jesus, Master, it is good for us to be here: and let us make three Tabernacles; one for You, and one for Moses, and one for Elijah (Peter compounds his error by placing Moses and Elijah in the same category as Jesus).

6 For he wist not what to say; for they were sore afraid (terrified).

7 And there was a cloud that overshadowed them (was the Shekinah Glory Cloud which guided Israel out of Egypt, and which rested above the Mercy Seat in the Holy of Holies in the Tabernacle): and a voice came out of the cloud (proclaims the actual voice of God), saying, This is My Beloved Son (in the Greek Text, "this is My Son, The Beloved One,"): hear Him (the phrase, "hear Him," refers to Christ; in other words, Moses and Elijah are not to be placed on the same par with Christ; the phrase actually means, "be constantly hearing Him"; it as well refers to obeying what is heard).

8 And suddenly (proclaims a sudden change), when they had looked round about, they saw no man any more, save Jesus only with themselves (they had just witnessed something which no other

human beings had ever seen).

9 And as they came down from the mountain, He charged them that they should tell no man what things they had seen, till the Son of Man were risen from the dead.

10 And they kept that saying with themselves *(meaning that they obeyed the Command of the Lord)*, questioning one with another what the rising from the dead should mean *(they still did not understand the purpose and reason for His coming to this world, which was to redeem man, which would necessitate His going to the Cross; in other words, the Cross was ever His destination)*.

11 And they asked Him, saying, Why say the Scribes that Elijah must first come? *(They were referring to Malachi 4:5.)*

12 And He answered and told them *(but with them still lacking in understanding)*, Elijah verily cometh first, and restoreth all things *(refers to this Prophet coming as one of the two witnesses not long before the Second Advent [Rev. 11:3-12])*; and how it is written of the Son of Man, that He must suffer many things, and be set at nought *(as predicted by the Prophet Isaiah, Chpt. 53)*.

13 But I say unto you, That Elijah is indeed come *(refers to John the Baptist who came in the spirit and power of Elijah [Lk. 1:17])*, and they have done unto him whatsoever they listed, as it is written of Him *(refers to John's execution by Herod)*.

LACK OF POWER

14 And when He came to *His Disciples (joined the other nine at the foot of the mountain after the Transfiguration)*, He saw a great multitude about them, and the Scribes questioning with them *(actually, taunting them)*.

15 And straightway *(immediately)* all the people, when they beheld Him, were greatly amazed, and running to *Him* saluted Him *(greeted Him with great warmth and admiration)*.

16 And He asked the Scribes *(supposed experts in the Law of Moses)*, What question ye with them? *(In effect, what is the problem?)*

17 And one of the multitude answered and said, Master, I have brought unto You my son, which has a dumb spirit *(a correct analysis of the situation; a demon spirit had bound the boy's tongue and vocal organs, plus as well, had tried to kill him several times)*;

18 And wheresoever he *(the demon spirit)* takes him, he tears him: and he foams, and gnasheth with his teeth, and pines away: and I spoke to Your Disciples that they should cast him

out; and they could not *(the idea is, they tried repeatedly, but without success; hence, the taunts of the Scribes)*.

19 He answered him, and said, O faithless generation *(rather, a misplaced faith; Galatians, Chpt. 5 will explain it)*, how long shall I be with you? *(Will My short time be enough?)* how long shall I suffer you? *(Is it possible for even the Twelve who are constantly with Me, to understand?)* bring him unto Me *(implies that the boy was not immediately with the father, but was being held by others a short distance away)*.

20 And they brought him unto Him: and when he *(the demon spirit)* saw Him *(Jesus)*, straightway *(immediately)* the spirit *(demon spirit)* tore him *(the boy)*; and he fell on the ground, and wallowed foaming.

21 And He *(Jesus)* asked his father, How long is it ago since this came unto him? And he said, Of a child *(the incident tells us that children can be oppressed or even possessed by demon spirits)*.

22 And ofttimes it has cast him into the fire, and into the waters, to destroy him *(reflects suicidal tendencies, as promoted by this spirit)*: but if You can do any thing, have compassion on us, and help us *(his faith was weak, due to the failure of the Disciples)*.

23 Jesus said unto him, If you can believe, all things *are* possible to him who believes *(if He has promised it, and you can believe it, you can have it)*.

24 And straightway *(immediately)* the father of the child cried out *(speaks of a loud cry that comes from the very depths of the man's soul)*, and said with tears, Lord, I believe *(proclaims belief, but yet imperfect belief!; the "tears" proclaimed the consternation of the battle that is raging in the man's soul)*; help Thou mine unbelief *(proclaims the deficiency of his faith; it is a prayer the Lord will always answer)*.

25 When Jesus saw that the people came running together *(He evidently was standing a little ways from the people, as He spoke with the man, with the Disciples holding the people back; but they can hold them no longer)*, He rebuked the foul spirit, saying unto him, You dumb and deaf spirit, I charge you, come out of him, and enter no more into him *(he was to come out, which he did, and was never to come back again)*.

26 And the spirit *(demon spirit)* cried, and rent him sore, and came out of him *(it seems that he attempted to kill the boy as he came out)*: and he was as one dead; insomuch that many said, He is dead *(the boy lay motionless and pallid as a corpse)*.

27 But Jesus took him by the

hand, and lifted him up; and he arose *(concerned more than just a helping hand; healing power flooded the boy's body, healing that which the demon had damaged).*

28 And when He was come into the house *(doesn't say which house)*, His Disciples asked Him privately, Why could not we cast him out? *(They had been successful at other times, so why not now? There is evidence that this demon was more powerful than any that Jesus had addressed.)*

29 And He said unto them, This kind *(demon spirits of this power)* can come forth by nothing, but by prayer and fasting *("fasting" includes not only, doing without food, but as well, denying one's own strength and ability, and looking exclusively to the Cross [I Cor. 1:17-18]).*

HIS DEATH AND RESURRECTION

30 And they departed thence, and passed through Galilee; and He would not that any man should know it *(by now there was terrible opposition against Him from the religious leaders of the area; in fact this would get progressively worse).*

31 For He taught His Disciples, and said unto them, The Son of Man is delivered into the hands of men *(means that His* betrayal in the heart of Judas had already begun)*, and they shall kill Him *(the crucifixion)*; and after that He is killed, He shall rise the third day *(the Resurrection was never in doubt).*

32 But they understood not that saying, and were afraid to ask Him *(stemmed back to Peter rebuking Him when He had previously made this announcement and His response, which had been strong indeed!).*

WHO IS GREATEST?

33 And He came to Capernaum: and being in the house *(Peter's house)* He asked them, What was it that you disputed among yourselves by the way? *(Concerned a very serious problem in their lives.)*

34 But they held their peace *(means they were ashamed to relate to Him what they had been, in fact, discussing)*: for by the way they had disputed among themselves, who *should* be the greatest *(it is not unlikely that the preference given by our Lord to Peter, James, and John, may have given occasion for this contention).*

35 And He sat down, and called the Twelve, and said unto them, If any man desire to be first *(in response to their question as to whom should be the great-*

est), the same shall be last of all, and servant of all *(means to think of one's self last, with all others first, to minister to others, which is the very opposite of the world).*

36 And He took a child, and set him in the midst of them: and when He had taken him in His arms, He said unto them *(will use the child as an example),*

37 Whosoever shall receive one of such children in My Name, receives Me *(in effect, says that if the person doesn't have a childlike spirit, he should not be received):* and whosoever shall receive Me, receives not Me, but Him Who sent Me *(the way to Christ is through a childlike spirit, and the way to the father is through Christ [Jn. 14:6]).*

38 And John answered Him, saying, Master, we saw one casting out devils in Your Name, and he followeth not us: and we forbad him, because he followeth not us *(portrays the sectarianism that is beginning to creep in).*

39 But Jesus said, Forbid him not *(Jesus did not say, "receive him," for the man's motive did not appear; however, he does say that the attitude toward such a one should at least be neutral):* for there is no man which shall do a miracle in My Name, that can lightly speak evil of Me *(providing it truly is a miracle).*

40 For he who is not against us is on our part *(the marks of false teachers are numerous in Scripture, so that no mistake need be made in detecting them [Mat. 7:15-20; 23:1-33; Acts 8:9; 13:8; Rom. 1:18-32; 16:17; I Cor. 1:18-31; I Tim. 4:1-8; II Tim. 3:1-13; 4:3-4; II Pet., Chpt. 2; III Jn. 9-10; Jude 4-19; Rev. 2:14, 20]).*

41 For whosoever shall give you a cup of water to drink in My Name, because you belong to Christ, verily I say unto you, He shall not lose His reward *(refers to helping take the Gospel to others; all help respecting this will be rewarded, no matter how small that help might be).*

CONCERNING OFFENCES

42 And whosoever shall offend one of *these* little ones who believe in Me, it is better for him that a millstone were hanged about his neck, and he were cast into the sea *(as the smallest help will be rewarded, likewise, the smallest offense will be likewise addressed; these admonitions had better be taken seriously).*

43 And if your hand offend you, cut it off *([symbolic], do not allow yourself to be placed in the position of opposing those who truly are of God):* it is better for you to enter into life maimed, than having two hands to go into hell, into the fire that never shall be quenched *(proves the reality of*

Hell, and of it being the destiny of those who oppose true Believers, who are truly doing the Work of God):

44 Where their worm dies not, and the fire is not quenched *(Christ is proclaiming what one faces who opposes true Believers; the punishment is eternal).*

45 And if your foot offend you, cut it off: it is better for you to enter halt into life, than having two feet to be cast into hell, into the fire that never shall be quenched:

46 Where their worm dies not, and the fire is not quenched.

47 And if your eye offend you, pluck it out: it is better for you to enter into the Kingdom of God with one eye, than having two eyes to be cast into hell fire:

48 Where their worm dies not, and the fire is not quenched *(when Christ gives an illustration of this magnitude, it is of extreme importance; when He doubles it, as He does here, it becomes extremely important; but when He triples it, as He definitely does, then its significance is of such magnitude as to defy description; most of the opposition against true Believers, and especially against those called of God for specific work, comes from the religious sector; to oppose that apostatized religious sector, may generate harm to one's person; but it is better to*

endure that harm, than to lose one's soul).

49 For every one shall be salted with fire *(whether tested to offend, or tested by the offender)*, and every sacrifice shall be salted with salt *(salt is a type of the Word of God; if the Sacrifice is to be true, it will be centered up in the Cross).*

50 Salt is good *(the Word of God which acts as a preservative)*: but if the salt have lost his saltness *(the Word of God has been diluted)*, wherewith will you season it? *(The preservation is now gone.)* Have salt in yourselves *(abide according to the Word of God)*, and have peace one with another *(abiding by the Word, will guarantee peace).*

CHAPTER 10

CONCERNING MARRIAGE AND DIVORCE

AND He arose from thence *(from Capernaum)*, and cometh into the coasts *(borders)* of Judaea by the farther side of Jordan *(the east side of the Jordan River; He will not come back to this region, but will be crucified in Jerusalem)*: and the people resort unto Him again *(it was the time of Passover and many people were on their way to Jerusalem)*; and, as He was wont *(accustomed* to doing), He taught them again *(they so much needed His teaching, but it was His death that would set them free)*.

2 And the Pharisees came to Him *(there were Pharisees in the crowd, going to Jerusalem)*, and asked Him, Is it lawful for a man to put away *his* wife? *(The question of divorce and remarriage was the great controversy at that time in Israel.)* tempting Him.

3 And He answered and said unto them, What did Moses command you? *(Took them to the Word, but not as they thought — not to the Law of Moses.)*

4 And they said, Moses suffered to write a bill of divorcement, and to put *her* away *([Deut. 24:1], but they misinterpreted Moses, even as many do)*.

5 And Jesus answered and said unto them, For the hardness of your heart he wrote you this precept *(the Lord does not deny that Moses permitted divorce; commanded he did not; consequently, for the Pharisees to shelter themselves under the temporary recognition of a necessary evil, was to confess that they had not outgrown the moral stature of their fathers)*.

6 But from the beginning of the creation God made them male and female *(not from the beginning of Creation per se, but rather, from the beginning of the creation of humankind)*.

7 For this cause *(has to do with the way man and woman were created and, therefore, meant to live)* shall a man leave his father and mother, and cleave to his wife *(completely debunks the homosexual lifestyle)*;

8 And they twain *(two)* shall be one flesh *(one of the reasons that adultery and fornication are so wicked)*: so then they are no more twain, but one flesh *(the Will of God carried out to its logical and beautiful conclusion)*.

9 What therefore God has joined together *(places the seal of God's approval on the marriage union; and we speak of the nuclear family of husband, wife, and children)*, let not man put asunder *(there are only two Scriptural grounds for divorce and remarriage: A. Fornication [Mat. 5:32]; and, B. Desertion on spiritual grounds [I Cor. 7:14-15])*.

10 And in the house *(where evidently they had stopped for the night on the way to Jerusalem)* His Disciples asked Him again of the same *matter (the matter of divorce and remarriage)*.

11 And He said unto them *(concerns marriage after divorce)*, Whosoever shall put away his wife *(refers to divorce)*, and marry another, commits adultery against her *(refers to having no Scriptural grounds; in doing such, he commits sin not only against God, but*

also against his wife).

12 And if a woman shall put away her husband *(divorce)*, and be married to another, she commits adultery *(again, has no Scriptural grounds; such constitutes the sin of adultery).*

JESUS BLESSES LITTLE CHILDREN

13 And they brought young children to Him, that He should touch them *(this custom finds its symbolism in Genesis 48:14-15)*: and *His* Disciples rebuked those who brought *them (presents a paradox; the Disciples were strongly rebuking the people for bringing their children to Jesus, while Jesus was strongly blessing those brought to Him).*

14 But when Jesus saw *it (saw what the Disciples were doing)*, He was much displeased *(was moved with strong indignation)*, and said unto them, Suffer the little children to come unto Me, and forbid them not: for of such is the Kingdom of God *(to start a child out right, is to insure its Salvation [Prov. 22:6]).*

15 Verily I say unto you, Whosoever shall not receive the Kingdom of God as a little child *(the simplicity of the little child is the model and the rule for everyone who desires, by the Grace of Christ, to obtain the Kingdom of Heaven)*,

he shall not enter therein *(presents a double negative in the Greek, and consequently, presents an emphatic denial).*

16 And He took them up in His arms, put *His* hands upon them, and blessed them *(He blessed them fervently).*

THE RICH YOUNG RULER

17 And when He was gone forth into the way *(refers to Him the next morning leaving the house, and going toward Jerusalem)*, there came one running, and kneeled to Him *(he is not asking for physical help, but rather for spiritual help)*, and asked Him, Good Master, what shall I do that I may inherit eternal life? *(In the first place, one cannot inherit eternal life. It is a free gift, which comes with the acceptance of Christ [Rom. 10:9-10,13].)*

18 And Jesus said unto him, Why do you call Me good? *there is* none good but one, *Who is*, God *(is not meant to state that Christ Himself wasn't good, but rather that the word "good" be placed in its proper perspective; Christ is God!).*

19 You know the Commandments *(draws the young man to the Word of God, in both a positive and negative sense; positive, because the Word alone holds the answer; and negative, because it will show*

him as a mirror where he is wrong), Do not commit adultery, Do not kill, Do not steal, Do not bear false witness, Defraud not, Honour your father and mother.

20 And he answered and said unto Him, Master, all these have I observed from my youth *(there is no eternal life in the keeping of the Commandments, as wonderful as that is; had there been, he would not be seeking the satisfaction of the conscience).*

21 Then Jesus beholding him loved him, and said unto him *(loved him despite the fact that he really had not kept the Commandments, as he was claiming; and of course, Jesus knew that!),* One thing you lack: go your way, sell whatsoever you have, and give to the poor, and you shall have treasure in Heaven *(puts the finger directly on the man's problem):* and come, take up the Cross, and follow Me *(without explanation, Christ here tells the young man, and all others for that matter, that Salvation is in the Cross alone; and it is only by and through the Cross, that we can truly follow Christ).*

22 And he was sad at that saying *(concerns the attitude of multiple millions; they, as he, desire Salvation, but on their own terms!),* and went away grieved: for he had great possessions *(the only possession that really matters is Eternal Life).*

WARNING TO THE RICH

23 And Jesus looked round about, and said unto His Disciples *(He looks searchingly at His Disciples),* How hardly shall they who have riches enter into the Kingdom of God! *(It's not the riches which constitute the sin, but the attitude toward them.)*

24 And the Disciples were astonished at His words *(the Jews of that time considered riches to be the approval of God; at the same time, they considered poverty to be His disapproval).* But Jesus answered again, and said unto them, Children *(using this word, He now takes them back to His dissertation concerning receiving the Kingdom of God as a little child; a child does not grasp after things),* how hard is it for them who trust in riches to enter into the Kingdom of God! *(As stated, it is the trust in riches, which constitutes the sin.)*

25 It is easier for a camel to go through the eye of a needle, than for a rich man to enter into the Kingdom of God *(the word that Jesus uses here for "needle," doesn't refer to a small hole in the wall as some think, but rather the type of needle used with thread).*

26 And they were astonished out of measure, saying among themselves, Who then can be saved? *(Presents their theology being completely turned over.)*

27 And Jesus looking upon them said *(knew that His statement would produce this type of reaction)*, With men *it is* impossible *(whether rich or poor, it is impossible to be saved without God)*, but not with God: for with God all things are possible *(only through God, is the Salvation process possible)*.

THE REWARDS OF CONSECRATION

28 Then Peter began to say unto Him, Lo, we have left all, and have followed You *(by this statement, Peter shows that they are still thinking in terms of material rather than spiritual riches)*.

29 And Jesus answered and said, Verily I say unto you *(concerns all Believers, not just the Twelve)*, There is no man who has left house, or brethren, or sisters, or father, or mother, or wife, or children, or lands, for My sake, and the Gospel's *(to many, Jesus is just a means to an end, in other words, to get what they want in the realm of material things; He completely debunks that here; contrary to that, He says here that everything must be placed secondary to Christ)*,

30 But he shall receive an hundredfold now in this time *(refers to this present life)*, houses, and brethren, and sisters, and mothers, and children, and lands *(we have the use of these things, and of that alone, we are to be concerned)*, with persecutions *(regrettably, most of the persecution will come from the Church)*; and in the world to come eternal life *(the world to come is eternal, and one must have eternal life to enter into that world. That alone is what counts!)*.

31 But many *who are* first shall be last; and the last first *(Israel, although first, will be last, because of rejection of Christ; the Church, although last, will be first because of acceptance of Christ)*.

JESUS AGAIN SPEAKS OF HIS COMING DEATH AND RESURRECTION

32 And they were in the way going up to Jerusalem; and Jesus went before them *(presents Christ walking ahead of His Disciples, and for a purpose and reason)*: and they were amazed *(there was something about Him that was now different — a great sadness)*; and as they followed, they were afraid *(speaks not only of the Disciples, but as well, of all who were near Him)*. And He took again the twelve *(apart from the others)*, and began to tell them what things should happen unto Him *(He had already told them this several times, but still they didn't understand)*,

33 *Saying*, Behold, we go up to

Jerusalem *(they had gone to Jerusalem several times in the past, but this time would be different)*; and the Son of Man shall be delivered unto the Chief Priests, and unto the Scribes *(betrayed by Judas)*; and they shall condemn Him to death *(the Sanhedrin would pass sentence upon Him)*, and shall deliver Him to the Gentiles *(to the Romans)*:

34 And they shall mock Him, and shall scourge Him, and shall spit upon Him *(both Jews and Gentiles would do such)*, and shall kill Him *(the Crucifixion)*: and the third day He shall rise again *(predicts His Resurrection, even as He had already done several times before; but they actually didn't believe it)*.

THE REQUEST OF JAMES AND JOHN

35 And James and John, the sons of Zebedee, come unto Him *(Matthew claims Salome, their mother, evidently traveling with them, as making the request [Mat. 20:20], the sons prompted her to do such)*, saying, Master, we would that You should do for us whatsoever we shall desire *(constitutes a most selfish request; how often do we approach Him in the same manner?)*.

36 And He said unto them, What would you that I should do for you? *(In effect, He is asking every Believer the same question!)*

37 They said unto Him, Grant unto us that we may sit, one on Your right hand, and the other on Your left hand, in Your glory *(concerned the most coveted positions; they were speaking of "glory," while He was speaking of "death")*.

38 But Jesus said unto them, You know not what you ask *(characterizes so many petitions made by Believers)*: can you drink of the cup that I drink of? and be baptized with the baptism that I am baptized with? *(Both of these questions signify the Cross!)*

39 And they said unto Him, We can *(a mere profession of moral courage, not a claim to spiritual power; they really didn't know what they were saying)*. And Jesus said unto them, You shall indeed drink of the cup that I drink of; and with the baptism that I am baptized withal shall you be baptized *(concerns not only the Twelve, but all who follow Christ, and for all time — the Cross demands this)*:

40 But to sit on My right hand and on My left hand is not Mine to give *(positions in the Kingdom are determined solely by the Will of God)*; but *it* shall be given to them for whom it is prepared *(Jerome said, "our Lord does not say, 'you shall not sit,' lest He put to shame these two; neither does He say, 'you shall sit,' lest the oth-*

ers should be envious; but by holding out the prize to all, He animates all to contend for it").

41 And when the ten heard *it*, they began to be much displeased with James and John (*the sons of Zebedee want to be first, and the ten were unwilling to be last!; such was the energy of the carnal nature in all Twelve*).

42 But Jesus called them *to Him*, and said unto them, You know that they which are accounted to rule over the Gentiles exercise lordship over them (*the way of the world*); and their great ones exercise authority upon them (*in the world, the greater the position, the greater the authority*).

43 But so shall it not be among you (*the way of the world, is not the way of the Lord*): but whosoever will be great among you, shall be your minister (*servant*):

44 And whosoever of you will be the chiefest (*hold the greater position*), shall be servant of all (*in the Kingdom of God the greatness of the individual comes from the lowly place he takes as a servant of all*).

45 For even the Son of Man came not to be ministered unto (*proclaims Christ as the example*), but to minister (*be a servant*), and to give His life a ransom for many (*He is Very God of Very God, but became incarnate in human flesh and a Servant to mankind;*

what a rebuke to His Disciples, and to us!*).

THE HEALING OF BLIND BARTIMAEUS

46 And they came to Jericho (*this is the only record of Him being in Jericho; it was to be a red-letter day for some*): and as He went out of Jericho with His Disciples and a great number of people, blind Bartimaeus, the son of Timaeus (*suggests the possibility of Bartimaeus coming from a family of some note*), sat by the highway side begging (*symbolic of all the sons of Adam's fallen race*).

47 And when he heard that it was Jesus of Nazareth (*he had, no doubt, long since prayed for this moment*), he began to cry out (*means in the Greek that he kept crying over, and over to Jesus*), and say, Jesus, *Thou* Son of David (*a title that referred to the Messiah; this blind beggar knew He was the Messiah, but the religious leaders of Israel didn't*), have mercy on me (*he pled the right kind of petition*).

48 And many charged him that he should hold his peace (*the word "charged" is strong, meaning to "censure severely"; in other words, they were telling him, and in no uncertain terms, to "shut up"*): but he cried the more a great deal *(proclaims their demand as having the opposite effect on him)*, **Thou** Son of David, have mercy on me.

49 And Jesus stood still *(faith caused Christ to stop; it will do the same presently!)*, and commanded him to be called *(constitutes the greatest moment in the life of this blind beggar)*. And they call the blind man, saying unto him, Be of good comfort, rise; He calls you *(should be the message of every single Believer to every single lost soul)*.

50 And he, casting away his garment *(this was a garment just for beggars; during the day he would spread it out, for people to throw coins on it, and would use it as a blanket at night; he knew he would never need it again)*, rose, and came to Jesus *(if the whole world came to Jesus, they would receive even more than Bartimaeus [spiritual sight])*.

51 And Jesus answered and said unto him, What will you that I should do unto you? *(That's the question asked of all Believers. Our answer reveals our spiritual condition.)* The blind man said unto Him, Lord, that I might receive my sight.

52 And Jesus said unto him, Go your way; your faith has made you whole *("whole" in the Greek is "sozo," it means, "to save"; it is used either as a physical healing* or of spiritual Salvation; consequently, the implication is that Bartimaeus was not only healed, but saved as well!)*. And immediately he received his sight, and followed Jesus in the way *(tradition says that he followed Jesus to Jerusalem, and became an ardent Disciple in the Early Church)*.

CHAPTER 11

THE TRIUMPHAL ENTRY INTO JERUSALEM

AND when they came near to Jerusalem, unto Bethphage and Bethany, at the Mount of Olives *(concerned two villages, suburbs of Jerusalem east of the city)*, He sent forth two of His Disciples *(tradition says Peter and John)*,

2 And said unto them, Go your way into the village over against you *(probably Bethphage, because it was nearer)*: and as soon as you be entered into it, you shall find a colt tied, whereon never man sat *(no one had ever ridden the colt)*; loose him, and bring *him*.

3 And if any man say unto you, Why do you this? *(Implying that this would be the case, and so it was.)* say you that the Lord has need of him *(as God, the Lord needs nothing; as the Son of Man, He did need certain things)*; and straightway *(immediately)* he will

send him hither *(will give permission to use the colt, all of this revealed to Christ by the Holy Spirit).*

4 And they went their way, and found the colt tied by the door without in a place where two ways met; and they loose him *("their way" was "His Way").*

5 And certain of them who stood there said unto them, What are you doing, loosing the colt? *(Represents that no prior arrangements had been made.)*

6 And they said unto them even as Jesus had commanded *(the Lord has need of him):* and they let them go *(an instant obedience; what a privilege these men had to lend their colt to Christ).*

7 And they brought the colt to Jesus, and cast their garments on him; and He sat upon him *(proclaims the beginning of the Triumphal Entry; this was a fulfillment of the Prophecy given by Zechariah [Zech. 9:9]).*

8 And many spread their garments in the way *(this was His formal presentation of Himself as the Messiah; as is obvious, it would be rejected):* and others cut down branches off the trees, and strawed *them* in the way *(probably palm fronds).*

9 And they who went before, and they who followed *(represents crowds both behind Christ and in front of Christ, as He went into Jerusalem),* cried, saying,

Hosanna; Blessed *is* He Who comes in the Name of the Lord *(taken from Psalms 118:25-26; this acclamation was given at the "Feast of Tabernacles," as the Priests marched once daily for seven days around the Altar with palm branches in their hands; on the eighth day they marched seven times, which was the "Great Hosanna"; the people believed that Jesus was now about to take the Throne; they felt the great Kingdom Age was now beginning; the truth is, it could have, but the religious leadership of Israel rejected Him):*

10 Blessed *be* the Kingdom of our father David *(should have been translated, "Blessed be the Kingdom that comes, the Kingdom of our Father David"),* that comes in the Name of the Lord *(should have been translated, "Who comes in the Name of the Lord"; Jesus was that Person!):* Hosanna in the Highest *(meant that He was the Highest One; consequently, the Only One Who could save them).*

11 And Jesus entered into Jerusalem, and into the Temple: and when He had looked round about upon all things *(He observed all the haggling, bartering, arguing, over prices, which probably was in the Court of the Gentiles; He would come back the next day, and cleanse the place),* and now the eventide was come, He went out unto Bethany with the Twelve

(it was probably Sunday, and if so, one week later Jesus would rise from the dead; consequently, the intervening week would be one of such magnitude of sorrow as to defy description).

JESUS PLACES A CURSE ON A BARREN FIG TREE

12 And on the morrow *(suggests it was Monday; Matthew says it was early, probably before 6 a.m., with the Disciples, He has probably spent the night in the open),* when they were come from Bethany, He was hungry:

13 And seeing a fig tree afar off having leaves, He came, if haply He might find any thing thereon *(according to all appearances, there should have been figs):* and when He came to it, He found nothing but leaves *(no fruit);* for the time of figs was not yet *(means that despite its appearance, which suggested fruit, and which there should have been fruit, it was barren).*

14 And Jesus answered and said unto it *(proclaims the Lord forgetting His natural hunger and the thought of a spiritual figure which the sight of this tree began to present to His mind),* No man eat fruit of you hereafter forever *(symbolic of the Jewish nation; a curse was placed on the fig tree, not necessarily for being barren, but for being false; as well, the* word "forever," should have been translated "for the age," that is, until the times of the Gentiles be fulfilled; this will be at the Second Coming). And His Disciples heard it *(they will learn a lesson from this, even as we shall see!).*

JESUS CLEANSES THE TEMPLE

15 And they come to Jerusalem: and Jesus went into the Temple *(refers to the fact that its condition, spiritually speaking, had been on His mind all night; He was probably in the Court of the Gentiles),* and began to cast out them who sold and bought in the Temple, and overthrew the tables of the moneychangers, and the seats of them who sold doves;

16 And would not suffer that any man should carry *any* vessel through the Temple *(He would have the whole of His Father's House regarded as sacred).*

17 And He taught, saying unto them *(no doubt to a large crowd of people who had gathered, watching, as it seems, with open-mouth astonishment!),* Is it not written *(took the people and His actions to the Word of God),* My House shall be called of all nations the House of Prayer? *(Signifying, as stated, that He was in the Court of the Gentiles, which had been turned into a market place. His statement is derived*

from Isaiah 65:7 and Jeremiah 7:11.) but you have made it a den of thieves (should have been translated "robbers," for the Greek word signifies operations on a large and systematic scale).

18 And the Scribes and Chief Priests heard it (they were the "robbers," because they were in charge of what was taking place there, and actually profited personally from what was being done), and sought how they might destroy Him (meant to not only kill Him, but to utterly destroy His influence as a great spiritual energy in the world): for they feared Him (feared that He would use His Power to upset their corrupted place and position), because all the people was astonished at His Doctrine (a "Doctrine" which was so different than their doctrine).

19 And when evening was come, He went out of the city (there is no indication that Jesus ever spent the night in Jerusalem, with the exception of the night that He was on trial).

THE LESSON FROM THE WITHERED FIG TREE

20 And in the morning (probably refers to Tuesday), as they passed by, they saw the fig tree dried up from the roots (means that it was completely withered away; Israel in a short time would do the same, actually ceasing to be a nation).

21 And Peter calling to remembrance said unto Him, Master, behold, the fig tree which You cursed is withered away (Jesus could have done the same thing with His enemies, had He so desired; but He never used His Power, except in the way that the Heavenly Father told Him to use it).

22 And Jesus answering said unto them (indicates Jesus dealing with what happened, rather than why it happened; they were not able yet to grasp the fig tree as a symbol of Israel; that would come later!), Have faith in God (literally says, "Have the Faith of God"; such a faith judges profession [the fig tree] removes difficulties [the mountain] forgives injuries).

23 For verily I say unto you, That whosoever shall say unto this mountain, Be thou removed, and be thou cast into the sea; and shall not doubt in his heart, but shall believe that those things which he says shall come to pass; he shall have whatsoever he says (the "mountain" is used as a symbol, i.e., "mountain of difficulties," etc.; God is a Miracle working God, and will do so for any of His Children, "whosoever"; however, every petition must be predicated as well on the Will of God).

24 Therefore I say unto you, What things soever you desire

(one seeking to do the Will of God, will want only what God desires), **when you pray** *(the value of prayer, without which these things cannot be done)*, **believe** *(have faith)* **that you receive** *them,* **and you shall have** *them (as is obvious here, the receiving of these things, whatever they might be, requires relationship, and that is the key).*

25 **And when you stand praying, forgive, if you have ought against any** *(implying, that the above Promises will not be honored, if we harbor unforgiveness):* **that your Father also which is in Heaven may forgive you your trespasses** *(forgiveness from the Lord on our part, is predicated on us forgiving others).*

26 **But if you do not forgive, neither will your Father which is in Heaven forgive your trespasses** *(implies, unforgiveness breaks down relationship, which destroys the whole program of God; in such a case, our sins are not forgiven, and neither can we expect God to answer prayer; these are extremely serious implications).*

JESUS' AUTHORITY QUESTIONED

27 **And they come again to Jerusalem: and as He was walking in the Temple** *(represents the third day in which He visits this edifice)*, **there come to Him the** Chief Priests, and the Scribes, and the Elders *(these were the religious leaders of Israel)*,

28 **And say unto Him, By what authority do You do these things? and who gave You this authority to do these things?** *(They were the custodians of the Temple. Our Lord, by forcibly ejecting those who were engaged in business in the Temple, was claiming a superior jurisdiction.)*

29 **And Jesus answered and said unto them, I will also ask of you one question** *(His question and the answer, will greatly simplify the issue)*, **and answer Me, and I will tell you by what authority I do these things** *(actually means that the correct response to His question will provide the answer to their questions).*

30 **The baptism of John, was** *it* **from Heaven, or of men? answer Me** *(John had introduced Christ as the Messiah; if they claimed the Prophet to be of God, then they would have to acknowledge the One he had introduced; they had tried to put Jesus on the spot, and now they are instead on the spot).*

31 **And they reasoned with themselves, saying, If we shall say, From Heaven; He will say, Why then did you not believe him?** *(Refers to believing what John said about Jesus.)*

32 **But if we shall say, Of men; they feared the people: for all** *men*

counted John, that he was a Prophet indeed *(the respect for John by the people had even deepened since his martyrdom; they feared if they denied John's calling, the people might stone them then and there)*.

33 And they answered and said unto Jesus, We cannot tell *(their answer was ridiculous to say the least!; they were the very ones who were supposed to know)*. And Jesus answering said unto them, Neither do I tell you by what authority I do these things *(in effect, "I will not answer you, because your answer to My question is the answer to your own"; Jerome says, "He thus shows that they knew, but would not answer; they saved themselves from this dilemma by professing ignorance")*.

CHAPTER 12

THE PARABLE OF THE WICKED HUSBANDMEN

AND He began to speak unto them by Parables *(represents the first time He had used this method in Jerusalem, although it had been used plentifully in Galilee)*. A *certain* man planted a vineyard *(constitutes no other than God Himself)*, and set an hedge about *it (the Power of God about the nation)*, and digged *a place* for the winefat *(better translation,*

"wine-vat"; *speaks of the product of the vineyard)*, and built a tower *(would contain a watchman, which was to guard the vineyard from plunderers; it spoke of the spiritual leaders of Israel)*, and let it out to husbandmen *(left it in the hands of the people)*, and went into a far country *(refers to God's residence being in Heaven)*.

2 And at the season *(harvest season)* he sent to the husbandmen a servant *(speaks of Old Testament Prophets)*, that he might receive from the husbandmen of the fruit of the vineyard *(respects that which was rightly his)*.

3 And they caught *him*, and beat him, and sent *him* away empty *(the failure to receive fruit points to the failure of Israel to heed the preaching of the Prophets)*.

4 And again he sent unto them another servant; and at him they cast stones, and wounded *him* in the head, and sent *him* away shamefully handled.

5 And again he sent another; and him they killed, and many others; beating some, and killing some *(proclaims an increase in the rebellion and its obvious results; barring repentance, sin never slows, but instead, increases)*.

6 Having yet therefore one son, his wellbeloved, he sent him also last unto them, saying, They will reverence my son *(refers to the Lord Jesus Christ)*.

7 But those husbandmen said among themselves *(in this case, the Sanhedrin)*, This is the heir *(it means that the religious leaders of Israel knew that Jesus was the Messiah)*; come, let us kill him, and the inheritance shall be ours *(constitutes the plan of Satan from the very beginning; he wants that which belongs to God, and will usually work through organized religion to further his purpose)*.

8 And they took him, and killed *him*, and cast *him* out of the vineyard *(this was the last effort of Divine Mercy — the sending of the incarnate God, whom the Jews put to death without the city)*.

9 What shall therefore the lord of the vineyard do? *(The Lord had the power to do whatever He desired; yet, they treated Him as if He had no power at all!)* He will come and destroy the husbandmen *(this is exactly what happened in A.D. 70)*, and will give the vineyard unto others *(speaks of the Church, made up mostly of Gentiles, and this being the channel through which God is operating temporarily while Israel is in dispersion, and until Israel will be regathered at the Second Advent, and restored to fellowship and usefulness to God)*.

10 And have you not read this Scripture *(refers to Psalms 118:22-23)*; The Stone which the builders *(the spiritual leaders of Israel)* rejected *(He was not the type of Messiah they wanted)* is become the Head of the Corner *(the "Corner" represents the Corner Stone which is the pivot point for the structure; Christ is the Head of the Church, and of the Work of God, due to what He did at the Cross [Zech. 4:7])*:

11 This was the Lord's doing *(refers to the Great Plan of God, which necessitated God becoming flesh and dwelling among men, in order to bring about the Redemption of man)*, and it is marvellous in our eyes? *(It wasn't marvelous in the eyes of Israel of Jesus' day, and the results were awful. As the Church, we should take a lesson, in what He has done. It had better be marvelous in our eyes.)*

12 And they sought to lay hold on Him *(they were growing even more incensed at Him)*, but feared the people *(whatever they did, would have to be done in secret)*: for they knew that He had spoken the Parable against them *(He predicted that they would kill Him, and as well what would happen to them; God would destroy them!; but still they wouldn't turn around)*: and they left Him, and went their way *(they definitely didn't go His Way)*.

TRIBUTE TO CAESAR

13 And they send unto Him certain of the Pharisees and of

the Herodians *(these two parties normally hated each other)*, to catch Him in His words *(something for which they could incriminate Him)*.

14 And when they were come, they say unto Him *(these were the most brilliant minds of the Pharisees and the Herodians)*, Master *([teacher] the word was not used without design)*, we know that You are true, and care for no man: for You regard not the person of men, but teach the Way of God in truth *(they didn't believe any of this, but they were baiting their trap)*: Is it lawful to give tribute to Caesar, or not? *(This question raged in Israel at that time. The Jews were not necessarily discussing the legality of paying a poll tax to Caesar, but whether a Jew should do so in view of his theocratic relationship to God.)*

15 Shall we give, or shall we not give? *(This placed the situation in strictly a "yes" or "no" mode, or so they thought! They would trap Him either way He answered.)* But He, knowing their hypocrisy, said unto them *(He knew they had no desire for the true answer, but only were attempting to embarrass Him before the crowd, or to have something in order to accuse Him to Rome)*, Why tempt you Me? *(This told them that He knew what they were doing.)* bring Me a penny, that I may see it *(refers to the Roman Denarius, the coin with which the tax was to be paid)*.

16 And they brought it *(there was no coin like this in the Temple, as such was not allowed, so one had to be brought in)*. And He said unto them, Whose is this image and superscription? *(Speaking of the image on the coin.)* And they said unto Him, Caesar's *(referred to the image of Tiberius Caesar, the then reigning Roman Emperor; consequently, the coin of the country proved the subjection of the country to him whose image was upon it, in this case, Caesar)*.

17 And Jesus answering said unto them *(in a sense, Jesus placed His approval by His answer on the separation of Church and State, which did not exist in Israel)*, Render to Caesar the things that are Caesar's, and to God the things that are God's. And they marvelled at Him *(the Jewish leaders had used the "give" respecting tribute or taxes paid to Caesar, while Jesus used the word, "render," which speaks of paying something as a debt; in other words, He was saying that Israel owed Rome certain obligations, such as taxes, etc.; it also means that Believers are obligated to pay taxes, and as well, to submit to Civil Government in every respect, providing its demands do not abrogate the Word of God)*.

THE RESURRECTION

18 Then come unto Him the Sadducees (*another party in Israel*), which say there is no Resurrection (*this denial was their major platform; it was a denial of the possibility of such a thing as a resurrection from the dead*); and they asked Him, saying,

19 Master (*their use of this title was purely formal; they in no way considered Jesus to be a great teacher*), Moses wrote unto us (*proclaims them quoting the Scripture, but attempting as many, to subvert it*), If a man's brother die, and leave *his* wife *behind him*, and leave no children, that his brother should take his wife, and raise up seed unto his brother (*quoted from Deuteronomy 25:5-6; this law was given, to prevent the family inheritance from being broken up, among other things*).

20 Now there were seven Brethren: and the first took a wife, and dying left no seed.

21 And the second took her, and died, neither left he any seed (*children*): and the third likewise.

22 And the seven had her, and left no seed: last of all the woman died also (*none of the above Text is in the Law of Moses; it is all a made-up story in order to prove, they think, their argument against the Resurrection; these skeptics will have a good laugh at Jesus' expense*).

23 In the Resurrection therefore, when they shall rise, whose wife shall she be of them? for the seven had her to wife (*this is the pivot point of their trap*).

24 And Jesus answering said unto them (*proclaims an answer they had never yet received, even though having argued about this matter with the Pharisees for many years*), Do you not therefore err, because you know not the Scriptures (*points to their ignorance which was inexcusable, seeing that most Sadducees were members of the Priesthood*), neither the Power of God? (*They assumed either that God could not raise the dead, or that He could raise them only to a life, which would be a counterpart of the present. Their failure to know "the Power of God" stems from unbelief.*)

25 For when they shall rise from the dead (*proclaims the guarantee by Christ of the coming Resurrection*), they neither marry, nor are given in marriage (*marriage was instituted by God to bring forth and perpetuate the human race; due to having glorified bodies in Heaven, which will take place in the Resurrection, there will be no death and, therefore, no need to perpetuate the race, therefore, no need for marriage*); but are as the Angels which are in Heaven (*only in the sense of which He speaks*).

26 And as touching the dead,

that they rise *(refers to dead bodies, and not the soul and spirit, which are already with the Lord, that is, if the person was saved when they died)*: have you not read in the Book of Moses, how in the bush God spoke unto him *(Ex. 3:5-6)*, saying, I *am* the God of Abraham, and the God of Isaac, and the God of Jacob? *(God did not say, "I was the God of Abraham . . ." referring to someone who was dead, out of existence, and was no more. He instead said, "I am the God of Abraham . . ." meaning that these individuals continued to be alive at the time of Moses, even though their bodies were dead.)*

27 He is not the God of the dead *(meaning that God is not the God of something which no longer exists)*, but the God of the Living *(meaning that no individual goes out of existence at death, but actually lives forever, whether redeemed or in a fallen state; the soul and the spirit of man are eternal)*: you therefore do greatly err *(not merely "err," but rather "greatly err")*.

THE GREAT COMMANDMENT

28 And one of the Scribes came *(probably a Pharisee)*, and having heard them reasoning together, and perceiving that He had answered them well, asked Him, Which is the first Commandment of all? *(Was not asked in sarcasm, but sincerely. He is one of the few who took advantage of the perfect knowledge of Christ. He was not really referring to the single most important Commandment of the Ten, but rather, which was the most important, the ritual or the ethical?)*

29 And Jesus answered him, The first of all the Commandments *is*, Hear, O Israel; The Lord our God is one Lord *(the word, "one" in the Hebrew is "echad," and means "to be united as one, one in number")*:

30 And you shall love the Lord Your God with all your heart, and with all your soul, and with all your mind, and with all your strength: this *is* the first Commandment *(this is the type of "love" which the world doesn't have, and in fact, cannot have, which only a Believer can have, and which can only be given by the Lord)*.

31 And the second *is* like, namely this, You shall love your neighbour as yourself. There is none other Commandment greater than these *(if we truly love God, we will as well, "love our neighbor"; this is the answer to all war, prejudice, hate, bias, racism, etc.)*.

32 And the Scribe said unto him, Well, Master, You have said the truth *(refers to a Pharisee, who for a change, spoke kindly to and of Jesus)*: for there is one God; and there is none other but He:

33 And to love Him with all the heart and with all the understanding, and with all the soul, and with all the strength, and to love *his* neighbour as himself, is more than all whole Burnt Offerings and Sacrifices *(proclaims the fact that this Pharisee understood what the Sacrifices actually were all about; in other words, they were not mere rituals).*

34 And when Jesus saw that he answered discreetly, He said unto him *(means that this man had a mind of his own, which means he did not blindly follow the religious leaders of his day)*, You are not far from the Kingdom of God *(not there yet, but close!; the distance from the "Kingdom of God" is measured neither by miles, nor by ceremonial standards, but by spiritual conditions; however, being close is not enough; regrettably, millions fall into this category).* And no man after that does ask Him any question *(none were able to match wits with Christ!; it is tragic that they approach Christ in this fashion, and not in worship and adoration; but how many, approach Christ presently in the same fashion!).*

DAVID'S SON

35 And Jesus answered and said, while He taught in the Temple *(is presented by Matthew as Jesus talking with the Pharisees [Mat. 22:41-42])*, How say the Scribes that Christ is the Son of David? *(This concerns the Incarnation, i.e., God becoming man, and dwelling among men.)*

36 For David himself said by the Holy Spirit *(affirms by Christ that David wrote Psalms 110; as well, it proclaims the fact that it was inspired by the Holy Spirit)*, The LORD said to my Lord *(the first "LORD" is the august title of God in the Hebrew Old Testament, i.e., "Jehovah"; so the first "LORD" refers to God the Father with the second "Lord" referring to God the Son; in effect, the entirety of the Trinity is here addressed; the Holy Spirit makes up the Third Person, the One Who inspired what was said)*, Sit thou on My Right Hand, till I make Your enemies Your footstool *(refers to the time after the Cross, when Christ is exalted, which speaks of the present time [Heb. 1:3]; in essence, all enemies were defeated at the Cross [Col. 2:14-15], but will be defeated in a practical sense by the end of the Kingdom Age [Rev. 20; 1 Cor. 15:24-28]).*

37 David therefore himself calls Him Lord *(recognizes Christ as Deity, actually, the Jehovah of the Old Testament)*; and whence is He *(Christ)* then his son? *(David's Son, which speaks of the Incarnation, God becoming man. Jesus is God,*

and at the same time, He is David's Son.) And the common people heard Him gladly *(means that the common people believed Him respecting His claim as Messiah, but the religious leaders did not; with this statement about David, He brings them face-to-face with His claim as Messiah, a claim they could not deny; so they said nothing [Mat. 22:46]).*

38 And He said unto them in His Doctrine *(specifies that His Doctrine was totally different than that of the Pharisees and the religious leaders),* Beware of the Scribes *(those who claim to be expert in the Law of Moses),* which love to go in long clothing *(priestly or royal robes),* and love salutations in the marketplaces *(to be called "Rabbi," or "Doctor"; He was not condemning these titles, but only the greedy grasping after them),*

39 And the chief seats in the Synagogues *(seats reserved for officials and persons of distinction)* and the uppermost rooms at feasts *(the place for the most honored guest at a feast):*

40 Which devour widows' houses *(for money),* and for a pretence make long prayers *(praying long and loud for these widows and in their presence, hoping they would make out a will in favor of the Scribes):* these shall receive greater damnation *(teaches degrees of punishment in the coming Judgment).*

THE WIDOW'S MITE

41 And Jesus sat over against the treasury *(He did so for a purpose),* and beheld how the people cast money into the treasury *(not the amount that they cast in, but rather "how" it was cast in):* and many who were rich cast in much *(made an ostentatious display of their gift, in order that all may know how much it was).*

42 And there came a certain poor widow *(proclaims her being noticed not at all, except by the Lord; the word, "poor," in the Greek Text is "ptochos," and is used to designate a pauper rather than a mere peasant; the woman was destitute),* and she threw in two mites, which make a farthing *(it was referred to as a "lepton," which was the smallest Greek copper coin, with both of them being presently worth about a dollar, if that, in 2003 currency).*

43 And He called *unto Him* His Disciples, and said unto them, Verily I say unto you, That this poor widow has cast more in, than all they which have cast into the treasury:

44 For all *they* did cast in of their abundance; but she of her want did cast in all that she had, *even* all her living *(God judges our gift, not only by the amount, but*

how much we have left, and our motives).

CHAPTER 13

DESTRUCTION OF THE TEMPLE FORETOLD

AND as He went out of the Temple *(He went out spiritually as well as physically, which guaranteed its doom),* one of His Disciples said unto Him *(concerns a conversation no doubt held on the Mount of Olives, as Jesus and the Disciples overlooked the Temple and surrounding area),* Master, see what manner of stones and what buildings *are here! (Josephus said that this building was one of the wonders of the world.)*

2 And Jesus answering said unto him, Seest thou these great buildings? *(This included the entire Temple enclosure, pertaining to several buildings.)* there shall not be left one stone upon another, that shall not be thrown down *(this was fulfilled in exact totality, in 70 A.D., by the Roman General Titus).*

SIGNS OF THE END TIME

3 And as He sat upon the Mount of Olives over against the Temple, Peter and James and John and Andrew asked Him privately *(it was extremely dangerous to* speak of the destruction of the Temple, or anything that resembled such, for fear of the Scribes and Pharisees; so they would "ask Him privately"),*

4 Tell us, when shall these things be? and what *shall be* the sign when all these things shall be fulfilled? *(They were speaking more than likely of the near future. His answer would incorporate the future of Israel, in essence, forever.)*

5 And Jesus answering them began to say *(there is a possibility that one or more of them was taking notes),* Take heed lest any *man* deceive you *(Jesus begins His discourse with a warning of deception; this is Satan's greatest weapon):*

6 For many shall come in My Name *(after the Ascension of Christ, a number of Jews appeared on the scene, claiming to be the Messiah, who would lead Israel out from under the dominion of the Romans; those false Messiahs led Israel to her destruction in A.D. 70),* saying, I am *Christ (carries the meaning as well, of saying "I am of Christ");* and shall deceive many.

7 And when you shall hear of wars and rumours of wars, be ye not troubled *(has to do with the mission at hand of Evangelizing the world; our Lord exhorts the Disciples and all who would follow, not to permit political and national upheavals to distract them from their work of Evangelism):*

for *such things* must needs be *(due to Israel rejecting Christ, the world was and is subjected to all of these problems)*; but the end *shall* not be yet *(means that the "end" will not be brought about until the Second Coming)*.

8 For nation shall rise against nation, and kingdom against kingdom *(two thousand years of education, culture, and experience have not ameliorated the problem)*: and there shall be earthquakes in divers places *(proclaims disturbance at the very foundation of the Earth [Rom. 8:22])*, and there shall be famines and troubles *(the natural product of the course taken by the human family and their rejection of Jesus Christ; and this problem will not be made right until Israel accepts Christ, which she will at the Second Coming)*: these *are* the beginnings of sorrows *(not short-lived, but of duration; as well, it speaks of the greatest "sorrow" of all, the coming Great Tribulation)*.

9 But take heed to yourselves *(leaves the national scope, and addresses all Believers on a personal basis)*: for they shall deliver you up to councils; and in the Synagogues you shall be beaten *(the Early Church records this)*: and you shall be brought before rulers and kings for My sake *(such has happened all over the world, from then until now)*, for a testimony against them *(should have been translated, "For a testimony to them")*.

10 And the Gospel must first be published among all nations *(it didn't say every person, but it did say "all nations"; to a great degree this has been done, and is being done, but yet there is so much more to be done)*.

11 But when they shall lead *you*, and deliver you up *(refers to persecution)*, take no thought beforehand what you shall speak, neither do you premeditate *(the Lord does not mean that we are not to premeditate a prudent and wise answer, seeking His Face for guidance, but that we are not to be anxious about it; He is speaking of fear, and that it is not to beset us)*: but whatsoever shall be given you in that hour, you speak that: for it is not you who speaks, but the Holy Spirit *(this concerns His constant leading, guidance, companionship, and counsel)*.

12 Now the brother shall betray the brother to death, and the father the son; and children shall rise up against *their* parents, and shall cause them to be put to death *(beginning with Verse 11, even though the admonition holds true for other times, it mostly speaks of the coming Great Tribulation; during that time, some Jews will come to Christ, and many of them will lose their lives, betrayed*

by even their close loved ones).

13 And you shall be hated of all men for My Name's sake (while Israel has been hated for so very long, that hatred will intensify in the coming Great Tribulation; all because of Christ; it is ironic, Israel proper hates the Name of Jesus, and they are hated for His Name's sake!): but he who shall endure unto the end, the same shall be saved (concerns the Jews during the coming Great Tribulation who accept Christ, which some few shall, and that they must be "faithful unto death"; if so, the Lord has said, "I will give you a Crown of Life" [Rev. 2:10]).

THE ABOMINATION OF DESOLATION

14 But when you shall see the abomination of desolation, spoken of by Daniel the Prophet (speaks of the Antichrist taking over Jerusalem and the Temple, actually declaring war on Israel [Dan. 9:27]), standing where it ought not (refers to this abomination, the image of the Antichrist, being set up in the Holy of Holies in the Temple), (let him who reads understand,) (means there is no reason to misunderstand, because Daniel has plainly foretold this happening) then let them who be in Judaea flee to the mountains (as stated, this refers to the time

that the Antichrist will show his true colors, and invade Israel, in which she will be defeated for the first time since becoming a nation again in 1948):

15 And let him who is on the housetop (in Israel, the tops of the houses are flat; during the summer time, people sleep, at times, in these areas) not go down into the house, neither enter therein, to take any thing out of his house (make haste):

16 And let him who is in the field not turn back again for to take up his garment.

17 But woe to them who are with child (pregnant women), and to them who give suck in those days! (Who have little babes in arms.)

18 And pray you that your flight be not in the winter (bad weather).

THE GREAT TRIBULATION

19 For in those days (the last three and one half years of the Great Tribulation) shall be affliction, such as was not from the beginning of the creation which God created unto this time, neither shall be (the last half of the Great Tribulation will be worse than the Earth has ever seen, and so bad in fact, that such will never be seen again).

20 And except that the Lord had shortened those days, no flesh

should be saved *(meaning that every Jew would be killed, and that could apply to the majority of the world)*: but for the elect's sake *(Israel's sake, not the Church, for the Church is now with the Lord)*, whom He has chosen *(the Lord chose these people, actually raising them up from the loins of Abraham and the womb of Sarah)*, He hath shortened the days *(by how much, we aren't told)*.

21 And then if any man shall say to you *(the word "then" refers to the last half of the Great Tribulation, a time period of some three and one half years)*, Lo, here is Christ *(Messiah)*; or, lo, He is there; believe him not *(the Lord is actually speaking here of the Antichrist who will make great claims)*:

22 For false Christs and false prophets shall rise, and shall show signs and wonders, to seduce, if it were possible, even the elect *(the word "elect" refers to the Jews, but as it is used here, to those who have accepted Christ)*.

23 But take ye heed *(repeated four times in this Chapter [Verses 5, 9, 23, 33]; "ye" is emphatic, specifically meaning that each individual must take heed)*: behold, I have foretold you all things *(this leaves no one with an excuse)*.

THE SECOND COMING

24 But in those days *(the Sec-*ond Coming)*, after that tribulation, the sun shall be darkened, and the moon shall not give her light *(pertains to the fifth time the planets will be affected in part, or in whole, during Daniel's 70th week)*,

25 And the stars of Heaven shall fall *(pertains to meteorites, but as well, can definitely pertain to spirit beings of the spirit world of darkness)*, and the powers that are in Heaven shall be shaken *(refers to the Satanic hosts that now rule the air [Eph. 2:1-3; 6:12])*.

26 And then shall they see *(it is quite possible that Television will portray the Second Coming and do so to the whole world)* the Son of Man coming *(the Second Coming)* in the clouds *(doesn't speak of clouds as we think of such, but rather, a great multitude of people who will be with Him, namely all the Saints who have ever lived)* with great power and glory *(in other words, when Christ truly comes back, no one will have to ask the question, is this really Him?; it will be overly obvious that it is)*.

27 And then shall He send His Angels, and shall gather together His elect from the four winds, from the uttermost part of the earth to the uttermost part of Heaven *(all the Jews then alive on Earth, will be brought to the land of Israel; they will gladly come, even helped by Angels, simply be-*

cause, they have finally accepted their Messiah, the Lord Jesus Christ, Whom they rejected so long ago).

THE PARABLE OF THE FIG TREE

28 Now learn a Parable of the fig tree (symbolic of Israel and the Second Coming); When her branch is yet tender, and putteth forth leaves (refers to the rebirth of Israel as it began in 1948; for about nineteen hundred years this "fig tree" produced nothing, now this tree, taking life from the roots, is beginning to "put forth leaves"), you know that summer is near (Israel is God's prophetic time clock; looking at Israel, we now know that summer is near, i.e., "the Endtime Prophecies are about to be fulfilled"):

29 So you in like manner, when you shall see these things come to pass (the beginning of these things predicted by Christ, has already begun), know that it is near, even at the doors (should have been translated, "He is near," because it refers to Christ).

30 Verily I say unto you, that this generation shall not pass (concerns the generation in existence at the time of these happenings, which will be the time of the Great Tribulation), till all these things be done (speaks of the events proclaimed in Revelation, Chapters 6-19).

31 Heaven and earth shall pass away (better translated, "Heaven and Earth shall pass from one condition to another"): but My Words shall not pass away (what Christ is saying will come to pass, and without fail!).

THE DAY OF CHRIST'S COMING UNKNOWN

32 But of that day and that hour knows no man, no, not the Angels which are in Heaven, neither the Son, but the Father (the Son of Man under the self-imposed limitations of the Incarnation, says that even He Himself did not at that time know the hour of the Second Advent, and of the time of the fulfillment of these other things grouped around that event; without a doubt, He now knows, and I'm sure the Angels now know as well; but then they didn't!).

33 Take ye heed, watch and pray (the idea is a state of watchfulness, which is seasoned by prayer): for you know not when the time is (the "time" itself is not that important, but "watchfulness" is!).

34 For the Son of Man is as a man taking a far journey (Christ is speaking of Himself, when He would go back to Heaven, which He did), Who left His house (refers to the Work He established on Earth, constituted as the "Church"

[Mat. 16:18]), and gave authority to his servants *(pertains to every Believer)*, and to every man his work *(every Believer is called by God for a particular task, no exceptions)*, and commanded the porter to watch *(conveys the idea of wakefulness)*.

35 Watch ye therefore: for you know not when the Master of the house cometh, at even, or at midnight, or at the cockcrowing, or in the morning *(Christ is not speaking here of the Rapture of the Church, but specifically to Israel; but yet, the admonition can definitely apply to modern Believers, and should apply as it regards the Rapture)*:

36 Lest coming suddenly He find you sleeping *(regrettably most of the modern Church is spiritually asleep; most little know and realize the lateness of the hour)*.

37 And what I say unto you *(the Disciples and Israel)* I say unto all *(includes the Church)*, Watch *(the last Word of Christ respecting this dissertation; we should take it very seriously)*.

CHAPTER 14

THE PLOT

AFTER two days was *the Feast of* the Passover *(the greatest Feast of the Jewish year, celebrating the deliverance from Egypt; it lasted one day)*, and of Unleavened Bread *(the Second Feast, which began on the day of the Passover, and continued for seven days; during that time no leaven was to be placed in bread or anything else; the "Passover" symbolized the price that Christ would pay on Calvary's Cross, and "Unleavened Bread" symbolized His Perfect Life and Perfect Body, which would be offered in Sacrifice)*: and the Chief Priests and the Scribes sought how they might take Him by craft *(deceit)*, and put *Him* to death *(in doing such, they would destroy themselves as well)*.

2 But they said, Not on the Feast *Day (Passover)*, lest there be an uproar of the people.

JESUS ANOINTED AT BETHANY

3 And being in Bethany *(a small village, actually a suburb of Jerusalem, to the east of the city)* in the house of Simon the leper *(a man whom Jesus had healed)*, as He sat at meat, there came a woman *(probably refers to Mary, the sister of Lazarus [Jn. 11:1-2])* having an alabaster box of ointment of spikenard very precious *(the Greek word, "pistikos," is used, meaning that it was genuine, not imitation or adulterated; it was very costly.)*; and she broke the box, and poured *it* on His head

(she broke the seal that kept the fragrance preserved; the pouring upon Him, spoke of her anointing Him for His burial; anointing Him now, which was generally done after death, testified to her belief in the Resurrection; she seems to have been the only one who did believe in His Resurrection before the fact).

4 And there were some who had indignation within themselves *(pertained to some, if not all, of the Disciples but with Judas Iscariot taking the lead)*, and said, Why was this waste of the ointment made? *(It is believed by some that this ointment would have been worth about $10,000 in 2003 currency. The truth is, nothing given to Christ is wasted, while much of the world's resources used otherwise, are in fact, wasted.)*

5 For it might have been sold for more than three hundred pence, and have been given to the poor *(originated with Judas [Jn. 12:4-6]; he probably had other things in mind, such as stealing it).* And they murmured against her *(no case of murmuring has ever been justified or sanctioned by God in Scripture regardless of how right the cause; and to make matters worse, this cause wasn't right).*

6 And Jesus said, Let her alone *(it appears from John 12:7 that Jesus here addressed Himself pointedly to Judas)*; why trouble ye her? *(Concerns the murmuring.)* she has wrought a good work on Me *(even though they didn't understand it, her action showed her faith in His Resurrection).*

7 For you have the poor with you always *(regrettably, portrays a condition resulting from the Fall in the Garden of Eden)*, and whensoever you will you may do them good *(the two, Himself and the poor, are equivalent in His sight [Mat. 25:40-45])*: but Me you have not always *(speaking of His present position, which was soon to change).*

8 She has done what she could *(she had been moved by the Holy Spirit to do this)*: she is come aforehand to anoint My Body to the burying *(His body had been prepared by God for Sacrifice [Heb. 10:5]).*

9 Verily I say unto you, Wheresoever this Gospel shall be preached throughout the whole world *(a prediction that it would go throughout the whole world, which it has)*, this also that she has done shall be spoken of for a memorial of her *(this act is connected with her and will never be forgotten).*

THE BETRAYAL

10 And Judas Iscariot, one of the Twelve *(is noted by design by the Holy Spirit, in that all will know that it is Judas who did this,*

and that he forfeited one of the most important offices ever given to a human being in the history of mankind), went unto the Chief Priests, to betray Him unto them.

11 And when they heard it (the religious leaders of Israel), they were glad, and promised to give him money (that amount was "thirty pieces of silver" [Mat. 26:15]). And he sought how he might conveniently betray Him (the word, "conveniently," refers to the fact that he would attempt to carry it out in a manner in which his part and activity would be concealed; however, it was not to be!).

PREPARATION FOR
THE PASSOVER

12 And the first day of Unleavened Bread, when they killed the Passover (the lamb was killed), His Disciples said unto Him, Where will You that we go and prepare that You may eat the Passover? (A place had to be prepared.)

13 And He sent forth two of His Disciples (refers to Peter and John [Lk. 22:8]), and said unto them, Go ye into the city (Jerusalem), and there shall meet you a man bearing a pitcher of water (this was seldom done by men): follow him (in a spiritual sense, this man was a Type of the Holy Spirit).

14 And wheresoever he shall go in, say ye to the goodman of the house (believed to have been owned by John Mark, or his family, who wrote the Gospel according to Mark), The Master says, Where is the guestchamber, where I shall eat the Passover with My Disciples? (Actually says, "My guestchamber.")

15 And He (the owner of the house) will show you a large upper room furnished and prepared (was in a state of readiness): there make ready for us (has to do with the preparation of the Passover ingredients).

16 And His Disciples went forth, and came into the city, and found as He had said unto them: and they made ready the Passover (meant that Peter and John took the Paschal Lamb to the Temple where it was there killed, with the Priests officiating, with the blood poured out at the base of the Brazen Altar; the carcass of the lamb would have then been brought back to this house, where it would have been roasted and prepared by the Disciples).

THE LAST PASSOVER

17 And in the evening He cometh with the Twelve (He would be arrested that night, after He had eaten the Passover).

18 And as they sat and did eat (on the first Passover in Egypt, they

were to eat standing, because they had not yet been delivered; now in the Promise Land, their inheritance, they were to eat "sitting," signifying that the work had been done), Jesus said, Verily I say unto you, One of you which eats with Me shall betray Me *(the words, "eateth with Me," are not merely to point to the individual who would betray Christ, but to the enormity of the offense)*.

19 And they began to be sorrowful, and to say unto Him one by one, *Is it I?* and another *said, Is it I?*

20 And He answered and said unto them, *It is* one of the Twelve, who dips with Me in the dish *(all were dipping with Him in the dish, so that statement really did not tell them very much)*.

21 The Son of Man indeed goeth, as it is written of Him *([Ps. 22; Isa., Chpt. 51; Gen. 3:15], actually, the tenor of the entirety of the Old Testament points to Christ giving His Life as a ransom for many, even to which all the Sacrifices pointed)*: but woe to that man by whom the Son of Man is betrayed! *(This predestined purpose of God did not make the guilt any the less of those who brought the Saviour to His Cross. The "woe" is not of vindictiveness, or even in the nature of a curse, but rather, "reveals a misery which love itself could not prevent.")* good were it for that man if he had never been born *(obedient to the Divine purpose, Christ must die as a Sacrifice for sin, but that necessity did not excuse the free agent who brought it about)*.

THE LORD'S SUPPER

22 And as they did eat, Jesus took bread, and blessed, and broke *it*, and gave to them *(this is typical of what the Lord has to do with us; He takes us, blesses us, and then breaks us, and only then can we be given to others)*, and said, Take, eat: this is My Body *(the word "is" means "represents")*.

23 And He took the cup, and when He had given thanks, He gave *it* to them: and they all drank of it *(signifies the shedding of the Saviour's Blood at Calvary, and that which it afforded, Eternal Life, at least to those who will take Christ as Saviour)*.

24 And He said unto them, This is *(represents)* My blood of the New Testament *(New Covenant)*, which is shed for many *(for the whole world [Jn. 3:16])*.

25 Verily I say unto you, I will drink no more of the fruit of the vine, until that day that I drink it new in the Kingdom of God *(the coming Kingdom Age)*.

26 And when they had sung an hymn *(Ps. 118)*, they went out into the Mount of Olives *(where He*

would be betrayed).

PETER'S DENIAL FORETOLD

27 And Jesus said unto them, All you shall be offended because of Me this night *(referred to His betrayal, and subsequent arrest by the Romans; "offended" means to, "find occasion of stumbling")*: for it is written, I will smite the Shepherd, and the sheep shall be scattered ([Zech. 13:7], all the Disciples would flee).

28 But after that I am risen *(Resurrection again foretold, but still they didn't believe)*, I will go before you into Galilee *(after the Resurrection, and two appearances in Jerusalem).*

29 But Peter said unto Him, Although all shall be offended, yet *will* not I *(constitutes presumption on his part, and an insult toward the others).*

30 And Jesus said unto him, Verily I say unto you, That this day, *even* in this night *(means that Peter would not even have the strength to last out the night)*, before the cock crow twice, you shall deny Me thrice *(three times).*

31 But he spoke the more vehemently *(he kept on speaking, disavowing that he would ever fail Christ)*, If I should die with You, I will not deny You in any wise *(Peter was so carried away by the fervor of his zeal and love for Christ*

that he regarded neither the weakness of his own flesh, nor the truth of his Master's word). Likewise also said they all.

THE GARDEN OF GETHSEMANE

32 And they came to a place which was named Gethsemane *(a garden at the foot of the Mount of Olives; "Gethsemane" means, "the place of the Olive-press")*: and He said to His Disciples, Sit ye here, while I shall pray *(if Jesus had to pray, what about us?).*

33 And He took with Him Peter and James and John *(the third time such a thing was done, in reference to the other Disciples)*, and began to be sore amazed, and to be very heavy *(Swet says: "The Lord was overwhelmed with sorrow, but His first feeling was one of terrified surprise; His foreseeing the passion was one thing, but when it came clearly into view, its terrors exceeded His anticipations" [Heb. 5:7-8]);*

34 And said unto them *(to Peter, James, and John)*, My Soul is exceeding sorrowful unto death *(means that grief, so overwhelmed Him that He was close to dying; in fact, Satan definitely tried to kill Him at this time!)*: tarry you here, and watch *(regrettably, they didn't watch very well, but rather went to sleep, but probably from*

spiritual and physical exhaustion, more than anything else).

35 And He went forward a little, and fell on the ground *(actually means that He fell on the ground repeatedly; it portrays the desperation of the struggle)*, and prayed that, if it were possible, the hour might pass from Him *(continued to put forth the same petition, saying it over and over; the "hour" spoken of here pertains to the Cross, and His terrible death in this fashion, which pertained to the bearing of the sin penalty of the world).*

36 And He said, Abba, Father *(is actually the expression of two languages; He thus in His agony cried to God in the name of the whole human family, the Jew first, and also the Gentile)*, all things *are* possible unto You *(tells us that God could have affected the Salvation and Redemption of humanity in another way; such was possible!; but such was not His Will!)*; take away this cup from Me *(if He had not offered this petition, He would not have been Who and What He was)*: nevertheless not what I will, but what You will *(proclaims the principle of Faith for all Believers; His Will was subject to the Will of the Father as our wills must be subject).*

37 And He comes, and finds them sleeping, and said unto Peter, Simon *(addressing him by his old name)*, sleepest thou? *(All of this was a part of the problem of Peter depending on self.)* could not you watch one hour? *(Pertains to the struggle between the flesh and the spirit.)*

38 Watch ye and pray, lest you enter into temptation *(this is not a suggestion, but actually, a Command!; prayer is imperative, if proper relationship is to be established).* The Spirit truly is ready *(the human spirit)*, but the flesh is weak *(the "flesh" pertains to our own personal strength, ability, and will power; these things within themselves are insufficient for the task; unless the Believer properly understands the Cross; as it regards Sanctification, he will inevitably fall back on the flesh).*

39 And again He went away, and prayed, and spoke the same words *(many times we have to pray the same thing over and over; this is not a sign of lack of faith, but rather of great faith).*

40 And when He returned, He found them asleep again, (for their eyes were heavy,) *(in the Greek Text means literally they were "weighed down"; their sleep was not deliberate, but the result of an oppressive sorrow)* neither wist they what to answer Him *(they couldn't account for their condition, so they said nothing).*

41 And He cometh the third time, and said unto them, Sleep

on now, and take *your* rest *(said in irony)*: it is enough, the hour is come *(this is the "hour" which had been planned even before the foundation of the world [Rev. 13:8])*; behold, the Son of Man is betrayed into the hands of sinners *(the word "sinners," expresses not only Judas, but the religious leaders as well)*.

42 Rise up, let us go *(this was His hour and He was there to meet it)*; lo, he who betrays Me is at hand.

THE ARREST OF JESUS

43 And immediately, while He yet spoke, cometh Judas, one of the Twelve *(speaks of their arrival, even while Jesus was speaking)*, and with Him a great multitude with swords and staves, from the Chief Priests and the Scribes and the Elders *(sadly this was the "Church" of that day!)*.

44 And he who betrayed Him had given them a token *(proclaims the scheme perpetrated by Judas and the religious leaders)*, saying, Whomsoever I shall kiss, that same is He; take Him, and lead *Him* away safely *(proclaims the most perfidious act in human history; Judas had told his co-conspirators that the one he kissed would be Jesus [Ps. 109:5-20])*.

45 And as soon as He was come, he went straightway to Him, and said, Master, Master; and kissed Him.

46 And they *(the religious leaders)* laid their hands on Him, and took Him *(they only could do so, because He allowed them to do so [Jn. 10:17-18])*.

47 And one of them who stood by *(Simon Peter)* drew a sword, and smote a servant of the High Priest, and cut off his ear *(the servant's name was "Malchus"; Luke is the only one who mentions the healing of the wound by our Lord [Lk. 22:51])*.

48 And Jesus answered and said unto them, Are you come out, as against a thief, with swords and *with* staves to take Me? *(The Lord protests the manner in which this act is carried out. He was not a thief, so why were they treating Him as one?)*

49 I was daily with you in the Temple teaching, and you took Me not *(they did not take Him then, because they did not have any legitimate charge to bring against Him; as well, they feared the people)*: but the Scriptures must be fulfilled *(the Holy Spirit through foreknowledge saw what would happen [Isa., Chpt. 53; Zech. 11:13; 13:7])*.

50 And they all forsook Him, and fled *(refers to the Eleven Disciples; not being allowed to fight, they fled; the flesh will fight or flee, but it will not "trust")*.

51 And there followed Him a

certain young man *(even though it is not known for sure, most think that this "young man" was Mark, who wrote this Gospel)*, having a linen cloth cast about his naked *body (the "linen cloth" was not that which people of poor circumstances could have owned; therefore, he belonged to a family of means)*; and the young men laid hold on him *(means the soldiers were setting about to arrest him)*:

52 And he left the linen cloth *(in the struggle, his garment was pulled from him)*, and fled from them naked *(probably means that he only had undergarments; there is no evidence that they pursued him)*.

THE TRIAL

53 And they led Jesus away to the High Priest *(refers to Caiaphas; however, we learn from John 18:13 that Jesus was first brought before Annas, the father-in-law of Caiaphas)*: and with him *(Caiaphas)* were assembled all the Chief Priests and the Elders and the Scribes *(proclaims the religious hierarchy of Israel)*.

54 And Peter followed Him afar off *(the Holy Spirit delineates the "afar off"; the idea is meant to call our attention to the boasts of Peter, which this following at a distance occasioned)*, even into the palace of the High Priest *(refers to the court of the palace where the guards and servants were assembled)*: and he sat with the servants, and warmed himself at the fire.

55 And the Chief Priests and all the Council *(the Sanhedrin, the ruling body of Israel)* sought for witness against Jesus to put Him to death *(they were attempting to legalize their vile action)*; and found none *(refers to the emptiness of their accusations)*.

56 For many bear false witness against Him, but their witness agreed not together *(proclaims such being contrary to the Law of Moses, which required a trial to begin with those things which would acquit the accused, instead of condemning Him)*.

57 And there arose certain *(speaks of two men, as given in Mat. 26:60)*, and bear false witness against Him, saying *(proclaims the Sanhedrin as thinking they finally had a proper accusation against Him; however, they were to see that this was false as well!)*,

58 We heard Him say, I will destroy this Temple that is made with hands, and within three days I will build another made without hands *(they had added the words, "that is made with hands, and I will build another made without hands"; they tried to make it*

seem as if Jesus was talking about the Jerusalem Temple, when actually what He did say, was speaking of His physical body; He really said: "destroy this Temple," and speaking of His Own body, "and in three days I will raise it up").

59 But neither so did their witness agree together *(the idea in the Greek Text is that they made repeated attempts to bring testimony that would warrant conviction, but without success).*

60 And the High Priest stood up in the midst *(this man had become exasperated by their inability to bring forth a credible witness, and sought to make up by bluster, the lack of evidence),* and asked Jesus, saying, Answerest Thou nothing? *(He didn't answer, because they had no desire to hear the Truth.)* what *is* it which these witness against You? *(He demanded an answer from Christ concerning the accusations, but Jesus said nothing, at least to that charge.)*

61 But He held His peace, and answered nothing *(He kept on maintaining His silence).* Again the High Priest asked Him, and said unto Him, Are You the Christ, the Son of the Blessed? *(Actually means, "Are You the Messiah?" namely, "The Anointed of God.")*

62 And Jesus said, I am *(constitutes a bold declaration of who He was; the pronoun "I" is used for emphasis; it is, "as for myself, in contradistinction to all others"; His answer left absolutely no doubt):* and you shall see *(proclaims the fact, that the entirety of the Jewish Sanhedrin, would ultimately "see" that what Jesus had said was absolutely true)* the Son of Man sitting on the Right Hand of Power, and coming in the clouds of Heaven *(refers to the Great White Throne Judgment, and the Second Coming, the latter happening first).*

63 Then the High Priest rent His clothes *(this was a sign that he considered what Jesus said to have been blasphemy),* and said, What need we any further witnesses? *(In their minds this was the sought for evidence. The prisoner had incriminated himself.)*

64 You have heard the blasphemy *(proclaims the High Priest rendering his conclusion even before testing the claims of Jesus; consequently, it becomes more and more obvious that this farce of a trial was not convened to seek for Truth, but instead, to find any way to condemn Christ):* what do you think? *(Actually, this is the question of the ages, and a question, that every person must answer.)* And they all condemned Him to be guilty of death *(Joseph of Arimathaea, and Nicodemus, although members of the Sanhedrin, were not present; so the "all" pertained to*

those present, and not those absent).

65 And some began to spit on Him, and to cover His face, and to buffet Him (the "some" included members of the Sanhedrin, as well as the Temple guards and soldiers. Actually, the evidence is that the latter did not join in these indignities until they observed the members of the Sanhedrin engaging in these vile acts), and to say unto Him, Prophesy (they now add spiritual abuse to the physical abuse): and the servants did strike Him with the palms of their hands (Isaiah, some eight hundred years before, had prophesied, "His visage was so marred more than any man" [Isa. 52:14]).

PETER DENIES JESUS

66 And as Peter was beneath in the palace (speaks of the porch of the palace; the trial of Jesus was held in an upper story), there cometh one of the maids of the High Priest:

67 And when she saw Peter warming himself, she looked upon him, and said, And you also was with Jesus of Nazareth (the very fact that Peter was there, shows that he did not want to desert Jesus; however, his actions will show that he will not desire to stand up for Him either!).

68 But he denied, saying, I know not, neither understand I what you say. And he went out into the porch; and the rooster crowed (Peter's test came in an unexpected form, and discovered a weak point — his lack of moral courage).

69 And a maid saw him again, and began to say to them who stood by, This is one of them (this is a different maid).

70 And he denied it again. And a little after, they who stood by said again to Peter, Surely you are one of them: for you are a Galilaean, and your speech agrees thereto.

71 But he began to curse and to swear, saying, I know not this man of whom you speak (this does not refer to profanity but rather "to declare anathema or cursed"; Peter thus declares himself subject to the Divine curse if he is not telling the truth when he disclaims all acquaintance with Jesus; in fact, what he did was much worse than the use of profanity).

72 And the second time the rooster crowed. And Peter called to mind the word that Jesus said unto him, Before the rooster crowed twice, you shall deny Me thrice. And when he thought thereon, he wept (the word "wept" refers to racking sobs, which came from the depths of his being; in fact, this was the time of Peter's repentance, which is portrayed by "a broken and a contrite heart" [Ps. 51:17]).

CHAPTER 15

JESUS BEFORE PILATE

AND straightway *(immediately)* in the morning the Chief Priests held a consultation with the Elders and Scribes and the whole Council, and bound Jesus, and carried *Him* away, and delivered *Him* to Pilate *(sentences of condemnation might not be legally pronounced on the day of trial; yet our Lord was tried, condemned, and crucified on the same day; as they took Him to Pilate, they continued to strike and beat Him)*.

2 And Pilate asked Him, Are You the King of the Jews? *(To him, this was a political question. He had no regard or concern for the religious controversy.)* And He answering said unto him, You say it *(Jesus answered in the affirmative; in effect, He said, "You say that which is true")*.

3 And the Chief Priests accused Him of many things: but He answered nothing *(He knew that to refute their erroneous and false charges, was a waste of time)*.

4 And Pilate asked Him again, saying, Answerest Thou nothing? behold how many things they witness against You *(Pilate had never seen a man, who would not defend himself; he didn't understand Christ!)*.

5 But Jesus yet answered noth-ing; so that Pilate marveled *(the silence of a blameless life pleads more powerfully than any defense, however elaborate)*.

6 Now at *that* feast *(Passover)* he *(Pilate)* released unto them *(Israel)* one prisoner, whomsoever they desired *(immediately before the situation concerning Barabbas, Pilate sent Jesus to Herod, which is omitted by Mark [in Luke, Chpt. 23]; the custom of releasing a prisoner regarding its origin is anyone's guess)*.

JESUS SENTENCED TO DIE

7 And there was *one* named Barabbas *(this man had been arrested for homicidal political terrorism; there is some evidence that he was referred to as "Jesus Barabbas"; if so, the Jews had the choice of "Jesus Barabbas" or "Jesus Christ")*, which *lay* bound with them who had made insurrection with him, who had committed murder in the insurrection.

8 And the multitude crying aloud began to desire *him (Pilate)* to do as he had ever done unto them *(concerned the releasing of a particular prisoner)*.

9 But Pilate answered them, saying, Will you that I release unto you the King of the Jews? *(Referred to Jesus, in that which Pilate hoped this crowd would do. He used the title "King of the Jews,"*

in sarcasm.)

10 For he knew that the Chief Priests had delivered Him for envy (*inasmuch as the "envy" was so obvious that even this pagan could see it, tells us exactly to what level these religious leaders had sunk*).

11 But the Chief Priests moved the people, that he should rather release Barabbas unto them.

12 And Pilate answered and said again unto them, What will you then that I shall do *unto Him* whom you call the King of the Jews?

13 And they cried out again, Crucify Him (*they wanted Him crucified, because they thought this would prove to the people that He was not of God*).

14 Then Pilate said unto them, Why, what evil has He done? (*It was not for "evil" that they wanted to Crucify Him, but because of His "good."*) And they cried out the more exceedingly, Crucify Him (*Luke says they repeated the cry again, and again [Lk. 23:23]*).

15 And *so* Pilate, willing to content the people (*he was willing to content the people, but not willing to content God; untold thousands of preachers do the same every week*), released Barabbas unto them (*presents a study in irony!; they accused Christ of being an insurrectionist, which He was not, and yet demanded Barab-* bas *be released, who had actually made insurrection!; such is evil!*), and delivered Jesus, when he had scourged *Him,* to be crucified (*the scourging was so severe, that many who experienced this ordeal didn't survive it*).

JESUS CROWNED
WITH THORNS

16 And the soldiers led Him away into the hall, called Praetorium (*this was actually the barracks of the soldiers, which could have numbered as many as six hundred*); and they call together the whole band (*they would now mock Him*).

17 And they clothed Him with purple (*they were mocking Him as King*), and platted a crown of thorns, and put it about His *Head* (*the Greek word for "crown" as used here, is "stephanos," and means the "the victor's crown"; in the Mind of God, the victory had already been won, because He knew that Calvary would pay the total price*),

18 And began to salute Him, Hail, King of the Jews! (*He was the King of the Jews, even though they didn't know it, but as well, He was the King of the whole world, which the world will recognize in the coming Kingdom Age.*)

19 And they smote Him on the head with a reed (*this was a stiff object which would have driven the thorns deep within His scalp*), and

did spit upon Him, and bowing *their* knees worshipped Him *(but in mockery)*.

20 And when they had mocked Him, they took off the purple from Him, and put His own clothes on Him, and led Him out to Crucify Him.

21 And they compel one Simon a Cyrenian *(due to the beatings, Jesus could no longer physically carry the Cross, so they pressed this particular man to carry it for Him)*, who passed by, coming out of the country *(means that he was not a part in any way to these insidious proceedings, but just happened to be standing near when Jesus came by)*, the father of Alexander and Rufus, to bear His Cross *(speaks of the sons of Simon who would give their hearts to Christ, becoming well-known Disciples, and all because of what happened here this day)*.

THE CRUCIFIXION

22 And they bring Him unto the place Golgotha, which is, being interpreted, The place of a skull *(two meanings: A. Some claim this is the place where Adam was buried, and his skull later found; however, there is no evidence whatsoever of this tradition; and, B. Others think the interpretation simply means that the rock face of the hill resembles a skull, which is probably the correct interpretation)*.

23 And they gave Him to drink wine mingled with myrrh *(referred to a strong narcotic made of sour wine and mingled with bitter herbs; it was supposed to dull the sense of pain; some think that Christ was offered the drink twice, but there is some indication that it was offered three times)*: but He received *it* not *(He would not seek alleviation of the agonies of the Crucifixion by any drug potion which might render Him insensible; He would bear the full burden consciously)*.

24 And when they had crucified Him *(referred to them nailing Him to the Cross)*, they parted His garments, casting lots upon them, what every man should take *(His garments, with the exception of the seamless Robe, were divided among the soldiers; not wanting to tear the seamless Robe apart, they cast lots with the winner taking ownership of the garment [Ps. 22:18])*.

25 And it was the third hour *(9 a.m. in the morning, the time of the morning Sacrifice)*, and they crucified Him.

26 And the superscription of His accusation was written over *(over the Cross)*, THE KING OF THE JEWS *(out of anger, no doubt toward the Jews, Pilate wrote the title himself [Jn. 19:19]; the Chief Priests were visibly angry over this, and strongly requested that it be changed to read, "He said, I am King of the

Jews"; Pilate answered by saying, "what I have written I have written" [Jn. 19:21-22]; so, Who, and What Jesus really was, were fitly placed over His Head on the Cross).

27 And with Him they crucify two thieves *(robbers)*; the one on His right hand, and the other on His left.

28 And the Scripture was fulfilled, which said, And He was numbered with the transgressors *([Isa. 53:12], He took the place of the transgressors; so His death, its manner, and with whom He died, were fitting!)*.

29 And they who passed by railed on Him *([Ps. 22:7-8], "they," referred to the religious leaders of Israel)*, wagging their heads, and saying, Ah, You Who destroyed the Temple, and build *it* in three days *(they were referring to the statement He did make, recorded in [Jn. 2:19-21], which referred to His Body the Temple, its Death, and Resurrection in three days; He wasn't talking about the Temple in Jerusalem)*,

30 Save Yourself, and come down from the Cross *(this jest was the harder to endure since it appealed to a consciousness of power held back only by the self-restraint of a Sacrificed will; had He saved Himself, no one else could have been saved)*.

31 Likewise also the Chief Priests mocking said among themselves with the Scribes, He saved others; Himself He cannot save *(they could not deny the fact that He saved others, but they attempted to turn that fact against Him, by alleging that He performed these miracles by the power of Satan, rather than by the Power of God)*.

32 Let Christ the King of Israel descend now from the Cross *(said in mockery)*, that we may see and believe *(they lied!; He rose from the dead after the third day, and they still didn't believe)*. And they who were crucified with Him reviled Him *(while both did revile Him, one shortly thereafter repented and was saved, which Mark did not mention)*.

THE DEATH OF JESUS

33 And when the sixth hour was come *(12 noon)*, there was darkness over the whole land until the ninth hour *(until 3 p.m.; as it was now the Passover time the moon was full, so that it could not have been caused by an eclipse; for when the moon is full it cannot intervene between the Earth and the sun; how far this darkness extended, we aren't told; we do know that it went as far as Egypt toward the south, and as far as Bithynia toward the north; it was at this time that He became the Burnt-offering, and the Sin-offering of*

Leviticus 1:4).

34 And at the ninth hour *(3 p.m.)* Jesus cried with a loud voice *(proving that He did not die from physical weakness, but that He purposely, laid down His Own life [Jn. 10:17-18])*, saying, Eloi, Eloi, lama sabachthani? which is, being interpreted, My God, My God, why have You forsaken Me? *(During this three hour period when darkness covered that part of the world, if not the whole Earth, He bore the sin penalty of mankind, on which the Heavenly Father could not look [Hab. 1:13; I Pet. 2:24].)*

35 And some of them who stood by *(refers to the Roman soldiers, even some of the religious leaders of Israel)*, when they heard it, said, Behold, He calls Elijah *(mockingly said by the religious leaders of Israel)*.

36 And one ran and filled a spunge full of vinegar *(according to John, this was placed on hyssop [Jn. 19:29] which fulfilled [Ex. 12:22])*, and put it on a reed, and gave Him to drink *(there is no record that He drank it)*, saying, Let alone; let us see whether Elijah will come to take Him down *(sarcasm!)*.

37 And Jesus cried with a loud voice *(once again, proving that His death was not brought about by physical weakness)*, and gave up the ghost *(should have been translated, "breathed out His life"; in* fact, He didn't die, until the Holy Spirit told Him to die [Heb. 9:14]).

38 And the Veil of the Temple was rent in twain from the top to the bottom *(this signified that the price had been paid, with all sin atoned; now, the way to the Holy of Holies was opened up that man might come, for the Veil hid the Holy of Holies)*.

39 And when the centurion *(he was the first Gentile to render this testimony of Faith; tradition affirms that his name was Longinus, and that he became a devoted follower of Christ, preached the Faith, and died a martyr's death)*, which stood over against Him *(beside Christ)*, saw that He so cried out, and gave up the ghost, he said, Truly this man was the Son of God *(in effect, he was saying, many have claimed to be God, but this One is God)*.

40 There were also women looking on afar off *(speaks of women from Galilee, and not women from Jerusalem)*: among whom was Mary Magdalene, and Mary the mother of James the less and of Joseph, and Salome *(there is no record that Mary the Mother of Jesus was there; no doubt, the strain was more than she could bear, and John undoubtly took her away)*;

41 (Who also, when He was in Galilee, followed Him, and ministered unto Him;) *(did what they could to help)* and many other

women which came up with Him unto Jerusalem *(who they were, we aren't told)*.

THE BURIAL OF JESUS

42 And now when the evening was come *(soon to come. It was now approximately 3 p.m. — the evening would be at about 6 p.m. so they had about three hours to work)*, because it was the preparation *(to prepare for the Passover, for it would begin at 6 p.m. that evening)*, that is, the day before the Sabbath *(this was the High Sabbath of the Passover Feast, which was Thursday, and not the ordinary weekly Sabbath, which was Saturday [Lev. 23:6-7]; Jesus was crucified on a Wednesday, and not on Friday, as many think, spending three full days and nights in the Tomb, and rose on the first day of the week, even as He had said He would do [Mat. 12:40])*,

43 Joseph of Arimathaea, an honourable counselor *(he was a member of the Grand Council of Jerusalem, the Sanhedrin)*, which also waited for the Kingdom of God *(spoke of his spiritual hunger, which was fulfilled in Jesus)*, came, and went in boldly unto Pilate *(means that such was not commonly done)*, and craved the body of Jesus *(he strongly requested that he be given the remains)*.

44 And Pilate marvelled if He *(Jesus)* were already dead *(it normally took several days for one to die on the cross; Jesus had only been on the cross for six hours, so Pilate was skeptical)*: and calling *unto him* the centurion, he asked him whether he had been any while dead *(how long He had been dead)*.

45 And when he knew *it* of the centurion *(it was affirmed by the Roman soldier)*, he gave the body to Joseph *(the word "body" in the Greek is "ptoma," and means "a corpse")*.

46 And he *(Joseph)* bought fine linen *(a piece of expensive cloth used to wrap around the body of Jesus)*, and took Him down *(took Him down from the Cross)*, and wrapped Him in the linen, and laid Him in a sepulchre which was hewn out of a rock *(the tomb was in the garden adjacent to the place of crucifixion, most certainly the property of Joseph)*, and rolled a stone unto the door of the sepulcher *(proving that the tomb had never before been used)*.

47 And Mary Magdalene and Mary *the mother* of Joseph beheld where He was laid.

CHAPTER 16

THE TESTIMONY OF THE ANGEL

AND when the Sabbath was past *(the regular weekly Sab-*

bath of Saturday), Mary Magdalene, and Mary the *mother* of
James, and Salome, had bought
sweet spices, that they might
come and anoint Him (*proving
that they really did not believe that
He would rise from the dead; if
so, it would have been pointless to
have wasted money on the purchase
of these expensive items*).

2 And very early in the morning the first *day* of the week (*Sunday morning*), they came unto the
sepulchre at the rising of the sun.

3 And they said among themselves (*means in the Greek Text that
"they kept on saying among themselves"*), Who shall roll us away
the stone from the door of the
sepulchre? (*The stone would have
to be rolled away, so they could
apply the spices to the corpse.*)

4 And when they looked, they
saw that the stone was rolled
away: for it was very great.

5 And entering into the sepulchre, they saw a young man sitting on the right side (*sitting on
the raised projection, which had
contained the body of Jesus; Him
"sitting" portrayed far more than
posture; it meant that the work of
the Resurrection was completed, and
death had been defeated*), clothed
in a long white garment (*the
"young man" was an Angel; Expositors remarked that no such robe
was worn by young men on Earth*);
and they were affrighted (*no won-

der, Matthew said, "his countenance
was like lightning" [Mat. 28:3]*).

6 And he said unto them, Be
not affrighted (*fear not*): You seek
Jesus of Nazareth, Who was crucified: He is risen (*without a doubt,
the greatest statement ever made in
the annals of human history*); He
is not here (*speaks of victory over
death, Hell, and the grave*): behold the place where they laid
Him (*signifies the empty tomb; in
other words, He definitely was dead,
but is now definitely alive!*).

7 But go your way, tell His
Disciples and Peter (*no censor or
reprimand concerning their unbelief; as well, "Peter" is added to
let him know that he is included,
despite his denial of Christ, because
Peter had repented*) that He goes
before you into Galilee: there
shall you see Him, as He said
unto you (*there were several appearances of Christ to the Disciples
in Jerusalem before the Galilee appearance, but it was only during
the latter appearance that He re-
commissioned them [Jn. 21]*).

THE TESTIMONY
OF THE WOMEN

8 And they went out quickly,
and fled from the sepulchre; for
they trembled and were amazed
(*proclaims them seeing more than
they could comprehend, digest, or
even accept for the moment*): nei-

ther said they any thing to any man; for they were afraid *(they were fearful that they would be accused of stealing the body)*.

9 Now when *Jesus* was risen early the first *day* of the week *(referred to some time after sundown Saturday, which would have been the beginning of the Jewish Sunday, the first day of the week)*, He appeared first to Mary Magdalene *(He appeared to her even before appearing to His Disciples)*, out of whom He had cast seven devils *(gives us at least a hint as to the cause of her love and devotion)*.

10 *And* she went and told them who had been with Him *(referred to His Disciples)*, as they mourned and wept *(as stated, they had not believed that He would rise from the dead, despite the fact that He had plainly told them so [Mat. 12:40])*.

11 And they, when they had heard that He was alive, and had been seen of her, believed not *(they flatly rejected her testimony; Luke said that it seemed to them "as idle tales" [Lk. 24:11]; the repeated unbelief of the Apostles concerning the Resurrection, destroys the theory that they invented the Resurrection)*.

THE TESTIMONY OF THE DISCIPLES

12 After that He appeared in another form unto two of them *("another form," in the Greek Text literally says, "In a different outward expression or appearance"; this is given in detail in Luke 24:13-35)*, as they walked, and went into the country *(outside of Jerusalem toward Emmaus; it is believed that the two were Cleophas, and Luke)*.

13 And they went and told *it* unto the residue *(to the Disciples)*: neither believed they them *(places them at the position of disbelieving two different and distinct sources)*.

14 Afterward He appeared unto the Eleven as they sat at meat *(could have been His appearance to them by the Sea of Galilee [Jn. 21:4-23])*, and upbraided them with their unbelief and hardness of heart, because they believed not them which had seen Him after He was risen *(He rebuked them, and did so sharply)*.

THE GREAT COMMISSION

15 And He said unto them, Go ye into all the world *(the Gospel of Christ is not merely a western Gospel, as some claim, but is for the entirety of the world)*, and preach the Gospel to every creature *("preaching" is God's method, as is here plainly obvious; as well, it is imperative that every single person have the opportunity to hear; this is the responsibility of every Believer)*.

16 He who believes *(believes in

Christ and what He did for us at the Cross) and is baptized *(baptized into Christ [Rom. 6:3-5] not water baptism)* shall be saved; but he who believes not shall be damned *(Jn. 3:16)*.

17 And these signs shall follow them who believe *(not these "sins" shall follow them who believe)*; In My Name shall they cast out devils *(demons — Jesus defeated Satan, fallen Angels, and all demon spirits at the Cross [Col. 2:14-15])*; they shall speak with new Tongues *(Baptism with the Holy Spirit with the evidence of speaking with other Tongues [Acts 2:4])*;

18 They shall take up serpents *(put away demon spirits [Lk. 10:19] has nothing to do with reptiles)*; and if they drink any deadly thing, it shall not hurt them *(speaks of protection; in no way does it speak of purposely drinking poison, etc., in order to prove one's faith; the word, "if," speaks of accidental ingestion)*; they shall lay hands on the sick, and they shall recover *(means to do so "in the Name of Jesus" [Acts 5:12; 13:3; 14:3; 19:11; 28:8; I Tim. 4:14; II*

Tim. 1:6; Heb. 6:2; James 5:14])*.

THE ASCENSION

19 So then after the Lord had spoken unto them, He was received up into Heaven *(the Ascension)*, and sat on the right Hand of God *([Heb. 1:3] signifying that the work of Redemption, was total and complete, i.e., "a finished work")*.

THE EARLY CHURCH

20 And they went forth *(refers to the entirety of the Early Church, and not just the Twelve Apostles)*, and preached everywhere *(at the end of the First Century, the Gospel of Christ had been taken to the greater majority of the Roman Empire)*, the Lord working with *them* (He will "work" if His Commands are followed), and confirming the Word *(the Word of God, what He had said)* with signs following *(if the "signs" are not "following," the Gospel is not being preached, but rather something else)*. Amen *(Truth)*.

THE GOSPEL ACCORDING TO
LUKE

CHAPTER 1

INTRODUCTION

FORASMUCH as many have taken in hand to set forth in order a declaration (*means many were attempting at that time to write accounts of the Life and Ministry of Christ, which proved to have no inspiration of the Holy Spirit, and consequently, were unreliable*) of those things which are most surely believed among us (*proclaims the Gospel as a narrative concerning facts fully established*),

2 Even as they delivered them unto us (*concerns those who were there, and actually observed what took place*), which from the beginning were eyewitnesses, and ministers of the Word (*probably concerned members of the "Twelve" and the "Seventy," as well as others*);

3 It seemed good to me also (*moved upon by the Holy Spirit to do such*), having had perfect understanding of all things from the very first (*means that he made absolutely certain of the reliability of these "eyewitness accounts"*), to write unto you in order (*refers to an orderly design, not necessarily in chronological order*), most excel-lent Theophilus (*it is not known exactly as to who this man was; he was evidently a Gentile of high rank in the Roman world of that day, who had accepted Christ as his Saviour*),

4 That you might know the certainty of those things (*means that he could rely on what Luke told him*), wherein you have been instructed (*he will now be able to sort the facts from the fiction; Luke writing this Gospel to Theophilus has helped millions to "know" the "certainty of these things"*).

JOHN THE BAPTIST

5 There was in the days of Herod, the king of Judaea (*Herod the Great; the event concerning the birth of John the Baptist took place towards the end of his reign*), a certain Priest named Zacharias (*should be pronounced, "Zechariah"; it means "remembered of Jehovah"*), of the course of Abia (*pertains to the twenty-four courses for Temple service; each of the twenty-four courses lasted for one week [I Chron. 24:1]; Zacharias was especially distinguished by belonging to the first of the twenty-four courses or families*): and his wife was of the daughters of Aaron, and

her name *was* Elisabeth *(meaning that both the husband and the wife traced their lineage back to Aaron, the first High Priest — a coveted distinction in Israel).*

6 And they were both Righteous before God *(tells us that at this time, there were precious few who were actually Righteous before God),* walking in all the Commandments and Ordinances of the Lord blameless *(proclaims a lifestyle of Righteousness which not many had; what an honor to be called by the Holy Spirit, "blameless!").*

7 And they had no child *(they desperately wanted children),* because that Elisabeth was barren *(placed her in the same category as Sarah),* and they both were *now* well stricken in years *(Elisabeth was now beyond the age of child bearing; consequently, John's birth was just as miraculous as that of Isaac [Rom. 4:17-21; Heb. 11:11]).*

8 And it came to pass, that while he *(Zacharias)* executed the Priest's office before God in the order of his course *(some think this was the month of July, if so, Jesus was conceived six months later [Lk. 1:26], which would have been in January, consequently, being born nine months later in October),*

9 According to the custom of the Priest's office, his lot was to burn Incense when he went into the Temple of the Lord *(this was done by coals of fire taken from the Brazen Altar, a Type of Christ and His Crucifixion, and taken to the Altar of Incense, with coals placed on the Altar, with Incense poured over the coals; this was done twice a day at the time of the morning and evening Sacrifices).*

10 And the whole multitude of the people were praying without at the time of Incense.

11 And there appeared unto him an Angel of the Lord *(Gabriel)* standing on the right side of the Altar of Incense *(the right side is the side of propitiation, which, in effect, means that God accepts the Sacrifice [Heb. 1:3]).*

12 And when Zacharias saw *him,* he was troubled, and fear fell upon him.

13 But the Angel said unto him, Fear not, Zacharias: for your prayer is heard *(the Greek translation should read, "was heard," implying that it was no longer offered because of their age; but every prayer prayed in the Will of God is always heard by the Lord, and will be answered in His due time);* and your wife Elisabeth shall bear you a son, and you shall call his name John *(John means, "Jehovah shows favor or Grace"; it was an apt description of the one who would introduce the Lord of Glory).*

14 And you shall have joy and gladness; and many shall rejoice

at his birth *(the rejoicing would be because he would introduce the Messiah)*.

15 For he shall be great in the sight of the Lord *(his greatness would come because of his introduction of Christ)*, and shall drink neither wine nor strong drink *(meant that he was a "Nazarite" [Num., Chpt. 6])*; and he shall be filled with the Holy Spirit, even from his mother's womb *(has no reference to the Acts 2:4 experience, which had not yet come to pass; he would have unusual help from the Holy Spirit due to his mission, which was to introduce Christ)*.

16 And many of the children of Israel shall he turn to the Lord their God *(he would be the first Prophet since Malachi, a time span of about four hundred years; there would be a great move of the Spirit under his Ministry)*.

RIGHTEOUSNESS

17 And he shall go before Him *(Christ)* in the spirit and power of Elijah *(John could have been Elijah to the people, thereby ushering in the Kingdom Age, if Israel had only accepted Christ)*, to turn the hearts of the fathers to the children *(that the Israel of John's day might have the Righteousness of the Godly Patriarchs of the past)*, and the disobedient to the wisdom of the just *(God and His Word)*; to make ready a people prepared for the Lord *(preparation for the coming Messiah, Whom John would introduce)*.

18 And Zacharias said unto the Angel, Whereby shall I know this? for I am an old man, and my wife well stricken in years *(a posture of unbelief)*.

19 And the Angel answering said unto him, I am Gabriel *(the same Angel who had come to Daniel [Dan. 8:16; 9:21], and shortly would be sent to Mary [Lk. 1:26])*, who stands in the Presence of God *(may well represent the highest rank of all among Angels)*; and am sent to speak unto you, and to show you these glad tidings *(sent from the Throne of God)*.

20 And, behold, you shall be dumb *(there is some indication in the Greek Text that he would be both deaf, and dumb)*, and not able to speak, until the day that these things shall be performed *(he had asked for a sign and had been given one most painful)*, because you believed not my words *(unbelief is a sin)*, which shall be fulfilled in their season *(irrespective of your unbelief, it shall happen)*.

21 And the people waited for Zacharias *(pertained to the usual custom of the Priest finishing his duties, then coming out and pronouncing a blessing upon the people)*, and marvelled that he tarried so long in the Temple *("mar-*

veled" does not show impatience, but rather anticipation; they were not to be disappointed!).

22 And when he came out, he could not speak unto them (the "sign" had already begun): and they perceived that he had seen a vision in the Temple (probably referred to a possible glow on his countenance): for he beckoned unto them, and remained speechless.

23 And it came to pass, that, as soon as the days of his ministration were accomplished (it was about a week), he departed to his own house.

24 And after those days his wife Elisabeth conceived (we aren't told how old she was, just "well-stricken in years" [Vs. 7]), and hid herself five months, saying (she hid herself in order to seek the Lord regarding how this child was to be raised, and how he should be trained),

25 Thus hath the Lord dealt with me in the days wherein he looked on me, to take away my reproach among men (she would no longer be childless, but, in fact, would give birth to the greatest Prophet who ever lived).

MARY

26 And in the sixth month (refers to six months after Elisabeth had conceived; consequently, John was six months older than Jesus) the Angel Gabriel was sent from God unto a city of Galilee, named Nazareth (strangely enough, Nazareth was held in scorn by Israel at that time),

27 To a virgin (in the Greek Text is "parthenos," which refers to a pure virgin who has never known a man, and never experienced a marriage relationship; in the Hebrew, the word is "Ha-alma," which means, "the Virgin — the only one who ever was, or ever will be a mother in this way") espoused (engaged) to a man whose name was Joseph, of the house of David (he was in the direct lineage of David through Solomon); and the Virgin's name was Mary (Mary went back to David through another of David's sons, Nathan; so their lineage was perfect as it regards the Prophecies that the Messiah would come from the House of David [II Sam., Chpt. 7]).

28 And the Angel came in unto her, and said (presents the greatest moment in human history, the announcement of the coming birth of the Lord of Glory in the Incarnation, i.e., "God becoming man"), Hail, you that are highly favoured (means "much engraced," not "full of grace," as the Catholic Church teaches, but one who, herself meritless, had received signal Grace from God), the Lord is with you (signals her position of humility): blessed are you among women (does

not say "above women," as the Catholics teach; however, she definitely was much blessed).

29 And when she saw *him*, she was troubled at his saying (*a total disturbance; not a partial, or light agitation*), and cast in her mind what manner of salutation this should be (*she in no way understood the reason that he addressed her as he did*).

30 And the Angel said unto her, Fear not, Mary: for you have found favour with God (*should have been translated, "you have received Grace from God"*).

31 And, behold, you shall conceive in your womb (*should have been translated, "You shall forthwith conceive in your womb," meaning immediately*), and bring forth a Son (*proclaims the Incarnation, "God manifest in the flesh, God with us, Immanuel" [Isa. 9:6]*), and shall call His name JESUS (*the Greek version of the Hebrew, "Joshua"; it means "Saviour," or "The Salvation of Jehovah"*).

32 He shall be great, and shall be called the Son of the Highest (*actually means "The Most High," and refers to "Jehovah"*): and the Lord God shall give unto Him the throne of His father David (*II Sam., Chpt. 7*):

33 And He shall reign over the house of Jacob for ever; and of His Kingdom there shall be no end (*this will begin at the Second Coming, and will last forever; it could have begun at the beginning of His Ministry, but He was rejected by Israel; but at the Second Coming, they will accept Him as their Saviour, Messiah, and King [Zech., Chpts. 12-14]*).

34 Then said Mary unto the Angel, How shall this be, seeing I know not a man? (*She was probably in her late teens.*)

35 And the Angel answered and said unto her, The Holy Spirit shall come upon you (*has the same connotation as, "the Spirit of God moved upon the face of the waters" [Gen. 1:2]*), and the power of the Highest shall overshadow you (*has the same reference as, "and God said, let there be light: and there was light" [Gen. 1:3]*): therefore also that holy thing which shall be born of you shall be called the Son of God (*constitutes the Incarnation, "God becoming Man"; He would be Very God and Very Man*).

36 And, behold, your cousin Elisabeth (*the word, "cousin," in the Greek Text is "suggenes," which means "countryman," and not necessarily a cousin in the sense of a blood relative; however, Mary definitely could have been personally kin to Elisabeth*), she has also conceived a son in her old age: and this is the sixth month with her, who was called barren.

37 For with God nothing shall

be impossible *(what is impossible with man is very much possible with God)*.

38 And Mary said, Behold the handmaid of the Lord *(beautifully portrays the humility of this young lady; I think she would be greatly grieved at the unscriptural manner in which Catholicism has elevated her — even to the place of Deity)*; be it unto me according to your word *(she gives this consent in a word that was simple and sublime, which involved the most extraordinary act of Faith that a woman ever consented to accomplish)*. And the Angel departed from her.

MARY VISITS ELISABETH

39 And Mary arose in those days *(concerned the time immediately after the appearance of the Angel Gabriel)*, and went into the hill country with haste, into a city of Judah *(tradition places this at Hebron)*;

40 And entered into the house of Zacharias, and saluted Elisabeth *(she was welcomed wholeheartedly)*.

41 And it came to pass, that, when Elisabeth heard the salutation of Mary *(the account that the Angel Gabriel had given to Mary concerning the birth of Jesus)*, the babe *(the one who would be known as John the Baptist)* leaped in her womb *(at the mention of Jesus,*

the Holy Spirit moved upon this unborn child and it responded; it doesn't mean that the unborn child had comprehension)*; and Elisabeth was filled with the Holy Spirit *("filled" in the Greek Text is "pletho," and means to "imbue, influence or supply"; it does not have the meaning of that which happened on the day of Pentecost, referring to Acts 2:4)*:

42 And she *(Elisabeth)* spake out with a loud voice and said, Blessed are you *(Mary)* among women *(not above women as the Catholics claim; however, Mary was truly blessed, as would be obvious)*, and blessed *is* the fruit of your womb *(Jesus Christ was that "fruit!")*.

43 And whence *is* this to me *(why am I honored in this way?)*, that the mother of my Lord should come to me? *(She used the word "Lord" in its highest sense; great as her own child was to be in the sight of the Lord, here was the mother of One yet greater, even the Lord Himself.)*

44 For, lo, as soon as the voice of your salutation sounded in my ears, the babe leaped in my womb for joy *(as stated, this was a manifestation of the Holy Spirit Who produced this response)*.

45 And blessed *is* she who believed *(refers to Mary and her faith)*: for there shall be a performance of those things which were

told her from the Lord *(the words "shall be" are a certitude of action)*.

THE MAGNIFICAT

46 And Mary said *(the following actually constitutes a song, and is in the tradition of the "song of Deborah" [Judg. 5:1-31]),* My soul doth magnify the Lord *(she "magnified the Lord," while the Catholic Church erroneously magnifies her),*

47 And my spirit has rejoiced in God my Saviour *(disproves the theory of the "Immaculate Conception," or the total absence of original sin in Mary; God was her Saviour, so she must have been a sinner, in order to be saved; the Scripture says, "all have sinned" [Rom. 3:23]).*

48 For He has regarded the low estate of His handmaiden *(humility)*: for, behold, from henceforth all generations shall call me blessed *(the word "blessed" is here a single syllable, and simply means "a recipient of Grace").*

49 For He Who is mighty has done to me great things; and Holy is His Name *("Holy" is the essence of His Being, and speaks of God the Father).*

50 And His Mercy is on them who fear Him from generation to generation *(mercy is extended to those who truly revere, i.e., "respect Him").*

51 He has showed strength with His arm *(proclaims the Power of God in the manner in which it is used)*; He has scattered the proud in the imagination of their hearts *(proclaims the Messianic reversal of man's conception of what is great and little).*

52 He has put down the mighty from *their* seats, and exalted them of low degree *(the Lord ignored the proud self-exaltation of the religious elite of Israel, and showered His attention on a little "handmaiden").*

53 He has filled the hungry with good things *(concerns they who hunger and thirst after righteousness [Mat. 5:6])*; and the rich He has sent empty away *(refers to those who claim to be rich and increased with goods, and have need of nothing [Rev. 3:17]).*

54 He has helped His servant Israel, in remembrance of *His* mercy *(regrettably, Israel didn't want His help, or His Mercy)*;

55 As He spoke to our fathers, to Abraham, and to his seed for ever *(Mary's song opens with "magnifying the Lord," and closes with the "Promises of God being remembered forever").*

56 And Mary abode with her *(Elisabeth)* about three months, and returned to her own house *(every indication is Joseph and Mary were married almost immediately after the appearance of the Angel*

Gabriel [Mat. 1:18-25]).

THE BIRTH OF JOHN
THE BAPTIST

57 Now Elisabeth's full time came that she should be delivered; and she brought forth a son.

58 And her neighbours and her cousins heard how the Lord had shown great mercy upon her; and they rejoiced with her.

59 And it came to pass, that on the eighth day they came to circumcise the child *(this was the Command originally given to Abraham by the Lord [Gen. 17:10-12]);* and they called him Zacharias, after the name of his father *("they" referred to friends and relatives, not Zacharias and Elisabeth).*

60 And his mother answered and said, Not *so*; but he shall be called John *(in obedience to what Gabriel had demanded).*

61 And they said unto her, There is none of your kindred who is called by this name.

62 And they made signs to his father, how he would have him called *(shows that he could not hear or speak).*

63 And he asked for a writing table, and wrote, saying, His name is John. And they marvelled all *(upon obedience, as the next verse proclaims, Zacharias could now hear and speak, and possibly related to them the account of the*

appearance of Gabriel).

64 And his mouth was opened immediately, and his tongue *loosed*, and he spoke, and praised God.

65 And fear came on all who dwelt round about them: and all these sayings were noised abroad throughout all the hill country of Judaea *(God was moving again in Israel; the four hundred year prophetic drought was being broken; once again, they would hear, "Thus saith the Lord . . .").*

66 And all they who heard them *(the predictions of Gabriel as related by Zacharias and Elisabeth)* laid *them* up in their hearts, saying, What manner of child shall this be! And the hand of the Lord was with him *(this is Luke's way of expressing all that would happen to John the Baptist through the entirety of his life).*

ZECHARIAH'S PROPHECY

67 And his father Zacharias was filled with the Holy Spirit *(pertains to the Holy Spirit helping him)*, and prophesied, saying *(concerned what John the Baptist would do and be in his Ministry)*,

68 Blessed *be* the Lord God of Israel; for He has visited and redeemed His people *(the word "Blessed," as here used, is a double syllable, "Bless-ed," and means that God is full of Grace, and actually*

the dispenser of Grace; the great Redemption had long been a promise; now it is to be a reality!),

69 And has raised up an Horn of Salvation for us in the house of His servant David ("an Horn of Salvation" is another name given to Christ by the Holy Spirit);

70 As He spoke by the mouth of his Holy Prophets, which have been since the world began (this began with Genesis 3:15):

71 That we should be saved from our enemies, and from the hand of all who hate us (proclaims Salvation by Grace, but as well to Israel, and will be fulfilled at the Second Coming);

72 To perform the mercy promised to our fathers, and to remember His Holy Covenant (Jesus is the bearer of that "Mercy," actually He is Mercy!);

73 The oath which He swore to our father Abraham (this "Oath" is found in Genesis 12:3; 17:4; 22:16-17),

74 That He would grant unto us, that we being delivered out of the hand of our enemies might serve Him without fear (pertains to Salvation, and as well to the coming Kingdom Age),

75 In Holiness and Righteousness before Him, all the days of our life (will totally be fulfilled in the coming Kingdom Age).

76 And you, child (John the Baptist), shall be called the Proph-et of the Highest: for you shall go before the Face of the Lord to prepare His ways (John the Baptist would be the forerunner of the King about Whom the Prophets had written);

77 To give knowledge of Salvation unto His people by the remission of their sins (which would be done by Jesus going to the Cross),

78 Through the tender Mercy of our God; whereby the Dayspring from on high has visited us (another name for Christ, "The Dayspring from on High"),

79 To give light to them who sit in darkness and in the shadow of death, to guide our feet into the way of peace (Jesus is the Light of the world).

80 And the child grew, and waxed strong in spirit (in the ways of the Lord), and was in the deserts till the day of his showing unto Israel (he remained there until he was thirty years of age, before beginning his Ministry, which was the fulfilling of the Law [Num. 4:3]).

CHAPTER 2

THE BIRTH OF JESUS CHRIST

AND it came to pass in those days, that there went out a decree from Caesar Augustus (Caius Octavius, the adopted son and successor of Julius Caesar; he reigned 29 B.C. to A.D. 14) that all the world should be taxed (*a figure of speech; a whole is put for a part; it was only the part of the world of which it spoke*).

2 (*And* this taxing was first made when Cyrenius was governor of Syria.) (*This Verse should have been translated, "This census was before Cyrenius was Governor of Syria."*)

3 And all went to be taxed, every one into his own city.

4 And Joseph also went up from Galilee, out of the city of Nazareth, into Judaea, unto the city of David, which is called Bethlehem; (because he was of the house and lineage of David:) (*It was a distance of about 80 miles.*)

5 To be taxed with Mary his espoused wife, being great with child (*the trip must have been very difficult for her*).

6 And so it was, that, while they were there, the days were accomplished that she should be delivered (*this concerned the most important delivery of a baby in human history; God would become flesh, and offer up Himself on the Cross as a perfect Sacrifice in order to deliver humanity*).

7 And she brought forth her Firstborn Son (*this is meant to emphasize the fact that there were no other children up to this time;*

as well, it refutes the error of the Catholic Church, which claims that Mary, thereafter, had no other children, and remained a Virgin throughout her life; actually, Jesus had four brothers, "James, Joseph, Simon, and Jude," as well as two or three sisters [Mat. 13:55-56]*), and wrapped Him in swaddling clothes, and laid Him in a manger (*spoke of a feeding place for animals*); because there was no room for them in the inn (*the Inn of Bethlehem was of ancient duration, being mentioned in Jeremiah 41:17; this type of "Inn" was for the poorest of the poor, and offered little more than the shelter of its walls and roof*).

THE ANGELIC ANNOUNCEMENT

8 And there were in the same country (*referred to the area around Bethlehem*) shepherds abiding in the field (*pertained to the lowest caste in society at that time*), keeping watch over their flock by night (*gives indication that December 25th was not the day on which Jesus was born; it was the custom to send flocks out after the Passover, which was in April, to stay until the first rain in October or November*).

9 And, lo, the Angel of the Lord came upon them (*proclaims the fact that the Birth of the Lord*

was not announced to the notables of Israel, but rather to obscure shepherds), and the glory of the Lord shone round about them: and they were sore afraid *(this was the visible token of the presence of the Eternal, which appeared first in the bush before Moses, and then in the pillar of fire and cloud, which guided the desert wanderings, and then in the Tabernacle and the Temple)*.

10 And the Angel said unto them, Fear not: for, behold, I bring you good tidings of great joy, which shall be to all people *(includes all races)*.

11 For unto you is born this day in the city of David a Saviour, which is Christ the Lord *(this Baby was not to become a King and a Saviour — He was born both)*.

12 And this *shall be* a sign unto you; You shall find the Baby wrapped in swaddling clothes, lying in a manger.

13 And suddenly there was with the Angel a multitude of the Heavenly Host praising God, and saying *(many other Angels had been with the Angel who spoke to the shepherds, but now the shepherds can see them as well; this presents sinless Angels praising God for sending the Redeemer; if they did so, certainly we should as well)*,

14 Glory to God in the highest, and on Earth peace, good will toward men *(Jesus is that "Peace";* *during His approximate 33 years of life on this Earth, the Roman Empire was relatively at peace; it was because the Prince of Peace was here; peace will not return until Jesus returns)*.

THE SHEPHERDS

15 And it came to pass, as the Angels were gone away from them into Heaven, the Shepherds said one to another, Let us now go even unto Bethlehem, and see this thing which is come to pass, which the Lord has made known unto us *(proclaims one of the greatest honors in the whole of human history; the Lord would dispatch Angels only to these lowly shepherds in exclusion of all others)*.

16 And they came with haste, and found Mary, and Joseph *(means they had to do a small amount of searching)*, and the baby lying in a manger.

17 And when they had seen *it (should have been translated, "and when they had seen Him"; theirs were the first human eyes to see Jesus after His Birth, other than His foster Father and His Mother)*, they made known abroad the saying which was told them concerning this Child *(they were the first Preachers to proclaim His Birth, as Mary Magdalene was the first to proclaim His Resurrection)*.

18 And all they who heard *it*

wondered at those things which were told them by the shepherds.

19 But Mary kept all these things, and pondered *them* in her heart (*means that she thought about them almost constantly, and no wonder!*).

20 And the shepherds returned (*to their flocks*), glorifying and praising God for all the things that they had heard and seen, as it was told unto them (*this proclaims the fact that these men truly knew the Lord, hence at least one of the reasons that the Angels appeared to them*).

THE NAMING OF JESUS

21 And when eight days were accomplished for the circumcising of the Child (*this was according to the Law of Moses; it is said that the blood did not properly coagulate in the little baby boy until he was eight days old*), His Name was called JESUS (*meaning Saviour*), which was so named of the Angel before He was conceived in the womb.

THE PRESENTATION

22 And when the days of her purification according to the Law of Moses were accomplished (*speaks of forty days after the Birth of Jesus; it was eighty days in the case of a daughter [Lev. 12:1-6]*),

they brought Him to Jerusalem, to present *Him* to the Lord (*all the firstborn of the boy babies belonged to the Lord, and were to be presented to Him as a token of His rightful claim to them [Num. 3:44; 18:15]*);

23 (As it is written in the Law of the Lord, Every male that opens the womb shall be called Holy to the Lord;) (*refers to the firstborn only*).

24 And to offer a sacrifice according to that which is said in the Law of the Lord (*Lev. 12:8*), A pair of turtledoves, or two young pigeons (*proclaimed that which could be offered in place of a "Lamb," providing the offerer could not afford the Lamb; this tells us that Mary and Joseph were poor, at least as far as this world's goods were concerned; it also tells us that Mary was not sinless, as claimed by the Catholic Church; if so, she would not have had to offer these Sacrifices for her impurity*).

THE PROPHECY OF SIMEON

25 And, behold, there was a man in Jerusalem, whose name *was* Simeon; and the same man *was* just and devout, waiting for the consolation of Israel (*is a term describing the Coming and Ministry of the Messiah*): and the Holy Spirit was upon him (*he was being led by the Spirit*).

26 And it was revealed unto him by the Holy Spirit, that he should not see death, before he had seen the Lord's Christ (consequently, each day he was anticipating this great event).

27 And he came by the Spirit into the Temple (the Spirit of the Lord had pressed upon him strongly that at this particular time he was to go to the Temple): and when the parents (Joseph and Mary) brought in the Child Jesus, to do for Him after the custom of the Law (Jesus was made of woman under the Law [Gal. 4:4]; the Law is mentioned five times in this Chapter, and so confirms the statement in Galatians; to save man justly doomed to death by the Law, it was necessary that Christ should be born under the Law),

28 Then took he Him up in his arms, and blessed God, and said (proclaims Simeon the first on record to have "handled the Word of Life," other than Mary and Joseph),

29 Lord, now let Thou Thy servant depart in peace, according to Your Word (indicates that it had been a number of years since the Lord had revealed to Simeon that he would actually see "the Lord's Christ"):

30 For my eyes have seen Your Salvation (Simeon didn't have to ask Mary Who the Child was; he recognized Him at once by inspiration as Jehovah's Anointed; Jesus is Salvation, and Salvation is Jesus),

31 Which You have prepared before the face of all people (opens the door of Salvation to every human being on the face of the Earth, regardless of color, nationality, or country);

32 A light to lighten the Gentiles (once again, the Holy Spirit includes all people), and the glory of Your people Israel (regrettably, Israel would not accept Him).

33 And Joseph and His mother marvelled at those things which were spoken of Him (if it is to be noticed, the Holy Spirit through Luke wrote "Joseph and His mother," and not "His father and mother"; the reason is obvious! Joseph was only His foster father, so to speak).

34 And Simeon blessed them (refers only to Joseph and Mary, and not Jesus; while Christ blesses all, none are qualified to bless Christ; sometimes the word, "blessed," is used in the sense of "praise," which then becomes not only acceptable, but desirable), and said unto Mary His mother, Behold, this Child is set for the fall and rising again of many in Israel (according to the acceptance or rejection of Christ); and for a sign which shall be spoken against (men who have agreed in nothing else have agreed in hating Christ);

35 (Yes, a sword shall pierce through your own soul also,) (pertained to the rejection of Jesus'

Ministry by the religious leaders of Israel, and ultimately His Crucifixion on the Cross) that the thoughts of many hearts may be revealed (presents the purpose of the Gospel of Christ; Mary's own heart, being carnal as all others, had to come under the rays of this great light, and her soul had to feel the piercing of the Divine Sword of the Word of God; she was indeed blessed as the chosen Vessel of the Incarnation, but all women who follow Jesus are as blessed [Lk. 11:27]).

THE ADORATION OF ANNA

36 And there was one Anna, a Prophetess, the daughter of Phanuel (presents this dear lady as a Preacher of the Gospel; in the Bible the first woman to Prophesy was Rachel, even though she is not called a Prophetess [Gen. 30:24]), of the Tribe of Aser (refers to the Tribe of Asher): she was of a great age, and had lived with an husband seven years from her virginity (means that her husband died seven years after they were married, and she never remarried);

37 And she was a widow of about fourscore and four years (it had been eighty-four years since her husband had died; consequently, she was well over one hundred years old), which departed not from the Temple (she had literally lived in the Temple, probably being provided a small room or chamber, and was assigned some small tasks), but served God with fastings and prayers night and day (notes her wonderful consecration to the Lord).

38 And she coming in that instant gave thanks likewise unto the Lord (proclaims the fact that the Holy Spirit revealed unto her that this Child was indeed the Messiah), and spoke of Him to all them who looked for redemption in Jerusalem (she related to all her experience at seeing the Child, and the Lord had revealed to her that He was the Messiah; they both, Simeon and Anna, loved the Courts of Jehovah's House, and He met them there).

39 And when they had performed all things according to the Law of the Lord (referred to the Law of Moses), they returned into Galilee, to their own city Nazareth (Luke does not mention the visit of the Wise men, or the flight into Egypt as Matthew does not mention the shepherds).

40 And the Child grew, and waxed strong in spirit (Jesus did not have a sin nature, so this means that He was never sick, and neither did He ever sin), filled with wisdom (there is every evidence that Jesus began studying the Bible from the time He learned to read): and the Grace of God was upon Him (the Goodness of God).

JESUS AS A BOY

41 Now His parents went to Jerusalem every year at the Feast of the Passover (the word, "went" means that they were accustomed to going, for they were Godly people).

42 And when He (Jesus) was twelve years old (refers to the age at which every Jewish boy became "a son of the Law"), they went up to Jerusalem after the custom of the Feast (Jerusalem was where the Feast was held, and in fact, must be held).

43 And when they had fulfilled the days (pertained to seven days, which actually incorporated three Feasts: the Feast of Passover, the Feast of Unleavened Bread, and the Feast of Firstfruits), as they returned (were leaving Jerusalem to go to Nazareth), the Child Jesus tarried behind in Jerusalem (at twelve years of age, every Jewish boy from henceforth was treated as an Adult, which meant that there was now much less supervision than had previously been); and Joseph and His mother knew not of it (Joseph and Mary were not being lax in their supervision; they were treating Jesus as an adult, which the custom then demanded, and felt that He would join up with them at a given point).

44 But they, supposing Him to have been in the company (with another group going to Nazareth), went a day's journey (again, this was the custom in those days, with all groups headed to a certain destination, meeting at a particular point, and then going together); and they sought Him among their kinsfolk and acquaintance.

45 And when they found Him not, they turned back again to Jerusalem, seeking Him (refers to a diligent search; it also speaks of concern and anxiety).

46 And it came to pass, that after three days they found Him in the Temple (probably refers to the third day after originally leaving Jerusalem; they spent the first day traveling from Jerusalem to the designated meeting point; upon not finding Jesus, they then journeyed back to Jerusalem the next day; on the third day, they found Him in the Temple), sitting in the midst of the doctors (included the most famous Bible Scholars of that day), both hearing them, and asking them questions (what a sight this must have been, these most famous doctors of the Mosaic Law with this twelve-year-old Boy sitting in their midst, and with most of the attention directed toward Him; it is believed that Nicodemus was in this group).

47 And all who heard Him were astonished at His understanding and answers (the word, "astonished" in the Greek Text refers to amazement to such an ex-

tent that one is beside one's self; in truth, His "understanding and answers" were far beyond that of these learned Doctors).

48 And when they saw Him, they were amazed (referring to His parents): and His mother said unto Him, Son, why have you thus dealt with us? (The possibility does exist that the Holy Spirit had Jesus to do this purposely, in order to awaken Mary and Joseph to His true mission and purpose, even though it would not truly begin until He was thirty years of age.) behold, Your father and I have sought You sorrowing (Mary used the phrase, "Your Father," and Jesus gently reminded her in the next Verse Who His Father actually was; legally, Joseph was His father, but only in the foster sense).

49 And He said unto them, How is it that you sought Me? (He gently reminded them that they should have known Who He was, and His Mission.) wist you not that I must be about My Father's business? (This was His first recorded utterance, with the words, "It is finished," His last recorded utterance before His Crucifixion [Jn. 19:30], which means He Finished the Father's Business.)

50 And they understood not the saying which He spoke unto them (they should have understood!).

51 And He went down with them, and came to Nazareth, and was subject unto them (concerns the next eighteen years): but His mother kept all these sayings in her heart (refers to all that pertained to Jesus).

52 And Jesus increased in wisdom and stature, and in favour with God and man (this means that He perfectly kept the Law of God, and did perfectly the Will of God).

CHAPTER 3

JOHN THE BAPTIST

NOW in the fifteenth year of the reign of Tiberius Caesar (the stepson of the Emperor Augustus, whom he succeeded; he reigned from 14 B.C. to A.D. 37, consequently covering the entire span of Jesus' Life and Ministry), Pontius Pilate being Governor of Judaea, and Herod being Tetrarch of Galilee (he was known as "Antipas"; he was a son of Herod the Great, and reigned for more than forty years), and his brother Philip Tetrarch of Ituraea and of the region of Trachonitis (the area northeast of the Sea of Galilee, which included Caesarea Philippi, which was actually built by him), and Lysanias the Tetrarch of Abilene (referred to the district now known as southern Lebanon; the title "Tetrarch" meant "ruler of a fourth part," but actually came to be used *of all Governors).*

2 Annas and Caiaphas being the High Priests *(the High Priests were supposed to be descendants of Aaron; however, the office was now controlled by Rome, with both men now serving somewhat in this capacity),* the Word of God came unto John the son of Zacharias in the wilderness *(it was now time for John to begin his Ministry).*

3 And he came into all the country about Jordan *(the location of his Ministry centered around the Jordan River),* preaching the baptism of repentance for the remission of sins *(he was preaching personal repentance which guaranteed remission of sins, which was to be followed by Water Baptism);*

4 As it is written in the Book of the words of Isaiah the Prophet *(Isa. 40:3-5),* saying, The voice of one crying in the wilderness *(John's Ministry was predicted by Isaiah some 800 years before),* Prepare you the Way of the Lord, make His paths straight *(Israel must come in line with the Word of God, inasmuch as the Messiah is about to be introduced).*

5 Every valley shall be filled, and every mountain and hill shall be brought low; and the crooked shall be made straight, and the rough ways *shall be* made smooth *(concerns a proper interpretation of the Word of God, which produces*

proper lives);

6 And all flesh shall see the Salvation of God *(all Israel would see the Lord Jesus Christ, their Messiah, Who is the "Salvation of God").*

7 Then said he to the multitude who came forth to be baptized of him *(Water Baptism in this fashion, was new to Israel),* O generation of vipers *(this is what the Holy Spirit through John said of the Israel of that time),* who has warned you to flee from the wrath to come? *(Wrath is guaranteed to come on all Christ rejecters; this means that one can flee that wrath only by accepting Christ.)*

8 Bring forth therefore fruits worthy of repentance *(in effect says that Water Baptism would do them no good unless there had first been repentance, and if there was true repentance, fruits would be evident),* and begin not to say within yourselves, We have Abraham to our father *(there is no such thing as a national salvation):* for I say unto you, That God is able of these stones to raise up children unto Abraham *(proclaims John striking boldly at the very root of Jewish pride).*

9 And now also the axe is laid unto the root of the trees *(the "trees" spoke of Israel, and the "axe" spoke of the Judgment of God; it did not say that the axe was then severing the roots, but that it was poised to do so, that is if repentance*

was not forthcoming): every tree therefore which brings not forth good fruit is hewn down, and cast into the fire *(this is a Law of God that applies to every individual person)*.

10 And the people asked him, saying, What shall we do then? *(We come again, as will be obvious, to the Fruits of Repentance.)*

11 He answered and said unto them, He who has two coats, let him impart to him who has none; and he who has meat, let him do likewise *(John's answer has no reference to the doing of these things as the cause of Salvation, but rather the result)*.

12 Then came also publicans to be baptized, and said unto him, Master, what shall we do? *(Publicans were tax-collectors, in a sense employees of Rome, and thereby looked at as traitors by Israel as a whole; most didn't even believe that publicans could be saved.)*

13 And he said unto them, Exact no more than that which is appointed you *(we find here that John treated the publicans no different than he did the Pharisees, who claimed to be so religious; the message was the same to all)*.

14 And the soldiers likewise demanded of him, saying, And what shall we do? *(Israel had no army, so these could very well have been Gentiles.)* And he said unto them, Do violence to no man, neither accuse *any* falsely; and be content with your wages *(these men, both publicans and soldiers, are not bidden by the inspired Prophet of the Highest to change their way of life, but only its manner)*.

JOHN'S PREDICTION OF JESUS

15 And as the people were in expectation *(proclaims the fact that all of Israel at that time were looking for the Messiah)*, and all men mused in their hearts of John, whether he were the Christ, or not *(had they known the Word, they would have known better)*;

16 John answered, saying unto *them* all, I indeed baptize you with water *(the best that mortal man can do, even one as holy as John the Baptist)*; but One mightier than I comes *(only the Almighty can set men free)*, the latchet of Whose shoes I am not worthy to unloose *(presents the humility of John, and the humility demanded of all)*: He shall baptize you with the Holy Spirit and with fire *(this was made possible by the Cross, and was fulfilled according to Acts 2:4, with untold millions having received this experience)*:

17 Whose fan *is* in His hand *(the fan used to blow the chaff away*

from the wheat), and He will thoroughly purge His floor *(will separate the chaff from the wheat, which is a violent process)*, and will gather the wheat into His garner *(the wheat alone is accepted)*; but the chaff He will burn with fire unquenchable *(all that's not of God will be consigned to Hell)*.

18 And many other things in his exhortation preached he unto the people *(preaching was God's way then, and preaching is God's now)*.

19 But Herod the Tetrarch, being reproved by him *(by John the Baptist)* for Herodias his brother Philip's wife *(Herod had taken Philip's wife for himself)*, and for all the evils which Herod had done *(an evil depraved man)*,

20 Added yet this above all, that he shut up John in prison *(the Holy Spirit says that this was the worst thing Herod did; he put his hand on the Lord's anointed)*.

JOHN BAPTIZES JESUS

21 Now when all the people were baptized *(were being baptized)*, it came to pass, that Jesus also being baptized *(this was to testify of His Death, Burial, and Resurrection, of which Water Baptism is a type)*, and praying *(as He came up out of the water, He came up praying)*, the Heaven was opened *(Heaven had been closed to man since the Fall; through Jesus it would now open)*,

22 And the Holy Spirit descended in a bodily shape like a Dove upon Him *(the Holy Spirit is a Person, the Third Person of the Godhead, separate from the Father and the Son)*, and a voice came from Heaven, which said *(the voice of God the Father)*, You are My Beloved Son *(literally, "as for You," in contradistinction to all others)*; in You I am well pleased *(God is pleased with us, only as long as we are in Christ)*.

THE GENEALOGY OF JESUS

23 And Jesus Himself began to be about thirty years of age *(at this age a Priest entered into his Office [Num. 4:3]; Jesus is our Great High Priest)*, being (as was supposed) *(should have been translated, "being by legal adoption")* the son of Joseph, which was *the son* of Heli *(Joseph was the son of Jacob [Mat. 1:16] by birth and the son of Heli by marriage; it was ordained in Numbers, Chpt. 36 that the man who married the daughter of a father having no son became the son of that father and inherited his property)*,

24 Which was *the son* of Matthat, which was *the son* of Levi, which was *the son* of Melchi, which was *the son* of Janna, which was *the son* of Joseph,

25 Which was *the son* of Mattathias, which was *the son* of Amos, which was *the son* of Naum, which was *the son* of Esli, which was *the son* of Nagge,

26 Which was *the son* of Maath, which was *the son* of Mattathias, which was *the son* of Semei, which was *the son* of Joseph, which was *the son* of Juda,

27 Which was *the son* of Joanna, which was *the son* of Rhesa, which was *the son* of Zorobabel, which was *the son* of Salathiel, which was *the son* of Neri,

28 Which was *the son* of Melchi, which was *the son* of Addi, which was *the son* of Cosam, which was *the son* of Elmodam, which was *the son* of Er,

29 Which was *the son* of Jose, which was *the son* of Eliezer, which was *the son* of Jorim, which was *the son* of Matthat, which was *the son* of Levi,

30 Which was *the son* of Simeon, which was *the son* of Juda, which was *the son* of Joseph, which was *the son* of Jonan, which was *the son* of Eliakim,

31 Which was *the son* of Melea, which was *the son* of Menan, which was *the son* of Mattatha, which was *the son* of Nathan, which was *the son* of David,

32 Which was *the son* of Jesse, which was *the son* of Obed, which was *the son* of Booz *(Boaz)*, which was *the son* of Salmon, which was *the son* of Naasson,

33 Which was *the son* of Aminadab, which was *the son* of Aram, which was *the son* of Esrom, which was *the son* of Phares, which was *the son* of Juda,

34 Which was *the son* of Jacob, which was *the son* of Isaac, which was *the son* of Abraham, which was *the son* of Thara, which was *the son* of Nachor,

35 Which was *the son* of Saruch, which was *the son* of Ragau, which was *the son* of Phalec, which was *the son* of Heber, which was *the son* of Sala,

36 Which was *the son* of Cainan, which was *the son* of Arphaxad, which was *the son* of Sem *(Shem)*, which was *the son* of Noe *(Noah)*, which was *the son* of Lamech,

37 Which was *the son* of Mathusala *(Methuselah)*, which was *the son* of Enoch, which was *the son* of Jared, which was *the son* of Maleleel, which was *the son* of Cainan,

38 Which was *the son* of Enos, which was *the son* of Seth, which was *the son* of Adam, which was *the Son* of God *(was a son of God by creation, and not by the bornagain experience; it was the intention of God that humanity bring sons and daughters of God into the world, which they could do by procreation; however, due to the Fall, children cannot be born in the likeness of God, but rather in the like-*

ness of Adam, *i.e., the sinful nature; as wonderful as being in the genealogy of Christ was, some, if not many, of these individuals were not saved; and in fact, some of them were ungodly; this proves that Salvation does not come by inheritance or genealogy; it comes only by accepting Christ as one's Saviour [Jn. 3:16]).*

CHAPTER 4

THE TEMPTATION OF JESUS

AND Jesus being full of the Holy Spirit *(in Christ's case, He received the Spirit without measure [Jn. 3:34; Acts 10:38])* returned from Jordan *(His Water Baptism),* and was led by the Spirit into the wilderness *(speaks of great urgency by the Spirit),*

2 Being forty days tempted of the devil *(refers to being tempted for the entirety of this time; "forty" is God's number for probation).* And in those days He did eat nothing *(speaks of Him fasting for forty days and nights)*: and when they were ended, He afterward hungered *(some claim that God suspended hunger during these forty days and nights regarding Christ, but that is not so; Jesus suffered hunger exactly as we do).*

3 And the devil said unto Him *(Satan is a fallen Angel, who led a revolution against God in eternity*

past; he is at least one of the most powerful Angels ever created by God, and served God in righteousness and holiness for an undetermined period of time before his Fall [Isa., Chpt. 14; Ezek., Chpt. 28]),* If You be the Son of God *(should have been translated, "since You are the Son of God"),* command this stone that it be made bread *(the temptation was that Jesus use His Power for personal gratification, which was outside the Will of God).*

4 And Jesus answered him, saying, It is written, That man shall not live by bread alone, but by every Word of God *([Deut. 8:3], Jesus answered Satan's temptation with the Word; merely quoting it will not garner the same results; Jesus also said, "you shall know the Truth, and the Truth shall make you free" [Jn. 8:32]).*

5 And the Devil, taking Him up into an high mountain *(constitutes that which was literally done, at least as it regards the mountain),* showed unto Him all the kingdoms of the world in a moment of time *(this was not literally, but rather was done by suggestion).*

6 And the Devil said unto Him, All this power will I give You, and the glory of them *(proclaims Satan's method of operation; he has captured many by the offer of a part of the glory of Earthly dominion)*: for that is delivered unto me *(referred back to the Gar-*

den of Eden when Satan gained such authority because of the default of Adam and Eve); and to whomsoever I will I give it (makes Satan the pseudo-ruler of this world [Jn. 12:31; II Cor. 4:4; Eph. 2:1-3; Rev. 13:2, 7]; however, even then his authority is limited, with the Lord actually having the final say in everything).

7 If You therefore will worship me, all shall be Yours *(was a lie; but yet, the world has fallen for this lie from the beginning of time; Satan was attempting to have Christ gain the world without going through the Cross; he is still proposing the same, and mostly going through the Church to do such; every Believer is an "heir of the world," but only through the Cross [Rom. 4:13]).*

8 And Jesus answered and said unto him, Get thee behind Me, Satan: for it is written, You shall worship the Lord your God, and Him only shall you serve *([Deut. 6:13; 10:20], the answer given by Christ addresses itself to worship, as the first addressed itself to desire; men desire the wrong thing, the opposite of the Word of God, and worship the wrong thing, that proposed by Satan).*

9 And he *(Satan)* brought Him *(Jesus)* to Jerusalem, and set Him on a pinnacle of the Temple *(seems to have been literally done, meaning that it was not a vision),* and

said unto Him, If You be the Son of God *(since You are the Son of God),* cast Yourself down from hence:

10 For it is written, He shall give His Angels charge over You, to keep You *(a misquote from Psalms 91:11-12; the correct quotation is, "to keep you in all Your ways," which refers to the "Ways of God"; protection is guaranteed under those circumstances, but not as Satan said):*

11 And in *their* hands they shall bear You up, lest at any time You dash Your foot against a stone *(Satan again misquoted the Text by adding the words "at any time," which changes the meaning altogether; this tells us that Satan knows the Word very well, and to his own advantage subtly changes it to make it say something it originally did not say; as well, if one is to notice, Satan didn't quote the thirteenth Verse in the 91st Psalm, for it predicts his destruction by the Lord Jesus Christ).*

12 And Jesus answering said unto him, It is said, You shall not tempt the Lord your God *(expresses the sin of presumption; presumption is an attitude or belief dictated by probability; in other words, God's Word is not probable, but certain).*

13 And when the devil had ended all the temptation, he departed from Him for a season *(means that he would return, which he no doubt did again and again;*

the implication is that Jesus was tempted by Satan throughout His Ministry).

14 And Jesus returned in the Power of the Spirit into Galilee *(there is no power without the Holy Spirit)*: and there went out a fame of Him through all the region round about *(concerned all the miracles being performed, which actually began with the changing of the water to wine at Cana [Jn. 2:1-11])*.

NAZARETH

15 And He taught in their Synagogues, being glorified of all *(this was the beginning; it would soon change)*.

16 And He came to Nazareth, where He had been brought up *(makes vivid the fact that Jesus was Very Man, even as He was Very God)*: and, as His custom was *(in our language presently He was faithful to Church)*, He went into the Synagogue on the Sabbath day, and stood up for to read *(it was common to ask visitors to expound on the Word)*.

17 And there was delivered unto Him the Book *(Scroll)* of the Prophet Isaiah. And when He had opened the Book, He found the place where it was written *(Isa. 61:1)*,

18 The Spirit of the Lord *is* upon Me *(we learn here of the absolute*

necessity of the Person and Work of the Holy Spirit within our lives)*, because He has anointed Me *(Jesus is the ultimate Anointed One; consequently, the Anointing of the Holy Spirit actually belongs to Christ, and the Anointing we have actually comes by His Authority [Jn. 16:14])* to Preach the Gospel to the poor *(the poor in spirit)*; He has sent Me to heal the brokenhearted *(sin breaks the heart, or else is responsible for it being broken; only Jesus can heal this malady)*, to Preach deliverance to the captives *(if it is to be noticed, He didn't say to "deliver the captives," but rather "Preach deliverance," which refers to the Cross [Jn. 8:32])*, and recovering of sight to the blind *(the Gospel opens the eyes of those who are spiritually blind)*, to set at liberty them who are bruised *(the vicissitudes of life at times place a person in a mental or spiritual prison; the Lord Alone, and through what He did at the Cross, can open this prison door)*,

19 To Preach the acceptable Year of the Lord *(it is believed that the day, on which Jesus delivered this Message was the first day of the Year of Jubilee)*.

20 And He closed the book, and He gave *it* again to the Minister, and sat down *(portrays the custom of that time)*. And the eyes of all them who were in the Synagogue were fastened on Him

(even though most there would fail to see it, this represented a moment far exceeding anything these people had ever known).

21 And He began to say unto them, This day is this Scripture fulfilled in your ears *(in effect, He is saying, "I am the Messiah," the fulfillment of these Scriptures).*

22 And all bear Him witness *(all understood exactly what He said, but all did not believe Him),* and wondered at the gracious words which proceeded out of His mouth *(means that we are given only a small portion of the things He actually said).* And they said, Is not this Joseph's Son? *(This refers to the fact that they could not equate these "gracious words" with the carpenter they had known for about thirty years.)*

23 And He said unto them, You will surely say unto Me this Proverb, Physician, heal Yourself *(how could this carpenter be the Messiah?):* whatsoever we have heard done in Capernaum, do also here in your country *(perform the same miracles; but they would give him no opportunity to do so).*

24 And He said, Verily I say unto you, No Prophet is accepted in his own country *(He predicts their unbelief).*

25 But I tell you of a truth *(will proclaim in no uncertain terms Israel's problem of self-righteousness resulting from pride),* many widows were in Israel in the days of Elijah, when the Heaven was shut up three years and six months, when great famine was throughout all the land *(proclaims the time of Ahab, and the great wickedness concerning the northern kingdom of Israel);*

26 But unto none of them was Elijah sent, save unto Sarepta, *a* city of Sidon, unto a woman *who was* a widow *(she was a Gentile as well).*

27 And many lepers were in Israel in the time of Elisha the Prophet; and none of them was cleansed, saving Naaman the Syrian *(another Gentile).*

28 And all they in the Synagogue, when they heard these words, were filled with wrath *(incensed that He would hold up two Gentiles as examples of receiving from the Lord, while the Jews were shut out; He, in effect, was telling them that this is what would happen to Israel; the Gentiles would receive Him but Israel would refuse Him; "wrath" is generally the response of unbelief),*

29 And rose up, and thrust Him out of the city *(means that they bodily seized Him, taking Him by force out of the Synagogue and out of the city; this was their response to their own Messiah, God's only Son, and their only Saviour),* and led Him unto the brow of the hill whereon their city was

built, that they might cast Him down headlong (*presents Nazareth, His Own village, as the first to seek His death*).

30 But He passing through the midst of them went His way (*did so by the Power of God, and left never to return*),

HEALINGS AND DELIVERANCE

31 And came down to Capernaum, a city of Galilee (*this would be His home and headquarters for the entirety of His Ministry of some three and one half years*), and taught them on the Sabbath days (*in their Synagogues*).

32 And they were astonished at His doctrine (*had to do with the manner in which He explained the Scriptures*): for His Word was with power (*pertained to the Anointing of the Holy Spirit, which they had never experienced before*).

33 And in the Synagogue there was a man, which had a spirit of an unclean devil (*demon*), and cried out with a loud voice (*the voice of this demon spirit using the vocal cords of the man*),

34 Saying, Let us alone (*refers to the fact that Jesus Alone has power over these spirits of darkness*); what have we to do with You, *Thou* Jesus of Nazareth? (*This portrays the total separation of the spirit world of Light from the spirit world of darkness.*) Are You come to destroy us? I know You Who You are; the Holy One of God (*knowing Who He was, they also knew that He had come to destroy their kingdom of darkness*).

35 And Jesus rebuked him (*rebuked the evil spirit in the man*), saying, Hold your peace (*shut up*), and come out of him (*a command that had to be obeyed*). And when the devil had thrown him in the midst (*threw him down*), he came out of him, and hurt him not (*meaning that he was commanded by the Lord to do no damage upon his exit*).

36 And they were all amazed, and spoke among themselves, saying, What a word *is* this! (*presents that which they had never before seen*) for with authority and power He Commands the unclean spirits, and they come out (*they recognized His "Authority" and "Power"*).

37 And the fame of Him went out into every place of the country round about.

PETER'S MOTHER-IN-LAW

38 And He arose out of the Synagogue, and entered into Simon's house (*this was His headquarters during the three and one half years of His public Ministry*). And Simon's wife's mother was

taken with a great fever *(was life threatening)*; and they besought Him for her *(asked Him to heal her)*.

39 And He stood over her, and rebuked the fever *(indicates that this was an evil spirit causing the fever)*; and it left her *(the spirit left along with the sickness)*: and immediately she arose and ministered unto them *(speaks of an instant recovery, with her probably helping to prepare an evening meal)*.

CASTING OUT DEMONS

40 Now when the sun was setting *(meaning the Sabbath was ending; each new day in Jewish reckoning at that time began at the setting of the sun, where ours begin at midnight)*, all they who had any sick with divers diseases brought them unto Him; and He laid His hands on every one of them, and healed them.

41 And devils *(demons)* also came out of many, crying out *(speaks of deliverances other than healings)*, and saying, You are Christ the Son of God *(speaks of these spirits having personalities and intelligence; they knew who He was, even though the religious leaders of Israel didn't)*. And He rebuking *them* suffered them not to speak: for they knew that He was Christ *(He wanted no testimony from them)*.

42 And when it was day *(insinuates that He Ministered all night long)*, He departed and went into a desert place *(He desired a place of solitude for privacy)*: and the people sought Him, and came unto Him, and stayed Him, that He should not depart from them *(they desired that He spend all His time in Capernaum and not go elsewhere)*.

43 And He said unto them, I must Preach the Kingdom of God to other cities also: for therefore Am I sent *(modern thought belittles Preaching and exalts ceremony; the Eternal Son of God was wholly a Preacher; this fact, and the opposition of Satan to Preaching, demonstrates its importance)*.

44 And He Preached in the Synagogues of Galilee.

CHAPTER 5

A BORROWED SHIP

AND it came to pass, that, as the people pressed upon Him to hear the Word of God, He stood by the lake of Gennesaret *(the Sea of Galilee)*,

2 And saw two ships standing by the lake *(two among the many)*: but the fishermen were gone out of them, and were washing *their* nets *(Peter, Andrew, James, and John had fished all night and caught nothing)*.

3 And he entered into one of the ships, which was Simon's *(proclaims Him borrowing this vessel to serve as a platform or pulpit)*, and prayed him that he would thrust out a little from the land. And He sat down *(the custom then)*, and taught the people out of the ship.

THE MIRACLE

4 Now when He had left speaking *(had finished preaching and teaching)*, He said unto Simon, Launch out into the deep, and let down your nets for a draught *(came as a surprise to these fisherman; they had fished all night and caught nothing, so they must have wondered as to what He was doing; in effect, He will pay for the use of the boat; God will owe man nothing)*.

5 And Simon answering said unto Him, Master, we have toiled all the night, and have taken nothing: nevertheless at Your Word I will let down the net *(the idea is that Peter would not have bothered himself to have let down the net on the word of anyone else other than Jesus)*.

6 And when they had this done, they inclosed a great multitude of fishes: and their net broke *(so many fish that it broke the net)*.

7 And they beckoned unto *their* partners *(Peter and Andrew beckoned to James and John)*, which were in the other ship, that they should come and help them. And they came, and filled both the ships, so that they began to sink *(Christ had the same power over the fish of the sea as He had over the frogs, and lice, and locusts of Egypt)*.

8 When Simon Peter saw *it (proclaims the effect of this lesson is not to give Simon high thoughts of himself, but low thoughts; such is ever the effect of a manifestation of Divine Power and Grace upon the conscience of fallen man)*, he fell down at Jesus' knees, saying, Depart from me; for I am a sinful man, O Lord *(proclaims this miracle revealing the hidden unbelief of Simon's heart, for without a doubt, when casting the nets he said to himself: "we shall catch nothing")*.

9 For he was astonished, and all who were with him, at the draught of the fishes which they had taken:

10 And so *was* also James, and John, the sons of Zebedee, which were partners with Simon. And Jesus said unto Simon, Fear not; from henceforth you shall catch men *(the first recorded instance of Jesus using the words, "fear not," with His Disciples; His statement elevated them to being fishers of men, and constituted their call to*

Discipleship, and as Apostles).

11 And when they had brought their ships to land, they forsook all, and followed Him *(means they immediately did so).*

JESUS HEALS A LEPER

12 And it came to pass, when He was in a certain city, behold a man full of leprosy *(the man was in the last stages of leprosy, actually close to death)*: who seeing Jesus fell on *his* face, and besought Him, saying, Lord, if You will, You can make me clean *(he expressed doubt about the willingness of Jesus, rather than His Power; many Jews at that time, knowing that leprosy was a type of sin, didn't even believe that a leper could be Saved; hence the statement of this leper concerning the willingness of Christ to cleanse Him).*

13 And He put forth *His* hand, and touched him, saying, I will: be thou clean *(His answer and action forever settled the question of God's Will regarding the healing of the sick).* And immediately the leprosy departed from him *(the Greek structure of the sentence proclaims the fact that it was Jesus' Word which healed the man, so when He touched him, healing had already been effected).*

14 And he charged him to tell no man: but go, and show yourself to the Priest, and offer for your cleansing, according as Moses commanded, for a testimony unto them *(this concerned the Law of the cleansing of the Leper [Lev., Chpt. 14]).*

15 But so much the more went there a fame abroad of Him: and great multitudes came together to hear, and to be healed by Him of their infirmities.

16 And He withdrew Himself into the wilderness, and prayed *(if Jesus had to pray, what about us!).*

HEALING AND FORGIVENESS

17 And it came to pass on a certain day, as He was teaching, that there were Pharisees and Doctors of the Law sitting by, which were come out of every town of Galilee, and Judaea, and Jerusalem *(now the great opposition will begin)*: and the power of the Lord was *present* to heal them *(the implication is that sick people were being healed without Jesus even addressing their sicknesses or infirmities; the Spirit of God emanating from Him overwhelmed the sicknesses and diseases; in other words, His mere Presence brought healing).*

18 And, behold, men brought in a bed a man which was taken with a palsy *(four men as Mark testified; the man had a type of "paralysis")*: and they sought

means to bring him in, and to lay *him* before Him *(the place was so thronged with people that they could not get into the house)*.

19 And when they could not find by what *way* they might bring him in because of the multitude, they went upon the housetop *(houses are normally flat on top in that part of the world)*, and let him down through the tiling with *his* couch into the midst before Jesus *(they probably enlarged a trap door that was in the ceiling)*.

20 And when He saw their faith *(true faith always has action)*, He said unto him, Man, your sins are forgiven you *(indicates that the wretched physical condition of the sick man was due to his sinful life; yet, Jesus treated him with the utmost of kindness)*.

21 And the Scribes and the Pharisees began to reason, saying, Who is this which speaks blasphemies? Who can forgive sins, but God alone? *(There was a hostile atmosphere in the room, and our Lord sensed it. What they thought in their hearts was expressed on their faces, and in their actions, and very personalities.)*

22 But when Jesus perceived their thoughts *(the Holy Spirit revealed to Him what they were thinking)*, He answering said unto them, What reason ye in your hearts? *(He not only could forgive sins, but He could read the minds of individuals as the Holy Spirit revealed it to Him, proving that He was also God.)*

23 Whether is easier, to say, Your sins be forgiven you; or to say, Rise up and walk? *(The idea of the question as posed by Christ is that God Alone could do both, "forgive and heal.")*

24 But that you may know that the Son of Man has power upon earth to forgive sins *(to prove that power)*, (He said unto the sick of the palsy,) I say unto you, Arise, and take up Your couch, and go into your house.

25 And immediately he rose up before them *(implying that he could not do so previously)*, and took up that whereon he lay *(carried his own bed)*, and departed to his own house, Glorifying God *(he had come sick, unable to walk, and left healed and well; no wonder he Glorified God)*.

26 And they were all amazed *(the Truth was incontestable)*, and they Glorified God *(insinuating that even the Scribes and Pharisees did so)*, and were filled with fear, saying, We have seen strange things today *(in fact, they had seen what no human beings had ever before seen)*.

JESUS CALLS MATTHEW

27 And after these things He went forth, and saw a Publican *(a*

tax-collector), named Levi (Matthew), sitting at the receipt of custom (this was a lucrative occupation, but one despised by the Jews; in other words, they hated tax-collectors because they represented Rome; the task was so odious that most Publicans hired others to physically collect the taxes; but it seemed that Matthew little cared what people thought of him): and He *(Jesus)* said unto him *(Matthew),* Follow Me *(it was not in Indian-file nature, with one following another, but a side-by-side walk down the same road).*

28 And he left all, rose up, and followed Him *(he left his tax-collectors position, and did so immediately).*

29 And Levi made Him *(Jesus)* a great feast in his own house *(speaks of the fact that Matthew was a person of consideration and position):* and there was a great company of Publicans and of others who sat down with them *(speaks of a group of people who were probably not even allowed in the Synagogues).*

THE PHARISEES

30 But their Scribes *(were supposed to be expert in the Law of Moses)* and Pharisees *(the fundamentalist religious party in Israel)* murmured against His Disciples, saying, Why do ye eat and drink with Publicans and sinners? *(They would not have even remotely considered having a meal with any of these people, much less treating them in a friendly fashion.)*

31 And Jesus answering said unto them, They who are whole need not a physician; but they who are sick *(the association with "Publicans and sinners" was not the Pharisees' problem, but rather their black hearts, which were more wicked in the sight of God even than the ones whom they were condemning).*

32 I came not to call the righteous, but sinners to repentance *(in other words, the very reason I have come is for these people you are condemning).*

FASTING

33 And they said unto Him, Why do the disciples of John fast often, and make prayers, and likewise *the disciples* of the Pharisees *(this question was probably asked by the disciples of John the Baptist);* but yours eat and drink? *(This referred to the Disciples of Jesus in comparison to the disciples of John.)*

34 And He said unto them, Can you make the children of the bridechamber fast, while the bridegroom is with them? *(The object of all that is done by the Believer, whether it be fasting or feasting, is Jesus. He Alone is the*

focal point of all. The fasting done previously under the Old Covenant was in relationship to His Coming, which speaks of the First Advent because, as is obvious, He was not with them at that time. He is now with them, so there is no need for fasting, at least at that particular time.)

35 But the days will come, when the bridegroom *(Christ)* shall be taken away from them *(Believers)*, and then shall they fast in those days *(it refers to the period of time of the Church Age, which has lasted now for about 2,000 years; while the reasons for fasting are varied and many, the main reason of all pertains to Him not being here, which involves many things; when He comes back, joy, prosperity, and feasting will then be the order of the entirety of the world).*

36 And He spoke also a Parable unto them; No man puts a piece of a new garment upon an old; if otherwise, then both the new makes a rent, and the piece that was *taken* out of the new agrees not with the old *(the New Covenant is to be complete within itself, and not a part of the Old; in other words, the New Covenant cannot be patched onto the Old Covenant).*

37 And no man puts new wine into old bottles *(wineskins)*; else the new wine will burst the

bottles, and be spilled, and the bottles shall perish *(to try to attach the New Covenant to the Old would destroy both Covenants).*

38 But new wine *(New Covenant)* must be put into new bottles *(new skins)*; and both are preserved *(the "new wine" is the New Covenant; the "new bottles" constitute the Church; this means that Judaism will have no place whatsoever in Christianity, even though the roots of Christianity are definitely in Judaism).*

39 No man also having drunk old *wine* straightway *(immediately)* desires new: for he says, The old is better *(the Old Covenant had to be done away with completely, or else the New would not have been accepted; Why? "Works" are always more appealing to men than "faith"; Why? "Works" appeals to pride, while "faith" appeals to the Cross).*

CHAPTER 6

THE SABBATH

A ND it came to pass on the second Sabbath after the first *(refers to the regular Saturday Sabbath that followed the special Sabbath, which began the Feast regardless of what day of the week on which it fell)*, that He went through the corn fields *(barley or wheat)*; and His Disciples plucked the ears of corn *(grain)*, and did eat, rubbing them in their hands *(they did this to shed the husks, and then would eat the grain raw, which was quite common at that time)*.

2 And certain of the Pharisees said unto them, Why do you that which is not lawful to do on the Sabbath Days? *(This means from the Greek Text that the Pharisees kept prodding Jesus and the Disciples by asking the question over and over again, until Jesus finally responded; in fact, there was nothing in the Law of Moses restricting this, the restriction being of their own making.)*

3 And Jesus answering them said, Have you not read so much as this, what David did, when himself was hungry, and they which were with him *(He took them to I Samuel 21:3-6)*;

4 How he went into the House of God *(refers to the Tabernacle at Nob, which was only a short distance from Jerusalem)*, and did take and eat the shewbread, and gave also to them who were with him *(pertained to the hallowed bread which, since it had evidently just been baked, meant it was the Sabbath)*; which it is not lawful to eat but for the Priests alone? *(Our Lord proclaims the fact here that necessity overrode rulings, even though they were the legitimate Law of Moses; however, that which the Disciples did, which the Phari-*sees condemned, was not of the Law of Moses, but rather a law made up by the Pharisees.)*

5 And He said unto them, That the Son of Man is Lord also of the Sabbath *(this statement by Christ, in effect, declares Him to be God, and to be sure, the Pharisees plainly understood His meaning)*.

HEALING ON THE SABBATH

6 And it came to pass also on another Sabbath, that He entered into the Synagogue and taught: and there was a man whose right hand was withered.

7 And the Scribes and Pharisees watched Him *(means they kept watching, so as to find something for which they could accuse Him, such is religion!)*, whether He would heal on the Sabbath Day; that they might find an accusation against Him *(if one is to notice, Jesus paid no attention whatsoever to the silly rules made up by men)*.

8 But He knew their thoughts *(the Holy Spirit told Him what they were thinking)*, and said to the man which had the withered hand, Rise up, and stand forth in the midst *(means that what was done was carried out for all to see)*. And he arose and stood forth *(it is said that this man's exact petition to Christ was preserved in the Early Church; it is as follows, as he stood before Jesus: "I was a stone-*

mason earning my livelihood with my own hands; I pray Thee, Jesus, restore me to health, in order that I may not with shame beg my bread").

9 Then said Jesus unto them, I will ask you one thing; Is it lawful on the Sabbath Days to do good, or to do evil? to save life, or to destroy it? *(To have the power to "do good," and not do it, is consequently "to do evil.")*

10 And looking round about upon them all *(with an astute gaze; Mark said, "with anger, being grieved for the hardness of their hearts" [Mk. 3:5]),* He said unto the man, Stretch forth your hand *(the withered hand).* And he did so: and his hand was restored whole as the other *(before their very eyes, a miraculous healing took place).*

11 And they *(Scribes and Pharisees)* were filled with madness *(constitutes their reaction to this great miracle; they had no regard whatsoever for the plight of this poor man, only for their petty rules; "madness" speaks of "folly");* and communed one with another what they might do to Jesus *(speaks of their hearts being filled with murder; they would kill Him simply because He had healed a man on the Sabbath; such is religion).*

TWELVE DISCIPLES

12 And it came to pass in those days, that He went out into a mountain to pray, and continued all night in prayer to God *(the record shows that Jesus prayed constantly; among other things, He was seeking the Will of His Father, as it regards the choice of the Twelve Disciples; many were following Him at that time).*

13 And when it was day, He called *unto Him* His Disciples *(could have been as many as a hundred or more):* and of them He chose Twelve *(the number of God's Government),* whom also He named Apostles *(one sent with a special Message, which will always be according to the Word of God, and will set the standard for the Church);*

14 Simon, (whom he also named Peter,) *(his name means, "fragment of rock," which designates how that Christ would take this man who was weak within himself, and make of him a pillar of faith; such would characterize all of His Disciples in one way or the other, and in fact, all Believers)* and Andrew his brother, James and John, Philip and Bartholomew,

15 Matthew and Thomas, James the *son* of Alphaeus, and Simon called Zelotes *(the Zealot),*

16 And Judas *the brother* of James *(he was also called "Lebbaeus" and "Thaddaeus"),* and Judas Iscariot, which also was the traitor *(this man leaves the Gos-*

pel story "a doomed and dammed man" because he chose it so, and God confirmed him in that dreadful choice).

HEALINGS

17 And He *(Jesus)* came down with them, and stood in the plain *(as He had delivered the Sermon on the Mount, He will now deliver the Sermon in the Plain)*, and the company of His Disciples *(as Jesus traveled from place to place, there were no doubt as many as fifty to a hundred people who traveled with Him most of the time)*, and a great multitude of people out of all Judaea and Jerusalem, and from the sea coast of Tyre and Sidon, which came to hear Him, and to be healed of their diseases;

18 And they who were vexed with unclean spirits *("vexed" means "to harass"; these things caused particular types of sicknesses among the people, and no doubt do so presently)*: and they were healed.

19 And the whole multitude sought to touch Him: for there went virtue *(power)* out of Him, and healed *them* all *(it was a sight and a scene that the world had never experienced in all of its history)*.

SERMON ON THE PLAIN

20 And He lifted up His eyes on His Disciples, and said *(could have been Luke's account of the Sermon on the Mount, and could have been another Message altogether; Jesus no doubt repeated Himself many times, in order that the Message not be lost)*, Blessed be the poor *(poor in spirit, denoting humility)*: for yours is the Kingdom of God *(the Kingdom of God and the Kingdom of Heaven are basically the same)*.

21 Blessed *are you who* hunger now *(hunger and thirst after Righteousness)*: for you shall be filled *(the Lord always rewards spiritual hunger)*. Blessed *are you who* weep now *(mourn, because of spiritual weakness)*: for you shall laugh *(defeat will be turned to victory)*.

22 Blessed are you *(happy are you)*, when men shall hate you, and when they shall separate you *from their company*, and shall reproach *you*, and cast out your name as evil, for the Son of Man's sake *(those who subscribe to the Cross will be treated accordingly)*.

23 Rejoice ye in that day, and leap for joy *(the rejection by the religious world is a great sign that one is on the right track, which gives occasion for great joy)*: for, behold, your reward *is* great in Heaven *(means the greater reward awaits your arriving there)*: for in the like manner did their fathers unto the Prophets *(if the religious establishment did such unto the Prophets,*

and they definitely did, then we can expect no less; the Cross is the great dividing line for the Church, and in fact has always been; to accept the Cross as the answer is to reject all of man's ways, which doesn't set well with religion [Gal: 6:14]).

FOUR WOES

24 But woe unto you who are rich! *(Rich and increased with goods, and claim to have need of nothing [Rev. 3:17].)* for you have received your consolation *(you have traded the Spirit of God for "things," and that is what you will have).*

25 Woe unto you who are full! *(Things of the world.)* for you shall hunger *(they will not satisfy).* Woe unto you who laugh now! *(Do not see your spiritual failure.)* for you shall mourn and weep *(mourn now over spiritual weakness, which all have, or mourn later over lost opportunity).*

26 Woe unto you, when all men shall speak well of you! for so did their fathers to the false prophets *(such have always had men singing their praises, and do so no less today; however, it is because they are telling men what they want to hear instead of what God wants them to hear).*

LOVE FOR ENEMIES

27 But I say unto you which

hear *(refers to the fact that many refuse to hear),* Love your enemies, do good to them which hate you *(begins the most revolutionary lifestyle ever known in the history of man; no religion in the world can remotely compare with this; for instance, compare this with the religion of Islam),*

28 Bless them who curse you *(speak well of),* and pray for them which despitefully use you *(pray that they will see God's way).*

29 And unto him who smites you on the *one* cheek offer also the other *(is meant to serve as a principle and not to be taken literally; for example: the Lord, Himself, did not offer Himself to be stricken again [Jn. 18:22-23], but firmly, though with courtesy, rebuked the one who struck Him; the principle is that one should not seek retaliation);* and him who takes away your cloak forbid not *to take your* coat also *(if one demands his rights too loudly, the loss could even be greater than the cloak and coat).*

30 Give to every man who asks of you *(speaks of those truly in need; it is not meant to reward slothfulness);* and of him who takes away your goods ask *them* not again *(portrays unselfishness, which ought to characterize every Believer).*

THE GOLDEN RULE

31 And as you would that men

should do to you, do ye also to them likewise *(this is the Verse referred to as the "Golden Rule"; it is also a teaching of the Law [Lev. 19:18]).*

32 For if you love them which love you, what thank have you? *(The idea is Jesus loved us when we were unlovable [Rom. 5:8], and we are to do the same for them who are unlovable.)* for sinners also love those that love them *(to love those who do not love us portrays Godliness).*

33 And if you do good to them which do good to you, what thank have you? for sinners also do even the same *(the rule of man is to return good for good and evil for evil; then beneath this there is the returning of evil for good, which is devilish; while above it there is the returning of good for evil, which is Divine — that commanded of the followers of Christ).*

34 And if you lend *to* them of whom you hope to receive, what thank have you? for sinners also lend to sinners, to receive as much again.

35 But love ye your enemies, and do good, and lend, hoping for nothing again *(how can we call it "lending," if it is not to be repaid? Solomon gave the answer: "He who has pity upon the poor lends unto the Lord; and that which he has given will He pay him again" [Prov. 19:17]);* and your

reward shall be great *(the idea is the Lord will repay, and He does so abundantly),* and you shall be the children of the Highest *(means that we will be like our Heavenly Father):* for He is kind unto the unthankful and *to* the evil *(what we should do as well).*

36 Be ye therefore merciful, as your Father also is merciful *(as He has been merciful to us, we are to be merciful to others; everything we do is to be based on what He has done for us).*

JUDGING OTHERS

37 Judge not *(do not judge one's motives),* and you shall not be judged *(implying that you will be judged by the Lord, if you do not obey this admonition):* condemn not *(do not pass sentence),* and you shall not be condemned *(meaning conversely, that if you pass sentence on others, the Lord will ultimately pass sentence on you):* forgive, and you shall be forgiven *(implying that if you do not forgive, God will not forgive you, which puts a person in a terrible dilemma):*

38 Give, and it shall be given unto you *(God's economy; it refers not only to the giving of money, but as well to mercy, grace, love, help, etc.);* good measure, pressed down, and shaken together, and running over, shall men give into

your bosom *(constitutes a remarkable Promise)*. For with the same measure that you mete withal it shall be measured to you again *(is a Law of God which everyone should take very seriously, for Christ means exactly what He says)*.

39 And He spoke a Parable unto them, Can the blind lead the blind? shall they not both fall into the ditch? *(These are false religious teachers.)*

40 The disciple is not above his master *(those who listen to false teachers will become as perfectly deluded as their masters, for pupils cannot see more clearly than their teachers; hence the disciples of Romanism, Mormonism, etc., become as wholly deluded as their teachers)*: but every one who is perfect shall be as his master *(would have been better translated, "but every one who has been perfected," i.e., "embraced this false doctrine," shall be as his teacher)*.

41 And why behold thou the mote that is in your brother's eye *(don't look for faults in others)*, but perceive not the beam that is in your own eye? *(If you want to inspect, inspect yourself. You have plenty there to inspect, which desperately needs improvement.)*

42 Either how can you say to your brother, Brother, let me pull out the mote that is in your eye, when you yourself behold not the beam that is in your own eye? *(This does not pertain to doctrine, which must be judged constantly [Mat. 7:15-20], but rather one's person and character. Once again, we have enough about ourselves that needs improving, rather than condemning others.)* Thou hypocrite, cast out first the beam out of your own eye, and then shall you see clearly to pull out the mote that is in your brother's eye *(if we deal with ourselves as we should, that we will then be able to "see clearly," which means we'll have no desire to find fault with others)*.

THE FRUIT

43 For a good tree brings not forth corrupt fruit *(is the method delineated by Jesus for separating the good from the bad)*; neither does a corrupt tree bring forth good fruit *(the manner in which we are to judge false doctrine)*.

44 For every tree is known by his own fruit *(for example, look at the fruit of Islam, or even the part of Christianity which is corrupt)*. For of thorns men do not gather figs, nor of a bramble bush gather they grapes *(it's impossible to get good fruit from a corrupt tree)*.

45 A good man out of the good treasure of his heart brings forth that which is good *(refers to the fact that all of this, whether good*

or evil, *begins in the heart*); and an evil man out of the evil treasure of his heart brings forth that which is evil *(no matter the claims, what is in the heart is going to ultimately come forth)*: for of the abundance of the heart his mouth speaks *(there can be an imitation of the fruit of the Spirit, as a paper rose may be so like a real one as to be indistinguishable; but a bee will make no mistake!)*.

46 And why do you call Me, Lord, Lord, and do not the things which I say? *(Both the True Prophet and the false prophet will freely use the title "Lord," but Christ is "Lord" only to those who obey His Word.)*

TWO FOUNDATIONS

47 Whosoever comes to Me *(truly accepts Christ)*, and hears My sayings *(the Word of God)*, and does them *(the hearing must culminate in the doing)*, I will show you to whom he is like *(the end result)*:

48 He is like a man which built an house *(we ought to grow in grace and knowledge)*, and digged deep *(deep into the Word)*, and laid the foundation on a rock *(that "Rock" is Christ and Him Crucified [I Cor. 1:23])*: and when the flood arose *(problems will arise)*, the stream beat vehemently upon that house *(Satan will try to destroy the house)*, and could not

shake it: for it was founded upon a rock *(once again, "that Rock" is "Jesus Christ and Him Crucified," which must ever be the object of our Faith)*.

49 But he who hears, and does not *(doesn't obey the Word)*, is like a man that without a foundation *(the object of his faith is not the Cross of Christ)* built an house upon the earth *(outwardly this one looked identical to the one built on the rock)*; against which the stream did beat vehemently, and immediately it fell; and the ruin of that house was great *(if our faith is not in the Cross of Christ, things may go well for awhile, but sooner or later the storm will come, and Satan will win the day)*.

CHAPTER 7

THE SPOKEN WORD

NOW when He had ended all His sayings in the audience of the people, He entered into Capernaum.

2 And a certain centurion's *(an officer in the Roman army, a Gentile)* servant, who was dear unto him, was sick, and ready to die.

3 And when he heard of Jesus *(better translated, "and when he had heard about Jesus")*, he sent unto Him the Elders of the Jews *(he evidently thought that they*

would have more sway on Christ than he would as a Gentile), beseeching Him that He would come and heal his servant.

4 And when they came to Jesus, they *(the Elders of the Jews)* besought Him instantly, saying, That he *(the centurion)* was worthy for whom He should do this *(portrays the basis on which most people expect an answer; but prayer is never answered on this basis):*

5 For he loves our nation, and he has built us a Synagogue *(evidently this Gentile was sick of the pagan ways of Rome, and had become very interested in the God of Abraham, Isaac, and Jacob).*

6 Then Jesus went with them. And when He was now not far from the house, the centurion sent friends to Him *(Matthew says the centurion came personally; Luke here states that he came by deputation; both statements are true; for his messengers represented him, and also the word "him" as is given in Verse 9 supports the belief that the centurion followed his messengers and, in his anxiety for his servant, repeated the message he had given them to deliver),* saying unto him, Lord, trouble not yourself: for I am not worthy that You should enter under my roof *(not knowing exactly what the Jews had told the Lord, he wanted Christ to know exactly who he was, a Gentile, which carried with it many connotations):*

7 Wherefore neither thought I myself worthy to come unto You *(seems to be the stage that the centurion now approaches Christ personally):* but say in a word, and my servant shall be healed *(proclaims a level of faith seldom if ever equaled by anyone in the Bible, at least of this nature).*

8 For I also am a man set under authority, having under me soldiers *(proclaims the meaning of spiritual authority, and from a Gentile at that!),* and I say unto one, Go, and he goes; and to another, Come, and he comes; and to my servant, Do this, and he does *it (the authority of this centurion came from Caesar; likewise, all authority possessed by Believers comes from the Lord; also, unlike the centurion, authority held by Believers is never to be exercised over other people, but rather over spirits of darkness [Lk. 10:19]).*

9 When Jesus heard these things, He marvelled at him *(records one of the two instances when Jesus marveled, the other being at unbelief [Mk. 6:6]),* and turned him about *(will use him as an example),* and said unto the people that followed Him *(who followed Jesus),* I say unto you, I have not found so great faith, no, not in Israel *(all of this tells us that only "unbelief" or "faith," with all their attendant results both*

negative and positive, are the occasion in the eyes of God for astonishment).

10 And they who were sent *(the friends of Verse 6)*, returning to the house, found the servant whole who had been sick.

RAISING THE DEAD

11 And it came to pass the day after *(after the healing of the centurion's servant)*, that He went into a city called Nain; and many of His Disciples went with Him, and much people *(recorded only by Luke)*.

12 Now when He came nigh to the gate of the city *(about to enter the city)*, behold, there was a dead man carried out, the only son of his mother, and she was a widow: and much people of the city was with her.

13 And when the Lord saw her, He had compassion on her, and said unto her, Weep not.

14 And He came and touched the bier *(refers to a wooden frame on which the dead were laid, wrapped in folds of linen, with the entire apparatus carried on the shoulders of four men; it was against the Mosaic Law to touch anything pertaining to death; however, this didn't apply to Jesus, for His touching the bier portrayed His touching and defeating death itself, which He would do on the Cross of Calvary)*: and they who bear *him* stood still *(in His presence, everything must stop, including death).* And he said, Young man, I say unto you *(presents His Deity)*, Arise *(speaks of His Resurrection Power, which will be used shortly to raise all of the Sainted dead [I Cor. 15:51-55]).*

15 And he who was dead sat up, and began to speak *(what a scene that must have been).* And He delivered him to his mother *(she could now dry her tears; as well, this represents the great meeting that will one day take place in Heaven between loved ones).*

16 And there came a fear on all *(such power was incomprehensible)*: and they Glorified God *(everything that Jesus did brought Glory to God)*, saying, That a great Prophet is risen up among us *(in that, they were correct, but only partially so; He was God and, therefore, their Messiah, but that they could not understand)*; and, That God has visited his people *(proclaims a Truth, but in far greater degree than they imagined).*

17 And this rumour of Him went forth throughout all Judaea, and throughout all the region round about *(pertained to the debate as to Who He actually was; in other words, was this the Messiah?).*

18 And the disciples of John showed him of all these things *(they told John all about Christ).*

JOHN THE BAPTIST

19 And John calling *unto him* two of his disciples sent *them* to Jesus, saying, Are You He Who should come? or look we for another? *(At times, Faith waivers, even in the strongest, as here evidenced by John. It is only the Master Who never turns aside from the path of right. Quite possibly, John the Baptist was puzzled. If Jesus was truly the Messiah, why didn't He deliver him from prison?)*

20 When the men were come unto Him *(unto Jesus)*, they said, John Baptist has sent us unto You, saying, Are You He Who should come? or look we for another? *(Even though John may have temporarily doubted, no criticism is in order, as the answer of Christ projects!)*

JESUS' ANSWER

21 And in that same hour *(when the disciples of John the Baptist came to Him)* He cured many of *their* infirmities and plagues, and of evil spirits; and unto many who *were* blind He gave sight *(miracles, as miracles, did not accredit Jesus to be the Promised Messiah; what did accredit Him was that He worked the miracles predicted of Him in the Scriptures [Isa. 29:18; 35:4-6; 61:1-3]; the false prophet will also work amazing miracles [Rev. 13:13])*.

22 Then Jesus answering said unto them *(proclaims Him not answering their question until everyone around Him had received their healing or deliverance)*, Go your way, and tell John what things you have seen and heard *(were things never "seen and heard" by any previous generation)*; how that the blind see, the lame walk, the lepers are cleansed, the deaf hear, the dead are raised, to the poor the Gospel is preached.

23 And blessed is *he (begins this mild rebuke regarding John's questions, and is actually given in the form of a Beatitude)*, whosoever shall not be offended in Me *(would not find an occasion of stumbling in the manner in which Christ had actually come)*.

JESUS SPEAKS OF JOHN THE BAPTIST

24 And when the messengers of John were departed, He began to speak unto the people concerning John *(Jesus did not want the people to think less of John because of these questions)*, What went you out into the wilderness for to see? A reed shaken with the wind? *(Christ will now build up John as no other man, and that despite his temporal doubting.)*

25 But what went you out for to see? A man clothed in soft

raiment? *(John was clothed with Camel's hair, a crude garment.)* Behold, they which are gorgeously apparelled, and live delicately, are in kings' courts *(if John had compromised his Message, he would have been Herod's preacher; instead, he was Herod's prisoner).*

26 But what went you out for to see? A Prophet? Yes, I say unto you, and much more than a Prophet *(this one statement places John in a category all to himself; at that moment, the people may have thought less of him, but not God!)*

27 This is *he,* of whom it is written *(Jesus always took people to the Word),* Behold, I send My messenger before Your face *(before the face of Christ),* which shall prepare Your way before You *(John the Baptist prepared the way for the Lord to be introduced).*

28 For I say unto you, Among those who are born of women there is not a greater Prophet than John the Baptist *(all the Prophets before said that Jesus was coming; John said, "Behold, He is here" [Jn. 1:29]; he introduced Christ, which made him greater):* but he who is least in the Kingdom of God is greater than he *(since the Cross, the New Covenant affords us far greater privileges than those had under the Old Covenant, of which John was a part [Heb. 8:6]).*

29 And all the people who heard *Him,* and the Publicans *(tax-collectors),* justified God *(proclaimed the fact that God had done a glorious thing by sending John to precede Christ, and prepare the way for Christ),* being baptized with the baptism of John *(the Baptism of Repentance; proclaims the fact that Jesus recognized the fact of the Salvation of those baptized by John because they truly had repented).*

30 But the Pharisees and lawyers *(those who argued the Law of Moses)* rejected the counsel of God against themselves, being not baptized of him *(they refused to admit they needed to repent).*

31 And the Lord said, Where unto then shall I liken the men of this generation? *(This was the generation of Jesus' day, which had rejected both the Ministry of John and Ministry of Christ.)* and to what are they like? *(The Lord will answer His Own question in the following Verses.)*

32 They *(the religious leaders of Israel)* are like unto children sitting in the marketplace, and calling one to another, and saying, We have piped unto you, and you have not danced; we have mourned to you, and you have not wept *(proclaims the two methods used by the Lord to reach Israel, His Ministry and the Ministry of John the Baptist, both to no avail).*

33 For John the Baptist came

neither eating bread nor drinking wine (*refers to John's austere lifestyle spent in the desert*); and you say, He has a devil (*presents the response of the religious leaders of Israel to the Message of John demanding Repentance*).

34 The Son of Man is come eating and drinking (*refers to the lifestyle of Jesus as being totally opposite to that of John*); and you say, Behold a gluttonous man, and a winebibber (*this was not what Jesus was, but what they said He was; they also claimed that He performed His miracles by the power of Satan*), a friend of Publicans and sinners! (*For a change, they now proclaim something truthful of Jesus. He was a friend to these groups; however, being their "friend" did not mean that He partook of their lifestyles, or even condoned them.*)

35 But wisdom is justified of all her children (*the children of wisdom in this case are the two methods used by the Holy Spirit, i.e., "wisdom," to reach Israel; we speak of the Ministry of John the Baptist and of Christ; both were rejected by Israel, and Israel went to her doom*).

JESUS AND THE WOMAN

36 And one of the Pharisees desired Him that He would eat with him (*constitutes the enemy of the "wisdom" mentioned in Verse 35; this incident is peculiar to Luke*). And He went into the Pharisee's house, and sat down to meat (*implies that Jesus was given no prominent place at the table and, as stated, had to find seating for Himself, which was an insult!*).

37 And, behold, a woman in the city (*probably was Nain*), which was a sinner (*we are given no further information*), when she knew that Jesus sat at meat in the Pharisee's house (*she evidently was determined to see Him*), brought an alabaster box of ointment (*very expensive, so she must have been a woman of means; however, her riches did not satisfy the hunger and thirst of her heart*),

38 And stood at His feet behind Him weeping (*signified repentance; she had possibly witnessed Him raising the young man from the dead, and maybe heard His Message to the Pharisees and the lawyers; His Words had found a place in her heart*), and began to wash His feet with tears (*these were tears of sorrow and of joy — sorrow because of her sins, and joy because this was the One Who could forgive those sins, and in fact did!*), and did wipe *them* with the hairs of her head, and kissed His feet (*this was then a custom among the Jews, Greeks, and Romans; it was a mark of affection and reverence*), and anointed *them* with the

ointment *(spoke of His feet; as a sinner washed and anointed His feet, likewise sinners gave Him the only crown He wore — a crown of thorns)*.

39 Now when the Pharisee which had bidden Him saw *it*, He spoke within Himself *(not out loud)*, saying, This Man, if He were a Prophet, would have known who and what manner of woman *this is* who touches Him: for she is a sinner *("this man" judged both Jesus and the woman; he was wrong on both counts; while she was a sinner, the Pharisee was in fact a greater sinner)*.

40 And Jesus answering said unto him, Simon, I have somewhat to say unto you *(the Holy Spirit told the Saviour what this man was thinking)*. And he said, Master, say on *(is laced with sarcasm; therefore, he little expects the words of wisdom he will receive; he has already revealed the unbelief of his heart by using the words, "this man, if he were a Prophet . . .")*.

THE PARABLE

41 There was a certain creditor *(a moneylender)* which had two debtors *(individuals to whom money had been loaned)*: the one owed five hundred pence *(about twenty thousand dollars in 2003 currency)*, and the other fifty *(about two thousand dollars)*.

42 And when they had nothing to pay, he frankly forgave them both *(refers to the moneylender writing off the debts)*. Tell me therefore, which of them will love him most? *(Now comes the point illustrated by the Parable.)*

43 Simon answered and said, I suppose that *he*, to whom he forgave most. And He said unto him, You have rightly judged *(Jesus was appealing to this man on his own level)*.

44 And He turned to the woman *(records the first instance of Jesus acknowledging the woman in any way)*, and said unto Simon, Do you see this woman? *(The Lord speaks of her as a trophy of Grace!)* I entered into your house, you gave Me no water for My feet *(proclaims the studied insult now being noted)*: but she has washed My feet with tears, and wiped *them* with the hairs of her head.

45 You gave Me no kiss *(was a custom in those days)*: but this woman since the time I came in has not ceased to kiss my feet *(Simon would not kiss the face of Jesus, which denoted His Kingship; however, the Holy Spirit had the woman to kiss the "feet" of Jesus, denoting His Authority, Power, and Rule)*.

46 My head with oil you did not anoint *(presents another custom of that day)*: but this woman

has anointed my feet with ointment *(this act, brought about by
the Holy Spirit, signified Jesus as
the Messiah [Lk. 4:18])*.

47 Wherefore I say unto you,
Her sins, which are many, are
forgiven *(Jesus is performing that
which only the Messiah could actually do, and which Simon had
denied, and Jesus now declares);
for she loved much (what is wanting in order to love much is not
sin, but the knowledge of it)*: but
to whom little is forgiven, *the
same* loves little *(every Believer
must realize that he has been forgiven much; consequently, he will
love much)*.

48 And He said unto her, Your
sins are forgiven *(the guiltiest who
believe upon Christ shall enjoy assurance of Salvation and the conscious forgiveness of sin)*.

49 And they who sat at meat
with Him began to say within
themselves, Who is this Who forgives sins also? *(His act of forgiving this woman, should have told
them, and in fact did tell them
that He was the Messiah.)*

50 And He said to the woman,
Your faith has saved you *(Jesus
did not say to the woman, "your
love has saved you" or "your tears
have saved you," but, "your faith
has saved you"); go in peace (should
have been translated, "go into
peace"; this was justifying peace,
meaning this woman was justified*

before God because of her faith in
Christ)*.

CHAPTER 8

THE GOSPEL

AND it came to pass afterward
*(refers to the events of the pre-
vious Chapter)*, that He went
throughout every city and village
*(His Love unchilled by unbelief and
hatred, He visited every city and
village with the glad tidings of the
Gospel)*, preaching *(man magnifies sacraments and ceremonies, and
belittles preaching; God magnifies
preaching)* and showing the glad
tidings *(Good News)* of the Kingdom of God *(the "Kingdom of
God" is the Gospel of Jehovah's
King, the Lord Jesus Christ; it is a
dispensational term and refers to
Messiah's Kingdom on Earth; it was
offered by both John and Jesus, but
was rejected and thus postponed
until Christ comes the Second Time
[Rev., Chpt. 19])*: and the Twelve
were with Him *(means that the
Twelve remained with Him constantly)*,

2 And certain women *(women
are prominent and honorably mentioned in Luke; it was not a woman
who sold the Lord for thirty pieces
of silver; it was not women who
forsook Him and fled, etc.; it was
women who were the first to visit
His Tomb on the Resurrection morn-*

ing), **which had been healed of evil spirits and infirmities** *(healed of that which had been caused by evil spirits)*, **Mary called Magdalene, out of whom went seven devils** *(she was from Magdala, a little town near Tiberias; she loved much because she had been forgiven much; there is no proof that she is the woman who anointed His feet with the ointment of Luke 7:37-38)*,

3 **And Joanna the wife of Chuza Herod's steward** *(is believed to be the family whose dying son was healed by Jesus [Jn. 4:46])*, **and Susanna, and many others, which ministered unto Him of their substance** *(some of these women were wealthy, and they used their money to minister to the Lord's necessities; He could with a few loaves feed thousands, but He did not feed Himself; thus, He proved that He was a man like His fellowmen; true disciples now as then minister to Him; mere professers do not)*.

THE PARABLE OF THE SOWER

4 **And when much people were gathered together, and were come to Him out of every city, He spoke by a Parable** *(Parables had a tendency to confuse His opposers, and to enlighten those who were truly His followers)*:

5 **A sower** *(in this case, the Evangelist)* **went out to sow his seed** *(the Word of God)*: **and as he sowed, some fell by the way side** *(referred to an area which had not been prepared for the seed)*; **and it was trodden down, and the fowls of the air devoured it** *(demon spirits)*.

6 **And some** *(seed)* **fell upon a rock** *(covered by a very shallow layer of soil)*; **and as soon as it was sprung up, it withered away, because it lacked moisture** *(due to the rock, the roots could not go down into the soil where the moisture was)*.

7 **And some** *(seed)* **fell among thorns** *(pertains to good ground, but yet the competition of the thorns would prove to be a debilitating factor)*; **and the thorns sprang up with it, and choked it.**

8 **And other fell on good ground** *(means ground that was not full of rocks or thorns)*, **and sprang up** *(refers to bountiful growth)*, **and bear fruit an hundredfold** *(presents a tremendous harvest)*. **And when He had said these things, He cried, He who has ears to hear, let him hear** *(many did not have "ears to hear" because their hearts were hardened; some few did, and they changed the world!)*.

9 **And His Disciples asked Him, saying, What might this Parable be?** *(This proclaims the story being understood perfectly well, but not its meaning.)*

10 And He said, Unto you *(all who sincerely seek to know the Lord, and have a deeper understanding of His Word)* it is given to know the mysteries *(the word implies knowledge withheld; however, Jesus is saying that the Scriptural significance to these mysteries is about to be revealed, at least to those who hunger and thirst after Righteousness)* of the Kingdom of God: but to others in Parables *(the Divine story would be veiled to the careless and indifferent);* that seeing they might not see, and hearing they might not understand *(pertained to a willful blindness and a willful lack of comprehension; they had no desire to know).*

11 Now the Parable is this: The seed is the Word of God.

12 Those by the way side are they who hear; then comes the devil, and takes away the Word out of their hearts *(he is able to do this simply because they have little regard for the Word),* lest they should believe and be saved *(a willful blindness resulted in a judicial blindness).*

13 They on the rock *are* they, which, when they hear, receive the Word with joy; and these have no root, which for a while believe, and in time of temptation fall away *(completely refutes the unscriptural doctrine of unconditional eternal security).*

14 And that which fell among thorns are they, which, when they have heard, go forth, and are choked with cares and riches and pleasures of *this* life, and bring no fruit to perfection *(actually means that there is a beginning of fruit, but it is not allowed to ripen and is, therefore, unusable; they believe for a while and then fall away; there are many like this).*

15 But that on the good ground *(constitutes the fourth group which will bring forth "fruit to perfection," i.e., "fruit to maturity")* are they, which in an honest and good heart *(tells us that the problem is with the heart and not with circumstances),* having heard the Word, keep *it,* and bring forth fruit with patience *(merely hearing the Word is not enough; one must "keep it" as well).*

THE CANDLE

16 No man, when he has lit a candle, covers it with a vessel, or puts *it* under a bed *(means that Christ using Parables is not meant to hide Truth from sincere, inquiring hearts, but rather the very opposite);* but sets *it* on a candlestick, that they which enter in may see the light *(the teaching of Christ was designed to appeal to the honest, seeking heart; He wants men to "see the light").*

17 For nothing is secret, that shall not be made manifest *(ad-*

dresses itself to the mysteries of the Gospel); neither *any thing* hid, that shall not be known and come abroad *(it would all be made known in the New Covenant)*.

18 Take heed therefore how you hear *(refers to not only what is heard, but how it is heard)*: for whosoever has, to him shall be given *(constitutes a Divine Law that whosoever accepts Truth will be given Truth)*; and whosoever has not, from him shall be taken even that which he seems to have *(light rejected is light withdrawn)*.

TRUE RELATIVES

19 Then came to Him *His* mother and His brethren *(refers to those of His immediate family)*, and could not come at Him for the press *(the crowd was so large that they simply could not get to Him)*.

20 And it was told Him *by certain* which said, Your mother and Your brethren stand without, desiring to see You.

21 And He answered and said unto them *(presents a principle which places God first in all things)*, My mother and My brethren are these which hear the Word of God, and do it *(plainly proclaims allegiance to God, is even more solemn than family ties; Jesus here refutes the Catholic contention that Mary is above all)*.

THE STORM

22 Now it came to pass on a certain day, that He went into a ship with His Disciples: and He said unto them, Let us go over unto the other side of the lake *(from the western shore of Galilee to the eastern shore)*. And they launched forth.

23 But as they sailed He fell asleep *(physical exhaustion from healing and delivering, as well as teaching; this portrayed His humanity)*: and there came down a storm of wind on the lake *(from the Greek Text a "furious storm or hurricane")*; and they were filled *with water*, and were in jeopardy *(they were actually in danger of sinking, and of even losing their lives)*.

24 And they came to Him, and awoke Him *(refers to them not doing so until the danger was acute)*, saying, Master, Master, we perish *(He Alone can stop the soul from perishing)*. Then He arose, and rebuked the wind and the raging of the water *(refers to an evil spirit behind the storm attempting to kill the Disciples; Satan knew that Jesus could not be killed, but he also knew the Disciples to be very mortal)*: and they ceased, and there was a calm *(the change was instant; no power on Earth can even begin to approach such Authority; as well, He can instantly calm the storm in a man's soul)*.

25 And He said unto them, Where is your faith? *(Christ is the answer concerning all the storms of life.)* And they being afraid wondered *(the Disciples had accepted His Messiahship, but had a most inadequate view of the same)*, saying one to another, What manner of man is this! *(They evidently did not recognize all the implications, which His office carried with it.)* for He commands even the winds and water, and they obey Him *(proclaims His total control not only over demon spirits, and sickness, and death, but as well, the elements)*.

DELIVERANCE

26 And they arrived at the country of the Gadarenes *(was on the eastern side of the Sea of Galilee)*, which is over against Galilee *(refers to the part of Decapolis which bordered the Sea of Galilee on the southern tip and the eastern side)*.

27 And when He went forth to land *(when they beached the boat)*, there met Him out of the city a certain man *(he was from the nearby city, but no longer lived there)*, which had devils *(demons)* long time *(had long been possessed)*, and wore no clothes *(a type of man in the spiritual who is naked to the Judgment of God because of being in rebellion against God)*, neither abode in *any* house, but in the tombs *(death is the end result of sin)*.

28 When he saw Jesus *(the spirit world of darkness is subservient to the Lord Jesus Christ)*, he cried out *(for fear)*, and fell down before Him *(an acknowledgment of Him as Lord and Master)*, and with a loud voice said, What have I to do with You, Jesus, *You* Son of God most High? *(Even though most of mankind professes not to know, demon spirits know Who Jesus is.)* I beseech You, torment me not *(proclaims them knowing and realizing that Jesus has the power to do with them whatsoever He desires; proper Faith in Christ and the Cross will put us in the position of tormenting demons, instead of them tormenting us)*.

29 (For He had commanded the unclean spirit to come out of the man *(speaks of the head spirit or demon who was the leader of all the others, a great host, as we shall see)*. For oftentimes it had caught him *(refers to this spirit or spirits taking control of this man and giving him, as we shall see, superhuman strength)*: and he was kept bound with chains and in fetters *(restraint was attempted, but to no avail)*; and he brake the bands, and was driven of the devil into the wilderness.) *(He was totally taken over by demons and had no choice but to do what they de-*

sired.)

30 And Jesus asked him, saying, What is your name? *(This proclaims these demons as personalities.)* And he said, Legion *(could refer to as many as 6,000; that this many demons could inhabit one human being is startling to say the least)*: because many devils *(demons)* were entered into him.

31 And they besought Him that He would not command them to go out into the deep *(refers to the "bottomless pit" [Rev. 20:1-3]).*

32 And there was there an herd of many swine feeding on the mountain *(is recorded as being "about 2,000" [Mk. 5:13])*: and they besought Him that He would suffer *(permit)* them to enter into them. And He suffered them *(if demons have to ask permission from the Lord to enter swine, surely it should be understood that He wouldn't allow them to enter the Sheep of His Pasture).*

33 Then went the devils *(demons)* out of the man, and entered into the swine *(refers to these demons doing exactly what the Lord told them to do)*: and the herd ran violently down a steep place into the lake, and were choked *(drowned).*

34 When they who fed *them* saw what was done, they fled, and went and told *it* in the city and in the country *(means they told not only the owners, but any and all who would hear them).*

35 Then they *(the owners and others)* went out to see what was done; and came to Jesus, and found the man, out of whom the devils *(demons)* were departed *(no doubt, as they had never witnessed him before)*, sitting at the feet of Jesus *(our Lord was teaching him)*, clothed *(no doubt the Disciples had loaned him some clothes, and he was also clothed with Salvation)*, and in his right mind *(perfectly sound of mind)*: and they were afraid *(they couldn't understand such power).*

36 They also which saw *it* told them by what means he who was possessed of the devils was healed *(they gave a blow-by-blow account to the owners of the hogs, plus others).*

37 Then the whole multitude of the country of the Gadarenes round about besought Him to depart from them *(presents one of the saddest episodes in the Gospels; they felt they could not keep both the Saviour and their swine, of the two they preferred the swine! What an indictment on the human race, for this mirrors most of humanity)*; for they were taken with great fear *(constituted fear, which should have brought them to the Lord, but instead they responded in the opposite manner)*: and He went up into the ship, and returned back again *(to the*

western side of the lake).

38 Now the man out of whom the devils *(demons)* were departed besought Him that he might be with Him *(proclaims the very opposite of his countrymen, which is quickly noted by the Holy Spirit)*: but Jesus sent him away, saying *(constitutes a denial regarding his request, but yet with a mission to perform; He carried it out to great distinction)*,

39 Return to your own house, and show how great things God has done unto you *(constitutes a commission for this man, and for all Believers; for all Believers, the Lord has done "great things"). And he went his way, and published throughout the whole city how great things Jesus had done unto him *(doesn't tell us exactly which city, but does proclaim this man's success; the day before, he was a demon-crazed maniac, totally insane; twenty-four hours later or less, he is an Evangelist for the Lord Jesus Christ)*.

HEALINGS AND MIRACLES

40 And it came to pass, that, when Jesus was returned *(to Capernaum)*, the people *gladly* received Him: for they were all waiting for Him.

41 And, behold, there came a man named Jairus, and he was a ruler of the Synagogue *(this man was a fair representative of the wealthy and highly Orthodox Jew)*: and he fell down at Jesus' feet, and besought Him that He would come into his house:

42 For he had one only daughter, about twelve years of age, and she lay a dying *(proclaims the acuteness of the situation)*. But as He *(Jesus)* went *(to the house of Jairus)* the people thronged Him.

43 And a woman having an issue of blood twelve years *(probably referred to a female disorder)*, which had spent all her living upon physicians, neither could be healed of any *(there was no earthly remedy for her sickness, as there is no earthly remedy for sin; but there is a remedy, as we soon shall see!)*,

44 Came behind *Him*, and touched the border of His garment *(pertained to one of the four tassels, which formed part of the Jewish mantle; the blue of the tassel, which was worn by most men, reminded Israel that their help came from above, and of their duty to keep the Law [Num. 15:28-41; Deut. 22:12])*: and immediately her issue of blood stanched *(her cure was permanent, and she would never be troubled with this problem again)*.

45 And Jesus said, Who touched Me? *(In fact, many were touching Jesus, but none with the Faith this woman had.)* When all denied, Peter and they who were with him said, Master, the multitude throng

You and press *You*, and You say, Who touched Me? *(This is actually as much an exclamation as it is a question.)*

46 And Jesus said, Somebody has touched Me: for I perceive that virtue *(Power)* is gone out of Me *(Jesus didn't touch the woman, she touched Him; this tells us that if the Lord doesn't touch us, we still can touch Him, and receive that which we need).*

47 And when the woman saw that she was not hid *(means that she evidently was trying to hide)*, she came trembling *(it startled her that Jesus would stop, in essence, calling for her, especially considering the great throng of people)*, and falling down before Him, she declared unto Him before all the people for what cause she had touched Him *(she withheld nothing, telling all)* and how she was healed immediately.

48 And He said unto her, Daughter *(at first she was referred to as "a woman," and now she is referred to as "Daughter"; this speaks of relationship, pertaining to both Salvation and healing)*, be of good comfort *(addresses itself to her fear concerning her previous uncleanliness; she need have no fear that anyone would judge her unclean now)*: your faith has made you whole *(Faith is the only requirement)*; go in peace *(Justifying Peace; she was now "just" in the sight of God because she had trusted Christ, Who Alone can bring about our Justification; tradition says her name was Veronica, and she lived at Caesarea Philippi).*

49 While He yet spoke, there came one from the ruler of the Synagogue's house, saying to him *(to Jairus)*, Your daughter is dead; trouble not the Master *(while sufferers and their friends, and even the Lord's Disciples in countless instances, asked Him to heal, etc., no one ever asked Him to raise the dead to life; to the last, despite what they had seen, none could persuade themselves that He was indeed the Lord of death as well as of life, until after the Resurrection).*

50 But when Jesus heard *it*, He answered him, saying, Fear not *(in essence saying, "despite death," everything is going to be alright)*: believe only, and she shall be made whole *(the only requirement is Faith in Christ).*

51 And when He came into the house *(refers to the home of Jairus)*, He suffered no man to go in, save Peter, and James, and John, and the father and the mother of the maiden *(represents the first time these three Disciples had been singled out; they would be singled out a total of three times [Lk. 9:28; Mat. 26:37]).*

52 And all wept, and bewailed her *(represents paid mourners, which was then the custom)*: but

He said, Weep not; she is not dead, but asleep *(in fact, she was physically dead, but to Jesus she was only "asleep")*.

53 And they laughed Him to scorn *(the paid mourners)*, knowing that she was dead.

54 And He put them all out *(the Greek Text proclaims the fact that it must have been very close to a forceful ejection, as in the case of the cleansing of the Temple)*, and took her by the hand *(a firm grip)*, and called, saying, Maid, arise *(continues the exhibition of His Authority)*.

55 And her spirit came again *(demonstrates the separate existence of the spirit as independent of the body; her spirit and soul were once again reunited with her body, with the body instantly coming alive)*, and she arose straightway *(immediately)*: and He commanded to give her meat *(food)*.

56 And her parents were astonished *(they were transfixed to the spot, actually barely able to move, if at all)*: but He charged them that they should tell no man what was done *(Jesus sought neither publicity nor admiration)*.

CHAPTER 9

THE TWELVE

THEN He called His Twelve Disciples together *(a Divine call)*, and gave them power and authority over all devils *(demons)*, and to cure diseases *(Spiritual Authority is never exercised over people, but always over the spirit world of darkness only [Lk. 10:19])*.

2 And He sent them to preach *(the great business of the true man of God is preaching)* the Kingdom of God *(they were then to preach that the Kingdom was now available, because the King was present; the King rejected, which He was; the Message now is "Jesus Christ and Him Crucified," which will ultimately usher in the Kingdom on Earth that will come about at the Second Coming [I Cor. 1:21, 23])*, and to heal the sick *(constituted a part of these missions, and continued all the days of the Early Church and unto the present; anyone under the New Covenant is allowed to pray for the sick and expect healing [Mk. 16:17])*.

3 And He said unto them, Take nothing for your journey *(referring to the Call of Ministry)*, neither staves, nor scrip *(a small bag for carrying things)*, neither bread, neither money; neither have two coats apiece *(instead of waiting until those things can be afforded, carry out the work of the Lord, and trust the Lord to provide)*.

4 And whatsoever house you enter into, there abide, and thence depart *(don't be gadding about from house to house; the idea of*

your business is the Preaching of the Gospel, not socializing).

5 And whosoever will not receive you *(be it a single house, or the entirety of a city),* when ye go out of that city, shake off the very dust from your feet for a testimony against them *(the Gospel refused always heralds judgment in one form or another, whether for a single person or the entirety of an area).*

6 And they departed *(the Twelve),* and went through the towns, preaching the Gospel, and healing everywhere *(anything less is not the True Gospel).*

JOHN THE BAPTIST

7 Now Herod the Tetrarch *(Herod Antipas)* heard of all that was done by Him *(pertained to Jesus)*: and he was perplexed, because that it was said of some, that John was risen from the dead *(presented a terrifying spectacle to the hurting conscience of Herod who had murdered John);*

8 And of some *(some were saying),* that Elijah had appeared *(in other words that Jesus was Elijah);* and of others, that one of the old Prophets was risen again *(all of this portrayed a graphic ignorance of the Word).*

9 And Herod said, John have I beheaded *(is not said of bravado or scorn, but rather of fear)*: but

who is this, of whom I hear such things? *(The "such things" brought great joy to many, but fear to Herod because of a guilty conscience.)* And he desired to see Him *(this desire would be gratified, but not at the present; he did see Him on the day of the Crucifixion when Pilate sent Christ to Herod for judgment).*

FIVE THOUSAND FED

10 And the Apostles, when they were returned *(from their preaching mission of Verse 1),* told Him all that they had done. And He took them, and went aside privately into a desert place belonging to the city called Bethsaida *(this refers to Bethsaida, Julias situated on the northeastern shore of the Sea of Galilee; it was only a short distance from Capernaum).*

11 And the people, when they knew it *(knew where He had gone),* followed Him *(went to where He was)*: and He received them, and spoke unto them of the Kingdom of God, and healed them who had need of healing.

12 And when the day began to wear away, then came the Twelve, and said unto Him, Send the multitude away, that they may go into the towns and country round about, and lodge, and get victuals *(food)*: for we are here in a desert place *(the world is a desert place,*

but where Jesus is, the need can be met).

13 But He said unto them, Give ye them to eat (*proclaims that which within themselves they could not do*). And they said, We have no more but five loaves and two fishes; except we should go and buy meat for all this people (*they were thinking in material terms, when He was thinking in spiritual terms; our thinking shouldn't be what can we do, but rather what can He do*).

14 For they were about five thousand men (*counting the women and children, it could easily have been ten thousand or more*). And He said to His Disciples, Make them sit down by fifties in a company (*this way they could all be fed, whereas otherwise it would have been bedlam; God always functions from the position of order*).

15 And they did so, and made them all sit down.

16 Then He took the five loaves and the two fishes (*in their hands, it was nothing; in His hands, they were everything*), and looking up to Heaven (*when will we learn that our help comes from above?*), He blessed them (*that which He takes, He blesses*), and broke (*unfortunately there's a lot of self-will left in all of us, which requires a "breaking" that is not pleasant to say the least*), and gave to the Disciples to set before the multitude (*before we can properly be given to the multitude, we must first be blessed, then broken; far too many try to ignore the "breaking," depending only on the "blessing"; such can never be honored by the Lord*).

17 And they did eat, and were all filled (*that which the Lord provides always satisfies*): and there was taken up of fragments that remained to them twelve baskets (*what man does subtracts; what God does adds*).

PETER'S CONFESSION

18 And it came to pass, as He was alone praying (*some eight times Luke alludes to Jesus praying, which should serve as a lesson to us; while He definitely was God, and never ceased to be God, He functioned on this Earth as "Man"; as such, He had to pray*), His Disciples were with Him: and He asked them, saying, Whom say the people that I am? (*The answer to this question held grave consequences.*)

19 They answering said, John the Baptist; but some *say,* Elijah; and others *say,* that one of the old Prophets is risen again (*the Bible does not teach reincarnation, neither does it teach transmigration of one's spirit to another*).

20 He said unto them, But whom say you that I am? (*He was looked at by the Disciples as the*

*Master of Masters, and a Mystery
over and above.)* Peter answering
said, The Christ of God *(proclaims
the correct answer; "Christ" is actually a title, and means "anointed,"
or more perfectly, "The Anointed,"
meaning "Messiah").*

HIS DEATH AND
RESURRECTION

21 And He straitly charged
them, and commanded *them* to
tell no man that thing *(why? the
religious leaders of Israel had already rejected Him, and for the
Disciples to herald it far and wide
Who He really was would have only
brought about great problems);*

22 Saying, The Son of Man must
suffer many things *(is mentioned
apart from the glory that follows the
sufferings),* and be rejected of the
Elders and Chief Priests and
Scribes *(concerned the entirety of
the religious leadership of Israel),*
and be slain *(refers to the Crucifixion of Christ; the religious leaders
would be guilty of His Death),* and
be raised the third day *(the Resurrection, which was never in doubt;
the purpose of God becoming man
was to go to the Cross because this is
the only way sin could be addressed,
and sin is the problem).*

DISCIPLESHIP

23 And He said to *them* all, If
any *man* will come after Me *(the
criteria for Discipleship),* let him
deny himself *(not asceticism as
many think, but rather that one
denies one's own willpower, self-
will, strength, and ability, depending totally on Christ),* and take
up his cross *(the benefits of the
Cross, looking exclusively to what
Jesus did there to meet our every
need)* daily *(this is so important,
our looking to the Cross; that we
must renew our Faith in what
Christ has done for us, even on a
daily basis, for Satan will ever try
to move us away from the Cross as
the object of our Faith, which always spells disaster),* and follow
Me *(Christ can be followed only
by the Believer looking to the Cross,
understanding what it accomplished, and by that means alone [Rom.
6:3-5, 11, 14; 8:1-2, 11; I Cor. 1:17-
18, 21, 23; 2:2; Gal. 6:14; Eph.
2:13-18; Col. 2:14-15]).*

24 For whosoever will save his
life shall lose it *(try to live one's
life outside of Christ and the Cross):*
but whosoever will lose his life
for My sake, the same shall save
it *(when we place our Faith entirely in Christ and the Cross, looking exclusively to Him, we have
just found "more abundant life"
[Jn. 10:10]).*

25 For what is a man advantag-
ed, if he gain the whole world,
and lose himself, or be cast away?
(One cannot have both Christ and

the world. One or the other must go. And if one gains the whole world and loses his soul, what has it profited him?)

26 For whosoever shall be ashamed of Me *(ashamed of the Cross of Christ)* **and of My Words** *(a demand for the denial of self and the taking up of the Cross daily),* **of him shall the Son of Man be ashamed** *(a denial of Christ and the Cross is a denial of Salvation),* **when He shall come in His Own Glory** *(those who accept Christ and the Cross will be with Him when He comes, otherwise they will be "cast away"),* **and** *in his* **Father's** *(the Glory of the Father),* **and of the Holy Angels** *(if one wants to be on the side of Christ, the Heavenly Father, and the Holy Angels, one must accept Christ and the Cross, which automatically denies perfidious ways).*

27 But I tell you of a truth, there be some standing here, which shall not taste of death, till they see the Kingdom of God *(speaking of the transfiguration which would shortly take place).*

THE TRANSFIGURATION

28 And it came to pass about an eight days after these sayings *(Mark says "six days" [Mk. 9:2]; there is no discrepancy; Mark's statement is exclusive, which means all the days and time are not in-cluded in the statement; Luke's statement is inclusive),* **He took Peter and John and James, and went up into a mountain to pray** *(the first time these three were singled out was the raising of the daughter of Jairus from the dead).*

29 And as He prayed, the fashion of His countenance was altered *(means that it took on a glow that was obvious to all; as well, the Glory He was now experiencing did not come from without, but from within),* **and His raiment** *was* **white** *and* **glistering** *(this inward Glory turned those homespun, peasant garments into a thing of such beauty that it was absolutely indescribable).*

30 And, behold, there talked with Him two men, which were Moses and Elijah *(Moses had been dead for about 1,500 years, and Elijah had been translated, and in fact had never died, but had been in Heaven or Paradise for about 900 years; all of this puts to rest the erroneous doctrine of "soul sleep," which teaches that the soul and the spirit sleep at death and will do so until the Resurrection):*

31 Who appeared in glory *(their "glory" is that which came from without, actually from God the Father, while the "Glory" of Christ came from within Him because He is God, the Second Person of the Godhead),* **and spoke of His decease which He should accom-**

plish at Jerusalem *(the "Cross" was the topic of this conversation, and should be the topic of ours as well)*.

32 But Peter and they who were with Him were heavy with sleep: and when they were awake, they saw His Glory, and the two men that stood with Him *(this portrays to us how the Child of God will die, simply going to sleep in Jesus and awakening in Heaven in His Presence)*.

33 And it came to pass, as they departed from Him *(pertains to Moses and Elijah disappearing from the scene)*, Peter said unto Jesus, Master, it is good for us to be here: and let us make three tabernacles; one for You, and one for Moses, and one for Elijah: not knowing what He said *(proclaims Peter placing these two on the same par with Christ, which was not looked at favorably by God)*.

34 While He thus spoke, there came a cloud *(the same as that which accompanied the Lord leading the Children of Israel in their wilderness wanderings, and as well that which rested over the Tabernacle, i.e., "the Glory of God")*, and overshadowed them: and they feared as they entered into the cloud *(Christ didn't fear, but rather the three Disciples)*.

35 And there came a voice out of the cloud *(the Voice of God the Father)*, saying, This is My Beloved Son: hear Him *(actually says, "be constantly hearing Him," as well meaning that no mortal must be put on the same par with Christ; the Catholics should note that He didn't say, "hear Mary," but rather, "hear Him")*.

36 And when the voice was past, Jesus was found alone *(proclaims the fact that the Voice did not come from a physical body)*. And they kept it close, and told no man in those days any of those things which they had seen *(meaning that they did not relate the account of this incident until after the Resurrection)*.

LESSONS

37 And it came to pass, that on the next day, when they were come down from the hill, much people met Him *(implies they were waiting for Him)*.

38 And, behold, a man of the company cried out *(a man in the crowd)*, saying, Master, I beseech You, look upon my son: for he is mine only child *(peculiar to Luke; he is the only one who mentions that this poor tormented boy was an only child)*.

39 And, lo, a spirit *(evil spirit)* takes him, and he suddenly cries out *(speaks of the demon spirit taking control of the boy)*; and it tears him that he foams again, and bruising him hardly departing from him *(constant occurrences)*.

40 And I besought Your Disciples to cast him out; and they could not (*Mark says that Jesus said that the reason was the "prayerlessness" of the Disciples; in fact, the emphasis in the Greek Text is on their "prayerlessness," rather than their "lack of fasting" [Mk. 9:29]*).

41 And Jesus answering said, O faithless and perverse generation (*was spoken to the whole of Israel*), how long shall I be with you, and suffer you? (*This portrays a human exasperation on the part of Jesus.*) Bring your son hither (*indicates that the boy was being restrained a short distance away*).

42 And as he was yet a coming, the devil threw him down, and tore him (*represents this demon's last effort to hurt this child*). And Jesus rebuked the unclean spirit, and healed the child, and delivered him again to his father (*Jesus cast the demon out, and healed that which the demon had damaged regarding the child's physical body*).

43 And they were all amazed at the mighty power of God. But while they wondered every one at all things which Jesus did, He said unto His Disciples (*portrays the idea coming up once again, as recorded in the next Verse, of Him being the Triumphant Messiah, and therefore being made King*),

44 Let these sayings sink down into your ears (*concerned that which they did not want to hear*): for the Son of Man shall be delivered into the hands of men (*presents that which He had already said to them, but which they did not understand*).

45 But they understood not this saying, and it was hid from them, that they perceived it not (*it was not purposely hidden from them, but was rather hidden because of their unbelief*): and they feared to ask Him of that saying (*means that what He had said did not line up with their thinking*).

46 Then there arose a reasoning among them, which of them should be greatest (*the spirit of self-will, which was the cause of them not understanding*).

47 And Jesus, perceiving the thought of their heart (*refers to the Holy Spirit revealing to Him this which the Apostles were discussing*), took a child, and set him by Him (*is thought to be Peter's child*),

48 And said unto them, Whosoever shall receive this child in My Name receives Me (*carries the idea of service to others, which addresses the argument of the Disciples as to who will be the greatest; to bless a child, one must do so strictly out of Love, because a child cannot return the favor*): and whosoever shall receive Me receives him Who sent Me (*unless one comes as

a little child, one cannot receive Christ; and when one receives Christ, one has received at the same time God the Father; everything is through Christ): for he who is least among you all, the same shall be great *(the work for which Christ's Gospel came into the world was no less than to put down the mighty from their seat, and to exalt the humble and the meek).*

49 And John answered and said, Master, we saw one casting out devils *(demons)* in Your Name; and we forbad him, because he followeth not with us *(this is the sin of sectarianism, which in essence means, "the exclusion of all others, outside of a particular group").*

50 And Jesus said unto him, Forbid *him* not: for he who is not against us is for us *(forbids all sectarianism).*

51 And it came to pass, when the time was come that He should be received up *(this particular "time" had been planned by the Godhead since before the foundation of the world [I Pet. 1:20; Rev. 13:8])*, He stedfastly set His face to go to Jerusalem *(this is where the terrible deed must be carried out),*

52 And sent messengers before His face *(referred to Disciples or others who went to make preparation for them to spend some time, at least one night, in this particular village)*: and they went, and entered into a village of the Sa-

maritans, to make ready for Him *(descendants of the pagans who settled in this particular part of Israel at the time of the captivities; they intermarried with a few Jews who remained in the land [II Ki. 17:24-34]).*

53 And they did not receive Him *(presents the greatest mistake they ever made, and regrettably the great mistake made by most)*, because His face was as though He would go to Jerusalem *(had to do with the ongoing argument between the Jews and the Samaritans; in other words, they allowed their religion to cause them to miss the greatest moment in their history, and their religion probably took them to hell).*

54 And when His Disciples James and John saw this *(probably proclaims the two sent to the village by Jesus seeking accommodations)*, they said, Lord, will You that we command fire to come down from heaven, and consume them, even as Elijah did? *(Zeal without knowledge and failure to rightly divide the Word of Truth cause well-meaning men to greatly err.)*

55 But He turned, and rebuked them *(is the same Word used by Jesus when He rebuked evil spirits [Mat. 17:18]; the spirit of the Disciples at that time and demon spirits were all the same, hence they were both rebuked accordingly)*, and said, you know not what

manner of spirit you are of *(portrays them operating in the spirit of the Evil One; how many modern Christians do the same?)*.

56 For the Son of Man is not come to destroy men's lives, but to save *them (proclaims the true mission of Christ)*. And they went to another village *(constituted the greatest moment the "other village" would ever know)*.

DISCIPLESHIP

57 And it came to pass, that, as they went in the way *(continuing the next morning their trip toward Jerusalem)*, a certain *man* said unto him, Lord, I will follow You whithersoever You go *(proclaimed this man, according to Matthew, as being a Scribe [Mat. 8:19])*.

58 And Jesus said unto him, Foxes have holes, and birds of the air *have* nests; but the Son of Man has not where to lay *His* head *(the implication regarding the Scribe is that he had not counted the cost, and when revealed, did not desire to pay the price)*.

59 And He said unto another, Follow Me *(to this man, Christ extends an invitation)*. But he said, Lord, suffer me first to go and bury my father *(proclaims the "cares of this life" robbing him of pre-eminence with Christ)*.

60 Jesus said unto him, Let the dead bury their dead *(was not meant to show disrespect for the dead, or of shirking of responsibility; it wasn't the idea of burying his father, but rather of placing such things first; Christ must come first in all things)*: but go thou and preach the Kingdom of God *(there were plenty of people to perform the other tasks, but precious few to preach the Word of God)*.

61 And another also said, Lord, I will follow You; but let me first go bid them farewell, which are at home at my house *(the Holy Spirit is here portraying to us the single-minded purpose which must be paramount in the life of every Believer, that is, if they are to follow Christ as they should)*.

62 And Jesus said unto him, No man, having put his hand to the plough, and looking back, is fit for the Kingdom of God *(attachment to Christ and to His Service must be unconditional)*.

CHAPTER 10

THE SEVENTY

AFTER these things *(the things of the previous Chapter)*, the Lord appointed other seventy also *(other than the Twelve; this was done toward the close of His Ministry; as well, it was the Lord Who appointed, and pertains to that which man cannot do; Why seventy? It is God's number repre-*

senting His Spirit-Anointed Ministry), and sent them two and two before His face into every city and place, whither He Himself would come (when the Lord sends Preachers to certain places, it is because He desires to come there; the people must not forget this).

2 Therefore said He unto them, The harvest truly is great, but the labourers are few (this tells us that the Salvation of souls is a priority with the Lord; in fact, for everyone who doesn't have the privilege to hear, as far as that person is concerned, Jesus died in vain; there are many engaged in the fishing business, but very few who are actually fishing): pray ye therefore the Lord of the harvest (prayer must be the foundation on which the harvest is gathered; as well, we must remember that it is Jesus Christ Who is the Lord of the harvest), that He would send forth labourers into His harvest (if there are no "labourers," the harvest cannot be gathered).

3 Go your ways (respects those whom the Lord has called, and concerns where they are sent): behold, I send you forth as lambs among wolves (no shepherd deliberately sends his sheep among wolves, but this shepherd can because He is almighty to save [Ps., Chpt. 23]).

4 Carry neither purse, nor scrip, nor shoes (God will provide): and salute no man by the way (do not be deterred from the mission at hand).

5 And into whatsoever house you enter, first say, Peace be to this house (proclaims a blessing promised by the Lord to any who aid and abet those He has called, providing they are carrying out the Great Commission).

6 And if the son of peace be there (refers to one who desires the blessings of the Lord, attempting to serve in any capacity possible), your peace shall rest upon it (the blessing will be given): if not, it shall turn to you again (any hindrance to this all-important task stops the blessings of God).

7 And in the same house remain, eating and drinking such things as they give (pertains not only to a single house, but the field of ministry assigned by the Lord): for the labourer is worthy of his hire (this is the only quotation in the Epistles from the Gospel [I Tim. 5:18]). Go not from house to house (in modern times, it refers to Preachers seeking better Churches simply because they pay more money; money is never to be the object, but rather the Call of God and wherever that leads).

8 And into whatsoever city you enter, and they receive you (implies that some will not receive the Gospel), eat such things as are set before you (and don't complain):

9 And heal the sick who are

therein *(pertains to both physical and spiritual, a Part of the blessing),* and say unto them, The Kingdom of God is come nigh unto you *(the greatest thing that could ever happen to any family or place).*

10 But into whatsoever city you enter *(to where the Lord has sent you),* and they receive you not *(implying that this will be the case at times),* go your ways out into the streets of the same, and say *(that which is not desired is not to be given),*

11 Even the very dust of your city, which cleaves on us, we do wipe off against you *(the idea is the Lord keeps a careful record):* notwithstanding be ye sure of this, that the Kingdom of God is come nigh unto you *(it is imperative that all have the opportunity to hear, but woe be unto those who reject Christ; the Great White Throne Judgment will record the rejection [Rev. 20:11-15]).*

12 But I say unto you, that it shall be more tolerable in that day *(the Great White Throne Judgment)* for Sodom, than for that city *(the cities of which Jesus speaks have heard the Gospel; Sodom did not have that opportunity).*

13 Woe unto You, Chorazin! woe unto You, Bethsaida! for if the mighty works had been done in Tyre and Sidon, which have been done in you, they had a great while ago repented, sitting in sackcloth and ashes *(these are two cities where Jesus had performed mighty works — the greatest works in the history of mankind; men will be judged not only for what they have done or failed to do, but their opportunities, their circumstances, their chances in life, will be strictly taken into account before they are judged).*

14 But it shall be more tolerable for Tyre and Sidon at the judgment, than for you *(these twin cities did not see the Power of God as did those spoken of by Christ; cities and places which have had little opportunity will not be spared, but will not be judged as harshly).*

15 And You, Capernaum, which are exalted to Heaven *(chosen by the Holy Spirit as the headquarters of Christ during His earthly Ministry),* shall be thrust down to hell *(constitutes the most severe pronounced punishment).*

16 He who hears you hears Me *(proclaims Spiritual Authority given to the Messenger of the Lord);* and He who despises you despises Me *(fearsome indeed!);* and he who despises Me despises Him Who sent Me *(God the Father; these are most serious statements; in fact, some of the most serious ever uttered by Christ).*

THE SEVENTY RETURN

17 And the seventy returned

again with joy, saying, Lord, even the devils *(demons)* are subject unto us through Your Name *(demons are subject to us only through His Name).*

18 And He said unto them, I beheld Satan as lightning fall from Heaven *(by the Power of the Holy Spirit, Jesus saw into the future, observing Satan as he will be cast out of Heaven at the approximate mid-point of the coming Great Tribulation).*

19 Behold, I give unto you power to tread on serpents and scorpions, and over all the power of the enemy: and nothing shall by any means hurt you *(this is the domain of Spiritual Authority; it is only over spirit beings, and not at all over humans).*

20 Notwithstanding in this rejoice not, that the spirits are subject unto you *(this should not be the occasion of our joy)*; but rather rejoice, because your names are written in Heaven *(tells us that the Salvation of the soul must always be the occasion for rejoicing; when the Church rejoices more over other things than people being saved, something is wrong).*

21 In that hour Jesus rejoiced in spirit *(actually means in the Greek Text that Jesus greatly exulted in the Holy Spirit, which spoke of a great joy like a fountain springing up that came from the depths of His soul; as the previous Verses pro-* claim, *He saw the total and complete victory that would come about as a result of the Cross)*, and said, I thank You, O Father, Lord of Heaven and earth *(Satan is not the lord of either place, but rather God the Father)*, that You have hid these things from the wise and prudent, and have revealed them unto babes *(the religious hierarchy never saw this of which Jesus spoke, but these fishermen chosen by Christ did)*: even so, Father; for so it seemed good in Your sight *(unfortunately, far too much of the modern Church labels things "good" that God labels otherwise).*

22 All things are delivered to Me of My Father *(refers to Jesus being given the responsibility by the Father for defeating Satan and putting down his evil revolution, which would be done at the Cross)*: and no man knows Who the Son is, but the Father *(means that Jesus is of the Father, and not of man)*; and Who the Father is, but the Son *(no man can reach the "Father," or even know Who the "Father" is, except through the "Son," i.e., the Lord Jesus Christ; Jesus Alone is the Door [Jn. 10:9])*, and he to whom the Son will reveal Him *(Salvation is not a matter of education, but of Revelation).*

23 And He turned Him unto His Disciples, and said privately *(refers to not only the "Twelve," but the "Seventy" also)*, Blessed

are the eyes which see the things that you see *(He is speaking of seeing "with the eye of faith," and believing what is seen):*

24 For I tell you, that many Prophets and Kings have desired to see those things which you see, and have not seen *them*; and to hear those things which you hear, and have not heard *them (He is speaking here of all the Old Testament greats who pointed to His Coming, but of course, did not live to see such; but they believed just the same! as well, tens of thousands during Jesus' public Ministry did see and hear, but still would not believe; this shows that faith is not in the senses, but rather in the heart).*

THE GOOD SAMARITAN

25 And, behold, a certain lawyer stood up *(one who was supposed to be expert in the Mosaic Law)*, and tempted Him *(means that he would test the Lord's knowledge of the Law; he did not know that Jesus was the Law)*, saying, Master, what shall I do to inherit eternal life? *(This so-called expert in the Law was evidently not much of an expert at all, or He would have used the word "merit" and not "inherit"; inheritance is by birth; eternal life is man's greatest interest, and no more tremendous question could be asked than that of*

this Verse.)

26 He said unto him, What is written in the Law? *(This presents Jesus immediately pointing to the Bible as the infallible authority.)* how readest thou? *(Jesus was speaking not only of knowing the Word, but properly understanding it as well.)*

27 And He answering said, You shall love the Lord Your God with all your heart, and with all your soul, and with all your strength, and with all your mind; and your neighbour as yourself *(this is quoted from Deut. 6:5 and Lev. 19:18).*

28 And He *(Jesus)* said unto him, You have answered right *(proclaims Christ in effect saying, "you know it, but you are not doing it")*: this do, and you shall live *(means that he was not doing what he knew to do; in fact, it wasn't possible for him, or anyone else for that matter, to fully obey the Law; so there was no Salvation in this direction).*

29 But he, willing to justify himself, said to Jesus, And who is my neighbour? *(This statement discovers the character of the lawyer. He was self-righteous. He was determined to win Heaven by religious self-efforts.)*

30 And Jesus answering said, A certain *man* went down from Jerusalem to Jericho, and fell among thieves, which stripped

him of his raiment, and wounded *him*, and departed, leaving *him* half dead.

31 And by chance there came down a certain Priest that way: and when he saw him, he passed by on the other side *(selfishness is the commanding force in human nature)*.

32 And likewise a Levite *(spoke of those who were of the tribe of Levi)*, when he was at the place, came and looked *on him*, and passed by on the other side *(proclaims this man at least looking on, while the Priest did not even bother with that)*.

33 But a certain Samaritan *(the Samaritans and the Jews normally were enemies)*, as he journeyed, came where he was *(where the wounded Israelite was)*: and when he saw him, he had compassion *on him,*

34 And went to *him*, and bound up his wounds, pouring in oil and wine *(in those days, a wound was cleansed with grape-juice with oil then applied, which aided healing)*, and set him on his own beast, and brought him to an inn, and took care of him *(tells us that this wounded traveler was not rich, and therefore could not possibly repay the kindness extended to him)*.

35 And on the morrow when he *(the good Samaritan)* departed, he took out two pence, and gave *them* to the host, and said unto him,

Take care of him; and whatsoever you spend more, when I come again, I will repay you.

36 Which now of these three *(the three men who came in contact with the wounded traveler)*, do you think, was neighbour unto him who fell among the thieves?

37 And he said, He who showed mercy on him. Then said Jesus unto him, Go, and do thou likewise *(another lesson taught in this Parable is that some need to be placed in the position of the wounded traveler in order that they be willing to receive help from anyone, even the hated Samaritan).*

MARY AND MARTHA

38 Now it came to pass, as they went, that He entered into a certain village *(speaks of Bethany [Jn. 11:1; 12:1-3], a suburb of Jerusalem)*: and a certain woman named Martha received Him into her house.

39 And she had a sister called Mary, which also sat at Jesus' feet, and heard His Word *(sitting at Jesus' feet is a safe refuge from assaults upon the authority and inspiration of the Scriptures).*

40 But Martha was cumbered about much serving, and came to Him, and said, Lord, do You not care that my sister has left me to serve alone? bid her therefore that she help me *(had Martha fully*

realized that Jesus was Jehovah, she never would have spoken so petulantly to Him).

41 And Jesus answered and said unto her, Martha, Martha (is said in pitying love), you are careful and troubled about many things (concerned things which were important, but not the most important!):

42 But one thing is needful (proclaims to us the Mind of God, and tells us where all victory is): and Mary has chosen that good part (means that this is a "choice"), which shall not be taken away from her (the greatest thing is communion with Christ).

CHAPTER 11

PRAYER

AND it came to pass, that, as He was praying in a certain place (Jesus here does what He had admonished Martha to do — have fellowship with the Father, which Mary did), when He ceased, one of His Disciples said unto Him (they evidently noted the ease with which He prayed), Lord, teach us to pray, as John also taught his disciples (the answer to their request as given by Christ forms the basis for all prayer).

2 And He said unto them, When you pray (meaning that there should be a set time for prayer each day), say, Our Father (this speaks of relationship, and that He Alone can supply our every need) which art in Heaven (help comes from Heaven; none comes from this Earth), Hallowed be Your Name (open with praise). Your Kingdom come (the Believer is to pray for this Kingdom to come, and for all the obvious reasons). Your will be done, as in Heaven, so in earth (the "Will of God," and not our Will, should be the supreme goal of every Believer; the Will of God is not being presently done on Earth, but it will be when the Kingdom comes; then war, sickness, and suffering will end).

3 Give us day by day our daily bread (physical sustenance and spiritual sustenance, which the Lord Alone can give).

4 And forgive us our sins (this proclaims the fact that there are no perfect Believers, only a perfect God; the best of us, whomever that may be, still live in a house of flawed flesh; consequently, we must constantly look to Christ); for we also forgive every one who is indebted to us (the Lord forgiving us is predicated as well on our forgiving others). And lead us not into temptation (in effect states help me in my weakness not to be led into temptation); but deliver us from evil (there is only One Deliverer, that is the Lord; man cannot deliver man, despite the claims of humanistic psychology; and God delivers

through what Jesus did at the Cross, and our Faith in that Finished Work).

5 And He said unto them (*a continuance of the explanation regarding prayer*), Which of you shall have a friend, and shall go unto him at midnight, and say unto him, Friend, lend me three loaves (*a meager request*);

6 For a friend of mine in his journey is come to me, and I have nothing to set before him? (*We as Believers must give the Message of Eternal Life to all of mankind, but the truth is, within ourselves, we have nothing to give.*)

7 And he from within shall answer and say, Trouble me not: the door is now shut, and my children are with me in bed; I cannot rise and give to you (*an obvious denial*).

8 I say unto you, Though he will not rise and give him, because he is his friend, yet because of his importunity he will rise and give him as many as he needs (*the argument of this Parable is that if a sufficiency for daily need can, by importunity, i.e., "persistence," be obtained from an unwilling source, how much more from a willing Giver, which and Who is the Lord*).

9 And I say unto you (*telling us how to approach the Lord for whatever we need*), Ask, and it shall be given you; seek, and you shall find; knock, and it shall be opened unto you (*all of this speaks of persistence and guarantees a positive answer, at least if it's in the Will of God*).

10 For everyone who asks receives; and he who seeks finds; and to him who knocks it shall be opened (*he says "everyone," and that includes you!*).

11 If a son shall ask bread of any of you who is a father, will he give him a stone? or if *he ask* a fish, will he for a fish give him a serpent?

12 Or if he shall ask an egg, will he offer him (*an egg containing*) a scorpion?

13 If you then, being evil, know how to give good gifts unto your children (*means that an earthly parent certainly would not give a child a stone who has asked for bread, etc.*): how much more shall *your* Heavenly Father give the Holy Spirit to them who ask Him? (*This refers to God's goodness, and the fact that everything from the Godhead comes to us through the Person and Agency of the Holy Spirit; and all that He does for us is based upon the Cross of Christ, and our Faith in that Finished Work.*)

BLASPHEMY

14 And He was casting out a devil (*demon*), and it was dumb (*the Greek Text implies a mute silence, which was a form of insan-*

ity). And it came to pass, when the devil *(demon)* was gone out, the dumb spoke; and the people wondered *(in a moment's time, the man was completely delivered and healed).*

15 But some of them said *(some of the religious leaders in Israel),* He casts out devils *(demons)* through Beelzebub the chief of the devils *(concerns a startling accusation, which constituted the terrible sin of blaspheming the Holy Spirit, for which there is no forgiveness; "Beelzebub" was the Philistine god of flies [II Ki. 1:2]; it meant "the dung god," or "lord of the dung hill"; a most contemptuous and vile idol).*

16 And others, tempting *Him (attempting to ensnare Christ in His speech or actions),* sought of Him a sign from Heaven *(strange, considering that they had just witnessed a sign of unprecedented proportions; they actually demanded a stunt, such as calling fire down from Heaven; what these foolish men didn't realize was, if He had done such, the fire would have fallen on them; but they were so spiritually insensitive, they couldn't see the danger they were in).*

17 But He, knowing their thoughts *(presents the Holy Spirit informing Him of what they were thinking, which means that they had not been saying these things so that the crowd of people could*

hear), said unto them, Every Kingdom divided against itself is brought to desolation; and a house *divided* against a house falls *(division based on dissension is the sure destroyer of all).*

18 If Satan also be divided against himself, how shall his kingdom stand? *(This tells us unequivocally of the existence of such a kingdom of evil, all armed and thoroughly organized to carry out its dread purposes.)* because you say that I cast out devils *(demons)* through Beelzebub *(presents the absurdity of such an accusation).*

19 And if I by Beelzebub cast out devils *(demons),* by whom do your sons cast *them* out? *(This means that by condemning Him, accordingly they were condemning themselves.)* therefore shall they be your judges *(the crowd knew that they had never heard of anyone casting out demons by the power of Satan).*

20 But if I with the Finger of God *(Power of God)* cast out devils *(demons)* *(they could not question the Healings, Miracles or Deliverances),* no doubt the Kingdom of God is come upon you *(every evidence said that He was of God; His Power was undeniable!).*

21 When a strong man *(Satan)* armed keeps his palace *(the world),* his goods are in peace *(represents freedom from hostile action, which*

Satan enjoyed until the First Advent of Christ):

22 But when a stronger than he *(Jesus Christ is stronger)* shall come upon him, and overcome him *(referred to what Jesus did at the Cross [Col. 2:14-15])*, He takes from him all his armour wherein he trusted *(Jesus Christ defeated Satan totally and completely at the Cross, where He atoned for all sin)*, and divides his spoils *(means that multiple millions have been Redeemed from Satan's clutches, and instead of being captives of Satan they are now captives of Jesus Christ [Eph. 4:8-9])*.

23 He who is not with Me is against Me *(presents the fact that there is no neutrality with Christ)*: and he who gathers not with Me scatters *(everything is either of the Devil or of Christ; there is no middle ground)*.

24 When the unclean spirit is gone out of a man *(concerns the efforts of man, whatever they may be, to save himself other than by Christ and Him Crucified)*, he walks through dry places, seeking rest *(concerns the "unclean spirit" which has gone out)*; and finding none, he says, I will return unto my house whence I came out *(unless Christ affects the work, whatever it might be, it is not truly affected)*.

25 And when he *(the evil spirit)* comes, he finds it swept and garnished *(means that it was filled with that other than Christ)*.

26 Then goes he, and takes to him seven other spirits more wicked than himself *(concerns the reoccupation by demon spirits)*; and they enter in, and dwell there *(proving that most of the world is controlled by demon spirits)*: and the last state of that man is worse than the first *(this was the state of Israel after they had rejected Christ, which ultimately led to their total destruction)*.

27 And it came to pass, as He spoke these things, a certain woman of the company lifted up her voice, and said unto Him *(the Lord was teaching the most solemn truths about the terrors of the spirit world of darkness, and this woman rudely interrupted with her carnal thoughts)*, Blessed is the womb that bear You, and the paps which You have sucked *(it was true what the woman said, but out of place at this time)*.

28 But He said, Yea rather, blessed are they who hear the Word of God, and keep it *(the Lord gently reproved her, pointing out that the natural man and natural relationships cannot be recognized in the kingdom of spiritual realities)*.

JONAH

29 And when the people were gathered thick together, He be-

gan to say, This is an evil generation *(proclaims the unbelief of Israel; they were extremely religious, and yet did not know God Whom they spoke of constantly)*: they seek a sign; and there shall no sign be given it, but the sign of Jonah the Prophet *(the sign of which Jesus spoke was the resurrection of Jonah from the belly of the whale; likewise, Jesus would be Resurrected from the dead, but regrettably, Israel did not believe that sign)*.

30 For as Jonah was a sign unto the Ninevites *(they must have heard of his deliverance from the great fish; he was entombed in this monster for three days and three nights; and so was a type of Him Who was three days and three nights in the heart of the Earth)*, so shall also the Son of Man be to this generation *(Nineveh was given forty days in which to repent; Jerusalem was given forty years; Repentance in the one case averted the judgment; unbelief in the other determined the destruction)*.

31 The queen of the south shall rise up in the judgment with the men of this generation, and condemn them: for she came from the utmost parts of the Earth to hear the wisdom of Solomon; and, behold, a Greater than Solomon *is* here.

32 The men of Nineveh shall rise up in the judgment with this generation, and shall condemn it: for they repented at the preaching of Jonah; and, behold, a greater than Jonah *is* here *(in Verses 29-32; the Lord Jesus testifies to the truthfulness of the Scriptures respecting the Queen of the South, plus Jonah and the men of Nineveh; and further, He affirms the fact of the Resurrection and the judgment to come, declaring that all those persons will rise from the dead; this supplemental statement establishes the historic truth of the Book of Jonah)*.

THE LIGHT

33 No man, when he has lit a candle, puts *it* in a secret place, neither under a bushel, but on a candlestick, that they which come in may see the light *(Christ is the Light of the world; He did not hide that light, it shone fully on every man; but few accepted it, for the majority were so willfully blind that they remained unilluminated)*.

34 The light of the body is the eye *(what a lamp is to a room, the eye is to the body)*: therefore when your eye is single, your whole body also is full of light *(the emphasis is on the word "single"; it means singleness of purpose, which keeps us from the snare of having a double treasure and consequently a divided heart)*; but when *your* eye is evil, your body also *is* full of darkness *(Jesus is the Light; if the "eye" does*

not see Him fully, moral and spiritual darkness prevails).

35 Take heed therefore that the light which is in you be not darkness *(this speaks of deception; the Verse could be translated, "take heed therefore that the light that is in you be not artificial light, and therefore darkness").*

36 If your whole body therefore *be* full of light, having no part dark, the whole shall be full of light, as when the bright shining of a candle does give you light *(the problem with the Church is "part dark" and "part light").*

PHARISEES

37 And as He spoke, a certain Pharisee besought Him to dine with him: and He went in, and sat down to meat.

38 And when the Pharisee saw it, he marvelled that He *(Jesus)* had not first washed before dinner *(the "washing" spoken of here had nothing to do with sanitation; the Pharisees taught that a demon sat on unwashed hands, and unless a certain ritual was performed, the demon could be ingested while eating).*

39 And the Lord said unto him, Now do you Pharisees make clean the outside of the cup and the platter *(outward show)*; but your inward part is full of ravening and wickedness *(presents a scath-ing denunciation).*

40 You fools *(what an indictment! and He said this to the man's face)*, did not He *(God)* Who made that which is without make that which is within also? *(The inward man must be changed as well, and can only be changed by the Power of God.)*

41 But rather give alms of such things as you have; and, behold, all things are clean unto you *(the Greek here reads: "But rather the things that are within, that is the heart, the will, the affections, then all other actions proceeding from a heart truly given to God, will be acceptable to Him; otherwise such actions will be 'dead works'; thus, the Lord perpetually taught the necessity of the New Birth").*

42 But woe unto you, Pharisees! *(Once again, this is a scathing denunciation.)* for you tithe mint and rue *(leaves of certain plants)* and all manner of herbs *(meaning that they were meticulous to pay their tithes)*, and pass over judgment and the Love of God *(the giving of money will not take the place of righteous living)*: these ought you to have done *(you ought to pay your tithes)*, and not to leave the other undone.

43 Woe unto you, Pharisees! for you love the uppermost seats in the Synagogues *(position of importance)*, and greetings in the markets *(to be greeted as a superior).*

44 Woe unto you, Scribes *(supposed to be experts in the Law of Moses)* and Pharisees *(supposed to be the religious leaders of Israel)*, hypocrites! *(You aren't what you claim to be.)* for you are as graves which appear not, and the men who walk over *them* are not aware of them *(according to the Mosaic Law, it was wrong to touch anything that pertained to death because it represented sin; Jesus was saying that these religious leaders of Israel were like covered-over graves, with men walking over them and being defiled, and not aware of it; in other words, the religious leaders of Israel were sin, and therefore death, and a defilement to Israel)*.

45 Then answered one of the lawyers *(supposed to be experts in the Law of Moses)*, and said unto Him, Master, thus saying You reproach us also *(insult us)*.

46 And He *(Jesus)* said, Woe unto you also, *you* lawyers! for you laden men with burdens grievous to be borne *(kept adding things to the original Law of Moses)*, and you yourselves touch not the burdens with one of your fingers *(they did not themselves live up at all to that which they demanded of the people; such is religion!)*.

47 Woe unto you! for you build the sepulchres of the Prophets, and your fathers killed them *(they built gorgeous tombs for the Prophets of Old who had long since died, but in truth their hearts were just as murderous as their fathers of the past who killed the Prophets)*.

48 Truly you bear witness that you allow the deeds of your fathers *(means they were following in the same vein)*: for they indeed killed them, and you build their sepulchres *(it is far easier to admire dead Saints than to identify one's self with living ones)*.

49 Therefore also said the Wisdom of God *(Christ [I Cor. 1:24])*, I will send them Prophets and Apostles, and *some* of them they shall slay and persecute *("I" is emphatic, and speaks of the Divine self-consciousness of Jesus; in other words, the Redeemer identifies Himself with God, and actually as God"; "they" refers to the religious leaders of Israel who killed the Prophets and the Apostles)*:

50 That the blood of all the Prophets, which was shed from the foundation of the world, may be required of this generation *(the "generation" of which Jesus spoke was the generation of His day; the reason such judgment was called down upon their heads, which was fulfilled in A.D. 70, was that they rejected the One Whom the Prophets had predicted would come, namely Christ)*;

51 From the blood of Abel unto the blood of Zachariah, which perished between the Altar and

the Temple (*God keeps an account of every injustice, no matter how large or small*): verily I say unto you, It shall be required of this generation.

52 Woe unto you, lawyers! for you have taken away the key of knowledge (*they took the Word of God from the people, substituting their own glosses; such characterizes much of the modern Ministry as well!*): you entered not in yourselves (*you are not even saved yourselves*), and them who were entering in you hindered (*by teaching error, they kept the True Word of God from the people, thereby hindering them; once again, it is the same presently!*).

53 And as He said these things unto them, the Scribes and the Pharisees began to urge *Him* vehemently (*trying to get Him to say something by which they could accuse Him*), and to provoke Him to speak of many things:

54 Laying wait for Him, and seeking to catch something out of His mouth, that they might accuse Him (*speaks of all types of verbal traps they laid for Him, but all to no avail!*).

CHAPTER 12

THE LEAVEN

IN the mean time, when there were gathered together an innumerable multitude of people, insomuch that they trode one upon another, He began to say unto His Disciples first of all (*rejected by the religious leaders of Israel, He confines His Words to His Disciples, at least at this time*), Beware ye of the leaven of the Pharisees, which is hypocrisy (*"leaven" was the interpretations and traditions of men, which they substituted for the Word of God; Jesus labels this as hypocrisy, which is the acting out of the part of a character, or being something other than what one really is; in fact, all religion is hypocrisy, for the rules of men, which is religion, cannot change the heart*).

2 For there is nothing covered, that shall not be revealed; neither hid, that shall not be known (*what is right or wrong will ultimately be revealed*).

3 Therefore whatsoever you have spoken in darkness shall be heard in the light (*wrong doctrine, which is darkness, will ultimately be revealed as to what it actually is by the light of the Word of God*); and that which you have spoken in the ear in closets shall be proclaimed upon the housetops (*the Pharisees plotted in secret to kill Christ; their secrets are now known all over the world; and so shall all ungodliness be ultimately found out*).

4 And I say unto you My friends,

Be not afraid of them who kill the body, and after that have no more that they can do (*Believers are not to fear men*).

5 But I will forewarn you whom you shall fear: Fear Him (*God*), which after He has killed (*life and death are in the Hands of God Alone*) has power to cast into hell (*the greater fear of God would banish the lesser fear of man; for man can only touch the body, but God can reach the soul and cast it into Hell*); yea, I say unto you, Fear Him (*presents the second time this is stated, and is therefore meant to be clearly understood*).

6 Are not five sparrows sold for two farthings (*an insignificant transaction*), and not one of them is forgotten before God? (*Every incident and transaction, no matter how small or seemingly insignificant, is known and recorded by God.*)

7 But even the very hairs of your head are all numbered (*presents a degree of knowledge which is beyond the ability of any human being to comprehend*). Fear not therefore: you are of more value than many sparrows (*for those who truly follow the Lord, these words should greatly comfort all Believers; our every action is known by Him, and He will superintend every action, if we will allow Him to do so*).

8 Also I say unto you, Whoso-ever shall confess Me before men, him shall the Son of Man also confess before the Angels of God (*if we confess Him before men, however painful that testimony might be, He will confess us before Angels*):

9 But he who denies Me before men shall be denied before the Angels of God (*if we disown Him before men, He will disown us before Angels; these Passages declare to all that Jesus Christ, the poor Galilee Rabbi is in truth King of kings and Lord of lords!*).

THE UNPARDONABLE SIN

10 And whosoever shall speak a word against the Son of Man, it shall be forgiven him (*that is, if forgiveness is sought [I Jn. 1:9]*): but unto him who blasphemes against the Holy Spirit it shall not be forgiven (*this "blasphemy" cannot be committed by those who make no profession of the Lord; this means that only professors of religion commit this sin; there is no forgiveness for this sin, and in fact, the perpetrators will not even seek forgiveness*).

OPPOSITION

11 And when they bring you unto the Synagogues, and unto magistrates, and powers (*officials*), take you no thought how or what thing you shall answer,

or what you shall say *(simply means not to be full of anxiety; it does not mean that no preparation should be made, but only that trust must be placed in the Lord to provide the suitable answers)*:

12 For the Holy Spirit shall teach you in the same hour what you ought to say *(the Believer should always look to the Holy Spirit for leading and guidance).*

COVETOUSNESS

13 And one of the company said unto Him, Master, speak to my brother, that he divide the inheritance with me *(the insensibility and rudeness of the natural heart is here exhibited; this man interrupted the Lord, making a ridiculous request).*

14 And He said unto him, Man, who made Me a judge or a divider over you? *(Had the Lord interfered in Civil Government, He would have placed Himself in the power of His enemies; that was not His place. He dealt with souls, and directed men's attention to another life that lies beyond the grave.)*

15 And He said unto them, Take heed, and beware of covetousness *(the desire of wrong things, or attempting to obtain right things in the wrong way)*: for a man's life consisteth not in the abundance of the things which he possesseth *(most of the world tries to find life* in possessions; however, there is no "life" in these things; "Life" is found only in Christ [Jn. 14:6]).*

THE RICH FOOL

16 And He spoke a Parable unto them, saying, The ground of a certain rich man brought forth plentifully *(riches, if rightly acquired, should be thought of as blessings from God, and treated accordingly)*:

17 And he thought within himself, saying, What shall I do, because I have no room where to bestow my fruits? *(The "fruits" had been given to him by God, and should be used accordingly. But instead he will heap them up unto himself, which regrettably, is what most do.)*

18 And he said, This will I do: I will pull down my barns, and build greater; and there will I bestow all my fruits and my goods *(he was meant to use these "fruits" for the Glory of God, which was to take the Gospel to the world, but instead he did the opposite).*

19 And I will say to my soul, Soul, you have much goods laid up for many years; take your ease, eat, drink, *and* be merry *(the truth was his soul had nothing; in fact, he had provided for the flesh, but he hadn't provided for the soul; how many rich Christians, regrettably, fall into this same category?).*

20 But God said unto him *(what is God saying to me and you?)*, **You fool** *(the Lord is saying the same to all who follow in the train of covetousness)*, **this night your soul shall be required of you** *(sooner or later, "this night" will come)*: **then whose shall those things be, which you have provided?** *(He didn't give them to God, and now "these things" are to be squandered.)*

21 So *is* he who lays up treasure for himself, and is not rich toward God *(if riches come, they can either be used for self or God; which are they?)*.

WORRY

22 And He said unto His Disciples, Therefore I say unto you, Take no thought for your life, what you shall eat; neither for the body, what you shall put on *(don't worry about these things)*.

23 The life is more than meat, and the body *is more* than raiment *(in other words, take care of the spiritual, and the Lord will take care of the material and the physical)*.

24 Consider the ravens *(an unclean fowl)*: for they neither sow nor reap; which neither have storehouse nor barn; and God feeds them *(no matter how lowly they are)*: how much more are you better than the fowls? *(If the Lord feeds buzzards, don't you think that* He will feed us, that is, if we truly trust Him!)

25 And which of you with taking thought *(by worry)* can add to his stature one cubit? *(Of all creation, man alone is given to worry, fear, rebellion, sin, and unbelief.)*

26 If you then be not able to do that thing which is least *(if we cannot change by worry even the smallest things)*, why take you thought for the rest?

27 Consider the lilies how they grow: they toil not, they spin not *(whirling around in a state of mental confusion)*; and yet I say unto you, that Solomon in all his glory was not arrayed like one of these *(the lily abides by God's creation, and if the Believer will do the same, he will enjoy the provision of that creation)*.

28 If then God so clothe the grass, which is to day in the field, and tomorrow is cast into the oven *(assures us of the fact that God even provides for that which is of short duration)*; how much more *will He clothe* you, O ye of little faith? *(Speaks of Believers being eternal, and consequently, of untold value; to observe God's glorious creation and how He cares for it, and then to doubt His care for us is an insult to the Lord of the highest magnitude.)*

29 And seek not ye what you shall eat, or what you shall drink

(trust the Lord for these things), neither be ye of doubtful mind *(a distracted state of mind, wavering between hope and fear).*

30 For all these things do the nations of the world seek after *(speaks of the world's economy, and not God's economy)*: and your Father knows that you have need of these things *(means that we are now in His Kingdom; therefore, we are in His creative care).*

31 But rather seek ye the Kingdom of God *(tells us what we are to truly seek)*; and all these things shall be added unto you *(when we come to Christ, we leave the world's economy and enter into God's economy, which the latter is a never failing economy).*

32 Fear not *(not a suggestion, but rather a Command)*, little flock *(expressing the Great Shepherd's tender care for His sheep)*; for it is your Father's good pleasure to give you the Kingdom *(this is the Kingdom of God, thereby far greater than the kingdoms of this world).*

RICHES

33 Sell that you have, and give alms *(the idea is not to hoard and covet such as the world does; as God blesses us, we should give liberally and generously to His work; however, we must make certain that it is His work to which we are giving)*; provide yourselves bags which wax not old, a treasure in the Heavens that fails not, where no thief approaches, neither moth corrupts *(lay up treasures in Heaven).*

34 For where your treasure is, there will your heart be also *(treasure here will fail because of thieves and corruption; however, treasure there, referring to Heaven, will never fail; the "heart" is one's very being; the implication is that if there is no treasure in Heaven, the person will not go there when he dies; no matter his profession, his heart is where his treasure is).*

WATCHING SERVANTS

35 Let your loins be girded about, and *your* lights burning *(working and waiting should characterize the Christian);*

36 And you yourselves like unto men who wait for their Lord *(refers to the Rapture of the Church)*, when He will return from the wedding *(in essence, means to "return from preparations for the wedding")*; that when He comes and knocks, they may open unto Him immediately *(speaks of readiness at all times).*

37 Blessed *are* those servants, whom the Lord when He comes shall find watching *(proclaims those ready for the Rapture)*: verily I say unto you, that He *(the Lord)* shall gird Himself, and make them to sit down to meat,

and will come forth and serve them (*speaks of the Marriage Supper of the Lamb, with Jesus as the Host*).

38 And if He shall come in the second watch (*9 p.m. to 12 midnight*), or come in the third watch (*12 midnight till 3 p.m.*), and find *them* so, blessed are those servants (*the idea is that we are to be ready for His coming at all times*).

THE GOODMAN OF THE HOUSE

39 And this know, that if the goodman of the house had known what hour the thief would come, he would have watched, and not have suffered his house to be broken through (*if one is truly watching for the Lord, then at the same time he will be watching as it respects Satan that the evil one not destroy his "house"*).

40 Be you therefore ready also: for the Son of Man comes at an hour when you think not (*regrettably, most of the modern Church doesn't think the Rapture will take place; this means that it will definitely take place, and very soon!*).

THE UNFAITHFUL SERVANT

41 Then Peter said unto Him, Lord, do You speak this Parable unto us, or even to all? (*Peter is

thinking of an earthly kingdom about to begin, with the Twelve paramount in that Kingdom; in fact, Jesus is speaking to all.*)

42 And the Lord said, Who then is that faithful and wise steward (*some have claimed that the "steward" refers to Ministers only; however, the very nature of the word pertains not to position, but to responsibility, which applies to all*), whom *his* lord shall make ruler over His household, to give *them their* portion of meat in due season? (*It is the steward who is "faithful and wise."*)

43 Blessed *is* that servant (*stewards and servants are the same*), whom his Lord when He comes shall find so doing (*being faithful in what the Lord has called us to do, proclaiming the fact that such are also wise*).

44 Of a truth I say unto you, that He will make him ruler over all that He has (*a ruler in the Kingdom of God, which is yet to come, is the reward which the "faithful and wise" will seek, and not things of this world*).

45 But and if that servant say in his heart, my lord delays his coming (*regrettably, most of the modern Church falls into this category*); and shall begin to beat the menservants and maidens (*to not properly love God is to not properly love our neighbor as ourselves*), and to eat and drink, and to be drunken

(proclaims Believers who have
ceased to believe and have thereby
lost their way, which will ultimately
conclude in the loss of their souls;
as well, this completely refutes the
Unscriptural Doctrine of Unconditional Eternal Security);

46 The lord of that servant will
come in a day when he looks not
for *Him*, and at an hour when he
is not aware, and will cut him in
sunder, and will appoint him his
portion with the unbelievers (this
clearly points to former Believers
who have ceased to believe, and will
thereby die eternally lost [Heb. 6:4-
6; 10:23-29]).

47 And that servant (one who
had formerly been saved), which
knew his Lord's will, and prepared not *himself*, neither did
according to His *(God's)* will,
shall be beaten with many *stripes*
(degrees of punishment; people who
have known God, but have turned
from Him, will suffer greater punishment in eternity than will those
who had little opportunity, if any,
to know the Lord).

48 But he who knew not (did
not know the way of the Lord), and
did commit things worthy of
stripes, shall be beaten with few
stripes (fewer stripes than his counterpart who had every opportunity).
For unto whomsoever much is
given, of him shall be much required: and to whom men have
committed much, of him they will
ask the more (from these Scriptures, Catholics claim the doctrine
of purgatory; but purgatory is said
to be purgative and not punitive;
hence these verses do not apply).

OPPOSITION

49 I am come to send fire on
the earth (the Work of the Lord
will bring about persecution; regrettably, most of it will come from
that which refers to itself as the
"Church"); and what will I, if it
be already kindled? (This speaks
of the terrible opposition of the
Pharisees and Scribes against Him,
which would mark the position of
the apostate Church, even as it continues unto this hour.)

50 But I have a baptism to be
baptized with (speaks of the baptism of suffering, which would lead
to the Cross); and how am I straitened (pressed) till it be accomplished!

51 Suppose ye that I am come
to give peace on earth? I tell you,
No; but rather division (His object was to bring peace, but the
effect was fire and sword; this effect was caused through the corruption of man's nature, for the
presence of Christ brought to the
surface the evil of the human heart;
the depth of that evil and the hatred of the heart for God were
manifested in the Cross; regarding "division," Christ is not the

cause of division, but the occasion of it; division is caused by the rebellion of men against the Gospel [II Cor. 2:14-17]):

52 For from henceforth there shall be five in one house divided, three against two, and two against three *(because of Christ, the "division" in families has been obvious from that time until the present).*

53 The father shall be divided against the son, and the son against the father; the mother against the daughter, and the daughter against the mother; the mother-in-law against her daughter-in-law, and the daughter-in-law against her mother-in-law *(blood ties are not strong enough to assuage this hatred; it may be addressed toward the individual, but it is actually toward Christ).*

THE PHARISEES

54 And He said also to the people *(all the previous instruction had been given solely to His Disciples)*, When you see a cloud rise out of the west, straightway you say, There comes a shower; and so it is.

55 And when *you see* the south wind blow, you say, There will be heat; and it comes to pass.

56 You hypocrites, you can discern the face of the sky and of the earth; but how is it that you do not discern this time? *(In these statements, the Lord warns the people of Israel of approaching judgment. He bases this warning upon two factors, signs and their own moral consciousness.)*

57 Yea, and why even of yourselves judge you not what is right? *(He accuses them of willful blindness to the Prophecies of Daniel, which define the actual appearing of the Messiah. This blindness was more inexcusable because of their intelligence in observing the weather. They could observe that, but they could not observe Him, and He was much more obvious than the weather.)*

58 When you go with your adversary to the Magistrate *(in this case, the Holy Spirit)*, as you are in the way, give diligence that you may be delivered from Him *(in other words, get right with God)*; lest He *(the Holy Spirit)* hale you to the Judge *(God the Father)*, and the Judge deliver you to the officer *(the Angels)*, and the officer cast you into prison *(into Hell)*.

59 I tell you, you shall not depart thence, till you have paid the very last mite *(the condition of release laid down in this Verse is impossible to the sinner, for he could never discharge his indebtedness of a perfect obedience to God's Law; the only answer is Jesus; He paid all the price that we may go free; simple trust in Him dis-*

charges all our spiritual debt; but Israel refused Him, even as most of the world refuses Him; consequently, if He is not allowed to pay the debt, then the individual must pay the debt, which is eternal Hell, and in fact, can never be paid).

CHAPTER 13

REPENTANCE

THERE were present at that season (*probably referred to the previous Passover when this event took place*) some who told Him of the Galilaeans, whose blood Pilate had mingled with their sacrifices (*something happened at the Temple, which is not here explained, with Pilate dispatching soldiers to quell the disturbance; whatever it was, some had been killed while they were offering up Sacrifices at the great Altar immediately in front of the Temple; as a result, their "blood" had mingled with the blood of the Sacrifices*).

2 And Jesus answering said unto them, Do you suppose that these Galilaeans were sinners above all the Galilaeans, because they suffered such things? (*This is exactly what the religious leaders thought.*)

3 I tell you, No: but, except you repent, you shall all likewise perish (*this is a Message of som-*ber note; evidently, they had assumed in their minds that the judgments suffered by these people was because of their great sins; they reasoned that they themselves were much more righteous, and would not suffer such — Jesus tells them differently).

4 Or those eighteen, upon whom the tower in Siloam fell, and slew them, think ye that they were sinners above all men who dwelt in Jerusalem? (*It is said that the Jews looked on the catastrophe as a judgment on the workmen who perished because Pilate paid them out of Temple money. It had to do with the pool of Siloam located in Jerusalem.*)

5 I tell you, No: but, except you repent, you shall all likewise perish (*if Christ says something one time, it is of extreme significance; if it is said twice, as here, then it takes on a consequence of unprecedented proportions; the tragedy is in A.D. 70; they did perish when Titus, the Roman General, completely destroyed Jerusalem*).

THE BARREN FIG TREE

6 He spoke also this Parable (*refers to it being said immediately after the demand for repentance*); A certain *man* had a fig tree planted in his vineyard (*the "fig tree" is symbolic of Israel*); and he came and sought fruit

thereon, and found none *(Israel had brought forth no fruit for the Lord at all, despite all their religiosity; this should be a lesson for the modern Church).*

7 Then said He unto the Dresser of His Vineyard *(portrays the "owner" as God, and the "Dresser" as Jesus; the "Vineyard," i.e., "belonged to God"; as well, the Church also belongs to Him [Mat. 16:18]),* Behold, these three years I come seeking fruit on this fig tree, and find none *(illustrates the three years of the Lord's Ministry up to now; despite the greatest miracles the world had ever seen, and by far, Israel remained spiritually blind and dumb; there was no fruit):* cut it down; why cumbereth it the ground? *(This was a warning to Israel that if no fruit was forthcoming, judgment was imminent. But still, they did not heed or listen.)*

8 And He *(the Lord Jesus)* answering said unto Him *(God the Father),* Lord, let it alone this year also, till I shall dig about it, and dung it *(represents the last months of the last year of the Master's Ministry, for it is thought that His Ministry lasted for about three and a half years; this portrays the fact that Christ had pleaded with the Father for a little more time):*

9 And if it bear fruit, *well:* and if not, *then* after that You shall cut it down *(in fact, the last few months of His public Ministry were opposed more than ever; Israel did not bear any fruit, and in A.D. 70 they were "cut down").*

THE SABBATH

10 And He was teaching in one of the Synagogues on the Sabbath *(by now, most Synagogues were closed to Him; this evidently was one of the few which still allowed Him to Minister).*

11 And, behold, there was a woman which had a spirit of infirmity eighteen years *(means that a demon spirit had caused this sickness, which no doubt is the cause of much sickness presently, as well),* and was bowed together, and could in no wise lift up *herself (constituted, some think, a curvature of the spine; she was an example of what Satan has done to the whole of humanity; mankind in general, at least in one way or the other, has "a spirit of infirmity" brought on by Satan, and is "bound together"; as well, man in no wise, can "lift up himself").*

12 And when Jesus saw her, He called *her* to Him *(means that this miracle, like that of Nain, was unsolicited),* and said unto her, Woman, you are loosed from your infirmity *(a declaration of deliverance, needed by the entirety of the human race).*

13 And He laid *His* hands on

her: and immediately she was made straight, and glorified God *(this portrays the fact that this woman knew the Lord, which means that she was right with God, but yet was bound by this "spirit of infirmity," proving to us that such can happen, even now, and no doubt does; this doesn't mean the woman was demon possessed, for she wasn't; it does mean that she was "oppressed by demon spirits," which can happen to any believer [Acts 10:38]).*

14 And the ruler of the Synagogue answered with indignation, because that Jesus had healed on the Sabbath Day *(there was nothing in the Law of Moses that said a person could not be healed on the Sabbath Day; this was an invention purely of man),* and said unto the people, There are six days in which men ought to work: in them therefore come and be healed, and not on the Sabbath Day *(proclaims this self-righteous bigot rebuking Christ; religious evil is the highest form of evil!).*

15 The Lord then answered him, and said, *You* hypocrite *(proclaims righteous indignation, and rightly so! and let it be understood that Christ said this out loud in front of all the people),* does not each one of you on the Sabbath loose his ox or *his* ass from the stall, and lead *him* away to watering? *(He vividly draws a contrast between animals and human beings, and made these Pharisees look like fools, which they were!)*

16 And ought not this woman, being a daughter of Abraham *(proclaims Covenant relationship),* whom Satan has bound, lo, these eighteen years *(Satan is the cause of all bondage, be it physical, mental, financial, or spiritual),* be loosed from this bond on the Sabbath Day? *(This proclaims the deliverance of this woman as more important than keeping some silly man-made rule.)*

17 And when He had said these things, all His adversaries were ashamed *(they were ashamed, but not changed, for they would not repent):* and all the people rejoiced for all the glorious things that were done by Him *(but this incensed these hypocrites even more!).*

THE MUSTARD SEED

18 Then said He, Unto what is the Kingdom of God like? *(This is meant to portray what Satan and religious men have done to the Great Plan of God as given to Abraham and Moses, as well as the Prophets. It would apply presently to the Church as well!)* and whereunto shall I resemble it? *(This presents God Himself revealing His judgment about that which professed to be His Kingdom.)*

19 It is like a grain of mustard seed, which a man took, and cast into his garden *(has to do with the humble beginnings of the Kingdom of God on Earth, going as far back as Abel; in fact, its beginnings were so small that the Bible only records two conversions up to Noah, a period of some 1600 years);* and it grew, and waxed a great tree *(speaks of the nation of Israel growing into millions of people);* and the fowls of the air lodged in the branches of it *(proclaims demon spirits making their home in this Kingdom; hence, this explains the spiritual attitude of the Ruler of the Synagogue where Jesus healed the woman, as well as the entirety of the religious leadership of Israel).*

THE LEAVEN

20 And again He said, Whereunto shall I liken the Kingdom of God?

21 It is like leaven *(meant to portray rot and corruption),* which a woman took *(the word "woman" as used here represents wickedness, fallacy, uncleanness, unfaithfulness, and false religion)* and hid in three measures of meal *(meal symbolizes the Word of God),* till the whole was leavened *(portrays Israel during the time of Christ as being thoroughly corrupted, and as well, refers to the modern Church).*

MERE PROFESSION

22 And He went through the cities and villages, teaching, and journeying toward Jerusalem *(infers that He was no longer welcome in any Synagogue; these were the last few months, or even weeks, of the Master's Ministry).*

23 Then said one unto Him, Lord, are there few that be saved? *(This question was asked no doubt because of the statements just made by Christ concerning the "mustard tree" and the "three measures of meal.")* And He said unto them,

24 Strive to enter in at the strait gate *(automatically narrows the opening for admittance to Salvation; it is not that God refuses people, but people refuse God, or at least God's way):* for many, I say unto you, will seek to enter in, and shall not be able *(proclaims the fact of many trying to enter in by a way other than the Cross, which is impossible!).*

25 When once the master of the house is risen up, and has shut to the door *(pertains to death),* and you begin to stand without *(refers to great multitudes, who thought they were within, but in reality, were "without"; there is nothing worse than a false way of Salvation),* and to knock at the door, saying, Lord, Lord, open unto us *(a prayer that could have been answered at any time before death,* but cannot be answered after death); and He shall answer and say unto you, I know you not whence ye are (Christ will say to all who have rejected the Cross, "I know you not"; there could be no more chilling announcement):

26 Then shall you begin to say, We have eaten and drunk in Your presence, and You have taught in our streets (pertains to the Israel of Jesus' day, who were so familiar with Christ, but rejected Him; it pertains now, to the vast multitudes, who are religious but lost).

27 But He shall say, I tell you, I know you not whence you are (proclaims Jesus Christ Alone as the Judge); depart from Me, all ye workers of iniquity (anyone who rejects the Cross, is a "worker of iniquity," whether they understand such or not; rejecting the Cross puts one in a state of rebellion).

28 There shall be weeping and gnashing of teeth (places the professors of religion on the same par as the atheist and Christ-rejecters), when you shall see Abraham, and Isaac, and Jacob, and all the Prophets, in the Kingdom of God (presents these as being with the Lord), and you yourselves thrust out (to be shut out from Heaven is to be shut into Hell).

29 And they shall come from the east, and from the west, and from the north, and from the south (proclaims an end of any type of exclusivity of the Gospel as practiced by the Jews in Jesus' day; it will go to the world, which it did), and shall sit down in the Kingdom of God (predicts the Gentile Church having the same rights as the Jews, at least the Jews who are saved [Eph. 2:13-18]).

30 And, behold, there are last which shall be first (refers basically to the Church which is "last," i.e., after Israel, but will come in "first," because of being the first to accept Christ), and there are first which shall be last (refers to Israel which was first in line to receive Christ, but instead rejected Him, and will consequently, be the "last" to accept Him, which they will do at the Second Coming).

HEROD

31 The same day there came certain of the Pharisees, saying unto Him, Get Thee out, and depart hence: for Herod will kill You (proclaims a pretense on their part at friendliness and concern, when their only true objective was to stop Christ in His Work and silence His Preaching; this was the same Herod who murdered John the Baptist).

32 And He said unto them, You go, and tell that fox (literally reads in the Greek Text, "she-fox," which was the most contemptuous name ever given anyone by Jesus), Be-

hold, I cast out devils *(demons)*, and I do cures today and tomorrow *(speaks of His Personal Ministry, i.e., "today," and this Ministry that would continue through His followers, i.e., "tomorrow"; in this statement, He is actually declaring Herod to be of the devil, and that the day is coming, when such as he, will no longer rule among the sons of men; this awaits the Second Coming, but is closer now than ever)*, and the third *day* I shall be perfected *(predicts His Death, Resurrection, Ascension, and Exaltation)*.

33 Nevertheless I must walk today, and tomorrow, and the *day* following *(simply meant that He was on His way to Jerusalem, which would take some three days)*: for it cannot be that a Prophet perish out of Jerusalem *(a terrible indictment on that city! Satan has contested this city as no other, because the Lord chose Jerusalem wherein His Name would be placed [II Chron. 6:6]; at the Second Coming there will finally be peace)*.

JERUSALEM

34 O Jerusalem, Jerusalem *(said as a cry of anguish and of love, but yet with a deep foreboding!)*, which kills the Prophets, and stones them who are sent unto you *(this affected not only Israel, but the entirety of the world; the rejection of Christ by His Own people, caused the "times of the Gentiles" to be continued, with the Government of God concerning this planet delayed)*; how often would I have gathered thy children together, as a hen *does gather* her brood under her wings, and you would not! *(Proclaims the countless opportunities given for repentance, but to no avail.)*

35 Behold, your house is left unto you desolate *(in effect speaks of the Temple, which with the rejection of Him, will now be rejected by God)*: and verily I say unto you, You shall not see Me *(having rejected Christ, they would see "Caesar," which would prove to be a catastrophic choice)*, until *the time* come when you shall say, Blessed *is* He Who comes in the Name of the Lord *(quoted from Psalms 118:26; it speaks of the coming Kingdom Age, which will begin with the Second Coming; at that time Israel will then accept Christ as Lord, Saviour, and Messiah)*.

CHAPTER 14

SABBATH

AND it came to pass, as He went into the house of one of the chief Pharisees to eat bread on the Sabbath Day *(concerns a very influential Rabbi, or even possibly a member of the vaunted Sanhedrin)*, that they watched Him *(suggests that this man was not a guest, but was brought there purposely by the Pharisees in order to accuse Jesus of Sabbath-breaking if He healed him)*.

2 And, behold, there was a certain man before Him which had the dropsy *(has reference to a disease causing swelling due to excess water)*.

3 And Jesus answering spoke unto the Lawyers and Pharisees, saying *(proclaims Jesus instantly recognizing the situation, and immediately judging the hypocrisy, which broke the Sabbath when their own interests were involved)*, Is it lawful to heal on the Sabbath Day? *(He turns the trap on their own heads.)*

4 And they held their peace *(means they did not know what to say)*. And He *(Jesus)* took *him (means that He zeroed in on the man, so there would be absolutely no doubt what was being done)*, and healed him, and let him go *(means that his healing was instantaneous, and easily observable by all; in other words, even miraculously, the excess fluid in the man's body disappeared; He did not "let him go" until the effects of this healing were obvious to all)*;

5 And answered them, saying, Which of you shall have an ass or an ox fallen into a pit, and will not straightway *(immediately)* pull him out on the Sabbath Day? *(The Lord was not criticizing them for doing such a thing, but rather their hypocrisy in condemning Him for a greater and nobler act.)*

6 And they could not answer Him again to these things *(their silence was the better part of wisdom; to have answered it at all would have shown them up even worse than they already looked)*.

HUMILITY

7 And He put forth a Parable to those which were bidden *(refers to the invited guests of this feast, which is obvious were the wealthy class)*, when He marked how they chose out the chief rooms *(after the healing of the man was completed, the invited guests were called to be seated for the banquet; evidently, there was an obvious scurrying for the "chief seats")*; saying unto them,

8 When you are bidden of any *man* to a wedding, sit not down in the highest room *(actually strikes at the very heart of these hypocrites, which was a love of praise as well as place and position)*; lest a more honourable man than you be bidden of him *(positions the Believer in God's hands, instead of the hands of self-seeking)*;

9 And He who bade you and him come and say to you, Give this man place; and you begin

with shame to take the lowest room *(the one who seeks self-willed position will ultimately be forsaken by the Lord, or put down by the Lord; this is a "shame" that can be avoided by letting the Lord do the doing; in other words, the Believer is to refrain from self-promotion).*

10 But when you are bidden, go and sit down in the lowest room *(is the place and position that the truly God-called will always take; to do so lets the Lord chart the course);* that when He who bade you comes, He may say unto you, Friend, go up higher *(places the Lord in the position of Leader and Guide):* then shall you have worship in the presence of them who sit at meat with you *(the idea in all of this is many do not advance because they do not allow the Lord to do the advancing, but seek to do such themselves).*

11 For whosoever exalteth himself shall be abased *(this speaks of self-exaltation, which the Lord cannot tolerate; its end result will always be "abasement");* and he who humbles himself shall be exalted *(humility, which can only come by a proper understanding of the Cross, is the requirement for advancement by the Lord).*

THE WEDDING FEAST

12 Then said He also to him who bade Him *(who invited Him to the Feast; the previous Parable had been spoken to the guests, while this is spoken to the host),* When you make a dinner or a supper, call not your friends, nor your brethren, neither your kinsmen, nor your rich neighbours; lest they also bid you again, and a recompence be made to you *(it is not the activity that is condemned, but rather its purpose).*

13 But when you make a feast, call the poor, the maimed, the lame, the blind *(that is, if you really want to do something good for people):*

14 And you shall be blessed *(is a single promise given by God, with His Word standing as surety);* for they cannot recompense you *(the idea is if we really want to be blessed by the Lord, we are to do good things for people who, in turn, cannot do good things for us; that is Christlike, because He has done so much for us when we in turn could not do anything for Him):* for you shall be recompensed at the resurrection of the just *(proclaims the fact that God keeps the account of all things, and to be sure, every good thing, at least that which He labels as "good," will be rewarded at the Resurrection, i.e., "the Judgment Seat of Christ").*

15 And when one of them who sat at meat with Him heard these things, he said unto Him *(proclaims a total lack of knowledge*

about what the Lord was saying),
Blessed *is* he who shall eat bread
in the Kingdom of God *(by using
the word "blessed," and directing
it toward himself, this Pharisee
loudly trumpets his self-righteousness; the Lord's answer will be very
revealing, as we shall see).*

THE GREAT SUPPER

16 Then said He unto him, A
certain man made a great supper, and bade many:

17 And sent his servant at supper time to say to them who were
bidden, Come; for all things are
now ready *(was the Message of
both John the Baptist and Christ
concerning entrance into the Kingdom of God).*

18 And they all with one *consent* began to make excuse *(proclaimed Israel then, and regrettably most of the Church now!).* The
first said unto Him, I have bought
a piece of ground, and I must
needs go and see it: I pray you
have me excused *(the purchase of
the ground wasn't wrong, but the
self-interest was wrong).*

19 And another said, I have
bought five yoke of oxen, and I
go to prove them: I pray you have
me excused *(as the previous was
self-interest, this one was that of
self-will).*

20 And another said, I have
married a wife, and therefore I
cannot come *(this spoke of self-
love).*

21 So that servant came, and
showed his Lord these things *(Jesus
is the "servant," and the "Lord" is
the Heavenly Father).* Then the
Master of the house being angry
said to His servant *(proclaims the
Just anger of God over the rejection by Israel to the great invitation to enter the Kingdom of God),*
Go out quickly into the streets and
lanes of the city, and bring in
hither the poor, and the maimed,
and the halt, and the blind *(this is
an apt description of the Gentile
world, spiritually speaking! but out
of this came the Church).*

22 And the servant said, Lord,
it is done as You have commanded,
and yet there is room *(proclaims
the vastness of the Gospel Message;
what Jesus did at Calvary was sufficient to cleanse the stain of every
sin, of every human being in the
entirety of the world, and for all
time, at least for those who will
come; "yet, there is room").*

23 And the Lord said unto the
servant *(proclaims Jesus as being
the Light of the World),* Go out
into the highways and hedges *(the
Gospel must be taken to the entirety of the world),* and compel
them to come in *(there is a compelling force about the Gospel when
it is preached under the Anointing of the Spirit),* that My house
may be filled *(irrespective of the*

fall of Israel, the Plan of God will not be thwarted; His House will be filled!).

24 For I say unto you, That none of those men which were bidden *(and wouldn't come)* shall taste of My supper *(this is the answer of Christ to the statement of the man of Verse 15).*

DISCIPLESHIP

25 And there went great multitudes with Him *(proclaims Him having left the home of this Pharisee, and now continuing His journey toward Jerusalem):* and He turned, and said unto them *(He was anxious now, at the end, clearly to make it known to all these multitudes what serving Him really signified),*

26 If any *man* come to Me *(no exceptions),* and hate *(prefer)* not his father, and mother, and wife, and children, and brethren, and sisters, yea, and his own life also *(no affection, however strong, must be permitted to compete with or displace Christ),* he cannot be My Disciple *(once again, no exceptions!).*

27 And whosoever does not bear his Cross *(this doesn't speak of suffering as most think, but rather ever making the Cross of Christ the object of our Faith; we are saved and we are victorious not by suffering, although that some-* times will happen, or any other similar things, but rather by our Faith, but always with the Cross of Christ as the object of that Faith), and come after Me *(one can follow Christ only by Faith in what He has done for us at the Cross; He recognizes nothing else),* cannot be My Disciple *(the statement is emphatic! if it's not Faith in the Cross of Christ, then it's faith that God will not recognize, which means that such people are refused [I Cor. 1:17-18, 21, 23; 2:2; Rom. 6:3-14; 8:1-2, 11, 13; Gal. 6:14; Eph. 2:13-18; Col. 2:14-15]).*

COUNTING THE COST

28 For which of you, intending to build a tower *(is the example that Jesus will use in order to explain the Cross-bearing, Christ-following life),* sits not down first, and counts the cost *(this is not meant that we can earn Salvation, but rather that there will be a price to pay for the acceptance of Christ and the Cross; sadly, most of the opposition will come from the Church, exactly as it came from Israel in Jesus' day),* whether he have sufficient to finish *it? (This proclaims that the race must be finished, before it can be said to have been run. This completely refutes the Unscriptural Doctrine of Unconditional Eternal Security.)*

29 Lest haply, after he has laid

the foundation, and is not able to finish *it*, *(regrettably, millions do not finish this race, i.e., "tower")* all who behold *it* begin to mock Him *(in the spiritual sense which Jesus here intends, the far greater degree of mocking will come from Satan himself and his evil spirits)*,

30 Saying, This man began to build, and was not able to finish *(not only does the Lord monitor our progress constantly, but Satan and his cohorts do as well)*.

31 Or what king, going to make war against another king *(Jesus continues to use illustrations from everyday life which are familiar to all)*, sits not down first, and consults whether he be able with ten thousand to meet him who comes against him with twenty thousand? *(This type of invitation is a far cry from the majority of the invitations given today regarding the acceptance of Christ. Presently it is, "come to Christ and get rich!" But the Message of Jesus was and is, "come to Christ, and face the opposition of the world and of organized religion.")*

32 Or else, while the other is yet a great way off, he sends an ambassador, and desires conditions of peace *(unfortunately, the modern Church has made peace with Satan; this means they have forsaken Christ and the Cross; however, the "peace" they have is a false peace)*.

33 So likewise, whosoever he be of you who forsakes not all that he has, he cannot be My Disciple *(the key to victory regarding the world is the gathering of great resources to one's self; however, the key to this spiritual conflict is the very opposite, the "forsaking of all that one has"; this refers to a denial of dependence on self, and total trust being placed in Christ and what He has done for us at the Cross)*.

34 Salt *is* good *(salt seasons and preserves, and so does the true Believer)*: but if the salt have lost his savour *(refers to salt no longer being salty, and consequently, good for nothing)*, wherewith shall it be seasoned? *(This means that there is no alternative to Christ. He and the Word are the saltiness of the salt. If that be removed from Israel, which it was, then Israel was of no more use. It is the same presently with individuals.)*

35 It is neither fit for the land *(means that it can no longer serve its intended purpose, because it no longer has that which gives it purpose)*, nor yet for the dunghill; but men cast it out *(many things, if not used for their intended purpose, can be used elsewhere; however, the savorless Christian does not fall into that category, actually becoming totally worthless)*. He who has ears to hear, let him hear *(meaning that only those who*

have spiritual ears will hear what He is saying, and thereby understand it).

CHAPTER 15

MURMURING

THEN drew near unto Him all the Publicans and sinners for to hear Him *(Publicans were tax-collectors, and looked at as traitors by the religious hierarchy of Israel; consequently, they were afforded no opportunity for Salvation whatsoever; they were classified with the "sinners"; but these desired to hear Jesus, and rightly so!).*

2 And the Pharisees and Scribes murmured *(presents them conducting themselves exactly as their Fathers in the wilderness, which brought plagues then and will bring the greatest plague of all now, the destruction of themselves and their country [Ex. 16:7-12; Num. 14:27; 17:5-10]),* saying, This man receives sinners, and eats with them *(if it is to be noticed, Jesus gave the Pharisees and Scribes no place or position at all, and for the obvious reasons; He did give place and position to the Publicans and sinners, and for the purpose of saving their souls).*

THE LOST SHEEP

3 And He spoke this Parable unto them, saying,

4 What man of you, having an hundred sheep, if he lose one of them *(proclaims the value the Lord places on just one soul),* does not leave the ninety and nine in the wilderness, but go after that which is lost, until he find it? *(This does not mean the ninety-nine are left alone, but rather that every effort is to be made to retrieve the one that is lost.)*

5 And when he has found *it,* he lays *it* on his shoulders, rejoicing *(the Parable of the lost sheep is also found in Matthew 18:12; there it expresses the love that seeks; here, the joy that finds).*

6 And when he comes home, he calls together *his* friends and neighbours *(should have been the religious leaders of Israel),* saying unto them, Rejoice with me *(is really the only occasion of rejoicing in Heaven other than rejoicing over the Work and Person of the Lord Jesus Christ [Rev. 5:11-14]);* for I have found my sheep which was lost *(according to Heaven, the greatest statement that could ever be made).*

7 I say unto you, that likewise joy shall be in Heaven over one sinner who repents *(while other things are certainly important, still, nothing can match a soul being saved),* more than over ninety and nine just persons, which need no repentance *(this*

must properly be understood; the ninety-nine were rejoiced over when they were saved, exactly as this sinner is now rejoiced over).

THE LOST COIN

8 Either what woman having ten pieces of silver, if she lose one piece *(points to something of value; the sheep was valuable, and the coin as well is valuable; both are like unto a lost soul),* does not light a candle, and sweep the house, and seek diligently till she find *it? (The "Light" of the Gospel, which is Jesus Christ and Him Crucified, can alone find the lost soul. Let it be understood, we didn't find Christ, He found us!)*

9 And when she has found *it,* she calls *her* friends and *her* neighbours together, saying, Rejoice with me; for I have found the piece which I had lost.

10 Likewise, I say unto you, there is joy in the presence of the Angels of God over one sinner who repents *(this Verse is very similar to Verse 7, but there is an addition; this takes us to the very throne of God, placing even more emphasis on the significance of the Salvation of a lost soul).*

THE PRODIGAL SON

11 And he said, A certain man had two sons *(it is possible that the sheep and coin represent the Gentiles who were eagerly sought after because they were helpless; the Prodigal represents the Jew who was not so much sought after, but had to come of his own accord, as will happen at the Second Coming):*

12 And the younger of them said to *his* Father *(will be treated as the Jewish people even though it definitely can apply to any and all),* Father, give me the portion of goods that falls *to me (was typical of Roman Law at that time).* And he divided unto them *his* living *(by the use of the pronoun "them," it seems that a certain amount was guaranteed by law to each; the younger one took his and left).*

13 And not many days after the younger son gathered all together *(concerned an inheritance that he really had not earned, but that had been freely given to him because of his relationship with his Father),* and took his journey into a far country *(the son fell while yet in the Father's house; he fell at the moment he desired the Father's goods without the Father's company; and it only needed a few days to find him in the far country; backsliding begins in the heart, and very soon places the feet with the swine; sin will take you further than you want to go, and cost you more than you can afford to pay),* and there wasted his substance with riotous living *(this characterizes the world).*

14 And when he had spent all *(Satan does not replenish; he only uses and abuses)*, there arose a mighty famine in that land *(ultimately the "famine" will come to the wayward Believer)*; and he began to be in want *(represents the first time in his life he had ever experienced such a malady; he always had plenty at his Father's house, but now the "want" will only increase)*.

15 And he went and joined himself to a citizen of that country *(the word "joined" translates into forcing himself upon an unwilling employer; in short, he was reduced to begging)*; and he sent him into his fields to feed swine *(represented the most degrading occupation in which any Jew could ever engage)*.

16 And he would fain have filled his belly with the husks that the swine did eat *(means that he not only fed the swine, but was forced to eat their swill as well! from so high, he had fallen so low!)*: and no man gave unto him *(in the Devil's country nothing is given, everything must be bought; and bought at a terrible price)*.

17 And when he came to himself *(fully admitted to what he was and where he was)*, he said, How many hired servants of my Father's have bread enough and to spare *(many have bought Satan's lie that living for God deprives one of so many good things; nothing could be further from the truth)*, and I perish with hunger! *(Even though the illustration is addressing itself to the physical sense, the spiritual lesson it conveys pertains to the soul of man, which hungers for the Lord and can only be satisfied by the Lord, and never by worldly things.)*

18 I will arise and go to my Father *(the first step for the penitent soul; until that step is taken, the realization of need, nothing can be done; the word "arise" tells us that the journey to God is always upward, while that with Satan is always downward)*, and will say unto him, Father, I have sinned against Heaven, and before you *(the young man did not plead extenuating circumstances, lay the blame on others, or plead wrongs done to him; he placed the blame squarely where it belonged, upon himself; confession of wrongdoing is always demanded by God [I Jn. 1:9])*,

19 And am no more worthy to be called your son *(this presents the second requirement — admitted unworthiness)*: make me as one of your hired servants *(presents the position of humility, which is necessary; however, God has never received one as such; in other words, He will never make a "hired servant" out of a "son")*.

20 And he arose, and came to

his Father *(anyone can do this if he so desires [Rev. 22:17])*. But when he was yet a great way off, his Father saw him, *(the Father was earnestly looking for him)*, and had compassion *(the Lord always has compassion)*, and ran *(the only occasion given in the Bible of God running, and that is to welcome home a lost soul)*, and fell on his neck, and kissed him *(this is what awaits every sinner who comes to the Lord)*.

21 And the son said unto him, Father, I have sinned against Heaven, and in Your sight, and am no more worthy to be called Your son *(this is as far as the young man got; he had intended to continue as Verse 19 proclaims, "make me as one of Your hired servants"; but the Father interrupted him)*.

22 But the Father said to his servants, Bring forth the best robe, and put it on him *(Grace ran to kiss the Prodigal in his rags, and Righteousness hasted to dress him in its robes; the robe was that of II Cor. 5:21)*; and put a ring on his hand *(the "ring" addressed here was a seal or signet ring, which was much the same as a modern credit card; the ring bore the crest of his Father's house)*, and shoes on his feet *(this denotes ownership, for slaves did not wear shoes; all these things were provided for him and declared his sonship; servants were not thus arrayed and feasted)*:

23 And bring hither the fatted calf, and kill it; and let us eat, and be merry *(signifies that the young man is now back in Covenant and celebrated by feasting; the true "merriment" is never in alcoholic beverage or other things, but only in Christ)*:

24 For this my son was dead, and is alive again; he was lost, and is found *(so beautifully portrays the Salvation experience)*. And they began to be merry *(once again, Christ proclaims the joy of a lost soul coming home)*.

25 Now his elder son was in the field *(inasmuch as the Father did not bring the elder son in for the celebration, tells us that he knew the heart of the elder son; so he left him "in the field")*: and as he came and drew near to the house, he heard musick and dancing *(signifies the celebration then taking place respecting the return of the Prodigal)*.

26 And he called one of the servants *(proclaims the servant knowing more about the Father's business than even he, the elder son, knew)*, and asked what these things meant *(proclaims him not knowing that which was dearest to the Father's heart)*.

27 And he *(the servant)* said unto him, Your brother is come *(it is astounding that an event of this magnitude was happening and he knew nothing of it; the reason

will be obvious shortly); **and your father has killed the fatted calf, because he has received him safe and sound** *(proclaims the celebration that takes place in Heaven upon the Salvation of souls, and should as well take place on Earth among Believers; however, much of the time, the joy and the energy are spent on other pursuits)*.

28 And he was angry *(shows the true nature of the heart, and why he didn't know what was going on; the elder brother portrayed the Pharisee; he neither understood nor shared in the Father's joy)*, **and would not go in** *(proclaims rebellion! Jesus said of the Scribes and Pharisees that they would not go in themselves, and would try to stop all others from going in [Mat. 23:13])*: **therefore came his father out, and intreated him** *(proclaims Jesus making every appeal to the Scribes and Pharisees, but as here, to no avail; the patience He had shown with the Prodigal, He shows with the rebellious as well; such is our Heavenly Father!)*.

29 And he answering said to his father *(will be an answer totally different than that given by his younger brother)*, **Lo, these many years do I serve you** *(is said in the realm of merit; he thought this way because he had no relationship with the Father; consequently, it was just a job to him; he "served" for all the wrong reasons)*, **neither transgress-**

ed I at any time Your Commandment *(self-righteous, he claimed to have given a perfect obedience)*: **and yet you never gave me a kid, that I might make merry with my friends** *(he wanted "merriment" for all the wrong reasons; this shows that morally he was as much lost to his Father as his younger brother had been)*:

30 But as soon as this your son was come *(now portrays him disowning any relationship with his younger brother; self-righteousness always feels this way!)*, **which has devoured your living with harlots** *(the two phrases, "You never gave me a kid (a lamb,) for a celebration," and "Your son, who has devoured your living with harlots," showed the hatred of his heart to his Father and to his brother)*, **you have killed for him the fatted calf** *(is a proclamation of self-righteousness, which cannot conceive of such a thing; instead of "making merry," the younger brother should be punished, and severely, or so the elder brother thought; not understanding Grace, this is the attitude, regrettably, of most modern Christians)*.

31 And he said unto him, Son, you are ever with me, and all that I have is yours *(in effect says that he really had not partaken of these riches, even though they were his for the asking; he had tried to earn them, which was unnecessary, and actually unacceptable; he missed*

the entirety of the point of what
Salvation really was).

32 It was meet (necessary) that
we should make merry, and be
glad: for this your brother was
dead (dead in trespasses and sins),
and is alive again (has come to
Christ); and was lost, and is found
(the death of the sinless calf was a
necessity ere the feast could be enjoyed; had the Prodigal refused this
raiment and claimed the right to
enter the Father's house in his rags
and nakedness, he, like Cain, would
have been rejected; but his was true
repentance, and so it accepted these
gifts assuring purity, perpetuity, position, and provision).

CHAPTER 16

THE UNJUST STEWARD

AND He said also unto His Disciples (someone has said that
Chapter 15 was addressed to the
Pharisees in the hearing of the Disciples; Chapter 16 to the Disciples
in the hearing of the Pharisees),
There was a certain rich man,
which had a steward (the moral
of the Parable seems to be found
in Verse 8); and the same was accused unto him that he had wasted his goods (the man had wasted
his employer's goods).

2 And He called him, and said
unto him, How is it that I hear
this of You? (That you have wasted

my goods.) give an account of your
stewardship (will be the very words
or similar which will be spoken to
every Believer at the Judgment Seat
of Christ); for you may be no longer steward (how many Believers
are wasting that which the Lord has
placed into their hands; in other
words, they are not attending very
well to the Lord's business).

3 Then the steward said within
himself, What shall I do? (This
proclaims him beginning to make
plans.) for my lord takes away
from me the stewardship: I cannot dig (has reference to digging
out stores of goods from stockpiles
to replace what was lost; the idea
is the goods which he was charged
with have been wasted, and there
is no more stockpile); to beg I am
ashamed (many Believers will be
ashamed at the Judgment Seat of
Christ).

4 I am resolved what to do (the
beginning of a plan or scheme to
provide for himself), that, when I
am put out of the stewardship,
they may receive me into their
houses (he will ingratiate himself
to those who owe money to his
former Master).

5 So he called every one of
his lord's debtors unto him (the
beginning of his scheme), and
said unto the first, How much
do you owe unto my lord? (It is
typical in one way or the other of
that which is happening all over

the world, each and every day, and millions of times over. The scheming and planning are the ordinary course of events in the world, and as Paul said, "They do it to obtain a corruptible crown" [I Cor. 9:25].)

6 And he said, An hundred measures of oil (this "steward" actually had the right, as given to him by his employer, to set the price of certain commodities; however, as we see here, he misused that right in order to ingratiate himself with these debtors). And he said unto him, Take your bill, and sit down quickly, and write fifty (he was wiping out half of their debt).

7 Then said he to another, And how much do you owe? And he said, An hundred measures of wheat. And he said unto him, Take your bill, and write fourscore (he reduced his by twenty measures).

8 And the lord (not the Lord of Glory, but rather his employer) commended the unjust steward, because he had done wisely (exclaimed as to his cleverness, inasmuch as his dishonesty could not now be proven): for the children of this world are in their generation wiser than the children of light (this closing statement is the entirety of the moral of this Parable as given by Christ; the "children of the world" are "wiser" because the diligence given, crooked or otherwise, is the very best effort they have; but all too often, the "children of light," even though possessing that which is far and away more important than anything the world has, still, most of the time pay precious little attention or diligence to the all important task of living for God).

GOD AND MAMMON

9 And I say unto you, Make to yourselves friends of the mammon of unrighteousness (simply means that Believers must learn to be faithful with money regarding others and the work of God; money is here called the "mammon of unrighteousness" simply because the love of such is the root of all forms of evil [I Tim. 6:10]); that, when ye fail (when you die), they (the Angels) may receive you into everlasting habitations (Heaven).

10 He who is faithful in that which is least is faithful also in much (implies that if a Believer is faithful with the money that God gives him, he will more than likely be faithful in all other aspects of his Christian endeavor): and he who is unjust in the least is unjust also in much (if the Believer will not allow the Lord to have first place respecting money, he will be unjust as well in spiritual matters).

11 If therefore you have not been faithful in the unrighteous mammon (*this tells us that the Lord judges the faithfulness of a Believer, at least in part, as to how he handles money, which our Lord refers to as "the mammon of unrighteousness"*), who will commit to your trust the true *riches*? (*If you can't handle the "least" money, than how can you handle the "much" — spiritual riches?*)

12 And if ye have not been faithful in that which is another man's (*strikes at our practical everyday living*), who shall give you that which is your own? (*This tells us that the Lord will not bless anyone who does not discharge their responsibilities as they should.*)

13 No servant can serve two masters (*we cannot serve the Lord and ourselves*): for either he will hate the one, and love the other; or else he will hold to the one, and despise the other (*mostly Jesus dealt with the Pharisees; here, He addresses the Publicans; they, plus every Believer, must be very careful about money, or anything for that matter that's not truly of the Lord*). Ye cannot serve God and mammon (*places God and money side by side, for this is what "mammon" means, at least in this case; money is not demeaned here by Christ; but the manner in which we hold or handle it; neither is the amount in question, but rather our faithfulness*).

14 And the Pharisees also (*His statements applied to the Pharisees, as well as the Publicans*), who were covetous, heard all these things: and they derided Him (*Israel had come to believe that riches equaled Godliness, and poverty equaled the curse of God; so they sneered at Christ, actually making fun of Him*).

15 And He said unto them, You are they which justify yourselves before men (*means they tried to do things to make themselves look Holy in the sight of men*); but God knows your hearts (*that's a powerful phrase, "God knows," and to be sure He does!*): for that which is highly esteemed among men is abomination in the sight of God (*religious works are highly esteemed among men, hence the adulation of the Catholic Nun called "Mother Teresa"; if men attempt to justify themselves with works, instead of by Faith in Christ and the Cross, God refers to it as "abomination"*).

16 The Law and the Prophets *were* until John (*actually means, "as far as John," which included that Prophet; in other words, John ministered unto the Law, but was the last Prophet of that era*): since that time the *Kingdom* of God is preached (*the "Kingdom of God" is obtained by being "born-again," which comes about by Faith in

Christ, and what Christ has done at the Cross), and every man presses into it ("every man" is welcome into the New Covenant).

17 And it is easier for Heaven and earth to pass, than one tittle of the Law to fail *(Jesus would fulfill the Law, and in every capacity, and in fact would be the only One Who ever did because He was the only One Who could).*

18 Whosoever puts away his wife, and marries another, commits adultery *(Jesus addresses the subject here, even though it seems out of place, because the Pharisees treated divorce lightly and were secretly covetous and immoral; this is why, when exposed by the Lord, they derided Him)*: and whosoever marries her that is put away from her husband commits adultery *(the Pharisees taught that if one was divorced, irrespective that they had no Scripture as grounds to do so, that they were then free to marry or to be married to such; Jesus refutes this, and does so pointedly).*

19 There was a certain rich man, which was clothed in purple and fine linen, and fared sumptuously every day *(the Jews of Jesus' day concluded that riches were the favor of God, and poverty was the curse of God; therefore, this illustration given by Christ ripped to shreds their false doctrine):*

20 And there was a certain beggar named Lazarus *(many claim this is a Parable not to be taken literally; however, as it is to be noticed, Jesus uses names in this illustration, meaning that it's not a Parable but actually, something that really happened; consequently, it is chilling indeed!),* which was laid at his gate, full of sores *(the rich man saw Lazarus constantly, but offered no help whatsoever; as stated, such concluded ones like Lazarus to be cursed of God, and to help such would be thwarting the Plan of God; how so much the Word of God is twisted by so many),*

21 And desiring to be fed with the crumbs which fell from the rich man's table *(probably means that this rich man felt very good with himself in even allowing "crumbs" to be given to this beggar):* moreover the dogs came and licked his sores *(proclaims the fact that this man was not only poverty stricken, but as well was sick; he would not fit the mold of the modern prosperity gospel, which in fact is no gospel at all; but he definitely did fit God's mold; we should consider all of this very carefully).*

22 And it came to pass, that the beggar died *(more than likely, no-one cared, but the Lord cared, as we shall see),* and was carried by the Angels into Abraham's bosom *(Paradise; where all Believers went before the Cross; as well, Jesus also tells us here that whenever a Believer dies, his soul and*

spirit are escorted by Angels into the presence of God): the rich man also died, and was buried (no Angels carried him away, for he died eternally lost; his being rich did not carry any weight as it regards his soul's Salvation);

23 And in Hell he lift up his eyes (Jesus here plainly proclaims the doctrine of eternal Hell; as well, He also proclaims the fact that the soul and the spirit immediately go to Heaven or Hell at the time of death, and that the soul and the spirit are totally conscious), being in torments (to say the least, Hell is not a pleasant place, and as stated, it is eternal), and sees Abraham afar off, and Lazarus in his bosom (all Believers before the Cross expressed faith in the Revelation given to Abraham by God as it regards Redemption, and in a sense, it is the same presently [Rom. 4:16]).

24 And he cried and said, father Abraham, have mercy on me (there are no unbelievers in Hell, nor is there any Salvation there; the rich man repented, but too late), and send Lazarus (he had no concern for Lazarus back on Earth, but his conscience now recalls many things, but too late), that he may dip the tip of his finger in water (evidently there is no water there), and cool my tongue; for I am tormented in this flame (the Bible teaches that the fires of Hell are literal; Jesus said so!).

25 But Abraham said, Son, remember that you in your lifetime received your good things (in no way does it mean that this was the cause of him being lost; it merely means that he was treated very well, but showed no thankfulness for his blessings), and likewise Lazarus evil things (the rich man didn't allow his blessings to bring him to the Lord, and Lazarus didn't allow his poverty to keep him from the Lord): but now he is comforted (because he had accepted the Lord), and you are tormented (the word "now" is that which is all-important; it speaks of the time after death; will it be one of "comfort" or "torment"?).

26 And beside all this, between us and you there is a great gulf fixed (this is in the heart of the Earth [Mat. 12:40]; before the Cross, even though all who went to Paradise were comforted, they were still captives of Satan, with him hoping that ultimately he would get them over into the burning pit [Eph. 4:8-9]; this means that when Believers died before the Cross, due to the fact that the blood of bulls and goats could not take away sins, the sin debt remained, and Satan still had a claim on them; so all those in Paradise were awaiting the Cross, which would deliver them): so that they which would pass from hence to you

cannot *(proclaims the fact that all opportunities for Salvation are on this side of the grave; this means that the Catholic doctrine of Purgatory is a "fool's hope"; there is no such place)*; neither can they pass to us, that *would come* from thence *(but yet it was possible for those in Hell to look over and see those in Paradise, and it seems to speak to them; that place, due to the Cross, is now empty, with all liberated by Christ after the price was paid [Eph. 4:8-9])*.

27 Then he said, I pray thee therefore, father, that you would send him *(send Lazarus)* to my father's house *(this is the only example of praying to a dead Saint in Scripture; let those who do so remember that prayer to all other dead Saints will avail just as much as this prayer did — nothing)*:

28 For I have five brethren; that he may testify unto them *(these statements proclaim the fact that this man had a working knowledge of God and more than likely even professed Salvation before his death; but he wasn't saved!)*, lest they also come into this place of torment *(he did not ask this grace for himself, for he knew that he was eternally entombed; it is easy to step into Hell, but impossible to step out)*.

29 Abraham said unto him, They have Moses and the Prophets; let them hear them *(doesn't mean that this event happened during the time of Moses, but that Abraham is referring to the Word of God; this tells us that at least a part of the Old Testament had then been written)*.

30 And he said, Nay, father Abraham: but if one went unto them from the dead, they will repent *(the Scriptures contain all that is necessary to Salvation; a returned spirit could add nothing to them; and a man who will not listen to the Bible would not listen to a multitude, if raised from the dead; in fact, a few days later, the Lord did raise a man named Lazarus from the grave, and the Pharisees went about to put him to death)*.

31 And he said unto him, If they hear not Moses and the *Prophets*, neither will they be persuaded, though one rose from the dead *(this illustration as given by Christ, actually happened and in fact presents a startling portrayal of life after death; we learn from this, and in stark reality, that the only thing that really matters in life is being right with God; there is a Heaven and there is a Hell, and every soul who has ever lived has gone or is going to one or the other; the only way to make Heaven one's eternal Home is to accept Christ; He Alone is the Door; everything else leads one to Hell, exactly as the rich man found out,*

and to his eternal dismay).

CHAPTER 17

FORGIVENESS AND FAITH

THEN said He unto the Disciples *(presents the teaching here given by Christ as immediately following the illustration given concerning the rich man in Hell)*, It is impossible but that offences will come *(refers to the fact of opposition against the Child of God, and from whom it will mostly come)*: but woe unto him, through whom they come! *(Strangely enough, most opposition will come from the religious sector! There is an offence to the Cross! And those who reject the Cross, which are the far greater majority, will oppose those who accept the Cross. To reject the Cross is to reject Christ! Judgment is guaranteed to follow such action.)*

2 It were better for him that a millstone were hanged about his neck, and he cast into the sea *(pronounces the judgment which awaits Christ-rejecters)*, than that he should offend one of these little ones *("little ones" mentioned here have nothing to do with children, but rather Believers who are clothed with humility, consequently allowing the Lord to defend them; they are "little" in their own eyes, judged to be the same by the offenders,* but held very dear by the Lord and watched over minutely by Him).

3 Take heed to yourselves *(speaking directly to His Disciples, warning them that this spirit of offence can come on anyone unless they are careful)*: If your brother trespass against you, rebuke him *(has to do with Matthew 18:15-17)*; and if he repent, forgive him.

4 And if he trespass against you seven times in a day, and seven times in a day turn again to you, saying, I repent; you shall forgive him *(while the untiring, fearless rebukers of all sin, at the same time, we must never tire of exercising forgiveness the moment the offender is sorry)*.

5 And the Apostles said unto the Lord, Increase our faith *(this is the request of many; however, the answer the Lord will give is extremely interesting)*.

6 And the Lord said, If you had faith as a grain of mustard seed *(a very small seed, telling us in effect that it's not really the amount of faith, but rather the correct object of faith; the correct object is the Cross [I Cor. 1:18])*, you might say unto this sycamine tree, Be thou plucked up by the root, and be thou planted in the sea; and it should obey you *(the removal of trees and mountains were proverbial figures of*

speech among the Jews at that time, expressing the overcoming of great difficulties).

THE FAITHFUL SERVANT

7 But which of you, having a servant plowing or feeding cattle, will say unto him by and by *(immediately)*, when he is come from the field, Go and sit down to meat?

8 And will not rather say unto him, Make ready wherewith I may sup, and gird yourself, and serve me, till I have eaten and drank; and afterward you shall eat and drink? *(A faithful servant will attend to his duties first, and himself second.)*

9 Does he thank that servant because he did the things that were commanded him? I trow not *(I think not!).*

10 So likewise, when you shall have done all those things which are commanded you, say, We are unprofitable servants: we have done that which was our duty to do *(the Lord, in essence, says that having fulfilled all these conditions, which were their duty to do, they would be no better than unprofitable servants; this is a fatal blow to the doctrine of Salvation by works; the Disciple is to say, "I am an unprofitable servant"; the Master will then say, "well done, good and faithful servant" [Mat. 25:21]).*

THE LEPERS

11 And it came to pass, as He went to Jerusalem, that He passed through the midst of *(between)* Samaria and Galilee *(the Lord was traveling eastward to the Jordan, which He would cross, and travel south toward Jerusalem on the eastward side, which was the longer route).*

12 And as He entered into a certain village, there met Him ten men who were lepers, which stood afar off *(Levitical Law stated that they had to remain approximately one hundred feet or so from other people [Lev. 13:21, 45-46; 14:2]):*

13 And they lifted up *their* voices *(they were not allowed to come closer to Christ, or anyone else for that matter, so they had to shout to make themselves heard),* and said, Jesus, Master, have mercy on us *(they had no doubt heard many wonderful things about Jesus, and now, miracle of miracles, he was standing not too far from them).*

14 And when He saw *them*, He said unto them *(they got His attention)*, Go show yourselves unto the Priests *(this command assured cleansing; for only a cleansed leper was to show himself to the Priests).* And it came to pass, that as they went, they were cleansed *(they knew they were unclean; but they*

believed Christ's Word, went away with the conviction that it was true, and were immediately healed on the way).

15 And one of them, when He saw that He was healed (concerned the Samaritan), turned back, and with a loud voice glorified God (every Believer should praise the Lord continually),

16 And fell down on his face at His feet, giving Him thanks: and he was a Samaritan (what Jesus did for him destroyed his national faith in Mount Gerizim, and rightly so, and pulled him into the right way [Jn. 4:22]).

17 And Jesus answering said, Were there not ten cleansed? but where are the nine? (The "nine" were indicative of most of Israel of that particular time, unthankful!)

18 There are not found who returned to give Glory to God, save this stranger (as well, the "stranger" who had been healed would be indicative of the Gentile Church, which was shortly to be brought about).

19 And He said unto him, Arise, go your way (Jesus lifts people up): your faith has made you whole (proclaims the fact that not only was he healed, but saved as well; all of them showed Faith by asking Christ for healing, which they received; however, only one, it seems, was given eternal life

because He Glorified God).

THE KINGDOM OF GOD

20 And when He was demanded of the Pharisees, when the Kingdom of God should come (the Lord, in effect, answered that the Kingdom of God was at that moment in their midst, for He was the Kingdom of God), He answered them and said, The Kingdom of God cometh not with observation (the Jews claimed that when the Messiah came, He would overthrow Rome, etc.; Jesus is telling them that their "observations" are wrong):

21 Neither shall they say, Lo here! or, lo there! (He is saying that all these outward signs they were talking about are not Scriptural, and really have no bearing on the Kingdom of God.) for, behold, the Kingdom of God is within you (would have been better translated, "the Kingdom of God is within your midst," for the Kingdom is Jesus, but Israel would not recognize Him; the "born-again" experience brings Christ into the heart, and thereby places the "Kingdom of God within the person").

SECOND COMING

22 And He said unto the Disciples, The days will come, when

you shall desire to see one of the days of the Son of Man, and you shall not see It *(after the day of Pentecost, all the followers of Christ, and especially the Disciples, would have a far greater understanding of all the things that Jesus said and did, and would love to have the opportunity to relive those former days)*.

23 And they shall say to you, See here; or, see there: go not after *them*, nor follow *them (He is speaking of the Second Coming)*.

24 For as the lightning, that lighteneth out of the one *part* under Heaven, shineth unto the other *part* under Heaven; so shall also the Son of Man be in His day *(in other words, He is saying that when He really does come back, there will be such a display of Heavenly Glory that no one will have to ask the question, "is it really Him?"; it will be overly obvious to all that it is He)*.

25 But first must He suffer many things, and be rejected of this generation *(the Glories of that coming day will have a relation to and will be the result of His Atoning Sufferings at Calvary)*.

WARNINGS

26 And as it was in the days of Noah, so shall it be also in the days of the Son of Man *(means that the world, at the time of the Second Coming, will be as indif-ferent and corrupt as in the days of Noah and Lot for that matter)*.

27 They did eat, they drank, they married wives, they were given in marriage *(proclaims business as usual; in other words, as the world did not expect the predictions of Noah to come to pass respecting the flood, neither will the world expect the Second Coming, which is proclaimed in the Bible)*, until the day that Noah entered into the ark *(means that up to that very moment they laughed at his predictions; they saw him enter the ark, and it was met with derision)*, and the flood came, and destroyed them all *(their negative response in no way altered the judgment that soon came)*.

28 Likewise also as it was in the days of Lot; they did eat, they drank, they bought, they sold, they planted, they built *(pertains to the destruction of Sodom and Gomorrah)*;

29 But the same day that Lot went out of Sodom it rained fire and brimstone from Heaven, and destroyed *them* all *(the Judgment did not come, however, until the Righteous concerning both Noah and Lot had been taken out; even though all of this pertains to the Second Coming, it could also pertain to the Rapture of the Church, which will take out the Believers and usher in tremendous Judgment as recorded in Revelation, Chapters 6-19)*.

30 Even thus shall it be in the day when the Son of Man is revealed *(this is the Second Coming)*.

31 In that day *(this definitely refers to the Second Coming, and not the Rapture)*, he which shall be upon the housetop, and his stuff in the house, let him not come down to take it away *(in the Middle East, almost all of the houses have flat roofs, and in Jesus' day, especially during the summer months, many would sleep on top of the house, even as some still do presently)*: and he who is in the field, let him likewise not return back *(these particular statements have nothing to do with the Rapture, inasmuch as that will be sudden, "in the twinkling of an eye"; Verses 31 through 37 pertain to the mobilization of Israel against the Antichrist; Ezekiel describes it in Chapters 38 and 39; that mobilization will be hurried)*.

32 Remember Lot's wife *(the emphasis is if Israel hesitates at that particular time, they will be destroyed exactly as was Lot's wife; incidentally, in this one Passage, Jesus proclaims the historical fact of Lot's wife being turned to salt [Gen. 19:26])*.

33 Whosoever shall seek to save his life shall lose it *(refers to the Jews at that time who will think fleeing in other directions will preserve them, but in reality it will have the opposite effect)*; and whosoever shall lose his life shall preserve it *(refers to those who go forward to the battle (Battle of Armageddon), and as a result, will have the protection of the Lord [Zech. 12:8])*.

34 I tell you, in that night there shall be two *men* in one bed; the one shall be taken, and the other shall be left.

35 Two *women* shall be grinding together *(grinding at the mill)*; the one shall be taken, and the other left.

36 Two *men* shall be in the field; the one shall be taken, and the other left *(once again, all of this speaks of the mobilization of Israel at the Battle of Armageddon; it does not speak of the Rapture as many have been led to believe)*.

37 And they answered and said unto Him, Where, Lord? *(They did not know where or what the Lord was talking about, at least at that time.)* And He said unto them, Wheresoever the body *is*, thither will the eagles be gathered together *(it refers directly to the Battle of Armageddon, and once again not the Rapture as some think! [Ezek. 39:17])*.

CHAPTER 18

PERSEVERING PRAYER

AND He spoke a Parable unto them *to this end*, that men

ought always to pray (without a proper prayer life, Faith cannot be truly exercised, irrespective to how much it is claimed) and not to faint (don't lose heart; believe and keep praying);

2 Saying, There was in a city a judge, which feared not God, neither regarded man (but yet a poor widow woman, without influence, was able to bend him to her will):

3 And there was a widow in that city; and she came unto him, saying, Avenge me of my adversary (do me justice).

4 And he would not for a while (at the beginning, he paid her no mind): but afterward he said within himself, Though I fear not God, nor regard man;

5 Yet because this widow troubles me, I will avenge her, lest by her continual coming she weary me (means that every time the judge looked up she was there, and he gave her that for which she asked!).

6 And the Lord said, Hear what the unjust judge says (if such a judge will in the end listen to the petition of a supplicant for whom he cares nothing, will not God surely listen to the repeated prayer of someone whom He loves with a deep, enduring love?).

7 And shall not God avenge His Own elect (especially considering that God is not unjust, as was that judge), which cry day and night unto Him (keep on praying),

though He bear long with them? (Even though the judge delayed for selfish indifference, God at times delays for an all-wise purpose, depending on what is asked, or whether one has faith or not.)

8 I tell you that He will avenge them speedily (is the assurance that God will answer prayer, and in comparison to man, He will answer "speedily"). Nevertheless when the Son of Man comes, shall He find faith on the earth? (Considering that the Church has been taken out of the world, at the Second Coming there won't be very much Faith in the world; nevertheless, this will not stop or hinder the Second Coming.)

THE PHARISEE AND THE PUBLICAN

9 And He spoke this Parable unto certain which trusted in themselves (self-righteousness) that they were righteous, and despised others (the twin curse of self-righteousness):

10 Two men went up into the Temple to pray (only one would be heard by God, who would probably be the very opposite of the one most men would choose); the one a Pharisee (a fundamentalist, who claimed to believe all the Bible), and the other a Publican (a tax-collector, referred to by Israel as traitors, and thereby beyond Sal-

vation).

11 The Pharisee stood and prayed thus with himself (meaning that his Prayer got no further than himself; even though it was directed toward God, it was not heard by God), God, I thank You, that I am not as other men are, extortioners, unjust, adulterers, or even as this Publican (he put himself on a much higher plane than the Publican; he actually asked the Lord for nothing, and that's exactly what he received; as far as he was concerned, he had everything, "have need of nothing" [Rev. 3:17]).

12 I fast twice in the week, I give tithes of all that I possess (Verse 11 portrays relative righteousness and this Verse portrays works righteousness, both rejected by the Lord).

13 And the Publican, standing afar off (means he did not feel free to come close to the Temple appointments as had the Pharisee), would not lift up so much as his eyes unto Heaven (refers to him realizing and admitting just how unclean he actually was), but smote upon his breast, saying, God be merciful to me a sinner (brought instant results because the plea was based upon Atonement and not on self-righteousness; every afternoon at 3 o'clock the evening Lamb was offered up as a propitiation for the sins of that day; the Publican pleaded forgiveness and acceptance because of the merit of that atoning blood; it foreshadowed the Atoning death of the Lamb of God, Who was Himself the propitiation, i.e., the "Mercy-Seat").

14 I tell you, this man went down to his house justified (declared a righteous man; there are no degrees in justification; one is either justified totally, or not justified at all!) rather than the other (the Pharisee who depended on his self-righteousness was not justified, and therefore, lost): for every one who exalts himself shall be abased (rejected); and he who humbles himself shall be exalted (proclaims the basis for acceptance by God).

LITTLE CHILDREN

15 And they brought unto Him also infants, that He would touch them: but when His Disciples saw it, they rebuked them (erroneously thinking that Jesus should not be bothered with such).

16 But Jesus called them unto Him (called the parents with their infants), and said, Suffer little children to come unto Me, and forbid them not: for of such is the Kingdom of God (Jesus is presenting an object lesson; a little child is completely dependent on its parents or guardians; likewise, we are to be totally dependent in the same manner on the Lord).

17 Verily I say unto you, Who-

soever shall not receive the Kingdom of God as a little child shall in no wise enter therein *(the greatest hindrance to entering the "Kingdom of God" is the refusal of many to humble themselves before God; it is the pride factor, which is the opposite of little children).*

THE RICH YOUNG RULER

18 And a certain ruler asked Him, saying, Good Master, what shall I do to inherit eternal life? *(Inasmuch as this is detailed three times [Mat. 19:16; Mk. 10:17; Lk. 18:18] tells us that the Holy Spirit strongly desires that the message be heeded. In the first place, eternal life cannot be inherited, it being a free gift from God upon Faith in Christ and His Atoning Work.)*

19 And Jesus said unto him, Why do you call Me good? *(He really did not conclude Jesus to be the Messiah, which is what the word "good" denotes.)* none is good, save One, that is, God *(this destroyed the entire myth of his belief; actually he thought of himself as "good").*

20 You know the Commandments, Do not commit adultery, Do not kill, Do not steal, Do not bear false witness, Honour your father and your mother *(why did Jesus take this tact, knowing that no one could keep all the Com-*mandments all the time? only Christ did that! Jesus addressed him in this fashion in order to show him that his ground for Salvation was faulty; if these things had saved him, why was he still unsure?).*

21 And he said, All these have I kept from my youth up *(he was serving as his own judge, which is always a sure sign of self-righteousness; and yet, Jesus, as recorded by Mark, "loved him," denoting a feeling beyond the normal love that God has for all men).*

22 Now when Jesus heard these things, He said unto him, Yet you lack one thing *(Jesus will now hit at the heart of the matter)*: sell all that you have, and distribute unto the poor, and you shall have treasure in Heaven: and come, follow Me *(this statement by Christ is not meant to institute a charity program for the poor; as needful as they may be, they are not the subjects of this conversation; this man's material possessions stood in-between him and obeying the Lord; consequently they proved a hindrance, and whatever they may have been had to be laid aside; that is, if he was to have eternal life).*

23 And when he heard this, he was very sorrowful: for he was very rich *(proclaims the heart attitude of multiple millions; they want the Lord, but they do not desire to pay the price the Lord demands; that price is the forsaking*

of all else in favor of Christ).

WARNING

24 And when Jesus saw that he was very sorrowful, he said, How hardly shall they who have riches enter into the Kingdom of God! *(This was a shock to His Disciples, because the Jews of Jesus' day thought that riches signified the favor of God.)*

25 For *it* is easier for a camel to go through a needle's eye *(means a literal needle)*, than for a rich man to enter into the Kingdom of God *(riches aren't necessarily wrong; it's the dependence on these things that constitutes the wrong).*

26 And they who heard *it* said, Who then can be saved? *(This question proclaims the fact that their idea of Salvation was totally confused, even as it is presently.)*

27 And He said, The things which are impossible with men are possible with God *(Salvation in any case is impossible with man; however, it is possible with God, and Jesus is that Salvation).*

CONSECRATION

28 Then Peter said, Lo, we have left all, and followed You *(the statement as given by Peter seems to indicate that when they first set out to follow Christ, they thought it would lead to great earthly riches; they are now seeing that they misunderstood many things).*

29 And He said unto them, Verily I say unto you, There is no man who has left house, or parents, or brethren, or wife, or children, for the Kingdom of God's sake *(God will owe no man anything),*

30 Who shall not receive manifold more *(many times more)* in this present time *(before Heaven),* and in the world to come life everlasting *(serving God is the greatest thing a person could ever do).*

DEATH AND RESURRECTION

31 Then He took *unto Him* the Twelve, and said unto them, Behold, we go up to Jerusalem *(which will bring Him to the end of His earthly Ministry),* and all things that are written by the Prophets concerning the Son of Man shall be accomplished *(pertaining to many things, but mostly the Crucifixion).*

32 For He shall be delivered unto the Gentiles *(that which would be done would have to be done by Rome, since the Jews had no authority to crucify anyone),* and shall be mocked, and spitefully entreated, and spit on *(how is it possible that they could hate Him?):*

33 And they shall scourge *Him* *(beat Him),* and put Him to death *(the Crucifixion):* and the third day He shall rise again *(His Res-*

urrection).

34 And they understood none of these things *(His Words fell upon deaf ears)*: and this saying was hid from them, neither knew they the things which were spoken *(the reason for this was that they had a Plan of God worked out in their minds, which was contrary to the Word of God).*

A BLIND BEGGAR

35 And it came to pass, that as He was come near unto Jericho *(Matthew and Mark speak of Jesus going out of Jericho when this healing took place; however, there is no discrepancy or contradiction; Luke is simply saying that as Jesus was coming into Jericho, at that particular time a blind man was sitting by the side of the highway begging, on the other side of Jericho),* a certain blind man sat by the way side begging *(Jesus will eventually get to him):*

36 And hearing the multitude pass by, he asked what it meant *(refers to a later time after Jesus had already entered the city, and was now actually departing).*

37 And they told him, that Jesus of Nazareth passes by *(this would be the greatest news that had ever fallen upon his ears).*

38 And he cried, saying *(points to his desperation and determination),* Jesus, *Thou* Son of David *(is a Messianic salutation, which means that irrespective as to what others might have said, Bartimaeus believed Jesus Christ was the Messiah),* have mercy on me *(seems to be a request he had studiously thought out; if Jesus did come his way, this is what he would say; in fact, this is the first recorded occasion of Jesus going to Jericho).*

39 And they which went before rebuked him, that he should hold his peace *(in other words, they told him to "shut up"):* but he cried so much the more *(he doubled his efforts),* Thou Son of David, have mercy on me *(it was a request that Christ would not deny).*

40 And Jesus stood *(stood still),* and commanded him to be brought unto Him *(proclaims Jesus answering Faith):* and when he was come near, He asked him,

41 Saying, What will you that I shall do unto you? *(What a question!)* And he said, Lord, that I may receive my sight *(one of the versions says, "That our eyes might be opened and we might see you," for Matthew said there were two blind men [Mat. 20:29-34]).*

42 And Jesus said unto him, Receive your sight: your faith has saved you *(means that he was not only healed, but saved as well).*

43 And immediately he received his sight, and followed Him, glorifying God *(tradition says that He followed Christ to Jerusa-*

lem, and was a staunch Believer in the Early Church; and no wonder!): and all the people, when they saw it, gave praise unto God (incidentally, this man was not only saved and healed, he was no longer a beggar, but rather a Child of God).

CHAPTER 19

ZACCHAEUS

A ND *Jesus* entered and passed through Jericho (He always left a place better than when He found it).

2 And, behold, *there was* a man named Zacchaeus, which was the chief among the Publicans (tax-collectors), and he was rich (we find that the blind beggar is here preferred, for he was healed first before the rich tax-collector; he is last but is put first; he was told to "rise," but Zacchaeus to "come down"; thus rich and poor meet on the one level as sinners before God).

3 And he sought to see Jesus who He was (as Bartimaeus he sought to see Jesus; also as Bartimaeus, he was lacking because money never satisfies the spiritual thirst of the human heart); and could not for the press (the great multitude of people), because he was little of stature (evidently means that he was head and shoulders shorter than most other men).

4 And he ran before (he ascer-

tained the direction Jesus was going, and sought to find a vantage point, which he did), and climbed up into a sycomore tree to see Him: for He was to pass that *way* (a statement of monumental proportions).

5 And when Jesus came to the place, He looked up, and saw him (all were orchestrated by the Holy Spirit; a hungry, seeking, heart will always find the Lord), and said unto him, Zacchaeus, make haste, and come down; for to day I must abide at your house (proclaims the Deity and Kingship of Jesus, although little used; He did not ask for lodging, but as King commanded such; the Salvation of Zacchaeus is one of the most striking in the Gospels; it was personal: "Zacchaeus"; it was pressing: "make haste"; it was humbling: "come down"; it was immediate: "today"; it was abiding: "I must abide"; it was social: "at thy house").

6 And he made haste, and came down, and received Him joyfully (the moral effect of the conversion was seen in Zacchaeus taking his stand along with Jesus in public).

7 And when they saw *it* (the multitude), they all murmured (murmuring is always a sin), saying, That He was gone to be guest with a man who is a sinner (Jesus never catered whatsoever to public whim, prevailing opinion, or conventional wisdom).

8 And Zacchaeus stood, and said unto the Lord; Behold, Lord, the half of my goods I give to the poor *(unlike the rich young ruler, he immediately volunteers such)*; and if I have taken any thing from any man by false accusation, I restore *him* fourfold *(Roman law required a fourfold restitution, but Levitical Law only demanded the principal and one-fifth part added [Num. 5:7]; but he imposed upon himself the severe measure of Exodus 22:1; thus, he judged himself, and true repentance acts as he did)*.

9 And Jesus said unto him, This day is Salvation come to this house *(Jesus is the answer to all problems)*, forsomuch as he also is a son of Abraham *(Jesus is saying that Zacchaeus has as much right to Salvation as any other person in Israel; because he was a tax-collector, the religious leadership may have shut him out, but the Lord didn't; we should think about that statement very carefully)*.

10 For the Son of Man is come to seek and to save that which was lost *(the "seeking of the lost," at least on the part of God, involves far more than a mere quest, but rather an extremely active participation; so much so in fact, that it took Christ to the Cross)*.

THE TEN POUNDS

11 And as they heard these things, He added and spoke a Parable, because He was near to Jerusalem, because they thought that the Kingdom of God should immediately appear *(His going to Jerusalem, and the recent happenings with Bartimaeus and Zacchaeus, probably exacerbated the feelings of the people; they didn't realize that He was on His way to be crucified; they thought He was about to take the Throne)*.

12 He said therefore, A certain Nobleman went into a far country to receive for himself a Kingdom, and to return *(this was Jesus Himself!)*.

13 And He called His ten servants *(the number "ten" in Jewish ideology pertains to an indefinite number and, therefore, includes all who would follow Him)*, and delivered them ten pounds *(about $10,000 in 2003 currency)*, and said unto them, Occupy till I come *(refers to the discharge of that responsibility on the part of each, until the Lord returns)*.

14 But His citizens hated Him *(refers to the Jews at His first coming)*, and sent a message after Him, saying, We will not have this *Man* to reign over us.

15 And it came to pass, that when He was returned *(speaks of the Second Coming)*, having received the kingdom *(Rev. 11:15)*, then He commanded these servants to be called unto Him, to

whom He had given the money, that He might know how much every man had gained by trading *(pertains to the Judgment Seat of Christ, which will take place immediately before the Second Coming; but the action of that Judgment will not be carried out until the Kingdom Age, which will commence with the Second Coming).*

16 Then came the first, saying, Lord, Your pound has gained ten pounds *(about $50,000 in 2003 U.S. currency).*

17 And He said unto him, Well, thou good servant: because you have been faithful in a very little *("faithfulness," or the lack thereof, constitutes the basis of all judgment),* have thou authority over ten cities *(some have claimed this pertains to the coming Kingdom Age, with Believers given rulership over particular cities; however, considering all Believers, there aren't that many cities in the world; so the statement merely has to do with the degree of reward).*

18 And the second came, saying, Lord, Your pound has gained five pounds.

19 And He said likewise to him, Be thou also over five cities.

20 And another came, saying, Lord, behold, *here is* Your pound, which I have kept laid up in a napkin *(represents the one who did nothing):*

21 For I feared You, because You are an austere man *(untrue)*: You take up that You laid not down, and reap that which You did not sow *(all of this is untrue).*

22 And He *(Jesus)* said unto him, Out of your own mouth will I judge you, *you* wicked servant *(doesn't seem to have been involved in gross sin, but seems to have been guilty of spiritual apathy, which characterizes so many Christians).* You knew that I was an austere man *(in other words, if you really believe that),* taking up that I laid not down, and reaping that I did not sow:

23 Wherefore then gave not you My money into the bank, that at My coming I might have received My Own with usury? *(With interest.)*

24 And He said unto them who stood by, Take from him the pound, and give *it* to him who has ten pounds *(he was judged not so much because of what he did, but because of what he failed to do).*

25 (And they said unto Him, Lord, he has ten pounds.) *(The people said this because they were aghast that the pound taken from the man would be given to the one who already had ten pounds.)*

26 For I say unto you, That unto every one which has shall be given; and from him who has not, even that he has shall be

taken away from him *(this is the "Law of Diminishing Returns"; light given and then rejected causes the person not only to lose what they could have had, but even what they presently have; this means that if the Message of the Cross is heard and rejected, not only will those particular individuals lose what they could have had, but they will lose what little they have previously had, which translates into spiritual wreckage).*

27 But those My enemies, which would not that I should reign over them, bring hither, and slay *them* before Me *(pertains to all who fall into this category, including the entirety of the Earth, and for all time; this will take place at the "Great White Throne Judgment" [Rev. 20:11-15]).*

THE TRIUMPHANT ENTRY

28 And when He had thus spoken, He went before, ascending up to Jerusalem *(is literally correct, for Jerusalem is approximately 3,500 feet higher in elevation than Jericho).*

29 And it came to pass, when He was come nigh to Bethphage and Bethany, at the Mount called *the Mount* of Olives *(the suburbs of Jerusalem)*, He sent two of His Disciples *(the identity of the two is not known exactly, but was believed to have been Peter and John)*,

30 Saying, Go ye into the village over against *you (was either Bethany or Bethphage)*; in the which at your entering you shall find a colt tied, whereon yet never man sat: loose him, and bring *him* hither *(proclaims that the triumphant entry would begin now, as predicted by the Prophet Zechariah [Zech. 9:9]).*

31 And if any man ask you, Why do ye loose *him? (This portrays that no previous preparation had been made for the borrowing of the animal. Why? Jesus as King, for this was what He represented at that time, does not, and in fact, must not ask permission. He is Sovereign.)* thus shall you say unto him, Because the Lord has need of him.

32 And they who were sent went their way, and found even as He had said unto them *(this will always be the case!).*

33 And as they were loosing the colt, the owners thereof said unto them, Why loose ye the colt?

34 And they said, The Lord has need of him *(evidently the owners immediately acquiesced; what a privilege it was for them to supply the animal — there were actually two animals — used by the Lord at this time).*

35 And they brought him *(the animal)* to Jesus: and they cast their garments upon the colt *(making a saddle of sorts)*, and they

set Jesus thereon.

36 And as He went, they spread their clothes in the way *(concerned the vast number of pilgrims who had come from all over Israel for the Passover; this road would have been filled with people).*

37 And when He was come near, even now at the descent of the Mount of Olives, the whole multitude of the Disciples *(all the followers of Christ, not merely the Twelve)* began to rejoice and praise God with a loud voice for all the mighty works that they had seen;

38 Saying, Blessed *be* the King Who comes in the Name of the Lord *(the Prophecy of Zechariah demanded this public presentation of Jesus as the King of Israel, even though He would be rejected)*: peace in Heaven, and glory in the highest *(these phrases are of great magnitude; Jesus was to suffer and die in a few hours; this would bring peace to Heaven as well as Earth; He completely defeated Satan, making it possible for all things to be reconciled in Heaven and Earth; this is not yet done, but because of the Cross, it most assuredly will be done [Col. 2:14-17; Heb. 2:14-15]).*

39 And some of the Pharisees from among the multitude said unto Him, Master, rebuke Your Disciples *(Satan will do all within his power to stop people from praising the Lord, and will mostly use the Church to carry out his devious designs).*

40 And He answered and said unto them, I tell you that, if these should hold their peace, the stones would immediately cry out *(God demands praise, and true Christians will definitely praise Him; this proclaims to the spirit world that God's Plan will succeed and Satan will be overthrown).*

JERUSALEM

41 And when He was come near, He beheld the city *(Jerusalem, at that time, was a city of unparalleled beauty; the Temple was gleaming white, and one of the most beautiful buildings in the world)*, and wept over it *(refers to loud crying, lamentations, even wailing; what must have been the reaction of people as they saw Him do this?),*

42 Saying, If you had known, even you, at least in this your day, the things *which belong* unto your peace! *(The things that Israel could have had, had they only obeyed the Word of God.)* but now they are hid from your eyes *(refers to willful blindness, which resulted in judicial blindness; Leadership will be given now unto the Gentiles).*

43 For the days shall come upon you, that your enemies shall cast a trench about you *(was fulfilled in totality in A.D. 70)*, and compass you round, and keep you

in on every side (the Romans surrounded Jerusalem with a stone wall, making escape impossible),

44 And shall lay you even with the ground (the Roman General Titus, with the Tenth Legion, reduced the city to rubble), and your children within you (concerning the siege, over one million were killed, with hundreds of thousands of others sold as slaves); and they shall not leave in you one stone upon another (this concerned the Temple, and was fulfilled in totality; every stone was removed and a plough run over the place where it had stood, fulfilling Micah 3:12); because you knew not the time of your visitation (refers to the life and Ministry of Jesus, which constituted the greatest visitation ever experienced by any people).

THE TEMPLE

45 And He went into the Temple (actually refers to the next day), and began to cast out them who sold therein, and them who bought (probably took place in the Court of the Gentiles);

46 Saying unto them, It is written (Isa. 56:7), My house is the house of prayer: but you have made it a den of thieves (Satan had done this by and through religious leaders).

47 And He taught daily in the Temple (pertained to the approximate five days before His arrest and trial on the sixth day). But the Chief Priests and the Scribes and the Chief of the people sought to destroy Him (concerns, as is obvious, the religious hierarchy of Israel; but no matter how powerful that hierarchy might be, to oppose God is a fight that cannot be won; they only succeeded in destroying themselves),

48 And could not find what they might do (couldn't find a way to destroy Him): for all the people were very attentive to hear Him (so whatever they would do could not be done in the open, but had to be done in secret, which it was).

CHAPTER 20

AUTHORITY

AND it came to pass, that on one of those days (probably was Monday; He was arrested Wednesday night, for the new day began at the going down of the sun rather than midnight as we now reckon time), as He taught the people in the Temple, and preached the Gospel ("preaching" and "teaching" are still God's way of proclaiming the Word), the Chief Priests and the Scribes came upon Him with the Elders (they were very angry with Him for several reasons, but the greatest reason of all was that they were full *of the Devil),*

2 And spoke unto Him, saying, Tell us, by what authority do You these things? *(This is a trap designed to force Him to openly claim a Divine Commission.)* or who is he who gave You this authority? *(They knew He claimed God as His sole Authority, but they wanted Him to say it publicly in the Temple. Of course, they did not believe His Source was God. Yet it was very difficult for them to explain away the miracles; therefore, they attributed these to Satan, which in fact was Blasphemy of the Holy Spirit [Mat. 12:24-32].)*

3 And He answered and said unto them, I will also ask you one thing; and answer Me *(in demanding an answer from them, the Lord was claiming an answer from authorized teachers, which they claimed to be; so the tables were now turned, with Him putting them on the spot):*

4 The baptism of John, was it from Heaven, or of men? *(His question was not a trick question as theirs had been, but rather a legitimate question, with a legitimate and obvious answer pointing to the Source of His Authority.)*

5 And they reasoned with themselves *(they went into a huddle; they were on the horns of a dilemma!),* saying, If we shall say, From Heaven; He will say, Why then believed you him not? *(If they ac-knowledged that John was a true Prophet of God, then they would have to acknowledge his Message, and more importantly the One he introduced, the Lord Jesus Christ.)*

6 But and if we say, Of men; all the people will stone us: for they be persuaded that John was a Prophet *(concerns the people being far ahead of their spiritual leaders).*

7 And they answered, that they could not tell whence *it was* *(in fact, they were the very ones who were supposed to be able to answer such a question; their lame answer showed that they had no spirituality at all; what a cop-out!).*

8 And Jesus said unto them, Neither tell I you by what authority I do these things.

THE WICKED HUSBANDMEN

9 Then began He to speak to the people this Parable *(will outline in graphic detail the answer to the question these religious leaders had asked);* A certain man *(God)* planted a Vineyard *(Israel),* and let it forth to husbandmen *(referred to the religious leaders of Israel, whomever they were, and for the entire time of the nation),* and went into a far country for a long time *(pertains from the time of Abraham up to Christ).*

10 And at the season He sent a servant to the husbandmen *(speaks*

of the Prophets who were sent at intervals), that they should give Him of the fruit of the vineyard: but the husbandmen beat him, and sent *him* away empty *(concerns the treatment of the Prophets)*.

11 And again He sent another servant *(another Prophet)*: and they beat him also, and entreated *him* shamefully, and sent *him* away empty.

12 And again He sent a third: and they wounded him also, and cast *him* out.

13 Then said the Lord of the Vineyard, What shall I do? *(The question does not lack of knowledge on the part of God as to what He will do, but in effect actually states what will be done.)* I will send My Beloved Son *(the Lord Jesus Christ)*: it may be they will reverence *Him* when they see Him *(the Son was the Heir, therefore, the Vineyard belonged to Him)*.

14 But when the husbandmen saw Him, they reasoned among themselves *(exactly as the religious leaders did)*, saying, This is the Heir *(proclaims in no uncertain terms that the Scribes and Pharisees knew exactly Who Jesus really was)*: come, let us kill Him *(even though they knew Who He was, their response to Him was one of murder)*, that the inheritance may be ours *(untold millions have said the same thing; they do not want the Plan of God for this world and for* their lives; they desire to chart their own course, which always leads to destruction; they have done nothing but wreck the inheritance).

15 So they cast Him out of the Vineyard, and killed *Him* *(says in no uncertain terms exactly what they would do, and in fact, did do!)*. What therefore shall the Lord of the Vineyard do unto them? *(Even though they are warned, even as the next Verse proclaims, they would not listen.)*

16 He shall come and destroy these husbandmen *(it happened some thirty-seven years later, exactly as He said it would, as Rome destroyed Jerusalem and did so completely)*, and shall give the Vineyard to others *(has reference to the Gentile Church)*. And when they heard *it*, they said, God forbid *(proclaims that they knew exactly what Jesus was saying, and exactly what He meant; their answer was "God forbid," meaning, "God will not allow such!"; their answer should have been, "God have mercy on us")*.

17 And He beheld them, and said, What is this then that is written *(Ps. 118:22)*, The Stone which the builders rejected *(that "Stone" is Christ)*, the same is become the Head of the Corner? *(Israel's rejection of Christ did not abrogate His position as "Cornerstone." He is that to the Church, and will ultimately be that to Israel.)*

18 Whosoever shall fall upon that Stone shall be broken (speaks of Israel, and any nation or people or a person for that matter who sets out to destroy Christ, i.e., "set Him aside"; instead, they are broken themselves; this is a battle that no one can win, for Jesus is God!); but on whomsoever it shall fall, it will grind him to powder (speaks of Christ ultimately smashing the Kingdoms of this world, which He will do at the Second Coming, making them His Own [Dan. 2:35]; Jesus presents Himself here as the principal figure of the entirety of humanity and the world, and proclaims their rise or fall based on their acceptance or rejection of Him).

TRIBUTE MONEY

19 And the Chief Priests and the Scribes the same hour sought to lay hands on Him (they were incensed at the Parable He had just related to them, and especially Him speaking of Himself as the "Stone," i.e., "Cornerstone"); and they feared the people: for they perceived that He had spoken this Parable against them (so what they did was not at all in ignorance, but rather from the position of rebellion).

20 And they watched Him (refers to the fact that they were trying to catch Him in His Words in order to level a charge of treason against Him), and sent forth spies, which should feign themselves just men, that they might take hold of His words (how foolish they were), that so they might deliver Him unto the power and authority of the Governor (Pilate).

21 And they asked Him, saying, Master, we know that You say and teach rightly, neither do You accept the person of any, but teach the Way of God truly (all of this was true, but they didn't believe it, only saying these words in order to attempt to snare Him):

22 Is it lawful for us to give tribute unto Caesar, or no? (This "tribute" was tax levied by Rome on every person in Israel at a Denarius a head. If He said "yes," He would be labeled a traitor by Israel, because they abhorred this tax inasmuch as it proclaimed them a subject of Rome. If He said "no," He could be branded an insurrectionist by Rome. So in their minds, either way He answered would incriminate Him.)

23 But He perceived their craftiness (He instantly recognized their treachery and trickery), and said unto them, Why do you tempt Me? (He lets them know that He knows exactly what they're doing, and their hypocrisy.)

24 Show Me a penny (the Roman Denarius; such was not normally brought into the Temple because there was an inscription of

Caesar on its face). Whose image and superscription has it? They answered and said, Caesar's.

25 And He said unto them, Render therefore unto Caesar the things which be Caesar's, and unto God the things which be God's *(Jesus is saying that debts to man and debts to God are both to be discharged, and the two spheres of duty are at once distinct and reconcilable; in effect, Jesus was here teaching in its beginning forms the separation of Church and State).*

26 And they could not take hold of His words before the people *(His answer was so perfect that they had no rebuttal)*: and they marvelled at His answer, and held their peace *(in their trickery, they were positive that His answer would incriminate Him in one way or the other, but to their amazement, it served no purpose at all for their evil designs).*

THE RESURRECTION

27 Then came to *Him* certain of the Sadducees *(the Modernists of Israel of that day, and who mostly controlled the High Priesthood and the Sanhedrin),* which deny that there is any Resurrection *(their false interpretation of the Word of God ruled out an after-life, consequently reducing the Plan of God to mere window dressing)*; and they asked Him,

28 Saying, Master, Moses wrote unto us, If any man's brother die, having a wife, and he die without children, that his brother should take his wife, and raise up seed unto his brother *([Deut. 25:5], they claimed to believe Genesis through Deuteronomy, but placed no credence in the balance of the Bible of that day, which was Joshua through Malachi).*

29 There were therefore seven brethren: and the first took a wife, and died without children.

30 And the second took her to wife, and he died childless.

31 And the third took her; and in like manner the seven also: and they left no children, and died.

32 Last of all the woman died also.

33 Therefore in the Resurrection whose wife of them is she? for seven had her to wife *(Deuteronomy does not contain this illustration, at least in this fashion; this is a hypothetical situation conjured up by the Sadducees, which they thought sealed their argument that there was no such thing as a Resurrection).*

34 And Jesus answering said unto them, The children of this world *(this life before death)* marry, and are given in marriage *(this places the institution of marriage solely in this present world, and not in the world to come):*

35 But they which shall be ac-

counted worthy to obtain that world (*eternal life, brought about by the "born-again" experience*), and the Resurrection from the dead (*proclaims unequivocally that there will be a "Resurrection"*), neither marry, nor are given in marriage (*this pertains to those who have part in the First Resurrection, which will include every Believer who has ever lived up unto the conclusion of the Great Tribulation*):

36 Neither can they die any more (*at that time, all Saints of God will have Glorified bodies; there will be no more death among them*): for they are equal unto the Angels (*speaking only of immortality*); and are the Children of God, being the Children of the Resurrection (*all Believers will be "Children of the Resurrection," simply because they are "Children of God" through the born-again experience [Jn. 3:3]*).

37 Now that the dead are raised, even Moses showed at the bush (*takes the Sadducees to the very part of the Bible they claim to believe*), when he called the Lord the God of Abraham, and the God of Isaac, and the God of Jacob (*presents a solid truth concerning life after death, which the next Verse will explain*).

38 For He is not a God of the dead (*meaning that there is life after death, whether in Heaven or Hell*), but of the living (*in effect, Moses was saying that Abraham, Isaac, and Jacob were even then alive, even though they had physically died many years before; it is the same with all Believers*): for all live unto Him (*He is not a God of dead beings, but of living beings; God cannot be the God of a being who does not exist*).

THE INCARNATION

39 Then certain of the Scribes answering said, Master, You have well said (*the Scribes were Pharisees, and did believe in the Resurrection*).

40 And after that they do not ask Him any *question at all (both Pharisees and Sadducees gave up this method of attack).*

41 And He said unto them, How say they that Christ is David's son? (*"Christ" means Anointed One" or "Messiah." This question, posed by Christ, had to do with the Incarnation.*)

42 And David himself said in the Book of Psalms, The LORD said unto My Lord, Sit Thou on My right hand (*[Ps. 110:1] this statement proclaims Deity on the part of the Messiah, which struck at the heart of the false belief of the Jews concerning Jesus, who expected their Messiah to be merely a "beloved man"; in essence, "God the Father says to God the Son . . ."*),

43 Till I make your enemies

your footstool (*Jesus did this through the Cross [Col. 2:14-15]*).

44 David therefore called Him Lord, how is He then His Son? (*With this question, Jesus placed the Incarnation, God becoming man, squarely before the Pharisees. Jesus is David's Lord because He is God. He is David's Son, in respect to His humanity, God becoming man.*)

45 Then in the audience of all the people He said unto His Disciples (*said the following in the hearing of all the people*),

46 Beware of the Scribes, which desire to walk in long robes, and love greetings in the markets, and the highest seats in the Synagogues, and the chief rooms at feasts (*their religion was a "show," and contained no substance; but yet, they were the Pastors of the people*);

47 Which devour widows' houses, and for a show make long prayers (*prayed these prayers in the presence of these particular women in order to get their money*): the same shall receive greater damnation (*refers to judgment; Hell will be the hottest for this type, who are mere professers, but do not actually possess*).

CHAPTER 21

THE TWO MITES

AND He looked up (*our Lord was in the covered colonnade of that part of the Temple which was open to the Jewish women; here was the treasury with its thirteen boxes on the wall, where the people could give offerings*), and saw the rich men casting their gifts into the treasury (*implying that they were making a show of their gifts, desiring to impress the people by the amount, etc.*).

2 And He saw also a certain poor widow casting in thither two mites (*was probably worth something less than a U.S. dollar in 2003 purchasing power*).

3 And He said, Of a truth I say unto you (*presents a new concept of giving*), that this poor widow has cast in more than they all (*the term "poor widow" means that she worked very hard for what little she received*):

4 For all these have of their abundance cast in unto the offerings of God (*means that they had much left, constituting very little given, at least in the eyes of God*): but she of her penury (*poverty*) has cast in all the living that she had (*spoke of her gift, as small as it was, being larger than all others combined because she gave all; God judges our giving by many factors; motive plays very heavily into the account*).

THE TEMPLE

5 And as some spoke of the

Temple (*was said on the Mount of Olivet, as Jesus and His Disciples left the city*), how it was adorned with goodly stones and gifts (*this building was one of the most beautiful in the world*), He said,

6 As for these things which you behold (*referred to the beauty of the Temple, which the Disciples were even then admiring*), the days will come, in the which there shall not be left one stone upon another, that shall not be thrown down (*this is exactly what happened in A.D. 70, when Titus destroyed the Temple and the city*).

7 And they asked Him, saying, Master, but when shall these things be? (*While Matthew, Chapter 24 deals primarily with the Second Coming, Luke addressed himself to the Words of Christ, which concerned the coming destruction by Titus the Roman General.*) and what sign *will there be* when these things shall come to pass? (*This is somewhat different than the question recorded by Matthew, "what shall be the sign of Your Coming and of the end of the world?"*)

SIGNS OF THE END TIME

8 And He said (*for the next four Verses, Luke deals with the signs of the times as it regards the Second Coming*), Take heed that you be not deceived (*presents the exact manner in which Matthew begins his account — the warning of deception; it is mainly in the realm of religion*): for many shall come in My Name, saying, I am Christ (*of Christ*); and the time draws near (*the Rapture of the Church*): go ye not therefore after them (*be very careful as to whom you follow*).

9 But when you shall hear of wars and commotions, be not terrified (*when Israel rejected Christ, this subjected the world to some 2,000 more years of terror*): for these things must first come to pass (*which in effect have characterized the world from then until now*); but the end is not by and by (*means that the end is not immediate*).

10 Then said He unto them, Nation shall rise against nation, and kingdom against kingdom (*refers to the time immediately preceding the Great Tribulation, and on into that particular time period*):

11 And great earthquakes shall be in divers places, and famines, and pestilences; and fearful sights and great signs shall there be from Heaven (*these things will take place on this particular scale during the Great Tribulation Period*).

JERUSALEM

12 But before all these (*speaking of the time very soon after

He made these statements), they shall lay their hands on you, and persecute *you,* delivering *you* up to the Synagogues, and into prisons, being brought before kings and rulers for My Name's sake *(the Book of Acts records these events, and history records that which followed the Book of Acts).*

13 And it shall turn to you for a Testimony *(Believers must not allow their "Testimony" to be hindered by persecution, but rather make it the cause of being strengthened).*

14 Settle *it* therefore in your hearts, not to meditate before what you shall answer *(does not condemn careful thought, but encourages total trust in the Lord without fear):*

15 For I will give you a mouth and wisdom *(speaks of the unction of the Holy Spirit in the heart and life of the Believer, giving the help that is needed),* which all your adversaries shall not be able to gainsay nor resist.

16 And you shall be betrayed both by parents, and brethren, and kinsfolks, and friends *(this portrays the power of demon religions and their control of their victims)*; and *some* of you shall they cause to be put to death *(some will not be delivered, but will rather die for their Testimony).*

17 And you shall be hated of all *men* for My Name's sake *(this one Verse is ample proof of the validity of Christianity, in that anything which could survive such opposition, and even grow — until it is now the largest in the world — proves the integrity of its Founder, the Lord Jesus Christ, and the sincerity of its converts).*

18 But there shall not an hair of your head perish *(our Lord is speaking now of the coming destruction of Jerusalem in A.D. 70; in that carnage, which resulted in over one million Jews being killed, not a single Christian lost his life because they read these very Verses, and did exactly what Jesus said to do).*

19 In your patience possess ye your souls *(if the situation does not seem to improve, the Believer is to be "patient," knowing that God has all things under control, and everything that He does is for the benefit of the Believer and not His hurt).*

20 And when you shall see Jerusalem compassed with armies *(speaks of the invasion by Titus in A.D. 70),* then know that the desolation thereof is near *(speaks of the moment that Titus would begin to surround Jerusalem, which would be the signal that Christians were to leave, which they did!).*

21 Then let them which are in Judaea flee to the mountains *(spoke of all those who believed this Word, which all Christians did);*

and let them which are in the midst of it depart out *(means that no part of Judaea would be safe from the Roman armies)*; and let not them who are in the countries enter thereinto *(speaks of Christians who lived in surrounding countries, who at this time were not to come into Judaea).*

22 For these be the days of vengeance *(refers to judgment; Israel had rejected Christ; now they must pay)*, that all things which are written may be fulfilled *(concerning the fulfillment of these very Words as given by Christ, as well as all prophecies; to be sure, every single Word of God will come to pass, exactly as predicted).*

23 But woe unto them who are with child, and to them who give suck, in those days! for there shall be great distress in the land, and wrath upon this people *(once again speaks of the terrible days which were to come on Jerusalem, and which did come in A.D. 70).*

24 And they shall fall by the edge of the sword, and shall be led away captive into all nations *(hundreds of thousands of Jews after the carnage of A.D. 70 were sold as slaves all over the world of that day; as well, the Jewish people as a whole were scattered all over the world, fulfilling exactly what Jesus said would happen)*: and Jerusalem shall be trodden down of the Gentiles, until the times of the Gentiles be fulfilled *(has actually proved the case since Jerusalem was destroyed by the Babylonians some six hundred years before Christ; in fact, it has continued unto this hour, and will for all practical purposes continue until the Second Coming; then the "times of the Gentiles will be fulfilled," with Israel once again becoming the premiere nation of the world, which they will do under Christ).*

25 And there shall be signs in the sun, and in the moon, and in the stars *(proclaims the Lord now returning to His former subject of signs concerning His Second Coming, which was first broached in Verses 8-11)*; and upon the earth distress of nations, with perplexity *(refers to problems without a solution, which will prevail in the coming Great Tribulation)*; the sea and the waves roaring *(does not pertain to bodies of water, but rather to nations roaring in discontent, anger, rebellion, and war [Rev. 17:15])*;

26 Men's hearts failing them for fear *(has nothing to do with heart disease, but rather men losing heart, i.e., having no more courage to continue)*, and for looking after those things which are coming on the earth *(Revelation, Chapters 6 through 19 give us in graphic detail an account of that which will happen)*: for the powers of Heaven shall be shaken

(proclaims the Judgment of God that will fall upon unbelieving Israel and the Gentile nations, which will have no precedent in all past history, and will have no counterpart in all succeeding history [Mat. 24:21]).

27 And then *(refers to the conclusion of the Great Tribulation)* shall they see the Son of Man coming *(refers to the Second Coming, and may very well be televised by News Agencies covering the Battle of Armageddon, raging at that time, which will portray this Coming all over the world)* in a cloud *(does not speak of the clouds of the Heavens, but rather clouds of Saints and Angels, which will be coming back with the Lord at that Coming)* with power and great glory *(as stated, when He comes the second time, the world will not have to ask if it is really Him; it will be overly obvious!).*

28 And when these things begin to come to pass *(refers to the "signs" of Verses 8-11, as well as Verses 25-26),* then look up, and lift up your heads; for your Redemption draws nigh *(does not refer to the Rapture, for that will have already happened years before, but rather the deliverance of Israel at the Second Coming when Christ comes with Raptured Saints [Isa. 11:10-12; 66:7-8; Zech., Chpt. 14; Mat. 24:29-31; Rom. 11:25-29; Rev., Chpt. 19]).*

THE FIG TREE

29 And He spoke to them a Parable; Behold the fig tree, and all the trees *(Jesus is using a simple illustration which is meant to point to the Second Coming);*

30 When they now shoot forth, you see and know of your own selves that summer is now nigh at hand *(the season of Spring tells us that the season of Summer is about to begin).*

31 So likewise ye, when you see these things come to pass *(once again speaks of the happenings of Verses 8 through 11, as well as Verses 25 and 26),* know ye that the Kingdom of God is near at hand *(points to the Second Coming, which will usher in the Kingdom Age).*

32 Verily I say unto you, This generation shall not pass away, till all be fulfilled *(the generation that will be alive at the time of these happenings).*

33 Heaven and earth shall pass away *(will pass from one condition to another)*: but My Words shall not pass away *(the Word of God is more sure of fulfillment even than the stability of Heaven and Earth).*

WATCH AND PRAY

34 And take heed to yourselves *(begins a portion of teaching that applies to the entirety of the body of Christ, and for all times),* lest

at any time your hearts be over-charged (weighed down) with surfeiting (debauchery), and drunkenness, and cares of this life (things which are not spiritual), and so that day come upon you unawares (actually points to the Second Coming, but can point as well to the Rapture and Death).

35 For as a snare shall it come on all them who dwell on the face of the whole Earth (in other words, things will not turn out as man thinks they will, for the Second Coming will change everything).

36 Watch ye therefore, and pray always (watch events which transpire, and equate them in whatever capacity with the Word, asking the Lord to give discernment), that you may be accounted worthy to escape all these things that shall come to pass (it speaks of the Rapture of the Church; the "worthiness" spoken of here by Jesus has nothing to do with self-righteousness, but rather the righteousness which is freely given to anyone who expresses Faith in Christ and the Cross; that and that alone is the key), and to stand before the Son of Man (refers to being taken to be with the Lord before the Coming Great Tribulation [I Thess. 4:13-18]).

37 And in the daytime He was teaching in the Temple (concerned His last hours before the Crucifixion); and at night He went out, and abode in the Mount that is called the Mount of Olives (we have here the Son of God, the Creator of all things, the Maker of Heaven and Earth, Who would actually have no place to lay His Head, with the exception of a rock; the humiliation He suffered has no comparison in the annals of human history).

38 And all the people came early in the morning to Him in the Temple (concerns the many thousands who filled Jerusalem, for it was the time of the Passover), for to hear Him (to hear the "Giver of Life," present the "Words of Life").

CHAPTER 22

THE PLOT

NOW the Feast of Unleavened Bread drew nigh, which is called the Passover (it began on April 14th; there were three Feasts held at this particular time, "Passover, Unleavened Bread, and First Fruits").

2 And the Chief Priests and Scribes sought how they might kill Him (represented the religious hierarchy of Israel; it is ironic; the world did not Crucify Him so much as did the Church, i.e., "Israel"); for they feared the people (they should have feared God!).

JUDAS ISCARIOT

3 Then entered Satan into Judas

surnamed Iscariot *(pertained to the present time, even though Satan had been working on Judas for quite some time)*, being of the number of the Twelve *(the Holy Spirit wanted all to know what an opportunity this man had, but threw it all away)*.

4 And he *(Judas)* went his way *(it was not God's way)*, and communed with the Chief Priests and Captains, how he might betray Him unto them *(proclaims the most evil deed ever carried out by a human being)*.

5 And they were glad *(portrays evil beyond belief; it is more tragic still when one realizes that this was the "Church" of Jesus' day; however, it hasn't changed; were Christ here now, institutionalized religion would do the same thing as was done then)*, and covenanted to give him money *(thirty pieces of silver, the price of a slave)*.

6 And he promised, and sought opportunity to betray Him unto them in the absence of the multitude *(they had to carry out this act when He was Alone, or at least in the presence of His Disciples only; Judas promised to provide this opportunity)*.

THE PASSOVER

7 Then came the day of Unleavened Bread, when the Passover must be killed *(Jesus, God's Passover, must be killed because the Scriptures predicted it; only His Atoning Death could expiate man's sin; all four Gospels record at great length His death, while only two briefly record His birth)*.

8 And He sent Peter and John, saying *(had to do with the preparation of the Passover, which constituted the Last Supper)*, Go and prepare us the Passover, that we may eat *(means that Peter and John, representing the Apostolic band, took a lamb to the Temple where it was killed)*.

9 And they said unto Him, Where will You that we prepare? *(At this time, they did not know where it would be eaten. In fact, Jesus would eat the Passover a day early.)*

10 And He said unto them, Behold, when you are entered into the city, there shall a man meet you, bearing a pitcher of water *(in those days, men seldom carried pitchers of water, that being reserved for women; consequently, such would be easy to spot)*; follow him into the house where he enters in *(would be the place where the Passover would be eaten; some think this was the home of John Mark, who wrote the Gospel that bears his name)*.

11 And you shall say unto the goodman of the house, The Master says unto you, Where is the guestchamber, where I shall eat

the Passover with My Disciples? *(If it is to be noticed, Jesus does not ask permission; for Kings tell instead of ask.)*

12 And he shall show you a large upper room furnished *(prepared)*: there make ready *(this could well be the same "upper room" from Acts 1:13, as it most probably was)*.

13 And they went, and found as He had said unto them *(will always be the case regarding anything He has spoken unto us)*: and they made ready the Passover *(means that they prepared the Lamb for roasting, along with the making of the Unleavened Bread, etc.)*.

THE LORD'S SUPPER

14 And when the hour was come *(was a little after sundown, which was Wednesday, at least as Israel then reckoned time)*, He sat down, and the Twelve Apostles with Him *(including Judas as is obvious)*.

15 And He said unto them, With desire I have desired to eat this Passover with you before I suffer *(it would be symbolic of the New Covenant, brought about by what He would suffer through the Cross)*:

16 For I say unto you, I will not any more eat thereof *(this would be the last Passover, at least which God would recognize, because Jesus,* Who was in reality the Passover, would meet its requirements on the Cross), until it be fulfilled in the Kingdom of God *(even though the total price was paid at Calvary, still all that Redemption affords has not yet been received, but will be received at the Resurrection of Life [I Cor. 15:49-58])*.

17 And He took the cup, and gave thanks *(evidently a large cup)*, and said, Take this, and divide *it* among yourselves *(a small portion was poured for each one)*:

18 For I say unto you, I will not drink of the fruit of the vine, until the Kingdom of God shall come *(same as Verse 16)*.

19 And He took bread, and gave thanks, and broke *it*, and gave unto them, saying, This is My Body which is given for you *(His Body was prepared by God, in order that it be a perfect Sacrifice [Heb. 10:5])*: this do in remembrance of Me *(in remembrance of His Death on the Cross of Calvary that purchased our Redemption, which we celebrate in that referred to as "the Lord's Supper")*.

20 Likewise also the cup after supper, saying, This cup *is* the New Testament *(New Covenant)* in My blood *(the terminology is symbolic and figurative, not literal; Leviticus 3:17 and Leviticus 7:26 forbade the eating of blood)*, which is shed for you *(which was done on the Cross*

of Calvary).

THE BETRAYAL FORETOLD

21 But, behold, the hand of him who betrays Me *is* with Me on the table *(it doesn't tell us much because the hands of all of the Apostles were on the table).*

22 And truly the Son of Man goes, as it was determined *(God's foreknowledge does not abrogate man's responsibility; God wills in the sense of permission, but not necessarily)*: but woe unto that man by whom He is betrayed! *(This tells us that it was not pre-determined who the man would be, even though it was predetermined that some man would do such a thing.)*

23 And they began to enquire among themselves, which of them it was that should do this thing *(at this time, none of the Disciples knew of the disposition of Judas).*

STRIFE

24 And there was also a strife among them *(took place almost immediately after Supper; "Strife" in this instance means "contention"),* which of them should be account-ed the greatest *(Christ was about to die, and His Disciples were ar-guing over place and position; they still did not have a clue as to what*

was about to happen to Him).

25 And He said unto them, The kings of the Gentiles exercise lordship over them *(proclaims the way of the world, which the Be-liever is not to emulate)*; and they that exercise authority upon them are called benefactors *(presents the means by which these dictators justify themselves; they claim to give all types of good things to the people, but most give nothing).*

26 But ye shall not be so *(the "lordship spirit" is the way of the world, and is not to be adopted by the Church)*: but he who is great-est among you, let him be as the younger; and he who is chief, as he who does serve *(all Believers, and especially those who will be greatly used by the Lord, must know and live as the "servant").*

27 For whether *is* greater, he who sits at meat, or he who serves? *(This is meant to point out the total contrast between the ways of the world and the Ways of God.)* is not he who sits at meat? *(The world looks at the one who is be-ing served as the Greatest, but now Jesus shows us true Greatness.)* but I am among you as He who serves *(as is obvious, Jesus lived by the servant principle, which as stated is the opposite of the world; and we must do the same).*

28 You are they which have continued with Me in My temp-tations *(He was the Man of Sor-*

rows; *His whole life was a series of trials, griefs, hatreds, and sufferings*).

29 And I appoint unto you a Kingdom (*though He foreknew that they would all forsake Him, yet in His most wonderful and tender love, He praised their fidelity and courage and promised them a recompense out of all proportion to their service*), as My Father has appointed unto Me (*we become a joint heir with Christ [Rom. 8:17]*);

30 That you may eat and drink at My Table in My Kingdom (*has reference to the coming Kingdom Age, mentioned in Verse 18*), and sit on thrones judging the Twelve Tribes of Israel (*is a privilege to be enjoyed only by the Twelve Apostles, with Matthias taking the place of Judas*).

PETER

31 And the Lord said, Simon, Simon, behold, Satan has desired *to have* you (*portrays to us a glimpse into the spirit world, which was very similar to the same request made by Satan concerning Job*), that he may sift *you* as wheat (*Satan tempts in order to bring out the bad, while God tests in order to bring out the good; the simple truth is God, at times using Satan as His instrument in addressing character, causes men to seek God's Holiness rather than their own*):

32 But I have prayed for you, that your Faith fail not (*Satan's attack is always delivered against Faith, for if that fails all fail*): and when you are converted, strengthen your brethren (*does not refer to being saved again, but rather coming to the right path of trust and dependence on the Lord, instead of on self; that lesson learned, one is then able to strengthen the brethren*).

33 And he (*Peter*) said unto Him, Lord, I am ready to go with You, both into prison, and to death (*most probably Peter's true feelings, but his confidence was in self, and self cannot perform the task*).

34 And He said, I tell you, Peter (*Jesus seldom addressed Peter by this name; it means "a rock"; so by Him referring to Peter in this fashion, in essence, told him that, despite the terrible denial which was coming, Peter would survive the onslaught*), the cock shall not crow this day, before that you shall thrice deny that you know Me (*pinpoints the time, and exactly the number of times this would happen*).

35 And He said unto them, When I sent you without purse, and scrip, and shoes, lacked you any thing? And they said, Nothing (*speaks of every need being met and abundantly so*).

36 Then said He unto them, But now, he who has a purse, let

him take *it*, and likewise *his* scrip *(a bag for carrying things, placed over the shoulder or around the waist; He is telling them that while the needs will always be met, it will not be nearly so easy as it had been in the past)*: and he who has no sword, let him sell his garment, and buy one *(all of these terms are symbolic; the "sword" has reference to the fact that Believers are to accept the protection of an ordered Government)*.

37 For I say unto you, that this that is written must yet be accomplished in Me *(refers to Isaiah, Chapter 53, and is the first time the Lord refers to that Text)*, And He was reckoned among the transgressors *(does not mean that He was actually a transgressor, but that Israel considered Him one even though they could find no wrong doing for which He could be charged)*: for the things concerning Me have an end *(He had come to fulfill all the Prophecies of the past, and this He would do shortly)*.

38 And they said, Lord, behold, here *are* two swords *(proclaims that they did not understand that to which He referred concerning the purchasing of a sword; they took it literally, whereas He was speaking symbolically respecting the authority of Gentile nations)*. And He said unto them, It is enough *(proclaims Him making no attempt to correct their* false assumption in this securing of two swords, knowing that the meaning would become abundantly clear after the Day of Pentecost)*.

GETHSEMANE

39 And He came out, and went, as He was wont *(accustomed)*, to the Mount of Olives *(constitutes the beginning of the agony in the Garden)*; and His Disciples also followed Him *(proclaims, it seems, that they did not quite know what He was going to do, and what the occasion would present)*.

40 And when He was at the place *(Gethsemane, the place of surrender)*, He said unto them, Pray that you enter not into temptation *(the temptation of subverting the Will of God)*.

41 And He was withdrawn from them about a stone's cast, and kneeled down, and prayed *(His prayer life was exceptional, and ours should be as well!)*,

42 Saying, Father, if You be willing, remove this cup from Me *(speaks of that which He would have to drink in the spiritual sense)*: nevertheless not My Will, but Thine, be done *(this is the price of surrender)*.

43 And there appeared an Angel unto Him from Heaven, strengthening Him *(this was the peace of surrender; as a human being, He suffered now as possibly*

no other has suffered, thereby desperately needing the help of the Angel).

44 And being in an agony He prayed more earnestly *(Hebrews 5:7 shows that the wrath of God was to judge Him as if He, and He Alone, were the only sinner who ever existed, even though He was no sinner at all; this caused that agony; so His death was not just a great example of resignation and self-sacrifice, as multitudes vainly think)*: and His sweat was as it were great drops of blood falling down to the ground *(portrays a recognized fact that under extreme mental pressure, the pores may become so dilated that blood may issue from them in the form of bloody sweat).*

45 And when He rose up from prayer, and was come to His Disciples *(signals the victory won, at least in this great struggle concerning the Will of God)*, He found them sleeping for sorrow *(the agony upon Him also affected His Disciples),*

46 And said unto them, Why sleep ye? *(This presents the moment He awakened them. He does not expect an answer.)* rise and pray, lest you enter into temptation *(would have been better translated, "lest you succumb to temptation").*

THE ARREST

47 And while He yet spoke, be-hold a multitude *(pertains to the group coming to arrest Jesus, consisting of Roman Legionnaires and of Levitical guards belonging to the Temple)*, and he who was called Judas, one of the Twelve, went before them *(proclaims the Holy Spirit purposely explaining who Judas was, so as not to confuse him with others of the same name)*, and drew near unto Jesus to kiss Him *(the prearranged design).*

48 But Jesus said unto him, Judas, you betrayest thou the Son of Man with a kiss? *(This was the most infamous "kiss" in history.)*

49 When they which were about Him saw what would follow *(saw that He was about to be arrested)*, they said unto Him, Lord, shall we smite with the sword? *(This presents the very opposite of what He wanted them to do.)*

50 And one of them smote the servant of the High Priest *(this was Simon Peter; as well, John gives the servant's name as Malchus)*, and cut off his right ear *(evidently, Peter was trying to kill him!).*

51 And Jesus answered and said, Suffer you thus far *(probably means, although it has been debated, "bear with My Disciples")*. And He touched his ear, and healed him *(presents the last miracle of healing He performed before the Crucifixion).*

52 Then Jesus said unto the Chief Priests, and Captains of the

Temple, and the Elders, which were come to Him *(represented the religious hierarchy of Israel, the very ones who should have welcomed Him instead)*, Be ye come out, as against a thief, with swords and staves? *(This presents two thoughts: 1. If I wanted to use My Power against you, your swords and staves would do you no good at all; and, 2. I am not a thief, as should be obvious, so why do you treat Me as one?)*

53 When I was daily with you in the Temple, you stretched forth no hands against Me *(presents the truth of His position, and the fallacy of theirs)*: but this is your hour *(refers to God allowing the religious leaders of Israel to do this dastardly thing)*, and the power of darkness *(means that the energy by which they were doing this thing was the energy of the "power of darkness," i.e., Satan himself!)*.

THE DENIAL

54 Then took they Him, and led *Him*, and brought Him into the High Priest's house *(the High Priest at this time was Caiaphas, son-in-law to Annas, who was the legal High Priest, but who had been deposed by the Romans some time before)*. And Peter followed afar off *(does not record the reason for Peter's failure, as some believe; his problem, as with us all, was self-will)*.

55 And when they had kindled a fire in the midst of the hall, and were set down together *(speaks of those who had arrested Jesus, bringing Him to the house of the High Priest)*, Peter sat down among them *(proclaims him arriving at the Palace with John who was able to procure admission for the both of them, due to John being known to the High Priest)*.

56 But a certain maid beheld him as he sat by the fire, and earnestly looked upon him *(provides the first occasion for the terrible denial)*, and said, This man was also with Him *(probably came as a surprise to Peter)*.

57 And he denied Him, saying, Woman, I know Him not *(the first of three denials)*.

58 And after a little while another saw him, and said, You are also of them. And Peter said, Man, I am not *(the second denial)*.

59 And about the space of one hour after another confidently affirmed, saying, Of a truth this *fellow* also was with Him: for he is a Galilaean *(represents the occasion for the third and final denial)*.

60 And Peter said, Man, I know not what you say. And immediately, while he yet spoke, the rooster crowed *(the third denial, and exactly the number that Jesus predicted)*.

61 And the Lord turned, and

looked upon Peter (*probably refers to the moment that Jesus was being led from the interrogation before Caiaphas, to be examined before the Sanhedrin*). And Peter remembered the Word of the Lord, how He had said unto him, Before the rooster crows, you shall deny Me three times (*presents this coming back to Peter in full force, with all its attendant implications*).

62 And Peter went out, and wept bitterly (*this type of "weeping" signals repentance [Ps. 51:17]*).

THE TRIAL

63 And the men who held Jesus mocked Him (*referred to them goading Jesus that He use His Power to stop them; that is, if He had any power*), and smote Him (*fulfilled the Prophecies of Isaiah [Isa. 52:14]*).

64 And when they had blindfolded Him, they struck Him on the face (*many struck Him, no doubt causing His face to swell*), and asked Him, saying, Prophesy, who is it who smote You? (*These mockers will one day stand before God, with each name being called out and exactly the number of blows that they delivered to the Face of Jesus.*)

65 And many other things blasphemously spoke they against Him.

66 And as soon as it was day (*the trial which had been conducted that night was actually illegal; so now the Sanhedrin will meet again during the day, to try to legitimize what they had already done*), the Elders of the people and the Chief Priests and the Scribes came together, and led Him into their council, saying (*was to constitute His trial they thought, but in reality it was their trial*),

67 Are You the Christ? (*Evidently, all who were present were aware that Jesus had admitted to this while before Caiaphas, which Luke incidentally passes over, but is recounted by both Matthew and Mark.*) tell us (*said with anger and determination*). And He said unto them, If I tell you, you will not believe (*constitutes an answer far broader than they had asked*):

68 And if I also ask you (*refers to questions that, if properly answered, would have proved His Messiahship*), you will not answer Me (*refers to the fact that they were not looking for Truth*), nor let Me go (*this meant that the trial was a farce*).

69 Hereafter shall the Son of Man (*presents the last time Jesus will refer to Himself as such; in effect, this answers their question*) sit on the right hand of the Power of God (*refers to the Great White Throne Judgment, in effect saying, "you are judging Me today, but tomorrow I will judge you"*).

70 Then said they all, Are you then the Son of God? *(This was said with sarcasm!)* And He said unto them, You say that I am *(even though not resident in the Greek, in the Hebrew denotes a strong affirmation; in other words, in the clearest possible language He said, "I am!").*

71 And they said, What need we any further witness? *(This proclaims exactly what they wanted.)* for we ourselves have heard of His Own mouth *(means they would all witness against Him to Pilate that He had made this claim).*

CHAPTER 23

JESUS BEFORE PILATE

AND the whole multitude of them arose *(included the entirety of the seventy members of the Sanhedrin, with the possible exception of Joseph of Arimathaea and Nicodemus, who were also members but loved Christ)* and led Him unto Pilate *(presents the second step which must be carried out if, in fact, they were to rid themselves of Jesus once and for all, or so they thought!).*

2 And they began to accuse Him *(presents their response to Christ, and from the very beginning of His Ministry),* saying, We found this *fellow* perverting the nation *(claiming that Christ was attempting to agitate the nation of Israel to enter into rebellion against Caesar; this was a total fabrication, with Him doing the very opposite),* and forbidding to give tribute to Caesar *(constituted their second accusation, which was also a lie!),* saying that He Himself is Christ a King *(they were claiming He was telling Israel that He was King instead of Caesar, which was another lie).*

3 And Pilate asked Him, saying, Are You the King of the Jews? *(This presents Pilate completely ignoring the first two accusations, seeing clearly that they were baseless.)* And He answered him and said, You say *it (in effect, He answered in the affirmative).*

4 Then said Pilate to the Chief Priests and *to* the people, I find no fault in this Man *(and neither has any other human being ever truly found any "fault" in Him).*

5 And they were the more fierce *(proclaims the fact that Pilate's position came somewhat as a surprise to these fanatics),* saying, He stirs up the people *(the Greek word "stirs" is somewhat like inciting a mob to riot; of course, what they were saying was basely false),* teaching throughout all Jewry, beginning from Galilee to this place.

HEROD

6 When Pilate heard of Galilee, he asked whether the man were a Galilaean.

7 And as soon as he knew that He belonged unto Herod's jurisdiction, he sent Him to Herod (*proclaims him thinking he could wash his hands of this affair*), who himself also was at Jerusalem at that time (*constituted the Passover Season, which brought Herod to the city; his usual residence was Capernaum, which had been the headquarters of Jesus, but yet seemingly without much impact upon this murderer*).

8 And when Herod saw Jesus, he was exceeding glad (*constitutes a gladness for all the wrong reasons*): for he was desirous to see Him of a long *season*, because he had heard many things of Him (*had to do somewhat with both of them headquartered at Capernaum*); and he hoped to have seen some miracle done by Him (*Jesus was to Herod Antipas, the slayer of John the Baptist, as a juggler is to a sated court — an object of curiosity; it seems he had very little interest in Him otherwise!*).

9 Then he questioned with Him in many words; but He answered him nothing (*tells us that the questions were trivial; this pompous egomaniac did not for a moment realize that the Lord of Glory, the Creator of all things, was standing before him*).

10 And the Chief Priests and Scribes stood and vehemently accused Him (*they all evidently followed in order to accuse Jesus before Herod; we have here before us secular devils and religious devils; as bad as the secular devils might be, the religious devils are worse!*).

11 And Herod with his men of war set Him at nought, and mocked *Him* (*records the attitude and thinking of this despot*), and arrayed Him in a gorgeous robe, and sent Him again to Pilate (*means, as well, that Herod found no cause for death in Him; consequently, we have a second record and public attestation of His innocence*).

12 And the same day Pilate and Herod were made friends together: for before they were at enmity between themselves (*worldly men with differences meet together, when opportunity offers itself for wounding Christ*).

BARABBAS

13 And Pilate, when he had called together the Chief Priests and the Rulers and the people (*once again at Pilate's judgment hall*),

14 Said unto them, You have brought this man unto me, as one who perverts the people: and, behold, I, having examined *Him* before you, have found no fault in this man touching those things whereof you accuse Him (*presents the second public confession of*

Pilate, who also publicly acknowledged that the civil rulers of Galilee had found no fault in Him as
well!):

15 No, nor yet Herod: for I sent
you to Him (refers to the Sanhedrin
being sent to Herod, along with
Jesus); and, lo, nothing worthy of
death is done unto Him (should
have been translated "by Him").

16 I will therefore chastise Him
(scourge Him; he would subject a
Man Whom he had pronounced
innocent to the horrible punishment
of scourging just to satisfy the clamor
of the Sanhedrists, because he was
fearful of what they might accuse
him of at Rome, where he knew he
had enemies), and release Him (was
said concerning the release of one
prisoner each year at the Passover).

17 (For of necessity he must
release one unto them at the
feast.) (This custom was probably
introduced at Jerusalem by the Roman power. There is no evidence
of such in Levitical Law.)

18 And they cried out all at
once (proclaims their strong opposition to his decision to release
Jesus), saying, Away with this Man,
and release unto us Barabbas
(this is exactly what they got, and
have had ever since; they preferred
a "robber," as John styled him, to
the Son of God; so they got the
robber, and they've had robbers ever
since; the nations of the world have
robbed them of their dignity, pride,

and lives for nearly 2,000 years):

19 (Who for a certain sedition
made in the city (tried to stir up
insurrection against Rome), and for
murder, was cast into prison.) (It
was bad enough to prefer a "robber" over Jesus, but to prefer a "murderer" was a horror, which would
be perpetrated upon them from that
day forward. History is replete with
the accounts!)

20 Pilate therefore, willing to
release Jesus, spoke again to them
(presents the Governor attempting
to release Jesus for the fourth time
as recorded by Luke, but to no
avail!).

21 But they cried, saying, Crucify Him, crucify Him (presents the
type of execution they demanded;
Why? the Levitical Law said that
one who was hung upon a tree for
gross crimes was cursed by God;
consequently, Him being Crucified
would prove to the people, or so
they thought, that He was not of
God; were He of God, they reasoned, God would not allow such
[Deut. 21:22-23]).

22 And he said unto them the
third time (refers to the times he
had attempted to free Jesus on the
premise of the custom of releasing
at the Passover each year; actually,
this was about the fifth time he
had made such an attempt over all),
Why, what evil has He done? (He
had done no evil, and Pilate knew
the accusations of the religious

hierarchy against Him to be false.) I have found no cause of death in Him *(little did the Governor know that of which He spoke; had there been a cause of death in Jesus, He could not have served as the Sacrifice for sin)*: I will therefore chastise Him, and let Him go *(sounds a note of desperation).*

23 And they were instant with loud voices, requiring that He might be crucified *(many have said that the same crowd who was crying, "Hosanna to the Highest" at the Triumphant Entry was now crying, "Crucify Him!"; that is incorrect; the rabble that joined the religious leaders that early morning hour was, for the most part, the night people, or lackeys of the Sanhedrin).* And the voices of them and of the Chief Priests prevailed *(presents their success, but a success they would ever rue; their prevailing sealed their own doom).*

24 And Pilate gave sentence that it should be as they required *(would prove to be the worst day of His life, but could have been the best).*

25 And he released unto them him who for sedition and murder was cast into prison, whom they had desired *(they got exactly that for which they asked, which has followed them unto this hour)*; but he delivered Jesus to their will *(was the worst thing that Pilate would ever do in all his life).*

26 And as they led Him away *(presents the horrifying trip to the place of Crucifixion, Golgotha, with Jesus carrying the Cross)*, they laid hold upon one Simon, a Cyrenian, coming out of the country *(as Mark tells us, this was the father of "Alexander, and Rufus," notable persons in the Early Church [Mk. 15:21])*, and on him they laid the cross, that he might bear it after Jesus *(probably means that Jesus, due to being beaten so severely, which no doubt resulted in a great loss of blood, ultimately became too weak to bear the weight of the Cross; so Simon was compelled; what an honor to carry it for Jesus).*

THE WOMEN

27 And there followed Him a great company of people *(there were many no doubt in the crowd whom He had healed)*, and of women, which also bewailed and lamented Him *(no woman is mentioned in the Gospels as having spoken against the Lord, or as having a share in His death).*

28 But Jesus turning unto them said *(represents the first time He spoke since His last interrogation before Pilate)*, Daughters of Jerusalem *(a fixture of the "Song of Solomon")*, weep not for Me, but weep for yourselves, and for your children *(proclaims His rejection by the religious leaders of Israel, and*

the subsequent judgment which will follow).

29 For, behold, the days are coming (would actually see fulfillment about thirty-seven years from this time), in the which they shall say, Blessed *are* the barren, and the wombs that never bear, and the paps which never gave suck (presents a strange Beatitude; He was speaking of the horror that was coming, which would be so bad that the dead would be blessed, along with the children never born).

30 Then shall they begin to say to the mountains, Fall on us; and to the hills, Cover us (this Prophecy speaks of the destruction of Jerusalem in A.D. 70).

31 For if they do these things in a green tree (He was the "Green Tree"), what shall be done in the dry? (When He would be gone! Concerns the great Tribulation, even yet to come.)

THE CRUCIFIXION

32 And there were also two others, malefactors (criminals; some think these were companions of Barabbas, who had just been released), led with Him to be put to death.

33 And when they were come to the place, which is called Calvary, where they crucified Him (the Cross, which was the most hor-rifying instrument of torture the world had ever known, became an emblem of beauty because of what Jesus did on that Cross), and the malefactors (the two criminals), one on the right hand, and the other on the left (may not have been the only ones crucified that day, but were the only ones in this particular position).

34 Then said Jesus, Father, forgive them; for they know not what they do (presents the only prayer ever prayed by Jesus, which was not answered; if men will not seek forgiveness, even Christ praying for them will not avail!). And they parted His raiment (divided up His garments), and cast lots (His robe was without seam, so rather than cutting it up, they would draw straws).

35 And the people stood beholding (who made up this crowd is not known). And the Rulers also with them derided Him (means that they "mocked Him"), saying, He saved others; let Him save Himself, if He be Christ, the Chosen of God (if He had saved His life, which He certainly could have done, He could not have saved others; in fact, the Cross had been planned from before the foundation of the world [I Pet. 1:18-20]).

36 And the soldiers also mocked Him (was probably carried out by these heathen simply because they heard the religious leaders mocking Him), coming to Him, and

offering Him vinegar (was in response to His plea for water [Jn.
19:28]),

37 And saying, If You be the
King of the Jews, save Yourself
(what they did not know was that
He was not only the "King of the
Jews," but the Creator of the Heavens and Earth, the Maker of all
things).

38 And a superscription also
was written over Him in letters
of Greek, and Latin, and Hebrew
(constituted that written by Pilate;
he probably did it to mock the religious leaders of Israel), THIS IS
THE KING OF THE JEWS.

THE PENITENT THIEF

39 And one of the malefactors
which were hanged railed on Him,
saying, If You be Christ, save Yourself and us (is reported by Matthew
and Mark as both doing this in the
beginning; however, at a point,
one, which we will read about momentarily, changed completely).

40 But the other answering rebuked Him, saying (proclaims the
spirit of true repentance), Do not
You fear God, seeing you are in
the same condemnation? (This
means that he is owning up to his
guilt, which is the first requirement of repentance.)

41 And we indeed justly; for we
receive the due reward of our
deeds (proclaims him making no
excuses, admitting to his sin, holding no enmity toward his executers,
which presents a powerful truth):
but this Man has done nothing
amiss (presents the only kind word
uttered about Christ at this time,
other than that spoken by the Centurion).

42 And He said unto Jesus
(speaks of recognition as to Who Jesus
really was), Lord, remember me
when You come into Your Kingdom (presents the simple prayer of
repentance; it is one of the most remarkable conversions recorded in the
Bible).

43 And Jesus said unto him,
Verily I say unto you, Today shall
you be with Me in Paradise (a
statement of fact, and not a question, as some claim; however, his
stay in Paradise would be very short;
some three days later, he would accompany Christ to Heaven, along
with every other person in Paradise, which included all the Old
Testament Saints).

THE DEATH OF JESUS

44 And it was about the sixth
hour (12 noon), and there was a
darkness over all the earth until
the ninth hour (3 p.m., this was
the time that Jesus bore the penalty of sin for the entirety of mankind, and for all time).

45 And the sun was darkened
(means that the darkness was so

deep that it literally blotted out the light of the sun; what He experienced during this 3-hour period, no one will ever know [Ps. 22:1-21]), and the Veil of the Temple was rent in the midst (probably referred to the approximate time He died, about 3 p.m.; this "Veil" separated the Holy Place in the Temple from the Holy of Holies, where God was supposed to dwell; the Veil being torn apart, in effect, stated that God had accepted the Sacrifice, and now the way was open for sinful man to come to God and be cleansed; but he would have to come by the Way of Christ and the Cross; there is no other way of Salvation [Jn. 14:6]).

46 And when Jesus had cried with a loud voice (proclaims the fact that He did not die from weakness; actually, they did not take His life, He gave it up freely [Jn. 10:17-18]), He said, Father, into Your hands I commend My Spirit (proclaims the last words He uttered): and having said thus, He gave up the ghost (He didn't die until the Holy Spirit told Him He could die [Heb. 9:14]).

47 Now when the Centurion saw what was done, he glorified God (this hard-bitten Roman Centurion knew that Jesus was the Son of God, but the religious leaders of Israel didn't!), saying, Certainly this was a Righteous Man (tradition says that his name was Longinus, and that he became an avid follower of Christ, and died a martyr to the cause).

48 And all the people who came together to that sight, beholding the things which were done (seems to indicate that quite a few were there when He died, standing in the darkness, hearing His last words, and thereby experiencing the earthquake; but yet, due to the darkness, they really did not see Him die; in fact, no one did!), smote their breasts, and returned (speaks of an agony of heart, knowing that something horrible has happened, and that a great wrong has been done).

49 And all His acquaintance (concerned His chosen Disciples and some chosen followers), and the women who followed Him from Galilee, stood afar off, beholding these things (seems to indicate that they stood near the Cross for a time [John 19:25-27], and then retired for whatever reason to a further distance [Mat. 27:55-56]).

THE BURIAL OF JESUS

50 And, behold, there was a man named Joseph, a Counsellor (this was Joseph of Arimathaea, a member of the Sanhedrin and a person of high distinction in Jerusalem and evidently of great wealth); and he was a good man, and a just:

51 (The same had not con-
sented to the counsel and deed
of them;) *(speaks of the illegal and
unjust decision of the Sanhedrin,
of which he was a part)* he was of
Arimathaea, a city of the Jews *(the
home of the Prophet Samuel; however, he now lived in Jerusalem due
to the fact of being a member of
the Sanhedrin)*: who also himself
waited for the Kingdom of God
*(he would be shown that Kingdom,
and would enter that Kingdom)*.

52 This *man* went unto Pilate
*(it seems that the Centurion who
had testified at the Death of Jesus
accompanied Joseph to an audience
with Pilate)*, and begged the body
of Jesus *(there is an urgency about
this because the High Sabbath of
the Passover would begin at sundown Thursday; if Jesus was not
taken down from the Cross before
then and placed in a tomb, they
would have to allow Him to remain
on the Cross for another twenty-
four hours)*.

53 And he took it down *(refers
to the body of Jesus, which says so
very much, while saying so very
little)*, and wrapped it in linen
*(pertained to a part of the burial
process, which was done very hur-
riedly because the High Sabbath of
the Passover would begin at sundown, necessitating that all work
must stop)*, and laid it in a sepulchre that was hewn in stone,
wherein never man before was
laid *(the tomb belonged to Joseph,
and was the very kind predicted by
Isaiah [Isa. 53:9])*.

54 And that day was the preparation *(spoke of the preparation
of the Passover, which was to be
eaten the next day, Thursday)*, and
the Sabbath drew on *(is not speaking of the regular weekly Sabbath
of Saturday, but rather the High
Sabbath of the Passover, which would
commence at sundown)*.

55 And the women also, which
came with Him from Galilee
*(Matthew records that there were
"many women who were there")*,
followed after, and beheld the
sepulchre, and how His body was
laid *(does not exactly say that they
participated in this which was done
by Joseph and Nicodemus, but possibly they did!)*.

56 And they returned, and prepared spices and ointments *(means
that they returned to the places
where they were staying while in
Jerusalem, and would have made
these preparations on Friday)*; and
rested the Sabbath day according
to the Commandment *(the next
day, Thursday, was the High Sabbath of the Passover, and so they
could not prepare these things that
day; they would have prepared them
on Friday; and then resting again
on the weekly Sabbath of Saturday
as required, would have come early
on Sunday morning to apply the
ingredients, but would be greatly

surprised at what they found).

CHAPTER 24

THE RESURRECTION

NOW upon the first *day* of the week *(Sunday)*, very early in the morning *(before the rising of the sun)*, they came unto the sepulchre *(speaks of the women of Verse 55 of the previous Chapter)*, bringing the spices which they had prepared *(proclaims that none of these women, or the Disciples, or anyone for that matter, believed that Jesus would rise from the dead; had they believed, they would not have been coming to the tomb with spices for the corpse)*, and certain *others* with them *(who they were, we aren't told)*.

2 And they found the stone rolled away from the sepulchre *(this "stone" weighed several hundred pounds, thereby requiring at least several men to roll it away from the door where it had been placed; so, the stone being rolled away was no doubt very strange to them)*.

3 And they entered in *(entered the tomb)*, and found not the body of the Lord Jesus *(His Resurrection Title is, "Lord Jesus")*.

4 And it came to pass, as they were much perplexed thereabout *(they did not know what to make of the situation)*, behold, two men stood by them in shining gar-

ments *(these were Angels, and their "shining garments" were literally unlike anything these women had ever seen, regarding glory)*:

5 And as they were afraid, and bowed down *their* faces to the earth *(implying that the appearance of these Angels was so dazzling that it blinded their eyes, causing them to look downward)*, they said unto them *(the Angels spoke to the women)*, Why seek ye the living among the dead? *(Notes a mild rebuke, with a touch of sarcasm.)*

6 He is not here, but is risen *(this phrase, or a derivative, became the watchword of the Early Church; "He is Risen")*: remember how He spoke unto you when He was yet in Galilee *(proclaims the Angels drawing these women back to the Words of Christ, when He had related to them and the Disciples how He would be killed in Jerusalem, and would rise from the dead; He had even told them how long He would be in the tomb [Mat. 12:40])*,

7 Saying, The Son of Man must be delivered into the hands of sinful men, and be crucified, and the third day rise again *([Luke 18:32-33] the Angels referred to the religious leaders of Israel and the Romans as "sinful men")*.

8 And they remembered His words *(recollection is more important than information)*,

THE TESTIMONY

9 And returned from the sepulchre, and told all these things unto the Eleven, and to all the rest *(records the fact that women were the first Preachers of the Resurrection).*

10 It was Mary Magdalene, and Joanna *(the wife of Chuza, Herod's steward [Lk. 8:3]),* and Mary *the mother* of James *(James and John),* and other *women who were* with them, which told these things unto the Apostles.

11 And their words seemed to them as idle tales *(means in the Greek, "silly nonsense"),* and they believed them not *(the reason for their unbelief, resulting in their demeanor, was a departure from the Word of God; every wrongdoing and wrong direction are always, and without exception, a departure from the Word; the persistence of the Apostles in Preaching the Resurrection everywhere after Pentecost proves that the Resurrection was a fact; for if not a fact, how could they confidently affirm to be true that which they had steadfastly refused to believe?).*

12 Then arose Peter, and ran unto the sepulchre *(he was accompanied by John [Jn. 20:3]);* and stooping down, he beheld the linen clothes laid by themselves *(this proved that His Body had not been stolen; if such had been the* case, the thief certainly would not have stopped to take all the time to unwrap the linen from around the corpse; as well, this linen wrapping was neatly folded and laid to the side, which no thieves would have done),* and departed, wondering in himself at that which was come to pass *(presents the beginning of Faith, but yet very weak).*

THE TWO DISCIPLES

13 And, behold, two of them *(one was Cleopas, the father of James the Less and husband of Mary, the sister of the Mother of Jesus [Jn. 19:25]; we are not told who the other man was; many ancient scholars hold that it was Luke himself, and they further say that he was one of the seventy, and the reason he did not mention himself was that he was the writer of this account)* went that same day to a village called Emmaus, which was from Jerusalem *about* threescore furlongs *(about seven miles).*

14 And they talked together of all these things which had happened *(pertaining to the Crucifixion and as well to the testimonies of the women concerning the appearance of Angels, etc.).*

15 And it came to pass, that, while they communed *together* and reasoned *(they were deep in thought),* Jesus himself drew near, and went with them *(this would*

not of itself have occasioned surprise; the roads in those days were
heavily trafficked with pedestrians,
and someone doing this would not
have been out of the ordinary).

16 But their eyes were holden
that they should not know Him
(was done purposely by the Lord so
they would not recognize Him; He
would not reveal Himself to these
two Disciples until He had brought
them into a fitting condition of soul).

17 And He said unto them,
What manner of communications
are these that you have one to
another, as you walk, and are sad?
(Many modern Christians are uselessly sad, even as here, because of
unbelief!)

18 And the one of them, whose
name was Cleopas, answering said
unto Him (had He known this was
Jesus, He would have conducted himself quite differently), Are You only
a stranger in Jerusalem, and have
not known the things which are
come to pass therein these days?
(This is asked with some sarcasm!)

19 And He said unto them, What
things? (The question is asked solely
for the purpose of drawing them
out.) And they said unto Him, Concerning Jesus of Nazareth, which
was a Prophet mighty in deed and
word before God and all the
people (if it is to be noticed, Cleopas
did not mention Jesus being the
Messiah; while they had once believed
this, their faith was now shaken):

20 And how the Chief Priests
and our Rulers delivered Him to
be condemned to death, and have
crucified Him (organized religion
did this!).

21 But we trusted that it had
been He which should have redeemed Israel (they had confined
their Bible study to that which the
Scriptures promised respecting the
Messiah's glory and Kingdom, but
they had been blind to the multitude of types and Prophecies foretelling His sufferings as an Atoning Saviour): and beside all this,
today is the third day since these
things were done (they dwelt on
the third day, and rightly so).

22 Yea, and certain women also
of our company made us astonished, which were early at the
sepulchre (speaks of their testimony of the tomb being empty);

23 And when they found not
His body, they came, saying, that
they had also seen a vision of Angels, which said that He was alive.

24 And certain of them which
were with us went to the sepulchre (Peter and John), and found
it even so as the women had said:
but Him they saw not (the last
phrase carries an element of doubt).

25 Then He said unto them, O
fools (should have been translated,
"foolish men!"), and slow of heart
to believe all that the Prophets
have spoken (proclaims the fact
that the Lord concludes as very

"foolish" those who do not make His Word as the basis for all actions and decisions; He pulls them back to the Bible; It alone is the criteria for all things):

26 Ought not Christ to have suffered these things (means the Bible predicted His sufferings, which should have been obvious to His followers and would have been had they only devoted time and attention to the Word of God), and to enter into His glory? (Proclaims that the Bible does outline the coming Kingdom of Glory, hence the "Triumphant Messiah;" however, it must be preceded by the mission of the "Suffering Messiah.")

27 And beginning at Moses and all the Prophets (the Lord here makes two declarations respecting the Bible: 1. It is the supreme authority as to Faith and Doctrine because it is inspired; and, 2. It's subject are the sufferings and glories of Christ — His sufferings as sin-bearer and His glories as sin-purger [Phil. 2:5-11; Heb. 1:3]), He expounded unto them in all the Scriptures the things concerning Himself (it may truly be said that Christ went into death Bible in hand, and that He came out from among the dead Bible in hand; He insisted that it predicted His Death and Resurrection in relation to sin and its judgment).

28 And they drew nigh unto the village, whither they went (Em-

maus): and He made as though He would have gone further (how many are there to whom He has drawn near, but with whom He has not tarried because they have allowed Him to "go away").

29 But they constrained Him, saying, Abide with us (they insisted, and strongly!): for it is toward evening, and the day is far spent. And He went in to tarry with them (He will tarry with any and all who sincerely desire Him to do so).

30 And it came to pass, as He sat at meat with them, He took bread, and blessed it, and break, and gave to them (symbolic of what He does with us; He "takes us," and then "blesses us," and then "breaks us," for the flesh must ultimately be broken, and then "gives us" to the Church; if this pattern is not followed, we will be of no blessing whatsoever).

31 And their eyes were opened (He now allowed them to truly see), and they knew Him (what joy must have filled their hearts; Jesus is alive!); and He vanished out of their sight (but only after He had revealed Himself to them).

32 And they said one to another, Did not our heart burn within us, while He talked with us by the way, and while He opened to us the Scriptures? (The business of Christ, through the Holy Spirit, is to help us understand the Word of God.)

33 And they rose up the same

hour, and returned to Jerusalem *(presents a joy they could not contain, and no wonder)*, and found the Eleven gathered together, and them who were with them *(presents a meeting that will quickly change from despair to great joy; admittedly, they had to arrive at this place by stages, but were on their way; praise God!)*,

34 Saying, The Lord is risen indeed *(presents a conversation of victory, in fact the greatest victory ever recorded in human history)*, and has appeared to Simon *(the Scripture does not give us the account of this appearance, but the likelihood is that Peter was the first man to see Jesus after His Resurrection)*.

35 And they told what things *were done* in the way *(an excited presentation)*, and how He was known of them in breaking of bread.

JESUS APPEARS

36 And as they thus spoke, Jesus Himself stood in the midst of them *(refers to an instant appearance and revelation; John added that "the doors were shut")*, and said unto them, Peace *be* unto you *(presents His first words to them as a group after the Resurrection)*.

37 But they were terrified and affrighted *(speaks to the suddenness of the event, and the manner in which it was done; one moment He is not there, and the next moment He is!)*, and supposed that they had seen a spirit *(this shows that they still didn't understand the Resurrection; they did not doubt the appearances, but did not really recognize these appearances for what they actually were)*.

38 And He said unto them, Why are you troubled? *(Being troubled robs us of peace.)* and why do thoughts arise in your hearts? *(This pertains to fear, doubt, discouragement and even despair, all brought on by lack of Faith in God's Word. We should, as well, take the questions to heart.)*

39 Behold My hands and My feet, that it is I Myself: handle Me, and see *(they will now understand what His Resurrection really was)*; for a spirit has not flesh and bones, as You see Me have *(in other words, Jesus was telling them that He was not a disembodied spirit; He, in fact, had a physical body of flesh and bones; no blood is mentioned because the Glorified Body has no blood; whereas now the life of the flesh is in the blood, then, when our bodies are glorified, the life will be in the Spirit, i.e., "Holy Spirit")*.

40 And when He had thus spoken, He showed them *His* hands and *His* feet *(John also adds that He had invited them as well to see the wound in His side; in fact, He will retain these wounds forever*

[Zech. 13:6; Rev. 5:6]).

41 And while they yet believed not for joy, and wondered *(indicates that their faith was still weak; we have a tendency to correct them, but would we have done any better?),* He said unto them, Have you here any meat? *(This is meant to further portray to them the fact that He still retained a human body, albeit Glorified, and that as such He could partake of food. A "spirit" does not have flesh and bones, and likewise does not eat.)*

42 And they gave Him a piece of a broiled fish, and of an honeycomb *(it is speculated that this was in the home of John Mark, who wrote the Book of Mark).*

43 And He took *it,* and did eat before them *(if it is to be noticed, Jesus did not ask His Disciples to believe anything that was contrary to their senses).*

44 And He said unto them, These *are* the words which I spoke unto you, while I was yet with you, that all things must be fulfilled, which were written in the Law of Moses, and *in* the Prophets, and *in* the Psalms, concerning Me *(the Jews divided the Old Testament into three parts — the Law of Moses, the Prophets, and the Psalms, which consisted of the Wisdom Books; the entire story of the Old Testament is the story of Jesus and the Cross, and what the Cross affords; in fact, if we do not understand that, we can-*

not fully understand the Word of God; as is here made plainly obvious, "Christ and Him Crucified" is the key to all understanding).

45 Then opened He their understanding, that they might understand the Scriptures *(he who doesn't understand the Scriptures, understands little or nothing; let us say it again: "Jesus Christ and Him Crucified," is the story of the Bible; every doctrine must be built upon that foundation, which constitutes the house built upon the Rock; otherwise, it's a house built upon sand),*

THE GREAT COMMISSION

46 And said unto them, Thus it is written *(proves what I have just stated concerning Christ and the Cross),* and thus it behoved Christ to suffer, and to rise from the dead the third day *(let us say it again, this is the story of the Bible):*

47 And that repentance and remission of sins should be preached in His Name *(presents God's method of proclaiming His Word, and carrying out His Work; any other method is unscriptural)* among all nations, beginning at Jerusalem *(God's Plan of Salvation is identical for all regarding race, color, or culture; it is for the whole world).*

48 And you are witnesses of these things *(Christianity was not begun as the result of an enlightened philosophy, as with all religions;*

it was begun by men and women who literally witnessed the incarnate Son of God in all His earthly Ministry, as well as His Death and Resurrection; consequently, they could say, "we have seen, and do testify").

49 And, behold, I send the Promise of My Father upon you *(the Baptism with the Holy Spirit, which would come on the Day of Pentecost [Acts 1:4-5]):* but tarry ye in the city of Jerusalem *(this was where the Temple was located, and where the Day of Pentecost was always celebrated, which would occasion the outpouring of the Spirit; this was only for the initial outpouring; since then, Jesus Baptizes with the Holy Spirit wherever the person might be [Acts, Chapters 8-10, 19]),* until you be endued with power from on high *(this is the Baptism with the Holy Spirit, which is always accompanied by the speaking with other tongues [Acts 2:4]; without being thus endued, the Believer and the Church are of little worth to the Kingdom of God).*

THE ASCENSION

50 And He led them out as far as to Bethany *(this little village was located on the far side of the Mount of Olives, and is actually a suburb of Jerusalem; it was the home of Jesus' beloved friends, Mary, Martha, and Lazarus),* and He lifted up His hands, and blessed them *(proclaims Him as Israel's High Priest, having made Atonement, consequently lifting up His Hands and blessing the people, which the High Priests of Israel had done for nearly 1,600 years; all is a type of what He would ultimately do; but let it be understood that His blessing is for all, and not merely the Jews).*

51 And it came to pass, while He blessed them *(implies continued blessing, which means that it continues even unto this hour, and will in fact continue forever),* He was parted from them, and carried up into Heaven *(pertains to the Ascension; He hastened to the Cross in order to Atone for His people's sins, but He did not hasten to Glory, for He was reluctant to leave His Beloved sheep).*

52 And they worshipped Him *(means His Presence was still with them, even though He had already ascended),* and returned to Jerusalem with great joy *(signaled a different group of people, at least regarding faith, spirit, and emotions, than at the Crucifixion; then all was darkness; now all is light):*

53 And were continually in the Temple, praising and blessing God *(due to the Promise of the Father being made real in our hearts, we now are the Temple [I Cor. 3:16] and should praise the Lord continually).* Amen *(all of the four Gospels close with the word "Amen," which means "Truth").*

THE GOSPEL ACCORDING TO

JOHN

CHAPTER 1

THE DEITY OF CHRIST

IN the beginning (*does not infer that Christ as God had a beginning, because as God He had no beginning, but rather refers to the time of Creation [Gen. 1:1]*) was the Word (*the Holy Spirit through John describes Jesus as "the Eternal Logos"*), and the Word was with God (*"was in relationship with God," and expresses the idea of the Trinity*), and the Word was God (*meaning that He did not cease to be God during the Incarnation; He "was" and "is" God from eternity past to eternity future*).

2 The same was in the beginning with God (*this very Person was in eternity with God; there's only one God, but manifested in three Persons — God the Father, God the Son, God the Holy Spirit*).

3 All things were made by Him (*all things came into being through Him; it refers to every item of Creation one by one, rather than all things regarded in totality*); and without Him was not any thing made that was made (*nothing, not even one single thing, was made independently of His cooperation and volition*).

4 In Him was Life (*presents Jesus, the Eternal Logos, as the first cause*); and the Life was the Light of men (*He Alone is the Life Source of Light; if one doesn't know Christ, one is in darkness*).

5 And the Light shines in darkness (*speaks of the Incarnation of Christ, and His coming into this world; His "Light," because it is derived from His Life, drives out "darkness"*); and the darkness comprehended it not (*should have been translated, "apprehended it not"; it means that Satan, even though he tried with all his might, could not stop "the Light"; today it shines all over the world, and one day soon, there will be nothing left but that "Light"*).

JOHN THE BAPTIST

6 There was a man sent from God, whose name *was* John.

7 The same came for a witness (*speaks of the Mission of the Prophet*), to bear witness of the Light (*spoke of Jesus and only Jesus*), that all *men* through Him might believe (*presents that Jesus is not only for Israel, but also for the entirety of the world*).

8 He was not that Light *(John the Baptist was not the Light)*, but *was sent* to bear witness of that Light *(presents the sum total that man can do)*.

THE INCARNATION

9 *That* was the True Light *(there are many false lights; Jesus is the only True Light)*, which lighteth every man who comes into the world *(if man is to find Light, it will be only in Christ, and it is for "every man")*.

10 He was in the world *(the Eternal Logos, the "Creator")*, and the world was made by Him *(as it was originally created before the fall of Lucifer and the Fall of man)*, and the world knew Him not *(the world cannot know Christ by wisdom, but only by Revelation)*.

11 He came unto His Own *(the world in general, but more specifically to the Jews)*, and His Own received Him not *(He came as the Heir unto His Own Possessions [Mat. 21:38], but His Own servants did not receive Him; on the contrary, they killed Him)*.

12 But as many as received Him *(some did receive Him, and some do receive Him)*, to them gave He power to become the sons of God *(constitutes one of the greatest Promises in the Word of God)*, *even* to them who believe on His Name *(Faith in Christ and in what He has done for us at the Cross alone can make a person a "son or daughter of God")*:

13 Which were born, not of blood *(means that men become God's children not by natural birth)*, nor of the will of the flesh *(man cannot earn Salvation, it is a free gift, received upon Faith)*, nor of the will of man *(refers to man's religious efforts)*, but of God *(Salvation is not at all of man, but altogether of God)*.

14 And the Word was made flesh *(refers to the Incarnation, "God becoming man")*, and dwelt among us *(refers to Jesus, although Perfect, not holding Himself aloft from all others, but rather lived as all men, even a peasant)*, (and we beheld His glory, the glory as of the only Begotten of the Father,) *(speaks of His Deity, although hidden from the eyes of the merely curious; while Christ laid aside the expression of His Deity, He never lost the possession of His Deity)* full of Grace and Truth *(as "flesh," proclaimed His humanity, "Grace and Truth" His Deity)*.

THE TESTIMONY

15 John bear witness of Him *(John the Baptist was raised up for this very purpose)*, and cried, saying, This was He of Whom I spoke *(concerns the Ministry of John regarding the Person of Jesus)*, He

who comes after me is preferred before me (*should have been translated, "existed before me"*): for He was before me (*once again, a testimony to the Deity of Christ; as God, He has always been*).

16 And of His fulness have all we received (*John has told us Who Jesus is, now he tells us what He does*), and Grace for Grace (*should have been translated, "Grace upon Grace;" this is the provision of His Love heaped one upon another in this supply of His people's needs*).

17 For the Law was given by Moses, *but* Grace and Truth came by Jesus Christ (*proclaims Him as the Representative Law Keeper for all humanity, i.e., to all who will believe; the Law manifested man [full of wickedness]; the Son manifested God [full of goodness]*).

18 No man has seen God at any time (*better translated, "No man has ever comprehended or experienced God at any time in all His fullness"*); the Only Begotten Son (*Jesus Christ and the Incarnation, Who Alone could perfectly declare the Father*), which is in the bosom of the Father (*proclaims the most intimate and loving fellowship with the Father*), He has declared *Him* (*in essence, God the Father and God the Son are One*).

19 And this is the record of John, when the Jews sent Priests and Levites from Jerusalem to ask him, Who are you? (*At the time, some thought that John the Baptist was the Messiah.*)

20 And he confessed (*there was absolutely no hesitation in his confession regarding who he actually was, and above all, his mission*), and denied not (*he did not deny that some were calling him "Christ," however, to not even the slightest degree did he encourage this, and in fact grandly repudiates the rumor*); but confessed, I am not the Christ (*in the Greek actually says, "I, for my part, am not the Christ," and is said with emphasis*).

21 And they asked him, What then? Are you Elijah? (*Malachi had predicted the coming again from Heaven of Elijah the Prophet [Mal. 4:5].*) And he said, I am not (*presents a categorical negative; some of the Jews were insinuating that He was the actual reincarnation of Elijah*). Are you that Prophet? (*This spoke of the Prophet mentioned by Moses in Deuteronomy 18:15-18. This was the Messiah. So again, they asked him if he was the Messiah?*) And he answered, No.

22 Then said they unto him, Who are you? that we may give an answer to them who sent us (*they were not really seeking proper information, or the Truth about the matter, but rather desired that he claim something of which they could accuse him*). What say you of yourself? (*His answer is extremely re-*

vealing!)

23 He said, I *am* the voice of one crying in the wilderness *(is taken from Isaiah 40:3)*, Make straight the Way of the Lord, as said the Prophet Isaiah *(proclaims his mission as the first phrase proclaims his identity)*.

24 And they which were sent were of the Pharisees *(the Holy Spirit is careful to delineate the source of these questions; the opposition now begins)*.

25 And they asked him, and said unto him, Why do you baptize then, if you be not that Christ, nor Elijah, neither that Prophet? *(They were indignant that John not only baptized without ecclesiastical authority, but baptized contrary to the practice of the Pharisees. In other words, he had not asked nor sought their permission, nor did it seem that he cared whether they agreed or not!)*

26 John answered them, saying, I baptize with water *(meaning that it was but a temporary symbol of the true, abiding, and effectual baptism of the One Who would baptize with the Holy Spirit)*: but there stands One among you, Whom you know not *(points to their spiritual ignorance; Christ was in their very midst, and they did not know!)*;

27 He it is *(the Messiah is already here, even though you do not know Him, and He, as stated, is not me)*, Who coming after me is

preferred before me *(Who existed before me, in fact, has existed eternally)*, Whose shoe's latchet I am not worthy to unloose *(by comparison to Christ, the greatest Prophet born of woman labels himself, and rightly so!)*.

28 These things were done in Bethabara beyond Jordan, where John was baptizing *(probably not far from Jericho)*.

29 The next day *(refers to the day after John had been questioned by the emissaries from the Sanhedrin)* John sees Jesus coming unto him *(is no doubt after the baptism of Jesus, and the temptation in the wilderness)*, and said, Behold the Lamb of God *(proclaims Jesus as the Sacrifice for sin, in fact the Sin-Offering, Whom all the multiple millions of offered lambs had represented)*, which takes away the sin of the world *(animal blood could only cover sin, it could not take it away; but Jesus offering Himself as the perfect Sacrifice took away the sin of the world; He not only cleansed acts of sin, but, as well, addressed the root cause [Col. 2:14-15])*.

30 This is He of Whom I said *(proclaims John making a positive identification; it is the One Who "takes away the sin of the world")*, After me comes a Man which is preferred before me *(affirms His essential humanity)*: for He was before me *(affirms His essential Deity)*.

31 And I knew Him not *(doesn't mean that he was not acquainted with Christ, but that he was not to introduce Christ until the Holy Spirit said so)*: but that He should be made manifest to Israel *(means that at a certain time, and not before, Jesus was to be introduced to Israel as the Messiah, which John carried out exactly as led)*, therefore am I come baptizing with water *(proclaims that which the Holy Spirit told him to do)*.

32 And John bear record *(means that this is exactly what the Holy Spirit said would happen, concerning the identity of Jesus as the Messiah)*, saying, I saw the Spirit descending from Heaven like a dove *(we must come to the conclusion that John saw something, which was the Holy Spirit; Luke recorded, "descending in a bodily shape like a dove upon Him," [Lk. 3:22]; we must conclude from these statements that the Holy Spirit has a Spirit Body of some nature)*, and it abode upon Him *(the Spirit coming upon Him signaled the beginning of His Ministry)*.

33 And I knew Him not *(is used the second time by John, and with purpose; the Holy Spirit wants all to know that John's introduction of Jesus as the Messiah was not according to the flesh, i.e., personal knowledge, circumstances, etc., but rather by Revelation from on High; no one can really know Jesus, un-less revealed by the Holy Spirit)*: but He Who sent me to baptize with water *(telling us that Water Baptism as instituted by John was not that Prophet's idea at all, but rather was given to him by Revelation from God)*, the same said unto me, Upon Whom you shall see the Spirit descending, and remaining on Him *(was to be the Revelation from God, which John was to heed, and he did)*, the same is He which baptizes with the Holy Spirit *(proclaims what Jesus would do after His Death and Resurrection; the Cross would make this possible!)*.

34 And I saw, and bear record that this is the Son of God *(John the Baptist had followed his instructions to the letter, and according to the Revelation, he knew without doubt that Jesus was the Son of God)*.

THE FIRST DISCIPLES

35 Again the next day after John stood *(the day after he made the previous statements)*, and two of his disciples *(was Andrew and no doubt John, who at that time were Disciples of the Baptist)*;

36 And looking upon Jesus as He walked *(takes us back to Verse 29, for both Verses speak of the same incident)*, he said, Behold the Lamb of God! *(This phrase is used here again, in order to develop the time frame for the account about to be*

given.)

37 And the two disciples heard Him speak, and they followed Jesus *(in essence, this was the beginning of their becoming Disciples of Christ).*

38 Then Jesus turned, and saw them following, and said unto them, What do you seek? *(It was a penetrating question that had eternal consequences.)* They said unto Him, Rabbi, (which is to say, being interpreted, Master,) where do You dwell? *(They were speaking of an earthly abode, while the full answer to that question incorporated a dimension that was beyond the comprehension of any mere mortal. His actual dwelling place was the Throne of God.)*

39 He said unto them, Come and see *(the journey they began that day has not stopped, even unto this hour, and in fact never will!).* They came and saw where He dwelt, and abode with Him that day: for it was about the tenth hour *(it has been debated for centuries as to whether John the Beloved was using Jewish time or Roman time; Jewish time would have been 4 p.m., while Roman time would have been 10 a.m.).*

40 One of the two which heard John *speak,* and followed him, was Andrew, Simon Peter's brother *(the manner in which "Andrew" is addressed, as the brother of "Simon Peter," tells us that Peter's name was* now recognized to a greater degree than any of the other Apostles).*

41 He *(Andrew)* first found his own brother Simon, and said unto him, We have found the Messiah, which is, being interpreted, the Christ *(was entirely the cause of Andrew's eagerness and excitement).*

42 And he brought him to Jesus. And when Jesus beheld him *(Jesus was enabled by the Holy Spirit to look into the very soul of Peter),* He said, You are Simon the son of Jonah *("Simon" means "hearing"; Peter was named after "Simeon," the second son of Jacob and Leah [Gen. 29:32-33]):* you shall be called Cephas, which is by interpretation, A stone *(proclaims the ability of Christ to change men fundamentally and characteristically — or rather to re-create men).*

43 The day following Jesus would go forth into Galilee *(seems to insinuate that His journey from the place of His Water Baptism and Wilderness Temptation, the latter which John does not mention, toward Galilee will now commence),* and found Philip, and said unto him, Follow Me *(doesn't exactly tell us where this happened; however, there is some small indication that it was in Galilee).*

44 Now Philip was of Bethsaida, the city of Andrew and Peter *(this town was located on the northern shore of the Sea of Galilee; it had*

been the home of these men before they moved to Capernaum, about six miles distant).

45 Philip found Nathanael (Nathanael is also called "Bartholomew"), and said unto him, We have found Him, of Whom Moses in the Law, and the Prophets, did write (in Philip's mind, Jesus met the criteria of the Word of God), Jesus of Nazareth, the son of Joseph (Jesus was really not the Son of Joseph, due to the Virgin Birth, but was referred to in this manner for the obvious reasons).

46 And Nathanael said unto him, Can there any good thing come out of Nazareth? (The town of Nazareth was not held by Israel as a distinguished place, but rather the opposite.) Philip said unto him, Come and see (proclaims within itself the basic thrust of Christianity).

47 Jesus saw Nathanael coming to Him, and said of him, Behold an Israelite indeed, in whom is no guile! (Jesus did not say that this man was sinless, but "guileless," which means, "to be without deceit.")

48 Nathanael said unto Him, From where do You know me? (This proclaims the potential Disciple as being startled.) Jesus answered and said unto him, Before that Philip called you, when you were under the fig tree, I saw you (the Holy Spirit revealed this to Him).

49 Nathanael answered and said unto Him, Rabbi, You are the Son of God; You are the King of Israel (Nathanael's faith will never possess more than it embraces at this moment).

50 Jesus answered and said unto him, Because I said unto you, I saw you under the fig tree, causes you to believe? You shall see greater things than these (to be sure, he certainly did!).

51 And He said unto him, Verily, verily, I say unto you, Hereafter you shall see Heaven open, and the Angels of God ascending and descending upon the Son of Man (has to do with Jacob's dream [Gen. 28:11-13]; it was fulfilled in Jesus; He Alone could open Heaven, because He Alone is the way to God).

CHAPTER 2

THE FIRST MIRACLE

AND the third day (speaks of the amount of time which had lapsed since Jesus left the Wilderness Temptation to begin His public Ministry) there was a marriage in Cana of Galilee (occasions the site of His very first Miracle); and the mother of Jesus Was there (indicates that she was already there when Jesus came):

2 And both Jesus was called, and His Disciples, to the mar-

riage *(He may have only had some five Disciples this early in His Ministry)*.

3 And when they wanted wine *(they had run out of wine; the Greek word for wine, as here used, is "oinos"; it means either fermented or unfermented, according to how it is used; every indication is it was unfermented, i.e., "grape juice")*, the mother of Jesus *(Mary)* said unto Him, They have no wine *(there was an indication in her spirit, placed there by the Holy Spirit, that she should appeal to her Son)*.

4 Jesus said unto her, Woman, what have I to do with you? *(The term "Woman," as then used, was basically the same as our present use of "Madam." The language implies that the period of subjection to Mary [it is believed that Joseph was now dead] was now at an end.)* My hour is not yet come *(He is meaning that if this is the hour when He is to begin His Miracle Ministry, such direction would have to come from God, and God Alone! in other words, as it regards spiritual things, He was not there to do what His mother wanted, but rather what God wanted; the Catholic Church should note this)*.

5 His mother said unto the servants *(indicates a Revelation to her by the Holy Spirit)*, Whatsoever He says unto you, do it *(represents the last recorded words of Mary; with this word she stepped aside, in effect telling the servants to turn from her to Him)*.

6 And there were set there six waterpots of stone, after the manner of the purifying of the Jews *("six" represents the number of man, and always falls short of perfection represented by the number "7," called "God's number")*, containing two or three firkins apiece *(referred to 18 to 27 gallons each, depending on the size; as is obvious, they were quite large)*.

7 Jesus said unto them, Fill the waterpots with water *(means that His hour had come, and He had been given instructions from His Heavenly Father as to what He should do)*. And they filled them up to the brim *(presented all that man could do; the balance was left up to our Lord)*.

8 And He said unto them, Draw out now, and bear unto the Governor of the feast *(that was all that was said and done)*. And they bear *it*.

9 When the Ruler of the feast had tasted the water that was made wine, and knew not whence it was *(evidently, this scenario had taken place only in the presence of a few people)*: (but the servants which drew the water knew;) the Governor of the feast called the bridegroom,

10 And said unto him, Every man at the beginning does set

forth good wine; and when men have well drunk *(doesn't mean that they were intoxicated, as some suppose, but that they had already consumed a lot)*, then that which is worse: *but* you have kept the good wine until now *(the best was saved until the last, but not intentionally!)*.

11 This beginning of miracles did Jesus in Cana of Galilee *(this was the first miracle He performed; there would be many more!)*, and manifested forth His glory *(this type of miracle was performed first in order to show that He could change things, and do so miraculously)*; and His Disciples believed on Him *(their faith increased due to the manifestation of His Glory in the changing of the water to wine)*.

12 After this He went down to Capernaum *(we aren't told why, but quite possibly He was thinking now of making it His headquarters)*, He, and His mother, and His brethren *(it seems that His brothers were not now opposed to Him, as they would later be; at least two of them, despite their former opposition, would become leaders in the Church; I speak of James and Jude; Joseph is not mentioned here, so he was possibly dead by now; as well, His sisters aren't mentioned, so they were probably married, and at their own respective houses)*, and His Disciples *(as stated, exactly how many He had*

at this time is not known): and they continued there not many days *(has reference to the "Passover," which was to commence shortly in Jerusalem)*.

THE TEMPLE

13 And the Jews' Passover was at hand *(it had been Jehovah's Passover, but corruption had permeated it and now it was "The Jew's Passover")*, and Jesus went up to Jerusalem *(proclaims Him making this trip, although as events will relate, not with enthusiasm)*,

14 And found in the Temple those who sold oxen and sheep and doves, and the changers of money sitting *(probably refers to the Court of the Gentiles; it was not the selling of the animals to which Jesus objected, but where they were being sold; the same would go for the money changers)*:

15 And when He had made a scourge of small cords *(represents the Lord's first cleansing of the Temple; the second and last cleansing was that of Matthew 21:12)*, He drove them all out of the Temple, and the sheep, and the oxen; and poured out the changers' money, and overthrew the tables *(what He did was Scriptural [Ps. 69:9]; spiritually, I suspect the modern Church is guilty of the same sin)*;

16 And said unto them who sold doves, Take these things

hence *(tradition says that He opened the cages, letting the doves loose,
with them flying over the heads of
the people, etc.)*; make not My
Father's House an house of merchandise *(His statement in essence
says that He is the "Son of God Most
High")*.

17 And His Disciples remembered that it was written, The zeal
of Your House has eaten Me up
*(this is a foreshadowing of the re-
proach and agony which will befall the Righteous Servant of God
in His Passion for God's Honor)*.

A SIGN

18 Then answered the Jews and
said unto Him *(concerns itself with
the opposition, which would only
grow in intensity)*, What sign do
You show us, seeing that You do
these things? *(The proper translation is, "what sign do You show
unto us that You are the Messiah,
seeing that You do these things?")*

19 Jesus answered and said
unto them, Destroy this Temple
*(referred to His physical Body, not
the structure built by Herod)*, and
in three days I will raise it up
*(speaks of His Resurrection and
exactly when it would be, three
days after His Death)*.

20 Then said the Jews, Forty
and six years was this Temple in
building, and will you rear it up
in three days? *(The last statement

is spoken in sarcasm.)*

21 But He spoke of the Temple
of His Body *(this is said after the
fact; however, when He originally
made the statement, more than likely He pointed to His Body, but still
they would have not understood His
meaning)*.

22 When therefore He was risen
from the dead, His Disciples remembered that He had said this
unto them *(realizing that it referred
to His Death and Resurrection, and
not the Temple built by Herod)*; and
they believed the Scripture, and
the Word which Jesus had said
*(perhaps they were referring here
to Psalms 16:10; a Divine Faith is
always based upon the Scriptures)*.

23 Now when He was in Jerusalem at the Passover, on the Feast
Day *(speaks of the same time in
which He had cleansed the Temple)*,
many believed in His Name, when
they saw the Miracles which He
did.

24 But Jesus did not commit
Himself unto them *(means that
He paid little attention to their
praises, which were occasioned by
the miracles; their faith was a shallow faith, and was rooted not necessarily in the Scriptures, but rather
in outward observances)*, because
He knew all *men (refers to the
fickleness of man, especially those
whose faith is as misplaced as these)*,

25 And needed not that any
should testify of man *(means that

He Alone properly discerned the true nature of man): for He knew what was in man *(total depravity).*

CHAPTER 3

NICODEMUS

THERE was a man of the Pharisees, named Nicodemus *(said to have been one of the three richest men in Jerusalem),* a ruler of the Jews *(a member of the Sanhedrin, the Ruling body of Israel):*

2 The same came to Jesus by night *(it is not known exactly as to why he came by night),* and said unto Him, Rabbi, we know that You are a Teacher come from God *(the pronoun "we" could indicate that Nicodemus represented several members of the Sanhedrin; Nicodemus addresses Christ here as a man, and not as God; the Cross would change him):* for no man can do these miracles that You do, except God be with Him *(in this, he is correct!).*

3 Jesus answered and said unto him *(presents an answer totally different from that which he expected),* Verily, verily, I say unto you, Except a man be born again *(the term, "born again," means that man has already had a natural birth, but now must have a Spiritual Birth, which comes by Faith in Christ, and what He has done for us at the Cross, and is available to all),* he cannot see the Kingdom of God *(actually means that without the New Birth, one cannot understand or comprehend the "Kingdom of God").*

4 Nicodemus said unto Him, How can a man be born when he is old? *(This proclaims this spiritual leader of Israel as having no knowledge at all of what Jesus is saying. Had he truly been "born-again," he would have understood these terms.)* can he enter the second time into his mother's womb, and be born? *(It seems he did not know the language of the Prophets concerning circumcision of the heart [Deut. 30:6; Jer. 4:4], and concerning a hard heart and right spirit [Ps. 51:10; Ezek. 36:26-27].)*

5 Jesus answered, Verily, verily, I say unto you, Except a man be born of water and of the Spirit *(the phrase, "born of water," speaks of the natural birth, which Jesus says in the next Verse, and pertains to a baby being born; being "Born of the Spirit" speaks of a Spiritual Birth, which is brought about by God Alone; and neither does it speak of Water Baptism),* he cannot enter into the Kingdom of God.

6 That which is born of the flesh is flesh *(has to do with the natural birth, and is illustrated, as stated, by the phrase, "born of Water");* and that which is born of the Spirit is spirit *(has to do with that which is solely of God;*

the one [flesh] has no relationship to the other [Spirit] and cannot be joined).

7 Marvel not that I said unto you, You must be born again *(evidently addresses itself to the surprise, which must have been registered on the countenance of Nicodemus).*

8 The wind blows where it listeth, and you hear the sound thereof, but cannot tell from where it comes, and whither it goes *(presents the way in which Jesus explains the "born-again" experience; He likens it to the wind which comes and goes, but is impossible to tell exactly how)*: so is every one who is born of the Spirit *(it is a spiritual birth, so it cannot be explained intellectually).*

9 Nicodemus answered and said unto Him, How can these things be? *(Not being "born-again" at this particular time, and despite his vast intelligence in other areas, he has no understanding of this great Truth; he is religious but lost!)*

10 Jesus answered and said unto him, Are you a Master of Israel *(was held in very high regard as one of the spiritual leaders of Israel)*, and knowest not these things? *(As a spiritual leader, he should have known the way of Salvation, but the sad fact was he didn't.)*

11 Verily, verily, I say unto you, We speak that we do know *(Jesus was speaking of the Triune Godhead, and as well of all the "Apostles and Prophets"; in essence, He is speaking of the Word of God, and is directing Nicodemus to that Source instead of tradition)*, and testify that we have seen *(means that one can actually "see" the fruit or benefits of this "Testimony," i.e., "The Word of God")*; and you receive not our witness *(has to do with the Jewish Sanhedrin).*

12 If I have told you earthly things, and you believe not *(refers to the earthly type and events in the Bible, such as the Sacrifices and Feast Days, etc., which Nicodemus no doubt read many times, but was so blind that he did not see nor believe their lessons)*, how shall you believe, if I tell you of Heavenly things? *(In effect, this tells us that if we are to know Jesus as God [Heavenly things], we must first know Jesus and the Incarnation [earthly things]. Nicodemus had addressed Jesus as merely a "Teacher." So until he understands God becoming flesh and dwelling among men, he will not understand Heavenly things.)*

13 And no man has ascended up to Heaven, but He who came down from Heaven *(He came down from Heaven and became Man, and approximately three and a half years later will ascend up to Heaven, when His mission is complete)*, even the Son of Man which is in Heaven *(better translated, "which is from Heaven").*

14 And as Moses lifted up the

serpent in the wilderness *(refers to Numbers 21:5-9; the "serpent" represents Satan who is the originator of sin)*, even so must the Son of Man be lifted up *(refers to Christ being lifted up on the Cross, which alone could defeat Satan and sin)*:

15 That whosoever *(destroys the erroneous hyper-Calvinistic explanation of predestination that some are predestined to be saved, while all others are predestined to be lost; the word "whosoever" means that none are excluded from being lost, and none are excluded from being saved)* believes in Him *(believes in Christ and what He did at the Cross; otherwise, one would perish)* should not perish, but have Eternal Life *(the Life of God, the Ever-Living One, Who has life in Himself, and Alone has immortality)*.

16 For God so loved the world *(presents the God kind of love)*, that He gave His only Begotten Son *(gave Him up to the Cross, for that's what it took to redeem humanity)*, that whosoever believes in Him should not perish, but have Everlasting Life.

17 For God sent not His Son into the world to condemn the world *(means that the object of Christ's Mission was to save, but the issue to those who reject Him must and can only be condemnation)*; but that the world through Him might be saved *(Jesus Christ is the only Salvation for the world; there is no other! as well, He is Salvation only through the Cross; consequently, the Cross must ever be the object of our Faith)*.

18 He who believes on Him is not condemned *(is not condemned to be eternally lost in the Lake of Fire forever and forever [Rev. 20:11-15])*: but he who believes not is condemned already, because he has not believed in the Name of the Only Begotten Son of God *(all of this refers to Christ and what He did at the Cross in order to redeem humanity; Salvation is never by works, but rather by Grace through Faith, with the Cross ever the object of that Faith)*.

19 And this is the condemnation, that Light is come into the world *(refers to Jesus as the "Light;" there is no other!)*, and men loved darkness rather than light, because their deeds were evil *(proclaims the fact that the great penalty of sin is sinful desire; the love of darkness is the consequence of man's wicked ways; the rejection of Jesus Christ is not the occasion of man's lostness, but rather the result of it)*.

20 For every one who does evil hates the Light *(presents a striking rebuke to Nicodemus with a keen thrust of the sharp sword, saying to him that evil-doers choose the darkness, so why did this Pharisee come

by night?), neither cometh to the Light, lest his deeds should be reproved *(to truly come to Jesus means the Revelation and condemnation of every evil way, which is totally unlike the religions of the world which reveal nothing; the "Light" automatically reveals what is hidden by the darkness).*

21 But he who does truth comes to the Light *(the desire for truth must be placed in the heart of man by the Holy Spirit, by the means of the revealed Word of God; if the person sincerely wants to "do truth," he must come to Christ, for Christ is the only "Light"),* that his deeds may be made manifest, that they are wrought in God *(proclaims the great change that takes place in the Believing sinner's life upon coming to Christ; the evil deeds are forever gone, with righteous deeds taking their place).*

22 After these things came Jesus and His Disciples into this land of Judaea *(means that Jesus and His Disciples left the metropolis of Jerusalem, where hostility was already beginning to mount, especially considering His cleansing of the Temple; they went to other parts of Judaea);* and there He tarried with them, and baptized *(He actually did not do any baptizing Himself; it was done by His Disciples, but no doubt under His direction; the Scripture seems to indicate that this practice wasn't carried forth too very long; no doubt it was done by Christ to further validate the Ministry of John the Baptist, whose great emphasis was Water Baptism).*

JOHN THE BAPTIST

23 And John also was baptizing in Aenon near to Salim, because there was much water there *(is believed to have been located about fifty miles north of Jerusalem in Samaria):* and they came, and were baptized *(means the crowds kept coming, but were actually diminishing by this time).*

24 For John was not yet cast into prison *(the Holy Spirit is here telling us that the Ministry of John the Baptist is about to conclude).*

25 Then there arose a question between *some* of John's disciples and the Jews about purifying *(it was a very angry debate! the debate was over the many laws and rituals which had been fabricated by the Pharisees; in other words, a great ado about nothing!).*

26 And they came unto John, and said unto him, Rabbi, He Who was with You beyond Jordan, to Whom you bear witness *(Jesus),* behold, the same baptizeth, and all *men* come to Him *(they were trying to instigate a rivalry between Christ and John, and more particularly to demean John).*

27 John answered and said, A

man can receive nothing, except it be given him from Heaven *(John's Ministry was from God, and therefore from Heaven; and the Ministry of Christ was from God, and therefore from Heaven; consequently, they complemented each other; there was no rivalry!)*.

28 You yourselves bear me witness, that I said, I am not the Christ *(means that he is subservient and submissive to the One Who is actually the Christ)*, but that I am sent before Him *(proclaims the fact that John is under the authority of Christ, and not the authority of the Pharisees, or any part of the religious hierarchy of Israel)*.

29 He who has the bride is the bridegroom *(he is saying that all the souls he has won in reality belong to Jesus, and not him, because Jesus is the "Bridegroom"; consequently, he takes no umbrage at the great crowds now going to Jesus, which had originally come to him)*: but the friend of the bridegroom *(that which John concludes himself to be)*, which stands and hears Him *(refers to the Ministry of Christ, which exceeds all that John could ever have surmised)*, rejoices greatly because of the bridegroom's voice *(refers to the Ministry of Christ)*: this my joy therefore is fulfilled *(John had not only "fulfilled" his mission, but he was "fulfilled")*.

30 He must increase *(He must ever "increase," not men, denominations, religious offices, the Virgin Mary, Apostles, etc.)*, but I must decrease *(the Ministers of the New Covenant must all take note of Divine Praise and self-depletion, as we prepare the way of the Lord to human hearts; we must hide ourselves behind the greater Glory of our Lord; we are successful, only as we succeed in doing this)*.

31 He who comes from above is above all *(refers to the fact that Christ was a man, but above all that He was more than man, in fact, God)*: he who is of the earth is earthly, and speaks of the earth *(refers to all men, even the great Prophets, which are of necessity limited)*: He who comes from Heaven is above all *(places Christ in a category above all men, even as He ever shall be!)*.

32 And what He has seen and heard, that He testifies *(refers to that which Jesus received from the Father, which testified of Him and He of it)*; and no man receives His Testimony *(means that no man contributed to His Testimony, but that it was all from God)*.

33 He who has received His Testimony *(refers to all who have believed on His Name and accepted Him as Lord and Saviour)* has set to His Seal that God is true *(has to do with man receiving the witness of the Son as the Giver of Eternal Life; as the witness of Jesus is true in every respect, such portrays

that God is true to His Word).

34 For He Whom God has sent speaks the Words of God *(refers to Christ Who always spoke the Mind of God, and thereby the Word of God)*: for God gives not the Spirit by measure *unto Him (refers to the fact that all others, whomever they may have been and even the very greatest, while having the Holy Spirit, did so by "measure," which was not so with Jesus; He had the Spirit in totality, hence the constant healings and miracles)*.

35 The Father loves the Son *(refers to the Incarnation, and what Christ would do to redeem humanity)*, and has given all things into His hand *(refers to the great Plan of Redemption and it being carried out by the Lord Jesus Christ)*.

36 He who believes on the Son has Everlasting Life *(proclaims to one and all the simple Plan of Salvation; the consequences are eternal)*: and he who believes not the Son shall not see life *(this means that there is only one way to be saved, and that is by trusting Christ and what He has done for us at the Cross)*; but the wrath of God abides on him *(the only way to be cleansed from sin is by the Precious Blood of Christ, and our Faith in that Finished Work; to not do that means that sin remains, and the Wrath of God must evermore be opposed to sin, and those who allow it to remain in their lives)*.

CHAPTER 4

SYCHAR

WHEN therefore the Lord knew how the Pharisees had heard that Jesus made and baptized more disciples than John *(Him hearing this information portrays His humanity; even though He was God, and never ceased to be God, He never used His Power of Personal Deity, but rather was led and guided by the Holy Spirit exactly as we are, or should be)*,

2 (Though Jesus Himself baptized not, but His Disciples,) *(His Baptism then was the same as that of John, the "Baptism of Repentance," which was carried out by His Disciples)*.

3 He left Judaea, and departed again into Galilee *(He did so at the behest of the Holy Spirit)*.

4 And He must needs go through Samaria *(this direction as well was instigated by the Holy Spirit; normally, Jews coming from Judaea up to Galilee went around Samaria, because they were not particularly enamored with Samaritans)*.

5 Then comes He to a city of Samaria, which is called Sychar *(is said by some to refer to the ancient city of Shechem)*, near to the parcel of ground that Jacob gave to his son Joseph *(proclaims, as is obvious, this spot having a long*

Bible history).

6 Now Jacob's well was there *(in fact, this well is still there, nearly four thousand years after Jacob).* Jesus therefore, being wearied with His journey, sat thus on the well *(proclaims His humanity; hence, John impresses upon us the full humanity, the definite human existence of Jesus; even as He was "the Only Begotten Son of the Father", He was "The Word made flesh"):* and it was about the sixth hour *(if using Jewish time, it would have been 12 o'clock noon).*

7 There comes a woman of Samaria to draw water *(would prove to be the greatest moment of her life):* Jesus said unto her, Give Me to drink *(this must have startled the woman, because most Jews, as she knew Jesus to be, would not even speak to a Samaritan, much less ask a favor).*

8 (For His Disciples were gone away unto the city to buy meat.) *(Some feel that John was the one Disciple who remained behind; it was his custom not to mention himself when relating these experiences, even though he was present.)*

9 Then said the woman of Samaria unto Him *(proclaims these two isolated hearts meeting — His isolated by Holiness, for He was separate from sinners, hers by sin, for she was separate from society),* How is it that You, being a Jew, askest drink of me, which am a woman of Samaria? *(She was perplexed that He would address her at all, much less ask of her a favor!)* for the Jews have no dealings with the Samaritans *(referred to hospitality, for ordinary buying and selling were, in fact, carried on; however, Jesus didn't have this animosity!).*

10 Jesus answered and said unto her, If you knew the Gift of God *(proclaims Jesus as that Gift, and the Salvation He Alone affords),* and Who it is Who says to you, Give me to drink *(proclaims her so close to Eternal Life, but yet at this moment, so far!);* you would have asked of Him, and He would have given you Living Water *(proclaims Him asking her for water to slake His physical thirst, while in turn He will give her "Living Water," which refers to Salvation that will forever slake her spiritual thirst).*

11 The woman said unto Him, Sir, You have nothing to draw with, and the well is deep *(she was right, the well was very deep, but we speak of the spiritual well!):* from where do You get this Living Water? *(She finds the phrase, "Living Water," to be intriguing!)*

12 Are You greater than our father Jacob, which gave us the well, and drank thereof himself, and his children, and his cattle? *(Her emphasis had always been on Jacob, as was the emphasis of most*

Samaritans; Jesus will have to draw her away from that, without denigrating Jacob.)

13 Jesus answered and said unto her, Whosoever drinks of this water *(water of the world)* shall thirst again *(presents one of the most simple, common, yet at the same time, profound statements ever uttered; the things of the world can never satisfy the human heart and life, irrespective as to how much is acquired)*:

14 But whosoever drinks of the water that I shall give him shall never thirst *("Whosoever" means exactly what it says! Christ accepted is spiritual thirst forever slaked!)*; but the water that I shall give him shall be in him a well of water springing up into Everlasting Life *(everything that the world or religion gives pertains to the externals; but this which Jesus gives deals with the very core of one's being, and is a perennial fountain)*.

15 The woman said unto Him, Sir, give me this water *(proclaims that she now has some understanding, although faint, of what Jesus is saying; she senses that it is not literal water of which He speaks, but rather something else altogether)*, that I thirst not, neither come hither to draw *(she knows now that the water of which He speaks cannot be drawn from Jacob's well)*.

16 Jesus said unto her, Go, call your husband, and come hither *(a profession of Faith in Christ that ignores the question of sin, the Holiness of God, the spirituality of worship as distinct from sacerdotal ceremonies, the need of pardon, and the condition of trust in an Atoning and Revealed Saviour — such a profession is worthless)*.

17 The woman answered and said, I have no husband *(presents a truth, but only partially so!)*. Jesus said unto her, You have well said, I have no husband *(bores to the very heart of her problem; it speaks to her domestic and spiritual life, and points out her problem and the solution)*:

18 For you have had five husbands *(must have come as a shock to her, especially considering that she knew He did not know her; as well, the Samaritans worship five gods, so He will show her that her worship of five heathen gods has a great deal to do with her domestic problems of having had five husbands)*; and he whom you now have is not your husband: in that said you truly *(the man she was now living with was not her husband, i.e., "not one of the five")*.

19 The woman said unto Him, Sir, I perceive that You are a Prophet *(had to do with the belief of the Samaritans and their interpretation of Whom the Messiah would be)*.

20 Our fathers worshipped in

this mountain (*speaks of Mount Gerizim, which was about fifty miles north of Jerusalem; in a sense, they worshipped "this mountain"*); and You say, that in Jerusalem is the place where men ought to worship (*she admitted that Jesus fit the profile of the Great Prophet Who would come as Moses had predicted, but she was perplexed because He was a Jew and worshipped in Jerusalem, which the Samaritans believed were false*).

21 Jesus said unto her, Woman, believe Me (*He is telling her to hear carefully what He is saying, and then to believe it*), the hour comes, when you shall neither in this mountain, nor yet at Jerusalem, worship the Father (*Calvary, which did away with the entire Jewish system, would introduce a new way of Worship*).

22 You worship you know not what (*He minced no words, telling her plainly that the Samaritan way of worship held no validity with God; regrettably it is the same with most presently*): we know what we worship: for Salvation is of the Jews (*meaning that through the Jewish people, came the Word of God and, as well, the Son of God, Who Alone brought Salvation, and did so by going to the Cross*).

23 But the hour comes, and now is, when the true worshippers shall worship the Father in spirit and in truth (*God is not looking for Holy Worship; He is looking for Holy Worshippers; as stated, Calvary would make possible an entirely different type of worship, which did not require ceremonies or rituals, etc.*): for the Father seeketh such to worship Him (*means that by the word "seeketh" such are not easily found*).

24 God is a Spirit (*simply means that "God is a Spirit Being"*): and they who worship Him must worship Him in spirit and in truth (*man worships the Lord through and by his personal spirit, which is moved upon by the Holy Spirit; otherwise it is not worship which God will accept*).

25 The woman said unto him, I know that Messiah comes, which is called Christ (*the Samaritans had adopted the Hebrew word of "Messiah," and they were looking for Him to come; "Christ" means the "Anointed One"*): when He is come, He will tell us all things (*constituted Truth, but not in the way this woman suspected*).

26 Jesus said unto her, I Who speak unto you am He (*it is nothing short of amazing that Jesus little revealed Himself to Nicodemus, except in a veiled way, but plainly and clearly reveals Himself to this woman — a Samaritan at that! and to the seeking soul . . .*).

27 And upon this came His Disciples, and marvelled that He talked with the woman (*as stated,

there were no dealings normally between Jews and Samaritans, and even above that, Rabbis did not converse with women in public or instruct them in the Law): yet no man said, What do You seek? or, Why do You talk with her? (This means that they kept their astonishment at Jesus' actions to themselves.)

28 The woman then left her waterpot, and went her way into the city (so a woman became the first Preacher of the Gospel to the Gentile nations, and so effective was her preaching that it caused a Revival), and said to the men (refers to the fact that she went directly to the leaders of the particular Samaritan religion),

29 Come, see a Man, which told me all things that ever I did (Christianity is not a philosophy nor a religion; it is really, as stated, a "Man," the Man Christ Jesus): is not this the Christ? (Her question presupposes that, as stated, her fellow Samaritans were looking for a Messiah.)

30 Then they went out of the city, and came unto Him (the Holy Spirit knew there were hungry hearts in this place, and so would have Christ go through Samaria).

31 In the mean while His Disciples prayed Him, saying, Master, eat (they urged Him to eat, out of concern for His health).

32 But He said unto them, I have meat to eat that you know not of (the insensibility of the Disciples to spiritual realities is again evidenced in Verses 31 through 38; and His "meat" and "harvest" were the Samaritans, who at the moment were leaving the city and coming to Him, and believing on Him).

33 Therefore said the Disciples one to another, Has any man brought Him ought to eat? (At this stage, the Disciples could only think in carnal terms, whereas Jesus spoke almost exclusively in spiritual terms.)

34 Jesus said unto them, My meat is to do the will of Him Who sent Me (this statement, although brief, constitutes the whole duty of man [Eccl. 12:13-14]), and to finish His Work (the work is His, and not ours!).

35 Say not ye, There are yet four months, and then cometh harvest? (The harvest is now!) behold, I say unto you, Lift up your eyes, and look on the fields (simply means that we don't have to go very far to see the need); for they are white already to harvest.

36 And He who reaps receives wages (the wages are souls), and gathers fruit unto life eternal (the Salvation of a soul will bring forth fruit forever, and will be marked to the credit of the Sowers and Reapers; what an investment!): that both he who sows and he who reaps may rejoice together (this speaks of all who play their parts,

and do so without failure).

37 And herein is that saying true, One sows, and another reaps *(God has a special Ministry for each individual; the "Sowers" are those who make it possible for the "reapers" to reap; the Preacher can only reap what has been sowed!).*

38 I sent you to reap that whereon you bestowed no labour *(whatever is done for Christ is brought to fruition as a result of much labor on the part of many different people)*: other men laboured, and you have entered into their labours *(He is actually speaking here of the Prophets of Old; in Christ, their Prophecies are now coming to pass, and the Apostles will reap what they sowed down through the many centuries; it is the same with us presently, as it regards both the Prophets and the Apostles, etc.).*

SALVATION

39 And many of the Samaritans of that city believed on Him for the saying of the woman, which testified *(this is a perfect example of true Christianity in action)*, He told me all that ever I did *(while Jesus did expose her sin, as the Gospel always does, it was not done in a negative, condemnatory fashion, but rather to deliver her from sin; He then gave her Eternal Life).*

40 So when the Samaritans were come unto Him *(bespoke hearts ready to receive from God)*, they besought Him that He would tarry with them *(presents a request that was not denied and, in fact, a request that will never be denied)*: and He abode there two days *(the greatest two days they would ever see and know).*

41 And many more believed because of His Own Word *(this is what happened during the two days);*

42 And said unto the woman, Now we believe, not because of your saying *(should have been translated, "not only because of your saying," because her saying was the testimony which originally brought them to Christ)*: for we have heard *Him* ourselves, and know that this is indeed the Christ, the Saviour of the world *(proclaims one of the most profound statements ever made, which occurs only one other time in the Bible [I Jn. 4:14]; it fell from the lips of Samaritans; regrettably, toward the end of His Ministry, there were some Samaritans who would not receive Him [Lk. 9:51-56]).*

GALILEE

43 Now after two days He departed thence, and went into Galilee.

44 For Jesus Himself testified, that a Prophet has no honour in His Own country *(He would later extend this statement to say, "and*

among His Own kin, and in His Own house" [Mat. 13:57; Mk. 6:4]).

45 Then when He was come into Galilee, the Galilaeans received Him (Faith based on outward observances is at best feeble; but as feeble as their Faith might be, He, obedient to His Father's Will, acted in Grace and Power whenever He met with Faith, however poor), having seen all the things that He did at Jerusalem at the Feast: for they also went unto the Feast (they needed the miracles to believe, with the evidence being that the Samaritans needed only His Word, for they had the greater Faith).

THE NOBLEMAN'S SON

46 So Jesus came again into Cana of Galilee, where He made the water wine (His first miracle). And there was a certain nobleman, whose son was sick at Capernaum (pertains to one who was an officer of Herod Antipas, Tetrarch of Galilee).

47 When he heard that Jesus was come out of Judaea into Galilee, he went unto Him (the news had spread to Capernaum that Jesus was back in Galilee, even at Cana, only about twenty miles distant), and besought Him that He would come down, and heal his son: for he was at the point of death (contains, buried within the text, the faint idea that due to his place and

position in the political structure of Galilee that Jesus would be impressed by who he was, an officer in Herod's Court; at any rate, he was desperate!).

48 Then said Jesus unto him, Except you see signs and wonders, you will not believe (proclaims Jesus knowing this man's heart and its unbelief, so He will draw him out; He will pull him to the highest Faith, taking Christ at His Word!).

49 The nobleman said unto Him, Sir, come down ere my child die (one can feel the pathos in this man's plea, with the mild rebuke preparing for what Jesus is about to say).

50 Jesus said unto him, Go your way; your son lives (presents a startling statement, and one which must have taken this man by surprise; his Faith is now being tested, and he will rise to the challenge). And the man believed the Word that Jesus had spoken unto him, and he went his way (back to Capernaum).

51 And as he was now going down, his servants met him, and told him, saying, Your son lives (the very words that Jesus had used).

52 Then enquired he of them the hour when he began to amend (portrays him putting the times together when Jesus had spoken the Word and when the boy was healed). And they said unto him, Yesterday at the seventh hour the fever left him (if Roman time, 7 p.m.

the day before).

53 So the father knew that *it was* at the same hour, in the which Jesus said unto him, Your son lives *(his Faith, ever how weak it had previously been, was greatly rewarded):* and himself believed, and his whole house *(all became converts to Christ).*

54 This *is* again the second Miracle that Jesus did *(was speaking only of Galilee; actually, He had performed quite a number of Miracles in the last few days in Jerusalem [Jn. 2:23]), when He was come out of Judaea into Galilee (proclaims that everywhere He went, Miracles followed, plus the changing of lives; such was Jesus then, and such is Jesus now!).*

CHAPTER 5

THE POOL OF BETHESDA

AFTER this there was a Feast of the Jews *(even though the Scriptures don't say, most think this was Passover; if correct, Jesus would have been little over a year into His public Ministry);* and Jesus went up to Jerusalem *(speaks of the express purpose of keeping this "Feast").*

2 Now there is at Jerusalem by the sheep *market* a pool *(should have been translated, "by the sheep gate"),* which is called in the Hebrew tongue Bethesda, having five porches *(means, "house of grace and mercy"; it was somewhat like a public infirmary).*

3 In these lay a great multitude of impotent folk, of blind, halt, withered *(presents a perfect description of humanity; due to the Fall, man is "impotent," helpless to save himself),* waiting for the moving of the water.

4 For an Angel went down at a certain season into the pool, and troubled the water *(not given by John as folklore, but rather as a fact):* whosoever then first after the troubling of the water stepped in was made whole of whatsoever disease he had *(earthly princes on entering a city resort to the houses of the great and rich, but the feet of the Prince of princes immediately turned to the abode of misery and suffering, the fruits of sin).*

5 And a certain man was there *(the healing of the impotent man contrasts the quickening Power of Christ with the powerlessness of the Law; it demanded strength on the part of the sinner in order to obtain the life it promised; but man is without strength [Rom. 5:6]),* which had an infirmity thirty and eight years *(a perfect type of Israel, which because of her sin was helpless, shut up in the desert for thirty-eight years; the similarity is not coincidental).*

6 When Jesus saw him lie *(presents a picture of Israel of Jesus'*

day but, as well, of all humanity), and knew that he had been now a long time *in that case (once again speaks of Israel)*, He said unto him, Will you be made whole? *(This must, beyond a doubt, be the greatest question of all time! Man is not "whole," and, in fact, cannot be "whole" without Jesus. This is where the great contention is.)*

7 The impotent man answered Him, Sir, I have no man, when the water is troubled, to put me into the pool *(proclaims his dependence on man, which has brought nothing but disappointment)*: but while I am coming, another steps down before me *(Love no doubt selected this man as being the most miserable, needy, and helpless in all that sad company; and wisdom chose him as a vessel of instruction to the Nation)*.

8 Jesus said unto him, Rise, take up your bed, and walk *(a single word from Christ sufficed)*.

9 And immediately the man was made whole, and took up his bed, and walked *(strength was given, that fact demonstrated by the man carrying his bed)*: and on the same day was the Sabbath *(and what a Sabbath of rest, relief, and joy for this man!)*.

10 The Jews therefore said unto him who was cured *(proclaims, as we shall see, no joy over his healing and deliverance, but rather the opposite, as religion always does)*, It is the Sabbath Day: it is not lawful for you to carry *your* bed *(pointed only to man's laws, and not God's Laws; Jesus paid absolutely no attention to the man-made laws, as numerous as they were)*.

11 He answered them, He Who made me whole *(proclaims the man using Jesus as his authority, which is what he should have done)*, the Same said unto me, Take up your bed, and walk *(Sabbath or no Sabbath, it was a command that he eagerly obeyed; it meant the Healing and Salvation of his physical body)*.

12 Then answered they him, What man is that which said unto you, Take up your bed, and walk?

13 And he who was healed knew not who it was *(it seems that after the healing, Jesus left instantly, so as not to create a scene; consequently, the man really did not know Who it was that had healed him)*: for Jesus had conveyed Himself away, a multitude being in *that* place *(He did so because He knew the hatred of the leaders and the result of His breaking their man-made laws; this is perhaps the reason He did not stay to heal others; at any rate, it was the Holy Spirit Who told Him what to do)*.

14 Afterward Jesus finds him *(the man He had healed)* in the Temple, and said unto him *(proclaims Jesus seeking him out, and*

for a purpose), Behold, you are made whole *(refers to the Salvation experience, as well as physical healing)*: sin no more, lest a worse thing come unto you *(this tells us first of all that his sickness of thirty-eight years had been brought up on him because of sin; as well, it tells us that disobedience to the Lord can open the door for "worse things")*.

15 The man departed, and told the Jews that it was Jesus, which had made him whole *(some have claimed that this man was ungrateful; however, he had no way of knowing of the animosity of the religious leaders against Jesus, so he probably thought he was doing the right thing)*.

16 And therefore did the Jews persecute Jesus *(the opposition from the religious hierarchy will do nothing but increase from now forward)*, and sought to kill Him, because He had done these things on the Sabbath day *(this is ironical; the religious leaders of Israel wanted to kill the Lord in the Name of the Lord; this is how blind they were!)*.

EQUALITY WITH GOD

17 But Jesus answered them *(proclaims that this was a face-to-face confrontation)*, My Father worketh hitherto, and I work *(this says two things: 1. He claims equality with God, and that He was God;* and, 2. *The very "Work" of the Father and the Son was to deliver mankind, whether physically or spiritually, or both, which brought the true Sabbath to the soul of man, for which it was originally intended)*.

18 Therefore the Jews sought the more to kill Him *(means that He not only did not seek any type of accommodations with these hypocrites, but rather reinforced His position to such an extent that no one had absolutely any doubt as to what He was saying or doing)*, because He not only had broken the Sabbath *(He had not really broken the Sabbath, but only one of their silly man-made rules)*, but said also that God was His Father, making Himself equal with God *(presents a charge not disclaimed by Jesus, because He did make Himself equal with God, and rightly so)*.

19 Then answered Jesus and said unto them, Verily, verily, I say unto you, The Son can do nothing of Himself *(proclaims the Humanity of Christ, with Him freely giving up the expression of His Deity while never losing its possession)*, but what He sees the Father do *(proclaims His total subservience to the Father, which as a Man He was to do and did do)*: for what things soever He does, these also do the Son likewise *(setting an example of humility and dependence, which the human family seriously lacked)*.

20 For the Father loves the Son

(the obedience of the Son is based on the love the Father has for the Son), and shows Him all things that Himself does (plainly says that everything Jesus did is that which the Father told Him to do): and He will show Him greater works than these, that you may marvel (has to do with Verses 28 and 29, which speak of the coming Resurrection).

21 For as the Father raises up the dead, and quickens them (proclaims as a fact the Truth of the coming Resurrection of Life); even so the Son quickens (makes spiritually alive) whom He will (portrays the truth that Salvation is not of him who wills [in the sense of willing Salvation by works, etc.], but of God Who shows Mercy).

22 For the Father judges no man (judges no one who has come to Christ, for all sin has been settled in Christ), but has committed all judgment unto the Son (Christ is the Saviour today, but will be the Judge tomorrow):

23 That all men should honour the Son, even as they honour the Father (claims equality with God in honor [Heb. 2:7-9]). He who honors not the Son honors not the Father which has sent Him (proclaims in no uncertain terms that if Jesus is dishonored, the Father is dishonored as well!).

24 Verily, verily, I say unto you, He who hears My Word (the Word of the Cross [Jn. 3:14-15]), and believes on Him Who sent Me (if one doesn't believe in Jesus, they cannot believe in God; to have the Son is to have the Father), has Everlasting Life (outside of Christ, there is no Spiritual Life), and shall not come into condemnation (Christ took the condemnation at the Cross); but is passed from death unto life (born-again).

25 Verily, verily, I say unto you (always signals a statement of the highest authority, and proclaims Jesus as that Authority), The hour is coming, and now is, when the dead shall hear the Voice of the Son of God: and they who hear shall live (has a double meaning: 1. It refers to people being Saved, thereby, coming from spiritual death to Spiritual Life and 2. It refers to the coming Resurrection of Life, when all Saints will be Resurrected).

26 For as the Father has Life in Himself (refers to God as the Eternal Fountain of Life, the Source Ultimate); so has He given to the Son to have Life in Himself (Jesus saying that He is not merely a participator in this "Life," but in fact is, as well, the Source of Life and, in Truth, the Ultimate Source exactly as the Father; consequently, He again claims Deity);

27 And has given Him Authority to execute judgment also (this speaks of "The Judgment Seat of Christ," which will be for all Believers and, as well, the "Great White

Throne Judgment," which will be for all the unsaved), because He is the Son of Man *(refers to Him paying the price on Calvary's Cross, and by the merit of such, He will also be the "Judge").*

28 Marvel not at this *(these statements, as given by Christ, left the religious leaders of Israel speechless):* for the hour is coming, in the which all who are in the graves shall hear His Voice *(speaks of the Resurrection of Life and the Resurrection of Damnation; again, these statements proclaim Christ as the Lord of both life and death),*

29 And shall come forth *(portrays both Resurrections as we shall see, and according to His "Voice");* they who have done good, unto the Resurrection of Life *(pertains to the First Resurrection, or as commonly referred, "The Rapture" [I Thess. 4:13-18]);* and they who have done evil, unto the Resurrection of Damnation *(this last Resurrection will take place approximately a thousand years after the First Resurrection of Life [Dan. 12:2; Rev., Chpt. 20]).*

30 I can of Mine Own Self do nothing *(in His humanity, He derived all Authority from the Father):* as I hear, I judge *(the Judgment He pronounced was that which He heard in His ear, as given by the Father [Isa. 50:4]):* and My Judgment is Just *(it is perfect, because it comes from the Throne of God);* because I seek not Mine Own Will, but the Will of the Father Who has sent Me *(proclaims the fact that the human consciousness of the Son becomes the basis for the Father's Judgment, which is uttered absolutely and finally through human lips of the Son of God; He sought only the Will of the Father, and we must seek only the Will of the Father, which is given in His Word).*

31 If I bear witness of Myself *(as to Who and What I am),* My witness is not true *(if I Alone bear witness; but as we shall see, there are also other witnesses).*

32 There is another Who bears witness of Me *(speaks of John the Baptist);* and I know that the witness which he witnesses of Me is true *(John's witness of Christ carried all the Authority of the Word of God).*

33 You sent unto John *(refers to the happenings of John 1:19-27),* and he bear witness unto the truth *(proclaims the things that John told them when they asked if he was the Messiah).*

34 But I receive not testimony from man *(in effect says, "even though John's testimony is true, I will not use a testimony from any man"):* but these things I say, that you might be Saved *(in effect, Jesus is telling the religious leaders of Israel that they are unsaved).*

35 He was a burning and a

shining light *(John the Baptist was "a light," but he wasn't "the Light," Who Alone is Christ)*: and you were willing for a season to rejoice in his light *(the religious leaders of Israel were willing for a brief period to listen to John, but when they saw that the major thrust of his Ministry was to introduce Jesus as the Son of God and Lamb of God, they turned away).*

36 But I have greater witness than *that* of John *(does not in any way demean the witness of John)*: for the works which the Father has given Me to finish *(the Miracles and Calvary)*, the same works that I do, bear witness of Me, that the Father has sent Me *(all the healings and miracles, which could not be refuted).*

37 And the Father Himself, which has sent Me, has borne witness of Me *(it is the Father, Who through the Holy Spirit gave Christ the Power to do these things [Lk. 4:18-19]).* You have neither heard His Voice at any time, nor seen His Shape *(in essence, Jesus is saying that these Jews to whom He was speaking believed that God existed, even though they had never heard His Voice or seen His Shape; therefore, why should they not believe the One sent by the Father, which the Miracles and Deliverances have proved?).*

38 And you have not His Word abiding in you *(if they truly knew God as they claimed, they would have His Word abiding in them, and would, therefore, believe the Son, for the Word spoke of the Son)*: for Whom He has sent, Him you believe not *(the rejection of Christ by the religious leaders of Israel demonstrated not only ignorance of God, but hostility to Him).*

THE SCRIPTURES

39 Search the Scriptures *(proclaims an imperative command, not a mere suggestion)*; for in them you think you have Eternal Life *(should have been translated, "You claim to believe the Scriptures, so believe what they say about Me")*: and they are they which testify of Me *(the entire story of the Bible is "Christ and Him Crucified").*

40 And you will not come to Me, that you might have Life *(all Life is in Christ; to have that Life, one must accept what Christ has done at the Cross).*

41 I receive not honour from men *(He sought honor from God Alone; that must be our criteria as well!).*

42 But I know you, that you have not the Love of God in you *(if one is truly Saved, one will truly have the Love of God).*

43 I am come in My Father's Name, and you receive Me not *(proclaims that the real reason they did not receive Him is because they*

did not know the Father, despite their claims): if another shall come in his own name, him you will receive (actually speaks of the coming Antichrist, as well as all other false Messiahs; shortly after the Rapture of the Church, Israel will receive a false Messiah, claiming that he is the one for whom they have long looked; they will find, to their dismay, how wrong they are!).

UNBELIEF

44 How can you believe, which receive honour one of another (proclaims that God does not minister to the pride of man, nor modify truth so as to please it and feed it), and seek not the honour that comes from God only? (To seek and receive such honor, which portrays itself in the Moving and Operation of the Holy Spirit, most of the time will incur the wrath of the religious establishment; consequently, most Preachers seek the honor that comes from men.)

45 Do not think that I will accuse you to the Father (means that they are already accused): there is one who accuses you, even Moses, in whom ye trust (they were claiming to abide by the Law of Moses, but in reality they were not).

46 For had you believed Moses, you would have believed Me (despite their claims, they did not keep the Law; for if they did they would

believe Christ): for he (Moses) wrote of Me (Gen. 3:15, 12; 17:18; 49:10; Deut. 18:5-18; Lk. 24:27, 44, etc.).

47 But if ye believe not his writings (bluntly tells them to their faces that despite their claims to the contrary, they were, in fact, unbelievers; all the religious machinery was but a show! at heart they did not believe the Bible any more than the heathen), how shall you believe My words? (This question proclaims the unity of Christ and the Scriptures.)

CHAPTER 6

JESUS FEEDS FIVE THOUSAND

AFTER these things (refers to the recent trip to Jerusalem where the tremendous exchange took place between Jesus and the religious leaders of Israel) Jesus went over the Sea of Galilee, which is the Sea of Tiberias (it was referred to by several names).

2 And a great multitude followed Him (there were at least 5,000 men, besides the women and children), because they saw His Miracles which He did on them who were diseased (and He turned none of them away, but healed all who came to Him despite their spiritual condition, because He is the "Bearer of Grace").

3 And Jesus went up into a mountain, and there He sat with

His Disciples *(contemplates a time of teaching and instruction).*

4 And the Passover, a Feast of the Jews, was near *(the Ministry of Christ had now passed the milestone of its first year).*

5 When Jesus then lifted up His Eyes, and saw a great company come unto Him *(represented this great multitude who had followed Him),* He said unto Philip, Where shall we buy bread, that these may eat? *(According to Matthew, Mark, and Luke, this had been preceded by a period of time given over to teaching and healing. This was not recorded by John.)*

6 And this He said to prove him *(carries the idea in the Greek of testing or examining Him; He would test the Faith of Philip):* for He Himself knew what He would do *(even though we do not know at times, He always knows; consequently, we must ever seek His face for leading and guidance).*

7 Philip answered Him *(presents carnal thinking, as all of us far too often do),* Two hundred pennyworth of bread is not sufficient for them, that every one of them may take a little *(this is the way the world plans, but it is not the way that the Child of God should plan).*

8 One of His Disciples, Andrew, Simon Peter's brother, said unto Him *(at least Andrew included Jesus in his thinking),*

9 There is a lad here, which has five barley loaves, and two small fishes *(some scholars believe that this boy traveled with the company of Christ for the purpose of bearing their food, considering that at times they were in places which were secluded, even as here):* but what are they among so many? *(In the boy's hands, they were nothing; but in the hands of Christ, they were everything.)*

10 And Jesus said, Make the men sit down *(Mark adds, "by hundreds, and by fifties" [Mk. 6:40]).* Now there was much grass in the place *(being the Passover season, this was spring, the month of April).* So the men sat down, in number about five thousand *(counting the women and children, the crowd probably totaled about ten to fifteen thousand).*

11 And Jesus took the loaves *(little is much if God be in it);* and when He had given thanks *(this He always did, and so must we!),* He distributed to the Disciples, and the Disciples to them who were set down; and likewise of the fish as much as they would *(exactly how this Miracle happened, we aren't told; however, at some point, it began to multiply, which obviously was a Miracle of astounding proportions).*

12 When they were filled *(all ate as much as they desired),* He said unto His Disciples, Gather

up the fragments that remain, that nothing be lost (*this bread in a sense represented Christ and the Gospel; none of it, therefore, must be wasted*).

13 Therefore they gathered *them* together, and filled twelve baskets with the fragments of the five barley loaves, which remained over and above unto them who had eaten (*presents a Law that is known only to God, of which man has no understanding; everything that man does depletes; everything that God does multiplies; the numbers "7" and "12" are brought to bear here; "7" [five loaves and two fish] speaks of perfection, while "12" speaks of God's Government; if we have His Government, we have His Perfection*).

14 Then those men, when they had seen the miracle that Jesus did, said (*presents a picture of Israel desiring to use Jesus for their own purposes, instead of realizing the true purpose for which He came*), This is of a truth that Prophet Who should come into the world (*refers to Deuteronomy 18:15; these people recognize Jesus as the Messiah, but for all the wrong reasons*).

15 When Jesus therefore perceived that they would come and take Him by force, to make Him a King (*represented the type of King that Israel did not need*), He departed again into a mountain Himself Alone (*refers to Him hav-ing already sent the Disciples away, actually back to Capernaum*).

WALKING ON THE WATER

16 And when evening was *now* come, His Disciples went down unto the sea (*that which happened before He went up into the mountain Alone*),

17 And entered into a ship, and went over the sea toward Capernaum (*where Jesus told them to go*). And it was now dark, and Jesus was not come to them (*John sets the stage for that which will now appear*).

18 And the sea arose by reason of a great wind that blew (*the Scripture does not say it was a storm, but that the wind was adverse; in other words, it was blowing against them to where they could not make any headway*).

19 So when they had rowed about five and twenty or thirty furlongs (*represents approximately four miles, and portrays them being pushed out into the middle of the lake*), they see Jesus walking on the sea, and drawing near unto the ship: and they were afraid (*and no wonder!*).

20 But He said unto them, It is I; be not afraid (*the literal translation is, "I Am; be not afraid"; in effect, He was telling them that He was the "I Am" of the Old Testament, i.e., "Jehovah!"*).

21 Then they willingly received Him into the ship *(without Jesus in the ship, their progress was difficult, if not impossible; with Him in the ship, all things change, and immediately!)*: and immediately the ship was at the land where they went *(at Capernaum, a distance of about four miles; this means that one second the ship was about four miles distance from the land, and the next second it was at the land).*

THE BREAD OF LIFE

22 The day following, when the people which stood on the other side of the sea saw that there was none other boat there, save that one whereinto His Disciples were entered *(no other boat from Capernaum)*, and that Jesus went not with His Disciples into the boat, but *that* His Disciples were gone away alone *(they saw that the boat left without Jesus)*;

23 (Howbeit there came other boats from Tiberias near unto the place where they did eat bread, after that the Lord had given thanks:) *(These particular boats were from Tiberias, not Capernaum.)*

24 When the people therefore saw that Jesus was not there, neither His Disciples *(despite the fact that Jesus did not go with His Disciples in the boat, the people could not find Him)*, they also took shipping, and came to Capernaum *(implies that some of them possibly hired some of the boats from Tiberias)*, seeking for Jesus *(regrettably, they were seeking Him, as the Text will portray, for all the wrong reasons).*

25 And when they had found Him on the other side of the sea *(in Capernaum)*, they said unto Him, Rabbi, when did You come here? *(The people, knowing the Disciples had left without Jesus, were puzzled as to how the Lord now came to be in Capernaum; Jesus little answered their question, for His Mission was a moral one, rather than an intellectual or material one.)*

26 Jesus answered them and said, Verily, verily, I say unto you *(presents an answer that is so startling as to defy all description)*, You seek Me, not because you saw the Miracles *(would have been better translated, "you seek Me, not because you properly understood the Miracles")*, but because you did eat of the loaves, and were filled *(reads perfectly their true motives; the modern "Word of Faith" message falls into the same category).*

27 Labour not for the meat which perishes *(regrettably, this is where much of the modern Church is presently [Rev. 3:17])*, but for that meat which endures unto Everlasting Life *(the idea is that our efforts must rest in things which are eternal, rather than things which*

are temporal), which the Son of Man shall give unto you ("Son of Man" refers to what Christ would do at the Cross, and the manner in which men will receive Eternal Life): for Him has God the Father sealed (refers to the One, and the only One Who can fill and, in fact, has filled, this role; all other claimants are spurious).

28 Then said they unto Him, What shall we do, that we might work the Works of God? (They wanted to do the Works of God, when in reality most of them did not even know God. This was because of erroneous leadership.)

29 Jesus answered and said unto them, This is the Work of God, that you believe on Him Whom He has sent (it offends the self-righteous to tell them that, without Faith, it is impossible to please God [Heb. 11:6]; the Great work that God requires is Faith in His Beloved Son Whom He has sent; otherwise, works, however pious, are "dead works").

30 They said therefore unto Him, What sign do You then show (presents these people ignoring what Jesus has just said concerning "Believing on Him," and at once demanding a "sign"), that we may see, and believe You? (Many of them had just seen the Miracle of the loaves and the fish, but seemingly to no avail!) what do You work? (The gross ignorance of the people was astounding to say the least! But is it any better presently?)

31 Our fathers did eat Manna in the desert; as it is written, He gave them bread from Heaven to eat (they were implying that the bread Jesus had multiplied didn't come from Heaven, as did the Manna).

32 Then Jesus said unto them, Verily, verily, I say unto you, Moses gave you not that bread from Heaven (setting the people straight that it was not Moses who sent the Manna from Heaven, but rather God the Father); but My Father gives you the true bread from Heaven (He was pulling their attention from the meat which perishes to the True Bread, which and Who is Himself, the Lord Jesus Christ).

33 For the Bread of God is He which comes down from Heaven (once again presents Himself as the Messiah, the True Lord of Israel), and gives life unto the world (the meat that perishes will not give Eternal Life; Christ Alone, gives such Life).

34 Then said they unto Him, Lord, evermore give us this Bread (strangely enough, when they find out that the Bread is Jesus, and the requirement for obtaining this Bread, many would leave Him, which follows through unto this very hour).

35 And Jesus said unto them, I am the Bread of Life (proclaims Him dropping all disguise, and gathering up into one burning Word all

the previous teaching which they might have fathomed, but did not): he who comes to Me shall never hunger (pertains to spiritual hunger); and he who believes on Me shall never thirst (pertains to spiritual thirst; Christ satisfies all spiritual desire).

36 But I said unto you, That you also have seen Me, and believe not (despite overwhelming evidence!).

37 All who the Father gives Me shall come to Me (refers to all, whomever they may be, whether Israelites, Gentiles, Pharisees, Scoffers, Harlots, or even the very Castaways of the Devil); and him who comes to Me I will in no wise cast out (proclaims to all a promise of unparalleled proportion; no one has ever been turned away, and no one will ever be turned away).

38 For I came down from Heaven (proclaims God becoming Man, thereby the "Incarnation"), not to do My Own Will, but the Will of Him Who sent Me (He is telling the Jews that Jehovah, Whom they claim to know and serve, is the Very One Who sent Him; and what He does and says is the Will of God, and to ignore it or reject it is to violate that Will).

39 And this is the Father's Will which has sent Me (pertains to the ultimate Blessing of Redemption), that of all which He has given Me I should lose nothing (what He came to do would be done), but should raise it up again at the last day (speaks of the coming Resurrection, when all Believers will have all the benefits of the Cross).

40 And this is the Will of Him Who sent Me (speaks of the Father's desires), that every one which sees the Son, and believes on Him, may have Everlasting Life (one must "see" or comprehend the Lord Jesus Christ, which refers to what He did at the Cross, and believe on Him; it is never doing, but rather "Believing"): and I will raise Him up at the last day (a guaranteed Resurrection).

THE BREAD OF LIFE

41 The Jews then murmured at Him (murmuring was one of the great sins of Israel, which denotes rebellious feelings against God [Ex. 16:7-9; Num. 11:1; 14:27]), because He said, I am the Bread which came down from Heaven (this means that the Jews did not misunderstand His meaning; they understood it perfectly and rebelled against it).

42 And they said, Is not this Jesus, the son of Joseph, whose father and mother we know? (They did not believe the Incarnation, despite the fact that Jesus met every single criteria.) how is it then that He says, I came down from Heaven? (Unbelief questions

everything, and cannot comprehend Truth.)

43 Jesus therefore answered
and said unto them, Murmur not
among yourselves *(their "murmuring" showed their disapproval
and rejection).*

44 No man can come to Me,
except the Father which has sent
Me draw him *(the idea is that all
initiative toward Salvation is on
the part of God toward the sinner
and not from the sinner himself;
without this "drawing of the Father," which is done by the Holy
Spirit, no one could come to God,
or even have any desire to come to
God)*: and I will raise him up at
the last day *(for the third time in
this Chapter alone, Jesus addresses
the Resurrection).*

45 It is written in the Prophets,
And they shall be all taught of God
*(this is found in Isaiah 54:13; God
draws sinners to Christ by a spiritual operation consonant to their
moral nature and enlightening
their rational conviction, and He
effects through the Scriptures as
written in the Prophets).* Every man
therefore who has heard, and has
learned of the Father, comes unto
Me *(our Lord is telling the Jews
that if they really knew the Father,
they would accept Christ).*

46 Not that any man has seen
the Father *("seen" in the Greek is
"horao," and means "to fully comprehend and understand with the
mind; to see Truth fully"),* save
He which is of God, He has seen
the Father *(the pronoun "He" refers to Christ; He Alone fully understands and comprehends the
Father; so all that is learned about
God, must be learned through Jesus
Christ, which will be according to
the Word).*

47 Verily, verily, I say unto you,
He who believes on Me has Everlasting Life *(this is obtained immediately upon "Believing"; it is not
something the Believer shall have,
but something the Believer presently has).*

48 I am that Bread of Life *(as
the Bread of Life, Christ gives Life
to the Believer, and He sustains that
Life; by using the words "I am,"
Jesus plainly identifies Himself as
the Jehovah of the Old Testament
[Ex. 3:14]).*

49 Your fathers did eat Manna
in the wilderness, and are dead
*(the Manna which God gave in the
wilderness was a type of Christ;
however, "types" had no life within
themselves and, therefore, could
not effect Salvation; Jesus was speaking of Spiritual Life and physical
life).*

50 This is the Bread which comes
down from Heaven *(quite possibly when Jesus said this, He was
pointing to Himself; in essence, He
would have been speaking of His
physical body, which was to be given
in Sacrifice for the purchase of lost*

humanity), that a man may eat thereof, and not die *(speaks of that which is spiritual, and means that man is restored to union with God, when previously he had been alienated; once again, our Lord is speaking of Spiritual Life).*

51 I am the Living Bread which came down from Heaven *(now proclaims Jesus presenting Himself as God ["I am"], while in the previous Verse He presented Himself as Man; and so He is the God-Man Jesus Christ):* if any man eat of this Bread, he shall live forever *(says the same thing as in the previous Verse, but in a different way; there He said, "and not die," now He says, "shall live forever"; the latter adds to the former):* and the Bread that I will give is My Flesh, which I will give for the life of the world *(this speaks of Him giving Himself on the Cross as a Sacrifice, which would guarantee Salvation for all who would Believe).*

52 The Jews therefore strove among themselves *(presents the inevitable results of unbelief),* saying, How can this man give us His Flesh to eat? *(This presents them thinking in the physical, while He is speaking in the Spiritual. Unredeemed man, despite all his intellectual loftiness, cannot think as God thinks, despite education and self-improvement; for all that. He thinks little above the level of a beast.)*

53 Then Jesus said unto them, Verily, verily, I say unto you *(instead of softening or modifying this seemingly harsh Doctrine, He instead intensified it by declaring it indispensable to Salvation),* Except you eat the Flesh of the Son of Man, and drink His Blood, you have no Life in you *(this terminology addresses the Cross; Christ would give Himself on the Cross for the Salvation of mankind; to fully believe in Him and what He did for us is what He means here; however, this Verse tells us the degree of believing that is required; it refers to the Cross being the total Object of one's belief; failing that, there is no Life in you).*

54 Whoso eats My Flesh, and drinks My Blood, has Eternal Life *(once again, Christ reiterates the fact that if the Cross is the total Object of one's Faith, such a person has "Eternal Life"); and I will raise him up at the last day (constitutes the fourth time this is spoken by Christ; consequently, the Believer has a fourfold assurance of the Resurrection).*

55 For My Flesh is meat indeed, and My Blood is drink indeed *(the idea is that one must continue eating and drinking even on a daily basis, which speaks of bearing the Cross daily [Lk. 9:23]).*

56 He who eats My Flesh, and drinks My Blood, dwells in Me, and I in him *(the only way that*

one can dwell in Christ and Christ in him, which guarantees a victorious, overcoming life, is for the Cross to ever be the Object of Faith and, as stated, on a daily basis).

57 As the Living Father has sent Me ("Life-giving Father"), and I live by the Father (speaks of the Incarnation): so he who eats Me, even he shall Live by Me (proclaims the Truth that as Jesus did not live an independent life apart from the Father, so the Believer does not, and in fact cannot, live an independent life apart from Christ; we obtain and maintain this "Life" by ever looking to the Cross; the Believer never departs from the Cross; to do so is to invite spiritual wreckage [Gal. 2:20]).

58 This is that Bread which came down from Heaven (once again points to Himself, and extols the outsized superiority over the Law, etc.): not as your fathers did eat Manna, and are dead (makes the comparison between that bread, a mere symbol of the True Bread which was to come, and the True Bread which now has come): he who eats of this Bread shall live for ever (He Alone, as the True Bread of Life, could give Eternal Life, but one had to "eat of this Bread" in order to have this Life, which means to accept Him as for Who He is and What He would do, which speaks of Calvary).

59 These things said He in the Synagogue, as He taught in Capernaum.

60 Many therefore of His Disciples, when they had heard this (spoke of those other than the Twelve), said, This is an hard saying; who can hear it? (They were unwilling to accept the bloody death of their Messiah, or to entrust themselves to a Divine Personality Whose most distinctive act would be His Sacrifice of Himself. This was the gross and terrible offence which made the Cross a stumblingblock to the Jews [Mat. 16:21; I Cor. 1:23; Gal. 5:11].)

61 When Jesus knew in Himself that His Disciples murmured at it (registered unbelief), He said unto them, Does this offend you? (In fact, the Cross is an offence to the entirety of the world, and regrettably even most of the Church [Gal. 5:11].)

62 What and if you shall see the Son of Man ascend up where He was before? (Jesus points out that if His Death were a stumblingblock to them, how much more would be His Resurrection? But would not that prove the reality and value of His Death, and the depth of their unbelief?)

63 It is the Spirit Who quickens (the Holy Spirit); the flesh profits nothing (in effect says, "If you could literally eat My Flesh, and drink My Blood, it would not save your souls"; the word "flesh" as it is used

here speaks of man's efforts, what-
ever they might be, apart from
Christ and the Cross): the words that
I speak unto you, *they* are spirit,
and *they* are Life *(of the Holy Spirit,
Who gives Life by and through the
Finished Work of Christ).*

64 But there are some of you
who believe not *(they did not believe what He said about Himself,
which referred to the Cross; millions presently in the Church fall
into the same category).* For Jesus
knew from the beginning who
they were who believed not *(not
the individuals per se, but rather
that which would occasion their
unbelief),* and who should betray
Him *(it is speaking here of Judas
Iscariot and the occasion of his betrayal, which was the Cross).*

65 And He said, Therefore said
I unto you, that no man can come
unto Me, except it were given unto
him of My Father *(the invitation is
to "whosoever will"; however, if the
person rejects the Cross, the Father
Commands the Holy Spirit to bar
all entrance [Eph. 2:18]).*

66 From that *time* many of His
Disciples went back, and walked
no more with Him *(the claims of
Christ were so profoundly different
from what they anticipated that they
now refused to accept Him at all!).*

PETER'S CONFESSION

67 Then said Jesus unto the
Twelve, Will you also go away?
*(The defection of these former Dis-
ciples must have deeply pained the
Lord's Heart. His question to the
original Twelve abrogates the Doctrine of Unconditional Eternal Security. In fact, Judas did go away.)*

68 Then Simon Peter answered
Him, Lord, to whom shall we go?
*(This presents the Apostle for the
second time confessing Who Jesus
is, but in more emphatic language.)*
You have the words of Eternal Life
*(other than Judas, they believed what
He said).*

69 And we believe and are sure
that You are that Christ, the Son
of the Living God *(we have believed,
and have got to know [have learned
by experience] that you are the Messiah, the Son of the Living God).*

70 Jesus answered them, Have
not I chosen you Twelve *(proclaims far more than random selection, but rather specific direction as given to Him by the Father),* and one of you is a devil?
*(Jesus chose Judas, and Judas as well
at first chose Christ; however, Judas' choice was turned by unbelief
as it has been with millions.)*

71 He spoke of Judas Iscariot
the son of Simon *(means that he
was "a man of Kerioth," a place in
Judah [Josh. 15:25]; as far as is
known, he was the only one of the
Twelve who came from Judah, the
Tribe of Jesus):* for he it was who
should betray Him, being one of

the Twelve *(it is said in this manner because the Holy Spirit will have all know what Judas threw away; it seems that with this Message as delivered by Christ, the Message of the Cross, rebellion began in Judas' heart)*.

CHAPTER 7

THE FEAST OF TABERNACLES

AFTER these things Jesus walked in Galilee *(covers a span of approximately six months, from the Passover in April to the Feast of Tabernacles in October)*: for He would not walk in Jewry, because the Jews sought to kill Him *(spoke of Jerusalem and Judaea; these were the religious leaders of the Nation, and are to be distinguished from the multitude of the people)*.

2 Now the Jews' Feast of Tabernacles was at hand.

3 His brethren therefore said unto Him *(refers to James, Joseph, Simon, and Jude [Mat. 13:55])*, Depart hence, and go into Judaea, that Your Disciples also may see the works that You do *(a proclamation of sarcasm; by the use of the Word, "Your Disciples," they were saying that they [His Brothers] are not His Disciples, and want all to know that they have no association with His group)*.

4 For *there is* no man *who* does any thing in secret, and he himself seeks to be known openly *(they knew full well the animosity of the religious leaders against Jesus; so they cannot help but know that He would be greatly exposing Himself if He went there at this time)*. If You do these things, show yourself to the world *(very similar to the temptations offered by Satan in the wilderness [Mat. 4:1-11])*.

5 For neither did His brethren believe in Him *(had His mother, brothers, and sisters presented themselves as moral lepers for cleansing from their sins, they would have learned Who and What He was, for knowledge of spiritual realities only reaches the soul through a sin-convicted heart, not through a religious intellect)*.

6 Then Jesus said unto them, My time is not yet come *(He was speaking of the time of His Crucifixion, which would take place in about six months; they did not understand this, and neither did His closest Disciples)*: but your time is always ready *(His statement proclaims that their ideas were akin to the world and, hence, the Devil)*.

7 The world cannot hate you *(their thinking at that time was in line with the thinking of the world, which was of Satan)*; but Me it hates *(the world of religion)*, because I testify of it, that the works thereof are evil *(pertains mostly to anything in the religious sense which is not Scriptural)*.

8 Go ye up unto this Feast *(pertains to the fact that most of the people who attended this Feast little understood its true spiritual meaning)*: I go not up yet unto this Feast; for My time is not yet full come *(His time for fulfilling what this Feast represented had not yet come, and will not come until the Millennium)*.

9 When He had said these words unto them, He abode *still* in Galilee *(waited there two or three days before He finally went to Jerusalem)*.

10 But when His brethren were gone up, then went He also up unto the Feast *(insinuates that Jesus did not want to travel with His brethren, considering their hostility, even though His other reasons for delay were far weightier)*, not openly, but as it were in secret *(proclaimed such being done for particular reasons)*.

11 Then the Jews sought Him at the Feast, and said, Where is He? *(This speaks of the religious hierarchy of Israel. To be sure, they were not seeking Him for the right reasons.)*

12 And there was much murmuring among the people concerning Him *(pertained to both negative and positive remarks)*: for some said, He is a good man: others said, No; but He deceives the people *(the latter group, no doubt, was attempting to curry favor with the religious leaders of Israel, whom they knew were in opposition to Christ)*.

13 Howbeit no man spoke openly of Him *(spoke favorably)* for fear of the Jews.

THE TEMPLE

14 Now about the midst of the Feast Jesus went up into the Temple, and taught.

15 And the Jews marveled *(spoke of the ruling and learned class)*, saying, How knows this man letters, having never learned? *(This spoke of the great theological schools in Jerusalem. In spite of their opposition to Him, the immediate effect of His Message was great astonishment. Despite themselves, they were moved by what He said and how He said it.)*

16 Jesus answered them, and said, My Doctrine is not Mine, but His who sent Me *(presents a far greater claim than any of the Prophets of Old; in other words, His Doctrine is of God)*.

17 If any man will do His Will *(is willing to do God's Will)*, he shall know of the Doctrine, whether it be of God, or *whether* I speak of Myself *(if you truly know God, and are striving to do His Will, you will instantly recognize My Words as Truth, thereby knowing them to be from God)*.

18 He who speaks of himself seeks his own glory *(refers to those*

who speak words of man's origin, whether of themselves or others): but he who seeks His Glory Who sent him (seeks to bring glory to God), the same is true, and no unrighteousness is in Him (Christ is saying that He is True and Righteous because He seeks that all Glory go to God).

19 Did not Moses give you the Law, and yet none of you keep the Law? (The idea is that they claimed they did keep the Law, and Jesus, in effect, is calling them liars to their faces.) Why go you about to kill Me? (This was in itself an indictment against their claims of Law-keeping, inasmuch as the Law forbade murder.)

20 The people answered and said, You have a devil (these were the people, and not the religious leaders): who goes about to kill You? (They were ignorant of the plot, and so were astonished at His statement.)

21 Jesus answered and said unto them, I have done one work, and you all marvel (He was speaking of a healing of a man on the Sabbath, which was done about a year and a half previous; more than likely, the religious leaders had brought up the subject).

22 Moses therefore gave unto you Circumcision (means that the Lord told Moses to include Circumcision in the Law); (not because it is of Moses, but of the fathers;)

(means that it actually had its beginning with Abraham [Gen. 17:9-14]) and you on the Sabbath Day circumcise a man (Jesus is pointing out that if Circumcision was lawful on the Sabbath Day, how much more lawful is an action which benefited a person greatly, such as healing).

23 If a man on the Sabbath Day receive Circumcision, that the Law of Moses should not be broken; are you angry at Me, because I have made a man every whit whole on the Sabbath Day? (The question meant that Jesus, Who was actually the fulfillment of these Laws, and to Whom they originally pointed, had done the very things these Laws symbolized, but could not perform.)

24 Judge not according to the appearance (in effect says, "if you think you have not violated the Sabbath in Circumcision, then how can you think I broke the Sabbath when I healed one of you who had been helpless for thirty-eight years?"), but judge righteous judgment (says that Judgment must be rendered according to the whole Word of God, and not merely by taking a part and perverting it to one's own satisfaction).

25 Then said some of them of Jerusalem (concerned natives of that city), Is not this He, Whom they seek to kill? (This means that the plot to kill Jesus by the religious

authorities was not a complete secret, at least to those in Jerusalem.)

26 But, lo, He speaks boldly, and they say nothing unto Him (Christ didn't pull any punches, and the rulers at this time said nothing to Him simply because of the massive crowds listening to Him). Do the rulers know indeed that this is the very Christ? (This proclaims how widespread and how detailed the idea of the Coming Christ was.)

27 Howbeit we know this man whence He is (this is said in a negative sense; they are meaning that they knew His parentage, the place of His early life, etc.; they gave Him no respect): but when Christ comes, no man knows whence He is (proclaims a common error of that time concerning the Messiah; the Bible taught the very opposite).

28 Then cried Jesus in the Temple as He taught, saying, You both know Me, and you know whence I am (in effect, says, "you think you know Me, and where I come from, but you actually do not"): and I am not come of Myself, but He Who sent Me is true (in effect, says, "you know Me as Jesus of Nazareth; and yet you do not know Me, for you do not know Him Who sent Me; but I am from Him and He did send Me"), Whom you know not (despite all their claims and great display of religion, He plainly tells them that they do not know God).

29 But I know Him (They were of the same essence): for I am from Him, and He has sent Me (means that He is from the Father in a unique way and position, as were no Prophets or Angels).

30 Then they sought to take Him (these were the religious leaders of Israel, and they were so incensed, so angry, and so empowered by Satan that they hated Him): but no man laid hands on Him, because His hour was not yet come (the Holy Spirit orchestrated events in holding back these jackals; it was not yet the time that Jesus should be Crucified, that coming about six months later).

31 And many of the people believed on Him (did not refer at all to the religious authorities, but instead to the crowds gathered for the Feast of Tabernacles, who had come from all over Israel and even other parts of the Roman Empire), and said, When Christ comes, will He do more miracles than these which this Man has done? (The evidence of the Power of God in delivering people was obvious to all. Consequently, the religious leaders are now on the horns of a dilemma.)

32 The Pharisees heard that the people murmured such things concerning Him (constituted a different group than the rulers, but equally opposed to Him); and the Pharisees and the Chief Priests sent officers to take Him (proclaims these two groups as joining

forces against Him).

33 Then said Jesus unto them, Yet a little while am I with you *(in effect, Jesus is saying that in about six months, which would actually be at the next Passover, He would become the Passover Lamb for all men),* and *then* I go unto Him Who sent Me *(back to God the Father, which He did do!).*

34 You shall seek Me, and shall not find *Me (refers to the time when they would desperately need Him, which would be about thirty-seven years in the future when Titus would destroy their city and the very Temple in which they now stand):* and where I am, *there* you cannot come *(actually means that they can come now, but they will not do so because of their unbelief and rebellion).*

35 Then said the Jews among themselves, Where will He go, that we shall not find Him? *(This presents minds that are darkened by unbelief and are, therefore, putting ironical and confusing meanings into His Words, in order to pour an air of contempt over His reply.)* will He go unto the dispersed among the Gentiles, and teach the Gentiles? *(Their question constituted the utter scorn of the Jewish mind for a pseudo Messiah Who, failing with His Own people and here in the Courts of the Lord's House, would instead turn to the Gentiles. However, even though they meant it as the insult of all insults, still they were far closer to the Truth than they ever would dare realize.)*

36 What *manner* of saying is this that He said, You shall seek Me, and shall not find *Me:* and where I am, *there* you cannot come? *(By the very tenor of its construction, their sarcasm proclaims the spiritual meaning to be completely lost on them.)*

THE FEAST

37 In the last day, that great *day* of the Feast *(spoke of the eighth day of the Feast of Tabernacles),* Jesus stood and cried, saying, If any man thirst, let him come unto Me, and drink *(presents the greatest invitation ever given to mortal man).*

38 He who believes on Me *(it is "not doing," but rather, "believing"),* as the Scripture has said *(refers to the Word of God being the Story of Christ and Him Crucified; all the Sacrifices pointed to Christ and what He would do at the Cross, as well as the entirety of the Tabernacle and Temple and all their appointments),* out of his belly *(innermost being)* shall flow rivers of Living Water *(speaks of Christ directly, and Believers indirectly).*

39 (But this spoke He of the Spirit *(Holy Spirit),* which they Who believe on Him should receive *(it would begin on the day of Pentecost):* for the Holy Spirit was not yet *given (He has now*

been given); **because that Jesus was not yet glorified.**) *(The time of which John wrote was shortly before the Crucifixion. When Jesus died on the Cross and was Resurrected three days later, He was raised with a Glorified Body, which was one of the signs that all sin had been atoned, now making it possible for the Holy Spirit to come in a new dimension.)*

DIVISION

40 Many of the people therefore, when they heard this saying, said *(as the Temple Mount was thronged with people at that time, many hundreds heard what Jesus said and, as well, felt the power of what He said)*, **Of a truth this is the Prophet** *(probably refers to Deuteronomy 18:15).*

41 Others said, This is the Christ *(this means "The Anointed," which alone, at least in this fashion, spoke of the Messiah).* **But some said, Shall Christ come out of Galilee?** *(This proclaims that they did not Scripturally connect Galilee with the Messiah. They evidently were overlooking the remarkable prediction in Isaiah 9:1.)*

42 Has not the Scripture said, That Christ comes of the Seed of David, and out of the town of Bethlehem, where David was? *(Christ was of the Seed of David, and was born in Bethlehem. However, it seems that they somewhat misun-*derstood Micah's prediction, thinking that the Messiah would make this little village his home. The Prophet Micah did not say that!)*

43 So there was a division among the people because of Him *(the "division" was caused by a lack of understanding of the Scriptures, plus a desire on the part of some to win the approval of the religious leaders [Jn. 7:48]).*

44 And some of them would have taken Him *(would have arrested Him)*; **but no man laid hands on Him** *(evidently they were stopped in some manner by the Holy Spirit).*

45 Then came the officers to the Chief Priests and Pharisees *(the officers who had been sent to arrest Him, as outlined in Verse 32)*; **and they said unto them** *(said to the officers)*, **Why have you not brought Him?** *(This means that they had firmly intended that He be arrested.)*

46 The officers answered, Never man spoke like this Man *(it was the Holy Spirit they were feeling and sensing, although they little understood that, if at all!).*

47 Then answered them the Pharisees *(seems to indicate that these men were the leading spirits in this assault upon Jesus)*, **Are you also deceived?** *(Even though this was directed to these officers, it was in reality their problem.)*

48 Have any of the rulers or of the Pharisees believed on Him?

(The Pharisees asked this question of these officers.)

49 But this people who know not the Law are cursed (should have been translated, "but this ignorant rabble, in speaking of the people, unlearned in the Law, are a cursed set"; this is what the religious leaders thought of the people!).

50 Nicodemus said unto them (presents this vaunted member of the Sanhedrin, who incidentally greatly outranked the Pharisees, now speaking up for Jesus), (he who came to Jesus by night, being one of them,) (this refers back some three years earlier, he was one of the rulers.)

51 Does our Law judge any man, before it hear him, and know what he does? (Although feeble and timid as was the plea of Nicodemus, yet was it precious to the Lord, and so is honorably recorded here by the Holy Spirit.)

52 They answered and said unto him (to Nicodemus), Are you also of Galilee? Search, and look: for out of Galilee arises no Prophet (they failed to check out the facts; Jesus was born in Bethlehem, not Galilee; also, had they searched the Scriptures, they would have found that Jonah, Hosea, Elijah, Elisha, and others were from the Northern Kingdom and not from Judaea).

53 And every man went unto his own house (even though these men had houses to which they could retire, Jesus had not place to lay His Head; so the next Verse says that He "went unto the Mount of Olives").

CHAPTER 8

ADULTERY

JESUS went unto the Mount of Olives (there, out in the open, He spent the night).

2 And early in the morning He came again into the Temple (speaks of daybreak), and all the people came unto Him; and He sat down, and taught them (proclaims Him revealing Himself as the "Word of God," the "Light of the World," and "Eternal Life"; this Chapter, plus those following will record His rejection in all these relationships).

3 And the Scribes and Pharisees brought unto him a woman taken in adultery (in the Greek, it means that she was "dragged by main force"); and when they had set her in the midst (proclaims the results of self-righteousness; they would subject her to great shame, caring not at all about her feelings),

4 They say unto Him, Master (was not meant at all as a term of endearment; they were merely referring to Him as a "teacher"), this woman was taken in adultery, in the very act (why wasn't the man brought as well?).

5 Now Moses in the Law com-

manded us, that such should be stoned *(was true, but for both the man and the woman [Lev. 20:10])*: but what do You say? *(In fact, His answer alone matters, and will always be according to the Word; therefore, how did He obey the Law, and at the same time, let her go free?)*

6 This they said, tempting Him, that they might have to accuse Him *(it was a trap!)*. But Jesus stooped down, and with *His* finger wrote on the ground, *as though He heard them not (actually meant that He wrote in the dust on the stone, for the Temple Court was paved; what did He write? had the Holy Spirit desired that we know, He would have told us; He may have written what He momentarily said to them)*.

7 So when they continued asking Him *(means they pressed the issue, demanding an answer)*, He lifted up Himself, and said unto them, He who is without sin among you, let him first cast a stone at her *(now turns the tables from her, and Him for that matter, onto the accusers; they didn't expect this!)*.

8 And again He stooped down, and wrote on the ground *(once again, we aren't told what He wrote)*.

9 And they which heard *it*, being convicted by *their own* conscience *(tells us that their position was so spiritually and mor-* *ally untenable that they could only vacate the premises)*, went out one by one, beginning at the eldest, *even* unto the last *(portrays them one by one dropping the stones held in their hands, and quietly retiring away from this Awful Presence)*: and Jesus was left alone, and the woman standing in the midst *(probably presented her continuing to cower in shame and mortal fear)*.

10 When Jesus had lifted up Himself, and saw none but the woman, He said unto her *(the accusers were gone, with the great multitude continuing to observe the proceedings)*, Woman, where are those your accusers? has no man condemned you? *(This actually means that none are qualified to "accuse.")*

11 She said, No man, Lord *(by her calling Him "Lord," she had made Him her Salvation)*. And Jesus said unto her, Neither do I condemn you: go, and sin no more *(records the sweetest words she had ever heard in all her life; He kept the Law perfectly by dying in her place, exactly as He did with all of us; that's how He could let her go free, as well as you and me)*.

THE LIGHT OF THE WORLD

12 Then spoke Jesus again unto them, saying, I am the Light of the world *(He is the Light of the*

world, because He is the Source of its Life): he who follows Me shall not walk in darkness, but shall have the Light of Life *(in effect says that all who do not follow Jesus, walk in darkness).*

13 The Pharisees therefore said unto Him, You bear record of Yourself; Your record is not true *(brings up the same argument used in Chapter 5).*

14 Jesus answered and said unto them, Though I bear record of Myself, *yet* My Record is true *(as He now nears the end of His Ministry, He no longer placates the Pharisees as He did in Chapter 5, but rather uses Himself as a Witness; He did not do this in Chapter 5, but He was certainly entitled to have done so):* for I know from where I came, and where I go *(proclaims His Deity);* but you cannot tell from where I come, and where I go *(is freighted with meaning respecting their unbelief).*

15 You judge after the flesh *(has reference to His Incarnation; they were of the flesh, which means that they did not understand spiritual things, and so they judged everything after the flesh);* I judge no man *(simply means that He did not come to judge, but rather to Save).*

16 And yet if I judge, My Judgment is true *(means that His previous statement of "judging no man" is not in any way meant to abrogate* His Position as the ultimate Judge of all men, but simply that this was not His Mission at present!):* for I am not alone, but I and the Father Who sent Me *(places an entirely different perspective on the claims of Christ; in effect, He is saying that any judgment rendered does not rest on mere human consciousness, but rather on the infallible decisions of God the Father).*

17 It is also written in your Law, that the testimony of two men is true *(is derived from Deuteronomy 17:6; 19:15; Jesus is merely saying that upon the common principles of jurisprudence as laid down in the Law of Moses, He is willing to rest His claim).*

18 I am One who bears witness of Myself *(reflects His Own Divine self-consciousness),* and the Father Who sent Me bears witness of Me *(did so through the Miracles and Healings, etc.).*

19 Then said they unto Him, Where is Your Father? *(They did not ask: "Who is He?" or "What is He?" Rather, "Where is He?" is asked with acute sarcasm!)* Jesus answered, You neither know Me, nor My Father *(bluntly He tells them that they are without God, and consequently without hope!):* if you had known Me, You should have known My Father also *(another utterance, implying the most intimate relation between Himself and the Father).*

20 These words spoke Jesus in

the treasury, as He taught in the Temple (where He stood teaching were two colossal golden Lampstands on which hung a multitude of lamps that were lit during the Feast of Tabernacles, and around which the people danced with great rejoicing; as He stands in the midst of these lamps, He declares Himself the "Light of Life," as proclaimed in Verse 12): and no man laid hands on Him; for His hour was not yet come (no one had any power over Him in any capacity, save only that which was given them by the Father).

21 Then said Jesus again unto them, I go My way, and you shall seek Me (refers to the fact that they had rejected Him, and would consequently continue to look for a Messiah, but obviously in vain!), and shall die in your sins (one of the most sobering statements ever made by our Lord; from then until now, they have died in their sins, because they rejected Him): Where I go, you cannot come (proclaims His departure to the Father by a blood-stained pathway by means of a violent death, but a death which would liberate mankind, at least those who will believe).

22 Then said the Jews, Will He kill Himself? (This query was one of harsh mockery, and its hurtful intent can hardly be exaggerated.) Because He said, Where I go, you cannot come (they had no spiritual understanding, so they did not comprehend what He said in the least).

23 And He said unto them, you are from beneath (meaning that they were of Satan); I am from above (speaks of Heaven): you are of this world; I am not of this world (in effect says that they are lost without God, because they would not accept Him Who Alone could save them).

24 I said therefore unto you, that you shall die in your sins (to be sure, this type of preaching arouses great animosity and even hatred on the part of those to whom such words are delivered): for if you believe not that I am He, you shall die in your sins (states the reason, and in no uncertain terms, for their spiritual depravity).

25 Then said they unto Him, Who are You? (This in effect says, "Who are You to deal out threats to us like this?") And Jesus said unto them, Even the same that I said unto you from the beginning (the beginning of this Message, referring to Verse 12).

26 I have many things to say and to judge of you (even though they dismissed His Words as inconsequential, the bitter consequences would be reaped nonetheless; their treatment of Him and Him Alone decided their destiny, as it does every man): but He Who sent Me is True (as God is True, so is Christ);

and I speak to the world those things which I have heard of Him *(he who accepts Christ accepts God the Father, and He Who rejects Christ rejects God the Father)*.

27 They understood not that He spoke to them of the Father *(not knowing the Son, speaks loudly that they did not know the Father as well)*.

28 Then said Jesus unto them, When you have lifted up the Son of Man *(speaks of the Cross)*, then shall you know that I am He *(that time has not even yet arrived, but will take place at the Second Coming when they look upon Him Whom they have pierced [Zech. 12:10; Rev. 1:7])*, and that I do nothing of Myself *(Christ was led totally by the Holy Spirit)*; but as My Father has taught Me, I speak these things *(even though He was God, still He was also Man, and functioned totally as a Man while on this Earth; as such, He had to learn exactly as we do)*.

29 And He Who sent Me is with Me *(speaks of a union that is beyond comprehension to mere mortals; He and the Father were indivisible; they were of the same essence)*: the Father has not left Me alone *(the Holy Spirit was constantly with Christ)*; for I do always those things that please Him *(Christ pleased the Father without fail, which no other human being can say)*.

ABRAHAM

30 As He spoke these words, many believed on Him *(their Faith, as we shall see, was misplaced and unacceptable!)*.

31 Then said Jesus to those Jews which believed on Him *(now presents a part of the Message upon which their Faith will falter; thus resides millions!)*, If you continue in My Word, *then* are you My Disciples indeed *(simply means that one has to believe all the Word, not just part, and then continue in that believing; regrettably, as the Parable of the Sower points out, many do not continue to believe; consequently, this refutes the Unscriptural Doctrine of Unconditional Eternal Security)*;

32 And you shall know the Truth, and the Truth shall make you free *(this is the secret of all abundant Life in Christ; the "Truth" is "Jesus Christ and Him Crucified," which alone is the answer to the problems of Man)*.

33 They answered Him, We be Abraham's seed, and were never in bondage to any man *(proclaims an ironical statement, inasmuch as they had been in bondage to the Egyptians, the Assyrians, the Babylonians, the Persians, the Greeks, and were even now in bondage to the Romans)*: why do you say, you shall be made free? *(This proclaims*

them not seeing nor admitting their true spiritual condition, which Jesus will now readily address.)

34 Jesus answered them, Verily, verily, I say unto you, Whosoever commits sin is the servant of sin *(and whosoever is the servant of sin is not free; there's only one way for the Believer to overcome sin, and that is the Cross of Christ ever being the Object of our Faith [Gal. 6:14]).*

35 And the servant abides not in the house for ever *(the servant of sin will ultimately be cast out of the house, i.e., "out of the Kingdom of God"): but* the Son abideth ever *(whosoever abides in the Son, will abide in the house; otherwise, he will be cast out).*

36 If the Son therefore shall make you free *(Christ Alone can make one free, and He does so through and by what He did at the Cross, and our Faith in that Finished Work),* you shall be free indeed *(a freedom which the world cannot give and, in fact, doesn't even understand).*

37 I know that you are Abraham's seed *(in effect, Jesus is saying that being "Abraham's seed" by physical birth contains no Salvation); but* you seek to kill Me *(this completely negated their spiritual claims),* because My Word has no place in you *(signifies the reason for their murderous hearts, despite their claims).*

38 I speak that which I have seen with My Father *(again and again Christ reiterates the fact that He did only the Father's Will):* and you do that which you have seen with your father *(signifying that their father was the Devil, despite their religious claims).*

39 They answered and said unto Him, Abraham is our father *(was true according to the flesh, but not true spiritually).* Jesus said unto them, If you were Abraham's children *(spiritual children),* you would do the works of Abraham *(means that Abraham loved God, had Faith in God, and longingly looked for God's Son, Who would ultimately come).*

40 But now you seek to kill Me *(that He could know their hearts should have told them Who He actually was),* a Man Who has told you the truth *(presents the first and only time that Jesus referred to Himself in this fashion; He did so to mark the contrast between Himself and the "man-slayer" of John 8:44; "murderer" is "man-slayer" in the Greek Text; Jesus is a "man-saver," while Satan is a "man-slayer"),* which I have heard of God *(the very highest representation of the very conception of a Divine Commission, and a Divine Message):* this did not Abraham *(proclaims the fact that while they may be Abraham's "seed," they were not his children, and he in this*

sense could not be their "father").

41 You do the deeds of your father *(while claiming to be Abraham's seed, they were not doing the deeds of Abraham, but rather the Devil).* Then said they to Him, We be not born of fornication *(has reference to the false worship and idolatry that so often characterized Israel of old; as well, they may, at the same time, have been accusing Jesus of having been thusly born);* we have one Father, *even* God *(presents the proud claim made still by those who are morally the children of Satan, even as untold millions do presently).*

42 Jesus said unto them, If God were your Father, you would love Me *(Jesus Alone is the yardstick):* for I proceeded forth and came from God *(He Alone has done this, with no other able to say such a thing);* neither came I of Myself, but He sent Me *(places the entirety of the Godhead in unison respecting the Redemption of mankind, and concerning that which Jesus would do).*

43 Why do ye not understand My speech? *(The unconverted man cannot understand the Word of the Lord [I Cor. 2:14].) even* because you cannot hear My Word *(they heard it physically, but did not hear it spiritually because they did not know the Lord).*

44 You are of *your* father the Devil, and the lusts of your father you will do *(presents the Lord repudiating in terrible language the spiritual claims made by these Jews respecting their association with Jehovah; this is the cause of all the problems in the world).* He was a murderer from the beginning *(refers to the fact that Satan originated sin, and sin brings forth death),* and abode not in the truth *(it means he was actually in truth, for a time, until he rebelled against God),* because there is no truth in him *(no truth in him since his rebellion).* When he speaks a lie, he speaks of his own: for he is a liar, and the father of it *(Satan is the originator of the "lie"; consequently, his entire kingdom of darkness, in totality, is built on the "lie").*

45 And because I tell *you* the truth, you believe Me not *(truth can only be believed and accepted by one's Faith being exclusively in Christ, and the price He paid on the Cross).*

46 Which of you convinces Me of sin? *(They could not point to any sin that He had committed, so that alone should have told them Who He was.)* And if I say the truth, why do you not believe Me? *(They didn't believe Him because they were not of God. This clearly and plainly showed them up for what they really were.)*

47 He who is of God hears God's Words *(could be said, "the closer to God one is, the more one* *hears and abides by the Word of God")*: **you therefore hear** *them* **not, because you are not of God** *(this is the reason for so much error in the modern Church; most aren't of God!).*

DECLARATION

48 Then answered the Jews, and said unto Him, Say we not well that You are a Samaritan, and have a devil? *(Calling Him a "Samaritan" was the grossest insult they could level at anyone. So, they were saying that His Doctrine was as the Samaritans — false, corrupt, and, in effect, a lie.)*

49 Jesus answered, I have not a devil *(presents Him making a simple denial, and taking no notice of the charge of being a Samaritan)*; **but I honour My Father, and you do dishonour Me** *(in effect says that by dishonoring Him, they were dishonoring the Father as well, Whom they claimed to serve).*

50 And I seek not My Own glory *(in effect says that He didn't come to this Earth for "Glory," but rather to Redeem mankind)*: **there is One who seeks and judges** *(actually means that God sought Glory for Jesus, and Judged Him worthy of Glory).*

51 Verily, verily, I say unto you, If a man keep My saying, he shall never see death *(means that he shall not see spiritual or eternal death).*

52 Then said the Jews unto Him, Now we know that You have a devil *(they were denying Him Who Alone could give Life!)*. **Abraham is dead, and the Prophets** *(portrays a total lack of understanding of what He had said; while these men were dead physically, they were very much alive spiritually, and actually in Paradise at that very moment)*; **and You say, If a man keep My saying, he shall never taste of death** *(they changed what He said by inserting the word "taste" in place of the word "see"; they had reduced His statement from the spiritual to the physical).*

53 Are You greater than our father Abraham, which is dead? and the Prophets are dead *(yes, He is greater than all of these!)*: **what do You make yourself?** *(He didn't make anything of Himself as the Man Christ Jesus! God made Him what He was.)*

54 Jesus answered, If I honour Myself, My honour is nothing *(He now addresses Himself to their question)*: **it is My Father who honors Me** *(His answer should have given them room for pause)*; **of Whom you say, that He is your God** *(He has repeatedly stated in every way possible that if they truly knew God, they would know Him)*:

55 Yet you have not known Him *(is blunt, and speaks exactly the Truth)*; **but I know Him** *(as no one has ever known Him)*: **and if I should**

say, I know Him not, I shall be a liar like unto you *(as is painfully obvious, Jesus pulled no punches)*: but I know Him, and keep His saying *(which is in contrast to these religious leaders)*.

56 Your father Abraham rejoiced to see My day: and he saw it, and was glad *(in the great revelation of Justification by Faith given to Abraham by God, he was made to understand that this great Redemption Plan was wrapped up, not in a philosophy, but rather a Man, the Man Christ Jesus, and what He would do at the Cross; the Patriarch rejoiced in that)*.

57 Then said the Jews unto Him, You are not yet fifty years old *(the Jews at that time believed that a man did not reach full maturity, regarding wisdom and intellect, until fifty years old)*, and have You seen Abraham? *(They were either misinterpreting His Words, or they, in fact, did understand what He said, but did not believe Him, consequently answering sarcastically.)*

58 Jesus said unto them, Verily, verily, I say unto you, Before Abraham was, I am *(in essence He said, "Before Abraham was brought into being, I was eternally existent"; He also said, "Abraham was," "I am")*.

59 Then took they up stones to cast at Him *(presents their response to their Messiah)*: but Jesus hid Himself, and went out of the Temple, going through the midst of them, and so passed by *(means that He slowly walked through them and went on His way, with them doing nothing; thus was the response of the religious leaders of Israel to their Messiah!)*.

CHAPTER 9

BORN BLIND

AND as *Jesus* passed by, He saw a man which was blind from his birth *(proclaims the only instance of such a healing being recorded; this is a picture of humanity born in sin, consequently spiritually blind from birth)*.

2 And His Disciples asked Him, saying, Master, who did sin, this man, or his parents, that he was born blind? *(Many believed, as evidenced by the question of the Disciples, that every peculiar disaster pointed to some special or particular sin. It seems they had not learned much from the Book of Job, which repudiates this type of thinking.)*

3 Jesus answered, Neither has this man sinned, nor his parents *(does not mean that our Lord asserts these people are sinless, but rather severs the supposed link between their conduct and the specific affliction before us)*: but that the Works of God should be made

manifest in Him *(means that Jesus did not come to the Earth to condemn men for their fallen condition because, in fact, they are already condemned; He came to set man free by the Power of God).*

4 I must work the Works of Him Who sent Me *("We" should be substituted for "I," simply because these Works are meant to be continued by all who follow Christ),* while it is day *(this life span)*: the night comes, when no man can work *(refers to the end of this life span).*

5 As long as I am in the world *(the span of His earthly Ministry),* I am the Light of the world *(proclaims Jesus as sublimely conscious of His Power to do for the moral world what the Sun was doing for the physical world).*

6 When He had thus spoken, He spat on the ground, and made clay of the spittle *(is meant to express to the morally blind eyes of men Christ in a body of lowly clay, animated by Divine Breath; the clay symbolized His humanity, and the moisture of His Lips the life that animated it),* and He anointed the eyes of the blind man with the clay *(was meant to serve as a symbol of the human Body of Christ serving as the Perfect Sacrifice for sin),*

7 And said unto him, Go, wash in the pool of Siloam *(symbolizing the shed Blood of Christ, which cleanses from all sin),* (which is by interpretation, Sent.) *(This refers to Jesus being sent from God for the Salvation of the world.)* He went his way therefore, and washed, and came seeing *(spiritually refers to all who are washed in the precious shed Blood of the Lord Jesus Christ; only then can we "see").*

8 The neighbours therefore, and they which before had seen him who was blind, said *(proclaims those who personally knew Him, witnessing the miraculous change which had taken place),* Is not this he who sat and begged? *(He would beg no more.)*

9 Some said, This is he: others *said,* He is like him: *but* he said, I am he *(he wants everyone to know who he is, and Who performed this Miracle; despite the religious leaders, he is not ashamed of Christ, neither does he fear them).*

10 Therefore said they unto him, How were your eyes opened?

11 He answered and said, A man Who is called Jesus made clay, and anointed my eyes, and said unto me, Go to the pool of Siloam, and wash *(proclaims this man repeating almost exactly what Jesus had told him to do; He began where all Disciples must, with the man, i.e., a "Man called Jesus"):* and I went and washed, and I received sight *(think of this! this man, born blind, had never seen anything, and now he can see).*

12 Then said they unto him, Where is He? *(This seems to be asked with some sarcasm.)* He said, I know not *(seems to be said with the thought in mind that even though he did not then know, he was determined to find out).*

THE PHARISEES

13 They *(seems to be those who are trying to cause trouble)* brought to the Pharisees him who aforetime was blind.

14 And it was the Sabbath Day when Jesus made the clay, and opened his eyes *(we now come to another confrontation over religious rules, which has plagued humanity almost from the beginning).*

15 Then again the Pharisees also asked him how he had received his sight. He said unto them, He put clay upon my eyes, and I washed, and do see *(it seems that this man is beginning to suspect that some charge is being trumped up against Jesus; therefore, he shrewdly omits the "saliva" and the "making of the clay," as well as the place where he had been sent to wash, which things the Pharisees claimed were the breaking of the Law of Moses).*

16 Therefore said some of the Pharisees, This man is not of God, because he keeps not the Sabbath Day *(as given in the Greek, it is especially contemptuous).* Others said, How can a man who is a sinner do such Miracles? *(This provides a dilemma for the Pharisees because the truth is that a sinner could not do such Miracles.)* And there was a division among them *(proclaims the obvious!).*

17 They say unto the blind man again, What do you say of Him, Who has opened your eyes? *(This portrays the idea as presented by the Pharisees that Jesus might have performed this Miracle through the agency of demon spirits.)* He said, He is a Prophet *(having scant knowledge of Jesus, he calls Him a "Prophet" because that is the highest title he can now apply).*

18 But the Jews did not believe concerning him, that he had been blind, and received his sight *(not only do the Pharisees deny Christ, they now deny what has been obviously done, claiming they need more proof),* until they called the parents of him who had received his sight.

19 And they asked them, saying, Is this your son, who you say was born blind? *(The question implies that they even somewhat doubted the testimony of the parents.)* how then does he now see? *(What a stupid question!)*

20 His parents answered them and said, We know that this is our son, and that he was born blind:

21 But by what means he now sees, we know not *(true, in that*

they only knew what their son had told them); or who has opened his eyes, we know not *(does not quite present all the truth; surely they knew it was Jesus, but experiencing the obvious animosity, they will not confess Christ)*: he is of age; ask him: he shall speak for himself *(actually presents them distancing themselves from the Miracle and, in a sense, from their own son)*.

22 These *words* spoke his parents, because they feared the Jews *(proclaims the man-fear which Jesus had earlier addressed)*: for the Jews had agreed already, that if any man did confess that He was Christ, He should be put out of the Synagogue *(excommunication, which cut them off from family, from socialities, from employment, literally everything)*.

23 Therefore said his parents, He is of age; ask him *(the Holy Spirit brings this out twice in order to highlight the position taken by the parents)*.

24 Then again called they the man who was blind, and said unto him, Give God the praise *(implies that they want the man to repudiate Jesus; in this type of instance, to give God praise was the equivalent of swearing to tell the truth [Josh. 7:19])*: we know that this man is a sinner *(their blasphemy and threats did not sway the former blind man in the least!)*.

25 He answered and said, Whether He be a sinner *or* no, I know not *(even though the translation seems to leave doubt, in the original Greek Text there is no hint of such; in effect, "you assert it, but the facts of my experience are altogether of a different kind")*: one thing I know, that, whereas I was blind, now I see *(pulls the attention back to the great Miracle which had been performed by Jesus; they had an argument, while he had an experience!)*.

26 Then said they to him again, What did He to you? *(This represents the third time they have asked him how he was healed.)* how opened He your eyes? *(Once again, the implication is that it was done by the power of demon spirits. In effect, these religious leaders were blaspheming the Holy Spirit.)*

27 He answered them, I have told you already, and you did not hear *(presents a courage that few in Israel had at that time)*: wherefore would ye hear it again? *(This actually says, "What is the point of telling you again?")* will ye also be His Disciples? *(The former blind man now uses sarcasm, and rightly so!)*

28 Then they reviled him *(means to vilify, to rail at, and to abuse by words)*, and said, You are His Disciple *(presents them telling the Truth for a change)*; but we are Moses' disciples *(despite their claims, they were no more the Disciples of Moses than they were of Christ)*.

29 We know that God spoke unto Moses *(that is true, but they did not at all obey what God spoke to Moses)*: as for this *fellow*, we know not from whence He is *(had they truly known Moses, they would have known Christ)*.

30 The man answered and said unto them, Why herein is a marvellous thing, that ye know not from whence He is, and *yet* He has opened mine eyes *(in effect says, "even you ought to know that only God can open blinded eyes!")*.

31 Now we know that God hears not sinners *(in effect says, "we know God does not listen to the cry of sinners, when, as sinners, they ask from the ground of their sin to secure their own sinful purpose)*: but if any man be a worshipper of God, and does His Will, him He hears *(proclaims the deepest Truth of the Divine Revelation about the conditions of acceptable prayer; it is obvious that this man had a knowledge of God that few people in Israel possessed at that time)*.

32 Since the world began was it not heard that any man opened the eyes of one who was born blind *(portrays the magnitude of this Miracle)*.

33 If this Man were not of God, He could do nothing *(thus the Pharisees are compelled for a few moments to hear from one known as a street beggar, words of teaching along the finest lines of a deep experience)*.

34 They answered and said unto him, You were altogether born in sins, and do you teach us? *(The question presents them unable to answer his Scriptural charge, so they have no other weapon to use but invectiveness and persecution.)* And they cast him out *(means they excommunicated him from the Synagogue)*.

JESUS

35 Jesus heard that they had cast him out; and when He had found him, He said unto him, Do you believe on the Son of God? *(Jesus is introducing Himself to this former beggar as the Messiah of Israel.)*

36 He answered and said, Who is He, Lord, that I might believe on Him? *(This question is asked with the idea that he already suspects Jesus is speaking of Himself!)*

37 And Jesus said unto him, You have both seen Him *(saw Him physically and spiritually)*, and it is He Who talks with you *(proclaims the greatest Revelation that could ever be given to any person at any time!)*.

38 And he said, Lord, I believe *(what did he believe? he believed that Jesus was and is the "Son of God," the Saviour of mankind, the Redeemer of the world, the Messiah of Israel)*. And he worshipped Him

(both for the great Miracle of Healing that he received and, as well, the Great Salvation he has now received, which was the greatest of all).

39 And Jesus said, For judgment I am come into this world *(what men think of Christ is the question that decides in every age their moral condition before God)*, that they which see not might see *(pertains mostly to the Gentile world)*; and that they which see might be made blind *(could be translated, "they which think they see, but in reality do not, and with the presentation of the Gospel, refuse to accept it, thinking they have no need of such")*.

40 And *some* of the Pharisees which were with Him heard these words, and said unto Him, Are we blind also? *(This seems to have been asked in sarcasm.)*

41 Jesus said unto them, If ye were blind, ye should have no sin *(doesn't mean that the absence of light abrogates their condition as sinners; all men are sinners [Rom. 3:9-18]; Jesus is saying that if they admitted they were spiritually blind, which they were, then this particular sin of rejecting the Light would not be attributed to them)*: but now you say, We see; therefore your sin remains *(therefore they were guilty of the terrible sin of refusing the True Light, which meant that the Light they did have would be taken away, with them being left totally "blind" in the* spiritual sense).

CHAPTER 10

THE GOOD SHEPHERD

VERILY, verily, I say unto you, He who enters not by the door into the sheepfold *(proclaims to us that there is a "door," and, in fact, only one "door!")*, but climbs up some other way, the same is a thief and a robber *(using a "way" other than Christ; He Alone is the Door)*.

2 But he who enters in by the Door *(Way)* is the Shepherd of the Sheep *(Jesus Alone is the True Shepherd)*.

3 To Him the porter opens *(means that the Law, the Doorkeeper, immediately admitted Him because He had perfectly kept the Law, and actually was the only One Who had done such a thing)*; and the Sheep hear His Voice *(means that True Sheep hear the Voice of the True Shepherd)*: and He calls His Own Sheep by name *(this speaks of relationship which Salvation automatically brings)*, and leads them out *(speaks of finding suitable pasture; the one who truly wants to know the Word of God will be led into all Truth [Jn. 16:13])*.

4 And when He puts forth His Own Sheep *(He is Owner as well as Shepherd of the Sheep, and has, therefore, so to speak, a double love for us)*, He goes before them *(He*

has planned everything), and the Sheep follow Him: for they know His Voice (the true heart will know His Voice, and the false heart will follow others).

5 And a stranger will they not follow, but will flee from him (refers to "thieves and robbers, and false prophets" [Mat. 7:15-20]): for they know not the voice of strangers (True Sheep cannot be deceived).

6 This Parable spoke Jesus unto them: but they understood not what things they were which He spoke unto them (the Pharisees did not understand because they were not true sheep).

EXPLANATION

7 Then said Jesus unto them again, Verily, verily, I say unto you, I am the door of the Sheep ("I am," exclusive of all others! there is only "One Door," and that "Door" is Christ).

8 All who ever came before Me are thieves and robbers (pertains to any and all before or after Christ, who claim to have the way of Salvation without Christ!): but the Sheep did not hear them (True Sheep cannot be deceived).

9 I am the Door (presents an emphatic statement; the Church is not the door to Christ, as the Catholics teach, but Christ is the Door to the Church): by Me if any man enter in, he shall be Saved (as the "Door," Jesus is the "Saviour"), and shall go in and out, and find pasture (they went in for safety and went out for pasture).

10 The thief comes not, but for to steal, and to kill, and to destroy (speaks of Satan and his emissaries who pedal a false way of Salvation): I am come that they might have life, and that they might have it more abundantly (the Source of this "Life" is Christ; all true Believers have such; however, all true Believers enjoy such only by constant Faith in Christ and the Cross).

11 I am the good Shepherd (speaks of Jesus dying for the Sheep; the "Good Shepherd" dies for the Sheep, the "Great Shepherd" lives for the Sheep [Heb. 13:20], and the "Chief Shepherd" comes for the Sheep [I Pet. 5:4]): the good Shepherd gives His life for the Sheep (the Cross: His "Life," if given for the Sheep, would guarantee "Eternal Life"; the "Cross" is ever the Central point of Christianity).

12 But he who is an hireling, and not the shepherd (presents the one who poses as a shepherd, but really is not), whose own the sheep are not (True Sheep do not belong to false shepherds), sees the wolf coming, and leaves the sheep, and flees (the purpose of the "hireling" is to fleece the sheep, not protect the sheep): and the wolf catches them, and scatters the sheep (de-

struction awaits those who follow false shepherds).

13 The hireling flees, because he is an hireling, and cares not for the sheep *(false apostles have no real concern for the sheep, but only for other things, mostly money).*

14 I am the good Shepherd, and know My *Sheep (the Lord approves those who are His because they have trusted Him for Salvation),* and am known of Mine *(I know My Sheep, and they know Me).*

15 As the Father knows Me, even so know I the Father *(in effect, Jesus is claiming omniscience exactly as God, for He is God!):* and I lay down My life for the Sheep *(once again speaks of the Crucifixion).*

16 And other Sheep I have, which are not of this fold *(speaks of the Gentile Church):* them also I must bring, and they shall hear My Voice *(the Apostle Paul was used by the Lord to help plant the Gentile Church);* and there shall be one fold *(one flock, made up of both Jews and Gentiles), and* one Shepherd *(the Lord Jesus Christ).*

17 Therefore does My Father love Me *(proclaims that what Christ was to do held a special value in God's Heart),* because I lay down My Life *(the entirety of the idea of the Incarnation was to purposely "lay down His Life"),* that I might take it again *(the Resurrection).*

18 No man takes it from Me, but I lay it down of Myself *(His death was not an execution nor an assassination, it was a Sacrifice; the idea is that He allowed His death to take place).* I have power to lay it down, and I have power to take it again *(proclaims that what He did, He did voluntarily; He did not step out of the path of obedience, for He died as commanded).* This Commandment have I received of My Father *(this means that God the Father gave Him the latitude to do what He desired, and His desire was to do the Will of God; so He purposely laid down His Life).*

DIVISION

19 There was a division therefore again among the Jews for these sayings *(this tells us of the fact of the division, while the cause of the division lay with the religious leadership of Israel).*

20 And many of them said, He has a devil *(proclaims the policy of the Pharisees and Scribes who claim that Jesus cast out demons by the power of Satan),* and is mad *(claiming He was insane);* why hear you Him? *(This portrays the Pharisees seeking to dissuade the people from paying attention to Christ.)*

21 Others said, These are not the words of Him Who has a devil *(demon).* Can a devil open the eyes of the blind? *(The answer* is an obvious "no.")

MESSIAH

22 And it was at Jerusalem the Feast of the Dedication, and it was winter (*this particular Feast was appointed by Judas Maccabaeus to commemorate the purification of the Temple, after Antiochus Epiphanes had defiled it; it took place in December, and actually was not a Biblical Feast*).

23 And Jesus walked in the Temple in Solomon's porch.

24 Then came the Jews round about Him (*portrays them doing such in a threatening manner, demanding an immediate answer*), and said unto Him, How long do You make us to doubt? (*It was not Christ Who made them doubt, but rather their own unbelief.*) If You are the Christ, tell us plainly (*actually, He had already told them in every conceivable way possible*).

25 Jesus answered them, I told you, and you believed not (*refers to their expectations of a type of Messiah, which role Jesus would not fill*): the works that I do in My Father's Name, they bear witness of Me (*this "witness" was Scriptural and, therefore, pointed Israel to the Bible [Isa. 61:1]*).

26 But you believe not, because you are not of My Sheep, as I said unto you (*they were not His Sheep because they did not desire to be His Sheep; the decision was theirs, and reached because of unbelief*).

27 My Sheep hear My Voice (*Christ is the head of the Church, not men*), and I know them (*refers to perfect and absolute knowledge, even on an individual basis*), and they follow Me (*proclaims what True sheep will do*):

28 And I give unto them Eternal Life (*carries with it a promise that cannot be matched elsewhere under any circumstances*); and they shall never perish (*means that no Believer need ever fear that God will change His Mind respecting their Salvation*), neither shall any man pluck them out of My hand (*refers to any and all outside forces; however, if one so desires, one can take one's self out of His hand, which regrettably millions have done*).

29 My Father, which gave them to Me, is greater than all (*proclaims the Power of God that is able to keep any and all, which He does through the Spirit by what Christ did at the Cross, and our Faith in that Finished Work*); and no man is able to pluck them out of My Father's hand (*when one has Christ, one at the same time has the Father, and the protection of the Father*).

30 I and My Father are One (*the Greek Text says, "We are One"; these simple words destroy the teaching of those who deny the distinction of

persons in the Godhead, and those who question the Deity of Christ).

THE JEWS

31 Then the Jews took up stones again to stone Him *(thus was the answer of "God's chosen people" to "God's chosen Gift," the Lord Jesus Christ!).*

32 Jesus answered them, Many good works have I showed you from My Father *(speaks of healing the sick, casting out demons, cleansing lepers, etc.);* for which of those works do you stone Me? *(This is a good question indeed!)*

33 The Jews answered Him, saying, For a good work we stone You not *(at the same time meant the Jews had no regard for His "Good Works," and in reality would have stopped them had they the power);* but for blasphemy *(the truth is they were the blasphemers, not Christ);* and because that You, being a man, make Yourself God *(it was true that He was a Man, but at the same time He was God!).*

DEITY

34 Jesus answered them, Is it not written in your Law *(presents the Lord taking up one illustration from among many in the Scriptures that the union between man and God lay at the heart of their Law; by Jesus using the word "your," He* was not implying that the Law was not His; actually there's not a shadow of disrespect cast on the Law by the pronoun, but it is used in such a sense that His hearers may identify with it), I said, you are gods? *(This is taken from Psalms 82:6; the word "gods" is used here in the sense of magistrates and Prophets appointed and energized by the Word of God. In this case, it did not refer to Deity.)*

35 If he called them gods, unto whom the Word of God came *(once again, "gods" as used here refer to "Magistrates and Judges," etc.),* and the Scripture cannot be broken *(proclaims to one and all the standard to which our Lord held the Scripture);*

36 Say ye of Him, Whom the Father has Sanctified, and sent into the world *(for the purpose of the Redemption of mankind),* You blaspheme *(presents a most serious charge indeed!);* because I said, I am the Son of God? *(This portrays Him presenting Himself in a far greater dignity than even they had aspired the Messiah would be.)*

37 If I do not the Works of My Father, believe Me not *(He tells them to judge Him on the basis of the Miracles He has performed, in effect telling them that everything He did was commanded Him by God).*

38 But if I do *(refers to the carrying out of these Mighty Works),*

though you believe not Me, believe the Works (actually says they are without excuse): that you may know, and believe, that the Father is in Me, and I in Him (further explains Verse 30, "I and My Father are One").

JESUS

39 Therefore they sought again to take Him (speaks of their efforts, but without success): but He escaped out of their hand (Reynolds said, "His escape was facilitated by the strange moral power He could exert to render their physical assaults upon Him in vain. They stretched out hands which dropped harmlessly at their side, verifying the solemn statement of Verse 18."),

40 And went away again beyond Jordan into the place where John at first baptized; and there He abode (our Lord had about three and a half months of Ministry remaining before the Crucifixion).

41 And many resorted unto Him (indicates that they did so in the right way), and said, John did no miracle: but all things that John spoke of this Man were true (they accepted Him as Lord and Saviour).

42 And many believed on Him there (these recognized the fact of sin and the need of pardon, which, no doubt, evidenced a True Faith that was different from the car-

nality of John 2:23 and 8:30).

CHAPTER 11

LAZARUS

NOW a certain man was sick, named Lazarus (was not the same Lazarus of Luke, Chapter 16, who had died sometime before now), of Bethany (a small village about two miles from Jerusalem, situated on the eastern slope of the Mount of Olives), the town of Mary and her sister Martha (the sisters of Lazarus).

2 (It was that Mary which anointed the Lord with ointment, and wiped His feet with her hair (the "anointing" took place very shortly before the Crucifixion, and after the event of Lazarus being raised from the dead), whose brother Lazarus was sick.)

3 Therefore his sisters sent unto Him, saying, Lord, behold, he whom You love is sick (refers to more than a mere malady, but a life-threatening affliction, which in fact did take his life, at least at the time).

4 When Jesus heard that, He said, This sickness is not unto death (the Greek Text actually says, "he shall not fall prey to death," which is the way it should have been translated), but for the Glory of God, that the Son of God might be glorified thereby (this tells us

that even though the Lord does not receive glory from sin or sickness, He definitely does receive glory in delivering men from sin, and from healing the sick).

5 Now Jesus loved Martha, and her sister, and Lazarus *(the result of a long acquaintance).*

6 When He had heard therefore that he *(Lazarus)* was sick *(seems to indicate that a messenger was sent before Lazarus died, with Lazarus dying shortly after he had left, but the messenger did not know this when he approached Christ),* He abode two days still in the same place where He was *(He did so on instructions from the Holy Spirit; in fact, the Spirit told Him that Lazarus had died).*

JUDAEA

7 Then after that said He to His Disciples, Let us go into Judaea again *(Reynolds said, "The use of the word 'again' points forcibly back to the last visit, when He told both friends and foes that the Good Shepherd would snatch His Sheep from the jaws of death, even though He lay down His Own Life in the doing of it).*

8 *His* Disciples said unto him, Master, the Jews of late sought to stone You; and You are going there again? *(How different this language is from that of His Own brothers [Jn. 7:3-5].)*

9 Jesus answered, Are there not twelve hours in the day? *(Our Lord is using this terminology as an analogy.)* If any man walk in the day, he stumbles not, because he sees the light of this world *(refers to the sun shining according to the rotation of the Earth).*

10 But if a man walk in the night, he stumbles *(using a natural expression to express a Spiritual Truth),* because there is no light in him *(destroys the doctrine of the "inner light" as claimed by man in natural birth; in truth, man within himself has no Spiritual Light).*

11 These things said He: and after that He said unto them, Our friend Lazarus sleeps *(Jesus is not teaching "soul sleep" here; at death, it is only the body of the Believer that sleeps, not the soul and the spirit, which immediately go to be with Christ; actually, the soul and spirit of Lazarus went down into Paradise at this time, because Jesus had not yet been glorified);* but I go, that I may awake him out of sleep *(refers to the fact that the Holy Spirit had told Jesus to raise this man from the dead).*

12 Then said His Disciples, Lord, if he sleep, he shall do well *(they did not know what Jesus was actually saying).*

13 Howbeit Jesus spoke of His Death *(this proclaims the fact that John, who wrote this account, does not hide the fact of the spiritual*

dullness of the Disciples): but they thought that He had spoken of taking of rest in sleep *(they put a carnal interpretation on His statements)*.

14 Then said Jesus unto them plainly, Lazarus is dead.

15 And I am glad for your sakes that I was not there *(portrays the fact that if Jesus had been there, Lazarus would not have died; Jesus would have healed him)*, to the intent you may believe *(has reference to the fact that the Holy Spirit instructed Jesus to perform the Miracle of raising Lazarus from the dead for a variety of reasons; among them, to teach the Disciples the fact of the coming Resurrection)*; nevertheless let us go unto him.

16 Then said Thomas, which is called Didymus, unto his fellow-Disciples, Let us also go, that we may die with him *(this statement, as given by Thomas, proclaims the fact that the Disciples had given up hope of a Messianic Kingdom, which they had thought would come immediately)*.

THE RESURRECTION

17 Then when Jesus came, He found that he *(Lazarus)* had lain in the grave four days already *(on the fourth day of death, decomposition begins to set in; so there was no doubt about the death of this man)*.

18 Now Bethany was near unto Jerusalem, about fifteen furlongs off *(about two miles from Jerusalem)*:

19 And many of the Jews came to Martha and Mary, to comfort them concerning their brother *(this shows that the family could well have been one of some wealth, position, and importance)*.

20 Then Martha, as soon as she heard that Jesus was coming, went and met Him *(implies that Jesus, upon coming close to Bethany, stopped short of coming into the town; knowing the animosity against Him, He did not desire to attract any undue disturbance, especially at this time; evidently He had sent someone to their home to inform them He had arrived, with information as to where He was)*: but Mary sat still in the house *(someone had to be in the house to meet the people who came to pay their respects)*.

21 Then said Martha unto Jesus, Lord, if You had been here, my brother had not died *(evidently she does not seem to think of Jesus as raising her brother from the dead)*.

22 But I know, that even now, whatsoever You will ask of God, God will give it You *(the terminology used by Martha shows it was still unclear to her exactly Who Jesus was)*.

23 Jesus said unto her, Your brother shall rise again *(very plainly, Jesus tells her what is about*

to happen; but in her doubt, she misunderstands).

24 Martha said unto Him, I know that he shall rise again in the Resurrection at the last day (proclaims what she had probably learned at the feet of Jesus [Dan. 12:2,13; Jn. 6:39-40, 44, 54; 12:48]).

25 Jesus said unto her, I am the Resurrection, and the Life (in effect He is saying, "Martha, look at Me, you are looking at the Resurrection and the Life"; this shows that "Resurrection" and "Life" are not mere doctrines, but in reality a Person, the Lord Jesus Christ): he who believes in Me, though he were dead, yet shall he live (speaks of the coming Resurrection of Life, when all the Sainted dead will rise [I Thess. 4:13-18]):

26 And whosoever lives and believes in Me shall never die ("whoever believes in Me will live Eternally"). Do you believe this? (The Resurrection is the end of death; consequently death has no more to do with the Redeemed; it has done all it can do; it is finished! the Redeemed live in the imparted life that put an end to it; for them, the old life, its death and judgment no longer exist.)

27 She said unto Him, Yes, Lord: I believe that You are the Christ, the Son of God, which should come into the world (proclaims her belief in the Lord in a different light than she had known Him previously; she now believes that Jesus is God!).

JESUS AND MARY

28 And when she had so said, she went her way, and called Mary her sister secretly (she relates to her sister what Jesus had just said), saying, The Master is come, and calls for you (has to be one of the most beautiful statements found in the entirety of the Word of God).

29 As soon as she heard that, she arose quickly, and came unto Him (she did such with a great spirit of anticipation).

30 Now Jesus was not yet come into the town, but was in that place where Martha met Him (probably a very short distance from the home of the sisters).

31 The Jews then which were with her in the house, and comforted her, when they saw Mary, that she rose up hastily and went out, followed her, saying, She goes unto the grave to weep there (they little knew what was about to happen!).

32 Then when Mary was come where Jesus was, and saw Him, she fell down at His Feet (represents, in a sense, her anticipation), saying unto Him, Lord, if You had been here, my brother had not died (the same words as uttered by her sister Mary; they believed, but I think it was still very difficult

for them to grasp the fact that He would raise their brother from the dead, even though he had been dead for some four days).

COMPASSION

33 When Jesus therefore saw her weeping, and the Jews also weeping which came with her, he groaned in the spirit, and was troubled (Reynolds said, "At that time, there flashed upon His Spirit all the terrible moral consequences of which death was the ghastly symbol."),

34 And said, Where have you laid him? They said unto Him, Lord, come and see (they would lead Him to the tomb).

35 Jesus wept (tears of sorrow because of the terrible specter of death, brought on the human race by sin).

36 Then said the Jews, Behold how He loved him! (However, His tears had to do with a far greater degree of misery than was evident here.)

37 And some of them said, Could not this Man, which opened the eyes of the blind, have caused that even this man should not have died? (This seems to have been said by some of the on-lookers with some sarcasm.)

38 Jesus therefore again groaning in Himself comes to the grave (if there is anything which symbol-izes all the pain and hurt resulting from the Fall of man, the "grave" or "tomb" is that example; Death is such an enemy!). It was a cave, and a stone lay upon it (presents the striking end of all men, for it is "appointed unto men once to die").

39 Jesus said, Take ye away the stone (presents one of the most poignant moments in human history). Martha, the sister of him who was dead, said unto Him, Lord, by this time he stinks: for he has been dead four days (her Faith seems to wane and weaken when she stands before the cold reality of this tomb).

40 Jesus said unto her, Said I not unto you, that, if you would believe, you should see the Glory of God? (Corruption, whether physical or moral, is no obstacle to Him Who is the Resurrection and the Life.)

PRAYER

41 Then they took away the stone from the place where the dead was laid. And Jesus lifted up His Eyes, and said, Father, I thank You that You have heard Me (proclaims this as a thanksgiving for that which had already been prayed and heard).

42 And I knew that You hear Me always (this speaks of relationship beyond our comprehension): but because of the people which stand by I said it, that they may

believe that You have sent Me *(the people heard Him pray to the Father, and now they will see the Father answer His Prayer; consequently, the proof of Who He is will be undeniable)*.

LAZARUS

43 And when He thus had spoken, He cried with a loud voice, Lazarus, come forth *(constitutes a Command, and from the Creator of the Ages; considering that He is the Resurrection and the Life, had He not called Lazarus by name all the other Sainted dead would have come forth as well!)*.

44 And he who was dead came forth *(constitutes the greatest Miracle in human history)*, **bound hand and foot with graveclothes** *(his legs were, no doubt, bound separately with him able to walk, but with some difficulty)*: and his face was bound about with a napkin *(concerns a cloth which had been tied over his face, but which he had probably partially removed)*. Jesus said unto them, Loose him, and let him go *(refers, as is obvious, to this burial shroud being taken off his body; Lazarus had been called up from Paradise where he had been for the past four days; one can only surmise as to what happened when the Voice of Jesus rang out in that place concerning Lazarus)*.

45 Then many of the Jews which came to Mary, and had seen the things which Jesus did, believed on Him *(Jesus would later say, "blessed are they who have not seen, and yet have believed" [Jn. 20:29])*.

46 But some of them went their ways to the Pharisees, and told them what things Jesus had done *(how is it that individuals could observe the type of Miracle just witnessed, and still oppose Christ?)*.

PHARISEES

47 Then gathered the Chief Priests and the Pharisees a Council, and said, What do we? *(This presents both the Pharisees and Sadducees joining in their denunciation of Jesus, even though they were normally bitter enemies between themselves.)* for this Man does many Miracles *(presents not all of them denying the Miracles, but some actually admitting to their veracity)*.

48 If we let Him thus alone, all *men* will believe on Him: and the Romans shall come and take away both our place and nation *(in fact, the Romans did exactly that; their rejection of Christ brought it all about; how spiritually blind they were!)*.

49 And one of them, *named* Caiaphas, being the High Priest that same year *(presents the political spectrum of this high office)*, said unto them, you know nothing at

all *(could be translated, "you do not understand the dangers we face!")*,

50 Nor consider that it is expedient for us, that one man should die for the people, and that the whole nation perish not *(Williams said, "the death of Jesus, proposed and commanded by the High Priest, was resolved upon that fearful moment; for the raising of Lazarus, had brought their malignity to a head.")*.

51 And this spoke He not of Himself *(actually means that their condemning Jesus to death, even though evil and wicked for which they would pay dearly, would be used of God for the Redemption of mankind)*: but being High Priest that year, he prophesied that Jesus should die for that Nation *(once again fell out to that which was ordained by God, but which in no way absolved these of blame)*;

52 And not for that Nation only *(refers to the fact that when Jesus died, He died for the entirety of the world, not for Israel only)*, but that also He should gather together in one *(one body consisting of both Jews and Gentiles)* the Children of God who were scattered abroad *(the Apostle Paul would be given the meaning of the New Covenant, which was the meaning of the Cross that would establish the Church)*.

53 Then from that day forth they took counsel together for to put Him to death *(if men reject Christ, the next step is to kill Him, i.e.,* repudiate Him for Who and What He is)*.

54 Jesus therefore walked no more openly among the Jews *(the raising of Lazarus from the dead was the great Miracle that brought all of this to a climax)*; but went thence unto a country near to the wilderness, into a city called Ephraim, and there continued with His Disciples *(seems to represent a place in connection with Bethel [II Chron. 13:19]; it was probably about fifteen miles north of the Jerusalem of that day)*.

55 And the Jews' Passover was nigh at hand *(He was the True Passover, and would fulfill the Type by dying on Calvary)*: and many went out of the country up to Jerusalem before the Passover, to purify themselves *(pertained to going through a Levitical, ceremonial cleansing from touching the dead and other unclean things [Num. 9:6-10])*.

56 Then sought they for Jesus *(seems to present the authorities seeking Him in order that He be arrested)*, and spoke among themselves, as they stood in the Temple, What think ye, that He will not come to the Feast? *(In almost every place, hundreds, if not thousands, of people seeking to hear Him or be healed by Him surrounded Him; so, their task of arresting Him would not be easy!)*

57 Now both the Chief Priests and the Pharisees had given a

commandment, that, if any man knew where He were, he should show it, that they might take Him *(they had determined that He must be stopped, and at all costs; the truth is that it cost them everything, both life and soul)*.

CHAPTER 12

MARY ANOINTS JESUS

THEN Jesus six days before the Passover came to Bethany *(represents the closing days of His Ministry and Work)*, where Lazarus was which had been dead, whom He raised from the dead *(He went to where He was welcome; He was not welcome in the Temple, even though it was His House; His Presence there would be looked at as an intrusion in a short time, as it is in most Churches presently)*.

2 There they made Him a supper *(probably in the house of Simon the Leper [Mat. 26:6; Mk. 14:3])*; and Martha served: but Lazarus was one of them who sat at the table with Him *(possibly Simon the Leper was there as well! if so, there would have been seated at the table two transcendent proofs of the Power of Jesus to save not only from the semblance of death as was Simon the Leper, but from the reality of death by the Resurrection of Lazarus)*.

3 Then took Mary a pound of ointment of spikenard, very costly *(probably worth about ten thousand dollars in 2003 currency)*, and anointed the Feet of Jesus, and wiped His Feet with her hair *(harmonious with the purpose of this Gospel and setting forth the Deity of the Lord Jesus, only the Anointing of His Feet is recorded)*: and the house was filled with the odour of the ointment *(it was testimony to His coming Resurrection, and she knew she would have no other opportunity; incidentally, Mary was not found at the empty Tomb; she was too spiritually intelligent to be there)*.

4 Then said one of His Disciples, Judas Iscariot, Simon's son, which should betray Him *(was not Simon the Leper in whose house this supper was prepared)*,

5 Why was not this ointment sold for three hundred pence, and given to the poor? *(Reynolds said, "sinful motive often hides itself under the mask of reverence for another virtue.")*

6 This he said, not that he cared for the poor *(this was not his real reason)*; but because he was a thief, and had the bag, and bear what was put therein *(had the ointment been sold and the money given to Christ, Judas would have stolen it; unfortunately, most of the money presently given for that which is supposed to be the Work of God is "stolen," i.e., "used for the wrong purposes")*.

7 Then said Jesus, Let her alone *(Jesus places His Seal of approval on what she is doing)*: against the day of My burying has she kept this *(indicating she had this ointment for quite some time)*.

8 For the poor always you have with you *(presents that which is regrettable, but true!)*; but Me you have not always *(Jesus would not be with them in the flesh very much longer)*.

THE PLOT

9 Much people of the Jews therefore knew that He was there *(at the home of Lazarus)*: and they came not for Jesus' sake only, but that they might see Lazarus also, whom He had raised from the dead *(no doubt, there were many and varied questions that people had concerning death, which they desired to ask Lazarus; and yet, the Scripture is silent on this subject)*.

10 But the Chief Priests consulted that they might put Lazarus also to death *(it had been about two months since Jesus had performed this greatest of Miracles; these religious leaders were not speaking of a judicial execution, but rather how they could hire some brigand to murder Lazarus in cold blood; religious evil is the worst evil of all!)*;

11 Because that by reason of Him many of the Jews went away, and believed on Jesus *(one cannot be in sympathy with Christ and at the same time remain in league with the evil of this religious hierarchy; one or the other must go!)*.

THE TRIUMPHANT ENTRY

12 On the next day much people who were come to the Feast *(the Passover)*, when they heard that Jesus was coming to Jerusalem *(their excitement is understandable)*,

13 Took branches of palm trees, and went forth to meet Him *(as was the custom; presents them waving these palm fronds in token of the approach of a conqueror)*, and cried, Hosanna *(in the Hebrew means, "saved we pray")*: Blessed is the King of Israel Who comes in the Name of the Lord *(is taken from Psalms 118:25-26; while the people at that moment were proclaiming Jesus as King, the religious leaders were plotting His Death)*.

14 And Jesus, when He had found a young ass, sat thereon; as it is written *(presents an animal that had never before been ridden; Matthew tells us that the foal was accompanied by its mother, and both animals satisfied the prediction of Zechariah, Chapter 9, and Isaiah 62:11)*,

15 Fear not, daughter of Sion: behold, The King comes, sitting

on an ass's colt *(is recorded by John from Zechariah 9:9).*

16 These things understood not His Disciples at the first *(refers to His Disciples being a part of this great celebration, but yet not knowing or realizing that they were fulfilling Prophecy)*: but when Jesus was glorified *(refers to the glorified body of Jesus after His Resurrection)*, then remembered they that these things were written of Him *(speaks of the time after the Day of Pentecost when they were baptized with the Holy Spirit, and He began to explain things to them)*, and *that* they had done these things unto Him *(the Scriptures portrayed what was to be done, and, in fact, what was done).*

17 The people therefore who was with Him when He called Lazarus out of his grave, and raised him from the dead, bear record *(they had been giving the testimony of what they had seen and heard from the moment it happened, with, no doubt, ready ears to listen).*

18 For this cause the people also met Him, for that they heard that He had done this Miracle *(proclaims the raising of Lazarus as the catalyst which instigated the Triumphant Entry).*

19 The Pharisees therefore said among themselves, Perceive ye how you prevail nothing? behold, the world is gone after Him *(John portrays the anger of the Pharisees as no other writer; this public entrance associated with the supreme Miracle of the raising of Lazarus compelled Priests and people to a decision; while the people were praising Him, the Priests decided to Crucify Him, but they could have "prevailed nothing" had He not voluntarily surrendered Himself).*

GREEKS

20 And there were certain Greeks among them who came up to worship at the Feast *(pertained to a large group of Gentiles)*:

21 The same came therefore to Philip, which was of Bethsaida of Galilee *(one of the Twelve Apostles)*, and desired Him, saying, Sir, we would see Jesus *(they were ready to plead with Him to go among them and offer His Message to the Gentiles!).*

22 Philip comes and tells Andrew: and again Andrew and Philip tell Jesus *(may present more, much more, than the passing on of information; but the time was wrong, which Jesus will now address).*

THE PREDICTION

23 And Jesus answered them *(answered the Greeks as well as His Disciples)*, saying, The hour is come *(the Crucifixion, which would*

pay the price for Adam's fallen race), that the Son of Man should be Glorified *(this statement guarantees the Resurrection, because Jesus could not be Glorified unless He was Resurrected)*.

24 Verily, verily, I say unto you *(the pronoun "you" is emphatic toward the Disciples that their idea of circumventing His death was a violation of the Word of God, and a hindrance to the very purpose and reason for which He came)*, Except a corn of wheat fall into the ground and die, it abideth alone *(says that His Atoning Death was a necessity)*: but if it die, it brings forth much fruit *(proclaims the very purpose for His death was to bring forth Life)*.

DISCIPLESHIP

25 He who loves his life shall lose it *(hits at the very heart of man's problem; it could be paraphrased, "He who loves self shall not see fulfillment")*; and he who hates his life in this world shall keep it unto Life Eternal *(refers to putting self last, and Christ first in all things)*.

26 If any man serve Me, let him follow Me *(follow Christ exclusively)*; and where I am, there shall also My Servant be *(actually means to be "Crucified together" [Romans 6:3-5], "Glorified together" [Romans 8:17])*: if any man serve Me,

him will My Father honour *(this is the true honor which comes from God)*.

JESUS PRAYS

27 Now is My soul troubled *(proclaims Him facing that which would come about in a very short time)*; and what shall I say? Father, save Me from this hour *(could be translated, "should I pray to the Father that He save Me from this hour?")*: but for this cause came I unto this hour *(could be translated, "No, for this cause came I unto this hour")*.

28 Father, glorify Your Name *(proclaims that which Jesus always sought to do)*. Then came there a Voice from Heaven, *saying*, I have both glorified *it*, and will glorify *it* again *(it was glorified at the raising of Lazarus, and it will be glorified again with the Resurrection of Christ)*.

29 The people therefore, who stood by, and heard *it*, said that it thundered *(does not mean that it was unintelligible, but that the Voice sounded with such Power that it was like thunder)*: others said, An Angel spoke to Him *(proclaims the fact that they did hear what was said, and did at least understand the words, even though they did not understand the meaning)*.

30 Jesus answered and said, This Voice came not because of

Me *(proclaims in no uncertain terms that Jesus was not in doubt as to Who and What He was)*, but for your sakes *(refers to God making this statement, and in an audible Voice that all who were there may hear and know)*.

31 Now is the Judgment of this world *(pertains to that which Jesus would do at Calvary; He would suffer the Wrath of God instead of the world)*: now shall the prince of this world be cast out *(Jesus would defeat Satan by atoning for all sin; sin is the legal means by which Satan keeps men in captivity; that means being removed, which it was by Christ, leaves the Evil One with no legal right, unless men freely give him that right; acceptance of Christ and the Cross defeats Satan and breaks his bondage)*.

32 And I, if I be lifted up from the Earth *(refers to His Death at Calvary; He was "lifted up" on the Cross; the "Cross" is the Foundation of all Victory)*, will draw all men unto Me *(refers to the Salvation of all who come to Him, believing what He did, and trusting in its atoning Work)*.

33 This He said, signifying what death He should die *(Reynolds says, "In these Words, we learn that the attraction of the Cross of Christ will prove to be the mightiest, and most sovereign motive ever brought to bear on the human will, and, when wielded by the Holy Spirit as a Revelation of the matchless Love of God, will involve the most sweeping judicial sentence that can be pronounced upon the world and its prince.")*.

34 The people answered Him *(proclaims an unsatisfactory answer, actually an answer of unbelief!)*, We have heard out of the Law that Christ abides forever *(refers to several passages out of the Old Testament being taken out of context)*: and how do You say, The Son of Man must be lifted up? *(This presents these people attempting to excuse their unwillingness to obey moral appeal to the conscience by raising some Bible difficulty.)* who is this Son of Man? *(If they did not now know, there is nothing that could be done that would ever help them to know.)*

35 Then Jesus said unto them, Yet a little while is the Light with you *(the warning is clearly given that their day was nearly gone, and the eternal darkness was coming)*. Walk while you have the Light, lest darkness come upon you *(presents a choice!)*: for he who walks in darkness knows not where he goes *(proclaims the majority of the world at present and, in fact, since the beginning of time)*.

36 While you have the Light *(Jesus is the Light)*, believe in the Light *(make Christ the central focus of your life and living)*, that you may be the Children of Light *(which*

at the same time means they were not the children of Light). These things spoke Jesus, and departed, and did hide Himself from them (this was the last public Word of Jesus; if the Word of God is rejected, ultimately the Lord will hide Himself, fulfilling Proverbs 1:24-30).

REJECTION

37 But though He had done so many Miracles before them (seems to be proclaimed with a sigh by the Holy Spirit), yet they believed not on Him (if people will not believe the Word of God, they will little believe Miracles, irrespective as to how powerful they may be):

38 That the saying of Isaiah the Prophet might be fulfilled, which he spoke (Isa., Chpt. 53), Lord, who has believed our report? (This doesn't mean no one believed, but it does mean that the number was few.) and to whom has the arm of the Lord been revealed? (This speaks of the Messiah being revealed to Israel, but they would not accept Him!)

39 Therefore they could not believe (means that Israel willfully shut their eyes to the Message of the Miracles), because that Isaiah said again (refers to where their unbelief led them),

40 He has blinded their eyes, and hardened their heart (God set in motion the "Law of Unbelief," which in effect is the "Law of Sowing and Reaping"); that they should not see with their eyes, nor understand with their heart, and be converted, and I should heal them (because they willfully refused to believe, God willed a judicial blindness and hardness accordingly).

41 These things said Isaiah, when he saw His Glory, and spoke of Him (in this Passage, John proclaims that the vision Isaiah had of the Lord [Isa. 6:1-2] was actually of the pre-Incarnate Christ; so we are told here that the Jehovah of the Old Testament was Jesus).

42 Nevertheless among the Chief Rulers also many believed on Him (does not relate exactly who they were, with the exception of Nicodemus and Joseph of Arimathea); but because of the Pharisees they did not confess Him, lest they be put out of the Synagogue (proclaims not only their excuses, but the excuses of many millions the world over):

43 For they loved the praise of men more than the praise of God (this means that they counted God as less than men; what an indictment!).

TEACHING

44 Jesus cried and said, he who believes on Me (claims the absolute necessity of believing on Christ as God manifest in the flesh and,

therefore, the Saviour of mankind, which He was through the Cross), believes not on Me *(believes not on Me Alone)*, but on Him Who sent Me *(to have the Son is to have the Father; to refuse the Son is to refuse the Father)*.

45 And he who sees Me sees Him Who sent Me *(had to be done by Faith, because Christ in His human form offered no expression of Deity)*.

46 I am come a Light into the world *(reveals all understanding, all purifying, all gracious influence which are shed on human affairs, nature, and destiny)*, that whosoever believes on Me should not abide in darkness *(the only way out of darkness is through Christ; He Alone is the Light!)*.

47 And if any man hear My Words, and believe not, I judge him not *(means that He is not pronouncing sentence now; He has come as Saviour)*: for I came not to judge the world, but to save the world *(proclaims His present Mission, which has lasted now for nearly 2,000 years)*.

48 He who rejects Me, and receives not My Words, has One Who Judges him *(presents a Truth that the Church desperately needs to hear and understand, and the entirety of the world for that matter)*: the Word that I have spoken, the same shall judge him in the last day *(speaks of the "Judgment Seat of Christ" for Believers, and the* "Great White Throne Judgment" *for unbelievers)*.

49 For I have not spoken of Myself *(His Words are not simply His Own, but rather from the Father, i.e., in effect the entirety of the Godhead)*; but the Father which sent Me *(He was sent by the Father for a distinct purpose and mission)*, He gave Me a Commandment, what I should say, and what I should speak *(in effect says, "in rejecting Me and My Words, men reject and insult the Father; His Word that they dare to renounce is as solemn and unalterable as the Word spoken on Sinai")*.

50 And I know that His Commandment is Life Everlasting *(as well says that Life Everlasting is found in the Words of no one else)*: whatsoever I speak therefore, even as the Father said unto Me, so I speak *(His Doctrine, its Substance, and the very Words used in its proclamation are all of Divine origin)*.

CHAPTER 13

THE LAST PASSOVER

NOW before the Feast of the Passover *(refers to the preparation day of the Passover, our Tuesday sunset to Wednesday sunset, with Wednesday being the day of the Crucifixion)*, when Jesus knew that His hour was come *(refers to the Cru-*

cifixion, which was the purpose for which He came) that He should depart out of this world unto the Father *(refers to the Resurrection and the Ascension)*, having loved His Own which were in the world, He loved them unto the end *(presents not so much an expression of time as of degree)*.

2 And supper being ended *(actually refers to the preparation for the Supper being ended, not the Supper itself; it was just beginning)*, the devil having now put into the heart of Judas Iscariot, Simon's *son*, to betray *Him (a short time before Satan did this thing)*;

HUMILITY

3 Jesus knowing that the Father had given all things into His Hands *(portrays two things in His Heart as He girded Himself, His conscious Deity and the heartless conduct of Judas)*, and that He was come from God, and went to God *(was something that He knew, at least from the time that He was twelve years old)*;

4 He rose from supper *(He rose from the table when the preparation had been completed)*, and laid aside His garments *(physically, His outer robe; spiritually, He laid aside the expression of His Deity, while never losing the possession of His Deity)*; and took a towel *(refers to the action of the lowliest slave or* servant in a household; it represents the servant spirit possessed by Christ)*, and girded Himself *(wrapped Himself in the towel; spiritually speaking, it refers to His Human Body provided for Him by the Father [Heb. 10:5] in order to serve as a Sacrifice on the Cross for sin)*.

5 After that He poured water into a basin *(spiritually, it referred to the Holy Spirit, which would pour from Him like a River [7:38-39])*, and began to wash the Disciples' feet *(presenting the servant principle which we are to follow, but even more particularly the cleansing guaranteed by the Holy Spirit concerning our daily walk, which comes about according to our Faith in Christ and what He did for us at the Cross)*, and to wipe *them* with the towel wherewith He was girded *(refers to the Incarnation, which made possible His Death on Calvary that atoned for all sin and made cleansing possible for the human race)*.

PETER'S RESPONSE

6 Then comes He to Simon Peter *(seems to indicate it was Peter to whom He first approached)*: and Peter said unto him, Lord, do you wash my feet? *("The flesh" cannot understand spiritual realities; it is too backward or too forward, too courageous or too cowardly; it is incapable of ever being right, and it is impossible to im-*

prove, consequently, it must "die.")

7 Jesus answered and said unto him, What I do you know not now; but you shall know hereafter *(when Peter was filled with the Spirit, which he was on the Day of Pentecost).*

8 Peter said unto Him, You shall never wash my feet *(the Greek Text actually says, "Not while eternity lasts"; Calvin said, "With God, obedience is better than worship").* Jesus answered him, If I wash you not, you have no part with Me *(the statement as rendered by Christ speaks to the constant cleansing needed regarding our everyday walk before the Lord, which the washing of the feet [our walk], at least in part, represented).*

9 Simon Peter said unto Him, Lord, not my feet only, but also *my* hands and *my* head *(Chrysostom said, "in his deprecation he was vehement, and his yielding more vehement, but both came from his love").*

10 Jesus said to him, he who is washed needs not save to wash *his* feet *(as stated, pertains to our daily walk before God, which means that the Believer doesn't have to get Saved over and over again; the "head" refers to our Salvation, meaning that we do not have to be repeatedly Saved, while the "hands" refer to our "doing," signifying that this doesn't need to be washed because Christ has already done what needs to be done; all of this is in the spiritual sense),* but is clean every whit *(refers to Salvation, and pertains to the Precious Blood of Jesus that cleanses from all sin; the infinite Sacrifice needs no repetition):* and you are clean, but not all *(refers to all the Disciples being Saved with one exception, which was Judas).*

11 For He knew who should betray Him *(portrays Him knowing this quite some time earlier);* therefore said He, You are not all clean *(actually presents Jesus making another appeal to Judas).*

12 So after He had washed their feet, and had taken His Garments, and was set down again *(now He is their Teacher and Lord)*, He said unto them, Do you know what I have done to you? *(Reynolds said, "There was no affectation [pretense] of humility about it; the purpose of the Lord was distinctly practical and ethical.")*

13 Ye call Me Master and Lord *(presents a double title which was not given except to the most accredited teachers):* and you say well; for *so* I am *(He is also telling them that, even though He has washed their feet, in no way does this diminish His position as the Lord God of Glory; we will not be diminished by such activity either, but rather exalted).*

14 If I then, *your* Lord and Master, have washed your feet *(speaks of and proclaims the example set);* you also ought to wash

one another's feet *(is not meant to be taken literally, but is to serve as an example of the Servant Principle).*

15 For I have given you an example *(meaning that "foot washing" is not meant to be a Church Ordinance, such as the Lord's Supper, etc.), that you should do as I have done to you (were it mere ceremony, they would have instantly known what He was doing).*

16 Verily, verily, I say unto you, The servant is not greater than his Lord *(Jesus, Who is Lord, has set the example that we must follow);* neither He who is sent greater than he who sends him *(He must ever increase, as we must ever decrease).*

17 If ye know these things, happy are you if you do them *(knowing and doing are often perilously divorced).*

JUDAS

18 I speak not of you all *(we are about to be presented with another attempt to bring Judas back from the crumbling edge, but sadly without success)*: I know whom I have chosen *(the Holy Spirit told Him whom to choose as His Personal Disciples)*: but that the Scripture may be fulfilled, He who eats bread with Me has lifted up his heel against Me *(in effect, He is saying, "I am the Person spoken of in Psalms 41:9).*

19 Now I tell you before it come *(proclaims Him knowing exactly what is going to happen, at least according to what the Scripture has foretold),* that, when it is come to pass, you may believe that I am He *(once again, proclaims Himself as being the One spoken of in Psalms 41:9).*

20 Verily, verily, I say unto you, He who receives whomsoever I send receives Me *(in effect says that we might be hated and betrayed as He the Master was, yet like Him our mission is Divine);* and he who receives Me receives Him Who sent Me *(proclaims the fact that acceptance or rejection reaches all the way to the Throne of God).*

21 When Jesus had thus said, He was troubled in spirit *(proclaims a strong expression used of the sorrows of Christ),* and testified, and said, Verily, verily, I say unto you, that one of you shall betray Me *(proclaims Jesus saying plainly that which He had previously hinted).*

22 Then the Disciples looked one on another, doubting of whom He spoke *(Judas was not suspected, showing that his actions of the past had not been those of treachery).*

23 Now there was leaning on Jesus' bosom one of His Disciples *(presents the manner in which they then reclined when dining; meals were then much more formal than now),* whom Jesus loved *(pertains*

to John the Beloved who wrote this Gospel).

24 Simon Peter therefore beckoned to him *(to John),* that he should ask who it should be of whom He spoke *(refers to Peter sitting far enough away from Jesus that he could not whisper to Him personally, so that others would not hear and would, therefore, ask John to do so for him).*

25 He then lying on Jesus' breast said unto Him, Lord, who is it? *(This proclaims none suspecting Judas.)*

26 Jesus answered, He it is, to whom I shall give a sop, when I have dipped it *(in its normal sense, this was a mark of honor for the guest who received it; it was another appeal to Judas).* And when He had dipped the sop, He gave *it* to Judas Iscariot, *the son* of Simon *(Verse 21 records Jesus appealing to the conscience of Judas, and now appealing to his heart, all to no avail!).*

27 And after the sop Satan entered into him *(he yielded to Satan).* Then said Jesus unto him, That you do, do quickly *(it was quickly done, but the results were not quickly done, as such results are never quickly done).*

28 Now no man at the table knew for what intent He spoke this unto him *(the remaining Eleven little knew, it seems, what was actually happening).*

29 For some *of them* thought, because Judas had the bag *(Judas was the treasurer of the group),* that Jesus had said unto him, Buy *those things* that we have need of against the Feast; or, that he should give something to the poor *(it seems they gave to the poor quite regularly).*

30 He then having received the sop went immediately out *(this means that Judas was not present when Jesus gave His discourse as given in the next four Chapters, which immediately followed the Supper):* and it was night *(dark as was the night upon Judas' head, there was a blacker night in his heart; all was darkness in his soul).*

A NEW COMMANDMENT

31 Therefore, when he was gone out *(refers to the fact that Jesus could not give His discourse to the Disciples, which now follows, until the traitor had left),* Jesus said, Now is the Son of Man Glorified, and God is Glorified in Him *(Christ Glorified God in death, and God Glorified Him in Resurrection).*

32 If God be Glorified in Him *(refers to the perfect obedience of Jesus Christ as the "Second Man," i.e., "Last Adam"),* God shall also Glorify Him in Himself, and shall straightway *(immediately)* Glorify Him *(the Son of Man was Glorified on the Cross in a much more*

admirable way than He will be by the Millennial Glories attaching to that title; for on the Cross as the Son of Man, He displayed all the Moral Glory of God).

33 Little children, yet a little while I am with you *(He would only be with them for about another forty-four days before the Ascension).* You shall seek Me *(simply made reference to the fact that He would be gone)*: and as I said unto the Jews, Where I go, you cannot come *(referring to Heaven, at least at that particular moment)*; so now I say to you *(presents an entirely different statement than that given to the faithless Jews).*

34 A new Commandment I give unto you, That you love one another *(is beyond the Old Commandment in Leviticus 19:18, "you shall love your neighbor as yourself")*; as I have loved you, that you also love one another *(in effect, He is saying, "I have loved each of you unto death; and in loving one another you are loving Me; you are loving an Object of My tender Love").*

35 By this shall all *men* know that you are My Disciples *(not only proclaims this "Love" as the foundation of the New Covenant, but, as well, proclaims it as the basis for recognition that one is truly in the New Covenant)*, if you have love one to another *(this type of Love is* the "God-Kind of Love," and is impossible for anyone to have without accepting Christ as one's Saviour; as well, "Love" and the "Cross" are indivisible).*

DENIAL

36 Simon Peter said unto Him, Lord, where are you going? *(As stated, the Disciples had no idea as to what Jesus was saying regarding His departure.)* Jesus answered him, Where I go, you cannot follow Me now; but you shall follow Me afterwards *(He assures them that where He is going, they would follow later, which they did!).*

37 Peter said unto Him, Lord, why cannot I follow You now? *(Their immaturity was so obvious at this time, but would change after the Day of Pentecost.)* I will lay down my life for Your sake *(Peter thought himself ready to die for His Lord, before His Lord had died for him).*

38 Jesus answered him, Will you lay down your life for My sake? *(This is a question that does not really expect an answer, because the answer was already known.)* Verily, verily, I say unto you, The rooster shall not crow, till you have denied Me thrice *(proclaims a coming terrible moment in the life of Peter, and one which was the very opposite of what he was claiming).*

CHAPTER 14

COMFORT AND PROMISE

LET not your heart be troubled *(is said by Christ immediately after predicting Peter's shameful denial)*: you believe in God, believe also in Me *(means simply to have Faith in Him, as they had Faith in God; this is His Highest and most complete Revelation of Himself as God)*.

2 In My Father's House are many mansions *(proclaims Heaven as a large place; a place so large actually, that its possibilities transcend one's imagination and exceed our comprehension)*: if it were not so, I would have told you *(has reference to the fact that He is speaking from firsthand knowledge)*. I go to prepare a place for you *(refers to Him Personally superintending this extra building project in Heaven)*.

3 And if I go and prepare a place for you, I will come again, and receive you unto Myself *(proclaims the first mention of the Rapture of the Church [I Thess. 4:13-18])*; that where I am, *there* you may be also *(refers to Heaven, where the Saints of God will go at the Resurrection)*.

4 And where I go you know *(He had just told them)*, and the Way you know *(actually spoke of Himself, for He is the "Way")*.

5 Thomas said unto Him, Lord, we know not where You go *(presents this Disciple striving after Truth and reality through intellectualism, and not Faith)*; and how can we know the way? *(Christ will answer immediately!)*

JESUS

6 Jesus said unto Him, I am the Way, the Truth, and the Life *(proclaims in no uncertain terms exactly Who and What Jesus is)*: no man comes unto the Father, but by Me *(He declares positively that this idea of God as Father, this approach to God for every man is through Him — through what He is and what He has done)*.

7 If you had known Me, you should have known My Father also *(means, "If you had learned to know Me Spiritually and experientially, you should have known that I and the Father are One," i.e., One in essence and unity, and not in number)*: and from henceforth you know Him, and have seen Him *(when one truly sees Jesus, one truly sees the Father; as stated, they are "One" in essence)*.

8 Philip said unto Him, Lord, show us the Father, and it suffices us *(like Philip, all, at least for the most part, want to see God, but the far greater majority reject the only manner and way to see Him, which is through Jesus)*.

9 Jesus said unto Him, Have I been so long with you, and yet have you not known Me, Philip? *(Reynolds says, "There is no right understanding of Jesus Christ until the Father is actually seen in Him.")* He who has seen Me has seen the Father *(presents the very embodiment of Who and what the Messiah would be; if we want to know what God is like, we need only look at the Son)*; and how do you say *then*, Show us the Father?

10 Do you believe not that I am in the Father, and the Father in Me? *(The key is "believing.")* the words that I speak unto you I speak not of Myself *(the words which came out of the mouth of the Master are, in fact, those of the Heavenly Father)*: but the Father Who dwells in Me, He does the works *(the Father does such through the Holy Spirit)*.

11 Believe Me that I *am* in the Father, and the Father in Me *(once again places Faith as the vehicle and Jesus as the Object)*: or else believe Me for the very works' sake *(presents a level which should be obvious to all, and includes present observation as well)*.

POWER

12 Verily, verily, I say unto you, He who believes on Me, the Works that I do shall he do also *(believing on Christ gives one access to the Father, Who does the Works)*; and greater *Works* than these shall he do; because I go unto My Father *(it respects quantity rather than quality; the Works of Christ were confined to greater Israel, while the works of Believers cover the entirety of the world)*.

13 And whatsoever you shall ask in My Name, that will I do *(the Christian is given the Power of Attorney to use the Name of Christ; but if one is to notice, all the usage of His Name is confined to the spirit world; Believers are never given authority over other Believers)*, that the Father may be glorified in the Son *(is accomplished through the great Work of Christ being extended through all Believers)*.

14 If you shall ask any thing in My Name, I will do *it (refers to that which is in harmony with His Character and Will)*.

THE HELPER

15 If you love Me, keep My Commandments *(His Commandments can be kept only in one way; the Believer must ever make Christ and the Cross the Object of his Faith, which will then give the Holy Spirit latitude to work within our lives and help us do these things which we must do)*.

16 And I will pray the Father, and He shall give you another

Comforter *("Parakletos," which means "One called to the side of another to help"),* that He may abide with you forever *(before the Cross, the Holy Spirit could only help a few individuals, and then only for a period of time; since the Cross, He lives in the hearts and lives of Believers, and does so forever);*

17 *Even* the Spirit of Truth *(the Greek says, "The Spirit of the Truth," which refers to the Word of God; actually, He does far more than merely superintend the attribute of Truth, as Christ "is Truth" [I Jn. 5:6]);* Whom the world cannot receive *(the Holy Spirit cannot come into the heart of the unbeliever until that person makes Christ his or her Saviour; then He comes in),* because it sees Him not, neither knows Him *(refers to the fact that only Born-again Believers can understand the Holy Spirit and know Him):* but you know Him *(would have been better translated, "But you shall get to know Him");* for He dwells with you *(before the Cross),* and shall be in you *(which would take place on the Day of Pentecost and forward, because the sin debt has been forever paid by Christ on the Cross, changing the disposition of everything).*

18 I will not leave you comfortless *(helpless):* I will come to you *(through the Person of the Holy Spirit).*

19 Yet a little while, and the world sees Me no more *(in a few days He would be taken back to Glory);* but you see Me *(after the Day of Pentecost, we will see Christ in the Person of the Holy Spirit):* because I live, you shall live also *(refers to His coming Resurrection, which guarantees the Work of the Cross).*

20 At that day *(after the Resurrection, and the coming of the Holy Spirit on the Day of Pentecost)* you shall know that I *am* in My Father *(speaks of Deity; Jesus is God!),* and you in Me *(has to do with our Salvation by Faith),* and I in you *(enables us to live a victorious life [Gal. 2:20]).*

21 He who has My Commandments, and keeps them, he it is who loves Me *(as stated, we can keep His Commandments only by allowing the Holy Spirit to work within our lives, which He does based on our Faith expressed in Christ and the Cross):* and he who loves Me shall be loved of My Father *(provides the criteria of approval by the Father),* and I will love him, and will manifest Myself to him *(means to fully disclose His Person and Nature and Goodness to the Believer).*

22 Judas said unto Him, not Iscariot, Lord, how is it that You will manifest Yourself unto us, and not unto the world? *(Also known as Lebbaeus or Thaddaeus.*

He was the brother of James the Less. His questions have implications of Israel being restored to her place of glory and grandeur.)

23 Jesus answered and said unto him, If a man love Me, he will keep My Words *(presents this of which Jesus speaks as based on Love, which is the exact opposite of what the Apostles were speaking, which was force; they wanted Jesus to use His Power to force Rome and other people of the world to recognize Israel as the Premier Nation):* and My Father will love him, and We will come unto him *(all through the Holy Spirit)*, and make Our abode with him *(Jesus explained that His manifestation of Himself was to the heart; it was inward and spiritual, so that the heart would consciously enjoy His abiding in it).*

24 He who loves Me not keeps not My sayings *(millions claim to love Jesus, but such is an empty claim if His "sayings" are ignored):* and the Word which you Hear is not Mine, but the Father's which sent Me *(Reynolds said, "Love involves obedience, and obedience involves Love. Consequently, obedience is the great proof of Love, and if Love is absent, this means that obedience of the Word is absent as well.").*

25 These things have I spoken unto you, being *yet* present with you *(tells us that His time is short in this capacity).*

26 But the Comforter *(Helper),* which is the Holy Spirit *(proclaims the Third Person of the Godhead),* Whom the Father will send in My Name *(because Jesus paid the price on the Cross, enabling the Holy Spirit to come in a completely new dimension),* He shall teach you all things, and bring all things *(proclaims the Holy Spirit as the Great Teacher of the Word of God, which is the only way one can learn the Word)* to your remembrance, whatsoever I have said unto you *(refers to the Holy Spirit helping the Apostles remember what Jesus had said and, as well, to understand what He had said).*

PEACE

27 Peace I leave with you *(Sanctifying Peace),* My Peace I give unto you *(there is a vast difference in "Peace with God," which all Believers have, and "The Peace of God" of which Jesus here speaks):* not as the world gives, give I unto you *(the peace of the world is but surface; that given by Christ is in the heart).* Let not your heart be troubled, neither let it be afraid *("The Peace of God" heals the troubled heart, and takes away fear).*

28 You have heard how I said unto you, I go away, and come *again* unto you *(He is speaking of sending the Holy Spirit, which He did!).* If you loved Me, you would rejoice, because I said, I go unto

the Father *(Christ going to the Father proclaimed the fact that His Great Sacrifice on the Cross had been accepted, and Righteousness could now be imputed to men, all carried out by the Holy Spirit)*: for My Father is greater than I *(speaks of Christ as it regards His Incarnation)*.

29 And now I have told you before it come to pass *(refers to all the things He would do, which pertained to the Crucifixion, the Resurrection, and the Ascension; as well, it spoke of Him sending back the Holy Spirit, Who in effect would take His place)*, that, when it is come to pass, you might believe *(has reference to the fact that the fulfillment would be very soon, actually beginning the next day)*.

30 Hereafter I will not talk much with you *(could be translated, "Hereafter I will not have much more time to talk with you")*: for the Prince of this world comes *(speaks of Satan)*, and has nothing in Me *(Satan had no hold over Jesus, no claim on Jesus, no sin in Jesus, nothing of evil about Jesus; He was totally Holy, completely, absolutely, and irrevocably above sin and Satan)*.

31 But that the world may know that I love the Father *(presents Himself in the same mode which He demanded of His Disciples)*; and as the Father gave Me Commandment, even so I do *(proclaims His Perfect Example; we are to follow accordingly!)*. Arise, let us go Hence *(it expressed haste to accomplish the Father's Will)*.

CHAPTER 15

THE TRUE VINE

I AM the True Vine *(the True Israel, as He is the True Church, and the True Man; more specifically, He Alone is the Source of Life)*, and My Father is the Husbandman *(refers to God the Father not simply as the Vinedresser, but also the Owner so to speak)*.

2 Every branch *(Believer)* in Me *(to have Salvation, we must be "in Christ" which refers to trusting in what He did at the Cross)* that beareth not fruit *(the Holy Spirit Alone can bring forth fruit within our lives, and He does such through the Finished Work of Christ, which demands that the Cross ever be the Object of our Faith)* He takes away *(if the Believer refuses the Cross, ultimately, he will be taken out of the Body of Christ)*: and every branch that bears fruit *(has some understanding of Christ and the Cross)*, He purges it *(uses whatever means necessary to make the Cross the total Object of one's Faith)*, that it may bring forth more fruit *(only when the Cross becomes the total Object of one's Faith can the Holy Spirit perform His Work of bringing forth proper fruit [Rom.*

8:1-2, 11]).

3 Now you are clean through the Word which I have spoken unto you *(the answer, as always, is found in the Word of God; the Story of the Bible is "Jesus Christ and Him Crucified").*

4 Abide in Me *(look to Him exclusively, and what He has done for us at the Cross),* and I in you *(if we properly abide in Him, which we can only do by ever making the Cross the Object of our Faith, then He will abide in us without fail).* As the branch *(Believer)* cannot bear fruit of itself *(one cannot Sanctify one's self! it is impossible!),* except it abide in the Vine *(abiding in Him refers to the fact that we understand that every solution we seek, for whatever the need might be, is found only in Christ and the Cross; we must never separate Christ from the Cross [I Cor. 1:23; 2:2]);* no more can you, except you abide in Me.

5 I am the Vine *(not the Church, not a particular Preacher, not even a particular Doctrine, but Christ Alone),* you *are* the branches *(Believers):* he who abides in Me, and I in him, the same brings forth much fruit *(let us say it again; the Believer must understand that everything we receive from God comes to us exclusively through Christ and the Cross; that being the case, the Cross must ever be the Object of our Faith; then the Holy Spirit can* develop fruit within our lives; it can be done no other way!)*: for without Me *(what He did for us at the Cross)* you can do nothing *(the Believer should read that phrase over and over).*

6 If a man abide not in Me *(refuses to accept the Cross, which means he is serving "another Jesus" [II Cor. 11:4]),* he is cast forth as a branch *(is removed from the Source of Life),* and is withered *(without proper Faith in Christ and the Cross, the Believer ultimately withers);* and men gather them, and cast *them* into the fire, and they are burned *(the implication is striking! if proper Faith in Christ and the Cross is not maintained, the ultimate result is eternal Hell).*

7 If you abide in Me *(keep your Faith anchored in Christ and the Cross),* and My Words abide in you *(in fact, the entirety of the Word of God is the Story of "Christ and the Cross"),* you shall ask what you will, and it shall be done unto you *(proper Faith in Christ and the Cross desires only the Will of God, which Will is guaranteed now to be carried forth).*

8 Herein is My Father Glorified *(that Believers totally and completely place their Faith exclusively in Christ and the Cross),* that you bear much fruit *(meaning that Jesus did not die in vain, but that His Death on the Cross will result in "much fruit");* so shall you be

My Disciples *(Lk. 9:23-24)*.

9 As the Father has loved Me *(the Heavenly Father loves us accordingly, as we abide in Christ)*, so have I loved you *(the Good Shepherd gives His Life for the sheep)*: continue ye in My Love *(we can continue in His Love, only as we continue in our Faith, which must ever have the Cross as its Object)*.

10 If you keep My Commandments *(this can be done only by the Holy Spirit working within us, which He does according to our Faith in Christ and the Cross)*, You shall abide in My Love *(this can be done <u>only</u> in the manner stated)*; even as I have kept My Father's Commandments, and abide in His Love *(the Father's Commandment regarding Christ was that He was to go to the Cross [Mat. 16:21-24]; His Commandment to us is that we ever make Christ and the Cross Alone the Object of our Faith [Jn. 6:53])*.

11 These things have I spoken unto you, that My Joy might remain in you *(His Joy remains in us, only as our Faith is properly placed in Him and the Cross)*, and that your joy might be full *(the Christian cannot know "full joy" until He properly understands the Cross, which means that he then properly understands Christ)*.

12 This is My Commandment, That you love one another *(we can only do so through a proper understanding of the Cross)*, as I have loved you *(He loved us enough to give His Life for us)*.

13 Greater love has no man than this *(the epitome of love)*, that a man lay down his life for his friends *(this portrays the Cross, as is obvious)*.

14 You are My friends *(consequently, I lay down My Life for you)*, if ye do whatsoever I Command you *(as stated, we can only do what He Commands, as we allow the Holy Spirit latitude within our lives, which is done by ever making the Cross the Object of our Faith)*.

15 Henceforth I call you not servants *(Faith in Christ and the Cross Alone can lift the Believer to a new status)*; for the servant knows not what his lord does *(with faith improperly placed, the Lord cannot confide in us)*: but I have called you friends; for all things that I have heard of My Father I have made known unto you *(therefore, we have no excuse!)*.

16 You have not chosen Me, but I have chosen you *(it is not really that we find the Lord; the truth is, He finds us)*, and ordained you *(has chosen us for a purpose)*, that you should go and bring forth fruit *(as stated, we can only do this by ever looking to the Cross [Gal. 6:14])*, and that your fruit should remain *(as our Faith remains in the Cross, the fruit will remain)*: that whatsoever you

shall ask of the Father in My Name *(using His Name always refers to the victory He won at the Cross)*, He may give it you.

17 These things I Command you, that you love one another *(if Faith is improperly placed, there is no love, even as there can be no love)*.

HATRED

18 If the world hate you *(as it definitely will, if you make Christ and the Cross the Object of your Faith)*, you know that it hated Me before *it* hated you. *(Why? The world refuses to admit it is so evil that God would have to become man and die on a Cross in order that men might be Saved. Therefore, Christ bears the brunt of that animosity.)*

19 If you were of the world *(looking to a way other than Christ and the Cross)*, the world would love his own *(the world loves its own, and its own love the world)*: but because you are not of the world *(refuse to accept the proposed solutions presented by the world)*, but I have chosen you out of the world *(brought us out of the system of the world, into the way of the Lord)*, therefore the world hates you *(the world hates us because we deny its proposed solutions, and claim that Christ is the only answer; this impacts the pride of man)*.

20 Remember the word that I said unto you, The servant is not greater than his Lord *([John 13:16], there it was used concerning humility; here it is used respecting opposition)*. If they have persecuted Me *(and they definitely did)*, they will also persecute you *(most of the persecution will come from the world of religion)*; if they have kept My saying *(they didn't)*, they will keep yours also *(meaning that the world, as the world, will not accept our solution of Christ and Him Crucified)*.

21 But all these things will they do unto you for My Name's sake *(the Name that is held with more love, and at the same time more contention, is the Name of Jesus)*, because they know not Him Who sent Me *(despite the claims of the religions of the world, if they reject Christ, it means they do not know God)*.

22 If I had not come and spoken unto them, they had not had sin *(the sin of rejecting Christ, which is the greatest sin of all)*: but now they have no cloak for their sin *(means that since the Cross, the world is without excuse)*.

23 He who hates Me hates My Father also *(in every way possible, Jesus repeatedly stated that it was impossible to separate Him from the Father or the Father from Him)*.

24 If I had not done among them the Works which none other

man did, they had not had sin (proclaims that His Preaching, Teaching, and Miracles all plainly revealed Who He was): but now have they Both seen and hated Both Me and My Father (the most awful condemnation that can be pronounced on mortal beings).

25 But this comes to pass, that the Word might be fulfilled that is written in their Law (doesn't mean that they were forced to do this thing, but that it was predicted they would), They hated Me without a cause (Ps. 35:19; 69:4).

26 But when the Comforter (Helper) is come (the Holy Spirit), Whom I will send unto you from the Father (presents Jesus as the Baptizer with the Holy Spirit [Mat. 3:11; Jn. 1:31-33]), even the Spirit of Truth (concerns the veracity of the Word of God; the Holy Spirit superintended its writing all the way from Moses, who began with Genesis, to the closing as given to John on the Isle of Patmos), which proceeds from the Father (proclaims the Father sending the Holy Spirit in the Name of Jesus and by the Authority of Jesus), He shall testify of Me (Who Christ is [God] and What Christ has done — the Cross):

27 And you also shall bear witness (the Apostles), because you have been with Me from the beginning (speaks of them observing all He did and all He said [Eph. 2:20]).

CHAPTER 16

PERSECUTION

THESE things have I spoken unto you, that you should not be offended (concerns all the warnings of the coming persecution).

2 They shall put you out of the Synagogues (religion, which refers to that which man has devised, will not accept Christ and the Cross): yes, the time comes, that whosoever kills you will think that he does God service (speaks of terrible religious deception [I Tim. 4:1]).

3 And these things will they do unto you (in one way or the other), because they have not known the Father, nor Me (despite their claims!).

THE HOLY SPIRIT

4 But these things have I told you, that when the time shall come, you may remember that I told you of them (if the world loves us, something is wrong with our testimony). And these things I said not unto you at the beginning (the beginning of His Ministry was not the time to reveal these things), because I was with you (but now He is about to leave them, so He reveals what is going to happen).

5 But now I go My way to Him Who sent Me (back to the Father in Heaven); and none of you asks

Me, Where do You go? *(They are not asking now, simply because it seems they are beginning to understand what He is saying, at least about leaving.)*

6 But because I have said these things unto you, sorrow has filled your heart *(they somewhat understood Him going back to the Father, but still they didn't understand the coming Resurrection).*

7 Nevertheless I tell you the truth; It is expedient for you that I go away *(the Mission and Ministry of the Holy Spirit to the Body of Christ depended upon the return of Christ to the Father)*: for if I go not away, the Comforter *(Holy Spirit)* will not come unto you *(concerns the respective Office Work of Both Jesus and the Holy Spirit — Jesus as the Saviour of men, and the Holy Spirit as the Power of the Church)*; but if I depart, I will send Him unto you *(a Finished Work on the Cross was demanded of Christ, before the Holy Spirit could be sent).*

8 And when He *(the Holy Spirit)* is come, He will reprove *(convict)* the world of sin *(the supreme sin of rejecting Christ)*, and of Righteousness *(Jesus is Righteousness, and declared so by the Resurrection)*, and of Judgment *(Satan was judged at Calvary, and all who follow him are likewise judged)*:

9 Of sin, because they believe not on Me *(to reject Christ and the Cross is to reject Salvation)*;

10 Of Righteousness, because I go to My Father *(Jesus presented a spotless Righteousness to the Father, namely Himself, which pertained to His Sacrifice at Calvary, that was accepted by God; consequently, that Righteousness is imputed to all who will believe in Him and His Work on the Cross)*, and you see me no more *(meaning that His Work was Finished)*;

11 Of Judgment, because the Prince of this world is judged *(Satan was completely defeated at Calvary, and thereby judged as eternally condemned; all who follow him will suffer his fate, the lake of fire, and that fate will be forever and forever [Rev. 20:12-15]).*

12 I have yet many things to say unto you *(pertained to the entirety of the New Covenant that would be given to the Apostle Paul, and which foundation had already been laid by Christ)*, but ye cannot bear them now.

13 Howbeit when He, the Spirit of Truth, is come *(which He did on the Day of Pentecost)*, He will guide you into all Truth *(if our Faith is properly placed in Christ and the Cross, the Holy Spirit can then bring forth Truth to us; He doesn't guide into some truth, but rather "all Truth")*: for He shall not speak of Himself *(tells us not only What He does, but Whom He represents)*; but whatsoever He shall hear, *that* shall

He speak (doesn't refer to lack of knowledge, for the Holy Spirit is God, but rather He will proclaim the Work of Christ only): and He will show you things to come (pertains to the New Covenant, which would shortly be given).

14 He shall glorify Me (will portray Christ and what Christ did at the Cross for dying humanity): for He shall receive of Mine (the benefits of the Cross), and shall show it unto you (which He did, when He gave these great Truths to the Apostle Paul [Rom., Chpts. 6-8, etc.]).

15 All things that the Father has are Mine (has always been the case; however, due to the Cross, all these things can now be given to the Believer as well): therefore said I, that He shall take of Mine, and shall show it unto you (the foundation of all the Holy Spirit reveals to the Church is what Christ did at the Cross [Rom. 6:3-14; 8:1-2, 11; I Cor. 1:17-18, 21, 23; 2:2; Gal., Chpt. 5, etc.]).

16 A little while, and you shall not see Me (refers to His Ascension, which would take place in a few days): and again, a little while, and you shall see Me (refers to the coming of the Holy Spirit, Who would be sent back by Christ), because I go to the Father (means that the great Plan of Redemption is completed).

17 Then said some of His Disciples among themselves, What is this that He said unto us, A little while, and you shall not see Me: and again, a little while, and you shall see Me: and, Because I go to the Father?

18 They said therefore, What is this that He said, A little while? we cannot tell what He says.

19 Now Jesus knew that they were desirous to ask Him, and said unto them, Do you inquire among yourselves of that I said (evidently the Holy Spirit informed Him of that which they were whispering among themselves), A little while, and you shall not see Me: and again, a little while, and you shall see Me?

20 Verily, verily, I say unto you, That you shall weep and lament (regarding His Crucifixion), but the world shall rejoice (the religious leaders of Israel would rejoice, because they were of the world and not of God): and you shall be sorrowful, but your sorrow shall be turned into joy (the Resurrection and the sending of the Holy Spirit).

21 A woman when she is in travail has sorrow, because her hour is come (speaks of the pain which accompanies the birth of a child): but as soon as she is delivered of the child, she remembers no more the anguish, for joy that a man is born into the world (the sorrow of the Cross will vanish away in the hearts of His followers, when

they see what the Cross has accomplished).

22 And you now therefore have sorrow: but I will see you again *(speaks of the Resurrection)*, and your heart shall rejoice, and your joy no man takes from you *(because you now know the Truth)*.

PRAYER

23 And in that day *(after the Day of Pentecost)* you shall ask Me nothing *(will not ask Me Personally, as you now do)*. Verily, verily, I say unto you, Whatsoever you shall ask the Father in My Name *(according to what He did at the Cross, and our Faith in that Finished Work)*, He will give it you *(He places us in direct relationship with the Father, enjoying the same access as He Himself enjoys)*.

24 Hitherto have you asked nothing in My Name *(while He was with them, the Work on the Cross had not been accomplished; so His Name could not be used then as it can be used now)*: ask, and you shall receive *(ask in His Name, which refers to the fact that we understand that all things are given unto us through and by what Christ did at the Cross)*, that your joy may be full *(it can only be full when we properly understand the Cross)*.

25 These things have I spoken unto you in Proverbs *(concerns the Parables and, as well, His portraying Truths to them in a veiled way, and for purpose)*: but the time comes, when I shall no more speak unto you in Proverbs, but I shall show you plainly of the Father *(this could not be done until the Cross was a Finished Work; then the Holy Spirit could reveal things plainly, but only if one properly understands the Cross)*.

26 At that day *(after the Day of Pentecost)* you shall ask in My Name *(in a sense, we are given the power of attorney)*: and I say not unto you, that I will pray the Father for you *(His very Presence before the Father guarantees that the Sacrifice of the Cross was accepted; therefore, all who truly follow Christ are instantly accepted as well; if Jesus had to pray to the Father for us, that would mean the Cross was not a Finished Work)*:

DEPARTURE

27 For the Father Himself Loves you, because you have loved Me *(acceptance of Christ is acceptance by the Father)*, and have believed that I came out from God *(concerns the Faith of the Believer as it is registered in Christ)*.

28 I came forth from the Father *(speaks of His Deity, and the Mission for which He was sent)*, and am come into the world *(but for one purpose, that was to go to the Cross that man might be Re-

deemed [I Pet. 1:18-20]): **again, I leave the world, and go to the Father** (the Mission is complete).

29 His Disciples said unto Him, Lo, now You are speaking plainly, and speak no Proverb (however, they still only understood in a partial sense).

30 Now are we sure that You know all things (they now strongly sense that nothing in their hearts was hidden from Him), and need not that any man should ask You (means that before they could ask particular questions, He, already discerning their thoughts, would begin to answer their proposed inquiry): by this we believe that You came forth from God (but still their Faith was imperfect, even as we shall see).

31 Jesus answered them, Do you now believe? (He will now tell them just how imperfect their Faith is.)

32 Behold, the hour comes, yes, is now come (the Crucifixion was just hours away), that you shall be scattered, every man to his own (proclaims their Faith weakening as to its power, but not its essential quality), and shall leave Me Alone (proclaims exactly what it says, at the end He was alone!): and yet I am not alone, because the Father is with Me (the Father would be with Him every moment, with the exception of the three hours between 12 noon and 3 p.m. when He was on the Cross, bearing the penalty of sin).

33 These things I have spoken unto you, that in Me you might have peace (in effect says to them, "Things may look dark, however, despite how they look, everything is under control; trust what I have said and believe Me!"). In the world you shall have tribulation (concerns the fundamental condition of Divine Life in this world; the world is totally opposed because its system is solely of Satan): but be of good cheer; I have overcome the world (He did this through the Cross [Col. 2:14-15], so may we overcome the world).

CHAPTER 17

INTERCESSION

THESE **words spoke Jesus, and lifted up His Eyes to Heaven, and said** (portrays in the following the longest of the Lord's Prayers in the four Gospels; as well, it is the only one stated to have been prayed with the Disciples), **Father, the hour is come** (the time for the Redemption of man, which would be accomplished at the Cross, and which had been planned from eternity past [I Pet. 1:18-20]); **Glorify Your Son** (the Cross, as horrible as it was, would Glorify Christ because it would effect the Redemption of untold millions), **that Your Son also**

may Glorify You *(refers to Him taking upon Himself all the burden of human sorrow and, as well, exhausting the poison of the sting of death, which He would do at the Cross and would Glorify God)*:

2 As You have given Him Power over all flesh *(presents Christ as the Channel through which Eternal Life may be given)*, that He should give Eternal Life to as many as You have given Him *(refers to those who meet the conditions laid down in Scripture concerning Faith [Jn. 3:16; I Tim. 2:4; II Pet. 3:9; Rev. 22:17])*.

3 And this is Life Eternal *(proclaims the true kernel of what Eternal Life actually is)*, that they might know You the Only True God, and Jesus Christ, Whom You have sent *(the Cross would make all of this possible!)*.

4 I have Glorified You on the Earth *(proclaims Christ carrying out the Will of God in all things)*: I have finished the Work which You gave Me to do *(that Work was the Cross of Calvary; He was so much committed to that Work that He could call it done, even though its conclusion was a few hours in the future)*.

5 And now, O Father, Glorify Thou Me with Thine Own Self *(proclaims that all True Glory exists only in God; when Christ as God became Man, He divested Himself of that Glory)* with the Glory which I had with You before the world was *(a request that He would be glorified as Man with the Glory which is Eternally His as God; this prayer was answered at the Resurrection, when He came forth with a Glorified Body)*.

HIS DISCIPLES

6 I have manifested Your Name unto the men which You gave Me out of the world *(proclaims the fact that the Name of God was but partially and imperfectly understood before)*: Yours they were, and You gave them to Me *(proclaims a precondition; it means that God had ordained them for this task long before they heard Jesus say, "follow Me," and, no doubt, long before they were even born; the Omniscience of God can do this, without affecting the free moral agency of man)*; and they have kept Your Word *(doesn't mean that they were perfect, but does mean that they were true to the Light)*.

7 Now they have known that all things whatsoever You have given Me are of You *(actually the Disciples, insensible and full of faults, and yet the Grace that loved them spoke of them in the admiring words of Verses 6 through 8)*.

8 For I have given unto them the Words which You gave Me *(over and over again, Jesus proclaims that He was led by the Fa-*

---

ther in all that He did, even to the very Words He spoke); **and they have received** *them* (does not necessarily mean that they understood them, at least at the time, but they did believe them, and later come to understand them), **and have known surely that I came out from You** (portrays the bedrock of their Faith), **and they have believed that You did send Me** (proclaims a core belief not only in His Person, but, as well, regarding His Mission, even though that knowledge at this time was imperfect).

UNITY

9 **I pray for them** (concerns His Intercession on their behalf, and is assured of an answer): **I pray not for the world** (only speaks of this moment, as He no doubt prayed much for the world in days past; actually, His entire Ministry was the expression of the Father's Love to the whole world [Jn. 3:16]), **but for them which You have given Me** (presents Grace which reveals these desires as wonderful, and the privileges that flow from His care for His Own); **for they are Thine** (presents all that Jesus had and did as First belonging to the Father).

10 **And all Mine are Thine** (proclaims total consecration in that they were the Father's before they were His), **and Thine are Mine** (a man can say, "all mine are Thine," but only Jesus could say, "all Thine are Mine"; this is a claim of perfect equality with the Father); **and I am Glorified in them** (the Lord is Glorified in Eternal Souls, and not in things).

11 **And now I am no more in the world** (speaks of His Mission being finished, with Him returning to the Father shortly), **but these are in the world** (speaks of a hostile environment, with God Alone able to keep them), **and I come to You** (the Ascension). **Holy Father, keep through Your Own Name those whom You have given Me** (this would be done by the means of the Cross, and our Faith in that Finished Work), **that they may be one, as We** *are* (one in love and unity).

12 **While I was with them in the world, I kept them in Your Name** (all who truly follow, referring to Faith anchored in the Cross, will be kept): **those who You gave Me I have kept, and none of them is lost, but the son of perdition** (it refers to the fact that Satan tried to destroy all the Disciples, as would be obvious); **that the Scripture might be fulfilled** (Judas was not lost that Prophecy might come to pass, but Prophecy foretold the fact of his willful sin and lost state [Ps. 41:9; 69:25-29; 109:8; Acts 1:20-25]).

13 **And now come I to You** (He set the example relative to prayer; we are meant to follow suit); **and**

these things I speak in the world
(He is praying this prayer in a hostile environment, and believes that the Father's Care will protect them in this hostile environment), that they might have My Joy fulfilled in themselves (this would be answered on the Day of Pentecost).

14 I have given them Your Word (speaks of a permanent endowment; we must live by the Word); and the world has hated them, because they are not of the world, even as I am not of the world (the spirit of the world is ruled by Satan, the Prince of Darkness, so it is greatly antagonistic toward the Lord).

KEPT FROM EVIL

15 I pray not that You should take them out of the world (in fact, we should be Light in the face of the darkness of this world), but that You should keep them from the evil (this is done through the Cross, and our Faith in that Finished Work).

16 They are not of the world (the calling and election of all Saints have nothing to do with the world or its systems), even as I am not of the world (reflects that the servants should be like their Lord).

17 Sanctify them through Your Truth (refers to the Word of God; it alone must ever be the criteria for all things): Your Word is Truth (means that the Bible does not merely contain Truth, but "is Truth").

18 As You have sent Me into the world (refers to a Commission which He carried out on the Cross), even so have I also sent them into the world (to preach and live the Cross [I Cor. 1:18, 23; 2:2]).

19 And for their sakes I Sanctify Myself (I separate Myself unto God in order to do His Will), that they also might be Sanctified through the Truth (no one can Sanctify one's self; this is a Work of the Holy Spirit, which is carried out as the Believer evidences Faith in the Cross of Christ [Rom. 8:1-2, 11]).

BELIEVERS

20 Neither pray I for these alone (Jesus is speaking not only of His present Disciples, but the multitudes in all ages who would believe their Testimony), but for them also which should believe on Me through their Word (has reference to the fact that all must take the Word to others);

21 That they all may be One (again He prays for unity among Believers, which can only be brought about by Love); as You, Father, are in Me (unity and "Communion"), and I in You (unity and "Purpose"), that they also may be One in Us (the pronoun "Us" proclaims the Trinity): that the world may believe that You have sent Me (proclaims the Father sending the Son into the world to save the world,

and the Son sending His Disciples into the world for the same purpose).

22 And the glory which You gave Me I have given them (unity and "Glory"); that they may be one, even as We are One (one in "Communion," "Purpose," and "Glory"):

23 I in them, and You in Me (spoken distinctly by Christ; Jesus is the mediating link of relation between the Father and Believers), that they may be made perfect in one (all of this can be done only through the Cross); and that the world may know that You have sent Me (proclaims what this unity brings about), and have Loved them, as You have Loved Me (that God loves His people will draw more people to Christ than anything else).

24 Father, I will that they also, whom You have given Me, be with Me where I am (one with the Father); that they may behold My Glory, which You have given Me (pertains to the Exaltation that He will receive at His Resurrection, which was only hours away): for You Loved Me before the foundation of the world (Jesus proclaims His preexistence with the Father and, therefore, His Deity).

25 O Righteous Father, the world has not known You (the reason: due to the Fall, it is spiritually dead): but I have known You (pertains to far more than mere acquaintance; it speaks of relationship beyond the pale of human comprehension), and

these have known that You have sent Me (refers to His Mission of Redeeming the world).

26 And I have declared unto them Your Name, and will declare it (they do now know, but they have more to learn, much more, which the Spirit will teach them): that the Love wherewith You have Loved Me may be in them, and I in them ("Love" is the Foundation of all which Christ speaks).

CHAPTER 18

THE BETRAYAL

WHEN Jesus had spoken these Words (probably refers to everything said in Chapters 14 through 17), He went forth with His Disciples over the brook Cedron (the brook Cedron [Kedron] runs in a deep valley between the Mount of Olivet and the City of Jerusalem), where was a garden, into the which He entered, and His Disciples (spoke of "Gethsemane").

2 And Judas also, which betrayed Him, knew the place: for Jesus ofttimes resorted thither with His Disciples (seems to be where He spent most nights while in the City of Jerusalem).

3 Judas then, having received a band of men and officers from the Chief Priests and Pharisees (proclaims John completely omitting the Passion of Christ in the Garden, and

cutting straight through to His ar-
rest), coming thither with lanterns
and torches and weapons *(being*
Passover, it was a full moon; but
treachery and hatred distrusted its
pure and gentle light; therefore, His
enemies brought torches and lan-
terns).

4 Jesus therefore, knowing all
things that should come upon
Him *(speaks of being perfectly led*
by the Father and through the Min-
istry of the Holy Spirit), went forth,
and said unto them, Whom seek
ye? *(This speaks of His arrest as He*
is met by the soldiers and Temple
guards; such is evil; and above all,
such is religious evil.)

5 They answered Him, Jesus
of Nazareth *(proclaims them speak-*
ing the Greatest Name in the an-
nals of human history). Jesus said
unto them, I am *He (should have*
been translated, "I am," for the
pronoun "He" was added by the
translators; as such, He was saying
the same thing He said to Moses
some 1600 years earlier [Ex. 3:14]).
And Judas also, which betrayed
Him, stood with them *(Judas had*
a choice to make; he could stand
with Jesus or with the religious hier-
archy; he could not stand with both!).

6 As soon then as He had said
unto them, I am *He (describes that*
Power and Force were in these
Words), they went backward, and
fell to the ground *(there could have*
been a hundred or more men present;

His answer and their response ful-
filled the prediction by David con-
cerning this moment [Ps. 27:2]).

7 Then asked He them again,
Whom seek ye? *(He asked this ques-*
tion again, because with this dem-
onstration of Power He wants them
to fully understand what they are
doing, and exactly Whom they are
arresting.) And they said, Jesus of
Nazareth *(it would seem that His*
display of power would have spo-
ken to them, and given them pause;
however, the human heart, in its hard-
ness, does not easily give way to Righ-
teousness).

8 Jesus answered, I have told
you that I am *He:* if therefore you
seek Me, let these go their way
(speaking of His Disciples, and pre-
sents a request which they dared
not disobey):

9 That the saying might be
fulfilled, which He spoke *(is an*
insertion into the Narrative given
by John), Of them which You gave
Me have I lost none *([John 17:12],*
the Lord is speaking of this mo-
ment concerning His arrest).

10 Then Simon Peter having a
sword drew it, and smote the
High Priest's servant, and cut off
his right ear *(presents Peter, I think,*
attempting to cleave the man's skull;
the Holy Spirit, no doubt, turned
aside his aim, with the sword sev-
ering the ear only). The servant's
name was Malchus *(the servant's*
name was given by John only; how-

ever, John does not mention the healing of the man's ear as did Luke [Lk. 22:51]).

11 Then said Jesus unto Peter, Put up your sword into the sheath (in one sentence, Jesus is proclaiming to the Church that the Gospel is not to be spread by the sword, and in fact, cannot be!): the cup which My Father has given Me, shall I not drink it? (This proclaims that which must be done.)

CAIAPHAS

12 Then the band and the captain and officers of the Jews took Jesus, and bound Him (this was a part of their procedure for all who were arrested),

13 And led Him away to Annas first (he was perhaps the head of the Sanhedrin, the ruling body of Israel); for he was father-in-law to Caiaphas, which was the High Priest that same year (this office was now by appointment of Roman authorities).

14 Now Caiaphas was he, which gave counsel to the Jews, that it was expedient that one man should die for the people (this "counsel" would destroy their Nation!).

PETER

5 And Simon Peter followed Jesus, and so did another Disciple (refers to John the beloved, who

wrote this account): that Disciple was known unto the High Priest, and went in with Jesus into the palace of the High Priest (how well John knew Caiaphas is not known).

16 But Peter stood at the door without (which probably meant that even though John had permission to enter, Peter did not). Then went out that other Disciple, which was known unto the High Priest, and spoke unto her who kept the door, and brought in Peter.

17 Then said the damsel that kept the door unto Peter, Are you not also one of this Man's Disciples? (This now begins the scenario that will be so hurtful to Peter and to Jesus.) He said, I am not (this was a terrible sin; and as sin does, the failure would become increasingly worse).

18 And the servants and officers stood there, who had made a fire of coals; for it was cold: and they warmed themselves: and Peter stood with them, and warmed himself (pictures Peter taking up position with the enemies of the Lord).

THE TRIAL

19 The High Priest then asked Jesus of His Disciples (refers to all followers of Christ), and of His Doctrine (pertained to the things

He taught).

20 Jesus answered him, I spoke openly to the world *(means that He had said nothing in secret)*; I ever taught in the Synagogue, and in the Temple, whither the Jews always resort *(in essence says, "if you are claiming that I preached or taught something wrong, why did you not arrest Me in one of the Synagogues, or in the Temple? Why did you not accuse Me before the people?")*; and in secret have I said nothing *(there was no sedition)*.

21 Why do you ask Me? *(In effect, this punches through their hypocrisy.)* ask them which heard Me, what I have said unto them: behold, they know what I said *(the spirit of Darkness in them fought against the Spirit of Light in Him; admittedly they were religious, but in truth, they were religious devils, which in one form or the other characterizes all religion)*.

22 And when He had thus spoken, one of the officers which stood by struck Jesus with the palm of his hand *(probably did this in order to curry favor with the High Priest)*, saying, Answerest Thou the High Priest so? *(This answers the fact that they were looking for a reason to strike Him.)*

23 Jesus answered him, If I have spoken evil, bear witness of the evil *(in essence says, "if I have spoken or committed some type of evil, tell Me what it is!)*: but if well, why do you smite Me? *(What have I said or done to deserve this?)*

24 Now Annas had sent Him bound unto Caiaphas the High Priest *(spoken in the past tense and, therefore, speaks of Jesus being sent from Annas to whom He had been sent first)*.

PETER

25 And Simon Peter stood and warmed himself *(now picks up the account of Peter as it ended in Verse 18)*. They said therefore unto him, Are you not also *one* of His Disciples? *(This presents others taking up the accusation, along with the damsel of Verse 17.)* He denied *it*, and said, I am not *(presents the second denial)*.

26 One of the servants of the High Priest, being *his* kinsman whose ear Peter cut off, said, Did not I see you in the garden with Him? *(This presents the occasion for the third denial.)*

27 Peter then denied again: and immediately the rooster crowed *(proclaims the fulfillment of the prediction of Jesus [Lk. 22:34])*.

PILATE

28 Then led they Jesus from Caiaphas unto the hall of judgment *(speaks of Pilate's judgment hall)*: and it was early *(represented the fourth watch of the night, which*

was between 3 and 6 a. m. in the morning, but closer to 6); and they themselves went not into the judgment hall, lest they should be defiled *(ironical! they could murder the Lord of Glory, but their religion forbade them to enter the house of a Gentile; such is self-righteousness!)*; but that they might eat the Passover *(has reference to the idea that cleansing from such defilement would take a period of time and, therefore, they would not be able to partake of the Passover that day; they did not even remotely realize that they were killing the True Passover)*.

29 Pilate then went out unto them, and said, What accusation bring you against this Man?

30 They answered and said unto him, If He were not a malefactor, we would not have delivered Him up to you *(actually records no answer at all, simply because they did not have a case against Him)*.

31 Then said Pilate unto them, Take you Him, and judge Him according to your Law *(proclaims him desiring to rid himself of this matter)*. The Jews therefore said unto him, It is not lawful for us to put any man to death *(they had already condemned Him in their hearts; they wanted Him dead!)*:

32 That the saying of Jesus might be fulfilled, which He spoke, signifying what death He should die *(Jesus had foretold this in John 3:14;* 8:28; 12:32; the Mind of God had long since settled this question [I Pet. 1:18-20])*.

33 Then Pilate entered into the judgment hall again, and called Jesus *(refers to him calling Jesus to his side, out of hearing of the crowd)*, and said unto him, Are You the King of the Jews? *(He expected a negative reply; should He answer in the affirmative, it might easily suggest to Pilate that He must be under some futile hallucination.)*

34 Jesus answered him, Do you say this thing of yourself, or did others tell it to you of Me? *(This question, as asked by Jesus, is meant to take the Governor beyond the hurled accusations of those who were thirsty for blood.)*

35 Pilate answered, Am I a Jew? *(The question is asked with some sarcasm, and is actually more of a statement than a question.)* Your Own nation and the Chief Priests have delivered You unto me *(in effect says, "I am not making the charge, they are!")*: what have you done? *(This is as much asked of himself as it is of Jesus.)*

36 Jesus answered, My Kingdom is not of this world *(in no way denies His Kingship, but does claim that the origin of His Kingdom and Kingship are not of this world)*: if My Kingdom were of this world, then would My servants fight, that I should not be delivered to the Jews *(in essence, says*

that if He was what the Jews claimed Him to be, a usurper over Rome, His followers would have long since been incited to use force): but now is My Kingdom not from hence *(now it's not of this world, but in the future it will be [Hab. 2:14; Rev., Chpt. 19]).*

37 Pilate therefore said unto Him, Are You a king then? *(This question is not exactly asked in sarcasm or sincerity; quite probably, there is a little of both!)* Jesus answered, You say that I am a King *(is the same as saying "yes, it is so!").* To this end was I born *(addresses the Incarnation, God becoming Man [Isa. 7:14]),* and for this cause came I into the world *(He is to be King in the hearts of all who believe Him),* that I should bear witness unto the Truth *(carries in its statement the entirety of the embodiment of the Ways of God).* Every one who is of the Truth hears My Voice *(only those who sincerely desire Truth will know Christ, i.e., "hear His Voice").*

BARABBAS

38 Pilate said unto Him, What is Truth? *(Pilate shows himself by his question to be a cynic.)* And when he had said this, he went out again unto the Jews, and said unto them *(is done so in the midst of tumult),* I find in Him no fault at all *(Pilate knew that Jesus was*

not guilty of treason against Rome, or any other type of infraction).*

39 But you have a custom, that I should release unto you one at the Passover *(seems to have taken place immediately upon Jesus being returned to him from Herod):* will you therefore that I release unto you the King of the Jews? *(This is said with some sarcasm, but yet as an appeal to the absurdity of these charges.)*

40 Then cried they all again, saying, Not this man, but Barabbas *(Pilate thought maybe he could get off the hook, thinking surely they would not prefer a robber over Jesus! he was to be sadly disappointed!).* Now Barabbas was a robber *(they chose a robber, and they have been mercilessly robbed ever since).*

CHAPTER 19

CROWN OF THORNS

THEN Pilate therefore took Jesus, and scourged *Him (Pilate seemed to hope that the scourging would satisfy their blood lust! he was again to be disappointed).*

2 And the soldiers platted a crown of thorns *(Victor's thorns),* and put *it* on His Head, and they put on Him a purple robe *(probably the one placed on Him by Herod),*

3 And said, Hail, King of the Jews! (*This was meant to insult not only Christ, but the Nation of Israel as well!*) and they smote Him with their hands (*means that they continued hitting Him in the face with their open palms or doubled-up fists*).

CRUCIFY HIM

4 Pilate therefore went forth again, and said unto them, Behold, I bring Him forth to you, that you may know that I find no fault in Him (*proclaims another fruitless appeal to the perverted humanity and justice of the maddened mob*).

5 Then came Jesus forth, wearing the crown of thorns (*again, the Governor hoped to mitigate their ferocity*), and the purple robe. And *Pilate* said unto them, Behold the Man! (*His appeal was in vain; not a voice in Jesus' favor broke the silence.*)

6 When the Chief Priests therefore and officers saw Him (*this Pagan, who knows not God, is moved to pity by this sight, but the religious leadership of Israel showed no pity at all; such is religion!*), they cried out, saying, Crucify *Him*, crucify *Him* (*registers the most hideous words that ever came out of the mouths of any human beings at any time*). Pilate said unto them, Take ye Him, and crucify *Him*: for I find no fault in Him (*proclaims the Governor once again attempting to absolve himself of blame*).

7 The Jews answered him, We have a law, and by our law He ought to die (*spoke of the Jewish Sanhedrin, the Ruling Body of Israel, both Civil and Religious*), because He made Himself the Son of God (*He did not make Himself the Son of God, but, in fact, was the Son of God*).

PILATE

8 When Pilate therefore heard that saying, He was the more afraid (*in the Greek, it means to be "exceedingly afraid"*);

9 And went again into the judgment hall (*he will question Jesus further*), and said unto Jesus, Who are You? (*Pilate was asking Jesus if He was God.*) But Jesus gave him no answer (*this fulfilled Isaiah 53:7*).

10 Then said Pilate unto Him, Do You refuse to speak unto Me? (*The Governor was irritated that Jesus did not answer him.*) *Do You* not know that I have power to crucify You, and have power to release You?

11 Jesus answered, You could have no power *at all* against Me, except it were given you from above (*tells us the degree of control exercised by God*): therefore he who delivered Me unto you

has the greater sin *(we learn from this that some sins are worse than others, thereby we learn that the Jews were held by God as more culpable than the Romans).*

12 And from thenceforth Pilate sought to release Him *(he has just said that he has the power to do so, but he is a spineless man)*: but the Jews cried out, saying, If you let this man go, you are not Caesar's friend *(ironical! they hated Caesar; however, they hated their own Messiah more!)*: whosoever makes himself a king speaks against Caesar *(hits at Pilate's weakest spot; the slightest hint of disloyalty to the Emperor would bring serious consequences).*

FINAL REJECTION

13 When Pilate therefore heard that saying, he brought Jesus forth *(presents Jesus brought out of the Judgment Hall to stand before the mob)*, and sat down in the judgment seat in a place that is called the Pavement, but in the Hebrew, Gabbatha *(was a stone platform in the open Court in front of the praetorium, the place of final sentence).*

14 And it was the preparation of the Passover *(was actually a Wednesday instead of Friday, as supposed by most)*, and about the sixth hour *(6 a.m.)*: and he said unto the Jews, Behold your King!

(This sounds like resignation on the part of Pilate, recognizing his tepid efforts to save Christ will not be realized.)

15 But they cried out, Away with *Him,* away with *Him,* crucify Him *(only Rome could crucify! they want Jesus crucified, hoping this would disprove that He was actually the Son of God; they were taking their cue from Deuteronomy 21:22-23).* Pilate said unto them, Shall I crucify your King? *(This was exactly what they wanted.)* The Chief Priests answered, We have no king but Caesar *(they elected Caesar to be their king; by Caesar they were destroyed).*

THE CRUCIFIXION

16 Then delivered he Him therefore unto them to be crucified *(he acquiesced to their wishes)*. And they took Jesus, and led *Him* away *(proclaims that which they wanted and they got).*

17 And He bearing His Cross *(this is the answer of humanity to the only good Man Who ever lived)* went forth into a place called *the place* of a skull, which is called in the Hebrew Golgotha *(undoubtedly speaks of that which is referred to presently as "Gordon's Calvary," named for the British General who discovered the place of Crucifixion and the Tomb)*:

18 Where they crucified Him

(crucifixion was one of the most hideous forms of death that the tortured mind of man could ever begin to conceive), and two other with Him, on either side one, and Jesus in the midst (proclaims such being designed purposely, placing Him between two criminals; however, in this His enemies fulfilled Isaiah 53:9).

19 And Pilate wrote a title, and put it on the Cross (it was done by Pilate, despite the Jews). And the writing was, JESUS OF NAZARETH THE KING OF THE JEWS (although intended as sarcasm, nevertheless it was the Truth, and so was engineered by the Holy Spirit).

20 This title then read many of the Jews (served its purpose exactly as Pilate hoped it would): for the place where Jesus was crucified was nigh to the city (means it was immediately outside the city limits and alongside a major highway): and it was written in Hebrew, and Greek, and Latin.

21 Then said the Chief Priests of the Jews to Pilate, Write not, The King of the Jews; but that He said, I am King of the Jews.

22 Pilate answered, What I have written I have written (in effect he was saying, "You have falsely charged Him with rebelling against Caesar, and you know that you have lied to my face").

23 Then the soldiers, when they had crucified Jesus (pertains to the gruesome work being completed of nailing Him to the Cross), took His garments, and made four parts, to every soldier a part (means that four soldiers were employed in the Crucifixion; this was their extra pay for so gruesome a detail); and also His coat: now the coat was without seam, woven from the top throughout (the value of this particular garment was that it was without seam, meaning it was all one piece of cloth).

24 They said therefore among themselves, Let us not rend it, but cast lots for it, whose it shall be (presents that which John evidently saw and heard with his own eyes and ears; actually it seems he was the only Disciple to stand near the Cross at this time): that the Scripture might be fulfilled, which said, They parted My raiment among them, and for My vesture they did cast lots (Ps. 22:18). These things therefore the soldiers did (little did they realize they were fulfilling Scripture).

25 Now there stood by the Cross of Jesus His Mother (the suffering she must have endured as she watched this spectacle is, no doubt, beyond comprehension!), and His Mother's sister, Mary (Maria) the wife of Cleophas, and Mary Magdalene.

26 When Jesus therefore saw His Mother, and the Disciple standing by, whom He loved (John,

the author of this Gospel), He said unto His Mother, Woman, behold your son! *(Due to His Own half-brothers not believing in Him, Jesus would place the care of Mary into the hands of John the Beloved; however, the Resurrection would cure this.)*

27 Then said He to the Disciple, Behold your mother! *(Jesus told John that from that moment on, he was to look at Mary exactly as his own Mother.)* And from that hour that Disciple took her unto his own *home (proclaims John speaking of himself in the third person; tradition says that John carried out the Master's Command in totality)*.

DEATH

28 After this, Jesus knowing that all things were now accomplished *(speaks of the last minutes before His death)*, that the Scripture might be fulfilled, said, I thirst *(Ps. 69:21)*.

29 Now there was set a vessel full of vinegar *(presents a type of wine, which was not an intoxicant)*: and they filled a sponge with vinegar, and put *it* upon hyssop, and put *it* to His Mouth *(it was "hyssop," which was also used to put the blood on the doorpost in Egypt at the First Passover; in a sense, it is symbolic of the Humanity of Christ)*.

30 When Jesus therefore had received the vinegar *(pertained to the moistening of the lips and tongue, which had dried up because of the loss of body fluid; most probably He asked for this in order that He might speak the last words)*, He said, It is finished *(proclaims the greatest Words, albeit at great price, that any sinner could ever hear; in effect, the world's debt was paid; every iota of the Law had been fulfilled)*: and He bowed His Head, and gave up the ghost *(Jesus did not die from His Wounds; He freely gave up His Life, in fact, dying when the Holy Spirit told Him to die [Heb. 9:14])*.

31 The Jews therefore, because it was the preparation *(concerned the preparation of the Passover meal, carried out the day before the actual Passover)*, that the bodies should not remain upon the Cross on the Sabbath Day, (for that Sabbath Day was an high day,) *(does not speak of the regular Jewish Sabbath of Saturday, but rather the "High Day" of the Passover, also called a Sabbath, which took place on a Thursday)* besought Pilate that their legs might be broken, and *that* they might be taken away *(the shock of the broken legs would kill the victims on the Cross, in order that they might be taken down, thereby not being left on the Cross on the Sabbath)*.

32 Then came the soldiers, and

broke the legs of the first, and of the other which was crucified with Him *(speaking of the two thieves)*.

33 But when they came to Jesus, and saw that He was dead already *(presents something unusual, because the victims usually hung on the Cross for days before expiring)*, they broke not His Legs:

34 But one of the soldiers with a spear pierced His Side *(along with the remainder of the Verses of this Chapter, is fundamentally valuable as affirming beyond controversy the actual Death of Jesus Christ)*, and forthwith came there out blood and water *(is proclaimed by some to be the result of a broken or ruptured heart)*.

35 And he that saw *it* bear record, and his record is true: and he knows what he says is true, that you might believe *(refers to John speaking of himself as an eyewitness)*.

36 For these things were done, that the Scripture should be fulfilled, A Bone of Him shall not be broken *(Exodus 12:46; Num. 9:12; Ps. 34:20; at this moment, the Jews were hurrying to eat their Paschal Lamb, not a bone of which could be legally broken, which was a type of Christ)*.

37 And again another Scripture said, They shall look on Him Whom they pierced *(Ps. 22:16-17; Zech. 12:10; Rev. 1:7)*.

THE BURIAL

38 And after this Joseph of Arimathaea *(he was a member of the Jewish Sanhedrin, along with Nicodemus)*, being a Disciple of Jesus *(a follower of Christ)*, but secretly for fear of the Jews *(speaks of fear of what others would say, and what they would do — the problem with millions presently)*, besought Pilate that he might take away the Body of Jesus *(it took the Cross to bring Joseph of Arimathaea to the place that he would now boldly and openly take a stand for Christ)*: and Pilate gave *him* leave *(allowed him to do so)*. He came therefore, and took the Body of Jesus *(foiled the plans of the Jews to remove the corpse to the Valley of Hinnom, which in reality was a garbage dump)*.

39 And there came also Nicodemus, which at the first came to Jesus by night *(as well, the Cross changed him)*, and brought a mixture of myrrh and aloes, about an hundred pound *weight (this pertained to the embalming process as it was then done by wealthy Jews; this would have been very costly! at the same time, it shows that they did not at all expect Jesus to be raised from the dead)*.

40 Then took they the Body of Jesus, and wound it in linen clothes with the spices, as the manner of the Jews is to bury

(whatever their thoughts concerning the Resurrection, both Joseph and Nicodemus were making the statement by their actions that they were friends of Christ).

41 Now in the place where He was Crucified there was a garden *(John alone mentions the "garden");* and in the garden a new sepulchre, wherein was never man yet laid *(among other things, this prevented the possibility of any confusion or the Lord's Sacred Body coming into contact with corruption).*

42 There laid they Jesus therefore because of the Jews' preparation day *(spoke of the Passover, which would commence at sundown);* for the sepulchre was near at hand *(was close to the place of Crucifixion).*

CHAPTER 20

THE RESURRECTION

THE first *day* of the week *(Sunday)* comes Mary Magdalene early, when it was yet dark, unto the sepulchre *(probably about 5 o'clock in the morning),* and sees the stone taken away from the sepulchre *(proclaims that which she did not expect to find).*

2 Then she ran, and came to Simon Peter, and to the other Disciple, whom Jesus loved *(John the Beloved),* and said unto them, They have taken away the Lord out of the sepulchre, and we know not where they have laid Him *(all of this shows that the women and the Disciples did not believe He would be Resurrected; maybe they thought Joseph and Nicodemus had moved the Body of Jesus to some other place).*

3 Peter therefore went forth, and that other Disciple *(John),* and came to the sepulchre *(had they really believed He would rise from the dead, they would have never left the sepulchre).*

4 So they ran both together: and the other Disciple *(John)* did outrun Peter, and came first to the sepulchre *(John arrived first).*

5 And he *(John)* stooping down, *and looking in,* saw the linen clothes lying *(referred to the "linen cloth" of Jn. 19:40; if someone had stolen His Body, they would not have bothered to take the linen from the remains);* yet went he not in.

6 Then came Simon Peter following him *(John),* and went into the sepulchre, and saw the linen clothes lie *(the "lie" indicates that this material was neatly folded),*

7 And the napkin, that was about His Head, not lying with the linen clothes *(presents that which is extremely interesting, considering that Jesus' Head and Face had been so maltreated He was hardly recognizable),* but wrapped together in a place by itself *(none of these actions speak of haste, which*

would have accompanied the moving or stealing of a body, but rather something done deliberately and with precision; this shouted "Resurrection!").

8 Then went in also that other Disciple, which came first to the sepulchre *(speaks of John also entering the Tomb now with Peter),* and he saw, and believed *(refers to what Mary Magdalene reported, and not that Jesus had risen from the dead, as the next Scripture reveals).*

9 For as yet they knew not the Scripture, that He must rise again from the dead *(evidently refers to Psalms 16:10-11).*

10 Then the Disciples went away again unto their own home *(the place where they were temporarily residing, respecting their coming to Jerusalem to keep the Passover).*

MARY MAGDALENE

11 But Mary stood without at the sepulchre weeping *(presents her staying after Peter and John had gone; evidently, she came back not long after them):* and as she wept, she stooped down, *and looked* into the sepulchre *(evidently represents the second time she had done this [Mat. 28:1-7; Mk. 16:1-7; Lk. 24:1-11]),*

12 And saw two Angels in white sitting *(apparently represents the second appearance of Angels),* the one at the head, and the other at the feet, where the Body of Jesus had lain *(in a sense, this represents the true Mercy-Seat, with the Angels representing the Cherubim; the Angels sat, but the Cherubim stood, for Redemption was now accomplished [Ex. 25:19]; obviously, these Angels were Princes, for the dignity and importance of the Resurrection demanded the Ministry of the highest Angels [Dan. 9:21; 10:21; 12:1; Lk. 1:19,26] — Williams).*

13 And they say unto her, Woman, why do you weep? *(The truth is that soon she will be shouting!)* She said unto them, Because they have taken away my Lord, and I know not where they have laid Him *(in essence, says, "wherever He is, even though it is only a dead Body, there I want to be").*

14 And when she had thus said, she turned herself back *(would have been better translated, "she was caused to turn back"; perhaps she noticed the Angels looking past her at someone else; Williams said, "to a wounded heart seeking Christ Himself, Angels, however glorious, have no interest"),* and saw Jesus standing, and knew not that it was Jesus *(regarding our Lord's appearances after the Resurrection, there seem to have been two reasons He was not easily recognizable; the first was unbelief, and the second was that His appearance was changed, at least to a small degree; but unbelief was the biggest problem!).*

15 Jesus said unto her, Woman, why do you weep? *(This is identical to that asked by the Angels. By virtue of His Death and Resurrection, He for all practical purposes had removed the cause of weeping.)* Whom do you seek? *(This presents the second question asked by Jesus, and really gets to the heart of the matter.)* She, supposing Him to be the gardener *(evidently means she thought this man worked for Joseph of Arimathaea, who owned this garden; still, there is no thou-ght of Resurrection!)*, said unto Him, Sir, if you have borne Him hence, tell me where you have laid Him *(in her mind, the Sacred Body was to be embalmed with the precious spices, which quite possibly she had spent her all to buy; she probably knew that the Jews desired to take His Body and place it in the garbage dump, so she was concerned)*, and I will take Him away *(simply means that if they will allow her, she will give Him a proper burial)*.

16 Jesus said unto her, Mary *(the first expression of "woman" makes her the representative of the whole of suffering humanity; the second expression of "Mary" proclaims the individuality of the Gospel and the manner in which our Lord deals with all who come to Him)*. She turned herself *(refers to her recognizing His Voice)*, and said unto Him, Rabboni; which is to say, Master *(the Greek Text says, "My Master!"; in this Fourth Gospel, the Holy Spirit records four appearances of the Lord after He rose from the dead, and these appearances banished four great enemies of the human heart — "sorrow, fear, doubt, and care")*.

17 Jesus said unto her, Touch Me not *(in effect says, "Do not hold onto Me, do not try to detain Me")*; for I am not yet ascended to My Father *(Reynolds said, "He, Who is Father of Christ and Father of men, is so in different ways. He is Father of Christ by nature, and of men by Grace." [Forty days later, He would ascend])*: but go to My brethren, and say unto them *(speaks not of those who were his half-brothers in the flesh, but rather His Chosen Disciples, minus Judas who was now dead)*, I ascend unto My Father, and your Father; and to My God, and your God *(this statement as given by Christ, portrays a great relationship between the Believer and the Heavenly Father; actually, the very purpose of Calvary and the Resurrection was to establish this relationship through Redemption, which it did!)*.

18 Mary Magdalene came and told the Disciples that she had seen the Lord, and that He had spoken these things unto her *(He appeared first of all to her! regrettably, her account was met with*

unbelief [Mk.16:9-11]).

THE TEN DISCIPLES

19 Then the same day at evening, being the first *day* of the week *(proclaims the first gathering on a Sunday),* when the doors were shut where the Disciples were assembled for fear of the Jews *(the "fear" expressed here pertained to the idea or thought that the religious authorities having now murdered Jesus, may very well seek to do the same to His closest Followers; the Day of Pentecost would remove this "fear"),* came Jesus and stood in the midst *(gives us no information as to how this was done; He just seems to have suddenly appeared),* and said unto them, Peace *be* unto you *(presents a common salutation, but coming from Him, and especially at this time, it spoke Volumes).*

20 And when He had so said, He showed unto them *His* Hands and His Side *(had to do with His Wounds, which proved He was not a spirit).* Then were the Disciples glad, when they saw the Lord *(means that the "Peace which they had not had, they now have"; Jesus is Alive!).*

21 Then said Jesus to them again, Peace *be* unto you *(is said again by design; the first "Peace" gave to all who were assembled a new Revelation; the second "Peace," a summons to service as we shall see):* as My Father has sent Me, even so send I you *(pertains to the Great Commission of taking the Gospel of Jesus Christ to the world).*

22 And when He had said this, He breathed on *them (presents the same act performed in Genesis 2:7; and to Adam He had breathed the Breath of Life, and now upon our Lord's sons and daughters He breathed the Holy Spirit),* and said unto them, Receive ye the Holy Spirit *(in essence, Jesus is saying to them that what He did at Calvary will now make it possible for them and all Believers to "receive" or to be Baptized with the Holy Spirit [Jn. 7:39; Acts 2:4]):*

23 Whose soever sins you remit, they are remitted unto them *(in its simplest form means that when the Gospel of Jesus Christ is preached and accepted by sinners, the Preacher of the Gospel, or any Believer for that matter, can announce unequivocally to the new Believer that all his sins are "remitted," i.e., forgiven);* and whose soever *sins* you retain, they are retained *(is the same as the former, but exactly opposite; if the Gospel is refused, the Believer has the obligation to inform the Christ-rejecter that, despite whatever else he might do, he is still in his sins, and barring repentance will suffer the consequences).*

24 But Thomas, one of the Twelve, called Didymus *(Judas*

had long since been replaced by Matthias by the time John wrote this Gospel), was not with them when Jesus came (this should be a lesson to us all! I'm sure it was a lesson to Thomas that he ever again be present).

25 The other Disciples therefore said unto Him, We have seen the Lord (was the greatest announcement they had ever made, at least since their conversion). But he said unto them, Except I shall see in His Hands the print of the nails, and put my finger into the print of the nails, and thrust my hand into His Side, I will not believe (unbelief ever takes us lower and lower; the problem with untold millions is that "they will not Believe").

THE ELEVEN DISCIPLES

26 And after eight days again His Disciples were within, and Thomas with them (presents Jesus meeting with them again on Sunday, the First Day of the week, the Day of His Resurrection): then came Jesus, the doors being shut, and stood in the midst (proclaims His Entrance exactly as eight days earlier), and said, Peace be unto you (all of these times, He is speaking of Sanctifying Peace).

27 Then said He to Thomas, Reach hither your finger, and behold My Hands; and reach hither your hand, and thrust it into My Side (presents Jesus, at least in the latter phrase, using the same words that Thomas had used, showing that He knew exactly what Thomas had said): and be not faithless, but believing (simply means, "have faith!"; every evidence is that Thomas did exactly that!).

28 And Thomas answered and said unto Him, My Lord and My God (there is no evidence that Thomas touched the wounds of the Master; however, he was the first to give this title to Jesus, other than the Prophets in predicting these events [Isa. 9:6-7; Ps. 45:6-7]).

29 Jesus said unto Him, Thomas, because you have seen Me, you have believed (presents the lowest form of Faith): blessed are they who have not seen, and yet have believed (concerns the entirety of the Church, and through all ages; they [we] believe even though we haven't personally seen Him; but one day we will!).

THIS GOSPEL

30 And many other signs truly did Jesus in the presence of His Disciples (refers to the entirety of His Ministry), which are not written in this Book (refers to the Gospel of John):

31 But these are written, that you might believe that Jesus is the Christ, the Son of God (pertains to the fact that John did not

feel led of the Spirit to record great numbers of Miracles, but rather in his Book is to make prominent the Eternal Life that all who believe in Him, apart from Miracles and material vision, receive); and that believing you might have Life through His Name (proclaims that the Holy Spirit desires that Faith accept the Testimony of the Scripture that Jesus of Nazareth is the Messiah officially, and the Son of God essentially; and that whosoever believes in Him shall Live Eternally in ever-enduring bliss).

CHAPTER 21

JESUS

AFTER these things Jesus showed himself again to the Disciples (proclaims the fact that Jesus only appeared, it seems, to those who were His Followers; Believers in Him were those alone who could see His Spiritual Body) at the Sea of Tiberias (Sea of Galilee); and on this wise showed He Himself (represents the fourth appearance of the Lord, at least in the context of His great victories over various life problems).

2 There were together Simon Peter, and Thomas called Didymus, and Nathanael of Cana in Galilee, and the sons of Zebedee, and two other of His Disciples.

3 Simon Peter said unto them,

I go a fishing (even though the Scripture is not clear, it seems this fishing expedition was not for pleasure, but rather the necessity of making a living for their families; however, a Ministry which originates in the energy of the carnal will is fruitless; but when under the Governance of the Head of the Church, it brings forth rich fruit). They say unto him, We also go with you (represents the other six Disciples present; we aren't told where the remaining four were at this time). They went forth, and entered into a ship immediately (probably referred to one of the vessels formerly used by Peter and the sons of Zebedee in their former fishing business); and that night they caught nothing (points to the fact that they were doing this for income, not for pleasure).

THE MIRACLE

4 But when the morning was now come (they had fished all night, but without success), Jesus stood on the shore (presents the beginning of a most valuable lesson): but the Disciples knew not that it was Jesus (once again portrays the same experience as had by others).

5 Then Jesus said unto them, Children, have you any meat? (This question was meant to draw them out, because their concern

at the time was making a living for their families.) They answered Him, No *(showed their lack of success for a night's work).*

6 And He said unto them, Cast the net on the right side of the ship, and you shall find *(what must have been their thoughts concerning the admonition of this stranger!).* They cast therefore *(seems to suggest that John may have suspected this was the Lord),* and now they were not able to draw it for the multitude of fishes *(this appearance of Christ addressed the life problem of "care").*

7 Therefore that Disciple whom Jesus loved *(John)* said unto Peter, It is the Lord *(without a doubt, it would be one of the greatest moments of their lives).* Now when Simon Peter heard that it was the Lord, he girded *his* fisher's coat *unto him,* (for he was naked,) *(does not refer to a total lack of clothing, but rather that he had laid aside his outer garment in order that it not be soiled),* and did cast himself into the sea *(presents such being done not to attend the overburdened net, but rather to come quickly to Jesus).*

8 And the other Disciples came in a little ship *(different than the main vessel);* (for they were not far from land, but as it were two hundred cubits,) *(approximately one hundred yards)* dragging the net with fish *(represents a tremen-*dous catch which took only a few minutes, versus their night-long efforts which had produced only an empty net; such is the effort with Christ, and such is the effort without Christ!).*

9 As soon then as they were come to land, they saw a fire of coals there, and fish laid thereon, and bread *(where did Jesus get these provisions? I personally believe He miraculously supplied them).*

10 Jesus said unto them, Bring of the fish which you have now caught *(this portrays the fact that the fish Jesus had cooked didn't come from this particular supply).*

11 Simon Peter went up, and drew the net to land full of great fish *(insinuating that each fish was larger than normal),* an hundred and fifty and three *(the exact number is given by the Holy Spirit for purpose and reason; the Disciples were to be fishers of men, not of fish per se; consequently, the number given of the fish portrays the fact that each soul is precious in the sight of God, and numbered accordingly):* and for all there were so many, yet was not the net broken *(presents a contrast with the miraculous catch given in Luke 5:6, where the net did break; symbolically speaking, the net broke then because the Holy Spirit had not yet come; with the Holy Spirit, the net won't break).*

12 Jesus said unto them, Come

and dine *(presents Him functioning as a Servant as usual, even in His Glorified State).* And none of the Disciples did ask Him, Who are You? knowing that it was the Lord *(regrettably, many today are asking, concerning certain religious phenomenon, "Who are You?"; meaning that the earmarks of the True Gospel are little present).*

13 Jesus then comes, and takes bread, and gives them, and fish likewise *(the "bread" was symbolic of Himself, with the fish, i.e., "meat," being symbolic of His Word).*

14 This is now the third time that Jesus showed Himself to His Disciples, after that He was risen from the dead *(third time to His Disciples; there is some discrepancy as to how many times He appeared, but the fact is He did appear to many after His Resurrection, before His Ascension).*

THE COMMISSION

15 So when they had dined, Jesus said to Simon Peter, Simon, *son* of Jonah, do you love Me more than these? *(This question is referring to Peter's boasts immediately before the Crucifixion that He loved Jesus more than the other Disciples [Mat. 26:31-35; Mk. 14:29].)* He said unto him, Yes, Lord; You know that I love You *(Jesus used the Greek verb "Agapao" for Love, which means "Ardent, Supreme, and Perfect," while Peter used the Greek verb "Phileo," which means "to be fond of, to feel friendship for another").* He said unto him, Feed My Lambs *(refers to the newest converts, which need special attention, and who will be entrusted to Peter).*

16 He said to him again the second time, Simon, *son* of Jonah, do you love Me? *(The question presents Jesus leaving off the words, "more than these"; however, He does continue to use the strong Greek word "Agapao" for Love; by leaving off these words, Jesus will draw Peter away from a boastful attitude.)* He said unto him, Yes, Lord; You know that I love You *(presents Peter continuing to use the same Greek verb "Phileo" for Love as He did the first time; this is not a negative, but rather a positive; he is finally seeing that he cannot trust the flesh).* He said unto him, Feed My Sheep *(by Christ using the word "Sheep," He now is speaking of strong, mature Believers).*

17 He said unto him the third time, Simon, *son* of Jonah, Do you love Me? *(Jesus now uses the weaker word "Phileo" for Love, as Peter had used.)* Peter was grieved because he said unto him the third time, Do you Love Me? *(Peter very well understands that Jesus has Himself now used the lesser word for Love, which says something to*

the Apostle.)   And he said unto Him, Lord, You know all things (the Apostle now knows that Jesus knows all things about him — that which he did, thought, and felt; he also knows that the Lord has wounded His heart in order to train and fit him for the high honor of shepherding that which was most precious to Himself, i.e., the Sheep of John, Chpt. 10); You know that I love You (and Jesus, of course, did know). Jesus said unto him, Feed My Sheep (expresses total and complete confidence).

PROPHECY

18 Verily, verily, I say unto you, When you were young, you girded yourself, and walked where you would (refers to his prime of life): but when you shall be old, you shall stretch forth your hands, and another shall gird you (predicted Peter's faithfulness unto death, which undoubtedly comforted and strengthened his pierced heart and, as well, prevented the other Disciples from scornfully reminding him of his former cowardice), and carry you where you would not (refers to the time and distant day when Peter would die).

19 This spoke He, signifying by what death he should glorify God (Tertullain and Eusebius said that the Apostle, upon facing death, preferred Crucifixion with his head downwards on the plea that to be Crucified as His Master was too great an honor for one who had denied his Lord). And when He had spoken this, He said unto him (said to Peter), Follow Me (with one word, the Lord now corrects every one of Peter's failings, and institutes him into His sublime Mission).

JOHN

20 Then Peter, turning about, seeing the Disciple whom Jesus loved following (spoke of John, and once more, even this soon, presents Peter's extraordinary characteristic to guide rather than to follow; old habits die hard!); which also leaned on His breast at supper, and said, Lord, which is he who betrays You? (This question presents John speaking of himself, and taking us back to the Last Supper.)

21 Peter seeing Him said to Jesus, Lord, and what shall this man do? (This presents Peter asking something for which He will be rebuked.)

22 Jesus said unto him, If I will that he tarry till I come, what is that to you? (In effect, Jesus is proclaiming to Peter that it is none of his business as to what the Will of God is for John.) You follow Me (the pronoun "you" is emphatic; the lesson we should learn from this is not the glory of any Church, but the Personal Glory of the Lord Jesus; we

are to follow Him, which means we follow nothing else; that alone will keep us occupied to the extent that, if done properly, we will not try to attend to the business of others).

23 Then went this saying abroad among the brethren, that that Disciple should not die *(proclaims the manner in which Scripture can be misinterpreted)*: yet Jesus said not unto him, He shall not die *(refers to John setting the record straight as to what Jesus had actually said to him)*; but, If I will that he tarry till I come, what *is that* to you? *(This presents Jesus in the words, "If I will," as the absolute disposer of human life, and as well reveals His Godhead. Jesus did come to him on the Isle of Patmos and gave him the great Revelation, which closed out the Canon of Scripture.)*

TESTIMONY

24 This is the Disciple which testifies of these things *(presents John as an eye-witness of all he relates)*, and wrote these things *(verifies John as the author of this Gospel)*: and we know that his testimony is true *(verifies the Inspiration of the Holy Spirit upon these accounts in that which we refer to as "The Gospel according to John")*.

25 And there are also many other things which Jesus did *(speaks, no doubt, of the many Miracles He performed, some which are not recorded in any of the four Gospels)*, the which, if they should be written every one *(lends credence to the idea that there were far more Miracles performed by Jesus and not recorded, than those which were recorded)*, I suppose that even the world itself could not contain the books that should be written. Amen *(Christ is infinite, the Earth finite; hence the supposition of the Verse is most reasonable)*.

THE
ACTS OF THE APOSTLES

CHAPTER 1

POST-RESURRECTION

THE former treatise have I made *(refers to the Gospel of Luke, which was probably finished a year or so before the writing of this account called, "The Acts of the Apostles")*, O Theophilus *(the same person addressed by Luke in that Gospel)*, of all that Jesus began both to do and teach *(is the Standard, the Principal, and the Foundation of the Gospel)*,

2 Until the day in which He was taken up *(the Resurrection)*, after that He through the Holy Spirit *(refers to the fact that the Spirit of God is the Speaker and Actor in this Book)* had given Commandments unto the Apostles whom He had chosen *(refers to our Lord's Ministry of some three and a half years, which the Apostles witnessed)*:

3 To whom also He showed Himself alive after His passion by many infallible proofs *(many people saw Him after His Resurrection, and before His Ascension)*, being seen of them forty days *(from the time of the Resurrection to the time of His Ascension)*, and speaking of the things pertaining to the Kingdom of God *(it seems that much teaching was included during this period of time)*:

HOLY SPIRIT

4 And, being assembled together with *them (speaks of the time He ascended back to the Father; this was probably the time of the "above five hundred" [I Cor. 15:6])*, Commanded them *(not a suggestion)* that they should not depart from Jerusalem *(the site of the Temple where the Holy Spirit would descend)*, but wait for the Promise of the Father *(spoke of the Holy Spirit which had been promised by the Father [Lk. 24:49; Joel 2])*, which, said *He*, you have heard of Me *(you have also heard Me say these things [Jn. 7:37-39; 14:12-17, 26; 15:26; 16:7-15])*.

PROPHECY

5 For John truly baptized with water *(merely symbolized the very best Baptism Believers could receive before the Day of Pentecost)*; but you shall be baptized with the Holy Spirit not many days hence *(spoke of the coming Day of Pentecost, although Jesus did*

not use that term at that time).

6 When they therefore were come together, they asked of Him, saying *(seemingly presents the last meeting before the Ascension)*, Lord, will You at this time restore again the Kingdom to Israel? *(He would later answer this question through the Apostle Paul [II Thess., Chpt. 2].)*

7 And He said unto them, It is not for you to know the times or the seasons, which the Father has put in His Own power *(the Master is saying that it is not the business of the followers of Christ to know this information, but rather to "occupy till I come" [Lk. 19:13]).*

POWER

8 But you shall receive power *(Miracle-working Power)*, after that the Holy Spirit is come upon you *(specifically states that this "Power" is inherent in the Holy Spirit, and solely in His domain)*: and you shall be witnesses *(doesn't mean witnessing to souls, but rather to one giving one's all in every capacity for Christ, even to the laying down of one's life)* unto Me *(without the Baptism with the Holy Spirit, one cannot really know Jesus as one should)* both in Jerusalem, and in all Judaea, and in Samaria, and unto the uttermost part of the earth *(proclaims the Work of God*

as being world-wide).

THE ASCENSION

9 And when He had spoken these things *(refers to His last instructions to His followers)*, while they beheld, He was taken up *(refers to Him ascending before their very eyes)*; and a cloud received Him out of their sight *(represents the Shekinah Glory of God, which enveloped Christ as He ascended).*

SECOND ADVENT

10 And while they looked stedfastly toward Heaven as He went up *(these statements are important because they affirm His actual Ascension testified to by eyewitnesses)*, behold, two men stood by them in white apparel *(these two "men" were actually Angels)*;

11 Which also said, You men of Galilee, why do you stand gazing up into Heaven? *(This does not mean that it was only men who were present, but rather that this was a common term used for both men and women.)* this same Jesus, which is taken up from you into Heaven *(refers to the same Human Body with the nail prints in His Hands and Feet, etc.)*, shall so come in like manner as you have seen Him go into Heaven *(refers to the same place, which is the Mount of Olivet).*

THE UPPER ROOM

12 Then returned they unto Jerusalem from the Mount called Olivet *(represents, as stated, the place of His Ascent, which will also be the place of His Descent)*, which is from Jerusalem a Sabbath Day's journey *(represents a little over half a mile)*.

13 And when they were come in, they went up into an upper room *(was probably the same room where they had eaten the Passover with Christ [Lk. 22:12])*, where abode both Peter, and James, and John, and Andrew, Philip, and Thomas, Bartholomew, and Matthew, James *the son* of Alphaeus, and Simon Zelotes, and Judas *the brother* of James *(this Judas is also called "Lebbaeus" and "Thaddaeus" [Mat. 10:3; Mk. 3:18])*.

14 These all continued with one accord in prayer and supplication *(proclaims the manner in which these meetings were conducted)*, with the women, and Mary the Mother of Jesus *(concerns the women who followed Christ from Galilee [Mat. 27:55-56])*, and with His Brethren.

THE SUCCESSOR TO JUDAS ISCARIOT

15 And in those days Peter stood up in the midst of the Disciples *(represents Peter taking the lead)*, and said, (the number of names together were about an hundred and twenty,) *(in essence forms the beginning of the "Church")*.

16 Men *and* brethren, this Scripture must needs have been fulfilled, which the Holy Spirit by the mouth of David spoke before concerning Judas, which was guide to them who took Jesus *(is derived from Psalms 69:25-28)*.

17 For he was numbered with us, and had obtained part of this Ministry *(means he was one of the Apostles, and chosen by the Lord)*.

18 Now this man purchased a field with the reward of iniquity *(refers to Pharisees taking the blood money from Judas, and buying his burying place [Mat. 27:6-8])*; and falling headlong, he burst asunder in the midst, and all his bowels gushed out *(he committed suicide [Mat. 27:3-8])*.

19 And it was known unto all the dwellers at Jerusalem *(actually means that it "became known")*; insomuch as that field is called in their proper tongue, Aceldama, that is to say, The field of blood *(was also known as the "Potter's Field")*.

20 For it is written in the Book of Psalms, Let his habitation be desolate, and let no man dwell therein *(the indication is that the name of Judas had been in the Book of Life, but had been blotted out because of his sin)*: and his

bishoprick let another take *(refers to his Apostleship)*.

21 Wherefore of these men which have companied with us all the time that the Lord Jesus went in and out among us *(probably spoke of the seventy [Lk. 10:17])*,

22 Beginning from the Baptism of John, unto that same day that He was taken up from us *(spans the entirety of the three and one half years of the Ministry of Christ)*, must one be ordained to be a witness with us of His Resurrection *(we learn from this that the Resurrection of Christ from the dead is a Cardinal Doctrine of the Gospel)*.

23 And they appointed two, Joseph called Barsabas, who was surnamed Justus, and Matthias *(they would present these two to the Lord for His choice)*.

24 And they prayed *(shows their utter dependence on the Lord for leading and guidance)*, and said, You, Lord, which knows the hearts of all men *(tells us where alone the Truth can be found)*, show whether of these two You have chosen *(proclaims their desire for God's Choice, and His Choice Alone)*,

25 That he may take part of this Ministry and Apostleship *(the Foundation of the Church)*, from which Judas by transgression fell *(tells us plainly that Judas once knew the Lord, for how can one fall from something to which one has never attained)*, that he might go to his own place *(self-will will take one to eternal hell, even as it did Judas)*.

26 And they gave forth their lots *(was similar to the Urim and Thummim with which the Disciples would have been familiar and the Lord, in Old Testament times, gave leading to His people [Deut. 33:8-10; Num. 27:21])*; and the lot fell upon Matthias *(probably means that the names of the two men were placed on two stones, pieces of parchment, or wood, and then placed into an urn, with one lot drawn out [Lev. 16:8-9; Josh. 14:2])*; and he was numbered with the Eleven Apostles *(indicates that he was God's Choice)*.

CHAPTER 2

PENTECOST

AND when the Day of Pentecost was fully come *(the Feast of Pentecost, one of the seven great Feasts ordained by God and practiced by Israel yearly; it took place fifty days after Passover)*, they were all with one accord in one place *(not the Upper Room where they had been previously meeting, but rather the Temple [Lk. 24:53; Acts 2:46])*.

2 And suddenly there came a sound from Heaven as of a rushing mighty wind *(portrays the com-*

ing of the Holy Spirit in a new dimension, all made possible by the Cross), and it filled all the house (the Temple) where they were sitting (they were probably in the Court of the Gentiles).

3 And there appeared unto them cloven tongues like as of fire (the only record of such in the New Testament, and was the fulfillment of the Prophecy of John the Baptist concerning Jesus [Mat. 3:11]), and it sat upon each of them (refers to all who were there, not just the Twelve Apostles; the exact number is not known).

4 And they were all filled with the Holy Spirit (all were filled, not just the Apostles; due to the Cross, the Holy Spirit could now come into the hearts and lives of all Believers to abide permanently [Jn. 14:16]), and began to speak with other tongues (the initial physical evidence that one has been Baptized with the Spirit, and was predicted by the Prophet Isaiah [Isa. 28:9-12], and by Christ [Mk. 16:17; Jn. 15:26; 16:13]), as the Spirit gave them utterance (meaning they did not initiate this themselves, but that it was initiated by the Spirit; as we shall see, these were languages known somewhere in the world, but not by the speaker).

5 And there were dwelling at Jerusalem Jews, devout men, out of every nation under Heaven (Jews were then scattered all over the Roman World, with thousands coming in from every nation to keep the Feast).

6 Now when this was noised abroad (multitudes who were in the Temple heard and saw the proceedings, and as well, began to tell others), the multitude came together (what was happening attracted a multitude), and was confounded, because that every man heard them speak in his own language (means that these onlooking Jews heard these people speaking in many different languages, in fact languages of the nations of their residence, wherever that might have been, proving that this was not gibberish or babble as some claim).

7 And they were all amazed and marveled (mostly centered upon this speaking with other tongues), saying one to another, Behold, are not all these which speak Galilaeans? (This means that the Galilaean accent was peculiar and well known [Mk. 14:70; Lk. 22:59].)

8 And how hear we every man in our own tongue, wherein we were born? (This proves once again that this was not babble, mere chatter, or gibberish, but rather a language known somewhere in the world, but not by the speaker.)

9 Parthians, and Medes, and Elamites, and the dwellers in Mesopotamia, and in Judaea, and

Cappadocia, in Pontus, and Asia, 10 Phrygia, and Pamphylia, in Egypt, and in the parts of Libya about Cyrene, and strangers of Rome, Jews and proselytes,

11 Cretes and Arabians, we do hear them speak in our tongues the wonderful Works of God (*this tells us what speaking in tongues actually is, a recitation of the "Wonderful Works of God"*).

12 And they were all amazed, and were in doubt (*should have been translated, "and were perplexed;" they had no rational answer to their perplexity*), saying one to another, What does this mean? (*This was more asking more in wonder than demanding an answer.*)

13 Others mocking said (*they scoffed; whether by gesture or word, they jeered at the Testimony of this given by the Holy Spirit*), These men are full of new wine (*was actually an accusation that they were drunk, i.e., "intoxicated"; some were amazed and some "mocked," which continues to be done even unto this hour*).

PETER

14 But Peter, standing up with the Eleven, lifted up his voice, and said unto them (*Peter will now preach the inaugural Message of the Church on that Day of Pentecost*), You men of Judaea, and all you who dwell at Jerusalem, be this known unto you, and hearken to my words (*the Message was probably delivered on Solomon's Porch, a part of the Court of the Gentiles; it was where debates and such like were commonly conducted*):

15 For these are not drunken, as you suppose (*in effect says they are drunk, but not in the common manner*), seeing it is *but* the third hour of the day (*9 a.m.*).

16 But this is that which was spoken by the Prophet Joel (*please notice that Peter did not say, "this fulfills that spoken by the Prophet Joel," but rather, "this is that . . ." meaning that it will continue*);

17 And it shall come to pass in the last days, saith God (*proclaims these "last days" as beginning on the Day of Pentecost, and continuing through the coming Great Tribulation*), I will pour out of My Spirit upon all flesh (*speaks of all people everywhere, and therefore not limited to some particular geographical location; as well, it is not limited respecting race, color, or creed*): and your sons and your daughters shall Prophesy (*includes both genders*), and your young men shall see visions, and your old men shall dream dreams (*all given by the Holy Spirit; the Hebrew language insinuates, "both your young men and old men shall see visions, and both your old men*

and young men shall dream dreams"; it applies to both genders as well):

18 And on My servants and on My handmaidens I will pour out in those days of My Spirit *(is meant purposely to address two classes of people who had been given very little status in the past, slaves and women)*; and they shall Prophesy *(pertains to one of the "Gifts of the Spirit" [I Cor. 12:8-10])*:

19 And I will show wonders in Heaven above, and signs in the earth beneath; blood, and fire, and vapour of smoke *(pertains to the fact that these "days of My Spirit" will cover the entirety of the Church Age, even into the coming Great Tribulation; that time limit has now been nearly two thousand years)*:

20 The sun shall be turned into darkness, and the moon into blood *(not meant to be literal, but rather that the moon will look blood red because of atmospheric conditions)*, before that great and notable Day of the Lord come *(the Second Coming)*:

21 And it shall come to pass, that whosoever shall call on the Name of the Lord shall be saved *(Joel 2:30-32; presents one of the most glorious statements ever made; it includes both Jews and Gentiles equally)*.

22 You men of Israel, hear these words *(the inaugural Message of the Church)*; Jesus of Nazareth, a Man approved of God among you *(Jesus must ever be the theme of our Message; He was approved of God, but not of men)* by miracles and wonders and signs, which God did by Him in the midst of you *(what Peter knew first hand, because he was there)*, as you yourselves also know *(so many of these things were done that there was absolutely no excuse for them not to know)*:

23 Him, being delivered by the determinate counsel and foreknowledge of God *(it was the Plan of God that Jesus would die on the Cross; however, it was not the Plan of God for the religious leaders of Israel to do this thing; that was of their own making and choice)*, you have taken, and by wicked hands have crucified and slain *(presents a charge so serious it absolutely defies description! but yet, if they will seek mercy and forgiveness, God will forgive them, even as we shall see)*:

24 Whom God has raised up *(concerns the Resurrection)*, having loosed the pains of death *(death could not hold Him because He atoned for all sin, which occasions death [Rom. 6:23])*: because it was not possible that He should be held by it *(death would liked to have held Him in its grip, but it could not because He had taken away its legal right; as stated, He atoned for all sin, which defeated death, Satan, and all principali-*

ties and powers [Col. 2:14-15]).

25 For David speaks concerning Him *(Ps. 16:8-11)*, I foresaw the Lord always before My face, for He is on My Right Hand, that I should not be moved *(through the Cross, Christ would gain this position at the Father's Right Hand, which speaks of power and authority, all on our behalf [Heb. 1:3])*:

26 Therefore did My heart rejoice *(concerns Christ rejoicing over His Father's guarantee and protection regarding His descent into the death world; He knew that the Father would bring Him out)*, and My tongue was glad *(refers to the things He said regarding His Resurrection [Mat. 16:21; 17:23; 20:17-19; Mk. 8:31])*; moreover also My flesh shall rest in hope *(refers to resting on the Promises of God relating to the Resurrection)*:

27 Because You will not leave My soul in hell *(it was not the burning part of Hell [Lk. 16:19-31]*, neither will You *(God the Father)* suffer Your Holy One to see corruption *(His physical body, being sinless, saw no corruption, which normally accompanies death; in fact, it was glorified and raised from the dead)*.

28 You have made known unto Me the ways of Life *(presents Christ as the Pattern, and as well presents the Resurrection not only of Himself, but all Believers)*; You shall make Me full of joy with Your countenance *(God's Face did shine upon Christ, and it shines upon us as well, as we are "in Christ")*.

29 Men *and* Brethren, let me freely speak unto you of the Patriarch David *(presents the only time David is referred to in Scripture as a "Patriarch")*, that he is both dead and buried, and his sepulchre is with us unto this day *(is given here to dispel the erroneous notions held by the Pharisees and religious leaders of Israel concerning the Messiah)*.

30 Therefore being a Prophet *(concerns the many Prophecies given by David in the Psalms regarding Christ)*, and knowing that God had sworn with an oath to him, that of the fruit of his loins, according to the flesh *(II Sam. 7:11-16)*, He *(God)* would raise up Christ to sit on his throne *(to sit on David's Throne, which has not yet happened, but most surely will in the coming Kingdom Age; all of this portrays the Incarnation, God becoming Man and doing so through the lineage of David)*;

31 He *(David)* seeing this before spoke of the Resurrection of Christ *(tells the religious leaders of Israel David plainly Prophesied that Jesus would be raised from the dead [Ps. 16:8-11])*, that His soul was not left in Hell *(as stated, He did not go to the burning side of Hell, but rather into Paradise [Lk. 16], and as well to some particu-*

lar prisons in that infernal region [I Pet. 3:19-20]), neither did His flesh see corruption (He was not tormented in Hell as some teach, neither was there any decay in His physical body; rather it was Glorified).

32 This Jesus (the One you Crucified) has God raised up (speaks of the physical Jesus and not some spirit), whereof we all are witnesses (Peter is telling them that despite what they say, all of Israel knows that Jesus was raised from the dead).

33 Therefore being by the Right Hand of God exalted (Christ is now exalted, not only as Creator, but as well as Saviour, the latter made possible by the Cross), and having received of the Father the Promise of the Holy Spirit (proves that Jesus was accepted by the Father because the Holy Spirit was sent back, even as Promised [Jn. 16:7]), He has shed forth this, which you now see and hear (they saw the people, and they heard them speak with tongues).

34 For David is not ascended into the Heavens (given by Peter to prove that these Prophecies were not given to David concerning himself, but rather the One Who was to come, namely the Lord Jesus Christ; evidently, some of the religious leaders of Israel were claiming that these Prophecies pertained to David, and had nothing to do with Jesus, which Peter here repudiates): but he (David) said himself, The LORD said unto My Lord (God the Father said to God the Son), Sit Thou on My Right Hand ([Psalms 110:1] this is where Jesus now abides [Heb. 1:3]),

35 Until I make Your foes Your footstool (all made possible by the Cross [Col. 2:14-15], but will not be fully realized until the conclusion of the Kingdom Age [Rev., Chpt. 20; I Cor. 15:24-25]).

36 Therefore let all the house of Israel know assuredly (is leveled by Peter directly toward the religious leadership of Israel, and is inspired by the Holy Spirit), that God has made that same Jesus, Whom you have Crucified, both Lord and Christ (Jesus was and is "Jehovah," and as well, Israel's "Messiah").

THE EFFECT

37 Now when they heard this, they were pricked in their heart (the convicting Power of the Holy Spirit), and said unto Peter and to the rest of the Apostles, Men and Brethren, what shall we do? (This proclaims these people, whomever they may have been, desiring to get right with God.)

38 Then Peter said unto them, Repent (admit that God is right, and we are wrong), and be baptized every one of you in the

Name of Jesus Christ *(by the authority of that Name; there is no baptismal formula given in the Book of Acts; the only formula given was given by Christ in Matthew 28:19)* for the remission of sins *(should have been translated, "because of remission of sins"; one is Baptized in Water because one's sins have already been remitted due to Faith in Christ, and not that sins should be remitted)*, and you shall receive the Gift of the Holy Spirit *(repentance guarantees Salvation, which makes the Believer ready to be Baptized with the Holy Spirit; one is not Baptized with the Spirit automatically at conversion; it is an experience that follows Salvation, and is always accompanied by speaking with other tongues [Acts 2:4; 10:44-46; 19:1-7]).*

39 For the Promise *(of the Baptism with the Holy Spirit)* is unto you *(directed toward the many Jews standing in the Temple listening to Peter that day)*, and to your children *(means that this great outpouring did not stop with the initial outpouring, but continues on)*, and to all who are afar off *(meaning that it's not only for those in Jerusalem, but the entirety of the world as well)*, *even* as many as the Lord our God shall call *(that "Call" is "whosoever will" [Jn. 7:37-39; Rev. 22:17]).*

40 And with many other words did he testify and exhort *(tells us that we only have a part of Peter's Message here)*, saying, Save yourselves from this untoward generation *(it is a call to Repentance).*

41 Then they who gladly received his word were baptized *(some believed what Peter said, gave their hearts to God, and repented of their sins; they were then baptized in water)*: and the same day there were added *unto them* about three thousand souls *(on the first Day of Pentecost, the Day the Law was given, some three thousand men died [Ex. 32:28]; on this Day of Pentecost, due to the Cross, some three thousand people were saved).*

THE EARLY CHURCH

42 And they continued stedfastly in the Apostles' Doctrine *(that Doctrine is found in Verse 38)* and fellowship, and in breaking of bread *(had to do with the celebration of the Lord's Supper, which was probably a much more informal setting than presently)*, and in prayers *(simply meant it was a praying Church).*

43 And fear came upon every soul *(speaks of the Moving and Operation of the Holy Spirit; seeing the things that the Spirit was doing, all had a sense of awe, wonder, and fear)*: and many wonders and signs were done by the Apostles *(the Holy Spirit did this*

in order to give the Church a great start; it continued, even as it is meant to continue, but on a more limited basis, as the latter part of the Book of Acts bears out).

44 And all who believed were together *(due to the great animosity of the Jews against the followers of Christ, Believers had to band together)*, and had all things common *(due to thousands losing their jobs because of persecution, those who had material goods shared with those who didn't)*;

45 And sold their possessions and goods *(they sold things they did not absolutely need, in order that they may be able to help those who were in great need)*, and parted them to all *men*, as every man had need *(proclaimed a Christlike community because of the great persecution at hand)*.

46 And they, continuing daily with one accord in the Temple *(in a sense, the Temple had been turned into a Church, which must have been extremely irritating to the religious authorities)*, and breaking bread from house to house *(means that the Church per se was actually ensconced in houses all over Jerusalem)*, did eat their meat with gladness and singleness of heart *(they had a joy that persecution could not hinder)*,

47 Praising God, and having favour with all the people *(Jerusalem as a whole was favorably im-*pressed by what they saw respecting these followers of Christ)*. And the Lord added to the Church daily such as should be saved *(many were coming to the Lord)*.

CHAPTER 3

HEALING

NOW Peter and John went up together into the Temple at the hour of prayer, *being* the ninth hour *(3 o'clock in the afternoon)*.

2 And a certain man lame from his mother's womb was carried, whom they laid daily *(seemed to be a daily occurrence which had taken place in one way or the other since the man was a child; little did he realize that this would be the greatest day of his life)* at the gate of the Temple which is called Beautiful *(according to Josephus, it was made of costly Corinthian brass; it was said to be about 62 feet wide and 31 feet high)*, to ask alms of them who entered into the Temple *(he was a beggar)*;

3 Who seeing Peter and John about to go into the Temple asked an alms.

4 And Peter, fastening his eyes upon him with John *(indicates they were moved upon by the Holy Spirit to do this thing)*, said, Look on us *(Peter wanted him to hear what he was about to say)*.

5 And he gave heed unto them,

expecting to receive something of them (*expecting to receive money*).

6 Then Peter said, Silver and gold have I none (*I wonder how this statement as given by Peter concerning silver and gold relates to the modern greed message?*); but such as I have give I thee (*presently, the modern Church has silver and gold, but doesn't have the Power of God*): In the Name of Jesus Christ of Nazareth rise up and walk (*it is not in the name of Mohammed, or Confucius, etc.*).

7 And he took him by the right hand, and lifted *him* up (*was not presumption, but rather Faith in action*): and immediately his feet and ankle bones received strength (*this was a Miracle*).

8 And he leaping up stood, and walked, and entered with them into the Temple, walking, and leaping, and praising God.

9 And all the people saw him walking and praising God (*constantly praising God*):

10 And they knew that it was he which sat for alms at the Beautiful Gate of the Temple (*he had been coming there no doubt for years*): and they were filled with wonder and amazement at that which had happened unto him (*his healing was indisputable*).

11 And as the lame man which was healed held Peter and John (*he didn't want to let Peter and John out of his sight; it was as if his* malady would return when they left, or so he thought*), all the people ran together unto them in the porch that is called Solomon's, greatly wondering (*it drew a crowd, which the Holy Spirit intended*).

THE SERMON

12 And when Peter saw it (*the crowd gathering*), he answered unto the people, You men of Israel, why do you marvel at this? (*In essence, he is saying that Jesus is alive, and His work is continuing.*) or why look you so earnestly on us, as though by our own power or holiness we have made this man to walk? (*He turns the attention from himself and John to the Lord Jesus Christ.*)

13 The God of Abraham, and of Isaac, and of Jacob, the God of our fathers, has glorified His Son Jesus (*Chrysostom said, "He thrust himself upon the Fathers of old, lest he should appear to be introducing a new doctrine."*); Whom you delivered up (*pertains to the Chief Priest delivering Jesus to Pilate to be Crucified*), and denied Him in the presence of Pilate, when he was determined to let Him go (*the Holy Spirit puts most of the blame on the religious leaders of Israel*).

14 But you denied the Holy One and the Just (*proclaims the

terrible sin of Israel, and the terrible sin of most of humanity as well, and for all time), and desired a murderer to be granted unto you *(speaks of Barabbas [Mat. 27:15-26], and murderers have ruled them ever since!)*;

15 And killed the Prince of Life *(Peter minced no words, not at all softening his Message)*, Whom God has raised from the dead *(the Resurrection, as would be obvious, ratified what was done at the Cross)*; whereof we are witnesses *(means that they had personally seen the Resurrected Christ; there is no greater witness than an eyewitness)*.

16 And His Name through Faith in His Name has made this man strong *(presents the key to all things!)*, whom you see and know *(there was no denying the Miracle)*: yes, the Faith which is by Him *(Jesus)* has given him *(the crippled man)* this perfect soundness in the presence of you all *(no partial healing, but a total healing, which is the way the Lord does things)*.

17 And now, brethren, I reckon that through ignorance you did it, as *did* also your Rulers *(while they were ignorant, regrettably it was a willful ignorance; in other words, they had no desire to know the Truth about Jesus)*.

18 But those things, which God before had showed by the mouth of all His Prophets *(in other words, had they known the Bible, which they certainly should have known, they would have known about Jesus)*, that Christ should suffer *(the entirety of the story of the Bible is "Jesus Christ and Him Crucified")*, He has so fulfilled *(proclaims that His death was predestined, but not who would commit the deed)*.

19 Repent ye therefore, and be converted *(Repentance is an admittance that God is right, and we are wrong; he was speaking to the Rulers as well as to the people)*, that your sins may be blotted out *(speaks of Justification by Faith)*, when the times of refreshing shall come from the Presence of the Lord *(should have been translated, "In order that the times of refreshing shall come from the Presence of the Lord")*;

20 And He shall send Jesus Christ *(pertains to the Second Coming [Rev., Chpt. 19])*, which before was preached unto you *(through the Prophets, and as well the public Ministry of Christ to Israel for some three and a half years)*:

21 Whom the Heaven must receive until the times of restitution of all things *(refers to Jesus remaining in Heaven until this Dispensation of Grace has run its course, after which He will return to this Earth)*, which God has spoken by the mouth of all His Holy Prophets since the world began

(once again, had they known the Word of God, which then consisted of Genesis through Malachi, they would have known all these things).

22 For Moses truly said unto the Fathers *(Deut. 18:15-19)*, A Prophet shall the Lord your God raise up unto you of your brethren, like unto me *(the Promise of the Messiah)*; Him shall you hear in all things whatsoever He shall say unto you *(could not be clearer)*.

23 And it shall come to pass, *that* every soul, which will not hear that Prophet *(refers to the entirety of the world)*, shall be destroyed from among the people *(will be eternally lost!)*.

24 Yes, and all the Prophets from Samuel *(even though there were Prophets before Samuel, he was the first one to stand in the office of the Prophet)*, and those who follow after, as many as have spoken, have likewise foretold of these days *(speaks of all the Prophets, at least in one way or another, pointing to the coming Redeemer, Who would be the Lord Jesus Christ)*.

25 You are the children of the Prophets *(means that they should have known what the Prophets had said)*, and of the Covenant which God made with our Fathers *(refers to the Abrahamic Covenant [Gen. 12:1-3])*, saying unto Abraham, And in your seed shall all the kindreds of the earth be blessed *(speaks of Jesus Christ as that "Seed")*.

26 Unto you first *(refers to the offer of Salvation being made first to the Jews [Lk. 24:47; Rom. 1:16; 2:10])* God, having raised up His Son Jesus *(refers to the Resurrection)*, sent Him to bless you, in turning away every one of you from his *(your)* iniquities *(only Jesus could do this, which He did by His Atoning Work at the Cross [Eph. 2:13-18])*.

CHAPTER 4

PERSECUTION

AND as they spoke unto the people, the Priests, and the captain of the Temple, and the Sadducees, came upon them *(the "Sadducees" almost completely controlled the High Priesthood, and actually most of the Priestly duties of the Temple)*,

2 Being grieved that they taught the people *(worried)*, and preached through Jesus the resurrection from the dead *(they were angry that Jesus and the Resurrection were being preached, which Doctrine the Sadducees denied [Lk. 20:27])*.

3 And they laid hands on them *(arrested them)*, and put *them* in hold unto the next day *(a small prison in the confines of the Temple)*: for it was now evening.

4 Howbeit many of them

which heard the Word believed *(they believed on Christ, thereby accepting Him as the Messiah of Israel and the Saviour of men)*; and the number of the men was about five thousand *(seems to speak only of men, so including women and children, it could have numbered ten thousand or more)*.

5 And it came to pass on the morrow, that their Rulers, and Elders, and Scribes,

6 And Annas the High Priest, and Caiaphas, and John *(probably was Johanan Ben Zakkai, a famous Rabbi of that time)*, and Alexander *(probably was Alexander Lysimachus, one of the richest Jews of his time who contributed very generously to the Temple)*, and as many as were of the kindred of the High Priest *(possibly all five sons of Annas were present)*, were gathered together at Jerusalem *(some of them probably didn't live in Jerusalem, but happened to be there at that time)*.

7 And when they had set them in the midst *(Peter and John)*, they asked, By what power, or by what name, have you done this? *(By the crippled man being healed, they already knew the answer.)*

8 Then Peter, filled with the Holy Spirit, said unto them *(the Holy Spirit is mentioned in one way or the other in the Book of Acts over fifty times)*, You Rulers of the people, and Elders of Israel *(the Holy Spirit, through Peter, is point-*ing out the responsibility these religious leaders hold as the spiritual guides of the people)*,

9 If we this day be examined of the good deed done to the impotent man *(proclaims Peter in effect asking as to how or why a good deed such as this should be questioned at all!)*, by what means he is made whole *(presents the cause of the attitude and action of the ruling body of Israel)*;

10 Be it known unto you all, and to all the people of Israel *(once again, Peter will not mince words)*, that by the Name of Jesus Christ of Nazareth *(he desired that there be no mistake as it regards the One of Whom He was speaking; since the Baptism with the Holy Spirit, Peter is not the same man he was when he denied Christ even before a young maiden; he will now boldly stand up for Christ in front of the entirety of the ruling body of Israel)*, Whom you Crucified *(places the emphasis on the word "you," thereby pointedly and directly fastening the terrible sin of Crucifying their Messiah squarely on their shoulders; as stated, he pulled no punches)*, Whom God raised from the dead *(proclaims words they certainly didn't want to hear)*, even by Him does this man stand here before you whole *(the man was evidently brought with Peter and John before the Council; in essence, Peter is say-*

ing that a dead man could not produce these results).

11 This is the Stone which was set at nought of you builders (Jesus is the Stone [Ps. 118:22-23]), which is become the Head of the Corner (Israel rejected Him, but it did not stop the Plan of God; Israel only succeeded in destroying themselves).

12 Neither is there Salvation in any other (proclaims unequivocally that Jesus Alone holds the key to Salvation, and in fact is Salvation): for there is none other name under Heaven given among men, whereby we must be saved (says it all!).

RELEASE

13 Now when they saw the boldness of Peter and John (pertains not only to what was spoken, but to the power with which it was spoken as well), and perceived that they were unlearned and ignorant men, they marveled (means they had not studied in the Rabbinical Schools; in fact, they were not "unlearned and ignorant," but rather the very opposite!); and they took knowledge of them, that they had been with Jesus (this explained it all).

14 And beholding the man which was healed standing with them (presents a beautiful picture!), they could say nothing against it (proclaims the proof which was obvious to all!).

15 But when they had commanded them to go aside out of the Council (proclaims the fact that God had left this Council a long time ago), they conferred among themselves (but not with the Scriptures),

16 Saying, What shall we do to these men? (Why would they want to do anything negative to these men?) for that indeed a notable miracle has been done by them is manifest to all them who dwell in Jerusalem; and we cannot deny it (infers that the news of this man's Miraculous Healing had spread far and wide, even in the last few hours).

17 But that it spread no further among the people (seems to present their greatest fear), let us straitly threaten them, that they speak henceforth to no man in this Name (automatically places the situation into a posture which cannot be obeyed).

18 And they called them, and commanded them not to speak at all nor teach in the Name of Jesus.

19 But Peter and John answered and said unto them, Whether it be right in the Sight of God to hearken unto you more than unto God, judge ye (in effect, Peter and John are saying that these religious leaders are not of God, are not doing the Work of God,

and consequently do not have the Mind of God, irrespective of their claims).

20 For we cannot but speak the things which we have seen and heard *(there are two groups of Christians, those who "cannot speak" and those who "cannot but speak").*

21 So when they had further threatened them, they let them go, finding nothing how they might punish them *(what had they done that warranted punishment?),* because of the people *(they feared an uprising):* for all men Glorified God for that which was done *(and rightly so!).*

22 For the man was above forty years old *(carries the idea that this man was mature, responsible, and therefore could be believed),* on whom this Miracle of Healing was showed.

PRAISE AND PRAYER

23 And being let go *(Peter and John were no longer under arrest),* they went to their own company *(probably the other Apostles and others, perhaps many others),* and reported all that the Chief Priests and Elders had said unto them *(presents the first account of opposition against the Early Church; it was not long in coming).*

24 And when they heard that *(heard the account),* they lifted up their voice to God with one accord, and said *(all were praying in one way or the other),* Lord, You *are* God, which has made Heaven, and earth, and the sea, and all that in them is *(a compendium of what was said):*

25 Who by the mouth of Your servant David has said *(refers to the Second Psalm),* Why did the heathen rage, and the people imagine vain things? *(This is used by the Holy Spirit to refer to these religious leaders concerning Jesus. This proclaims the fact that the Messiah is the Person spoken of in the Second Psalm.)*

26 The Kings of the earth stood up, and the Rulers were gathered together against the Lord, and against His Christ *(this Psalm speaks of all the opposition against Christ from the very beginning, but more particularly speaks of the coming Antichrist).*

27 For of a truth against Your Holy Child Jesus, Whom You have anointed *(proclaims Jesus as the fulfillment of all the Prophecies, the Son of God, the Incarnate One, the Saviour of Men),* both Herod, and Pontius Pilate, with the Gentiles *(the Romans),* and the people of Israel, were gathered together *(they were "gathered together" for the express purpose of Crucifying Christ),*

28 For to do whatsoever Your Hand and Your Counsel determined before to be done *(speaks*

of predestination concerning Christ, His Death on Calvary's Cross, and His Resurrection from the dead; but again we state that those who were to Crucify Him were not determined by God; they did this cruel deed by their own choice).

29 And now, Lord, behold their threatenings *(proclaims those praying turning over these rulers and others to the Lord, in order that He may handle the situation)*: and grant unto Your servants, that with all boldness they may speak Your Word *(proclaims the very opposite of that demanded by the religious leaders of Israel),*

30 By stretching forth Your Hand to heal *(proclaims the request for more Healings and Miracles)*; and that signs and wonders may be done by the Name of Your Holy Child Jesus *(all speak of the Power of God, but in the "Name of Jesus").*

31 And when they had prayed, the place was shaken where they were assembled together *(this literally happened; the assembly place shook, and did so by the Power of God)*; and they were all filled with the Holy Spirit *(it means the Holy Spirit was leading and guiding them)*, and they spoke the Word of God with boldness *(the Lord answered their prayer by giving them more boldness, and they did not hesitate to speak accordingly; this is something the modern* Church *desperately needs as well, and would have if the Holy Spirit were prevalent and present).*

BELIEVERS

32 And the multitude of them who believed were of one heart and of one soul *(speaks of unity which can only be brought about by the Holy Spirit; man's efforts to do such always fall short)*: neither said any *of them* that ought of the things which he possessed was his own; but they had all things common *(once again, this refers to the great persecution suffered by the Believers in Jerusalem at that time; many who came to Christ lost their jobs because they were excommunicated from the Synagogue; many were put out of their apartments, etc.; so, others who did not suffer such losses had to share, which they gladly did).*

33 And with great power gave the Apostles witness of the Resurrection of the Lord Jesus *(this was done by the Holy Spirit greatly anointing the Apostles to attest to the Resurrection of Christ, and by signs and wonders being performed as well)*: and great Grace was upon them all *(is a portrayal of the beginning of the great dispensation of Grace, which actually began on the Day of Pentecost).*

34 Neither was there any among them who lacked *(those*

*who lost their employment, etc.,
had their needs met)*: for as many
as were possessors of lands or
houses sold them, and brought
the prices of the things that were
sold *(refers to extra possessions, etc.)*,

35 And laid *them* down at the
Apostles' feet *(they were entrusted
with this largesse)*: and distribution was made unto every man
according as he had need *(no hint
of communism here, as some have
suggested)*.

36 And Joseph, who by the
Apostles was surnamed Barnabas
*(Barnabas became a Prophet and
an Apostle [Acts 13:1; 14:14],
(which is, being interpreted, The
son of consolation,) a Levite, and
of the country of Cyprus (he was a
Jew who had been born in Cyprus
and lived there for a considerable
period of time, as likely his father
had done before him; being a Levite,
he was of the Priestly class, although
not a Priest)*,

37 Having land, sold *it*, and
brought the money, and laid *it* at
the Apostles' feet *(probably refers
to property in Cyprus)*.

CHAPTER 5

ANANIAS AND SAPPHIRA

BUT a certain man named Ananias, with Sapphira his wife,
sold a possession *(the story of this
man and his wife was placed here*

*in graphic detail by the Holy Spirit
as a warning)*,

2 And kept back *part* of the
price, his wife also being privy *to
it (instantly proclaims the conception of this great sin and its deception in being carried out)*, and
brought a certain part, and laid *it*
at the Apostles' feet *(a detailed
plan with a very wide application;
it was done with a certain purpose
in mind)*.

3 But Peter said, Ananias,
why has Satan filled your heart
to lie to the Holy Spirit *(presents
two Gifts of the Spirit in operation: "Discerning of Spirits," and
"A Word of Knowledge"; how many
millions of professing Christians
are presently lying to the Holy
Spirit?)*, and to keep back *part* of
the price of the land? *(This details their insidious plan.)*

4 While it remained, was it not
your own? and after it was sold,
was it not in your own power?
*(This means simply that God did
not require of them to sell the land,
or to give all the money received to
the Work of the Lord.)* why have
you conceived this thing in your
heart? *(This proclaims to us where
sin originates.)* you have not lied
unto men, but unto God *(actually
portrays the object of all sin; it is
against God!)*.

5 And Ananias hearing these
words fell down, and gave up the
ghost *(he was stricken dead on the*

spot): and great fear came on all them who heard these things *(this is the type of healthy fear of God that all men should have)*.

6 And the young men arose, wound him up, and carried *him* out, and buried *him (prepared him for burial)*.

7 And it was about the space of three hours after, when his wife, not knowing what was done, came in.

8 And Peter answered unto her, Tell me whether you sold the land for so much? And she said, Yes, for so much *(all of this seems to indicate that these were not strangers among the thousands who had gotten saved, but were fairly well known; she had an opportunity to tell the truth, but didn't!)*.

9 Then Peter said unto her, How is it that you have agreed together to tempt the Spirit of the Lord? *(Peter's question concerning the tempting of the Holy Spirit seems to imply that the Spirit of God dealt with them greatly so, but to no avail. They pushed aside His Warnings.)* behold, the feet of them which have buried your husband *are* at the door, and shall carry you out *(seems to imply that the Lord had already told Peter what her reaction would be, and that the same young men who had attended her husband were waiting to do the same with her)*.

10 Then fell she down straight-way at his feet, and yielded up the ghost *(presents the Judgment of God striking her exactly as it had stricken her husband)*: and the young men came in, and found her dead, and, carrying *her* forth, buried *her* by her husband *(prepared her for burial)*.

11 And great fear came upon all the Church, and upon as many as heard these things *(inasmuch as the Holy Spirit again makes the same statement as He had made in Verse 5, we are made to realize that God is to be feared as well as praised; also, if it is to be known, the same Judgment is happening presently, but not so dramatic; the Holy Spirit is the same, so the results have to be the same)*.

POWER

12 And by the hands of the Apostles were many signs and wonders wrought among the people *(the Church was founded on the Power of God, and is meant to continue by the Power of God)*; (and they were all with one accord in Solomon's porch *(portrays a roofed colonnade bearing Solomon's name, which ran along the eastern wall in the Court of the Gentiles of Herod's Temple)*.

13 And of the rest does no man join himself to them *(to the Apostles)*: but the people magnified them *(they knew the Apostles*

were of the Lord and that the Lord was greatly using them, so they found no fault with them).

14 And Believers were the more added to the Lord, multitudes both of men and women.) *(It could have been as many as forty or fifty thousand, or even more.)*

15 Insomuch that they brought forth the sick into the streets, and laid *them* on beds and couches *(evidently refers to two or three different streets on which Peter and the Apostles came to the Temple each day; the crowds were so large they could not all get into the Temple Court)*, that at the least the shadow of Peter passing by might overshadow some of them *(implying that when this happened, healing resulted)*.

16 There came also a multitude *out* of the cities round about unto Jerusalem, bringing sick folks *(proclaims the extent to which this Move of God had reached)*, and them which were vexed with unclean spirits *(probably implying that much of the sickness was caused by demon spirits)*: and they were healed every one *(delivered and healed)*.

PERSECUTION

17 Then the High Priest rose up *(either speaks of Annas or Caiaphas, which one is not clear)*, and all they who were with him,

(which is the sect of the Sadducees,) and were filled with indignation *(refers here to "envy" or "jealousy")*,

18 And laid their hands on the Apostles *(refers to all Twelve)*, and put them in the common prison.

DELIVERANCE

19 But the Angel of the Lord by night opened the prison doors *(should have been translated, "an Angel"; it was one of the many Angels who serve as Ministering Spirits to Believers [Heb. 1:14]*, and brought them forth, and said *(brought them out of the prison)*,

20 Go, stand and speak in the Temple to the people all the words of this life *(presents instructions directly opposite of those the religious leaders had given; these were "Words" announcing Eternal Life to dying men)*.

21 And when they heard *that*, they entered into the Temple early in the morning, and taught *(proclaims it was the night before that they were released by the Angel)*. But the High Priest came, and they who were with Him, and called the Council together, and all the senate of the children of Israel *(the entirety of the Jewish Sanhedrin, the ruling body of Israel)*, and sent to the prison to have them brought *(they were in for quite a surprise)*.

22 But when the officers came, and found them not in the prison, they returned, and told (*presents a scenario which is absolutely unbelievable, but yet totally true!*),

23 Saying, The prison truly found we shut with all safety (*presents the fact that nothing seemed unusual, and that the locks had not been tampered with*), and the keepers standing without before the doors (*presents the fact that the guards had no idea what had happened*): but when we had opened, we found no man within (*what must these jailers have thought?*).

24 Now when the High Priest and the Captain of the Temple and the Chief Priests heard these things (*imagine their surprise!*), they doubted of them whereunto this would grow (*they were thoroughly perplexed; no one could explain what had happened or where it would stop!*).

ON TRIAL

25 Then came one and told them, saying, Behold, the men whom you put in prison are standing in the Temple, and teaching the people (*they obeyed exactly what the Angel had said do*).

26 Then went the Captain with the officers, and brought them without violence (*means they did not bind them, but simply asked that they follow*): for they feared the people, lest they should have been stoned (*they feared the people, but they did not fear Him Who manifested His Power in opening the prison, for their hearts and consciences were hardened with hatred against Him and His followers*).

27 And when they had brought them, they set *them* before the Council (*implies the full Sanhedrin of seventy-one members, plus onlookers*): and the High Priest asked them,

28 Saying, Did not we straitly Command you that you should not teach in this Name? and, behold, You have filled Jerusalem with your doctrine (*proclaims the success of their Preaching and Teaching*), and intend to bring this Man's blood upon us (*seems to now seek to avoid their own imprecation, having previously prayed that "His Blood might be on them and on their children" [Mat. 27:25]*).

29 Then Peter and the *other* Apostles answered and said (*represents their answer being instant and unequivocally clear*), We ought to obey God rather than men (*in this brave reply there was neither pride nor self-will; there was faithfulness, subjection to Truth, and intelligence in the Scriptures;*

Hervey said, "The rule is a golden one for all men, all circumstances, and all time.").

30 The God of our fathers raised up Jesus *(Peter links Jesus with the Patriarchs and Prophets of old, as well with God),* Whom you slew and hanged on a tree *(places the responsibility of the murder of Christ squarely on the shoulders of the Sanhedrin).*

31 Him has God exalted with his Right Hand *(refers to the fact that the Power of God not only raised Jesus from the dead, but as well has seated Him at His Own Right Hand in the Heavenlies [Rom. 8:34; Eph. 1:20]) to be a Prince and a Saviour (as "Prince," He is the Titular Leader of Israel and the Church; as "Saviour," He is the "Deliverer," and there is no other),* for to give repentance to Israel, and forgiveness of sins *(tells us that not only is the Lord Jesus the Medium of Forgiveness and Life, but He is the Dispenser of both; as well, He "Gives," not sells!").*

32 And we are His witnesses of these things *(in effect says that their Doctrine was not a mere philosophy, but rather eyewitness accounts);* and *so is* also the Holy Spirit, Whom God has given to them who obey Him *(the witness of the Holy Spirit in the hearts and lives of Believers guarantees the veracity of all that Christ has done at the Cross).*

33 When they heard *that,* they were cut *to the heart (Peter's words were said with powerful conviction),* and took counsel to slay them *(is the reaction which normally comes from the world of religion).*

GAMALIEL

34 Then stood there up one in the Council, a Pharisee, named Gamaliel, a Doctor of the Law, had in reputation among all the people *(constitutes one of the most celebrated and honored Jewish Rabbis; He was Grandson of Hillel and succeeded as President of the Sanhedrin on the death of His Father, Rabbi Simeon, son of Hillel),* and commanded to put the Apostles forth a little space *(in order that his word of wisdom may be given to the members of the Sanhedrin);*

35 And said unto them, You men of Israel, take heed to yourselves what you intend to do as touching these men *(evidently, the Holy Spirit moved upon him to take this position).*

36 For before these days rose up Theudas, boasting himself to be somebody *(evidently concerns a particular insurrection led by this man, which had recently taken place);* to whom a number of men, about four hundred, joined themselves: who was slain; and

all, as many as obeyed him, were scattered, and brought to nought *(refers to those who were dupes of this self-pronounced Messiah, or some such)*.

37 After this man rose up Judas of Galilee in the days of the taxing, and drew away much people after him *(another insurrectionist)*: he also perished; and all, *even* as many as obeyed him, were dispersed *(proclaims these as coming to the same end as those under Theudas)*.

38 And now I say unto you, Refrain from these men, and let them alone *(in effect, Gamaliel was saying, "let them alone, Rome will handle the problem")*: for if this counsel or this work be of men, it will come to nought *(in this case, such advice was correct)*:

39 But if it be of God, you cannot overthrow it *(presents a great Truth as given by Gamaliel)*; lest haply you be found even to fight against God *(presents the very worst position in which anyone can find themselves)*.

PERSECUTION

40 And to him they agreed *(at least about not killing them)*: and when they had called the Apostles, and beaten *them (presents a cruel and brutal punishment which was cowardly and unjust)*, they commanded that they should not speak in the Name of Jesus, and let them go *(presents the second command not to Preach in this Name [Acts 4:17-18])*.

REJOICING

41 And they departed from the presence of the Council *(proclaims that from which the Lord had long since departed)*, rejoicing that they were counted worthy to suffer shame for His Name *(presents the first sharp stroke of persecution; it was bitter and painful to the flesh, but caused rejoicing in the spirit; shame is Glory if suffered for the Name)*.

42 And daily in the Temple *(presents them boldly and properly disregarding their illegal Judges, as they kept on preaching that Jesus was the Promised Messiah)*, and in every house, they ceased not to teach and preach Jesus Christ *(tells us that the Churches then were in houses for the most part, if not altogether)*.

CHAPTER 6

THE FIRST DEACONS

AND in those days, when the number of the Disciples was multiplied *(the followers of Christ were multiplying)*, there arose a murmuring of the Grecians against the Hebrews *(refers* to Jews who spoke Greek as a result of having once lived in various countries where Greek was spoken), because their widows were neglected in the daily ministration (speaks of relief in the form of food and money given to "widows" in the Church in Jerusalem who had no way to provide for themselves).

2 Then the Twelve (Twelve Apostles) called the multitude of the Disciples unto them, and said (constitutes probably the very first business meeting in the Early Church), It is not reason that we should leave the Word of God, and serve tables (refers to the voluminous administrative duties which accompanied the great growth of the Early Church in Jerusalem).

3 Wherefore, brethren, look ye out among you seven men of honest report, full of the Holy Spirit and wisdom (is thought by some to represent the first Deacons, even though they are not called that in this Chapter), whom we may appoint over this business (the Holy Spirit told the "Twelve" what to do, the number to choose, and how they were to be chosen).

4 But we will give ourselves continually to prayer, and to the Ministry of the Word (tells us that "Prayer" is mentioned first, and is more important than "Preaching"; without a proper Prayer Life, there can be no proper Ministry).

5 And the saying pleased the whole multitude (proclaims wisdom the people could not fault, for it was wisdom from above): and they chose Stephen, a man full of Faith and of the Holy Spirit, and Philip, and Prochorus, and Nicanor, and Timon, and Parmenas, and Nicolas a proselyte of Antioch (presents the seven men):

6 Whom they set before the Apostles (now presented for acceptance and confirmation): and when they had prayed (sought the Lord's approval of these men, which evidently they received), they laid their hands on them (the laying on of hands was to designate them for an office, work, or Ministry, as Moses did Joshua [Num. 27:18-23]).

7 And the Word of God increased (means that more and more men were Preaching the Gospel of Jesus); and the number of the Disciples multiplied in Jerusalem greatly (could have been as many as one hundred thousand people who had accepted the Lord); and a great company of the Priests were obedient to the Faith (presents one of the greatest Testimonies to date of the Power of God).

STEPHEN

8 And Stephen, full of faith and power (speaks of a great

knowledge of the Word of God, and of the Holy Spirit controlling this man, and thereby using him), did great wonders and miracles among the people (these things were Divinely done).

9 Then there arose certain of the Synagogue, which is called *the Synagogue* of the Libertines (speaks of Jews who had been taken as slaves to Rome or elsewhere in the Roman Empire, but now had been set free, consequently coming back to Jerusalem; they had a Synagogue in Jerusalem, and perhaps several), and Cyrenians, and Alexandrians, and of them of Cilicia and of Asia (pertains to each one of these groups of Jews who had a Synagogue in Jerusalem), disputing with Stephen (it is thought by some that Paul, then known as Saul, was the leading disputer against Stephen; he could have been associated with the Synagogue that pertained to Cilicia, as Tarsus, the hometown of Paul, was in that region).

10 And they were not able to resist the wisdom and the spirit by which he spoke (if it was Paul who led the dispute against Stephen, it would have been most interesting, considering that Paul was the hope of the Pharisees at that time, and therefore reputed to have great knowledge of the Word; the difference is that the Holy Spirit anointed Stephen!).

11 Then they suborned men (they planned and formed a scheme together, which held no validity or truth), which said, We have heard him speak blasphemous words against Moses, and *against* God (concerns their concocted scheme).

12 And they stirred up the people, and the Elders, and the Scribes (refers to the lies they told and kept telling respecting Stephen), and came upon *him*, and caught him, and brought *him* to the Council (refers to them getting permission from the Sanhedrin to arrest Stephen, which they did),

13 And set up false witnesses, which said (proclaims the similarity of Stephen's trial with that of our Lord), This man ceases not to speak blasphemous words against this holy place, and the Law (this was their charge, which was false):

14 For we have heard him say (represents a distortion of what Stephen had probably said; they probably based their accusation upon some semblance of Truth, but totally distorted its meaning), that this Jesus of Nazareth (said in such a way as to be most contemptuous) shall destroy this place (probably referred to the Words said by Jesus in the Olivet discourse [Mat. 24:2]), and shall change the customs which Moses delivered us (it is true that the customs were to be changed as a result of the New

Covenant, and in fact were meant to be changed).

15 And all that sat in the Council *(Sanhedrin)*, looking stedfastly on him *(gazed intently, and for purpose and reason)*, saw his face as it had been the face of an Angel *(pertains to the Glory of the Lord shining on the face of Stephen)*.

CHAPTER 7

STEPHEN'S DEFENSE

THEN said the High Priest, Are these things so? *(This was asked concerning the charges!)*

2 And he said *(Stephen)*, Men, brethren, and fathers, hearken *(addresses and is meant to address the religious hierarchy of Israel)*; The God of Glory appeared unto our father Abraham, when he was in Mesopotamia, before he dwelt in Charran *(doesn't tell us exactly what this appearance was, whether visible or that the Lord may have used someone else to deliver the Message; the exact place in that land was Ur of the Chaldees [Gen. 15:7])*,

3 And said unto him, Get thee out of your country *(pertained to a land of idol worship)*, and from your kindred *(in effect says they were idol-worshippers as well)*, and come into the land which I shall show you *(refers to the land of Canaan)*.

4 Then came he out of the land of the Chaldaeans, and dwelt in Charran *(about 700 miles north of Ur of the Chaldees; he stayed there approximately two or three years)*: and from thence, when his father was dead, he removed him into this land, wherein you now dwell *(the Land of Canaan)*.

5 And He *(God)* gave him none inheritance in it, no, not *so much as* to set his foot on *(means that Abraham personally never owned any of the Land of Canaan, except the "Cave of Machpelah," which was used for a burial place for he and Sarah [Gen. 23])*: yet he promised that he would give it to him for a possession, and to his seed after him *(refers to the seed of Isaac, not Ishmael [Gen. 17:19])*, when as yet he had no child *(for all of this to be done, Abraham and Sarah must have an heir, which they ultimately did have in Isaac)*.

6 And God spoke on this wise *(concerns the Prophecy given to Abraham by the Lord respecting the future of his seed)*, That his seed should sojourn in a strange land *(Egypt)*; and that they should bring them into bondage, and entreat *them* evil four hundred years *(the whole length of the Dispensation of Promise [Abraham to Moses] was 430 years [Ex. 12:40; Gal. 3:14-17]; the 400 years of Genesis 15:13 and Acts 7:6 are to*

be reckoned from the confirmation of Isaac as the seed when Ishmael was cast out [Gen. 21:12; Gal. 4:30]; this was five years after the birth of Isaac).

7 And the nation to whom they shall be in bondage will I judge, said God (speaks of Egypt [Ex. 1:1-14; 31]): and after that shall they come forth, and serve Me in this place (the Children of Israel were delivered from Egyptian bondage and given the Promised Land, which Stephen refers to as "this place").

8 And He (God) gave him (Abraham) the Covenant of Circumcision (refers to the Abrahamic Covenant of Genesis 12:1-3; 17:9-27, and not the Mosaic Covenant which continued Circumcision, but did not originate it): and so Abraham begat Isaac, and circumcised him the eighth day; and Isaac begat Jacob; and Jacob begat the Twelve Patriarchs (speaks of his sons as the Twelve Heads of the Tribes of Israel, and who came under the same Covenant of Circumcision).

9 And the Patriarchs, moved with envy, sold Joseph into Egypt (they were jealous of him, in that he was chosen by his father Jacob to inherit the Birthright [I Chron. 5:1-2]): but God was with him (men rule, but God overrules!),

10 And delivered him out of all his afflictions (does not say

there were no afflictions, but that the Lord delivered Joseph out of every snare set for him by Satan), and gave him favour and wisdom in the sight of Pharaoh king of Egypt; and he made him Governor over Egypt and all his house (portrays, for a change, a wise ruler!).

11 Now there came a dearth over all the land of Egypt and Canaan (refers to the seven year famine), and great affliction: and our fathers found no sustenance (all of this was orchestrated purposely by the Lord, in order that His Plan be carried out respecting the nation of Israel).

12 But when Jacob heard that there was corn in Egypt, he sent out our fathers first (he sent his sons).

13 And at the second time Joseph was made known to his brethren (refers to their second trip to Egypt with Joseph testing them [Gen. 45:1-28]); and Joseph's kindred was made known unto Pharaoh (they were introduced to Pharaoh, with Joseph seeking permission for his family to come into Egypt).

14 Then sent Joseph, and called his father Jacob to him (this is symbolic of the Second Coming, when Israel will finally come to Jesus), and all his kindred, threescore and fifteen souls (seventy-five souls; Stephen was including the five sons of Manasseh and Ephraim; Gen-

esis 46:27 and Deuteronomy 10:22 mention seventy people who went into Egypt, but did not include these five).

15 So Jacob went down into Egypt, and died, he, and our fathers *(while his life and Ministry were in Egypt, his heart was in Canaan),*

16 And were carried over into Sychem, and laid in the sepulchre that Abraham bought for a sum of money of the sons of Emmor the father of Sychem *(refers to "Shechem" [Gen. 23:6-20; 33:19; 47:30; 49:29; 50:5; Ex. 13; 19; Josh. 24:32]; this was in Canaan).*

17 But when the time of the Promise drew near *(God's timing is just as important as His Promise),* which God had sworn to Abraham *(the Promise of God concerned the Land of Canaan being given to the Children of Israel),* the people *(Israelites)* grew and multiplied in Egypt,

18 Till another king arose *(another Pharaoh),* which knew not Joseph *(means that this new Pharaoh had no regard for Egypt's past respecting Joseph, and consequently had no regard for Joseph's people, the Israelites!).*

19 The same dealt subtilly with our kindred, and evil entreated our fathers *(proclaimed such being allowed by the Lord, and for purpose and reason; had they been treated kindly by this* Pharaoh, they would not have desired to leave Egypt),* so that they cast out their young children, to the end they might not live *(speaks of the demand ordered by Pharaoh that all the boy babies of the Israelites be killed when they were born).*

20 In which time Moses was born *(presents another step in the Plan of God for Israel's deliverance),* and was exceeding fair *(describes the appearance of the child),* and nourished up in his father's house three months *(pertained to the time he was hidden by his parents, in order that he not be killed as was demanded by Pharaoh of all newly-born baby boys):*

21 And when he was cast out *(speaks of the time when he could not be hidden any longer),* Pharaoh's daughter took him up, and nourished him for her own son *(again, this was orchestrated by the Lord).*

22 And Moses was learned in all the wisdom of the Egyptians *(highly educated),* and was mighty in words and in deeds *(Josephus says that Moses ultimately became a General in the Egyptian Army, and defeated the Ethiopians).*

23 And when he was full forty years old *(pertains to the years Moses spent in Pharaoh's Court),* it came into his heart to visit his brethren the Children of Israel *(before now it seems that he had not been too occupied with the plight*

of "his brethren").

24 And seeing one *of them* suffer wrong, he defended *him (the Holy Spirit begins to move Moses in this direction)*, and avenged him who was oppressed, and smote the Egyptian *(Moses had the right motive, but this was the wrong way)*:

25 For he supposed his brethren would have understood how that God by his hand would deliver them *(the sentence structure here tells us that the Lord was definitely dealing with Moses about the deliverance of the Children of Israel; however, the people were not ready and neither was Moses!)*: but they understood not.

26 And the next day he showed himself unto them as they strove, and would have set them at one again *(these two Israelites were angry with each other)*, saying, Sirs, you are brethren; why do ye wrong one to another? *(This will bring forth an answer he was not anticipating.)*

27 But he who did his neighbour wrong thrust him *(Moses)* away *(plainly proclaims the man rejecting the leadership of Moses)*, saying, Who made you a ruler and a judge over us? *(As stated, neither Moses nor the people were yet ready for deliverance.)*

28 Will you kill me, as you did the Egyptian yesterday? *(Evidently, Moses did not realize that* his killing of the Egyptian was known; however, he had been seen!)*

29 Then fled Moses at that saying *(Moses was soon to find out that Pharaoh also knew and was angry, so he fled Egypt [Ex. 2:14-15])*, and was a stranger in the land of Madian, where he begat two sons *(their names were Gershom and Eliezer [Ex. 2:22; 18:3-4])*.

30 And when forty years were expired *(it only took a very short time to get Moses out of Egypt, but forty years to get Egypt out of Moses; the flesh dies hard!)*, there appeared to him in the wilderness of Mount Sina an Angel of the Lord in a flame of fire in a bush *(this was actually God Himself appearing to Moses [Ex. 3:2; 4:17])*.

31 When Moses saw *it (the burning bush)*, he wondered at the sight: and as he drew near to behold *it*, the Voice of the Lord came unto him *(after forty years, the Lord now speaks)*,

32 *Saying*, I *am* the God of your fathers, the God of Abraham, and the God of Isaac, and the God of Jacob *(in essence says that He was the same One Who had spoken to them; it also means they were alive at that very time, actually in Paradise)*. Then Moses trembled, and turned his face away *(Ex. 3:6)*.

33 Then said the Lord to him *(begins a scenario that would only end some forty years later)*, Put off

your shoes from your feet: for the place where you stand is Holy Ground (*the pulling off of the shoes signified that Moses was relinquishing ownership to everything; slaves do not wear shoes, and he in effect would be a slave of Christ, exactly as Paul*).

34 I have seen, I have seen the affliction of My people which is in Egypt (*God sees all and knows all*), and I have heard their groaning (*groaning under the burden imposed by the Egyptian taskmasters, who were types of Satan*), and am come down to deliver them (*He delivered them by the means of the slain lamb and the blood applied to the doorposts, in essence the Cross; the Cross is still the only manner of deliverance [Ex. 12:13]*). And now come, I will send you into Egypt (*presents one of the most appalling commissions ever given to any man*).

35 This Moses whom they refused, saying, Who made you a ruler and a judge? (*This is meant by the Holy Spirit through Stephen to show that the Jesus they had rejected and Crucified was their only Present and Eternal Saviour.*) the same did God send *to be* a ruler and a deliverer by the hand of the Angel which appeared to him in the bush (*the Sanhedrin were overly familiar with this; however, they surely understood the implication*).

36 He brought them out (*speaks of Egypt, but is meant to convey as well the deliverance effected regarding every believing sinner upon coming to Christ*), after that he had showed wonders and signs in the land of Egypt (*he manifested His great Power to Egypt, so that the Egyptians were without excuse*), and in the Red Sea (*speaks of the greatest Miracle that had ever been performed up to that time*), and in the wilderness forty years (*presents the Divine protection of God for this length of time, even though it was His Will that they only be there about two years, if that!*).

37 This is that Moses, which said unto the Children of Israel (*portrays Stephen now presenting the fact of Christianity, even though it was not even called such then*), A Prophet shall the Lord your God raise up unto you of your brethren, like unto me; Him shall you hear (*points directly to Jesus as the fulfillment of that Prophecy given by Moses so long before*).

38 This is he (*Moses*), who was in the Church in the wilderness with the Angel which spoke to him in the Mount Sinai (*actually refers to God Himself, Who gave Moses the Law*), and *with* our fathers (*refers to the fact that the Elders of Israel, were to help Moses, but rather, did the opposite!*): who received the lively oracles to give unto us (*refers to the Law of Moses*):

39 To whom our fathers would not obey *(marks the history of Israel, which ultimately led to their destruction)*, but thrust him from them *(had God not intervened, at least several times, they would have killed Moses)*, and in their hearts turned back again into Egypt *(puts the finger right square on the problem; their "hearts" were still in Egypt, just like the hearts of many Believers presently are still in the world)*,

40 Saying unto Aaron, Make us gods to go before us *(proclaims the sin which ultimately destroyed Israel)*: for as for this Moses, which brought us out of the land of Egypt, we know not what is become of him *(while God was preparing great things for them, they were preparing to worship idols!)*.

41 And they made a calf in those days *(this was their idol)*, and offered sacrifice unto the idol *(probably represented a lamb, but in times to come would include human sacrifice)*, and rejoiced in the works of their own hands *(it is still the problem presently, with the Church little desiring to lean solely on Christ and what He has done at the Cross; many prefer a Salvation "of their own hands")*.

42 Then God turned, and gave them up to worship the host of Heaven *(refers to the sun, moon, and stars)*; as it is written in the Book of the Prophets, O ye house of Israel, have you offered to Me slain beasts and sacrifices by the space of forty years in the wilderness? *(While Israel did offer up Sacrifices, they were not always to God. "To Me" is emphatic!)*

43 Yes, you took up the tabernacle of Moloch *(refers to the name of the main Ammonite Deity to whom children were offered by fire [Lev. 18:21; 20:2; Deut. 18:10; II Ki. 16:3; 26:6; 23:10; Jer. 19:5; 32:35])*, and the star of your god Remphan, figures which you made to worship them *(this was the star-god of Babylon)*: and I will carry you away beyond Babylon *(Stephen quotes from Amos 5:25-27; however, he used the name "Babylon" while Amos used the name "Damascus"; both were correct)*.

44 Our fathers had the tabernacle of witness in the wilderness, as He had appointed *(means that God gave them the "Tabernacle" plus the articles of Sacred Vessels, in order that His people may have a way to worship Him)*, speaking unto Moses, that he should make it according to the fashion that he had seen *(presents the design exclusively by the Lord, which means that Moses was not to deviate from that design)*.

45 Which also our fathers who came after brought in with Jesus *(Joshua)* into the possession of the Gentiles *(refers to the Land of

Canaan), whom God drove out before the face of our fathers, unto the days of David *(refers to a time span of approximately five hundred years; during that time, victories were sparse);*

46 Who found favour before God *(referring to David),* and desired to find a Tabernacle for the God of Jacob *(speaks of the Ark of the Covenant being brought into Jerusalem, after being untended for approximately seventy years [II Sam. 6:12; Ps. 132:6]).*

47 But Solomon built Him *(God)* an house *(the plans were given to David, but it is Solomon, his son, who built the house).*

48 Howbeit the most High dwells not in Temples made with hands *(speaks of the prayer offered by Solomon at the dedication of the Temple [I Ki. 8:27]);* as said the Prophet *(this phrase should have been in the next Verse, because it speaks of Isaiah),*

49 Heaven *is* My Throne, and earth *is* My Footstool *(God is bigger and greater than anything):* what house will you build Me? says the Lord *(the Temple was to be merely a stopgap measure until Christ would come):* or what *is* the place of My rest? *(Israel had come to the place where they believed the Temple was all in all. They didn't see it as a step toward an ultimate goal. The "rest" is found only in Christ [Mat. 11:28-30].)*

50 Has not My Hand made all these things? *(He has made the Heavens and the Earth and all that is therein, so why would He want to confine Himself totally to one small building on Earth?)*

51 You stiffnecked and uncircumcised in heart and ears *(presents Stephen using the same language as Moses when he conveyed God's rebuke to Israel [Deut. 10:16]),* you do always resist the Holy Spirit: as your fathers *did,* so *do* you *(everything carried out by God on Earth is through the Person and Office of the Holy Spirit; to resist Him is to resist God, for He is God; they resisted Him by resisting the Plan of God, Who and what was Jesus Christ).*

52 Which of the Prophets have not your fathers persecuted? *(This is very similar to that stated by Christ [Mat. 5:12; 23:30-31, 34-37; Lk. 13:33-34].)* and they have slain them which showed before of the coming of the Just One *(they killed the Prophets who pointed to the One Who was to come, namely Jesus);* of Whom you have been now the betrayers and murderers *(is about as strong as anything that could be said; how different this is from most of the modern Preaching!):*

53 Who *(Israel)* have received the Law *(Law of Moses)* by the disposition of Angels *(speaks of the myriads of Angels who were present*

and were used to help give the Law of Moses to Israel [Ps. 68:17]), and have not kept it (contradicted their claims!).

THEIR ANSWER

54 When they heard these things, they were cut to the heart (refers to the depth to which the Holy Spirit took Stephen's words, which in effect were the "Words of the Lord"), and they gnashed on him with their teeth (proclaims their answer to Stephen and the Holy Spirit).

55 But he, being full of the Holy Spirit (the second time this is said of him [Acts 6:5]), looked up stedfastly into Heaven (means that Stephen saw something in Heaven which immediately seized his attention), and saw the Glory of God (he saw the Throne of God), and Jesus standing on the Right Hand of God (Christ is usually presented as sitting at the Right Hand of God [Heb. 1:3], but here He is seen standing, as rising to welcome His Faithful martyr and to place on his head the Crown of Life),

56 And said, Behold, I see the Heavens opened (proclaims Jesus in His Glory as God, just as the Heavens had opened to see Jesus in His humiliation on Earth as Man [Jn. 1:51]), and the Son of Man standing on the Right Hand of God (proclaims His rightful place by virtue of His Achievements and Exaltation to original Glory [Jn. 17:5; Eph. 1:20-23; Phil. 2:9-11; Heb. 1:3-4]).

57 Then they (members of the Sanhedrin) cried out with a loud voice (had they cried out in Repentance, the future of Israel could have been drastically changed for the better), and stopped their ears (means that they no longer desired to hear anything he desired to say), and ran upon him with one accord (all of the religious leadership of Israel were guilty),

58 And cast him out of the city, and stoned him (this was their answer to the plea of God for their souls): and the witnesses laid down their clothes at a young man's feet (they took off their outer garments so as to be free to hurl the stones at their victim with greater force), whose name was Saul (presents the first mention of this man who would have a greater positive impact on Christianity than any other human being who has ever lived; the death of Stephen, no doubt, played a part in the later conversion of Paul).

59 And they stoned Stephen, calling upon God (presents a monstrous offense on the part of his murderers; we must remember, he was murdered by the religious leaders of Israel), and saying, Lord Jesus, receive my spirit (presents

Stephen rendering Divine Worship to Jesus Christ in the most sublime form, and in the most solemn moment of his life).

60 And he kneeled down, and cried with a loud voice, Lord, lay not this sin to their charge *(presents him dying on his knees, without malice toward his murderers).* And when he had said this, he fell asleep *(portrays the body falling asleep, while his soul and spirit instantly went to be with Jesus; due to what Jesus did at the Cross; death is now looked at as merely going to sleep).*

CHAPTER 8

SAUL

A ND Saul *(Paul)* was consenting unto his death *(means that he expressed hearty approval of the stoning of Stephen).* And at that time there was a great persecution against the Church which was at Jerusalem *(the Church, as far as we know, was then confined to Jerusalem);* and they were all scattered abroad throughout the regions of Judaea and Samaria *(the persecution helped take the Gospel to these particular regions; so Satan's plan backfired),* except the Apostles *(they stayed in Jerusalem, no doubt at the behest of the Holy Spirit; for the Apostles to leave at that time could have destroyed the infant*

Church).

2 And devout men carried Stephen to his burial *(proclaims the high esteem with which they held this man, and rightly so!),* and made great lamentation over him *(what a difference between his death and that of Ananias and Sapphira).*

3 As for Saul, he made havoc of the Church *(it seems he was the leader of this persecution),* entering into every house *(referring to those houses he knew contained followers of Christ),* and haling men and women committed *them* to prison *(he spared no age or gender, but forced them all before magistrates).*

4 Therefore they who were scattered abroad *(refers to a result of the persecution)* went every where preaching the Word *(as stated, the persecution backfired; instead of stopping the "Word" it rather scattered the "Word!"; Satan dreads the preaching of the Gospel by the Anointing of the Holy Spirit, but has no controversy with either ritualism or philanthropy).*

PHILLIP

5 Then Philip went down to the city of Samaria *(should have been translated, "a city of Samaria," which was probably "Sychem;" this was the Philip of Acts 6:5),* and preached Christ unto them *(refers to him proclaiming Jesus as*

the Messiah, God manifest in the flesh, and being raised from the dead; He would not have understood much about the Cross at this particular time; that awaiting the conversion of Paul).

6 And the people with one accord gave heed unto those things which Philip spoke (proclaims a great acceptance of the Gospel), hearing and seeing the miracles which he did (verified the Message he preached).

7 For unclean spirits, crying with loud voice, came out of many who were possessed with them (the Name of Jesus was used to cast out demons): and many taken with palsies, and who were lame, were healed.

8 And there was great joy in that city (when the Message of Christ is accepted, it always brings "great joy").

THE SORCERER

9 But there was a certain man, called Simon, which beforetime in the same city used sorcery (pertained to the practice of the rites of the art of the Magi; it is of Satan), and bewitched the people of Samaria, giving out that himself was some great one (it seemed they believed his claims):

10 To whom they all gave heed, from the least to the greatest (proclaims that all were duped by his sorceries), saying, This man is the great power of God (they attributed his magic and stunts to being done by the Power of God, when in reality it was of Satan; much in the modern Church which claims to be the Power of God falls into the same category).

11 And to him they had regard, because that of long time he had bewitched them with sorceries (the word "bewitched" refers to the fact that the person or persons are deprived of the ability to think or order their thoughts correctly).

12 But when they believed Philip preaching the things concerning the Kingdom of God (they now encountered a Power which was greater than the powers of darkness), and the Name of Jesus Christ (Salvation is in that Name and what it refers to, which speaks of the Cross; the very Name "Jesus" means "Saviour"), they were baptized, both men and women (they were baptized in water after they were saved, not baptized in order to be saved).

13 Then Simon himself believed also (every evidence is that Simon truly gave his heart and life to the Lord Jesus; the word "believed" is used here exactly as it was in the previous Verse, which signifies Salvation [Jn. 3:16; Rom. 10:9-13]): and when he was baptized (plainly informs us that Philip saw enough evidence of Re-

pentance and Faith in Christ that he baptized Simon exactly as he did the others), he continued with Philip, and wondered, beholding the miracles and signs which were done *(he watched carefully what Philip was doing, and noted that there was no trickery involved).*

THE HOLY SPIRIT

14 Now when the Apostles which were at Jerusalem heard that Samaria had received the Word of God *(many had been saved),* they sent unto them Peter and John *(for a reason which we will see):*

15 Who, when they were come down, prayed for them, that they might receive the Holy Spirit *(this was their purpose for coming, and this is how important it is for Believers to be Baptized with the Spirit):*

16 (For as yet He *(the Holy Spirit)* was fallen upon none of them *(evidently Philip had strongly preached Salvation, but had not preached the Baptism with the Holy Spirit):* only they were baptized in the Name of the Lord Jesus.) *(This is meant to infer that they had been baptized in water, but not the Baptism with the Spirit.)*

17 Then laid they *their* hands on them *(presents one of the ways Believers can be Baptized with the*

Spirit, but this is not necessary in order to be filled [Acts 2:4; 10:44-48]), *and they received the Holy Spirit (doesn't give any more information, but we know from Acts 2:4; 10:44-48; 19:1-7 that they also spoke with tongues).*

THE SINFUL PROPOSAL

18 And when Simon saw that through laying on of the Apostles' hands the Holy Spirit was given *(what did he see? he saw and heard them speak with tongues),* he offered them money *(he would not have offered money for the mere laying on of hands),*

19 Saying, Give me also this power, that on whomsoever I lay hands, he may receive the Holy Spirit *(money cannot purchase these Gifts, or anything else of God for that matter).*

20 But Peter said unto him, Your money perish with you, because you have thought that the Gift of God may be purchased with money *(every Preacher must be extra careful that money not be made a part of the equation; God has nothing for sale; everything He has is a "Gift" [Jn. 3:16]).*

21 You have neither part nor lot in this matter *(the word "matter" in the Greek, as it is used here, is "Logos," and means "a word or speech"; Peter is referring to these Believers speaking with other tongues):* for your

heart is not right in the Sight of God (*self-will is the cause of the evil heart*).

22 Repent therefore of this your wickedness (*proclaims just how bad the sin was, but yet that hope is offered*), and pray God, if perhaps the thought of your heart may be forgiven you (*tells us that God Alone could remedy this situation, and He always will upon proper Repentance, which says that He is right and I am wrong*).

23 For I perceive (*refers to the Holy Spirit informing Peter of the exact cause, and not mere symptoms*) that you are in the gall of bitterness (*condition of extreme wickedness*), and in the bond of iniquity (*a bondage of greed for money, power, and control over other men*).

24 Then answered Simon, and said, Pray ye to the Lord for me (*suggests a right attitude on the part of Simon*), that none of these things which you have spoken come upon me (*has reference to him potentially perishing, that is if he remained on that particular course*).

25 And they, when they had testified and preached the Word of the Lord (*they no doubt saw a Church established there*), returned to Jerusalem, and preached the Gospel in many villages of the Samaritans (*on their way to Jerusalem, they preached in many towns and villages, probably taking several weeks to do so*).

PHILIP

26 And the Angel of the Lord spoke unto Philip (*proclaims another mission entirely for Philip, rather than going back to Jerusalem with Peter and John*), saying, Arise, and go toward the south unto the way that goes down from Jerusalem unto Gaza, which is desert (*probably referred to the road that led to the Old Testament Gaza, which was destroyed in 93 B.C.*).

27 And he arose and went (*a distance of approximately one hundred miles; He immediately obeyed*): and, behold, a man of Ethiopia, an Eunuch of great authority under Candace Queen of the Ethiopians (*evidently presents a Gentile who was proselyte to the Covenant of Israel*), who had the charge of all her treasure (*he was the treasurer of that African country*), and had come to Jerusalem for to worship (*could refer to the Feast of Tabernacles, which was held in October; Eusebius says, "He was the very first Gentile to convert to Christ, at least in the Early Church."*),

28 Was returning (*returning to Ethiopia*), and sitting in his chariot read Isaiah the Prophet (*more than likely spoke of a trans-*

lation into Greek).

29 Then the Spirit *(Holy Spirit)* said unto Philip *(the Holy Spirit will lead and guide all who desire such a relationship),* Go near, and join yourself to this chariot.

30 And Philip ran thither to him *(the driver had probably stopped to water the horses),* and heard him read the Prophet Isaiah *(means that he was reading aloud),* and said, Do you understand what you are reading? *(This was perhaps asked because the Holy Spirit told him to ask such a question.)*

31 And he said, How can I, except some man should guide me? *(This is the reason the God-called Preacher is so very important!)* And he desired Philip that he would come up and sit with him *(he wanted Philip to explain the Scripture to him).*

32 The place of the Scripture which he read was this *(as well presents an orchestration carried out by the Holy Spirit),* He was led as a sheep to the slaughter; and like a lamb dumb before his shearer, so opened He not His mouth *(this refers to the Cross and the manner of approach by our Lord to this Sacrifice):*

33 In His humiliation His judgment was taken away *(means that all justice was suspended concerning the trial and Crucifixion of Christ):* and who shall declare His generation? *(This means that the Jewish Sanhedrin had tried to blot out His memory, but with no success at all.)* for His life is taken from the earth *(despite their evil intentions, the Plan of God was carried out to total fulfillment).*

34 And the Eunuch answered Philip, and said, I pray thee, of whom speaks the Prophet this? *(This presents, as will become obvious, a heart hungry for God.)* of himself, or of some other man? *(This presents the correct question, which Philip will answer.)*

35 Then Philip opened his mouth, and began at the same Scripture, and preached unto him Jesus *(refers to Isaiah 53:7-8; He explains to the Ethiopian that the Prophet Isaiah is speaking of Jesus).*

36 And as they went on *their* way, they came unto a certain water *(as they journeyed a little ways, with Philip explaining to him all of this time, they come to a place where there was water; evidently, Philip had explained to him that Water Baptism was the outward sign that Jesus had been accepted in the heart):* and the Eunuch said, See, *here* is water; what does hinder me to be baptized? *(He had accepted Christ, and was now eager to follow the Lord in Water Baptism.)*

37 And Philip said, If you believe with all your heart, you may *(presents the only Scriptural re-*

quirement for Salvation). And he answered and said, I believe that Jesus Christ is the Son of God *(this shows that Philip had explained the Gospel Program to this man very well!)*.

38 And he *(the Ethiopian)* commanded the chariot to stand still: and they went down both into the water, both Philip and the Eunuch *(this tells us that Water Baptism is by immersion, and not by mere sprinkling as taught by some)*; and he *(Philip)* baptized him.

39 And when they were come up out of the water, the Spirit of the Lord caught away Philip *(means exactly what it says)*, that the Eunuch saw him no more *(this would have been quite an experience)*: and he *(the Ethiopian)* went on his way rejoicing *(his trip had been well worthwhile)*.

40 But Philip was found at Azotus *(this was the old Ashdod, situated on the Mediterranean)*: and passing through he preached in all the cities, till he came to Caesarea *(about sixty miles north of Azotus)*.

CHAPTER 9

SAUL

AND Saul, yet breathing out threatenings and slaughter against the Disciples of the Lord *(presents Paul as the Leader of the persecution against the Early Church)*, went unto the High Priest *(if it was A.D. 35, Caiaphas was the High Priest; once again, we see the evil of religion)*,

2 And desired of him letters to Damascus to the Synagogues *(proclaims the persecution led by Paul branching out to other cities)*, that if he found any of this way *(portrays the description of the Early Church [Jn. 14:6; Acts 18:25-26; 19:9, 23; 22:4; 24:14, 22])*, whether they were men or women, he might bring them bound unto Jerusalem *(refers to them appearing before the Sanhedrin, the same group that Crucified Christ)*.

3 And as he journeyed, he came near Damascus *(approximately 175 miles from Jerusalem)*: and suddenly there shined round about him a light from Heaven *(proclaims the appearance of Christ in His Glory)*:

4 And he fell to the earth *(implies that the Power of God knocked him down)*, and heard a voice saying unto him, Saul, Saul, why do you persecute Me? *(To touch one who belongs to the Lord in a negative way is to touch the Lord!)*

5 And he said, Who are You, Lord? *(Paul uses this in the realm of Deity, not merely as respect as some have claimed.)* And the Lord said, I am Jesus Whom you persecute *(presents the Lord using the Name that Paul hated)*: it is hard

for you to kick against the pricks *(has reference to sharp goads, which were placed immediately behind the oxen and were attached to the plow; to kick against it, would cause sharp pain).*

6 And he trembling and astonished said *(he was stupefied and astounded)*, Lord, what will You have me to do? *(This constitutes the moment that Paul was Saved.)* And the Lord *said* unto him, Arise, and go into the city, and it shall be told you what you must do *(pertains to the plan of God for Paul, which in effect would change the world).*

7 And the men which journeyed with him stood speechless *(they were very much aware that something had happened, but they did not know exactly what)*, hearing a voice, but seeing no man *(but Paul saw the Man, and that Man was Christ).*

SAUL BLINDED

8 And Saul arose from the earth; and when his eyes were opened, he saw no man *(it seems that his eyes had been blinded by the Glory of the Lord)*: but they led him by the hand, and brought *him* into Damascus *(Paul, the champion of the persecutors, is now led like the blind man he temporarily is).*

9 And he was three days without sight *(speaks only of the physical sense; in fact, for the very first time he was now able to see)*, and neither did eat nor drink *(presents him fasting three days and nights).*

ANANIAS

10 And there was a certain Disciple at Damascus, named Ananias *(the word "Disciple," as used without exception in the Book of Acts, refers to followers of Christ)*; and to him said the Lord in a vision, Ananias *(he actually saw the Lord, but in Vision form)*. And he said, Behold, I *am* here, Lord *(proclaims an extensive familiarity with the Lord, far beyond the normal).*

11 And the Lord *said* unto him, Arise, and go into the street which is called Straight *(proclaims the street, which still exists even after nearly two thousand years)*, and enquire in the house of Judas for *one* called Saul of Tarsus *(expresses the name of the man who was the most notorious scourge of the followers of Christ in the world of that time)*: for, behold, he prays *(Paul had much to pray about)*,

12 And has seen in a vision a man named Ananias coming in *(proclaims the second Vision that Paul had in a very short period of time)*, and putting *his* hand on him, that he might receive his sight.

13 Then Ananias answered, Lord, I have heard by many of this man (*how empty our fears often are! how ignorant we are of where our chief good lies hid! but God knows; let us trust Him*), how much evil he has done to Your Saints at Jerusalem (*but yet, the Lord has changed this man, and he will become the greatest blessing to the Saints of anyone in history*):

14 And here he has authority from the Chief Priests to bind all who call on Your Name (*Paul's evil intentions had preceded him; but the Lord invaded those intentions, completely changing them*).

15 But the Lord said unto him, Go your way (*presents an urgency which demands instant obedience by Ananias*): for he is a chosen vessel unto Me (*it means, "Divine Selection"*), to bear My Name before the Gentiles, and kings, and the Children of Israel (*"Gentiles" are placed first; that was Paul's principal calling*):

16 For I will show him how great things he must suffer for My Name's sake (*this is altogether different from much of the modern Gospel, which in fact is no Gospel at all!*).

THE HOLY SPIRIT

17 And Ananias went his way, and entered into the house (*he obeyed the Command of the Lord*); and putting his hands on him (*on Paul*) said, Brother Saul (*he addressed Paul in this manner because Paul was already saved, and had been so for the last three days and nights*), the Lord, *even* Jesus, Who appeared unto you in the way as you came, has sent me, that you might receive your sight, and be filled with the Holy Spirit (*this proclaims the fact that one is not Baptized with the Holy Spirit at conversion, as many teach; in fact, the Baptism with the Holy Spirit is a separate work of Grace, which takes place after conversion [Acts 2:4; 8:14-17; 19:1-7]*).

18 And immediately there fell from his eyes as it had been scales: and he received sight forthwith, and arose, and was baptized (*was baptized with water, after he was Baptized with the Holy Spirit*).

PREACHING CHRIST

19 And when he had received meat, he was strengthened (*refers to him ending his three-day fast*). Then was Saul certain days with the Disciples which were at Damascus (*probably means that Ananias introduced him to these followers of Christ; he had come to arrest them, and now he joins them; what a mighty God we serve!*).

20 And straightway *(immediately)* he preached Christ in the Synagogues *(these were the very Synagogues to which letters of the High Priest were addressed, empowering Paul to arrest any Jewish Believers who called upon the Name of Jesus)*, that He is the Son of God *(the first time in Acts that Jesus is referred to by this title)*.

21 But all who heard *him* were amazed, and said; Is not this he who destroyed them which called on this Name in Jerusalem, and came hither for that intent, that he might bring them bound unto the Chief Priests? *(This means that those in the Synagogues had been expecting him, but not what he is now saying.)*

22 But Saul increased the more in strength *(refers to his greater understanding of the Word of God as the days wore on; in fact, for the first time, he understands the Word)*, and confounded the Jews which dwelt at Damascus, proving that this is very Christ *(proving from the Word of God that Jesus was the Messiah)*.

JEWISH LEADERS

23 And after that many days were fulfilled, the Jews took counsel to kill him *(the persecutor is now persecuted)*:

24 But their laying await was known of Saul *(presents Believers informing him of the proposed action of the Jews)*. And they watched the gates day and night to kill him *(which he was informed of as well; therefore, he will escape by a different route)*.

25 Then the Disciples *(followers of Christ)* took him by night, and let *him* down by the wall in a basket.

JERUSALEM

26 And when Saul was come to Jerusalem *(presents his first visit there after his conversion)*, he assayed to join himself to the Disciples: but they were all afraid of him, and believed not that he was a Disciple *(they thought it was a ploy!)*.

27 But Barnabas took him *(presents the same one mentioned in Acts 4:36)*, and brought *him* to the Apostles *(actually only refers to Peter and James, the Lord's brother [Gal. 1:19])*, and declared unto them how he *(Paul)* had seen the Lord in the way *(the Vision on the road to Damascus)*, and that He *(Jesus)* had spoken to him, and how he had preached boldly at Damascus in the Name of Jesus *(Barnabas had heard this report, and now testifies to its veracity)*.

28 And he *(Paul)* was with them *(the Apostles)* coming in and going out at Jerusalem *(probably refers to the approximate fifteen*

days he spent there, most of it with Simon Peter *[Gal. 1:18]*).

29 And he spoke boldly in the Name of the Lord Jesus *(he did this, as is obvious, in the very center or core of Jesus hate)*, and disputed against the Grecians *(he disputed with the Grecian Jews, probably preaching in the very Synagogues in which he had heard Stephen, and maybe even had debated him)*: but they went about to kill him *(presents the same spirit now against him that he had presented against Stephen)*.

30 Which when the brethren knew *(knew about the efforts to kill him)*, they brought him down to Caesarea, and sent him forth to Tarsus *(speaks of his home; as a result, we hear no more of Paul until Acts 11:25)*.

31 Then had the Churches rest throughout all Judaea and Galilee and Samaria *(the attention of the Jews was diverted at this time from the Believers to other things, thereby giving the Churches rest from persecution, at least for a while)*, and were edified *(without interruption, the Lord now builds His house)*; and walking in the fear of the Lord, and in the comfort of the Holy Spirit, were multiplied *(many people were saved)*.

PETER'S MINISTRY

32 And it came to pass, as Pe-ter passed throughout all *quarters (now shifts the attention to this Apostle, and for a reason)*, he came down also to the Saints which dwelt at Lydda *(refers to a town about thirty miles west of Jerusalem)*.

33 And there he found a certain man named Aeneas, which had kept his bed eight years, and was sick of the palsy *(portrays, as is obvious, his helplessness)*.

34 And Peter said unto him, Aeneas, Jesus Christ makes you whole *(refers to Peter staunchly giving Christ the credit for these Miracles)*: arise, and make your bed *(as a token of his Miraculous Cure)*. And he arose immediately *(he was healed instantly, and healed completely)*.

35 And all who dwelt at Lydda and Saron saw him, and turned to the Lord *(the word "all," as it is given in the original Greek, does not necessarily mean every single person in these areas, but rather to those who "saw him," which no doubt numbered many)*.

TABITHA

36 Now there was at Joppa a certain Disciple named Tabitha, which by interpretation is called Dorcas *(it was "Tabitha" in Syrian and "Dorcas" in the Greek; both names mean "a gazelle")*: this woman was full of good works

and almsdeeds which she did *(she was a lady of fine reputation and love for God)*.

37 And it came to pass in those days, that she was sick, and died *(refers to the days in which Peter was at Lydda; her death was unexpected)*: whom when they had washed, they laid *her* in an upper chamber *(it means that they laid her out for viewing)*.

38 And forasmuch as Lydda was near to Joppa, and the Disciples *(followers of Christ)* had heard that Peter was there *(tells us that there was a Church in Joppa)*, they sent unto him two men, desiring *him* that he would not delay to come to them *(it seems that they were expecting a Miracle, irrespective that the woman was dead)*.

39 Then Peter arose and went with them *(indicates that he was led by the Lord to do so)*. When he was come, they brought him into the upper chamber: and all the widows stood by him weeping, and showing the coats and garments which Dorcas made, while she was with them *(seems to indicate that Dorcas was a widow as well!)*.

40 But Peter put them all forth, and kneeled down, and prayed; and turning *him* to the body said, Tabitha, arise *(exactly the same as that said by Jesus when He raised the daughter of Jairus from the dead [Mk. 5:41])*. And she opened her eyes: and when she saw Peter, she sat up *(presents the first person being raised from the dead in the Early Church)*.

41 And he gave her *his* hand, and lifted her up *(a common courtesy)*, and when he had called the Saints and widows, presented her alive *(she is one of few in human history who has actually died, and then come back to tell the story; all who did so were connected with the Lord)*.

42 And it was known throughout all Joppa *(one can well imagine the impact this Miracle had)*; and many believed in the Lord.

43 And it came to pass, that he tarried many days in Joppa with one Simon a tanner *(probably referred to several months; about eight years had passed now since Pentecost, during which time the Gospel had been preached only to the Jews; that is about to change)*.

CHAPTER 10

CORNELIUS

THERE was a certain man in Caesarea called Cornelius *(presents the beginning of one of the great turning points of history)*, a centurion of the band called the Italian *band (in charge of about a hundred men)*,

2 A devout *man (but unsaved!)*,

and one who feared God with all his house *(but unsaved!)*, which gave much alms to the people *(but unsaved!)*, and prayed to God always *(but unsaved! all of these things were wonderful, and certainly noticed by the Lord; but they did not save the man, even as they do not save anyone now; being religious does not constitute Salvation; there must be an acceptance of Christ and His Finished Work, if one is to be saved [Jn. 3:16; Rom. 10:9-10, 13])*.

3 He saw in a vision evidently about the ninth hour of the day *(but which did not save him)* an Angel of God coming in to him *(this as well did not save him!)*, and saying unto him, Cornelius *(the Angel knowing his name did not save him!)*.

4 And when he *(Cornelius)* looked on him *(the Angel)*, he was afraid, and said, What is it, Lord? *(The title "Lord," in the manner in which Cornelius used it, does not refer to Deity, but rather refers to respect or honor.)* And he *(the Angel)* said unto him, Your prayers and your alms are come up for a memorial before God *(a seeking heart will find the Lord)*.

5 And now send men to Joppa *(proclaims the Angel telling Cornelius what to do in order to hear the Gospel, but not presenting the Gospel himself; that privilege is given to man and not to Angels)*, and call for *one* Simon, whose surname is Peter *(through Peter, the Lord will open the door to the Gentile world, for whom Christ died)*:

6 He lodges with one Simon a tanner, whose house is by the sea side *(presents, as should be obvious, the Lord knowing at all times exactly where His people are)*: he shall tell you what you ought to do *(all he had previously done, as commendable as it was, did not save him)*.

7 And when the Angel which spoke unto Cornelius was departed *(signals the beginning of this scenario which will shake the world)*, he called two of his household servants, and a devout soldier of them who waited on him continually *(concerns the three who would go to fetch Peter; it was about thirty-five miles from Caesarea to Joppa)*;

8 And when he had declared all *these* things unto them *(no doubt referred to the visitation by the Angel, and what the Angel had said)*, he sent them to Joppa.

THE VISION

9 On the morrow, as they went on their journey, and drew near unto the city *(probably means that they left Caesarea very shortly after being given instructions by*

Cornelius the day before), Peter went up on the housetop to pray about the sixth hour *(12 noon):*

10 And he became very hungry, and would have eaten *(proclaims that he was about to quit praying and have lunch):* but while they made ready, he fell into a trance *(a state in which one ceases to be aware of surroundings, but sees only what is portrayed to him),*

11 And saw Heaven opened *(before Jesus, Heaven had been closed; due to the Cross, it is now open!),* and a certain vessel descending unto him, as it had been a great sheet knit at the four corners, and let down to the earth *(an object lesson):*

12 Wherein were all manner of fourfooted beasts of the earth, and wild beasts, and creeping things, and fowls of the air *(they all seemed to be unclean animals and fowls as listed in Leviticus, Chpt. 11).*

13 And there came a Voice to him *(proclaims the Lord now speaking to Peter),* Rise, Peter; kill, and eat *(literally says in the Greek Text, "sacrifice and eat").*

14 But Peter said, Not so, Lord *(Peter will now have to be taught a lesson);* for I have never eaten any thing that is common or unclean *(refers to that which is defiled and forbidden by the Law of Moses [Lev. 11; Deut. 14; Mk. 7:2]).*

15 And the voice *spoke* unto him again the second time *(proclaims a correction tended toward Peter by the Lord),* What God has cleansed, *that* call not thou common *(struck at the very heart of present Jewish beliefs; as stated, the Lord is giving Peter an object lesson, proclaiming the fact that what He did on the Cross was for the Gentile world as well as the Jewish world, with Gentiles being symbolized by the unclean animals).*

16 This was done thrice *(meant to impress the significance of what is being said):* and the vessel was received up again into Heaven *(the Vision ended).*

17 Now while Peter doubted in himself what this vision which he had seen should mean *(proclaims that, at this stage, Peter did not actually know what the Lord was telling him),* behold, the men which were sent from Cornelius had made enquiry for Simon's house, and stood before the gate *(he will soon know what the Vision meant, and will understand perfectly what the Lord is telling him),*

18 And called, and asked whether Simon, which was surnamed Peter, were lodged there *(specifies emphatically, so that only Peter would do!).*

19 While Peter thought on the Vision *(trying to understand what the Lord had told him),* the Spirit *(Holy Spirit)* said unto him, Be-

hold, three men seek you.

20 Arise therefore, and get thee down *(pertains to Peter being on the housetop, which in those days, as now, in that area are flat)*, and go with them, doubting nothing *(do not waver or hesitate to obey)*: for I have sent them *(now he will begin to understand what the Lord was telling him)*.

21 Then Peter went down to the men which were sent unto him from Cornelius; and said, Behold, I am he whom you seek: what *is* the cause wherefore you are come? *(The Holy Spirit didn't tell Peter what they wanted or the reason for their coming. He just told Peter to go with them, "doubting nothing.")*

22 And they said, Cornelius the Centurion *(portrays to Peter immediately that this man is a Gentile)*, a just man, and one who fears God, and of good report among all the Nation of the Jews, was warned from God by an Holy Angel to send for you into his house, and to hear words of you *(what Cornelius must hear in order to be saved; Peter had been chosen to deliver to those "Words," and now it was up to Cornelius to "hear them")*.

23 Then called he them in, and lodged *them* *(tells us that Peter now knows what the Vision meant, or at least has a good idea)*. And on the morrow Peter went away with them, and certain brethren from Joppa accompanied him *(six Jewish brethren accompanied him [Acts 11:1-18; 15:7])*.

PETER

24 And the morrow after they entered into Caesarea *(they probably had spent the night at Apollonia, which was about halfway along on the coast road)*. And Cornelius waited for them, and had called together his kinsmen and near friends *(probably was quite a crowd)*.

25 And as Peter was coming in, Cornelius met him *(this meeting probably took place outside the house, at the gate)*, and fell down at his feet, and worshipped *him* *(does not necessarily mean that Cornelius was worshipping Peter, but was merely worshipping, inasmuch as the pronoun "him" was added by the translators)*.

26 But Peter took him up *(better translated, "but Peter raised him up")*, saying, Stand up; I myself also am a man *(he is not to be bowed before or worshipped)*.

27 And as he *(Peter)* talked with him *(portrays Peter putting himself on the same level as Cornelius)*, he went in, and found many who were come together *(implies that they were awe-struck when they saw him)*.

28 And he said unto them, You know how that it is an unlawful thing for a man who is a Jew to

keep company, or come unto one of another nation (*proclaims him relating something that was quite well known by all Gentiles who had resided in Israel for any length of time*); but God has showed me that I should not call any man common or unclean (*tells us that Peter now fully understands what the Vision was all about, concerning the sheet let down from Heaven*).

29 Therefore came I *unto you* without gainsaying, as soon as I was sent for (*means he questioned nothing, but obeyed as the Holy Spirit had told him to*): I ask therefore for what intent you have sent for me? (*This actually pertains to that which he already knew, but wanted to hear from Cornelius.*)

30 And Cornelius said, Four days ago I was fasting until this hour; and at the ninth hour I prayed in my house (*3 p.m.*), and, behold, a man stood before me in bright clothing (*the Angel who radiated with the Presence of God*),

31 And said, Cornelius, your prayer is heard, and your alms are had in remembrance in the sight of God (*God remembers both the bad and the good; in His time, He rewards both accordingly!*).

32 Send therefore to Joppa, and call hither Simon, whose surname is Peter (*second time related, which tells us how important all of this is*); he is lodged in the house of one Simon a tanner by the sea side: who, when he comes, shall speak unto you (*refers to the Way of Salvation made clear by Peter; this signifies that God uses men in this capacity, and not Angels*).

33 Immediately therefore I sent to you (*implies that such was done within the hour*); and you have well done that you are come (*means that they are so very pleased that Peter has come, and that he came as soon as possible*). Now therefore are we all here present before God, to hear all things that are Commanded you of God (*they were ready!*).

THE GENTILES

34 Then Peter opened *his* mouth, and said (*proclaims a profound truth, as simple as it was; the Gospel will now break the bounds of Judaism, despite the efforts of man to do otherwise*), Of a truth I perceive that God is no respecter of persons (*not meant to be implied by Peter that this Truth is new, for it is not [II Sam. 14:14], but up to this time Peter had applied it to Jews only, not Gentiles*):

35 But in every Nation (*the Gospel is for all*) he who fears Him, and works righteousness, is accepted with Him (*the pronoun "Him" refers to Christ; God accepted the Sacrifice of Christ on the Cross, and all who accept Christ and the Cross are accepted with

"Him").

36 The Word which *God* sent unto the Children of Israel, preaching peace by Jesus Christ *(this is justifying Peace, which comes instantly upon the acceptance of Christ)*: (He is Lord of all:) *(Jesus Christ is Lord because He has made Salvation possible for all who will believe [Phil. 2:11])*.

37 That word, *I say,* you know *(refers to the Life, Ministry, Death, Resurrection, and Ascension of Christ)*, which was published throughout all Judaea, and began from Galilee, after the Baptism which John preached *(John introduced Christ)*;

38 How God anointed Jesus of Nazareth with the Holy Spirit and with Power *(as a Man, Christ needed the Holy Spirit, as we certainly do as well! in fact, everything He did was by the Power of the Spirit)*: Who went about doing good *(everything He did was good)*, and healing all who were oppressed of the devil *(only Christ could do this, and Believers can do such only as Christ empowers them by the Spirit)*; for God was with Him *(God is with us only as we are "with Him")*.

39 And we *(the Apostles and others)* are witnesses of all things which He did both in the land of the Jews, and in Jerusalem *(Jerusalem is inferred because it was the center of religious authority;*

so they were without excuse); Whom they slew and hanged on a tree *("they" referred to "the Sanhedrin," the religious leaders of Israel)*:

40 Him God raised up the third day *(Peter is affirming the Resurrection of Christ)*, and showed Him openly *(Jesus revealed Himself after the Resurrection to quite a number of people)*;

41 Not to all the people *(not to all of Israel)*, but unto witnesses chosen before of God *(refers to those who had Faith in Him and Believed)*, *even* to us, who did eat and drink with Him after He rose from the dead *(proclaims that Jesus was not a spirit, or mere apparition, but rather real, physical, and alive)*.

42 And He Commanded us to preach unto the people *(presents God's Way of spreading the Gospel)*, and to testify that it is He which was ordained of God *to be* the Judge of the quick *(living)* and dead *(today Jesus is the Saviour, tomorrow He will be the Judge)*.

43 To Him give all the Prophets witness *(means that He fulfilled all of the Prophecies)*, that through His Name *(His Name Alone)* whosoever *(anyone in the world)* Believes in Him *(Believes in Who and What He has done, referring to the Cross)* shall receive remission of sins *(freedom, deliverance, forgiveness)*.

THE HOLY SPIRIT

44 While Peter yet spoke these words *(concerning Believing in Him)*, the Holy Spirit fell on all them which heard the Word *(even though we are given very little information here, this is the moment when Cornelius and his household accepted Christ, and were saved)*.

45 And they of the Circumcision *(Jews)* which believed *(Believed in Christ)* were astonished *(at what they saw the Lord doing, which could not be denied)*, as many as came with Peter, because that on the Gentiles also was poured out the Gift of the Holy Spirit *(Cornelius and his household were saved, and then moments later Baptized with the Holy Spirit; it was quite a meeting!)*.

46 For they heard them speak with tongues *(this is the initial, physical evidence that one has been Baptized with the Holy Spirit; it always and without exception accompanies the Spirit Baptism)*, and magnify God *(means that some of them would stop speaking in tongues momentarily, and then begin to praise God in their natural language, magnifying His Name)*. Then answered Peter *(presents the Apostle about to take another step)*,

47 Can any man forbid water, that these should not be baptized *(they had accepted Christ and had been Baptized with the Spirit, so now they should be Baptized in Water, which they were)*, which have received the Holy Spirit as well as we? *(Multiple millions of Gentiles since that day have been Baptized with the Holy Spirit.)*

48 And he Commanded them to be baptized in the Name of the Lord *(simply means, "by the Authority of the Lord")*. Then prayed they him to tarry certain days *(which he possibly did!)*.

CHAPTER 11

THE GENTILE QUESTION

AND the Apostles and brethren who were in Judaea *(refers to the Eleven other than Peter, as well as others)* heard that the Gentiles had also received the Word of God *(this type of news travels fast)*.

2 And when Peter was come up to Jerusalem *(presents a time of great significance)*, they who were of the Circumcision *(Jewish Believers)* contended with him *(it means, at least at the outset, that they were not accepting Peter's explanation, feeling he had made himself unclean by associating with Gentiles)*,

3 Saying, you went in to men uncircumcised *(Gentiles)*, and did eat with them *(there is nothing in the Law of Moses which forbids eating with Gentiles; this was an ad-

dition made by men, not God).

PETER'S DEFENSE

4 But Peter rehearsed *the matter* from the beginning *(proclaims the Apostle being very patient, and for cause; if it is to be remembered, the Lord had been patient with him)*, and expounded *it* by order unto them, saying *(portrays him taking the entire episode step-by-step)*,

5 I was in the city of Joppa praying: and in a trance I saw a Vision, A certain vessel descending, as it had been a great sheet, let down from Heaven by four corners; and it came even to me *(proclaims what he saw, and that he knew it was meant for him)*:

6 Upon the which when I had fastened my eyes, I considered, and saw fourfooted beasts of the earth, and wild beasts, and creeping things, and fowls of the air.

7 And I heard a Voice saying unto me, Arise, Peter; kill and eat *(this was not a suggestion, but rather a Command; therefore, intended to be obeyed).*

8 But I said, Not so, Lord: for nothing common or unclean has at any time entered into my mouth.

9 But the Voice answered me again from Heaven *(he didn't see a form, but only heard a Voice)*, What God has cleansed, *that* call not thou common.

10 And this was done three times: and all were drawn up again into Heaven.

GENTILES AND THE GOSPEL

11 And, behold, immediately there were three men already come unto the house where I was, sent from Caesarea unto me.

12 And the Spirit *(Holy Spirit)* bade me go with them, nothing doubting. Moreover these six brethren accompanied me *(he now tells how many went with him)*, and we entered into the man's house *(the house of Cornelius)*:

13 And he showed us how he had seen an Angel in his house, which stood and said unto him, Send men to Joppa, and call for Simon, whose surname is Peter *(all of this proclaims that God works through men)*;

14 Who shall tell you words, whereby you and all your house shall be saved *(proclaims unequivocally that they were not saved before Peter came and preached the Gospel, even though Cornelius had done many good things).*

15 And as I began to speak *(had gotten a little way into the Message)*, the Holy Spirit fell on them, as on us at the beginning *(speaks of Cornelius and his household being Baptized with the Spirit, exactly as the Apostles and others had been on the Day of Pentecost).*

16 Then remembered I the

Word of the Lord, how that He said *(pertains to something that Peter had not mentioned in the actual happening)*, John indeed baptized with water; but you shall be Baptized with the Holy Spirit *(Acts 1:5; Mat. 3:11)*.

17 Forasmuch then as God gave them *(the Gentiles)* the like Gift *(Salvation and the Holy Spirit Baptism)* as He did unto us, who believed on the Lord Jesus Christ *(the requirement)*; what was I, that I could withstand God? *(To not go would be to disobey God.)*

18 When they heard these things, they held their peace, and glorified God *(they not only stifled their own thoughts of opposition, but glorified God as well for what had been done)*, saying, Then has God also to the Gentiles granted Repentance unto Life *(proclaims in no uncertain terms that they were given such "Life" strictly on Faith, which included none of the rituals and Ceremonies of Judaism)*.

ANTIOCH

19 Now they which were scattered abroad upon the persecution that arose about Stephen *(concerns that which happened in Acts, Chpt. 8, about six or seven years before)* travelled as far as Phenice *(Lebanon)*, and Cyprus, and Antioch *(a city of Syria)*, preaching the Word to none but unto the Jews only *(pertained basically to proclaiming Jesus as the Messiah of Israel and the Saviour of the world, and that He had risen from the dead)*.

20 And some of them were men of Cyprus and Cyrene *(implies that they were late comers to Antioch)*, which, when they were come to Antioch, spoke unto the Grecians *(pertains to Gentiles, not Greek-speaking Jews as some claim)*, preaching the Lord Jesus *(indicates that Jews who preached to them were not demanding that they also keep the Law of Moses)*.

21 And the Hand of the Lord was with them *(signifies that God was pleased with the Gospel being preached to these Gentiles)*: and a great number believed, and turned unto the Lord *(they gave their hearts and lives to the Lord Jesus Christ)*.

22 Then tidings of these things came unto the ears of the Church which was in Jerusalem *(which was then the headquarters Church; these "tidings" spoke of good news)*: and they sent forth Barnabas, that he should go as far as Antioch *(Barnabas was the right man! therefore, they were led by the Spirit in sending him)*.

23 Who, when he came, and had seen the Grace of God *(refers to the fact that Barnabas saw the changed lives of these Gentiles)*, was glad, and exhorted them all, that with purpose of heart they

would cleave unto the Lord *(be led by the Holy Spirit)*.

24 For he was a good man *(this is what the Holy Spirit said)*, and full of the Holy Spirit and of Faith *(describes Barnabas in the same manner as Stephen [Acts 6:5])*: and much people was added unto the Lord *(many Jews and Gentiles were coming to Christ)*.

25 Then departed Barnabas to Tarsus, for to seek Saul *(this is one of the single most important Verses in the entirety of the Word of God; the Holy Spirit led him to do this; as well, the Text implies that he had some difficulty in finding Paul; this was around the year A.D. 43, about ten years after the Crucifixion)*:

26 And when he had found him, he brought him unto Antioch. And it came to pass, that a whole year they assembled themselves with the church, and taught much people *(could well signal the beginning of teaching of the New Covenant as it had been given to Paul by Christ)*. And the Disciples were called Christians first in Antioch *(they received the name of "Christians," as followers of Christ, from the outside world and accepted it [Acts 26:28; I Pet. 4:16])*.

27 And in these days came Prophets from Jerusalem unto Antioch *(probably refers to near the conclusion of the year spent by Paul and Barnabas in Antioch at that time)*.

28 And there stood up one of them named Agabus *(proclaims Agabus giving forth a Prophetic Utterance, as he did in Acts 21:10 as well)*, and signified by the Spirit that there should be great drought throughout all the world *(the known world of that day)*: which came to pass in the days of Claudius Caesar *(the Holy Spirit informed them of this for a reason, as we shall see)*.

29 Then the Disciples, every man according to his ability, determined to send relief unto the Brethren which dwelt in Judaea *(there was already great hardship in Jerusalem due to multiple thousands of Believers being excommunicated from the Synagogue, and now this drought added extra strain, as would be obvious)*:

30 Which also they did, and sent it to the Elders by the hands of Barnabas and Saul *(they took the offering to Jerusalem)*.

CHAPTER 12

PERSECUTION

NOW about that time *(pertains to the time Paul and Barnabas went to Jerusalem)* Herod the king *(speaks of Herod Agrippa, the son of Aristobulus, grandson of Herod the Great, who murdered the ba-*

bies of Bethlehem) stretched forth his hands to vex certain of the Church (was probably done to ingratiate himself with the Jewish Leadership).

2 And he killed James the brother of John with the sword (the first of the Apostles to die; no successor for James was ever chosen; in fact, with the exception of Judas who was replaced by Matthias, no others ever followed any of the Twelve in Office; in other words, there is no such thing as Apostolic Succession, as taught by some).

PETER

3 And because he saw it pleased the Jews, he proceeded further to take Peter also. (Then were the days of Unleavened Bread.) (It was the time of the Passover, i.e., April.)

4 And when he had apprehended him, he put him in prison (represents the third time Peter was arrested [Acts 4:3; 5:18-19]), and delivered him to four quaternions of soldiers to keep him (represented sixteen soldiers, four to the watch); intending after Easter to bring him forth to the people (should have been translated, "Intending after Passover . . .").

5 Peter therefore was kept in prison: but prayer was made without ceasing of the Church unto God for him (presents the greatest weapon at the Church's disposal).

6 And when Herod would have brought him forth (Herod had probably spread the word all over Jerusalem that he was going to put on a show, which would be the death of the great Apostle Peter), the same night Peter was sleeping between two soldiers, bound with two chains: and the keepers before the door kept the prison (Peter was sleeping, even though he was supposed to die the next day; he wasn't worried because the Lord had told him that he would not die young, but old [Jn. 21:18]).

THE ANGEL

7 And, behold, the Angel of the Lord came upon him (should have been translated, "An Angel of the Lord"), and a light shined in the prison (meaning there was no doubt this being was "from the Lord"): and he smote Peter on the side, and raised him up, saying, Arise up quickly (simply means that the Angel awakened him). And his chains fell off from his hands (great power!).

8 And the Angel said unto him, Gird yourself, and bind on your sandals. And so he did. And he said unto him, Cast your garment about you, and follow me (speaks of the outer garment, with

Peter now being fully dressed).

9 And he went out, and followed him *(presents Peter doing something, which at the moment he is not certain is real);* and wist not that it was true which was done by the Angel; but thought he saw a Vision *(he had difficulty making the transition to the supernatural; he kept thinking that he was seeing a Vision).*

10 When they were past the first and the second ward *(probably means that Herod had placed Peter in the inner prison; as well, they went through the doors and passed the guards without them knowing what was happening; in some way, the Angel made all of this invisible to these individuals),* they came unto the iron gate that leads unto the city *(pertained to the gate of the Prison);* which opened to them of his own accord *(means that it opened automatically):* and they went out, and passed on through one street; and forthwith the Angel departed from him *(so Miraculous that it actually defies description).*

11 And when Peter was come to himself *(meaning he now knows that this had not been a vision or a dream, but that he had been truly delivered by an Angel),* he said, Now I know of a surety, that the Lord has sent His Angel, and has delivered me out of the hand of Herod *(proclaims Peter giving God all the Glory),* and *from* all the expectation of the people of the Jews *(Herod would be deprived of his show, and all who were expecting to see the bloodletting).*

PETER'S ACCOUNT

12 And when he had considered *the thing,* he came to the house of Mary the mother of John, whose surname was Mark *(the John Mark mentioned here is the one who wrote the Gospel which bears his name);* where many were gathered together praying *(proclaims they were praying for Peter around the clock; most think that Peter was rescued between 3 a.m. and 6 a.m.).*

13 And as Peter knocked at the door of the gate *(not the door to the house, but the gate at the fence that surrounded the house, which was normally kept locked),* a damsel came to hearken, named Rhoda *(pertains to this lady who was a servant in this house, with a part of her duties being to welcome guests).*

14 And when she knew Peter's voice *(tells us that the wall and gate were tall, with her unable to see who was knocking),* she opened not the gate for gladness, but ran in, and told how Peter stood before the gate *(presents her message as being so astounding, as to be unbelievable!).*

15 And they said unto her, You are mad (*in other words, they not only did not believe her, but concluded that she was losing touch with reality*). But she constantly affirmed that it was even so (*pertains to her claim being made with more and more conviction*). Then said they, It is his Angel (*proclaims a belief in that day that all Jews had a Guardian Angel*).

16 But Peter continued knocking (*refers to Peter knocking ever harder*): and when they had opened the door, and saw him, they were astonished (*they were speechless, even to the extent of putting them in a daze*).

17 But he, beckoning unto them with the hand to hold their peace (*they were all speaking to him at one time*), declared unto them how the Lord had brought him out of the prison. And he said, Go show these things unto James, and to the Brethren (*referred to the Lord's half-brother and the Elders of the Church in Jerusalem, plus any other of the Twelve who may have been in Jerusalem at that time*). And he departed, and went into another place (*evidently he didn't tell anyone where he was going*).

HEROD

18 Now as soon as it was day, there was no small stir among the soldiers, what was become of Peter (*losing their prisoner meant certain death for them*).

19 And when Herod had sought for him, and found him not, he examined the keepers (*means that he did not believe their story; it was, in fact, quite a story!*), and commanded that *they* should be put to death. And he went down from Judaea to Caesarea, and *there* abode (*has reference to the fact that he had been embarrassed before the people, not being able to put forth his spectacle concerning Peter; so he left Jerusalem*).

JUDGMENT

20 And Herod was highly displeased with them of Tyre and Sidon (*gives us no clue for the reason of this displeasure*): but they came with one accord to him, and, having made Blastus the king's chamberlain their friend, desired peace (*they tried to make peace with Herod because of some disruption, which history failed to mention*); because their country was nourished by the king's *country* (*pertains to trade agreements regarding food, etc.*).

21 And upon a set day Herod, arrayed in royal apparel, sat upon his throne (*all of this was done with great fanfare and ceremony*), and made an oration unto them (*concerns him speaking with great

pride about the agreement he had just made with Tyre Sidon; he made it appear that he was the saviour of these cities).

22 And the people gave a shout *(means that whatever he was saying greatly pleased them),* saying, It is the voice of a god, and not of a man *(means they kept shouting this over and over!).*

23 And immediately the Angel of the Lord smote him *(may have been the same Angel who delivered Peter),* because he gave not God the glory *(in other words, he accepted the acclamations of the people that he was a "little god"):* and he was eaten of worms *(Josephus said that he lingered for five days with agonizing pains in his stomach),* and gave up the ghost *(he died; this took place A.D. 44).*

24 But the Word of God grew and multiplied *(didn't say the "Church grew," but rather "the Word of God grew . . .").*

25 And Barnabas and Saul returned from Jerusalem *(proclaims such happening, but does not tell us exactly when),* when they had fulfilled *their* Ministry *(speaks of the offerings brought to Jerusalem from the Saints in Antioch, and possibly elsewhere as well),* and took with them John, whose surname was Mark *(Mark would join with them on the very first Missionary Journey).*

CHAPTER 13

FIRST MISSIONARY JOURNEY

NOW there were in the Church that was at Antioch certain Prophets and Teachers *(the Holy Spirit, as we shall see, shifts the emphasis from Jerusalem to this Syrian city);* as Barnabas, and Simeon who was called Niger, and Lucius of Cyrene, and Manaen, which had been brought up with Herod the Tetrarch, and Saul.

2 As they ministered to the Lord, and fasted *(refers to worship),* the Holy Spirit said *(the Holy Spirit still speaks, at least to all who have the right type of relationship, and anyone can who so desires),* Separate Me Barnabas and Saul for the work whereunto I have called them *(expresses a strong Command; in other words, it is not a suggestion; the Lord does the calling, not man).*

CYPRUS

3 And when they had fasted and prayed *(the Early Church was a praying Church; it is a shame that the same cannot be said for the modern Church),* and laid *their* hands on them *(it signified the Blessings of the Church upon Paul and Barnabas),* they sent *them* away *(represents, as far as is known, the very first Missionary trip to new*

places for the expressed purpose of planting new Churches).

4 So they, being sent forth by the Holy Spirit *(presents the Spirit not only calling them, but sending them as well; due to the Cross, the Holy Spirit now has far greater latitude to work within our lives)*, departing unto Seleucia; and from thence they sailed to Cyprus *(represented a journey of approximately one hundred miles; as well, Cyprus was the boyhood home of Barnabas, where he no doubt still had many friends [Acts 4:36])*.

5 And when they were at Salamis *(one of the principal cities on the Island of Cyprus)*, they preached the Word of God in the Synagogues of the Jews *(upon arriving in a new city, Paul would normally first go to the Synagogue and minister; it was the Jew first, and then the Gentile)*: and they had also John to *their* minister *(speaks of John Mark, who wrote one of the Four Gospels which bears his name; he was their helper)*.

6 And when they had gone through the isle unto Paphos *(the Capitol of Cyprus)*, they found a certain sorcerer, a false prophet, a Jew, whose name was Bar-jesus *(this man claimed to be of God, but in reality was of Satan)*:

7 Which was with the deputy of the country, Sergius Paulus, a prudent man *(he had this sorcerer with him; being a pagan, he did* not know the difference between sorcery and that which was legitimately of God)*; who called for Barnabas and Saul, and desired to hear the Word of God *(the news of these men had gotten around)*.

8 But Elymas the sorcerer (for so is his name by interpretation) withstood them *(he saw a threat in Paul and Barnabas)*, seeking to turn away the deputy from the faith *(means that the Governor was believing the Message of Jesus Christ, as presented by Paul and Barnabas)*.

9 Then Saul, (who also is *called* Paul,) *(presents here the change of name; he will be referred to as Paul from now on; "Paul" is the Roman derivative of the Hebrew "Saul")*, filled with the Holy Spirit *(not only speaks of an ongoing state, but seems to imply a special new Anointing)*, set his eyes on him *(did so according to the leading of the Holy Spirit)*,

10 And said, O full of all subtilty and all mischief, *you* child of the devil, *you* enemy of all Righteousness *(this was the Gift of "Discerning of spirits" [I Cor. 12:10])*, will you not cease to pervert the Right Ways of the Lord? *(This glaringly proclaims that this sorcerer who claimed to be of God was not of God at all, but rather of Satan.)*

11 And now, behold, the Hand of the Lord is upon you *(would have been better translated, "is against you")*, and you shall be

blind, not seeing the sun for a season *(there is indication that there was opportunity for Repentance; in other words, it was a remedial chastisement)*. And immediately there fell on him a mist and a darkness *(was used by the Holy Spirit to teach this man that his message was "darkness")*; and he went about seeking some to lead him by the hand *(indicates that he now has no followers due to the fact that he has been shown up for what he truly is, an imposter!)*.

12 Then the deputy, when he saw what was done, believed *(he accepted the Lord Jesus Christ as his Saviour)*, being astonished at the Doctrine of the Lord *(speaks to the fact that this "Doctrine" was not mere rhetoric, but was accompanied by Power as well)*.

13 Now when Paul and his company loosed from Paphos, they came to Perga in Pamphylia *(presents them going back to the mainland from the Island of Cyprus)*: and John departing from them returned to Jerusalem *(speaks of Mark who wrote the Gospel which bears his name; even though the Holy Spirit is silent regarding why Mark did this, we do know that his departure caused hardship on this Missionary Team [Acts 15:37-39])*.

PISIDIA

14 But when they departed from Perga, they came to Antioch in Pisidia *(proclaims an Antioch other than the Antioch of Syria, where the home Church was located [Acts 13:1])*, and went into the Synagogue on the Sabbath Day, and sat down *(has reference to special seats, thus intimating that they were willing to speak if invited, as was the custom in the Synagogue)*.

15 And after the reading of the Law and the Prophets the Rulers of the Synagogue sent unto them *(proclaims the custom)*, saying, *You* men *and* Brethren, if you have any word of exhortation for the people, say on *(as stated, this was generally the manner in which Paul began his Evangelism in any given area; he would first go to the Jewish Synagogue, and then to the Gentiles)*.

SALVATION BY FAITH

16 Then Paul stood up, and beckoning with *his* hand said, Men of Israel, and you who fear God *(Gentiles who attended Jewish Synagogues were given a particular place to sit, and were called "God-fearers")*, give audience *(the gist of Paul's Message is given here, but doesn't go into much detail in the record of later sermons)*.

17 The God of this people of Israel chose our Fathers *(presents Paul beginning his Message much as Steven had years before)*, and

exalted the people when they dwelt as strangers in the land of Egypt, and with an high arm brought He them out of it.

18 And about the time of forty years suffered He their manners in the wilderness (bad manners).

19 And when He had destroyed seven nations in the land of Canaan (referred to the Canaanites, Hittites, Girgashites, Amorites, Havites, Perizzites, and Jebusites), He divided their land to them by lot (speaks of the Urim and Thummim; gave different portions to different Tribes).

20 And after that He gave unto them judges about the space of four hundred and fifty years, until Samuel the Prophet (Samuel was the last Judge, and the first man to stand in the Office of the Prophet).

21 And afterward they desired a king: and God gave unto them Saul the son of Cis, a man of the Tribe of Benjamin, by the space of forty years (meaning that he ruled for forty years).

22 And when He (God) had removed him (removed Saul), He raised up unto them David to be their king (David was meant to be the first king of Israel, but the people jumped the gun, so to speak; they demanded a king and got Saul, which proved to be a disaster); to whom also He gave testimony, and said, I have found David the son of Jesse, a man after Mine own heart, which

shall fulfil all My Will.

23 Of this man's seed (David's seed) has God according to His Promise raised unto Israel a Saviour, Jesus (proclaims the Apostle now introducing the One Who is the Cause and Reason for everything; He is the only "Saviour"):

24 When John had first preached before His coming the Baptism of Repentance to all the people of Israel (the Ministry of John the Baptist).

25 And as John fulfilled his course, he said, Whom think ye that I am? I am not He. But, behold, there comes One after me, Whose shoes of His feet I am not worthy to loose (John bluntly announces the fact that he is not the Messiah, but rather Jesus).

26 Men and Brethren, children of the stock of Abraham (the Jews), and whosoever among you fear God (the Gentiles), to you is the word of this Salvation sent (presents Paul, without apology, including the Gentiles in this great plan of Salvation).

27 For they who dwell at Jerusalem, and their Rulers (pinpoints the murderers of Christ), because they knew Him not (implies a willful ignorance that brought about a willful blindness), nor yet the voices of the Prophets which are read every Sabbath Day (the Prophets told them of Christ, but they would not believe), they have

fulfilled *them* in condemning Him *(Isa., Chpt. 53)*.

28 And though they found no cause of death *in Him (they opposed Him from the very beginning; they heard Him with closed minds, and as a result closed their ears)*, yet desired they Pilate that He should be slain.

29 And when they had fulfilled all that was written of Him *(pertained to that which the Prophets had predicted)*, they took *Him* down from the tree *(speaks of the Cross; if it is to be noticed, both Paul and Peter used the term "tree" regarding the Cross; it is derived from Deuteronomy 21:23)*, and laid *Him* in a sepulchre.

30 But God raised Him from the dead *(as Paul proclaimed the Crucifixion of Jesus, he now proclaims His Resurrection)*:

31 And He was seen many days of them which came up with Him from Galilee to Jerusalem *(concerns a number of appearances over a time span of some forty days)*, who are His witnesses unto the people *(Paul is making the case that there were too many appearances for His Resurrection to be denied)*.

32 And we declare unto you Glad Tidings *(speaks of the Good News of the Gospel, all wrapped up in Christ)*, how that the Promise which was made unto the Fathers *(had its beginnings in Genesis 3:15, and spanned the entirety of Old Testament history)*,

33 God has fulfilled the same unto us their children *(means simply that the Lord did exactly what He had Promised)*, in that He has raised up Jesus again *(the Resurrection)*; as it is also written in the Second Psalm, You are My Son, this day have I begotten You *(refers to the Incarnation when the Second Person of the Divine Trinity took a perfect human body, in order that it would be offered up as Sacrifice to Redeem humanity [Isa. 7:14; 9:6; Phil. 2:5-11])*.

34 And as concerning that He raised Him up from the dead, *now* no more to return to corruption *(this phrase proclaims the fact that Jesus was raised from the dead in greater form than when He went into the abode of death; He died with a regular, although perfect, human body, but was raised with a glorified body)*, He said on this wise, I will give You the sure mercies of David *(actually refers to the Lord Jesus Christ, Who embodies all of these great "Mercies" [Isa. 55:3])*.

35 Wherefore He said also in another *Psalm*, You shall not suffer Your Holy One to see corruption *(refers to Psalms 16:10; this passage, as many others, shoots down the "Jesus died Spiritually Doctrine"; if Jesus had gone to the burning side of Hell when He died, and suffered there for three days and nights as*

some claim, He would definitely have seen corruption; but this He did not do).

36 For David, after he had served his own generation by the Will of God, fell on sleep *(refers to David's death)*, and was laid unto his Fathers, and saw corruption *(this shows that the great Davidic Covenant pertained to the greater son of David, and not David himself)*:

37 But He, Whom God raised again, saw no corruption *(Paul's Message here is very similar to that of Peter in Acts, Chpt. 2).*

38 Be it known unto you therefore, men *and* Brethren, that through this Man is preached unto you the forgiveness of sins *(presents Jesus as having paid the price for man's Redemption, and through Him Alone can be "forgiveness of sins")*:

39 And by Him *(what He did at the Cross)* all who believe *(place our Faith in what He did at the Cross)* are justified from all things *(the Scripture here plainly says, "all things," not just some things)*, from which you could not be justified by the Law of Moses *(dogmatically and without apology sets aside the Law of Moses as being empty of any ability to justify one with God).*

40 Beware therefore, lest that come upon you, which is spoken of in the Prophets *(speaks of the Judgment of God, and plainly says that it will come upon rejecters of Truth)*;

41 Behold, you despisers, and wonder, and perish *([Hab. 1:5] spoke of Israel which rejected Christ, and holds true for all Christ Rejecters, whomever and wherever they might be)*: for I work a work in your days, a work which you shall in no wise believe, though a man declare it unto you *(predicts the unbelief of mankind respecting Jesus Christ as the source of all Salvation).*

42 And when the Jews were gone out of the Synagogue *(indicates that some had gotten angry at Paul's statements)*, the Gentiles besought that these words might be preached to them the next Sabbath *(speaks of those Gentiles referred to as "God-fearers," who were in the Synagogue and heard Paul's Message).*

43 Now when the congregation was broken up, many of the Jews and religious proselytes *(Gentiles who had accepted Judaism)* followed Paul and Barnabas *(wanted to hear more)*: who, speaking to them, persuaded them to continue in the Grace of God *(not only must they accept Christ, they must also continue in Christ).*

OPPOSITION

44 And the next Sabbath Day

came almost the whole city together to hear the Word of God *(during the intervening week, it seems the new converts quickly spread the Message of Grace through Jesus Christ; consequently, there is a great crowd on this particular Sabbath Day to hear the Gospel).*

45 But when the Jews saw the multitudes, they were filled with envy *(they did not expect this large a crowd),* and spoke against those things which were spoken by Paul, contradicting and blaspheming *(the Synagogue leaders were trying to contradict Paul, and blaspheming Christ as well).*

46 Then Paul and Barnabas waxed bold *(this boldness was given to them by the Holy Spirit),* and said, It was necessary that the Word of God should first have been spoken to you *(should be first given to the Jews)*: but seeing you put it from you, and judge yourselves unworthy of Everlasting Life, lo, we turn to the Gentiles *(proclaims a statement of far-reaching magnitude; one might say this was the beginning of Western Civilization).*

47 For so has the Lord Commanded us *(speaks not only of His Personal Call, but of the Prophecy given by Isaiah as well),* saying, I have set you to be a Light of the Gentiles *(is taken from Isaiah 49:6, and refers to the Messiah),* that you should be for Salvation unto the ends of the earth *(the Salvation afforded by Christ is intended for the entirety of the world).*

48 And when the Gentiles heard this, they were glad, and glorified the Word of the Lord *(they knew this meant them, and it brought great joy, even as it should)*: and as many as were ordained to Eternal Life believed *(means that God has appointed and provided Eternal Life for all who will believe [Jn. 3:15-20; Rom. 1:16; 10:9-10; I Tim. 2:4; II Pet. 3:9; Rev. 22:17]).*

49 And the Word of the Lord was published throughout all the region *(it didn't say the Church, or some religious institution, etc., but "the Word of the Lord"; this shows us where the emphasis must be).*

50 But the Jews *(those who opposed the Gospel)* stirred up the devout and Honourable women *(seems to indicate female Gentile Proselytes),* and the Chief men of the city, and raised persecution against Paul and Barnabas *(means that these individuals believed the lies they were told about these two),* and expelled them out of their coasts *(they were not merely requested to leave, but forcibly ejected; there is no evidence of physical violence, but definite evidence that physical violence was threatened).*

51 But they shook off the dust of their feet against them *(presents that which Jesus Commanded*

His Disciples to do under these circumstances [Mat. 10:14; Mk. 6:11; Lk. 9:5; 10:11]), and came unto Iconium *(a city in the southern part of the Roman Province of Galatia)*.

52 And the Disciples were filled with joy *(proclaims the fact that the Holy Spirit informed them that the problem in Antioch was not their fault; this brings them great joy)*, and with the Holy Spirit *(means that the Spirit of God was the Author of this "joy")*.

CHAPTER 14

ICONIUM

AND it came to pass in Iconium, that they went both together *(Paul and Barnabas)* into the Synagogue of the Jews, and so spoke *(presents them continuing with their custom of going to the Jews first)*, that a great multitude both of the Jews and also of the Greeks believed *(they accepted Christ)*.

2 But the unbelieving Jews *(as obvious, some of the Jews didn't believe)* stirred up the Gentiles *(means that these Gentiles were not of the ruling class)*, and made their minds evil affected against the brethren *(the unbelieving Jews used any lie they could tell)*.

3 Long time therefore abode they speaking boldly in the Lord *(the unbelieving Gentiles who were stirred up by the unbelieving Jews*

did not have immediate sway, as those Gentiles in the previous city; so Paul and Barnabas were able to minister there for some weeks)*, which gave testimony unto the Word of His Grace *(this "Grace" speaks of God's unmerited favor in sending Jesus to save us from our sins)*, and granted signs and wonders to be done by their hands *(healings, miracles, and deliverances)*.

4 But the multitude of the city was divided *(though Grace be its keynote, the Message causes dissension and disrupts families, communities and nations)*: and part held with the Jews, and part with the Apostles *(proclaims the extent of this division)*.

5 And when there was an assault made both of the Gentiles, and also of the Jews with their rulers, to use *them* despitefully, and to stone them *(constitutes their plan, but with Paul and Barnabas leaving before it was put into motion)*,

LYSTRA

6 They were ware *(made aware)* of *it*, and fled unto Lystra and Derbe, cities of Lycaonia, and unto the region that lies round about *(doesn't mean that Paul and Barnabas were afraid, but that these were the instructions of the Lord)*:

7 And there *(Lystra and Derbe)* they preached the Gospel *(preach-*

ing is the method chosen by God to reach people, irrespective of their locality or circumstances).

8 And there sat a certain man at Lystra, impotent in his feet, being a cripple from his mother's womb, who never had walked:

9 The same heard Paul speak *(seems that Paul was preaching in the town square)*: who stedfastly beholding him, and perceiving that he had faith to be healed *(presents Paul being drawn to this man by the Holy Spirit, because the man apparently believed what he heard Paul saying about Christ; evidently Paul referred to Christ in his Message, not only as the Saviour, but the Healer as well)*,

10 Said with a loud voice *(Paul spoke loudly)*, Stand upright on your feet *(this was no doubt in front of a great crowd)*. And he leaped and walked *(proclaims him being healed immediately)*.

11 And when the people saw what Paul had done, they lifted up their voices, saying in the speech of Lycaonia *(presents their native language)*, The gods are come down to us in the likeness of men *(Greek Mythology pointed to many gods, and their coming down to Earth in human form)*.

12 And they called Barnabas, Jupiter; and Paul, Mercurius *(presents their two principal gods)*, because he *(Paul)* was the chief speaker.

13 Then the priest of Jupiter, which was before their city *(speaks of the temple of Jupiter, which was constructed just outside the gates)*, brought oxen and garlands unto the gates, and would have done sacrifice with the people *(spoke of offering up the animals and actually worshiping Paul and Barnabas)*.

14 *Which* when the apostles, Barnabas and Paul, heard *of (probably means the people were speaking in their native language, so the Apostles at first did not know what was happening)*, they rent their clothes, and ran in among the people, crying out *(this was to show their disapproval of what was happening)*,

15 And saying, Sirs, why do you these things? *(Why do people in India bathe in the filth of the Ganges River, thinking that such will guarantee them some type of eternal life? Why do many in Africa smear cow dung over their bodies, working themselves into a frenzy as someone beats a drum?)* We also are men of like passions with you *(Paul and Barnabas disavowed the ridiculous claims of these people that they are gods)*, and preach unto you that you should turn from these vanities unto the living God *(other than the Living God Who can only be found through Jesus Christ, all is vanity)*, which made Heaven, and earth, and the sea, and all things that are therein:

16 Who in times past *(before the Cross)* suffered all nations to walk in their own ways *(means that He did not destroy them despite their evil ways, as abominable as they were)*.

17 Nevertheless He left not Himself without witness, in that He did good, and gave us rain from Heaven, and fruitful seasons, filling our hearts with food and gladness *(however powerful Creation may be as a "witness," it is not a Saviour; while it could point men toward God, it within itself could not save men; despite that "witness", they died eternally lost)*.

18 And with these sayings scarce restrained they the people *(the people were still somewhat fearful of not heeding Paul and Barnabas)*, that they had not done sacrifice unto them *(the people were restrained at the last moment)*.

PERSECUTION

19 And there came thither *certain* Jews from Antioch and Iconium, who persuaded the people *(this evidently took place some days after the situation concerning the proposed Sacrifice; these Jews persuaded the people to turn against Paul and Barnabas)*, and, having stoned Paul, drew *him* out of the city, supposing he had been dead *(they considered Paul to be the leader, with Barnabas, it seems,* being spared from the stoning; Paul was near death)*.

20 Howbeit, as the Disciples stood round about him *(speaks of those who had come to Christ in the last few days or weeks)*, he rose up *(indicates that however serious the situation was, there is some evidence that he was instantly healed)*, and came into the city *(means that Paul's detractors had now left, thinking he was dead)*: and the next day he departed with Barnabas to Derbe *(presents a distance of about forty miles)*.

21 And when they had preached the Gospel to that city *(proclaims their Evangelism not slowing at all despite the persecution)*, and had taught many *(preaching had brought them to Christ, and now they needed to be taught)*, they returned again to Lystra, and *to* Iconium, and Antioch *(they were led by the Holy Spirit to go back to these places of their persecution; as such, Satan would not be able to kill them)*,

22 Confirming the souls of the Disciples *(pertained to the new converts in these areas)*, and exhorting them to continue in the Faith *(it is not he who begins, but he who finishes)*, and that we must through much tribulation enter into the Kingdom of God *(quite a different Message than that being presently proposed)*.

23 And when they had ordained them Elders *(Preachers)*

in every Church *(by the help of the Holy Spirit, a Pastor from the local congregation was selected to lead the local flock)*, and had prayed with fasting *(means that Paul, Barnabas, and others sought the Lord earnestly as to His Will in these matters)*, they commended them to the Lord *(seeking the Lord's Blessings on them after the appointment)*, on Whom they believed *(believing that He would lead and guide them, which He did!)*.

THE HOME CHURCH

24 And after they had passed throughout Pisidia, they came to Pamphylia *(Pamphylia is southwest of Pisidia)*.

25 And when they had preached the Word in Perga, they went down into Attalia *(there is no record that they ministered in Attalia)*:

26 And thence sailed to Antioch *(the home Church)*, from whence they had been recommended to the Grace of God for the work which they fulfilled *(the Holy Spirit here says that Paul and Barnabas did exactly what the Lord wanted them to do regarding this Missionary journey)*.

THE REPORT

27 And when they were come, and had gathered the Church together *(at Antioch)*, they rehearsed all that God had done with them *(related it all to the congregation)*, and how He had opened the door of Faith unto the Gentiles *(how receptive the Gentiles were)*.

28 And there *(Antioch, Syria)* they abode long time with the Disciples *(with the congregation, possibly as long as two years)*.

CHAPTER 15

THE COUNCIL

AND certain men which came down from Judaea taught the Brethren *(presents the greatest crisis of the Early Church)*, and said, Except you be circumcised after the manner of Moses, you cannot be Saved *(they were attempting to refute Paul's Message of Grace through Faith; in other words, they were attempting to circumvent the Cross, trying to add the Law of Moses to the Gospel of Grace)*.

2 When therefore Paul and Barnabas had no small dissension and disputation with them *(seems to indicate that these men came to Antioch not long after Paul and Barnabas had returned from their first Missions tour)*, they *(the Elders of the Church at Antioch)* determined that Paul and Barnabas, and certain other of them, should go up to Jerusalem unto the Apostles and Elders

about this question *(no doubt refers to the trip mentioned by Paul in Galatians 2:1-10)*.

3 And being brought on their way by the Church *(means that the Church at Antioch paid the expenses of the Brethren respecting this trip)*, they passed through Phenice and Samaria, declaring the conversion of the Gentiles *(indicates that they stopped to visit Churches all along the way)*: and they caused great joy unto all the Brethren *(seems to indicate that the Judaizers had not brought their false doctrine to these Churches)*.

4 And when they had come to Jerusalem, they were received of the Church *(indicates they were received with open arms)*, and of the Apostles *(refers to the Twelve, minus James the brother of John who had been martyred)* and Elders *(other Preachers)*, and they declared all things that God had done with them *(gave a report of their recent Missions trip)*.

5 But there rose up certain of the sect of the Pharisees which believed *(refers to them as having accepted Christ as their Saviour; they were in the Church at Jerusalem)*, saying, That it was needful to circumcise them, and to command *them* to keep the Law of Moses *(speaking of new converts; this was the great controversy; even though this was a different group, it was the same erroneous message)*.

6 And the Apostles and Elders came together for to consider of this matter *(this was not a closed meeting, but was rather played out before many Believers)*.

PETER

7 And when there had been much disputing *(much questioning and discussion)*, Peter rose up, and said unto them *(portrays the Apostle, at least now and at this particular meeting, in the position of Leadership)*, Men *and* Brethren, you know how that a good while ago God made choice among us, that the Gentiles by my mouth should hear the word of the Gospel, and believe *(harks back some ten to twelve years earlier to Peter's experience with Cornelius [Acts, Chpt. 10])*.

8 And God, Who knows the hearts *(speaks of this action concerning Cornelius being of the Lord and not of Peter)*, bear them witness *(witnessed to the validity of their conversion)*, giving them the Holy Spirit, even as *he* did unto us *(all of this without Circumcision and Law-keeping)*;

9 And put no difference between us and them *(in other words, these Gentiles were just as Saved as Jews, and without all of the Laws of the Jews)*, purifying their hearts by Faith *(Faith in Christ and Faith in Christ alone, not by Law-keeping)*.

10 Now therefore why do you tempt God *(calls into question that which God has done)*, to put a yoke upon the neck of the Disciples *(followers of Christ)*, which neither our Fathers nor we were able to bear? *(Peter was not speaking disparagingly of the Law of Moses, but stating that its demands were beyond the ability of human beings to meet because of man's fallen condition.)*

11 But we *(the Apostles)* believe that through the Grace of the Lord Jesus Christ we shall be Saved *(without Law-keeping)*, even as they *(even as the Gentiles)*.

THE GENTILES

12 Then all the multitude kept silence *(refers to the introduction of both "Barnabas and Paul" to the audience)*, and gave audience to Barnabas and Paul *(Barnabas is listed first because he was known to the Church at Jerusalem; he probably spoke first)*, declaring what miracles and wonders God had wrought among the Gentiles by them *(they simply gave an account, which refers to the fact that Paul and Barnabas preached Grace and Faith to the Gentiles, and didn't preach the Law at all; God honored it by giving them signs and wonders, which would not have been the case had He been displeased)*.

13 And after they had held their peace *(concluding their remarks)*, James answered, saying, Men *and* Brethren, hearken unto me *(presents the Lord's Brother as the presiding Elder of the Church in Jerusalem)*:

14 Simeon has *(Peter)* declared how God at the first did visit the Gentiles *(refers to the conversion of Cornelius and his household)*, to take out of them a people for His Name *(presents this as the Plan of God, which it surely was!)*.

15 And to this agree the words of the Prophets *(James now appeals directly to the Word of God, which verifies all that has been said)*; as it is written *(Amos 9:11)*,

16 After this I will return *(speaks of the Church Age and the Second Coming of the Lord)*, and will build again the Tabernacle of David, which is fallen down; and I will build again the ruins thereof, and I will set it up *(speaks of the restoration of Israel and the coming Kingdom Age, in which all the Prophets declare [Isa. 9:6-7; Dan. 7:13-14; Hos. 3:4-5; Lk. 1:32-33; Rom., Chpts. 9-11; Rev. 11:15; 20:1-10; 22:4-5])*:

17 That the residue of men might seek after the Lord, and all the Gentiles *(a world-wide harvest of souls during the Kingdom Age)*, upon whom My Name is called, saith the Lord *(refers to the Gentile world which has been favorable toward the Lord to a de-*

gree), Who does all these things (refers to the Power of God in performing all of this).

18 Known unto God are all His works from the beginning of the world *(the Plan of God regarding the human family was known from "the beginning of the world" [Gen., Chpt. 4]).*

19 Wherefore my sentence is *(would have been better translated, "I think it good"),* that we trouble not them, which from among the Gentiles are turned to God *(carries the idea that it does not make any sense to demand certain other things of them, claiming such things are needed in order to be saved, when in fact the people are already saved!)*:

20 But that we write unto them, that they abstain from pollutions of idols *(this was common in the heathen world of that day),* and *from* fornication *(all forms of immorality),* and *from* things strangled *(which refers to the blood not being properly drained from the flesh),* and *from* blood *(not to eat blood, which was somewhat common among the heathen during those days; in any case, blood was not to be imbibed, but this did not refer to transfusion; man is saved by the shed Blood of Christ, so blood must be treated accordingly).*

21 For Moses of old time has in every city them who preach him, being read in the Synagogues every Sabbath Day *(the idea is that Gentiles who desire to know more about the Law of Moses need only to go to one of the Synagogues on the Sabbath, which was every Saturday).*

THE DECISION

22 Then pleased it the Apostles and Elders, with the whole Church, to send chosen men of their own company to Antioch with Paul and Barnabas *(proclaims the fact that all of the Church at Jerusalem, or at least the greater majority, totally agreed with what James had said respecting Gentiles and the Law of Moses);* namely, Judas surnamed Barsabas, and Silas, Chief men among the Brethren *(Silas was to play a very important part regarding his help to Paul with respect to future Evangelism):*

23 And they wrote *letters* by them after this manner; The Apostles and Elders and Brethren *send* greeting unto the Brethren which are of the Gentiles in Antioch and Syria and Cilicia:

24 Forasmuch as we have heard, that certain which went out from us have troubled you with words, subverting your souls *(evidently speaks of those mentioned in Verse 1 of this Chapter),* saying, *You must* be circumcised, and keep the Law: to whom we gave no *such* Commandment *(specifies*

exactly what the error was; these individuals, whomever they may have been, were not sent by the Church in Jerusalem, nor were they given any Commandment to teach any type of false doctrine):

25 It seemed good unto us, being assembled with one accord *(proclaims the unity of the Brethren in Jerusalem)*, to send chosen men unto you with our beloved Barnabas and Paul *(places a gracious and kind endearment toward Paul and Barnabas, which spoke volumes as well)*,

26 Men who have hazarded their lives for the Name of our Lord Jesus Christ *(tells us for Whom it was done!).*

27 We have sent therefore Judas and Silas, who shall also tell *you* the same things by mouth *(with these two men accompanying this letter, and verifying its contents, no false prophet could claim that the letter was forged, etc.).*

28 For it seemed good to the Holy Spirit, and to us *(proclaims without a doubt that the Holy Spirit led and guided these proceedings)*, to lay upon you no greater burden than these necessary things *(when men leave the Word of God, they get into a lot of "unnecessary things")*;

29 That you abstain from meats offered to idols, and from blood, and from things strangled, and from fornication: from which if you keep yourselves, you shall do well. Fare ye well.

30 So when they *(possibly six or seven Brethren)* were dismissed *(sent away with great love)*, they came to Antioch: and when they had gathered the multitude together, they delivered the Epistle *(we aren't told how large the Church was in Antioch; however, it could have numbered several hundred; that being the case, they would have met outdoors for this Epistle to be read to them)*:

31 *Which* when they had read, they rejoiced for the consolation *(tells us that the Law/Grace issue had been very serious; now this settles the dispute, at least for the time being).*

32 And Judas and Silas, being Prophets also themselves *(means that they stood in the Office of the Prophet [Eph. 4:11])*, exhorted the Brethren with many words, and confirmed *them (they addressed the multitude with words of great encouragement).*

33 And after they *(Judas and Silas)* had tarried *there* a space, they were let go in peace from the Brethren unto the Apostles *(refers to Judas returning to Jerusalem, but not Silas).*

34 Notwithstanding it pleased Silas to abide there still *(it was the Holy Spirit Who moved on him to remain in Antioch).*

SECOND MISSIONARY JOURNEY

35 Paul also and Barnabas continued in Antioch, teaching and preaching the Word of the Lord, with many others also *(this Church was blessed, to say the least!)*.

36 And some days after *(could have been as much as a year)* Paul said unto Barnabas, Let us go again and visit our Brethren in every city where we have preached the Word of the Lord, *and see* how they do *(refers to the Churches they had planted on the first missionary journey)*.

37 And Barnabas determined to take with them John, whose surname was Mark *(the word "determined" implies a "deliberate action," which means that Barnabas was adamant on the subject)*.

38 But Paul thought not good to take him with them, who departed from them from Pamphylia *(suggests a rupture)*, and went not with them to the work *(he did not go with them to the work to which God called them, as he ought to have done)*.

39 And the contention was so sharp between them *(means to dispute to the point of anger)*, that they departed asunder one from the other *(it created an abrupt and severe rupture; it is my feeling that Barnabas should have acquiesced to Paul; the Holy Spirit* had said "separate Me Barnabas, and Paul for the work where unto I have called them"; the Holy Spirit didn't mention Mark)*: and so Barnabas took Mark, and sailed unto Cyprus *(Barnabas will not be mentioned again in the great Book of Acts, and yet, we dare not take away from the godliness of this man)*;

PAUL AND SILAS

40 And Paul chose Silas, and departed *(proclaims the beginning of the second missionary journey; this is the reason the Holy Spirit had Silas remain behind in Antioch)*, being recommended by the Brethren unto the Grace of God *(he wholeheartedly approved of the great Covenant of Grace, which was absolutely necessary if he was to be of help to Paul)*.

41 And he *(Paul)* went through Syria and Cilicia, confirming the Churches *(teaching in each Church, which obviously was so very much needed)*.

CHAPTER 16

TIMOTHY

THEN came he *(Paul)* to Derbe and Lystra *(the second missionary journey will have a greater effect on civilization than anything that has ever happened, other than* the First Advent of Christ): and, behold, a certain Disciple was there, named Timothy, the son of a certain woman, which was a Jewess, and believed (speaks of Timothy and his mother as being followers of Christ); but his Father was a Greek (it seems he was not a Believer):

2 Which was well reported of by the Brethren who were at Lystra and Iconium (Timothy's consecration is obvious here).

3 Him would Paul have to go forth with him (which was undoubtedly a leading of the Spirit); and took and circumcised him because of the Jews which were in those quarters (this was wisdom on Paul's part, which he felt led by the Holy Spirit to do): for they knew all that his Father was a Greek (Paul would do all he could to appease people, but not at the expense of compromising the Gospel).

4 And as they went through the cities, they delivered them the decrees for to keep, that were ordained of the Apostles and Elders which were at Jerusalem (pertained to copies of the decision concerning the Law/Grace issue, which came out of the Council at Jerusalem).

5 And so were the Churches established in the Faith (Jesus Christ and Him Crucified), and increased in number daily (many were being Saved).

6 Now when they had gone throughout Phrygia and the region of Galatia (implies a time frame of probably several months), and were forbidden of the Holy Spirit to preach the Word in Asia (refers to the area now known as northwestern Turkey; while the Holy Spirit definitely wanted the Gospel to go to this area, there was another place He desired first),

7 After they were come to Mysia, they assayed to go into Bithynia (represented an area east of the Ephesus area): but the Spirit suffered them not (proclaims the door being closed to this area as well!).

8 And they passing by Mysia came down to Troas (this area would be closed for the time being also).

THE MACEDONIAN CALL

9 And a Vision appeared to Paul in the night (proclaims the Holy Spirit now telling the Apostle exactly where He wanted him to go); there stood a man of Macedonia (the northern part of modern Greece, from the Adriatic to the Hebrus River), and prayed him, saying, Come over into Macedonia, and help us (thus was ushered in the most momentous event in the history of the world, the going forth of Paul to take the

Gospel to the nations of the West).

10 And after he had seen the Vision, immediately we endeavored to go into Macedonia *(by the use of the pronoun "we," we know that Luke, the writer of this Book of Acts, now joins Paul here at Troas)*, assuredly gathering that the Lord had called us for to preach the Gospel unto them *(they knew they now had the Mind of the Lord)*.

PHILIPPI

11 Therefore loosing from Troas, we came with a straight course to Samothracia, and the next *day* to Neapolis *(this would be the very first presentation of the Gospel on European soil, which would have such a bearing on what is presently referred to as "Western Civilization")*;

12 And from thence to Philippi, which is the chief city of that part of Macedonia *(Paul's destination)*, and a colony *(was a colony of Rome)*: and we were in that city abiding certain days *(represents tremendous hardships, but a Church was established here)*.

FIRST CONVERT

13 And on the Sabbath we went out of the city by a riverside, where prayer was wont to be made *(evidently meant there was no synagogue in the city; what few Jews were there met by the riverside)*; and we sat down, and spoke unto the women which resorted *thither (seems to tell us that no men were present other than Paul and his party)*.

14 And a certain woman named Lydia, a seller of purple, of the city of Thyatira *(she was a businesswoman)*, which worshipped God *(proclaims her as a Gentile who had probably begun visiting a Jewish Synagogue in Thyatira)*, heard us *(Paul evidently was asked to speak to these women, thus proclaiming the story of Jesus Christ and His Redemption afforded by the Cross of Calvary)*: whose heart the Lord opened *(presents her hungry for God)*, that she attended unto the things which were spoken of Paul *(she gave her heart to Christ, and was thereby the first convert on European soil)*.

15 And when she was baptized *(evidently took place some days later)*, and her household *(refers to the fact that all of those with her accepted the Lord as well, and were baptized)*, she besought *us*, saying, If you have judged me to be faithful to the Lord, come into my house, and abide *there (as well, her house was probably the first Church on European soil)*. And she constrained us *(means they did not acquiesce at first, feeling perhaps that it may be an im-*

position on her; but she would not take no for an answer).

DELIVERANCE

16 And it came to pass, as we went to prayer *(does not tell us exactly where this was, but does specify that it was a certain place, more than likely the home of Lydia),* a certain damsel possessed with a spirit of divination met us *(speaks of the girl being demon possessed),* which brought her masters much gain by soothsaying *(claiming to give advice and counsel from the spirit world, which brought quite a sum of money to her owners):*

17 The same followed Paul and us, and cried, saying *(implies that this went on for some time, possibly several days),* These men are the servants of the Most High God, which show unto us the way of Salvation *(should have been translated, "a way of Salvation," because that's the way it is in the original Text).*

18 And this did she many days *(for some reason, the Holy Spirit didn't give Paul latitude to pray for the girl until now).* But Paul, being grieved, turned and said to the spirit *(addressed himself to the evil spirit, and not directly to the girl),* I command you in the Name of Jesus Christ to come out of her. And he *(the evil spirit)* came out the same hour *(means*

that the spirit came out instantly).

19 And when her masters saw that the hope of their gains was gone *(meaning that the girl could no longer function as she had previously done),* they caught Paul and Silas, and drew *them* into the marketplace unto the Rulers *(these men evidently had some sway with these Rulers),*

20 And brought them to the Magistrates *(pertained to Romans appointed by Rome),* saying, These men, being Jews, do exceedingly trouble our city *(the manner in which the word "Jews" is used implies contempt),*

21 And teach customs, which are not lawful for us to receive, neither to observe *(a gross untruth! actually, Judaism was a legal religion in the Roman Empire; even though Paul and Silas were not actually teaching Judaism, but rather proclaiming Jesus, still the Romans would not have been able to distinguish the difference),* being Romans *(implying superiority).*

22 And the multitude rose up together against them *(presents a stacked audience against Paul and Silas):* and the Magistrates rent off their clothes *(took off Paul and Silas' clothes, at least to the waist),* and commanded to beat *them* *(Paul recalls this in First Thessalonians 2:2; scourging under Roman Law was a most brutal and cruel punishment).*

23 And when they had laid many stripes upon them (*the lectors were egged on by the mob, with the Apostles being beaten almost to death*), they cast *them* into prison (*prisons then were far worse than anything we can now imagine*), charging the jailor to keep them safely (*contains the implication that Paul and Silas were desperados*):

24 Who, having received such a charge (*means that he could punish them even more if he so desired, which he did*), thrust them into the inner prison (*reserved for the most violent of criminals*), and made their feet fast in the stocks (*the legs were pulled wide apart, with the individual laying on their back on the floor; after a short time, the muscles in the legs would begin to constrict, causing severe pain*).

THE CONVERSION

25 And at midnight Paul and Silas prayed (*doesn't mean they began to pray at midnight, but rather that they were still praying at midnight having begun some time earlier*), and sang praises unto God (*the Greek Text suggests that bursts of song broke out from time to time as they prayed; their song was probably one of the Psalms*): and the prisoners heard them (*means they prayed and sang so loud that other prisoners heard them*).

26 And suddenly there was a great earthquake (*this was no ordinary earthquake*), so that the foundations of the prison were shaken (*presents the Lord as the Instigator of this upheaval, not a normal force of nature*): and immediately all the doors were opened, and every one's bands were loosed (*this implies no normal earthquake, but rather something supernatural*).

27 And the keeper of the prison awaking out of his sleep, and seeing the prison doors open (*automatically causes him to assume that all the prisoners had fled*), he drew out his sword, and would have killed himself, supposing that the prisoners had been fled (*meaning that under the penalty of death, he was responsible for the prisoners*).

28 But Paul cried with a loud voice (*Paul sees what the jailer is about to do to himself*), saying, Do yourself no harm: for we are all here (*tells us that none of the prisoners, ever how many there were, took the opportunity to escape; this also tells us that quite possibly some, if not all, had given their hearts to the Lord*).

29 Then he called for a light, and sprang in, and came trembling (*proclaims that something powerful was happening to this man, over and above the shock of the*

earthquake and his thoughts of suicide), and fell down before Paul and Silas (the jailer treated Paul with great brutality, but Paul treated him with great humanity),

30 And brought them out (brought Paul and Silas out of the prison), and said, Sirs, what must I do to be Saved? (This presents terminology that shows some familiarity with the Gospel; quite possibly before the arrest of the Apostle, the jailer had heard him preach)

31 And they said, Believe on the Lord Jesus Christ, and you shall be Saved (presents the most beautiful explanation of Salvation that could ever be given), and your house (means that Salvation is not limited merely to the jailer, but is available to the entirety of his family as well, that is if they will meet the conditions of Faith in Christ required of them).

32 And they spoke unto him the Word of the Lord (pertained to a fleshing out of the answer given in the previous Verse, explaining what believing in Christ really meant), and to all that were in his house (presents this service being conducted sometime after midnight, which resulted in all of his family giving their hearts to Christ; what a beautiful night it turned out to be!).

33 And he (the jailer) took them (Paul and Silas) the same hour of the night, and washed their stripes (speaks of the terrible beating they had suffered a short time before); and was baptized, he and all his, straightway (immediately).

34 And when he had brought them into his house, he set meat before them (proclaims, as obvious, a meal prepared for them), and rejoiced, believing in God with all his house (a night of misery turned into a night of great joy, and joy which would last forever for this jailer and his family).

THE MAGISTRATES

35 And when it was day, the Magistrates sent the serjeants (probably refers to the same men who had administered the beating to Paul and Silas), saying, Let those men go (the Codex Bezae says that the Magistrates came into Court that morning feeling that their treatment of Paul and Silas had brought on the earthquake; they were right!).

36 And the keeper of the prison told this saying to Paul, The Magistrates have sent to let you go: now therefore depart, and go in peace.

37 But Paul said unto them, They have beaten us openly uncondemned, being Romans (presents a scenario which puts an entirely different complexion on the matter; it was against Roman

Law for Romans to be beaten; so, in beating them, the Magistrates had broken the law, evidently not realizing they were Romans), and have cast *us* into prison; and now do they thrust us out privily? *(They were treated as common criminals.)* No verily; but let them come themselves and fetch us out *(in this way, the city of Philippi would know that the charges were false)*.

38 And the serjeants told these words unto the Magistrates: and they feared, when they heard that they were Romans *(if Paul and Silas so desired, they could have brought charges against these individuals, which could have resulted in severe consequences)*.

39 And they came and besought them, and brought *them* out *(refers to the fact that the "Magistrates" now came to Paul and Silas)*, and desired *them* to depart out of the city *(has reference to the fact that they were pleading with the Apostles not to bring charges against them, but rather depart in peace)*.

40 And they went out of the prison, and entered into *the house of* Lydia *(they were somewhat the worse for wear in the physical sense, but greatly encouraged in the spiritual sense)*: and when they had seen the Brethren, they comforted them, and departed *(these were new converts in the Philippian Church)*.

CHAPTER 17

THESSALONICA

NOW when they had passed through Amphipolis and Apollonia, they came to Thessalonica *(presents Paul's destination evidently directed here by the Holy Spirit)*, where was a synagogue of the Jews *(presents Paul once again taking the Gospel first of all to the Jews)*:

2 And Paul, as his manner was, went in unto them *(should have been translated, "as his custom was")*, and three Sabbath Days reasoned with them out of the Scriptures *(the Old Testament, and concerning Christ)*,

3 Opening and alleging *(to expound and present)*, that Christ must needs have suffered *(had to go to the Cross in order that all sin might be atoned [Gen. 3:15; Ex. 12:13; Isa., Chpt. 53])*, and risen again from the dead *(Lev. 14:1-7; Ps. 16:10)*; and that this Jesus, whom I preach unto you, is Christ *(is the Messiah, the One pointed to in the Scriptures)*.

4 And some of them believed *(some Jews)*, and consorted with Paul and Silas *(wanted to hear more about Jesus)*; and of the devout Greeks a great multitude *(many Gentiles were Saved)*, and

of the chief women not a few *(could have referred to the wives of some of the Civil Rulers in the city, or at least wives of influential men).*

5 But the Jews which believed not, moved with envy *(presents a perfect example of religious people who refuse the Light of the Gospel, and then set about to stop the propagation of that Light)*, took unto them certain lewd fellows of the baser sort, and gathered a company, and set all the city on an uproar *(presents these Jews as being unable to Scripturally counter Paul's Message, so they now resort to other measures)*, and assaulted the house of Jason, and sought to bring them out to the people *(evidently refers to where Paul and his associates were staying)*.

6 And when they found them not *(evidently Paul and Silas were not there at the time)*, they drew Jason and certain Brethren unto the Rulers of the city *(proclaims the mob determined to take their anger out on someone, if not Paul!)*, crying, These who have turned the world upside down are come hither also *(tells us that the Jews had prepped certain people in this mob thoroughly)*;

7 Whom Jason has received *(charges Jason as being a part of the alleged conspiracy)*: and these all do contrary to the decrees of Caesar, saying that there is another King, *One* Jesus *(presents that which is blatantly false, and the Jews knew it was false).*

8 And they troubled the people and the Rulers of the city, when they heard these things *(by their lies, they created a commotion).*

9 And when they had taken security of Jason *(probably means that Jason put up a security bond of some sorts)*, and of the other *(probably refers to a guarantee on the part of Jason and others that Paul and his party would leave the city, even though they were not to blame)*, they let them go *(implies that the authorities were now satisfied).*

BEREA

10 And the Brethren immediately sent away Paul and Silas by night unto Berea *(this town is about fifty miles from Thessalonica; they left by night, because to remain longer could have caused more problems)*: who coming thither went into the Synagogue of the Jews *(presents, as stated, Paul's custom, but which this time will turn out better, for a change).*

11 These were more noble than those in Thessalonica *(we now learn God's definition of "noble")*, in that they received the Word with all readiness of mind *(this is the meaning of the word "noble")*, and searched the Scriptures daily,

whether those things were so *(tells us why they so eagerly accepted the Message of Jesus Christ)*.

12 Therefore many of them believed *(speaks of Jews who accepted Christ as Saviour)*; also of Honourable women which were Greeks, and of men, not a few *(speaks of Gentiles who had been attending the Jewish Synagogue, and as well, accepted Christ)*.

13 But when the Jews of Thessalonica had knowledge that the Word of God was preached of Paul at Berea *(these Jews in Thessalonica, not content with what they had done in their city, now attempt to stop that which is happening in Berea)*, they came thither also, and stirred up the people *(shows how effective a lie can be)*.

14 And then immediately the Brethren sent away Paul to go as it were to the Sea *(speaks of the Aegean, which was about seventeen miles from Berea)*: but Silas and Timotheus abode there still *(remained in Berea)*.

15 And they who conducted Paul brought him unto Athens *(presents the chief city of Greece, famed for its learning)*: and receiving a commandment unto Silas and Timotheus for to come to him with all speed, they departed *(Paul sends the Message back with these men that Silas and Timothy are to come to Athens as soon as possible)*.

ATHENS

16 Now while Paul waited for them at Athens, his spirit was stirred in him, when he saw the city wholly given to idolatry *(means it was full of idols)*.

17 Therefore disputed he in the synagogue with the Jews *(from the Scriptures, he would preach Jesus; the Scriptures then, at least as far as the Jews were concerned, were the Old Testament)*, and with the devout persons *(singles out the Jews who really seemed to be devoted to the Scriptures)*, and in the market daily with them that met with him *(this was a place in Athens, where speakers generally gave forth)*.

18 Then certain philosophers of the Epicureans *(those who claimed that gratification of the appetites and pleasures was the only end in life)*, and of the Stoics *(they taught that man was not to be moved by either joy or grief)*, encountered him *(challenged his statements about Christ)*. And some said, What will this babbler say? *(This presents the highest insult of which they could think.)* other some, He seems to be a setter forth of strange gods *(in their minds, anything outside of Greek philosophy was of no consequence)*: because he preached unto them Jesus, and the Resurrection *(they didn't want a Resur-*

rection, simply because they did not desire the idea of living this life over again; this shows they totally misunderstood what Paul said).

19 And they took him, and brought him unto Areopagus (refers to Mars Hill which faces the Acropolis; this was the Supreme Court of Athens), saying, May we know what this new doctrine, whereof you speak, is? (This presents Paul facing this Supreme Court Justices' of Athens.)

20 For you bring certain strange things to our ears (it's strange that those who brought Paul to this place labeled what he said as mere babblings, but yet think it important enough to be taken to the highest Court in Athens): we would know therefore what these things mean (presents a noble request to Paul, and an unparalleled opportunity).

21 (For all the Athenians and strangers which were there spent their time in nothing else, but either to tell, or to hear some new thing.) (With the great philosophers now dead, Athens was attempting to live off the glory of former times.)

MARS' HILL

22 Then Paul stood in the midst of Mars' hill, and said, You men of Athens, I perceive that in all things you are too supersti-tious (in this one sentence, he debunks all of their philosophies; they are guided by superstition, which is no way to live).

23 For as I passed by, and beheld your devotions (has reference to their objects of worship), I found an altar with this inscription, TO THE UNKNOWN GOD (by addressing the situation in this way, he could not be accused of preaching a foreign god to them). Whom therefore you ignorantly worship, Him declare I unto you (refers to them acknowledging that maybe they did not have the last word on gods! actually, they did not have any word at all).

24 God Who made the world and all things therein (presents God as the Creator), seeing that he is Lord of Heaven and earth (proclaims Him not only as Creator, but the constant Manager of all that He has created as well), dwells not in Temples made with hands (He is bigger than that!);

25 Neither is worshipped with men's hands (the Second Commandment forbids the making of any graven image of God, or the worship of any type of statue, etc.), as though He needed any thing (God needs nothing!), seeing He gives to all life, and breath, and all things (presents His Creation needing what He provides, which is provided by no other source);

26 And has made of one blood

all nations of men for to dwell on all the face of the Earth *(proclaims all having their origin in Adam)*, and has determined the times before appointed, and the bounds of their habitation *(pertains to particular parts of the world, and those who occupy these areas; however, the statement, "one blood all nations of men," eliminates any type of racial superiority)*;

27 That they should seek the Lord *(presents the chief end of all God's dealings with men [I Pet. 2:24; II Pet. 3:9; Jn. 3:15-20; Rev. 22:17])*, if haply they might feel after Him, and find Him *(Paul is appealing to the action of logic and common sense in trying to address these Pagans)*, though He be not far from every one of us *(speaks of the Creator being very close to His Creation)*:

28 For in Him we live, and move, and have our being *(proclaims God as the source of all life [Heb. 1:3])*; as certain also of your own poets have said, For we are also His offspring *(presents a direct quote from Aratus of Tarsus, Paul's own country)*.

29 Forasmuch then as we are the offspring of God *(is offered by Paul in the sense of Creation; it does not mean the "Fatherhood of God, and the Brotherhood of Man," as many contend)*, we ought not to think that the Godhead is like unto gold, or silver, or stone,

graven by art and man's device *(Paul is saying that God is not a device of man, as all the Greek gods in fact were)*.

30 And the times of this ignorance God winked at *(does not reflect that such ignorance was Salvation, for it was not! before the Cross, there was very little Light in the world, so God withheld Judgment)*; but now commands all men every where to repent *(but since the Cross, the "Way" is open to all; it's up to us Believers to make that "Way" known to all men)*:

31 Because He has appointed a day *(refers to the coming of the Great White Throne Judgment [Rev. 20:11-15])*, in the which He will Judge the world in Righteousness by *that* Man Whom He has ordained *(this Righteousness is exclusively in Christ Jesus and what He has done for us at the Cross, and can be gained only by Faith in Him [Eph. 2:8-9; Rom. 10:9-10,13; Rev. 22:17])*; whereof He has given assurance unto all *men*, in that He has raised Him from the dead *(refers to the Resurrection ratifying that which was done at Calvary, and is applicable to all men, at least all who will believe!)*.

32 And when they heard of the Resurrection of the Dead, some mocked *(the "mocking" was caused by sheer unbelief)*: and others said, We will hear you again of this matter *(many were touched by*

Paul's Message, but regrettably procrastinated).

33 So Paul departed from among them (they ascertained that he had broken none of their laws, so he was free to go, which he did!).

34 Howbeit certain men clave unto him, and believed (these believed wholeheartedly, recognizing in Paul the true Words of Life): among the which was Dionysius the Areopagite (he was a member of the Great Court of Athens; tradition says that he became the Pastor of the Church in Athens), and a woman named Damaris (a person of prominence), and others with them.

CHAPTER 18

CORINTH

AFTER these things Paul departed from Athens (seems to imply that he departed alone, with Silas and Timothy joining him later at Corinth), and came to Corinth (one of the great cities of the Roman Empire);

2 And found a certain Jew named Aquila, born in Pontus, lately come from Italy, with his wife Priscilla (pertains to a husband and wife who became very close friends to Paul); (because that Claudius had commanded all Jews to depart from Rome:) (believed to have occurred in about A.D. 49 or 50) and came unto them (Paul came to them).

3 And because he was of the same craft, he abode with them, and wrought (evidently means that Paul had inquired concerning those involved in this occupation): for by their occupation they were tentmakers (tentmakers wove the black cloth of goat or camel's hair with which tents were made).

4 And he reasoned in the synagogue every Sabbath (preached Christ from the Old Testament), and persuaded the Jews and the Greeks (his argument was ironclad).

SILAS AND TIMOTHY

5 And when Silas and Timothy were come from Macedonia (probably means that Silas had come from Berea, with Timothy coming from Thessalonica; Macedonia was a Province which included both places), Paul was pressed in the spirit, and testified to the Jews that Jesus was Christ (the Holy Spirit told him to bear down even harder!).

6 And when they opposed themselves, and blasphemed (proclaims the response of some of these Jews to the Paul's claim that Christ was the Messiah), he shook his raiment, and said unto them, Your blood be upon your own heads; I am clean (in other words,

he had delivered his soul): from henceforth I will go unto the Gentiles (does not mean that he would no longer minister to Jews if given the opportunity, which he did do at Ephesus [Acts 19:8], but that the thrust would be toward the Gentiles).

THE HOUSE

7 And he departed thence (out of the synagogue), and entered into a certain man's house (a meeting place for Church), named Justus, one who worshipped God, whose house joined hard to the synagogue (evidently points to Justus in the recent past as having accepted Christ under Paul's Ministry).

8 And Crispus, the Chief Ruler of the synagogue, believed on the Lord with all his house (this must have been galling to the Jews to have their Chief Ruler of the synagogue converted to Christ); and many of the Corinthians hearing believed, and were baptized (speaks of many Gentiles now being Saved).

9 Then spoke the Lord to Paul in the night by a Vision (does not clarify whether Paul saw the Lord, or only heard Him speak, it being a "Vision" implies that he was awake), Be not afraid, but speak, and hold not your peace (there evidently was fear in Paul's heart regarding the tremendous opposition against him; he was told by the Lord to speak with boldness):

10 For I am with you, and no man shall set on you to hurt you (speaks to the idea that Paul had threats on his life, threats which were not empty, but rather deadly serious): for I have much people in this city (concerns the great Church which will be raised up at Corinth).

11 And he continued there a year and six months, teaching the Word of God among them (records the longest time that Paul spent in any place other than Ephesus, where he spent some three years).

12 And when Gallio was the deputy of Achaia (it is believed that he was Proconsul in A.D. 52-53), the Jews made insurrection with one accord against Paul, and brought him to the judgment seat (Jews had no power to punish any person in a Roman Province, so they were obliged to bring Paul before the Roman Governor),

13 Saying, This fellow persuades men to worship God contrary to the Law (does not pertain to Roman Law as some claim, but rather the Law of Moses).

14 And when Paul was now about to open his mouth (refers to him waiting for his accusers to cease their tirade against him), Gallio said unto the Jews (proclaims the Proconsul interrupting

Paul), If it were a matter of wrong or wicked lewdness, O *you* Jews, reason would that I should bear with you *(proclaims the Governor putting everything in its proper perspective immediately!)*:

15 But if it be a question of words and names, and *of* your Law, look ye *to it (in effect tells them to settle this thing themselves because it had no place in a Roman Court); for I will be no judge of such matters (in essence says, "you will not use a Roman Court to carry forth your personal schemes!")*.

16 And he drove them from the judgment seat *(implies the humiliating dismissal of the case, without even being tried or further heard)*.

17 Then all the Greeks took Sosthenes, the Chief Ruler of the synagogue *(presents the man who took the place of Crispus, with the latter having given his heart to the Lord)*, and beat *him* before the judgment seat *(gives us little clue as to why this was done, unless they had refused to dissemble)*. And Gallio cared for none of those things *(means that he considered the whole matter outside his jurisdiction)*.

EPHESUS

18 And Paul *after this* tarried *there* yet a good while *(could have referred to several months)*, and then took his leave of the Brethren *(was done strictly according to the timing of the Lord)*, and sailed thence into Syria, and with him Priscilla and Aquila *(they had now become fast friends of Paul)*; having shorn *his* head in Cenchrea: for he had a vow *(Cenchrea was the Port of Corinth; there was a Church there as well; we aren't told what this "vow" was)*.

19 And he came to Ephesus *(Ephesus was the most important city in the Roman Province of Asia)*, and left them there *(has to do with Priscilla and Acquila remaining in Ephesus when Paul left some days later)*: but he himself entered into the synagogue, and reasoned with the Jews *(has no reference to the previous phrase; no doubt, Priscilla and Acquila were with him during this meeting)*.

20 When they *(the Jews in the Synagogue)* desired *him* to tarry longer time with them, he consented not *(Paul left, but Priscilla and Acquila remained, and no doubt continued teaching these Jews about Christ)*;

ANTIOCH

21 But bade them farewell *(speaks of Priscilla and Acquila, and possibly some few Jews who had accepted Christ)*, saying, I must by all means keep this Feast that comes in Jerusalem *(probably was*

the Passover): but I will return again unto you, if God will *(portrays the manner in which all Believers should conduct everything)*. And he sailed from Ephesus *(places him on his way to Jerusalem)*.

22 And when he had landed at Caesarea *(puts him about sixty-five miles northwest of Jerusalem)*, and gone up, and saluted the Church *(refers to the Mother Church at Jerusalem)*, he went down to Antioch *(refers to Antioch, Syria)*.

THIRD MISSIONARY JOURNEY

23 And after he had spent some time *there*, he departed *(portrays the beginning of his Third Missionary Journey)*, and went over *all* the country of Galatia and Phrygia in order, strengthening all the Disciples *(probably lasted about six months; it is believed that Timothy, Erastus, Gaius, and Aristarchus may have been traveling with Paul at this time; Titus may have been included as well)*.

APOLLOS

24 And a certain Jew named Apollos, born at Alexandria, an eloquent man, *and* mighty in the Scriptures, came to Ephesus *(introduces a man whom Paul came to hold in high esteem)*.

25 This man was instructed in the Way of the Lord *(however, his knowledge was greatly limited respecting Grace and the Baptism with the Holy Spirit)*; and being fervent in the spirit *(spoke of his own spirit and not the Holy Spirit)*, he spoke and taught diligently the things of the Lord, knowing only the Baptism of John *(speaks of Repentance and Water Baptism)*.

26 And he began to speak boldly in the Synagogue: whom when Aquila and Priscilla had heard *(presents that which was all in the providence of God)*, they took him unto *them*, and expounded unto him the Way of God more perfectly *(no doubt pertained to the full complement of Salvation by the Grace of God exclusively, correct Water Baptism, and the Baptism with the Holy Spirit with the evidence of speaking with other Tongues)*.

27 And when he *(Apollos)* was disposed to pass into Achaia *(refers to Greece, across the Aegean Sea, and Corinth in particular)*, the Brethren wrote, exhorting the Disciples to receive him: who, when he was come, helped them much which had believed through Grace *(he is now proficient in this most excellent Message of the Grace of God that comes through the Cross)*:

28 For he mightily convinced the Jews, *and that* publickly, showing by the Scriptures that Jesus

was Christ *(had reference more than likely to ministering in their Synagogue).*

CHAPTER 19

EPHESUS

AND it came to pass, that, while Apollos was at Corinth *(pertains to Acts 18:27)*, Paul having passed through the upper coasts came to Ephesus *(refers back to Acts 18:23)*: and finding certain Disciples *(they were followers of Christ, but deficient in their understanding)*,

2 He said unto them, Have you received the Holy Spirit since you believed? *(In the Greek, this is literally, "having believed, did you receive?" We know these men were already Saved because every time the word "Disciples" is used in the Book of Acts, it refers to individuals who have accepted Christ. Paul could tell that these individuals, although Saved, had not yet been baptized with the Holy Spirit.)* And they said unto him, We have not so much as heard whether there be any Holy Spirit *(doesn't mean that they didn't know of the existence of the Holy Spirit, but they were not aware that the Age of the Spirit had come, and that Believers could literally be baptized with Him; at Salvation, the Holy Spirit baptizes Believing* sinners into Christ; at the Spirit Baptism, Jesus baptizes Believers into the Holy Spirit [Mat. 3:11]).*

3 And he said unto them, Unto what then were you baptized? *(After asking about the Holy Spirit Baptism, Paul was met with a blank stare, so to speak.)* And they said, Unto John's Baptism *(this was the Baptism of Repentance).*

4 Then said Paul, John verily baptized with the Baptism of Repentance *(which in effect was all that could be done at that particular time)*, saying unto the people, that they should believe on Him which should come after him, that is, on Christ Jesus *(proclaims John the Baptist lifting up Jesus as the Saviour of mankind).*

5 When they heard *this (no doubt, Paul said much more; however, the evidence is they instantly believed and accepted what Paul said, and they then desired what he said)*, they were baptized in the name of the Lord Jesus *(means, "by the authority of the Lord Jesus"; the only Baptismal formula in the Word of God is Mat. 28:19).*

6 And when Paul had laid *his* hands upon them *(constitutes a Biblical principle [Acts 8:17; 9:17-18])*, the Holy Spirit came on them *(refers to them being Baptized with the Holy Spirit)*; and they spoke with tongues, and prophesied *(proclaims Tongues as*

the initial physical evidence that one has been Baptized with the Holy Spirit; sometimes there is Prophesying at that time, and sometimes not [Acts 8:17; 9:17; 10:46]).

7 And all the men were about twelve (it seems that no women were involved at this particular time).

THE SYNAGOGUE

8 And he (Paul) went into the Synagogue, and spoke boldly for the space of three months (it seems that he lasted longer here than he had in most Synagogues), disputing and persuading the things concerning the Kingdom of God (he would have brought reasonable proofs from the Old Testament Scriptures to show that the Kingdom [ruled authority] of God is revealed in Jesus, Who is now Ascended to the Right Hand of the Father and seated at the Father's Throne [Acts 2:30-33]).

THE CHURCH

9 But when divers were hardened, and believed not, but spoke evil of that way before the multitude (they rebelled against the Gospel of Christ), he departed from them, and separated the Disciples (proclaims the break with the Synagogue), disputing daily in the school of one Tyrannus (is thought to be the Lecture Hall of a Greek Philosopher).

10 And this continued by the space of two years (probably referred to most every night and, at times, during the day as well; he spent a total of three years in Ephesus [Acts 20:31]); so that all they which dwelt in Asia heard the Word of the Lord Jesus, both Jews and Greeks (does not refer to every single person, but rather to people from all walks of life, and from all surrounding areas).

MIRACLES

11 And God wrought special Miracles by the hands of Paul (the Lord did these things, not Paul):

12 So that from his body were brought unto the sick handkerchiefs or aprons (there is no indication in the Text that he purposely sent these things out, although he definitely may have, but rather that people on their own simply picked them up; they took them to the diseased or demon-possessed, evidently placing the cloth on the person, with them receiving healing and/or deliverance), and the diseases departed from them, and the evil spirits went out of them (it was not the pieces of cloth which did this, but rather the Power of God using these cloths as a point of contact regarding Faith).

13 Then certain of the vaga-

bond Jews, exorcists (speaks of individuals who practiced divination, and who were not of God, but rather of Satan), took upon them to call over them which had evil spirits the name of the Lord Jesus (apparently these people had heard Paul minister and observed him praying for the sick and casting out demons; they evidently noted that he used "The Name of Jesus," which had a powerful effect), saying, We adjure you by Jesus Whom Paul preaches (seems to be their own formula or incantation they cooked up by observing Paul).

14 And there were seven sons of one Sceva, a Jew, and Chief of the Priests, which did so (infers that this man may have been a member of the Jewish Council at Ephesus).

15 And the evil spirit answered and said (points to a man who was demon-possessed, and that some or all of these seven sons had been hired to exorcise this spirit), Jesus I know, and Paul I know; but who are you? (This represents two different and distinct Greek verbs regarding the word "know." Referring to Jesus, it implied fear! Referring to Paul, there was much less action.)

16 And the man in whom the evil spirit was leaped on them, and overcame them, and prevailed against them (probably involved all seven sons being soundly whipped by the demon-possessed man), so that they fled out of that house naked and wounded (the Greek Text indicates that they suffered wounds severe enough to effect them for a while).

17 And this was known to all the Jews and Greeks also dwelling at Ephesus ("all" does not mean every single person, but rather quite a number); and fear fell on them all (they now knew not to trifle with the Name of Jesus), and the Name of the Lord Jesus was magnified (presents the constant idea of the Holy Spirit that Jesus will always be Glorified [Jn. 16:14]).

18 And many who believed came (speaks of those who had trusted the Lord for Salvation, but as of yet had not given up particular sins), and confessed, and showed their deeds (concerns the Holy Spirit now leading these Believers to Holiness and Righteousness, even as He had led them to Salvation previously).

19 Many of them also which used curious arts brought their books together, and burned them before all men ("curious arts" refers to the practicing of magic; so the Holy Spirit was mightily working in people's lives, just as He desires to do always; if we will allow Him, He will clean us up; He does it through our Faith in Christ and the Cross [Rom. 8:2]): and they counted the price of them,

and found it fifty thousand *pieces* of silver *(it must have been many, many books, etc., for the amount in 2003 dollars would be approximately $2,000,000).*

20 So mightily grew the Word of God and prevailed *(it doesn't say that the Church grew mightily, but rather the "Word of God . . .").*

21 After these things were ended, Paul purposed in the Spirit *(refers to the Holy Spirit),* when he had passed through Macedonia and Achaia, to go to Jerusalem *(he wanted to be there for the Feast of Pentecost [Acts 20:16]),* saying, After I have been there, I must also see Rome *(the Greek Text indicates a Divine hand laid upon Paul).*

22 So he sent into Macedonia two of them who ministered unto him, Timothy and Erastus *(concerned preparations they would make in the Churches for Paul's visit a short time later);* but he himself stayed in Asia for a season *(stayed in Ephesus a little longer, maybe two or three months).*

EPHESUS

23 And the same time there arose no small stir about that Way *("that Way" is the "Pentecostal Way," which characterizes the entirety of the Book of Acts).*

24 For a certain *man* named Demetrius, a silversmith *(he was probably the guild-master of the silversmith guild or trade union),* which made silver shrines for Diana *(speaks of miniatures of the Temple of Diana with the goddess in the middle of the Temple background),* brought no small gain unto the craftsmen *(speaks of those who made their living by this particular craft);*

25 Whom he called together with the workmen of like occupation *(whom Demetrius called together),* and said, Sirs, you know that by this craft we have our wealth *(tells us that their chief concern was not really the worship or the honor of this goddess, but their own prosperity).*

26 Moreover you see and hear, that not alone at Ephesus, but almost throughout all Asia *(presents a powerful Testimony, from an enemy no less, to the power and effectiveness of Paul's labors and his Message),* this Paul has persuaded and turned away much people, saying that they be no gods, which are made with hands *(proclaims that which Paul had preached, and which many people had come to believe, and rightly so):*

27 So that not only this our craft is in danger to be set at nought *(follows the idea that it would fall in disrepute);* but also that the Temple of the great goddess Diana should be despised, and her magnificence should be

destroyed, whom all Asia and the world worships *(there was quite a bit of exaggeration here)*.

28 And when they heard *these sayings*, they were full of wrath *(the accusations of Demetrius had the desired effect)*, and cried out, saying, Great *is* Diana of the Ephesians *(actually, the great wealth and prominence of the city of Ephesus were largely due to its great Temple of Diana, but it was basically localized to that city)*.

29 And the whole city was filled with confusion *(the mob is forming)*: and having caught Gaius and Aristarchus, men of Macedonia, Paul's companions in travel, they rushed with one accord into the theatre *(recognizing these two men as Paul's associates, they dragged them into the amphitheater)*.

30 And when Paul would have entered in unto the people *(Paul was determined to go into the theater and address the mob)*, the Disciples suffered him not *(these were the Believers who were a part of the Church at Ephesus, and who knew the danger that awaited Paul)*.

31 And certain of the chief of Asia, which were his friends *(these were men of high rank and great wealth, which presents another striking proof of the enormous influence of Paul's preaching in Asia)*, sent unto him, desiring *him*

that he would not adventure himself into the theatre *(seems to mean that they sent Paul word, but did not come to him in person)*.

32 Some therefore cried one thing, and some another *(presents the actions and mannerisms of a mob)*: for the assembly was confused; and the more part knew not wherefore they were come together *(means that a few were agitating the many)*.

33 And they drew Alexander out of the multitude, the Jews putting him forward *(exactly as to who this Alexander was is not clear)*. And Alexander beckoned with the hand, and would have made his defence unto the people *(presents that which is to no avail)*.

34 But when they knew that he was a Jew *(proclaims the reason for their outburst which followed)*, all with one voice about the space of two hours cried out, Great *is* Diana of the Ephesians *(despite all of this, history records that the Gospel, which Paul preached, had such an effect that the worshipers of the goddess Diana came in ever fewer numbers, while the Church in Ephesus continued to flourish)*.

35 And when the townclerk had appeased the people *(presents an office of influence)*, he said, *You* men of Ephesus, what man is there who knows not how that the city of the Ephesians is a worshipper of the great goddess

Diana, and of the *image* which fell down from Jupiter? *(The idea is that Ephesus is the proud possessor of this goddess, of which no other city in the world could boast.)*

36 Seeing then that these things cannot be spoken against *(appeals to the pride of these individuals, as to Diana being so great)*, you ought to be quiet, and to do nothing rashly *(represents good advice, although coming from a heathen)*.

37 For you have brought hither these men *(speaking of Gaius and Aristarchus)*, which are neither robbers of Churches, nor yet blasphemers of your goddess *(means that Paul had not directed attention to this particular idol, but had no doubt referred to idols made by men's hands [Vs. 26])*.

38 Wherefore if Demetrius, and the craftsmen which are with him, have a matter against any man, the law is open *(reflects the common sense of the townclerk)*, and there are deputies: let them implead one another *(he was saying that if Demetrius really had a case against Paul and those with him, he should pursue it in open Court)*.

39 But if you inquire any thing concerning other matters *(in effect is saying, if there are other complaints against Paul than that mentioned, it should be addressed correctly, and not by mob action)*, it shall be determined in a lawful assembly *(open Court)*.

40 For we are in danger to be called in question for this day's uproar *(refers to Roman peace being disturbed for no good reason)*, there being no cause whereby we may give an account of this concourse *(proclaims the townclerk wondering how this mob action could be explained to Roman authorities, if called to account)*.

41 And when he had thus spoken, he dismissed the assembly *(common sense prevailed, and Gaius and Aristarchus were released forthwith)*.

CHAPTER 20

MACEDONIA AND GREECE

AND after the uproar was ceased *(the mob had dispersed)*, Paul called unto *him* the Disciples, and embraced *them* *(speaks of some of the Believers of the Church in Ephesus)*, and departed for to go into Macedonia *(pertained to his care for the Churches in that region)*.

2 And when he had gone over those parts *(no doubt included Philippi, Thessalonica, and Berea)*, and had given them much exhortation *(refers to the teaching of the Word of God, as is obvious)*, he came into Greece *(probably refers to a repeat visit to Athens,*

Corinth, and Cenchrea, as well as other places),

3 And there abode three months (he probably spent most of this time at Corinth [I Cor. 16:6]). And when the Jews laid wait for him, as he was about to sail into Syria (these were most probably Jews from the Synagogue at Corinth, who planned to kill him), he purposed to return through Macedonia (basically presents the opposite direction, actually to Philippi, from where he would then turn toward Syria).

4 And there accompanied him into Asia Sopater of Berea; and of the Thessalonians, Aristarchus and Secundus; and Gaius of Derbe, and Timothy; and of Asia, Tychicus and Trophimus (some expositors believe that some of these men where chosen by various Churches to travel with Paul, and take their offerings for the poor in Jerusalem [Acts 19:29; 27:2; Rom. 15:25-28; I Cor. 16:3; II Cor. 8:19-23]).

5 These going before tarried for us at Troas (by the use of the pronoun "us," Luke indicates that he has once again joined Paul and his party).

PAUL AT TROAS

6 And we sailed away from Philippi after the days of unleavened bread (speaks of the Passover Week), and came unto them to Troas in five days (evidently portrays the length of time it took to make the voyage by ship); where we abode seven days.

7 And upon the first day of the week (Sunday), when the Disciples came together to break bread (Sunday had become the main day of worship), Paul preached unto them, ready to depart on the morrow; and continued his speech until midnight (proclaims him preaching possibly for several hours).

8 And there were many lights in the upper chamber (evidently spoke of a third story room, which would seat two or three hundred people), where they were gathered together (this was the meeting place or Church in Troas).

9 And there sat in a window a certain young man named Eutychus, being fallen into a deep sleep: and as Paul was long preaching, he sunk down with sleep, and fell down from the third loft, and was taken up dead (the Greek Text declares that he was a lifeless corpse; the fall had killed him).

10 And Paul went down, and fell on him, and embracing him said (presents the example of Elijah in this, which is probably what Paul intended [I Ki. 17:17-21]), Trouble not yourselves; for his life is in him (does not mean, as

some claim, that the boy had merely been knocked unconscious, but rather that he had been dead, and that the Lord had infused life back into him; he was raised from the dead!).

11 When he (Paul) therefore was come up again, and had broken bread, and eaten, and talked a long while, even till break of day (this all night Message was interrupted only by the raising of the boy from the dead; he had much to tell them, and there was much they needed to hear), so he departed.

12 And they brought the young man alive, and were not a little comforted (what a night it had been!).

PAUL

13 And we went before to ship (refers to Luke and the men of Verse 4, but not Paul, at least at this time), and sailed unto Assos (a short distance of about forty miles around Cape Electum), there intending to take in Paul: for so had he appointed, minding himself to go afoot (by land it was about twenty miles; he would walk this distance alone, no doubt desiring to be alone with the Lord in prayer).

14 And when he met with us at Assos, we took him in, and came to Mitylene (presented another approximate forty miles by ship).

15 And we sailed thence, and came the next day over against Chios (presents another Island about the size of Lesbos; it lay due west of both Smyrna and Ephesus, about a hundred miles in distance); and the next day we arrived at Samos, and tarried at Trogyllium; and the next day we came to Miletus.

16 For Paul had determined to sail by Ephesus (not stop there), because he would not spend the time in Asia (tells us, I think, he did not want to tarry, having settled this thing with the Lord respecting this eventful trip): for he hasted, if it were possible for him, to be at Jerusalem the Day of Pentecost (the Holy Spirit has warned him of the coming difficulties he will face on this trip, and it is almost as if he must haste, lest he draw back because of these coming difficulties).

EPHESIAN ELDERS

17 And from Miletus he sent to Ephesus, and called the Elders of the Church (it was about thirty miles to Ephesus; he wanted the Elders to come meet him at Melitus before he left).

18 And when they were come to him (probably represents two or three days from the time the Messenger was originally sent), he

said unto them, You know, from the first day that I came into Asia *(takes them back to the very beginning of the Church at Ephesus)*, after what manner I have been with you at all seasons *(indicates him nurturing them with the Gospel of Jesus Christ)*,

19 Serving the Lord with all humility of mind *(presents that which was the very opposite of the Judaizers and other false teachers, who were attempting to draw a following after themselves)*, and with many tears *(Paul's emotions ran deep)*, and temptations *(a provocation to deal with a situation outside the Ways of the Lord)*, which befell me by the lying in wait of the Jews *(the constant plots against Paul by the Jews were never ceasing)*:

20 *And* how I kept back nothing that was profitable *unto you (he did not allow anything to silence his voice respecting the great Doctrine of Jesus Christ and Him Crucified)*, but have showed you *(explained the Scriptures)*, and have taught you publickly, and from house to house *(most Churches were then in houses)*,

21 Testifying both to the Jews, and also to the Greeks *(the Gospel is the same for all)*, repentance toward God, and Faith toward our Lord Jesus Christ *(presents the Gospel in the proverbial nutshell; Faith in Christ pertains to Faith* in what He did at the Cross*)*.

22 And now, behold, I go bound in the spirit unto Jerusalem *(speaks of the Holy Spirit, and the desire of the Spirit that Paul take this trip, irrespective of the coming difficulties)*, not knowing the things that shall befall me there *(the Holy Spirit tells him to go to Jerusalem and that there will be great problems, but doesn't tell him exactly what they will be)*:

23 Save that the Holy Spirit witnesses in every city *(tells us that such happened, but gave no information about the actual events)*, saying that bonds and afflictions abide me *(the Holy Spirit didn't tell Paul exactly how these things would come about)*.

24 But none of these things move me *(proclaims Paul putting himself entirely in the hands of the Lord)*, neither count I my life dear unto myself *(his life belonged to the Lord, and the Lord could do with it as He so desired)*, so that I might finish my course with joy *(and that he ultimately did)*, and the ministry, which I have received of the Lord Jesus, to testify the Gospel of the Grace of God *(proclaims basically what this "course" actually is; his Message was Jesus Christ and Him Crucified)*.

25 And now, behold, I know that you all, among whom I have gone preaching the Kingdom of

God *(he had faithfully preached the Message to these Ephesians)*, shall see my face no more *(he knew this would be the last time he would see them, and therefore, the reason he had sent for them)*.

26 Wherefore I take you to record this day *(the Heavenly record will show)*, that I *am* pure from the blood of all *men (means that he had delivered the Gospel to everyone who heard him preach, exactly as it was given to him by the Lord)*.

27 For I have not shunned to declare unto you *(refers to the fact that the temptation was always there to trim the Message)* all the Counsel of God *(all the Word of God, holding back nothing)*.

28 Take heed therefore unto yourselves, and to all the Flock *(this word is directed to the Pastors who had come from Ephesus to meet him)*, over the which the Holy Spirit has made you overseers *(Elders, Bishops, Overseers, Shepherds, and Presbyters all mean the same thing, "Pastor")*, to feed the Church of God *(to tend as a Shepherd)*, which He has purchased with His Own Blood *(Christ bought us at a great price)*.

29 For I know this, that after my departing shall grievous wolves enter in among you, not sparing the flock *(presents a perfect description of those who merchandise the Body of Christ, and in whatever way)*.

30 Also of your own selves shall men arise *(will not come from the outside, but from the inside)*, speaking perverse things, to draw away Disciples after them *(not to Christ, but to themselves)*.

31 Therefore watch *(be spiritually vigilant)*, and remember, that by the space of three years I ceased not to warn every one night and day with tears *(Paul not only preached the Truth of the Word, but warned of and pointed out false doctrine and false apostles as well)*.

32 And now, Brethren, I commend you to God *(he has planted enough of the Gospel in them that they will not turn from the Lord)*, and to the Word of His Grace *(that "Word" is "the Cross")*, which is able to build you up *(the Gospel of Grace alone can build one up)*, and to give you an inheritance among all them which are Sanctified *(the Believer is Sanctified only by making the Cross the object of His Faith, which gives the Holy Spirit the latitude to carry out this work within our hearts and lives; the Believer cannot Sanctify himself)*.

33 I have coveted no man's silver, or gold, or apparel *(he was not after their money as were these grievous wolves of Verse 29)*.

34 Yes, you yourselves know, that these hands have ministered

unto my necessities, and to them who were with me *(refers to Paul repairing tents to support himself [Acts 18:3])*.

35 I have showed you all things *(means that this particular aspect of unselfishness is to serve as an example)*, how that so labouring you ought to support the weak *(everything the Believer does is to set a spiritual example)*, and to remember the Words of the Lord Jesus, how He said, It is more blessed to give than to receive *(these words are not recorded in the Gospels; however, we know that only a tiny part of what He said and did is recorded; Peter, or one of the other Apostles who were with Jesus, evidently related this to Paul)*.

36 And when he had thus spoken *(represented the last time they would ever hear him speak to them)*, he kneeled down, and prayed with them all *(as well, concerns the last time he will pray with them, even though he will continue to pray for them)*.

37 And they all wept sore *(concerns their great love for the Apostle)*, and fell on Paul's neck, and kissed him *(his Message had brought them from death to life)*,

38 Sorrowing most of all for the words which he spoke, that they should see his face no more *(so far as is known, these Ephesians never saw the Apostle again until they saw him in Glory)*. And they

accompanied him unto the ship *(this was at the port of Melitus)*.

CHAPTER 21

TYRE

AND it came to pass, that after we *(Luke is with the party)* were gotten from them, and had launched *(left the Elders from Ephesus)*, we came with a straight course unto Coos, and the *day* following unto Rhodes, and from thence unto Patara *(located on the West Coast of Lucia and Pamphylia)*:

2 And finding a ship sailing over unto Phenicia, we went aboard, and set forth *(they changed ships at Patara)*.

3 Now when we had discovered Cyprus, we left it on the left hand *(means they did not stop at this Island)*, and sailed into Syria, and landed at Tyre: for there the ship was to unlade her burden.

4 And finding Disciples *(followers of Christ)*, we tarried there seven days *(during this time, his teaching was invaluable to them)*: who said to Paul through the Spirit, that he should not go up to Jerusalem *(would have been better translated, "who said to Paul in consequence of the Spirit"; the idea is that due to what the Spirit of God was portraying to these Believers concerning the coming problems in Jerusalem, the indi-*

viduals themselves were voicing their own feelings that he should not go; it was not the Holy Spirit saying, "don't go"; the Spirit was actually constraining him to go [Acts 20:22]).

CAESAREA

5 And when we had accomplished those days (the past seven days), we departed and went our way; and they all brought us on our way, with wives and children, till we were out of the city (shows the love and affection Paul continued to gain in these last few days, even from the children): and we kneeled down on the shore, and prayed (I think the strength of Paul's prayer life is now obvious).

6 And when we had taken our leave one of another, we took ship; and they returned home again (these Believers at Tyre returned to their homes, but with a full heart and an exercised soul).

7 And when we had finished our course from Tyre, we came to Ptolemais (about thirty miles from Tyre; proclaims the end of Paul's voyage by ship), and saluted the Brethren, and abode with them one day.

8 And the next day we who were of Paul's company departed, and came unto Caesarea (approximately sixty miles; they evidently walked this distance; the "company" could have been as many as nine): and we entered into the house of Philip the Evangelist (presents the same Philip of Acts 8:40), which was one of the seven (Acts 6:5); and abode with him (his house was evidently quite large).

9 And the same man had four daughters, virgins (insinuates they had given themselves over to perpetual virginity, meaning they would not marry, but would give their lives totally in serving the Lord), which did Prophesy (the idea is that they were Evangelists exactly as their father, which strikes down the idea that women cannot preach).

10 And as we tarried there many days (waiting for the Day of Pentecost), there came down from Judaea a certain Prophet (the same Brother mentioned in Acts 11:28), named Agabus.

11 And when he was come unto us, he took Paul's girdle (a sash worn around the waist like a belt), and bound his own hands and feet (presents that which the Holy Spirit told him to do as an object lesson), and said, Thus saith the Holy Spirit, So shall the Jews at Jerusalem bind the man who owns this girdle, and shall deliver him into the hands of the Gentiles (this was designed by the Holy Spirit to test Paul's resolution to obey the inward voice which bound him to go, even as Elijah tested

Elisha).

12 And when we heard these things, both we, and they of that place, besought him not to go up to Jerusalem (*but Paul must listen to the Holy Spirit, not men*).

13 Then Paul answered, What mean you to weep and to break mine heart? (*They kept trying to persuade him, becoming emotionally distraught with some of them weeping.*) for I am ready not to be bound only, but also to die at Jerusalem for the Name of the Lord Jesus (*proclaims the consecration already settled in Paul's heart and mind respecting these coming events*).

14 And when he would not be persuaded, we ceased, saying, The Will of the Lord be done (*means that all had now come to the place where they realized what Paul was doing and the direction he was going were indeed the Will of God; Paul was a chosen vessel to offer the Kingdom to Israel, as well as to proclaim it among the Gentiles; the final offer he would shortly give to Israel was a Divine necessity; but as we shall see, they rejected that offer and went to their doom*).

JERUSALEM

15 And after those days we took up our carriages (*referred to their baggage, whatever that may have been*), and went up to Jerusa-lem (*it was approximately sixty miles, and they probably walked*).

16 There went with us also *certain of the Disciples of Caesarea (meant that the party is now quite large, possibly numbering fifteen to twenty people, or even more*), and brought with them one Mnason of Cyprus (*he was originally from Cyprus, but now lived in Jerusalem, or nearby*), an old Disciple (*does not necessarily mean old in age, but thought by some to have been one of the original group Baptized with the Holy Spirit on the Day of Pentecost*), with whom we should lodge (*Mnason had invited Paul and his party to stay at his home while in Jerusalem*).

17 And when we were come to Jerusalem, the Brethren received us gladly (*indicates some of the Saints in Jerusalem, but not necessarily the leaders of the Church at this particular time; that would come the next day*).

GENTILES

18 And the *day* following Paul went in with us unto James (*refers to James, the Lord's Brother, who was the Senior Pastor of the Church in Jerusalem*); and all the Elders were present (*refers to the many Pastors who served with James concerning the Church in Jerusalem; the Church was quite large, perhaps numbering as many as*

thirty thousand members or more).

19 And when he *(Paul)* had saluted them *(greeted them)*, he declared particularly what things God had wrought among the Gentiles by his Ministry *(gave an account of his second and third Missionary Journeys with the planting of many Churches)*.

20 And when they heard *it*, they glorified the Lord *(praised the Lord for what had been done)*, and said unto him, you see, brother, how many thousands of Jews there are which believe *(probably spoken by James, and referring to the Church in Jerusalem, made up almost exclusively of Jews)*; and they are all zealous of the Law *(meaning their newfound Faith in Christ stirred them up to serve the Lord with a new zeal, which they channeled in the direction of attempting to obey the Law of Moses to an even greater degree than ever)*:

21 And they are informed of you *(concerned itself with charges against Paul relative to what he was teaching concerning the Law/Grace issue)*, that you teach all the Jews which are among the Gentiles to forsake Moses *(was not correct, at least in the manner in which it was being said; in fact, Paul preached almost exclusively from the Old Testament, holding up all that it stated as pointing to Christ)*, saying that they ought not to Circumcise *their* children, neither to walk after the customs *(once again, this was not exactly what Paul was saying; he taught that Circumcision did not save the soul, and that no flesh shall be justified by the deeds of the Law [Rom. 3:24-31; 4:21; Gal. 3:19-25])*.

22 What is it therefore? *(I think this illustrates that James himself was not settled on the matter, respecting Paul.)* the multitude must needs come together: for they will hear that you are come *(we aren't told anything about this particular meeting of which James spoke)*.

23 Do therefore this that we say to you *(proclaims a plan James, it seems, thought might defuse the situation)*: We have four men which have a vow on them *(pertained to the Nazarite Vow [Num. 6:14-20])*;

24 Them take, and purify yourself with them, and be at charges with them, that they may shave *their* heads *(proclaims the fact that Paul was to pay for all of these sacrifices out of his own pocket, which in 2003 money amounted to several thousands of dollars)*: and all may know that those things, whereof they were informed concerning you, are nothing *(the thought here is that if Paul was as opposed to the Law as it was claimed, he certainly would not be in the Temple carrying out a Nazarite Vow, which was a part of the Mosaic Law)*; but *that* you yourself

also walk orderly, and keep the Law *(no answer from Paul is recorded; we know that Paul didn't keep the Law as it regarded all of its rituals and ceremonies; in fact, all of that was fulfilled in Christ; the only answer we can give concerning Paul's action in doing what James said is that he was trying to prevent a split in the Church; it is my opinion that James didn't understand the Message of Grace as he should, and was still trying to hold to the Law; about ten years later, the Lord made it impossible for the Law to be kept anymore, in that the Temple was totally destroyed by the Roman Army).*

25 As touching the Gentiles which believe, we have written *and* concluded that they observe no such thing *(releases Gentiles from obligation to the Mosaic Law; it is obvious here, however, that James didn't include the Jews in this freedom, which presented a dichotomy and caused great problems in the Early Church),* save only that they keep themselves from *things* offered to idols, and from blood, and from strangled, and from fornication *(this was right; but as stated, James didn't include the Jews, which made that part wrong).*

PERSECUTION

26 Then Paul took the men *(the four men of Verse 23),* and the next day purifying himself with them entered into the Temple, to signify the accomplishment of the days of purification *(presents something which Paul had, no doubt, done at times in the past),* until that an offering should be offered for every one of them *(speaks of the Sacrifices to be offered at the conclusion of the seven days).*

27 And when the seven days were almost ended *(seven days of purification),* the Jews which were of Asia *(Jews came from all over the Roman Empire to keep the various Feasts; Ephesus was in Asia, so these Jews knew Paul and were not happy with him at all),* when they saw him in the Temple, stirred up all the people, and laid hands on him *(they bodily seized him),*

28 Crying out, Men of Israel, help *(Paul was in the innermost Court with other men)*: This is the man, who teaches all *men* every where against the people, and the Law, and this place *(once again portrays one of Satan's favorite tactics of twisting what has actually been said to make it mean something else entirely)*: and further brought Greeks also into the Temple, and has polluted this Holy Place *(was an entirely false accusation; the four men with Paul were Jews).*

29 (For they had seen before

with him in the city Trophimus an Ephesian, whom they supposed that Paul had brought into the Temple.) *(They jumped to conclusions!)*

30 And all the city was moved *(the claim that Paul had brought a Gentile into the Innermost Court spread like wildfire)*, and the people ran together: and they took Paul, and drew him out of the Temple *(actually means they dragged him out, beating him as they went; he was dragged into the Court of the Gentiles, which was the Outer Court)*: and forthwith the doors were shut *(referred to the doors of the Court of the Gentiles, and the Court of Women)*.

31 And as they went about to kill him *(such is religion!)*, tidings came unto the Chief Captain of the band, that all Jerusalem was in an uproar *(pertained to the Roman Tribune who commanded a cohort of approximately a thousand soldiers)*.

32 Who immediately took soldiers and centurions, and ran down unto them *(probably represented about two hundred men)*: and when they saw the Chief Captain and the soldiers, they left beating of Paul *(which no doubt saved Paul's life)*.

ARRESTED

33 Then the Chief captain came near, and took him, and commanded *him* to be bound with two chains *(refers to him being bound to a soldier on each side)*; and demanded who he was, and what he had done *(speaking to the Jews)*.

34 And some cried one thing, some another, among the multitude *(generally proclaims the conduct of a mob, for this is what the crowd now was!)*: and when he could not know the certainty for the tumult, he commanded him to be carried into the castle *(he gave instructions for Paul to be taken into the Fortress, or Tower of Antonia)*.

35 And when he came upon the stairs, so it was, that he was borne of the soldiers for the violence of the people *(in order to protect him the soldiers were forced to lift him up, possibly even above their heads)*.

36 For the multitude of the people *(the Jews)* followed after, crying, Away with him *(presents the cry of those who had also thirsted for the Blood of Jesus Christ [Lk. 23:18])*.

PAUL

37 And as Paul was to be led into the castle, he said unto the Chief Captain, May I speak unto you? *(This presents Paul speaking to the Captain in the Greek lan-*

guage, which was actually the major language of the Roman Empire.) Who said, Can you speak Greek? (The next Verse explains the reason for this question.)

38 Are not you that Egyptian, which before these days made an uproar, and led out into the wilderness four thousand men who were murderers? (This question portrays how this Captain was mistaken about Paul's identity.)

39 But Paul said, I am a man which am a Jew of Tarsus, a city in Cilicia, a citizen of no mean city (presents an entirely different scenario to this Roman Captain, inasmuch as Tarsus was famous for philosophy and learning): and, I beseech you, suffer me to speak unto the people (Paul was, no doubt, impressed by the Holy Spirit to do this).

40 And when he (the Roman Captain) had given him licence (told him he could address the crowd), Paul stood on the stairs, and beckoned with the hand unto the people (presents the last time the Holy Spirit will appeal to Israel as a Nation, at least as far as is recorded). And when there was made a great silence, he spoke unto them in the Hebrew tongue, saying (it is possible that Paul was speaking in the ancient Biblical Hebrew, which was read every week in the synagogues; as stated, it was the last appeal by the Spirit),

CHAPTER 22

PAUL'S DEFENSE

MEN, Brethren, and Fathers (presents the beginning of Paul's final address to Israel, at least which is recorded, which will culminate the next day with the Sanhedrin), hear you my defence which I make now unto you (presents some of the greatest words they will ever hear; Paul was the instrument, but the Holy Spirit was the Speaker).

2 (And when they heard that he spoke in the Hebrew tongue to them, they kept the more silence: and he said,)

3 I am verily a man which am a Jew, born in Tarsus, a city in Cilicia, yet brought up in this city at the feet of Gamaliel (automatically gave Paul credibility), and taught according to the perfect manner of the Law of the Fathers, and was zealous toward God, as you all are this day (all of this means Paul was a scholar in the Mosaic Law).

4 And I persecuted this Way (the Way of the Lord Jesus Christ) unto the death (his persecution of Believers had resulted in the death of some), binding and delivering into prisons both men and women (proclaims that he showed no mercy).

5 As also the High Priest does bear me witness, and all the es-

tate of the Elders (*even though this happened some twenty-five years before, there no doubt were some Jewish Leaders present who knew what he was talking about*): from whom also I received letters unto the Brethren (*Acts 9:1-2*), and went to Damascus, to bring them which were there (*followers of Christ*) bound unto Jerusalem, for to be punished.

CONVERSION

6 And it came to pass, that, as I made my journey, and was come near unto Damascus about noon (*a day Paul would never forget*), suddenly there shone from Heaven a great light round about me (*would later be described by him as brighter than the noonday sun [Acts 26:13]*).

7 And I fell unto the ground (*knocked down by the Power of God*), and heard a Voice saying unto me, Saul, Saul, why do you persecute Me? (*When we oppose those who truly belong to the Lord, and I speak of opposing their Righteousness, we are at the same time opposing God.*)

8 And I answered, Who are You, Lord? (*Paul knew that it was Deity to Whom he was speaking.*) And He said unto me, I am Jesus of Nazareth, Whom you persecute (*describes the Lord using the very Name so hated by Paul*).

9 And they who were with me saw indeed the light, and were afraid (*tells us that all of Paul's Testimony could be confirmed by witnesses*); but they heard not the Voice of Him Who spoke to me (*should have been translated, "they did not hear what the Voice said, they only heard the sound"*).

10 And I said, What shall I do, Lord? (*At this moment, Paul accepted Christ as his Lord and Saviour.*) And the Lord said unto me, Arise, and go into Damascus; and there it shall be told you of all things which are appointed for you to do (*proclaims the Plan of God for Paul's life and Ministry*).

11 And when I could not see for the Glory of that Light (*the Light shining from Christ was so bright that it blinded Paul*), being led by the hand of them who were with me, I came into Damascus (*presents Paul coming into the city in an entirely different posture than he had heretofore reckoned*).

12 And one Ananias, a devout man according to the Law, having a good report of all the Jews which dwelt *there* (*he was a follower of Christ, but still was loved and respected by the Jews who were not friendly to Christ*),

13 Came unto me, and stood, and said unto me, Brother Saul (*referred to him in this manner because Paul was already saved*), receive your sight (*he was healed*

immediately, and it seems at that moment Baptized with the Holy Spirit, with the evidence of speaking with other Tongues [Acts 9:17]). And the same hour I looked up upon him (Acts 9:18 says, "there fell from his eyes as it had been scales").

14 And he said, The God of our Fathers has chosen you (Paul was chosen by the Lord for a particular task), that you should know His Will (what the Lord wanted, not what Paul wanted), and see that Just One (Jesus Christ was to be the focal point of all things), and should hear the Voice of His Mouth (this made Paul a witness to His Resurrection on the same level as those who saw Him alive before His Ascension).

15 For you shall be His witness unto all men of what you have seen and heard (this speaks of his Great Commission to take the Gospel to the world of that day).

16 And now why do you tarry? (In essence, this presents Ananias telling Paul that it is time to begin.) arise, and be Baptized, and wash away your sins (refers to a present action being done because of a past action; he was being Baptized in water because his sins had already been washed away by the Blood of Jesus), calling on the Name of the Lord (your sins were washed when you called on the Name of the Lord).

THE GENTILES

17 And it came to pass, that, when I was come again to Jerusalem (pertains to Acts 9:26), even while I prayed in the Temple, I was in a trance (speaks of his high regard for the Temple, and at the same time refutes the accusation by some of the Jews that he would pollute the Temple);

18 And saw Him (Jesus) saying unto Me, Make haste, and get thee quickly out of Jerusalem (presents the Lord once more indicting this city, His city, but now in total rebellion against Him): for they will not receive your testimony concerning Me (they not only have rejected the Message of Christ, but would kill Paul as well, if given the opportunity).

19 And I said, Lord, they know that I imprisoned and beat in every Synagogue them who believed on You:

20 And when the blood of your martyr Stephen was shed (presents this event which undoubtedly had a lasting effect on Paul), I also was standing by, and consenting unto his death, and kept the raiment of them who killed him (this made Paul a party to the death of this man).

21 And he (Jesus) said unto me, Depart: for I will send you far hence unto the Gentiles (this was the particular calling of Paul, even

as he had been told by Ananias at the time of his conversion [Acts 9:15]).

22 And they gave him audience unto this word *(speaks of the word "Gentiles"),* and *then* lifted up their voices, and said, Away with such a *fellow* from the earth: for it is not fit that he should live *(presents these people claiming they are Scriptural in their demand for Paul's life).*

23 And as they cried out, and cast off *their* clothes, and threw dust into the air *(portrayed their anger),*

24 The Chief Captain commanded him to be brought into the castle, and bade that he should be examined by scourging *(a most terrible form of torture);* that he might know wherefore they cried so against him *(considering that Paul was speaking in Hebrew, the Roman Captain little knew what was taking place).*

A ROMAN CITIZEN

25 And as they bound him with thongs *(getting him ready for the beating that would now be inflicted),* Paul said unto the centurion who stood by, Is it lawful for you to scourge a man who is a Roman, and uncondemned? *(Paul did not shrink from torture when it was directly connected with the Name of Jesus, but he quietly and with much dignity avoided it when ordered by official ignorance.)*

26 When the centurion heard *that,* he went and told the Chief Captain, saying, Take heed what you do: for this man is a Roman *(the rights of Roman citizens were guarded as something sacred by Rome).*

27 Then the Chief Captain came, and said unto him, Tell me, are you a Roman? He said, Yes *(in fact, the Chief Captain had broken the Law even by binding Paul).*

28 And the Chief Captain answered, With a great sum obtained I this freedom *(proclaims one of the ways Roman citizenship could be gained).* And Paul said, But I was *free* born *(Paul was born a Roman citizen, either through some service performed for Rome by his family, or else because of living in the city of Tarsus).*

29 Then straightway *(immediately)* they departed from him which should have examined him *(refers to those who were going to scourge Paul quickly retiring):* and the Chief Captain also was afraid, after he knew that he was a Roman, and because he had bound him.

30 On the morrow, because he would have known the certainty wherefore he was accused of the Jews, he loosed him from *his* bands *(he was no longer restricted, but at the same time held in custody that the Captain may hopefully gain some information),* and command-

ed the Chief Priests and all their Council to appear *(the Jewish Sanhedrin, the highest Jewish Council, and ruling Civil and Religious body)*, and brought Paul down, and set him before them.

CHAPTER 23

THE SANHEDRIN

A ND Paul, earnestly beholding the Council *(evidently speaks of all seventy-one members of the Sanhedrin, with the High Priest Ananias serving as its President)*, said, Men *and* Brethren, I have lived in all good conscience before God until this day *(means that whatever he had been doing, he had thought it right at the time, whether true or not)*.

2 And the High Priest Ananias commanded them who stood by him to smite him on the mouth *(this man would have hated Paul; history records he was appointed about nine years before this through political influence; he ruled like a tyrant in Jerusalem, and was a glutton according to the Jewish Talmud; Zealots assassinated him in A.D. 66 for his pro-Roman sympathies)*.

3 Then said Paul unto him, God shall smite you, *you* whited wall *(in effect says, "you whitewashed wall," meaning that the whitewash covered a black heart)*: for you sit to judge me after the Law,

and command me to be smitten contrary to the Law? *(This presents Paul knowing the Law of Moses to a far greater degree than any of these members of the Sanhedrin.)*

4 And they who stood by said, Do you revile God's High Priest? *(Paul did not know this man was the High Priest.)*

5 Then said Paul, I did not know, Brethren, that he was the High Priest *(it was very difficult at that time for a visitor to Jerusalem, as Paul was, to know who was High Priest; the Romans made and unmade them at their pleasure, in addition to those made and unmade by the Sanhedrin; in other words, the High Priest was no longer a son of Aaron, as Scripturally they should have been)*: for it is written, You shall not speak evil of the Ruler of your people *(Ex. 22:28)*.

6 But when Paul perceived that the one part were Sadducees, and the other Pharisees *(we aren't told how he came about this information)*, he cried out in the Council, Men *and* Brethren, I am a Pharisee, the son of a Pharisee *(expresses the party with which Paul had been associated before his conversion, and his Father having been the same)*: of the hope and resurrection of the dead I am called in question *(the whole Christian Faith is built around Christ, His Death on the Cross, and His Bodily*

Resurrection; without Faith in both, men are lost).

7 And when he had so said, there arose a dissension between the Pharisees and the Sadducees: and the multitude was divided *(speaks of the Sanhedrin itself, but typifies the majority of the Church world presently).*

8 For the Sadducees say that there is no Resurrection, neither Angel, nor spirit *(they were the modernists of that present time)*: but the Pharisees confess both *(they were the fundamentalists of that time, which means to profess belief in all the Bible).*

9 And there arose a great cry: and the Scribes *who were* of the Pharisees' part arose, and strove, saying, We find no evil in this man *(proclaims the situation being decided on the basis of Doctrine, and not on Paul personally)*: but if a spirit or an Angel has spoken to him, let us not fight against God.

10 And when there arose a great dissension, the Chief Captain, fearing lest Paul should have been pulled in pieces of them, commanded the soldiers to go down, and to take him by force from among them, and to bring *him* into the castle *(portrays the fact that the situation had gotten completely out of hand).*

11 And the night following the Lord stood by him, and said *(presents another appearance by Jesus Christ to Paul [Acts 22:8, 14, 18; I Cor. 9:1; 15:8; II Cor. 12:1-4])*, Be of good cheer, Paul *(evidently, Paul was greatly discouraged at this time, hence, the needed admonition given by Christ)*: for as you have testified of Me in Jerusalem, so must you bear witness also at Rome *(this meant that despite the hatred and great efforts of his enemies, the Jews in Jerusalem would not be able to take his life, which they didn't).*

THE JEWS

12 And when it was day, certain of the Jews banded together, and bound themselves under a curse *(their "curse" was a religious curse, which sought to put God in a position where He would have to do their will; their thinking was ridiculous!)*, saying that they would neither eat nor drink till they had killed Paul *(such is religion!).*

13 And they were more than forty which had made this conspiracy.

14 And they came to the Chief Priests and Elders, and said, We have bound ourselves under a great curse, that we will eat nothing until we have killed Paul *(they now seek to make their efforts official).*

15 Now therefore you with the Council signify to the Chief Cap-

tain that he bring him down unto you tomorrow, as though you would enquire something more perfectly concerning him: and we, or ever he come near, are ready to kill him *(proclaims the depth of infamy to which the religion of the carnal heart can sink cultured and religious people)*.

THE PLOT DISCOVERED

16 And when Paul's sister's son heard of their lying in wait *(presents Paul's Nephew and all we know of his family other than references in Romans 16:7, 11, 21)*, he went and entered into the castle, and told Paul *(we aren't told how he came by this knowledge)*.

17 Then Paul called one of the Centurions unto *him*, and said, Bring this young man unto the Chief Captain: for he has a certain thing to tell him.

18 So he *(the Centurion)* took him *(Paul's Nephew)*, and brought *him* to the Chief Captain, and said, Paul the prisoner called me unto *him*, and prayed me to bring this young man unto you, who has something to say unto you.

19 Then the Chief Captain took him by the hand, and went *with him* aside privately, and asked *him*, What is that you have to tell me? *(This portrays an honest effort on the Chief Captain's part to obtain the Truth in all these matters.)*

20 And he said, The Jews have agreed to desire you that you would bring down Paul tomorrow into the Council, as though they would enquire something of him more perfectly.

21 But do not thou yield unto them: for there lie in wait for him of them more than forty men, which have bound themselves with an oath, that they will neither eat nor drink till they have killed him: and now are they ready, looking for a promise from you *(a plot to which the Tribune would probably have innocently agreed had the young man not warned him; in fact, what the Jews were doing was totally against Roman Law)*.

22 So the Chief Captain *then* let the young man depart, and charged *him, See you* tell no man that you have showed these things to me *(it is believed, although not stated, that the young man went and related to Paul his ready acceptance by the Tribune, which no doubt encouraged Paul greatly)*.

CAESAREA

23 And he called unto *him* two Centurions, saying, Make ready two hundred soldiers to go to Caesarea, and horsemen threescore and ten *(seventy)*, and spearmen two hundred, at the third

hour of the night *(9 p.m.)*;

24 And provide *them* beasts, that they may set Paul on *(probably placed the Apostle next to one of the Centurions in the very midst of the force)*, and bring *him* safe unto Felix the Governor *(not exactly a man of kind disposition to whom Paul must answer)*.

25 And he wrote a letter after this manner:

26 Claudius Lysias *(the Roman Tribune)* unto the most excellent Governor Felix *sends* greeting.

27 This man was taken of the Jews, and should have been killed of them: then came I with an army, and rescued him, having understood that he was a Roman.

28 And when I would have known the cause wherefore they accused him, I brought him forth into their Council *(Sanhedrin)*:

29 Whom I perceived to be accused of questions of their *Law (Law of Moses)*, but to have nothing laid to his charge worthy of death or of bonds.

30 And when it was told me how that the Jews laid wait for the man, I sent straightway *(immediately)* to you, and gave commandment to his accusers also to say before you what *they had* against him. Farewell.

31 Then the soldiers, as it was commanded them, took Paul, and brought *him* by night to Antipatris *(about forty miles from Jerusalem, with about twenty miles left to Caesarea; the soldiers must have marched without stopping for about fifteen hours)*.

32 On the morrow they left the horsemen to go with him *(the infantry of about four hundred soldiers returned to Jerusalem, while the Cavalry, consisting of some seventy horsemen, took Paul the balance of the way to Caesarea)*, and returned to the castle:

33 Who, when they came to Caesarea, and delivered the epistle to the Governor *(the letter written by the Roman Tribune)*, presented Paul also before him.

34 And when the Governor had read *the letter*, he asked of what province he was *(the home of Paul)*. And when he understood that *he was* of Cilicia *(this automatically gave the Governor jurisdiction; the fact that Paul was a Roman citizen from this important Province, meant that Felix could not ignore him)*;

35 I will hear you *(he speaks to Paul)*, said he, when your accusers are also come *(pertained to members or representatives of the Sanhedrin)*. And he commanded him to be kept in Herod's Judgment Hall *(a part of the lavish Palace built by Herod the Great; it served as the Capitol Building as well as the official residence of the Roman Governors; it evidently had some prison cells within its con-*

fines).

CHAPTER 24

PAUL BEFORE FELIX

AND after five days Ananias the High Priest descended with the Elders *(represented members of the Sanhedrin who were Sadducees)*, and *with* a certain orator *named* Tertullus, who informed the Governor against Paul *(he served as the prosecutor for the Jews).*

2 And when he was called forth, Tertullus began to accuse *him*, saying, Seeing that by you *(Felix)* we enjoy great quietness, and that very worthy deeds are done unto this nation by your providence *(Josephus said that even though Felix did suppress some of the robbers and murderers in Judaea, he was himself "more hurtful than them all"),*

3 We accept *it* always, and in all places, most noble Felix, with all thankfulness.

4 Notwithstanding, that I be not further tedious unto you, I pray you that you would hear us of your clemency a few words *(Felix was not a man of clemency).*

5 For we have found this man a pestilent *fellow,* and a mover of sedition among all the Jews throughout the world, and a ringleader of the sect of the Nazarenes *(presents the name for followers of Christ coined by the Jews):*

6 Who also has gone about to profane the Temple *(Paul didn't profane the Temple in any manner):* whom we took, and would have judged according to our Law *(presents another outright lie; they had no intention of giving him a trial as the word "judge" implies, but rather were attempting to beat him to death before he was rescued by the Tribune).*

7 But the Chief Captain Lysias came *upon us*, and with great violence took *him* away out of our hands *(is meant to throw the Roman Tribune in a bad light; it was a bad mistake on the part of Tertullus; no doubt, the Holy Spirit had him go in this direction),*

8 Commanding his accusers to come unto you: by examining of whom yourself may take knowledge of all these things, whereof we accuse him *(refers to the fact that the situation is now in the Court of the Governor, even though the Jews do not think it should be here; for all their plotting, they have not helped their cause).*

9 And the Jews also assented, saying that these things were so *(refers to the High Priest and those with him who joined Tertullus with their voices of approval respecting their hired prosecutor's statements; as stated, it was a mistake on their*

part).

PAUL'S DEFENSE

10 Then Paul, after that the Governor had beckoned unto him to speak, answered *(presents that which the Holy Spirit had said that Paul would do, "to bear My Name before the Gentiles, and Kings, and the Children of Israel" [Acts 9:15]),* Forasmuch as I know that you have been of many years a judge unto this nation, I do the more cheerfully answer for myself *(there was no one in the world at that time who knew Mosaic Law any better than Paul; as well, being a Roman citizen, he was also quite knowledgeable of Roman Law):*

11 Because that you may understand, that there are yet but twelve days since I went up to Jerusalem for to worship *(in essence, Paul is stating that what they were accusing him of was impossible, considering the short period of time).*

12 And they neither found me in the Temple disputing with any man, neither raising up the people, neither in the synagogues, nor in the city *(refers to the fact that absolutely nothing had been done that could be misconstrued in any way, referring to these charges):*

13 Neither can they prove the things whereof they now accuse me *(they couldn't prove their charge because they never happened).*

14 But this I confess unto you, that after the way which they call heresy *(following Christ),* so worship I the God of my Fathers *(places Christianity as the fulfillment of the great Promises and Predictions given to the "Fathers," i.e., all the Old Testament Worthies),* believing all things which are written in the Law and in the Prophets *(the entirety of the Old Testament):*

15 And have hope toward God *(in essence states that the Law and the Prophets were not complete within themselves, only pointing to the One Who was to come),* which they themselves also allow *(even his enemies among the Jews believed in the coming Messiah, but not that He was Jesus),* that there shall be a resurrection of the dead, both of the just and unjust *(proclaims, as is obvious, two Resurrections).*

16 And herein do I exercise myself *(diligence constantly practiced by Paul so that his life and conduct please the Lord in all things),* to have always a conscience void of offence toward God, and *toward* men *(Mat. 22:37-40).*

17 Now after many years I came to bring alms to my nation, and offerings *(probably refers to the six or seven years Paul had been away from Jerusalem).*

18 Whereupon certain Jews from Asia found me purified in the Temple, neither with multitude, nor with tumult *(refers to the fact that absolutely nothing was going on at that time which could have given any type of credence to these accusations)*.

19 Who ought to have been here before you, and object, if they had ought against me *(the ones who accused him were not present here; the High Priest and the members of the Sanhedrin who were present had not witnessed any of these so-called infractions)*.

20 Or else let these same *here* say *(now puts the High Priest and those with him on the spot)*, if they have found any evil doing in me, while I stood before the Council *(shifts the attention away from those not present to those who are)*,

21 Except it be for this one voice, that I cried standing among them, Touching the resurrection of the dead I am called in question by you this day *(this had to do with Jewish Law, which interested the Romans not at all)*.

22 And when Felix heard these things, having more perfect knowledge of *that way (Felix had greater knowledge of Christianity than Tertullus, and the Jews present at that trial were willing to give him credit)*, he deferred them, and said *(means simply that he refused to give a verdict at this time)*, When Lysias the Chief Captain shall come down, I will know the uttermost of your matter *(he was trying to delay the matter, hoping it would defuse the situation; moreover, there is no record he ever sent for Lysias)*.

23 And he commanded a Centurion to keep Paul, and to let *him* have liberty *(tells us that Felix considered Paul someone above the ordinary; he was under house arrest, but basically had the run of the place)*, and that he should forbid none of his acquaintance to minister or come unto him *(he could have as many visitors as he liked, with no restraint on such activity)*.

24 And after certain days, when Felix came with his wife Drusilla, which was a Jewess *(his wife was the young daughter of Herod Agrippa I, the Herod who killed James [the Brother of John] with a sword [Acts 12:1-2])*, he sent for Paul, and heard him concerning the Faith in Christ *(it seems to imply that his interest was sincere)*.

25 And as he *(Paul)* reasoned of Righteousness *(Righteousness can only come through Christ)*, temperance *(the bondages and vices which affect humanity)*, and judgment to come *(all must one day stand before God)*, Felix trembled, and answered *(proclaims tremendous Holy Spirit Conviction)*, Go your way for this time; when I

have a convenient season, I will call for you *(presents the sinner's excuse when under Conviction and refusing to surrender)*.

26 He hoped also that money should have been given him of Paul, that he might loose him *(the love of money was probably one of the reasons he would not give his heart to the Lord)*: wherefore he sent for him the oftener, and communed with him *(there is no record that he ever came to Christ; so close, but so far off!)*.

SILENCE

27 But after two years *(gives us no hint as to what took place during this particular time)* Porcius Festus came into Felix' room *(means that Festus now replaced Felix as Governor)*: and Felix, willing to show the Jews a pleasure, left Paul bound *(presents a terrible travesty of Justice)*.

CHAPTER 25

PAUL BEFORE FESTUS

NOW when Festus was come into the Province *(refers to him taking the position of Governor at Caesarea)*, after three days he ascended from Caesarea to Jerusalem *(according to topography, he ascended; but according to geography, he descended; Jerusalem is about 2,500 feet above sea level, while Caesarea, situated on the coast, is just a few feet above the level of measurement)*.

2 Then the High Priest and the Chief of the Jews informed him against Paul, and besought him *(they began to besiege Festus with repeated accusations against Paul)*,

3 And desired favour against him, that he would send for him to Jerusalem, laying wait in the way to kill him *(proclaims the idea, as thought by some, that this was to be done by the same forty men who had originally made the vow to kill Paul [Acts 23:16])*.

4 But Festus answered, that Paul should be kept at Caesarea, and that he himself would depart shortly thither *(seems to imply that the Governor had about had his fill of the hatred and hypocrisy of these Jews)*.

5 Let them therefore, said he, which among you are able, go down with *me*, and accuse this man, if there be any wickedness in him *(in effect, he is saying Paul is a Roman citizen and must be treated as such)*.

6 And when he had tarried among them more than ten days, he went down unto Caesarea; and the next day sitting on the judgment seat commanded Paul to be brought *(this meant the Governor was calling for a new official trial; Festus could do this because Felix*

had never officially handed down a decision).

7 And when he was come, the Jews which came down from Jerusalem stood round about *(evidently some Jews from Jerusalem had immediately come to Caesarea in order to testify against Paul),* and laid many and grievous complaints against Paul, which they could not prove *(undoubtedly proclaims the same complaints they had registered some two years before; they charged that Paul had indeed violated Roman Law in some manner at which in the next Verse hints, but which Luke did not specify).*

8 While he answered for himself, Neither against the Law of the Jews, neither against the Temple, nor yet against Caesar, have I offended any thing at all *(it seems they were claiming that Paul had instigated a new religion, which, if true, would have been against Roman Law).*

9 But Festus, willing to do the Jews a pleasure, answered Paul, and said *(Festus feared these Jewish leaders, knowing that if they were willing to bring these types of false charges against Paul, they would not hesitate to do the same against him to Rome),* Will you go up to Jerusalem, and there be judged of these things before me? *(This presents the compromise of the Governor.)*

CAESAR

10 Then said Paul, I stand at Caesar's judgment seat, where I ought to be judged *(proclaims the Apostle seeing through this ploy, knowing that if he went to Jerusalem the Jews would find some way to kill him):* to the Jews have I done no wrong, as you very well know *(proclaims that which is true, and which Paul hammers home, and rightly so!).*

11 For if I be an offender, or have committed any thing worthy of death, I refuse not to die *(in effect, Paul is attempting not so much to save his life, but rather to declare his innocence):* but if there be none of these things whereof these accuse me, no man may deliver me unto them. I appeal unto Caesar *(means it is the Will of God for him to stand before Caesar, not the Jews).*

12 Then Festus, when he had conferred with the Council, answered *(refers to the legal advisory Council of the Governor, which evidently advised Festus that he acquiesce to Paul because of Roman Law),* Have you appealed unto Caesar? unto Caesar shall you go.

AGRIPPA AND FESTUS

13 And after certain days king Agrippa *(pertains to the second son*

of Herod Agrippa who is mentioned in Acts 12:1) and Bernice *(she was Agrippa's sister)* came unto Caesarea to salute Festus *(to pay their respects to the new Governor).*

14 And when they had been there many days, Festus declared Paul's cause unto the king, saying *(Festus thought Herod had a better understanding of Jewish Law than he did, which was true),* There is a certain man left in bonds by Felix *(speaks of Paul):*

15 About whom, when I was at Jerusalem, the Chief Priests and the Elders of the Jews informed me, desiring to have judgment against him *(means that the Jews did not really want another trial for Paul, but rather that Festus accept their accusations at face value and pronounce the death sentence on Paul without any further trial or investigation).*

16 To whom I answered, It is not the manner of the Romans to deliver any man to die, before that he which is accused have the accusers face to face *(presents this heathen as having a better sense of justice than the religious Jews who, of all people, should have known better),* and have licence to answer for himself concerning the crime laid against him *(portrays the justice of the heathen Government of Rome, with Israel, who was supposed to be God's chosen, having no justice whatsoever).*

17 Therefore, when they were come hither, without any delay on the morrow I sat on the judgment seat *(proclaims, as is obvious, the recounting of this episode to King Agrippa by Festus),* and commanded the man to be brought forth.

18 Against whom when the accusers stood up, they brought none accusation of such things as I supposed *(he really didn't understand their accusations):*

19 But had certain questions against him of their own superstition *(he was actually saying, "against him of their own religion"),* and of One Jesus *(shows that Paul, in his defense, readily preached Jesus to the Governor and these Jewish leaders; in this account as given by Luke, we only have a capsule sketch),* which was dead, Whom Paul affirmed to be alive *(proclaims the Resurrection which, in its manner, was the most astounding Miracle the world had ever known; Jesus had been Crucified; the Roman records could show this, and Festus could check if he so desired; as well, Roman soldiers made the Tomb secure; all of this, as stated, was a matter of record).*

20 And because I doubted of such manner of questions *(he was at a loss as to how to decide such questions),* I asked him whether he would go to Jerusalem, and there be judged of these matters.

21 But when Paul had appealed to be reserved unto the hearing of Augustus *(Nero)*, I commanded him to be kept till I might send him to Caesar.

22 Then Agrippa said unto Festus, I would also hear the man myself. To morrow, said he *(Festus)*, you shall hear him.

23 And on the morrow, when Agrippa was come, and Bernice, with great pomp, and was entered into the place of hearing, with the Chief Captains, and principal men of the city *(the King and his sister took this opportunity to let the city of Caesarea see their glory)*, at Festus' commandment Paul was brought forth *(it is suggested that Luke was in attendance this particular day as well, and was a witness of all the proceedings)*.

24 And Festus said, King Agrippa, and all men which are here present with us, you see this man, about whom all the multitude of the Jews have dealt with me, both at Jerusalem, and *also* here, crying that he ought not to live any longer.

25 But when I found that he had committed nothing worthy of death, and that he himself has appealed to Augustus, I have determined to send him.

26 Of whom I have no certain thing to write unto my lord *(once again refers to Nero; the Governor is complaining that he is going to send a man to Caesar for a trial, but he has no idea what to tell the Emperor he has done)*. Wherefore I have brought him forth before you, and especially before you, O king Agrippa, that, after examination had, I might have somewhat to write *(he hopes the King, being a Jew, might be able to define the charges a little better)*.

27 For it seems to me unreasonable to send a prisoner, and not withal to signify the crimes *laid* against him *(the Roman world found no fault in Paul, even as Pilate found no fault in Jesus; but the world of religion did, as the world of religion always does!)*.

CHAPTER 26

PAUL'S DEFENSE

THEN Agrippa said unto Paul, You are permitted to speak for yourself. Then Paul stretched forth the hand, and answered for himself:

2 I think myself happy, king Agrippa, because I shall answer for myself this day before you touching all the things whereof I am accused of the Jews:

3 Especially *because I know* you to be expert in all customs and questions which are among the Jews *(this was not offered as flattery; in fact, Agrippa's Father, King Agrippa I, was zealous for*

the Jewish Law up to almost the end of his life): wherefore I beseech you to hear me patiently.

4 My manner of life from my youth, which was at the first among mine own nation at Jerusalem, know all the Jews *(concerns Paul being immersed in Jewish Ritual and Law from the time he was old enough to begin his advanced studies, which was probably about twelve years of age)*;

5 Which knew me from the beginning *(means simply that what he is saying can be easily proven)*, if they would testify, that after the most straitest sect of our religion I lived a Pharisee *(pertains to this group being the most strict in doctrines and moral practices)*.

6 And now I stand and am judged for the hope of the promise made of God unto our Fathers *(this "hope" was the Messiah, the Lord Jesus Christ Whom the Jews rejected)*:

7 Unto which *promise* our Twelve Tribes, instantly serving God day and night, hope to come. For which hope's sake, king Agrippa, I am accused of the Jews *(many of the Jews were looking forward to the fulfillment of the Prophecies regarding the coming Messiah; the great dissension was over Jesus)*.

8 Why should it be thought a thing incredible with you, that God should raise the dead? *(Israel's his-*

tory was one of Miracles, so the dead being raised, as extraordinary as it is, should not come as a surprise.)

9 I verily thought with myself, that I ought to do many things contrary to the Name of Jesus of Nazareth *(presents Paul taking himself back to his dreadful time of unbelief)*.

10 Which thing I also did in Jerusalem: and many of the Saints did I shut up in prison, having received authority from the Chief Priests; and when they were put to death, I gave my voice against *them (we know of Stephen; however, there may have been more)*.

11 And I punished them oft in every Synagogue, and compelled *them* to blaspheme *(should have been translated, "and attempted to compel them to blaspheme," because the Greek Text implies that he was not successful in this effort)*; and being exceedingly mad against them, I persecuted *them* even unto strange cities *(indicates that Damascus was not the only city, other than Jerusalem, where Paul was practicing his deadly wares)*.

12 Whereupon as I went to Damascus with authority and commission from the Chief Priests *(intending to continue his persecution in that city)*,

HIS CONVERSION

13 At midday, O king, I saw in

the way a Light from Heaven *(pro-claims one of, if not, the most dramatic Conversions the world has ever known)*, above the brightness of the Sun, shining round about me and them which journeyed with me *(this was the Glory of Jesus Christ)*.

14 And when we were all fallen to the earth *(the Power of God was so strong that Paul and all his associates with him fell to the ground)*, I heard a Voice speaking unto me, and saying in the Hebrew tongue *(actually speaks of all hearing the Voice, but only Paul knowing what was said [Acts 9:7])*, Saul, Saul *(his Hebrew name)*, why do you persecute Me? *(This proclaims the fact that when we persecute those who belong to the Lord, we in fact persecute the Lord.) it is* hard for you to kick against the pricks *(proclaims a common idiom of that day and even now; in other words, you will only succeed in hurting yourself; you will not stop the Plan of God)*.

15 And I said, Who are you, Lord? *(This proclaims the fact that Paul knew he was speaking to Deity.)* And He said, I am Jesus Whom you persecute *(proclaims the Lord using the Name Paul hated the most — Jesus)*.

16 But rise, and stand upon your feet *(very similar to what the Lord had said to Job many years before [Job 38:3])*: for I have appeared unto you for this purpose *(specifies that the Lord has a very important work for Paul to do)*, to make you a Minister and a witness both of these things which you have seen, and of those things in the which I will appear unto you *(in fact, it would be to Paul that the Lord would give the meaning of the New Covenant, which in effect was the meaning of the Cross [II Cor. 12:1-12])*;

17 Delivering you from the people *(refers to the Jews)*, and from the Gentiles, unto whom now I send you *(the Lord would not allow the death of the Apostle until he had finished his Mission; his primary Mission was to take the Gospel to the Gentiles, which he did)*,

18 To open their eyes, *and* to turn *them* from darkness to light, and *from* the power of Satan unto God, that they may receive forgiveness of sins, and inheritance among them which are Sanctified by Faith that is in Me *(the Apostle pointed out that man is blind, enslaved, impure, immoral, poverty-stricken, and unholy, but he can receive sight, liberty, forgiveness, true wealth and holiness upon the Principle of Faith in Christ and what Christ has done at the Cross)*.

LIGHT

19 Whereupon, O king Agrippa, I was not disobedient unto the

Heavenly Vision *(Paul had faithfully carried out that which the Lord had called him to do)*:

20 But showed first unto them of Damascus *(he preached Christ in Damascus immediately after being saved)*, and at Jerusalem, and throughout all the coasts of Judaea *(pertains to Paul going to Jerusalem immediately after Damascus, and then later to other areas of Judaea)*, and *then* to the Gentiles *(speaks of the far greater majority of his Ministry, even up to this particular time)*, that they should repent and turn to God, and do works meet for repentance *(turn from the heathen idols to God)*.

21 For these causes the Jews caught me in the Temple, and went about to kill *me (Paul is saying that the Jews do not hate him because of their stated reasons, but rather because of his preaching Jesus)*.

22 Having therefore obtained help of God, I continue unto this day, witnessing both to small and great *(proclaims the fact that God has sustained him through some very difficult times)*, saying none other things than those which the Prophets and Moses did say should come *(Paul claims total Scripturality for his Message, which it certainly was)*:

23 That Christ *(the Messiah)* should suffer *(means that he would die; in other words that was the rea-* son *He came [Isa., Chpt. 53])*, *and* that he should be the first who should rise from the dead *(Jesus is the "Firstfruits" of the Resurrection, and therefore the guarantee of the Resurrection of all Believers [I Cor. 15:1-23; Rev. 1:5])*, and should show light unto the people, and to the Gentiles *(refers to the Lord Jesus Christ as being the only "Light," and for all people)*.

FESTUS

24 And as he thus spoke for himself, Festus said with a loud voice, Paul, you are beside yourself; much learning does make you mad *(as a heathen, Festus could not understand as Agrippa could the great argument that the Atoning Death and Resurrection of the Messiah fulfilled the predictions of the Prophets, and were necessary in order to effect the Salvation of sinful men)*.

25 But he said, I am not mad *(insane)*, most noble Festus; but speak forth the Words of Truth and soberness *(presents the only "Truth" the Governor and others present had ever heard)*.

26 For the king *(Agrippa)* knows of these things, before whom also I speak freely: for I am persuaded that none of these things are hidden from him; for this thing was not done in a corner *(King Agrippa most certainly knew of Jesus; it*

would have been impossible for him not to have known).

ALMOST PERSUADED

27 King Agrippa, do you believe the Prophets? *(This presents an Altar Call being given to this King and his Sister, which drilled straight to the heart of this profligate Jew.)* I know that you believe *(presents the Apostle answering for the King, which saved him from embarrassment).*

28 Then Agrippa said unto Paul, Almost thou persuadest me to be a Christian *(the Greek Text does not give any more indication of what the King actually said; it is not known if he was really moved and then said sincerely, "you almost persuade me to be a Christian!" or "do you think you can easily make me a Christian!").*

29 And Paul said, I would to God, that not only you, but also all who hear me this day, were both almost, and altogether such as I am *(the Apostle, through and by the Gospel of Jesus Christ, proclaims the position of the Believer in Christ as being above any other office or position in the world),* except these bonds *(this must have been a dramatic moment when, coupled with the majesty of his words, Paul lifts up his manacled hands forming a picture of arresting grandeur).*

30 And when he had thus spoken, the King rose up, and the Governor, and Bernice, and they who sat with them *(they did not want to hear anymore, so they rose and thus closed the audience, and their opportunity for Eternal Life):*

31 And when they were gone aside, they talked between themselves, saying, This man does nothing worthy of death or of bonds *(they had been brought face-to-face with themselves, and above all with God; as such, they would never be the same again, even though they had rejected the appeal and the plea).*

32 Then said Agrippa unto Festus, This man might have been set at liberty, if he had not appealed unto Caesar *(implies that the appeal had already been registered, and now must be carried out; behind it all, the Lord wanted the Apostle to go to Rome).*

CHAPTER 27

PAUL SAILS FOR ROME

AND when it was determined that we *(Luke is still with Paul)* should sail into Italy *(the time has now arrived when Paul will now go to Rome),* they delivered Paul and certain other prisoners unto *one* named Julius, a centurion of Augustus' band *(this was an elite "band" directly re-*

sponsible to the Emperor).

2 And entering into a ship of Adramyttium, we launched, meaning to sail by the coasts of Asia; *one* Aristarchus, a Macedonian of Thessalonica, being with us *(proclaims another of Paul's converts being with him along with Luke; consequently, Festus allowed Paul two traveling associates [Acts 20:4]).*

3 And the next *day* we touched at Sidon *(a port about seventy miles north of Caesarea).* And Julius courteously entreated Paul, and gave *him* liberty to go unto his friends to refresh himself *(Paul and his associates were allowed to stay with these people in Sidon until the ship sailed; this shows how much trust the Centurion placed in Paul).*

4 And when we had launched from thence *(from Sidon)*, we sailed under Cyprus, because the winds were contrary.

5 And when we had sailed over the sea of Cilicia and Pamphylia, we came to Myra, *a city* of Lycia.

6 And there the centurion found a ship of Alexandria sailing into Italy; and he put us therein *(they changed ships).*

7 And when we had sailed slowly many days, and scarce were come over against Cnidus, the wind not suffering us, we sailed under Crete, over against Salmone *(the winds were not favorable, so they were not making good time);*

8 And, hardly passing it, came unto a place which is called The fair havens; near whereunto was the city *of* Lasea *(there was no town at Fair Havens for them to replenish their stores, with Lasea being about five miles distant).*

9 Now when much time was spent *(spoke of several days with still no favorable winds)*, and when sailing was now dangerous *(pertained to any time after September 14th)*, because the fast was now already past, Paul admonished them *(pertained to the Great Day of Atonement, and was actually a one day fast which Paul and his two associates no doubt kept)*,

10 And said unto them, Sirs, I perceive that this voyage will be with hurt and much damage, not only of the lading *(cargo)* and ship, but also of our lives *(presents that which the Lord had evidently already related to Paul).*

11 Nevertheless the Centurion believed the master and the owner of the ship, more than those things which were spoken by Paul *(they would find to their chagrin that they had chosen wrong).*

12 And because the haven *(Fair Havens)* was not commodious to winter in, the more part advised to depart thence also, if by any means they might attain to

Phenice, *and there* to winter; *which is* an haven of Crete, and lies toward the southwest and northwest *(pertains to a harbor which in fact was commodious, and where some imperial grain ships actually did tie up for the winter; it was about fifty miles west of Fair Havens)*.

13 And when the south wind blew softly, supposing that they had obtained *their* purpose, loosing *thence*, they sailed close by Crete *(pertains to a wind direction for which they had been waiting)*.

THE STORM

14 But not long after there arose against it a tempestuous wind, called Euroclydon *(this was a hurricane)*.

15 And when the ship was caught, and could not bear up into the wind, we let *her* drive *(means that the helmsman simply could not hold the wheel for the force of the wind; so he could do nothing but let the ship drive toward whatever the direction the wind wanted it to go)*.

16 And running under a certain island which is called Clauda, we had much work to come by the boat *(the "boat" of which Luke speaks was a little skiff they were pulling, which was the custom then and remained so for many centuries; due to the storm, they had great difficulty getting this small* boat on board)*:

17 Which when they had taken up, they used helps, undergirding the ship *(these were large ropes which were pulled under the ship and made sure, helping to hold the vessel together in the storm)*; and, fearing lest they should fall into the quicksands, strake sail, and so were driven *(this way they would be driven by the wind, but with few or no sails stretched at all; hopefully the wind would change before they were driven onto the rocks)*.

18 And we being exceedingly tossed with a tempest, the next *day* they lightened the ship *(they had to throw certain things overboard)*;

19 And the third *day* we cast out with our own hands the tackling of the ship *(pertains to the third day after leaving Clauda; they now threw overboard ship equipment, even that which was desperately needed)*.

20 And when neither sun nor stars in many days appeared, and no small tempest lay on *us*, all hope that we should be saved was then taken away *(now all on board knew that they should have listened to Paul)*.

THE VISION

21 But after long abstinence *(does not refer to a "fast" as some claim, but rather that they hadn't had a prepared meal for some days)*

Paul stood forth in the midst of them, and said, Sirs, you should have hearkened unto me, and not have loosed from Crete, and to have gained this harm and loss *(is not really meant as a reprimand by the Apostle, but rather to give foundation to what he is about to say)*.

22 And now I exhort you to be of good cheer: for there shall be no loss of *any man's* life among you, but of the ship *(plainly tells us that the ship will be lost with its cargo of wheat, but not a person will lose their life)*.

23 For there stood by me this night the Angel of God, Whose I am, and Whom I serve *(the statements "Whose I am," "Whom I serve," and "I believe God" [Vs. 25] form a noble confession of Faith)*,

24 Saying, Fear not, Paul *(said in this manner because there had been fear in Paul's heart, as well as everyone else on board)*; you must be brought before Caesar *(not because of Paul's appeal to Caesar, or because of the charges brought against him by the Jews, but rather because of the Divine Plan)*: and, lo, God has given you all them who sail with you *(every Saint had better know as to what Preacher he is "with")*.

25 Wherefore, sirs, be of good cheer: for I believe God, that it shall be even as it was told me *(insinuates that possibly some did not believe what Paul was saying)*.

26 Howbeit we must be cast upon a certain island *(the Angel evidently did not tell Paul what Island!)*.

THE SHIPWRECK

27 But when the fourteenth night was come *(pertained to the length of time after leaving Fair Havens; so the storm had lasted now for about two weeks)*, as we were driven up and down in Adria, about midnight the shipmen deemed that they drew near to some country *(they could hear waves breaking on the beach, or rocks, at some distance)*;

28 And sounded, and found *it* twenty fathoms *(a depth of about 120 feet)*: and when they had gone a little further, they sounded again, and found *it* fifteen fathoms.

29 Then fearing lest we should have fallen upon rocks, they cast four anchors out of the stern, and wished for the day *(were anxious for the night to be over, so they could see where they were)*.

30 And as the shipmen were about to flee out of the ship, when they had let down the boat into the sea *(portrays some, if not all, the ship's crew about to take the only small boat they had and attempt to escape to shore, in effect deserting the ship)*, under cover as though they would have cast anchors out

of the foreship *(presents their deception, but Paul was watching)*,

31 Paul said to the Centurion and to the soldiers, Except these abide in the ship, you cannot be saved *(to obtain God's Promises, we must abide by his conditions).*

32 Then the soldiers cut off the ropes of the boat, and let her fall off *(the Centurion now believes Paul).*

33 And while the day was coming on, Paul besought *them* all to take meat, saying, This day is the fourteenth day that you have tarried and continued fasting, having taken nothing *("nothing!" the Greek word used here means they had eaten no regular meal).*

34 Wherefore I pray you to take *some* meat: for this is for your health *(they should attempt to force at least some food down, irrespective of their seasickness, which no doubt some of them still had)*: for there shall not an hair fall from the head of any of you *(that is, if you will do what I say).*

35 And when he had thus spoken, he took bread, and gave thanks to God in presence of them all *(which every Believer should do at every meal, as well)*: and when he had broken *it*, he began to eat.

36 Then were they all of good cheer, and they also took *some* meat *(some food).*

37 And we were in all in the ship two hundred threescore and sixteen souls *(276 people on board, which meant the ship was quite large).*

38 And when they had eaten enough, they lightened the ship, and cast out the wheat into the sea *(what was left of the cargo still on board).*

39 And when it was day, they knew not the land *(they did not know where they were)*: but they discovered a certain creek with a shore, into the which they were minded, if it were possible, to thrust in the ship *(they wanted to take the ship as close to the shore as possible).*

40 And when they had taken up the anchors, they committed *themselves* unto the sea, and loosed the rudder bands, and hoised up the mainsail to the wind, and made toward shore *(once again, trying to get as close as possible!).*

41 And falling into a place where two seas met, they ran the ship aground; and the forepart stuck fast, and remained unmoveable, but the hinder part was broken with the violence of the waves *(they had not gotten in as close as they desired).*

42 And the soldiers' counsel was to kill the prisoners, lest any of them should swim out, and escape *(the reason for this being that Roman Law condemned guards to death if prisoners escaped under their watch).*

43 But the Centurion, willing

to save Paul, kept them from *their* purpose *(presents this man now knowing Paul was not just another prisoner)*; and commanded that they which could swim should cast *themselves* first *into the sea,* and get to land:

44 And the rest, some on boards, and some on *broken pieces* of the ship. And so it came to pass, that they escaped all safe to land *(fulfilled exactly that which the Angel had conveyed to Paul).*

CHAPTER 28

MELITA

AND when they were escaped, then they knew that the island was called Melita *(it is now called Malta, and is about fifty miles south of Sicily in the Mediterranean).*

2 And the barbarous people showed us no little kindness *(is not meant by Luke to be an insult; it just referred to people who were not influenced by Greek culture)*: for they kindled a fire, and received us every one, because of the present rain, and because of the cold.

THE MIRACLE

3 And when Paul had gathered a bundle of sticks, and laid *them* on the fire, there came a viper out of the heat, and fastened on his hand *(presents Satan, having been unsuccessful in killing Paul with a storm, now trying another tactic).*

4 And when the barbarians saw the *venomous* beast hang on his hand, they said among themselves, No doubt this man is a murderer, whom, though he has escaped the sea, yet vengeance suffers not to live *(they knew that the poison of this particular type of viper would kill any man).*

5 And he shook off the beast into the fire, and felt no harm *(doesn't mean that he did not feel the pain of the bite, but rather did not begin to swell, as instantly was the case normally!).*

6 Howbeit they looked when he should have swollen, or fallen down dead suddenly *(they had personally seen the snake bite Paul, even hanging on his hand; so, they knew the reptile had bitten full force)*: but after they had looked a great while, and saw no harm come to him, they changed their minds, and said that he was a god *(probably referred to Hercules; he was one of the gods of the Phoenicians and was worshiped on Malta under the title of "dispeller of evil").*

7 In the same quarters were possessions of the Chief man of the island, whose name was Publius *(this man had a Roman name, so it probably means he was the Roman official on this Island);*

who received us, and lodged us three days courteously.

HEALING

8 And it came to pass, that the father of Publius lay sick of a fever and of a bloody flux (*presents a medical term which Luke would have used, being a Physician; the man had a reoccurring fever and dysentery*): to whom Paul entered in, and prayed, and laid his hands on him, and healed him (*the Lord is still the Healer*).

9 So when this was done, others also, which had diseases in the island, came, and were healed:

10 Who also honoured us with many honours (*evidently indicates material things such as clothing, food, and even gifts of money, etc.*); and when we departed, they laded *us* with such things as were necessary (*no doubt refers to the entirety of the 276 people who had been shipwrecked*).

11 And after three months we departed in a ship of Alexandria, which had wintered in the isle, whose sign was Castor and Pollux (*evidently portrayed another grain ship from the same city where the wrecked ship had been based [Acts 27:6]; the two signs mentioned here were the favorite divinities of Mediterranean seamen at that time; it was the custom to have their images, whatever they were, on the head and stern of their ships*).

12 And landing at Syracuse, we tarried *there* three days (*Syracuse was the capitol of Sicily, about eighty miles north of Malta*).

13 And from thence we fetched a compass (*took a heading*), and came to Rhegium: and after one day the south wind blew, and we came the next day to Puteoli (*Puteoli was the chief port on the Bay of Naples*):

14 Where we found Brethren (*those who were followers of Christ*), and were desired to tarry with them seven days (*the Centurion allowed Paul to remain with these Brethren, and no doubt preach the Gospel to them for this length of time*): and so we went toward Rome (*finds them finishing this perilous journey on foot*).

15 And from thence, when the Brethren (*from Rome*) heard of us, they came to meet us as far as Appii forum, and The Three Taverns (*a runner evidently went to the Capitol informing the Brethren that Paul was coming; consequently, it seems a group went to meet Paul*): whom when Paul saw, he thanked God, and took courage (*refers to the fellowship the Apostle and those with him greatly enjoyed*).

ROME

16 And when we came to Rome, the Centurion delivered the pris-

oners to the Captain of the Guard *(pertained to the Commander of Nero's Praetorian Guard)*: but Paul was suffered to dwell by himself with a soldier who kept him *(obviously means Paul was treated differently from the other prisoners; he was evidently granted special favors)*.

17 And it came to pass, that after three days Paul called the Chief of the Jews together *(not only refers to the main Jewish Leader in Rome, but the other leaders as well)*: and when they were come together, he said unto them, Men and Brethren *(the following account seems to indicate that the Brethren of Verse 15 had no connection with these Jewish leaders)*, though I have committed nothing against the people, or customs of our Fathers, yet was I delivered prisoner from Jerusalem into the hands of the Romans *(proclaims the Apostle relating the situation exactly as it had happened)*.

18 Who, when they had examined me, would have let *me* go, because there was no cause of death in me *(pertained to the Romans, not the Jews, as the next Verse explains)*.

19 But when the Jews spoke against *it*, I was constrained to appeal unto Caesar *(proclaims the Apostle having done this in order to save his life)*; not that I had ought to accuse my nation of *(he was in no way in Rome to bring charges against the Jews or to cause them problems in any manner)*.

20 For this cause therefore have I called for you, to see *you*, and to speak with *you*: because that for the hope of Israel I am bound with this chain *(in effect he is saying that all of this is because of his proclamation of Christ as the Messiah of Israel, and the Saviour of the world)*.

PAUL

21 And they said unto him, We neither received letters out of Judaea concerning you, neither any of the Brethren who came showed or spoke any harm of you *(probably pertained to the fact that Roman Law punished unsuccessful prosecutors of Roman citizens; it is difficult to comprehend that these Jewish leaders in Rome had never heard of Paul, but it seems somewhat that this was the case, or else their knowledge of him was scant)*.

22 But we desire to hear of you what you think *(proclaims a great opportunity now presented to Paul)*: for as concerning this sect *(Christianity)*, we know that everywhere it is spoken against *(true Bible Christianity continues to be "everywhere spoken against")*.

23 And when they had appointed him a day, there came many to him into *his* lodging *(it is believed that he was allowed to rent*

a house, and there abide during his stay in Rome); to whom he expounded and testified the Kingdom of God, persuading them concerning Jesus, both out of the Law of Moses, and *out of* the Prophets, from morning till evening *(they heard the "Word" as they had never heard the "Word" before; above all, they heard about Jesus, to Whom the Word pointed)*.

24 And some believed the things which were spoken, and some believed not *(some embraced Christ as Lord, Messiah, and Saviour, and some did not)*.

THE JEWS

25 And when they agreed not among themselves, they departed, after that Paul had spoken one word, Well spoke the Holy Spirit by Isaiah the Prophet unto our Fathers *(proclaims the instrument as Isaiah, but the Speaker as the Holy Spirit)*,

26 Saying, Go unto this people, and say, Hearing you shall hear, and shall not understand; and seeing you shall see, and not perceive *(Isa. 6:9-10; presents the sixth of seven times this is recorded by the Holy Spirit [Isa. 6:9; Mat. 13:14; Mk. 4:12; Lk. 8:10; Jn. 12:40; Acts 28:26; Rom. 11:8])*:

27 For the heart of this people is waxed gross, and their ears are dull of hearing, and their eyes have they closed; lest they should see with *their* eyes, and hear with *their* ears, and understand with *their* heart, and should be converted, and I should heal them *(this is a willful rejection of Truth, which brings about a willful judgment of the hardening of the heart)*.

28 Be it known therefore unto you, that the Salvation of God is sent unto the Gentiles, and *that* they will hear it *(presents Paul's last statement to the Jewish leadership of Rome that day; in effect, he says that the "Salvation of God" is found only in Jesus)*.

29 And when he had said these words, the Jews departed, and had great reasoning among themselves *(discussing greatly what he had said)*.

ROME

30 And Paul dwelt two whole years in his own hired house *(rented house)*, and received all who came in unto him *(no doubt strengthened the Church mightily in Rome)*,

31 Preaching the Kingdom of God *(refers to the Rule of God in the human heart and life)*, and teaching those things which concern the Lord Jesus Christ, with all confidence, no man forbidding him *(it is said that even some from Caesar's household were converted [Phil. 4:22])*.

THE EPISTLE OF PAUL THE APOSTLE TO THE
ROMANS

CHAPTER 1

INTRODUCTION

PAUL *(the only Bible writer who discarded his Jewish name [Saul] for his Gentile name [Paul])*, a servant *(a voluntary Bondslave)* of Jesus Christ, called *to be* an Apostle *(he puts "Bondslave" ahead of Apostle)*, separated unto the Gospel of God *(means that Paul was separated by God from all mankind for his Apostleship)*,

2 (Which He *(God)* had promised afore by His Prophets in the Holy Scriptures,) *(He promised the Redeemer, Who would be the Lord Jesus Christ.)*

3 Concerning His Son Jesus Christ our Lord *(speaks of Jesus being the Core Message of the Old Testament)*, which was made *(signifies entrance into a new condition)* of the Seed of David *(through the family of David)* according to the flesh *(the Incarnation, God becoming man)*;

4 And declared *to be* the Son of God with power *(He was the Son of David regarding His humanity, and the Son of God regarding His Deity)*, according to the Spirit of Holiness *(presents another Name for the Holy Spirit)*, by the Resurrection from the dead *(the Jews Crucified Jesus because He claimed to be the Son of God; God Resurrected Him because He was the Son of God)*:

5 By Whom *(by God)* we have received Grace *(unmerited favor)* and Apostleship *(the Call)*, for obedience to the Faith *(Jesus Christ and Him Crucified)* among all nations *(one Gospel for the entirety of the world)*, for His Name *(He is the One Who has purchased our Redemption, by and through the Cross of Calvary)*;

6 Among whom *(all Believers)* are you also the called of Jesus Christ *(every person who is saved has been called of the Lord from something to something)*:

7 To all who be in Rome, Beloved of God, called *to be* Saints *("to be" was improperly supplied by the Translators; every person who is saved is a Saint, and made so by Jesus Christ and what He did at the Cross)*: Grace to you *(which comes through the Cross)* and peace *(Sanctifying Peace)* from God our Father, and the Lord Jesus Christ *(presents the Trinity, with the Holy Spirit inspiring these words to be written)*.

THANKSGIVING

8 First, I thank my God through Jesus Christ for you all, that your faith is spoken of throughout the whole world *(speaks of the Roman Empire)*.

9 For God is my witness, whom I serve with my spirit *(his human spirit)* in the Gospel of His Son *(Jesus Christ and Him Crucified)*, that without ceasing I make mention of you always in my prayers *(Paul had a strong prayer life)*;

10 Making request *(has to do with seeking the Lord about a certain thing, in this case the privilege of ministering to the Church at Rome)*, if by any means now at length I might have a prosperous journey by the Will of God to come unto you *(Acts, Chpts. 27 and 28, record that journey; it was very prosperous spiritually, but not prosperous in other ways)*.

11 For I long to see you, that I may impart unto you some spiritual gift *(does not mean, as some think, that Paul could impart one or more of the nine Gifts of the Spirit, but rather speaks of explaining to them more perfectly the Word of God)*, to the end you may be established *(spiritual Gifts, as valuable as they are, do not establish anyone; it is the Truth of the Word which establishes, and that alone [Jn. 8:32])*;

12 That is, that I may be comforted together with you by the mutual faith both of you and me *(carries the idea of a mutual strengthening brought about by his Ministry among them, and their Love shown to him)*.

13 Now I would not have you ignorant, Brethren *(a phrase often used by Paul)*, that oftentimes I purposed to come unto you, (but was let hitherto,) *(something hindered)* that I might have some fruit among you also, even as among other Gentiles *(he knew that his teaching concerning the Cross would help them to grow in Grace)*.

14 I am debtor *(true of every Believer)* both to the Greeks, and to the Barbarians; both to the wise, and to the unwise *(to all people, whomever they might be, and wherever they might be)*.

15 So, as much as in me is, I am ready to preach the Gospel to you who are at Rome also.

THE POWER

16 For I am not ashamed of the Gospel of Christ *(is said in reference to the Cross)*: for it is the Power of God unto Salvation to every one who believes; to the Jew first, and also to the Greek *(through the Cross, and the Cross alone, man is reconciled unto God)*.

17 For therein *(through the Cross)* is the Righteousness of God *(Right with God)* revealed from faith to faith *("from Faith" relates to God as the Provider and "to Faith" relates to man as the receiver)*: as it is written, The just shall live by Faith *(proclaims Paul showing that Righteousness by Faith is no new idea, but found in the Prophets [Hab. 2:4])*.

GUILT

18 For the Wrath of God *(God's Personal Emotion with regard to sin)* is revealed from Heaven *(this anger originates with God)* against all ungodliness and unrighteousness of men *(God must unalterably be opposed to sin)*, who hold the truth in unrighteousness *(who refuse to recognize Who God is, and what God is)*;

19 Because that which may be known of God is manifest in them *(speaks of the universal objective knowledge of God as the Creator, which is more or less in all men)*; for God has showed *it* unto them *(means that His Signature is in Creation)*.

20 For the invisible things of Him from the creation of the world are clearly seen *(explains Verse 19)*, being understood by the things that are made *(Creation demands a Creator)*, *even* His Eternal Power and Godhead; so that

they are without excuse *(the Creation tells us of the Eternal Power of God, and is obvious to all)*:

APOSTASY

21 Because that, when they knew God, they glorified *Him* not as God *(if men do not understand God in the realm of Creation, they will not understand Him in anything else)*, neither were thankful *(refusing to honor Him resulted in a lack of gratitude for His Gifts)*; but became vain in their imaginations *(presents the only direction that fallen man can go, considering he has rejected God)*, and their foolish heart was darkened *(speaks of the rejection of Light)*.

22 Professing themselves to be wise, they became fools *(lays waste to all so-called wisdom which is not of God)*,

23 And changed the glory of the uncorruptible God *(presents the sin of the ages, and points not only to the heathen of old, but also much of modern Christendom)* into an image made like to corruptible man, and to birds, and fourfooted beasts, and creeping things *(proclaims the degeneration of man, which is the opposite of evolution)*.

RESULTS OF APOSTASY

24 Wherefore God also gave

them up to uncleanness through the lusts of their own hearts (*not merely permissive, but God judicially delivered them over*), to dishonour their own bodies between themselves (*speaks of every type of immorality*):

25 Who changed the Truth of God into a lie (*refers back to Verse 23, which speaks of spiritual and sexual uncleanness*), and worshipped and served the creature more than the Creator (*this refers to man worshiping the creation of his own hands, which means that he is worshiping something less than himself*), Who is blessed forever. Amen (*should have been translated "Bless-ed" [two syllables], because it refers to the one doing the blessing, in this case the Lord*).

26 For this cause God gave them up unto vile affections (*the Lord removed His restraints and, therefore, gave them unimpeded access to their desires*): for even their women did change the natural use into that which is against nature (*in short speaks of Lesbianism*):

27 And likewise also the men (*homosexuality*), leaving the natural use of the woman (*speaks of the sex act which is performed between the man and his wife*), burned in their lust one toward another (*raging lust*); men with men working that which is unseemly (*specifies its direction, which is total perversion*), and receiving in themselves that recompence of their error which was meet (*refers to the penalty attached to wrongdoing*).

28 And even as they did not like to retain God in *their* knowledge (*carries the idea of the human race putting God to the test for the purpose of approving or disapproving Him*), God gave them over to a reprobate mind (*Light rejected is Light withdrawn*), to do those things which are not convenient (*which are not fitting*);

APOSTATES

29 Being filled with all unrighteousness, fornication, wickedness, covetousness, maliciousness; full of envy, murder, debate, deceit, malignity; whisperers,

30 Backbiters, haters of God, despiteful, proud, boasters, inventors of evil things, disobedient to parents,

31 Without understanding, covenant breakers, without natural affection, implacable, unmerciful (*these things listed are the end results of forsaking God, which is the reason for all the strife in the world*):

32 Who knowing the judgment of God (*in essence saying, "do Your worst, and it will not*

stop us"), that they which commit such things are worthy of death *(Divine Judgment is implied),* not only do the same, but have pleasure in them who do them *(proclaims the result of the "reprobate mind").*

CHAPTER 2

CRITICS

THEREFORE you are inexcusable, O man, whosoever you are who judges *(presents this segment as directed to the Jews):* for wherein you judge another, you condemn yourself *(in effect says that God judges one who judges another in the same manner in which he himself has judged, hence, "condemning himself" [Mat. 7:1-2]);* for you who judge do the same things *(in effect, says that the Jews were no better than the Gentiles, whom they constantly berated).*

GOD'S JUDGMENT

2 But we are sure that the Judgment of God is according to Truth *(proclaims that which is never of presumption)* against them which commit such things *(proclaims a perfect Judgment, because it comes from Truth).*

3 And do you think this, O man, who judges them which do such things, and do the same *(you, the Jew),* that you shall escape the Judgment of God? *(Many Jews thought the privilege of birth as a Jew would of itself insure his entrance into the Kingdom [Mat. 3:8-9].)*

4 Or despise you the riches of his goodness and forbearance and longsuffering *(presents the Jew as holding these things in contempt, thinking that they were worthy of such);* not knowing that the goodness of God leads you *(trying to lead you)* to Repentance?

5 But after your hardness and impenitent heart *(speaks of a hardness toward God, with a refusal to repent)* treasured up unto yourself wrath against the day of wrath and revelation of the Righteous Judgment of God *(Judgment was building up, and ultimately exploded over the Jews; we speak of A.D. 70);*

6 Who will render to every man according to his deeds *(we reap what we sow!):*

7 To them who by patient continuance in well doing *(portrays those who are not trusting in place or position for their Salvation, but rather in Christ)* seek for glory and honour and immortality, Eternal Life *(this speaks of that which comes exclusively from God):*

8 But unto them who are contentious *(carries the idea of contending with God),* and do not

obey the Truth *(attempt to devise a way other than Christ and Him Crucified)*, but obey unrighteousness, indignation and wrath *(the opposite of Truth)*,

9 Tribulation and anguish, upon every soul of man who does evil *(presents the natural results of the unnatural act of sin)*, of the Jew first *(held more responsible)*, and also of the Gentile *(will answer as well!)*;

NO RESPECTER OF PERSONS

10 But glory, honour, and peace, to every man who works good *(presents God's logic, which proclaims if certain things are done, certain things will follow)*, to the Jew first, and also to the Gentile *(is given again to show the place of prominence respecting the Jew, but which they forfeited)*:

11 For there is no respect of persons with God *(literally translated, the Verse reads, "for there is not a receiving of face in the Presence of God"; it means that God doesn't receive or accept anyone's face, irrespective as to whom they might be)*.

12 For as many as have sinned without Law shall also perish without Law *(while the Lord will not hold the Gentiles accountable to the Law of Moses regarding Old Testament times, this in no way means that He will not hold them accountable for their sin; the fact of sin is not abrogated in any case respecting ignorance)*: and as many as have sinned in the Law shall be judged by the Law *(in effect places the Jew in a more responsible and even fearful situation)*;

13 (For not the hearers of the Law *are* just before God *(the mere having of the Law, or even hearing the Law, saves no one)*, but the doers of the Law shall be justified *(is used by Paul in this manner to make a point; he is not meaning that the keeping of the Law of Moses could actually bring Justification; in fact, due to man's fallen condition, he could not keep the Law)*.

14 For when the Gentiles, which have not the Law *(Law of Moses)*, do by nature the things contained in the Law *(their conscience told them some semblance of right and wrong)*, these, having not the Law, are a Law unto themselves *(at the Great White Throne Judgment, God will Judge the Gentile world which existed before the Law according to that which they did know; once again, this has nothing to do with Salvation; ignorance has never brought Salvation)*:

15 Which show the work of the Law written in their hearts *(means that no one, whomever they might be and wherever they might be, is absent of all Light)*, their conscience also bearing witness *(but*

which can be seared), and their thoughts the mean while accusing or else excusing one another (conscience does not prove a reliable guide, as is proclaimed here);)

16 In the day when God shall Judge the secrets of men by Jesus Christ (lays to rest any idea that Judgment will be on any other basis; while many other things, such as conscience, may be a witness, still Jesus Alone is the criteria) according to my Gospel (Jesus Christ and Him Crucified).

GUILT

17 Behold, you are called a Jew (implying special favor from God), and rest in the Law (presents the picture of a blind and mechanical reliance on the Mosaic Law which could not save, and had never been meant to save), and make your boast of God (glorying in who they were),

18 And know His Will (Israel had the literal Word of God, which no other Nation in the world had at that time), and approve the things that are more excellent (they had proved the Word over and over), being instructed out of the Law (in essence means that they were instructed by the very Mouth of God);

19 And are confident that you yourself are a guide of the blind (the Jews were meant by God to be the guides of the Gentiles, to lead them to the Lord), a light of them which are in darkness (it was always God's Will that His Word, Will, and Way, be given to the entirety of mankind),

20 An instructor of the foolish (the Gentile world was foolish in their worship of their gods of human invention), a teacher of babes (presents the Holy Spirit looking at Greek Philosophers as no more than infants), which have the form of knowledge and of the truth of the Law (the Jews had the Word of God, which put them light years ahead of the balance of mankind).

21 You therefore which teach another, do you not teach yourself? (The Jews made fun of the Gentile world, but little applied themselves to the Law, at least as they should have.) you who preach a man should not steal, do you steal? (Most of them did!)

22 You who say a man should not commit adultery, do you commit adultery? (Many did!) you who abhor idols, do you commit sacrilege? (In a sense, the Holy Spirit through Paul is placing Israel in the same state as the Gentile world.)

23 You who make your boast of the Law, through breaking the Law you dishonor God? (In other words, due to having the Law and not keeping the Law, they were dishonoring God, even more than the

Gentiles were.)

24 For the Name of God is blasphemed among the Gentiles through you *(proclaims the Jews bringing reproach upon the Lord by living in open contradiction to their own profession)*, as it is written *(Isa. 52:5)*.

25 For Circumcision verily profits, if you keep the Law *(in other words, Circumcision profited nothing if they were breaking the Law of God)*: but if you be a breaker of the Law, your Circumcision is made uncircumcision *(proclaims the fact that religious rites, no matter how much God-given, contain no properties of Salvation)*.

26 Therefore if the uncircumcision *(Gentiles)* keep the Righteousness of the Law *(through Jesus Christ)*, shall not his uncircumcision be counted for Circumcision? *(This proclaims that one's trust in Jesus satisfies the demands of the Law, and thereby secures the "Righteousness of the Law," which in fact is the only way it can be secured.)*

27 And shall not uncircumcision which is by nature, if it fulfil the Law, judge you *(proclaims the obvious results of the changed life upon Faith in Christ)*, who by the letter and Circumcision do transgress the Law? *(This speaks of the Jews who, outside of Christ, try to keep the letter of the Law by engaging in all of its Rituals, but*

continue to transgress the Law. In other words, what they are doing doesn't change their lives.)*

DEFINITION

28 For he is not a Jew, which is one outwardly *(completely destroys national Salvation)*; neither is that Circumcision, which is outward in the flesh *(the mere Ritual is no true Circumcision at all, and spiritually affords nothing)*:

29 But he is a Jew, which is one inwardly *(it is only the work carried out by Christ inwardly which constitutes Salvation)*; and Circumcision is that of the heart, in the spirit *(refers to the "heart" of the individual being changed, which is done in one's spirit and speaks of being "Born-again")*, and not in the letter *(refers to the rules and regulations of the Law of Moses, or even such in the Church)*; whose praise is not of men, but of God *(keeping religious Rituals garners the praise of men, but not of God; men can truly praise God only when they truly accept Christ, which means to truly trust Christ and not men's religious Rituals)*.

CHAPTER 3

THE JEW

WHAT advantage then has the Jew? *(This proclaims the Apo-*

stle asking such after he has shown that the mere possession of the Law does not exempt the Jew from Judgment.) or what profit *is there* of Circumcision? *(The rite of Circumcision symbolizes the entirety of the Law.)*

2 Much every way *(proclaims tremendous advantages, but none which could save their souls, other than simple Faith in Christ and the Cross, which all the Sacrifices of the Law symbolized)*: chiefly, because that unto them were committed the Oracles of God *(presents the title for the Old Testament as given by the Holy Spirit).*

3 For what if some did not believe? *(This proclaims the unbelief which rejected the Bible, but by no means nullified its Truthfulness.)* shall their unbelief make the Faith of God without effect? *(The unbelief of Israel in no way affected the Great Plan that God has provided for humanity, which is built on the premise of Faith.)*

4 God forbid *(proclaims Paul's answer to the questions of Verse 3)*: yes, let God be true, but every man a liar *(shows us that the problem is always of man, never of God)*; as it is written, That you might be justified in your sayings, and might overcome when you are judged *([Ps. 51:4] this statement is from David's Repentance regarding the matter of Uriah, in which David absolves God from all* blame and takes the blame on himself; this is a pattern for True Repentance).

5 But if our unrighteousness commend the Righteousness of God, what shall we say? *(In no way does this mean that God places an approval upon sin of any nature.)* Is God unrighteous Who takes vengeance? *(The answer is "No!")* (I speak as a man) *(This is meant apologetically in that only a foolish man would ask such a question.)*

6 God forbid *(once again serves as Paul's answer to the preposterous question of the previous Verse)*: for then how shall God Judge the world? *(This is the Great White Throne Judgment [Rev. 20:11-15]. The fact that this Judgment cannot be avoided means the hypothesis of man is foolish indeed.)*

7 For if the Truth of God has more abounded through my lie unto His Glory *(is meant to be answered in the negative, for such a thing cannot be done)*; why yet am I also judged as a sinner? *(This is meant to portray the foolishness of such thinking.)*

8 And not *rather*, (as we be slanderously reported, and as some affirm that we say,) Let us do evil, that good may come? *(This presents the reason Paul is addressing this subject. Because of his strong teaching on Grace, his detractors were slandering him*

by claiming he was teaching something he wasn't.) whose damnation is just *(proclaims the Apostle saying that those who report such slander are liable to a just damnation)*.

GUILT

9 What then? are we better than they? *(Are Jews better than Gentiles?)* No, in no wise: for we have before proved both Jews and Gentiles, that they are all under sin *(points to the supposed claim of the Jews of superiority, which is refuted)*;

10 As it is written *(Ps. 14:1-3)*, There is none righteous, no, not one *(addresses the complaint of the Jews and clinches the argument with the Scriptures, which the Jews could not deny)*:

11 There is none who understands *(proclaims total depravity)*, there is none who seek after God *(man left on his own will not seek God, and in fact cannot seek God; he is spiritually dead)*.

12 They are all gone out of the Way *(speaks of the lost condition of all men; the "Way" is God's Way)*, they are together become unprofitable *(refers to the terrible loss in every capacity of wayward man)*; there is none who does good, no, not one *(the Greek Text says, "useless!")*.

13 Their throat *is* an open sepulcher *(the idea is of an open grave, with the rotting remains sending forth a putrid stench)*; with their tongues they have used deceit *(speaks of guile, deception, hypocrisy, etc.)*; the poison of asps *is* under their lips *(man cannot be trusted in anything he says)*:

14 Whose mouth *is* full of cursing *(wishing someone evil or hurt)* and bitterness *(bitter and reproachful language)*:

15 Their feet *are* swift to shed blood *(the world is filled with murder, killing, and violence)*:

16 Destruction and misery *are* in their ways *(all brought about by sin)*:

17 And the way of peace have they not known *(and cannot know until Christ returns)*:

18 There is no fear of God before their eyes *(there is no fear of God, because unbelieving man does not know God)*.

19 Now we know that what things soever the Law says, it says to them who are under the Law *(is meant first of all to inform the Jews that Verses 10 through 18 apply to them as well as the Gentiles)*: that every mouth may be stopped *(the Gentiles were claiming ignorance, while the Jews were claiming exception from Judgment)*, and all the world may become guilty before God *(states the case exactly as it is, meaning all need a Saviour)*.

20 Therefore by the deeds of the Law there shall no flesh be justified in His sight *(should read, "by works of the Law")*: for by the Law *is* the knowledge of sin *(the Law in itself was only meant to define sin, it in no way delivered from sin, nor was it designed to do so!).*

THE REMEDY

21 But now the Righteousness of God without the Law is manifested *(should read, "apart from Law, i.e., "from works of merit"),* being witnessed by the Law and the Prophets *(Testimony of the Law to the Divine Principle of Justification by Faith is found in Genesis 15:6; the Testimony of the Prophets in Habakkuk 2:4);*

22 Even the Righteousness of God *which is* by Faith of Jesus Christ *(concerns Imputed Righteousness, and tells how it is obtained)* unto all and upon all them who believe *(the criteria is believing, and believing in Christ and Him Crucified)*: for there is no difference *(Salvation is by Faith, whether the person is a Jew or a Gentile)*:

23 For all have sinned *(presents all men placed in the same category),* and come short of the Glory of God *(the Greek Text infers that even the most Righteous among us continue to come short of the Glory of God on a continuing basis);*

24 Being justified freely by His Grace *(made possible by the Cross)* through the Redemption that is in Christ Jesus *(carried out at the Cross)*:

25 Whom God has set forth *to be* a propitiation *(Atonement or Reconciliation)* through Faith in His Blood *(again, all of this is made possible by the Cross)*, to declare His Righteousness for the remission of sins that are past *(refers to all who trusted Christ before He actually came, which covers the entirety of the time from the Garden of Eden to the moment Jesus died on the Cross)*, through the forbearance *(tolerance)* of God *(meaning that God tolerated the situation before Calvary, knowing the debt would be fully paid at that time);*

26 To declare, *I say*, at this time His Righteousness *(refers to God's Righteousness which must be satisfied at all times, and is in Christ and only Christ)*: that He *(God)* might be just *(not overlooking sin in any manner)*, and the Justifier of him which believes in Jesus *(God can justify a believing [although guilty] sinner, and His Holiness not be impacted, providing the sinner's Faith is exclusively in Christ; only in this manner can God be "just" and at the same time "Justify" the sinner).*

27 Where *is* boasting then? *(This refers primarily to the Jews boasting of themselves as a result of the Law of God given to them, but the principle is true for modern Christians as well!)* It is excluded *(not only means that God will not accept such boasting [outside of Christ], but that it actually serves to keep one from Salvation).* By what Law? of works? *(In a sense, this tells us where and how the boasting, God will not accept, originates).* No: but by the Law of Faith *(refers to trust exclusively in Christ and what He did at the Cross; Faith in Christ and Him Crucified is more than a principle; it is a Law, meaning that God will not deviate at all from this proclamation).*

28 Therefore we conclude that a man is justified by Faith *(and only by Faith, with the Cross ever being the object of such Faith)* without the deeds of the Law *(faith in works is out).*

29 *Is He* the God of the Jews only? *is He* not also of the Gentiles? Yes, of the Gentiles also *(it is one Salvation for all, and all gain this Salvation by Faith)*:

30 Seeing *it is* One God, which shall justify the Circumcision by Faith *(places the Jew on the same level as the Gentile)*, and uncircumcision through faith *(Jews and Gentiles are all saved alike, through Faith in Christ and what Christ has done at the Cross).*

31 Do we then make void the Law *(Law of Moses)* through faith? God forbid: yes, we establish the Law *(the Law ever pointed to Faith in Christ).*

CHAPTER 4

ABRAHAM

WHAT shall we say then that Abraham our father, as pertaining to the flesh, has found? *(Having stated that the Old Testament teaches that God justifies the sinner on the Faith principle as opposed to the merit principle, the Holy Spirit now brings forward Abraham.)*

2 For if Abraham were justified by works *(which he wasn't)*, he has *whereof* to glory; but not before God *(the boasting of Salvation by works, which God will not accept).*

3 For what says the Scripture? Abraham believed God, and it was counted unto him for Righteousness *([Gen. 15:6] if one properly understands this Verse, he properly understands the Bible; Abraham gained Righteousness by simple Faith in God, Who would send a Redeemer into the world [Jn. 8:56]).*

4 Now to him who works *(tries to earn Salvation)* is the reward *(Righteousness)* not reckoned of

Grace (the Grace of God), but of debt (claiming that God owes us something, which He doesn't!).

5 But to him who works not (doesn't trust in works for Salvation), but believes on Him Who Justifies the ungodly (through Christ and the Cross), his faith is counted for Righteousness (God awards Righteousness only on the basis of Faith in Christ and His Finished Work).

6 Even as David (both Abraham and David were progenitors of the Promised Messiah, and as such they held a unique place in the Faith and veneration of the Work of God) also describes the blessedness of the man (a blessed man), unto whom God imputes Righteousness without works (works will never gain the Righteousness of God),

7 Saying, Blessed are they whose iniquities are forgiven ([Ps. 32:1-2] iniquities can only be forgiven by Faith in Christ), and whose sins are covered (the Cross made this possible).

8 Blessed is the man to whom the Lord will not impute sin (the Lord will not impute sin to the person who places his Faith solely in Christ and what Christ did at the Cross).

9 Comes this blessedness then upon the Circumcision only, or upon the uncircumcision also? (It comes on all alike!) for we say that Faith was reckoned to Abraham for Righteousness (presents Faith alone as the ingredient).

10 How was it then reckoned? (This may be the greatest question of all time.) when he was in Circumcision, or in uncircumcision? Not in Circumcision, but in uncircumcision (because of his Faith, Abraham was declared Righteous by God before the Covenant of Circumcision [Gen. 15:6]).

11 And he received the sign of Circumcision (Gen. 17:9-14), a seal of the Righteousness of the Faith which he had yet being uncircumcised (plainly states that his Righteousness was by Faith, and was received long before Circumcision): that he might be the father of all them who believe (Jews and Gentiles), though they be not Circumcised (places the ground or Foundation of Salvation squarely on Faith instead of works); that Righteousness might be imputed unto them also (Righteousness has never been imputed on the ground of works, but always on the ground of Faith):

12 And the father of Circumcision to them who are not of the Circumcision only (presents Abraham as being the father of all Believers, whether Jews or Gentiles), but who also walk in the steps of that Faith of our father Abraham (refers to him simply believing God, and God accounting his Faith to

him for Righteousness [Gen. 15:6]), which *he had* being *yet* uncircumcised *(clinches the argument and opens up Salvation to all who come by Faith in Christ, irrespective as to whom they may be).*

THE PROMISE

13 For the Promise, that he should be the heir of the world, *was* not to Abraham, or to his seed, through the Law *(the Law of Moses, which had not even been given during the time of Abraham)*, but through the Righteousness of Faith *(when Paul uses the word "Faith," without exception, he is speaking of Faith in Christ and what Christ did at the Cross; in fact, Christ must never be separated from the Cross, as it regards His Redemptive Work).*

14 For if they which are of the Law *be* heirs *(only those in the Law)*, faith is made void *(Salvation cannot exist in both works and Faith; either one cancels out the other)*, and the Promise made of none effect *(faith in works cancels out Christ and all that He has done for us)*:

15 Because the Law works wrath *(Law has a penalty, so it must work wrath)*: for where no Law is, *there* is no transgression *(Christ has satisfied the Law, thereby taking away all transgression).*

16 Therefore *it is* of Faith, that

it *might be* by Grace *(Grace functions only on Faith, and we speak of Faith in Christ; otherwise, Grace stops)*; to the end the Promise might be sure to all the seed *(refers to the whole of humanity, at least those who will believe)*; not to that only which is of the Law *(Jews)*, but to that also which is of the faith of Abraham *(everything is by Faith)*; who is the father of us all *(proclaims the Patriarch being used as an example of Faith [Gen. 15:6])*,

JUSTIFICATION

17 (As it is written, I have made you a father of many nations *[Genesis 12:1-3; 17:4-5]*,) before Him Whom he believed, *even* God *(refers to Abraham believing God)*, who quickens the dead *(makes spiritually alive those who are spiritually dead)*, and calls those things which be not as though they were *(if God has said it to us personally, we can call it; otherwise, it is presumption).*

18 Who against hope believed in hope *(a description of Abraham's Faith, as it regarded the birth of Isaac)*, that he might become the father of many nations; according to that which was spoken *(the Promise of God)*, So shall your seed be *(Gen. 15:5).*

19 And being not weak in faith *(strong Faith)*, he considered not

his own body now dead, when he was about an hundred years old *(no longer able to have children)*, neither yet the deadness of Sarah's womb *(placed her in the same situation as her husband)*:

20 He staggered not at the Promise of God through unbelief *(he did not allow difficulties to deter him from the intended conclusion)*; but was strong in Faith, giving Glory to God *(his Faith came from the Word of God)*;

21 And being fully persuaded *(no turning back)* that, what He *(God)* had Promised, He was able also to perform *(whatever it was, God could do it!)*.

22 And therefore it was imputed to him for Righteousness *(simple Faith in God brought Abraham a spotless Righteousness)*.

23 Now it was not written for his sake alone *(his struggle of Faith was meant to serve as an example)*, that it was imputed to him *(serves as the example of how we receive from God, whether it be Salvation or anything else)*;

24 But for us also, to whom it shall be imputed *(we can have that which Abraham had, a perfect Righteousness)*, if we believe on Him Who raised up Jesus our Lord from the dead *(proclaims the condition for Salvation)*;

25 Who was delivered for our offences *(had to do with Jesus dying on the Cross for our sins; He*

had no sins), and was raised again for our Justification *(we were raised with Him in newness of life [Rom. 6:4-5])*.

CHAPTER 5

JUSTIFICATION BY FAITH

THEREFORE being justified by Faith *(this is the only way one can be justified; refers to Faith in Christ and what He did at the Cross)*, we have peace with God *(justifying peace)* through our Lord Jesus Christ *(what He did at the Cross)*:

2 By Whom also we have access by Faith into this Grace *(we have access to the Goodness of God by Faith in Christ)* wherein we stand *(wherein alone we can stand)*, and rejoice in hope *(a hope that is guaranteed)* of the Glory of God *(our Faith in Christ always brings Glory to God; anything else brings glory to self, which God can never accept)*.

3 And not only so, but we glory in tribulations also *(in the fact that tribulations do not hurt us)*: knowing that tribulation works patience *(points to the characteristic of a man who is unswerved from his deliberate purpose and his loyalty to Faith, even by the greatest trials and sufferings)*;

4 And patience, experience *(points to an end result)*; and experience, hope *(presents the natural*

product of an approved experience).

5 And hope makes not ashamed *(in effect tells us that this is not a false hope)*; because the Love of God is shed abroad in our hearts *(God's Love brings all of this about)* by the Holy Spirit which is given unto us *(all of this is wholly a work of the Holy Spirit)*.

6 For when we were yet without strength *(before we were saved)*, in due time *(at the appointed time)* Christ died for the ungodly *(the entirety of humanity fell into this category)*.

7 For scarcely for a Righteous man will one die *(not many would do such)*: yet peradventure for a good man some would even dare to die *(some few might)*.

8 But God commend His Love toward us *(Christ dying for the ungodly is a proof of Love immeasurable)*, in that, while we were yet sinners, Christ died for us *(Jesus died for those who bitterly hate Him)*.

9 Much more then *(if Christ died for us while we were yet sinners, how much more will He do for us now that we are Redeemed, and thereby reconciled to Him!)*, being now Justified by His Blood *(we are justified now, and the Blood of Christ stands as the guarantee for that Justification)*, we shall be saved from wrath through Him *(the Wrath of God, which is always manifested against sin)*.

10 For if, when we were enemies, we were reconciled to God by the Death of His Son *(the only way we could be reconciled; this Verse shoots down the "Jesus died spiritually" doctrine)*, much more, being reconciled, we shall be saved by His life *(does not speak of His Perfect Life, but rather the pouring out of His Life's Blood at Calvary)*.

11 And not only *so*, but we also joy in God through our Lord Jesus Christ *(we are to boast of our Reconciliation to God, for it is a true confidence [I Cor. 1:31; II Cor. 10:17])*, by Whom we have now received the Atonement *(Reconciliation)*.

ADAM

12 Wherefore, as by one man sin entered into the world *(by Adam)*, and death by sin *(both spiritual and physical death)*; and so death passed upon all men *(for all were in Adam)*, for that all have sinned *(all are born in sin, because of Adam's transgression)*:

13 (For until the Law *(Law of Moses)* sin was in the world *(caused by Adam's Fall)*: but sin is not imputed when there is no Law *(before the Law was given, sin and its immediate Judgment were not imputed to the account of those who were then alive; but by the fact of Adam's Fall, they were still*

sinners).

14 Nevertheless death reigned from Adam to Moses *(because of the sin nature that was in all men due to Adam's Fall)*, even over them who had not sinned after the similitude of Adam's transgression *(irrespective that all did not in essence commit high treason against God, as did Adam, they were still sinners)*, who is the figure of Him Who was to come *(Adam was the fountainhead of all sin and death, while Christ is the Fountainhead of all Redemption and Life)*.

CONTRASTS

15 But not as the offence, so also *is* the free gift *(would have probably been better translated, "as the offence, much more the Free Gift"; the "Free Gift" refers to Christ and what He did at the Cross, which addressed all that was lost at the Fall)*. For if through the offence of one *(Adam)* many be dead, much more the Grace of God *(proclaims the inexhaustible Power of this attribute)*, and the Gift by Grace *(presents Jesus as that "Gift")*, which is by One Man, Jesus Christ *(what He did at the Cross)*, has abounded unto many *(this "One Man," the Lord Jesus Christ, nullified the offence of the "one man" Adam)*.

16 And not as *it was* by one who sinned, *so is* the Gift *(so much greater is the Gift)*: for the judgment *was* by one to condemnation *(by Adam)*, but the Free Gift is of many offences unto Justification *(cleanses from all sin)*.

17 For if by one man's offence death reigned by one *(Adam's Fall)*; much more they which receive abundance of Grace *(not just "Grace," but "Abundance of Grace"; all made possible by the Cross)* and of the Gift of Righteousness *(Righteousness is a Gift from God which comes solely through Jesus Christ, and is received by Faith)* shall reign in life by One, Jesus Christ.) *(This proclaims the Believer "reigning," even as death had reigned, but from a position of much greater power than that of death.)*

18 Therefore as by the offence of one *judgment came* upon all men to condemnation *(Judged by God to be lost)*; even so by the Righteousness of One *(Christ)* the Free Gift came upon all men unto Justification of life *(received by simply believing in Christ and what He did at the Cross, which is the only answer for sin)*.

19 For as by one man's disobedience many were made sinners *(the "many" referred to all)*, so by the obedience of One *(obedient unto death, even the death of the Cross [Phil. 2:8])* shall many be made Righteous *("many" refers to all who will believe)*.

20 Moreover the Law entered, that the offence might abound (the Law of Moses, that the offence might be identified). But where sin abounded, Grace did much more abound (where sin increased, Grace super-abounded, and then some on top of that):

21 That as sin has reigned unto death (sin reigns as an absolute monarch in the being of the unredeemed), even so might Grace reign through Righteousness unto Eternal Life by Jesus Christ our Lord (Grace reigns unto Life, but it reigns "through Righteousness," i.e., because of God's Righteous Judgment of sin at Calvary executed in the Person of His Son Jesus Christ).

CHAPTER 6

THE CROSS

WHAT shall we say then? (This is meant to direct attention to Rom. 5:20.) Shall we continue in sin, that grace may abound? (Just because Grace is greater than sin doesn't mean that the Believer has a license to sin.)

2 God forbid (presents Paul's answer to the question, "Away with the thought, let not such a thing occur"). How shall we, who are dead to sin (dead to the sin nature), live any longer therein? (This portrays what the Believer is now in Christ.)

3 Know you not, that so many of us as were baptized into Jesus Christ (plainly says that this Baptism is into Christ and not water [I Cor. 1:17; 12:13; Gal. 3:27; Eph. 4:5; Col. 2:11-13]) were baptized into His Death? (When Christ died on the Cross, in the Mind of God, we died with Him; in other words, He became our Substitute, and our identification with Him in His Death gives us all the benefits for which He died; the idea is that He did it all for us!)

4 Therefore we are buried with Him by baptism into death (not only did we die with Him, but we were buried with Him as well, which means that all the sin and transgression of the past were buried; when they put Him in the Tomb, they put all of our sins into that Tomb as well): that like as Christ was raised up from the dead by the Glory of the Father, even so we also should walk in Newness of Life (we died with Him, we were buried with Him, and His Resurrection was our Resurrection to a "Newness of Life").

5 For if we have been planted together (with Christ) in the likeness of His death (Paul proclaims the Cross as the instrument through which all Blessings come; consequently, the Cross must ever be the object of our Faith, which gives the Holy Spirit latitude to work within our

lives), we shall be also *in the likeness* of His Resurrection *(we can have the "likeness of His Resurrection," i.e., "live this Resurrection Life," only as long as we understand the "likeness of His Death," which refers to the Cross as the means by which all of this is done)*:

6 Knowing this, that our old man is Crucified with *Him (all that we were before conversion),* that the body of sin might be destroyed *(the power of sin broken),* that henceforth we should not serve sin *(the guilt of sin is removed at conversion, because the sin nature no longer rules within our hearts and lives).*

7 For he who is dead *(He was our Substitute, and in the Mind of God, we died with Him upon Believing Faith)* is freed from sin *(set free from the bondage of the sin nature).*

8 Now if we be dead with Christ *(once again pertains to the Cross, and our being Baptized into His Death),* we believe that we shall also live with Him *(have Resurrection Life, which is more Abundant Life [Jn. 10:10])*:

9 Knowing that Christ being raised from the dead dies no more *(means that His Work was a Finished Work, and will require nothing else)*; death has no more dominion over Him *(because all sin has been Atoned; inasmuch as Christ is our Substitute, if death* has no more dominion over Him, it has no more dominion over us; this means that the power of the sin nature is broken).

10 For in that He died, He died unto sin *(the sin nature)* once *(actually means, "He died unto the sin nature, once, for all")*: but in that He lives *(the Resurrection),* He lives unto God *(refers to the fact that all life comes from God, and that we receive that life by virtue of the Cross and our Faith in that Finished Work).*

11 Likewise reckon *(account)* you also yourselves to be dead indeed unto *(the)* sin *(while the sin nature is not dead, we are dead unto the sin nature by virtue of the Cross and our Faith in that Sacrifice, but only as long as our Faith continues in the Cross),* but alive unto God *(living the Resurrection Life)* through Jesus Christ our Lord *(refers to what He did at the Cross, which is the means of this Resurrection Life).*

SANCTIFICATION

12 Let not sin *(the sin nature)* therefore reign *(rule)* in your mortal body *(showing that the sin nature can once again rule in the heart and life of the Believer, if the Believer doesn't constantly look to Christ and the Cross; the "mortal body" is neutral, which means it can be used for Righteousness or*

unrighteousness), that you should obey it in the lusts thereof *(ungodly lusts are carried out through the mortal body, if Faith is not maintained in the Cross [I Cor. 1:17-18])*.

13 Neither yield you your members *(of your mortal body)* as instruments of unrighteousness unto sin *(the sin nature)*: but yield yourselves unto God *(we are to yield ourselves to Christ and the Cross; that alone guarantees victory over the sin nature)*, as those who are alive from the dead *(we have been raised with Christ in "Newness of Life")*, and your members *as* instruments of Righteousness unto God *(this can be done only by virtue of the Cross and our Faith in that Finished Work, and Faith which continues in that Finished Work from day-to-day [Lk. 9:23-24])*.

14 For sin shall not have dominion over you *(the sin nature will not have dominion over us if we as Believers continue to exercise Faith in the Cross of Christ; otherwise, the sin nature most definitely will have dominion over the Believer)*: for you are not under the Law *(means that if we try to live this life by any type of law, no matter how good that law might be in its own right, we will conclude by the sin nature having dominion over us)*, but under Grace *(the Grace of God flows to the Believer on an unending basis only* as long as the Believer exercises Faith in Christ and what He did at the Cross; Grace is merely the Goodness of God exercised by and through the Holy Spirit, and given to undeserving Saints)*.

15 What then? *(This presents Paul going back to the first question he asked in this Chapter.)* shall we sin, because we are not under the Law, but under Grace? *(If we think such a thing, then we're completely misunderstanding Grace. The Grace of God gives us the liberty to live a Holy life, which we do through Faith in Christ and the Cross, and not license to sin as some think.)* God forbid *(every true Believer hates sin; so the idea of living under its dominion is abhorrent to say the least!)*.

16 Know you not, that to whom you yield yourselves servants to obey, his servants you are to whom you obey *(the Believer is either a slave to Christ, for that's what the word "servant" means, or else a slave to sin, which he will be if he doesn't keep his Faith in Christ and the Cross)*; whether of sin unto death *(once again allow us to state the fact that if the Believer attempts to live for God by any method other than Faith in the Finished Work of Christ, the Believer will fail, no matter how hard he otherwise tries)*, or of obedience unto Righteousness? *(The Believer is required to obey the Word of the

Lord. He cannot do that within his own strength, but only by understanding that he receives all things through what Christ did at the Cross and his continued Faith in that Finished Work, even on a daily basis. Then the Holy Spirit, Who Alone can make us what we ought to be, can accomplish His work within our lives.)

17 But God be thanked, that you were the servants of sin *(slaves to the sin nature, what we were before we were saved)*, but you have obeyed from the heart that form of Doctrine *(Jesus Christ and Him Crucified; understanding that all things come to the Believer from God by the means of the Cross)* which was delivered you *(the Lord gave this "form of Doctrine" to Paul, and he gave it to us in his Epistles)*.

18 Being then made free from sin *(being made free from the sin nature; it has no more power over the Believer, but only as we continue to look to the Cross)*, you became the servants of Righteousness *(whereas you were formerly a slave to the sin nature, you are now a slave to Righteousness; if Faith is maintained in the Cross, there is a constant pull of the Believer toward Righteousness)*.

19 I speak after the manner of men because of the infirmity of your flesh *("the manner of men"* pertains to the Fall, which has made the flesh weak; this speaks of our own personal strength and ability)*: for as you have yielded your members servants to uncleanness *(which the Believer will do, if the object of his Faith is anything but the Cross)* and to iniquity unto iniquity *(without constant Faith in the Cross, the Believer's situation regarding sin will get worse and worse)*; even so now yield your members servants to Righteousness unto Holiness *(which, as repeatedly stated, can only be done through constant Faith in the Cross; understanding that it is by and through the Cross that we receive all things, and that the Holy Spirit, Who Alone can develop Righteousness and Holiness in our lives, works exclusively through the Cross)*.

20 For when you were the servants of sin *(slaves to sin)*, you were free from Righteousness *(speaking of our lives before conversion to Christ)*.

21 What fruit had you then in those things whereof you are now ashamed? *(This means that absolutely nothing of any value can come out of the sinful experience. It is impossible for there to be any good fruit.)* for the end of those things is death *(if the Believer refuses to look to the Cross, but rather looks to something else regarding his Sanctification, domination by the sin nature is going to be the*

result, and spiritual death will be the conclusion; the Cross is the only answer for sin!).

22 But now *(since coming to Christ)* being made free from sin *(set free from the sin nature)*, and become servants *(slaves)* to God *(but this yoke is a light yoke [Mat. 11:28-30])*, you have your fruit unto Holiness *(which the Holy Spirit will bring about, providing the Cross is ever the object of our Faith)*, and the end Everlasting Life *(so the Believer has the choice of "death," which is the end result of trusting something other than Christ and the Cross, or "Everlasting Life," which is the result of trusting Christ and the Cross)*.

23 For the wages of sin *is* death *(speaks of spiritual death, which is eternal separation from God)*; but the Gift of God *is* Eternal Life through Jesus Christ our Lord *(as stated, all of this, without exception, comes to us by the means of what Christ did at the Cross, which demands that the Cross ever be the Object of our Faith, thus giving the Holy Spirit latitude to work within our lives and bring forth His Fruit)*.

CHAPTER 7

THE LAW AND SIN

KNOW you not, Brethren *(Paul is speaking to Believers)*, (for I speak to them who know the Law,) *(he is speaking of the Law of Moses, but it could refer to any type of religious Law)* how that the Law has dominion over a man as long as he lives? *(The Law has dominion as long as he tries to live by Law. Regrettably, not understanding the Cross regarding Sanctification, virtually the entirety of the Church is presently trying to live for God by means of the Law. Let the Believer understand that there are only two places he can be, Grace or Law. If he doesn't understand the Cross as it refers to Sanctification, which is the only means of victory, he will automatically be under Law, which guarantees failure.)*

2 For the woman which has an husband is bound by the Law to *her* husband so long as he lives *(presents Paul using the analogy of the marriage bond)*; but if the husband be dead, she is loosed from the Law of *her* husband *(meaning that she is free to marry again)*.

3 So then if, while *her* husband lives, she be married to another man, she shall be called an adulteress *(in effect, the woman now has two husbands, at least in the eyes of God; following this analogy, the Holy Spirit through Paul will give us a great truth; many Christians are living a life of spiritual adultery; they are married to Christ, but they are in effect serv-

*ing another husband, "the Law";
it is quite an analogy!)*: but if her
husband be dead *(the Law is dead
by virtue of Christ having fulfilled
the Law in every respect)*, she is
free from that Law *(if the husband
dies, the woman is free to marry
and serve another; the Law of Moses,
being satisfied in Christ, is now
dead to the Believer and the Believer is free to serve Christ without the Law having any part or
parcel in his life or living)*; so that
she is no adulteress, though she
be married to another man *(presents the Believer as now married
to Christ, and no longer under
obligation to the Law)*.

4 Wherefore, my Brethren,
you also are become dead to the
Law *(the Law is not dead per se,
but we are dead to the Law because
we are dead to its effects; this means
that we are not to try to live for God
by means of "Law," whether the Law
of Moses, or Laws made up by other
men or of ourselves; we are to be
dead to all Law)* by the body of
Christ *(this refers to the Crucifixion of Christ, which satisfied the
demands of the broken Law, which
we could not satisfy; but Christ did
it for us; having fulfilled the Law
in every respect, the Christian is not
obligated to Law in any fashion,
only to Christ and what He did at
the Cross)*; that you should be
married to another *(speaking of
Christ)*, even to Him Who is raised
from the dead *(we are raised with
Him in newness of life, and we
should ever understand that Christ
has met, does meet, and shall meet
our every need; we look to Him
exclusively, referring to what He
did for us at the Cross)*, that we
should bring forth fruit unto God
*(proper fruit can only be brought
forth by the Believer constantly
looking to the Cross; in fact, Christ
must never be separated from the
Work of the Cross; to do so is to produce "another Jesus" [II Cor. 11:4])*.

5 For when we were in the
flesh *(can refer to the unsaved state
or to the Believer who is attempting to overcome the powers of sin
by his own efforts, i.e., "the flesh")*,
the motions of sins *(denotes being under the power of the sin nature, and refers to the "passions of
the sin nature")*, which were by
the Law *(the effect of the Law is to
reveal sin, which Law is designed
to do whether it's the Law of God
or Laws made up of ourselves; that
doesn't mean its evil, for it isn't;
it just means that there is no victory in the Law, only the revelation of sin and its penalty)*, did
work in our members to bring
forth fruit unto death *(when the
Believer attempts to live for the
Lord by means of Law, which regrettably most of the modern church
does, the end result is going to be
sin and failure; in fact, it can be
no other way; let us say it again!*

if the Believer doesn't understand the Cross, as it refers to Sanctification, then the Believer is going to try to live for God by means of Law; the sadness is that most of the modern church thinks it is under Grace, when in reality it is living under Law because of not understanding the Cross).

6 But now we are delivered from the Law (*delivered from its just demands, meaning that Christ has paid its penalty*), that being dead (*dead to the Law by virtue of having died with Christ on the Cross*) wherein we were held (*we were once held down by the sin nature*); that we should serve in newness of Spirit (*refers to the Holy Spirit and not man's spirit; the Believer has a completely new way of living, which is Faith in Christ and what He did at the Cross on our behalf; this guarantees perpetual victory*), and not in the oldness of the letter (*this refers to the Law of Moses; most modern Believers would argue that they aren't living after the Law of Moses; but, as we have stated, the truth is if they do not understand the Cross as it refers to Sanctification, then in some way they're still living under that old Law*).

THE STRUGGLE AGAINST SIN

7 What shall we say then? (*In Verses 1 through 6 of this Chapter, Paul has shown that the Believer is no longer under Law; in the remainder of the Chapter, he shows that a Believer putting himself under Law, thus failing to avail himself of the resources of Grace, is a defeated Christian.*) Is the Law sin? God forbid (*man's condition is not caused by the Law of God, for the Law is Holy; rather it is exposed*). No, I had not known sin, but by the Law (*means that the Law of Moses defined what sin actually is, but gave no power to overcome sin*): for I had not known lust, except the Law had said, You shall not covet (*tells us that the desire for what is forbidden is the first conscious form of sin; this is the sin nature at work!*).

8 But sin (*the sin nature*), taking occasion by the Commandment, wrought in me all manner of concupiscence ("*concupiscence*" is "*evil desire*," meaning if the Believer attempts to live for God by means other than the Cross, he will be ruled by "*evil desires*"; and no matter how dedicated he might be otherwise, he will not be able to stop the process in that manner, with it getting worse and worse). For without the Law sin *was* dead (*means that the Law of Moses fully exposed what was already in man's heart; that's one of the reasons God gave the Law*).

9 For I was alive without the

Law once (*Paul is referring to himself personally and his conversion to Christ; the Law, he states, had nothing to do with that conversion; neither did it have anything to do with his life in Christ*): but when the Commandment came (*having just been saved, and not understanding the Cross of Christ, he tried to live for God by keeping the Commandments through his own strength and power; in his defense, no one else at that time understood the Cross; in fact, the meaning of the Cross, which is actually the meaning of the New Covenant, would be given to Paul*), sin revived (*the sin nature will always, without exception, revive under such circumstances, which results in failure*), and I died (*he was not meaning that he physically died, as would be obvious, but that he died to the Commandment; in other words, he failed to obey no matter how hard he tried; let all Believers understand that if the Apostle Paul couldn't live for God in this manner, neither can you!*).

10 And the Commandment, which *was ordained* to life (*refers to the Ten Commandments*), I found to be unto death (*means that the Law revealed the sin, as it always does, and its wages which are death; in other words, there is no victory in trying to live by Law; we are to live by Faith, referring to Faith in Christ and the Cross*).

11 For sin (*the sin nature*), taking occasion by the Commandment (*in no way blames the Commandment, but that the Commandment actually did agitate the sin nature, and brought it to the fore, which it was designed to do*), deceived me (*Paul thought, now that he had accepted Christ, by that mere fact alone he could certainly obey the Lord in every respect; but he found he couldn't, and neither can you, at least in that fashion*), and by it slew me (*despite all of his efforts to live for the Lord by means of Law-keeping, he failed; and again, I say, so will you!*).

12 Wherefore the Law is Holy (*points to the fact that it is God's Revelation of Himself; the problem is not in the Law of God, the problem is in us*), and the Commandment Holy, and just, and good (*the Law is like a mirror which shows man what he is, but contains no power to change him*).

13 Was then that which is good made death unto me? God forbid (*once again, it is not the Law that is at fault, but rather the sin in man which is opposed to the Law*). But sin (*the sin nature*), that it might appear sin (*proclaims the Divine intention of the Law, namely that sin might show its true colors*), working death in me by that which is good (*the Law was good, and is good, but if one attempts to keep its moral precepts by means other than constant Faith in the

Cross, the end result will be the "working of death" instead of life; all of this can be done, but only by Faith in Christ and the Cross); **that sin** (the sin nature) **by the Commandment might become exceeding sinful** (this greatly confuses the Believer; he is trying to live for God, and trying for all of his strength and might, but continually fails; he doesn't understand why! the truth is that no one can live for God in this fashion; it is not God's Prescribed Order; that Order is the Cross).

14 For we know that the Law is spiritual (refers to the fact that the Law is totally of God and from God): **but I am carnal, sold under sin** (refers to Adam's Fall, which has affected all of mankind and for all time; this means that no one, even Spirit-filled Believers, can keep the Law of God if they attempt to do so outside of Faith in the Cross; in other words, it is all in Christ).

15 For that which I do (the failure) **I allow not** (should have been translated, "I understand not"; these are not the words of an unsaved man, as some claim, but rather a Believer who is trying and failing): **for what I would, that do I not** (refers to the obedience he wants to render to Christ, but rather fails; why? as Paul explained, the Believer is married to Christ, but is being unfaithful to Christ by spiritually cohabiting with the Law, which frustrates the Grace of God; that means the Holy Spirit will not help such a person, which guarantees failure [Gal. 2:21]); **but what I hate, that do I** (refers to sin in his life, which he doesn't want to do and, in fact, hates, but finds himself unable to stop; unfortunately, due to the fact of not understanding the Cross as it refers to Sanctification, this is the plight of most modern Christians).

16 If then I do that which I would not (presents Paul doing something against his will; he doesn't want to do it, and is trying not to do it, whatever it might be, but finds himself doing it anyway), **I consent unto the Law that it it is good** (simply means that the Law of God is working as it is supposed to work; it defines sin, portraying the fact that the sin nature will rule in man's heart if not addressed properly).

17 Now then it is no more I that do it (this has been misconstrued by many! it means, "I may be failing, but it's not what I want to do"; no true Christian wants to sin because now the Divine Nature is in his life and it is supposed to rule, not the sin nature [II Pet. 1:4]), **but sin** (the sin nature) **that dwells in me** (despite the fact that some Preachers claim the sin nature is gone from the Christian, Paul here plainly says that the sin nature is still in the Christian; however, if our Faith remains constant in the Cross, the sin nature will be dormant, causing us no problem; otherwise, it will cause us great problems; while the sin nature "dwells" in us, it is not to "rule" in us).

18 For I know that in me (that is, in my flesh,) dwells no good thing (speaks of man's own ability, or rather the lack thereof in comparison to the Holy Spirit, at least when it comes to spiritual things): for to will is present with me (Paul is speaking here of his willpower; regrettably, most modern Christians are trying to live for God by means of willpower, thinking falsely that since they have come to Christ, they are now free to say "no" to sin; that is the wrong way to look at the situation; the Believer cannot live for God by the strength of willpower; while the will is definitely important, it alone is not enough; the Believer must exercise Faith in Christ and the Cross, and do so constantly; then he will have the ability and strength to say "yes" to Christ, which automatically says, "no" to the things of the world); but how to perform that which is good I find not (outside of the Cross, it is impossible to find a way to do good).

19 For the good that I would I do not (if I depend on self, and not the Cross): but the evil which I would not (don't want to do), that I do (which is exactly what every Believer will do no matter how hard he tries to do otherwise, if he tries to live this life outside of the Cross [Gal. 2:20-21]).

20 Now if I do that I would not (which is exactly what will happen if the Believer tries to live this life outside of God's prescribed order), it is no more I that do it, but sin (the sin nature) that dwells in me (this emphatically states that the Believer has a sin nature; in the original Greek Text, if it contains the definite article before the word "sin" which originally did read "the sin," it is not speaking of acts of sin, but rather the sin nature or the evil nature; the idea is not getting rid of the sin nature, which actually cannot be done, but rather controlling it, which the Apostle has told us how to do in Romans, Chapters 6 and 8; when the Trump sounds, we shall be changed and there will be no more sin nature [Rom. 8:23]).

21 I find then a Law (does not refer in this case to the Law of Moses, but rather to the "Law of Sin and Death" [Rom. 8:2]), that, when I would do good, evil (the evil nature) is present with me (the idea is that the sin nature is always going to be with the Believer; there is no hint in the Greek that its stay is temporary, at least

until the Trump sounds; we can successfully address the sin nature in only one way, and that is by Faith in Christ and the Cross, which Paul will detail in the next Chapter).

22 For I delight in the Law of God (refers to the moral Law of God ensconced in the Ten Commandments) **after the inward man** (refers to the spirit and soul of man which has now been regenerated):

23 But I see another Law in my members (the Law of Sin and Death desiring to use my physical body as an instrument of unrighteousness), **warring against the Law of my mind** (this is the Law of desire and willpower), **and bringing me into captivity to the Law of sin** (the Law of Sin and Death) **which is in my members** (which will function through my members, and make me a slave to the Law of Sin and Death; this will happen to the most consecrated Christian if that Christian doesn't constantly exercise Faith in Christ and the Cross, understanding that it is through the Cross that all powers of darkness were defeated [Col. 2:14-15]).

24 O wretched man that I am! (Any Believer who attempts to live for God outside of God's prescribed order, which is "Jesus Christ and Him Crucified," will, in fact, live a wretched and miserable existence. This life can only be lived in one way, and that way is the Cross.) **who shall deliver me from the body of this death?** (The minute he cries "Who," he finds the path to Victory, for he is now calling upon a Person for help, and that Person is Christ; actually, the Greek Text is masculine, indicating a Person).

25 I thank God through Jesus Christ our Lord (presents Paul revealing the answer to his own question; deliverance comes through Jesus Christ and Christ Alone, and more particularly what Jesus did at Calvary and the Resurrection). **So then with the mind I myself serve the Law of God** (the "will" is the trigger, but it within itself can do nothing unless the gun is loaded with explosive power; that Power is the Cross); **but with the flesh the Law of sin** (if the Believer resorts to the "flesh," [i.e., "self-will, self-effort, religious effort"] which refers to his own ability outside of Christ and the Cross, he will not serve the Law of God, but rather the Law of sin).

CHAPTER 8

LIFE IN THE SPIRIT

THERE **is** therefore now no condemnation (guilt) **to them which are in Christ Jesus** (refers back to Romans 6:3-5 and our being Baptized into His Death, which speaks of the Crucifixion), who walk not after the flesh (depending on one's personal strength and ability or great religious efforts in order to overcome sin), but after the Spirit (the Holy Spirit works exclusively within the legal confines of the Finished Work of Christ; our Faith in that Finished Work, i.e., "the Cross," guarantees the help of the Holy Spirit, which guarantees Victory).

2 For the Law (that which we are about to give is a Law of God, devised by the Godhead in eternity past [I Pet. 1:18-20]; this Law, in fact, is "God's prescribed order of Victory") of the Spirit (Holy Spirit, i.e., "the way the Spirit works") of Life (all life comes from Christ, but through the Holy Spirit [Jn. 16:13-14]) in Christ Jesus (any time Paul uses this term or one of its derivatives, he is, without fail, referring to what Christ did at the Cross, which makes this "life" possible) has made me free (given me total Victory) from the Law of Sin and Death (these are the two most powerful Laws in the Universe; the "Law of the Spirit of Life in Christ Jesus" alone is stronger than the "Law of Sin and Death"; this means that if the Believer attempts to live for God by any manner other than Faith in Christ and the Cross, he is doomed to failure).

3 For what the Law could not do, in that it was weak through the flesh (those under Law had only their willpower, which is woefully insufficient; so despite how hard they tried, they were unable to keep the Law then, and the same inability persists presently; any person who tries to live for God by a system of laws is doomed to failure, because the Holy Spirit will not function in that capacity), God sending his own Son (refers to man's helpless condition, unable to save himself and unable to keep even a simple Law and, therefore, in dire need of a Saviour) in the likeness of sinful flesh (this means that Christ was really human, conformed in appearance to flesh which is characterized by sin, but yet sinless), and for sin (to atone for sin, to destroy its power, and to save and Sanctify its victims), condemned sin in the flesh (destroyed the power of sin by giving His Perfect Body as a Sacrifice for sin, which made it possible for sin to be defeated in our flesh; it was all through the Cross):

4 That the Righteousness of the Law might be fulfilled in us (the Law finding its full accomplishment in us can only be done by Faith in Christ, and what Christ has done for us at the Cross), who walk not after the flesh (not after our own strength and ability), but after the Spirit (the word "walk" refers to the manner in which we

order our life; *when we place our Faith in Christ and the Cross, understanding that all things come from God to us by means of the Cross, ever making it the object of our Faith, the Holy Spirit can then work mightily within us, bringing about the Fruit of the Spirit; that is what "walking after the Spirit" actually means!).*

5 For they who are after the flesh do mind the things of the flesh *(refers to Believers trying to live for the Lord by means other than Faith in the Cross of Christ);* but they who are after the Spirit the things of the Spirit *(those who place their Faith in Christ and the Cross, do so exclusively; they are doing what the Spirit desires, which alone can bring Victory).*

CONTRAST

6 For to be carnally minded is death *(this doesn't refer to watching too much Television, as some think, but rather to trying to live for God outside of His prescribed order; the results will be sin and separation from God);* but to be Spiritually minded is life and peace *(God's prescribed order is the Cross; this demands our constant Faith in that Finished Work, which is the Way of the Holy Spirit).*

7 Because the carnal mind is enmity against God *(once again, this refers to attempting to live for God by means other than the Cross, which places one "against God"):* for it is not subject to the Law of God, neither indeed can be *(in its simplest form means that what is being done, whatever it may be, is not in God's Prescribed Order, which is the Cross).*

8 So then they that are in the flesh cannot please God *(refers to the Believer attempting to live his Christian Life by means other than Faith in Christ and the Cross).*

9 But you are not in the flesh *(in one sense of the word is asking the question, "since you are now a Believer and no longer depending on the flesh, why are you resorting to the flesh?"),* but in the Spirit *(as a Believer, you now have the privilege of being led and empowered by the Holy Spirit; however, He will do such for us only on the premise of our Faith in the Finished Work of Christ),* if so be that the Spirit of God dwell in you *(if you are truly saved).* Now if any man have not the Spirit of Christ, he is none of His *(Paul is saying that the work of the Spirit in our lives is made possible by what Christ did at Calvary, and the Resurrection).*

10 And if Christ *be* in you *(He is in you through the Power and Person of the Spirit [Gal. 2:20]),* the body *is* dead because of sin *(means that the physical body has been rendered helpless because of the Fall; consequently, the Believer*

trying to overcome by willpower presents a fruitless task); but the Spirit *is* life because of Righteousness *(only the Holy Spirit can make us what we ought to be, which means we cannot do it ourselves; once again, He performs all that He does within the confines of the Finished Work of Christ).*

11 But if the Spirit *(Holy Spirit)* of Him *(from God)* who raised up Jesus from the dead dwell in you *(and He definitely does),* He who raised up Christ from the dead shall also quicken your mortal bodies *(give us power in our mortal bodies that we might live a victorious life)* by His Spirit Who dwells in you *(we have the same power in us, through the Spirit, that raised Christ from the dead, and is available to us only on the premise of the Cross and our Faith in that Sacrifice).*

12 Therefore, Brethren *(means that Paul is addressing Believers),* we are debtors *(refers to what we owe Jesus Christ for what He has done for us on the Cross),* not to the flesh *(we do not owe anything to our own ability, meaning that such cannot save us or give us victory),* to live after the flesh *("living after the flesh" pertains to our works, which God can never accept, and which can never bring us victory, but rather defeat).*

13 For If you live after the flesh *(after your own strength and abil-*ity, which is outside of God's prescribed order),* you shall die *(you will not be able to live a victorious, Christian life):* but if you through the Spirit *(by the Power of the Holy Spirit)* do mortify the deeds of the body *(which the Holy Spirit Alone can do),* you shall live *(shall walk in victory; but once again, even at the risk of being overly repetitive, we must never forget that the Spirit works totally and completely within the confines of the Cross of Christ; this means that we must ever make the Cross the object of our Faith, giving Him latitude to work).*

DELIVERANCE

14 For as many as are led by the Spirit of God *(the Spirit will always lead us to the Cross),* they are the sons of God *(we live as sons of God, which refers to total victory within every aspect of our lives; if the sin nature is dominating a person, he certainly isn't living as a Son of God).*

15 For you have not received the spirit of bondage *(to try to live after a system of works and laws will only succeed in placing one in "bondage")* again to fear *(such living creates a perpetual climate of fear in the heart of such a Believer);* but you have received the Spirit of Adoption *(the Holy Spirit has adopted us into the Family of God),*

whereby we cry, Abba, Father *(the Holy Spirit enables the Child of God to call God "Father," which is done so because of Jesus Christ).*

16 The Spirit itself *(Himself)* bears witness with our spirit *(means that He is constantly speaking and witnessing certain things to us),* that we are the Children of God *(meaning that we are such now, and should enjoy all the privileges of such; we can do so if we will understand that all these privileges come to us from God, by the means of the Cross):*

17 And if children *(Children of God),* then heirs *(a privilege);* heirs of God *(the highest enrichment of all),* and joint-heirs with Christ *(everything that belongs to Christ belongs to us through the Cross, which was done for us); if* so be that we suffer with *Him (doesn't pertain to mere suffering, but rather suffering "with Him," referring to His suffering at the Cross which brought us total victory),* that we may be also glorified together *(He has been glorified, and we shall be glorified; all made possible by the Cross).*

18 For I reckon that the sufferings of this present time *(speaks of the world and its condition because of the Fall) are* not worthy *to be compared* with the glory *(the glory of the coming future time will bear no relation to the misery of this present time)* which shall be revealed in us *(our glory will be a reflective glory, coming from Christ).*

19 For the earnest expectation of the creature *(should have been translated, "for the earnest expectation of the Creation")* waits for the manifestation of the sons of God *(pertains to the coming Resurrection of Life).*

20 For the creature *(Creation)* was made subject to vanity *(Adam's Fall signaled the fall of Creation),* not willingly *(the Creation did not sin, even as such cannot sin, but became subject to the result of sin which is death),* but by reason of Him Who has subjected *the same* in Hope *(speaks of God as the One Who passed sentence because of Adam's Fall, but at the same time gave us a "Hope"; that "Hope" is Christ, Who will rectify all things),*

21 Because the creature *(Creation)* itself also shall be delivered *(presents this "Hope" as effecting that deliverance, which He did by the Cross)* from the bondage of corruption *(speaks of mortality, i.e., "death")* into the glorious liberty of the Children of God *(when man fell, Creation fell! when man shall be delivered, Creation will be delivered as well, and is expressed in the word "also").*

22 For we know that the whole Creation *(everything has been affected by Satan's rebellion and*

Adam's Fall) groans and travails in pain together until now *(refers to the common longing of the elements of the Creation to be brought back to their original perfection).*

23 And not only they *(the Creation, and all it entails)*, but ourselves also *(refers to Believers)*, which have the Firstfruits of the Spirit *(even though Jesus addressed every single thing lost in the Fall at the Cross, we only have a part of that possession now, with the balance coming at the Resurrection)*, even we ourselves groan within ourselves *(proclaims the obvious fact that all Jesus paid for in the Atonement has not yet been fully realized)*, waiting for the Adoption *(should be translated, "waiting for the fulfillment of the process, which Adoption into the Family of God guarantees")*, to wit, the Redemption of our body *(the glorifying of our physical body that will take place at the Resurrection).*

24 For we are saved by hope *(means that the greater part of our Salvation is yet future)*: but hope that is seen is not hope *(proclaims in another way the great Truth that all Salvation affords is not yet given unto the Believer)*: for what a man sees, why does he yet hope for? *(In effect, this bluntly tells us that what is coming is so far beyond that which is here at the present, as to be no comparison.)*

25 But if we hope for that we see not *(plainly tells us that more, much more, is coming)*, then do we with patience wait for it *(proclaims the certitude of its coming, because the Holy Spirit has promised it would).*

26 Likewise the Spirit *(Holy Spirit)* also helps our infirmities *(the help given to us by the Holy Spirit is made possible in its entirety by and through what Jesus did at the Cross)*: for we know not what we should pray for as we ought *(signals the significance of prayer, but also that without the Holy Spirit, all is to no avail)*: but the Spirit itself *(Himself)* makes intercession for us *(He petitions or intercedes on our behalf)* with groanings which cannot be uttered *(not groanings on the part of the Holy Spirit, but rather on our part, which pertains to that which comes from the heart and cannot properly be put into words).*

27 And He Who searches the hearts *(God the Father)* knows what is the Mind of the Spirit *(what the Spirit wants done, and not what we want done)*, because He *(Holy Spirit)* makes intercession for the Saints according to the Will of God *(the overriding goal of the Spirit is to carry out the Will of God in our lives, not our personal wills; in other words, the Spirit is not a glorified bellhop).*

CONQUERORS

28 And we know that all things work together for good *(but only if certain conditions are met)* to them who love God *(the first condition)*, to them who are the called according to *His* purpose *(this means it's "His purpose, and not ours," which is the second condition; otherwise, all things will not work together for our good)*.

29 For whom He *(God)* did foreknow *(God's foreknowledge)*, He also did predestinate *to be* conformed to the Image of His Son *(it is never the person that is predestined, but rather the Plan)*, that He *(Jesus)* might be the Firstborn among many Brethren *(doesn't mean that Jesus was Born-Again as a sinner, as some teach, but rather that He is the Father of the Salvation Plan, having paid the price on the Cross, which made it all possible)*.

30 Moreover whom He *(God)* did predestinate *(to be conformed to the Image of His Son)*, them He also called *(without that "Call," man cannot be saved; sadly, many refuse the "Call" [Prov. 1:24-33])*: and whom He called, them He also justified *(those who responded faithfully to the Call)*: and whom He justified, them He also glorified *(shall glorify at the Resurrection; Justification guarantees it will be done)*.

31 What shall we then say to these things? *(This refers to the suffering presently endured [Vss. 17-18] in comparison to "the Glory which shall be revealed in us.")* If God *be* for us *(should have been translated, "since God is for us")*, who *can be* against us? *(It is who can be against us that will really matter.)*

32 He Who spared not His Own Son *(concerns the Great Gift of God, i.e., the Lord Jesus Christ)*, but delivered Him up for us all *(the Cross)*, how shall He not with Him also freely give us all things? *(We can have all things that pertain to Life and Godliness, which Jesus paid for at the Cross, providing our Faith is ever in Christ and the Cross [II Pet. 1:3-7].)*

33 Who shall lay any thing to the charge of God's elect? *(In effect means, "Who shall pronounce those guilty whom God pronounces Righteous?")* It is God who justifies *(it is God Who sets the rules for Justification, not man)*.

34 Who is he who condemns? *(No man has the right to condemn God's Justification Plan.)* It is Christ Who died *(if one condemns a Believer who is trusting Christ solely for Justification and Sanctification, he is at the same time condemning Christ and His Death on the Cross)*, yea rather, Who is risen again *(the Resurrection ratified the fact that Jesus was the Perfect Sac-*

rifice, and that God accepted Him as such), Who is even at the Right Hand of God (refers to the exaltation of Christ), Who also makes intercession for us (at the Right Hand of God, showing that His Sacrifice has been accepted, which guarantees intercession for us).

35 Who shall separate us from the Love of Christ? (This speaks of the Love of Christ for the Believer, instead of the Believer's Love for Christ.) shall tribulation, or distress, or persecution, or famine, or nakedness, or peril, or sword? (We are protected against all outside influence, but not from ourselves. If a person so desires, he can separate himself from the Love of Christ by rejecting the Cross.)

36 As it is written (Ps. 44:22), For Your sake we are killed all the day long (the world has always been opposed to Christ and what He did at the Cross; regrettably, so is most of the Church); we are accounted as sheep for the slaughter (the way the world looks at us; in their eyes, we are fit only for slaughter).

37 Nay, in all these things we are more than conquerors (it is a Holy arrogance of Victory and the Might of Christ) through Him Who loved us (He loved us enough to give His Life on the Cross, which alone makes us "more than conquerors").

38 For I am persuaded (the Apostle has faced the things of which he now speaks), that neither death, nor life, nor Angels, nor principalities, nor powers, nor things present, nor things to come,

39 Nor height, nor depth, nor any other creature, shall be able to separate us from the Love of God, which is in Christ Jesus our Lord (this Love of God extended to us is made possible solely by Christ, and what He has done for us at the Cross; once again, this is God's Love for us, which never wavers because we are "in Christ Jesus").

CHAPTER 9

REJECTION

I say the Truth in Christ, I lie not (Paul refutes the accusation in preaching to the Gentiles; he is not animated by hostility to the Jews), my conscience also bearing me witness in the Holy Spirit (his own spirit is exactly in tune with the Holy Spirit),

2 That I have great heaviness and continual sorrow in my heart (grieving over the plight of the Israel of his day; they were in this state because they rejected Christ and the Cross; regrettably, the Church, with some exceptions, is doing the same).

3 For I could wish that myself were accursed from Christ for my Brethren (presents a moot point,

for such is impossible), my kinsmen according to the flesh *(Jews):*

4 Who are Israelites *(God's chosen people, yet who rejected the Lord);* to whom *pertains* the Adoption *(refers to the selection of Israel to be God's peculiar people [Ex. 19:5]),* and the glory *(refers to the Divine Presence which was always with them, at least until they rejected God [Ex. 16:7, 10; 24:16-17; Lev. 9:6; Num. 14:10, 21; Deut. 5:24]),* and the Covenants *(various Covenants God made with Israel, such as the Abrahamic, first of all promising Salvation by Faith [Gen. 15:6]),* and the giving of the Law *(the Mosaic Law),* and the service *of God (Tabernacle, offerings, Priesthood, etc.),* and the Promises *(the Messianic Promises);*

5 Whose *are* the fathers *(refers basically to Abraham, Isaac, and Jacob),* and of whom as concerning the flesh Christ *came (through the Jews),* Who is over all *(the very purpose of Israel was to bring the Redeemer into the world),* God blessed forever *(Jesus is the Redeemer, Who is God).* Amen *(Truth).*

6 Not as though the Word of God has taken none effect *(even though Israel failed, the Word of God didn't fail; the Redeemer came).* For they *are* not all Israel, which are of Israel *(is meant to denounce national Salvation; in other words, one is not saved just because he is an Israelite):*

7 Neither, because they are the seed of Abraham, *are they* all children *(further debunks the nationalistic Salvation theory):* but, In Isaac shall your seed be called *(Ishmael was not included, even though a son of Abraham; this means that all works of the flesh are rejected).*

THE DISTINCTION

8 That is, They which are the children of the flesh, these *are* not the Children of God *(are not Children of God merely because they are Jews):* but the Children of the Promise are counted for the seed *(those who believe in "the Promise," Who is Christ).*

9 For this *is* the Word of Promise *(pertains to Faith, not works),* At this time will I come, and Sarah shall have a son *(Abraham is not the principle figure, neither is Sarah or Isaac for that matter; only the "Promise," which would ultimately figure into Christ).*

10 And not only this *(he will now give another example);* but when Rebecca also had conceived by one, *even* by our father Isaac *(Paul further shoots down the idea of nationalistic Salvation, as we shall see);*

11 (For *the children* being not yet born, neither having done any good or evil *(refers to Esau and Jacob, who were twins),* that the

purpose of God according to election might stand *(speaks of God's foreknowledge)*, not of works, but of Him Who calls;) *(This pronounces the entire basis of God's dealings with men and His manner of operation.)*

12 It was said unto her *(refers to the Lord speaking to Rebecca, found in Genesis 25:23)*, The Elder shall serve the younger *(in the spiritual analysis, the Sin Nature, which is the oldest in the Believer because the Believer is born with such, will serve the Divine Nature, which is younger; that is, if the Believer properly follows Christ)*.

13 As it is written *(Mal. 1:2-3)*, Jacob have I loved, but Esau have I hated *(was not done capriciously; God did not indiscriminately love Jacob, nor did He indiscriminately hate Esau; both passions, love and hate, were based on the attitudes of both men toward God)*.

14 What shall we say then? *(This is meant to counter the claim that God was unfair in His disposition toward Jacob and Esau.)* Is there unrighteousness with God? God forbid *(there is no unrighteousness with God, Who, through foreknowledge, sees the attitude of both these boys and judges accordingly)*.

15 For He said to Moses, I will have Mercy on whom I will have Mercy, and I will have Compassion on whom I will have Compassion *([Ex. 33:19] God has Mercy and Compassion on those who meet His conditions)*.

16 So then *it is* not of him who wills, nor of him who runs *(Mercy and Compassion cannot be earned or merited by the sinner; consequently, this completely rules out a "works" Salvation)*, but of God Who shows Mercy *(God shows Mercy on the basis of man's acceptance of Christ and the Cross; otherwise, there is no Mercy)*.

17 For the Scripture said unto Pharaoh *(Ex. 9:16)*, Even for this same purpose have I raised you up *(presents the Lord using what is available, but not forcing the issue; in other words, God did not predestine Pharaoh to take a position of rebellion, leaving him having no choice in the matter)*, that I might show My Power in you, and that My Name might be declared throughout all the earth *(as stated, God used the stubbornness of Pharaoh, which was Pharaoh's own choice, to glorify His Name — God's Name)*.

18 Therefore has He Mercy on whom He will *have Mercy (God will always have Mercy on those who meet His conditions)*, and whom He will He hardens *(stubbornness towards God will be met with God forcing the issue by providing the setting which will make the heart even harder; in other words, if one wants hardness, one will get hardness)*.

JUSTICE AND MERCY

19 You will say then unto me *(Paul knows the argument of the Jews),* Why does He yet find fault? *(Why does God find fault with man?)* For who has resisted His Will? *(Untold numbers have resisted His Will, but never with success!)*

20 No but, O man, who are you who replies against God? *(Man finds fault with God!)* Shall the thing formed say to Him Who formed *it*, Why have you made me thus? *(Man wants to blame God for his predicament!)*

21 Has not the potter power over the clay *(God is likened to a "Potter"),* of the same lump to make one vessel unto honour, and another unto dishonour? *(He has the power to make it possible for man to choose honor or dishonor. The fault is never with God, but always with man. God is not to blame simply because He gives man the power of choice, and man chooses the way of dishonor!)*

22 What if God, willing to show *his* wrath, and to make His power known *(in effect is saying, inasmuch as there are vessels of dishonor; there is a Divine necessity that God should demonstrate the Power of His Wrath, as well as the riches of His Mercy),* endured with much longsuffering the vessels of wrath fitted to destruction *(those who choose dishonor will* ultimately *be destroyed, but God in His longsuffering will bear long with them, even though He knows beforehand their fate):*

23 And that He might make known the riches of His Glory on the Vessels of Mercy *(pertains to those, whether Jews or Gentiles, who accept the "riches of His Glory" unto Salvation),* which He had afore prepared unto Glory *(doesn't mean that God predestined these for Salvation, but does mean that those who accepted His Mercy and Grace would be "prepared unto Glory"),*

24 Even us, whom He has called *(God initiates the Call, but regrettably many, if not most, refuse),* not of the Jews only, but also of the Gentiles? *(The Lord had always intended that the Gentiles be included as well.)*

25 As He said also in Hosea *(Hos. 2:23),* I will call them My people, which were not My people; and her beloved, which was not beloved *(is used by Paul in the context of the Gentiles, even though it was originally meant for the Jews).*

26 And it shall come to pass, *that* in the place where it was said unto them *(Hos. 1:9-10),* You *are* not My people; there shall they be called the Children of the Living God *(once again, the Apostle is taking a Passage that was given exclusively to Israel, and broadening it in order that it cover the Gen-*

tiles).

27 Isaiah also cried concerning Israel *(Isa. 10:22)*, Though the number of the Children of Israel be as the sand of the sea, a remnant shall be saved *(despite the vast number of Israelites down through the many centuries, only a small number were actually saved; it is the same in the modern Church)*:

28 For He will finish the work *(which He did at the Cross)*, and cut *it* short in Righteousness *(God's Righteousness demands such! however, what is short to Him is not necessarily short to mankind)*: because a short work will the Lord make upon the earth *(by comparison to Eternity, the six thousand years we have now seen constitute a short time)*.

29 And as Isaiah said before *(Isa. 1:9)*, Except the Lord of Sabaoth *(the Lord of Hosts)* had left us a seed *(the Remnant)*, we had been as Sodom, and been made like unto Gomorrha *(completely destroyed)*.

30 What shall we say then? *(Paul wants to say something good about the spiritual condition of the Jews, but finds there is nothing good to say.)* That the Gentiles, which followed not after Righteousness *(has reference to the fact that these Pagans did not pursue after God or Righteousness, of which their history is re-*

plete; they were idol worshippers)*, have attained to Righteousness *(because they accepted Christ)*, even the Righteousness which is of Faith *(Faith in Christ and what He did at the Cross, which Israel rejected)*.

31 But Israel, which followed after the Law of Righteousness *(presents Israel following in the wrong way, by works)*, has not attained to the Law of Righteousness *(couldn't attain to Righteousness by works; it can only be attained by trusting in Christ and the Cross)*.

32 Wherefore? *(Why?)* Because *they sought it* not by faith *(proper Faith can only be exercised by accepting Christ and the Cross, which Israel rejected)*, but as it were by the works of the Law *(by their performance, which can never measure up)*. For they stumbled at that stumblingstone *(presents the necessity of Faith in the Lord Jesus Christ, the One Whom all the Sacrifices had symbolized)*;

33 As it is written *(Isa. 8:14)*, Behold, I lay in Sion *(Israel)* a stumblingstone and rock of offence *(refers to Jesus Christ; He was not the type of Saviour they wanted; they needed Salvation from sin, but they wanted something else)*: and whosoever believes on Him shall not be ashamed *(portrays that Salvation is open to all, not a select predestined few, as*

many teach).

CHAPTER 10

ISRAEL

BRETHREN, my heart's desire and prayer to God for Israel is, that they might be saved *(Israel, as a nation, wasn't saved, despite their history; what an indictment!).*

2 For I bear them record that they have a zeal of God *(should read, "for God"; they had a zeal which had to do with God as its object)*, but not according to knowledge *(pertains to the right kind of knowledge).*

3 For they being ignorant of God's Righteousness *(spells the story not only of ancient Israel, but almost the entirety of the world, and for all time; "God's Righteousness" is that which is afforded by Christ, and received by exercising Faith in Him and what He did at the Cross, all on our behalf; Israel's ignorance was willful!)*, and going about to establish their own Righteousness *(the case of anyone who attempts to establish Righteousness by any method other than Faith in Christ and the Cross)*, have not submitted themselves unto the Righteousness of God *(God's Righteousness is ensconced in Christ and what He did at the Cross).*

4 For Christ *is* the end of the Law for Righteousness *(Christ fulfilled the totality of the Law)* to everyone who believes *(Faith in Christ guarantees the Righteousness which the Law had, but could not give).*

RIGHTEOUSNESS

5 For Moses described the Righteousness which is of the Law *(tells us plainly that the Law did contain Righteousness, but Righteousness to which man could not attain due to his fallen condition)*, That the man which does these things shall live by them *(Paul is saying that no matter how hard a person tries to render perfect obedience, he will not be able).*

6 But the Righteousness which is of Faith speaks on this wise *(will proclaim the wonderful and beautiful simplicity found only in Christ)*, Say not in your heart, Who shall ascend into Heaven? (that is, to bring Christ down *from above:*) *(For one to be saved, one does not have to perform some great task such as bring Christ down in Person from Heaven. As we shall see, God's Word is enough.)*

7 Or, Who shall descend into the deep? (That is, to bring up Christ again from the dead.) *(Christ does not need to be brought down from Heaven or up from the abyss to impart to the sinner forgiveness and Holiness. The Chris-*

tian Message contains no impossibilities.)

8 But what does it say? *(In other words, it says how to be saved!)* The Word is near you *(the Word of God), even* in your mouth *(speaks of the confession which must come from the mouth in order for one to be saved, even as Paul will say in the next Verse),* and in your heart *(proclaims the part of man in which Faith begins)*: that is, the Word of Faith, which we preach *(presents the declaration by Paul that Justification is on the Faith-Principle, as opposed to the Works-Principle; it speaks of Faith in Christ and what He did at the Cross; in other words, every Preacher should "Preach Christ and Him Crucified")*;

HOW TO RECEIVE

9 That if you shall confess with your mouth the Lord Jesus *(confess that Jesus is the Lord of Glory, and the Saviour of men, and that He died on the Cross that we might be saved),* and shall believe in your heart that God has raised Him from the dead *(pertains to the Bodily Resurrection of Christ, as is obvious),* you shall be saved *(it is that simple!).*

10 For with the heart man believes unto Righteousness *(presents the word "believing" in a mode of "thinking," not of feel-*ing; the "believing" has to do with believing Christ, and that His Sacrifice of Himself Atoned for all sin)*; and with the mouth confession is made unto Salvation *(when Faith comes forth from its silence to announce itself and proclaim the Glory and the Grace of the Lord, its voice "is confession").*

11 For the Scripture says *(combining parts of Isaiah 28:16 with 49:23),* Whosoever believes on Him *(proclaims the fact that Salvation is reachable by all)* shall not be ashamed *(in essence says, "shall not be put to shame," but rather will receive what is promised).*

12 For there is no difference between the Jew and the Greek *(should read, "between the Jew and the Gentile"; all must come the same way, which is by and through Christ and what He did at the Cross on our behalf)*: for the same Lord over all is rich unto all who call upon Him *(the riches of Grace will be given to all who truly call upon the Lord).*

13 For whosoever *(anyone, anywhere)* shall call upon the Name of the Lord shall be saved *(speaks of the sinner coming to Christ, but can refer to any Believer and with whatever need; the Cross is the means by which all of this is done).*

14 How then shall they call on Him in Whom they have not be-

lieved? *(The great sin of mankind is the sin of "unbelief.")* and how shall they believe in Him of Whom they have not heard? *(Ignorance is not Salvation. It is the business of the Church to take the Gospel to the world.)* and how shall they hear without a Preacher? *(This reveals God's method of proclaiming His Message.)*

15 And how shall they Preach, except they be sent? *(Those who send the Preacher are just as important as the Preacher.)* as it is written *(Isa. 52:7)*, How beautiful are the feet of them who Preach the Gospel of Peace *(presents the Message which, if accepted, will make things right between the sinner and God)*, and bring glad tidings *(Good News)* of good things! *(It's all made possible by the Cross.)*

16 But they have not all obeyed the Gospel *(all who hear the Gospel will not heed the Gospel)*. For Isaiah said, Lord, who has believed our report? *([Isa. 53:1] despite the fact of Who Christ was and what He did, only a few accepted Him as the Messiah.)*

17 So then Faith *comes* by hearing *(it is the publication of the Gospel which produces Faith in it)*, and hearing by the Word of God *(Faith does not come simply by hearing just anything, but rather by hearing God's Word, and believing that Word)*.

NO EXCUSE

18 But I say, Have they not heard? *(This proclaims Paul bringing the subject matter back to the Jews.)* Yes verily, their sound went into all the earth, and their words unto the ends of the world *(plainly proclaims the fact that Israel knew about Christ, and rejected Him anyway)*.

19 But I say, Did not Israel know? *(There was no excuse for Israel not to know. They had the Word of God for their guide.)* First Moses said *(Deut. 32:21)*, I will provoke you to jealousy by *them who are* no people, *and* by a foolish nation I will anger you *(some 1,600 years before Paul's day, Moses Prophesied the acceptance of the Gospel by the Gentiles)*.

20 But Isaiah is very bold, and said *(Isa. 65:1-2)*, I was found of them who sought Me not; I was made manifest unto them who asked not after Me *(as Moses, the Prophet Isaiah predicted that the Gentiles would hear and receive the Gospel)*.

21 But to Israel He said, All day long I have stretched forth My hands unto a disobedient and gainsaying people *(by their rejection of Christ and the Cross, the majority of Israel fashioned themselves into vessels of wrath through their self-will and unbelief; is the Church presently doing*

the same?).

CHAPTER 11

GOD'S PURPOSE

I say then, Has God cast away His people? *(This is phrased in the Greek Text so that it requires a negative answer.)* God forbid. For I also am an Israelite, of the seed of Abraham, *of* the Tribe of Benjamin *("Israelite" is the most august title of the three names).*

2 God has not cast away His people which He foreknew *(refers to Israel as a Nation, and the many Promises made respecting the future of these ancient people).* Do you not know what the Scripture says of Elijah? *(I Ki. 19:10, 14)* how he makes intercession to God against Israel, saying *(carries the thought that the Prophet should have pleaded for Israel, not against Israel),*

3 Lord, they have killed your Prophets, and dug down your Altars *(the true worship of God at that time was forsaken, and in its place idols were substituted [I Ki. 12:28-33]);* and I am left alone, and they seek my life *(in fact, Elijah was not alone, even as we shall see).*

4 But what was the answer of God unto him? I have reserved to myself seven thousand men, who have not bowed the knee to the image of Baal *(this tells us that*

True Faith always has the attachment of spiritual action).

A REMNANT

5 Even so then at this present time *(Paul's day)* also there is a Remnant according to the election of Grace *(definitely speaks of Predestination, but not as many think; it is the "Remnant" that is elected or predestined, not who will be in the Remnant).*

6 And if by Grace *(the Goodness of God, all made possible by the Cross),* then is it no more of works *(no one can point to their works as grounds for Salvation):* otherwise Grace is no more Grace *(if works are mixed with Grace, they nullify Grace).* But if it be of works, then is it no more Grace *(works can never produce Grace):* otherwise work is no more work *(for example, Water Baptism, if acted upon wrongly, nullifies its true meaning; this holds true as well for all other great Ordinances of the Lord).*

REBELLION AND UNBELIEF

7 What then? *(This was asked regarding Israel, but can also apply to the Church as well!)* Israel has not obtained that for which he seeks *(emphatically states that Salvation cannot be obtained in any manner or way other than God's*

Way, which is the Cross); but the election has obtained it *(refers to the Jews who did not attempt to claim Salvation by Merit, but rather by Grace)*, and the rest were blinded *(refers to a judicial blindness)*.

8 (According as it is written *(Isa. 29:10)*, God has given them the spirit of slumber *(that's what they wanted, so that's what they got!)*, eyes that they should not see, and ears that they should not hear;) *(This refers to not being able to "see" even though the evidence is plainly visible, or to "hear" even though the words are plainly spoken.)* unto this day *(refers to a condition that will not correct itself, but will actually grow worse)*.

9 And David said *(Ps. 69:22)*, Let their table be made a snare *(refers to their prosperity)*, and a trap *(pertains to the end result of the "snare")*, and a stumblingblock *(Israel stumbled over the very blessings which were intended for her betterment)*, and a recompence unto them *(a negative end result)*:

10 Let their eyes be darkened, that they may not see *(they didn't want to "see," so the Lord gave them what they wanted)*, and bow down their back always *(refers to them coming under the burden of captivity, which is exactly what happened)*.

GENTILES

11 I say then, Have they stum-bled that they should fall? *(Never to rise again?)* God forbid: but *rather* through their fall Salvation *is come* unto the Gentiles *(is another manner of expressing the formation or building of the Church)*, for to provoke them to jealousy *(harks back to the Prophecy of Noah after the flood, "God shall enlarge Japheth [Gentiles], and he shall dwell in the tents of Shem," i.e., "Israel"; Japheth will receive the blessings intended for Shem, which is exactly what has happened [Gen. 9:26-27])*.

12 Now if the fall of them *be* the riches of the world *(the idea is that their Fall did not stop the Gospel from coming to the world; the manner of the translation makes it seem as if the world has been greatly enriched by the Fall of Israel; however, that is not the case!)*, and the diminishing of them the riches of the Gentiles *(the Blessings that were supposed to go to Israel came to the Gentiles, and we speak of the Church, i.e., "The True Church")*; how much more their fulness? *(In this one question, Paul implies Israel's rightful place in the Kingdom of God yet to come, which will then bring everything into line, with Israel being the great Blessing that God always intended.)*

13 For I speak to you Gentiles *(it speaks of nations which are distinct from Israel)*, inasmuch as I am the Apostle of the Gentiles

(speaks of Paul's special Calling by the Lord), I magnify my office *(the office of the Apostle, which refers to the Message of Grace that would affect every Believer)*:

14 If by any means I may provoke to emulation *them which are* my flesh, and might save some of them *(Paul hoped Israel might see the Blessings of the Lord on the Gentiles, and, desiring those Blessings, accept Christ and thereby be saved)*.

15 For if the casting away of them *be* the reconciling of the world *(refers to the Act of God in setting Israel aside temporarily as a channel through which to bring the Good News of Salvation to the world, and in their place the substitution of the Church)*, what *shall* the receiving *of them be,* but life from the dead? *(All of this is with a view to bringing Israel back into fellowship with Himself and service in the coming Millennium. Their conversion is likened to a Resurrection.)*

16 For if the Firstfruit *be* Holy *(refers to the Patriarchs of Israel, who were Abraham, Isaac, and Jacob)*, the lump *is* also Holy *(does not refer to personal attributes, but simply that Israel has been Called of God, and set apart by God for a special task which will ultimately be performed)*: and if the root *be* Holy, so *are* the branches *(this pertains to their work, their rea-son for being; they are even now in the beginning stages of being brought back "from the dead")*.

17 And if some of the branches be broken off *(not all the branches, but some; referring to the fact that Israel will ultimately be brought back)*, and you *(refers to the Church, i.e., "the Gentiles")*, being a wild olive tree *(inferior)*, were grafted in among them *(presents the inferior being grafted into the superior, which is totally against nature)*, and with them partake of the root and fatness of the olive tree *(means that the Church derives its life from the common Root that was originally given to Israel of long ago)*;

18 Boast not against the branches *(the Church has not replaced Israel in the Plan of God, even though the Church is included in the Plan of God due to Israel's rejection of Christ)*. But if you boast, you bear not the root, but the root you *(as stated, the Church was grafted in, and is built upon the Promises originally given to Israel, which still apply to Israel and one day will be fulfilled)*.

19 You will say then, The branches were broken off, that I might be grafted in *(the Church must ever know and understand that it was and is second choice)*.

20 Well; because of unbelief they *(Israel)* were broken off *(unbelief respecting Christ and the*

Cross), and you stand by Faith *(proclaims that the Church was brought in because of Faith and not merit, and stands in its present position by Faith and not merit)*. Be not highminded, but fear *(the reason is given in the next Verse)*:

21 For if God spared not the natural branches *(Israel)*, *take heed* lest He also spare not you *(again refers to the Church, as is obvious)*.

22 Behold therefore the goodness and severity of God *(don't mistake the Goodness of God for license)*: on them which fell, severity *(speaks of Judgment which came on Israel, God's chosen people)*; but toward you, goodness, if you continue in *His* Goodness *(proclaims the condition; the continuing of that "Goodness" pertains to continued Faith in Christ and the Cross)*: otherwise you also shall be cut off *(is the modern Church on the edge of that even now? Revelation 3:15-22 tells us this is the case!)*.

23 And they also *(Israel)*, if they abide not still in unbelief, shall be grafted in *(Israel's unbelief will end at the Second Coming)*: for God is able to graft them in again *(and that He will do!)*.

24 For if you were cut out of the olive tree which is wild by nature *(refers to the Gentile world, and in this case the Church)*, and were grafted contrary to nature into a good olive tree *(the inferior into the superior)*: how much more shall these, which be the natural *branches*, be grafted into their own olive tree? *(Israel failed, but the Plan did not fail. Israel will ultimately be brought back and will Evangelize the world as originally planned. This will take place in the coming Kingdom Age [Isa. 66:19].)*

RESTORATION

25 For I would not, Brethren, that you should be ignorant of this mystery *(what has happened to Israel)*, lest you should be wise in your own conceits *(the Gentiles were not pulled in because of any merit or Righteousness on their part, but strictly because of the Grace of God)*; that blindness in part is happened to Israel *(is the "mystery" of which Paul speaks)*, until the fulness of the Gentiles be come in *(refers to the Church; in fact, the Church Age is even now coming to a close)*.

26 And so all Israel shall be saved *(when the Church Age ends, and the Second Coming commences; then Israel will accept Christ and be saved)*: as it is written *(Isa. 27:9; 59:20-21)*, There shall come out of Sion the Deliverer *(Jesus Christ will be the Deliverer)*, and shall turn away ungodliness from Jacob *(Christ will deliver Israel*

from the Antichrist, and more importantly will deliver them from their sins):

27 For this *is* my Covenant unto them *(a Promise)*, when I shall take away their sins *(as stated, it will be done at the Second Coming [Zech. 13:1]).*

28 As concerning the Gospel, *they are* enemies for your sakes *(refers to the Gospel of Jesus Christ)*: but as touching the election, *they are* beloved for the fathers' sakes *(speaks of their Calling).*

29 For the Gifts and Calling of God *are* without Repentance *(the Gifts and Calling of God are not subject to a change of mind on God's part).*

30 For as you in times past have not believed God *(concerns the Gentile world which lived outside of the Promises of God for about 4,000 years)*, yet have now obtained Mercy through their unbelief *(refers to the unbelief of Israel, but their unbelief did not stop Mercy being granted to the Gentiles, which God had planned all along):*

31 Even so have these also now not believed *(pertains once again to Israel, and the fact that even though they are now in unbelief; this will ultimately change)*, that through your Mercy *(the Church)* they also may obtain Mercy *(the Mercy which was extended to the Gentiles will ultimately bring Is-* rael back as well, with the entirety of the Plan of God now coming full circle).

32 For God has concluded them all in unbelief *(both Jews and Gentiles; the Jews were loath to accept this conclusion)*, that he might have Mercy upon all *(proclaims God's condition of dealing with the entirety of the human family, both Jew and Gentile).*

GREATNESS OF GOD

33 O the depth of the riches both of the wisdom and knowledge of God! *(This depth is beyond our comprehension.)* how unsearchable *are* His Judgments, and His Ways past finding out! *(They cannot be found out by the intellect, only by Revelation which comes by the Spirit.)*

34 For who has known the Mind of the Lord? *(As stated, the only way the Mind of the Lord can be known is for it to be revealed by the Holy Spirit.)* or who has been His counsellor? *(It would have to be, "no one.")*

35 Or who has first given to Him *(Job 41:11)*, and it shall be recompensed unto him again? *(What we sow, we reap!)*

36 For of Him *(refers to Creation)*, and through Him *(refers to His Perfect Knowledge)*, and to Him *(His Presence is everywhere)*, are all things *(He Alone is the First*

Cause): to Whom be Glory forever (He Alone deserves the Glory). Amen (Truth).

CHAPTER 12

CONSECRATION

I beseech you therefore, Brethren (I beg of you please), by the Mercies of God (all is given to the Believer, not because of merit on the Believers part, but strictly because of the "Mercy of God"), that you present your bodies a Living Sacrifice (the word "Sacrifice" speaks of the Sacrifice of Christ, and means that we cannot do this which the Holy Spirit demands unless our Faith is placed strictly in Christ and the Cross, which then gives the Holy Spirit latitude to carry out this great work within our lives), holy (that which the Holy Spirit Alone can do), acceptable unto God (actually means that a holy physical body, i.e., "temple," is all that He will accept), which is your reasonable service (reasonable if we look to Christ and the Cross; otherwise impossible!).

2 And be not conformed to this world (the ways of the world): but be ye transformed by the renewing of your mind (we must start thinking spiritually, which refers to the fact that everything is furnished to us through the Cross, and is obtained by Faith and not works), that you may prove what is that good (is put to the test and finds that the thing tested meets the specifications laid down), and acceptable, and perfect, Will of God (presents that which the Holy Spirit is attempting to bring about within our lives, and can only be obtained by ever making the Cross the object of our Faith).

SPIRITUAL GIFTS

3 For I say, through the grace given unto me (refers to Paul's Apostleship given by the Grace of God [Eph. 3:8]), to every man who is among you, not to think of himself more highly than he ought to think (Israel had fallen, and the reason at least in part was because of this very thing — a prideful, unscriptural evaluation of themselves); but to think soberly (don't be high-minded), according as God has dealt to every man the measure of Faith (this is given by the Holy Spirit at conversion).

4 For as we have many members in one body (refers to every person who is in the body of Christ), and all members have not the same office (a mode of acting or function):

5 So we, being many, are one body in Christ (speaks of the unity which ought to be prevalent within the Body), and every one members

one of another (*in effect says that whatever is true according to one is also true according to the other; this does not speak of "offices," but rather being a member of the Body*).

6 Having then gifts differing according to the grace that is given to us (*speaks of different "Gifts" or "Offices"*), whether Prophecy, *let us Prophesy* according to the proportion of Faith (*has to do with "the measure of Faith"*);

7 Or Ministry (*one who serves*), *let us wait* on *our* Ministering (*would have been better translated, "let us Minister according to the proportion of Faith"*): or he who teaches, on teaching (*carries the same idea; it is a wise man who stays within the sphere of service for which God, the Holy Spirit, has fitted him, and does not invade some other field of service for which he is not fitted*);

8 Or he who exhorts, on exhortation: he who gives, *let him do it* with simplicity (*proclaims "giving" as a "Gift" or "Office"*); he who rules, with diligence (*a position of authority*); he who shows mercy, with cheerfulness (*the Holy Spirit says that this is a "Gift" as well*).

COMMANDS

9 *Let* love be without dissimulation (*real, not feigned or hypocritical*). Abhor that which is evil (*the Christian is to express his ha-tred of evil by a withdrawal from it and a loathing of it*); cleave to that which is good (*fasten, and firmly*).

10 Be kindly affectioned one to another with brotherly love (*speaks of the Brotherhood of Believers, which is even closer than the blood ties of relatives who aren't saved*); in honour preferring one another (*the respect shown another, which is measured by one's evaluation of another*);

11 Not slothful in business (*must be done with fervency, diligence, and attention to detail, with responsibility*); fervent in Spirit (*should have been translated, "fervent in the Holy Spirit"; looking to the Spirit constantly for leading and guidance*); serving the Lord (*serving Him in everything we do*);

12 Rejoicing in hope (*constantly rejoicing in the sphere of hope, always believing God*); patient in tribulation (*to remain under the test in a God-honoring manner; not seeking to escape it, but eager to learn the lessons it was sent to teach*); continuing instant in prayer (*the idea is that we pray about everything continually, and be quick to do so*);

13 Distributing to the necessity of Saints (*pertains to concern and generosity*); given to hospitality (*kindness toward all, even strangers*).

14 Bless them which persecute

you (speak well of such a one): bless, and curse not (the Christian is to only bless, and not pronounce judgment on others, even our most strident enemies; we must leave judgment to the Lord).

15 Rejoice with them who do rejoice (speaks of the Believer being sincerely glad for the Blessings of others), and weep with them who weep (expresses the Believer being sincerely sorry for and with those who experience tribulation and sorrow).

16 Be of the same mind one toward another (have the same mind toward all, whether great or small, rich or poor). Mind not high things, but condescend to men of low estate (the manner in which a Believer treats a person who occupies the lowest station of life [whatever that might be] when no one else is seeing or hearing shows what you are). Be not wise in your own conceits (proclaims the antipathy felt by the Apostle to every sort of spiritual aristocracy, and to every caste-distinction within the Church).

CONDUCT

17 Recompense to no man evil for evil (we are not to repay evil in like kind, but rather with the very opposite). Provide things honest in the sight of all men (the Christian is exhorted to take care-ful forethought that his manner of life and his outward expression conforms to, and is honestly representative of, what he is, a Child of God).

18 If it be possible, as much as lieth in you, live peaceably with all men (the Believer has no control over the conduct of another, but the idea is that the initiative in disturbing the peace is never to lie with the Christian).

19 Dearly beloved, avenge not yourselves (proclaims action respecting fellow human beings), but rather give place unto wrath (speaks of God's Wrath, and means to leave room for it and not take God's proper work out of His Hands): for it is written, Vengeance is Mine; I will repay, saith the Lord ([Lev. 19:18] the righting of wrong is to be committed to the Lord).

20 Therefore if your enemy hunger, feed him; if he thirst, give him drink (we should treat our enemies with goodness): for in so doing you shall heap coals of fire on his head (coals of fire were taken from the Brazen Altar, a type of the Cross, and placed on the Altar of Incense; the Cross diverted judgment to intercession, of which the Altar of Incense was a type; by showing kindness to an enemy, we are diverting judgment, and showing mercy which God has shown us).

21 Be not overcome of evil

(don't meet evil with evil, which only breeds more evil), but overcome evil with good *(the initiative has changed from evil to good)*.

CHAPTER 13

HONOR AUTHORITY

L ET every soul be subject unto the higher powers *(refers to Human Government)*. For there is no power but of God *(refers to the fact that God has ordained Government)*: the powers that be are ordained of God *(refers to Human Government being a permanent institution, brought into being by God for the regulation of human affairs)*.

2 Whosoever therefore resists the power, resists the Ordinance of God *(anarchy is not of God)*: and they who resist shall receive to themselves damnation *(the Law of the Land is to always to be obeyed, providing it does not offend our conscience or the Word of God; the "damnation" mentioned here does not necessarily refer to such coming from God, but rather from men)*.

3 For rulers are not a terror to good works, but to the evil *(concerns the Divine right of Government to oppose crime and to protect its citizens)*. Will you then not be afraid of the power? *(This means that Civil Government should*

be respected, and all should fear breaking the Law.) do that which is good, and you shall have praise of the same *(refers to obeying the Law, as all Christians ought to do; as well, it assumes that the Laws are right and just)*:

4 For he *(the Civil Magistrate)* is the minister of God to you for good *(proclaims Government as a Divine Institution)*. But if you do that which is evil, be afraid; for he bears not the sword in vain *(the sword is the symbol of the right of the State to inflict Capital punishment for Capital crimes)*: for he is the minister of God *(not a Preacher of the Gospel, but a servant of the State)*, a revenger to *execute* wrath upon him who does evil *(proclaims the right of the State, as ordained by God, to use whatever force is necessary to stop "evil," i.e., crime)*.

5 Wherefore *you* must needs be subject *(plainly tells us that Christians are subject to the Law of the Land; that is, if it does not violate the Word of God)*, not only for wrath, but also for conscience sake *(refers to the fact that the Believer has a higher principle than that of the unbeliever)*.

6 For for this cause pay ye tribute also *(refers to the paying of taxes)*: for they are God's ministers, attending continually upon this very thing *(refers to public servants)*.

7 Render therefore to all their dues *(means that it is proper and right for all people to pay taxes, Christians as well!)*: tribute to whom tribute *is due (refers to that which is owed, and should be paid)*; custom to whom custom *(addresses hidden taxes, which we should pay as well)*; fear to whom fear; honour to whom honour *(Government is an Institution to be respected, extending to all Civil servants from the lowest to the highest)*.

PUBLIC RELATIONSHIPS

8 Owe no man any thing *(carries the idea that Christians do not "owe" their Brethren in the Lord the same obedience that is owed Civil Rulers)*, but to love one another *(proclaims the only requirement between Believers)*: for he who loves another has fulfilled the Law *(pertains to what the Law of Moses intended, but wasn't able to bring about; it can be done under Christ, and Christ Alone)*.

9 For this, You shall not commit adultery *(sex in any form outside of marriage is unlawful [Gen. 2:23-24])*, You shall not kill *(should have been translated, "murder")*, You shall not steal *(don't take what's not yours)*, You shall not bear false witness *(don't lie)*, You shall not covet *(do not try to unlawfully take that which belongs to another)*; and if *there be* any

other Commandment, it is briefly comprehended in this saying, namely, You shall love your neighbour as yourself *(Divine Love produced by the Holy Spirit is self-sacrificial in its nature)*.

10 Love works no ill to his neighbour *(will not hurt his neighbor)*: therefore love *is* the fulfilling of the Law *(proclaims the fact that this is all the Law formally requires, but can only be done in Christ)*.

11 And that, knowing the time *(the Believer is to do everything with the Judgment Seat of Christ in view)*, and now *it is* high time to awake out of sleep *(spiritual apathy and lethargy must be shaken off)*: for now *is* our Salvation nearer than when we believed *(actually speaks of the coming Rapture of the Church, and the Believer at that time being Glorified)*.

12 The night is far spent, the day is at hand *(refers to everything up until the coming Resurrection as "night"; all after the Resurrection is referred to as "day," with both day and night used as symbols)*: let us therefore cast off the works of darkness *(could be translated, "let us therefore cast off the clothes of darkness"; former bad habits of life are here, as elsewhere, regarded as clothing once worn, but now to be put off)*, and let us put on the armour of light *(could be translated, "and let us put on*

the clothes of Light").

13 Let us walk honestly, as in the day *(we should conduct ourselves in a manner befitting our high station in life as Saints of the Most High God)*; not in rioting and drunkenness *(the ways of the world)*, not in chambering and wantonness *(speaks of sexual immorality of every nature)*, not in strife and envying *(speaks of constant manipulation and exploitation to best others regarding business, place, or position)*.

14 But put ye on the Lord Jesus Christ *(avail yourself of all that Christ has accomplished at the Cross, which is available to all Believers)*, and make not provision for the flesh, to *fulfil* the lusts *thereof (Faith in the Cross will give the Holy Spirit latitude within our lives, which alone gives us victory over the flesh)*.

CHAPTER 14

DOUBTFUL THINGS

HIM who is weak in the faith receive ye *(refers to the Believer not understanding the Cross as he should)*, but not to doubtful disputations *(is directed toward the strong Believers and those "weak in the Faith"; it means that the strong, who welcome those of weak Faith into the fellowship of the Church, are to do so unreservedly* and not with the purpose of judging and attempting to rule their minds)*.

2 For one believes that he may eat all things *(pertains to the strength of one's Faith, based on a proper understanding of what Jesus did for us at the Cross)*: another, who is weak, eats herbs *(this latter group doesn't properly understand the Finished Work of Calvary, and think that eating or not eating certain things gauge their Sanctification and Holiness, etc.)*.

3 Let not him who eats despise him who eats not *(speaks of the spirit of spiritual superiority)*; and let not him which eats not judge him who eats *(is the same thing in reverse; spiritual superiority or spiritual pride is no respecter of persons; it can fasten itself to either group with equal tenacity)*: for God has received him *(speaks of the individuals in either case, strong or weak)*.

4 Who are you who judges another man's servant? *(This actually says, "As for you, who are you to judge God's Servant?")* to his own master he stands or falls *(the Lord Alone is to be the judge)*. Yes, he shall be held up: for God is able to make him stand *(has reference to the fact that God Alone can hold us up, and He is able to do so; the idea is that brow beating an individual will never help the person!)*.

5 One man esteems one day above another *(is actually referring back to the Jewish Sabbaths)*: another esteems every day *alike (subject every day to scrutiny; this is the proper course)*. Let every man be fully persuaded in his own mind *(the Apostle is not speaking of things here that are morally wrong and which the Word of God has already condemned; he is speaking of Rituals only)*.

6 He who regards the day, regards *it* unto the Lord *(whatever Ritual someone may be attempting to keep, he is supposed to be doing it unto the Lord, and not for some personal satisfaction)*; and he who regards not the day, to the Lord he does not regard *it (the interests of the Lord should be in view in either case)*. He who eats, eats to the Lord, for he gives God thanks *(his Faith is sufficient and whatever the food might be is of no consequence)*; and he who eats not, to the Lord he eats not, and gives God thanks *(has the same end in view, or at least it should, to please the Lord)*.

7 For none of us lives to himself, and no man dies to himself *(no Christian is his own end in life; what is always present in his mind as a rule of his conduct is the will and interest of his Lord)*.

8 For whether we live, we live unto the Lord; and whether we die, we die unto the Lord *(every-thing in our lives is to be, "unto the Lord")*: whether we live therefore, or die, we are the Lord's *(reflects the Lord having total control over our lives and deaths, which we must desire He use to the fullest)*.

9 For to this end *(refers to the fact of Christ's absolute ownership of the Believer, spirit, soul, and body)* Christ both died, and rose, and revived *(a price was paid for us of such magnitude that it absolutely defies description)*, that he might be Lord both of the dead and living *(refers to the Lordship of Christ over all Saints, whether alive or having passed on)*.

10 But why do you judge your brother? *(Is any Believer qualified to judge another Believer? "Your Brother" is another reason for not judging. It is inconsistent with the recognition of the Brotherhood of Believers.)* or why do you set at nought your brother? *(There is only one reason for refusing fellowship, and that reason is unconfessed, unrepentant, habitual sin in a person's life [I Cor., Chpt. 5].)* for we shall all stand before the Judgment Seat of Christ *(we will be judged there, not for our sins, those having been handled at the Cross, but as it regards our stewardship and our motives, etc.; gain or loss of reward will be the result)*.

11 For it is written *(Isa. 45:23)*,

As I live, saith the Lord (*God cannot die*), every knee shall bow to me, and every tongue shall confess to God (*to make a confession of God's honor, and as well, to praise Him*).

12 So then every one of us shall give account of himself to God (*each is responsible, meaning that the blame cannot be shifted elsewhere*).

RESPONSIBILITY

13 Let us not therefore judge one another any more (*can be translated, "let us no longer have the habit of criticizing one another"*): but judge this rather, that no man put a stumblingblock or an occasion to fall in *his* brother's way (*tells us what is in fact permissible to judge; as Believers, we are to judge every Brother and Sister and situation which surrounds them, irrespective what it might be, as to how we can help them, instead of harming them*).

14 I know, and am persuaded by the Lord Jesus (*means that this declaration is of the Lord, not merely of Paul's reasoning power*), that there is nothing unclean of itself (*speaks of ceremonial impurity, not of actual immorality; in the manner in which everything was originally created by the Lord and intended to be used, there is nothing unclean*): but to him who esteems any thing to be unclean, to him *it* is unclean (*is this way because of Faith placed in things other than the Cross*).

15 But if your brother be grieved with *your* meat, now walkest thou not charitably (*do not take that as an occasion to be uncharitable toward him*). Destroy not him with your meat, for whom Christ died (*our actions should always be motivated by the fact that Jesus died for this person, and this person belongs to Christ; we should treat him accordingly!*).

16 Let not then your good be evil spoken of (*our "good" must be exercised with a gracious spirit, always considering others*):

17 For the Kingdom of God is not meat and drink (*actually refers to rules, regulations, ceremonies, or rituals, etc.*); but Righteousness, and Peace, and Joy in the Holy Spirit (*a right spirit, which refers to a spirit that is controlled by the Holy Spirit, will always produce Righteousness, Peace, and Joy, not argument, etc.*).

18 For he who in these things serves Christ *is* acceptable to God (*Righteousness, Peace, and Joy are acceptable to the Lord; but not contention, quarreling, and fighting in the Church*), and approved of men (*Righteousness, Peace, and Joy alone will bring men together*).

19 Let us therefore follow after the things which make for

Peace *(following that which is of God, and not that devised by men)*, and things wherewith one may edify another *(refers to that which is produced by the Holy Spirit, and not by man)*.

20 For meat destroy not the Work of God *(let's not fight over incidental things, which are what most Church fights are all about)*. All things indeed *are* pure *(refers to that which is created by God, and used for its intended purpose)*; but *it is* evil for that man who eats with offence *(refers to the man who is "weak in Faith")*.

21 *It is* good neither to eat flesh, nor to drink wine, nor *any thing* whereby your brother stumbles, or is offended, or is made weak *(the idea is that love is to be the ruling guide, not our freedom of liberties)*.

22 Have you faith? *(This is addressed to the strong.)* have it to yourself before God *(don't run the risk of injuring a Brother's conscience merely for the sake of exercising in a special way the spiritual freedom we have the happiness to possess)*. Happy *is* he who condemns not himself in that thing which he allows *(refers to this being joy enough, without us taking our liberty further, and thereby hindering a weaker Brother or Sister)*.

23 And he who doubts is damned if he eat, because *he eats* not of faith *(Faith, that is proper Faith, is the criteria for all things)*: for whatsoever *is* not of faith is sin *(the type of Faith addressed here is Faith in "Jesus Christ and Him Crucified"; any other type of faith is "sin")*.

CHAPTER 15

UNITY IN CHRIST

WE then who are strong ought to bear the infirmities of the weak *(has the end result in mind of these weaker Brethren also becoming strong in Faith and knowledge of the Lord)*, and not to please ourselves *(pleasing self ruins our Christian fellowship)*.

2 Let every one of us please his neighbour for *his* good to edification *(refers to the Believer foregoing a legitimate act because a weaker Christian thinks it to be wrong)*.

3 For even Christ pleased not Himself *(the entirety of the Life and Ministry of Christ was to do the Will of the Father)*; but, as it is written *(Ps. 69:9)*, The reproaches of them who reproached You fell on Me *(Christ suffered this reproach for our sakes, and surely not to please Himself; this should be our example)*.

4 For whatsoever things were written aforetime were written for our learning *(refers to the*

whole of Old Testament Scriptures), that we through patience and comfort of the Scriptures might have hope *(the Word of God must always be our criteria, and not our own self-will).*

5 Now the God of Patience and Consolation grant you to be likeminded one toward another *(presents God as the Author of the Patience and Consolation lodged in the Scriptures, which nourish the Hope of Believers)* according to Christ Jesus *(once again, if we place our Faith exclusively in Christ and the Cross, these admonitions will not be difficult to obey):*

6 That you may with one mind and one mouth glorify God *(proclaims the Christlikeness of the previous Verse as the only manner in which differences can be correctly settled),* even the Father of our Lord Jesus Christ *(contains the rendering of Christ pleasing the Father, Whom we must desire to please accordingly).*

7 Wherefore receive ye one another *(to take into friendship and fellowship),* as Christ also received us to the Glory of God *("Us" covers all parties in the Church, however they may be distinguished; if Christ receives both, we are bound to receive each other).*

ONE IN CHRIST

8 Now I say that Jesus Christ was a Minister of the Circumcision for the Truth of God *(proclaims the fact that Jesus was obligated first of all to the Jews, and for particular reasons),* to confirm the Promises *made* unto the Fathers *(proclaims the fulfillment of the Messianic Promises to Israel):*

9 And that the Gentiles might Glorify God for His Mercy *(we Gentiles are grafted in, not because of any merit on our part, but strictly because of "Mercy" on His part);* as it is written *(Ps. 18:49),* For this cause I will confess to You *(to God)* among the Gentiles, and sing unto Your Name *(Christ is assumed here to be the Speaker, even as He is in all the Psalms; He gives thanks to God among the Gentiles, when the Gentiles give thanks to God through Him [Heb. 2:12]).*

10 And again He says, Rejoice, you Gentiles, with His people *(by joining "Gentiles" with Israel, "His People," Moses predicts the grafting of the "wild olive tree" into the "good olive tree" [Rom. 11:17-24]).*

11 And again *(Ps. 117:1),* Praise the Lord, all you Gentiles; and laud Him, all you people *(this predicted the day about a thousand years in the future that the Gentiles would Praise the Lord and "Laud Him," meaning to extol His Grace and Virtue).*

12 And again *(Isa. 11:1)*, Isaiah said, There shall be a root of Jesse *(concerns Jesus coming from the family of David, regarding the Incarnation)*, and He Who shall rise to reign over the Gentiles *(this Passage predicts that Jesus will ultimately "reign" as King over the entirety of the Earth)*; in Him shall the Gentiles trust *(the Church is almost entirely made up of Gentiles)*.

MINISTRY

13 Now the God of Hope fill you with all Joy and Peace in believing *(that which the Lord imparts to Believers rests on Faith)*, that you may abound in Hope, through the Power of the Holy Spirit *(the Holy Spirit will help us have all these things if we place our Faith exclusively in Christ and the Cross [I Cor. 1:18])*.

14 And I myself also am persuaded of you, my Brethren *(has faith in these Believers)*, that you also are full of goodness *(means that they had such because of Christ)*, filled with all knowledge *(knowledge of the Word)*, able also to admonish one another *(they could correct each other if need be, because of their knowledge of the Word)*.

15 Nevertheless, Brethren, I have written the more boldly unto you in some sort *(with greater confidence than otherwise)*, as putting you in mind, because of the Grace that is given to me of God *(his peculiar Mission as Apostle to the Gentiles gave him the right to admonish them)*,

16 That I should be the Minister of Jesus Christ to the Gentiles *(Paul presents his Calling as an Apostle to the Church)*, Ministering the Gospel of God *(the word "Ministering" is used in the sense of the Priests and Levites of old, who were busied with the Sacred Rites in the Tabernacle and Temple)*, that the offering up of the Gentiles might be acceptable *(presents Paul perceiving himself as presenting to God the Gentile Church as an "Offering")*, being Sanctified by the Holy Spirit *(the Holy Spirit, through Paul, pictures the Apostle offering up the Gentiles as a pure Sacrifice acceptable to God, because they were washed in the Blood and Sanctified by the Holy Spirit)*.

17 I have therefore whereof I may glory through Jesus Christ *(everything is through Christ, and what Christ has done at the Cross)* in those things which pertain to God *(the idea is that all of Paul's Ministry, and in whatever capacity, is ordered and directed by the Holy Spirit, signifying the Divine Order)*.

18 For I will not dare to speak of any of those things which

Christ has not wrought by me *(as the Apostle, in fact the first Apostle, to the Gentiles, he is here claiming inspiration in the writing of this Epistle, and rightly so)*, to make the Gentiles obedient, by word and deed *(it is not on his own impulse that he write this Epistle, but in Christ that he does it; the Romans as Gentiles, lie within this sphere in which Christ works through him)*,

19 Through mighty signs and wonders, by the Power of the Spirit of God *(proclaims the Mighty Power of God in operation)*; so that from Jerusalem, and round about unto Illyricum, I have fully Preached the Gospel of Christ *(he preached all the Gospel, compromising it not at all)*.

20 Yes, so have I strived to Preach the Gospel *(speaks of his earnest zeal)*, not where Christ was named *(means that Paul never sought to Evangelize where Christianity was already established)*, lest I should build upon another man's foundation *(Jesus, as the Head of the Church, gives direction through and by the Holy Spirit to particular workers; that "direction," must not be impugned by others)*:

21 But as it is written *(Isa. 52:15)*, To whom He was not spoken of, they shall see: and they who have not heard shall understand *(refers to the Message of Redemption going to the Gentiles, as is obvious)*.

ROME

22 For which cause also *(refers to Paul preaching these number of years in areas that did not have the Gospel)* I have been much hindered from coming to you *(his desire to minister in Rome was not born out of personal ambition, but was directed by the Holy Spirit concerning his Apostleship)*.

23 But now having no more place in these parts *(meaning he had finished his work in the places mentioned)*, and having a great desire these many years to come unto you *(proclaims that which had been strong within his heart, and placed there by the Holy Spirit)*;

24 Whensoever I take my journey into Spain, I will come to you *(there is no record in Scripture or history that Paul ever fulfilled this proposed journey to Spain)*: for I trust to see you in my journey, and to be brought on my way thitherward by you *(implies that he hoped to take a select number from the Church in Rome to Spain with him)*, if first I be somewhat filled with your *company (refers to his proposed stop in the Imperial City on his way to Spain)*.

25 But now I go unto Jerusalem to Minister unto the Saints *(to take offerings from the Gen-*

tile Churches to Jerusalem to minister to many Saints who were in dire need).

26 For it has pleased them of Macedonia and Achaia to make a certain contribution for the poor Saints which are at Jerusalem *(had to do with the persecution leveled at the Church in Jerusalem by the Jewish Sanhedrin)*.

27 It has pleased them verily; and their debtors they are *(refers to the Jews of Antiquity being the bearers of Salvation, which was a great Blessing to the Gentile world)*. For if the Gentiles have been made partakers of their spiritual things, their duty is also to minister unto them in carnal things *(this goes for the entirety of the Gospel, and for all time; if we are ministered to spiritually, we should in turn minister back in material things)*.

28 When therefore I have performed this *(to take the Offerings to Jerusalem)*, and have sealed to them this fruit *(everything the Believer does for the Lord is looked at by the Holy Spirit as "fruit")*, I will come by you into Spain *(there is a tradition that Paul did ultimately go to Spain; but as stated, there is no historical or Scriptural proof)*.

29 And I am sure that, when I come unto you, I shall come in the fulness of the Blessing of the Gospel of Christ *(proclaims the fact of great Truths held by Paul, actually given to him by Christ [Gal. 1:11-12], which he wished to give to the Roman Church)*.

PRAYER

30 Now I beseech you, Brethren, for the Lord Jesus Christ's sake *(refers to the Work of God; even though the Lord has paid the price on the Cross for man's Redemption, it is up to us to take the Message to the world)*, and for the Love of the Spirit *(that he would always be led by the Spirit)*, that you strive together with me in *your* prayers to God for me *(proclaims the humility of this man, and the Power of Prayer)*;

31 That I may be delivered from them who do not believe in Judaea *(the Nation of Israel, which had rejected Christ)*; and that my service which *I have* for Jerusalem may be accepted of the Saints *(concerns the Offering for the poor Saints in Jerusalem who were in desperate need)*;

32 That I may come unto you with joy by the Will of God *(refers to the fact that it definitely was the Will of God for Paul to go to Rome)*, and may with you be refreshed *(reveals that Paul had many friends in Rome, hence the warmness of his statements)*.

33 Now the God of Peace *be* with you all. Amen.

CHAPTER 16

COMMENDATIONS

I commend unto you Phebe our sister, which is a servant of the Church which is at Cenchrea (the word "servant" in the Greek is "diakonos," with our words "Deacon" and "Deaconess" derived from it; this shows that it is Scriptural for a woman to serve in this capacity as well as a man; Cenchrea was the Port of Corinth, about nine miles from that city):

2 That you receive her in the Lord, as becometh Saints (refers to receiving her into companionship and fellowship; in fact, she delivered the Epistle to the Romans to the Church in Rome; of this, Renan says: "Phoebe carried under the folds of her robe the whole future of Christian Theology), and that you assist her in whatsoever business she has need of you (suggests that she may have had business in Rome of a legal nature): for she has been a succourer of many, and of myself also (Phoebe was a great Blessing to the Work of God).

PERSONAL GREETINGS

3 Greet Priscilla and Aquila my helpers in Christ Jesus (Paul first met them at Corinth, but evidently they had now gone back to Rome):

4 Who have for my life laid down their own necks (means they risked their lives for Paul; exactly where and how aren't known): unto whom not only I give thanks, but also all the Churches of the Gentiles (all the Churches of the Gentiles thanked Priscilla and Aquila as well).

5 Likewise greet the Church that is in their house (evidently, they had one of the house Churches in Rome). Salute my well-beloved Epaenetus, who is the Firstfruits of Achaia unto Christ (this man was among the first in Corinth to give his heart to Christ).

6 Greet Mary, who bestowed much labour on us (other than this statement, no information is given concerning this dear lady).

7 Salute Andronicus and Junia, my kinsmen (probably refers to fellow Jews, and not blood relatives), and my fellow-prisoners (implies that these two had been, like himself, imprisoned at some time for the Faith), who are of note among the Apostles (doesn't mean they were Apostles themselves, but that they were well-known to the original Twelve), who also were in Christ before me (their conversion predated his).

8 Greet Amplias my beloved in the Lord.

9 Salute Urbane, our helper in Christ, and Stachys my beloved (it seems these men had been Paul's

helpers in earlier times).

10 Salute Apelles approved in Christ. Salute them which are of Aristobulus' *household (probably refers to slaves who had once belonged to this man).*

11 Salute Herodion my kinsman *(another Jew).* Greet them who be of the *household* of Narcissus, which are in the Lord *(does not refer to Narcissus personally, but to slaves of his household, at least those who were followers of the Lord).*

12 Salute Tryphena and Tryphosa, who labour in the Lord *(presents two more slaves, for theirs are slave names).* Salute the beloved Persis, which laboured much in the Lord *(refers to a woman).*

13 Salute Rufus chosen in the Lord, and his mother and mine *(he was probably the son of Simon of Cyrene who helped Jesus bear the Cross).*

14 Salute Asyncritus, Phlegon, Hermas, Patrobas, Hermes, and the Brethren which are with them.

15 Salute *(greet)* Philologus, and Julia, Nereus, and his sister, and Olympas, and all the Saints which are with them.

16 Salute one another with an holy kiss *(presents that which was the custom of all Oriental people at that time, not only Christians).* The Churches of Christ salute you *(refers to the Churches planted by Paul who in turn were greeting the Church in Rome).*

ADMONITION

17 Now I beseech you, brethren, mark them which cause divisions and offences contrary to the doctrine which you have learned *(refers to the fact that false teachers are to be identified);* and avoid them *(turn away from and shun these).*

18 For they who are such serve not our Lord Jesus Christ, but their own belly *(the satisfaction of creature needs, and not the Work of God);* and by good words and fair speeches deceive the hearts of the simple *(refers to those who have little true understanding of the Word of God).*

OBEDIENCE

19 For your obedience is come abroad unto all *men (refers to Paul not linking the Saints in the Church in Rome with these false teachers, whomever they may have been).* I am glad therefore on your behalf *(expresses his joy at their maturity in the Lord):* but yet I would have you wise unto that which is good, and simple concerning evil *(he wanted them to be so grounded in the Word that they would instantly know false doctrine when it came their way).*

20 And the God of Peace shall bruise Satan under your feet shortly *(all who trust Christ and*

what He has done at the Cross are guaranteed victory, and in every capacity). The grace of our Lord Jesus Christ be with you. Amen (presents the standard Benediction of Paul, which he uses in one form or the other in all of his Epistles, even Hebrews).

GREETINGS

21 Timothy my workfellow *(refers to Paul's young understudy and fellow worker)*, and Lucius, and Jason, and Sosipater, my kinsmen *(fellow Jews)*, salute you.

22 I Tertius, who wrote *this* Epistle, salute you in the Lord *(he was Paul's Scribe to whom he dictated the letter to the Romans)*.

23 Gaius my host, and of the whole Church, salutes you *(probably means that Paul was staying in this man's home in Corinth)*. Erastus the chamberlain of the city salutes you *(probably the one mentioned in II Timothy 4:20 and Acts 19:22)*, and Quartus a brother.

24 The Grace of our Lord Jesus Christ *be* with you all. Amen.

BENEDICTION

25 Now to Him Who is of power to stablish you according to my Gospel *(Paul's Gospel was, "Jesus Christ and Him Crucified")*, and the Preaching of Jesus Christ *(Paul Preached the Cross [I Cor. 1:23; 2:2])*, according to the Revelation of the Mystery, which was kept secret since the world began *(proclaims that which is now revealed in his Gospel, the story of Redemption)*,

26 But now is made manifest *(the actual Greek reads, "but now has been made known through Prophetic writings")*, and by the Scriptures of the Prophets *(refers to the Old Testament, which Scriptures constantly pointed to the coming of Christ)*, according to the Commandment of the Everlasting God *(actually means that, according to the appointment of God, the "Mystery" should now at last be made known)*, made known to all nations for the Obedience of Faith *(it must be Preached to the whole world)*:

27 To God only wise, *be* Glory through Jesus Christ forever. Amen *(the Great Price Jesus paid by giving himself in Sacrifice will forever bring Glory to God, in that it has brought about the Salvation of untold numbers of souls)*.

THE FIRST EPISTLE OF PAUL THE APOSTLE TO THE
CORINTHIANS

CHAPTER 1

INTRODUCTION

PAUL, called *to be* an Apostle *(this Calling presents the titular leader of the Church, and pertains to the Message; in other words, every God-called Apostle has been given a special emphasis by the Holy Spirit regarding his Message)* of Jesus Christ through the Will of God *(by God's Own Appointment and Will)*, and Sosthenes *our* brother *(Acts 18:17)*,

2 Unto the Church of God which is at Corinth *(this form of address shows the absence of any fixed Ecclesiastical Government)*, to them who are Sanctified in Christ Jesus *(set apart unto Christ)*, called *to be* Saints *(means that everyone who is "in Christ" is a "Saint")*, with all who in every place call upon the Name of Jesus Christ our Lord *(pertains to the fact that this Epistle is meant not only for the Church at Corinth, but for all other Churches and for all time)*, both theirs and ours *(deals a death blow to Christians who claim a monopoly on Christ for themselves and their own sects, etc.)*:

3 Grace *be* unto you, and Peace *(Grace is the beginning of all Blessings, while Peace is the end of all Blessings; all are made possible by the Cross)*, from God our Father, and *from* the Lord Jesus Christ *(places the "Father" first; in this paternal role, He is the Source of every good gift and every perfect gift, but does so through Jesus Christ and what He did at the Cross)*.

THANKSGIVING

4 I thank my God always on your behalf *(the natural overflow of a full heart)*, for the Grace of God which is given you by Jesus Christ *(as stated, all Grace, which is the Goodness of God, is made possible by the Cross, and the Cross alone!)*;

5 That in every thing you are enriched by Him *(meant to exclaim the Source of "every good thing," Who is Christ Jesus)*, in all utterance *(is not speaking of the Gift of Tongues as some think, but rather all the Promises of God which He has uttered or given since the beginning of time)*, and in all knowledge;

6 Even as the Testimony of Christ was confirmed in you *(what Christ did at the Cross had*

played out in the lives of some of these Corinthians):

7 So that you come behind in no Gift *(is not limited to the nine Gifts of the Spirit, but rather every single thing given by the Lord, which He paid for at the Cross)*; waiting for the Coming of our Lord Jesus Christ *(pertains here to the Rapture of the Church [I Thess. 4:13-18])*:

8 Who shall also confirm you unto the end *(refers to the keeping power of "our Lord Jesus Christ," which is done by the Holy Spirit as the Believer ever makes the Cross the object of his Faith)*, that you may be blameless in the day of our Lord Jesus Christ *(once again, such a life can only be attained by constant Faith in the Cross of Christ)*.

9 God *is* Faithful *(was a favorite expression of the integrity of God among Jews [II Cor. 1:18; I Thess. 5:24; II Thess. 3:3])*, by Whom you were called unto the fellowship of His Son Jesus Christ our Lord *("called" refers to Predestination, but of the Plan and not the person)*.

DIVISIONS

10 Now *(implies the transition from thanksgiving to reproof)* I beseech you *(I beg you)*, Brethren, by the Name of our Lord Jesus Christ *(proclaims the Lord as the Head of the Church)*, that you all speak the same thing *(de-*mands unity with respect to the Person of Christ, and what He has done to Redeem us through the Cross)*, and *that* there be no divisions among you *(as it regards Christ and the Cross)*; but *that* you be perfectly joined together in the same mind and in the same judgment *(presents that which can only be done by the Cross ever being the object of one's Faith, which then gives the Holy Spirit the latitude to bring about these things in our lives)*.

11 For it has been declared unto me of you, my Brethren, by them which are of the House of Chloe *(Paul wisely and kindly mentions his authority for these reports)*, that there are contentions among you. *(We will see that these contentions centered on disagreements concerning the Cross.)*

12 Now this I say, that every one of you says *(refers to a self-assertive manner)*, I am of Paul; and I of Apollos; and I of Cephas *(Simon Peter)*; and I of Christ. *(In effect, this latter group was saying they didn't need any Preachers at all, which is wrong.)*

13 Is Christ divided? *(Is there a Baptist Christ, a Pentecostal Christ, or a Holiness Christ? The answer is a solid "No.")* was Paul crucified for you? *(The Apostle rebukes the partisanship, which attached itself to his own name.)* or were you baptized in the name of Paul?

(This proclaims the idea that he had never attempted to draw away Disciples after himself, but rather to Christ.)

14 I thank God that I baptized none of you, but Crispus and Gaius *(if Water Baptism were essential to Salvation, as some claim, I hardly think Paul would have blatantly announced that he had only baptized these few, as he did here);*

15 Lest any should say that I had baptized in mine own name *(nothing must be done to draw away allegiance from Christ).*

16 And I baptized also the household of Stephanas: besides, I know not whether I baptized any other *(informs us that the inspiration of the Apostles in writing the Scriptures involved none of the mechanical infallibility ascribed to them by popular dogma).*

17 For Christ sent me not to baptize *(presents to us a Cardinal Truth)*, but to preach the Gospel *(the manner in which one may be Saved from sin)*: not with wisdom of words *(intellectualism is not the Gospel)*, lest the Cross of Christ should be made of none effect. *(This tells us in no uncertain terms that the Cross of Christ must always be the emphasis of the Message.)*

WISDOM

18 For the Preaching *(Message)* of the Cross is to them who perish foolishness *(Spiritual things cannot be discerned by unredeemed people, but that doesn't matter; the Cross must be preached just the same, even as we shall see)*; but unto us which are Saved it is the Power of God. *(The Cross is the Power of God simply because it was there that the total sin debt was paid, giving the Holy Spirit, in Whom the Power resides, latitude to work mightily within our lives.)*

19 For it is written *(Isa. 29:14)*, I will destroy the wisdom of the wise, and will bring to nothing the understanding of the prudent *(speaks to those who are wise in their own eyes, in effect having forsaken the ways of the Lord).*

20 Where is the wise? *(This presents the first of three classes of learned people who lived in that day.)* where is the Scribe? *(This pertained to the Jewish Theologians of that day.)* where is the disputer of this world? *(This speaks of the Greeks, who were seekers of mystical and metaphysical interpretations.)* has not God made foolish the wisdom of this world? *(This pertains to what God did in sending His Son to Redeem humanity, which He did by the Cross. All the wisdom of the world couldn't do this!)*

21 For after that in the Wisdom of God the world by wisdom knew not God *(man's puny wis-*

dom, *even the best he has to offer, cannot come to know God in any manner*), it pleased God by the foolishness of Preaching *(Preaching the Cross)* to save them who believe. *(Paul is not dealing with the art of preaching here, but with what is preached.)*

22 For the Jews require a sign *(the sign of the Messiah taking the Throne and making Israel a great Nation once again)*, and the Greeks seek after wisdom *(they thought that such solved the human problem; however, if it did, why were they ever seeking after more wisdom?)*:

23 But we Preach Christ Crucified *(this is the Foundation of the Word of God, and thereby of Salvation)*, unto the Jews a stumblingblock *(the Cross was the stumblingblock)*, and unto the Greeks foolishness *(both found it difficult to accept as God a dead Man hanging on a Cross, for such Christ was to them)*;

24 But unto them who are called *(refers to those who accept the Call, for the entirety of mankind is invited [Jn. 3:16; Rev. 22:17])*, both Jews and Greeks *(actually stands for both "Jews and Gentiles")*, Christ the Power of God *(what He did at the Cross Atoned for all sin, thereby making it possible for the Holy Spirit to exhibit His Power within our lives)*, and the Wisdom of God.

(This Wisdom devised a Plan of Salvation which pardoned guilty men and at the same time vindicated and glorified the Justice of God, which stands out as the wisest and most remarkable Plan of all time.)

25 Because the foolishness of God is wiser than men *(God achieves the mightiest ends by the humblest means)*; and the weakness of God is stronger than men *(refers to that which men take to be weak, but actually is not — the Cross)*.

26 For you see your calling, brethren *(refers to the nature and method of their Heavenly Calling)*, how that not many wise men after the flesh, not many mighty, not many noble, *are Called (are Called and accept)*:

27 But God has chosen the foolish things of the world to confound the wise *(the preaching of the Cross confounds the wise because it falls out to changed lives, which nothing man has can do)*; and God has chosen the weak things of the world to confound the things which are mighty *(the Cross is looked at as weakness, but it brings about great strength and power, regarding those who accept the Finished Work of Christ)*;

28 And base things of the world, and things which are despised, has God chosen *(it is God working in the base things and the*

despised things, which brings about *miraculous things*), yes, and things which are not, to bring to naught things that are (*God can use that which is nothing within itself, but with Him all things become possible*):

29 That no flesh (*human effort*) should glory in His Presence.

30 But of Him are you in Christ Jesus (*pertains to this great Plan of God, which is far beyond all wisdom of the world; we are "in Christ Jesus," by virtue of the Cross — what He did there*), Who of God is made unto us Wisdom, and Righteousness, and Sanctification, and Redemption (*we have all of this by the Holy Spirit, through Christ and what He did at the Cross; this means the Cross must ever be the object of our Faith*):

31 That, according as it is written (*Jer. 9:23*), he who glories, let him glory in the Lord. (*He who boasts, let him boast in the Lord, and not in particular preachers.*)

CHAPTER 2

TRUE WISDOM

A ND I, brethren, when I came to you, came not with excellency of speech or of wisdom (*means that he depended not on oratorical abilities, nor did he delve into philosophy, which was all the rage of that particular day*), declaring unto you the Testimony of God (*which is Christ and Him Crucified*).

2 For I determined not to know any thing among you (*with purpose and design, Paul did not resort to the knowledge or philosophy of the world regarding the Preaching of the Gospel*), save Jesus Christ, and Him Crucified (*that and that alone is the Message which will save the sinner, set the captive free, and give the Believer perpetual victory*).

3 And I was with you in (*personal*) weakness (*an expression of utter dependence on God*), and in fear (*fear that he might not properly preach the Cross*), and in much trembling. (*He realized the significance of what he was preaching, and his inadequacy regarding his own person.*)

4 And my speech and my preaching was not with enticing words of man's wisdom (*he knew that would not set anyone free; the modern church should take a lesson from this*), but in demonstration of the Spirit and of Power (*which speaks of what the Holy Spirit can do in the hearts and lives of Believers, if the Cross is properly preached*):

5 That your Faith should not stand in the wisdom of men (*speaks of any proposed way other than the Cross*), but in the Power

of God *(made possible only by the Cross)*.

6 Howbeit we speak wisdom among them who are perfect *(only the spiritually mature can understand the Wisdom of God, which is the Cross)*: yet not the wisdom of this world *(the Wisdom of God pertaining to Salvation has absolutely no relationship whatsoever to the "wisdom of this world")*, nor of the princes of this world, that come to naught *(the great Sages and Philosophers of the world contributed nothing to Paul, nor do they to us as well)*:

7 But we speak the Wisdom of God in a mystery, *even* the hidden *wisdom (God's Wisdom leads sinful men to the great Sacrifice of history, the offering up of Jesus on the Cross of Calvary, which paid the terrible sin debt of man, at least for all who will believe)*, which God ordained before the world unto our glory *(in the Mind of God, Christ was offered up on the Cross even before the Foundation of the world [I Pet. 1:18-20])*:

8 Which none of the princes of this world knew *(pertains to their ignorance being a willful ignorance, which was their judgment for rejecting Christ [Acts 3:17; 13:27])*: for had they known *it (had they desired to know)*, they would not have Crucified the Lord of Glory. *(These words bring in juxtaposition the lowest humiliation and the most splendid exaltation.)*

THE HOLY SPIRIT

9 But as it is written *(Isa. 64:4)*, Eye has not seen, nor ear heard, neither have entered into the heart of man *(the purpose is to show that we cannot come to a knowledge of God through these normal ways of learning)*, the things which God has prepared for them who love Him.

10 But God has revealed *them* unto us by His Spirit *(tells us the manner of impartation of spiritual knowledge, which is Revelation)*: for the Spirit searches all things, yes, the deep things of God. *(The Holy Spirit is the only One amply qualified to reveal God because He is God, and He is the member of the Godhead Who deals directly with man.)*

11 For what man knows the things of a man, save the spirit of man which is in him? *(The spirit of a man can know some things about another man, but within itself cannot know anything about God.)* even so the things of God knows no man, but the Spirit of God. *(Men cannot learn about God through scientific investigation or human reasoning, but only as the Spirit of God reveals such to the Believer.)*

12 Now we have received, not the spirit of the world *(which is of Satan)*, but the Spirit which is

of God (upon conversion, the Believer receives the Spirit of God); that we might know the things that are freely given to us of God (the only way we can truly know).

13 Which things also we speak, not in the words which man's wisdom teaches (corrupted wisdom), but which the Holy Spirit teaches (which is an understanding of the Word of God); comparing spiritual things with spiritual (communicating spiritual Truths to spiritual men by the Spirit).

14 But the natural man receives not the things of the Spirit of God (speaks of the individual who is not Born-again): for they are foolishness unto him (a lack of understanding): neither can he know them (fallen man cannot understand spiritual Truths), because they are spiritually discerned (only the Regenerated spirit of man can understand the things of the Spirit).

15 But he who is spiritual judges all things (portrays only the spiritual person as capable of proper judgment), yet he himself is judged of no man (refers to judgment which God will accept).

16 For who has known the Mind of the Lord, that he may instruct him? (The answer is no one! [Isa. 40:14].) But we have the Mind of Christ. (They who have the Mind of Christ see things as God sees them.)

CHAPTER 3

THE CARNAL STATE

AND I, Brethren, could not speak unto you as unto spiritual, but as unto carnal (a solemn rebuke; they were carnal because they had shifted their Faith from the Cross to other things), even as unto babes in Christ. (Ironically enough, this is spoken to people who considered themselves to be spiritual giants.)

2 I have fed you with milk, and not with meat (because of their carnality): for hitherto you were not able to bear it, neither yet now are you able. (They were still functioning in spiritual immaturity. Their spiritual growth had stopped.)

3 For you are yet carnal (in the short version, carnality is the placing of one's faith in that other than the Cross; in other words, such a one makes the Cross of Christ of none effect [1:17]): for whereas there is among you envying, and strife, and divisions, are you not carnal, and walk as men? (They acted and spoke in the same way men of the world act and speak; in other words, as the unconverted.)

4 For while one said, I am of Paul; and another, I am of Apollos; are you not carnal? (This is the party spirit, which has wrecked so many Churches.)

LABORERS

5 Who then is Paul, and who is Apollos *(the idea is these men, though used greatly by God, were still mere men)*, but Ministers by whom you believed *(better translated, "Though whom you believed")*, even as the Lord gave to every man? *(Whatever Gifts each Preacher had came from the Lord, and was not due to their own, abilities or merit.)*

6 I have planted *(refers to Paul being the founder of the Church per se under Christ)*, Apollos watered *(the strengthening of the Faith of wavering Churches)*; but God gave the increase *(pertains to souls and their spiritual growth)*.

7 So then neither is he who plants any thing, neither he who waters *(the Planter and the Waterer are nothing by comparison to the Lord)*; but God Who gives the increase. *(Man by his own ability cannot bring about the increase, no matter how much he plants or waters, spiritually speaking.)*

8 Now he who plants and he who waters are one *(literally means in the Greek, "one thing")*: and every man shall receive his own reward according to his own labour. *(Paul did not say, "according to his own success," but rather "labor." God hasn't called us to be successful, but He has called us to be Faithful.)*

9 For we are labourers together with God *(pertains to Labor in the harvest)*: you are God's husbandry *(God's field, God's tilled land)*, you are God's building *(Vineyard)*.

10 According to the Grace of God which is given unto me, as a wise masterbuilder *(in essence Paul, under Christ, founded the Church)*, I have laid the foundation *(Jesus Christ and Him Crucified)*, and another builds thereon *(speaks of all Preachers who followed thereafter, even unto this very moment, and have built upon this Foundation)*. But let every man take heed how he builds thereupon. *(All must Preach the same Doctrine Paul Preached, in essence, "Jesus Christ and Him Crucified.")*

FOUNDATION

11 For other foundation can no man lay than that is laid *(anything other than the Cross is another foundation and, therefore, unacceptable to the Lord)*, which is Jesus Christ *(Who He is, God manifest in the flesh, and what He did, Redemption through the Cross)*.

12 Now if any man build upon this foundation gold, silver, precious stones *(presents Paul using symbols; the first three are materials which will stand the test of*

fire, *symbolic of the Word of God which is the Standard)*, wood, hay, stubble *(will not stand the test of fire)*;

13 Every man's work shall be made manifest *(at the Judgment Seat of Christ)*: for the day shall declare it *(the time of the Judgment Seat of Christ)*, because it shall be revealed by fire *(the fire of God's Word)*; and the fire shall try every man's work of what sort it is. *("Fire" in the Greek is "puri," and speaks of the ability of Christ, Who will be the Judge and Who sees through everything we do [Rev. 2:18]. He Alone knows our very motives!)*

14 If any man's work abide which he has built thereupon *(assuming it to be true)*, he shall receive a reward *(pertains to that which will be eternal, although we aren't told what it will be)*.

15 If any man's work shall be burned, he shall suffer loss *(refers to the loss of reward, but not Salvation)*: but he himself shall be saved; yet so as by fire. *(Actually, this means the person is saved "despite the fire." While the fire of the Word of God will definitely burn up improper works, it will not touch our Salvation, that being in Christ and the Cross.)*

THE TEMPLE

16 Know you not that you are the Temple of God *(where the Holy Spirit abides)*, and that the Spirit of God dwells in you? *(That makes the Born-again Believer His permanent home.)*

17 If any man defile the Temple of God *(our physical bodies must be a living Sacrifice, which means that we stay Holy by ever making the Cross the object of our Faith [Rom. 12:1])*, him shall God destroy *(to fail to function in God's prescribed Order [the Cross], opens the Believer up to Satan, which will ultimately result in destruction)*; for the Temple of God is Holy, which Temple you are. *(We are "Holy" by virtue of being "in Christ." We remain Holy by the Work of the Holy Spirit, Who demands that our Faith ever be in the Cross, which has made all of this possible.)*

18 Let no man deceive himself *(proclaims that which is possible, or the admonition would not have been given)*. If any man among you seems to be wise in this world *(is not meant to denigrate education, but rather to portray the Truth that neither God nor His Ways can be found through the wisdom of this world, i.e., higher education, etc.)*, let him become a fool *(let the person accept the Lord as his Saviour, and then go to the Word of God to learn about the Lord, which the world thinks is foolish)*, that he may be wise *(concerns itself with True wisdom)*.

19 For the wisdom of this world is foolishness with God *(because it's all wrong)*. For it is written *(Job 5:13)*, He takes the wise in their own craftiness. *(God will see to it that such people are caught in the traps they set for other people.)*

20 And again *(Ps. 94:11)*, The Lord knows the thoughts of the wise *(the worldly wise)*, that they are vain *(empty nothings)*.

21 Therefore let no man glory in men *(but rather the Lord)*. For all things are yours *(everything given by God is available to every single Believer, providing it is the Will of God; God does not play favorites)*;

22 Whether Paul, or Apollos, or Cephas, or the world, or life, or death, or things present, or things to come *(the Lord Rules all things)*; all are yours *(nothing can happen to us, but that the Lord directs the action)*;

23 And you are Christ's *(we are bought with a price, the Cross)*; and Christ is God's *(refers to what Christ has done to Redeem humanity by means of the Cross, which was the Plan of God [I Pet. 1:18-20])*.

CHAPTER 4

JUDGMENT

LET a man so account of us, as of the Ministers of Christ *(Christians should form some estimate of the position of Ministers of the Gospel, and Paul tells us what that estimate should be)*, and Stewards *(literally a house-manager)* of the Mysteries of God. *(These are Truths once hidden, but now revealed.)*

2 Moreover it is required in Stewards, that a man be found Faithful *(as stated, God doesn't demand success, but He does demand Faithfulness)*.

3 But with me it is a very small thing that I should be judged of you *(judged regarding his motives)*, or of man's judgment *(refers to any man judging him regarding motives)*: yes, I judge not mine own self. *(In effect, this says a Believer is not actually even qualified to properly judge himself, much less others.)*

4 For I know nothing by myself *(in effect, "the verdict of my own conscience acquits me of all intentional unfaithfulness"; but this is insufficient, because God sees with clearer eyes than ours)*; yet am I not hereby justified *(I know of nothing in my life or Ministry that is contrary to the Lord, still it is not my judgment that counts in this case, but rather that of the Lord)*: but He who judges me is the Lord *(refers to the Lord as the final Command, in fact the only True Judge)*.

5 Therefore judge nothing

before the time, until the Lord come *(refers to the coming "Judgment Seat of Christ")*, Who both will bring to light the hidden things of darkness, and will make manifest the counsels of the hearts *(at that time, the Lord will reveal the true motives behind the actions of His people)*: and then shall every man have praise of God *(actually means "such praise as he deserves")*.

HUMILITY

6 And these things, Brethren, I have in a figure transferred to myself and *to* Apollos for your sakes *(he has used himself and Apollos as examples)*; that you might learn in us not to think *of men* above that which is written *(refers to the Scriptures)*, that no one of you be puffed up for one against another *(an inflation of pride)*.

7 For who makes you to differ *from another? (All are on the same level, in desperate need of God.)* and what have you that you did not receive? *(Whatever we have is a Gift, not a merit.)* now if you did receive *it*, why do you glory, as if you had not received *it? (This presents a fake boast!)*

8 Now you are full, now you are rich *(presents the Apostle using irony)*, you have reigned as kings without us *(you are acting as if you do not need our Ministry)*: and I would to God you did reign, that we also might reign with you *(in effect says he wished they were actually in the Millennium)*.

9 For I think that God has set forth us the Apostles last, as it were appointed to death *(gladiators in the arena, appointed to die)*: for we are made a spectacle unto the world, and to Angels, and to men. *(God-called men and women are exhibited as a spectacle in a theatre to the world of men and to Angels.)*

10 We *are* fools for Christ's sake *(continuing to be the spectacle)*, but you *are* wise in Christ *(telling the Corinthians, and all others for that matter, that if they truly walk close to Christ, they will meet with the same contempt and hatred men showed to Christ)*; we *are* weak *(all Believers are weak, at least as far as the flesh is concerned)*, but you *are* strong *(these Corinthians were busy telling everyone just how strong they were in the Lord)*; you *are* honourable, but we *are* despised. *(The more popular the Church is, the further away from God it is. True Believers are despised!)*

11 Even unto this present hour *(speaks of the moment in which he was writing this particular Epistle)* we both hunger, and thirst, and are naked, and are buffeted, and have no certain dwellingplace *(perhaps this homelessness was*

among the severest of all trials);

12 And labour, working with our own hands *(spoke of his tent-making, which he did in order to meet his needs in places where he was attempting to plant a Church):* being reviled, we bless *(presents the correct spiritual stance for the Child of God);* being persecuted, we suffer it *(put it in the hands of the Lord):*

13 Being defamed, we intreat *(irrespective as to how evil the response to the Message was, the Apostle would not allow his spirit to be affected by the opposition):* we are made as the filth of the world *(could be translated, "we are treated as the filth of the world"),* and are the offscouring of all things unto this day *(shoots down popularity).*

COUNSEL

14 I write not these things to shame you *(carries the idea that he is not merely venting his spleen, so to speak; there is a lesson the Holy Spirit desires that he teach),* but as my beloved sons I warn you. *(These four Chapters are not merely presenting the hurt feelings of a Preacher who has been rejected, but rather proclaiming that these Corinthians were completely getting off track, which would fall out to their hurt if continued.)*

15 For though you have ten thousand instructors in Christ *(refers to Teachers),* yet *have you* not many fathers *(speaks of one who has brought the Gospel to the sinner so that he might be saved):* for in Christ Jesus I have begotten you through the Gospel. *(This presents far more than merely preaching. It actually speaks of the entirety of the Call of God on a man's life, resulting in souls.)*

16 Wherefore I beseech you *(I beg you),* be ye followers of me *(should have been translated, "be ye imitators of me"; Paul preached the Cross, lived the Cross, and knew if victory was to be had by anyone, it would have to be by the Cross; unfortunately, all Preachers then, as now, were not Preaching the Cross; hence the admonition of the Apostle).*

17 For this cause have I sent unto you Timothy *(Paul knew that the letter would arrive before Timothy),* who is my beloved son, and Faithful in the Lord *(his son in the Lord; Paul had won him to Christ some years before),* who shall bring you into remembrance of my ways which be in Christ, as I teach every where in every Church. *(Timothy would Preach the Cross, exactly as did Paul [I Cor. 1:17-18, 23; 2:2].)*

18 Now some are puffed up *(prideful attitudes),* as though I would not come to you *(should*

have been translated, "as though they would not eventually have to face me in person").

19 But I will come to you shortly, if the Lord will *(expresses a humble spirit of dependence)*, and will know, not the speech of them which are puffed up, but the power. *(He addresses these remarks to those who actually thought their spirituality was greater than his.)*

20 For the Kingdom of God is not in word, but in power. *(The Message of the Cross changes lives, and does so by the Power of God.)*

21 What will you? *(This actually comes from the Holy Spirit, and delivers an ultimatum.)* shall I come unto you with a rod, or in love, and in the spirit of meekness? *(If the Cross is rejected, trouble ultimately is in the offing. Accepted? The opposite!)*

CHAPTER 5

MORAL STANDARDS

IT is reported commonly *that there is* fornication among you *(fornication speaks of all types of immorality; it seemed to have been more widespread than just a case or two)*, and such fornication as is not so much as named among the Gentiles *(meaning this type was not common among the Gentiles)*, that one should have his father's wife *(refers to the man's* stepmother; it also seems the father was alive [II Cor. 7:12]).

2 And you are puffed up *(it seems that some were attempting to say such was allowed under the guise of Christian liberty)*, and have not rather mourned *(presents that which should have been the norm, but seemingly was not)*, that he who has done this deed might be taken away from among you *(the idea is the individual repent, thereby ceasing such activity or be disfellowshiped)*.

JUDGMENT OF SIN

3 For I verily, as absent in body, but present in spirit *(means that even though he is not present personally in Corinth, the direction he will now give is still to be taken just as seriously as if he were there personally)*, have judged already, as though I were present, *concerning* him who has so done this deed. *(Does not, as some think, contradict Jesus' instructions to not judge [Mat. 7:1-5]. Paul is judging an action here, as all Believers are called upon to do, i.e., "Fruit" [Mat. 7:15-20].)*

4 In the Name of our Lord Jesus Christ *(refers to Christ as the Head of the Church)*, when you are gathered together *(presents the authority of the local Church)*, and my spirit *(refers to Paul being there in spirit, even though he*

could not be there in the flesh), with the power of our Lord Jesus Christ. *(The authority is in the "Name," and the "Power" is in the Person of Christ. This recognizes Him totally as the Head of the Church.)*

5 To deliver such an one *(the one committing the sin of incest)* unto Satan for the destruction of the flesh *(it refers to ceasing all prayer for such an individual, and can be done by the local Body, providing the Church is correct in its position; God will no more honor wrong committed by the Church than He will by an individual),* that the spirit may be saved in the day of the Lord Jesus *(it is hoped that such action will cause the person to repent).*

LEAVEN

6 Your glorying is not good *(these people had taken liberty into license).* Do you not know that a little leaven leaveneth the whole lump? *(Leaven is figurative of such that is minuscule in quantity, but extremely pervasive in its penetrating force.)*

7 Purge out therefore the old leaven *(spoken in Old Covenant terminology, but with the same meaning carried over in the hearts and lives of New Testament Believers),* that you may be a new lump *(start acting like what you are, "a new creation"),* as you are unleav-ened *(speaks of the position that one has in Christ; that is our "standing"; it is the business of the Spirit to bring our "state" up to our "standing").* For even Christ our Passover is Sacrificed for us *(the Believer can have victory over all sin by placing his Faith exclusively in the Cross of Christ, which Sacrifice addressed all sin):*

8 Therefore let us keep the feast *(is meant to serve as a symbol of the Jewish Passover, when all leaven was purged from the household),* not with old leaven *(old sins committed before conversion),* neither with the leaven of malice and wickedness *(refers to the ways of the world from which the Child of God has been delivered);* but with the unleavened *bread* of sincerity and truth *(can only be attained by one's Faith being anchored solely in the Sacrifice of Christ).*

SOCIAL RELATIONS

9 I wrote unto you in an Epistle *(refers to a previous letter written to the Church of Corinth, which has been lost)* not to company with fornicators *(actually means, "not to be mingled up among"):*

10 Yet not altogether with the fornicators of this world *(places a difference between those in the world and those in the Church),* or with the covetous, or extor-

tioners, or with idolaters; for then must you needs go out of the world *(refers to normal commerce and activity with those who are unsaved, which is different than those who profess Christ).*

11 But now I have written unto you not to keep company *(Believers must not condone such immoral activity in other Christians, considering that they refuse to repent),* if any man who is called a brother be a fornicator, or covetous, or an idolater, or a railer, or a drunkard, or an extortioner *(plainly tells us that many will call themselves "Christian" or "Brother," who practice these type of sins);* with such an one no not to eat *(speaks more so of the Lord's Supper than anything else).*

12 For what have I to do to judge them also who are without? *(The idea is that we have no right to apply these standards to people who have not professed Christ as Saviour.)* do not you judge them who are within? *(As Believers, we have enough on our plate without having to call unbelievers to task. That is not our obligation.)*

13 But them who are without (unsaved) God judges *(so lets leave the unredeemed to Him).* Therefore put away from among yourselves that wicked person *(If the Believer will not repent of obvious wrongdoing, and we speak of scandalous sins, then that person must be disfellowshiped).*

CHAPTER 6

CIVIL LAW

DARE any of you, having a matter against another, go to Law before the unjust *(this situation had evidently been brought to Paul's attention by the House of Chloe [1:11]),* and not before the Saints? *(This portrays what our Lord proclaimed as He laid down the rule for "Believers" to settle quarrels among themselves [Mat. 18:15-17].)*

2 Do you not know that the Saints shall judge the world? *(This refers to the Millennial and Eternal Reigns of Jesus Christ and His Saints.)* and if the world shall be judged by you, are you unworthy to judge the smallest matters? *(This presents a fitting rebuke.)*

3 Know you not that we shall judge Angels? *(This only pertains to those Angels who fell with Lucifer [II Pet. 2:4; Jude, Vs. 6; Rev. 20:10].)* how much more things that pertain to this life? *(The statement regards this present life as being elementary in comparison to that life to come.)*

4 If then you have judgments of things pertaining to this life *(seems like there were many quarrels in the Church at Corinth),* set them to judge who are least esteemed in the Church *(presents Paul again using irony).*

5 I speak to your shame *(I shouldn't have to say these things).* Is it so, that there is not a wise man among you? *(The question drips with sarcasm.)* No, not one who shall be able to judge between his Brethren? *(This is asked in the Greek in a manner which demands an affirmative answer. "Of course there is!")*

6 But brother goes to Law with brother, and that before the unbelievers *(a bad example!).*

7 Now therefore there is utterly a fault among you, because you go to Law one with another *(should not be among Christians).* Why do you not rather take wrong? *(This portrays the perfect example of uncrucified self.)* why do ye not rather *suffer yourselves* to be defrauded? *(It is better to suffer material loss, than to suffer spiritual loss.)*

8 No, you do wrong, and defraud, and that *your* Brethren *(to defraud anyone is bad enough, but to defraud a fellow Brother in the Lord is worse still!).*

PURITY

9 Do you not know that the unrighteous shall not inherit the Kingdom of God? *(This shoots down the unscriptural doctrine of Unconditional Eternal Security.)* Be not deceived *(presents the same words of our Lord, "let no man de-ceive you" [Mk. 13:5]):* neither fornicators, nor idolaters, nor adulterers, nor effeminate, nor abusers of themselves with mankind *(the proof of true Christianity is the changed life),*

10 Nor thieves, nor covetous, nor drunkards, nor revilers, nor extortioners, shall inherit the Kingdom of God *(refers to those who call themselves "Believers," but yet continue to practice the sins mentioned, whom the Holy Spirit says are not Saved, irrespective of their claims).*

11 And such were some of you *(before conversion)*: but you are washed *(refers to the Blood of Jesus cleansing from all sin),* but you are sanctified *(one's position in Christ),* but you are justified *(declared not guilty)* in the Name of the Lord Jesus *(refers to Christ and what He did at the Cross, in order that we might be Saved),* and by the Spirit of our God *(proclaims the Third Person of the Triune Godhead as the Mechanic in this great Work of Grace).*

12 All things are Lawful unto me *(refers to the fact that Christianity is not a religion which consists of rules, etc.),* but all things are not expedient *(not profitable):* all things are Lawful for me, but I will not be brought under the power of any *(Grace does not give a license to sin, but rather liberty to live a Holy Life).*

13 Meats for the belly, and the belly for meats *(food contains no spiritual application)*: but God shall destroy both it and them *(don't make a god out of your belly; it won't set well with the Lord)*. Now the body is not for fornication, but for the Lord *(our physical bodies are Temples of the Holy Spirit [3:16])*; and the Lord for the body *(if we keep the Temple pure, which we can only do by His Grace, He will keep it well)*.

14 And God has both raised up the Lord *(the Resurrection of our Lord)*, and will also raise up us by His Own Power *(carries the idea that the human body belongs to God, not just the soul and spirit, because it will also participate in the physical Resurrection of Believers)*.

15 Do you not know that your bodies are the members of Christ? *(When a person is saved, they are saved holistically, meaning spirit, soul, and body. We become a member of Christ as a unity, with the Holy Spirit looking at the triune being of man as "one.")* shall I then take the members of Christ, and make *them* the members of an harlot? *(This constitutes every part of the physical body, including the sex organs, as belonging to Christ.)* God forbid *("may it never be!")*.

16 What? *(How could anyone, especially a Believer, think the Holy Spirit would sanction the terrible sin of fornication!)* do you not know that he which is joined to an harlot is one body? *(Involves an argument against this sin which is the most original and impressive that could have been used.)* for two, said He, shall be one flesh *([Gen. 2:24] this means that no type of sexual intercourse between the sexes is free from sin, except under the sanction of marriage)*.

17 But he who is joined unto the Lord *(indicates the closest possible union, symbolized by the sexual union of a Christian husband and wife)* is one spirit *(reflects the same union with Christ, albeit in a spiritual sense, as a husband and wife have in a physical sense)*.

18 Flee fornication *(is not a suggestion, but a Command; fornication, as an abbreviated definition, pertains to any type of immorality)*. Every sin that a man does is without the body *(speaks of all sins other than fornication; gluttony, drunkenness, or drug addiction, etc., while affecting the body in a negative way, originate from without; with fornication, the source of uncleanness is in the heart)*; but he who commits fornication sins against his own body *(presents in the physical sense a type of the spiritual union of man with devils; that's the reason God referred to Israel worshiping idols as "spiritual adultery or fornication" [Jer. 3:1-9; Ezek. 23:1-45; Hos., Chpt. 4])*.

19 What? *(By this time, you should

know!) do you not know that your body is the Temple of the Holy Spirit *which is* in you *(actually refers to the human body of the Born-again Believer as being a Sanctuary of the Holy Spirit)*, which you have of God *(means that it's all of God and must be treated accordingly)*, and you are not your own? *(We belong to the Lord.)*

20 For you are bought with a price *(the price was the shed Blood of Christ at Calvary)*: therefore Glorify God in your body *(the house of the Spirit)*, and in your spirit *(the use of the house)*, which are God's *(because we were created by God, and have been purchased at great price)*.

CHAPTER 7

UNMARRIED CHRISTIANS

NOW concerning the things whereof you wrote unto me *(the Apostle will now address things he was asked in a letter; the previous Chapters addressed things he had been told)*: It is good for a man not to touch a woman *(it is not wrong for a man not to marry, providing the Lord desires this for the man's personal life)*.

2 Nevertheless, *to avoid* fornication, let every man have his own wife, and let every woman have her own husband *(this is a rule, not merely permission)*.

MARRIED CHRISTIANS

3 Let the husband render unto the wife due benevolence *(it refers to the husband respecting the sexual needs of his wife, and to meet them accordingly; of course, we speak of legitimate needs)*: and likewise also the wife unto the husband *(proclaims the same duty imposed upon the wife regarding the husband)*.

4 The wife has not power of her own body, but the husband: and likewise also the husband has not power of his own body, but the wife *(refers to the fact that the husband and wife belong to each other, meaning neither has the right to refuse normal demands)*.

5 Defraud you not one the other *(it seems that some married couples in that day were refraining from sexual activity, which they erroneously thought enabled them to live more spiritual lives; man seems to go from one extreme to the other!)*, except it be with consent for a time, that ye may give yourselves to fasting and prayer *(not mandatory, but given as a suggestion)*; and come together again, that Satan tempt you not for your incontinency *(the idea is that the Believer not unnecessarily place himself or herself into a self-tormenting repression beyond what God demands)*.

6 But I speak this by permission, *and* not of Commandment. *(The Holy Spirit, through Paul, leaves*

the details of lives, whether celibate or married, to the individual consciences, though with large-hearted wisdom and charity. He would emancipate them from human and unauthorized restrictions.)

THE UNMARRIED

7 For I would that all men were even as I myself *(is not said by Paul to denigrate marriage as some have claimed; in effect, he is saying that he wished for the Coming Resurrection, when all would be as he was then)*. But every man has his proper Gift of God, one after this manner, and another after that *(speaks of different types of Ministry)*.

8 I say therefore to the unmarried and widows *(advice evidently given in response to a question)*, It is good for them if they abide even as I *(is explained in Verse 26, where he says, "for the present distress," speaking of the hostility of Rome)*.

9 But if they cannot contain, let them marry *(refers to the sex drive)*: for it is better to marry than to burn *(refers to burning with passion)*.

REGULATIONS

10 And unto the married I command, *yet* not I, but the Lord *(means that this is not mere permission as* in Verse 6, but rather a Commandment), Let not the wife depart from *her* husband *(pertains to departing on grounds which were not Scriptural; in other words, the husband being unsaved did not give the wife the right to divorce him on those grounds)*:

11 But and if she depart, let her remain unmarried, or be reconciled to *her* husband *(refers to her getting a divorce or else Paul would not have restricted her to remain single, not remarrying unless it was to her former husband)*: and let not the husband put away *his* wife *(places the same restriction on the husband as it does the wife; the Holy Spirit, through the Apostle, gives women the same rights as men)*.

12 But to the rest speak I, not the Lord *(doesn't mean this is not inspired! the Apostle is merely saying that Jesus did not teach anything about what to do with mixed marriages, i.e., "Believers and unbelievers")*: If any brother has a wife who believes not *(not a Christian)*, and she be pleased to dwell with him, let him not put her away *(such a situation does not provide grounds for divorce)*.

13 And the woman which has an husband who believes not, and if he be pleased to dwell with her, let her not leave him *(same as the previous Verse)*.

14 For the unbelieving husband is Sanctified by the wife, and

the unbelieving wife is Sanctified by the husband *(means that the Believer, by virtue of being one flesh with his or her unbelieving spouse, is not considered living in an unlawful relationship; "Sanctified" means that God looks at the home as a Christian home and marriage, even though one or the other partner is unsaved)*: else were your children unclean; but now are they holy *(looked at by the Lord as being born in a Christian home, despite the fact that either the Mother or Dad is unsaved).*

15 But if the unbelieving depart, let him depart *(speaks of desertion, and desertion for the sole purpose of the Cause of Christ).* A brother or a sister is not under bondage in such *cases (means there is nothing the Believer could have done to stop the unbelieving spouse from departing, and in that case, the Believer is free to remarry)*: but God has called us to peace. *(An unbelieving husband or wife who doesn't want to keep the marriage together destroys all peace, which creates an untenable situation.)*

16 For what knowest thou, O wife, whether you shall save *your* husband? or how knowest thou, O man, whether you shall save *your* wife? *(Everything should be done to keep the marriage together, believing that eventually the unsaved spouse will come to the Lord, which may be their only opportunity.)*

17 But as God has distributed to every man *(refers to the rule that the circumstances of our lives are regulated by the Providence of God, and must not be arbitrarily altered on our own caprice)*, as the Lord has called every one, so let him walk *(the Lord allocates our way, so don't try to change the position unless it is obviously wrong, or there's nothing you can do about the change).* And so ordain I in all Churches *(the instructions given are applicable to all Believers everywhere and for all time).*

18 Is any man called being Circumcised? *(Jews)* let him not become uncircumcised. Is any called in uncircumcision? *(Gentiles)* let him not be Circumcised.

19 Circumcision is nothing, and uncircumcision is nothing *(Paul is saying that Christ has fulfilled all the old Levitical Law, so it is no longer binding)*, but the keeping of the Commandments of God. *(Those Commandments are found in Matthew 22:36-40. They can only be kept by the Believer understanding that all power and strength come through the Cross, which must ever be the object of our Faith. That gives the Holy Spirit latitude to work in our lives, helping us to do that which needs to be done.)*

20 Let every man abide in the same calling wherein he was

called. *(The idea pertains to the state or position one is in when one comes to Christ, respecting positions or particular jobs that are honorable.)*

21 Are you called *being* a servant? care not for it *(actually refers to a slave; the Holy Spirit can make His home in the heart of a slave just as much as He can anyone else)*: but if you may be made free, use it rather *(refers to freedom as a preference, if such can be obtained; otherwise, serve God as a slave; slaves were the majority of the population in those days).*

22 For he who is called in the Lord, *being* a servant *(slave)*, is the Lord's freeman *(in the Lord such a one is free, despite their station in life; that's all that really matters)*: likewise also he who is called, *being* free, is Christ's servant *(means that a person who is not a slave becomes a Bond Slave of Christ).*

23 You are bought with a price *(refers to the ransom price which was the Precious Shed Blood of Jesus at Calvary's Cross)*; be not ye the servants of men. *(Liberation by Jesus Christ not only frees us from sin, but also from the fear of man and what man can do to us.)*

24 Brethren, let every man, wherein he is called, therein abide with God. *(The third time Paul says this [Vss. 17, 20]; the Holy Spirit places everybody in Christendom on the same level.)*

VIRGINS

25 Now concerning virgins I have no Commandment of the Lord *(meaning that the Old Testament or the Lord in His earthly Ministry did not say anything about this question; yet what He will now say is definitely inspired of God)*: yet I give my judgment, as one who has obtained mercy of the Lord to be faithful. *(Paul seems to imply here that he had been celibate all his life, and the Lord had given him Grace as it regards the sex drive.)*

26 I suppose therefore that this is good for the present distress *(persecution by Rome)*, I say, that it is good for a man so to be. *(He is speaking primarily of Preachers and the hardships they would encounter regarding a family concerning the "present distress.")*

27 Are you bound unto a wife? seek not to be loosed *(as stated, he is primarily speaking to Preachers).* Are you loosed from a wife? seek not a wife. *(In other words, if you aren't married, it might be best that you stay that way. But understand that Paul was speaking only of that particular time, which as well would have bearing on certain future times.)*

28 But and if you marry, you have not sinned *(speaks of the men whose wives had deserted them be-*

cause of accepting Christ and Preaching the Gospel; it is not a sin for that man [or woman] to remarry); and if a virgin marry, she has not sinned (refers to young ladies who had thought to remain so for the balance of their lives, but found they were in love with a young man, etc.). **Nevertheless such shall have trouble in the flesh** (refers to the "present distress," i.e., "persecution"): **but I spare you** (wants to spare them some problems if he can!).

MARRIED CHRISTIANS

29 But this I say, Brethren, the **time is short** (we must make the most of the time we have and not unnecessarily burden ourselves, thereby, hindering our life for the Lord): **it remains, that both they who have wives be as though they had none** (Christians should sit loose to earthly interest; the Lord is to come first in all things);

30 **And they who weep, as though they wept not** (all earthly things are transient; we must remember that!); **and they who rejoice, as though they rejoiced not; and they who buy, as though they possessed not;**

31 **And they who use this world, as not abusing It** (we are just passing through): **for the fashion of this world passes away** (it is like a melting vapor, therefore, Christians shouldn't anchor in it).

RESPONSIBILITIES

32 **But I would have you without carefulness** (we are not to be burdened down with care). **He who is unmarried cares for the things that belong to the Lord, how he may please the Lord** (refers once again to Preachers of the Gospel, and especially considering the "present distress"):

33 **But he who is married cares for the things that are of the world, how he may please his wife.** (Once again, the "present distress" concerned what Nero was about to do, which would result in many Christians losing their lives.)

34 **There is difference also between a wife and a virgin** (concerns only the manner of availability for the Lord). **The unmarried woman cares for the things of the Lord, that she may be Holy both in body and in spirit** (Paul is not speaking to all Christian women, only those who are called to Ministry, and more specifically only those for which this would be the Will of God): **but she who is married cares for the things of the world, how she may please her husband** (actually means that her interest is divided between the Lord and her husband, whereas that of an unmarried woman is only of the Lord, or at least it is supposed to be!).

35 **And this I speak for your**

own profit; not that I may cast a snare upon you *(means that his words are not binding, but are meant to serve as advice and counsel; each individual is to seek the Lord respecting his own life and Ministry)*, but for that which is comely, and that you may attend upon the Lord without distraction *(whatever the Will of the Lord might be in each individual case)*.

36 But if any man think that he behaves himself uncomely toward his virgin *(does not speak of a sweetheart as it seems here, but rather the Father of this young lady)*, if she pass the flower of *her* age *(was considered to be twenty years old at that time; as such, she must now be allowed to make her own decision concerning marriage, etc.)*, and need so require, let him do what he will, he sins not *(due to the daughter now being an adult, she is free to make her own decisions, with the Father no longer responsible)*: let them marry.

37 Nevertheless he who stands stedfast in his heart, having no necessity *(the daughter doesn't desire to marry; therefore the Father could continue with his dedication respecting her)*, but has power over his own will, and has so decreed in his heart that he will keep his virgin, does well *(concerns his dedication of her to the Lord, which is her desire as well, with the understanding that he will bear the expense of caring for her all of his life)*.

38 So then he who gives *her* in marriage does well *(if that is what she wants)*; but he who gives *her* not in marriage does better *(is not meant to state that it is better morally, but rather "better relative to the Work of God")*.

CHRISTIAN WIDOWS

39 The wife is bound by the law as long as her husband lives; but if her husband be dead, she is at liberty to be married to whom she will; only in the Lord *(to marry another Christian)*.

40 But she is happier if she so abide, after my judgment *(remain single)*: and I think also that I have the Spirit of God *(places Paul's advice out of the realm of mere human judgment and into the realm of the Divine)*.

CHAPTER 8

FOOD SACRIFICED TO IDOLS

NOW as touching things offered unto idols *(lambs and oxen were offered up and Sacrificed to idols, with part of the meat then offered for sale in the market place)*, we know that we all have knowledge *(but our consecration must not stop there)*. Knowledge puffs up *(knowledge without love)*, but charity *(love)* edifies *(builds up)*.

2 And if any man think that he knows anything *(refers to the fact that we never know as much about the Word of God as we think we know)*, he knows nothing yet as he ought to know *(we ought to know much more)*.

3 But if any man love God, the same is known of him. *(We all should have knowledge of the Word, but the emphasis must be on Love.)*

4 As concerning therefore the eating of those things that are offered in Sacrifice unto idols, we know that an idol *is* nothing in the world *(in effect, Paul is saying that the eating of such meat contains no offense to the Lord or His Word)*, and that *there is* none other God but one. *(The gods the heathen worshiped actually didn't exist.)*

5 For though there be that are called gods, whether in Heaven or in earth, (as there be gods many, and lords many,)

6 But to us *there is* but one God *("One" in unity and not "One" in number; it can refer to either)*, the Father *(speaks of relationship)*, of whom *are* all things *(refers to God as the Creator of all things)*, and we in Him *(which we are by virtue of Christ and the Cross)*; and one Lord Jesus Christ *(our Sav-*

iour*)*, by whom *are* all things *(what He did at the Cross made it all possible)*, and we by Him. *(Everything we have from God comes to us from Christ, with the Cross being the means by which it is done.)*

7 Howbeit *there is* not in every man that knowledge *(the knowledge of the Cross was deficient, even as Paul said in I Cor. 1:17)*: for some with conscience of the idol unto this hour eat *it* as a thing offered unto an idol *(means some could not dismiss from their minds the painful sense that, by eating the idol-sacrifice, they are participating in idol-worship)*; and their conscience being weak is defiled *(refers to these Gentiles who until recently had been idolaters)*.

8 But meat commendeth us not to God: for neither, if we eat, are we the better; neither, if we eat not, are we the worse *(has nothing to do with spirituality)*.

CHRISTIAN FREEDOM

9 But take heed lest by any means this liberty of yours become a stumblingblock to them who are weak. *(We make men worse if, by our example, we teach them to act in contradiction to their conscience.)*

10 For if any man see you which has knowledge sit at meat in the idol's temple *(speaks of those who*

knew and understood true Christian Liberty, but yet lacked wisdom), shall not the conscience of him which is weak be emboldened to eat those things which are offered to idols *(contains the idea that such action on the part of the "strong" could very well fall out to the spiritual destruction of the one who is "weak");*

11 And through your knowledge shall the weak brother perish, for whom Christ died? *(Paul could use no word that would more effectually point his warning.)*

12 But when you sin so against the Brethren, and wound their weak conscience, you sin against Christ *(to sin against a brother in any capacity is to sin against Christ).*

13 Wherefore, if meat make my brother to offend, I will eat no flesh while the world stands, lest I make my brother to offend. *(Everything we do must be done always with the idea of how it affects others.)*

CHAPTER 9

PAUL'S APOSTLESHIP

A M I not an Apostle? *(The idea is not so much to defend his Apostleship, as it is to show how he has abnegated his own rights in order to be a proper example to others.)* am I not free? *(Being free, he has liberty, but he did not use* that liberty in every case, even as he will further discuss.)* have I not seen Jesus Christ our Lord? *(This refers to the Vision on the Road to Damascus [Acts 9:3, 17; 22:7-8].)* are not you my work in the Lord? *(The Fruit was abundant!)*

2 If I be not an Apostle unto others *(meaning that some in the Early Church did not regard Paul's Apostleship),* yet doubtless I am to you *(the Corinthians knew, or at least should have known, he was an Apostle):* for the seal of my Apostleship are you in the Lord *(presents Paul using an example which was undeniable).*

A NORMAL LIFE

3 My answer to them who do examine me is this *(those who question his Ministry),*

4 Have we not power to eat and to drink? *(He could have asked them for financial help. He had every right to do so, but didn't, even though others who had no right did.)*

5 Have we not power to lead about a sister, a wife, as well as other Apostles, and as the Brethren of the Lord, and Cephas? *(The Churches, it seems, helped other Apostles with expenses, but Paul asked for none.)*

6 Or I only and Barnabas *(presents Paul mentioning Barnabas after the quarrel [Acts, Chpt. 15],*

which shows the Apostle regarded him with love and esteem), have not we power to forbear working? *(This means to give up the manual labor by which he maintained himself.)*

7 Who goeth a warfare any time at his own charges? *(The idea is if a soldier would expect to receive rations and wages from the Government he is serving, a Minister of the Gospel should expect the same.)* who plants a vineyard, and eats not of the fruit thereof? or who feeds a flock, and eats not of the milk of the flock?

8 Say I these things as a man? *(This presents Paul making the case that his statements are not merely his own thoughts, but are rather of God.)* or saith not the Law the same also? *(This refers to the Law of Moses, and is given in the next Verse.)*

SUPPORT

9 For it is written in the Law of Moses *(Deut. 25:4),* you shall not muzzle the mouth of the ox that treads out the corn *(presents basically what Jesus said in Luke 10:7).* Does God take care for oxen? *(If the Lord cares for a lowly beast, and He certainly does, would He not do much more for those who are taking His Gospel to the world?!)*

10 Or said He *it* altogether for our sakes? For our sakes, no doubt, *this* is written: that he who plows should plow in hope; and that he who threshes in hope should be partaker of his hope.

11 If we have sown unto you spiritual things, *is it* a great thing if we shall reap your carnal things? *(The pronoun "we" proclaims the fact that the argument applies not only to Paul's own case, but as well to all Preachers of the Gospel.)*

12 If others be partakers of *this* power over you, *are* not we rather? *(It seems these other Teachers, whomever they may have been, were well paid, while Paul received nothing.)* Nevertheless we have not used this power *(this privilege);* but suffer all things, lest we should hinder the Gospel of Christ *(that which should ever be foremost in the heart and mind of every Preacher of the Gospel).*

13 Do you not know that they which Minister about Holy things live *of the things* of the Temple? *(This pertains to the Old Economy of God, which Paul is using as an example.)* and they which wait at the Altar are partakers with the Altar? *(This pertained to certain portions of the Sacrifices given to the Priests [Num. 18:8-13; Deut. 18:1].)*

14 Even so has the Lord ordained that they which Preach the Gospel should live of the

Gospel. *(The idea, as is obvious, is that those who Minister in spiritual things should be supported financially by those to whom they Minister.)*

15 But I have used none of these things *(he had the right to be supported financially, but he never exercised that right, except in a limited way)*: neither have I written these things, that it should be so done unto me *(as well, he's not making these statements in order to spur the people to send him offerings)*: for it were better for me to die, than that any man should make my glorying void. *(In essence, this says he would rather die than stoop to such a level as that. To do such a thing would be manipulation, which the Lord can never bless.)*

16 For though I Preach the Gospel, I have nothing to glory of *(within himself; even though he is an Apostle, boasting of these gifts is out)*: for necessity is laid upon me *(the Preaching of the Gospel is not merely a choice on his part, but rather a Command from the Lord)*; yes, woe is unto me, if I Preach not the Gospel! *(This proclaims an overwhelming moral compulsion.)*

17 For if I do this thing willingly, I have a reward *(the reward comes from the Lord)*: but if against my will, a dispensation *of the Gospel* is committed unto me. *(The word "dispensation" means "administration or stewardship." It actually refers back to the "Parable of the Talents" [Mat. 25:14-30]. In other words, the Preaching of the Gospel must never be looked at in any manner except that we give it our very best. Otherwise, we will lose the reward.)*

18 What is my reward then? *(This is different than the reward of Verse 17.)* Verily that, when I Preach the Gospel, I may make the Gospel of Christ without charge *(a price must never be put on the Gospel)*, that I abuse not my power in the Gospel. *(The Preacher must make double certain that he does not exploit the people, but rather that he edify the people.)*

PAUL'S POLICY

19 For though I be free from all *men (Christ is Lord and Master, not man)*, yet have I made myself servant unto all *(a voluntary submission, which is the Way of the Spirit)*, that I might gain the more. *(This is God's Way. Men rule, but the Lord serves! We must emulate our Lord.)*

20 And unto the Jews I became as a Jew, that I might gain the Jews *(Paul here describes the innocent concessions which arise from the harmless and generous condescension of a loving spirit)*; to them who are under the Law, as under

the Law, that I might gain them who are under the Law *(him having Timothy to be Circumcised is a perfect example [Acts 16:3])*;

21 To them who are without Law *(Gentiles)*, as without Law, (being not without Law to God, but under the Law to Christ,) *(being "under the Law to Christ" satisfies every Law of God; it is simple Faith in Christ and what He has done for us at the Cross)* that I might gain them who are without Law *(gain the Gentiles)*.

22 To the weak became I as weak, that I might gain the weak *(refers to Paul not availing himself of some of his Christian Liberties simply because of the possibility of causing weak Christians to stumble)*: I am made all things to all *men*, that I might by all means save some. *(As stated, he is speaking of innocent concessions, never of compromising the Gospel.)*

23 And this I do for the Gospel's sake *(the Gospel of Christ being the only means of Salvation, it must take first place in all things)*, that I might be partaker thereof with you. *(This is the love every Preacher ought to show.)*

CONDITIONS

24 Know ye not that they which run in a race run all, but one receives the prize? So run, that you may obtain. *(In athletic events,*

only one receives the prize. However, all who run for Christ, spiritually speaking, win the Crown. There are no losers!)*

25 And every man who strives for the mastery is temperate in all things. *(The Apostle is saying we should let the athlete striving and training to win a temporary crown be a lesson to us Christians regarding diligence.)* Now they *do* it to obtain a corruptible crown; but we an incorruptible. *(If they will do such for the "corruptible," how much more should we do the same for the "incorruptible"?)*

26 I therefore so run, not as uncertainly *(all Believers who run and continue to run, spiritually speaking, are certain of winning)*; so fight I, not as one who beats the air *(the Apostle now switches from the metaphor of running a race to boxing; he is not fighting uselessly, but rather the good fight of Faith, which speaks of Faith anchored exclusively in the Cross; regrettably, far too many Christians in this Christian endeavor are simply "beating the air")*:

27 But I keep under my body, and bring *it* into subjection *(which he does by understanding that all victory is in the Cross)*: lest that by any means, when I have Preached to others, I myself should be a castaway. *(This means that even if a man is a Preacher of the Gospel, if he doesn't look to Christ and the Cross, and ever make the Cross the*

emphasis, he will conclude as a castaway, i.e., "disapproved." The Lord has one way of victory, which is the same for both Preachers and the laity. It is "Jesus Christ and Him Crucified.")

CHAPTER 10

ISRAEL

MOREOVER, Brethren, I would not that you should be ignorant *(this means the Holy Spirit doesn't want us to be ignorant about these Truths)*, how that all our fathers were under the cloud *(the Presence of God, which led Israel)*, and all passed through the Sea *(the Red Sea, typifying passing from death to life)*;

2 And were all baptized unto Moses *(the Law-Giver was a type of Christ)* in the cloud *(a type of the Presence of the Lord)* and in the sea *(a type of Water Baptism)*;

3 And did all eat the same spiritual meat *(speaking of the Manna as a type of the "Lord's Supper")*;

4 And did all drink the same spiritual drink *(refers to the Smitten Rock [Ex. 17:6; Num. 20:11; Ps. 78:15])*: for they drank *(says literally, "they were drinking," implying a continuous gift)* of that spiritual Rock that followed them *(there is a Jewish legend that says the original Smitten Rock at*

Rephidim [Ex. 17:6] followed them throughout their entire Wilderness Journey and supplied water for them; every evidence is that it was true): and that Rock was Christ *(the Rock typified Christ)*.

5 But with many of them God was not well pleased *(should have been translated, "most of them")*: for they were overthrown in the wilderness. *(This actually refers to God purposely designing their destruction because of their rebellion.)*

6 Now these things were our examples *(we are to learn from them, and not make the same mistakes)*, to the intent we should not lust after evil things, as they also lusted *(proclaims the same results of destruction for modern Christians as for the Israelites of old, that is if modern Believers insist upon living in sin)*.

7 Neither be ye idolaters, as *were* some of them *(religion is the greatest idolatry of all)*; as it is written *(Ex. 32:6)*, The people sat down to eat and drink, and rose up to play. *(I am afraid much of the modern Church is "playing," exactly as Israel of Old.)*

8 Neither let us commit fornication, as some of them committed, and fell in one day three and twenty thousand *(a warning against immorality [Num. 25:1-9])*.

9 Neither let us tempt Christ, as some of them also tempted *(refers to questioning the Word of*

God), and were destroyed of serpents *(Num. 21:5-9)*.

10 Neither murmur ye, as some of them also murmured *(refers to finding fault with the way God is doing things)*, and were destroyed of the destroyer. *(God is the ultimate Destroyer, even though He may use many other things as His instrument.)*

11 Now all these things happened unto them for examples *(as a warning; we had best heed those warnings)*: and they are written for our admonition, upon whom the ends of the world are come *(should have been translated, "to whom the fulfillment of the ages has arrived," i.e., "the Church Age")*.

WARNING

12 Wherefore let him who thinks he stands *(is addressed to all Believers)* take heed lest he fall. *(This means to not merely fall from fellowship as some teach, but to fall from Eternal Salvation. This won't happen if the Cross is ever in view.)*

13 There has no temptation taken you but such as is common to man *(refers to the limitations God has placed upon Satan respecting that which he can or cannot do)*: but God is faithful, who will not suffer you to be tempted above that you are able *(we have His Promise; all temptation is overcome by our Faith remaining constant in Christ and the Cross, which gives the Power of the Holy Spirit to help us [Rom. 8:2])*; but will with the temptation also make a way to escape, that you may be able to bear it. *(As stated, the "way of escape" is always the Cross [Eph. 6:10-18].)*

14 Wherefore, my dearly beloved, flee from idolatry. *(Anything in which we place our Faith, other than the Cross of Christ, becomes an idol.)*

15 I speak as to wise men *(whether they were or not, this is what they should have been)*; judge ye what I say *(meaning in this case, "what I am about to say")*.

16 The Cup of Blessing which we bless, is it not the Communion of the Blood of Christ? *(The Lord's Supper is a Blessing, if it is understood properly.)* The bread which we break, is it not the Communion of the Body of Christ? *(The "Blood" and the "Body" refer to the price Christ paid on the Cross.)*

17 For we *being* many are one bread, *and* one body *(Christ is the "Bread," and the only "Bread" which produces one Body, i.e., "the Church")*: for we are all partakers of that one Bread. *(This speaks of Jesus Christ as being the only "Bread of Life." There is no other!)*

18 Behold Israel after the flesh *(the Law of Moses)*: are not they which eat of the Sacrifices par-

takers of the Altar? *(This would probably have been better translated, "have they not Communion with the Altar?" It has reference to the next Verse.)*

19 What say I then? *(What am I saying?)* that the idol is anything, or that which is offered in Sacrifice to idols is anything? *(As a strict point, the idol is nothing, nor is the Sacrifice offered to idols anything.)*

20 But *I say*, that the things which the Gentiles Sacrifice, they Sacrifice to devils, and not to God *(proclaims in blunt terms the powers of darkness behind these idols)*: and I would not that you should have fellowship with devils. *(In effect, he is saying, "I do not want to be sharers or partakers in demons." The same could be said for most modern movies, plus most modern entertainment.)*

21 You cannot drink the Cup of the Lord, and the cup of devils *(if we are going to associate with demons, the Lord will not remain)*: you cannot be partakers of the Lord's table *(the Lord's Supper)*, and of the table of devils *(that which the world offers)*.

22 Do we provoke the Lord to jealousy? *(He is definitely jealous of anything in our lives which competes with Him, as ought to be obvious [James 4:5].)* are we stronger than He? *(This proclaims the warning that God's "jealousy" can-* not be challenged with impunity.)*

THE GLORY OF GOD

23 All things are Lawful for me, but all things are not expedient *(addresses Christian Liberty, and as well the manner in which it should be attended)*: all things are Lawful for me, but all things edify not. *(This addressed the contention of some of the Corinthians who claimed their Christian "rights" gave them the freedom to act as they saw fit.)*

24 Let no man seek his own, but every man another's *wealth. (This should have been translated, "every man another's good," meaning we should think of others regarding all things that we do. Freedom doesn't mean to seek my own good, but rather the good of others.)*

25 Whatsoever is sold in the shambles *(refers to the market place or the meat market)*, that eat, asking no question for conscience sake *(don't bother to inquire whether or not it was originally offered to idols)*:

26 For the earth *is* the Lord's, and the fulness thereof. *(Paul uses this Text to justify eating all foods, providing they are desired [Ps. 24:1].)*

27 If any of them who believe not *(unsaved)* bid you *to a* feast, and you be disposed to go *(per-*

tains to the homes of these individuals, *not to idol Temples*); whatsoever is set before you, eat, asking no question for conscience sake *(don't investigate, just eat it and be thankful for it)*.

28 But if any man say unto you, This is offered in Sacrifice unto idols, eat not for his sake who showed it, and for conscience sake *(this stand is to be taken only if the information is revealed by the host)*: for the earth *is* the Lord's, and the fulness thereof *(meaning that this fullness, speaking of meat offered to idols, is not being used in the way the Lord intends)*:

29 Conscience, I say, not your own, but of the other *(refers to the fact that we must always be conscious of others)*: for why is my liberty judged of another *man's* conscience? *(Meaning all that we do must be done with the thought in mind of how it will affect others.)*

30 For if I by Grace be a partaker, why am I evil spoken of for that for which I give thanks? *(The Apostle is saying we cannot please everyone. Some will find fault irrespective what we do.)*

31 Whether therefore you eat, or drink, or whatsoever you do, do all to the Glory of God. *(With anything and everything we do, we should always ask ourselves the question: "does this bring Glory to God?")*

32 Give none offence, neither to the Jews, nor to the Gentiles, nor to the Church of God:

33 Even as I please all *men* in all *things*, not seeking my own profit *("seek to please all men in all things")*, but the *profit* of many, that they may be saved *(always with the view in mind of the Salvation of souls)*.

CHAPTER 11

ADMONITION

BE ye followers *(imitators)* of me, even as I also *am* of Christ. *(Those who imitate Christ have a right to call upon others to imitate them.)*

2 Now I praise you, Brethren, that you remember me in all things *(Paul is thanking the Corinthians for seeking his Counsel)*, and keep the Ordinances, as I delivered *them* to you *(refers to the whole Body of Truth of the Gospel)*.

3 But I would have you know, that the Head of every man is Christ *(refers to authority)*; and the Head of the woman *is* the man *(pertains to the creation model)*; and the Head of Christ *is* God *(speaks here of two separate and distinct Persons [I Tim. 2:5])*.

REGULATIONS

4 Every man praying or Proph-

esying *(refers either to the Gift of Prophecy or Preaching [I Cor. 12:10])*, having *his* head covered, dishonors his Head *(dishonors Christ; such portrays a covering other than Christ)*.

5 But every woman who prays or Prophesies *(tells us that women did pray and Preach in the Church, or wherever)* with *her* head uncovered dishonors her Head *(portrays the fact that, due to the Creation model, the woman should have long hair, at least longer than that of the man)*: for that is even all one as if she were shaven. *(Refers to the fact that some women in those days had their heads shaved as a punishment for whoredom or adultery. The Apostle is saying that Christian women should not insist upon their rights so much that they begin to look like the worst of the world.)*

6 For if the woman be not covered, let her also be shorn *(in effect says, "if the woman wants to wear her hair short like a man, why not go all the way and be shorn")*: but if it be a shame for a woman to be shorn or shaven, let her be covered. *(This refers to the fact that if she does not want to look like an adulteress, let her be covered, i.e., "have long hair.")*

7 For a man indeed ought not to cover *his* head *(while praying or Preaching)*, forasmuch as he is the Image and Glory of God: but the woman is the Glory of the man. *(This refers to the fact that Eve was not "God's Image and Glory" in the same sense as Adam.)*

8 For the man is not of the woman *(Adam was not in any way derived from woman)*; but the woman of the man. *(In fact, the woman was derived from man by the Power of God.)*

9 Neither was the man created for the woman; but the woman for the man. *(This probably would have been better translated, "for also man was not created on account of the woman; on the contrary, woman on account of the man.")*

10 For this cause *(refers again to the creation model that "the woman is for the man")* ought the woman to have power on *her* head *(long hair, i.e., "authority")* because of the Angels. *(This has to do with her submission to God's Plan as a constant reminder to the fallen Angels, who rebelled against God's Plan and the Revolution led by Lucifer, which took place long before Adam.)*

11 Nevertheless neither is the man without the woman *(needs the woman)*, neither the woman without the man *(the woman also needs the man)*, in the Lord. *(This refers to the fact that this is the manner in which the Lord created the original model, and demands that it continue.)*

12 For as the woman *is of the* man *(refers to the fact that Eve was originally created from Adam [Gen. 2:21-22]),* even so *is the* man also by the woman *(by or through the medium of natural birth);* but all things of God. *(This puts everything on an even keel, meaning that men are no more important than women, or women than men.)*

13 Judge in yourselves *(refers to common sense):* is it comely that a woman pray unto God uncovered? *(This doesn't refer to a hat nearly so much as it refers to long hair, or at least hair that's longer than that of a man.)*

14 Does not even nature itself teach you, that, if a man have long hair, it is a shame unto him? *(A man wearing long hair is really not in accord with the nature of a man.)*

15 But if a woman have long hair, it is a glory to her *(is a way of saying that such manifests woman's voluntary submission to God's Will):* for *her* hair is given her for a covering. *(This points to the idea that man is the head or covering of the woman under Christ.)*

16 But if any man seem to be contentious *(refers to both men and women, who were insisting on conducting themselves wrongly),* we have no such custom *(we have no custom other than what I have said),* neither the Churches of God. *(What I have said is being* done in all the other Churches.)*

DIVISIONS

17 Now in this that I declare unto you I praise you not *(what he is about to say),* that you come together not for the better, but for the worse. *(This refers to the Church Services. They were being conducted in a manner which did not bring Glory to God.)*

18 For first of all, when you come together in the Church, I hear that there be divisions among you *(these "divisions" did not come about over Doctrine, at least at this time, but rather along sociological lines);* and I partly believe it. *(He is loathe to believe the worst, even on Testimony that is good.)*

19 For there must be also heresies among you *(a departure from the Word of God),* that they which are approved may be made manifest among you. *(Contains the idea that those who were prosperous, were claiming that they were "the approved ones." Sounds familiar doesn't it?)*

THE LORD'S SUPPER

20 When you come together therefore into one place *(refers to the Assembly of Believers),* this is not to eat the Lord's Supper. *(This has reference to the fact that they may have called it such, but the way*

it was being done was not recognized as such by the Holy Spirit.)

21 For in eating every one takes before *other* his own supper *(some brought lavish meals)*: and one is hungry *(some were slaves, and had nothing to bring)*, and another is drunken *(means intoxicated)*.

22 What? *(This shows the indignation of the Apostle.)* have ye not houses to eat and to drink in? *(This is directed toward the wealthy.)* or despise you the Church of God, and shame them who have not? *(The very poor were shamed by their lack in the midst of such plenty, of which they were offered little or nothing at all.)* What shall I say to you? shall I praise you in this? I praise *you* not. *(He seems to ask himself; "do these people really realize what they are doing?")*

23 For I have received of the Lord that which also I delivered unto you *(refers to the instructions he is about to give concerning the Lord's Supper)*, That the Lord Jesus the *same* night in which He was betrayed took bread *(recalls the sacred occasion)*:

24 And when He had given thanks, He broke *it*, and said, Take, eat *(the remarkable thing about this is the interpretation our Lord gives)*: this is My Body, which is broken for you *(is meant to symbolize the Death of Christ on the Cross)*: this do in remembrance of Me. *(This pertains to the Be-*

liever actually partaking of that Sacrifice by Faith. In brief, this is the meaning of the New Covenant.)*

25 After the same manner also *He took* the cup, when He had supped, saying, This cup is the New Testament in My Blood *(the New Covenant would be ratified by the shedding of Jesus' Own Blood, which forever satisfied the sin debt)*: this do you, as oft as ye drink *it*, in remembrance of Me *(never forgetting what He has done for us, speaking of the Cross)*.

26 For as often as you eat this bread, and drink this cup *(symbolic gestures)*, you do show the Lord's death till He come. *(This is meant to proclaim not only the Atoning Sacrifice necessary for our Salvation, but as well as an ongoing cause of our continued victory in life.)*

27 Wherefore whosoever shall eat this bread, and drink *this* cup of the Lord, unworthily *(tells us emphatically that this can be done, and is done constantly, I'm afraid)*, shall be guilty of the Body and Blood of the Lord *(in danger of Judgment, subject to Judgment)*.

28 But let a man examine himself *(examine his Faith as to what is its real object)*, and so let him eat of *that* bread, and drink of *that* cup *(after careful examination)*.

29 For he who eats and drinks unworthily, eats and drinks dam-

nation to himself (does not necessarily mean the loss of one's soul, but rather temporal penalties, which can become much more serious), not discerning the Lord's Body. (Not properly discerning the Cross refers to a lack of understanding regarding the Cross. All of this tells us that every single thing we have from the Lord, comes to us exclusively by means of the Cross of Christ. If we do not understand that, we are not properly "discerning the Lord's Body.")

30 For this cause (not properly discerning the Lord's Body) many (a considerable number) are weak and sickly among you (the cause of much sickness among Christians), and many sleep. (This means that many Christians die prematurely. They don't lose their souls, but they do cut their lives short. This shows us, I seriously think, how important properly understanding the Cross is.).

31 For if we would judge ourselves (we should examine ourselves constantly, as to whether our Faith is properly placed in the Cross of Christ), we should not be judged (with sickness, and even premature death).

32 But when we are judged (by the Lord, because we refuse to judge ourselves), we are chastened of the Lord (Divine discipline), that we should not be condemned with the world (lose our soul).

33 Wherefore, my Brethren, when you come together to eat, tarry one for another. (This proclaims the idea that all must share, and share alike.)

34 And if any man hunger, let him eat at home (the wealthy should prepare their sumptuous meals at home, but not in the context of the gathered assembly where some "have nothing"); that you come not together unto condemnation. (This refers to this "love feast" turning into a detriment instead of a Blessing. I would certainly think Paul's admonition would be heeded after the warning given.) And the rest will I set in order when I come (probably other instructions which needed to be given).

CHAPTER 12

SPIRITUAL GIFTS

NOW concerning Spiritual Gifts, Brethren (in this case, this has to do with the nine Gifts of the Spirit outlined in Verses 8 through 10), I would not have you ignorant (proclaims the Spirit of God, through Paul, saying He wanted the entirety of the Church to know about these Gifts).

2 You know that you were Gentiles (meaning that, before their conversion, they had no knowledge of God), carried away unto these dumb idols, even as you were led. (They were primarily led by super-

stition and witchcraft.)

3 Wherefore I give you to understand, that no man speaking by the Spirit of God calls Jesus accursed *(the True Spirit of God would never do such a thing; so those who did such, were not of God)*: and *that* no man can say that Jesus is the Lord, but by the Holy Spirit. *(Any other manner will be incorrect. It is the Holy Spirit Alone, Who reveals the Lordship of Christ to the Believer.)*

DIVERSITIES

4 Now there are diversities of Gifts *(different types of Gifts)*, but the same Spirit *(all of this means the Holy Spirit never contradicts Himself)*.

5 And there are differences of Administrations *(different Services, Ministries, Offices)*, but the same Lord. *(Christ is the One Who assigns the different Ministries, with the Holy Spirit then carrying out the function. As well, Christ never contradicts Himself.)*

6 And there are diversities of Operations *(different ways the Gifts work)*, but it is the same God which works all in all *(has reference to the fact it is God the Father Who energizes all things and all ways)*.

PURPOSE

7 But the manifestation of the Spirit *(pertains to that which the Gifts make manifest or reveal)* is given to every man to profit withal. *(If the Gifts are allowed to function properly, which they definitely will if the Holy Spirit has His Way, all will profit.)*

NINE GIFTS

8 For to one is given by the Spirit *(proclaims the Holy Spirit as being the One Who carries out the instructions of Christ, relative to who gets what)* the Word of Wisdom *(pertains to information concerning the future, whether of people, places, or things)*; to another the Word of Knowledge *(concerns the past or the present, relative to persons, places, or things; it is to be noted that it's "the Word of," which means a small amount)* by the same Spirit *(it is the Holy Spirit Who functions in all of these Gifts)*;

9 To another Faith *(special Faith)* by the same Spirit; to another the Gifts of Healing *(prayer for the sick)* by the same Spirit;

10 To another the working of Miracles *(extraordinary things)*; to another Prophecy *(this is for "edification, exhortation, and comfort [I Cor. 14:3]"; this has nothing to do with the Office of the Prophet)*; to another discerning of spirits *(whether the Spirit of God, human spirits, or evil spirits)*; to another

divers kinds of tongues *(meant to be interpreted)*; to another the interpretation of tongues:

DISTRIBUTION

11 But all these work that one and the selfsame Spirit *(refers to the fact that all the abilities and powers of the Gifts are produced and operated by the energy of the Spirit)*, dividing to every man severally as He *(the Holy Spirit)* will. *(All the distribution is within the discretion of the Holy Spirit, which means that men or women cannot impart Gifts to other individuals. That is the domain of the Spirit Alone!)*

ONE BODY

12 For as the Body *(Church)* is one, and has many members, and all the members of that one Body, being many, are one Body *(refers to the Church as being the "Body of Christ")*: so also is Christ *(presents the Saviour as oneness in multiplicity, as is the Church)*.

13 For by one Spirit *(the Holy Spirit Alone does this)* are we all baptized into one Body *(at Salvation, the Holy Spirit Baptizes the Believing sinner into the Body of Christ, which is the Born-again experience; it doesn't refer to Water Baptism)*, whether *we be* Jews or Gentiles, whether *we be* bond or free *(all must come in the same manner, "by and through Jesus Christ and what He did for us at the Cross")*; and have been all made to drink into one Spirit. *(The Holy Spirit is the agent Who affects the work of Redemption carried out in our lives, which is made possible by the Death, Burial, Resurrection, Ascension, and Exaltation of Christ.)*

14 For the body *(human body)* is not one member, but many.

15 If the foot shall say, Because I am not the hand, I am not of the body; is it therefore not of the body?

16 And if the ear shall say, Because I am not the eye, I am not of the body; is it therefore not of the body? *(Just because these various organs are different in their functions does not make them any less necessary for the successful working of the entirety of the human body.)*

17 If the whole body *were* an eye, where *were* the hearing? If the whole *were* hearing, where *were* the smelling? *(For a human body to be whole, it has to have the various different organs.)*

18 But now has God set the members every one of them in the body *(human body)*, as it has pleased Him.

19 And if they were all one member, where *were* the body? *(If the human body were one great* eye or one large ear, etc., it would no longer be a body, but rather a monstrosity.)

20 But now *are they* many members, yet but one body.

21 And the eye cannot say unto the hand, I have no need of you: nor again the head to the feet, I have no need of you *(proclaims a mutual interdependence in the human body, which beautifully typifies the interdependence in the Body of Christ).*

22 No, much more those members of the body, which seem to be more feeble, are necessary *(all play their important part, without which there would be serious repercussion)*:

23 And those *members* of the body, which we think to be less honourable, upon these we bestow more abundant honour *(probably speaks of the internal organs)*; and our uncomely *parts* have more abundant comeliness *(in reference to covering and dress).*

24 For our comely *parts* have no need *(being "comely," they do not need the same attention as others)*: but God has tempered the body together *(giving dignity to all, but special dignity to the inferior parts)*, having given more abundant honour to that *part* which lacked:

25 That there should be no schism in the body *(refers to disunion and disruption)*; but *that* the members should have the same care one for another *(refers to the fact that all should be treated alike).*

26 And whether one member suffer, all the members suffer with it *(presents it the way it ought to be)*; or one member be honoured, all the members rejoice with it.

27 Now you are the Body of Christ *(refers to the Church)*, and members in particular. *(This refers to every single individual in the Church who is truly Born-again.)*

28 And God has set some in the Church *(man or religious denominations cannot do the "setting," that being God's domain in its entirety)*, first Apostles *(God-called Apostles set the tone for the Church because of the special Message God has given them)*, secondarily Prophets *(is meant to include Evangelists as well, even as Teachers are meant to include Pastors; Prophets have the same function under the New Covenant as the Old, with one exception; Apostles have taken their place in the realm of Leadership; as well, this is the Office of the Prophet)*, thirdly Teachers *(those who explain the Word)*, after that Miracles *(pertains to this particular Gift of the Spirit)*, then Gifts of Healings *(examples of Gifts of the Spirit which should operate in the Ministry)*,

Helps (*refers to every kind of help God sets in the Church, whatever it might be*), Governments (*those who endeavor to hold the Church strictly in the Government of God, with all its many functions*), Diversities (*many different languages, but unknown by the speaker and normally unknown by the hearer*) of Tongues (*the Gift which requires interpretation*).

29 Are all Apostles? are all Prophets? are all Teachers? are all workers of Miracles? (*There are different Offices and Gifts, but all are needed.*)

30 Have all the Gifts of Healing? (*The answer is obviously, "no."*) do all speak with tongues? (*Paul is not addressing himself here to the initial Baptism with the Spirit, which is always and without exception accompanied by speaking with other Tongues, but rather is addressing the Gift of Tongues, which all do not have, although Baptized with the Spirit.*) do all Interpret? (*Again, the answer is "no," but some do!*)

31 But covet earnestly the best Gifts (*in essence speaks of that which the Holy Spirit wants a particular Believer to have*): and yet show I unto you a more excellent way. (*This refers to the Foundation of Love that must undergird all we have and do in the Lord, which the Apostle addresses in the next Chapter.*)

CHAPTER 13

LOVE

THOUGH I speak with the tongues of men and of Angels (*actually says in the Greek, "If it were possible to speak with the tongues of men and of Angels"; as well, Paul is not denigrating speaking with Tongues, as some have claimed [I Cor. 14:18]*), and have not charity (*love*), I am become as sounding brass, or a tinkling cymbal (*does not refer to our modern musical instrument which we call by that name, but that which made no more than a clattering sound*).

2 And though I have the Gift of Prophecy, and understand all mysteries, and all knowledge; and though I have all Faith, so that I could remove mountains (*tells us that the Gifts of the Spirit can be had by less than perfect people, as should be obvious*), and have not charity (*love*), I am nothing. (*We now see the basis on which everything must be built — it is love. If not, we are nothing!*)

3 And though I bestow all my goods to feed the poor, and though I give my body to be burned (*shifts from Gifts to "Works"*), and have not charity (*love*), it profits me nothing. (*As commendable as the acts may be, they bring a grade of zero unless God's Love motivates them.*)

CHARACTERISTICS

4 Charity (*love*) suffers long (*refers to patience*), *and* is kind (*represents the second side of the Divine attitude toward human kind*); charity (*the God kind of Love*) envies not (*does not want that which belongs to others*); Love vaunts not itself (*is never a braggart*), is not puffed up (*is not prideful*),

5 Does not behave itself unseemly (*is forgetful of self and thoughtful of others*), seeks not her own (*is unselfish*), is not easily provoked (*is not embittered by abuse, insult, or injury*), thinks no evil (*takes no account of evil*);

6 Rejoices not in iniquity (*never gossips about the misdeeds of others*), but rejoices in the Truth (*proclaims that which the Word of God identifies as Truth*);

7 Bears all things (*never complains*), believes all things (*takes the kindest views of all men*), hopes all things (*keeps believing for the best*), endures all things (*puts up with everything*).

ETERNAL

8 Love never fails (*because love cannot fail*): but whether *there be* Prophecies, they shall fail; whether *there be* Tongues, they shall cease; whether *there be* Knowledge, it shall vanish away. (*This refers to the fact that the Gifts of the Spirit will not be needed in the coming Resurrection, as well as many other things we could name.*)

9 For we know in part (*pertains to the "Word of Knowledge," which is just part Knowledge*), and we Prophesy in part (*falls into the same category*).

10 But when that which is perfect is come (*refers to the Rapture of the Church and the Resurrection*), then that which is in part shall be done away (*as should be obvious*).

11 When I was a child, I spoke as a child, I understood as a child, I thought as a child: but when I became a man, I put away childish things. (*The Apostle is comparing our present state, "as a child," to that which is coming, symbolized by a mature adult. That is the difference between the present state and the coming Resurrection.*)

12 For now (*before the Resurrection*) we see through a glass, darkly (*can only see the dim outline*); but then (*after the Resurrection*) face to face (*we can look and see openly and clearly*): now I know in part (*have some knowledge*); but then shall I know even as also I am known (*then everything will be perfect and complete*).

13 And now (*before the Resurrection*) abides Faith, Hope, Love, these three (*all three will abide forever*); but the greatest of these *is* Love (*it is the greatest because Love alone makes us like God [I Jn. 4:7]*).

CHAPTER 14

PROPHECY AND TONGUES

FOLLOW after Love *(let Love be the motivating factor in everything)*, and desire spiritual *Gifts (means to covet, but in the right way)*, but rather that you may Prophesy. *(This does not mean that "Prophecy" is the greatest Gift of all, but rather that it is the greater of the two vocal Gifts of utterance in Tongues and Prophecy.)*

2 For he who speaks in an *unknown* Tongue speaks not unto men, but unto God *(this is speaking of "Tongues" as one of the nine Gifts, and not the prayer language that every Believer receives upon being Baptized with the Spirit; as is obvious here, when one speaks in Tongues, whether in his prayer language or as a Gift, he is speaking directly to God)*: for no man understands *him (unless it is interpreted)*; howbeit in the Spirit he speaks mysteries *(that which pertains to God and is a mystery to all, unless revealed by the Holy Spirit)*.

3 But he who Prophesies *(speaks of the sixth Gift of the Spirit [I Cor. 12:8-10])* speaks unto men *(the opposite of Tongues, which speaks unto God)* to Edification *(builds up)*, and Exhortation *(to implore)*, and Comfort *(consolation)*.

4 He who speaks in an *unknown* tongue edifies himself *(whether the Gift of Tongues or one's prayer language)*; but he who Prophesies edifies the Church *(is meant for the Edification of the entirety of the Body, not just for the speaker)*.

5 I would that you all spoke with Tongues *(refers here in this instance to one's prayer language)*, but rather that you Prophesied *(now reverts to this particular Gift of the Spirit)*: for greater is he who Prophesies than he who speaks with Tongues, except he Interpret, that the Church may receive Edifying. *(This is obvious because Prophecy is given in the language of the people, and is thereby understood by all. Tongues cannot be understood unless Interpreted. Once again, we are speaking here of Church Services, and not one's private devotion.)*

6 Now, Brethren, if I come unto you speaking with Tongues, what shall I profit you *(does not refer to the "Gift of Tongues" as one of the nine Gifts of the Spirit, which is meant to be interpreted, but rather Believers praising and worshiping the Lord in Tongues out loud during the Service)*, except I shall speak to you either by Revelation, or by Knowledge, or by Prophesying, or by Doctrine? *(These things reveal Truth to the people, whereas one worshiping the Lord aloud in Tongues, not meant to be interpreted, edifies no one but*

the speaker. Paul is not demeaning Tongues, but only insisting that they be used in the right way.)

7 And even things without life giving sound, whether pipe or harp, except they give a distinction in the sounds, how shall it be known what is piped or harped? *(Unless a melody is followed, it is just noise!)*

8 For if the trumpet give an uncertain sound, who shall prepare himself to the battle? *(Paul is not denigrating the trumpet, but only stating that it be used properly.)*

9 So likewise ye, except you utter by the tongue words easy to be understood, how shall it be known what is spoken? *(This refers to Believers in the Church blurting out in Tongues and quite often creating confusion. No one knows what is being said. So, even though the person speaking may be blessed, no one else is.)* for you shall speak into the air *(of no significance, at least at that time).*

10 There are, it may be, so many kinds of voices in the world *(speaks of the many and varied languages which make up the entirety of mankind)*, and none of them is without signification. *(The language, whatever it might be, is important to the people who speak and understand it.)*

11 Therefore if I know not the meaning of the voice, I shall be unto him who speaks a barbar-ian, and he who speaks *shall be* a barbarian unto me *(nothing is accomplished)*.

12 Even so ye, forasmuch as you are zealous of Spiritual *Gifts (Paul is not criticizing their desire for such, inasmuch as he has already told them to "desire Spiritual Gifts")*, seek that you may excel to the Edifying of the Church *(presents the real foundation of all that is being said).*

13 Wherefore let him who speaks in an *unknown* Tongue *(the eighth Gift of the Spirit)* pray that he may Interpret *(also have that particular Gift, which is the ninth Gift).*

14 For if I pray in an *unknown* Tongue, my spirit prays *(speaks of the prayer language, not the Gift of the Spirit, and states that it comes from one's spirit and not one's mind)*, but my understanding is unfruitful *(signifying that it doesn't come from the mind).*

15 What is it then? *(This is meant to put the proper face on that which Paul has been saying.)* I will pray with the spirit *(pray in Tongues from my spirit, which speaks of one's prayer language)*, and I will pray with the understanding also *(pray in my regular language, which for me is English)*: I will sing with the spirit *(sing from my spirit in other Tongues)*, and I will sing with the understanding also *(sing unto the Lord in English; Paul is speaking here of one's own private devo-*

tions, and not regular Church Services).

16 Else when you shall bless with the spirit, how shall he who occupies the room of the unlearned say Amen at the giving of thanks, seeing he understands not what you say? *(This refers to blessing someone or saying grace at meals. If one does so in Tongues, the others there, not knowing what is being said, can hardly be blessed.)*

17 For you verily give thanks well, but the other is not edified.

18 I thank my God, I speak with Tongues more than you all *(as is here obvious, the Apostle is not denigrating Tongues, but rather regulating Tongues, and by the Spirit of God)*:

19 Yet in the Church *(when it's time to give instruction)* I had rather speak five words with my understanding, that *by my voice* I might teach others also *(which is the purpose of the assembly)*, than ten thousand words in an *unknown* Tongue *(which the people cannot understand, and thusly will not be edified)*.

20 Brethren, be not children in understanding *(meaning that what he has said is easy to understand)*: howbeit in malice be ye children *(children do not normally wish pain on others)*, but in understanding be men *(be adult, mature)*.

21 In the Law it is written *(Isa. 28:11)*, With *men of* other tongues and other lips will I speak unto this people *(concerns a Prophecy given by Isaiah nearly 800 years before Christ, which concerns the Baptism with the Holy Spirit with the evidence of speaking with other Tongues)*; and yet for all that will they not hear Me, saith the Lord *(predicts that many, if not most, will refuse to heed this which is of the Lord)*.

22 Wherefore Tongues are for a sign, not to them who believe, but to them who believe not *(a sign to the world that we are living in the last days)*: but Prophesying serves not for them who believe not, but for them which believe *(speaks of Edification, Exhortation, and Comfort to the Church)*.

ORDER

23 If therefore the whole Church be come together into one place, and all speak with Tongues, and there come in *those who are* unlearned, or unbelievers, will they not say that you are mad? *(I think that would be obvious!)*

24 But if all Prophesy *(speaking words that can be understood by all)*, and there come in one who believes not, or *one* unlearned, he is convinced of all, he is judged of all *(he can understand what is being said, whether he believes it or not)*:

25 And thus are the secrets of his heart made manifest *(he can*

understand what is being said, and it speaks to him personally); and so falling down on *his* face he will worship God, and report that God is in you of a truth *(that is, if he heeds the Message)*.

26 How is it then, Brethren? when you come together *(a Church Service)*, every one of you has a Psalm, has a Doctrine, has a Tongue, has a Revelation, has an Interpretation *(speaks of very good things which used in the wrong way, telling us that it is not Tongues alone which can be used in the wrong way)*. Let all things be done unto edifying. *(Everything done in the Church is meant to edify the entirety of the Body, irrespective what it is.)*

27 If any man speak in an *unknown* Tongue *(speaks of the Gift of the Spirit and how it is to be used in public meetings)*, let it be by two, or at the most *by* three *(is not speaking of the utterances, but rather the individuals who are giving out the utterances)*, and *that* by course *(simply means that these two or three should not interrupt each other)*; and let one interpret. *(The Tongues are meant to be interpreted. This doesn't necessarily mean that one should interpret all Messages, although they may. But rather that only "one" should interpret at a time, which should be obvious.)*

28 But if there be no interpreter, let him keep silence in the Church *(what good does it do if there is no one there to interpret)*; and let him speak to himself, and to God *(speak in Tongues to himself, which all Believers ought to do very often)*.

29 Let the Prophets speak two or three *(speaks not only of those who have the simple Gift of Prophecy, but also of those who stand in the Office of the Prophet)*, and let the other judge. *(This refers to the fact that everything should be judged according to Scriptural validity.)*

30 If *anything* be revealed to another who sits by *(refers to someone who feels the Lord is giving him a Revelation which should be given to the Church)*, let the first hold his peace. *(Those giving Prophecies should not interrupt each other.)*

31 For you may all Prophesy one by one *(in due order)*, that all may learn, and all may be comforted. *(The Holy Spirit ever has the entirety of the Body in mind.)*

32 And the spirits of the Prophets are subject to the Prophets. *(This means that if the individual claims to be compelled to blurt out at any time, such is out of order. The Holy Spirit works with the individual's spirit, with both deciding the right time.)*

33 For God is not *the author* of confusion, but of peace *(the Holy Spirit will never contradict Himself)*, as in all Churches of the

Saints. *(These instructions given by Paul pertain to all Churches, and not merely the Church at Corinth.)*

34 Let your women keep silence in the Churches: for it is not permitted unto them to speak *(is not referring to women being used by the Lord in the Gifts [Acts 2:17; I Cor. 11:5]; in Churches at that time, men and women did not normally sit together, but rather on opposite sides of the room; the women would call out to their husbands asking for an explanation concerning certain things, which was interrupting the Services)*; but they are commanded to be under obedience, as also says the Law *(refers back to Gen. 3:16 and the Creation Model)*.

35 And if they will learn any thing, let them ask their husbands at home *(proving what we've said in the previous Verse)*: for it is a shame for women to speak in the Church *(to speak out in the manner Paul has just mentioned; it doesn't refer to women Teachers or Preachers, etc.; if so, it would be wrong for a women to sing or say anything in the Church, which we know is not correct)*.

36 What? *(Paul is ready to end this discussion respecting order in the Church.)* came the Word of God out from you? or came it unto you only? *(The Apostle is telling the Corinthians that their lack of order is not of the Lord.)*

37 If any man think himself to be a Prophet, or Spiritual, let him acknowledge that the things that I write unto you are the Commandments of the Lord. *(If they really are Prophets, and they really are Spiritual, they will know that what the Apostle is saying is of the Lord)*.

38 But if any man be ignorant, let him be ignorant. *(In other words, if they will not accept what Paul is saying, there is no way they will ever learn the Truth. They will remain ignorant, and could lose their souls.)*

39 Wherefore, Brethren, covet to Prophesy *(desire the Gift of Prophecy)*, and forbid not to speak with Tongues. *(This proclaims the fact that all the instructions he has given are not meant to disallow Tongues, but rather to put them in their rightful order. So where does that put the so-called religious leaders who ignore this particular statement, which is actually a "Commandment of the Lord"?)*

40 Let all things be done decently and in order. *(This is the purpose for the all the instructions included in this Chapter.)*

CHAPTER 15

THE RESURRECTION

MOREOVER, Brethren, I declare unto you the Gospel which I Preached unto you *(it was* to Paul that the meaning of the New Covenant was given, which in effect was the meaning of the Cross and the Resurrection), which also you have received (unto Salvation), and wherein you stand (live a victorious life);

2 By which also you are saved (means that belief in the Resurrection is absolutely indispensable to one's Salvation), if ye keep in memory what I Preached unto you (Heb. 2:1), unless ye have believed in vain. (This refers to believing at first and then drawing back, which will cause one to lose one's soul. This also causes the unscriptural Doctrine of Unconditional Eternal Security to fall to the ground.)

3 For I delivered unto you first of all that which I also received (the meaning of the New Covenant), how that Christ died for our sins according to the Scriptures ([Ps. 22:15], speaks of the Cross of Christ);

4 And that He was buried (because He really died, not merely swoon as some claim), and that He rose again the third day according to the Scriptures ([Isa. 53:10; Hos. 6:2], the Resurrection of Christ was the demonstration of the perfection and efficacy of His Atonement):

5 And that He was seen (after His Resurrection) of Cephas (Peter), then of the Twelve (proving that Paul was not meant to be the Twelfth Apostle, as some claim):

6 After that (after those appearances), He was seen of above five hundred Brethren at once (many think this appearance took place in Galilee); of whom the greater part remain unto this present (are still alive), but some are fallen asleep (have died).

7 After that, He was seen of James (the Lord's Brother, who did not believe on Him during His earthly Ministry [Jn. 7:5]); then of all the Apostles [Lk. 24:50].

8 And last of all He was seen of me also (this was after the Ascension of Christ), as of one born out of due time. (He did not mean the timing was wrong, but rather that he was not worthy of what the Lord did for him.)

9 For I am the least of the Apostles (not mock modesty, but rather the most deep humility), that am not meet (worthy) to be called an Apostle, because I persecuted the Church of God (before his conversion).

10 But by the Grace of God I am what I am (concerns the Favor or Mercy of God): and His Grace which was bestowed upon me was not in vain (it was not without effect, telling us that it is without effect with many); but I laboured more abundantly than they all (proclaims that which Grace enabled Paul to do because he had a

*greater grasp of Grace than any-
one else, which speaks of the Cross,
the means of Grace): yet not I, but
the Grace of God which was with
me (is with all Believers who look
toward the Cross [I Cor. 1:17]).*

11 Therefore whether *it were* I
or they *(in this case, the other
Apostles)*, so we Preach *(what they
Preached)*, and so you believed.
*(False teachers had been attempt-
ing to turn their Faith away from
the coming Resurrection. Let the
reader understand that the Resurrection and the Rapture are one
and the same!)*

IMPORTANCE OF THE
RESURRECTION

12 Now if Christ be preached
that He rose from the dead, how
say some among you that there
is no Resurrection of the dead?
*(Some were actually repudiating
the Doctrine of the Resurrection.)*

13 But if there be no Resurrection of the dead, then is Christ not
risen *(Atonement and Resurrection
are the two great foundation stones
of the Gospel, and if either of them
is denied, then the Gospel ceases to
exist; once again, let us state the
Truth that if one doesn't believe in
the Rapture, then one doesn't believe in the Resurrection because
they are one and the same)*:

14 And if Christ be not risen
(if even one sin had been left un-
*atoned, then Christ could not have
risen from the dead, "for the wages
of sin is death" [Rom. 6:23]; the
fact of His Resurrection proves the
Atonement of all sin, past, present,
and future, at least for those who
will believe [Jn. 3:16])*, then is our
Preaching vain, and your Faith *is*
also vain *(empty nothings)*.

15 Yea, and we are found false
witnesses of God; because we
have testified of God that He
raised up Christ: Whom He raised
not up, if so be that the dead rise
not. *(The Resurrection of all the
Saints hinges completely upon the
Resurrection of Christ. The former
guarantees the latter, and without
the former there is no latter.)*

16 For if the dead rise not *(if
there is no Resurrection of all the
Saints)*, then is not Christ raised
*(a repetition of Verse 13 to empha-
size the argument that the Christian Faith in the Resurrection rests
not on philosophical theory, but on
historic fact)*:

17 And if Christ be not raised,
your Faith *is* vain *(all who do not
believe in the Atonement and the
Resurrection have a useless faith)*;
you are yet in your sins. *(Sins are
forgiven and cleansed only by and
through what Christ did at the Cross
and in the Resurrection, and our
Faith in that Finished Work. Otherwise the sins remain, which presents a situation of calamitous proportions.)*

18 Then they also which are fallen asleep in Christ are perished *(lost forever).*

19 If in this life only we have hope in Christ, we are of all men most miserable. *(That which is coming in the Resurrection is so far ahead of that which presently is, that there is no comparison.)*

RESURRECTION OF BELIEVERS

20 But now is Christ risen from the dead *(so says the Holy Spirit),* and become the Firstfruits of them who slept. *(The Resurrection of Christ guarantees the Resurrection of all Saints.)*

21 For since by man *came* death *(refers to Adam and the Fall in the Garden of Eden, and speaks of spiritual death, separation from God),* by Man *came* also the Resurrection of the dead. *(This refers to the Lord Jesus Christ Who Atoned for all sin, thereby making it possible for man to be united once again with God, which guarantees the Resurrection.)*

22 For as in Adam all die *(spiritual death, separation from God),* even so in Christ shall all be made alive. *(In the first man, all died. In the Second Man, all shall be made alive, at least all who will believe [Jn. 3:16].)*

23 But every man in his own order *(Christ first, and then all Believers thereafter):* Christ the Firstfruits *(He was the First One to be raised from the dead, never to die again);* afterward they who are Christ's at His coming. *(This pertains to the Rapture of the Church, not the Second Coming [I Thess. 4:13-18].)*

24 Then *comes* the end *(does not refer to the time immediately following the Rapture or even the Second Coming, but rather to when all Satanic rule and authority have been put down, which will take place at the conclusion of the Millennial Reign [Rev., Chpt. 20]),* when He *(Jesus)* shall have delivered up the Kingdom to God, even the Father; when He shall have put down all rule and all authority and power. *(He will have put down all of Satan's rule, etc.; the means of which were made possible by the Cross and the Resurrection.)*

25 For He *(Jesus)* must reign *(refers to the 1,000 year reign of Christ on Earth after He returns),* till He has put all enemies under His Feet *(the subjugation of all evil powers, which will take place at the conclusion of the Millennial Reign [Rev., Chpt. 20]).*

26 The last enemy *that* shall be destroyed *(abolished)* is death *(Death is the result of sin [Rom. 6:23], and the Cross addressed all sin. After the Resurrection, when all Saints are given glorified bodies, it will be impossible to sin. Even*

during the Millennial Reign, sin will still be in the world, but not in the Glorified Saints. It will be eradicated when Satan and all his fallen Angels and demon spirits, plus all people who followed him, are cast into the Lake of Fire, where they will remain forever [Rev., Chpt. 20]. Death will then be no more.)

27 For He has put all things under His feet. (God the Father has put all things under the Feet of Jesus.) But when He said all things are put under *Him, it is* manifest that He is excepted, which did put all things under Him. (This has reference to the fact that "all things" do not include God the Father being made subject to Jesus. God is excepted, as should be obvious.)

28 And when all things shall be subdued unto Him (implies that in Paul's day, this total dominion had not yet been exercised, and in fact has not done so unto this present hour; but the time will come when it definitely shall be, which will be at the close of the Millennial Reign), then shall the Son also Himself be subject unto Him Who put all things under Him, that God may be all in all. (There will be no trace of evil left anywhere in the Universe.)

29 Else what shall they do which are baptized for the dead, if the dead rise not at all? why are they then baptized for the dead? (Paul is actually saying, "It is a fruitless point to Baptize for the dead, which is unscriptural anyway, if there is no Resurrection as some are teaching.")

IMPLICATIONS

30 And why stand we in jeopardy every hour? (The idea is he wouldn't live a life of constant jeopardy if there were no Resurrection.)

31 I protest by your rejoicing which I have in Christ Jesus our Lord (the Corinthians were able to rejoice in the Lord because Paul had brought the Message of Redemption to them), I die daily. (The Apostle is referring here to his life being in constant danger on a daily basis. He is not referring to dying out to sin daily. He argued that we should become dead to sin once, and then stay dead to sin always [Rom. 6:6-11; Gal. 2:20].)

32 If after the manner of men I have fought with beasts at Ephesus, what does it advantage me, if the dead rise not? (It is not to be taken literally. He is actually saying, "I am risking my life daily, just as surely as those who fight the wild beast in the arenas; as well, as surely as these gladiators will sooner or later be killed, so will I.") let us eat and drink; for to morrow we die. (These words present the fatalism of those who do not believe in a coming Resurrection. So the

Apostle is saying, if there is no Resurrection there is no Hope.)

33 Be not deceived *(the statement actually says, "Do not go on being deceived!" meaning that many Corinthians had already been deceived into believing there was no Resurrection)*: evil communications corrupt good manners *(should have been translated, "evil occasions corrupt excellent morals").*

34 Awake to Righteousness, and sin not *(in effect says, "come to your senses");* for some have not the Knowledge of God *(in effect says, "for some are ignorant of God and His Ways"):* I speak this to your shame. *(I am speaking to shame you.)*

THE RESURRECTED BODY

35 But some man *(skeptic)* will say, How are the dead raised up? *(The skeptics use sarcasm.)* and with what body do they come? *(This refers to the form, shape, size, etc. False teachers were making fun of the Doctrine of the Resurrection of the human body.)*

36 You fool *(the Holy Spirit's answer to those who taught this false doctrine),* that which you sow is not quickened, except it die *(Paul takes this from the Words of Christ, when He spoke of the seed falling to the ground and dying, and then bringing forth much fruit, which is the nature of harvest [Jn. 12:24]):*

37 And that which you sow, you sow not that body that shall be, but bear grain *(the little seed, when sown, will bring forth a beautiful plant),* it may chance of wheat, or of some other *grain (one cannot tell from the seed exactly what the plant will be):*

38 But God gives it a body as it has pleased Him *(the Resurrection process is in the Hands of God, Who can do all things),* and to every seed his own body. *(This thwarts every evolutionary speculation. Every person will have their own body, not that of another. They will have their own color, appearance, etc., minus imperfections.)*

39 All flesh *is* not the same flesh *(once again, a point that definitely contradicts the theory of evolution):* but *there is* one *kind of* flesh of men, another flesh of beasts, another of fish, *and* another of birds *(refers to all being "flesh," but of different types).*

40 *There are* also celestial bodies *(Heavenly bodies, such as the Sun, Moon, etc.),* and bodies terrestrial *(earthly bodies, which refer to human beings, animals, trees, etc.):* but the glory of the celestial *is* one, and the *glory* of the terrestrial *is* another *(the glory differs).*

41 *There is* one glory of the Sun, and another glory of the Moon, and another glory of the Stars: for *one* Star differs from *another* Star in glory. *(Paul has a point here,*

which we will see in the next Verse.)

42 So also *is* the Resurrection of the dead. *(Some Saints, due to greater faithfulness, will have greater glory than others, which is the point of the previous Verse.)* It is sown in corruption *(refers to the grave)*; it is raised in incorruption *(refers to the Glorified Form and the type of Body God will provide)*:

43 It is sown in dishonour *(refers to the awful indignity of "dust to dust")*; it is raised in glory *(the same body, but glorified)*: it is sown in weakness *(death)*; it is raised in power *(life)*:

44 It is sown a natural body *(was energized by "blood," before death)*; it is raised a Spiritual Body *(energized by the Holy Spirit, not blood, and will be of immortal substance)*. There is a natural body *(which we now have)*, and there is a Spiritual Body. *(The Glorified Body of our Lord is the example, and our Glorified Body will be like His [I Jn. 3:2].)*

NECESSITY

45 And so it is written *(Gen. 2:7)*, The first man Adam was made a living soul *(the natural body)*; the last Adam *(Christ)* was made a quickening Spirit. *(The word "last" is used. No other will ever be needed. "Quickening" refers to making all alive who trust Him.)*

46 Howbeit that *was* not first which is spiritual, but that which is natural *(Adam came first)*; and afterward that which is spiritual. *(Christ, as the Last Adam, came second in order to undo that which occurred at the Fall.)*

47 The first man *(Adam)* is of the earth, earthy *(materialistic)*: the Second Man *(Christ)* is the Lord from Heaven *(a vast difference between the "first man" and the "Second Man")*.

48 As is the earthy, such *are* they also who are earthy *(it is the body and its present condition to which Paul points with the term "earthy")*: and as is the Heavenly, such *are* they also who are Heavenly. *(Christ is "the Heavenly One," and all who are "the Heavenly ones" are like Him. Paul is continuing to speak of the Resurrection, and what it will be like.)*

49 And as we have borne the image of the earthy *(refers to the fact that as our first father, we are frail, decaying, and dying)*, we shall also bear the image of the Heavenly. *(This tells us what we will be like in the Resurrection, i.e., "like Him.")*

50 Now this I say, Brethren, that flesh and blood cannot inherit the Kingdom of God *(pertains to our present physical bodies as they are now)*; neither does corruption inherit incorruption. *("Flesh and blood" comes under*

"corruption," while "the Kingdom of God" comes under "incorruption.")

THE ULTIMATE VICTORY

51 Behold, I show you a mystery (a new Revelation given by the Holy Spirit to Paul concerning the Resurrection, i.e., Rapture); We shall not all sleep (at the time of the Resurrection [Rapture], many Christians will be alive), but we shall all be changed (both those who are dead and those who are alive),

52 In a moment, in the twinkling of an eye (proclaims how long it will take for this change to take place), at the last trump (does not denote by the use of the word "last" that there will be successive trumpet blasts, but rather denotes that this is the close of things, referring to the Church Age): for the trumpet shall sound (it is the "Trump of God" [I Thess. 4:16]), and the dead shall be raised incorruptible (the Sainted dead, with no sin nature), and we shall be changed (put on the Glorified Body).

53 For this corruptible (sin nature) must put on incorruption (a Glorified Body with no sin nature), and this mortal (subject to death) must put on immortality (will never die).

54 So when this corruptible (sin nature) shall have put on incorruption (the Divine Nature in total control by the Holy Spirit), and this mortal (subject to death) shall have put on immortality (will never die), then shall be brought to pass the saying that is written, Death is swallowed up in Victory ([Isa. 25:8], the full benefits of the Cross will then be ours, of which we now have only the Firstfruits [Rom. 8:23]).

55 O death, where is your sting? (This presents the Apostle looking ahead, and exulting in this great coming victory. Sin was forever Atoned at the Cross, which took away the sting of death.) O grave, where is your victory? (Due to death being conquered, the "grave" is no more and, once again, all because of what Christ did at the Cross [Col. 2:14-15].)

56 The sting of death is sin (actually says, "The sting of the death is the sin"; the words "the sin" refer to the sin nature, which came about at the Fall, and results in death [Rom. 6:23]); and the strength of sin is the Law. (This is the Law of Moses. It defined sin and stressed its penalty, which is death [Col. 2:14-15].)

57 But thanks be to God, which gives us the victory through our Lord Jesus Christ. (This victory was won exclusively at the Cross, with the Resurrection ratifying what had been done.)

58 Therefore, my beloved Brethren, be ye stedfast (established, with your Faith firmly attached to

the Cross of Christ), unmoveable (not allowing your Faith to be moved from the Cross of Christ), always abounding in the Work of the Lord (telling others of what Jesus has done, regarding His great victory of the Cross), forasmuch as you know that your labour is not in vain in the Lord. (This is proclaiming that the Word of the Cross will always bring glorious results [I Cor. 1:18].)

CHAPTER 16

FINANCIAL HELP

NOW concerning the collection (offering) for the Saints (refers specifically to Jerusalem), as I have given order to the Churches of Galatia, even so do you (refers to this matter being the responsibility of all the Churches).

2 Upon the first day of the week (Sunday, which replaced the Jewish Sabbath of Saturday) let every one of you (no exceptions) lay by him in store, as God has prospered him (give to the Work of the Lord on this day), that there be no gatherings when I come (refers to their systematic giving).

3 And when I come (to the Church at Corinth), whomsoever you shall approve by your letters (means that the congregation at Corinth was to select one or more persons to take these funds to Jerusa-lem), them will I send to bring your liberality unto Jerusalem (those chosen by the Churches).

4 And if it be meet (necessary) that I go also, they shall go with me. (At this time, it seems Paul is uncertain as to whether he will also go to Jerusalem with this Gift. However, by the time he wrote II Corinthians, he had decided to go and, as stated, have these men accompany him [II Cor. 1:16; Rom. 15:25].)

PAUL'S FUTURE PLANS

5 Now I will come unto you, when I shall pass through Macedonia (presents the Apostle visiting the Churches in this area): for I do pass through Macedonia (not to linger, to spend only a little time at each of the Churches).

6 And it may be that I will abide, yes, and winter with you (he felt he needed to spend more time at Corinth than elsewhere, at least at this time), that you may bring me on my journey whithersoever I go. (The Corinthians would help him with finances, etc.)

7 For I will not see you now by the way (refers to him not being able to come to them immediately); but I trust to tarry a while with you, if the Lord permit (but when he does come, he hopes to stay a while).

8 But I will tarry at Ephesus until Pentecost. (Paul is writing

a short time before the Jewish Passover, and intends to leave Ephesus after the Jewish Feast of Pentecost, a period of about two months.)

9 For a great door and effectual is opened unto me *(refers to spreading the Gospel)*, and there are many adversaries *(those who opposed his Ministry, there seemed to have been many).*

TIMOTHY AND APOLLOS

10 Now if Timothy come, see that he may be with you without fear *(because of his youth, let no one intimidate him)*: for he works the Work of the Lord, as I also *do*. *(Inasmuch as Timothy is with Paul, he is to be treated accordingly.)*

11 Let no man therefore despise him *(refers to his youth and inexperience)*: but conduct him forth in peace, that he may come unto me *(I don't want him to come to me with a bad report)*: for I look for him with the Brethren. *(This pertains to those who accompanied Timothy, whomever they may have been.)*

12 As touching *our* brother Apollos, I greatly desired him to come unto you with the Brethren *(a previous visit)*: but his will was not at all to come at this time *(for whatever reason)*; but he will come when he shall have convenient time *(when a good opportunity offers itself to him; the Church at Corinth greatly respected Apollos).*

EXHORTATIONS

13 Watch ye *(a military command, be vigilant)*, stand fast in the Faith *(don't let the devil move your Faith from the Cross to other things)*, quit you like men *(act like mature men)*, be strong *(strong in the Faith, which makes one strong against the Devil).*

14 Let all your things be done with charity *(love)*.

15 I beseech you, Brethren, (ye know the house of Stephanas, that it is the Firstfruits of Achaia *(in all of Greece, the family of Stephanas was the first to come to Christ as a consequence of Paul's Ministry)*, and *that* they have addicted themselves to the Ministry of the Saints,) *(used of the Lord, and greatly so!)*

16 That you submit yourselves unto such *(let Stephanas and those like him be the ones you follow, instead of these false teachers)*, and to every one who helps with *us*, and labors *(because they Preach the same Gospel as Paul, the Gospel of the Cross and the Resurrection).*

17 I am glad of the coming of Stephanas and Fortunatus and Achaicus *(refers to them coming from Corinth to Paul at Ephesus)*: for that which was lacking on your part they have supplied. *(This probably means he wished he could have spoken to the entire Church at Corinth, but these Breth-*

ren *who represented that Church would be sufficient for the present.)*

18 For they have refreshed my spirit and yours *(eased my spirit, and as your representatives, eased your spirits as well)*: therefore acknowledge ye them who are such. *(This refers to these three men, and that what they will say to the Church at Corinth will be correct and right.)*

19 The Churches of Asia salute you *(speaking of the Churches in that area).* Aquila and Priscilla salute you much in the Lord, with the Church that is in their house *(a husband and wife, with one of the meeting places for worship in Ephesus being in their house; there were no Church buildings as such, at that time, as Rome was not allowing such).*

20 All the Brethren greet you. *(Paul is speaking not only of those at Ephesus, but all the Churches of Asia, etc., as well.)* Greet you one another with an holy kiss *(culture for that day and time, but which now is a handshake or embrace).*

SALUTATION AND BENEDICTION

21 The salutation of *me* Paul with my own hand. *(Paul had dictated the letter up to this point, with a Scribe doing the writing. However, the Apostle now takes the pen and, as we may say, signs the letter.)*

22 If any man love not the Lord Jesus Christ, let him be Anathema *(accursed)* Maranatha *(the Lord comes).*

23 The Grace of our Lord Jesus Christ *be* with you. *(Refers to the favor of the Lord, which comes in an uninterrupted flow to all who have Christ and the Cross as the object of their Faith.)*

24 My love *be* with you all in Christ Jesus. Amen. *(Paul includes this last statement because he has had to write some very strong things in the body of this Letter. He is saying that it was love for them, which occasioned the necessity.)*

THE SECOND EPISTLE OF PAUL THE APOSTLE TO THE
CORINTHIANS

CHAPTER 1

INTRODUCTION

PAUL, an Apostle of Jesus Christ by the Will of God, and Timothy our brother *(the Calling of the Apostle is meant by the Lord to serve as the defacto leader of the Church, and does so by the Message given to the Apostle; the salutation presents a high honor for Timothy)*, unto the Church of God which is at Corinth *(his second Epistle to this Church, of which we have record)*, with all the Saints which are in all Achaia *(refers to all of Greece)*:

2 Grace *be* to you *(which comes by the Cross)* and Peace *(Sanctifying Peace, which is the result of Grace)* from God our Father, and from the Lord Jesus Christ *(Who paid the price for this at the Cross)*.

THANKSGIVING

3 Blessed *be* God, even the Father of our Lord Jesus Christ *(presents Jesus as Deity and God as His Own Unique Father, which cannot be said of anyone else)*, the Father of Mercies *(Merciful Father)*, and the God of all comfort *(solace and consolation)*;

4 Who comforts us in all our tribulation *(does not deny the fact of tribulation, but does guarantee comfort in the midst of tribulation)*, that we may be able to comfort them which are in any trouble, by the comfort wherewith we ourselves are comforted of God *(we will comfort others by the same means which we have been comforted)*.

5 For as the sufferings of Christ abound in us *(pertains to Faith being placed in the Cross, and us experiencing its glorious benefits)*, so our consolation also abounds by Christ. *(We can offer this consolation of the Cross to any Believer.)*

6 And whether we be afflicted *(the offence of the Cross [Gal. 5:11])*, *it is* for your consolation and Salvation *(what the Lord has shown us about the Cross will be greatly to your benefit)*, which is effectual in the enduring of the same sufferings which we also suffer *(you will suffer the offence of the Cross as well)*: or whether we be comforted, *it is* for your consolation and Salvation. *(The "comfort" is in the Cross, which always guarantees that which is needed.)*

7 And our hope of you *is* stedfast, knowing, that as you are partakers of the sufferings, *you shall be* also of the consolation. *(They who suffer the offence of the Cross will also experience the comfort of the Cross.)*

8 For we would not, Brethren, have you ignorant of our trouble which came to us in Asia *(doesn't say exactly what)*, that we were pressed out of measure, above strength, insomuch that we despaired even of life *(if Satan hates anything, he hates the Cross; so he will attack those who Preach "Christ and Him Crucified," and do so powerfully)*:

9 But we had the sentence of death in ourselves *(Paul thought he was going to die)*, that we should not trust in ourselves, but in God which raises the dead *(the trial was meant to teach not only submission, but absolute trust in God [Jer. 17:5])*:

10 Who delivered us from so great a death *(the Believer cannot die until the Lord deems his work as finished)*, and does deliver *(the former spoke of past tense, while this speaks of present tense)*: in whom we trust that He will yet deliver us *(we trust the Lord for the future)*;

11 You also helping together by prayer for us *(proclaims Paul's deep conviction of the effectiveness of intercessory prayer [Rom. 15:30-31; Phil. 1:19; Phile., Vs. 22])*, that for the gift *bestowed* upon us by the means of many persons thanks may be given by many on our behalf. *(He felt that the prayers of these Believers contributed greatly toward his deliverance, and no doubt it did!)*

POSTPONEMENT

12 For our rejoicing is this *(boasting in the Lord)*, the testimony of our conscience *(a good conscience)*, that in simplicity and Godly sincerity *(the simplicity of Christ, which refers to the Cross [II Cor. 11:3])*, not with fleshly wisdom *(that which is outside of the Cross)*, but by the Grace of God *(made possible by the Cross)*, we have had our conversation *(conduct)* in the world, and more abundantly to you-ward. *(What the Cross has made possible in my life is meant for your abundant benefit.)*

13 For we write none other things unto you, than what you read or acknowledge *(what we write to you is what we are)*; and I trust you shall acknowledge even to the end *(the Message of the Apostle wouldn't change, and he wouldn't change)*;

14 As also you have acknowledged us in part *(some in the Corinthian Church did not acknowledge Paul's Apostleship, so they didn't acknowledge all that he wrote as*

being from God), that we are your rejoicing *(rejoicing in the fact that they had Paul as their Teacher)*, even as you also *are* ours *(rejoicing in the fact that he was able to teach them and watch them grow in Grace)* in the Day of the Lord Jesus. *(This refers to the "Judgment Seat of Christ.")*

15 And in this confidence I was minded to come unto you before *(the Apostle had every confidence that the majority in the Church at Corinth would receive him favorably)*, that you might have a second benefit *(that he may give them more teaching on the Cross)*;

16 And to pass by you into Macedonia *(he planned to stop at Corinth on his way)*, and to come again out of Macedonia unto you *(refers to a second visit he had hoped to make; neither one actually came to fruition at that time)*, and of you to be brought on my way toward Judaea *(to leave from Corinth to Judaea; the new plan is now to not divide his visit at Corinth, but to make one stay in that city as presented in I Cor. 16:6)*.

17 When I therefore was thus minded, did I use lightness? *(This refers to him changing his mind concerning the proposed visit to Corinth, at least regarding the date.)* or the things that I purpose, do I purpose according to the flesh *(evidently Paul was being accused by some of not knowing the Mind of the Spirit)*, that with me there should be yes yes, and no no? *(Some were saying that his "yes" didn't mean yes, and his "no" didn't mean no!)*

18 But *as* God *is* true, our word toward you was not yes and no *(not fickle)*.

19 For the Son of God, Jesus Christ, Who was Preached among you by us *(places the argument over Paul's integrity squarely on the Gospel he Preached)*, *even* by me and Silas and Timothy, was not yes and no, but in Him was yes *(carries the idea of One Who changes not [I Sam. 15:29; Mal. 3:6])*.

20 For all the Promises of God in Him *(in Christ) are* yes, and in Him Amen *(means these Promises will not change)*, unto the Glory of God by us *(our Preaching the Cross to you will bring Glory to God)*.

21 Now He *(God)* which stablishes us with you in Christ *(God is capable of keeping the people He saves)*, and has Anointed us, is God *(we have these benefits because of what Jesus did at the Cross)*;

22 Who has also sealed us *(a seal of ownership)*, and given the earnest of the Spirit in our hearts. *(This presents a guarantee that God will ultimately give us the balance of all He has Promised, which Jesus paid for at the Cross [Rom. 8:23].)*

23 Moreover I call God for a record upon my soul *(gives the*

reason for delaying his visit), that to spare you I came not as yet unto Corinth. (He had opted instead to send his First Epistle to Corinth, which would prepare the way for a visit when he did come. He felt by the leading of the Spirit that this would be the best way to address the problems at Corinth.)

24 Not for that we have dominion *(domination)* over your Faith *(actually a reference to the previous phrase of "not sparing them"),* but are helpers of your joy *(rather, he wanted to be a Blessing):* for by Faith you stand. *(Faith in Christ and the Cross presents the only way one can stand.)*

CHAPTER 2

THE APOSTLE'S LOVE

BUT I determined this with myself *(concerns a settled question),* that I would not come again to you in heaviness. *(On his second visit to Corinth, it seems things had happened which caused hurt to the Apostle. This was before I Corinthians was written.)*

2 For if I make you sorry *(a stand he had to take regarding one who had refused to repent, but did repent later because of Paul's stand),* who is he then who makes me glad *(refers to the person who had sinned),* but the same which is made sorry by me? *(The same man, whom Paul*

had made sorry, now repents and makes the Apostle glad. Some claim this was not the same man of I Cor., Chpt. 5. Whether it was or not, the principle is the same.)

3 And I wrote this same unto you, lest, when I came, I should have sorrow from them of whom I ought to rejoice *(had he gone to Corinth when he had first intended, he may not have been met with rejoicing due to sin in the Church; that situation has now changed);* having confidence in you all, that my joy is *the* joy of you all. *(Things have now taken a turn for the better.)*

4 For out of much affliction and anguish of heart I wrote unto you with many tears *(pertains to the writing of I Cor.);* not that you should be grieved, but that you might know the love which I have more abundantly unto you *(presents the greatest proof of all — that of tears).*

FORGIVENESS

5 But if any have caused grief, he has not grieved me, but in part *(presents the Apostle dealing with the person who is probably the incestuous one of I Cor., Chpt. 5):* that I may not overcharge you all. *(He didn't want everyone in the Church at Corinth to think he was putting all in the same category of wrong direction.)*

6 Sufficient to such a man *is* this

punishment *(means that turning him over to Satan had accomplished all that was desired [I Cor. 5:4-5])*, which *was inflicted* of many. *(Most in the Church obeyed Paul by turning the man over to Satan for the destruction of the flesh. Some few didn't, which means they didn't go along with what Paul had said.)*

7 So that contrariwise you *ought* rather to forgive *him*, and comfort *him (show love toward the man who had sinned and now repented)*, lest perhaps such a one should be swallowed up with overmuch sorrow *(sink into despair)*.

8 Wherefore I beseech you that you would confirm *your* love toward him *(do more than just say you love him, but rather show your love to him)*.

9 For to this end also did I write, that I might know the proof of you, whether you be obedient in all things. *(In I Cor., Chpt. 5, the man was on trial. Now the Church is on trial.)*

10 To whom you forgive any thing *(forgive the man)*, I *forgive* also *(I forgive you for taking the wrong direction at the beginning)*: for if I forgave any thing, to whom I forgave *it*, for your sakes *forgave I it* in the Person of Christ *(forgiveness is a great part of the Christian Faith, and is demanded by Christ [Mat. 6:14-15])*;

11 Lest Satan should get an advantage of us *(if we obey the Word, Satan will have no advantage)*: for we are not ignorant of his devices *(his ways, which take advantage of the Christian's wrong direction)*.

12 Furthermore, when I came to Troas to *Preach* Christ's Gospel, and a door was opened unto me of the Lord *(concerned an opportunity for Ministry in this place)*,

13 I had no rest in my spirit *(due to the problems in Corinth, which he addressed in his First Epistle, he could not take advantage of this open door; he was too troubled at the thought of the Church at Corinth possibly being lost, with perhaps other Churches following suit)*, because I found not Titus my brother *(evidently refers to a prearranged meeting at which Titus was to give him some information regarding Corinth; the meeting did not occur because Titus was delayed for some reason, which caused even greater anxiety with Paul)*: but taking my leave of them *(leaving Troas)*, I went from thence into Macedonia. *(He, no doubt, met Titus at Philippi, who then gave him some good news concerning Corinth.)*

TRIUMPHANT IN CHRIST

14 Now thanks *be* unto God, which always causes us to triumph in Christ *(we triumph only by constantly exhibiting Faith in the Cross, which gives the Holy*

Spirit latitude to work in our lives and bring about the victory), and makes manifest the savour of His Knowledge by us in every place *(the Preaching of the Cross [I Cor. 1:23; 2:2])*.

15 For we are unto God a sweet savour of Christ *(referring to what the Cross has done in lives)*, in them who are saved *(by trusting in Christ and the Cross)*, and in them who perish *(those who reject the Cross [I Cor. 1:18])*:

16 To the one *we are* the savour of death unto death *(continuing to refer to those who reject the Cross)*; and to the other the savour of life unto life. *(All life comes through the Spirit, from Christ and by the Cross [Rom. 8:2].)* And who is sufficient for these things? *(This refers to the Gospel, which is so mighty to save from death.)*

17 For we are not as many, which corrupt the Word of God *(Preach something other than the Cross)*: but as of sincerity, but as of God, in the sight of God speak we in Christ. *(God is observing all our efforts and will accept only that which is "in Christ," which always refers to the Cross.)*

CHAPTER 3

MINISTRY

D O we begin again to commend ourselves? *(This was in order to prove his Apostleship.)* or need we, as some *others*, Epistles of commendation to you, or *letters* of commendation from you? *(Paul is presenting this contention as an obscurity to suppose that he or Timothy should need such letters, either from the Corinthians or to them.)*

2 You are our Epistle written in our hearts, known and read of all men *(refers to the Saints at Corinth who had been saved under his Ministry, which were Epistle enough)*:

3 Forasmuch as you are manifestly declared to be the Epistle of Christ ministered by us *(Christ was the Author of this "Epistle" of which Paul speaks, i.e., "souls saved from sin and darkness")*, written not with ink, but with the Spirit of the Living God *(which is the highest commendation of all)*; not in tables of stone, but in fleshy tables of the heart *(referring to changed hearts)*.

4 And such trust have we through Christ to God-ward *(refers to the personal confidence Paul had that he was appointed by God, and God accepted his work)*:

5 Not that we are sufficient of ourselves to think any thing as of ourselves *(Paul was confident that he possessed that competency through Christ in the sight of God, though personally absolutely incompetent, as are all men for that matter)*; but our sufficiency is of God *(it

can either be in God or self; it cannot be in both);

NEW TESTAMENT

6 Who also has made us able Ministers of the New Testament (the New Covenant); not of the letter (the old Law of Moses), but of the Spirit (Holy Spirit): for the letter kills (refers to the Law; all the Law can do is kill), but the Spirit gives life (and does so through Christ, due to what Christ did at the Cross [Rom. 8:1-2]).

7 But if the ministration of death (the Law of Moses), written and engraved in stones, was glorious (and it was), so that the children of Israel could not stedfastly behold the face of Moses for the glory of his countenance; which glory was to be done away (the glory on Moses' face faded, just as the Law faded, as it was intended to when Christ came):

8 How shall not the ministration of the Spirit be rather glorious? (It is a much better Covenant, based on better Promises [Heb. 8:6].)

GLORY AND RIGHTEOUSNESS

9 For if the ministration of condemnation be glory (the Law of Moses), much more does the ministration of Righteousness exceed in glory (due to what Christ did for us at the Cross, which made it possible for the Holy Spirit to do great things within our lives, providing we keep our Faith in the Cross; evidently, some false teachers had come from Jerusalem, attempting to extol the so-called virtues of the Law; in other words, they were trying to mix Law with Grace, which cannot be done).

10 For even that which was made glorious had no glory in this respect, by reason of the glory that excels. (The glory of the Law of Moses could not begin to compare with the Glory of the New Covenant.)

11 For if that which is done away was glorious (the Law), much more that which remains is glorious. (This pertains to the Gospel of Christ, which is forever [Heb. 13:20].)

TRANSFORMATION

12 Seeing then that we have such hope (which only the Cross could bring about), we use great plainness of speech (doesn't mince words):

13 And not as Moses, which put a veil over his face, that the children of Israel could not stedfastly look to the end of that which is abolished (as stated, the glory on Moses' face faded, and was meant to show that the Law would fade as well, which it did with Christ Who fulfilled it all):

14 But their minds were blinded *(they didn't understand the Law was meant to be phased out)*: for until this day remains the same veil untaken away in the reading of the Old Testament *(Israel was still trying to live by the Law, and some were trying to force it into the New Covenant)*; which *veil* is done away in Christ. *(The Law was meant to be fulfilled by Christ, and it was fulfilled by Christ.)*

15 But even unto this day, when Moses is read *(the Old Testament)*, the veil is upon their heart. *(This refers to Israel not seeing the true meaning and beauty of their own Scriptures, which portrayed Christ.)*

16 Nevertheless when it shall turn to the Lord, the veil shall be taken away *(which will be done at the Second Coming).*

17 Now the Lord is that Spirit *(Holy Spirit)*: and where the Spirit of the Lord is *(He is with all who Preach the Cross)*, there is Liberty *(Liberty to live a Holy life by placing one's Faith in the Cross, which gives the Holy Spirit the latitude to work mightily in our hearts and lives).*

18 But we all, with open face *(all who do not know Christ are veiled, i.e., "shut off")* beholding as in a glass *(looking into a mirror)* the Glory of the Lord *(because the Holy Spirit lives within our hearts)*, are changed into the same image from glory to glory *(changed into Christ-likeness, with the glory getting* greater and greater, while it became dimmer and dimmer with Moses), even as by the Spirit of the Lord *(the Holy Spirit Alone can make us what we ought to be, which He does within the parameters of the Finished Work of Christ and our Faith in that Sacrifice).*

CHAPTER 4

SINCERITY

THEREFORE seeing we have this Ministry *(refers to the great Covenant of Grace, made possible by the Cross)*, as we have received mercy, we faint not *(we will not fail to Preach the Gospel of Jesus Christ and Him Crucified)*;

2 But have renounced the hidden things of dishonesty *(all Gospel outside of the Cross is dishonest, because it's untrue)*, not walking in craftiness *(to do Holy deeds in an unholy way, or unholy deeds in a supposedly Holy way)*, nor handling the Word of God deceitfully *(refers to using it for one's own purpose and agenda)*; but by manifestation of the truth *(Preaching the Cross)* commending ourselves to every man's conscience in the sight of God. *(If these Corinthians will only listen to their conscience, they will know Paul's Message is true.)*

3 But if our Gospel be hid *(Christ and Him Crucified)*, it is

hid to them who are lost *(lost because they will not accept the Message of the Cross)*:

4 In whom the god of this world *(Satan)* has blinded the minds of them which believe not *(a willful blindness)*, lest the light of the Glorious Gospel of Christ *(the Message of the Cross)*, Who is the Image of God *(Who Alone is the Image of God)*, should shine unto them. *(If men reject the Cross, they have in effect rejected Christ.)*

5 For we Preach not ourselves *(not their own philosophies)*, but Christ Jesus the Lord *(what Christ did at the Cross)*; and ourselves your servants for Jesus' sake. *(This goes back to Christ's teaching on the servant principle [Mat. 20:25-28; Jn. 13:12-17].)*

6 For God, Who Commanded the light to shine out of darkness *(a reference to Genesis 1:3)*, has shined in our hearts *(His Preached Word)*, to give the Light of the Knowledge of the Glory of God *(the Cross was planned as carefully as Creation was planned; it is as necessary to our way of life as the Sun is to the Solar System)* in the Face of Jesus Christ. *(Previously, Christ was spoken of as the Image of God. Here, He is spoken of as the Light of God.)*

POWER

7 But we have this treasure *(the Light of the Gospel)* in earthen vessels *(man is never more than an earthen vessel, frail and humble)*, that the excellency of the Power may be of God, and not of us. *(Salvation and Victorious Living come to us entirely by and through what Christ did at the Cross. It is all of Christ and none of us.)*

8 We are troubled on every side, yet not distressed *(always confident of victory)*; we are perplexed, but not in despair *(never utterly at a loss)*;

9 Persecuted, but not forsaken *(pursued, but not actually caught)*; cast down, but not destroyed *(at times we are knocked down, but not knocked out)*;

10 Always bearing about in the body the dying of the Lord Jesus *(referring to the victory we have through the Cross of Christ)*, that the life also of Jesus might be made manifest in our body. *(We live the Resurrection Life by understanding that we have been planted together [Christ and ourselves] in the likeness of His Death.)*

11 For we which live are always delivered unto death for Jesus' sake *(the Holy Spirit delivers us unto the Death of Christ, which guarantees us the benefits of Calvary [Rom. 6:3-5])*, that the life also of Jesus might be made manifest in our mortal flesh. *(We have victory by exercising Faith in the Cross, which guarantees us the Life*

of Christ [Gal. 2:20].)

12 So then death works in us,
but life in you. (The "death" Paul
speaks of here concerns the Death
of Christ at Calvary, and its benefits as played out in his life. He
preached this to others, which
brought life to them as well.)

A FAITHFUL MINISTRY

13 We having the same Spirit
(Holy Spirit) of Faith (in Christ
and the Cross), according as it is
written (Ps. 1:16:10), I believed,
and therefore have I spoken (so
the Psalmist said); we also believe,
and therefore speak (believe what
Christ did at the Cross, and thereby
speak those words of Faith);

14 Knowing that He (God the
Father) which raised up the Lord
Jesus shall raise up us also by
Jesus (the Resurrection, whether
dead or alive), and shall present
us with you (a great assembly!).

15 For all things are for your
sakes (what Jesus did at the Cross),
that the abundant Grace might
through the thanksgiving of many
redound to the Glory of God.
(The price of the Cross has resulted,
and will result, in untold millions
finding Eternal Life, which brings
Glory to God.)

16 For which cause we faint not
(the stakes are too high); but though
our outward man perish (takes a
beating from overwork and persecution), yet the inward man is
renewed day by day (is renewed
by denying self and taking up the
Cross daily [Lk. 9:23-24]).

17 For our light affliction (in
view of the reward, the worst of
afflictions are referred to as "light"),
which is but for a moment (compared to Eternity), works for us a
far more exceeding and eternal
weight of glory (a greater reward,
which will be received at the Resurrection);

18 While we look not at the
things which are seen (the trials
and tests we presently endure), but
at the things which are not seen
(not seen by the eyes, but definitely
seen by Faith): for the things which
are seen are temporal (transient);
but the things which are not seen
are Eternal (the things of God, and
what He has prepared for us [I Cor.
2:9-10]).

CHAPTER 5

WITH THE LORD

FOR we know that if our earthly
house of this Tabernacle were
dissolved (our physical body, which
is not permanent), we have a building of God (refers to the Glorified
Body, which all Saints will gain at
the Resurrection), an house not
made with hands, eternal in the
Heavens. (This Glorified Body is
Created by God, and will last and

live forever.)

2 For in this *(this present physical body)* we groan *(not complaining, but rather seeing by Faith that which is to come, and thereby longing for it to arrive)*, earnestly desiring to be clothed upon with our house which is from Heaven *(concerns the coming Resurrection, when the corruptible shall put on incorruption and the mortal will put on immortality)*:

3 If so be that being clothed we shall not be found naked *(will not be destitute of covering, but will be clothed with light [I Cor. 15:41-42])*.

4 For we who are in *this* Tabernacle do groan, being burdened *(not for death, for death is an enemy, but rather for the coming Resurrection)*: not for that we would be unclothed *(we do not desire to die, nor are we unwilling to bear these burdens as long as God shall appoint)*, but clothed upon, that mortality might be swallowed up of life. *(This refers to putting on immortality [I Cor. 15:35-54].)*

5 Now He Who has wrought us for the selfsame thing *is* God *(is preparing us for Resurrection)*, Who also has given unto us the earnest of the Spirit *(a down payment that the totality is coming shortly)*.

6 Therefore *we are* always confident *(proclaims a guarantee)*, knowing that, while we are at home in the body *(makes an im-portant distinction between the person and his physical body)*, we are absent from the Lord *(but will be with Him forever at the Resurrection)*:

7 (For we walk by Faith *(has reference to the fact that life is a journey, and the Christian is traveling to another country)*, not by sight:) *(This refers to the things we can presently see. It is Faith that controls us, not sight.)*

8 We are confident, *I* say, and willing rather to be absent from the body *(this physical body is merely a house in which the real person resides)*, and to be present with the Lord. *(Death holds no terror for the Child of God.)*

LABOR

9 Wherefore we labour *(are ambitious)*, that, whether present *(with Christ)* or absent *(still in this world)*, we may be accepted of Him *(approved by Him, which we will be if our Faith is in Christ and the Cross)*.

10 For we must all appear before the Judgment Seat of Christ *(this will take place in Heaven, and will probably transpire immediately before the Second Coming)*; that every one may receive the things *done* in *his* body, according to that he has done, whether *it be* good or bad. *(This concerns our life lived for the Lord. Sins*

will not be judged here, but rather our motivation and faithfulness, for sin was judged at Calvary.)

11 Knowing therefore the terror of the Lord *(should have been translated, "fear"),* we persuade men; but we are made manifest unto God *(what we do, we do before Him, seeking only to have His leading, guidance, direction, and approval);* and I trust also are made manifest in your consciences. *(If our Message is acceptable to the Lord, it surely should be acceptable to Believers.)*

12 For we commend not ourselves again unto you *(shouldn't have to, because they knew Paul),* but give you occasion to glory on our behalf *(to stand up for us),* that you may have somewhat to *answer* them which glory in appearance, and not in heart. *(This presents Paul desiring no false praise from anyone, but wanting true recognition.)*

13 For whether we be beside ourselves, *it is* to God *(pertain to the idea that his detractors were accusing him of being mentally unbalanced):* or whether we be sober, *it is* for your cause. *(This refers to being of sound mind, and to be thought of as such. Some said he was insane, and some said he was too sober.)*

RECONCILIATION

14 For the Love of Christ con-

strains us *(what Christ did for us at the Cross);* because we thus judge, that if one died for all *(Christ died for the whole world, and for all time),* then were all dead *(we are all dead in trespasses and sins):*

15 And *that* He died for all *(brings the reader back to the supreme Sacrifice paid by Christ),* that they which live *(accept Christ)* should not henceforth live unto themselves *(we now belong to Christ),* but unto Him which died for them, and rose again *(to do His Will in our lives).*

16 Wherefore henceforth know we no man after the flesh *(pertains to any and all things that characterize humanity in this present world):* yea, though we have known Christ after the flesh, yet now henceforth know we *Him* no more. *(We are to know Him exclusively as Saviour, which was accomplished by the Cross.)*

17 Therefore if any man *be* in Christ *(saved by the Blood), he is* a new creature *(a new creation):* old things are passed away *(what we were before Salvation);* behold, all things are become new. *(The old is no longer useable, with everything given to us now by Christ as "new.")*

18 And all things *are* of God *(all these new things),* Who has reconciled us to Himself by Jesus Christ *(which He was able to do as a result of the Cross),* and has

given to us the Ministry of Reconciliation (*pertains to announcing to men the nature and conditions of this Plan of being Reconciled, which is summed up in the "Preaching of the Cross" [I Cor. 1:21, 23]*);

19 To wit, that God was in Christ (*by the agency of Christ*), reconciling the world unto Himself (*represents the Atonement as the work of the Blessed Trinity and the result of love, not of wrath*), not imputing their trespasses unto them (*refers to the fact that the penalty for these trespasses was imputed to Christ instead*); and has committed unto us the Word of Reconciliation. (*All Believers are to Preach the Cross in one way or the other [I Cor. 1:18].*)

20 Now then we are Ambassadors for Christ (*one empowered to deliver a message for another*), as though God did beseech you by us (*it is to be understood that our Message is to be regarded as the Message of God*): we pray you in Christ's stead (*as though He were performing the task*), be ye reconciled to God. (*It can only be done by accepting Christ and what He did for us at the Cross.*)

21 For He (*God the Father*) has made Him (*Christ*) to be sin for us (*the Sin-Offering [Isa. 53:6, 10; I Pet. 2:24]*), Who knew no sin (*He was not guilty; He was perfectly Holy and Pure*); that we might be made the Righteousness of God in Him (*made so by accepting what He did for us at the Cross*).

CHAPTER 6

THE MINISTRY

WE then, as workers together with Him (*with Christ*), beseech you also that you receive not the Grace of God in vain. (*All who turn away from the Cross, the means by which Grace is given, make it all vain.*)

2 (For He said (*Isa. 49:8*), I have heard You (*refers to God hearing the prayers of the Messiah; it is prayer for the Salvation of the heathen world*) in a time accepted (*refers to this Day of Grace*), and in the Day of Salvation (*which has been afforded by Christ, and what He did at the Cross*) have I succoured You (*God the Father upheld the Messiah, despite His many enemies*): behold, now is the accepted time (*Christ has made it all possible*); behold, now is the Day of Salvation.) (*In a sense, this "day" will end at the coming Resurrection.*)

3 Giving no offence in any thing (*we are to give no occasion for condemning or rejecting the Gospel*), that the Ministry be not blamed (*that the Finished Work of Christ be not blamed*):

4 But in all *things* approving ourselves as the Ministers of God

(in both word and deed), in much patience, in afflictions, in necessities, in distresses,

5 In stripes, in imprisonments, in tumults, in labours, in watchings, in fastings *(in all of this, the Grace of God can keep us)*;

6 By pureness, by knowledge, by longsuffering, by kindness, by the Holy Spirit, by love unfeigned *(the Holy Spirit Alone can help us to overcome, and to experience these graces as well; our part pertains to our constant Faith in the Cross; the Spirit will then do what needs to be done)*,

7 By the Word of Truth *(the Word of God)*, by the Power of God *(through the Holy Spirit)*, by the armour of Righteousness on the right hand and on the left *(speaks of being completely armed, which pertains to simple Faith in the Cross of Christ)*,

8 By honour and dishonour *(some people honor us and some don't)*, by evil report and good report *(it is very trying to human nature to have one's name slandered and cast out as evil, when we are conscious only of a desire to do good)*: as deceivers, and *yet* true *(we are labeled by some as a "deceiver," but God knows its not true)*;

9 As unknown, and *yet* well known *(despite being true, some will not know, but yet a few will)*; as dying, and, behold, we live *(we must*

be willing to face death, and willingly place our lives in the hands of the Lord)*; as chastened *(by the Lord)*, and not killed *(the Holy Spirit desires to "kill" many things in our lives which are wrong; this is a portrayal of the purging of the branch [Jn. 15:2]; we may think the purging is going to kill us, but it won't!)*;

10 As sorrowful, yet always rejoicing *(the evidence of an inner triumph which puts tears to flight by the Smiles of Praise)*; as poor, yet making many rich *(irrespective of our financial status [and I speak of lack], we can make many rich with the Gospel, spiritually speaking)*; as having nothing, and *yet* possessing all things. *(If one is saved, one has all things.)*

11 O *you* Corinthians *(Corinth was known for vice, but the Gospel changed it to Righteousness, at least for those who would believe)*, our mouth is open unto you, our heart is enlarged. *(The Apostle spoke straight, mincing no words, but it was because of love.)*

12 You are not straitened in us *(they did not possess a narrow place in his affections, but rather a large place)*, but you are straitened in your own bowels. *(This should have been translated, "you are straitened in your own hearts." It means the Corinthians didn't have a large place in their hearts for Paul, as they should have had.)*

13 Now for a recompence in the

same *(Paul asked the Corinthians to reciprocate by expanding their hearts wide as toward him as he had toward them)*, (I speak as unto *my* children,) be ye also enlarged *(simply means, "love me as I love you")*.

SEPARATION

14 Be you not unequally yoked together with unbelievers *(there are two fellowships in the world, and only two; all men belong either to one or to the other; no one can belong to both and claim to be a Christian; one is with the world, and one is with the Lord)*: for what fellowship has Righteousness with unrighteousness? *(None!)* and what communion has light with darkness? *(None!)*

15 And what concord has Christ with Belial? *(This presents another name for Satan.)* or what part has he who believes with an infidel? *(Those who make a profession of Salvation should resolve to separate themselves from the world. However, it is separation and not isolation.)*

16 And what agreement has the Temple of God with idols? *(God and idols cannot mix.)* for you are the Temple of the Living God *(speaking of all Believers)*; as God has said *(Ex. 29:45; Lev. 26:12; Ezek. 37:27)*, I will dwell in them, and walk in *them*; and I will be their God, and they shall be My people. *(The Believer is the*

Sanctuary of the Holy Spirit, all made possible by the Cross.)

17 Wherefore come out from among them, and be ye separate, saith the Lord *(as stated, the Word of God emphatically teaches separation from the world, but not isolation)*, and touch not the unclean thing *(refers to Christians avoiding all unholy contact with a vain and polluted world)*; and I will receive you *(at the same time, means if the person disobeys these injunctions the Lord will not receive us; the Christian can walk clean in this world only by constantly evidencing Faith in the Cross of Christ, which makes it possible for the Holy Spirit to do His work within our lives)*,

18 And will be a Father unto you *(but only under the conditions mentioned in the above Scriptures)*, and you shall be My sons and daughters, saith the Lord Almighty. *("Lord Almighty" in the Hebrew is "Jehovah Shaddai." The Hebrew word "Shad" means a woman's breast. The title "Shaddai" suggests that we must never resort to the world, but rather draw all nourishment from the Lord Who can provide all things, which the world can never provide.)*

CHAPTER 7

A HOLY MINISTRY

HAVING therefore these Promises *(that we can draw all*

nourishment from the Lord), dearly beloved, let us cleanse ourselves from all filthiness of the flesh and spirit *(when one sins, he sins spirit, soul, and body; there is no such thing as the body sinning, and not the spirit, etc.)*, perfecting holiness in the fear of God *(to bring to a state of completion; we can do this only by "walking after the Spirit" [Rom. 8:1-2], which refers to looking to the Cross, and looking to the Cross exclusively).*

PAUL'S JOY

2 Receive us *(don't turn a deaf ear to what we are saying)*; we have wronged no man, we have corrupted no man, we have defrauded no man. *(This is insinuating that false teachers with their false doctrine would definitely wrong, corrupt, and defraud their followers.)*

3 I speak not *this* to condemn *you (I do not speak this with any desire to reproach you)*: for I have said before, that you are in our hearts to die and live with *you (refers to the Corinthians having such a place in his affections).*

4 Great *is* my boldness of speech toward you *(they were his children in the Lord)*, great *is* my glorying of you *(even though he used boldness when addressing them personally, behind their backs he "gloried" in them by praising them)*:

I am filled with comfort, I am exceeding joyful in all our tribulation. *(The tribulation, whatever it might have been, did not take away the joy.)*

5 For, when we were come into Macedonia, our flesh had no rest *(he had written his First Epistle to the Church at Corinth, and was not certain if they would accept his admonitions; if not, the Church would be lost)*, but we were troubled on every side; without *were* fightings, within *were* fears. *(Like the rest of us, Paul was human. As such, he had all of these emotions, all in regard to the Church at Corinth.)*

6 Nevertheless God, Who comforts those who are cast down *(God comforts the lowly, while He will not comfort the proud; that is, if the lowly will trust Christ and what Christ did at the Cross)*, comforted us by the coming of Titus *(Titus gave happy news regarding Paul's First Epistle to the Corinthians; they had accepted Paul's admonitions; as well, Paul puts himself in the place of the "lowly")*;

7 And not by his coming only, but by the consolation wherewith he was comforted in you *(what his coming brought, which was good news)*, when he told us your earnest desire, your mourning *(over the sin being committed in the Church, and it not being properly addressed)*, your fervent mind to-

ward me *(their expressed love for Paul)*; so that I rejoiced the more.

8 For though I made you sorry with a Letter *(his First Epistle to them)*, I do not repent, though I did repent *(not a contradiction! he had to send the Letter, but he was sorry it had to be sent)*: for I perceive that the same Epistle has made you sorry, though *it were* but for a season. *(They repented, and the sorrow was lifted.)*

9 Now I rejoice, not that you were made sorry, but that you sorrowed to Repentance *(which is what the Holy Spirit intended)*: for you were made sorry after a Godly manner *(toward Repentance)*, that you might receive damage by us in nothing. *(This presents the grief of Repentance as never a loss in any way.)*

10 For godly sorrow *(sorrow instigated by the Holy Spirit over wrong doing)* works Repentance to Salvation not to be repented of *(means that such action will never be regretted)*: but the sorrow of the world works death. *(This presents a sorrow that is merely remorse, often despair.)*

11 For behold this selfsame thing *(refers to the happy effects of Godly sorrow)*, that you sorrowed after a Godly sort *(they did what true Repentance required)*, what carefulness it wrought in you *(they wanted to correct the wrong immediately)*, yes, what clearing of yourselves *(an apology for their laxness in respect to these problems being left unattended)*, yes, what indignation *(a decided hatred of sin)*, yes, what fear *(speaks of the fear of God they should have had all along, but did not)*, yes, what vehement desire *(the fervent effort to carry out that which Paul had proclaimed)*, yes, what zeal *(setting about the reformation in great earnest)*, yes, what revenge *(a determination to right the wrongs perpetrated against Paul)*! In all *things* you have approved yourselves to be clear in this matter. *(Their Repentance was sincere, resulting in certain things taking place.)*

12 Wherefore, though I wrote unto you, *I did it* not for his cause who had done the wrong, nor for his cause who suffered wrong *(the one who was committing the sin of incest [I Cor., Chpt. 5], and his father who had been wronged, the husband of the woman in question)*, but that our care for you in the sight of God might appear unto you. *(The entirety of the Church at Corinth needed direction.)*

13 Therefore we were comforted in your comfort *(refers to the joy and comfort the Corinthians experienced when they obeyed the Word of the Lord)*: yes, and exceedingly the more joyed we for the joy of Titus, because his spirit

was refreshed by you all *(refers to Titus being so kindly received and hospitably entertained)*.

14 For if I have boasted any thing to him of you, I am not ashamed *(the Apostle's boast to Titus had proven to be true)*; but as we spoke all things to you in Truth, even so our boasting, which I *made* before Titus, is found a Truth *(refers to the fact that Faith is never idle boasting)*.

15 And his inward affection is more abundant toward you, while he remembered the obedience of you all *(it is natural that the stock of this Church went up in the eyes of Titus)*, how with fear and trembling you received him. *(This suggests he had not expected to be received accordingly.)*

16 I rejoice therefore that I have confidence in you in all *things*. *(This refers not only to the present, but the future as well!)*

CHAPTER 8

GIVING

MOREOVER, Brethren, we do you to wit of the Grace of God bestowed on the Churches of Macedonia *(northern Greece)*;

2 How that in a great trial of affliction *(Macedonia was greatly impoverished due to political and military problems)* the abundance of their joy and their deep poverty abounded unto the riches of their liberality. *(Despite their deep poverty, they gave liberally to the Work of God.)*

3 For to *their* power, I bear record *(Paul knew their financial circumstances)*, yes, and beyond *their* power *they were* willing of themselves *(they gave beyond what it seemed they could give)*;

4 Praying us with much entreaty that we would receive the gift *(knowing their impoverished circumstances, Paul didn't want to take the gift, but they insisted)*, and *take upon us* the fellowship of the Ministering to the Saints. *(Paul was receiving an Offering from all the Churches for the poor Saints at Jerusalem.)*

5 And *this they did (gave far beyond what seemed to be their ability)*, not as we hoped *(meaning much greater than he had hoped)*, but first gave their own selves to the Lord *(this means it was the Will of the Lord for them to do what they did)*, and unto us by the Will of God. *(They had great confidence in Paul and his Ministry. As we see here, the Holy Spirit used Macedonia as an example.)*

6 Insomuch that we desired Titus, that as he had begun, so he would also finish in you the same Grace also. *(As the Lord had Blessed Macedonia, the Church at Corinth is to be Blessed also, that is if they*

will follow the example of Macedonia.)

7 Therefore, as you abound in every *thing, in* Faith, and utterance, and knowledge, and *in* all diligence, and *in* your love to us, *see* that you abound in this Grace also *(abound in the Grace of Giving).*

JERUSALEM

8 I speak not by Commandment *(the Grace of "Giving" cannot be by "Commandment," or it is no longer Giving)*, but by occasion of the forwardness of others *(proclaims grandly that Giving inspires Giving)*, and to prove the sincerity of your love. *(If we truly love God, we will give liberally to His Work.)*

9 For we know the Grace of our Lord Jesus Christ *(the Giving of Himself)*, that, though He was rich, yet for your sakes He became poor, that you through His poverty might be rich. *(We can only imagine what He left to come to this world. But because of what He did, we now have the riches of Eternal Life.)*

10 And herein I give *my* advice *(Paul was not commanding, but rather giving advice)*: for this is expedient for you *(it will be profitable)*, who have begun before, not only to do, but also to be forward a year ago. *(They had started this a year before, but had gotten sidetracked by problems, which the Devil desired to do.)*

11 Now therefore perform the doing *of it*; that as *there was* a readiness to will, so *there may be* a performance also out of that which you have. *(Don't just talk about it, do it!)*

12 For if there be first a willing mind *(the first consideration)*, *it is* accepted according to that a man has, *and* not according to that he has not. *(Our obligations to the Lord in all cases are limited to our ability.)*

13 For *I mean* not that other men be eased *(all should do their part, whatever it might be)*, and you burdened *(he was only asking that they give their fair share)*:

14 But by an equality, *that* now at this time your abundance *may be a supply* for their want *(Corinth had much more material wealth than those in Jerusalem, so they are asked to share)*, that their abundance also may be a *supply* for your want *(Paul was speaking of the fact that the Church in Jerusalem was at least partly responsible for the great Spiritual Blessing now held by the Corinthians)*: that there may be equality *(Jerusalem gave Spiritual Blessings, while Corinth gave material blessings, which made everything equal)*:

15 As it is written *(Ex. 16:18)*, He who *had gathered* much had nothing over *(hoarding money*

doesn't set well with the Lord); and he who *had gathered* little had no lack. *(Giving to the Work of God, and doing so generously, guarantees Blessing.)*

ARRANGEMENTS

16 But thanks *be* to God, which put the same earnest care into the heart of Titus for you. *(Titus had a heart very similar to Paul, as it regards the Gospel.)*

17 For indeed he accepted the exhortation *(to go back to Corinth to receive the Offering)*; but being more forward, of his own accord he went unto you. *(Since the Church at Corinth had experienced Revival, everything is now changed for the better. Titus was now eager to go back to them.)*

18 And we have sent with him the Brother, whose praise *is* in the Gospel throughout all the Churches *(we are not told exactly who the Brother was)*;

19 And not *that* only, but who was also chosen of the Churches to travel with us with this Grace *(with the Offering)*, which is administered by us to the Glory of the same Lord, and *declaration of* your ready mind *(the design was to promote the Glory of the Lord by showing the Love of God respecting this particular need)*:

20 Avoiding this, that no man should blame us in this abundance which is administered by us *(that everything be done honestly)*:

21 Providing for honest things, not only in the sight of the Lord, but also in the sight of men *(so as not to give the devil room for accusation)*.

22 And we have sent with them our Brother *(presents another man in conjunction with the Brother mentioned in Verse 18)*, whom we have oftentimes proved diligent in many things *(lends credence to thought that this man, whomever he may have been, was the companion and fellow-laborer of Paul)*, but now much more diligent, upon the great confidence which I have in you. *(He was happy to go to Corinth, as well.)*

23 Whether *any do* enquire of Titus, *he is* my partner and fellowhelper concerning you *(Paul placed Titus in charge respecting those who were to go to Corinth)*: or our Brethren be enquired of, they are the Messengers of the Churches, *and* the Glory of Christ. *(It seems these other Brethren were Apostles as well, for the word "Messengers" in the Greek is "Apostoloi" and means "Apostle.")*

24 Wherefore show you to them, and before the Churches *(set a good example before the other Churches)*, the proof of your love *(a good Offering for Jerusalem)*, and of our boasting on your behalf. *(The Apostle believes the*

Corinthians would surely do their part.)

CHAPTER 9

ENCOURAGEMENT

F OR as touching the Minister-ing to the Saints *(Paul con-tinues to address himself to the Of-fering which is to be received for the poor Saints in Jerusalem)*, it is superfluous for me to write to you *(he means he believes the Corinthians are already very much aware of their obligations)*:

2 For I know the forwardness of your mind *(eagerness to help)*, for which I boast of you to them of Macedonia, that Achaia *(Corinth)* was ready a year ago *(problems in the Church that hindered, which is what Satan desires to do)*; and your zeal has provoked very many *(excited others to give)*.

3 Yet have I sent the Brethren *(refers to those mentioned in II Cor. 8:18, 22-23)*, lest our boasting of you should be in vain in this be-half *(means he believes they will finish what they had grandly started)* that, as I said, you may be ready *(that should be asked of every Be-liever, "are you ready?")*:

4 Lest haply if they of Mace-donia come with me, and find you unprepared *(the Holy Spirit is here teaching "preparation")*, we (that we say not, you) should be ashamed in this same confident boasting. *(In essence, the Apostle says, "lest perhaps we be put to shame, not to say you.")*

5 Therefore I thought it nec-essary to exhort the Brethren, that they would go before unto you *(speaks of the three Brethren which included Titus)*, and make up beforehand your bounty *(Of-fering)*, whereof you had notice before, that the same might be ready, as *a matter of* bounty *(the Corinthians were to understand that not only would their Offering be a Blessing to the poor Saints in Jerusa-lem, but to the giver as well)*, and not as *of* covetousness. *(Although God abundantly blesses the giver, our giving should always be to prove the sincerity of our love, and not as a matter of greed.)*

THE BLESSINGS

6 But this *I say*, He which sows sparingly shall reap also sparingly *(if we give little to the Lord, He will bless little)*; and he which sows bountifully shall reap also boun-tifully. *(If we give bountifully, He will bless bountifully. This is a Prom-ise of the Lord.)*

7 Every man according as he purposes in his heart, *so let him give (without compulsion)*; not grudgingly, or of necessity *(if it is not willing giving, it is not really Christian Giving!)*: for God loves a

cheerful giver. *(This actually means "a hilarious giver.")*

8 And God *is* able to make all Grace abound toward you *(presents the ability of God)*; that you, always having all sufficiency in all *things (mental, physical, economical, and spiritual)*, may abound to every good work *(using God's Blessings for the good of others)*:

9 (As it is written *(Ps. 112:9)*, He has dispersed abroad *(the Promises of God apply to all of mankind, at least all who will believe)*; He has given to the poor *(Jesus is the only hope for the poor)*: his Righteousness remains forever. *(This refers to the Righteousness of Christ.)*

10 Now he who Ministers seed to the sower *(speaks of the Lord)* both Minister bread for *your* food *(both natural and spiritual)*, and multiply your seed sown *(presents the harvest)*, and increase the fruits of your Righteousness;) *(Giving to the Work of the Lord is the Fruit of Righteousness, unless it's done through covetousness.)*

11 Being enriched in every thing to all bountifulness *(the Blessings of God include everything regarding life and Godliness)*, which causes through us thanksgiving to God. *(We are to constantly thank the Lord for His Blessings.)*

12 For the administration of this service not only supplies the want of the Saints *(speaks of the poor Saints in Jerusalem)*, but is abun-dant also by many thanksgivings unto God *(the Giver is to constantly thank God as well, that God has supplied his giving in the first place)*;

13 While by the experiment of this ministration they Glorify God for your professed subjection unto the Gospel of Christ *(the thanksgiving which will come from the Saints in Jerusalem will be for more than the mere gift, but rather for the consecration of the Corinthians which made the gift possible)*, and for *your* liberal distribution unto them, and unto all *men (Paul is saying that what Corinth is doing will be an example to all the Churches)*;

14 And by their prayer for you *(the Saints in Jerusalem will now greatly pray for the Corinthians, which they should)*, which long after you for the exceeding Grace of God in you. *(Those in Jerusalem will know the Corinthians have done this thing because of the Grace of God.)*

15 Thanks *be* unto God for His unspeakable gift. *(While we may give, it is God Who has given the most in His Giving of the Lord Jesus Christ to the whole of humanity.)*

CHAPTER 10

WARFARE

NOW I Paul myself beseech you by the meekness and

gentleness of Christ (*I appeal to you on the basis of love*), who in presence *am* base among you (*probably presents the Apostle using the actual taunts of his adversaries*), but being absent am bold toward you:

2 But I beseech *you*, that I may not be bold when I am present with that confidence, wherewith I think to be bold against some (*refers to the fact that Paul would only use boldness if it was absolutely necessary*), which think of us as if we walked according to the flesh. (*Paul's enemies thought this way because they functioned in the flesh themselves, which means that they didn't have the Power of God.*)

3 For though we walk in the flesh (*refers to the fact that we do not yet have Glorified Bodies*), we do not war after the flesh (*after our own ability, but rather by the Power of the Spirit*):

4 (For the weapons of our warfare *are* not carnal (*carnal weapons consist of those which are man devised*), but mighty through God (*the Cross of Christ [I Cor. 1:18]*) to the pulling down of strong holds;)

5 Casting down imaginations (*philosophic strongholds; every effort man makes outside of the Cross of Christ*), and every high thing that exalts itself against the Knowledge of God (*all the pride of the human heart*), and bring-ing into captivity every thought to the obedience of Christ (*can be done only by the Believer looking exclusively to the Cross, where all Victory is found; the Holy Spirit will then perform the task*);

6 And having in a readiness to revenge all disobedience (*refers to that which is opposed to the Cross, where alone all Victory is found*), when your obedience is fulfilled (*is fulfilled when looking exclusively, as stated, to Christ and the Cross*).

7 Do ye look on things after the outward appearance? (*It is Faith alone that counts.*) If any man trust to himself that he is Christ's, let him of himself think this again (*refers to the false teachers who laid claims to being followers of Christ by way of eminence*), that, as he is Christ's, even so *are* we Christ's. (*Paul is simply saying that he is of Christ as well!*)

8 For though I should boast somewhat more of our authority (*what the Lord had called him to do*), which the Lord has given us for edification, and not for your destruction (*the true purpose of Spiritual Authority*), I should not be ashamed (*no shame shall ever accrue to me from my "boast" being proved false*):

9 That I may not seem as if I would terrify you by letters (*probably I and II Corinthians*).

10 For *his* letters, say they, *are*

weighty and powerful *(presents the description given by his critics)*; but *his* bodily presence *is* weak, and *his* speech contemptible. *(This presents slander concerning his person. His detractors didn't believe what he wrote or preached, especially as it concerned the Cross.)*

11 Let such an one think this *(directed at the individual of Verse 10, who made the accusation)*, that, such as we are in word by letters when we are absent, such *will we be* also in deed when we are present. *(This referred to the fact that the Spirit of God would be with him.)*

PAUL'S AUTHORITY

12 For we dare not make ourselves of the number *(the dividing line of the Church)*, or compare ourselves with some who commend themselves *(but the Lord didn't commend them)*: but they measuring themselves by themselves, and comparing themselves among themselves, are not wise *(self-righteousness)*.

13 But we will not boast of things without *our* measure *(refers to the Call of God on his life)*, but according to the measure of the rule which God has distributed to us, a measure to reach even unto you. *(This refers to God's measurement as it concerned Ministry. In other words, where he would take the Gospel.)*

14 For we stretch not ourselves beyond *our measure*, as though we reached not unto you: for we are come as far as to you also in *preaching* the Gospel of Christ *(apparently Asia Minor and Europe were apportioned to the Apostle Paul as his Missionary field of Gospel Service)*:

15 Not boasting of things without *our* measure, *that is*, of other men's labours *(proclaims Paul stating that his Ministry had not overlapped into others' field of endeavors)*; but having hope, when your Faith is increased, that we shall be enlarged by you according to our rule abundantly *(Paul was believing the Faith of the Corinthians would be increased in order that they might help him take the Gospel elsewhere, even as it had been brought to them)*,

16 To Preach the Gospel in the *regions* beyond you, *and* not to boast in another man's line of things made ready to our hand. *(He would Preach the Gospel where others had not ventured, and there build Churches. The truth is false apostles with false doctrines cannot get people saved, so these detractors would have to parasite Paul's converts.)*

17 But he who glories, let him Glory in the Lord. *(The Apostle is saying that man has nothing to glory about, unless he Glory in the Lord.)*

18 For not he who commends

himself is approved *(proclaims God's standard of approval)*, but whom the Lord commendeth. *(This tells us that the Lord does not accept man's recommendations or accommodations. They mean nothing to Him.)*

CHAPTER 11

GODLY JEALOUSY

WOULD to God you could bear with me a little in *my* folly: and indeed bear with me. *(In effect, the Apostle is saying, "indulge me.")*

2 For I am jealous over you with Godly jealousy *(refers to the "jealousy of God" [Ex. 20:5; 34:14; Nah. 1:2])*: for I have espoused you to one husband *(not jealous of the Corinthians' affection for himself, but of their affection for Christ)*, that I may present *you* as a chaste virgin to Christ. *(They must not commit spiritual adultery, which refers to trusting in things other than Christ and the Cross.)*

3 But I fear, lest by any means, as the serpent beguiled Eve through his subtilty *(the strategy of Satan)*, so your minds should be corrupted from the simplicity that is in Christ. *(The Gospel of Christ is simple, but men complicate it by adding to the Message.)*

4 For if he who comes Preaching another Jesus *(a Jesus who is not of the Cross)*, whom we have not Preached *(Paul's Message was "Jesus Christ and Him Crucified"; anything else is "another Jesus")*, or if you receive another spirit *(which is produced by preaching another Jesus)*, which you have not received *(that's not what you received when we Preached the True Gospel to you)*, or another gospel, which you have not accepted *(anything other than "Jesus Christ and Him Crucified" is "another gospel")*, you might well bear with *him*. *(The Apostle is telling the Corinthians they have in fact sinned because they tolerated these false apostles who had come in, bringing "another gospel" which was something other than Christ and the Cross.)*

APOSTLESHIP

5 For I suppose I was not a whit behind the very Chiefest Apostles. *(Apparently, this critic was claiming that Paul was not one of the original Twelve, so his Ministry was of little significance.)*

6 But though *I* be rude in speech *(the truth is he was not a poor speaker)*, yet not in knowledge *(what his critics were really opposing was his Message)*; but we have been thoroughly made manifest among you in all things. *(In other words, the Corinthians knew Paul, so they should not believe*

the ridiculous accusations.)

7 Have I committed an offence in abasing myself that you might be exalted, because I have preached to you the Gospel of God freely? *(He is using irony.)*

8 I robbed other Churches *(received Offerings from other Churches)*, taking wages *of them*, to do you service *(meaning he asked no monetary help from the Corinthians while he was establishing their Church)*.

9 And when I was present with you, and wanted *(in need)*, I was chargeable to no man *(meaning he did not make his need the Corinthians' responsibility)*: for that which was lacking to me the Brethren which came from Macedonia supplied *(other Churches supplied help)*: and in all *things* I have kept myself from being burdensome unto you, and *so* will I keep *myself*. *(He wasn't after their money.)*

10 As the Truth of Christ is in me *(he is declaring this in the Presence of Christ)* no man shall stop me of this boasting in the regions of Achaia. *(This actually means no man can disprove what the Apostle is saying.)*

11 Wherefore? because I love you not? *(This is actually meant to have the opposite meaning "I do what I do, because I love you.")* God knows. *(This refers to the fact that what he is saying is true.)*

FALSE APOSTLES

12 But what I do, that I will do *(I will continue to pursue the course of life I have been pursuing)*, that I may cut off occasion from them which desire occasion *(he will not do anything that will give his enemies occasion to find fault, at least, truthfully)*; that wherein they glory *(they claim to not be interested in your money, but that's not true)*, they may be found even as we. *(If they aren't interested in your money, let them conduct themselves as we do and not take your money.)*

13 For such *are* false apostles, deceitful workers *(they have no rightful claim to the Apostolic Office; they are deceivers)*, transforming themselves into the Apostles of Christ. *(They have called themselves to this Office.)*

14 And no marvel *(true Believers should not be surprised)*; for Satan himself is transformed into an angel of light. *(This means he pretends to be that which he is not.)*

15 Therefore *it is* no great thing if his ministers *(Satan's ministers)* also be transformed as the ministers of righteousness *(despite their claims, they were "Satan's ministers" because they preached something other than the Cross [I Cor. 1:17-18, 21, 23; 2:2; Gal. 1:8-9])*; whose end shall be according to their works *(that "end" is spiri-*

tual destruction [Phil. 3:18-19]).

SUFFERINGS

16 I say again, Let no man think me a fool (proclaims the Apostle's embarrassment at having to deal with this issue); if otherwise, yet as a fool receive me, that I may boast myself a little. (Whatever you think of me, hear what I have to say simply because it is very important.)

17 That which I speak, I speak it not after the Lord (not commanded, but permitted), but as it were foolishly, in this confidence of boasting (because it is necessary).

18 Seeing that many glory after the flesh, I will glory also. (The flesh is that which pertains to human ability.)

19 For you suffer fools gladly (speaking of the false apostles), seeing you yourselves are wise (presents the highest of irony).

20 For you suffer, if a man bring you into bondage, if a man devour you, if a man take of you (speaks of bringing one into slavery, which is exactly what these false apostles were doing to the Believers at Corinth, and anywhere else they were allowed to intrude), if a man exalt himself (these false teachers exalted self, not Christ), if a man smite you on the face (meaning these false teachers treated them with such little respect as if they smote them on the face).

21 I speak as concerning reproach (the Apostle had suffered terrible reproach at the hands of these detractors), as though we had been weak. (These false apostles referred to Paul as a "weak sister.") Howbeit whereinsoever any is bold, (I speak foolishly,) I am bold also. (He will now speak of the qualifications he has.)

22 Are they Hebrews? so am I. Are they Israelites? so am I. Are they the seed of Abraham? so am I.

23 Are they Ministers of Christ? (They claim to be, but they really were not.) (I speak as a fool) I am more (proclaims the Apostle stooping to a level in which he is not comfortable); in labours more abundant, in stripes above measure, in prisons more frequent, in deaths oft (means that he was exposed to death often).

24 Of the Jews five times received I forty stripes save one.

25 Thrice was I beaten with rods (different from the beatings listed in the previous Verse), once was I stoned, thrice I suffered shipwreck, a night and a day I have been in the deep (probably refers to a particular time when the Apostle was adrift on the open sea for a night and a day, and was in constant danger of drowning);

26 In journeyings often, in per-

ils of waters, *in* perils of robbers, *in* perils by *mine own* countrymen, *in* perils by the heathen, *in* perils in the city, *in* perils in the wilderness, *in* perils in the sea, *in* perils among false brethren *(this probably represents the crowning danger)*;

27 In weariness and painfulness, in watchings often, in hunger and thirst, in fastings often, in cold and nakedness.

28 Beside those things that are without, that which comes upon me daily, the care of all the Churches. *(All the Churches he had planted needed his constant supervision, as would be obvious.)*

29 Who is weak, and I am not weak? *(This presents the Apostle carrying the burden of each and every member of these Churches.)* who is offended, and I burn not? *(This concerns those who fail in times of temptations and trial.)*

30 If I must needs glory, I will glory of the things which concern my infirmities. *(If I have to glory, I will glory in my weaknesses, which force me toward total dependence on the Lord.)*

31 The God and Father of our Lord Jesus Christ, which is blessed for evermore, knows that I lie not. *(If his detractors call him a liar, they are at the same time calling God a liar.)*

32 In Damascus the Governor under Aretas the King kept the city of the Damascenes with a garrison, desirous to apprehend me *(he is speaking of the time he was first saved, recorded in Acts, Chpt. 9)*:

33 And through a window in a basket was I let down by the wall, and escaped his hands.

CHAPTER 12

THE THORN

IT is not expedient for me doubtless to glory *(but necessary!)*. I will come to Visions and Revelations of the Lord *(refers to that given to Paul by the Lord)*.

2 I knew a man in Christ above fourteen years ago *(speaking of himself)*, (whether in the body, I cannot tell; or whether out of the body, I cannot tell: God knows;) *(He doesn't know if he was actually taken to Heaven in his physical body, or only saw these things in a Vision.)* such an one caught up to the third Heaven. *(The first Heaven is the clouds, etc. The second Heaven is the starry space. The third Heaven is the Planet Heaven, the Abode of God.)*

3 And I knew such a man, (whether in the body, or out of the body, I cannot tell: God knows;) *(This is the second time he said this, and not without purpose.)*

4 How that he was caught up into Paradise *(presents the word "Paradise" being used by Paul in

a general manner), and heard unspeakable words *(it was not possible for the Apostle to properly put what he saw into words)*, which it is not lawful for a man to utter *(not permissible)*.

5 Of such an one will I glory *("of such a thing will I glory")*: yet of myself I will not glory, but in my infirmities *(that I was counted worthy to suffer for Christ)*.

6 For though I would desire to glory, I shall not be a fool *(knowing that God knows all things, and we have nothing to glory about)*; for I will say the truth: but *now* I forbear, lest any man should think of me above that which he sees me *to be*, or *that* he hears of me. *(In effect says, "I will not relate more about this Vision, and for the obvious reasons." He wanted the eyes of all Believers on Christ, and not on him at any time.)*

7 And lest I should be exalted above measure through the abundance of the Revelations *(presents the reasons for the thorn in the flesh)*, there was given to me a thorn in the flesh *(I think it was all the difficulties of II Cor. 11:23-27)*, the messenger of Satan to buffet me *(an angel of Satan)*, lest I should be exalted above measure. *(This has the Apostle concluding this sentence as it began.)*

8 For this thing I besought the Lord thrice, that it might depart from me. *(The Apostle knew it was the Lord allowing this, but he didn't understand why.)*

9 And He said unto me *(the Lord responded, but did not agree)*, My Grace is sufficient for you *(speaks of enabling Grace, which is really the Goodness of God carried out by the Holy Spirit)*: for My Strength is made perfect in weakness. *(All Believers are weak, but the Lord tends to make us weaker, with the intention being that we then depend solely upon Him, thereby obtaining His strength.)* Most gladly therefore will I rather glory in my infirmities *(because of the end result)*, that the Power of Christ may rest upon me. *(If Paul needed so humbling and painful an experience of what the carnal nature is, it is evident that all Christians need it. Whatever weakens, belittles, and humiliates that proud and willful nature should be regarded by the Believer as most worthwhile.)*

10 Therefore I take pleasure in infirmities, in reproaches, in necessities, in persecutions, in distresses for Christ's sake: for when I am weak, then am I strong *(then the strength of Christ can be exhibited through me, but only when I know I am weak)*.

DEMONSTRATION

11 I am become a fool in glo-

rying; you have compelled me *(it was necessary for him to vindicate his character)*: for I ought to have been commended of you *(the Corinthians should have stood up for Paul, instead of him having to stand up for himself)*: for in nothing am I behind the very Chiefest Apostles, though I be nothing. *(This is regarding all true Apostles, even the original Twelve.)*

12 Truly the signs of an Apostle were wrought among you in all patience, in signs, and wonders, and mighty deeds. *(As is obvious, his Apostleship had been questioned.)*

13 For what is it wherein ye were inferior to other Churches *(this question arose because Paul's detractors claimed the Church at Corinth was inferior because of Paul's inability)*, except it be that I myself was not burdensome to you? *(This refers to the fact that he did not take any financial support from the Corinthians, which he had already addressed.)* forgive me this wrong *(drips with sarcasm, even as it should!)*.

A PROPOSED VISIT

14 Behold, the third time I am ready to come to you *(there is little explanation as it regards "the third time")*; and I will not be burdensome to you: for I seek not yours, but you *(I seek your Salva-tion, not your property)*: for the children ought not to lay up for the parents, but the parents for the children. *(This presents the Apostle speaking to the Corinthians as a father to his children. The false apostles did the very opposite, as all false apostles do!)*

15 And I will very gladly spend and be spent for you *(be spent for your souls)*; though the more abundantly I love you, the less I be loved *(is designed as a gentle reproof)*.

16 But be it so, I did not burden you *(Paul's detractors claimed that even though he didn't take money from the Corinthians, he imposed upon them in other ways)*: nevertheless, being crafty, I caught you with guile. *(This should have been translated, "nevertheless, you say, being crafty, I caught you with guile." Paul is not saying he was "crafty" or using "guile," but that he was accused of these things.)*

17 Did I make a gain of you by any of them whom I sent unto you? *(The answer is a firm "No"!)*

18 I desired Titus, and with him I sent a Brother. Did Titus make a gain of you? *(This was answered with a firm "No!" as well.)* walked we not in the same spirit? *walked we* not in the same steps? *(Titus and the Brother conducted themselves exactly as did Paul.)*

REPENTANCE

19 Again, do you think that we excuse ourselves unto you? *(He has something far more in mind than defending himself.)* we speak before God in Christ *(it is God Who is the Judge of all this)*: but *we do* all things, dearly beloved, for your edifying. *(Everything he has said has been for their good.)*

20 For I fear, lest, when I come, I shall not find you such as I would *(the Corinthians must address every wrong)*, and *that* I shall be found unto you such as you would not *(the Apostle doesn't desire to have to continue in the correcting mode)*: lest *there be* debates, envyings, wraths, strifes, backbitings, whisperings, swellings, tumults *(presents what will happen if they do not heed that given by the Apostle)*:

21 *And* lest, when I come again, my God will humble me among you *(refers to the fact that, if his counsel is ignored, Judgment will come, which will inflict great pain on Paul)*, and *that* I shall bewail many which have sinned already, and have not repented of the uncleanness and fornication and lasciviousness which they have committed. *(The Apostle is lamenting the fact that if these sins were continued, which means these people had abandoned the Cross, they would lose their souls.)*

CHAPTER 13

THE PROPOSED VISIT

THIS *is* the third *time* I am coming to you *(a proposed visit)*. In the mouth of two or three witnesses shall every word be established *(Deut. 19:15)*.

2 I told you before, and foretell you, as if I were present, the second time *(I told you these things on my second visit to you)*; and being absent now I write to them which heretofore have sinned *(he is telling them to repent)*, and to all other, that, if I come again, I will not spare *(if his counsel is ignored, which in reality is the Counsel of God, Judgment will come)*:

3 Since you seek a proof of Christ speaking in me *(his Apostleship was being questioned)*, which to you-ward is not weak, but is mighty in you. *(The Gospel Paul preached had changed their lives. That was proof enough!)*

4 For though He was Crucified through weakness *(Christ purposely did not use His Power)*, yet He lived by the Power of God *(was Resurrected; we have this power at our disposal as well [Rom. 8:11])*. For we also are weak in Him *(regarding our personal strength and ability)*, but we shall live with Him by the Power of God toward you. *(This refers to our everyday life and living, which we*

do by constant Faith in the Cross. This gives the Holy Spirit latitude to work mightily in our lives.)

WARNING OF SIN

5 Examine yourselves, whether you be in the Faith *(the words, "the Faith," refer to "Christ and Him Crucified," with the Cross ever being the object of our Faith);* prove your own selves. *(Make certain your Faith is actually in the Cross, and not other things.)* Know you not your own selves, how that Jesus Christ is in you *(which He can only be by our Faith expressed in His Sacrifice),* except you be reprobates? *(Rejected.)*

6 But I trust that you shall know that we are not reprobates. *(If he was a reprobate, as his skeptics claimed, then they were as well, which of course is preposterous.)*

7 Now I pray to God that you do no evil *(Paul is speaking specifically about the Corinthians siding with the opponents who claimed him to be a reprobate);* not that we should appear approved *(the Apostle is saying he is not interested in whether people approve of him or not, but that he be approved of Christ),* but that you should do that which is honest *(the Corinthians must follow correct Doctrine),* though we be as reprobates *(irrespective that some may think we are reprobates).*

8 For we can do nothing against the Truth *(will not shade the Truth of the Cross in order to appease some),* but for the Truth. *(We must stand firm for the Truth.)*

9 For we are glad, when we are weak, and you are strong *(his recognized weakness caused him to depend on the Lord, meaning he trusted in the Cross and was able to impart this knowledge of the Cross to the Corinthians, which made them strong):* and this also we wish, *even* your perfection *(maturity).*

10 Therefore I write these things being absent, lest being present I should use sharpness *(when he comes to Corinth, he doesn't want to have to use sharpness, believing the problems will have been solved),* according to the power which the Lord has given me to edification, and not to destruction. *(If they accept that which the Lord gave him, they would be edified. If not, destruction would be the result.)*

BENEDICTION

11 Finally, Brethren, farewell. Be perfect *(mature),* be of good comfort, be of one mind, live in peace; and the God of Love and Peace shall be with you. *(All of this can be done by constant Faith evidenced in the Cross of Christ.)*

12 Greet one another with an holy kiss *(the custom at that time).*

13 All the Saints *(probably those in Philippi)* salute *(greet)* you.

14 The Grace of our Lord Jesus Christ *(made possible by the Cross)*, and the Love of God *(shown by the fact of the Cross)*, and the Communion of the Holy Spirit *(which we can constantly have by continually exhibiting Faith in the Cross)*, be with you all. Amen.

13 All the Saints (probably those in the midst of the Church, and the Congregation in Philippi saluted Paul, and he in turn here greeted them).

14 The Grace of our Lord Jesus Christ (that which we have by coming to Christ, made possible by the Cross), and the Love of God (always by Faith in the Cross), and the Love of God (always be with you all. Amen.

THE EPISTLE OF PAUL THE APOSTLE TO THE
GALATIANS

CHAPTER 1

INTRODUCTION

PAUL, an Apostle, (not of men, neither by man, but by Jesus Christ, and God the Father, Who raised Him from the dead;) *(This means Paul did not submit the authority of his Apostleship to men, neither was it conferred on him by man.)*

2 And all the Brethren which are with me, unto the Churches of Galatia *(refers to all in that region)*:

3 Grace *be* to you and Peace from God the Father *(made possible by the Cross)*, and *from* our Lord Jesus Christ *(Who made it possible)*,

4 Who gave Himself for our sins *(the Cross)*, that He might deliver us from this present evil world *(the Cross alone can set the captive free)*, according to the Will of God and our Father *(the standard of the entire process of Redemption)*:

5 To Whom *be* Glory forever and ever *(Divine Glory)*. Amen.

NO OTHER GOSPEL

6 I marvel that you are so soon removed from Him *(the Holy Spirit) Who* called you into the Grace of Christ *(made possible by the Cross)* unto another Gospel *(anything which doesn't have the Cross as its object of Faith)*:

7 Which is not another *(presents the fact that Satan's aim is not so much to deny the Gospel, which he can little do, as to corrupt it)*; but there be some who trouble you, and would pervert the Gospel of Christ *(once again, to make the object of Faith something other than the Cross)*.

8 But though we *(Paul and his associates)*, or an Angel from Heaven, preach any other Gospel unto you than that which we have preached unto you *(Jesus Christ and Him Crucified)*, let him be accursed *(eternally condemned; the Holy Spirit speaks this through Paul, making this very serious)*.

9 As we said before, so say I now again *(at some time past, he had said the same thing to them, making their defection even more serious)*, If any *man* preach any other Gospel unto you *(anything other than the Cross)* than that you have received *(which Saved your souls)*, let him be accursed *("eternally condemned," which means*

the loss of the soul).

10 For do I now persuade men, or God? *(In essence, Paul is saying, "Do I preach man's doctrine, or God's?")* or do I seek to please men? *(This is what false apostles do.)* for if I yet pleased men, I should not be the Servant of Christ *(one cannot please both men and God at the same time).*

REVELATION

11 But I certify you, Brethren *(make known)*, that the Gospel which was preached of me *(the Message of the Cross)* is not after man. *(Any Message other than the Cross is definitely devised by man.)*

12 For I neither received it of man *(Paul had not learned this great Truth from human teachers)*, neither was I taught it *(he denies instruction from other men)*, but by the Revelation of Jesus Christ. *(Revelation is the mighty Act of God whereby the Holy Spirit discloses to the human mind that which could not be understood without Divine Intervention.)*

13 For you have heard of my conversation *(way of life)* in time past in the Jews' religion *(the practice of Judaism)*, how that beyond measure I persecuted the Church of God, and wasted it *(Acts 9:1-2)*:

14 And profited in the Jews' religion above many my equals in my own nation *(he outstripped* his Jewish contemporaries in Jewish culture, etc.)*, being more exceedingly zealous of the traditions of my fathers *(a zeal from his very boyhood).*

THE GOSPEL

15 But when it pleased God, Who separated me from my mother's womb *(presents the idea that God had set Paul apart, devoting him to a special purpose from before his birth)*, and called me by His Grace *(called, not because of any merit on his part, but rather because of the Grace of God)*,

16 To reveal His Son in me *(the meaning of the New Covenant, which is the meaning of the Cross)*, that I might preach Him among the heathen *(Gentiles)*; immediately I conferred not with flesh and blood *(his Commission and Message came to him from God, and neither was affected in any way by human intervention)*:

17 Neither went I up to Jerusalem to them who were Apostles before me *(did not get this Revelation from the original Twelve)*; but I went into Arabia *(according to the Holy Spirit)*, and returned again unto Damascus. *(There would not have been any Apostles in Damascus. There he preached the Message of the Cross.)*

18 Then after three years I went up to Jerusalem to see Peter

(showing his independence from the Jerusalem Apostles), and abode with him fifteen days (when he no doubt revealed to Peter the Revelation of the Cross, which the Lord had given to him).

19 But other of the Apostles saw I none, save James the Lord's Brother. (James didn't refer to himself as an Apostle, but Paul did.)

20 Now the things which I write unto you, behold, before God, I lie not.

21 Afterwards I came into the regions of Syria and Cilicia;

22 And was unknown by face unto the Churches of Judaea which were in Christ (had he been a Disciple of the Twelve, the Churches in Judaea would have known him):

23 But they had heard only (were constantly hearing), That he which persecuted us (Believers) in times past now Preaches the Faith which once he destroyed (Faith in Christ).

24 And they Glorified God in me. (As he had "constantly persecuted," and now was "constantly preaching," they were "constantly glorifying.")

CHAPTER 2

THE CHURCH

THEN fourteen years after I went up again to Jerusalem with Barnabas (was probably the Jerusalem Council [Acts 15:1-35]), and took Titus with me also.

2 And I went up by Revelation (the Lord told him to go), and communicated unto them that Gospel which I Preach among the Gentiles (the Message of the Cross), but privately to them which were of reputation (to at least some of the original Twelve), lest by any means I should run, or had run, in vain. (If the Twelve, or even James the Lord's Brother, repudiated His Gospel of Grace, at least as far as the Gentiles were concerned, this would create an insurmountable barrier.)

3 But neither Titus, who was with me, being a Greek (a Gentile), was compelled to be circumcised (Paul probably took him as a test case):

4 And that because of false brethren unawares brought in (suggests they were fellow Believers, but their insistence upon the necessity of the Law constituted a denial of Christ in Paul's eyes), who came in privily (subtly) to spy out our liberty which we have in Christ Jesus (the Truth of the Gospel was at stake), that they might bring us into bondage (forsaking the Cross always results in bondage):

5 To whom we gave place by subjection, no, not for an hour (Paul would not yield one iota, nor

compromise in the slightest); that the Truth of the Gospel might continue with you. *(Justification by Faith was on trial.)*

6 But of these *(false brethren)* who seemed to be somewhat, (whatsoever they were, it makes no matter to me: God accepts no man's person:) for they who seemed *to be somewhat* in conference added nothing to me *(there was nothing anyone there could add to the Revelation given to him by the Lord, as it regards the Cross)*:

7 But contrariwise, when they saw that the Gospel of the uncircumcision *(the Gentiles)* was committed unto me *(presents the Jerusalem Apostles championing the cause of Paul after they heard the issue discussed in private conference)*, as *the Gospel* of the Circumcision *was* unto Peter *(the Jews)*;

8 (For He Who wrought effectually in Peter to the Apostleship of the Circumcision *(the Jews)*, the same was mighty in me toward the Gentiles:)

9 And when James *(the Lord's Brother)*, Cephas *(Peter)*, and John, who seemed to be pillars *(a metaphor)*, perceived the Grace that was given unto me *(the Message of Grace)*, they gave to me and Barnabas the right hands of fellowship *(a pledge of friendship and agreement)*; that we *should go* unto the heathen *(Gentiles)*, and they unto the Circumcision *(Jews)*.

10 Only *they would* that we should remember the poor *(the poor Saints in Jerusalem, who had suffered terrible hardships because of persecution)*; the same which I also was forward to do. *(Paul saw the need, and felt he must respond favorably, which he did.)*

PETER

11 But when Peter was come to Antioch *(Antioch Syria, the city used by God to spearhead world Evangelism)*, I withstood him to the face *(means Paul openly opposed and reproved him, even though Peter was the eldest)*, because he was to be blamed *(for abandoning the Cross and resorting to Law)*.

12 For before that certain came from James *(gives us all too well another example as to why Apostles, or anyone else for that matter, are not to be the final word, but rather the Word of God itself)*, he *(Peter)* did eat with the Gentiles *(Peter knew the Gospel of Grace)*: but when they were come *(those from James in Jerusalem)*, he withdrew and separated himself, fearing them which were of the Circumcision. *(The problem was "man fear." Some of the Jewish Christians were still trying to hold to the Law of Moses, which means they accepted Jesus as the Messiah, but gave no credence to the Cross whatsoever.*

This ultimately occasioned the necessity of Paul writing the Epistle to the Hebrews.)

13 And the other Jews *(in the Church at Antioch)* dissembled likewise with him *(with Peter)*; insomuch that Barnabas also was carried away with their dissimulation *(hypocrisy).*

14 But when I saw that they walked not uprightly according to the Truth of the Gospel *(they were forsaking the Cross)*, I said unto Peter before *them* all *(Paul's rebuke was in the presence of everybody, the whole Antioch Church)*, If you, being a Jew, live after the manner of Gentiles, and not as do the Jews, why do you compel the Gentiles to live as do the Jews? *(Hypocrisy!)*

JUSTIFICATION

15 We *who are* Jews by nature *(we ought to know better)*, and not sinners of the Gentiles *(who only know what we tell them because they were not privileged to have the Law as we did)*,

16 Knowing that a man is not justified by the works of the Law *(such is impossible)*, but by the Faith of Jesus Christ *(Faith in what He did at the Cross)*, even we have believed in Jesus Christ *(the object of Faith must always be the Cross)*, that we might be Justified by the Faith of Christ, and not by

the works of the Law: for by the works of the Law shall no flesh be justified *(emphatically so! it cannot be done).*

17 But if, while we seek to be Justified by Christ *(by trusting in what Christ did at the Cross)*, we ourselves also are found sinners *(if we fail, thereby sinning in some way)*, is therefore Christ the minister of sin? *(Is Christ to blame for our failure?)* God forbid. *(The Cross hasn't failed. It's we who have failed.)*

18 For if I build again the things which I destroyed *(revert back to the Law)*, I make myself a transgressor. *(To revert to any type of Law is a departure from God's prescribed Order of Victory [the Cross], and is sin).*

19 For I through the Law *(Christ has perfectly kept the Law and suffered its just penalty, all on my behalf)* am dead to the Law *(the Law is not dead, but I am dead to the Law by virtue of having died with Christ [Rom. 6:3-5])*, that I might live unto God. *(This presents that which can only be done through Christ, and never by the Law.)*

20 I am Crucified with Christ *(as the Foundation of all Victory; Paul, here, takes us back to Romans 6:3-5)*: nevertheless I live *(have new life)*; yet not I *(not by my own strength and ability)*, but Christ lives in me *(by virtue of me dying with Him on the Cross,*

and being raised with Him in newness of life): and the life which I now live in the flesh (my daily walk before God) I live by the Faith of the Son of God (the Cross is ever the object of my Faith), Who loved me, and gave Himself for me (which is the only way that I could be saved).

21 I do not frustrate the Grace of God (if we make anything other than the Cross of Christ the object of our Faith, we frustrate the Grace of God, which means we stop its action, and the Holy Spirit will no longer help us): for if Righteousness come by the Law (any type of religious Law), then Christ is dead in vain. (If I can successfully live for the Lord by any means other than Faith in Christ and the Cross, then the Death of Christ was a waste.)

CHAPTER 3

BY FAITH

O foolish Galatians (failure to use one's powers of perception), who has bewitched you (malignant influence), that you should not obey the truth (refers to "Jesus Christ and Him Crucified"), before whose eyes Jesus Christ has been evidently set forth, crucified among you? (Paul Preached the Cross with such vividness that his hearers could see Jesus Christ Crucified among them. Regrettably, only a few modern Preachers follow his example.)

2 This only would I learn of you (I will convince you of your error by this one argument), Did you receive the Spirit by the works of the Law, or by the hearing of Faith? (This refers to being Born-Again, at which time the Spirit of God comes into the heart and life of the new Believer. It is received simply by trusting Christ, and what He did at the Cross.)

3 Are you so foolish? having begun in the Spirit (do you think you can now be brought to a state of spiritual maturity by means of self effort?), are you now made perfect by the flesh? (These Galatians were practicing Salvation by "Faith," and Sanctification by "self," which is also the state of most modern Christians.)

4 Have you suffered so many things in vain? (You have suffered persecution because of your acceptance of Christ. Don't throw it away.) if it be yet in vain (in essence saying, "I trust it is not in vain").

5 He (the Lord Jesus) therefore Who Ministers to you the Spirit, and works Miracles among you, does He it by the works of the Law, or by the hearing of Faith? (It is obvious that everything the Lord does is done on the basis of the Believer exhibiting Faith. It is never by works of the Law.)

ABRAHAM

6 Even as Abraham believed God *(proclaims the fact that the Patriarch was justified by Faith, not works)*, and it was accounted to him for Righteousness. *(The Righteousness of God is imputed to a person only on the basis of Faith in Christ, and what Christ has done at the Cross [Jn. 8:56].)*

7 Know you therefore that they which are of Faith *(presents Faith, and Faith alone, as the foundation; but the object of Faith must ever be the Cross)*, the same are the children of Abraham *(the legitimate sons of Abraham)*.

8 And the Scripture, foreseeing that God would justify the heathen through Faith *(proclaims the Word of God as the Foundation of all Things)*, Preached before the Gospel unto Abraham, saying, In you shall the nations be blessed *(Gen. 12:1-3)*.

9 So then they *(whomsoever they might be)* which be of Faith *(in Christ and the Cross)* are blessed with Faithful Abraham. *(He received Justification by Faith, and so do we!)*

FAITH ALONE

10 For as many as are of the Works of the Law are under the curse *(the Believer can only be under Law or Grace; it is one or the other; one can only come to Grace through the Cross; if one is trusting in Law, whatever kind of Law, one is cursed)*: for it is written, Cursed is every one who continues not in all things which are written in the Book of the Law to do them *(Deut. 27:26)*. *(To attain the Righteousness of the Law, one must keep the Law perfectly, thereby never failing. Such is impossible, so that leaves only the Cross as the means of Salvation and Victory.)*

11 But that no man is justified by the Law in the sight of God, it is evident *(because it is impossible for man to perfectly keep the Law)*: for, The just shall live by Faith *([Hab. 2:4], Faith in Christ and what He did at the Cross)*.

12 And the Law is not of Faith *(the two principles of Law and of Faith as a means of Justification are mutually exclusive of one another)*: but, The man who does them shall live in them. *(The Believer has a choice. He can attempt to live this life by either Law or Faith. He cannot live by both.)*

13 Christ has redeemed us from the curse of the Law *(He did so on the Cross)*, being made a curse for us *(He took the penalty of the Law, which was death)*: for it is written, Cursed is every one who hangs on a tree *(Deut. 21:23)*:

14 That the blessing of Abraham *(Justification by Faith)* might

come on the Gentiles through Jesus Christ *(what He did at the Cross)*; that we might receive the Promise of the Spirit through Faith. *(All sin was atoned at the Cross which lifted the sin debt from believing man, making it possible for the Holy Spirit to come into the life of the Believer and abide there forever [Jn. 14:16-17].)*

THE COVENANT

15 Brethren, I speak after the manner of men *(now presents an argument to show that the Covenant God made with Abraham is still in force)*; Though *it be* but a man's covenant, yet *if it be* confirmed, no man disannulleth, or adds thereto. *(In other words, the Covenant of Justification by Faith cannot be broken or set aside.)*

16 Now to Abraham and his Seed were the Promises made *(to all those who are brought into Salvation by Faith in Christ)*. He said not, And to Seeds, as of many; but as of One, And to your Seed, which is Christ. *(Abraham's Seed was Christ, and Christ is both God and Man. Therefore, the Covenant cannot be broken.)*

17 And this I say, *that* the Covenant, that was confirmed before of God in Christ *(refers to the Abrahamic Covenant, which is Justification by Faith)*, the Law *(the Law of Moses)*, which was four hundred and thirty years after, cannot disannul, that it should make the Promise of none effect. *(In other words, the Law of Moses did not annul the Abrahamic Covenant. In fact that Covenant is still in force.)*

18 For if the inheritance *be* of the Law, *it is* no more of Promise *(the inheritance cannot come from both Covenants, and in fact it cannot come by the Law)*: but God gave *it* to Abraham by Promise. *(The verb "gave" is in a perfect tense, which means that God gave the Promise about Christ as a permanent Promise that cannot be superseded or modified.)*

THE LAW

19 Wherefore then *serves* the Law? *(What good is the Law?)* It was added because of transgressions *(was given to define sin)*, till the seed should come to whom the Promise was made *(Christ is the Promise)*; and it was ordained by Angels in the hand of a mediator. *(Moses was the mediator of the Law.)*

20 Now a mediator is not *a mediator* of one *(for there to be a mediator, there has to be more than one person involved; in other words, the mediator is the middle person between two or more people who are at enmity with each other)*, but God is one. *(God is the Mediator of the*

New Covenant, but in a different way than Moses. Jesus is God, and Jesus is also Man. Consequently, the New Covenant doesn't depend upon man as such, but rather the man Christ Jesus. Therefore, this Covenant cannot fail!)

21 Is the Law then against the Promises of God? *(This demands a negative answer.)* God forbid: for if there had been a Law given which could have given life, verily Righteousness should have been by the Law. *(The Law of Moses could show a man what he was, but had no power to change the man.)*

22 But the Scripture has concluded all under sin *(means that the Law could not give Eternal Life; it could only exact its penalty, which was death)*, that the Promise by Faith of Jesus Christ might be given to them who believe. *(Eternal Life comes by Faith in the Promise, Who is Jesus Christ and what He did at the Cross. In other words, the word "believe" demands that Christ and the Cross ever be the object of our Faith.)*

23 But before Faith came *(actually says in the Greek, "before the Faith"; in short, it refers to "Jesus Christ and Him Crucified")*, we were kept under the Law *(actually means, "to keep inward under lock and key")*, shut up unto the Faith which should afterwards be revealed. *(This proclaims the fact that the Law pointed to Christ, al-ways to Christ.)*

24 Wherefore the Law was our schoolmaster *(should have been translated, "guardian")* to bring us unto Christ *(proclaims what the end result of the Law was intended to be)*, that we might be justified by Faith. *(This proclaims to us that the Law had no permanent function, but served only until Christ would come. It is only by Faith in Christ that one can be justified.)*

25 But after that Faith is come *(Paul is speaking about the Finished Work of Christ on the Cross)*, we are no longer under a schoolmaster. *(This should actually say, "We are no longer under the guardianship of the Law." The Law was totally fulfilled in Christ.)*

FAITH

26 For you are all the Children of God by Faith in Christ Jesus. *(Every person who is saved, and every person who has ever been or ever will be saved, is saved only by "Faith in Christ Jesus," which refers to what He did at the Cross.)*

27 For as many of you as have been baptized into Christ *(refers to the Baptism into His Death at Calvary [Rom. 6:3-5]; the reference is not to Water Baptism)* have put on Christ *(means to be clothed with Him [Jn. 14:20])*.

28 There is neither Jew nor Greek, there is neither bond nor

free, there is neither male nor female (all have a common life in Christ Jesus): for you are all one in Christ Jesus. (This proclaims an end of all class, status, and social distinction. This phrase alone answers all racism.)

29 And if you be Christ's, then are you Abraham's seed (Christ is Abraham's Seed, so my union with Christ makes me Abraham's seed as well), and heirs according to the Promise (heirs of God, and joint heirs with Jesus Christ [Rom. 8:17]).

CHAPTER 4

HEIRSHIP ILLUSTRATED

NOW I say, That the heir, as long as he is a child, differs nothing from a servant, though he be lord of all (Paul continues the argument for the inferiority of the condition under Law using an illustration from contemporary life);

2 But is under tutors and governors until the time appointed of the father. (This refers to the fixed time when he would be of legal age and, therefore, able to accept the inheritance.)

3 Even so we, when we were children, were in bondage under the elements of the world (refer to passions and pride which enslave humanity):

4 But when the fulness of the time was come (which completed the time designated by God that should elapse before the Son of God would come), God sent forth His Son (it was God who acted; the Law required man to act; this requirement demonstrated man's impotency; the Son of God requires nothing from man other than his confidence), made of a woman (pertains to the Incarnation, God becoming man), made under the Law (refers to the Mosaic Law; Jesus was subject to the Jewish legal economy, which He had to be, that is if He was to redeem fallen humanity; in other words, He had to keep the Law perfectly, which no human being had ever done, but He did),

5 To redeem them who were under the Law (in effect, all of humanity is under the Law of God which man, due to his fallen condition, could not keep; but Jesus came and redeemed us by keeping the Law perfectly, and above all satisfying its penalty on the Cross, which was death), that we might receive the adoption of sons (that we could become the sons of God by adoption, which is carried out by Faith in Christ and what He did at the Cross).

6 And because you are sons (we now have many privileges), God has sent forth the Spirit of his Son into your hearts (because we are sons, the Holy Spirit has been sent to take up His permanent residence in our hearts), crying, Abba, Fa-

ther. *(This means it is the Holy Spirit Who is doing the crying, and does so to the Father on our behalf.)*

7 Wherefore you are no more a servant, but a son *(refers to the standing one has in Christ because of one's Faith in Christ)*; and if a son, then an heir of God through Christ. *(This proclaims the fact that all the privileges, which belong to Christ, now belong to us as well.)*

LEGALISM

8 Howbeit then, when you knew not God *(refers to the former unredeemed state)*, you did service unto them which by nature are no gods. *(They were slaves to heathenistic superstition.)*

9 But now, after that you have known God *(refers to Saving Grace, Knowing God through the acceptance of Jesus Christ, which is the only way He can be known)*, or rather are known of God *(refers to the Lord knowing us in a saving way)*, how turn you again to the weak and beggarly elements *(when the substance is reached and sonship established, going back to the "rudiments," i.e., symbols and sacraments, is not progress, but ignorance)*, whereunto you desire again to be in bondage? *(Bondage to the sin nature! It refers to leaving the Cross, and making other things the object of Faith.)*

10 You observe days, and months, and times, and years. *(The Judaizers were attempting to get the Galatians to go into Law-keeping in conjunction with Christ, which cannot work.)*

11 I am afraid of you *(afraid for your spiritual welfare)*, lest I have bestowed upon you labour in vain. *(If one leaves Faith in Christ and the Cross and embraces other things, which means to look to those other things for life and victory, the Holy Spirit will have bestowed upon such a person labor in vain.)*

12 Brethren, I beseech you, be as I *am (free from all the bondage of Salvation by works and sacraments, which is no Salvation at all)*; for I am as you are *(means that even though he is an Apostle, he is subject to the same Biblical Doctrines as they are)*: you have not injured me at all. *(My motive is not one of personal complaint, but because of the great harm that could come to you.)*

13 You know how through infirmity of the flesh *(doesn't say what it is)* I preached the Gospel unto you at the first *(evidently, when these Churches were first founded)*.

14 And my temptation which was in my flesh you despised not, nor rejected *(should have been translated, "my trial"; but once again, we do not know what it was, so speculation is useless)*; but re-

ceived me as an Angel of God, *even* as Christ Jesus. *(They accepted him and what he preached.)*

15 Where is then the blessedness you spoke of? *(This speaks of the wonderful prosperity of Salvation, which had come to them as a result of Paul bringing the Gospel to this region.)* for I bear you record, that, if *it had* been possible, you would have plucked out your own eyes, and have given them to me. *(This doesn't necessarily mean Paul had an eye disease, as some claim. This was an idiom used often to express extreme affliction.)*

16 Am I therefore become your enemy, because I tell you the truth? *(A real friend is one who will tell his friend the truth, even though it hurts.)*

17 They zealously affect you *(speaks of the Judaizers attempting to subvert the Galatians in order to win them over to themselves)*, *but* not well *(not for your good)*; yes, they would exclude you *(they would shut the Galatians out from the benefits of the Gospel of Grace)*, that you might affect them *(means to be drawn to their side)*.

18 But *it is* good to be zealously affected always in *a* good thing *(Paul wanted the Galatians to be as zealous over Christ and the Cross as it seems they were tending to be over false doctrine)*, and not only when I am present with you. *(Their zeal for the right thing should be present at all times.)*

19 My little children *(presents the language of deep affection and emotion)*, of whom I travail in birth again *(deliver to you again the rudiments of the great Message of Christ and Him Crucified, as though you had never heard it to begin with)* until Christ be formed in you *(presents the work only the Holy Spirit can do, and does exclusively within the parameters of the Sacrifice of Christ, which must always be the object of our Faith)*,

20 I desire to be present with you now *(as a loving parent wants to be at the side of a sick child)*, and to change my voice *(refers to the fact that his true love for them would more profitably come through were he only standing before them in person)*; for I stand in doubt of you. *(The Apostle was perplexed as to how the Galatians could have forsaken the Holy Spirit, substituting in His place the cold issues of dead Law. Any Christian who presently has as his object of Faith anything but the Cross is following the same course as the Galatians of old.)*

HAGAR AND SARAH

21 Tell me, you who desire to be under the Law *(the Law of Moses or any type of Law)*, do you not hear the Law? *(Do you actually know what the Law demands?)*

22 For it is written *(Gen. 16:15;*

21:2-3), that Abraham had two sons *(Ishmael and Isaac)*, the one by a bondmaid *(Hagar)*, the other by a freewoman *(Sarah)*.

23 But he *who was* of the bondwoman was born after the flesh *(by the scheming of Abraham and Sarah)*; but he of the freewoman *was* by Promise *(by an action of the Holy Spirit)*.

24 Which things are an allegory *(a figure of speech in which spiritual facts are presented in physical terms)*: for these are the two Covenants *(represents Law [Hagar] and Grace [Sarah])*; the one from the mount Sinai, which gendereth to bondage, which is Hagar. *(This presents the Apostle plainly saying he is using Hagar as a symbol of the Law of Moses. As is obvious, it was given at Mt. Sinai.)*

25 For this Hagar is Mount Sinai in Arabia, and answers to Jerusalem which now is *(refers to that city at the time of Paul; it was subject to Laws, rites, and customs, according to the Law of Moses)*, and is in bondage with her children. *(Israel was in bondage to sin because of having rejected Christ.)*

26 But Jerusalem which is above is free *(presents the origin of Salvation, which is Heaven, and proclaims its results, which are "freedom")*, which is the mother of us all. *(This refers to all who are true Christians, whether Jews or Gentiles.)*

27 For it is written *(Isa. 54:1)*, Rejoice, *you* barren who bears not; break forth and cry, you who travail not *(speaks of the Church, grafted in because of Grace, in the place of Israel, which demanded Law and which God would not accept)*: for the desolate has many more children than she which has an husband. *(This pertains to Sarah who was barren which, in one sense of the word and the culture of that day, was the same as not having a husband, even though she was married to Abraham. It also refers to the Church, which in effect had no husband, as did Israel, i.e., "God." The Church has many more children than Israel ever had!)*

28 Now we *(Believers)*, Brethren, as Isaac was, are the Children of Promise. *(The Promise is a picture of the Messiah, Who came through the lineage of Isaac to grant deliverance to people bound in sin.)*

29 But as then he who was born after the flesh *(Ishmael)* persecuted him *who was born* after the Spirit *(Isaac)*, even so *it is* now. *(Isaac and Ishmael symbolized the new and the old nature in the Believer. Hagar and Sarah typified the two Covenants of works and Grace, of bondage and Liberty, even as Paul is explaining here.)*

30 Nevertheless what says the Scripture? *(Gen. 21:10)* Cast out the bondwoman and her son *(the birth of the new nature demands the expulsion of the old; it is im-*

possible to improve the old nature; it must be cast out, i.e., "placed in a dormant position"; this can only be done by the Believer evidencing constant Faith in the Cross, which then gives the Holy Spirit latitude to bring about this necessary work): for the son of the bondwoman shall not be heir with the son of the freewoman. (Paul is giving a dramatic illustration of the irreconcilable conflict between Salvation by works and Salvation by Faith.)

31 So then, Brethren, we are not children of the bondwoman (Hagar, Ishmael, and the Law), but of the free. (We are not children of the Law, but rather free children of Faith.)

CHAPTER 5

BONDAGE

STAND fast therefore in the liberty wherewith Christ has made us free (we were made free, and refers to freedom to live a Holy life by evidencing Faith in Christ and the Cross), and be not entangled again with the yoke of bondage. (To abandon the Cross and go under Law of any kind guarantees bondage once again to the sin nature.)

CHRIST OF NO EFFECT

2 Behold ("mark my words!"),

I Paul say unto you (presents the Apostle's authority regarding the Message he brings), that if you be circumcised, Christ shall profit you nothing. (If the Believer goes back into Law, and Law of any kind, what Christ did at the Cross on our behalf will profit us nothing. One cannot have it two ways.)

3 For I testify again to every man who is circumcised (some of the Galatian Gentiles were being pressured by false teachers to embrace the Law of Moses, which meant they would have to forsake Christ and the Cross, for it's not possible to wed the two; as well, it's not possible to wed any Law to Grace), that he is a debtor to do the whole Law (which of course is impossible; and besides, the Law contained no Salvation).

4 Christ is become of no effect unto you (this is a chilling statement, and refers to anyone who makes anything other than Christ and the Cross the object of his faith), whosoever of you are justified by the Law (seek to be Justified by the Law); you are fallen from Grace (fallen from the position of Grace, which means the Believer is trusting in something other than the Cross; it actually means, "to apostatize").

5 For we through the Spirit (the Holy Spirit works exclusively within the parameters of the Sacrifice of Christ; consequently, He

demands that we place our Faith exclusively in the Cross of Christ) wait for the Hope of Righteousness *(which cannot come about until the Resurrection)* by Faith *(refers to Faith in Christ and what He did for us at the Cross)*.

6 For in Jesus Christ neither Circumcision avails anything, nor uncircumcision *(has no spiritual bearing on anything)*; but Faith which works by Love. *(The evidence of true Faith is the fact of the Love which emanates from such Faith.)*

GRACE

7 You did run well *(under the Ministry of Paul, the Galatians had begun well)*; who did hinder you that you should not obey the truth? *(Paul is referring to false teachers who were attempting to pull the Galatians away from the Cross to other things.)*

8 This persuasion *comes* not of Him *(the Holy Spirit)* Who calls you. *(What you are doing is not Biblical!)*

9 A little leaven *(corruption)* leaveneth *(corrupts)* the whole lump. *(The introduction of a small amount of false doctrine will ultimately consume the entirety of the belief system.)*

10 I have confidence in you through the Lord, that you will be none otherwise minded *(that* the Galatians would not abandon the Cross for this false doctrine)*: but he who troubles you shall bear his judgment, whosoever he be. *(Judgment will ultimately come on those who attempt to present a way of Salvation other than Christ and the Cross.)*

11 And I, Brethren, if I yet Preach Circumcision, why do I yet suffer persecution? *(Any message other than the Cross draws little opposition.)* then is the offence of the Cross ceased. *(The Cross offends the world and most of the Church. So, if the Preacher ceases to Preach the Cross as the only way of Salvation and Victory, then opposition and persecution will cease. But so will Salvation!)*

12 I would they were even cut off which trouble you. *(They might cease from the land, but unfortunately false teachers seem to ever plague the landscape.)*

LIBERTY

13 For, Brethren, you have been called unto liberty *(liberty from the Law, and to live a Holy life)*; only *use* not liberty for an occasion to the flesh *(because you are living under Grace, do not think sin is inconsequential)*, but by love serve one another. *(This is Paul's constant concern. How will you use your freedom? How will you live your new life?)*

14 For all the Law is fulfilled in one word, *even* in this *(presents the Apostle telling us how the Law is fulfilled in our lives)*; You shall love your neighbour as yourself. *(In this, the whole Law stands fully obeyed. This can be done, and in fact will be done, providing the Believer ever makes the Cross of Christ the object of his Faith. Accordingly, the Holy Spirit will then provide the power for us to do what we should do.)*

15 But if you bite and devour one another *(which will be done if the Believer seeks to live under Law)*, take heed that you be not consumed one of another. *(If Love is absent, this tells us that the Cross is absent. Fighting and quarreling always follow the Law.)*

VICTORY

16 *This* I say then, Walk *(order your behavior)* in the Spirit *(we do so by placing our Faith exclusively in Christ and the Cross, through which the Spirit works exclusively [Rom. 8:1-2])*, and you shall not fulfil the lust of the flesh. *(This proves the existence of the sin nature in the Believer. It declares the consciousness of corrupt desires. As stated, the only way to not fulfill the lust of flesh is for our Faith to be placed exclusively in the Cross.)*

17 For the flesh *(in this case, evil desires)* lusteth against the spirit *(is the opposite of the Holy Spirit)*, and the Spirit against the flesh *(it is the Holy Spirit Alone, who can subdue the flesh; He does so, as we have repeatedly stated, by our Faith being placed exclusively in the Cross)*: and these are contrary the one to the other *(these two can never harmonize; as Paul has stated, the old nature must be cast out, which the Holy Spirit Alone can do)*: so that you cannot do the things that you would. *(Without the Holy Spirit, Who works by the Cross, the Believer cannot live a Holy life.)*

18 But if you be led of the Spirit, you are not under the Law. *(One cannot follow the Spirit and the Law at the same time, but regrettably that's what most modern Christians are attempting to do. Unless one properly understands the Cross as it regards Sanctification, one cannot be properly "led of the Spirit," Who works exclusively within the framework of the Finished Work of Christ.)*

19 Now the works of the flesh are manifest, which are *these (if one attempts to function by means of Law of any nature, the "works of the flesh" will be manifested in one's life)*; Adultery, fornication, uncleanness, lasciviousness,

20 Idolatry, witchcraft, hatred, variance, emulations, wrath, strife, seditions, heresies,

21 Envyings, murders, drunkenness, revellings, and such like *(if one is walking after the flesh [Rom. 8:1], one or more of these sins will manifest themselves in one's life; the only way, and I mean the only way, one can walk in perpetual victory is to understand that everything we receive from God comes to us by means of the Cross; consequently, the Cross must ever be the object of our Faith; this being the case, the Holy Spirit, Who works exclusively within the confines of the Sacrifice of Christ, will exert His mighty Power on our behalf, which will enable us to live a Holy life)*: of the which I tell you before, as I have also told *you* in time past *(refers to the fact that the Apostle was not afraid to name specific sins)*, that they which do such things shall not inherit the Kingdom of God. *(This tells us in no uncertain terms that if our Faith is not everlastingly in Christ and the Cross, we simply won't make it. God doesn't have two ways of Salvation and Victory, only one, and that is "Jesus Christ and Him Crucified.")*

FRUIT OF THE SPIRIT

22 But the Fruit of the Spirit *(are not "fruits" but rather "Fruit"; they are to be looked at as a "whole," which means they grow equally)* is love, joy, peace, longsuffering, gentleness, goodness, Faith,

23 Meekness, temperance: against such there is no Law. *(Against such there doesn't need to be a Law. But let the Reader understand that this "Fruit" is of the "Holy Spirit," and not of man. It can only develop as we are "led of the Spirit." And we can only be led by the Spirit by making the Cross the object of our Faith.)*

A SPIRITUAL LIFE

24 And they who are Christ's have Crucified the flesh with the affections and lusts. *(This can be done only by the Believer understanding it was carried out by Christ at the Cross, and our being "Baptized into His Death" [Rom. 6:3-5]. That being the case, and as repeatedly stated, the Cross must ever be the object of our Faith, which alone will bring about these results.)*

25 If we live in the Spirit, let us also walk in the Spirit *("walk" refers to our lifestyle; this Passage declares both life and Holiness to be the work of the Holy Spirit; He operates Salvation and He operates Sanctification; both are realized on the Principle of Faith, and that refers to the Cross ever being the object of our Faith; many know they have received spiritual life, as it regards Salvation through Faith, but they think they can only secure Sanctification by works; this is a great*

error; it never brings victory; believing in Christ and the Cross for Sanctification, as well as for Justification, introduces one into a life of power and victory, which is the only way it can be accomplished.)

26 Let us not be desirous of vain Glory *(which is a sign that one is functioning according to Law)*, provoking one another *(self-righteousness)*, envying one another. *(These are works of the flesh, and will manifest themselves if our Faith is in things other than the Cross.)*

CHAPTER 6

RESTORATION

BRETHREN, if a man be overtaken in a fault *(pertains to moral failure, and is brought about because one has ignorantly placed himself under Law; such a position guarantees failure)*, you which are Spiritual *(refers to those who understand God's Prescribed Order of Victory, which is the Cross)*, restore such an one *(tell him he failed because of reverting to Law, and that Victory can be his by placing his Faith totally in the Cross, which then gives the Holy Spirit latitude to work, Who Alone can give the Victory)* in the spirit of meekness *(never with an overbearing, holier-than-thou attitude)*; considering yourself, lest you also be tempted *(the implica-* tion is that if we do not handle such a case Scripturally, we thereby open the door for Satan to attack us in the same manner as he did the failing brother).*

2 Bear ye one another's burdens *(refers to sharing the heartache and shame of one who has spiritually failed)*, and so fulfil the Law of Christ *(which is Love!)*.

3 For if a man think himself to be something, when he is nothing *(refers to a Believer who puts himself above the one who has failed in his own eyes)*, he deceives himself. *(This presents one who has the conceited idea he is morally and spiritually superior to what he actually is.)*

4 But let every man prove his own work *(to put his Faith in the Cross to the test for the purpose of approving, which is done by seeing how well one obeys the Word of the Lord)*, and then shall he have rejoicing in himself alone *(the spiritual man sees himself as he really is, totally dependent on Christ and the Cross)*, and not in another. *(He will not then be rejoicing over the other man's failure.)*

5 For every man shall bear his own burden. *(When each Believer sees his own failings, which we all have, he will have no inclination to compare himself with others, at least as it regards a superior position.)*

6 Let him who is taught in the

Word (*refers to the act of receiving instruction*) communicate unto him who teaches in all good things. (*Let us not make the load of the God-called Teacher heavier by hindering him in some way, but rather let us encourage him.*)

TWO DESTINIES

7 Be not deceived (*refers to the fact that a Believer can definitely be deceived; Paul is speaking primarily of Believers allowing false teachers to move their faith from the Cross to other things*); God is not mocked (*God, in fact, is mocked when we substitute something else in place of the Cross*): for whatsoever a man sows, that shall he also reap (*the Law of sowing and reaping, which will unfailingly come to pass*).

8 For he who sows to his flesh shall of the flesh reap corruption (*those who make something else the object of their Faith, rather than the Cross, which means they are now depending on self-will*); but he who sows to the Spirit (*does so by trusting exclusively in Christ and what Christ did at the Cross*) shall of the Spirit reap life everlasting (*God's prescribed Order of Victory*).

GLORIFY GOD

9 And let us not be weary in well doing (*Paul continues to speak of "sowing to the Spirit"*): for in due season we shall reap (*in God's time, our Faith in Christ and the Cross will not go unrewarded, but will bring forth exactly that which is Promised by the Lord*), if we faint not. (*Many start the race, but do not finish. They give up after a while, exclaiming that the "Cross" doesn't work. Let all know and understand that we might fail, but the Cross never fails!*)

10 As we have therefore opportunity, let us do good unto all *men* (*the Holy Spirit will help us do this, providing our Faith is ever in the Cross; otherwise, we will fail*), especially unto them who are of the household of Faith. (*There are many who are of the Faith, but really do not understand the Faith, so they walk in defeat. We are to give them the Message of the Cross, in order that they might walk in perpetual Victory [Rom. 8:2].*)

11 You see how large a letter I have written unto you with my own hand. (*This refers to the fact that Paul had written the entirety of the Epistle to the Galatians himself, which he normally did not do. Scribes generally wrote as he dictated, with him writing the postscript and signing his name.*)

THE CROSS

12 As many as desire to make

a fair show in the flesh, they constrain you to be Circumcised *(the Judaizers were attempting to get the Galatians to embrace the Law along with Christ)*; only lest they should suffer persecution for the Cross of Christ. *(The Message of the Cross brings forth persecution from both the world and the Church. It strikes at the very heart of all spiritual pride and self-righteousness.)*

13 For neither they themselves who are Circumcised keep the Law *(engaging in the rite of Circumcision, which was the seal of the Law of Moses, didn't help anyone keep the Law)*; but desire to have you Circumcised, that they may Glory in your flesh. *(Many in the Church glory in self-effort, but few glory in the Cross because it puts self-effort in its proper place.)*

14 But God forbid that I should Glory *(boast)*, save in the Cross of our Lord Jesus Christ *(what the opponents of Paul sought to escape at the price of insincerity is the Apostle's only basis of exultation)*, by Whom the world is Crucified unto me, and I unto the world. *(The only way we can overcome the world, and I mean the only way, is by plac-*ing our Faith exclusively in the Cross of Christ and keeping it there.)*

15 For in Christ Jesus neither Circumcision availeth any thing, nor uncircumcision *(blows all of man's religious ceremonies to pieces)*, but a new creature *(new in every respect, which can only be brought about by trusting Christ and what He did for us at the Cross)*.

16 And as many as walk *(to direct one's life, to order one's conduct)* according to this rule *(the principle of the Cross)*, peace *be* on them, and mercy *(which comes only by means of the Cross)*, and upon the Israel of God. *(This refers to all who look to the Cross for their Redemption. They alone are the true Israel.)*

17 From henceforth let no man trouble me *(don't listen to these false teachers)*: for I bear in my body the marks of the Lord Jesus. *(This concerns the persecution he suffered because of the "offence of the Cross" [5:11].)*

18 Brethren, the Grace of our Lord Jesus Christ *(which comes by our Faith in the Cross)* be with your spirit. *(We worship the Lord in Spirit and in Truth, and the Cross is that Truth.)* Amen.

THE EPISTLE OF PAUL THE APOSTLE TO THE
EPHESIANS

CHAPTER 1

INTRODUCTION

PAUL, an Apostle of Jesus Christ *(the Apostle stands as the de facto leader of the Church, and does so by the special Message he brings; with Paul, it was Grace)* by the Will of God *(the Foundation of Paul's Calling)*, to the Saints *(which one instantly becomes upon accepting Christ)* which are at Ephesus *(to those Saints and all others as well, and for all time)*, and to the Faithful in Christ Jesus *(ever Faithful in making the Cross the object of one's Faith)*:

2 Grace *be* to you, and peace *(which come by means of the Cross)*, from God our Father *(a privilege of untold proportions)*, and *from* the Lord Jesus Christ *(proclaims the Saviour in association with the Father)*.

SPIRITUAL BLESSINGS

3 Blessed *be* the God *(we should ever bless the Lord for what He has done for us)* and Father of our Lord Jesus Christ *(God is the Father of Christ, as Christ is seen in His humanity)*, Who has blessed us with all spiritual blessings *(every benefit of the Atonement)* in Heavenly *places* in Christ *(the Divine Blessing has its ground and reason in Christ; it is ours by reason of our being "in Him," which was brought about by the Cross)*:

4 According as He has chosen us in Him *(does not refer to the person being chosen, but rather the purpose for which the person is chosen)* before the foundation of the world *(the Creator, in laying His Plans for the world, had the purpose of Redeeming Grace in view)*, that we should be Holy and without blame before Him in Love *(presents the purpose of the "chosen")*:

5 Having predestinated us unto the adoption of children *(does not refer to the individual being predestinated as to whether he will be saved or lost, but rather the manner in which one becomes a Child of God)* by Jesus Christ to Himself *(by means of the Cross)*, according to the good pleasure of His Will *(it is an act of sovereignty, but an act based on love)*,

6 To the praise of the Glory of His Grace *(the ultimate reason)*, wherein He has made us accepted *(made possible by the*

Cross) in the beloved *(in Christ)*.

7 In Whom *(in Christ)* we have Redemption through His Blood *(the outpoured Blood of the Son of God at the Cross is the price for Redemption)*, the forgiveness of sins *(a remission of their penalty)*, according to the riches of His Grace *(the riches of that Grace gave us the Cross)*;

8 Wherein He has abounded toward us *(refers to God's Grace being manifested toward us in superabundance, again made possible by the Cross)* in all wisdom *(insight)* and prudence *(to solve the problems of each moment of time)*;

9 Having made known unto us the mystery of His Will *(refers to the secret purposes and counsels God intends to carry into effect in His Kingdom)*, according to His good pleasure *(extended to Believers)* which He has purposed in Himself *(originated in His Own Mind)*:

10 That in the dispensation of the fulness of times *(concerns itself with a well ordered plan)* He might gather together in one all things in Christ *(the Atonement addressed not only man's Fall, but the revolution of Lucifer as well)*, both which are in Heaven *(where the revolution of Lucifer began)*, and which are on earth *(the Fall of man)*; even in Him *(made possible by what Christ did at the Cross)*:

11 In Whom *(Christ)* also we have obtained an inheritance *(the best Greek Texts have, "we were designated as a heritage"; thus, the Saints are God's Heritage, His Possession through the Work of Christ on the Cross)*, being predestinated according to the purpose of Him *(pertains to the inheritance being predestinated, not the individual who would obtain the inheritance)* Who works all things after the Counsel of His Own Will *(therefore it is perfect)*:

12 That we should be to the praise of His Glory *(proclaims that which is guaranteed to be, not what is hoped to be)*, who first trusted in Christ. *(We will attain all of this by first trusting in Christ, which means accepting what He did for us at the Cross.)*

13 In Whom *(Christ)* you also trusted, after that you heard the Word of Truth *(pertains to the Message of the Cross [I Cor. 1:18])*, the Gospel of your Salvation *(the good news provided by the Cross)*: In Whom *(Christ)* also after that you believed *(believed in what Christ did for us at the Cross)*, you were sealed with that Holy Spirit of Promise *(made possible by the Cross)*,

14 Which is the earnest *(down payment)* of our inheritance *(but with a guarantee that it all will come at the Resurrection)* until the Redemption of the purchased

possession *(bought by the Blood of Christ, and will be totally fulfilled at the Resurrection)*, unto the praise of His Glory. *(This refers to that which God has done, and will do, which is a victory of astounding proportions.)*

PRAYER

15 Wherefore I also, after I heard of your Faith in the Lord Jesus *(day-by-day Faith exercised in the Lord Jesus for daily living)*, and love unto all the Saints *(it is only those who do not depend on the Finished Work of the Cross, who lack in love)*,

16 Cease not to give thanks for you *(is used some 23 times in one way or the other in Paul's Epistles)*, making mention of you in my prayers *(a habit of the Apostle — his intercessory prayer life)*;

17 That the God of our Lord Jesus Christ, the Father of Glory *(refers to our Lord in His humanity as worshiping and being obedient to God the Father)*, may give unto you the Spirit of Wisdom and Revelation in the knowledge of Him *(knowledge of Christ, which we receive through the Word, enables the Holy Spirit to increase our "Wisdom and Revelation")*:

18 The eyes of your understanding being enlightened *(could be translated, "The eyes of your heart having been enlightened with the present result that they are in a state of illumination")*; that you may know what is the hope of His calling *(in a sense, actually points to what the hope really is)*, and what the riches of the glory of His inheritance in the Saints *(speaks now not of the Saint's inheritance, but rather God's inheritance; the Saints are that inheritance)*,

19 And what *is* the exceeding greatness of His power to usward who believe *(power to live a Holy life; who believe in Christ and what He has done at the Cross)*, according to the working of His mighty power *(it works for us according to our Faith in the Finished Work of Christ, and by no other means)*,

20 Which He *(God the Father)* wrought in Christ, when He raised Him from the dead *(which He did by the Power of the Holy Spirit)*, and set *Him* at His Own Right Hand in the Heavenly *places (refers to the highest place of honor, dignity, and authority, and means that the Sacrifice of Christ was totally accepted)*,

21 Far above all principality, and power, and might, and dominion *(proclaims the exalted position of Christ)*, and every name that is named, not only in this world, but also in that which is to come *(Christ is given this exalted position, and will retain it*

forever, because of the Cross):

22 And has put all *things* under His feet *(He thus fulfills the destiny for which man was originally created)*, and gave Him *to be* the Head over all *things* to the Church *(He is the absolute, ultimate authority, because of the Cross)*,

23 Which is His Body *(the Church has its Source of Life in Him, sustained and directed by His Power, the instrument also by and through which He works)*, the fulness of Him that fills all in all. *(As Christ was the True Israel, and is the True Man, He is also the True Church.)*

CHAPTER 2

ALIVE IN CHRIST

A ND you *has He quickened (made alive)*, who were dead in trespasses and sins *(total depravity due to the Fall and original sin)*;

2 Wherein in time past you walked according to the course of this world *(refers to the fact that the unredeemed order their behavior and regulate their lives within this sphere of trespasses and sins)*, according to the prince of the power of the air *(pertains to the fact that Satan heads up the system of this world)*, the spirit that now works in the children of disobedience *(the spirit of Satan, which fills all unbelievers, thereby working disobedience)*:

3 Among whom *(the children of disobedience)* also we all had our conversation *(manner of life)* in times past in the lusts of our flesh *(evil cravings)*, fulfilling the desires of the flesh and of the mind *(the minds of the unredeemed are the laboratory of perverted thoughts, impressions, imaginations, etc.)*; and were by nature the children of wrath, even as others. *God's wrath is unalterably opposed to sin, and the only solution is the Cross.)*

4 But God, Who is rich in Mercy *(His Mercy comes to us by means of the Cross)*, for His great love wherewith He loved us *(the Love shown at Calvary)*,

5 Even when we were dead in sins *(speaks of a state in which we could by no means help ourselves)*, has quickened us together with Christ *(this new life is imparted to us through our identification with Christ in His Death and Resurrection)*, (by Grace you are saved;) *(Grace is made possible solely by the Cross, and comes to us in an uninterrupted flow as we ever make the Cross the object of our Faith.)*

6 And has raised *us* up together *(the Resurrection of Christ from the Tomb was our Resurrection as well, spiritually speaking, and gave us "newness of life" [Rom. 6:3-5])*, and made *us* sit together in Heavenly *places (made possible by the Cross)* in Christ Jesus *(it is all done in Christ, and refers to the*

way He did it, which is through the Cross):

7 That in the ages to come *(in the ages that are coming, one upon another, unending)* He might show the exceeding riches of His Grace *(presents the Believer's golden age is always future, never past)* in His kindness toward us through Christ Jesus. *(God is able to show us kindness only through the Cross. The Bible Student must realize the Cross is the oldest Doctrine in the Bible [I Pet. 1:18-20], and is in fact the Foundation on which all Doctrine must be built.)*

REDEMPTION

8 For by Grace *(the Goodness of God)* are you Saved through Faith *(Faith in Christ, with the Cross ever as its object)*; and that not of yourselves *(none of this is of us, but all is of Him)*: it is the Gift of God *(anytime the word "Gift" is used, God is speaking of His Son and His substitutionary work on the Cross, which makes all of this possible)*:

9 Not of works *(man cannot merit Salvation, irrespective what he does)*, lest any man should boast *(boast in his own ability and strength; we are allowed to boast only in the Cross [Gal. 6:14])*.

10 For we are His workmanship *(if we are God's workmanship, our Salvation cannot be of*

ourselves), created in Christ Jesus unto good works *(speaks of the results of Salvation, and never the cause)*, which God has before ordained that we should walk in them. *(The "good works" the Apostle speaks of has to do with Faith in Christ and the Cross, which enables the Believer to live a Holy life.)*

UNITY

11 Wherefore remember, that you *being* in time past Gentiles in the flesh, who are called Uncircumcision *(referred to the Gentiles not being in Covenant with God; physical Circumcision under the Old Economy was its external sign)* by that which is called the Circumcision in the flesh made by hands *(is said by Paul in this manner, regarding the Jews, in contradistinction from the Circumcision of the heart)*;

12 That at that time you were without Christ *(describes the former condition of the Gentiles, who had no connection with Christ before the Cross)*, being aliens from the commonwealth of Israel, and strangers from the Covenants of Promise, having no hope, and without God in the world *(all of this argues a darkened and perverted heart; the Gentiles had no knowledge of God at that time)*:

13 But now in Christ Jesus *(proclaims the basis of all Salvation)*

you who sometimes *(times past)* were far off *(far from Salvation)* are made nigh *(near)* by the Blood of Christ. *(The Sacrificial Atoning Death of Jesus Christ transformed the relations of God with mankind. In Christ, God reconciled not a nation, but "a world" to Himself [II Cor. 5:19].)*

14 For He *(Christ)* is our peace *(through Christ and what He did at the Cross, we have peace with God)*, Who has made both one *(Jews and Gentiles)*, and has broken down the middle wall of partition *between us (between Jews and Gentiles)*;

15 Having abolished in His Flesh *(speaking of His Death on the Cross, by which He Redeemed humanity, which also means He didn't die spiritually, as some claim)* the enmity *(the hatred between God and man, caused by sin)*, *even* the Law of Commandments *contained* in Ordinances *(pertains to the Law of Moses, and more particularly the Ten Commandments)*; for to make in Himself of twain *(of Jews and Gentiles)* one new man, *so* making peace *(which again was accomplished by the Cross)*;

16 And that He *(Christ)* might reconcile both *(Jews and Gentiles)* unto God in one body *(the Church)* by the Cross *(it is by the Atonement only that men ever become reconciled to God)*, having slain the enmity thereby *(removed the bar-rier between God and sinful man)*:

17 And came and preached peace to you which were afar off *(proclaims the Gospel going to the Gentiles)*, and to them who were nigh. *(This refers to the Jews. It is the same Message for both.)*

18 For through Him *(through Christ)* we both *(Jews and Gentiles)* have access by One Spirit unto the Father. *(If the sinner comes by the Cross, the Holy Spirit opens the door, otherwise it is barred [Jn. 10:1].)*

19 Now *(speaks of the present state of Believers)* therefore you are no more strangers and foreigners *(pertains to what Gentiles once were)*, but fellowcitizens with the Saints *(speaks of Gentiles now having access the same as Jews, all due to the Cross)*, and of the Household of God *(a progressive relationship with God in Christ)*;

20 And are built upon the Foundation *(the Cross)* of the Apostles and Prophets *(Apostles serve as leadership under the New Covenant, with Prophets having served in that capacity under the Old)*, Jesus Christ Himself being the Chief Corner Stone *(presents the part of the Foundation which holds everything together; Jesus Christ is the "Chief Corner Stone" by virtue of what He did at the Cross)*;

21 In Whom *(Christ)* all the building fitly framed together

grows unto an Holy Temple in the Lord:

22 In Whom you also are built together *(Jews and Gentiles)* for an habitation of God through the Spirit. *(This is all made possible by what Jesus did at the Cross.)*

CHAPTER 3

REVELATION

FOR this cause I Paul, the prisoner of Jesus Christ *(Paul wrote this Epistle from prison in Rome; as well, he didn't consider himself a prisoner of Nero, but rather of Jesus Christ; in other words, for whatever purpose and reason, the Lord wanted him at this time in prison, and that's the way that Paul looked at the situation)* for you Gentiles *(refers to the beginning of the Church, which was made up mostly of Gentiles, and the giving of the Gospel to the world),*

2 If you have heard of the dispensation of the Grace of God which is given me to you-ward *(presents the Apostle as having oversight or management over the New Covenant, and the proper administration of its presentation):*

3 How that by Revelation He *(Christ)* made known unto me the mystery *(the Cross, which in essence is the New Covenant, was a "mystery" before its meaning was given to Paul);* (as I wrote afore in few words *(evidently the Apostle*

had written a previous letter to the Ephesians concerning this great Truth, of which we now have no record),*

4 Whereby, when you read *(what we are now reading, as it regards this Epistle)*, you may understand my knowledge in the Mystery of Christ) *(The Lord wants us to understand the Mystery of the Cross, as it was given to Paul. In other words, we are not to deviate from what he taught.)*

5 Which in other ages was not made known unto the sons of men *(speaks of the entirety of time, up unto the Apostle Paul)*, as it is now revealed unto His Holy Apostles and Prophets by the Spirit *(Paul was given this Revelation first [Gal. 1:11-12], with the Spirit of God then using the Message as given to Paul to enlighten other Apostles and Prophets, etc.);*

6 That the Gentiles should be fellowheirs *(refers to the fact that all differences between Jews and Gentiles, regarding Redemption, have been erased)*, and of the same body *(everyone in the same Church, i.e., "Body of Christ")*, and partakers of His Promise in Christ by the Gospel *(should have been translated, "In Christ Jesus by the Gospel," for the best Greek Texts include the Name "Jesus"; if that latter Name wasn't there, Paul would be saying the Gentiles were fellowpartakers of the Jewish Messianic*

Promises, which are not true):

7 Whereof I was made a Minister *(refers to one who serves),* according to the Gift of the Grace of God given unto me *(all of this was granted to Paul strictly according to the Grace of God, which means it was not because of his merit, for he had none)* by the effectual working of His power. *(This is the Power of the Holy Spirit, made available to us by the Cross and our Faith in that Finished Work [Gal. 1:18].)*

8 Unto me, who am less than the least of all Saints, is this Grace given *(humility is made evident here, which can only be made possible by the Cross, through which Grace comes to us),* that I should Preach among the Gentiles the unsearchable riches of Christ *(the "riches of Christ" come to us exclusively by and through the Cross, and are inexhaustible, with greater and greater enlargement which will last forever);*

9 And to make all *men* see *(to bring to light something which had previously been hidden)* what *is* the fellowship of the Mystery *(could be translated, "the fellowship of the dispensation of the Revelation of the Mystery"; in other words, the Mystery is no more, having now been revealed),* which from the beginning of the world has been hid in God *(proclaims to us the fact that this was not a new kind of action* on the part of God, forced upon Him by the developments in human history; the Cross was His Plan from before the Foundation of the World [I Pet. 1:18-20]),* Who created all things by Jesus Christ *(God the Father officiates; God the Son orchestrates; God the Holy Spirit executes):*

10 To the intent that now unto the Principalities and Powers in Heavenly *places (concerns Righteous Angels)* might be known by the Church the manifold Wisdom of God *(presents the Church proclaiming to the Angelic Host a part of the Wisdom of God not previously known to the Angels),*

11 According to the eternal purpose *(the purpose of the ages)* which He purposed in Christ Jesus our Lord *(God has formed a Plan which is Eternal in reference to the Salvation of men, and the Plan is centered on the Lord Jesus and what He did at the Cross):*

12 In Whom *(refers to Christ, but more particularly to what He did at the Cross for us)* we have boldness *(because of the Cross, we can now have a boldness in our approach to God [Heb. 4:16])* and access *(the only way we can have access to the Throne of God is by and through Jesus Christ and His Atoning Work on the Cross)* with confidence by the Faith of Him. *("The Faith" is wrapped up in Jesus Christ and His Cross.)*

BLESSINGS

13 Wherefore I desire that you faint not at my tribulations for you *(don't let your Faith weaken because of my imprisonment)*, which is your glory. *(Whatever happens to me will ultimately fall out to a greater proclamation of the Gospel, which will be for your good.)*

14 For this cause *(the spread of the Gospel)* I bow my knees unto the Father of our Lord Jesus Christ *(Paul is saying he bows to the Will of God, whatever that Will might be)*,

15 Of Whom *(the Lord Jesus Christ)* the whole family *(all who have accepted Christ)* in Heaven and earth is named *(all Believers who have gone on to be with the Lord, and all Believers now alive on Earth)*,

16 That He *(Christ Jesus)* would grant you, according to the riches of His Glory *(refers to all the revealed perfections of God, not merely His Grace and Power)*, to be strengthened with might by His Spirit *(this will be done, providing our Faith is ever in the Cross, by and through which the Holy Spirit works)* in the inner man *(the spirit of man)*;

17 That Christ may dwell in your hearts by Faith *(which is accomplished by our Faith in the Cross)*; that you, being rooted and grounded in love *(securely settled and deeply founded)*,

18 May be able to comprehend with all Saints *(means not only to understand, but as well, "to lay hold of so as to make one's own")* what is the breadth, and length, and depth, and height *(metaphors used by Paul to explain the vastness of God's Love for the Saints)*;

19 And to know the Love of Christ *(speaks of knowledge gained by experience)*, which passes knowledge *(the Believer can know the Love of Christ, but cannot exhaust the knowledge of that Love)*, that you might be filled with all the fulness of God *(can come to us only through Christ, and what Christ did for us at the Cross)*.

20 Now unto Him Who is able *(presents God as the Source of all Power)* to do exceeding abundantly above all that we ask or think *(so far beyond our comprehension that the Holy Spirit could give us this explanation only in these terms)*, according to the power that works in us *(the word "according" refers to the fact that this Power can work in us only as we follow God's prescribed Order of Victory, which is the Cross and our Faith in that Finished Work; this then gives the Holy Spirit the latitude to use His Great Power on our behalf)*,

21 Unto Him be Glory *(Christ and the Church as one Body will be the vehicle of that eternal demonstration)* in the Church *(the*

Body of Christ) by Christ Jesus *(made possible by our Lord and what He did at the Cross)* through- out all ages, world without end *(Eternal).* Amen.

CHAPTER 4

OUR DAILY WALK

I therefore, the prisoner of the Lord *(as stated, the Apostle is in prison in Rome; he regards himself as having been made a prisoner be- cause the Lord so willed and ordered it),* beseech you that you walk wor- thy of the vocation wherewith you are called *(refers to the order of one's behavior; to walk right, the Believer must "walk after the Spirit," which can only be done by understanding that all strength and help come to us through the Cross, thereby ever making the Cross the object of our Faith),*

2 With all lowliness and meek- ness, with longsuffering, forbear- ing one another in love *(once again, all of these things are works of the Spirit, which means they cannot be done within our own ability; the help of the Spirit comes to us by our Faith being constant in the Cross [I Cor. 1:17-18, 23]);*

3 Endeavouring to keep the unity of the Spirit *(speaks of unity as it regards Faith in Christ and the Cross)* in the bond of peace *(Faith in things other than Christ and the*

Cross destroys peace, because it en- genders self-righteousness).

4 *There is* one body *(the body of called-out Believers),* and one Spirit *(one Holy Spirit, Who always works through Christ and the Cross [Jn. 16:13-14]; this means that Faith in things other than the Cross is not of the Holy Spirit, but rather of spir- its),* even as you are called in one hope of your calling *(our total hope is in Christ Jesus and what He has done for us at the Cross; that is our "one" and only "hope");*

5 One Lord *(Jesus Christ),* one Faith *(what He did at the Cross),* one Baptism *(our Salvation, re- ferring to Believers Baptized into Christ, which was done at the Cross; it has nothing to do with Water Baptism [Rom. 6:3-5]),*

6 One God and Father of all *(speaks of the Redeemed only; God is not the Father of the unsaved, as Jesus plainly said; their father is actually the Devil [Jn. 8:44]),* Who is above all *(refers to supremacy),* and through all *(God's creative abilities),* and in you all *(by vir- tue of what Christ did for us at the Cross, and our Faith in that Fin- ished Work).*

THE GIFT OF CHRIST

7 But unto every one of us is given Grace *(however, this Grace can be frustrated by Believers turn- ing away from the Cross to other*

things [Gal. 2:21]) according to the measure of the Gift of Christ (*measured to each Saint according to need unless, as stated, it is frustrated*).

8 Wherefore He said (*Ps. 68:18*), When He ascended up on high (*the Ascension*), He led captivity captive (*liberated the souls in Paradise; before the Cross, despite being Believers, they were still held captive by Satan because the blood of bulls and goats could not take away the sin debt; but when Jesus died on the Cross, the sin debt was paid, and now He makes all of these His captives*), and gave Gifts unto men. (*These "Gifts" include all the Attributes of Christ, all made possible by the Cross.*)

9 (Now that He ascended (*mission completed*), what is it but that He also descended first into the lower parts of the earth? (*Immediately before His Ascension to Glory, which would be done in total triumph, He first went down into Paradise to deliver all the believing souls in that region, which He did!*)

10 He Who descended is the same also Who ascended (*this is a portrayal of Jesus as Deliverer and Mediator*) up far above all Heavens (*presents His present location, never again having to descend into the nether world*), that He might fill all things.) (*He has always been the Creator, but now He is also the Saviour.*)

11 And He gave (*our Lord does the calling*) some, Apostles (*has reference to the fact that not all who are called to be Ministers will be called to be Apostles; this applies to the other designations as well; "Apostles" serve as the de facto leaders of the Church, and do so through the particular Message given to them by the Lord for the Church*); and some, Prophets (*who stand in the Office of the Prophet, thereby foretelling and forthtelling*); and some, Evangelists (*to gather the harvest*); and some, Pastors (*Shepherds*) and Teachers (*those with a special Ministry to teach the Word to the Body of Christ; "Apostles" can and do function in all of the callings*);

PURPOSE OF THE GIFTS

12 For the perfecting of the Saints (*to "equip for service"*), for the work of the Ministry (*to proclaim the Message of Redemption to the entirety of the world*), for the edifying of the Body of Christ (*for the spiritual building up of the Church*):

13 Till we all come in the unity of the Faith (*to bring all Believers to a proper knowledge of Christ and the Cross*), and of the knowledge of the Son of God (*which again refers to what He did for us at the Cross*), unto a perfect man (*the Believer who functions in maturity*), unto the measure of the stat-

ure of the fulness of Christ *(the "measure" is the "fullness of Christ," which can only be attained by a proper Faith in the Cross)*:

14 That we *henceforth* be no more children *(presents the opposite of maturity, and speaks of those whose Faith is in that other than the Cross)*, tossed to and fro, and carried about with every wind of doctrine, by the sleight of men *(Satan uses Preachers)*, and cunning craftiness *(they make a way, other than the Cross, which seems to be right)*, whereby they lie in wait to deceive *(refers to a deliberate planning or system)*;

15 But speaking the Truth in Love *(powerfully proclaiming the Truth of the Cross, but always with Love)*, may grow up into Him in all things *(proper Spiritual Growth can take place only according to proper Faith in the Cross [I Cor. 1:21, 23; 2:2])*, which is the Head, *even* Christ *(Christ is the Head of the Church, and is such by virtue of the Cross)*:

16 From Whom *(Christ Jesus)* the whole body *(Christ as the Head, and the Church as the Body)* fitly joined together *(presents the foot in the place it ought to be, and the eye in its proper place, etc.)* and compacted by that which every joint supplies *(one part is dependent on the other)*, according to the effectual working in the measure of every part *(every part labors to* produce a great result)*, making increase of the body unto the edifying of itself in love *(building itself up; will happen when we function according to God's prescribed order, which is the "unity of the Faith"; again, refers to a proper understanding of the Cross)*.

MORAL STANDARDS

17 This I say therefore, and testify in the Lord *(given to him by the Lord as it regards our everyday lifestyle)*, that you henceforth walk not as other Gentiles walk *(how one orders one's behavior)*, in the vanity of their mind *(refers to living in the sphere of emptiness; it denotes an ignorance of Divine things, a moral blindness)*,

18 Having the understanding darkened *(speaks of a process completed in the past [the Fall] but having results in the present)*, being alienated from the life of God *(proclaims the only true life there is)* through the ignorance that is in them *(does not refer merely to intellect, but denotes an ignorance of Divine things)*, because of the blindness of their heart *(it is a "willful ignorance" which brings about a "willful blindness," i.e., "spiritual blindness")*:

19 Who being past feeling *(moral insensibility, which brings about man's inhumanity to man)* have given themselves over unto

lasciviousness (*a complete surrender of self unto evil*), to work all uncleanness with greediness (*such a person is greedy for such a lifestyle*).

20 But you have not so learned Christ (*stands in contrast to the insensitive, passion-dominated pagans who exist only to satisfy their lower nature; in other words, the Lord saves us from sin, not in sin*);

21 If so be that you have heard Him (*the point is, "Since it was Christ you heard Preached"*), and have been taught by Him (*should have been translated, "in Him," i.e., "in this sphere of Christ"*), as the Truth is in Jesus (*the Truth is not only "in Jesus," it as well "is Jesus" [Jn. 14:6]*):

22 That you put off (*which can be done only by one placing his Faith exclusively in the Cross*) concerning the former conversation (*concerning the former manner of life*) the old man (*refers to the unsaved person dominated by the totally depraved nature [Rom. 6:6]*), which is corrupt according to the deceitful lusts (*the unsaved person is subject to a continuous process of corruption, which grows worse as time goes on*);

23 And be renewed (*a continuous act*) in the spirit of your mind (*has to do with the human will; the mind of the Believer must be pulled from a dependence on self to a total dependence on Christ, which can only be done by making*

the Cross, ever the Cross, the object of one's Faith [Rom. 12:1-2]*);

24 And that you put on the new man (*we are a "new man" by virtue of being Baptized into His Death, Buried with Him by Baptism into Death, all speaking of the Crucifixion, and being Raised with Him in "newness of life" [Rom. 6:3-5]*), which after God is created in Righteousness and true Holiness. (*This is what the "new man" is supposed to be, and what he can be, but only by reckoning himself to be dead indeed unto the sin nature [which was done at the Cross], but alive unto God through Jesus Christ our Lord [Rom. 6:11].*)

25 Wherefore putting away lying (*the first item to be included in the putting off of the "old self" is falsehood, which refers to believing something other than Christ and the Cross; in other words, everything other than Christ and Him Crucified is a "lie"*), speak every man truth with his neighbour (*the Truth is Christ and the Cross, which brings about Righteousness and True Holiness*): for we are members one of another. (*Therefore, we should all speak the same thing, which is Christ and the Cross.*)

26 Be ye angry, and sin not: let not the sun go down upon your wrath (*the only "anger" allowed is Righteous anger; all other anger is a result of the "old man," and must be "put off"; it has to do ba-*

sically with our emotions, which can only be properly settled by the Holy Spirit; meaning for Him to work, we must ever have the Cross as the object of our Faith):

27 Neither give place to the Devil. (Faith properly placed in the Cross gives Satan no place.)

28 Let him who stole steal no more (Christlikeness gives high moral standards): but rather let him labour, working with his hands the thing which is good (we are to earn our living by whatever honest method is at our disposal), that he may have to give to him who needs. (Instead of taking from others, we can now give to others.)

29 Let no corrupt communication proceed out of your mouth (let no slander or faithlessness proceed out of your mouth), but that which is good to the use of edifying (does what we are saying build up or tear down?), that it may Minister Grace unto the hearers (a Blessing).

30 And grieve not the Holy Spirit of God (proclaims the fact that the utterance of evil or worthless words is repugnant to the Holiness of the Spirit), whereby you are sealed unto the Day of Redemption. (This should have been translated, "In Whom you are sealed unto the Day of Redemption." The Holy Spirit is Himself the Seal God has placed on us.)

31 Let all bitterness, and wrath, and anger, and clamour, and evil speaking, be put away from you, with all malice (as the Believer puts His Faith in the Cross and keeps his Faith in the Cross, giving the Holy Spirit latitude to work, these evil things can then be "put away" from our lives):

32 And be you kind one to another, tenderhearted, forgiving one another (be quick to forgive), even as God for Christ's sake has forgiven you. (Christ's forgiveness of us is to always be the basis of our forgiveness of others.)

CHAPTER 5

COMMANDS

BE ye therefore followers of God, as dear children (we do so by obeying the Word of God, and we do that by keeping our Faith in the Cross);

2 And walk in love (be constantly ordering your behavior within the sphere of love), as Christ also has loved us (presents the Apostle passing from the Father to the Son as our example), and has given Himself for us an Offering and a Sacrifice to God for a sweetsmelling Savour. (Christ fulfilled all the symbolic Blood Offerings of the Levitical system [Heb. 10:8]. He fulfilled those by becoming an Offering for sin on the Cross. The "sweetsmelling Savor" describes the aton-

ing Sacrifice as accepted by God.)

SINS

3 But fornication, and all uncleanness, or covetousness, let it not be once named among you, as becomes Saints;

4 Neither filthiness, nor foolish talking, nor jesting, which are not convenient *(out of character)*: but rather giving of thanks. *(The Believer's protection against all these sins is the Cross of Christ, and the Cross alone. Keeping the Cross as the object of one's Faith guarantees Victory [Gal. 6:14], and for that we are ever to give thanks to God.)*

BE NOT PARTAKERS

5 For this you know, that no whoremonger, nor unclean person, nor covetous man, who is an idolater, has any inheritance in the Kingdom of Christ and of God *(Paul is speaking to Believers! if the Cross is not the object of Faith for the Believer, but rather something else, these Passages plainly tell us such a Believer will actually come to the place of unbelief and lose his soul; the only answer for the "Law of sin and death" is the "the Law of the Spirit of Life in Christ Jesus" [Rom. 8:2]).*

6 Let no man deceive you with vain words *(by trying to pull you away from the Cross)*: for because of these things comes the Wrath of God upon the children of disobedience *(the Cross alone stops the Wrath of God).*

7 Be not ye therefore partakers with them. *(Never forsake the Cross, no matter how enticing the other things might look.)*

COMMANDS

8 For you were sometimes darkness *(everyone who doesn't know Christ is in spiritual darkness)*, but now *(since coming to Christ) are you* light in the Lord *(we are a reflection of the Light of Christ)*: walk as children of Light *(order your behavior accordingly)*:

9 (For the Fruit of the Spirit *(Gal. 5:22-23) is* in all goodness and Righteousness and Truth;) *(This proclaims the end results of the "Fruit of the Spirit.")*

10 Proving what is acceptable unto the Lord *(put to the test, and the Cross alone will stand the test).*

11 And have no fellowship with the unfruitful works of darkness *(the Scripture teaches separation, but not isolation)*, but rather reprove them *(speak out boldly and forcibly against them).*

12 For it is a shame even to speak of those things which are done of them in secret. *(Paul's writings always emphasized the exceeding sinfulness of sin, but never more evidently than here.)*

13 But all things that are reproved are made manifest by the Light *(it is only Christ and the Cross which can adequately portray what sin actually is; that's the reason much of the Church doesn't care for the Cross!)*: for whatsoever does make manifest is light. *(The Cross alone manifests sin and all its evil effects.)*

14 Wherefore He said *(Isa. 60:1)*, Awake thou who sleeps *(the Apostle is warning Christians that they should stir themselves from lethargy and apathy)*, and arise from the dead *(dead to the things of the Spirit)*, and Christ shall give you Light. *(Christ will pour upon you the Light of Divine Truth as the Sun gives light to men aroused from sleep.)*

15 See then that you walk circumspectly *(carefully taking heed)*, not as fools *(a person who doesn't avail himself of all Christ has to offer is a fool)*, but as wise *(draw close to the Lord)*,

16 Redeeming the time *(take advantage of the opportunities that present themselves)*, because the days are evil. *(The Cross must be our Foundation. Only then can we overcome the "evil," and carry out that which the Lord has called us to do.)*

17 Wherefore be ye not unwise *(time is precious because God has given us only a few short days to make choices that will bring Eternal consequences)*, but understanding what the will of the Lord is.

(We can do this if we look exclusively to Christ and the Cross.)

18 And be not drunk with wine *(speaks of being controlled by alcoholic beverage, which Paul desires to use as an example)*, wherein is excess; but be filled with the Spirit *(being controlled by the Spirit constantly, moment by moment)*;

19 Speaking to yourselves in Psalms and Hymns and Spiritual Songs *(refers to worship as it regards songs and singing)*, singing and making melody in your heart to the Lord *(places the approval of the Holy Spirit on the same forms of music and styles of worship as were begun in the Old Testament)*;

20 Giving thanks always for all things unto God and the Father *(all things which come from God)* in the Name of our Lord Jesus Christ *(proclaims in this Verse the Source of all Blessings, and the means by which these Blessings have come upon the human race as well)*;

21 Submitting yourselves one to another *(this tells us that proper spiritual submission is always horizontal and never vertical as it refers to Believers, meaning that we submit one to another)* in the fear of God *(meaning that all vertical submission must be to God Alone, never to man)*.

WIVES

22 Wives, submit yourselves

unto your own husbands *(the Holy Spirit, through the Apostle, is relating to the spiritual leadership of the family)*, as unto the Lord. *(First of all, the submission is to be to Christ as Lord and Master, and not to the husband. If the husband's supremacy had been in view, it would have been expressed in a different manner, so say the Greek Scholars. If the wife properly submits to the Lord, she will properly submit to her husband as it regards spiritual leadership, that is if he knows the Lord. If he doesn't know the Lord, such submission cannot be tendered, as would be obvious.)*

23 For the husband is the head of the wife, even as Christ is the Head of the Church *(suggests the obedience the wife renders to her husband is to be regarded as obedience rendered to Christ, which she can do if her husband is properly following the Lord)*: and He is the Saviour of the Body. *(This refers to the Lord being the Saviour of Believers, who make up the Church. While the husband cannot be the Saviour of his wife in redemptive terms, he can be her protector and provider.)*

24 Therefore as the Church is subject unto Christ *(as its Head)*, so *let* the wives *be* to their own husbands in everything. *(This presupposes that the husband is conducting himself even as Christ.)*

HUSBANDS

25 Husbands, love your wives *(with a God kind of love)*, even as Christ also loved the Church *(presents the qualifier; if a husband conducts himself accordingly toward his wife, she will have no problem whatsoever submitting to him, even as she should)*, and gave Himself for it *(presents the great Sacrifice which characterizes the God kind of love; the answer for marriage problems is not marriage seminars, but rather that both husband and wife place their Faith and confidence totally in Christ and what He has done for us at the Cross; in other words, the Cross alone, which refers to what Jesus did there, is the answer)*;

26 That He might sanctify and cleanse it *(speaks of the view to the final presentation of the Church in perfect Holiness at the Coming Great Day)* with the washing of water by the Word *(actually means the "Word" washes and cleanses one exactly as water)*,

27 That He might present it to Himself *(it is Christ Himself Who is to present the Church, and He is to present it to Himself)* a glorious Church *(made possible by the Cross)*, not having spot, or wrinkle, or any such thing *(which the Cross alone can do)*; but that it should be Holy and without blemish. *(This is our position in Christ, made possible by the Cross.)*

28 So ought men to love their wives as their own bodies *(is proclaimed in this manner because "they are one flesh," even as Paul will say in Verse 31)*. He who loves his wife loves himself *(proclaims the oneness of the Sacred union of marriage)*.

29 For no man ever yet hated his own flesh; but nourishes and cherishes it, even as the Lord the Church *(the Holy Spirit here is using the union of husband and wife to symbolize the union of Christ and the Church)*:

30 For we are members of His Body, of His Flesh, and of His Bones. *(We are visible parts of that Body of which He is Head, and this is the reason He nourishes and cherishes the Church. "His Flesh" and "His Bones" speak of the Incarnation, and the giving of Himself on the Cross, which made it possible for us to become part of Him [Rom. 6:3-5].)*

31 For this cause shall a man leave his father and mother *(while he certainly continues to love his father and mother, his primary love is now for his wife)*, and shall be joined unto his wife, and they two shall be one flesh. *(The union that is meant to symbolize Christ and the Church.)*

32 This is a great Mystery *(had not been heretofore revealed)*: but I speak concerning Christ and the Church. *(This presents the spiritual fact that a Believer can become one with Christ as a member of His Body, symbolized by the husband-wife relationship.)*

33 Nevertheless let every one of you in particular so love his wife even as himself *(the husband is to love the wife as being part and parcel of himself, according to the Divine idea of the marriage union)*; and the wife *see* that she reverence *her* husband. *(This means to recognize and respect his position as spiritual leader of the family. If the husband or wife makes demands on the partner Christ Alone can meet, which is the cause of most problems in marriages, the pressure will become intolerable. No human being can fulfill what Christ Alone can do.)*

CHAPTER 6

DUTIES OF CHILDREN

CHILDREN, obey your parents in the Lord: for this is right. *(This means to be under authority. As well, it refers to parents who know God. If not, they are to be obeyed as far as possible, but not in that which violates the Scripture.)*

2 Honour your father and mother *(all of this is important because family Government is designed to be an imitation of the Government of God)*; (which is the first Commandment with Promise;)

3 That it may be well with you, and you may live long on the earth ([Deut. 5:16; Ex. 20:12], as should be obvious, failure to obey carries a penalty).

FATHERS

4 And, you Fathers, provoke not your children to wrath (refers to the fact that Fathers are to raise their children in love and not the opposite): but bring them up in the nurture and admonition of the Lord (raised according to the ways of the Lord, i.e., His Word).

SERVANTS AND MASTERS

5 Servants (slaves), be obedient to them who are your masters according to the flesh (the slave owners were masters as it pertained to the task at hand, but that only; the Lord was the Master of the soul and the spirit of the individual, and the eternal well-being also), with fear and trembling (actually refers to fear and trembling before the Lord), in singleness of your heart, as unto Christ (consider an order by the slave master as an order from Christ);

6 Not with eyeservice, as menpleasers (pertains to service which is done only when one is under the Master's eye, but something else when he is not watching); but as the Servants of Christ (they were to look at themselves as servants of Christ, not of men; this spirit will render excellent service to men), doing the Will of God from the heart (it is the Will of God that we conduct ourselves like Christ);

7 With good will doing service, as to the Lord, and not to men (this means every employee, irrespective whom his employer might be, is to function in his task, whatever it might be, as though he is doing it to the Lord):

8 Knowing that whatsoever good thing any man does, the same shall he receive of the Lord, whether he be bond or free. (Even though conscientious service may not always be rewarded by earthly employers, it definitely will not be overlooked by the Lord.)

9 And, you masters, do the same things unto them, forbearing threatening (means that Christian Masters, of which there definitely were some, were to treat their Christian slaves, or any slave for that matter, with kindness and respect): knowing that your Master also is in Heaven (thereby overlooking both the employer and the employee in using today's terminology); neither is there respect of persons with Him. (He looks at one as he looks at the other.)

SPIRITUAL WARFARE

10 Finally, my Brethren, be

strong in the Lord *(be continually strengthened, which one does by constant Faith in the Cross)*, and in the power of His Might. *(This power is at our disposal. The Source is the Holy Spirit, but the means is the Cross [I Cor. 1:18].)*

11 Put on the whole armour of God *(not just some, but all)*, that you may be able to stand against the wiles of the Devil. *(This refers to the "stratagems" of Satan.)*

12 For we wrestle not against flesh and blood *(our foes are not human; however, Satan constantly uses human beings to carry out his dirty work)*, but against principalities *(rulers or beings of the highest rank and order in Satan's kingdom)*, against powers *(the rank immediately below the "Principalities")*, against the rulers of the darkness of this world *(those who carry out the instructions of the "Powers")*, against spiritual wickedness in high *places. (This refers to demon spirits.)*

RESOURCES

13 Wherefore take unto you the whole armour of God *(because of what we face)*, that you may be able to withstand in the evil day *(refers to resisting and opposing the powers of darkness)*, and having done all, to stand. *(This refers to the Believer not giving ground, not a single inch.)*

14 Stand therefore, having your loins gird about with Truth *(the Truth of the Cross)*, and having on the breastplate of Righteousness *(the Righteousness of Christ, which comes strictly by and through the Cross)*;

15 And your feet shod with the preparation of the Gospel of Peace *(peace comes through the Cross as well)*;

16 Above all, taking the shield of Faith *(ever making the Cross the object of your Faith, which is the only Faith God will recognize, and the only Faith Satan will recognize)*, wherewith you shall be able to quench all the fiery darts of the wicked. *(This represents temptations with which Satan assails the Saints.)*

17 And take the Helmet of Salvation *(has to do with the renewing of the mind, which is done by understanding that everything we receive from the Lord, comes to us through the Cross)*, and the Sword of the Spirit, which is the Word of God *(the Word of God is the story of Christ and the Cross)*:

18 Praying always with all prayer and supplication in the Spirit *(an incessant pleading until the prayer is answered [Lk. 18:1-8])*, and watching thereunto *(being sensitive to what the Holy Spirit desires)* with all perseverance *(don't stop)* and supplication *(petitions and requests)* for all Saints *(Saints pray-*

ing for other Saints);

19 And for me *(pray for me),* that utterance may be given unto me *(pray that the Lord would anoint him to Preach and Teach),* that I may open my mouth boldly *(refers to being fearless and confident in the presentation of the Gospel),* to make known the Mystery of the Gospel *(to properly Preach and Teach the New Covenant, which is the story of the Cross),*

20 For which I am an Ambassador *(for Christ)* in bonds *(a prisoner):* that therein I may speak boldly, as I ought to speak *(that he would not allow the persecution to stop him from Preaching as he should Preach).*

BENEDICTION

21 But that you also may know my affairs, *and* how I do, Tychicus, a beloved Brother and Faithful Minister in the Lord, shall make known to you all things *(evidently, Tychicus was with Paul for a period of time while he was imprisoned in Rome; he would inform the Ephesians of Paul's state):*

22 Whom I have sent unto you for the same purpose, that you might know our affairs, and *that* he might comfort your hearts.

23 Peace *be* to the Brethren, and Love with Faith *(presents Love springing forth from Faith, which ever speaks of the Cross as its object),* from God the Father and the Lord Jesus Christ. *(This refers to the fact that what all Believers receive from God the Father comes through the Lord Jesus Christ, with the Cross being the means of such things.)*

24 Grace *be* with all them who love our Lord Jesus Christ in sincerity. *(If the Love is sincere, it will be based strictly in the Cross of Christ.)* Amen.

THE EPISTLE OF PAUL THE APOSTLE TO THE
PHILIPPIANS

CHAPTER 1

INTRODUCTION

PAUL and Timothy, the servants of Jesus Christ *(refers to both men being bound to Jesus Christ by the bands of a constraining love)*, to all the Saints in Christ Jesus which are at Philippi *(to those who are "set apart" unto Christ)*, with the Bishops *(Pastors)* and Deacons:

2 Grace *be* unto you, and peace, from God our Father, and *from* the Lord Jesus Christ. *(The Cross makes both attributes possible.)*

THANKSGIVING

3 I thank my God upon every remembrance of you *(does not refer to disconnected recollections, but his total past experience with the Philippians)*,

4 Always in every prayer of mine for you all *(proclaims the Apostle continually praying for these people, even as he prayed for all the other Churches)* making request with joy *(Paul was not interceding for this Church because of problems, but rather for continued Blessing)*,

5 For your fellowship in the Gospel *(the idea is the Philippians supported Paul with their prayers and finances while he went about his Missionary labors)* from the first day until now *(refers to the faithfulness of these Philippians)*;

6 Being confident of this very thing *(refers to both their growth in Christ and their continued financial support)*, that He *(the Holy Spirit)* which has begun a good work in you will perform *it* until the Day of Jesus Christ *(the Rapture of the Church)*:

7 Even as it is meet *(necessary)* for me to think this of you all, because I have you in my heart; inasmuch as both in my bonds, and in the defence and confirmation of the Gospel *(the ground of his confidence)*, you all are partakers of my Grace *(God had indeed made them His Own)*.

8 For God is my record *(One Who bears Testimony)*, how greatly I long after you all in the bowels of Jesus Christ. *(This refers to the compassion of Christ.)*

9 And this I pray *(Paul prayed about everything)*, that your love may abound yet more and more *(the Love that God is)* in knowledge *(knowledge of the Cross)* and

in all judgment *("discernment,"*
which is a spiritual and moral sense
or feeling);

10 That you may approve things
that are excellent *(to approve by*
testing); that you may be sincere
(pure) and without offence *(noth-*
ing in one's life that would give
cause to stumble, which can only
be done by exhibiting Faith in the
Cross) till the Day of Christ *(the*
Rapture of the Church);

11 Being filled with the Fruits
of Righteousness *(should have*
been translated, "Fruit of Righteous-
ness"), which are by Jesus Christ
(through what He did at the Cross),
unto the Glory and Praise of God.
(When we place our Trust in Christ
and the Cross, it brings "Glory and
Praise to God.")

TRIUMPH

12 But I would you should
understand, Brethren, that the
things *which happened* unto me
have fallen out rather unto the
furtherance of the Gospel *(Paul*
wrote this Epistle from prison in
Rome);

13 So that my bonds in Christ
(he was a prisoner because of his
relationship to Christ; the next
question would be, "who is Christ?")
are manifest in all the palace, and
in all other *places (not only the*
members of the Praetorian guard
who had custody of Paul, but the
whole Praetorium itself, and all its
judges and officials are included in
this statement);

14 And many of the Brethren
in the Lord, waxing confident by
my bonds *(many Christians in*
Rome had been persuaded by the
brave example of Paul in prison),
are much more bold to speak the
Word without fear. *(This refers to*
having overcome the tendency to-
wards silence.)

15 Some indeed Preach Christ
even of envy and strife *(in other*
words, they were opposed to Paul
in their Preaching, and for what-
ever reason); and some also of
good will *(some tried to help Paul*
in their Preaching):

16 The one preach Christ of
contention, not sincerely *(they*
have an agenda which is not of God),
supposing to add affliction to my
bonds *(these Preachers, whomever*
they may have been, were seeking
to make Paul's imprisonment even
worse than it already was):

17 But the other of love *(by*
pointing to those Preachers who in
fact did have Love, Paul is at the
same time saying the Preachers of
the previous Verse did not have
love), knowing that I am set for
the defence of the Gospel. *(The*
Gospel must not only be preached,
it must be defended against false
doctrine as well. This, most Preach-
ers will not do!)

18 What then? *(This does not*

mean Paul condoned the activities of these rogue Preachers, but that he did not allow it to bother him.) notwithstanding, every way, whether in pretence, or in truth, Christ is Preached (Paul was quite satisfied that the servant should be denounced and the Master announced; at least some good is being done! even though these rogue Preachers would have silenced Paul, he would not have reciprocated in kind, which is the attitude of the true Preacher); and I therein do rejoice, yes, and will rejoice. (This presents the idea that some people will get some knowledge of Christ, even from these rogue Preachers, which is better than nothing.)

19 For I know that this shall turn to my Salvation through your prayer (should have been translated "deliverance"), and the supply of the Spirit of Jesus Christ (Paul is referring to the Holy Spirit, and that He will supply whatever is needed, but that He is able to do such only through Christ and what He did at the Cross, which makes it all possible; hence him using the terminology he did),

CHRIST

20 According to my earnest expectation and my hope (describes a person with head erect and outstretched, whose attention is turned away from all other objects and riveted upon just one), that in nothing I shall be ashamed (whichever way it goes, his release or his execution, he will hold up Christ to the end), but that with all boldness, as always, so now also Christ shall be magnified in my body, whether it be by life, or by death. (Whatever the Lord wants is what the Apostle wants. This is total consecration!)

21 For to me to live is Christ (Paul being allowed to live longer makes it possible for him to continue to Preach Christ), and to die is gain. (He is saying it would be gain for him, but not for the Work of God.)

22 But if I live in the flesh (refers to him continuing to live in his physical body, which tells us it will be different in Heaven), this is the Fruit of my labour (souls being saved and lives being changed by the Message of the Cross): yet what I shall choose I wot not. (This actually means that if he had his choice, he is not certain which he would choose, to remain here longer or to go on to be with Christ.)

23 For I am in a strait betwixt two (refers to equal pressure being exerted from both sides; he is speaking here of his personal desires, and not necessarily that which the Lord would desire; however, he has already made it clear his personal will is to be swallowed up in the sweet Will of God), having a

desire to depart, and to be with Christ; which is far better *(the centerpiece of all of this is Christ; if one draws any other conclusions, one misses the point entirely)*:

24 Nevertheless to abide in the flesh *is* more needful for you. *(For Paul to continue to live and Preach the Gospel would be of great value to the Church, as would be obvious, at least until his work was finished.)*

25 And having this confidence *(he believes the Lord has told him he will be released from prison)*, I know that I shall abide and continue with you all for your furtherance and joy of Faith *(the Apostle is saying, "The Servant of the Lord is immortal until his work is done")*;

26 That your rejoicing may be more abundant in Jesus Christ for me *(presents Paul as the human instrument through which this teaching would come as it referred to Jesus Christ)* by my coming to you again. *(Without Paul, this advance in the Faith would probably not be brought about.)*

EXHORTATION

27 Only let your conversation *(lifestyle)* be as it becomes the Gospel of Christ *(refers to their behavior; they were to conduct themselves in a manner worthy of the Gospel, and could do so by ever look-* *ing to the Cross)*: that whether I come and see you, or else be absent, I may hear of your affairs, that you stand fast in one spirit, with one mind *(not be moved from Christ and the Cross, to other things)* striving together for the Faith of the Gospel *("The Faith" is "Christ and Him Crucified," and we must strive to hold it true; every attack by Satan, and in whatever capacity, is against the Cross and our Faith in that Finished Work)*;

28 And in nothing terrified by your adversaries *(those who would Preach another Jesus, by another spirit, presenting another Gospel [II Cor. 11:4])*: which is to them an evident token of perdition, but to you of Salvation, and that of God. *(Salvation from God, which is through Christ and the Cross, is evidenced by persecution.)*

29 For unto you it is given in the behalf of Christ, not only to believe on Him, but also to suffer for His sake *(the world opposes the Cross, and so does most of the Church)*;

30 Having the same conflict which you saw in me *(in essence speaks of the Christian struggle of Faith; the struggle is never so much with sin, as it is of Faith [I Tim. 6:12])*, and now hear *to be* in me *(refers to his present incarceration in Rome, which was a test of his Faith)*.

CHAPTER 2

EXALTATION

IF *there be* therefore any consolation in Christ *(should have been translated, "since there is consolation [encouragement] in Christ"),* if any comfort of love *(having the God kind of love),* if any fellowship of the Spirit *(refers to a common interest and a mutual and active participation in the things of God, in which the Believer and the Holy Spirit are joint-participants),* if any bowels and mercies *(being tenderhearted and having compassion),*

2 Fulfil ye my joy *(the Spiritual Growth of the Philippians would be his joy),* that you be likeminded *(unity of mind and of heart),* having the same love *(the God kind of Love),* being of one accord, of one mind. *(If the Cross of Christ is the object of such Faith, these things will be done.)*

3 *Let* nothing *be done* through strife or vainglory *(forming sides);* but in lowliness of mind let each esteem other better than themselves *(which a correct viewpoint of the Cross will bring about).*

4 Look not every man on his own things *(means to look only at one's own things),* but every man also on the things of others *(an interest in the affairs of others).*

5 Let this mind be in you *(refers to the self-emptying of Christ),* which was also in Christ Jesus *(portrays Christ as the supreme example):*

6 Who, being in the form of God *(refers to Deity, which Christ always was),* thought it not robbery to be equal with God *(equality with God refers here to our Lord's co-participation with the other members of the Trinity in the expression of the Divine Essence):*

7 But made Himself of no reputation *(instead of asserting His rights to the expression of the Essence of Deity, our Lord waived His rights to that expression),* and took upon Him the form of a servant *(a bond slave),* and was made in the likeness of men *(presents the Lord entering into a new state of Being when He became Man; but His becoming Man did not exclude His position of Deity; while in becoming Man, He laid aside the "expression" of Deity, He never lost "possession" of Deity):*

8 And being found in fashion as a man *(denotes Christ in men's eyes),* He humbled Himself *(He was brought low, but willingly),* and became obedient unto death *(does not mean He became obedient to death; He was always the Master of Death; rather, He subjected Himself to death),* even the death of the Cross. *(This presents the character of His Death as one of disgrace and degradation, which*

was necessary for men to be re-deemed. This type of death alone would pay the terrible sin debt, and do so in totality.)

9 Wherefore God also has highly exalted Him *(to a place of supreme Majesty; Jesus has always been Creator, but now He is Sav-iour as well)*, and given Him a Name which is above every name *(actually says, "The Name," refer-ring to a specific Name and Title; that Name, as Verse 11 proclaims, is "Lord")*:

10 That at the Name of Jesus every knee should bow *(in the sphere of the Name, which refers to all it entails; all of this is a result of the Cross, the price paid there, and the Redemption conse-quently afforded)*, of *things* in Heaven, and *things* in Earth, and *things* under the earth *(all Cre-ation will render homage, whether animate or inanimate)*;

11 And *that* every tongue should confess that Jesus Christ *is* Lord *(proclaims "Lord" as the "Name" of Verse 9; it means "Master" of all, which again has been made possible by the Cross)*, to the Glory of God the Father. *(The acknow-ledgment of the Glory of Christ is the acknowledgment of the Glory of the Father.)*

LIGHTS

12 Wherefore, my beloved, as you have always obeyed *(he com-mends them for their constant obe-dience)*, not as in my presence only, but now much more in my absence *(they continued to obey the Gospel, even though Paul was not personally present among them)*, work out your own Salvation with fear and trembling. *(This refers to going on to maturity, to the ulti-mate conclusion of total Christlike-ness.)*

13 For it is God which works in you *(Divine enablement)* both to will and to do of *His* good plea-sure. *(This refers to the Holy Spirit, Who energizes the Saint, making him not only willing, but also ac-tively desirous of doing God's sweet Will.)*

14 Do all things without mur-murings *(mutterings of discontent)* and disputings *(questioning the Word of God, which is brought on by "murmurings")*:

15 That you may be *(may be-come)* blameless and harmless, the sons of God, without rebuke, in the midst of a crooked and perverse nation *(what the Holy Spirit expects of us)*, among whom you shine as lights in the world *(the Saints are to be luminaries, which can only be done by constant-ly exhibiting Faith in the Cross)*;

16 Holding forth the Word of Life *(holding forth so as to offer)*; that I may rejoice in the Day of Christ *(Rapture of the Church)*,

that I have not run in vain, neither laboured in vain (*that the Gospel has not been wasted on these people; regrettably, it is wasted with many, if not most*).

17 Yes, and if I be offered upon the Sacrifice and service of your Faith (*I'll give myself for you*), I joy, and rejoice with you all. (*The rejoicing is in their Faith properly placed in the Cross of Christ.*)

18 For the same cause also do you joy, and rejoice with me.

COMMENDATION

19 But I trust in the Lord Jesus to send Timothy shortly unto you (*he was a disciple of Paul*), that I also may be of good comfort, when I know your state. (*The Apostle desired up-to-date information regarding the Church at Philippi.*)

20 For I have no man likeminded (*the Apostle is saying most Preachers had wrong agendas*), who will naturally care for your state (*speaks of a heart that has one thing in mind, that is doing the Will of God*).

21 For all seek their own (*doesn't mean there were no genuine Preachers in Rome, but there were none of the caliber he needed*), not the things which are Jesus Christ's (*again pertains to the Will of God in all matters*).

22 But you know the proof of him (*Timothy's character has met the test, and has been approved*), that, as a son with the father, he has served with me in the Gospel (*the original Greek says, "as a son to a Father"*).

23 Him therefore I hope to send presently (*refers to a delay, but it is hoped it will not be long*), so soon as I shall see how it will go with me. (*As soon as he knows his status, as it regards his release or continued incarceration, he will send Timothy.*)

24 But I trust in the Lord that I also myself shall come shortly. (*It seems this expectation was fulfilled, for Paul was released a short time later.*)

25 Yet I supposed it necessary to send to you Epaphroditus (*presents the Brother who brought the Love-Offering from the Philippians to Paul in Rome*), my Brother, and companion in labour, and fellow-soldier, but your messenger (*accolades given by Paul, but yet sanctioned by the Holy Spirit*), and he who ministered to my wants. (*The Apostle held the service of Epaphroditus in high regard.*)

26 For he longed after you all, and was full of heaviness (*due to his sickness*), because that you had heard that he had been sick. (*This indicates that Epaphroditus is now much improved.*)

27 For indeed he was sick nigh unto death (*he almost died*): but God had mercy on him (*proclaims

the manner in which everything is received from God — all by the Mercy of God); and not on him only, but on me also, lest I should have sorrow upon sorrow. *(This proclaims the fact that if the man had died, it would have been a great loss to the Apostle and to the Work of God.)*

28 I sent him therefore the more carefully *(Paul hopes to send Epaphroditus to Philippi very soon),* that, when ye see him again, you may rejoice *(presents the fact of the recovery or the healing of this man),* and that I may be the less sorrowful *(Paul's sorrow has been alleviated).*

29 Receive him therefore in the Lord with all gladness *(it seems there had been a problem in the Church in Philippi as it regards Epaphroditus, but the man has so proven himself to Paul that the Apostle can recommend him highly);* and hold such in reputation *(give honor to whom honor is due, and Epaphroditus is to be held in honor):*

30 Because for the work of Christ he was nigh unto death, not regarding his life *(it seems he became very ill because of overwork),* to supply your lack of service toward me. *(This evidently refers to something the Philippians couldn't do because of circumstances, but which Epaphroditus did on their behalf.)*

CHAPTER 3

FALSE TEACHERS

FINALLY, my Brethren, rejoice in the Lord *(as long as they keep their eyes on Christ and the Cross, they can keep rejoicing).* To write the same things to you, to me indeed *is* not grievous, but for you *it is* safe. *(This presents the Apostle now turning his attention to the Judaizers, who might at any time turn their attention toward Philippi.)*

2 Beware of dogs *(the Apostle is addressing the Judaizers, who were Jews from Jerusalem that claimed Christ, but insisted on Believers keeping the Law as well; all of this was diametrically opposed to Paul's Gospel of Grace, in which the Law of Moses had no part; as well, by the use of the word "dogs," the Apostle was using the worst slur),* beware of evil workers *(they denigrated the Cross),* beware of the concision. *(This presents a Greek word Paul uses as a play upon the Greek word "Circumcision," which was at the heart of the Law Gospel of the Judaizers.)*

3 For we are the Circumcision *(refers to the true Circumcision, which is that of the heart),* which worship God in the Spirit *(would have been better translated, "which worship by the Spirit of God"),* and rejoice in Christ Jesus *(refers not*

only to Who Christ is, but what He has done for us at the Cross), and have no confidence in the flesh *(in things other than the Cross, which alone is the guarantee of Salvation and Victory).*

4 Though I might also have confidence in the flesh *(refers to human attainments).* If any other man thinks that he has whereof he might trust in the flesh, I more *(the Apostle knows what he's talking about regarding Judaism):*

PAUL

5 Circumcised the eighth day, of the stock of Israel *(he was a pure-blooded Jew),* of the Tribe of Benjamin *(Benjamin was the only Tribe that stayed with Judah at the time of the division of the nation),* an Hebrew of the Hebrews *(goes all the way back to Abraham);* as touching the Law, a Pharisee *(in fact, Paul had been the hope of the Pharisees, touted to take the place of Gamaliel);*

6 Concerning zeal, persecuting the Church *(he thought he was doing God a service);* touching the Righteousness which is in the Law, blameless. *(He thought he was earning merit with God by persecuting the Church.)*

7 But what things were gain to me *(Paul was speaking of his privileges as a Jew),* those I counted loss for Christ. *(All must be given up for Christ, and Christ is worth all we give up, and a thousand times more.)*

8 Yes doubtless, and I count all things *but* loss for the excellency of the knowledge of Christ Jesus my Lord *(the knowledge of the Lord Jesus which Paul gained through the experience of intimate companionship and communion with Him):* for Whom I have suffered the loss of all things *("For Whose Sake I have been caused to forfeit"),* and do count them *but* dung, that I may win Christ *(next to Christ, everything else is nothing),*

9 And be found in Him *(to be united with Christ by a living Faith, which has as its object the Cross of Christ),* not having my own Righteousness *("not having any Righteousness which can be called my own"),* which is of the Law *(pertains to Law-keeping; he was done with that),* but that which is through the Faith of Christ *(what He did at the Cross),* the Righteousness which is of God by Faith *(a spotless Righteousness made possible by the Cross, and imputed by God to all who exhibit Faith in Christ and the Cross):*

10 That I may know Him *(referring to what Christ did at the Cross),* and the power of His Resurrection *(refers to being raised with Him in "Newness of Life" [Rom. 6:3-5]),* and the fellowship of His sufferings *(regarding our*

Trust and Faith placed in what He did for us at the Cross), being made conformable unto His death *(to conform to what He did for us at the Cross, understanding that this is the only means of Salvation and Sanctification)*;

11 If by any means I might attain unto the Resurrection of the dead. *(This does not refer to the coming Resurrection, but rather the Believing sinner being baptized into the death of Christ [refers to the Crucifixion], and raised in "Newness of Life," which gives victory over all sin [Rom. 6:3-5, 11, 14].)*

12 Not as though I had already attained, either were already perfect *(the Apostle is saying he doesn't claim sinless perfection)*: but I follow after *(to pursue)*, if that I may apprehend *(Paul is pursuing absolute Christlikeness)* that for which also I am apprehended of Christ Jesus. *(He was Saved by Christ for the purpose of becoming Christlike, and so are we!)*

13 Brethren, I count not myself to have apprehended *(in effect, repeats what he said in the previous Verse)*: but this one thing I do, forgetting those things which are behind *(refers to things the Apostle had depended upon to find favor with God, and the failure that type of effort brought about [3:5-6])*, reaching forth unto those things which are before *(all our attention must be on that which*

is ahead, and not on what is past; "those things" consists of all the victories of the Cross)*,

14 I press toward the mark *(this represents a moral and Spiritual target)* for the prize of the high calling of God *(Christlikeness)* in Christ Jesus *(proclaims the manner and means in which all of this is done, which is the Cross [I Cor. 1:17-18; 2:2])*.

UNITY

15 Let us therefore, as many as be perfect *(mature)*, be thus minded *(have our minds on what Christ has done at the Cross, and was done for us)*: and if in anything you be otherwise minded, God shall reveal even this unto you. *(This means some were actually otherwise minded. But through the words of Paul, the Holy Spirit was going to show them the right way, which is to pull them back to the Cross.)*

16 Nevertheless, whereto we have already attained *(progress)*, let us walk by the same rule, let us mind the same thing. *(Let us walk the same path, that of the Cross [Lk. 9:23-24].)*

ENEMIES OF THE CROSS

17 Brethren, be followers together of me *(be "fellow-imitators")*, and mark them which walk so as you have us for an ensample

(observe intently).

18 (For many walk *(speaks of those attempting to live for God outside of the victory and rudiments of the Cross of Christ)*, of whom I have told you often, and now tell you even weeping *(this is a most serious matter)*, that they are the enemies of the Cross of Christ *(those who do not look exclusively to the Cross of Christ must be labeled "enemies")*:

19 Whose end *is* destruction *(if the Cross is ignored, and continues to be ignored, the loss of the soul is the only ultimate conclusion)*, whose god *is* their belly *(refers to those who attempt to pervert the Gospel for their own personal gain)*, and *whose* glory *is* in their shame *(the material things they seek, God labels as "shame")*, who mind earthly things.) *(This means they have no interest in Heavenly things, which signifies they are using the Lord for their own personal gain.)*

20 For our conversation *(citizenship)* is in Heaven *(meaning the other ways will have no place in Heaven)*; from whence also we look for the Saviour, the Lord Jesus Christ *(the Rapture)*:

21 Who *(the Lord)* shall change our vile body *(the Resurrection)*, that it may be fashioned like unto His Glorious Body *(every Saint will have a Glorified Body)*, according to the working whereby He is able even to subdue all things unto Himself. *("All things" are done through the Cross.)*

CHAPTER 4

STAND FAST

THEREFORE, my Brethren dearly beloved and longed for *(proclaims this Apostle's love for the Philippians)*, my joy and crown *(Paul took great delight in this Church)*, so stand fast in the Lord, *my* dearly beloved *(one can do this only by making the Cross the object of his Faith, which will then give the Holy Spirit latitude to bring about such a victory)*.

REJOICE

2 I beseech Euodias *(should have been translated "Euodia," because "Euodias" is a man's name)*, and beseech Syntyche *(the Apostle beseeches both these ladies because it seems there had been a rupture between them, which had affected the entirety of the Church)*, that they be of the same mind in the Lord. *(They both needed a fresh look at the Cross, which is the answer to all things as it regards the Lord.)*

3 And I intreat you also, true yokefellow *(does not identify this man)*, help those women which laboured with me in the Gospel,

with Clement also, and *with* other my fellowlabourers *(help settle the problem)*, whose names *are* in the Book of Life *(refers to the roster of Believers kept in Heaven)*.

4 Rejoice in the Lord always *(not for all things, but in all things)*: *and* again I say, Rejoice. *(Paul's teaching on emotional well-being, which follows, begins with rejoicing in the Lord.)*

DON'T WORRY

5 Let your moderation *(being satisfied with less than one's due)* be known unto all men *(even our enemies)*. The Lord *is* at hand *(is near; actually refers to the Rapture)*.

6 Be careful for nothing *(don't worry about anything)*; but in everything by prayer and supplication *(presents the cure for worry, which is believing prayer)* with thanksgiving *(takes in all God has done for us in the past, what He is doing at present, and shall do in the future)* let your requests be made known unto God. *(This speaks of all things, material, physical, and spiritual.)*

7 And the Peace of God *(Sanctifying Peace)*, which passes all understanding *(beyond the pale of human comprehension)*, shall keep your hearts and minds through Christ Jesus *(through what Christ did at the Cross)*.

THINK

8 Finally, Brethren, whatsoever things are true, whatsoever things *are* honest, whatsoever things *are* just, whatsoever things *are* pure, whatsoever things *are* lovely, whatsoever things *are* of good report; if *there be* any virtue, and if *there be* any praise, think on these things. *(This can be done, providing the Cross is the object of our Faith, which then gives the Holy Spirit latitude to help us.)*

9 Those things, which you have both learned, and received, and heard, and seen in me, do *(Paul had given them the Gospel of the Cross, and they had seen it work in his life; so they had the correct teaching, and they had the correct example)*: and the God of Peace shall be with you. *(Sanctifying Peace will be ours, if our Faith is properly placed in the Cross and remains in the Cross.)*

THANKSGIVING

10 But I rejoiced in the Lord greatly *(concerning the gift they had sent him)*, that now at the last your care of me has flourished again *(it seems that for a period of time, the Philippians had ceased to help the Apostle)*; wherein you were also careful *(the Church at Philippi had not forgotten Paul, but lacked the means to get the*

gift to him), but ye lacked opportunity *(thank the Lord, opportunity had finally presented itself)*.

11 Not that I speak in respect of want *(declares his independence from creature comforts)*: for I have learned, in whatsoever state I am, *therewith* to be content *(to be independent of external circumstances)*.

12 I know both how to be abased *(to keep rejoicing when there is no money)*, and I know how to abound *(to keep rejoicing when there is money)*: everywhere and in all things I am instructed both to be full and to be hungry, both to abound and to suffer need. *(All will come sooner or later, and the negative is not for a lack of Faith, but rather for our instruction in Righteousness.)*

13 I can do all things *(be abased or abound)* through Christ which strengtheneth me *(from Whom I draw strength)*.

14 Notwithstanding you have well done *(he is not meaning to disparage the gift of the Philippian Church)*, that you did communicate with my affliction. *(They helped Paul with his needs, as it regards the offering they sent him.)*

15 Now you Philippians know also, that in the beginning of the Gospel *(refers to the time when Paul first Preached the Word to them, about ten years previously)*, when I departed from Macedonia, no Church communicated with me as concerning giving and receiving, but you only *(proclaims the fact that the Philippians had always been generous)*.

16 For even in Thessalonica *(when he was starting the Church there)* you sent once and again unto my necessity *(proclaims their faithfulness)*.

17 Not because I desire a gift *(presents the Apostle defending himself against the slanderous assertion that he is using the Gospel as a means to make money)*: but I desire fruit that may abound to your account. *(God keeps a record of everything, even our gifts, whether giving or receiving.)*

18 But I have all, and abound: I am full *(proclaims the fact that the Philippian gift must have been generous)*, having received of Epaphroditus the things *which were sent* from you *(Epaphroditus had brought the gift from Philippi to Rome)*, an odour of a sweet smell *(presents the Old Testament odors of the Levitical Sacrifices, all typifying Christ)*, a Sacrifice acceptable, well-pleasing to God. *(For those who gave to Paul, enabling him to take the Message of the Cross to others, their gift, and such gifts presently, are looked at by God as a part of the Sacrificial Atoning Work of Christ on the Cross. Nothing could be higher than that!)*

19 But my God shall supply all

your need *(presents the Apostle assuring the Philippians, and all other Believers as well, that they have not impoverished themselves in giving so liberally to the cause of Christ)* according to His riches in Glory *(the measure of supply will be determined by the wealth of God in Glory)* by Christ Jesus *(made possible by the Cross)*.

BENEDICTION

20 Now unto God and our Father *be* Glory forever and ever. Amen. *(All the Glory belongs to God, and rightly so!)*

21 Salute *(greet)* every Saint in Christ Jesus. The Brethren which are with me greet you. *(This no doubt included Timothy, and several others. We are not told who all of them were.)*

22 All the Saints salute you *(refers to the Believers in the Church at Rome)*, chiefly they that are of Caesar's household. *(This presents the fact that Paul's work had operated notably to produce results, even in the most unlikely of places.)*

23 The Grace of our Lord Jesus Christ *be* with you all *(made possible by the Cross)*. Amen.

THE EPISTLE OF PAUL THE APOSTLE TO THE
COLOSSIANS

CHAPTER 1

INTRODUCTION

PAUL an Apostle of Jesus Christ *(it is through the Apostle that the Holy Spirit leads the Church, and does so according to the Message given him, which in Paul's case was the Message of Grace)* by the Will of God *(only the Lord can set a person in the Office of the Apostle; man cannot do such)*, and Timothy *our* Brother,

2 To the Saints *(the moment a person accepts Christ, they become a Saint)* and Faithful Brethren in Christ *(proclaims the fact that some in Colosse were faithful to the Gospel Paul had brought to them, but at the same time others, it seems, were somewhat shaken in their allegiance)* which are at Colosse *(was written from Rome by Paul, while he was in prison)*: Grace *be* unto you, and peace *(made possible by the Cross)*, from God our Father and the Lord Jesus Christ.

THANKSGIVING

3 We give thanks to God and the Father of our Lord Jesus Christ *(thanksgiving presents a character-istic quality of the type of prayer offered by Paul)*, praying always for you *(a proper understanding of the Cross gives one a proper prayer life)*,

4 Since we heard of your Faith in Christ Jesus *(Paul did not found the Church at Colosse; in fact, it was probably founded by Epaphras, who gave him the information recorded here)*, and of the love *which you have* to all the Saints *(Agape Love)*,

5 For the hope which is laid up for you in Heaven *(presents the last of the trilogy, "Faith, Love, and Hope")*, whereof you heard before in the Word of the Truth of the Gospel *(is meant to contrast the true Gospel of Epaphras with a false gospel of false teachers)*;

6 Which is come unto you *(meant to differentiate it from the false message of the Gnostics)*, as *it is* in all the world *(refers to the True Gospel being the same the world over)*; and brings forth fruit, as *it does* also in you, since the day you heard *of it (the True Gospel of Jesus Christ and Him Crucified will always bring forth fruit in the capacity of changed lives)*, and knew the Grace of God in

Truth *(the "Grace of God" cannot function accept in "Truth," which is "Jesus Christ and Him Crucified")*:

7 As you also learned of Epaphras our dear fellowservant *(as stated, he was a disciple of Paul)*, who is for you a faithful Minister of Christ *(reflects the fact that Epaphras was the spiritual father of the Colossian Saints)*;

8 Who also declared unto us your love in the Spirit *(it was "Love" produced by the Spirit of God, made possible by the Cross)*.

GRACE

9 For this cause we also, since the day we heard it, do not cease to pray for you *(the "cause" refers to the "fruit" they were bearing for Christ, with "prayer" offered for them that this fruit would continue, and not be stifled by a false message)*, and to desire that you might be filled with the knowledge of His Will *("His Will," and not that of others)* in all wisdom and spiritual understanding *(proclaims that which proceeds only from the inspiration of the Holy Spirit)*;

10 That you might walk worthy of the Lord unto all pleasing *("walk" refers to one's behavior and that it can be accomplished only by making the Cross the object of one's Faith, which gives the Holy Spirit the latitude to perfect our "walk")*, being fruitful in every good work *(which is guaranteed, if Faith is properly placed in the Cross)*, and increasing in the Knowledge of God *(presents the knowledge of the Cross, which pertains to the Finished Work of Christ)*;

11 Strengthened with all might, according to His Glorious Power *(power to live a Holy life, which comes through Grace, with the Cross as the means)*, unto all patience and longsuffering with joyfulness *(joy, because proper Faith guarantees Victory)*;

12 Giving thanks unto the Father *(which all should do constantly)*, which has made us meet *(qualified)* to be partakers of the inheritance of the Saints in Light *(presents the "standing" of the Believer in Christ)*:

13 Who has delivered us from the power of darkness *(refers to being rescued by His strong arm as a mighty conqueror, made possible by the Cross)*, and has translated us into the Kingdom of His Dear Son *(while the Cross is not the Source [that being Christ] the Cross is the "means")*:

DOCTRINE

14 In Whom we have Redemption through His Blood *(proclaims the price that was paid for our Salvation)*, even the forgiveness of sins *(at the Cross, the Lord*

broke the power of sin, and took away its guilt *[Rom. 6:6]*):

15 Who is the Image of the invisible God *(the Son is the exact reproduction of the Father; a derived Image)*, the Firstborn of every creature *(actually means Jesus is the Creator of all things)*:

HIS CREATIVE WORK

16 For by Him were all things created *(presents the Justification of the title given Christ in the preceding Verse)*, that are in Heaven, and that are in earth, visible and invisible *(things seen and not seen)*, whether *they be* thrones, or dominions, or principalities, or powers *(refers to both Holy and fallen Angels)*: all things were created by Him, and for Him *(Christ is the Creator of all [Jn. 1:3])*:

HIS PREEXISTENCE

17 And He is before all things *(preexistence)*, and by Him all things consist. *(All things come to pass within this sphere of His Personality, and are dependent upon it.)*

18 And He is the Head of the Body, the Church *(the Creator of the world is also Head of the Church)*: Who is the Beginning *(refers to Christ as the Origin or Beginning of the Church)*, the firstborn from the dead *(does not refer to Jesus* being Born-again as some teach, but rather that He was the first to be raised from the dead as it regards the Resurrection, never to die again)*; that in all *things* He might have the preeminence. *(He is the First and Foremost as it relates to the Church.)*

19 For it pleased *the Father* that in Him should all fulness dwell *(this "fullness" denotes the sum total of the Divine Powers and Attributes)*;

THE MEDIATORSHIP OF CHRIST

20 And, having made peace *(justifying peace)* through the Blood of His Cross *(presents His Blood as being that which satisfied the just demands of the broken Law)*, by Him to reconcile all things unto Himself *(speaks of the result of Faith in the Cross)*; by Him, *I say*, whether *they be* things in earth, or things in Heaven. *(The Cross not only addressed the Fall of man, but as well the Fall of Lucifer.)*

21 And you, who were sometime *(in times past)* alienated and enemies in *your* mind by wicked works *(total depravity)*, yet now has He reconciled *(made possible by the Cross)*.

22 In the Body of His flesh *(the Incarnation, God becoming flesh)* through death *(refers to the fact*

that the reconciling act of Christ is not by His Incarnation, but by His dying [II Cor. 5:21]), to present you Holy and unblameable and unreproveable in His sight (all made possible by the Cross):

SERVICE

23 If you continue in the Faith (at the same time says it is possible not to continue in the Faith; "the Faith" is "Christ and Him Crucified") grounded and settled (the foundation of the Faith, which object must always be the Cross), and be not moved away (moved away from the Cross) from the Hope of the Gospel, which you have heard (pertains to the fact that they had been brought in right), and which was preached to every creature which is under Heaven (the Message of the Cross is the same for all); whereof I Paul am made a Minister (the meaning of the New Covenant was actually given to Paul, which is the meaning of the Cross [Gal. 1:11-12]);

24 Who now rejoice in my sufferings for you (Paul was in prison when this Epistle was written), and fill up that which is behind of the afflictions of Christ in my flesh (suffering for Righteousness' sake) for His Body's sake, which is the Church (Satan opposes the Message of the Cross like nothing else):

25 Whereof I am made a Minis-

ter (says plainly that he is a Minister and not a Mediator, which some have attempted to read into the previous Verse), according to the Dispensation of God which is given to me for you (the way and manner of administrating the Work), to fulfil the Word of God (presents the Apostle not wanting to become sidetracked on some minor issue that did not emphasize the centrality of the Gospel, which is the Cross);

26 Even the Mystery which has been hid from ages and from generations (refers to the Gentiles who would be partakers with the Jews of the Gospel, and actually in the same Church), but now is made manifest to His Saints (manifested to Believers, but not to the world):

27 To whom (the Saints) God would make known (desire to make known) what is the riches of the glory of this mystery among the Gentiles (refers to the fact that the Cross is for all, and is not limited by racial or national lines); which is Christ in you (made possible by the Cross), the Hope of Glory (the full realization will materialize at the coming Resurrection):

28 Whom we preach, warning every man, and teaching every man in all wisdom (tells us the Bible is the only revealed Truth in the world, and in fact ever has been); that we may present every man perfect (mature) in Christ

Jesus *(refers to the Cross, and what He did there)*:

29 Whereunto I also labour, striving according to His working *(refers to Christ working in Paul through the Might and Power of the Holy Spirit)*, which works in me mightily *(which will work mightily in anyone, if the object of Faith is always the Cross)*.

CHAPTER 2

THE CHURCH

FOR I would that you knew what great conflict I have for you, and *for* them at Laodicea *(deep concern as it regards false doctrine)*, and *for* as many as have not seen my face in the flesh *(those in Colosse and Laodicea were not personally acquainted with Paul, as many others in the Churches were, due to the fact that he didn't plant these particular Churches in Colosse and Laodicea)*;

2 That their hearts might be comforted *(doesn't concern the physical organ, but rather the hypothetical seat of the emotions; in effect, the soul and the spirit)*, being knit together in love *(proclaims the only manner in which true unity can be obtained)*, and unto all riches of the full assurance of understanding *(the idea is that we know the "Truth" about all things concerning the Word of God)*, to the acknowledgment of the Mystery of God, and of the Father, and of Christ *(presents Christ as that Mystery)*;

3 In Whom *(Christ)* are hid all the treasures of Wisdom and Knowledge. *(This presents a direct rebuttal to the Gnostics, which claimed otherwise. The Gnostics over-humanized Christ and deified themselves.)*

FALSE TEACHING

4 And this I say *(points directly to the false teachers)*, lest any man should beguile you with enticing words *(refers to being deceived by subtle reasoning)*.

5 For though I be absent in the flesh, yet am I with you in the spirit *(refers to Paul's human spirit)*, joying and beholding your order, and the stedfastness of your Faith in Christ *(speaks of "holding rank," and refers to maintaining one's Faith in the Cross)*.

6 As you have therefore received Christ Jesus the Lord *(refers to the manner of one's Salvation, which is Christ and Him Crucified)*, so walk ye in Him *(behavior is to be ordered in the sphere of Christ and the Cross)*:

7 Rooted and built up in Him *(pertains to a proper foundation)*, and stablished in the Faith *(in Christ and the Cross)*, as you have been taught *(refers to the Colossians*

coming in the right way, but some of them considering the false message of the Gnostics), abounding therein with thanksgiving. (This refers to the fact that the Gospel of the Cross, which had brought them to Christ, had also brought them untold benefits.)

8 Beware lest any man spoil you through philosophy and vain deceit (anything that pulls the Believer away from the Cross is not of God), after the tradition of men (anything that is not of the Cross is of men), after the rudiments of the world, and not after Christ. (If it's truly after Christ, then it's after the Cross.)

9 For in Him (Christ) dwells all the fulness of the Godhead bodily. (This is Godhead as to essence. Christ is the completion and the fullness of Deity, and in Him the Believer is complete.)

10 And you are complete in Him (the satisfaction of every spiritual want is found in Christ, made possible by the Cross), which is the Head of all principality and power (His Headship extends not only over the Church, which voluntarily serves Him, but over all forces that are opposed to Him as well [Phil. 2:10-11]):

11 In Whom also you are circumcised with the Circumcision made without hands (that which is brought about by the Cross [Rom. 6:3-5]), in putting off the body of the sins of the flesh by the Circumcision of Christ (refers to the old carnal nature that is defeated by the Believer placing his Faith totally in the Cross, which gives the Holy Spirit latitude to work):

12 Buried with Him in Baptism (does not refer to Water Baptism, but rather to the Believer baptized into the death of Christ, which refers to the Crucifixion and Christ as our substitute [Rom. 6:3-4]), wherein also you are risen with Him through the Faith of the operation of God, Who has raised Him from the dead. (This does not refer to our future physical Resurrection, but to that Spiritual Resurrection from a sinful state into Divine Life. We died with Him, we are buried with Him, and we rose with Him [Rom. 6:3-5], and herein lies the secret to all spiritual victory.)

13 And you, being dead in your sins and the uncircumcision of your flesh (speaks of Spiritual death [i.e., "separation from God"], which sin does!), has He quickened together with Him (refers to being made Spiritually alive, which is done through being "Born-again"), having forgiven you all trespasses (the Cross made it possible for all manner of sins to be forgiven and taken away);

14 Blotting out the handwriting of Ordinances that was against us (pertains to the Law of Moses, which was God's Standard of Righ-

teousness that man could not reach), which was contrary to us *(Law is against us, simply because we are unable to keep its precepts, no matter how hard we try)*, and took it out of the way *(refers to the penalty of the Law being removed)*, nailing it to His Cross *(the Law with its decrees was abolished in Christ's Death, as if Crucified with Him)*;

15 *And* having spoiled principalities and powers *(Satan and all of his henchmen were defeated at the Cross by Christ atoning for all sin; sin was the legal right Satan had to hold man in captivity; with all sin atoned, he has no more legal right to hold anyone in bondage)*, He *(Christ)* made a show of them openly *(what Jesus did at the Cross was in the face of the whole universe)*, triumphing over them in it. *(The triumph is complete and it was all done for us, meaning we can walk in power and perpetual victory due to the Cross.)*

16 Let no man therefore judge you in meat, or in drink, or in respect of an holyday, or of the new moon, or of the Sabbath Days *(the moment we add any rule or regulation to the Finished Work of Christ, we have just abrogated the Grace of God)*:

17 Which are a shadow of things to come *(the Law, with all of its observances, was only meant to point to the One Who was to come,* Namely Christ); but the Body *(Church) is* of Christ *(refers to "substance and reality," as opposed to shadow)*.

18 Let no man beguile you of your reward *(concerns false doctrine)* in a voluntary humility *(refers to self-abasement)* and worshipping of Angels *(pertained to the Gnostic teaching; this false teaching claimed man could not go directly to God through Jesus Christ, but rather must reach after God through successive grades of intermediate beings, i.e., "Angels!")*, intruding into those things which he has not seen *(refers to going outside the revealed Word of God)*, vainly puffed up by his fleshly mind *("mind of the flesh," which means it's not the Mind of God)*,

19 And not holding the Head *(failure to look totally to Christ and the Cross will ultimately lead to destruction)*, from which all the body by joints and bands having nourishment ministered *(Christ is the source of all nourishment, which comes by the means of the Cross)*, and knit together, increases with the increase of God *(proper Faith in the Cross guarantees spiritual increase)*.

20 Wherefore if you be dead with Christ *(actually says, "in view of the fact that you died with Christ")* from the rudiments of the world *(the way of the world)*, why, as though living in the world, are

you subject to Ordinances *(refers to trusting something other than Christ and the Cross for Salvation and Victory)*,

21 (Touch not; taste not; handle not *(there is no Salvation or Victory in rules and regulations)*;

22 Which all are to perish with the using;) *(This refers to the fact that they don't work because they are of human origin. Therefore, new ones are made that work no better than the old, which is the way of man.)* after the commandments and doctrines of men? *(This means it is not of God, and must be avoided at all cost.)*

23 Which things have indeed a show of wisdom in will worship *(refers to worship devised and prescribed by man, which characterizes most of the modern Church)*, and humility *(false humility)*, and neglecting of the body *(speaks of the human body)*; not in any honour to the satisfying of the flesh. *(All ascetic observances, while they appeal to men as indications of superior wisdom and piety, have no value as remedies against sensual indulgence. That can be handled only at the Cross.)*

CHAPTER 3

NEW LIFE

IF you then be risen with Christ *(presents the New Life [Rom. 6:3-5])*, seek those things which are above *(which come directly from the Lord, not man)*, where Christ sits on the Right Hand of God. *(This is referring to the fact that the great Work is a Finished Work, meaning man doesn't have to go elsewhere.)*

2 Set your affection on things above *(refers to directing one's mind to a thing)*, not on things on the earth *(everything on this Earth is temporal; as well, our help comes from above)*.

3 For you are dead *(dead to the old life by virtue of the fact of Christ dying on the Cross as our Substitute, and in effect us dying with Him [Rom. 6:3-5])*, and your life is hid with Christ in God *(all made possible by the Cross [Jn. 14: 20])*.

4 When Christ, Who is our life, shall appear *(refers to the Rapture of the Church)*, then shall you also appear with Him in Glory. *(This refers to every Saint at that time being given a Glorified Body [I Cor. 15:51-57; I Thess. 4:13-18].)*

PUT OFF

5 Mortify therefore your members *(of your physical body)* which are upon the earth *(can be done only by the Believer understanding that everything he receives from the Lord comes strictly through the Cross, which must ever be the ob-*

ject of our Faith, *thus giving the Holy Spirit latitude to work in our lives)*; fornication, uncleanness, inordinate affection, evil concupiscence, and covetousness, which is idolatry *(works of the flesh, which will in one way or the other show themselves, unless the Believer follows the pattern laid down by the Holy Spirit regarding Victory over the flesh, which is the Cross)*:

6 For which things' sake the Wrath of God comes on the children of disobedience *(God cannot abide sin in any form, even in His children, and especially in His children; the Cross is the only solution for sin)*:

7 In the which you also walked some time *(in times past)*, when you lived in them *(before coming to Christ)*.

8 But now you also put off all these *(can do so by evidencing Faith in Christ and His Cross)*; anger, wrath, malice, blasphemy, filthy communication out of your mouth.

9 Lie not one to another *(the Greek actually says, "lie not to yourself," and speaks of accepting a way other than the Cross)*, seeing that you have put off the old man with his deeds *(the "old man" died with Christ on the Cross [Rom. 6:6])*;

PUT ON

10 And have put on the new man *(in Christ, we are a "New Creation" [II Cor. 5:17])*, which is renewed in knowledge *(the learning of Christ [Mat. 11:28-30])* after the image of Him Who created him *(man's re-created self is thus after the image of Christ)*:

11 Where there is neither Greek nor Jew, Circumcision nor uncircumcision, Barbarian, Scythian, bond nor free *(in Christ, there is no distinction)*: but Christ is all, and in all. *(Christ occupies the whole sphere of human life and permeates all its developments.)*

12 Put on therefore, as the Elect of God *(refers to those who have been elected by God, because they elected to know God [Rev. 22:17])*, Holy and Beloved, bowels of mercies, kindness, humbleness of mind, meekness, longsuffering *(Fruit of the Spirit)*;

13 Forbearing one another *(exhibiting patience)*, and forgiving one another, if any man have a quarrel against any: even as Christ forgave you, so also *do* you.

14 And above all these things *put on* charity *(Love)*, which is the bond of perfectness *(complete growth)*.

15 And let the Peace of God rule in your hearts *(Sanctifying Peace)*, to the which also you are called in one body *(the Church)*; and be ye thankful *(show one's self thankful)*.

16 Let the Word of Christ dwell

in you richly in all wisdom *(the meaning of the New Covenant as given to Paul, which is the meaning of the Cross)*; teaching and admonishing one another in Psalms and Hymns and Spiritual Songs *(our songs of worship must proclaim the Word of God, thereby teaching us)*, singing with grace in your hearts to the Lord. *(This presents the real purpose of Spirit-Anointed Music, which tells how important music and singing are as it refers to worship.)*

17 And whatsoever you do in word or deed, *do* all in the Name of the Lord Jesus *(everything is to be done in the Name of our Lord, irrespective of what it is)*, giving thanks to God and the Father by Him. *(If properly obeyed, everything will take on a brand-new complexion.)*

DOMESTIC LIFE

18 Wives, submit yourselves unto your own husbands, as it is fit in the Lord *(only as the husband functions in the sphere of the Lord).*

HUSBANDS

19 Husbands, love *your* wives, and be not bitter against them. *(The idea is that the husband loves the wife with the same type of love with which he loves God. Consequently, there will be no bitterness.)*

CHILDREN

20 Children, obey *your* parents in all things *(pertains to that which is Scriptural)*: for this is well pleasing unto the Lord *(children properly obeying parents are taught thusly to obey the Lord).*

FATHERS

21 Fathers, provoke not your children *to anger*, lest they be discouraged. *(Children's obedience must be fed on love and praise. Fear paralyzes activity and kills service.)*

SERVANTS

22 Servants *(slaves)*, obey in all things *your* masters according to the flesh *(presents Christian slaves of that day working, for the most part, in the service of pagan masters)*; not with eyeservice, as menpleasers *(represents good work when the employer is watching, and the opposite otherwise)*; but in singleness of heart, fearing God *(means a person has one heart, and that is to please God, which will render proper service whether the Master is watching or not)*:

23 And whatsoever you do, do *it* heartily, as to the Lord, and not unto men *(the Lord now becomes the Master, with everything taking on a brand-new complexion)*;

24 Knowing that of the Lord

you shall receive the reward of the inheritance *(proclaims the fact that the Lord Who is being faithfully served will, at the same time, render just dues)*: for you serve the Lord Christ. *(Everything we do, irrespective what it is, is to be done with the idea that it is for the Lord and the Lord Alone!)*

25 But he who does wrong shall receive for the wrong which he has done *(indicates the Law of Divine Retribution [Mat. 7:1-2])*: and there is no respect of persons. *(God looks at all alike, playing favorites with no one.)*

CHAPTER 4

MASTERS

MASTERS, give unto *your* servants that which is just and equal *(speaking to Christian Masters)*; knowing that you also have a Master in Heaven *(presents the great principle on which all Christianity reposes)*.

PRAYER

2 Continue in prayer *(prayer should be a habit with every Believer)*, and watch in the same *(don't let the habit of prayer be broken)* with thanksgiving *(most prayer should be made up of thanksgiving)*;

3 Withal praying also for us,

that God would open unto us a door of utterance *(reminds us that even though the spread of the Gospel is under Divine direction [Acts 16:7], it is also subject to Satanic hindrances [I Thess. 2:18])*, to speak the Mystery of Christ *(concerns that which had been previously hidden, but now has been made fully known — the Cross and what it means)*, for which I am also in bonds *(refers to Paul's imprisonment in Rome)*:

4 That I may make it manifest *(preach Christ)*, as I ought to speak *(manifest Christ as Christ ought to be manifested)*.

5 Walk in wisdom toward them who are without *(refers to "ordering one's behavior")*, redeeming the time *(make wise and sacred use of every opportunity to present Christ)*.

6 Let your speech *be* alway with Grace *(gracious and pleasant)*, seasoned with salt *("salt" represents the incorruptible Word of God)*, that you may know how you ought to answer every man *(as it regards Christ)*.

BRETHREN

7 All my state shall Tychicus declare unto you, *who is* a beloved Brother, and a faithful Minister and fellowservant in the Lord *(this Brother was evidently with Paul in Rome, at least for a period of time)*:

8 Whom I have sent unto you

for the same purpose *(apparently, Tychicus had already left Rome to go to Colosse)*, that he might know your estate, and comfort your hearts *(implies the news Tychicus would bring about the Apostle; as well, he was entrusted with three Epistles: Ephesians, Colossians, and the short note to Philemon)*;

9 With Onesimus, a faithful and beloved Brother, who is *one* of you *(a runaway slave, who has now found Christ, accompanies Tychicus)*. They shall make known unto you *(the Church at Colosse)* all things which *are done* here *(Rome)*.

10 Aristarchus my fellow-prisoner salutes you *(is not known if Paul is speaking literally or spiritually concerning this man being a fellow-prisoner)*, and Marcus, sister's son to Barnabas *(refers to John Mark, the writer of the Gospel which bears his name among the four Gospels; he was the cousin of Barnabas)*, (touching whom you received commandments: if he come unto you, receive him;) *(It is not known exactly what Paul meant here. At any rate, he is recommending this young man, which tells us that the problem they had had some years before was now made right [Acts 15:37-40].)*

11 And Jesus, which is called Justus, who are of the Circumcision. These only *are my* fellow-workers unto the Kingdom of God, which have been a comfort unto me *(three Jews: Aristarchus, Mark, and Justus)*.

12 Epaphras, who is *one* of you, a servant of Christ, salutes you *(probably the founder of the Colossian Church, who is now with Paul for a period of time)*, always labouring fervently for you in prayers *(refers to strong intercession)*, that you may stand perfect and complete in all the Will of God *(spiritual maturity)*.

13 For I bear him record, that he has a great zeal for you, and them *who are* in Laodicea, and them in Hierapolis. *(Epaphras probably founded all three of these Churches, for these three towns were very close together.)*

14 Luke, the beloved physician *(this is Luke, the writer of the Gospel that bears his name, plus the Book of Acts; we also learn here that he was a medical doctor, although it seems he no longer practiced his craft)*, and Demas, greet you. *(Unfortunately, this man Demas, who had such a good beginning, lost his way [II Tim. 4:10].)*

BENEDICTION

15 Salute *(greet)* the Brethren which are in Laodicea, and Nymphas *(the Pastor, it seems, of the Church in Laodicea)*, and the Church which is in his house *(almost all Churches then were located in houses)*.

16 And when this Epistle (Colossians) is read among you, cause that it be read also in the Church of the Laodiceans (history records the fact that many copies were made of these Epistles, which circulated among the Churches); and that you likewise read the *Epistle* from Laodicea. (This evidently refers to an Epistle lost to us.)

17 And say to Archippus, Take heed to the Ministry which you have received in the Lord, that you fulfil it. (This speaks of the same man mentioned in Philemon, Verse 2. Tradition says he was the son of Philemon, and maybe the Pastor of the Church that was in their house in the city of Colosse.)

18 The salutation by the hand of me Paul (presents him, as stated, writing this closing word himself). Remember my bonds (in effect, he is asking for prayer that he will be released from prison). Grace *be* with you (the sum of the Gospel Message). Amen.

THESSALONIANS

CHAPTER 1

INTRODUCTION

PAUL, and Silas, and Timothy, unto the Church of the Thessalonians *(believed to be the first Epistle written by Paul; consequently, the first time in history this salutation concerning the Church is used)* which is in God the Father and *in* the Lord Jesus Christ *(has reference to the fact that God cannot address fallen, sinful humanity, except through the Cross of Christ)*: Grace *be* unto you, and Peace, from God our Father, and the Lord Jesus Christ *(presents the Source; but the means is the Cross).*

THANKSGIVING

2 We give thanks to God always for you all, making mention of you in our prayers *(prayer was the atmosphere of Paul's life, and should be ours as well);*

THIS CHURCH

3 Remembering without ceasing your work of faith, and labour of love, and patience of hope in our Lord Jesus Christ *(what Jesus did for us at the Cross makes all of this possible), in the sight of God and our Father (all things are under the scrutiny of His eye);*

4 Knowing, Brethren beloved, your election of God. *(This refers to the rejection of Israel as Gospel representatives, and to the election of the Gentiles to take their place [Mat. 21:43; 23:37-39; Rom. 11:11-29].)*

5 For our Gospel came not unto you in word only *(refers to the New Covenant)*, but also in power, and in the Holy Spirit *(tells us where the power is)*, and in much assurance *(proclaims the results which accrue as a result of the Gospel being properly presented)*; as you know what manner of men we were among you for your sake. *(Paul and those with him were living examples of what the Gospel can do in a person's life.)*

6 And you became followers of us, and of the Lord *(if the wrong Preacher is followed, the Lord will not be found)*, having received the Word in much affliction *(proclaims the opposition of former friends or even relatives)*, with joy of the Holy Spirit *(the more Satan afflicts, the more the Holy Spirit pours in joy):*

7 So that you were examples to all who believe in Macedonia and Achaia *(they were examples of*

evidencing the Joy of the Lord despite persecution).

8 For from you sounded out the Word of the Lord not only in Macedonia and Achaia *(pertains to the Message of the Cross, which had changed their lives)*, but also in every place your Faith to Godward is spread abroad *(nothing advertises the Gospel like changed lives)*; so that we need not to speak any thing. *(They were adhering to the Gospel he preached.)*

9 For they themselves show of us what manner of entering in we had unto you *(the Spiritual Fruit of the Thessalonians testified to the character of the laborers)*, and how you turned to God from idols to serve the Living and True God *(all idolatry is a lie; in fact, all religion is idolatry)*;

10 And to wait for His Son from Heaven *(refers to the Rapture of the Church)*, Whom He raised from the dead, *even* Jesus *(the Resurrection of Christ guarantees the Resurrection of the Saints)*, which delivered us from the wrath to come *(by means of the Cross, and meaning that judgment will ultimately come to all who reject Christ and the Cross).*

CHAPTER 2

PAUL

FOR yourselves, Brethren, know our entrance in unto you *(pre-*sents his defense, a justifiable defense of his personal Ministry for the sake of Truth)*, that it was not in vain *(it brought forth much fruit)*:

2 But even after that we had suffered before, and were shamefully treated, as ye know, at Philippi *(high motives are required for men to continue a true, and therefore costly, Gospel Ministry)*, we were bold in our God to speak unto you the Gospel of God with much contention. *(The triumph of the Gospel by an effort of only the highest kind and overcoming the most formidable opposition.)*

3 For our exhortation *was* not of deceit *(no ulterior motives)*, nor of uncleanness *(impure motives)*, nor in guile *(trickery)*:

4 But as we were allowed of God to be put in trust with the Gospel *(the testing had been completed, and thus signified an approval by God)*, even so we speak; not as pleasing men *(presents the biggest problem in the Ministry, pleasing men and not God)*, but God, which tries our hearts. *(This constant scrutiny by Omniscience is a great comfort to those who aim to please God, rather than men.)*

5 For neither at any time used we flattering words, as you know *(refers to the attempt to gain selfish ends by insincere speech)*, nor a cloak of covetousness; God *is* witness *(refers to pretense)*:

6 Nor of men sought we glory, neither of you, nor *yet* of others *(refers to conduct designed to elicit or extract praise)*, when we might have been burdensome, as the Apostles of Christ. *(This refers to the fact that as Apostles, they might have demanded certain things, but didn't!)*

7 But we were gentle among you, even as a nurse cherishes her children *(refers to a Mother feeding her children)*:

8 So being affectionately desirous of you, we were willing to have imparted unto you, not the Gospel of God only, but also our own souls, because you were dear unto us *(is literally in the Greek, "because you became beloved ones to us")*.

9 For you remember, Brethren, our labour and travail *(refers to his self-sacrificing as it concerns the Gospel)*: for labouring night and day, because we would not be chargeable unto any of you, we Preached unto you the Gospel of God. *(This probably refers to a mixture of preaching the Gospel and the repairing of tents to support himself.)*

10 You *are* witnesses, and God also *(it is important that conduct appear right in the eyes of men; however, only God's Judgment is infallible)*, how holily and justly and unblameably we behaved ourselves among you who believe *(concerns the lifestyles of the Apostle plus Silas, Timothy, and anyone else who may have been laboring with him)*:

11 As you know how we exhorted and comforted and charged every one of you *(pertains to dealing with the Thessalonians with encouragement, as well as by solemn injunctions)*, as a father *does* his children *(presents the image being changed from that of motherly tenderness to that of fatherly direction)*,

12 That you would walk worthy of God *(has to do with our daily living, which can only be done by proper Faith evidenced in the Cross)*, Who has called you unto His Kingdom and Glory *(should have been translated, "Who is calling you into His Kingdom and Glory")*.

RECEPTION

13 For this cause also thank we God without ceasing *(refers to the manner in which the Thessalonians had received the Word)*, because, when you received the Word of God which you heard of us, you received it not *as* the word of men, but as it is in Truth, the Word of God *(the Word of God was faithfully delivered to the Thessalonians, and they faithfully believed it)*, which effectually works also in you who believe. *(This refers to the fact that the Word "is working" only in those*

who "are believing," which refers to the Cross and makes the working of the Spirit possible.)

14 For you, Brethren, became followers of the Churches of God which in Judaea are in Christ Jesus (identifies all who are truly "in Christ Jesus" as being "True Churches"): for you also have suffered like things of your own countrymen, even as they have of the Jews (pertains to persecution):

15 Who both killed the Lord Jesus, and their own Prophets (presents the crime of the ages), and have persecuted us (the Jews tried repeatedly to kill Paul); and they please not God (is, in fact, a monumental understatement), and are contrary to all men (refers to their sectarian, self-righteous spirit and attitude):

16 Forbidding us to speak to the Gentiles that they might be saved (means the Jews, as a nation, had rejected Christ and the Cross, and would thereby never admit Gentiles could now be saved as well), to fill up their sins always (there is a limit beyond which God will not go): for the wrath is come upon them to the uttermost. (This is used in the past tense, simply because it is so sure of fulfillment. In fact, it was fulfilled totally in A.D. 70.)

PAUL'S CONCERN

17 But we, Brethren, being taken from you for a short time in presence, not in heart (refers to the Apostle having to leave the city before he desired to because of the Jews' action against him [Acts 17:1-10]), endeavoured the more abundantly to see your face with great desire. (This presents no want of affection, but from causes beyond control.)

18 Wherefore we would have come unto you, even I Paul, once and again; but Satan hindered us. (This proclaims the fact that the Evil One is a real personality, and not a mere figure of speech.)

19 For what is our hope, or joy, or crown of rejoicing? (This presents the Apostle pointing beyond, far beyond, the minor annoyances now, to the great coming time when there will be no more separation and no more hindrances by Satan.) Are not even you in the presence of our Lord Jesus Christ at His coming? (This points to the coming Rapture of the Church.)

20 For you are our glory and joy (what Christ had made of them).

CHAPTER 3

TIMOTHY

WHEREFORE when we could no longer forbear (refers to Paul strongly desiring to know the spiritual situation back at Thessa-

lonica), we thought it good to be left at Athens alone *(refers to Timothy being sent back to Thessalonica, with no mention of Silas)*;

2 And sent Timothy, our brother, and minister of God, and our fellowlabourer in the Gospel of Christ, to establish you *(the Thessalonians needed more teaching, so Timothy was sent to carry this out)*, and to comfort you concerning your Faith *(suggests encouragement)*:

3 That no man should be moved by these afflictions *(refers to the fact that we should not allow these things to discourage or hinder us)*: for yourselves know that we are appointed thereunto. *(We are destined for afflictions because of Satan's opposition to the Gospel.)*

4 For verily, when we were with you, we told you before that we should suffer tribulation *(Faith placed totally in the Cross of Christ brings opposition from both the world and the Church, but mostly from the Church)*; even as it came to pass, and you know *(means tribulation is inevitable)*.

5 For this cause *(speaks of the persecution, and their response)*, when I could no longer forbear *(presents the Apostle repeating for emphasis what he has already said in Verses 1 and 2)*, I sent to know your faith *(that their Faith was remaining steadfast in the Cross)*,

lest by some means the tempter have tempted you, and our labour be in vain. *(This tempted them to move their Faith to something other than the Cross, which would mean spiritual wreckage.)*

THE REPORT

6 But now when Timothy came from you unto us *(refers to Timothy coming from Thessalonica to Corinth, where Paul now was)*, and brought us good tidings of your faith and charity *(refers to an excellent report on their Faith and Love)*, and that you have good remembrance of us always, desiring greatly to see us, as we also *to see* you *(meaning the Thessalonians had not been pulled away from Paul by false teachers)*:

7 Therefore, Brethren, we were comforted over you in all our affliction and distress by your faith *(their Faith remaining strong greatly encouraged the Apostle)*:

8 For now we live *(are comforted)*, if you stand fast in the Lord. *(Refuse to allow your Faith to be moved from the Cross to other things.)*

9 For what thanks can we render to God again for you *(in essence says, "How can we thank our God enough concerning you!")*, for all the joy wherewith we joy for your sakes before our God *(presents that which produces joy in the*

heart of the Apostle, which is success in the Work of God, and pertains to the Spiritual Growth of these Believers);

10 Night and day praying exceedingly that we might see your face (has to do with the Apostle's desire to once again visit this fledgling Church, which he did sometime later [Acts 20:1-2]), and might perfect that which is lacking in your faith? (Strengthen them more firmly in the Cross, which must always be the object of our Faith.)

PAUL'S PRAYER

11 Now God Himself and our Father, and our Lord Jesus Christ (the Cross of Christ alone has made this relationship possible), direct our way unto you (the Will of God is sought, and the way being made as the Will of God comes to the fore).

12 And the Lord make you to increase and abound in love one toward another, and toward all men, even as we do toward you (which will come to pass as the Cross of Christ is more and more understood):

13 To the end He may stablish your hearts (be without blame at the Judgment Seat of Christ) unblameable in Holiness before God, even our Father (refers to the fact that it is God Who is the Judge of these things), at the coming of our Lord Jesus Christ with all His Saints. (This refers to the Rapture of the Church.)

CHAPTER 4

WALK GODLY

FURTHERMORE then we beseech you, Brethren, and exhort you by the Lord Jesus, that as you have received of us how you ought to walk and to please God (pertains to the whole manner of living), so you would abound more and more (the manner of Spiritual Growth).

2 For you know what Commandments we gave you by the Lord Jesus. (This is a Command to be Holy that can only be carried out by a constant and abiding Faith in Christ and the Cross, which gives the Holy Spirit the latitude to work.)

SANCTIFICATION

3 For this is the Will of God, even your Sanctification (the work of making one Holy, which can only be done by the Holy Spirit), that you should abstain from fornication (refers to all types of immorality):

4 That every one of you should know how to possess his vessel (the physical body, which is the Temple of the Holy Spirit [I Cor. 3:16]) in Sanctification and

honour *(morally clean, which can only be done by Faith exhibited constantly in the Cross of Christ)*;

5 Not in the lust of concupiscence *(evil passions and desires in the thought life)*, even as the Gentiles which know not God *(speaks of the Gentile world which walked in darkness before the advent of the Gospel)*:

6 That no *man* go beyond and defraud his brother in *any* matter *(refers to anything regarding fraud, however, the inference is to sexual misconduct; such must not be)*: because that the Lord is the avenger of all such *(presents the fact that the Judgment of God upon all impurity is sure and terrible, and will ultimately come)*, as we also have forewarned you and testified. *(This presents the possibility that sexual misconduct could have been a besetting temptation for the Thessalonians.)*

7 For God has not called us unto uncleanness, but unto Holiness. *(God has called us from "uncleanness," i.e., "sexual impurity," unto "Holiness.")*

LOVE

8 He therefore who despises *(despises the Commands of the Lord)*, despises not man, but God *(treating the words of men lightly is one thing; treating the Word of God lightly is something else altogether)*,

Who has also given unto us His Holy Spirit. *(The Holy Spirit is given to Believers in order that we might live a Holy Life, which is done by us evidencing a constant Faith in the Cross of Christ.)*

9 But as touching brotherly love you need not that I write unto you *(presents the Apostle with customary tactfulness beginning in a complimentary manner and then proceeding to the admonition)*: for you yourselves are taught of God to love one another *(Believers who have the Holy Spirit, Who definitely teaches us such, and constantly)*.

10 And indeed you do it toward all the Brethren which are in all Macedonia *(for the Thessalonians, Macedonia was home; if we cannot love those at home, how can we love others far away?)*: but we beseech you, Brethren, that you increase more and more *(presents the Apostle not admonishing them, but definitely exhorting them)*;

11 And that you study to be quiet *(is the opposite of aspiring to be prominently seen and heard)*, and to do your own business *(mind your own business, and not the business of others)*, and to work with your own hands, as we commanded you *(work; don't steal, and don't sponge off others)*;

12 That you may walk honestly toward them who are without *(set an example for unbelievers)*, and that you may have lack of noth-

ing. *(If we truly follow the Lord, there will be no lack.)*

THE RAPTURE

13 But I would not have you to be ignorant, Brethren, concerning them which are asleep *(refers to Believers who have died)*, that you sorrow not, even as others which have no hope. *(This concerns those who do not know the Lord who will have no part in the First Resurrection of Life and, therefore, no hope for Heaven.)*

14 For if we believe that Jesus died and rose again *(the very Foundation of Christianity is the Death and Resurrection of Christ; it is the proof of life after death in a glorified state for all Saints in that life, which incidentally will never end)*, even so them also which sleep in Jesus will God bring with Him. *(This refers to the Rapture of the Church, or the Resurrection of all Believers, with both phrases meaning the same thing, even as Paul describes in I Cor., Chpt. 15. At death, the soul and the spirit of the Child of God instantly go to be with Jesus [Phil. 1:23], while the physical body goes back to dust. At the Rapture, God will replace what was the physical body with a Glorified Body, united with the soul and the spirit. In fact, the soul and the spirit of each individual will accompany the Lord down close to this Earth to be united with a Glorified Body, which will then make the Believer whole.)*

15 For this we say unto you by the Word of the Lord *(presents the Doctrine of the Rapture of the Church as the "Word of the Lord")*, that we which are alive *and* remain unto the coming of the Lord *(all Believers who are alive at the Rapture)* shall not prevent them which are asleep. *(This refers to the fact that the living Saints will not precede or go before the dead Saints.)*

16 For the Lord Himself shall descend from Heaven with a shout *(refers to "the same Jesus" which the Angels proclaimed in Acts 1:11)*, with the voice of the Archangel *(refers to Michael, the only one referred to as such [Jude, Vs. 9])*, and with the Trump of God *(doesn't exactly say God will personally blow this Trumpet, but that it definitely does belong to Him, whoever does signal the blast)*: and the dead in Christ shall rise first *(the criteria for being ready for the Rapture is to be "in Christ," which means that all who are truly Born-again will definitely go in the Rapture)*:

17 Then we which are alive *and* remain shall be caught up *(Raptured)* together with them *(the Resurrected dead)* in the clouds *(clouds of Saints, not clouds as we normally think of such)*, to meet the Lord in the air *(the Greek word for "air" is "aer," and refers to the*

lower atmosphere, or from about 6,000 feet down; so, the Lord will come at least within 6,000 feet of the Earth, perhaps even lower, with all the Saints meeting Him there; but He, at that time, will not come all the way to the Earth, that awaiting the Second Coming, which will be seven or more years later): **and so shall we ever be with the Lord.** *(This presents the greatest meeting humanity will have ever known.)*

18 **Wherefore comfort one another with these words.** *(This pertains to the future of the Child of God, which is Glorious indeed!)*

CHAPTER 5

THE DAY OF THE LORD

BUT of the times and the seasons *(introduces the recurring question of the curious and the anxious: how long before Christ comes? at what point in history?),* **Brethren, you have no need that I write unto you.** *(The Apostle mentions this to repress that vain curiosity, which is natural to man.)*

2 **For yourselves know perfectly that the Day of the Lord so comes** *(it will begin with the Great Tribulation, and carry on through the Millennium; it will end with the Advent of the New Heavens and the New Earth)* **as a thief in the night.**

3 **For when they shall say,** Peace and safety *(refers to Israel, but will as well characterize the world; it pertains to the Antichrist signing the seven-year pact with Israel and other nations [Dan. 9:27]);* **then sudden destruction comes upon them** *(at the mid-point of the seven-year period, the Antichrist will break his pact, actually invading Israel [Rev. 12:1-6]),* **as travail upon a woman with child; and they shall not escape.** *(The Great Tribulation is definitely coming upon this world [Mat. 24:21].)*

4 **But you, Brethren, are not in darkness** *(Christians have spiritual enlightenment, which comes only from the Word of God),* **that that day should overtake you as a thief.** *(No Believer should be caught unawares, but regrettably, it seems many will.)*

5 **You are all the children of light, and the children of the day** *(refers to knowing Jesus Christ, Who is "the Light of the World" [Jn. 8:12]):* **we are not of the night, nor of darkness.** *(The Believer is to be in a totally different sphere of operation.)*

6 **Therefore let us not sleep, as do others** *(be overcome by lethargy and apathy);* **but let us watch and be sober.** *(The Christian is to maintain his relationship with Christ by continued watchfulness, even as it regards his personal life and Prophetic events.)*

7 **For they who sleep sleep in**

the night *(those who are in spiritual darkness have no idea what is coming upon this world)*; and they who be drunken are drunken in the night. *(Paul is not speaking here of alcoholic beverage, only using the word "drunken" as a metaphor to describe a spiritual condition.)*

8 But let us *(Believers)*, who are of the day *(who have spiritual light)*, be sober *(speaks of "assurance")*, putting on the breastplate of Faith and Love *(proper Faith in Christ and the Cross, which produces Love)*; and for an helmet, the Hope of Salvation *(the guarantee of deliverance from this present evil world, which pertains to the Rapture)*.

9 For God has not appointed us to wrath *(has not appointed Believers to go through the Great Tribulation)*, but to obtain Salvation by our Lord Jesus Christ *(again, pertains to the Rapture of the Church)*,

10 Who died for us, that, whether we wake or sleep, we should live together with Him *(again, the Rapture, all made possible by the Cross)*.

11 Wherefore comfort yourselves together *(it refers to comfort in view of the coming Rapture and the escape from wrath, which will be poured out upon the world in the coming Great Tribulation)*, and edify one another, even as also you do. *(This refers to cheering and strengthening one another.)*

PRACTICAL TEACHING

12 And we beseech you, Brethren, to know them which labour among you, and are over you in the Lord, and admonish you *(know for sure that the Preacher you are following is truly Preaching the Word)*;

13 And to esteem them very highly in love for their work's sake. *(This carries more reference to the work they do, than to the person in question.)* And be at peace among yourselves. *(This proclaims the esteem just mentioned as helping to produce such peace.)*

PAUL

14 Now we exhort you, Brethren, warn them who are unruly *(speaks of those who leave the ranks)*, comfort the feebleminded *(should have been translated, "comfort the fainthearted")*, support the weak *(refers to those who do not have proper understanding regarding the Cross of Christ, and what it means to their everyday walk before God)*, be patient toward all *men*. *(This refers to all the categories just mentioned.)*

15 See that none render evil for evil unto any *man* *(presents Biblical Christianity as the only system of such noble practice)*; but

ever follow that which is good, both among yourselves, and to all *men (even to our enemies)*.

16 Rejoice evermore. *(The Believer has every reason to do such, and irrespective of everyday problems.)*

17 Pray without ceasing. *(We should pray about everything.)*

18 In every thing give thanks *(not necessarily for everything)*: for this is the Will of God in Christ Jesus concerning you. *(No matter what happens, or how negative things may seem to be, we are to never stop giving thanks to the Lord, which is the Will of God.)*

19 Quench not the Spirit. *(To disobey these admonitions is to quench the Spirit.)*

20 Despise not Prophesyings. *(This Gift has been abused more so than any other Gift. Irrespective, we are to ever recognize the value of the true operation of this Gift [I Cor. 14:3].)*

21 Prove all things *(when Prophecies are given, or anything that claims to be of the Lord, it should be put to the test; the test is, "is it Scriptural?")*; hold fast that which is good. *(This refers to the sifting process of accepting that which is definitely of the Lord, and rejecting that which isn't!)*

22 Abstain from all appearance of evil. *(The question is, "Does this please God"?)*

23 And the very God of Peace

Sanctify you wholly *(this is "progressive Sanctification," which can only be brought about by the Holy Spirit, Who does such as our Faith is firmly anchored in the Cross, within which parameters the Spirit always works; the Sanctification process involves the whole man)*; and *I pray God* your whole spirit and soul and body *(proclaims the make-up of the whole man)* be preserved blameless unto the coming of our Lord Jesus Christ. *(This refers to the Rapture. As well, this one Verse proclaims the fact that any involvement, whether Righteous or unrighteous, effects the whole man, and not just the physical body or the soul as some claim.)*

24 Faithful *is* He Who calls you *(God will do exactly what He has said He will do, if we will only Believe Him)*, Who also will do it *(will Sanctify us wholly)*.

25 Brethren, pray for us. *(The great Apostle was ever humbly conscious of his own weakness in himself [I Cor. 2:1-5].)*

26 Greet all the Brethren with an holy kiss *(the custom then, with handshaking the custom presently)*.

27 I charge you by the Lord that this Epistle be read unto all the Holy Brethren *(and for all the obvious reasons)*.

28 The Grace of our Lord Jesus Christ *be* with you *(all made possible by the Cross)*. Amen.

THE SECOND EPISTLE OF PAUL THE APOSTLE TO THE
THESSALONIANS

CHAPTER 1

INTRODUCTION

PAUL and Silas, and Timothy, unto the Church of the Thessalonians *(this is probably the second Epistle written by the great Apostle)* in God our Father and the Lord Jesus Christ *(God is our Father, by Virtue of Christ and what He has done for us at the Cross)*:

2 Grace unto you, and Peace *(Sanctifying Peace)*, from God our Father and the Lord Jesus Christ *(all made possible by the Cross)*.

SPIRITUAL GROWTH

3 We are bound to thank God always for you, Brethren, as it is meet, because that your Faith grows exceedingly *(Faith grows as the Word is properly applied, with the Cross ever being the object of Faith)*, and the charity *(love)* of every one of you all toward each other abounds *(presents the first hallmark of Christianity, that we love the Brethren)*;

4 So that we ourselves glory in you in the Churches of God *(they had taken what little teaching Paul had been able to give*

them, which was no doubt the Cross, and used it to its full extent) for your patience and faith in all your persecutions and tribulations that you endure *(suggests continued and repeated sufferings which were still going on)*:

5 Which is a manifest token of the Righteous Judgment of God *(the sense of this phrase is that the endurance of affliction by the Righteous, in a proper manner, is a proof that there will be Righteous Judgment of God at the last day)*, that you may be counted worthy of the Kingdom of God, for which you also suffer *(could be translated, "God purposes to account His Children worthy of the Kingdom of God, for which they also suffer" [Acts 5:41; I Pet. 4:12-16])*:

6 Seeing it is a Righteous thing with God to recompense tribulation to them who trouble you *(we are not to attempt to defend ourselves as it regards getting even, but must leave such in the hands of the Lord)*;

THE SECOND COMING

7 And to you who are troubled rest with us *(unfortunately, the trouble will continue until Jesus*

comes; *we will then "rest")*, when the Lord Jesus shall be revealed from Heaven with His mighty Angels *(refers to the Second Coming, which is different from the Rapture)*,

8 In flaming fire taking vengeance on them who know not God *(gives us the manner of the Second Coming)*, and who obey not the Gospel of our Lord Jesus Christ *(who have rejected Christ and the Cross)*:

9 Who shall be punished with everlasting destruction from the Presence of the Lord *(pertains to the Lake of Fire, which will be everlasting)*, and from the Glory of His Power *(power to save, but rejected, and, therefore, the end is "everlasting destruction")*;

10 When He shall come to be Glorified in His Saints *(all Saints will praise Him, and will do so continually)*, and to be admired in all them who believe *(Christ will be the Center and Focal Point of all Things)* (because our testimony among you was believed) in that day. *(They believed the Testimony of Paul regarding Christ and the Cross and, therefore, will be with Christ forever.)*

PRAYER

11 Wherefore also we pray always for you *(presents the idea that the hope of Believers cannot be realized except through supernatural help)*, that our God would count you worthy of this calling *(presents the fact that it is Holy Character as evidence of Saving Faith which will qualify men "that day")*, and fulfil all the good pleasure of His goodness *(refers to all the wonderful things the Holy Spirit desires to do for us, and in fact will do for us if we will only cooperate with Him)*, and the work of Faith with power *(Faith in the Cross, which gives the Holy Spirit the latitude to work, in Whom is the Power)*:

12 That the Name of our Lord Jesus Christ may be glorified in you *(presents the object of the Holy Spirit)*, and you in Him *(in Christ)*, according to the Grace of our God and the Lord Jesus Christ. *(All are made possible by the Cross, which are then freely given to us by the means of Grace.)*

CHAPTER 2

THE SECOND COMING

NOW we beseech you, Brethren, by the coming of our Lord Jesus Christ *(refers to both the Rapture and the Second Coming)*, and by our gathering together unto Him *(this phrase refers strictly to the Rapture)*,

2 That you be not soon shaken in mind, or be troubled *(false doctrine does this)*, neither by spirit

(messages in tongues and interpretation, which purport to be of the Lord, but really were not), **nor by word** *(pertaining to those who claimed to have a word from the Lord)*, **nor by letter as from us** *(someone had written a letter claiming certain prophetic things, and evidently had signed Paul's name to it, which means it was a forgery)*, **as that the Day of Christ is at hand** *(should have been translated, "the Day of the Lord," because this is how the best manuscripts read; the "Day of the Lord" refers to all events after the Rapture; some were claiming, even in Paul's day, that the Second Coming was about to take place, which of course was wrong)*.

3 Let no man deceive you by any means *(in other words, don't listen to that which is Scripturally incorrect)*: **for that day shall not come, except there come a falling away first** *(should have been translated, "for that day shall not come, except there come a departure first"; this speaks of the Rapture, which in essence says the Second Coming cannot take place until certain things happen)*, **and that man of sin be revealed, the son of perdition** *(this speaks of the Antichrist, who must come upon the world scene before the Second Coming)*;

4 Who opposes and exalts himself above all that is called God *(pertains to his declaration of himself as Deity)*, **or that is worshipped** *(the Antichrist will put down all religions, at least in the area which he controls, making himself alone the object of worship)*; **so that he as God sits in the Temple of God** *(refers to the Jewish Temple, which will be rebuilt in Jerusalem; the Antichrist will take over the Temple, making it his religious headquarters)*, **showing himself that he is God.** *(This proclaims his announcement of Deity as it regards himself.)*

5 Don't you remember, that, when I was yet with you, I told you these things? *(So, there was no excuse for the Thessalonians to be drawn away by false doctrine.)*

6 And now you know what withholds *(speaks of the Church)* **that he might be revealed in his time.** *(This speaks of the Antichrist who will be revealed or made known after the Rapture of the Church.)*

7 For the mystery of iniquity does already work *(concerns false teaching by false teachers)*: **only he** *(the Church)* **who now lets** *(who now hinders evil)* **will let** *(will continue to hinder)*, **until he** *(the Church)* **be taken out of the way.** *(The pronoun "he" confuses some people. In Verses 4 and 6, the pronoun "he" refers to the Antichrist, while in Verse 7 "he" refers to the Church.)*

8 And then *(after the Rapture of the Church)* **shall that Wicked**

(the Antichrist) **be revealed** *(proving conclusively that the Rapture takes place before the Great Tribulation [Mat. 24:21])*, **whom the Lord shall consume with the spirit of His Mouth** *(should have been translated, "the Breath of His Mouth" [Isa. 11:4])*, **and shall destroy with the brightness of His Coming** *(both phrases refer to the Second Coming)*:

9 Even him *(the Antichrist)*, **whose coming is after the working of Satan** *(means that Satan is the sponsor of the Antichrist)* **with all power and signs and lying wonders** *(proclaims the fact that the Antichrist's rise to power, at least in the beginning, will be very religious)*,

10 And with all deceivableness of unrighteousness in them who perish *(refers to the fact that "all lying powers and lying signs and lying wonders" will be used to deceive the world)*; **because they received not the love of the Truth, that they might be saved** *(they rejected Christ and the Cross)*.

11 And for this cause *(the rejection of Christ and the Cross)* **God shall send them strong delusion** *(if one doesn't want "the Truth," God will see to it one receives a "delusion")*, **that they should believe a lie** *(should have been translated, "that they should believe the lie"; the Greek Text has the definite article "the lie," which refers to a specific lie; that "lie" pertains to* anything that leads a person away from the Cross)*:

12 That they all might be damned who believed not the Truth *(who would not accept the Cross)*, **but had pleasure in unrighteousness.** *(The Greek has the definite article, which actually says, "the unrighteousness," specifying a particular unrighteousness; it is really referring to the results of rejection of the Cross of Christ.)*

THANKSGIVING

13 But we are bound to give thanks always to God for you *(refers to those who did not succumb to the lies of false teachers)*, **Brethren beloved of the Lord, because God has from the beginning chosen you to Salvation through Sanctification of the Spirit** *(Holy Spirit)* **and belief of the Truth** *(concerns itself not with the "who" of Salvation [in other words, who will be saved], but rather the "manner" of Salvation and Sanctification; people are saved by trusting Christ and the Cross; Believers are Sanctified by continuing to trust Christ and the Cross; the "Cross" is the means of all things pertaining to God, as it relates to humanity)*:

14 Whereunto He *(God)* **called you by our Gospel** *(Jesus Christ and Him Crucified [I Cor. 1:17-18, 21; 2:2])*, **to the obtaining of the Glory of our Lord Jesus Christ.** *(This per-*

tains to the wonder that comes with Salvation, and all because of what Christ did at the Cross.)

15 Therefore, Brethren, stand fast (refers to standing fast in the Gospel Paul had Preached unto them), and hold the traditions which you have been taught (refers to what Paul had taught them, which was the Truth), whether by word, or our Epistle. (This is what he had preached to them when he was personally with them, and as well by the Epistle he had already sent them, and the second one he is now writing.)

16 Now our Lord Jesus Christ Himself (proclaims the Apostle giving the Resurrection Name of our Lord), and God, even our Father (refers to relationship), which has loved us, and has given us everlasting consolation and good hope through Grace (all made possible by the Cross),

17 Comfort your hearts (the Holy Spirit comforts us), and stablish you in every good word and work. (The foundation principle for this accomplishment is a proper understanding of the Cross of Christ.)

CHAPTER 3

PRAYER

FINALLY, Brethren, pray for us, that the Word of the Lord may have free course (will accomplish its intended purpose; this depends largely on the proper intercession of the Saints, hence Paul asking for prayer), and be glorified (bringing forth its full power, which speaks of a positive effect in people's lives), even as it is with you (the Gospel had changed the lives of the Thessalonians):

2 And that we may be delivered from unreasonable and wicked men (these false teachers gave undue prominence to things other than the Cross [I Cor. 1:17]): for all men have not Faith. (This should have been translated, "for all men have not the Faith." It speaks of the Finished Work accomplished at the Cross.)

3 But the Lord is Faithful (though some men cannot be trusted, God can be depended on), Who shall stablish you, and keep you from evil. (The Cross of Christ and one's Faith in the Cross guarantee the help of the Holy Spirit, and protects the Believer from both the Evil One and his evil designs.)

4 And we have confidence in the Lord touching you (pertaining to the Thessalonians), that you both do and will do the things which we command you. (Growth in Grace can be realized only as Believers maintain an attitude of obedience towards God, actually an attitude that is motivated by a love for Him that transcends all other objects of affection.)

5 And the Lord direct your

hearts into the Love of God (tells us the Lord wants total control within our lives, but it is control which must be freely given by us to Him), and into the patient waiting for Christ. (This pertains to our waiting for Him to rectify the situation, whatever it might be.)

THE EXAMPLE

6 Now we command you, brethren, in the Name of our Lord Jesus Christ (the Apostle is saying that what he is telling the people is "the Word of God," and must be heeded!), that you withdraw yourselves from every brother who walks disorderly (literally means, "to walk out of the ranks of the Word of God"; in abbreviated form, it means we should withdraw fellowship from those who teach something other than the Cross; it does not speak of excommunication), and not after the tradition which he received of us (after the teaching which Paul had given, which was definitely from the Lord; "tradition," as it is used here, does not mean "unwritten doctrines," as this word normally means; the Apostle is referring to what the Lord had given him, which he had faithfully taught to the people).

7 For yourselves know how you ought to follow us (it was to Paul the meaning of the New Covenant was given, which is the mean-ing of the Cross [Gal. 1:11-12]; so, what he was saying was the Word of the Lord; people had better make sure the Preacher they are following is of God): for we behaved not ourselves disorderly among you (the opposite of "disorderly" is a Sanctified life, in that sin has no dominion over the individual [Rom. 6:14]);

8 Neither did we eat any man's bread for nought (the Apostle didn't make himself a burden to others); but wrought with labour and travail night and day, that we might not be chargeable to any of you (he worked at his craft of tent making in order to meet his material needs):

9 Not because we have not power (refers to the fact that he was a Preacher of the Gospel, and by all rights should have been supported by the people; however, he did not avail himself of that privilege in Thessalonica, and for a purpose), but to make ourselves an example unto you to follow us. (The heathen priests in this Gentile city were constantly scheming in order to get money from the people. Paul wanted nothing in his Ministry to resemble that. However, he did receive two offerings from Philippi when he was in Thessalonica [Phil. 4:15-16].)

EXHORTATION

10 For even when we were with

you, this we commanded you, that if any would not work, neither should he eat. *(If a person is lazy and won't work, then let them do without. In other words, it's wrong to give money to someone of this nature.)*

11 For we hear that there are some which walk among you disorderly, working not at all, but are busybodies *(sponging off others)*.

12 Now them who are such we command and exhort by our Lord Jesus Christ *(refers to the Apostle having the Mind of the Lord, and the authority of the Lord in making these statements)*, that with quietness they work, and eat their own bread. *(Quit being busybodies, attempting to meddle in other people's affairs. Let them tend to their own business.)*

13 But you, Brethren, be not weary in well doing. *(The idea is that while they were to refuse to support those who were busybodies and lazy, they were not to forget the worthy poor.)*

14 And if any man obey not our word by this Epistle, note that man, and have no company with him, that he may be ashamed. *(This doesn't actually speak of excommunication, but rather a withdrawal of fellowship within the local Body. In some sense, after being repeatedly warned, the individual was to be pointed out.)*

15 Yet count *him* not as an enemy *(means to not count him out-side of Christ, but only as an erring Brother, which means he's going in the wrong direction)*, but admonish *him* as a Brother. *(Admonish him not as one lost, but as one who belongs to the Lord, but yet erring.)*

BENEDICTION

16 Now the Lord of Peace Himself give you Peace always by all means. *(This is "Sanctifying Peace." It doesn't refer to an absence of problems or troubles, but rather to an unending Peace in the midst of problems and troubles, etc., which can only be given by the Lord, and is a result of Grace which comes through the Cross.)* The Lord be with you all. *(It means all can have this "Sanctifying Peace." In fact, the pronoun "all" includes even the offending ones whom Paul has been addressing, that is if they will turn to the right way.)*

17 The salutation of Paul with my own hand *(it seems that Paul dictated this Letter to a Scribe up to this particular Verse; at this point, he took the pen in his own hand to add a closing greeting)*, which is the token in every Epistle: so I write. *(This presents the Apostle saying that this is his style. That is, the signature is "sign" or "proof" of the genuineness of the Epistle.)*

18 The Grace of our Lord Jesus Christ be with you all *(made possible by the Cross)*. Amen.

THE FIRST EPISTLE OF PAUL THE APOSTLE TO
TIMOTHY

CHAPTER 1

INTRODUCTION

PAUL, an Apostle of Jesus Christ *(the Office of the Apostle is, in effect, the de facto leader of the Church under Christ, and is so by the particular Message given to him by the Holy Spirit, which in Paul's case was the Message of Grace)* by the Commandment of God our Saviour, and Lord Jesus Christ *(places such a calling in the very highest councils)*, which is our hope *(Christ Alone and what He did at the Cross is "our hope")*;

2 Unto Timothy, *my* own son in the Faith *(refers to Timothy having more than likely been saved under Paul's Ministry)*: Grace, Mercy, *and* Peace, from God our Father and Jesus Christ our Lord *(all made possible by the Cross)*.

FALSE DOCTRINE

3 As I besought you to abide still at Ephesus *(Paul desired that Timothy remain at Ephesus for a period of time because of false teachers attempting to spread false doctrine among the people)*, when I went into Macedonia *(into Greece)*, that you might charge some that they teach no other doctrine *(the Doctrine must be "Jesus Christ and Him Crucified")*,

4 Neither give heed to fables and endless genealogies *(Jewish fables and Jewish genealogies; so, the false teachers were Judaizers who insisted that Law must be added to Grace, and who placed no stock in the Cross at all; in a sense, they were very similar to the modern "Word of Faith" teachers)*, which minister questions, rather than Godly edifying which is in Faith *(this speaks of the fact that Faith, not Law, is the sphere or element in which our Salvation functions; such Faith always has the Cross as its object, and thereby edifies)*: so do. *(Don't leave the Cross.)*

5 Now the end of the Commandment *(charge)* is charity *(love)* out of a pure heart *(which alone can produce love)*, and *of* a good conscience, and *of* Faith unfeigned *(feigned faith is pretended faith, which means it doesn't have the Cross as its object)*:

6 From which some having swerved have turned aside *(refers to missing the mark; in other words, they left the Cross)* unto vain jangling *(useless talk)*;

7 Desiring to be teachers of the Law (*refers to the Law of Moses, and speaks of the Judaizers*); understanding neither what they say, nor whereof they affirm. (*These individuals claimed to be professional interpreters of the Law, when in reality they had only a surface knowledge of the Law.*)

THE LAW

8 But we know that the Law *is* good (*the Apostle says this to show he definitely was not an enemy of the Law of Moses*), if a man use it lawfully (*understanding that the Law of Moses pointed strictly to Christ; when He came, He fulfilled it in totality*);

9 Knowing this, that the Law is not made for a Righteous man (*should have been translated, "Law is not made . . ."; the word "the" was inserted by the translators, and should not have been added; consequently, the way Paul uses the word, it refers to any type of Law, whether the Law of Moses or Law made up by religious men; the Believer is not to function after Law, but rather Grace, which refers to Faith placed exclusively in the Cross*), but for the lawless and disobedient, for the ungodly and for sinners, for unholy and profane, for murderers of fathers and murderers of mothers, for manslayers (*true Believers do not fall into these categories*),

10 For whoremongers, for them who defile themselves with mankind (*homosexuality*), for menstealers (*slave traders*), for liars, for perjured persons (*those who swear falsely*), and if there be any other thing that is contrary to sound Doctrine (*actually refers to all that is contrary to the Word of God*);

11 According to the Glorious Gospel (*refers to its moral Glory*) of the Blessed God (*pertains to His Blessed Gift of Forgiveness offered to all sinners who accept His Gospel of Love*), which was committed to my trust. (*The Lord chose Paul as the recipient and bearer of the New Covenant.*)

PAUL

12 And I thank Christ Jesus our Lord, Who has enabled me (*presents the One Who calls and blesses*), for that He counted me faithful, putting me into the Ministry (*the Lord knew Paul would be faithful, and that the Gospel committed to him would not be compromised*);

13 Who was before a blasphemer, and a persecutor, and injurious (*what he was before he was saved*): but I obtained Mercy, because I did *it* ignorantly in unbelief (*could be translated, "I was shown Mercy because, being igno-*

rant, I acted in unbelief").

14 And the Grace of our Lord was exceeding abundant (proclaims that which God stands ready to give to any honest, and earnest seeker) with Faith and Love which is in Christ Jesus (presents that which was produced in Paul, as a result of the Grace of God).

15 This is a faithful saying, and worthy of all acceptation (means the Gospel of Christ dying to save sinners is worthy of being accepted by the whole world), that Christ Jesus came into the world to save sinners (which He did through the Cross); of whom I am chief. (What he is saying is that his offense against God had been so great, and his sin of guilt so overwhelming, that he felt himself to be the number one sinner of all time.)

16 Howbeit for this cause I obtained Mercy (one might say it in this way: "because Christ came to save sinners, I obtained Mercy"), that in me first Jesus Christ might show forth all longsuffering (the representative instance of God's longsuffering to a high-handed transgressor), for a pattern (the Apostle is saying that if the Lord would do such for Paul, He will do it for anyone) to them which should hereafter believe on Him (on Christ and what He did at the Cross) to Life Everlasting (without beginning or end, that which has always been and always will be).

17 Now unto the King eternal (the Greek says, "Now, to the King of the Ages"), immortal (imperishable), invisible (as it regards His Glory), the only wise God (should have been translated, "the only God," with the word "wise" not being included in most of the Manuscripts; there is no other God), be honour and glory forever and ever. (This refers to respect and praise, and that it be done forever.) Amen (Truth).

TIMOTHY

18 This charge I commit unto you, son Timothy (refers to a command or injunction), according to the Prophecies which went before on you (probably refers to the time frame of Acts 16:1-3), that you by them might war a good warfare (we aren't told exactly what the Prophecies were, but that they spoke of an assignment to leadership in the army of King Jesus);

19 Holding Faith (maintaining Faith in Christ and the Cross), and a good conscience (speaks of following the Word of the Lord exactly as it is given); which some having put away concerning Faith have made shipwreck (a metaphor used by Paul, pointing to those who had abandoned the Cross):

20 Of whom is Hymenaeus and Alexander (presents two examples of one not "holding the Faith");

whom I have delivered unto Satan *(I Cor. 5:5)*, that they may learn not to blaspheme. *(This tells us that all who depart from "the Faith," which is Jesus Christ and Him Crucified, can only be concluded as "blaspheming.")*

CHAPTER 2

EXHORTATION

I exort therefore *(resumes and develops Paul's charge to Timothy, which began in I Tim. 1:18)*, that, first of all *(it is as if Paul said, "the most important point in this exhortation concerns the universal scope of prayer")*, supplications *(personal needs)*, prayers *(petitions)*, intercessions *(in this case, an approach to God on the basis of an accepted relationship)*, and giving of thanks *(Praise and Worship)*, be made for all men *(lends credence to the idea that we should pray about everything)*;

2 For kings, and for all who are in authority *(Civil Government)*; that we may lead a quiet and peaceable life in all Godliness and honesty. *(This speaks of Government that's free of turmoil, about which prayer can have a great effect.)*

3 For this is good and acceptable in the sight of God our Saviour *(refers to this being the Will of God, and for all the obvious reasons)*;

GOD'S WILL

4 Who will have all men to be saved *(presents Salvation, which is universal in virtue and aim)*, and to come unto the knowledge of the Truth. *(This pertains to Salvation through Jesus Christ and what He did at the Cross [Jn. 3:16; Rom. 6:3-6; 10:9-10].)*

ONE MEDIATOR

5 For there is one God *(manifested in three Persons — God the Father, God the Son, and God the Holy Spirit)*, and one Mediator between God and men, the Man Christ Jesus *(He can only be an adequate Mediator Who has sympathy with and an understanding of both parties, and is understandable by and clear to both; in other words, Jesus is both God and Man, i.e., "Very God and Very Man")*;

6 Who gave Himself a ransom for all *(refers to the fact that our Lord's Death was a spontaneous and voluntary Sacrifice on His part; the word "ransom" refers to the price He paid, owed by man to God, which was His Precious Blood [I Pet. 1:18-20])*, to be testified in due time. *(This refers to the planning of this great Work, which took place "before the Foundation of the World" [I Pet. 1:18-20], unto the "due time" of its manifestation, which refers to when Christ*

was Crucified).

TRUTH

7 Whereunto I am ordained a Preacher, and an Apostle *(presents the highest calling of the fivefold Ministry [Eph. 4:11]),* **(I speak the Truth in Christ,** *and* **lie not;)** *(was said because it seems some were denying his Apostleship)* **a teacher of the Gentiles in Faith and verity** *(in Faith and Truth).*

8 I will therefore that men pray everywhere *(proclaims the absolute necessity of prayer on the part of the Child of God),* **lifting up Holy hands** *(a surrendered spirit),* **without wrath and doubting.** *(This speaks of an angry spirit, which is caused by doubting the Word of God.)*

WOMEN

9 In like manner also *(refers to the fact that women should pray to the Lord in like manner as the men),* **that women adorn themselves in modest apparel** *(presents that which is consistent with what she is, a Child of God),* **with shamefacedness** *(Christian women should not be bold or forward toward men)* **and sobriety** *(the idea of self-restraint);* **not with broided hair** *(not the same meaning as now, but rather an extremely ostentatious display),* **or gold, or pearls** *(the Apostle is not condemning these things, but rather promoting the adornment of Christian character, which is to be the attraction of Christian women),* **or costly array** *(tells us that when either men or women live primarily for dress and outward show, then it is wrong);*

10 But (which becomes women professing Godliness) with good works.

11 Let the woman learn in silence *(its meaning is made clear in I Corinthians 14:34-35)* **with all subjection** *(Eph.5: 22-25).*

12 But I suffer not a woman to teach, nor to usurp authority over the man *(if a male teacher is more qualified, he should take the lead; otherwise the woman can do so),* **but to be in silence** *(silent regarding teachings unless there is no qualified man, which is the case at times.)*

13 For Adam was first formed, then Eve *(the creation model).*

14 And Adam was not deceived *(seems to imply the man is stronger regarding the will),* **but the woman being deceived was in the transgression.** *(This facility of deception on her part seems to suggest to the Apostle her inferiority to man in intellectual strength, and the consequent wrongness of allowing the woman an intellectual supremacy over man as it regards authority.)*

15 Notwithstanding she shall

be saved in childbearing *(pertains to protection from the Lord regarding the woman, and her offspring; the greater meaning of "childbearing" as used here refers to "Jesus being born into the world through the Virgin Mary, who would save lost humanity"),* if they continue in Faith and Charity *(love)* and Holiness with sobriety. *(A Godly life must be the example if the great Promise of God, as given here, is to be claimed.)*

CHAPTER 3

BISHOPS

THIS *is* a true saying, If a man desire the Office of a Bishop *(the Office of the Bishop is the same as the Office of the Pastor; they are one and the same),* he desires a good work. *(Most Pastors during Paul's day were raised up out of the local Church.)*

2 A Bishop *(Pastor)* then must be blameless *(he presents to the world at large such a Christian life that he furnishes no grounds for accusation; it speaks of the present, not the past),* the husband of one wife *(is a caution, I believe, against polygamy, which in fact posed a serious problem for the Church in those days),* vigilant, sober, of good behaviour, given to hospitality, apt to teach *(these are qualities, and not qualifications as some*

claim*)*;

3 Not given to wine *(refers to alcoholic beverage),* no striker *(not quarrelsome),* not greedy of filthy lucre *(not money hungry);* but patient, not a brawler, not covetous;

4 One who rules well his own house *(carries no idea of a dictatorial attitude, but rather sets the spiritual tone),* having his children in subjection with all gravity *(refers to obedience);*

5 (For if a man know not how to rule his own house, how shall he take care of the Church of God?) *(The case is clear and incontrovertible.)*

6 Not a novice *(it is used metaphorically for a new convert),* lest being lifted up with pride *(describes a person who is in a clouded or stupid state of mind as a result of pride)* he fall into the condemnation of the Devil. *(Satan is under the condemnatory sentence of God because of his original sin of rebellion against God, which sin it seems was motivated by pride.)*

7 Moreover he must have a good report of them which are without *(refers to the non-Christian world in the midst of which the Saints must live);* lest he fall into reproach and the snare of the Devil. *(The "Cross" is the only protection against these things of which we have been so carefully warned.)*

DEACONS

8 Likewise *must* the Deacons be grave *(a seriousness of purpose and self-respect in conduct)*, not doubletongued *(saying one thing and meaning another)*, not given to much wine *(Verse 3)*, not greedy of filthy lucre;

9 Holding the Mystery of the Faith in a pure conscience. *(This actually refers to the "Mystery of the Cross," which was not at all understood until its meaning was given to Paul. It is called "the Faith," and must not be diluted.)*

10 And let these also first be proved *(mature Christians)*; then let them use the Office of a Deacon *(serve well)*, being *found* blameless *(the Cross alone can guarantee such)*.

11 Even so *must their* wives be grave *(should have been translated, "even so must women be grave," pertaining to women who aspire to the Office of Deaconess)*, not slanderers, sober, faithful in all things. *(This is made possible by a proper Faith in the Cross.)*

12 Let the Deacons be the husbands of one wife *(identical to Verses 2, 4-5)*, ruling their children and their own houses well.

13 For they who have used the Office of a Deacon well purchase to themselves a good degree *(refers to acquiring or obtaining; it speaks of a position of trust and* influence in the Church, accompanied by the Blessings of the Lord)*, and great boldness in the Faith which is in Christ Jesus *(refers to a strong Faith in Christ)*.

JESUS

14 These things write I unto you, hoping to come unto you shortly *(hoping to meet Timothy soon)*:

15 But if I tarry long, that you may know how you ought to behave yourself in the House of God *(is not actually referring to Timothy, because he knows how to conduct himself, but how the members of the Church should conduct themselves)*, which is the Church of the Living God *(the True Church, bought and paid for by the Blood of Jesus)*, the pillar and ground of the Truth. *(The True Church proclaims the Cross [I Cor. 1:17-18, 21, 23; 2:2; Eph. 2:13-18].)*

16 And without controversy great is the mystery of Godliness *(refers to the Truth of the Cross previously hidden, but now fully revealed)*: God was manifest in the flesh *(refers to the Incarnation of Christ)*, justified in the Spirit *(vindicated, endorsed, proved, and pronounced by the Holy Spirit)*, seen of Angels *(refers to the fact that Angels witnessed every capacity of His Birth, Life, Passion, Resurrection, and Ascension)*, Preached

unto the Gentiles *(would have been better translated, "Preached unto the Nations"; His atonement was for the entirety of mankind, which Message is to be proclaimed to the entirety of the world)*, believed on in the world *(accepted by many)*, received up into Glory. *(His Mission was accomplished, finished, and accepted in totality by God.)*

CHAPTER 4

APOSTASY

NOW the Spirit *(Holy Spirit)* speaks expressly *(pointedly)*, that in the latter times *(the times in which we now live, the last of the last days, which begin the fulfillment of Endtime Prophecies)* some shall depart from the Faith *(anytime Paul uses the term "the Faith," in short he is referring to the Cross; so, we are told here that some will depart from the Cross as the means of Salvation and Victory)*, giving heed to seducing spirits *(evil spirits, i.e., "religious spirits," making something seem like what it isn't)*, and doctrines of devils *(should have been translated, "doctrines of demons"; the "seducing spirits" entice Believers away from the true Faith, causing them to believe "doctrines inspired by demon spirits")*;

2 Speaking lies in hypocrisy *(concerns the teachers of these "doc-*trines of demons," which pertain to anything that leads one away from the Cross)*; having their conscience seared with a hot iron *(refers to the fact that these deceivers are not acting under delusion, but deliberately and against conscience)*;

3 Forbidding to marry *(is an attack against the home, even against God's original Command that a husband and wife is His Plan for society [Gen. 2:23-24])*, and commanding to abstain from meats *(claiming the keeping of certain man-made Laws brings about Holiness)*, which God has created to be received with thanksgiving of them which believe and know the Truth. *(The reason for the error — these have rejected Truth, i.e., "the Cross.")*

4 For every creature of God *is* good, and nothing to be refused *(that is if it's used for the right purpose)*, if it be received with thanksgiving *(proclaims the fact that every kind of food and drink may become hateful in the eyes of the all-pure God if misused, or if partaken of without any sense of gratitude to the Divine Giver)*:

5 For it is Sanctified *(made clean)* by the Word of God *(realizing our Sanctification and Holiness come by our Faith in Christ and the Cross, and not by the keeping of particular rules and regulations)* and prayer *(a prayer of thanksgiving)*.

A GOOD MINISTER

6 If you put the Brethren in remembrance of these things *(call attention to it)*, you shall be a good Minister of Jesus Christ *(at the same time, in effect says if attention is not called to "these things," one will not be a good Preacher of the Gospel)*, nourished up in the words of Faith and of good doctrine, whereunto you have attained *(constantly nourishing one's self on the Word)*.

7 But refuse profane and old wives' fables *(that which does not have the true character of the Word of God)*, and exercise yourself *rather* unto Godliness. *(Paul's thought moves on immediately to a contrast between the discipline of the body and the discipline of the soul.)*

8 For bodily exercise profits little *(should have been translated, "profitable for a little")*: but Godliness is profitable unto all things *(covers every aspect of life and living)*, having Promise of the life that now is, and of that which is to come. *(Godliness affects our life and living now, and also the life that is to come, proving life after death.)*

9 This *is* a Faithful saying and worthy of all acceptation. *(The Apostle is referring to the statement made in Verse 8. It must be faithfully accepted and attended.)*

10 For therefore we both labour and suffer reproach *(neither the Devil nor his followers are in sympathy with the Believer)*, because we trust in the Living God *(the Salvation afforded by God through His Son, the Lord Jesus Christ)*, Who is the Saviour of all men *(refers to all men who will believe [Jn. 3:16; Rom. 5:4; 10:9-10, 13; Eph. 2:8-9])*, specially of those who believe. *(This refers to conditions laid down for Salvation.)*

11 These things command and teach. *(Jesus Christ Alone is the Saviour, and is so by virtue of what He did at the Cross.)*

EXAMPLES

12 Let no man despise your youth *(he had been well developed by Paul)*; but be thou an example of the Believers, in word, in conversation *(in lifestyle)*, in charity, in spirit, in Faith, in purity *(which can only be brought about by the Cross ever being the object of our Faith, with the Holy Spirit then able to bring about these graces)*.

COMMANDS

13 Till I come, give attendance to reading *(to the simple reading of the Word of God)*, to exhortation *(proclaiming the Truth or preaching the Gospel)*, to doctrine. *(This refers to properly teaching the Word.)*

14 Neglect not the Gift that is

in you *(refers to the Call of God, and the Anointing of the Holy Spirit upon the individual to carry out the "Call!")*, which was given you by Prophecy *(the "Prophecy" verified what the Lord had already done; Paul is reminding Timothy of this verification)*, with the laying on of the hands of the Presbytery. *(This actually refers to the Pastors of that particular local Church, in this instance either at Lystra or Derbe [Acts 16:1-3].)*

15 Meditate upon these things *(attend carefully)*; give yourself wholly to them *(total devotion)*; that your profiting may appear to all *(better translated, "so that your progress may be evident to all")*.

16 Take heed unto yourself, and unto the Doctrine *(keep on paying attention to yourself, what you believe, and also to what you're teaching)*; continue in them *(refers to not allowing any false doctrine to enter in, or sin to enter the personal life)*: for in doing this you shall both save yourself, and them who hear you. *(Unfortunately, most Believers are hearing Preachers who are leading them in the wrong direction.)*

CHAPTER 5

ELDERS

REBUKE not an Elder *(does not refer to a Pastor as it usually does, but rather an older person who is mature in both age and experience)*, but intreat *him* as a father *(appeal to him as if he were your father)*; *and* the younger men as Brethren *(in Christ, we are family)*;

2 The Elder women as mothers; the younger as sisters, with all purity. *(Failure to heed the word "purity" has caused untold problems and difficulties.)*

WIDOWS

3 Honour widows who are widows indeed. *(Help those financially who are truly widows. There was no Governmental welfare net of any kind in those days.)*

4 But if any widow have children or nephews *(should read, "children or grandchildren," for that's what the Greek word actually means)*, let them learn first to show piety at home, and to requite their parents *(refers to the family bearing the responsibility instead of the Church)*: for that is good and acceptable before God *(portrays this as being God's Way; each family is responsible for its own members, and should care for each of them accordingly)*.

5 Now she who is a widow indeed *(truly)*, and desolate *(meaning she has no relatives to help care for her)*, trusts in God *(has her hopes settled permanently on God)*,

and continues in supplications and prayers night and day. *(This presents an individual who is priceless, and who is most important to the Kingdom of God.)*

6 But she who lives in pleasure is dead while she lives *(portrays the contrast with one totally dedicated to God)*.

7 And these things give in charge *(give the people these instructions)*, that they may be blameless *(refers to the widows who are maintained by the Church; it is important that the support be reserved for those truly worthy of it)*.

8 But if any provide not for his own, and specially for those of his own house *(presents the Apostle speaking particularly of the duty of children towards a widowed Mother)*, he has denied the Faith *(refers to the fact that if one is truly saved, one will function according to these things laid down by the Holy Spirit through Paul)*, and is worse than an infidel. *(This carries the meaning that even an infidel, which refers to one who has no belief in Christ, abides in many cases by a code that cares for his own.)*

9 Let not a widow be taken into the number *(cared for by the Church)* under threescore years old *(60 years old)*, having been the wife of one man *(not a polygamist, but having been legally married to one man)*,

10 Well reported of for good works *(not a busybody)*; if she have brought up children *(pertains to the idea that she love children whether she had any of her own or not)*, if she have lodged strangers, if she have washed the Saints' feet *(hospitable)*, if she have relieved the afflicted *(those in distress)*, if she have diligently followed every good work *(her life portrays this)*.

11 But the younger widows refuse *(regarding the widows under 60 years of age, the Church should not be responsible for their upkeep)*: for when they have begun to wax wanton against Christ, they will marry *(insinuates such women were not really intending to totally give themselves to the Cause of Christ, but were only seeking support until they could find a husband)*;

12 Having damnation *(should have been translated, "condemnation")*, because they have cast off their first faith. *(This probably refers to the original impulse of Faith, which led such a lady to join the widows.)*

13 And withal they learn *to be* idle, wandering about from house to house *(doing so with no practical purpose or aim in mind, but rather for the purpose of gossip)*; and not only idle, but tattlers also and busybodies, speaking things which they ought not. *(It refers*

to young widows who would pry into the private affairs of others.)

14 I will therefore that the younger women marry (should have been translated, "younger widows"), bear children (those young enough to do such), guide the house (refers to the management of family affairs, which the wife seems to do better), give none occasion to the adversary to speak reproachfully. (If it is to be noticed, Paul's practical mind, guided by the Spirit of God, has left us no impossible rules of perfection, but rather injunctions that all, not a few, can obey.)

15 For some are already turned aside after Satan. (They follow the great tempter, rather than the Lord Jesus.)

16 If any man or woman who believes have widows, let them relieve them (places the responsibility of such on the family), and let not the Church be charged (don't put unnecessary responsibility on the Church); that it may relieve them who are widows indeed (refers to those who are in dire need).

PASTORS

17 Let the Elders (Pastors in this case) who rule well be counted worthy of double honour (respect and regard), especially they who labour in the Word and Doctrine (Preaching and Teaching; such Pastors are to be deeply appreciated, as should be obvious).

18 For the Scripture says (Deut. 25:4), You shall not muzzle the ox that treads out the corn. And, The labourer is worthy of his reward. ([Lev. 19:13; Deut. 24:14] In I Cor. 9:9, Paul argued from this Text the right of a Minister to be maintained by those to whom he Ministers.)

19 Against an Elder (Pastor) receive not an accusation, but before two or three witnesses. (If the Church were to follow this principle faithfully, no member or Minister would ever become the victim of one vengeful individual. Even if there is only one witness and the Preacher lies about the situation [as some will], it would still be better to adhere to the Word, knowing for certain the Lord will handle the situation. While men may fool other men, no one fools God.)

A SINNING BROTHER

20 Them who sin (continues to refer to Preachers, those who are sinning and will not repent) rebuke before all (it is to be done before other Preachers, and not the entire Body of the Church, as the next phrase bears out), that others also may fear. (As stated, refers to other Preachers only, and not the entirety of the Body of the Church.)

TIMOTHY

21 I charge *you* before God, and the Lord Jesus Christ, and the elect Angels *(presents a Command, and the fact that Heaven is witnessing our actions),* that you observe these things without preferring one before another, doing nothing by partiality. *(This refers to the fact that there must be no prejudice when judgment is rendered, meaning not one way or the other.)*

22 Lay hands suddenly on no man *(refers to approval; True Repentance will soon bring about True results, and will be obvious),* neither be partaker of other men's sins *(if a person refuses to repent and approval is given to that person, the Preacher giving the approval then becomes a partaker of the sins being committed):* keep yourself pure *(which can be done only by understanding that our Faith must ever be in the Cross, which then gives the Holy Spirit the latitude to give us Victory).*

23 Drink no longer water *(means "water exclusively"; water was not treated at all in those days, and in many cases and from many sources was impure),* but use a little wine for your stomach's sake and your often infirmities. *(Evidently Timothy's physical constitution was not quite as strong as Paul's. During those days, all grape juice and alcoholic beverage were referred to as "wine." It could only be determined by the context as to which it was. We have no way here of knowing, but it was probably grape juice.)*

24 Some men's sins are open beforehand *(should have been translated, "openly manifested to all eyes"),* going before to judgment *(meaning judgment in such a case is easy because everything is out in the open);* and some *men* they *(the sins)* follow after *(refers to the fact that some sins are never confessed or repented of, but to be sure will be dealt with at the Judgment; the only answer for sin is the Cross; sinful man can take the Judgment that was placed upon Christ, which was done in our place, or he can face the Judgment; the Cross alone stops the coming Judgment.).*

25 Likewise also the good works of *some* are manifest beforehand *(presents that which is open and obvious to all);* and they that are otherwise cannot be hid. *(At the Judgment Seat of Christ, every secret will be made manifest. Every hidden thing will be revealed. All things will then be made clear.)*

CHAPTER 6

SERVANTS

LET as many servants *(slaves)* as are under the yoke *(the yoke of slavery)* count their own masters worthy of all honour *(in*

Paul's day, slaves were common, possibly making up the majority of the population; irrespective of whether the master was good or bad, Christian slaves were to function and do their work exactly as if they were doing it for the Lord Himself, and not men), that the Name of God and *His* Doctrine be not blasphemed. *(Everything the slave did, and everything we do, must be done with the view of Christ in mind.)*

MASTERS

2 And they who have believing masters, let them not despise *them*, because they are Brethren *(because they are equals in Christ; this doesn't mean the slave is to think less of his Christian master)*; but rather do *them* service *(literally means in the Greek, "slave for them all the more")*, because they are faithful and beloved, partakers of the benefit *(refers to the fact that if a Christian slave was to show obedience and grace to an unbelieving master, even as they certainly should, how much more should they show the same to a Master who is now a Believer and, therefore, greatly beloved of the Lord!)*. These things teach and exhort *(suggests the touchiness of the issue)*.

MONEY

3 If any man teach otherwise *(proclaims the fact that some were teaching things opposed to Paul's teaching)*, and consent not to wholesome words, *even* the Words of our Lord Jesus Christ *(Lk. 20:25; Mat. 5:44; 11:28-30)*, and to the Doctrine which is according to Godliness *(refers to the teaching concerning the proper attitude of the individual towards God)*;

4 He is proud *(the false teacher)*, knowing nothing *(despite his claims)*, but doting about questions and strifes of words *(the profitless debating of which has rent asunder whole Churches, and even entire denominations)*, whereof comes envy, strife, railings, evil surmisings *(proclaims the results of these useless questions as tendered by the false teachers)*,

5 Perverse disputings of men of corrupt minds *(should have been translated, "of men corrupted in mind")*, and destitute of the Truth *(refers to the fact that they had once possessed the Truth, which is the Cross, but had turned away to other things)*, supposing that gain is Godliness *(should have been translated, "supposing that Godliness is a way or source of gain")*: from such withdraw yourself *(have no dealings with these Preachers)*.

6 But Godliness with contentment *(content with what we have, which means we are thankful to God for what we have)* is great gain *(true gain)*.

7 For we brought nothing into this world, *and it is* certain we can carry nothing out. *(This speaks of worldly possessions. The only thing a person can keep is their Faith, that is if it's true Faith, which refers to Faith in Christ and the Cross.)*

8 And having food and raiment let us be therewith content. *(The Lord can never bless grasping greed.)*

9 But they who will be rich fall into temptation and a snare, and *into* many foolish and hurtful lusts *(speaks of the sacrifice of principle)*, which drown men in destruction and perdition. *(This refers to the wreck and ruin of the mind and body, but more particularly to the awful ruin of the eternal soul.)*

10 For the love of money is the root of all evil *(there is no conceivable evil that can happen to the sons and daughters of men, which may not spring from covetousness — the love of gold and wealth)*: which while some coveted after, they have erred from the Faith *(speaking of Believers who have lost sight of the True Faith, which is the Cross, and have ventured into a false faith, trying to use it to garner much money)*, and pierced themselves through with many sorrows *(the end result of turning in that direction; let all understand that the Word of God is true, and what it says will happen!)*.

FAITH

11 But you, O man of God, flee these things *(the Holy Spirit is unequivocally clear in His Command; we can follow the Lord, or we can follow other things; we can't follow both!)*; and follow after Righteousness, Godliness, Faith, Love, Patience, Meekness. *(In a sense, this is Fruit of the Spirit, or at least that which the Spirit Alone can bring about in our lives, which He does by the Cross ever being the object of our Faith.)*

12 Fight the good fight of Faith *(in essence, the only fight we're called upon to engage; every attack by Satan against the Believer, irrespective of its form, is to destroy or seriously weaken our Faith; he wants to push our Faith from the Cross to other things)*, lay hold on Eternal Life *(we do such by understanding that all Life comes from Christ, and the means is the Cross)*, whereunto you are also Called *(Called to follow Christ)*, and have professed a good profession before many witnesses. *(This does not refer to a particular occasion, but to the entirety of his life for Christ.)*

13 I give you charge in the sight of God *(in essence, the mantle is soon to be passed to this young Preacher)*, who quickens *(makes*

alive) all things *(presents Christ here as the Preserver, rather than the Creator)*, and *before* Christ Jesus *("I charge you before Christ")*, who before Pontius Pilate witnessed a good confession *(the confession of Christ was the model confession for all martyrs, insofar as it was a bold confession of the Truth, even with the sentence of death before His eyes)*;

14 That you keep *this* Commandment without spot, unrebukeable *(the Gospel of Christ and Him Crucified must not be compromised in any fashion)*, until the appearing of our Lord Jesus Christ *(the statement refers to both the Rapture and the Second Coming)*:

15 Which in His times *(an epoch-making period, foreordained of God)* He shall show, *Who is* the Blessed and only Potentate, the King of kings, and Lord of lords *(the Second Coming; refers to the fact that there will be absolutely no doubt as to the identity of the One Who will appear)*;

16 Who only has immortality *(in a sense says God is the Source of all immortality)*, dwelling in the Light which no man can approach unto *(the Person of God is wholly concealed by His Dwelling, which is Light; and this Dwelling is Itself unapproachable)*; Whom no man has seen, nor can see *(refers to the fact that "flesh and blood cannot inherit the Kingdom of God" [I Cor. 15:50])*: to Whom *be* honour and power everlasting. Amen. *(The great names and titles which the Holy Spirit, through Paul, has ascribed here to Christ, while definitely including His Deity, more than all direct attention to His great Redemption Work, which He accomplished at the Cross of Calvary.)*

THE USE OF RICHES

17 Charge them *(Believers)* who are rich in this world *(limits the riches to the here and now, and shows that one can be rich in this world and not in the other world)*, that they be not highminded *(proud)*, nor trust in uncertain riches *(presents the fact that it's very difficult to have great wealth without in some measure trusting in it)*, but in the Living God, Who gives us richly all things to enjoy *(God is the Source, not money!)*;

18 That they do good, that they be rich in good works *(use the money to take the Gospel to the world)*, ready to distribute, willing to communicate *(looking for the True Gospel, which can be supported, and which they will support)*;

19 Laying up in store for themselves a good foundation against the time to come *(laying up treasures on the other side)*, that they

may lay hold on Eternal Life. *(This should have been translated, "that they may hold to that which is truly Life.")*

BENEDICTION

20 O Timothy, keep that which is committed to your trust *(refers to the deposit of Truth delivered to him; actually, it would be the entirety of the New Covenant as it was given to Paul; what a responsibility!)*, avoiding profane *and* vain babblings *(pertains to that which is devoid of godliness, and empty of content)*, and oppositions of science falsely so called *(should have been translated, "and oppositions of knowledge falsely so-called," and speaks of the Gnostics)*:

21 Which some professing have erred concerning the Faith *(have turned away from Christ and the Cross)*. Grace *be* with you. Amen. *(Grace will always be with the Believer who places his Faith exclusively in Christ and His Finished Work.)*

THE SECOND EPISTLE OF PAUL THE APOSTLE TO
TIMOTHY

CHAPTER 1

INTRODUCTION

PAUL, an Apostle of Jesus Christ by the Will of God *(the Office of the Apostle carries the leadership of the Church, and does so by a special Message given to the Apostle, which in Paul's case was Grace)*, according to the Promise of Life which is in Christ Jesus *(Life, and more particularly Eternal Life is found only in Christ Jesus, and comes by means of the Cross)*,

2 To Timothy, *my* dearly beloved son: Grace, Mercy, *and* Peace, from God the Father and Christ Jesus our Lord *(all made possible by the Cross)*.

TIMOTHY

3 I thank God, Whom I serve from *my* forefathers with pure conscience *(in effect says he was seeking to please God even while he persecuted the Church through ignorance)*, that without ceasing I have remembrance of you in my prayers night and day *(in this we see the depth of this man's prayer life)*;

4 Greatly desiring to see you *(Paul was in prison in Rome when he wrote this Epistle, his last)*, being mindful of your tears *(Timothy was probably present when Paul was arrested the second time, and transported to Rome for his final imprisonment)*, that I may be filled with joy *(knowing his time was short, he desired to see Timothy)*;

5 When I call to remembrance the unfeigned Faith that is in you *(he recalls the time he first met Timothy, and the young man was invited to join his Evangelistic team [Acts 16:1-3])*, which dwelt first in your grandmother Lois, and your mother Eunice; and I am persuaded that is in you also *(proclaims here a tremendous heritage)*.

THE CHARGE

6 Wherefore I put you in remembrance that you stir up the Gift of God *(refers to the entirety of the Call of God upon Timothy's life)*, which is in you by the putting on of my hands. *(This doesn't mean Paul bestowed this Gift upon young Timothy, but that he verified what he knew to already be there.)*

7 For God has not given us the spirit of fear *(refers to a disposition of the mind; the Apostle is*

telling the young Evangelist not to fear); but of power *(could be said, "the spirit of power," for such comes from the Holy Spirit)*, and of love *(again, given by the Holy Spirit)*, and of a sound mind *(a "spirit of self-control," all made possible by the Holy Spirit, Who demands that we ever keep our Faith in the Cross [Rom. 8:1-2, 11, 13])*.

8 Be not thou therefore ashamed of the Testimony of our Lord *(the Christian, instead of being ashamed of his "profession of Faith," must before the world show fearlessly that its Hopes and its Promises are his most precious treasure)*, nor of me his prisoner *(even though Paul was a prisoner in a Roman cell, he in no way considered himself a prisoner of Nero, but rather of the Lord)*: but be thou partaker of the afflictions of the Gospel according to the Power of God *(actually means to take one's share of the ill-treatment, which will always be accompanied by the Power of God, which gives us Grace to stand the test)*;

9 Who has saved us *(through what He did at the Cross)*, and called *us* with an Holy Calling *(we didn't call Him, rather He Called us)*, not according to our works *(Salvation is by Grace through Faith, not of works [Eph. 2:8-9])*, but according to His Own Purpose and Grace *(refers to the rea-*

son and the means)*, which was given us in Christ Jesus *(through what He did at the Cross)* before the world began *(the Cross of Christ is the very first Doctrine of the Bible, actually "foreordained before the foundation of the world" [I Pet. 1:18-20]; consequently, every true Doctrine is built on the Foundation of the Cross, or else it's not true)*,

10 But is now made manifest by the appearing of our Saviour Jesus Christ *(everything is wrapped up in Jesus and what He did at the Cross)*, Who has abolished death *(the wages of sin is death [Rom. 6:23], thus when Jesus atoned for all sin on the Cross, this removed the means of death, i.e., "spiritual death")*, and has brought life and immortality to light through the Gospel *(the Gospel is the Cross, which made "life" and "immortality" possible, and will see its total fulfillment at the coming Resurrection)*:

11 Whereunto I am appointed a Preacher *(to Preach the Gospel)*, and an Apostle *(of Grace)*, and a Teacher of the Gentiles. *(Although the Apostle also preached to the Jews, his major thrust was ever to the Gentiles, whose Salvation the Cross made possible.)*

12 For the which cause *(to establish the Church)* I also suffer these things *(imprisonment, etc.)*: nevertheless I am not ashamed *(pro-*

claims the fact that some were ashamed of Paul, regarding his imprisonment): for I know Whom I have believed *(refers to the Lord Jesus Christ)*, and am persuaded that He is able to keep that which I have committed unto Him against that day. *(This refers to the soul with all its immortal interests.)*

13 Hold fast the form of sound words *(forms the correct Doctrine, which is "Jesus Christ and Him Crucified)*, which you have heard of me *(refers to the fact that the Lord gave Paul the meaning and understanding of the New Covenant, which is the Cross [Gal. 1:11-12])*, in Faith and Love which is in Christ Jesus. *(Anytime Paul uses the phrase "in Christ Jesus" or one of its derivatives, without exception, he is speaking of what Christ did at the Cross.)*

14 That good thing which was committed unto you *(presents in such simple words the single most important thing in the world, the Gospel of Jesus Christ)* keep by the Holy Spirit *(has the help of the Holy Spirit respecting the purity of the Message)* which dwells in us. *(He is constantly present and, therefore, constantly available!)*

15 This you know, that all they which are in Asia be turned away from me *(one of the most sorrowful trials the great hearted Paul had to endure in the agony of his last witnessing for his Lord was the* knowledge that his name and teaching were no longer held in honor in some of these Asian Churches so dear to him; this turning away was a turning away from the Cross); of whom are Phygellus and Hermogenes. *(How sad that these two would be placed in the Sacred Texts, not in the realm of faithfulness, but rather "faithlessness"!)*

ONESIPHORUS

16 The Lord give Mercy unto the house of Onesiphorus *(from the terminology, it seems this man had died a short time before)*; for he oft refreshed me, and was not ashamed of my chain *(once again, it seems many Believers were in fact ashamed of Paul and his situation, but not Onesiphorus)*:

17 But, when he was in Rome, he sought me out very diligently, and found me. *(This man, so kind to the great Apostle, will be among those at the final Judgment to whom the Saviour will say, "I was in prison, and you came unto Me" [Mat. 25:36].)*

18 The Lord grant unto him that he may find Mercy of the Lord in that day *(speaks of the "Judgment Seat of Christ," which will commence after the Rapture of the Church; only Believers will be there; as well, it will not involve sin, for that was handled at Calvary, but rather our motives, etc.)*: and in

how many things he ministered unto me at Ephesus, you know very well. *(It seems this man had ever been a help to Paul. Therefore, his name will be proclaimed favorably and forever on the pages of Sacred Writ.)*

CHAPTER 2

A GOOD SOLDIER

THOU therefore, my son, be strong *(one carries this out by ever making the Cross the Object of Faith)* in the Grace that is in Christ Jesus. *(The Source of Grace is the Lord, but the means is the Cross.)*

2 And the things that you have heard of me among many witnesses *(the integrity of the mighty deposit of Truth)*, the same commit thou to Faithful men *(refers to others called of God, who would Preach this great Gospel)*, who shall be able to teach others also. *(While many turned away from Paul, the evidence here is that some didn't; they were Faithful.)*

3 You therefore endure hardness *(take your part in suffering hardship if called upon to do so)*, as a good soldier of Jesus Christ. *(The Roman Legionnaires suffered hardship in the service of the Emperor. Why not the Christian in the service of the King of kings?)*

4 No man who wars entangles himself with the affairs of *this* life *(a soldier has one thing on his mind, and that is to carry out his duty; the Christian is to have the same motive, the same spirit, and the same consecration; hence the Apostle using the word "soldier")*; that he may please Him Who has chosen him to be a soldier. *(We are to please Christ, not men.)*

5 And if a man also strive for masteries *(now presents the manner in which the Believer strives)*, yet is he not crowned, except he strive lawfully. *(It is the preparation for the contest that is in question, not the contest itself. What is the Apostle saying?)*

6 The husbandman who labors *(the sowing of seed in order that a crop may ultimately be harvested)* must be first partaker of the fruits. *(If he doesn't "strive lawfully," which means to walk after the Spirit which leads to the Cross, there aren't going to be any "fruits.")*

7 Consider what I say *(refers to the fact that what Paul is saying is actually the "Word of the Lord")*; and the Lord give you understanding in all things. *(The Holy Spirit will always help the sincere seeker understand the tenor of the Word of God.)*

8 Remember that Jesus Christ of the seed of David *(the Incarnation)* was raised from the dead *(out from among the dead)* according to my Gospel *(that which*

was given to him by the Lord [Gal. 1:11-12]):

SUFFERING

9 Wherein I suffer trouble, as an evil doer, *even* unto bonds (*proclaims the fact that it was because of his Preaching of the Gospel that Paul had suffered severe trouble*); but the Word of God is not bound. (*This presents the fact that the Gospel, as it had been given to Paul, had been preserved by that Apostle in that he could pass it on undiluted and uncompromised.*)

10 Therefore I endure all things for the elect's sakes (*refers to all who have accepted Christ, whether Jews or Gentiles*), that they may also obtain the Salvation which is in Christ Jesus with Eternal Glory. (*If the Message of the Cross was diluted in any way, there would be no Eternal Glory. We should vividly remember that.*)

11 *It is* a Faithful saying: For if we be dead with *Him* (*refers to Christ as our Substitute dying on the Cross, with our Faith placing us in the position of dying "with Him" [Rom. 6:3-8]*), we shall also live with *Him* (*the Greek says, "We shall live by means of Him"; our "living with Him," which speaks of Resurrection Life and thus speaks of perpetual victory, is attained only by us understanding that we have been "planted together [Christ and*

the Believer] in the likeness of His Death"; in other words, it was all done at the Cross!*):

12 If we suffer, we shall also reign with *Him* (*the "suffering" has to do with "fighting the good fight of Faith"; to "reign" means to "reign as a king," so the stakes are very high!*): if we deny *Him*, He also will deny us (*refers to denying what He did for us at the Cross*):

13 If we believe not (*believe what He did at the Cross*), *yet* He abides Faithful (*despite the unbelief of many, He will be Faithful to Redeem all who come to Him in Faith*): He cannot deny Himself. (*Heaven will never change the Plan of Redemption and Victory, which is the Cross.*)

INSTRUCTIONS

14 Of these things put *them* in remembrance (*has special reference to the issues of life and death set out in the previous three Verses*), charging *them* before the Lord that they strive not about words to no profit (*if the Cross is abandoned, "Christ shall profit you nothing" [Gal. 5:2]*), *but* to the subverting of the hearers (*refers to overthrowing their Faith*).

15 Study to show yourself approved unto God (*refers to a workman who has been put to the test and, meeting these specifica-*

tions, has won the approval of the one who has subjected him to the test), a workman who needs not to be ashamed (Faith placed exclusively in the Cross will never bring shame; faith placed elsewhere will, without fail, bring shame), rightly dividing the Word of Truth. (If one doesn't properly understand the Cross, one cannot rightly divide the Word of Truth.)

16 But shun profane and vain babblings (this means no false doctrine leaves its victims as they were found, but rather worse, much worse!): for they will increase unto more ungodliness. (If the Preacher is teaching anything other than the Cross of Christ, it is construed by the Holy Spirit as no more than "vain babblings," and is guaranteed to increase ungodliness more and more. In fact, it cannot be any other way!)

17 And their word will eat as does a canker (false doctrine, which constitutes anything other than the Cross, will ultimately corrupt the whole): of whom is Hymenaeus and Philetus (as is obvious, Paul is here "marking them, which caused divisions and offences contrary to sound Doctrine" [Rom. 16:17]; if we as Preachers are to be true to the Gospel, we must do the same);

18 Who concerning the Truth have erred (there is only one "Truth," and that is "Jesus Christ and Him Crucified" [I Cor. 1:17-18, 23; 2:2]), saying that the Resurrec-

tion is past already (this is very similar to some modern Christians who claim there will be no Rapture, especially considering that the Rapture and the Resurrection are one and the same); and overthrow the Faith of some. (The Death and Resurrection of Christ have made everything possible, including the coming Resurrection of all Saints. To be confused about Christ's Atoning Work is to be confused about everything.)

19 Nevertheless the Foundation of God stands sure (proclaims the truth that this foundation is secure, despite the fact that some make shipwrecks of their Faith), having this seal, The Lord knows them who are His. (This "seal" guarantees the "security of the Church" and the "purity of the Church." The two go together. The purity of the Church is indispensable to its security.) And, Let every one who names the Name of Christ depart from iniquity. (One can "depart from iniquity," only as one makes the Cross the object of his Faith, which then gives him Holy Spirit Power.)

20 But in a great house there are not only vessels of gold and of silver, but also of wood and of earth (presents the Apostle using metaphors); and some to honour, and some to dishonour. (This refers to the fact that there is no such thing as sinless perfection this side of the Resurrection. There are

problems in every Christian life, which only the Cross can cure.)

21 If a man therefore purge himself from these *(he can only do so by ever making the Cross the object of his Faith, which will then give him Holy Spirit Power that alone can accomplish the task; the "purging" cannot come about by any other manner)*, he shall be a vessel unto honour, Sanctified, and meet *(qualified)* for the Master's use, *and* prepared unto every good work.

22 Flee also youthful lusts *(refers to the evil attracted to one when they are young, which is then very difficult to free one's self from when they are older)*: but follow Righteousness, Faith, Charity *(Love)*, Peace, with them who call on the Lord out of a pure heart *(attributes of the Spirit, which He Alone can produce within our hearts and lives, and He does according to our Faith anchored firmly in the Cross)*.

23 But foolish and unlearned questions avoid *(if it's not "Christ and Him Crucified," forget it!)*, knowing that they do gender strifes. *(This proclaims agitation, and much ado about nothing.)*

24 And the servant of the Lord must not strive *(pertains to being drawn aside into endless discussions which serve no purpose, and can only conclude in "strife!")*; but be gentle unto all *men (Fruit of the Spirit [Gal. 5:22])*, apt to teach *(teach correct Doctrine)*, patient *(show patience to those who do not easily and quickly understand that which is being taught)*,

25 In meekness instructing those who oppose themselves *(refers to those who place themselves in opposition to the true servant of the Lord and to True Doctrine)*; if God peradventure will give them Repentance to the acknowledging of the Truth *(hoping those in error will repent and come to the Truth, and we might quickly say, "The Truth of the Cross")*;

26 And *that* they may recover themselves out of the snare of the Devil *(if one is placing his Faith and Hope in anything other than Christ and the Cross, he has been "snared by the Devil," which is serious indeed!)*, who are taken captive by him at his will. *(Unless the Believer makes the Cross the object of his Faith, which then gives him the help of the Holy Spirit, he is helpless against Satan, who will make him his captive, i.e., "in bondage to sin" [Gal. 5:1].)*

CHAPTER 3

APOSTASY

THIS know also, that in the last days *(the days in which we now live)* perilous times shall come. *(This speaks of difficult dangerous times, which Christians living just before the Rapture will encounter.)*

2 For men *(those who call them-selves Christians)* shall be lovers of their own selves, covetous, boasters, proud, blasphemers, disobedient to parents, unthank-ful, unholy,

3 Without natural affection, trucebreakers, false accusers, in-continent, fierce, despisers of those who are good,

4 Traitors, heady, highmind-ed, lovers of pleasures more than lovers of God *(and remember, this is describing the Endtime Church, which has been totally corrupted [Mat. 13:33; Rev. 3:14-22])*;

5 Having a form of Godliness *(refers to all the trappings of Chris-tianity, but without the power)*, but denying the power thereof *(the modern Church, for all practical purposes, has denied the Cross; in doing this, they have denied that through which the Holy Spirit works, and in Whom the power resides [Rom. 8:1-2, 11; I Cor. 1:18])*: from such turn away. *(No half measures are to be adopted here. The com-mand is clear! It means to turn away from churches that deny or ignore the Cross.)*

6 For of this sort are they which creep into houses *(pro-claims the methods of false teach-ers)*, and lead captive silly women laden with sins, led away with divers lusts *(due to Eve succumb-ing to temptation and deception,* *women are the easiest prey for these false teachers; the idea is that "silly women" will support these false teach-ers, and do so grandly; they are drawn to these false Preachers through "divers lusts")*,

7 Ever learning *(proclaims learn-ing that which is wrong)*, and never able to come to the knowledge of the Truth. *(This proclaims the fact that they really do not want the Truth.)*

8 Now as Jannes and Jambres withstood Moses *([Ex. 7:11-12], the names of these men are found in the Targum of Jonathan)*, so do these also resist the Truth *(they have been shown the Truth, but have rejected the Truth, which they did purposely; it pertains to a rejection of the Cross of Christ)*: men of cor-rupt minds, reprobate concerning the Faith. *(If it's not "Christ and Him Crucified," then it is corrupt and reprobate [I Cor. 2:2].)*

9 But they shall proceed no further *(means the Holy Spirit will allow this error to go so far, and no further)*: for their folly shall be manifest unto all men *(error will ultimately manifest itself for what it really is because the True Gospel is more powerful)*, as theirs also was *(referring to the two men who attempted to withstand Moses)*.

PAUL

10 But you have fully known

my doctrine *(better translated, "But as for you, in distinction from others, have fully known my Doctrine")*, manner of life, purpose, faith, longsuffering, charity, patience *(Timothy knew Paul's example, which the Gospel had wrought in his life)*,

11 Persecutions, afflictions, which came unto me at Antioch, at Iconium, at Lystra *(presents Churches being built in these areas at great personal price)*; what persecutions I endured *(the persecutions were necessary in order that these Churches be built)*: but out of *them* all the Lord delivered me. *(The Lord will always deliver until the person's work is finished.)*

12 Yes, and all who will live Godly in Christ Jesus shall suffer persecution. *(It is because of the "offence of the Cross" [Gal. 5:11].)*

13 But evil men and seducers shall wax worse and worse *(this problem of seduction in the last days is so acute that the word Paul uses here [seducers] occurs no where else in the New Testament; this means that such an effort is unique to this particular time)*, deceiving, and being deceived. *(Truth opens the door to even more Truth, while deception opens the door to even more deception.)*

THE SCRIPTURES

14 But you continue in the things which you have learned and have been assured of *(the Message of the Cross)*, knowing of whom you have learned *them (Timothy had learned the Word of God from Paul, even as all others did, in fact, at that particular time, including the original Twelve. The meaning of the New Covenant was given to Paul, so it had to be learned from him)*;

15 And that from a child you have known the Holy Scriptures *(presents the greatest education any boy or girl could ever have)*, which are able to make you wise unto Salvation through Faith which is in Christ Jesus. *(The entirety of the Word of God points directly to Christ and what He did on the Cross. The Old Testament points forward to His Coming and what He would do. The New Testament points backward to what He has already done. And at the center of it all is the Cross.)*

16 All Scripture *is* given by Inspiration of God *(the Greek says, "all Scripture is God-breathed," which means it is the Word of God, and thereby infallible!)*, and is profitable for Doctrine *(all we believe, teach, and do must be based squarely on the Scriptures)*, for reproof *(proclaims the use of the Word of God in setting direction)*, for correction *(refers to restoration to an upright state)*, for instruction in Righteousness *(pre-*

sents the Bible as the only guide for such instruction):

17 That the man of God may be perfect (refers to maturity), throughly furnished unto all good works (properly understands the Word, which then produces "good works," i.e., "godly lives").

CHAPTER 4

LAST CHARGE

I charge you therefore (has the weight of a legal affirmation) before God, and the Lord Jesus Christ (should have been translated, "Our God, even Christ Jesus), who shall judge the quick (living) and the dead (refers to the fact that all Believers will stand at the Judgment Seat of Christ) at His appearing and His Kingdom (refers here to the Second Advent);

2 Preach the Word (refers to the whole body of revealed Truth, which means the entirety of the Word of God); be instant in season, out of season (presents the idea of the Preacher holding himself in constant readiness to proclaim the Word); reprove (the Preacher is to deal with sin, both in the lives of his unsaved hearers and in those of the Saints to whom he Ministers, and he is to do so in no uncertain tones and terms), rebuke (a suggestion in some cases of impending penalty), exhort with all longsuffering and Doc-

trine. (This tells us that the "reproving" and the "rebuking" must be done with gentleness. As well, the "longsuffering" refers to a gentleness that continues even when the Message is met with rejection. However, the "Doctrine" is not to change, even though it is rejected.)

3 For the time will come when they will not endure sound Doctrine ("sound Doctrine" pertains to overriding principles: the Salvation of the sinner, and the Sanctification of the Saint; the Cross is the answer for both, and is the only answer for both); but after their own lusts shall they heap to themselves teachers, having itching ears (refers to the people who have ears that "itch" for the smooth and comfortable word, and are willing to reward handsomely the man who is sufficiently compromising to speak it; hearers of this type have rejected the Truth and prefer to hear the lie);

4 And they shall turn away their ears from the Truth (those who follow false teachers not only turn away their ears from the Truth, but see to it that the ears are always in a position such that they will never come in contact with the Truth), and shall be turned unto fables. (If it's not the "Message of the Cross," then it is "fables" [I Cor. 1:18].)

5 But watch thou in all things (carries the idea of watching one's

own life, Ministry, and the Doctrine which we are proclaiming), **endure afflictions** (*carries the idea of not allowing hardships, difficulties, or troubles to hinder one's carrying forth of one's Ministry; it is a sharp command given with military snap and curtness; Wuest says, "How we in the Ministry of the Word need that injunction today. What a 'softy' we sometimes are, afraid to come out clearly in our proclamation of the Truth and our stand as to false doctrine, fearing the ostracism of our fellows, the Ecclesiastical displeasure of religious leaders so-called, or even the cutting off of our immediate financial income." ["I would rather walk a lonely road with Jesus than be in a crowd, without His fellowship"]*), **do the work of an Evangelist** (*keep trying to get people saved*), **make full proof of your Ministry** (*does it match up with the Word of God?*).

PAUL

6 For I am now ready to be offered (*the word "ready" signifies that the Holy Spirit had already told the Apostle the time had now come; the word "offered" speaks of the Drink-Offering poured out upon the Sacrifice about to be offered, which in effect was the lesser part poured out upon the most important part; only one who considered himself less than the least of all Saints could write in such deep humility*), **and the time of my departure is at hand.** (*This presents the fact that the servant of the Lord is immortal until his work is done.*)

7 I have fought a good fight (*should have been translated, "I have fought the good fight"; Paul fought his fight with sin to a finish, and was resting in a complete victory*), **I have finished** *my* **course** (*he had been faithful in carrying out that which had been assigned to him*), **I have kept the Faith** (*refers here to the deposit of Truth regarding the meaning of the Cross and the Resurrection of Christ, with which the Lord had entrusted Paul*):

8 Henceforth there is laid up for me a Crown of Righteousness (*the Victor's Crown*), **which the Lord, the Righteous Judge, shall give me at that day** (*at the Judgment Seat of Christ*): **and not to me only, but unto all them also who love His appearing.** (*This Victor's Crown will go to all who consider His appearing precious.*)

INSTRUCTIONS

9 Do your diligence to come shortly unto me (*Timothy was in Ephesus, about 1,000 miles from Rome; consequently, it was a journey which at best would take several weeks; whether the young Apostle made it there in time or made it at all, is not known*):

10 For Demas has forsaken me, having loved this present world, and is departed unto Thessalonica *(presents a sad Commentary regarding one who had been blessed with such a golden opportunity)*; Crescens to Galatia *(mentioned here only; tradition says he founded the Church in France)*, Titus unto Dalmatia *(modern Yugoslavia)*.

11 Only Luke is with me *(presents the one who wrote the Gospel that bears his name, as well as the Book of Acts)*. Take Mark, and bring him with you *(John Mark, who wrote the Gospel of Mark, the nephew of Barnabas)*: for he is profitable to me for the Ministry. *(This presents a tremendous commendation by the Apostle concerning Mark.)*

12 And Tychicus have I sent to Ephesus. *(It is believed Tychicus conveyed this very Epistle, the last one written by Paul, to Timothy and was perhaps instructed to replace Timothy at Ephesus, while the young Apostle came to Rome.)*

13 The cloak that I left at Troas with Carpus, when you come, bring *with you (quite possibly it was summer when Paul wrote this Epistle, and if he survived till winter, he would need this cloak)*, and the Books, *but* especially the Parchments *(refers to the Old Testament Books)*.

14 Alexander the coppersmith did me much evil *(it is the Work of God Paul laments, which causes him to mention this person)*: the Lord reward him according to his works *(barring Repentance, Judgment will ultimately come most assuredly on all those who attempt to hinder the Work of God, and do so by attempting to hinder the worker for God)*:

15 Of whom you beware also *(presents this individual as a tool of Satan; incidentally, he lived in Ephesus where Timothy was now Ministering)*; for he has greatly withstood our words *(strongly opposed our Message of the Cross)*.

16 At my first answer no man stood with me, but all *men* forsook me *(when one is down, and anyone can do any negative thing to him or her they so desire without any fear of reprimand or censure, but will rather be applauded, one quickly finds exactly how many true Christians there really are; regrettably, there aren't many!)*: I pray God that it may not be laid to their charge. *(The Apostle pleads to the Lord for these weak, unnerved friends of his who, solely through fear and not ill will to the cause, had deserted him, that their actions not be laid to their charge.)*

17 Notwithstanding the Lord stood with me, and strengthened me *(presents the fact that the Apostle experienced an unusual degree of the Presence of the Lord during this*

time); that by me the preaching might be fully known (that he might give a full proclamation of the Gospel before Nero, not compromising it at all), and that all the Gentiles might hear (in his defense before Nero, the trial room would have been filled with Gentiles, important dignitaries from all over the Roman Empire; from the lips of Paul, they would hear the Gospel): and I was delivered out of the mouth of the lion. (This phrase has been debated almost from the time it was uttered by Paul. It does not refer to being delivered from Nero, because he was not acquitted. As well, it had no bearing that he would be thrown to the lions, as thought by some, because Roman citizens, which Paul was, did not suffer such a fate. It probably referred to the entire situation at hand, and Satan's efforts to hinder the Message of Paul, which Satan was not able to do.)

18 And the Lord shall deliver me from every evil work (which harks back to the previous Verse), and will preserve me unto His Heavenly Kingdom (even though said in the future tense, actually has to do with the entirety of his life): to Whom be Glory forever and ever. Amen. (This presents the Apostle bursting to an ascrip-

tion of praise to the Lord Who he has loved so long and so well and, in all his troubles and perplexities, had never left him friendless.)

BENEDICTION

19 Salute (greet) Priscilla and Aquila (two of Paul's earliest friends), and the household of Onesiphorus. (This presents the same Brother mentioned in II Tim. 1:16.)

20 Erastus abode at Corinth (probably means he had now gone back to that city, which in effect was his home): but Trophimus have I left at Miletum sick.

21 Do your diligence to come before winter (hence bringing the cloak). Eubulus greets you, and Pudens, and Linus, and Claudia, and all the Brethren. (This presents some of the Christians in Rome whose names have been immortalized by their being included in Paul's Letter.)

22 The Lord Jesus Christ be with your spirit (invokes the Resurrection Name of our Lord). Grace be with you. Amen. (The first Epistle written by Paul was I Thessalonians, which was addressed to the Church. This last one was addressed to a Preacher. This tells us that for the Church to be right, the Preacher must first be right.)

THE EPISTLE OF PAUL THE APOSTLE TO

TITUS

CHAPTER 1

INTRODUCTION

PAUL, a servant of God, and an Apostle of Jesus Christ *(the designation of "servant" is given here first, even before the designation of "Apostle"; the Holy Spirit would have it this way; if the man cannot be a true servant, he cannot be a true Apostle; those who have the calling of "Apostle" serve as the de facto leaders of the Church by virtue of the Message they Preach, which for Paul was the Message of Grace),* according to the Faith *(refers to the Cross as the Foundation on which all other Doctrines are built)* of God's elect *(refers to the Church, which took the place of the Jews as the elect of God during the time of their being cut off [Rom., Chpts. 9-11]),* and the acknowledging of the truth which is after Godliness *(the idea is that proper Faith in the Cross of Christ will produce "Godliness!");*

2 In hope of Eternal Life *(Eternal Life is now given to everyone who is in Christ on condition of remaining in Him [Jn. 15:1-8; Gal. 1:6-8; 4:19; 5:4; I Jn. 5:11-12]),* which God, Who cannot lie *(says in the Greek, "un-lieable God"),* promised before the world began *(says in the Greek, "before the times of the ages");*

3 But has in due times manifested his Word through Preaching *(God's secret purposes in Salvation have been brought to light in the Preaching of the Apostle),* which is committed unto me according to the Commandment of God our Saviour *(Paul is the one to whom the meaning of the New Covenant was given, which is actually the meaning of the Cross [Gal. 1:11-12]);*

4 To Titus, *mine* own son after the common Faith *("Faith in the great Sacrifice of Christ"):* Grace, Mercy, *and* Peace, from God the Father and the Lord Jesus Christ our Saviour. *(This is all made possible by what Christ did at the Cross.)*

QUALITIES

5 For this cause left I you in Crete *(Paul was in Crete with Titus for a period of time),* that you should set in order the things that are wanting *(refers mainly to Church Government),* and ordain Elders *(Pastors)* in every city, as I had appointed you *(should have been*

translated, *"appoint Pastors in every city"*):

6 If any be blameless, the husband of one wife *(no polygamists)*, having Faithful children not accused of riot or unruly. *(This refers to children who are Believers and have proven to be such by proper conduct.)*

7 For a Bishop *(Pastor, Bishop, Elder, Shepherd, and Presbyter are all interchangeable, and refer to the Pastor of a local Church)* must be blameless, as the steward of God *(refers to a man who seeks to be totally consecrated to the Lord)*; not selfwilled, not soon angry, not given to wine, no striker *(doesn't have a spirit of contention)*, not given to filthy lucre *(not money hungry)*;

8 But a lover of hospitality, a lover of good men, sober, just, holy, temperate *(self-control)*;

9 Holding fast the Faithful Word as he has been taught *(suggests the notion of withstanding opposition, and not compromising the Word)*, that he may be able by sound Doctrine *(proper teaching)* both to exhort and to convince the gainsayers. *(The "gainsayers" are those who deny and contradict the Truth of the Cross.)*

FALSE TEACHERS

10 For there are many unruly and vain talkers and deceivers *(refers to those who make their false doctrine sound so right)*, specially they of the Circumcision *(the Judaizers who ignored the Cross, and tried to mix Law with Grace)*:

11 Whose mouths must be stopped *(means to be reduced to silence, or at least to be made ineffective, which the True Message of the Cross can do)*, who subvert whole houses *(refers to the effect of false teaching)*, teaching things which they ought not, for filthy lucre's sake. *(Money is their object, as it is with most false teachers.)*

12 One of themselves, *even* a Prophet of their own, said, The Cretians *are* always liars, evil beasts, slow bellies. *(This presents a striking indictment, but one desired by the Holy Spirit.)*

13 This witness is true. *(This proclaims not the mere opinion of Paul, but actually the inspired words of the Spirit.)* Wherefore rebuke them sharply *(refers to proclaiming the Truth and clearly pointing out the error as well, and doing so in no uncertain terms)*, that they may be sound in the Faith *(refers to the fact that there is only one Faith, and that is "Jesus Christ and Him Crucified" [I Cor. 2:2])*;

14 Not giving heed to Jewish fables *(didn't endear the Apostle to most Jews)*, and commandments of men *(means they were not given by God)*, that turn from the Truth. *(This presents the fact that anything that turns men from the Truth of the*

Cross must be rejected out of hand.)

15 Unto the pure all things *are* pure *(is to be understood in its proper context)*: but unto them who are defiled and unbelieving *is* nothing pure *(proclaims those who attempt to find Salvation outside of Faith in the Cross of Christ)*; but even their mind and conscience is defiled. *(Salvation by Law, as this was, can only defile, it cannot save.)*

16 They profess that they know God *(they loudly proclaimed their profession)*; but in works they deny Him *(refers to them trying to earn Salvation by their works, which at the same time denies the "Finished Work of Christ")*, being abominable, and disobedient, and unto every good work reprobate. *(This is the manner in which the Holy Spirit labels all who attempt to serve God outside of the Cross of Christ.)*

CHAPTER 2

AGED MEN

BUT you speak the things which become sound Doctrine *(the Foundation of the Christian Faith, "Jesus Christ and Him Crucified" [I Cor. 2:2])*:

2 That the aged men be sober, grave, temperate, sound in Faith, in charity *(love)*, in patience. *(At every point, the Christian exceeded by far the so-called high standards the pagan world knew.)*

AGED WOMEN

3 The aged women likewise, that *they be* in behaviour as becomes Holiness *(refers to the fact that this end should always be in view)*, not false accusers, not given to much wine, teachers of good things *(teaching by their consecrated lives)*;

YOUNG WOMEN

4 That they may teach the young women to be sober *(by their example)*, to love their husbands, to love their children,

5 *To be* discreet, chaste, keepers at home, good, obedient to their own husbands, that the Word of God be not blasphemed *(not mocked)*.

YOUNG MEN

6 Young men likewise exhort to be sober minded *(exercise self-control)*.

7 In all things shewing yourself a pattern of good works: in Doctrine *showing* uncorruptness, gravity, sincerity,

8 Sound speech, that cannot be condemned *(refers to that being Preached and taught as being absolutely Scriptural)*; that he who is of the contrary part may be ashamed, having no evil thing to say of you. *(This concerns evil*

things, which are true.)

SERVANTS

9 *Exhort* servants *(slaves)* to be obedient unto their own masters, *and* to please *them* well in all things; not answering again *(don't argue; irrespective of the conduct or attitude of the Master, every task was to be done as unto the Lord; it is the same now for modern Christian employees)*;

10 Not purloining *(don't steal anything, not even time)*, but showing all good fidelity *(trustworthiness in all situations)*; that they may adorn the Doctrine of God our Saviour in all things *(means simply "we ought to practice what we Preach!")*.

THE CHRISTIAN LIFE

11 For the Grace of God that brings Salvation has appeared to all men *(is available to all on the basis of Faith in Christ and what He did at the Cross)*,

12 Teaching us that, denying ungodliness and worldly lusts *(tells us that it can be done)*, we should live soberly, righteously, and godly, in this present world *(this can only be done by the Believer making the Cross the object of his Faith, which gives the Holy Spirit latitude to work in our lives, bringing about these graces)*;

13 Looking for that Blessed Hope *(refers to the Rapture of the Church [I Thess. 4:13-18])*, and the glorious appearing of the Great God and our Saviour Jesus Christ *(the "Blessed Hope" is the glorious appearing of our Lord)*;

14 Who gave Himself for us *(on the Cross)*, that He might redeem us from all iniquity *(on the Cross, Christ atoned for every sin — past, present, and future, at least for all who will believe [Jn. 3:16])*, and purify unto Himself a peculiar people, zealous of good works. *(The Sanctified life is strictly a Work of the Spirit, Who works exclusively within the parameters of the Sacrifice of Christ, which must ever be the object of our Faith.)*

15 These things speak, and exhort, and rebuke with all authority. *(The idea is that Titus and all other preachers are to minister decidedly, which means that everyone knows exactly what is being said.)* Let no man despise you *(refers to the fact that no man is to tell another man what he can or cannot preach)*.

CHAPTER 3

CITIZENSHIP

PUT them in mind to be subject to principalities and powers, to obey Magistrates *(refers to Civil Government)*, to be ready to every good work *(the Christian counts it as a privilege to have the opportunity to do good),*

2 To speak evil of no man *(refers to the employment of the principle of Grace, which excludes all violence of thoughts, language, or action),* to be no brawlers *(don't be contentious),* but gentle *(a Fruit of the Spirit [Gal. 5:22-23]),* showing all meekness unto all men. *(This portrays the inwrought Grace of the soul, which can only be brought about in the life of the Believer by the Holy Spirit. He does these things strictly on the premise of our Faith in Christ and the Cross.)*

SINNERS

3 For we ourselves also were sometimes *(in time past)* foolish *(refers to a lack of understanding of spiritual things),* disobedient *(disobedient to God and His Word),* deceived *(because of the Fall, unredeemed man sees nothing in its true light),* serving divers lusts and pleasures *(the lifestyle of the unbeliever),* living in malice and envy, hateful, *and* hating one another. *(Outside of Christ, there is not true love for anyone.)*

JUSTIFICATION

4 But after that *(refers to the lost condition of the unredeemed)* the kindness and love of God our Saviour toward man appeared *(presents Christ Himself, and what He did by dying on the Cross to redeem lost humanity),*

5 Not by works of righteousness which we have done *(presents the utter impossibility of man performing works of Righteousness which will save him),* but according to His Mercy He saved us *(the initiative of Salvation springs entirely from the Lord, and is carried out by means of the Cross),* by the washing of Regeneration *(in effect, the Born-again Believer is regened, which is brought about by a cleansing process, with the Blood having cleansed from all sin, both its power and its guilt [I Jn. 1:7]),* and renewing of the Holy Spirit *(proclaims the Member of the Godhead Who actually carries out the work of Regeneration in the heart and life of the Believing sinner, which He does by exhibited Faith in Christ on the part of the individual);*

6 Which He shed on us abundantly *(kindness and Love)* through Jesus Christ our Saviour *(takes us back to the Cross);*

7 That being justified by His Grace *(we can only be justified by Grace, and not at all by works [Eph. 2:8-9]),* we should be made heirs according to the hope of Eternal Life. *(This presents the culminating effect of Justification by Faith.)*

FINAL CHARGES

8 *This is* a Faithful saying *(refers to the fact that it is trustworthy)*, and these things I will that you affirm constantly *(proclaims in undeniable terminology that the Preacher and Teacher of the Gospel should constantly Preach the Cross)*, that they which have believed in God might be careful to maintain good works *(the greatest "good work" of all is to tell people about Jesus)*. These things are good and profitable unto men.

9 But avoid foolish questions, and genealogies, and contentions, and strivings about the Law *(refers in this case to the Law of Moses, but could refer to any philosophy or religious ramblings — in other words, anything but the Cross)*; for they are unprofitable and vain. *(Faith in Christ and the Cross alone will bring about profitable results. Everything else is unprofitable.)*

10 A man who is an heretic *(refers to someone who has obviously departed from the Word of God)* after the first and second admonition reject *(if they will not listen after two warnings about false doctrine, they and their Ministry are to be rejected, which means they are to be avoided; that being the case, there should be no further action outside of praying for the individual)*;

11 Knowing that he who is such is subverted *(spiritually turned inside out)*, and sins *(states that all false doctrine is sin)*, being condemned of himself *(brings an automatic condemnation)*.

12 When I shall send Artemas unto you, or Tychicus *(Paul was thinking of sending either Artemas or Tychicus to relieve Titus at Crete)*, be diligent to come unto me to Nicopolis: for I have determined there to winter. *(This possibly presents the place where the Epistle to Titus was written.)*

13 Bring Zenas the lawyer and Apollos on their journey diligently *(evidently, these two were to stop by Crete on their way elsewhere)*, that nothing be wanting unto them. *(The Apostle is telling Titus to receive an offering for them. As well, there is even a probability that they were the bearers of this Epistle from Paul to Titus.)*

14 And let ours also learn to maintain good works for necessary uses *(proclaims the fact that the Apostle was training Believers to give of their financial resources in order to help take the Gospel to others)*, that they be not unfruitful. *(To be "fruitful" carries the idea that we are giving our money to that which is winning souls and truly doing a work for God.)*

15 All who are with me salute you. Greet them who love us in the Faith. *(The words "the Faith" always and without exception refer to the Sacrifice of Christ.)* Grace *be* with you all. Amen.

THE EPISTLE OF PAUL THE APOSTLE TO
PHILEMON

INTRODUCTION

PAUL, a prisoner of Jesus Christ, *(even though in prison in Rome, Paul concludes himself as being a prisoner of Christ, not Nero)*, and Timothy our brother *(the young Apostle was with Paul in Rome at this time)*, unto Philemon our dearly beloved, and fellowlabourer *(this person was a man of some standing and wealth, and was a convert of Paul)*,

2 And to *our* beloved Apphia *(said to be the wife of Philemon)*, and Archippus *(believed to be the son of Philemon and Apphia)* our fellowsoldier, and to the Church in your house *(the location of most Churches during that time)*:

3 Grace to you, and Peace, from God our Father and the Lord Jesus Christ. *(This implies that all these Blessings proceed from God the Father, with the Lord Jesus Christ being the means, which refers to the Cross.)*

THANKSGIVING

4 I thank my God, making mention of you always in my prayers *(speaks of Philemon)*,

5 Hearing of your Love and Faith *(concerns the two pillars of Christianity)*, which you have toward the Lord Jesus, and toward all Saints *(refers to the fact that Christ is the center of all things in this man's life)*;

6 That the communication of your Faith may become effectual *(Faith which doesn't bring about the development of the Fruit of the Spirit, with such Grace extended to others, is really not proper Faith)* by the acknowledging of every good thing which is in you in Christ Jesus. *(This proclaims the source of all this, and more particularly that this Source is the Cross of Christ.)*

7 For we have great joy and consolation in your Love *(part of Paul's strength came from hearing encouraging reports of those such as Philemon)*, because the bowels of the Saints are refreshed by you, Brother. *(Philemon was an encouragement to the Saints in that area of Colosse.)*

ONESIMUS

8 Wherefore, though I might be much bold in Christ *(could speak from Apostolic authority, but will not do so)* to enjoin you that

which is convenient *(speaking of the release of Onesimus, but he will seek that release in another way)*,

9 Yet for love's sake I rather beseech you *(proclaims the manner in which a true Apostle conducts himself, and any Believer for that matter)*, being such an one as Paul the aged *(this was at the close of Paul's first imprisonment in Rome; he must have been about 63 years old at the time)*, and now also a prisoner of Jesus Christ *(proclaims again that which he wore as a badge of honor)*.

10 I beseech you for my son Onesimus *(presents the first time this man's name is mentioned, even though he is the reason for the letter; he was owned by Philemon, and had run away from his master to Rome, a distance of about 1,000 miles; this was a most serious offense!)*, whom I have begotten in my bonds *(after arriving in Rome, this runaway slave had gotten in touch with Paul, and had given his heart to Christ)*:

11 Which in time past was to you unprofitable *(not knowing the Lord, Onesimus didn't provide very good service for Philemon)*, but now profitable to you and to me *(presents that which only Christ can do; He can make one "profitable!")*:

12 Whom I have sent again *(he is coming back home, in effect giving himself up, which is what he should have done now that he had come to Christ)*: you therefore receive him *(in effect pleads with Philemon to take back his formerly worthless servant, and assures him that he will not find Onesimus worthless now, but rather helpful!)*, that is, mine own bowels *(is the same as saying, "receive him as me, as my offspring")*:

13 Whom I would have retained with me *(presents a graceful expression of Paul's confidence in Onesimus)*, that in your stead he might have ministered unto me in the bonds of the Gospel *(proclaims the fact that he had been very helpful to Paul, even though there only a short time; conversion to Christ had totally changed the man)*:

14 But without your mind would I do nothing *(refers to the consent of Philemon)*; that your benefit should not be as it were of necessity, but willingly. *(This refers to the fact that the Apostle desires Philemon not feel he is under some type of constraint. Whatever Philemon does, Paul wants it to be "willingly," and not at all of necessity.)*

15 For perhaps he therefore departed for a season *(proclaims in the original Greek that there was a Divine Providence in the departure of Onesimus, or rather that the Holy Spirit used the occasion to bring the man to Christ; in fact, the Holy*

Spirit uses many such occasions), that you should receive him for ever *(the relationship will now be totally different)*;

16 Not now as a servant *(no more as a slave)*, but above a servant, a Brother beloved *(Paul is asking that Onesimus not be received as a slave; perhaps he will still be a slave insofar as the outward fact goes, but a new spirit is now breathed into the relationship, all because of Christ)*, specially to me, but how much more unto you, both in the flesh, and in the Lord? *("In the flesh, Philemon has the Brother for his slave; in the Lord, Philemon has the slave for his Brother.")*

17 If you count me therefore a partner *(places both Paul and Philemon in the same status, i.e., the same category)*, receive him as myself *(now brings Onesimus up to the level of Paul and Philemon)*.

18 If he has wronged you, or owes *you* ought, put that on my account *(I am asking you to forgive this debt; but if you feel you cannot do so, I will personally pay the debt)*;

19 I Paul have written *it* with my own hand, I will repay it *(presents the Apostle's Promise as ironclad; in other words, it is a contract!)*: albeit I do not say to you how you owe unto me even your own self besides. *(Whatever hope of Eternal Life this businessman cherished was to be traced to Paul's Ministry.)*

FELLOWSHIP

20 Yes, Brother, let me have joy of you in the Lord *(refers to the fact that what Paul is asking is not at all for himself, but rather for the Lord)*: refresh my bowels in the Lord. *(The granting of this request will be of the Lord also!)*

21 Having confidence in your obedience I wrote unto you *(expresses Faith that Philemon will do exactly as he has requested)*, knowing that you will also do more than I say *(hints at emancipation for Onesimus)*.

22 But withal prepare me also a lodging *(proclaims the fact that the Apostle felt his release would come very shortly)*: for I trust that through your prayers I shall be given unto you *(he thanks Philemon for praying for him)*.

BENEDICTION

23 There salute thee Epaphras, my fellowprisoner in Christ Jesus *(a native of Colosse)*;

24 Mark, Aristarchus, Demas, Luke, my fellow-labourers.

25 The Grace of our Lord Jesus Christ *be* with your spirit. Amen.

THE EPISTLE OF PAUL THE APOSTLE TO THE
HEBREWS

CHAPTER 1

JESUS CHRIST

GOD, Who at sundry times and in divers manners *(refers to the many and varied ways)* spoke in time past unto the fathers by the Prophets *(refers to Old Testament Times)*,

2 Has in these last days *(the dispensation of Grace, which is the Church Age)* spoken unto us by His Son *(speaks of the Incarnation)*, Whom He has appointed Heir of all things *(through the means of the Cross)*, by Whom also He made the worlds *(proclaims His Deity, as the previous phrase of Him being the "Heir of all things" proclaims His humanity)*;

3 Who being the brightness of His Glory *(the radiance of God's Glory)*, and the express Image of His Person *(the exact reproduction)*, and upholding all things by the Word of His Power *(carries the meaning of Jesus not only sustaining the weight of the universe, but also maintaining its coherence and carrying on its development)*, when He had by Himself purged our sins *(which He did at the Cross, dealing with sin regarding its cause, its power, and its guilt)*, sat down on the Right Hand of the Majesty on high *(speaks of the Finished Work of Christ, and that the Sacrifice was accepted by the Father)*;

ANGELS

4 Being made so much better than the Angels *(He was better than the Angels, which refers to the Incarnation, the price paid at Calvary [the reason for the Incarnation], and then His Exaltation as Saviour; as God, Jesus has always been greater than the Angels, but this is speaking of Him here as man)*, as He has by inheritance obtained a more excellent Name than they. *(This refers to what Christ did at the Cross, with the present result being that the inheritance is in His permanent possession.)*

5 For unto which of the Angels said He *(God the Father)* at any time, You are My Son *(Son of God)*, this day have I begotten You? *(This speaks of the Incarnation. God never said such of Angels, only of His Son [Ps. 2:7].)* And again, I will be to Him a Father, and He shall be to Me a Son?

(When uttered, referred to the future tense, but now is past tense. All had to do with Redemption, and all for you and me.)

6 And again, when He *(God the Father)* brought in the First-begotten into the world *(refers to Jesus being born of the Virgin Mary)*, He said, And let all the Angels of God worship Him. *(The idea is only Deity can be worshiped. Jesus is God!)*

7 And of the Angels He said, Who makes His Angels spirits *(the emphasis upon the variableness of the Angelic nature)*, and His Ministers a flame of fire. *(This does not speak of Preachers, as some have suggested, but continues to address itself to Angels.)*

8 But unto the Son *He said,* Your Throne, O God, *is for ever and ever (Thrones typify dominion, which in this case can only be occupied by Deity):* a sceptre of Righteousness *is* the sceptre of Your Kingdom *(totally unlike any other Kingdom that has ever existed, and was made possible by the Cross).*

9 You have loved Righteousness, and hated iniquity *(proclaims the True Man, Christ Jesus);* therefore God, *even* your God, has anointed You with the oil of gladness above Your fellows *(refers to the Holy Spirit).*

10 And, You, Lord, in the beginning have laid the foundation of the earth *(proclaims Jesus the Messiah as the Creator as well!);* and the Heavens are the Works of Your Hands *(presents the fact that only Deity could do such a thing):*

11 They shall perish *(means to wax old as a garment);* but You remain *(Christ is exalted because of the Cross, and will remain thus forever);* and they all shall wax old as does a garment *(proclaims the fact that there is going to have to be a change regarding the Creation);*

12 And as a vesture shall You fold them up, and they shall be changed *(changed from one condition to another):* but You are the same, and Your years shall not fail *(refers to the superiority of the Creator over the Creation).*

13 But to which of the Angels said He *(God the Father)* at any time, Sit on My Right Hand *(Angels stand before God; it is a mark of superior dignity that the Son sits),* until I make Your enemies Your footstool? *(This refers to God rendering all Christ's enemies utterly powerless, which is carried out by the Cross.)*

14 Are they not all Ministering spirits *(the function of Angels),* sent forth to Minister for them Who shall be heirs of Salvation? *(This proclaims that they attend only those who have made Christ their Saviour.)*

CHAPTER 2

COVENANT

THEREFORE we ought to give the more earnest heed to the things which we have heard (*actually refers to the New Testament Message of the Cross*), lest at any time we should let *them* slip. (*In the Greek Text, it carries the idea of a ring slipping from a finger. Regrettably, the Church presently has let the Message of the Cross slip and, as a result, the Church hardly knows where it's been, where it is, or where it's going.*)

2 For if the word spoken by Angels was stedfast (*actually refers to the Law of Moses, which had many Angels in attendance*), and every transgression and disobedience received a just recompence of reward (*sin is either addressed at the Cross, or else it is addressed in Judgment; so, each person has a choice*);

3 How shall we escape, if we neglect so great Salvation (*if we neglect the Cross, we have destroyed ourselves*); which at the first began to be spoken by the Lord (*announced by Christ when He said, "repent: for the Kingdom of Heaven is at hand" [Mat. 4:17]*), and was confirmed unto us by them who heard *Him* (*confirmed by healings and miracles which were witnessed by the original Twelve, plus untold numbers of others*);

4 God also bearing *them* witness (*presents the highest evidence of all, actually that which is absolutely indisputable*), both with signs and wonders, and with divers miracles (*which began with Christ, and continued on through His Apostles*), and Gifts of the Holy Spirit (*has to do with those listed in I Cor. 12:8-10*), according to His Own Will? (*These things were the Will of God then, and are the Will of God now!*)

REDEMPTION

5 For unto the Angels has He not put in subjection the world to come, whereof we speak. (*The Lord hasn't given the Angels dominion and rulership as He has Christ.*)

6 But one in a certain place testified, saying (*Ps. 8:4-6*), What is man, that You are mindful of him? (*This delves into the reason God has given man so much notice.*) or the son of man, that You visit him? (*This refers to looking upon in order to help or benefit. This clearly indicates the "son of man" spoken of here is the human race and not Christ.*)

7 You made him a little lower than the Angels (*should have been translated, "You made him a little lower than the Godhead"; the Hebrew word translated "Angels" is*

"Elohim" which means "God," and should have been translated accordingly); You crowned him with glory and honour (proclaims that which was never said of Angels), and did set him over the works of Your hands (some of that dominion is retained despite the Fall; however, as would be obvious, much has been lost; but to be sure, it has all been regained in Christ, and will ultimately be realized in Christ):

8 You have put all things in subjection under his feet. (This speaks of Adam before the Fall, but more particularly it speaks of Christ and what He did at the Cross on our behalf.) For in that He (God) put all in subjection under him (man), He (God) left nothing that is not put under him. (Once again speaks of the original Adam, but more than all speaks of the "Last Adam," the Lord Jesus Christ.) But now we see not yet all things put under him. (Due to the Fall, we do not now see what was originally intended for man, but through Christ it will ultimately be seen.)

9 But we see Jesus, Who was made a little lower than the Angels (the Incarnation) for the suffering of death (unequivocally proclaims the fact that Jesus came to this world for one specific purpose — to die upon a Cross, which was planned even before the foundation of the world [I Pet. 1:18-20]), crowned with glory and honour (the mission was accomplished, and now Christ is exalted); that He by the Grace of God should taste death for every man. (This proclaims the fact that He needed the Grace of God to accomplish this task, because He was a man, "the Man, Christ Jesus.")

10 For it became Him (refers to God's Way, as it concerns the Redemption of mankind), for Whom are all things (God is the final reason for all things), and by Whom are all things (through Whose agency), in bringing many sons unto Glory (speaks of the Divine Purpose), to make the Captain of their Salvation perfect through sufferings. (This carries the idea that Christ had to suffer the Cross in order to bring about Redemption for humanity.)

11 For both He Who Sanctifies and they who are Sanctified are all of One (of Christ): for which cause He is not ashamed to call them Brethren (refers to the fact that Jesus became one of us, but only in the sense of humanity, not in the sense of sin),

12 Saying, I will declare Your Name unto My Brethren ([Ps. 22:22] meaning that Christ will declare the Name of God to all the Brethren, in effect owning them), in the midst of the Church will I sing praise unto You. (Christ will praise God because of this great

Victory, which has brought many sons into the Kingdom, all made possible by the Cross.)

13 And again (II Sam. 22:3), I will put My trust in Him. (Christ puts His trust totally in God.) And again (Isa. 8:18), Behold I and the Children which God has given Me. (The Cross makes it possible for us to become a Child of God.)

14 Forasmuch then as the children are partakers of flesh and blood (refers to the fact that this Creation has a human, not Angelic, nature), He (Jesus) also Himself likewise took part of the same (the Incarnation, God becoming man); that through death (the Cross) He (Jesus) might destroy him (Satan) who had the power of death, that is, the Devil (the wages of sin is death, which speaks of separation from God; Jesus atoned for all sin at the Cross, thereby removing the cause of spiritual death, at least for all who will believe [Jn. 3:16]);

15 And deliver them (speaks of mankind held in captivity by Satan) who through fear of death were all their lifetime subject to bondage. (It has been well said that the two terrors from which none but Christ can deliver men are guilt of sin and fear of death. The latter is the offspring of the former.)

16 For verily He took not on Him the nature of Angels (Christ did not come to be the Saviour of fallen Angels; they are of another creation); but He took on Him the seed of Abraham. (This refers to His humanity, which He became and was the manner in which Redemption would be brought about.)

17 Wherefore in all things it behoved Him to be made like unto His Brethren (refers to our Lord laying hold of the human race for the purpose of saving those who would accept Salvation by Faith), that He might be a merciful and faithful High Priest in things pertaining to God (as our High Priest, He is our Representative to God, which He could be by becoming a Man and going to the Cross as well, which He did), to make reconciliation for the sins of the people (to make an atoning Sacrifice in order to regain the favor and goodwill of God on behalf of the human race).

18 For in that He Himself has suffered being tempted (in His Incarnation as the last Adam, our Lord was put to the test, and was also solicited to do evil [Mat. 4:1-11]), He is able to succour them who are tempted. (The Cross alone is the answer to temptation and sin. We overcome temptation by placing our Faith strictly in Christ and the Cross, which is the only way it can be overcome, thus giving the Holy Spirit latitude to strengthen us, as He always stands ready

to do [Rom. 8:2, 11].)

CHAPTER 3

MOSES

WHEREFORE, Holy Brethren, partakers of the Heavenly Calling *(pertains to all Believers)*, consider the Apostle *(presents the only time Christ is referred to as an "Apostle")* and High Priest of our profession, Christ Jesus *(among the Jews, the High Priest was also considered to be the Apostle of God; consequently, the two Apostles are now compared, the High Priest of Israel and Christ Jesus)*;

2 Who was faithful to Him Who appointed Him *(should read, "Christ was faithful to God Who appointed Him as Apostle and High Priest")*, as also Moses was faithful in all his house. *(This presents the Holy Spirit through Paul handling Moses delicately; however, there are vast differences in the two.)*

3 For this Man *(Christ Jesus)* was counted worthy of more glory than Moses *(finds Paul proclaiming the humanity of Christ, by which measurement he compares Moses)*, inasmuch as He *(God)* Who has built the house has more honour than the house. *(This proclaims the fact that the Lord built the House of Israel.)*

4 For every house is built by some *man (presents the fact that even though men are the instruments used by God, they are in fact only instruments)*; but He Who built all things *is* God. *(Christ, although humbling Himself to the likeness of sinful flesh, is still the Builder of all things, which means he is far greater than Moses [Jn. 1:1-3].)*

5 And Moses verily *was* faithful in all his house, as a servant *(proclaims the position of the great Lawgiver as it relates to God)*, for a testimony of those things which were to be spoken after *(pertained to Moses and the entirety of the Law with all its ceremonies, etc., all pointing to Christ and the Cross, Who was to come)*;

6 But Christ as a Son over His Own house *(presents a clear distinction made between the Old Testament House of God and the New Testament House)*; Whose house are we *(refers to the Church)*, if we hold fast the confidence and the rejoicing of the hope firm unto the end *(if we keep our confidence in Christ and the Cross)*.

ISRAEL

7 Wherefore (as the Holy Spirit says *(Ps. 95:7-11)*, Today if you will hear His Voice *(presents words which were originally a warning to Israel not to provoke God, lest they be excluded from the "rest" He had promised them; this same warning*

is now given to Christians),

8 Harden not your hearts *(as Israel hardened their hearts against God in the wilderness, it is likewise possible for modern Christians to do the same)*, as in the provocation *(Israel provoked God)*, in the day of temptation in the wilderness *(the Lord didn't tempt Israel, they tempted Him!)*:

9 When your fathers tempted Me *(they tempted God through unbelief and rebellion)*, proved Me *(registered unbelief toward God)*, and saw My works forty years. *(The proof was all around them regarding the miracle working power of God that was exhibited daily, even for forty years, but they still wouldn't believe.)*

10 Wherefore I was grieved with that generation *(and because of their unbelief)*, and said, They do always err in *their* heart *(proclaims the seat of obedience or disobedience)*; and they have not known My Ways. *(They could have known, but had no desire to know.)*

11 So I swore in My wrath *(is figurative, and denotes a determined purpose)*, They shall not enter into My rest.) *(This refers here to a particular "rest," which pertained to the land of Canaan, but was undoubtedly regarded as emblematic of the "rest" afforded by Salvation.)*

12 Take heed, Brethren *(proclaims Paul warning Believers by* the examples of Israel's failures in the wilderness)*, lest there be in any of you an evil heart of unbelief *(the Greek order of words is, "a heart evil with reference to unbelief")*, in departing from the Living God. *(As stated, the problem is unbelief, and in modern terminology it refers to unbelief in Christ and the Cross.)*

13 But exhort one another daily *(proclaims a constant frequency, which means the Preacher should preach the Cross, and do so constantly)*, while it is called Today *(it must be done today; in other words, start now talking and speaking about the Cross, which is the only answer [I Cor. 1:17; Gal. 6:14])*; lest any of you be hardened through the deceitfulness of sin. *(This actually says, "the deceitfulness of the sin," which refers to a rejection of the Sacrifice of Christ.)*

14 For we are made partakers of Christ *(refers to Rom. 6:3-5)*, if we hold the beginning of our confidence stedfast unto the end *(if our confidence remains steadfast in Christ and the Cross)*;

15 While it is said, Today if you will hear His Voice, harden not your hearts, as in the provocation *(Vss. 7-8)*.

16 For some, when they had heard, did provoke *(should have been translated, "For who when they had heard did provoke"; all*

did except Joshua and Caleb [Num. 14:6-9]): howbeit not all who came out of Egypt by Moses. *(This should have been translated, "Was it not all who came out of Egypt through Moses?")*

17 But with whom was He grieved forty years? *(This refers to God's wrath continuing simply because their unbelief continued.)* was it not with them who had sinned, whose carcases fell in the wilderness? *(Unbelief caused the deaths of approximately two million people.)*

18 And to whom swore He that they should not enter into His rest, but to them who believed not? *(They lost everything because of unbelief, and the modern Church is doing the same, which is the very reason that Paul wrote this Epistle.)*

19 So we see that they could not enter in because of unbelief *(and if the modern Believer registers unbelief toward Christ and the Cross, the results will be the same as it was with Israel of Old).*

CHAPTER 4

UNBELIEF

LET us *(modern Believers)* therefore fear *(refers to the fact that Salvation can be lost if the Believer ceases to believe)*, lest, a Promise being left us of entering into His rest *(the Promise of Salvation)*, any of you should seem to come short of it. *(This proves it is possible for such to be done, which means the loss of the soul.)*

2 For unto us was the Gospel Preached, as well as unto them *(there is only one Gospel, and that is "Jesus Christ and Him Crucified")*: but the Word preached did not profit them *(if the Cross is abandoned as the object of Faith, Christ will profit no one anything [Gal. 5:2])*, not being mixed with Faith in them who heard it. *(The Israelites had Faith, but not in the right object. It must be Faith in Christ and the Cross, or it's not valid Faith.)*

3 For we which have believed do enter into rest *(proclaims unequivocally that Faith is the key, but let it be understood that it's Faith in Christ and the Cross)*, as He said, As I have sworn in My wrath, if they shall enter into My rest *(the condition is Faith)*: although the works were finished from the foundation of the world. *(This refers to this great Plan of Salvation through Christ and the Cross having been formulated even before the world was created [I Pet. 1:18-20].)*

4 For He *(God)* spoke in a certain place of the seventh *day* on this wise *(Gen. 2:3)*, And God did rest the seventh day from all His Works. *(God ceased from the Work*

of Creation simply because the Creation was finished.)

5 And in this *place* again *(Ps. 95:7-11),* If they shall enter into My rest *(conditions are to be met).*

6 Seeing therefore it remains that some must enter therein *(speaks of the New Covenant and the Church),* and they to whom it was first preached entered not in because of unbelief *(proclaims from Verse 2 that the Israelites of Old had the same Gospel preached unto them as we do, but to no avail):*

7 Again, He *(God)* limited a certain day *(proclaims in no uncertain terms that even though the Call of God is unlimited, the opportunity to accept that Call is definitely limited),* saying in David, Today, after so long a time *(the Holy Spirit said "today" then, and He is continuing to say "today" at present, referring to the fact that tomorrow may be too late);* as it is said, Today if you will hear His Voice, harden not your hearts *(once again refers to unbelief).*

8 For if Jesus *(should have been translated, "Joshua")* had given them Rest *(refers to the fact that even though Joshua was able to lead Israel into the land of Canaan by the power of the Holy Spirit, this was only a symbol of the true Rest which was to come, namely the Lord Jesus Christ),* then would He *(God)* not afterward have spoken of another day *(meaning the Law*

could not bring about what was desired, but definitely did point to that which was to come, namely the Lord Jesus Christ).

9 There remains *(what the Law couldn't do, Christ would do)* therefore a Rest to the People of God. *(This is found only in Christ and through what He did at the Cross, to which everything in the Old Testament pointed.)*

10 For he who is entered into His *(God's)* Rest *(due to what Christ did at the Cross, anyone can enter into this "Rest"),* he also has ceased from his own works *(we enter in by Faith, which refers to Faith in Christ and what He did at the Cross),* as God did from His. *(God rested on the seventh day when Creation was finished. And we can Rest in Christ because the Plan of Redemption is finished, of which God's Rest was a type.)*

11 Let us labour therefore to enter into that Rest *(could be translated, "let us hasten therefore to enter into that Rest"),* lest any man fall after the same example of unbelief. *(This tells us that the root cause of the "fall" of any Believer is unbelief, and it refers to unbelief in the Cross, which was the true Mission of Christ.)*

12 For the word of God *is* quick *(alive),* and powerful *(active, energizing),* and sharper than any two-edged sword *(refers to the ability of the Word of God to "probe"),*

piercing even to the dividing asunder of soul and spirit, and of the joints and marrow (*doesn't mean the dividing asunder of soul from spirit or joints from marrow, but rather that the Word of God pierces the soul and the spirit, adequately proclaiming what man ought to be and can only be in Christ; as well, the Word of God portrays to us the Holy Spirit and His Power, and proclaims the fact that He Alone can "quicken our mortal bodies" [Rom. 8:11], which refers to giving us power to yield this physical body to that which is Righteous [Rom. 6:12-13]*), and is a discerner of the thoughts and intents of the heart (*carries the idea of "sifting out and analyzing evidence"*).

13 Neither is there any creature that is not manifest in His sight (*refers to God as the Creator of all things*): but all things *are* naked and opened unto the eyes of Him with Whom we have to do (*to Whom we must give account*).

HIGH PRIEST

14 Seeing then that we have a Great High Priest (*Christ acts on our behalf to God*), Who is passed into the Heavens (*has to do with a legal process*), Jesus the Son of God (*presents the fact that Jesus is not only man, but is God as well*), let us hold fast *our* profession. (*Let us hold fast to Christ and the Cross, which was necessary for our Lord to be our High Priest.*)

15 For we have not an High Priest who cannot be touched with the feeling of our infirmities (*being Very Man as well as Very God, He can do such*); but was in all points tempted like as we are, yet without sin (*His temptation, and ours as well, was to leave the prescribed Will of God, which is the Word of God; but He never did, not even one time.*)

16 Let us therefore come boldly unto the Throne of Grace (*presents the Seat of Divine Power, and yet the Source of boundless Grace*), that we may obtain Mercy (*presents that which we want first*), and find Grace to help in time of need (*refers to the Goodness of God extended to all who come, and during any "time of need"; all made possible by the Cross*).

CHAPTER 5

MELCHISEDEC

FOR every High Priest taken from among men is ordained for men in things *pertaining* to God (*"from among men" pertains to the frailty of men*), that he may offer both Gifts and Sacrifices for sins (*the "Gifts" referred to "Thank-Offerings, while the "Sacrifices" referred to certain animals being offered, all types of Christ*):

2 Who can have compassion on the ignorant *(refers to having feelings for those on whose behalf he officiates)*, and on them who are out of the way *(refers to those who have sinned, and who know they have sinned)*; for that He Himself also is compassed with infirmity. *(This refers to the condition of all men, even the High Priest in the old Judaistic economy.)*

3 And by reason hereof he ought *(refers to the very purpose of his office, which is to offer Sacrifice for sins)*, as for the people *(proclaims the High Priest serving as a Mediator)*, so also for himself, to offer for sins. *(This refers to the fact that he was a sinful man as well, and had to offer to Sacrifice even for himself, which would make Atonement that would provide reconciliation with God.)*

4 And no man takes this honour unto himself, but he who is called of God, as *was* Aaron. *(Under the Old Law, the only ones who could offer Sacrifices were Priests, who had to be sons of Aaron, and whose order was ordained by God and not man.)*

5 So also Christ Glorified not Himself to be made an High Priest *(proclaims the fact that this was no personal ambition on the Messiah's part that resulted in His becoming a High Priest, but rather the fact that God called Him to that position)*; but He who said unto Him, You are My Son, today have I begotten You. *(The Priesthood of Christ was planned by God from the very beginning, which meant the Incarnation was absolutely necessary.)*

6 As He said also in another place (Ps. 110:4), You are a Priest forever after the order of Melchisedec. *(This is the distinguishing characteristic of this order of Priesthood, and proclaims it as an Eternal One.)*

7 Who in the days of His flesh *(proclaims the Incarnation of Christ)*, when He had offered up prayers and supplications with strong crying and tears unto Him *(presents the prayer life of the Master)* Who was able to save Him from death *(presents the prayer for Resurrection)*, and was heard *(proclaims the fact that God heard and answered His prayer)* in that He feared *(the picture in the word "feared" is that of a cautious taking hold of, and a careful and respectful handling; it is Christ taking into account all things, not only His Own desire, but the Will of the Father)*;

8 Though He were a Son *(stresses Deity, but at the same time the role of Christ as "Son of Man")*, yet learned He obedience *(doesn't mean He had to learn to obey, for that would mean He had sinned; it means He actively sought out the path of obedience, and then un-*

failingly walked therein) by the things which He suffered (concerned the entire course of His Life, but more so the Cross);

9 And being made perfect (refers to being brought to the goal fixed by God, which had to be if He was to be the Perfect Sacrifice), He became the Author of Eternal Salvation (proclaims a perfect Salvation, because He was and is the Perfect Redeemer, because He was the Perfect Sacrifice) unto all them who obey Him (we obey Him by exhibiting Faith in the Cross, which then gives the Holy Spirit latitude to work; this Truth was given to Paul [Rom. 6:3-5, 11, 14; Gal. 1:11-12]);

10 Called of God an High Priest (the Title is conferred on Him by God the Father) after the order of Melchisedec. (Christ was not to be a great High Priest merely for the Jews, but for the Gentiles as well; in order for this to be, His Priesthood would have to rest in something other than the Levitical Order; being after the Order of Melchisedec satisfied both demands, because Melchisedec preceded Israel as a people [Gen. 14:18-20; Ps. 110:4].)

FAITH

11 Of Whom we have many things to say (refers to Christ), and hard to be uttered (his difficulty was in adapting the interpretation to the capacity of his readers), seeing you are dull of hearing. (These Jewish Christians were slow and sluggish regarding their understanding of the teaching of New Testament Truth. This made it difficult to teach them.)

12 For when for the time you ought to be teachers (refers to the fact that they had been saved long enough to be mature in the Word by now), you have need that one teach you again which be the first principles of the Oracles of God (pertains to the Old Testament and what it really meant, instead of the way it was being erroneously taken by these Christian Jews); and are become such as have need of milk, and not of strong meat (refers to their lack of maturity).

13 For every one who uses milk (doesn't refer to one who has just been saved, but rather to those who have been saved for quite some time, and should have advanced in the Word of the Lord) is unskilful in the Word of Righteousness (refers to the benefits of the Cross, from which Righteousness is derived): for he is a babe. (This refers to the individual who does not understand or know all the benefits of what Jesus did at the Cross.)

14 But strong meat belongs to them who are of full age (refers to those mature in the Lord), even those who by reason of use have

their senses exercised to discern both good and evil. *(Such a person is walking after the Spirit. This refers to placing one's Faith in the Cross and not after the flesh, the flesh refers to depending on other things [Rom. 8:1-2, 11].)*

CHAPTER 6

APOSTASY

THEREFORE leaving the Principles of the Doctrine of Christ *(speaks of the "first principles," which refers to the Old Testament; Christ is the Centerpiece of the entirety of the Bible)*, let us go on unto perfection *(speaks of the New Testament Sacrifice, the Lord Jesus, and the Testament He inaugurated with His Work on the Cross)*; not laying again the Foundation of Repentance from dead works *(refers to these Jewish Christians going back to the Old Sacrificial System, etc.)*, and of Faith toward God *(refers to Faith toward God in the realm of the Old Testament Way, which God will not accept now inasmuch as Jesus has fulfilled the Old Testament Law)*,

2 Of the Doctrine of Baptisms *(should have been translated, "the Doctrine of Washings"; this concerned the many "washings" contained in the Old Testament Sacrificial System)*, and of laying on of hands *(goes back to the Levitical Offerings of the Old Testament; when the person brought the animal for Sacrifice, he had to lay his hands on the head of the innocent victim, confessing his sins, thereby transferring them to the innocent animal which would be slain [Lev. 16:21])*, and of Resurrection of the dead *(refers to Resurrection as taught in the Old Testament; there, this Doctrine was very incomplete, even as all Doctrine in the Old Testament was incomplete; the true meaning could not be given until after the Cross and the Resurrection of Christ, which the Lord gave to Paul [I Cor., Chpt. 15])*, and of Eternal Judgment. *(In the Old Testament, the Lord was looked at more so as a Judge than anything else. Since the Cross, He is looked at more as the Saviour.)*

3 And this will we do *(in other words, if we don't do this [refers to going on to the perfection of Christ], the results will be disastrous)*, if God permit. *(This refers to the fact that all dependence must be in Christ and the Cross. God will not allow any other type of Faith.)*

4 For *it is* impossible for those who were once enlightened *(refers to those who have accepted the Light of the Gospel, which means accepting Christ and His great Sacrifice)*, and have tasted of the Heavenly Gift *(pertains to Christ and what He did at the Cross)*, and were made partakers of the Holy

Spirit *(which takes place when a person comes to Christ)*,

5 And have tasted the good Word of God *(is not language that is used of an impenitent sinner, as some claim; the unsaved have no relish whatsoever for the Truth of God, and see no beauty in it)*, and the powers of the world to come *(refers to the Work of the Holy Spirit within hearts and lives, which the unsaved cannot have or know)*,

6 If they shall fall away *(should have been translated, "and having fallen away")*, to renew them again unto Repentance *("again" states they had once repented, but have now turned their backs on Christ)*; seeing they crucify to themselves the Son of God afresh *(means they no longer believe what Christ did at the Cross, actually concluding Him to be an imposter; the only way any person can truly repent is to place his Faith in Christ and the Cross; if that is denied, there is no Repentance)*, and put *Him* to an open shame *(means to hold Christ up to public ridicule; Paul wrote this Epistle because some Christian Jews were going back into Judaism, or seriously contemplating doing so)*.

7 For the earth which drinks in the rain that comes oft upon it *(presents the Apostle using natural things to represent spiritual realities, which is common throughout Scripture)*, and brings forth herbs *(presents the natural result of ground that is properly cultivated and receives rain; there will be a harvest)* meet for them by whom it is dressed *(received by individuals who do the cultivating of the land, etc.)*, receives Blessing from God *(presents the inevitable result of proper Faith)*:

8 But that which bears thorns and briers *is* rejected *(this speaks of Believers who have turned their backs on Christ and the Cross, and now bring forth no proper fruit, but rather "thorns and briars")*, and is nigh unto cursing *(refers to judgment)*; whose end *is* to be burned. *(This refers to the simple fact that if a person who was once a Believer remains in that state, he will lose his soul.)*

9 But, Beloved *(presents the fact that these Christian Jews were not only the object of God's love, but also of Paul's care and concern)*, we are persuaded better things of you *(he is speaking specifically to those who were seriously contemplating turning their backs on Christ)*, and things that accompany Salvation *(the Blessings which will come if the Believer properly anchors his Faith in Christ and the Cross)*, though we thus speak. *(The Apostle is not speaking from guesswork, but from many years of experience.)*

10 For God *is* not unrighteous to forget your work and labour

of love *(presents a glorious and wonderful Promise)*, which you have showed toward His Name *(reflects that everything must be done in His Name)*, in that you have Ministered to the Saints, and do Minister. *(The Apostle is telling these Christian Jews to not turn their backs on what they have previously done.)*

11 And we desire that every one of you do show the same diligence to the full assurance of hope unto the end *(don't stop now!)*:

12 That you be not slothful *(means to be sluggish and lazy toward the things of the Lord)*, but followers of them who through faith and patience inherit the Promises *(refers to the Faith worthies of the Old Testament)*.

GOD'S PROMISE

13 For when God made Promise to Abraham *(presents the Patriarch as the most illustrious example of those who "inherit the Promises" [Jn. 8:58])*, because He (God) could swear by no greater *(refers to the solemnity and power of this Promise)*, He swore by Himself *(a guarantee with resources of Heaven behind it that the Promise will be kept)*,

14 Saying, Surely blessing I will bless you *(refers to "Justification by Faith," and is taken from Genesis 22:17)*, and multiplying I will multiply you. *(This refers to his seed becoming a nation, and more importantly, every Believer being a "Child of Promise" [Gal. 4:28].)*

15 And so, after he had patiently endured *(there's always a distance between the Promise and the Possession, and that distance is never uneventful)*, he obtained the Promise. *(The immediate meaning was the birth of Isaac. However, the eternal meaning was Justification by Faith, which would come about from Isaac's seed, Who is Christ [Gal. 3:16].)*

16 For men verily swear by the greater *(men never swear by one who is inferior to themselves)*: and an oath for confirmation *is* to them an end of all strife. *(In our modern terminology, this means a contract has been agreed upon and signed by all parties, which ends all strife.)*

17 Wherein God, willing more abundantly to show unto the heirs of Promise *(refers to the Lord working in accordance with this universal custom)* the immutability *(refers to the fact that God will not change His position as to His Promise)* of His counsel, confirmed *it* by an oath *(refers to the guarantee of the Pledge or Promise)*:

18 That by two immutable things *(they are the Promise to Abraham of the coming Redeemer, and the Oath given as it regards Christ be-

ing a Priest forever after the Order of Melchisedec), in which it was impossible for God to lie (refers to the moral impossibility of such), we might have a strong consolation (refers to assurance), who have fled for refuge to lay hold upon the hope set before us (carries the idea of the sinner fleeing to one of the Cities of Refuge in Israel; in effect, he was fleeing to the High Priest who has offered Atonement for him and his sin [Deut. 4:42]; using that as a type, we are to flee as well to our High Priest, the Lord Jesus Christ):

19 Which hope we have as an anchor of the soul, both sure and stedfast (presents the Apostle changing the illusion from safety in the Cities of Refuge to a ship reaching harbor after a tempestuous voyage, knowing that her anchor is sure and steadfast), and which enters into that within the Veil (refers to the Holy of Holies, which Jesus has entered on our behalf);

20 Whither the Forerunner is for us entered, even Jesus (presents the imagery of the Great Day of Atonement, when the High Priest entered the most Holy Place on behalf of the people; all of that was a type of Christ, Who has entered the Holiest for us), made an High Priest forever after the order of Melchisedec. (This presents Christ as not in the line of Aaron, but another Order altogether. The old Levitical Order had an ending. This Order has no ending. Christ is an Eternal High Priest.)

CHAPTER 7

MELCHISEDEC

FOR this Melchisedec, King of Salem (an ancient name for Jerusalem [Ps. 76:2; 122:3]), Priest of the Most High God (tells us what He was, but gives us almost no information after that [Gen. 14:18]), who met Abraham returning from the slaughter of the kings (Gen. 14:14-15), and blessed him (presents Melchisedec in a superior spiritual position);

2 To whom also Abraham gave a tenth part of all (the first mention of Tithes in the Bible; this means that if Abraham paid Tithe to Melchisedec, his natural and spiritual seed, which includes every Believer, should continue to pay Tithes to this Priesthood [namely Christ, i.e., "His Work"], since it has now replaced the Aaronic Priesthood); first being by interpretation King of Righteousness (Melchisedec was a type, and thereby meant to portray the true "King of Righteousness," the Lord Jesus Christ), and after that also King of Salem, which is, King of Peace (Jesus is also the "Prince of Peace," once again of which Melchisedec was a type [Isa. 9:6]);

3 Without father, without mother *(only means there was no record made of the name of his father, his mother, or any of his posterity)*, without descent, having neither beginning of days, nor end of life *(means the Holy Spirit intended Melchisedec to be without genealogy, in order that he may serve as the Type)*; but made like unto the Son of God *(actually says, "to be likened to the Son of God")*; abideth a Priest continually. *(This refers to Christ of Whom Melchisedec was a Type.)*

4 Now consider how great this man *was (the Text plainly tells us here that Melchisedec was a man, not an Angel, etc., as taught by some)*, unto whom even the Patriarch Abraham gave the tenth of the spoils. *(By use of the word "Patriarch" regarding Abraham, we know this speaks of Abraham's position as "Father of the Faithful." As well, we are told here how the standard is set as it regards the financing of the Work of God on Earth.)*

5 And verily they who are of the sons of Levi *(proclaims the Apostle now showing the difference between Law and Grace, and that the former is vastly inferior to the latter)*, who receive the Office of the Priesthood *(specifying those of the Tribe of Levi who were Priests; all were not! only the sons of Aaron were)*, have a commandment to take Tithes of the people according to the Law, that is, of their Brethren *(refers to the fact that the people were to pay Tithes to the Priesthood under the old Mosaic economy)*, though they come out of the loins of Abraham *(the Jews were fond of boasting that they had Abraham as their father, meaning they were his descendants; so, using him as an example, Paul proves that the Aaronic system was much inferior to the Order of Melchisedec, or else Abraham would not have paid Tithes to this man)*:

6 But he *(Melchisedec)* whose descent is not counted from them *(from Israel)* received Tithes of Abraham, and blessed him who had the Promises. *(This proclaims the fact that Melchisedec blessed Abraham, despite the fact that it was Abraham to whom the great Promises of God had been given. The only way one could be greater than Abraham is that he would be a type of Christ, which Melchisedec was.)*

7 And without all contradiction *(means that what he is saying cannot be contradicted)* the less *(Abraham)* is blessed of the better *(Melchisedec, who was a Type of Christ; this has Paul saying that Christ is better than any other system, and is the only One Who can properly Bless)*.

8 And here men who die re-

ceive Tithes *(refers to the Levitical Priesthood, which in fact was still being carried on at the time Paul wrote these words)*; but there he receives them *(refers back to the Passage in Genesis where Melchisedec is recorded as having received Tithes)*, of whom it is witnessed that he lives. *(This refers to the Eternal Priesthood of Christ, of which Melchisedec was the Type.)*

9 And as I may so say, Levi also, who receives Tithes *(because Tithes were paid to Levi, i.e., "the Priestly Order," in no way means this was the superior Order)*, paid Tithes in Abraham. *(This struck a telling blow in Paul's argument regarding the superiority of the Priestly Order of Melchisedec. If Abraham paid Tithes to Melchisedec [which he was instructed by the Lord to do], and Abraham is the father of the Jewish people [meaning Levi was in his loins], then Levi also paid Tithes to Melchisedec. This placed the whole of the Jewish system as second to that of Christ.)*

10 For he *(Levi)* was yet in the loins of his father *(Abraham)*, when Melchisedec met him. *(This makes the New Covenant better than the Old, which is the argument of the Book of Hebrews.)*

CHRIST'S PRIESTHOOD

11 If therefore perfection were by the Levitical Priesthood *(in effect, says this was not the case)*, (for under it the people received the Law,) *(This proclaims the fact that if the Levitical Priesthood [which was a part of the Law] was changed, which it was, then the Law had to be changed also.)* what further need was there that another Priest should rise after the Order of Melchisedec *(since the Levitical Priesthood brought nothing to completion, not merely another Priest was needed, but another Priest of a different kind altogether)*, and not be called after the Order of Aaron? *(This presents the fact that the Order of Aaron must give way to the Order of Melchisedec, a better Priesthood, which it was always meant to do.)*

12 For the Priesthood being changed *(refers to the Priestly Order of Aaron now being abrogated to make way for the original Priesthood that preceded it, which in effect had predicted this very thing)*, there is made of necessity a change also of the Law. *(The connection between the Priesthood and the Law means a change in one involves a change in the other.)*

13 For He *(Christ)* of Whom these things are spoken pertains to another Tribe *(Christ was not of the Tribe of Levi, from which all Levitical Priests had to come, but rather was of the Tribe of Judah)*, of which no man gave attendance at the Altar. *(This carries the ob-*

vious meaning that none of the Tribe of Judah officiated at the Altar, as it pertained to the Sacrifices, that being the domain of the Levites exclusively.)

14 For *it is* evident that our Lord sprang out of Judah *(presents a fact that was not questioned, even by the most ardent of the enemies of our Lord)*; of which Tribe Moses spoke nothing concerning Priesthood. *(The Tribe of Judah had nothing to do with the Priesthood, and the Priesthood had nothing to do with the Tribe of Judah.)*

15 And it is yet far more evident *(something plainly obvious, which speaks here of the Priesthood of Christ)*: for that after the similitude of Melchisedec there arises another Priest *(refers to the necessity of such, and that God had chosen Melchisedec to be the Type of Christ)*,

16 Who *(the Lord Jesus)* is made *(made a High Priest through His Atoning Sacrifice of Himself)*, not after the Law of a carnal commandment *(the idea is that the Levitical Priesthood was weak and frail, due to man's frailty of which it was made, and thereby needed a replacement)*, but after the power of an endless life. *(This refers to Christ, Who was raised from the dead and lives forever, and will thereby be the "High Priest" forever.)*

17 For He *(God)* testifies *(Ps.* 110:4), You *(Christ)* are a Priest forever after the Order of Melchisedec. *(This Order of Priesthood was made in this way so that it might address the entirety of mankind, both Jews and Gentiles. The Levitical Priesthood only addressed the Jews.)*

18 For there is verily a disannulling of the Commandment *(presents the end of the Law, which was all done by Christ, and was intended all the time)* going before for the weakness and unprofitableness thereof. *(This refers to the problems with the Old Law, and that it was of temporary character.)*

19 For the Law *(Law of Moses)* made nothing perfect *(the Law was a mirror which showed what man was, but had no power to change man)*, but the bringing in of a better hope did *(refers to Christ and what He did for us at the Cross)*; by the which we draw near unto God. *(The Law of Moses could not open the door to the Holy of Holies for all of mankind, but the Cross did!)*

A BETTER SACRIFICE

20 And inasmuch as not without an oath *(earthly Jewish Priests were not sworn in by an oath, simply because they were temporary)* He *(Christ)* was made Priest *(when Jesus was made a High Priest, God*

took an oath guaranteeing the unending character of His Priesthood):

21 (For those Priests were made
without an oath (the Jewish Priests);
but this (the Lord Jesus Christ) with
an oath by Him (by God the Father) Who said unto Him (said
unto Christ), The Lord sware and
will not repent (means the Lord
will not change His Mind), You are
a Priest for ever after the order of
Melchisedec:) (Ps. 110:4)

22 By so much was Jesus (proclaims the fact that all of Redemption is bound up totally and completely in Christ) made a surety
(guarantee) of a better Testament
(a better Covenant).

23 And they truly were many
Priests (many Priests were needed
under the Mosaic economy because
the Sacrifices were vastly inferior),
because they were not suffered
to continue by reason of death
(portrays the inferiority of the Old
Jewish system):

24 But this Man (the Lord Jesus
Christ), because He continues
ever (proclaims the Priesthood of
Christ as Eternal, while death was
inevitable as it regarded the Aaronic
Priests), has an unchangeable
Priesthood. (This not only refers
to that which is Eternal, but to
that which will not change as far
as its principle is concerned as
well. The reason is the Finished
Work of the Cross is an "Everlasting Covenant" [Heb. 13:20].)

25 Wherefore He (the Lord Jesus
Christ) is able also to save them
to the uttermost (proclaims the
fact that Christ Alone has made
the only true Atonement for sin;
He did this at the Cross) who come
unto God by Him (proclaims the
only manner in which man can
come to God), seeing He ever lives
to make intercession for them.
(His very Presence by the Right Hand
of the Father guarantees such, with
nothing else having to be done
[Heb. 1:3].)

26 For such an High Priest became us (presents the fact that no
one less exalted could have met the
necessities of the human race), Who
is Holy, harmless, undefiled, separate from sinners (describes the
spotless, pure, perfect character of
the Son of God as our Great High
Priest; as well, this tells us Christ
did not become a sinner on the
Cross, as some claim, but was rather
the Sin-Offering), and made higher
than the Heavens (refers to the
fact that He is seated at the Right
Hand of the Father, which is the
most exalted position in Heaven or
Earth);

27 Who needs not daily (refers
to the daily Sacrifices offered by
the Priests under the old Jewish
economy), as those High Priests,
to offer up Sacrifice, first for His
Own sins, and then for the people's
(refers to the work of the Jewish
High Priest on the Great Day of

Atonement, which specified their unworthiness; Christ did not have to function accordingly): for this He did once, when He offered up Himself. (This refers to His death on the Cross, which Atoned for all sin — past, present, and future, making no further Sacrifices necessary.)

28 For the Law (Law of Moses) makes men High Priests which have infirmity (refers to the fact that the system was imperfect because it depended on frail men); but the word of the oath (the Promise of God that He was going to institute a superior Priesthood, far superior to the old Levitical Order [Ps. 110:4]), which was since the Law (refers to the fact that the Oath was given some five hundred years before the Law was given to Moses), makes the Son (the Lord Jesus), Who is consecrated (means that He, and He Alone, can function in this capacity) for evermore. (This Covenant is perfect because the Son is Perfect, because what He did at the Cross is Perfect, which means it will never have to be replaced.)

CHAPTER 8

HIGH PRIEST

NOW of the things which we have spoken this is the sum (refers to what Paul will now give

as it regards the meaning of all this): We have such an High Priest, Who is set on the Right Hand of the Throne of the Majesty in the Heavens (the very fact that Christ is now seated in the Heavens at the Right Hand of God proves His Work is a Finished Work);

2 A Minister of the Sanctuary (as Paul uses the word "Minister," it speaks both of Priestly service to God and of service to man), and of the True Tabernacle (the true dwelling place of God, which is in the Heavens), which the Lord pitched, and not man. (This refers to the fact that Moses pitched the earthly Tabernacle, but God formed the True Tabernacle.)

3 For every High Priest is ordained to offer Gifts and Sacrifices (portrays the High Priests of old serving as mediators between God and men): wherefore it is of necessity that this Man (Christ Jesus) have somewhat also to offer. (A Priest must have a Sacrifice to offer. Christ offered Himself. This was His one great and all embracing Sacrifice, satisfying all the Types of the Old Covenant and abolishing all its Offerings for sin.)

4 For if He (the Lord Jesus) were on earth, He should not be a Priest (refers to the fact that He was not of the Levitical Order, and due to His Sacrifice of Himself, no more earthly Priests are now needed, which as should be obvi-

ous completely abrogates the Catholic Priesthood), seeing that there are Priests who offer Gifts according to the Law (due to His Eternal Priesthood, and the Offering of Himself in Sacrifice, the Law is done):

5 Who (the Levitical Priesthood) serve unto the example and shadow of Heavenly things (refers to a suggestive replica, which in fact had no substance within itself), as Moses was admonished of God when he was about to make the Tabernacle (proclaims the fact that this was but a poor replica of the reality Who is Christ): for, See, said He (Ex. 25:40; Num. 8:4), that you make all things according to the pattern showed to you in the Mount (meaning the Tabernacle on Earth was merely a replica of something far better in the Heavens).

MEDIATOR

6 But now (since the Cross) has He (the Lord Jesus) obtained a more excellent Ministry (the New Covenant in Jesus' Blood is superior, and takes the place of the Old Covenant in animal blood), by how much also He is the Mediator of a Better Covenant (proclaims the fact that Christ officiates between God and man according to the arrangements of the New Covenant), which was established upon better Promises. (This presents the New Covenant, explicitly based on the cleansing and forgiveness of all sin, which the Old Covenant could not do.)

7 For if that first Covenant had been faultless (proclaims the fact that the First Covenant was definitely not faultless; as stated, it was based on animal blood, which was vastly inferior to the Precious Blood of Christ), then should no place have been sought for the Second (proclaims the necessity of the New Covenant).

8 For finding fault with them (the First Covenant was actually designed to glaringly portray the fault of the people, which it successfully did), He said (Jer. 31:31), Behold, the days come, saith the Lord, when I will make a New Covenant with the House of Israel and with the House of Judah (that New Covenant was in Christ and what He did at the Cross; regrettably, Israel rejected Him):

9 Not according to the Covenant that I made with their fathers (refers to the Law of Moses, which was given some fifty days after Israel was delivered from Egypt) in the day when I took them by the hand to lead them out of the land of Egypt (speaks to the immaturity of Israel at that time; consequently, she was treated as a minor); because they continued not in My Covenant (Israel was not

true to the Covenant regarding the Old Law), and I regarded them not, says the Lord. *(Israel rejected God's First Covenant, so God rejected them.)*

10 For this *is* the Covenant that I will make with the House of Israel *(refers as stated to the "New Covenant")* after those days *(refers to the Old Covenant having run its course, which it did at the time of the Cross),* saith the Lord; I will put My Laws into their mind, and write them in their hearts *(proclaims in abbreviated detail the glorious fact of what the New Covenant would do because the sin debt was paid by Christ on the Cross, which made it possible for the Holy Spirit to abide forever in the hearts and lives of Believers [Jn. 14:16-17]):* and I will be to them a God, and they shall be to Me a people *(refers to relationship under the New Covenant that was not possible under the Old Covenant [Zech. 8:8]):*

11 And they shall not teach every man his neighbour, and every man his brother, saying, Know the Lord *(refers to the complicated process of the Old Covenant):* for all shall know Me, from the least to the greatest. *(This presents the fact that the Holy Spirit will teach every Believer, as He does, and which Jesus also said would be [Jn. 16:13-15]).*

12 For I will be merciful to their unrighteousness *(the Cross made this possible),* and their sins and their iniquities will I remember no more. *(Due to the Cross, sins and iniquities no longer exist, at least for those who trust Christ.)*

13 In that He said *(Jer. 31:31),* A New *Covenant (all in Christ and what He did at the Cross),* He *(God)* has made the first old *(it was designed to be temporary).* Now that which decays and waxes old *is* ready to vanish away. *(Since the Cross, which introduced the New Covenant, there is no more need for the Old, which is vastly inferior.)*

CHAPTER 9

CONTRAST

THEN verily the First *Covenant (is meant to describe the Tabernacle in which the Service of God was celebrated under the former dispensation, and to show it had a reference to what was future)* had also Ordinances of Divine Service *(Ordinances adapted for Divine Service),* and a worldly Sanctuary. *(The word "worldly" is used here as a contrast to the Heavenly world.)*

2 For there was a Tabernacle made *(refers to what Moses had made in the wilderness, which pattern was given to him by God);*

the first, wherein *was* the Candle-stick *(Golden Lampstand)*, and the table, and the shewbread *(refers to the "first room," which was the Holy Place where the Sacred Vessels were situated)*; which is called the Sanctuary. *(This should have been translated, "which is called the Holy Place." The name "Sanctuary" was commonly given to the whole edifice.)*

3 And after the Second Veil *(pertains to the Veil which separated the Holy Place and the Holy of Holies)*, the Tabernacle which is called the Holiest of all *(refers to the Holy of Holies, which contained the Ark of the Covenant and the Mercy Seat)*;

4 Which had the Golden Censer *(should have been translated, "the Golden Incense Altar," which sat immediately in front of the Veil in the Holy Place)*, and the Ark of the Covenant overlaid round about with gold *(presents the most Glorious and Mysterious Vessel of the Tabernacle)*, wherein *was* the Golden Pot that had Manna *(presents that which was a Type of Christ as the Bread of Life [Jn. 6:32-33, 35])*, and Aaron's rod that budded *(represents Christ Alone as Saviour, and proof that God would raise Him from the dead)*, and the Tables of the Covenant *(the two stone Tables containing the Ten Commandments, five to each Table)*;

5 And over it *(the Ark of the Covenant)* the Cherubims of Glory *(Living Creatures)* shadowing the Mercyseat *(they looked down upon the Mercyseat)*; of which we cannot now speak particularly *(cannot go into great detail)*.

6 Now when these things were thus ordained *(refers to the fact that all of this was of God, and every part and parcel of the Tabernacle in some way pointed to Christ)*, the Priests went always into the First Tabernacle *(into the first of the two rooms of the Tabernacle called the "Holy Place")*, accomplishing the Service *of God. (This refers to the daily, even constant, rituals that had to be carried out.)*

7 But into the second *(the second room of the Tabernacle called the "Holy of Holies," where the Ark of the Covenant was)* went the High Priest alone once every year *(pertained to the Great Day of Atonement [Lev. 16:14; 23:27])*, not without blood, which he offered for himself, and *for* the errors of the people *(presents him going in twice on this particular day, each time taking the blood of the Sacrificial animal which had been killed — once for himself, and once for the people — with the blood sprinkled on the Mercy Seat)*:

8 The Holy Spirit this signifying *(the Holy Spirit was both the Divine Author of the Levitical system of worship, and its Interpreter)*, that the way into the Holiest of

all was not yet made manifest *(proclaims the fact [and by the Holy Spirit, at that] that access to God was blocked while the Law was enforced, except in the most limited way)*, while as the First Tabernacle was yet standing *(show the limitations of the Levitical system)*:

9 Which *was* a figure for the time then present *(refers to the Tabernacle being a representation of Heavenly realities)*, in which were offered both Gifts and Sacrifices, that could not make him who did the service perfect, as pertaining to the conscience *(portrays the weakness of the First Covenant, in that it was based on animal blood, which was insufficient; in other words, the conscience of the Jew was still heavy with realization that sin had only been covered, not taken away; only the Cross could take away sin [Jn. 1:29])*;

10 Which stood only in meats and drinks, and divers washings, and carnal Ordinances *(refers to the entirety of the Levitical system, which could only present types and shadows)*, imposed on them until the time of Reformation. *(The Cross, to which all of this pointed, would address all of this once and for all.)*

11 But Christ being come *(the little word "but" is the pivot upon which all the arguments swing)* an High Priest *(presented by the Apostle to show how marvelously the one* Offering of our Lord Jesus Christ transcends all the types and shadows of the old) of good things to come *(should have been translated, "of the good things realized")*, by a greater and more perfect Tabernacle *(presents Christ Himself as the more perfect Tabernacle)*, not made with hands, that is to say, not of this building *(Christ is not a flimsy structure like the Tabernacle of old)*;

12 Neither by the blood of goats and calves *(proclaims by the fact of the continued need of more Sacrifices that it was not properly effected)*, but by His Own Blood *(presents the price paid)* He entered in once into the Holy Place *(presents Christ doing what no other Priest had ever done; He offered a Sacrifice that was complete, which means it would never have to be repeated; thereby the Heavenly Tabernacle was opened to Him; and if opened to Him, it was opened to us as well)*, having obtained Eternal Redemption for us. *(This proclaims what was accomplished by the giving of Himself on the Cross.)*

13 For if the blood of bulls and of goats *(presents Paul turning again to the Levitical Sacrifices as an example)*, and the ashes of an heifer sprinkling the unclean, Sanctifies to the purifying of the flesh *(in these animal Sacrifices, Paul proclaims the effect of an exter-*

nal purification, a cleansing from ritual defilement, but that was as far as it went; as should be obvious, animal Sacrifices could not take away sins):

14 How much more shall the Blood of Christ (while the Sacrifice of animals could cleanse from ceremonial defilement, only the Blood of Christ could cleanse from actual sin; so that throws out every proposed solution other than the Cross), Who through the Eternal Spirit offered Himself without spot to God (in this phrase, we learn Christ did not die until the Holy Spirit told Him to die; in fact, no man took His Life from Him; He laid it down freely [Jn. 10:17-18]; as well, the fact that Jesus "offered Himself without spot to God" shoots down the unscriptural Doctrine that "Jesus died Spiritually" on the Cross; had He died Spiritually, meaning He became a sinner on the Cross, He could not have offered Himself without spot to God, as should be obvious; God could only accept a perfect Sacrifice; when He died on the Cross, He took upon Himself the sin penalty of the human race, which was physical death; inasmuch as His Offering of Himself was Perfect, God accepted it as payment in full for all sin — past, present, and future, at least for those who will believe [Jn. 3:16]), purge your conscience from dead works to serve the Living God? ("Dead works" are anything other than simple Faith in the Cross of Christ, i.e., "the Blood of Christ.")

15 And for this cause (to purge our conscience) He is the Mediator (He Alone can be the Mediator) of the New Testament (the New Covenant), that by means of death (the death of Christ on the Cross, which atoned for all sin, and was necessary if man was to be saved), for the Redemption of the transgressions that were under the First Testament (proclaims the fact that the death of Christ pertained just as much to those before the Cross as those after the Cross; His Sacrifice of Himself guaranteed their Redemption, and we speak of all who had died in the Faith), they which are called might receive the Promise of Eternal Inheritance. (This continues to address those who had died in the Faith before the Cross. They are referred to as "the called." The reason their Salvation depended on the Cross was that the blood of bulls and goats, which was all they had before the Cross, was insufficient to take away sins [10:4].)

THE NEW COVENANT

16 For where a Testament is (Covenant), there must also of necessity be the death of the testator. (This refers to the death of

Christ, Who was charged to make a New Covenant on the part of man.)

17 For a Testament is of force after men are dead *(this tells us in no uncertain terms that the death of Christ on the Cross was a legal matter)*: otherwise it is of no strength at all while the testator lives. *(This simply means it is not valid until the individual to whom the Will belongs dies, as is the case of any Testament or Will.)*

18 Whereupon neither the First *Testament (Old Covenant)* was dedicated without blood *(but it was only the blood of animals).*

19 For when Moses had spoken every Precept to all the people according to the Law *(this was referred to as the "Law of Moses"),* he took the blood of calves and of goats *(proclaims the seal of the Old Covenant, which was "shed blood"; of course, it was a Type of the Shed Blood of Christ),* with water *(as the blood witnessed to the nature of His Atoning Death [Jn. 19:34], the water witnessed to His full and proper humanity [Jn. 19:34]),* and scarlet wool *(wool is normally white, which symbolizes the Righteousness of Christ; however, it was dyed red, which portrayed the fact that it took the Blood of Christ to make this Righteousness available to man),* and hyssop *(a bushy plant, which typified His death on the Cross as a man;*

in Egypt the blood was applied to the doorpost with hyssop [Ex. 12:22]),* and sprinkled both the Book, and all the people *(referred to the Book of Leviticus, with the Tribe of Levi Ordained for Tabernacle Service, pertaining to the people; the sprinkling of the blood was the ratification of the Covenant, and symbolized the Blood of Christ which would ultimately be shed and applied by Faith to the hearts and lives of believing sinners [the blood was mixed with water]),*

20 Saying, This is the Blood of the Testament *(presents that which made the Old Covenant valid)* which God has enjoined upon you. *(This presents the fact that everything in the First Covenant, exactly as in the New Covenant, is all of God and not at all of man.)*

21 Moreover he sprinkled with Blood both the Tabernacle, and all the Vessels of the Ministry. *(This particular Verse portrays the awfulness of sin, and that it has contaminated everything on this Earth.)*

22 And almost all things are by the Law purged with blood *(some few things were purged with water, but almost all with blood);* and without shedding of blood is no remission. *(The shed Blood of Christ on the Cross is the only solution for the sins, the ills, and the problems of this world. The problem of the world, and of the Church* as well, is that it has ever sought to substitute something else. But let all know, it is alone the Cross! the Cross! the Cross!)

23 It was therefore necessary that the patterns of things in the Heavens should be purified with these (everything that pertained to the Tabernacle and all of its Sacred Vessels was a copy of that which was in Heaven; inasmuch as the Vessels and the Tabernacle were touched by men, they had to be purified by Blood, i.e., "animal blood"); but the Heavenly things themselves with better Sacrifices than these. (If man were to enter Heaven, the abode of God, there would have to be a better Sacrifice than that of animal blood.)

24 For Christ is not entered into the Holy Places made with hands (Christ did not enter the earthly Tabernacle or Temple, regarding the offering up of His Precious Blood on the Mercy Seat), which are the figures of the true (presents the fact that these "figures" were only temporary); but into Heaven itself, now to appear in the Presence of God for us (presents the purpose and reason for the Cross; all of it was done "for us"):

25 Nor yet that He should offer Himself often (refers to the fact that the one Sacrifice of Christ, which was the Offering of Himself on the Cross, was eternally suffi-

cient for the cleansing from all sin — past, present, and future; It will never need to be repeated), as the High Priest enters into the Holy Place every year with blood of others (refers to the High Priest of Israel of Old, who went into the Holy of Holies once a year on the Great Day of Atonement, carrying animal blood);

26 For then must He (the Lord Jesus) often have suffered since the foundation of the world (presents the fact that He wasn't functioning as the High Priests of Israel who, as stated, had to offer Sacrifice yearly): but now once in the end of the world has He appeared to put away sin by the Sacrifice of Himself. (This presents the One Sacrifice of Christ as sufficient for all time. The phrase, "in the end of the world," should have been translated, "in the consummation of the ages." As well, by the Sacrifice of Himself, He didn't merely cover sin, but rather "took it away" [Jn. 1:29].)

27 And as it is appointed unto men once to die (due to the Fall, all men are under the sentence of death, and in fact all have died Spiritually, which means to be separated from God), but after this the Judgment (the answer to the Spiritual death of man is Christ and what He did at the Cross; if Christ the Saviour is rejected, all will face Christ the Judge; for as death was

inevitable, the Judgment is inevitable as well):

28 So Christ was once offered to bear the sins of many (the Cross was God's answer to sin, and in fact the only answer); and unto them who look for Him shall He appear the second time without sin unto Salvation. (This refers to the Second Coming. "Without sin" refers to the fact that the Second Coming will not be to atone for sin, for that was already carried out at the Cross at His First Advent. The Second Coming will bring all the results of Salvation to this world, which refers to all that He did at the Cross. We now only have the "Firstfruits" [Rom. 8:23].)

CHAPTER 10

THE OLD COVENANT

FOR the Law (the Law of Moses) having a shadow of good things to come (the Law of Moses was only meant to be temporary; it portrayed Christ Who was to come), and not the very image of the things (it was quite impossible for the Law to present a proper image of Who and what Christ would be; it suggested such, but was only a suggestion), can never with those Sacrifices which they offered year by year continually make the comers thereunto perfect. (The animal Sacrifices could only cover sins, they couldn't take away sins. That remained for Christ to do [Jn. 1:29].)

2 For then would they not have ceased to be offered? (Paul asked this question simply because the fact that the animal Sacrifices had to be offered over and over proclaimed their insufficiency. They were, in reality, only a stopgap measure.) because that the worshippers once purged should have had no more conscience of sins. (This proclaims what the Proper Sacrifice of Christ could do, and in fact did do, but which the Sacrifice of bulls and goats could not do. The phrase, "no more conscience of sin," should not be misunderstood as "no more consciousness of sin.")

3 But in those Sacrifices (animal Sacrifices) there is a remembrance again made of sins every year. (That the High Priest of Israel had to go into the Holy of Holies once a year with animal blood proclaimed the fact that this system was basically flawed, and was meant only to point to Christ Who was to come.)

4 For it is not possible that the blood of bulls and of goats should take away sins. (The word "impossible" is a strong one. It means there is no way forward through the blood of animals. As well, it applies to all other efforts

made by man to address the problem of sin, other than the Cross.)

5 Wherefore when He *(the Lord Jesus)* comes into the world *(presents Christ coming as the Saviour, Who undertakes in Grace to meet every claim the Throne of God has against penitent sinners)*, He said, *(Ps. 40:6)* Sacrifice and Offering You would not *(refers to the fact that He would pay for sin, but not with animal Sacrifices)*, but a Body have You prepared Me *(God became man with the full intention that His Perfect Physical Body was to be offered up in Sacrifice on the Cross, which it was; the Cross was ever His destination)*:

6 In Burnt Offerings and *Sacrifices* for sin *(proclaims the root of the problem which besets mankind — it is "sin"; the idea is, that the Sacrifices were not sufficient as it regards "sin"; therefore, God took no pleasure in them in that capacity)* You have had no pleasure.

7 Then said I, Lo, I come (in the Volume of the Book it is written of Me,) *(The entirety of the Old Testament points exclusively to Christ, and in every capacity.)* to do Your Will, O God. *(The Cross was the Will of God because it had to be if man was to be Redeemed.)*

8 Above when He said, Sacrifice and Offering and Burnt Offerings and *Offering* for sin You would not *(refers to the fact that*

animal Sacrifices could not cleanse from sin)*, neither had pleasure therein *(concerns the insufficiency of the Sacrifices)*; which are offered by the Law *(refers to the fact that all these Offerings were included in the Mosaic Law; even though instigated by God, they were meant to point to Christ)*;

9 Then said He, Lo, I come to do Your Will, O God. *(The doing of the Will of God, as it regards Christ, pertained totally and completely to His Sacrifice of Himself on the Cross.)* He takes away the First *(the Old Covenant, which He did by the Sacrifice of Himself)*, that He may establish the Second *(the New Covenant which He did by going to the Cross, the only way it could be established)*.

10 By the which will *(the Sacrifice of Christ took away the First Covenant, satisfying its demands, and established the New Covenant)* we are Sanctified through the Offering of the Body of Jesus Christ once *for all. (This proclaims unequivocally that the only way the Believer can live a victorious life is by the Cross ever being the object of his Faith.)*

11 And every Priest stands daily Ministering and offering oftentimes the same Sacrifices, which can never take away sins *(proclaiming the insufficiency of this method)*:

12 But this Man *(this Priest,*

Christ Jesus), **after He had offered One Sacrifice for sins forever** *(speaks of the Cross)*, **sat down on the Right Hand of God** *(refers to the great contrast with the Priests under the Levitical system, who never sat down because their work was never completed; the Work of Christ was a "Finished Work," and needed no repetition)*;

13 From henceforth expecting till His enemies be made His footstool. *(These enemies are Satan and all the fallen Angels and demon spirits, plus all who follow Satan.)*

14 For by one Offering He has perfected forever them who are Sanctified. *(Everything one needs is found in the Cross [Gal. 6:14].)*

15 *Whereof* **the Holy Spirit also is a witness to us** *(a witness to the Cross)*: **for after that He had said before** *(refers to the fact that the Holy Spirit has always witnessed to the veracity of the Finished Work of Christ)*,

16 This *is* **the Covenant that I will make with them after those days** *(proclaims its distinctive feature as being the Sanctifying Work of the Holy Spirit Who would be caused to take up His permanent abode in the Believer, all made possible by the Cross)*, **says the Lord, I will put My Laws into their hearts, and in their minds will I write them** *(the work of the New Covenant, which accompanies the Born-again experience)*;

17 And their sins and iniquities will I remember no more. *(He has taken them all away, and did so by the Cross.)*

18 Now where remission of these *is* *(with all sins Atoned, the argument is settled)*, **there is no more Offering for sin.** *(No more offering is necessary, for Christ paid it all.)*

FAITH

19 Having therefore, Brethren, boldness to enter into the Holiest by the Blood of Jesus *(the Cross has made it possible for any and every Believer to come into the presence of the very Throne of God, and at any time so desired)*,

20 By a new and living way *(presents the New Covenant)*, **which He has consecrated for us** *(by the Cross)*, **through the Veil** *(contains an allusion to the Veil which separated the Holy of Holies from the Holy Place in the Tabernacle)*, **that is to say, His flesh** *(refers to giving Himself on the Cross, which opened up the way to God)*;

21 And *having* **an High Priest over the House of God** *(the actual Greek says, "a Priest, a Great One"; He is the Head [Col. 1:18])*;

22 Let us draw near with a true heart in full assurance of Faith *(Faith in the Finished Work of Christ)*, **having our hearts sprinkled**

from an evil conscience, and our bodies washed with pure water. *(This portrays Paul using Old Testament Types to represent the reality we now have in Christ [Lev., Chpts. 8-9].)*

23 Let us hold fast the profession of our Faith without wavering *(Faith in Christ and the Cross)*; (for He *is* faithful Who Promised;) *(This refers to the fact that everything the New Covenant promises, which is Salvation and total victory over all sin, will be realized in totally.)*

24 And let us consider one another to provoke unto love and to good works *(that which will naturally follow true Faith in the Cross)*:

25 Not forsaking the assembling of ourselves together, as the manner of some *is (it is important that Believers assemble together, ever how the meeting might be conducted)*; but exhorting one another *(encouraging one another in the Faith):* and so much the more, as you see the day approaching *(especially during these last days)*.

CONSEQUENCES

26 For if we sin wilfully *(the "willful sin" is the transference of Faith from Christ and Him Crucified to other things)* after that we have received the knowledge of the Truth *(speaks of the Bible way of Salvation and Victory, which is "Jesus Christ and Him Crucified" [I Cor. 2:2])*, there remains no more Sacrifice for sins *(if the Cross of Christ is rejected, there is no other Sacrifice or way God will accept)*,

27 But a certain fearful looking for of judgment and fiery indignation *(refers to God's anger because of men rejecting Jesus Christ and the Cross)*, which shall devour the adversaries. *(It is hellfire, which will ultimately come to all who reject Christ and the Cross.)*

28 He who despised Moses' Law died without mercy under two or three witnesses *(there had to be these many witnesses to a capital crime before the death sentence could be carried out, according to the Old Testament Law of Moses [Deut. 17:2-7])*:

29 Of how much sorer punishment, suppose ye, shall he be Thought worthy, who has trodden under foot the Son of God *(proclaims the reason for the "sorer punishment")*, and has counted the Blood of the Covenant, wherewith he was Sanctified, an unholy thing *(refers to a person who has been saved, but is now expressing unbelief toward that which originally saved him)*, and has done despite unto the Spirit of Grace? *(When the Cross is rejected, the*

Holy Spirit is insulted.)

30 For we know Him Who has said, Vengeance *belongs* unto Me, I will recompense, says the Lord *(is meant to imply that every single thing is going to be judged by the Lord, Who Alone is the righteous Judge).* And again, The Lord shall Judge His people *(chastise His people [Deut. 32:35-36]).*

31 *It is* a fearful thing to fall into the hands of the Living God. *(This refers to those who have once known the Lord, but now express no Faith in the Cross.)*

REWARD

32 But call to remembrance the former days *(the earlier proofs of faithfulness and love),* in which, after you were illuminated *(refers to the enlightenment the Gospel brings to the mind of the Believer),* you endured a great fight of afflictions *(refers to the persecutions that came their way after conversion);*

33 Partly, while you were made a gazingstock both by reproaches and afflictions *(refers, as well, to public ridicule);* and partly, while you became companions of them who were so used. *(This refers to Christian Jews, who tried to be of help to newly converted Jews, coming under severe persecution.)*

34 For you had compassion of me in my bonds *(evidently refers to the time Paul was in prison in Rome, as recorded in Acts 8:28; as well, another proof that Paul wrote the Book of Hebrews),* and took joyfully the spoiling of your goods *(many Jews suffered great financial loss upon acceptance of Christ),* knowing in yourselves that you have in Heaven a better and an enduring substance. *(The loss of earthly treasure did not hinder their Heavenly treasure.)*

35 Cast not away therefore your confidence *(confession of Faith and Christ in the Cross),* which has great recompence of reward *(eternal reward, while earthly persecution is temporary).*

36 For you have need of patience *(proper Faith will always have proper patience),* that, after you have done the Will of God, you might receive the Promise. *(If we carry out the Will of God in our lives, we don't have to worry about the Promise being fulfilled.)*

37 For yet a little while, and He Who shall come will come, and will not tarry. *(This refers to the Rapture of the Church. If the Holy Spirit deemed the time frame short some 2,000 years ago, then how much closer are we presently?)*

38 Now the just shall live by Faith *(Faith in Christ and the Cross [Hab. 2:4]):* but if *any man* draw back *(proclaims the fact that such can be done, and refers to Believers transferring their Faith from*

Christ and the Cross to other things), My soul shall have no pleasure in him. *(As should be obvious, God is grieved over the conduct of any person who would do such.)*

39 But we are not of them who draw back unto perdition *(Paul is saying that he is not going to draw back, and that those who do will lose their souls)*; but of them who believe to the saving of the soul. *(Believe in Christ and Him Crucified.)*

CHAPTER 11

FAITH DEFINED

NOW Faith is the substance *(the title deed)* of things hoped for *(a declaration of the action of Faith)*, the evidence of things not seen. *Faith is not based upon the senses, which yield uncertainty, but rather on the Word of God.)*

2 For by it *(by Faith, and as we shall see, it is Faith in the Cross)* the Elders obtained a good report *(the approval of the Lord)*.

3 Through Faith we understand that the worlds were framed by the Word of God *(refers to Creation, along with everything that goes with Creation)*, so that things which are seen were not made of things which do appear. *(God began with nothing, thereby speaking into existence the* things needed to create the universe.)

PATRIARCHS

4 By Faith Abel offered unto God a more excellent Sacrifice than Cain *(immediately proclaims the fact that the object of our Faith must be "Jesus Christ and Him Crucified" [I Cor. 2:2])*, by which he obtained witness that he was Righteous *(proclaims the fact that Righteousness comes exclusively from Christ, and is obtained by the Cross being the object of our Faith)*, God testifying of his gifts *(referring to the fact that the Sacrifice of the Lamb which represented Christ was accepted by God; at the dawn of time it was "the Cross," and it is still "the Cross")*: and by it he being dead yet speaks *(speaks of that alone God will accept)*.

5 By Faith Enoch was translated that he should not see death *(refers to God transferring Enoch to Heaven in his physical body while he was yet alive)*; and was not found, because God had translated him *(refers to his translation being well known at that time)*: for before his translation he had this testimony, that he pleased God. *(He pleased God because he placed his Faith exclusively in Christ and the Cross.)*

6 But without Faith *(in Christ*

and the Cross; anytime Faith is mentioned, always and without exception, its root meaning is that its object is Christ and the Cross; otherwise, it is Faith God will not accept) it is impossible to please Him *(faith in anything other than Christ and the Cross greatly displeases the Lord):* for he who comes to God must believe that He is *(places Faith as the foundation and principle of the manner in which God deals with the human race),* and *that* He *(God)* is a rewarder of them who diligently seek Him *(seek Him on the premise of Christ and Him Crucified).*

7 By Faith Noah, being warned of God of things not seen as yet *(the Lord told Noah He was going to send a flood upon the Earth),* moved with fear *(stand in awe),* prepared an ark to the saving of his house *(refers to him doing exactly what God told him to do);* by the which he condemned the world *(the Righteousness of Christ always clashes with self-righteousness),* and became heir of the Righteousness which is by Faith *(Faith in Christ and the Cross).*

ABRAHAM

8 By Faith Abraham, when he was called to go out into a place which he should after receive for an inheritance, obeyed *(his posterity would receive the inheritance);* and he went out, not knowing whither he went. *(While he knew where to go [Canaan], he knew nothing about the place.)*

9 By Faith he sojourned in the Land of Promise *(the Greek says "the Land of the Promise," speaking of a particular Promise),* as in a strange country *(he lived in this land not as its owner, but as a resident alien),* dwelling in Tabernacles with Isaac and Jacob, the heirs with him of the same Promise *(what God promised to Abraham, He promised as well to those who would follow him, including us presently):*

10 For he looked for a city which has foundations *(Abraham knew all of this would lead to something Heavenly),* whose Builder and Maker is God. *(This actually refers to Christ as the great Architect, Designer, and Fabricator of all material creations [Jn. 1:3; Eph. 3:9], plus all moral creations [Col. 1:15-18].)*

11 Through Faith also Sarah herself received strength to conceive seed *(this speaks of Isaac),* and was delivered of a child when she was past age *(her bringing forth this child had to do with the coming Redeemer, the Lord Jesus Christ, Who would die on the Cross in order to Redeem lost humanity),* because she judged Him *(God)*

Faithful Who had promised. *(While we aren't always faithful, God is always faithful.)*

12 Therefore sprang there even of one, and him as good as dead *(refers to the hopelessness of Abraham's situation, which brought forth the multitude; God did exactly what He said He would do!),* so many as the stars of the sky in multitude, and as the sand which is by the sea shore innumerable. *(True Faith is immeasurable, and thereby brings forth immeasurable results.)*

13 These all died in Faith *(believing Christ would come and would pay the price in order that humanity might be redeemed),* not having received the Promises *(Christ did not come in their lifetimes),* but having seen them afar off *(they continued to believe, despite the fact that the Promises were "afar off"),* and were persuaded of them *(they traded that which they could see for that which they could not see),* and embraced them *(they claimed these Promises as their own, even though they were "afar off"),* and confessed that they were strangers and pilgrims on the earth. *(It is the same with modern Believers.)*

14 For they who say such things declare plainly that they seek a country. *(This refers to that which is not here, and has no reference to that which is here.)*

15 And truly, if they had been mindful of that *country* from whence they came out *(they never looked back),* they might have had opportunity to have returned. *(It never occurred to them to go back to the old life. They had received a vision of Jesus, and the things of the world had lost their glow.)*

16 But now *(since the vision)* they desire a better *country,* that is, an Heavenly *(all of this is attainable only through and by what Jesus did at the Cross, and our Faith in that Finished Work):* wherefore God is not ashamed to be called their God *(because they have commended themselves to God by their Faith):* for He has prepared for them a city *(not that He will, but that He has already done so).*

17 By Faith Abraham, when he was tried, offered up Isaac *(even though God stopped the event, in the mind of Abraham it was already done):* and he who had received the Promises offered up his only begotten *son (the Lord had already told Abraham He would send the Redeemer into this world in order to Redeem mankind, but now He shows the Patriarch "how" it was to be done, which was by death, i.e., "Sacrifice"),*

18 Of whom it was said, That in Isaac shall your seed be called *(refers to the fact that the posterity of Abraham was to be named after Isaac, not Ishmael [Gen. 21:12]):*

19 Accounting that God *was* able to raise *him* up, even from the dead *(the Lord had told Abraham to offer up Isaac as a Sacrifice; the Patriarch proceeded to obey, which God stopped at the last minute; but in his mind, he had already offered up Isaac, reasoning that God would raise him from the dead, because it was through Isaac that the Redeemer would come)*; from whence also he received him in a figure. *(The Greek actually says, "and figuratively speaking, he did receive Isaac back from death.")*

20 By Faith Isaac blessed Jacob and Esau concerning things to come. *(Isaac blessed his two sons because his Faith looked beyond death.)*

21 By Faith Jacob, when he was a dying, blessed both the sons of Joseph *(pertains to Manasseh and Ephraim, both born to Joseph in Egypt)*; and worshipped *(and for many reasons, but primarily because of the Redeemer Who was going to come through his posterity)*, leaning upon the top of his staff. *(On this staff was carved all the great happenings of the past years, which in effect was "the Word of God." So, he was leaning on "the Word of God.")*

22 By Faith Joseph, when he died, made mention of the departing of the Children of Israel *(he knew what God had in store for Israel)*; and gave Commandment concerning his bones. *(He was in Egypt when he died, but his heart was in Canaan. When the Children of Israel would be delivered from Egypt in the future, which they were, they would take the bones of Joseph with them to the Promised Land. His Faith knew it would happen.)*

23 By Faith Moses, when he was born, was hid three months of his parents, because they saw *he was* a proper child *(the Greek says, "he was comely with respect to God")*; and they were not afraid of the king's commandment. *(Pharaoh had mandated that all male children of the Israelites be killed at birth. They felt God would protect their child, which He did!)*

MOSES

24 By Faith Moses, when he was come to years *(refers to him coming to the age of 40 [Ex. 2:11])*, refused to be called the son of Pharaoh's daughter *(in effect, he refused the position of Pharaoh of Egypt, for which he had been trained because he had been adopted by Pharaoh's daughter)*;

25 Choosing rather to suffer affliction with the people of God *(proclaims the choice Moses made; He traded the temporal for the Eternal)*, than to enjoy the pleasures of sin for a season *(presents*

the choice which must be made, affliction or the pleasures of sin);

26 Esteeming the reproach of Christ greater riches than the treasures in Egypt *(he judged the reproach was greater than the throne of Egypt):* for he had respect unto the recompence of the reward. *(Moses habitually "looked away" from the treasures in Egypt, and purposely fixed his eye on the Heavenly Reward.)*

27 By Faith he forsook Egypt *(which, spiritually speaking, every Believer must do),* not fearing the wrath of the king *(Pharaoh tried to kill him at that time [Ex. 2:15]):* for he endured, as seeing Him Who is invisible. *(This speaks of Christ, Whom Moses saw by Faith.)*

28 Through Faith he kept the Passover *(means that he "instituted the Passover" according to the Work of the Lord,),* and the sprinkling of blood *(referred to the Blood of the Paschal Lamb on the lentils and doorposts of the houses [Ex. 12:22]),* lest He Who destroyed the firstborn should touch them. *(Every Israelite's house was safe that night because of the blood being applied to the doorposts, a type of the Blood of Christ applied to our hearts, which stops the Judgment of God.)*

RAHAB

29 By Faith they *(the Children of Israel)* passed through the Red Sea as by dry *land (presents that body of water becoming a temple to Israel, but a tomb to Egypt; the Faith that sprinkled the blood and the unbelief that refused its shelter fixed this great gulf between them):* which the Egyptians assaying to do were drowned. *(God, Who opened the Red Sea for the Israelites, closed it on the Egyptians, thereby destroying their army.)*

30 By Faith the walls of Jericho fell down, after they were compassed about seven days *(proclaims obedience).*

31 By Faith the harlot Rahab perished not with them who believed not *(while Jericho was totally destroyed, Rahab was spared because of her Faith in the God of Israel),* when she had received the spies with peace. *(She found out who they were, and instead of turning them over to the King of Jericho, she sought to know Israel's God.)*

EXAMPLES

32 And what shall I more say? *(This refers to the fact that enough has now been said to guide all who are willing to search the Scriptures for themselves.)* for the time would fail me to tell of Gideon, and *of* Barak, and *of* Samson, and *of* Jephthae; *of* David also, and Samuel, and *of* the Prophets:

33 Who through Faith subdued Kingdoms, wrought Righteousness, obtained Promises, stopped the mouths of lions,

34 Quenched the violence of fire, escaped the edge of the sword, out of weakness were made strong, waxed valiant in fight, turned to flight the armies of the aliens.

35 Women received their dead raised to life again: and others were tortured, not accepting deliverance; that they might obtain a better Resurrection (the Resurrection afforded by Christ):

36 And others had trial of cruel mockings and scourgings, yes, moreover of bonds and imprisonment:

37 They were stoned, they were sawn asunder, were tempted, were slain with the sword: they wandered about in sheepskins and goatskins; being destitute, afflicted, tormented (Faith in Christ and the Cross guarantees miracles of deliverance, or miracles of endurance if that is in fact what the Lord desires; it can be done no other way!);

38 (Of whom the world was not worthy:) (This refers to the fact that the few true Christians in this world are of far greater worth than all the balance of the world put together, and in every sense.) they wandered in deserts, and in mountains, and in dens and caves of the earth. (This refers to the lot of some Believers; not all of the time, but some of the time.)

39 And these all (Old Testament Saints), having obtained a good report through Faith (refers to being Judged accordingly by the Holy Spirit), received not the Promise (the Messiah didn't come during their times, but they had Faith He ultimately would come, and so He did!):

40 God having provided some better thing for us (presents that which God had originally promised to Abraham [Gen. 22:14]), that they (Old Testament Saints) without us (the Church) should not be made perfect. (This lays the stress on Christ Who made it all possible for both the Old Testament and the New Testament Saints.)

CHAPTER 12

JESUS

WHEREFORE seeing we also are compassed about with so great a cloud of witnesses (refers to the Old Testament Saints who looked forward to the coming Promise, Who is the Lord Jesus Christ, and what He would do at the Cross to Redeem mankind), let us lay aside every weight, and the sin which does so easily beset us (we can do this only as we understand

that all things come to us through
the Cross, and that the Cross must
ever be the object of our Faith, which
then gives the Holy Spirit latitude
to work within our lives), and let
us run with patience the race that
is set before us (the only "weight"
God will allow in the running of
this race is our taking up and bearing the Cross, and doing so constantly
[Lk. 9:23-24]),

2 Looking unto Jesus the Author and Finisher of our Faith
(Jesus will carry us through till
the end, for this is what the word
"Finisher" means, providing we keep
our eyes on Him and what He did
at the Cross; He is the Source, while
the Cross is the means); who for
the joy that was set before Him
endured the cross, despising the
shame (but the Cross was necessary, that is if man was to be redeemed), and is set down at the
Right Hand of the Throne of God.
(Him being "set down" refers to
His work at the Cross being a "Finished Work," and the fact that He
is set down at the "Throne of God"
means God has fully accepted His
Sacrifice.)

3 For consider Him Who endured such contradiction of sinners against Himself (means to
consider by way of comparison; it
speaks primarily of Israel's religious leaders who bitterly opposed
Him), lest you be wearied and
faint in your minds. ("Consider

Him" instead of yourself, and there
will be victory!)

4 Ye have not yet resisted unto
blood, striving against sin. (The
Lord doesn't call upon Believers to
go to the Cross and shed their blood,
regarding the resistance of sin. Jesus
has already done that for us.)

CHASTISEMENT

5 And you have forgotten the
exhortation which speaks unto
you as unto children (the Apostle's
objective in introducing this here
is to show that afflictions are designed, on the part of God, to produce positive effects in the lives of
His people), My son, despise not
you the chastening of the Lord,
nor faint when you are rebuked
of Him (everything that happens
to a Believer is either caused or
allowed by the Lord; consequently,
we should learn the lesson desired
to be taught):

6 For whom the Lord loves He
chastens (God disciplines those He
loves, not those to whom He is indifferent), and scourges every son
whom He receives. (This refers to
all who truly belong to Him.)

7 If you endure chastening,
God deals with you as with sons
(chastening from the Lord guarantees the fact that one is a Child of
God); for what son is he whom
the father chastens not? (If an
earthly father truly cares for his

son, he will use whatever measures necessary to bring the boy into line. If an earthly father will do this, how much more will our Heavenly Father do the same?)

8 But if you be without chastisement, whereof all *(all true Believers)* are partakers, then are you bastards, and not sons. *(Many claim to be Believers while continuing in sin, but the Lord never chastises them. Such shows they are illegitimate sons, meaning they are claiming faith on a basis other than the Cross. The true son, without doubt, will be chastised at times.)*

9 Furthermore we have had fathers of our flesh which corrected *us,* and we gave *them* reverence *(earthly parents)*: shall we not much rather be in subjection unto the Father of Spirits, and live? *("Father of Spirits" is contrasted to "Fathers of the flesh." The latter concerns our earthly parents. Their relation to us is limited. His is universal and eternal.)*

10 For they verily for a few days chastened *us* after their own pleasure *(the use of the word "pleasure" indicates that the chastening may or may not have been proper, as it regards our earthly parents)*; but He for *our* profit *(presents the difference between human liability of error and the perfect knowledge of our Heavenly Father; He seeks our profit, and* cannot err in the means He employs), that *we* might be partakers of His Holiness. *(This presents the objective of the chastening and correction of God.)*

11 Now no chastening for the present seems to be joyous, but grievous *(presents the fact that the trials we are at times exposed to do not give joy at that moment, and are often hard indeed to bear)*: nevertheless afterward it yields the peaceable fruit of Righteousness unto them which are exercised thereby. *(All of this is carried out by the Holy Spirit for a specific purpose [Jn. 15:1-9].)*

DISOBEDIENCE

12 Wherefore lift up the hands which hang down *(stop being discouraged)*, and the feeble knees *(the knees, which speak of our walk and direction, are feeble because of discouragement)*;

13 And make straight paths for your feet *(refers to the "right path," which the chastisement designed by the Lord desires to bring about)*, lest that which is lame be turned out of the way *(to be spiritually lame, which refers to our Faith being in something other than the Cross)*; but let it rather be healed *(which will be done when the Believer's Faith is once again anchored in the Cross)*.

14 Follow peace with all men,

and Holiness *(every effort must be made to live peacefully with all men, but not at the expense of Holiness, i.e., "the compromising of the Word"),* without which no man shall see the Lord *(Holiness cannot be brought about by Law; it can only be brought about by Grace, which is made possible by the Cross):*

15 Looking diligently lest any man fail of the Grace of God *(we frustrate the Grace of God, and can even fall from Grace, if we function outside the Cross [Gal. 2:21; 5:4]); lest any root of bitterness springing up trouble* you *(to try to live for God outside of His prescribed order, which is the Cross, will bring nothing but failure, thereby providing fertile ground for "roots of bitterness"),* and thereby many be defiled *(speaks of works of the flesh [Gal. 5:19-21]);*

16 Lest there be any fornicator, or profane person, as Esau *(he was "profane" because he rejected God's Way, i.e., the Cross, and which results are inevitable),* who for one morsel of meat sold his birthright. *(He was in the Family of God, but was not of the Family of God, which characterizes untold millions presently.)*

17 For you know how that afterward, when he would have inherited the Blessing, he was rejected *(proclaims Esau, as millions, desiring the Blessing without the Blesser):* for he found no place of repentance, though he sought it *(the Blessing)* carefully with tears. *(He wanted the Blessing, but did not want to repent of placing his Faith in things other than Christ.)*

18 For you are not come unto the Mount that might be touched *(in effect is saying to these Christian Jews, "you had better carefully consider the Law you are proposing once again to embrace"),* and that burned with fire, nor unto blackness, and darkness, and tempest *(the idea is that we can face God respecting His Law according to the symbols given here, or we can face Him through the Blood of His Son and our Saviour, the Lord Jesus Christ),*

19 And the sound of a trumpet, and the voice of words *(that which accompanied the giving of the Law on Mt. Sinai [Ex. 20:19]);* which *voice* they that heard entreated that the word should not be spoken to them any more *(relates the fact that the Voice of God sounded with such power it could not be stood by the people [Ex. 20:19; Deut. 5:22-27]):*

20 (For they could not endure that which was commanded *(they feared they would die),* And if so much as a beast touch the mountain, it shall be stoned, or thrust through with a dart *(all of this portrays the Holiness of God):*

21 And so terrible was the sight, *that* Moses said, I exceedingly fear and quake:) *(This proclaims in the strongest language possible that no lasting blessing can come to fallen man through the Law.)*

22 But you are come unto Mount Sion, and unto the city of the Living God, the Heavenly Jerusalem *(no one has ever reached this city by Law, but only by Grace)*, and to an innumerable company of Angels *(it refers to countless numbers)*,

23 To the General Assembly and Church of the Firstborn, which are written in Heaven *(pertains to every Born-again Believer from the time of Abel up to the Second Coming; the price was the Cross!)*, and to God the Judge of all *(God has judged all who are in the "Church of the First Born" as perfectly justified in His sight)*, and to the spirits of just men made perfect *(Justification by Faith)*,

24 And to Jesus the Mediator of the New Covenant *(which was made possible by the Cross)*, and to the blood of sprinkling *(Christ is the Mediator of the New Covenant, through the shedding of His Blood; it was typified by the Blood of the Old Covenant with which Moses sprinkled all the people [Ex. 24:4-8; Heb. 9:19])*, that speaks better things than *that* of Abel. *(This refers to Abel's animal Sacrifice as recorded in Gen., Chpt. 4.)*

25 See that you refuse not Him Who speaks. *(This refers implicitly to Christ and what He did at the Cross.)* For if they escaped not who refused Him Who spoke on earth *(refers to God giving the Law on Mt. Sinai)*, much more *shall not* we *escape*, if we turn away from Him Who *speaks* from Heaven *(if we reject Christ and the Cross, Judgment is sure!)*:

26 Whose Voice then shook the earth *(the Voice of God at Mt. Sinai was meant to impress upon Israel the solemnity of the moment)*: but now He has promised, saying, Yet once more I shake not the earth only, but also Heaven. *(This phrase refers to the First Advent of Christ, Whose Death on the Cross shook both Heaven and Earth. His Death, because it atoned for all sin, broke the legal claim of Satan on humanity.)*

27 And this *Word (refers to the "Word of the Cross" [I Cor. 1:18])*, Yet once more, signifies the removing of those things that are shaken, as of things that are made *(refers to the Act of God transferring this present universe which is under the curse of Adam's sin to a new basis; that new basis being a new and perfect universe, which will ultimately come)*, that those things which cannot be shaken may remain. *(This refers to all Jesus paid for at the Cross. Only Faith in Christ and the Cross cannot be shaken. It will remain!)*

28 Wherefore we receiving a Kingdom which cannot be moved *(refers to our entrance into this Kingdom, all made possible by the Cross)*, let us have Grace, whereby we may serve God acceptably with reverence and Godly fear *(one can serve God only by the means of Grace, which Source is Christ and which means is the Cross)*:

29 For our God *is* a consuming fire. *(The fire of God will consume everything that is not Faith in Christ and the Cross [I Cor. 3:10-17].)*

CHAPTER 13

INSTRUCTION

L ET brotherly love continue. *(This type of love refers to our social actions, one might say, toward our Brothers and Sisters in the Lord.)*

2 Be not forgetful to entertain strangers *(hospitality)*: for thereby some have entertained Angels unawares *(definitely would have a tendency to provide a positive incentive)*.

3 Remember them who are in bonds *(refers to Christians who were even then beginning to be imprisoned for their Faith)*, as bound with them *(become one with them, not forgetting to pray for them)*; *and* them which suffer adversity, as being yourselves also in the Body. *(Refers to the Body of Christ, and that if one suffers, in a sense all suffer.)*

4 Marriage *is* honourable in all, and the bed undefiled *(lawful sex between a husband and wife holds no defilement)*: but whoremongers and adulterers God will judge. *(This proclaims all sexual conduct outside of marriage to be absolutely defiled.)*

5 Let your conversation *(lifestyle) be* without covetousness *(in a sense, covetousness is idolatry [Col. 3:5])*; *and be* content with such things as you have *(Christ-dependent)*: for He has said, I will never leave you, nor forsake you. *(The Greek actually says, "He Himself has said," meaning the Lord Jesus Himself has Personally made this Promise [Josh. 1:5; I Chron. 28:20].)*

6 So that we may boldly say, The Lord *is* my helper *(there is no higher authority and power [Ps. 118:6])*, and I will not fear what man shall do unto me. *(Man can do no more to me than the Lord permits.)*

MINISTERS

7 Remember them which have the rule over you *(should have been translated, "Remember them which are your leaders")*, who have spoken unto you the Word of God *(refers to preaching and teaching)*: whose faith follow *(providing its*

Faith that ever makes the Cross its object), considering the end of their conversation (lifestyle; proper Faith will always produce a proper lifestyle).

JESUS CHRIST

8 Jesus Christ the same yesterday, and today, and forever. (He will never change, and this covers the entire range of time.)

9 Be not carried about with divers and strange doctrines. (This refers to anything that changes the object of Faith from the Cross to something else.) For it is a good thing that the heart be established with Grace (actually means this is the only way the heart can rightly be established); not with meats (is meant to refer to all types of religious ceremonies), which have not profited them who have been occupied therein. (This proclaims everything other than simple Faith in Christ and His Finished Work as having no value.)

ALTARS

10 We have an Altar (is used in this sense by Paul to describe all Christ has done at the Cross on behalf of lost humanity), whereof they have no right to eat which serve the Tabernacle. (This bluntly and plainly says that one cannot serve Christ and the Levitical Order at the same time. As well, one cannot function in Law and Grace at the same time!)

11 For the bodies of those beasts (refers to the animal Sacrifices of various kinds), whose blood is brought into the Sanctuary by the High Priest for sin (refers to this particular man bringing the blood of these Sacrificed animals into the Holy of Holies on the Great Day of Atonement, and applying it to the Mercy Seat and the Horns of the Altar of Incense), are burned without the camp. (The carcass of the animal was burned outside the camp, thus symbolizing God's Wrath against sin.)

12 Wherefore Jesus also, that he might sanctify the people with His Own Blood (presents the price that was paid so that man might be "Sanctified", i.e., "set free from sin"), suffered without the gate. (The Sin-Offering was burned "without the camp." Jesus, Who in all other points fulfilled the Law of Atonement, fulfilled it in this point also [Mat. 27:32; Jn. 19:20].)

13 Let us go forth therefore unto Him without the camp (presents Christ as the only bearer of Salvation), bearing His reproach (refers to sharing in the rejection He has undergone).

14 For here have we no continuing city (portrays earthly Jerusalem as having finished its course, at least at that particular time and

as it referred to the Law,), **but we seek one to come.** *(The hopes of mankind are now bound up with no abiding earthly Sanctuary, but rather we seek after the Heavenly Jerusalem.)*

15 By Him therefore let us offer the Sacrifice of Praise to God continually *(we must understand that we are able to praise God and He is able to accept our praises due to the Cross, hence "Praise" being linked to "Sacrifice"; as well, the word "continually" proclaims the fact that this will never change, meaning the Cross will ever abide as the foundation of all things pertaining to God)*, **that is, the fruit of our lips giving thanks to His Name.** *(His Name is "Jesus," which means "Saviour," and speaks of His Sacrificial Offering of Himself on the Cross.)*

16 But to do good and to communicate forget not *(Paul is saying here that our obligations to the Lord are not exhausted with Praise; good deeds must also be included)*: **for with such Sacrifices God is well pleased.** *(Such action and attitude symbolizes the Cross.)*

17 Obey them who have the rule over you *(has reference to Pastors; however, the emphasis is not on the Pastor, but rather on the Gospel he Preaches)*, **and submit yourselves** *(refers to submitting to the True Gospel that is being Preached by True Pastors)*: **for they watch for your souls** *(refers to Preachers who truly have the spiritual welfare of the people at heart)*, **as they that must give account, that they may do it with joy, and not with grief** *(every Preacher will give account to God for His Ministry)*: **for that is unprofitable for you.** *(If people will not heed the true Gospel being Preached, the Gospel will be of no profit to these particular individuals, whomever they might be, no matter how profitable it is to others. This brings "grief" to the True Preacher.)*

PRAYER

18 Pray for us *(presents a common request by Paul [Rom. 15:30; Eph. 6:18; Col. 4:3; I Thess. 5:25; II Thess. 3:1])*: **for we trust we have a good conscience** *(concerns all things; however, I personally think the Apostle is speaking here of the way he has handled the Law of Moses regarding this Epistle to the Hebrews)*, **in all things willing to live honestly.** *(This refers to his daily living for the Lord.)*

19 But I beseech you the rather to do this *(refers back to His request that they pray for him)*, **that I may be restored to you the sooner.** *(This lends credence to the thought that Paul may have been in prison when this Epistle to the Hebrews* *was written.)*

BENEDICTION

20 Now the God of Peace *(proclaims that Peace has been made between God and fallen man, and done so through what Jesus did on the Cross on man's behalf)*, that brought again from the dead our Lord Jesus *(presents the only mention of the Resurrection of Christ in this Epistle to the Hebrews)*, that Great Shepherd of the sheep *(presents the One Who died for us, and Whom God raised from the dead)*, through the Blood of the Everlasting Covenant *(points to the Cross and proclaims the fact that this Covenant, being perfect, is Eternal)*,

21 Make you perfect in every good work to do His Will *(refers to that which the Holy Spirit has been sent to do, and Who will do such through Christ)*, working in you that which is wellpleasing in His sight, through Jesus Christ *(proclaims the fact that men can do what is acceptable to God only through Jesus Christ)*; to Whom *be* Glory forever and ever. Amen.

(This is because of what He did at the Cross.)

22 And I beseech you, Brethren, suffer the word of exhortation *(this refers to the arguments and counsels in this entire Epistle)*: for I have written a Letter unto you in few words. *(Considering the subject matter, the Letter is short.)*

23 Know ye that *our* Brother Timothy is set at liberty *(presents another strong proof that Paul wrote this Epistle)*; with whom, if he come shortly, I will see you. *(This phrase gives no clue whatsoever if this actually happened.)*

24 Salute *(greet)* all them who have the rule over you *(more than likely refers to their Pastors and other Saints in that particular Church or Churches)*, and all the Saints. They of Italy salute you. *(This proves this Epistle was written from Italy, and more than likely Rome. As well, the manner of this Benediction is Paul's style. Also, whoever wrote the Epistle to the Hebrews had to know two things extensively so, and I speak of the Law of Moses and the Cross of Christ. Only Paul fit this description.)*

25 Grace *be* with you all. Amen.

THE EPISTLE GENERAL OF
JAMES

CHAPTER 1

INTRODUCTION

JAMES *(the Brother of our Lord)*, a servant of God and of the Lord Jesus Christ *(he never referred to himself as an Apostle, even though he definitely was one [Gal. 1:19])*, to the Twelve Tribes which are scattered abroad, greeting. *(This proclaims the fact that the Twelve Tribes of Israel were still in existence, so ten of them were not lost as some claim.)*

VICTORY

2 My Brethren, count it all joy when you fall into divers temptations *(refers not so much to the allurement of sin, as it does testing and trials)*;

3 Knowing *this*, that the trying of your Faith works patience. *(If it is genuine Faith, testing serves to develop its persistence.)*

4 But let patience have *her* perfect work *(means we must not grow discouraged regarding the test or trial we are going through)*, that you may be perfect and entire, wanting nothing. *(The goal in view is that Believers "may be ma-* ture and complete.")

FAITH

5 If any of you lack wisdom *(pertains to proper knowledge of the Word of God)*, let him ask of God, Who gives to all *men* liberally *(the Lord gives to those who ask, providing they ask the right thing; a greater knowledge of the Word of God is always the right thing)*, and upbraideth not; and it shall be given him. *(This means when we ask wisdom of Him, He will not reproach or chide us for our past conduct. He permits us to come in the freest manner, and meets us with a spirit of entire kindness, and with promptness in granting our requests.)*

6 But let him ask in Faith *(some accuse James of denigrating Faith; however, he actually does the very opposite, making Faith a criteria for all things)*, nothing wavering *(nothing doubting)*. For he who wavers is like a wave of the sea driven with the wind and tossed. *(He who continuously veers from one course to another only reveals his own instability and lack of a sense of being under Divine control.)*

7 For let not that man think that he shall receive any thing of the Lord. (*This points to a particular type of individual, one who has a "doubting heart."*)

8 A double minded man *is* unstable in all his ways. (*One cannot place one's Faith in the Cross and something else at the same time. Such produces instability, a type of Faith that will never be honored by the Lord.*)

HUMILITY

9 Let the Brother of low degree (*refers to one who is "lowly, insignificant, weak, and poor"*) rejoice in that he is exalted (*refers to the greatest place and position of all, one's position in Christ*):

10 But the rich, in that he is made low (*is meant to point toward trust in riches, which lowers one in the sight of God*): because as the flower of the grass he shall pass away. (*Worldly riches are temporal. We lose them quickly, or else we die and leave them.*)

11 For the sun is no sooner risen with a burning heat, but it withers the grass, and the flower thereof falls, and the grace of the fashion of it perishes (*presents an apt illustration for all things that are of this world*): so also shall the rich man fade away in his ways. (*The man fades, whether the riches do or not.*)

ENDURANCE

12 Blessed *is* the man who endures temptation (*refers to the test of Faith*): for when he is tried, he shall receive the Crown of Life (*refers to a reward much greater than the price paid*), which the Lord has promised to them who love Him. (*If we truly love Him, we will truly keep His Commandments [Jn. 14:15], which we can do with the help of the Holy Spirit, Who requires that our Faith ever rest in the Cross [Rom. 6:3-5, 11, 14].*)

TEMPTATION

13 Let no man say when he is tempted, I am tempted of God (*we must not assume that enticement to sin comes from God; it never does!*): for God cannot be tempted with evil, neither tempts He any man (*God's omnipotent Holy Will fully resists any direction toward sin*):

14 But every man is tempted, when he is drawn away of his own lust, and enticed. (*The temptation to sin appeals to a moral defect in us, even in the best, for none are perfect.*)

15 Then when lust has conceived (*speaks of evil lust*), it brings forth sin (*as stated, these temptations do not come from God, but from the appetites of man's*

sinful nature, which is a result of the Fall; the sin nature can be held at bay, and is meant to be held at bay by the Believer anchoring his Faith in the Cross of Christ, which will then give the Holy Spirit latitude to help): and sin, when it is finished, brings forth death. (This refers to spiritual death, because sin separates man from God.)

16 Do not err, my beloved Brethren (James is saying to Believers, "don't be deceived; sin is the ruin of all that is good.")

GOD'S GOODNESS

17 Every good gift and every perfect gift is from above (presents the Gift of His Son, the Lord Jesus Christ, by Whom every "Perfect Gift" is given), and comes down from the Father of Lights (evil is darkness; light is goodness), with Whom is no variableness, neither shadow of turning. (This is what God is, and He will never change.)

18 Of His Own Will begat He us with the Word of Truth (presents the imparting of Divine Life through the Word, and is of unspeakable significance), that we should be a kind of Firstfruits of His creatures. ("Firstfruits" represent not only what we have received, which in effect is a promise of what we are to receive in the future, but as well recognizes the principle of Divine Ownership and all that we possess.)

CHRISTIAN LIVING

19 Wherefore, my beloved Brethren, let every man be swift to hear (refers to the Word of God), slow to speak (could be translated, "slow to murmur"; we shouldn't murmur at all, but knowing the human heart, "slow to murmur" is more within our reach), slow to wrath (all of these things can be handled at the Cross, and only at the Cross):

20 For the wrath of man worketh not the Righteousness of God. (This proclaims the fact that the anger and irritation of the natural heart do not produce anything God accepts as Righteous.)

21 Wherefore lay apart all filthiness (refers to moral impurity) and superfluity of naughtiness (increased evil to which moral impurity will lead; these things can be laid aside only by the Believer understanding that all things come to him through Christ and what He did at the Cross, which demands that the Cross ever be the object of our Faith; in this capacity, the Holy Spirit, without Whom we cannot function, will use His Power on our behalf in order to give us victory), and receive with meekness the engrafted word, which is able to save your souls. (The story of the

Bible, i.e., "the Word," is the story of the Cross.)

22 But be ye doers of the Word *(the "Word" has the potential to do great and mighty things within our lives)*, and not hearers only *(while hearing the Word is definitely necessary, at the same time it must be heard properly, and that refers to a heart that wants to receive)*, deceiving your own selves. *(It's bad enough to be deceived by others, but worse yet to purposely deceive ourselves. If we think we can live this life without total Faith in Christ and the Cross, we are doing exactly what James said not to do, "deceiving ourselves.")*

23 For if any be a hearer of the word, and not a doer, he is like unto a man beholding his natural face in a glass *(he sees only that which is external, and therefore cannot make a proper evaluation)*:

24 For he beholds himself, and goes his way *(which is not God's way)*, and straightway forgets what manner of man he was. *(An evaluation of ourselves is necessary. However, it is God Alone Who knows the heart which the Word of God, properly presented, reveals.)*

25 But whoso looks into the perfect Law of Liberty *(defines the whole body of revealed truth concerning the Word of God)*, and continues *therein (there must be a continuous abiding in the Word)*,

he being not a forgetful hearer, but a doer of the work, this man shall be blessed in his deed. *(Obeying the Word of God brings great Blessing. However, the only way it can be obeyed is for the Believer to unequivocally place his Faith in Christ and the Cross.)*

26 If any man among you seem to be religious *(would have been better translated, "if any man among you seem to be spiritual")*, and bridles not his tongue *(again, only the Holy Spirit within our lives can do this)*, but deceives his own heart, this man's religion *is* vain. *(This would have been better translated, "profession is vain.")*

27 Pure religion *(should have been translated, "pure spirituality")* and undefiled before God and the Father is this *(refers to that which pleases God)*, To visit the fatherless and widows in their affliction *(proper Faith will always produce proper works)*, and to keep himself unspotted from the world *(Victory in everyday life and living, which again must have the help and power of the Holy Spirit)*.

CHAPTER 2

BROTHERLY LOVE

MY Brethren, have not the Faith of our Lord Jesus Christ, *the* Lord of Glory *(should have been* translated, "My Brethren, you have not the Faith of our Lord Jesus Christ"; *in other words, the ones James was writing to were not conducting themselves as the Lord),* with respect of persons. *(If the Lord doesn't show respect of persons, then we should not as well!)*

2 For if there come unto your assembly a man with a gold ring, in goodly apparel *(addresses the rich),* and there come in also a poor man in vile raiment *(refers to the obvious);*

3 And you have respect to him who wears the gay clothing, and say unto him, Sit you here in a good place *(show him partiality);* and say to the poor, you stand there, or sit here under my footstool *(proclaims a terrible attitude and spirit):*

4 Are you not then partial in yourselves *(answers itself),* and are become judges of evil thoughts? *(To show "respect of persons" is looked at by God as "evil.")*

5 Hearken, my beloved Brethren, Has not God chosen the poor of this world rich in Faith, and heirs of the Kingdom which He has promised to them who love Him? *(This demands a positive answer. Not many mighty, not many noble, answer the Call [I Cor. 1:26-29].)*

6 But you have despised the poor. *(This refers to the fact that some Christians had despised those* whom God had chosen.) Do not rich men oppress you, and draw you before the judgment seats? *(This proclaims a worldwide problem that has existed from the beginning of time, and continues unto this present hour.)*

7 Do not they blaspheme that worthy name by the which you are called? *(Those who place their Faith and trust in money will ultimately blaspheme the Name of the Lord.)*

8 If you fulfil the Royal Law according to the Scripture *(Lev. 19:18; Mat. 22:39),* You shall love your neighbour as yourself, you do well *(show favor to everyone, whether rich or poor):*

9 But if you have respect to persons, you commit sin *(there are many things of this nature which God constitutes as sin, but to which many Believers pay little heed),* and are convinced of the Law as transgressors. *(Refers to the Law of Moses, which was the only acceptable moral Law in the world of that day. To be sure, its moral precepts continue to be binding on the entirety of the human race, but Jesus fulfilled them in totality.)*

FAITH AND WORKS

10 For whosoever shall keep the whole Law *(Law of Moses),* and yet offend in one *point,* he is

guilty of all. *(This proclaims in no uncertain terms the impossibility of the Believer finding Victory through the Law, whether the Law of Moses, or any type of Law. It simply cannot be done!)*

11 For he who said, Do not commit adultery, said also, Do not kill. Now if you commit no adultery, yet if you kill, you are become a transgressor of the Law. *(The breaking of even one Commandment puts the person in the position of a "transgressor.")*

12 So speak ye, and so do *(what we say, we ought to do)*, as they who shall be judged by the Law of Liberty. *(This pertains to the coming Judgment Seat of Christ.)*

13 For he shall have judgment without Mercy, who has shown no Mercy *(if we withhold Mercy here, or whatever that is right, we will face the same at the Judgment Seat of Christ)*; and Mercy rejoices against Judgment. *(This presents the fact that one who shows Mercy in this life will have nothing to fear at the Judgment Seat of Christ.)*

14 What *does it* profit, my Brethren, though a man say he has Faith, and have not works? *(This presents the fact that proper Faith will always produce proper works.)* can Faith save him? *(This should have been translated, "is that Faith able to save him?" The truth is God will not recognize that type of Faith.)*

15 If a Brother or sister be naked, and destitute of daily food,

16 And one of you say unto them, Depart in Peace, be *ye* warmed and filled; notwithstanding you give them not those things which are needful to the body; what *does it* profit? *(This refers to claimed Faith which blesses no one, simply because it's not true Faith. True Faith will help the person.)*

17 Even so Faith, if it has not works, is dead, being alone. *(As stated, proper Faith will produce proper works. If not, the Holy Spirit says here that it is "dead faith.")*

18 Yes, a man may say, You have Faith, and I have works *(proclaims the efforts by some to divide the two)*: show me your Faith without your works, and I will show you my Faith by my works. *(This proclaims the fact that the profession of a lifeless Faith is profitless.)*

19 You believe that there is one God *(presents the type of Faith held by hundreds of millions, but in which there is no saving grace)*; you do well *(you think you do well!)*: the Devils also believe, and tremble. *(Simply believing there is a God says no more than what demons believe. Proper Faith will accept the Lord as one's Saviour.)*

20 But will you know, O vain man, that Faith without works is dead? *(In effect, James bluntly*

says anyone who trusts in an empty Faith has, in effect, an empty head.)

21 Was not Abraham our father Justified by works, when he had offered Isaac his son upon the Altar? *(Any Faith that doesn't have the Cross as its proper object is dead Faith. The Holy Spirit had James choose this example of Abraham offering Isaac to portray one of the most vivid illustrations of the Sacrifice of Christ.)*

22 Seest thou how Faith wrought with his works, and by works was Faith made perfect? *(James is making it clear that he is not talking about works as the sole source of Abraham's Justification as Verse 21, if taken out of context, might lead one to believe. Abraham's Faith and his actions were working together.)*

23 And the Scripture was fulfilled which said *(Gen. 15:6)*, Abraham believed God, and it was imputed unto him for Righteousness *(proclaims the fact that Abraham's Faith was genuine)*: and he was called the Friend of God *(Isa. 41:8)*.

24 You see then how that by works a man is Justified *(could be better understood by saying, "You see then, how that by works a man's Justification is proven")*, and not by Faith only. *(This must be understood in the context of the entire Passage. The Apostle is merely saying that no one can claim Justi-*fication on the basis of Faith alone, which produces no qualifying works. Such an individual is deceiving himself.)*

25 Likewise also was not Rahab the harlot Justified by works, when she had received the messengers, and had sent *them* out another way? *(This presents one of the most beautiful stories of Faith found in the annals of human history. This was proper Faith, which produced proper works.)*

26 For as the body without the spirit is dead, so Faith without works is dead also. *(In closing our comments on this Chapter, I must remind you with Paul that works without dynamic living Faith in the Lord Jesus cannot produce Salvation or Victory. On the other hand, I must also remind you with James that Faith in the form of declaring a dogma or confessing a creed, which fails to produce life and labor according to the Word of God, will likewise condemn you.)*

CHAPTER 3

THE TONGUE

MY Brethren, be not many masters *(should have been translated, "be not many Teachers")*, knowing that we shall receive the greater condemnation. *(This refers to the fact that mis-*

handling the Word of God will ultimately bring one tremendous problems. God holds the Teacher more responsible than the student.)

2 For in many things we offend all. *(This refers to the universality of sin and failure, even among Believers.)* If any man offend not in word, the same *is* a perfect man, *and* able also to bridle the whole body. *(The Holy Spirit Alone can control the Believer's tongue.)*

3 Behold, we put bits in the horses' mouths, that they may obey us; and we turn about their whole body. *(The Holy Spirit is saying our mouths should obey us, instead of us obeying our mouths.)*

4 Behold also the ships, which though *they be* so great, and *are* driven of fierce winds, yet are they turned about with a very small helm, whithersoever the governor lists. *(This refers here to the "helm" being likened unto the "tongue.")*

5 Even so the tongue is a little member *(it is small, but it exerts a powerful influence)*, and boasts great things *(responsible for great things, whether good or bad)*. Behold, how great a matter a little fire kindles! *(The image projected here by James is the picture of a vast forest in flames, all begun by the falling of a single spark.)*

6 And the tongue is a fire *(speaks of fire in a negative way, that which destroys)*, a world of iniquity *(the tongue in some way is responsible for all the iniquity in the world)*: so is the tongue among our members *(body members)*, that it defiles the whole body *(constantly speaking in a negative way can bring about physical illness in the body)*, and sets on fire the course of nature *(the tongue sets us on a particular path, and in this case the wrong path)*; and it is set on fire of Hell. *(By using the word "Hell," we are made to understand not only the wickedness of the tongue, but, as well, its destructive power.)*

7 For every kind of beasts, and of birds, and of serpents, and of things in the sea, is tamed, and has been tamed of mankind *(a proven fact)*:

8 But the tongue can no man tame *(this is the Word of the Lord; however, the tongue can most definitely be tamed by the Holy Spirit; the way it is done has to do with the Cross of Christ; the Holy Spirit works within the parameters of the Finished Work of Christ on the Cross; He demands that we ever make the Cross the object of our Faith, and then He can do mighty things within our lives [Rom. 8:1-2, 11])*; it *is* an unruly evil, full of deadly poison. *(The Believer must realize this. It means that just because he is Saved, such doesn't necessarily guarantee a change in this problem. As stated, it defi-*

nitely can be, and in fact must be, changed, but it can only be so by and through the Cross.)

9 Therewith bless we God, even the Father; and therewith curse we men (proclaims the inconsistency, to say the least, of blessing God one moment and cursing men the next), which are made after the similitude of God. (In a sense, when we curse men, which refers to wishing them hurt, we are cursing God. To curse the Creation is to curse the Creator.)

10 Out of the same mouth proceeds blessing and cursing (presents the tongue devoted to uses so different). My Brethren, these things ought not so to be. (If the Lord has His Way in our hearts and lives, they won't be.)

11 Does a fountain send forth at the same place sweet water and bitter? (Of necessity, this question must be answered in the negative.)

12 Can the fig tree, my Brethren, bear olive berries? either a vine, figs? so can no fountain both yield salt water and fresh. (This speaks of nature. However, man can do what nature cannot do.)

WISDOM

13 Who is a wise man and endued with knowledge among you? (This refers to a true teacher of the Word of God.) let him show out of a good conversation (life-style) his works with meekness of wisdom (refers to the conduct of the Believer).

14 But if you have bitter envying and strife in your hearts (proclaims the "sin nature" springing to life, thereby ruling in the Believer's life [Rom. 6:12-13]), Glory not (boast not), and lie not against the truth. (This refers to the fact that if we do boast of anything other than the Cross, we are "lying," pure and simple [Gal. 6:14].)

15 This wisdom descends not from above (any wisdom that claims Salvation or Victory in any way or manner other than the Cross is not wisdom from above), but is earthly, sensual, devilish. (Whatever its appeal, if it's not the Cross, it is of Satan. This covers humanistic psychology, plus anything else devised by men, i.e., "demons.")

16 For where envying and strife is, there is confusion and every evil work. (If it's not the "Cross," it is "confusion, and every evil work.")

17 But the wisdom that is from above is first pure (it is found in all its fullness in Christ, and in Christ Alone), then peaceable, gentle, and easy to be intreated, full of mercy and good fruits, without partiality, and without hypocrisy. (These things present the work of the Holy Spirit, with the Cross as the means and Christ as the Source.)

18 And the Fruit of Righteous-

ness is sown in Peace of them who make Peace *(presents the Law of sowing and reaping).*

CHAPTER 4

WORLDLINESS

FROM whence *come* wars and fightings among you? *(When Believers look to anything other than the Cross, strife is the result.)* come they not hence, *even* of your lusts that war in your members? *(Once again, the only solution for this problem, which besets every Christian, is that we understand all things come to us from God through the Cross. Making the Cross the object of our Faith gives the Holy Spirit latitude to work within our lives, in order that we might live the life we ought to live [Rom. 6:3-5, 12-13].)*

2 You lust, and have not *(such a person is not looking to God, but rather operating from self-will):* you kill, and desire to have, and cannot obtain *(the word "kill" refers to destroying the reputation of another in order to gain advantage, and to do so by slander, etc.):* you fight and war, yet you have not, because you ask not. *(This refers to Believers who little seek the Lord for anything, but rather depend upon other sources that are irregular to say the least!)*

3 You ask, and receive not *(and* there is a reason)*, because you ask amiss, that ye may consume *it* upon your lusts. *(Such a person is not asking in the Will of God, but rather from his or her own selfish desires.)*

4 You adulterers and adulteresses *(presents James using the same terminology as Paul [Rom. 7:1-4]; the Believer is to look exclusively to Christ and the Cross regarding all his needs; to look elsewhere, or rather for one's Faith to be placed in that other than the Cross, presents the person as committing spiritual adultery),* know ye not that the friendship of the world is enmity with God? *(If the Cross of Christ is not strictly the object of our Faith, God looks at everything else as "worldliness.")* whosoever therefore will be a friend of the world is the enemy of God. *(Allow me to once again make the statement that if the Cross of Christ is not our object of Faith, no matter how religious our efforts may be otherwise, it is still looked at by the Lord as "friendship with the world." This means the Believer in essence becomes an "enemy of God.")*

5 Do you think that the Scripture says in vain *(James was quoting several Scriptures [Gen. 15:6; 49:10; Ex. 17:6; Ps. 78:16; Ezek. 47:9; Joel 2:28-29]),* The Spirit Who dwells in us lusts to envy? *(This refers to the Holy Spirit,*

which means that the word "Spirit" should have been capitalized. The word "lusteth" here means "to earnestly or passionately desire." Of what is He envious, and what does He passionately desire? The Holy Spirit is envious of any control the fallen nature might have over the Believer, and is passionately desirous that He control all our thoughts, words, and deeds. He is desirous of having the Believer depend upon Him for His Ministry to Him, so that He might discharge His responsibility to the One Who sent Him, Namely God the Father.)

6 But He gives more Grace. *(Providing the Believer ever makes the Cross the object of His Faith, by which Grace comes from the Lord.)* **Wherefore he said** *(Job 22:29; Ps. 138:6; Prov. 3:34)*, **God resists the proud, but gives Grace unto the humble.** *(God resists those who look to that other than the Cross, and blesses those who humble themselves by looking strictly to Christ and the Cross, which develops humility.)*

PRAYER

7 Submit yourselves therefore to God *(to the Plan He has provided, which is the Cross).* **Resist the Devil, and he will flee from you.** *(We do this by strictly looking to Christ, and what He has done for us at the Cross, where Satan was totally defeated [Col. 2:14-15].)*

8 Draw near to God, and He will draw near to you. *(Once again and ever so, this is done only by Faith which ever makes the Cross its object.)* **Cleanse** *your* **hands,** *you* **sinners; and purify** *your* **hearts,** *you* **double minded.** *(Without a proper knowledge of the Cross regarding the Sanctification of the Saint, it is impossible for the Believer to live a Victorious, Christian life.)*

9 Be afflicted, and mourn, and weep *(refers to consternation over our having looked to that other than Christ and the Cross)*: **let your laughter be turned to mourning, and** *your* **joy to heaviness.** *(This refers to true Repentance, which means we confess our sin of looking to that other than the Cross, thereby seeking forgiveness. We must repent not only for the bad, but for the good as well. By that, I'm referring to our dependence on good things for victory in our lives, but yet that which is not the Cross.)*

10 Humble yourselves in the sight of the Lord, and He shall lift you up. *(As we have constantly stated, it refers to looking to Christ and the Cross, which is the only humbling process in which the Believer can truthfully engage.)*

JUDGING

11 Speak not evil one of an-

other, brethren *(refers to self-appointed Judges [Mat. 7:1-5])*. He who speaks evil of *his* Brother, and judges his brother, speaks evil of the Law, and judges the Law *(pertains to the Law of Moses, to which James is pointing; when a Believer judges another, he has taken himself out from under Grace and placed himself under Law, where he will only find condemnation)*: but if you judge the Law, you are not a doer of the Law, but a Judge. *(In other words, such a person has placed himself in the position of God.)*

12 There is one Lawgiver, Who is able to save and to destroy *(presents God as the only One Who can fill this position)*: who are you who judges another? *(The Greek actually says, "but you — who are you?" In other words, "who do you think you are?")*

THE SELF-WILLED

13 Go to now, you who say, Today or tomorrow we will go into such a city, and continue there a year, and buy and sell, and get gain *(proclaims the planning of individuals who don't include God)*:

14 Whereas you know not what *shall be* on the morrow *(proclaims the fact that we don't, while God does!)*. For what *is* your life? *(Making plans without God proclaims* the fact that we consider ourselves to be our own master.) It is even a vapour, that appears for a little time, and then vanishes away. *(This means that if the Lord doesn't guide our lives, then all is a waste.)*

15 For that ye *ought* to say *(presents the opposite of the "we will go" in Verse 13)*, If the Lord will, we shall live, and do this, or that *(proclaims our absolute dependence on God)*.

16 But now you rejoice in your boastings *(pertains to rejoicing in one's self-made plans)*: all such rejoicing is evil. *(All rejoicing should be in the Lord, and only in the Lord.)*

SIN

17 Therefore to him who knows to do good, and does *it* not, to him it is sin. *(Sin is an offence against God, which He cannot tolerate. If we do not abide by the Word of God, then we sin.)*

CHAPTER 5

THE RICH

GO to now, *you* rich men, weep and howl for your miseries that shall come upon *you*. *(This warning is to the wealthy who have gained their riches by fraud and deceit.)*

2 Your riches are corrupted,

and your garments are motheaten. *(These types of riches will do no one any good, and above all the person who has such.)*

3 Your gold and silver is cankered *(the idea is gold and silver laid up and not put to any use that is good)*; and the rust of them shall be a witness against you, and shall eat your flesh as it were fire. *(The having of money is not wrong. The question is what are we doing with this which God has given us? If we do not use it for His Glory, making certain that it is for His Glory, the Lord warns us here that such riches will consume us.)* You have heaped treasure together for the last days *(which means the treasure is not being laid up in Heaven [Mat. 6:19-20])*.

4 Behold, the hire of the labourers who have reaped down your fields, which is of you kept back by fraud, cries *(this Passage tells us, and rightly so, that far too much treasure is heaped up at the expense of others)*: and the cries of them which have reaped are entered into the ears of the Lord of Sabaoth *(the Lord of Hosts)*.

5 You have lived in pleasure on the earth, and been wanton *(luxury and self-indulgence at the expense of others is a great sin in God's eyes)*; you have nourished your hearts, as in a day of slaughter. *(James uses graphic imagery to indicate that the wicked rich, who have gained their riches at the expense of others, are always on the brink of Judgment.)*

6 You have condemned *and* killed the just; *and* he does not resist you. *(In hoarding such gain, some of the Righteous are victims. The Lord takes careful note of this, and especially of their helplessness.)*

PATIENCE

7 Be patient therefore, Brethren, unto the Coming of the Lord. *(This tells us the cure, and in fact the only cure for the injustices in this world. It is the Coming of the Lord.)* Behold, the husbandman waits for the precious fruit of the earth, and has long patience for it, until he receive the early and latter rain. *(The Holy Spirit, through James, tells us in a few words that the Coming of the Lord will take place shortly after the "Latter Rain," which in fact the world is now experiencing. This means the Second Coming is very near, and the Rapture is even at the door. The Second Coming will definitely address the gross injustices of this planet.)*

8 Be you also patient; stablish your hearts *(draw close to the Lord, which can only be done by making the Cross the object of our Faith)*: for the Coming of the Lord draws near. *(The Rapture of the Church should ever be in our minds.)*

9 Grudge not one against

another, Brethren, lest you be condemned *(the unjust Judgment of fellow Christians is sometimes more painful than the hatred of unbelievers)*: behold, the Judge stands before the door. *(This refers to the Lord Jesus and His readiness to avenge all wrong).*

10 Take, my Brethren, the Prophets, who have spoken in the Name of the Lord, for an example of suffering affliction, and of patience. *(Even though they were Prophets, which means they stood in a high and holy Office, they were not exempt from affliction.)*

11 Behold, we count them happy which endure. *(The word "endure" refers to the fact that the test or trial may last for some time.)* You have heard of the patience of Job, and have seen the end of the Lord; that the Lord is very pitiful, and of tender mercy. *(This is meant to proclaim the fact that whatever the Lord allows is meant for our good. We should understand that, and seek to learn the lesson desired to be taught.)*

TRUTH

12 But above all things, my Brethren, swear not, neither by Heaven, neither by the earth, neither by any other oath *(refers to the fact that the Lord is guiding every Believer, even in times of trial, and correspondingly we must* not lose Faith, thereby taking matters into our own hands)*: but let your yes be yes; and *your* no, no; lest you fall into condemnation. *(Even though we do not understand the reason for the situation, whatever it might be, we aren't to question the Lord!)*

HEALING

13 Is any among you afflicted? let him pray. *(Prayer is the recommendation of the Holy Spirit concerning affliction. But how many Christians take advantage of this privilege?)* Is any merry? let him sing Psalms. *(In effect refers to singing as a form of prayer, which it actually is, that is if we sing songs that rightly glorify the Lord.)*

14 Is any sick among you? *(This refers to physical or emotional illness of any nature.)* let him call for the Elders *(Pastors)* of the Church; and let them pray over him *(refers to asking the Lord for healing regarding the need)*, anointing him with oil in the Name of the Lord *(the "oil" has no medicinal purpose, but is rather meant to symbolize the Holy Spirit, and is used as a point of contact concerning our Faith; prayer is to be offered in the Name of Jesus [Jn. 16:23])*:

PRAYER OF FAITH

15 And the prayer of Faith

shall save the sick *(the "prayer of Faith" is simply the belief that God hears and answers prayer)*, and the Lord shall raise him up *(proclaims the Lord as the Healer, as is obvious, with the Cross being the means of all this; it is the Holy Spirit Who carries it out)*; and if he have committed sins, they shall be forgiven him. *(The conditional clause, "if he has sinned," makes it clear that not all sickness is the result of sin, but some definitely is. That being the case, the Lord will both heal and forgive upon believing Faith.)*

16 Confess your faults one to another *(refers to being quick to admit fault, if such be the case)*, and pray one for another, that you may be healed. *(The Holy Spirit, through James, broadens the aspect of prayer for the sick as applicable to any Believer.)* The effectual fervent prayer of a Righteous man avails much *(from any "Righteous man," Preacher or otherwise; "Righteousness" pertains to the fact that the Faith of the individual is strictly in Christ and the Cross, and not in other things.)*.

17 Elijah was a man subject to like passions as we are *(is said in this manner because the Holy Spirit wants us to know that what is in the reach of one is as well in the reach of the other)*, and he prayed earnestly that it might not rain: and it rained not on the earth by the space of three years and six months *(showing us the power of prayer, that is if we pray in the Will of God)*.

18 And he prayed again, and the Heaven gave rain, and the earth brought forth her fruit *(refers to the effect of one man's prayers)*.

THE TRUTH

19 Brethren, if any of you do err from the Truth *(James is speaking here of Believers, and of them straying from the Truth of the Cross)*, and one convert him *(refers to strengthening the individual, turning him back to the right way of Truth, which is back to Christ and the Cross)*;

20 Let him know, that he which converts the sinner from the error of his way *(bluntly proclaims any way other than the Cross as the "way of sin," which then makes the one traveling such a way "a sinner")* shall save a soul from death, and shall hide a multitude of sins. *(This refers to the fact that if the Believer leaves the Cross, thereby transferring his Faith to something else, and such an erring way is continued, it will result in the loss of the soul. To pull one back to the Cross saves that soul, which the Cross Alone can do!)*

THE FIRST EPISTLE GENERAL OF
PETER

CHAPTER 1

INTRODUCTION

PETER *(the name means "rock," and is used metaphorically here to describe Peter as a man like a rock by reason of his firmness and strength of soul)*, **an Apostle of Jesus Christ** *(presents the authoritative tone of this Epistle)*, **to the strangers** *(strangers to Peter because he had not previously met them)* **scattered throughout Pontus, Galatia, Cappadocia, Asia, and Bithynia** *(describes this Epistle being sent to Christian Jews who had settled in certain parts of the Roman Empire; however, it is also meant for the Gentiles)*,

2 **Elect** *(those who elect to favorably respond to the Call of the Holy Spirit, are the elect of God)* **according to the foreknowledge of God the Father** *(refers to God seeing ahead that He would have to send a Saviour to redeem man from the Fall; all who accept the Saviour are the "elect")*, **through Sanctification of the Spirit** *(elected to be Sanctified by the Holy Spirit)*, **unto obedience and sprinkling of the Blood of Jesus Christ** *(pertains to the fact that the Holy Spirit Sancti-* fies us on the basis of the Finished Work of Christ, where our Faith must reside; as the Cross is everything concerning Salvation, it is also everything concerning Sanctification)*: **Grace unto you, and Peace, be multiplied.** *(Both attributes come through the Cross, and will continue to multiply as long as our Faith is firmly anchored in the Cross of Christ.)*

THANKSGIVING

3 **Blessed** *be* **the God and Father of our Lord Jesus Christ** *(we are to Bless God at all times because of what He has done for us through Jesus Christ)*, **which according to His abundant Mercy** *(presents the fact that the Law and vengeance are no longer before us, but rather pure Mercy)* **has begotten us again unto a lively hope** *(proclaims the fact that we are transplanted from Adam's heritage into the heritage of God)* **by the Resurrection of Jesus Christ from the dead** *(this refers to us being raised with Christ to "newness of life," which enables us to live a Holy Life [Rom. 6:3-5])*,

4 **To an inheritance incorruptible, and undefiled, and that**

fades not away *(we, as begotten Children of God, are Heirs of God and Joint-heirs with His Son, the Lord Jesus Christ [Rom. 8:17])*, reserved in Heaven for you *(carries the idea that God is guarding our inheritance for us under constant surveillance)*,

5 Who are kept by the Power of God through Faith *(refers to the Holy Spirit exerting His Power on our behalf, as our Faith is ever planted in the Cross [Rom. 6:5])* unto Salvation ready to be revealed in the last time *(ready for the Rapture)*.

FAITH

6 Wherein you greatly rejoice *(refers to the time when this earthly sojourn will be finished, the Trump of God sounds, and "we shall be changed" [I Cor. 15:51-54])*, though now for a season, if need be, you are in heaviness through manifold temptations *(this life is the dress rehearsal for Eternity)*:

7 That the trial of your Faith *(all Faith is tested, and great Faith must be tested greatly)*, being much more precious than of gold that perishes *(the emphasis is the testing of our Faith to show whether or not it is genuine; the Holy Spirit says such is more precious than the testing of gold, which is the most precious commodity in the world; is our Faith really in the Cross or*

not?), though it be tried with fire *(the fire of temptation, trouble, etc.; such are meant to show the weakness)*, might be found unto Praise and Honour and Glory *(which can only be done if the Cross of Christ is the sole object of our Faith)* at the appearing of Jesus Christ *(we are being prepared by the Holy Spirit as fit subjects for the appearing of our Lord, as it regards the Rapture)*:

JOY UNSPEAKABLE

8 Whom *(Jesus Christ)* having not seen, you love *(we haven't personally seen the Lord, but the Holy Spirit has made Him real to our hearts)*; in Whom, though now you see *Him* not, yet believing *(proclaims total and complete Faith in Christ, though He has not been seen by the natural eyes, but Whom we shall one day see)*, you rejoice with Joy unspeakable and full of Glory *(the intended state for every Believer, and which can be attained despite trials and afflictions if Faith is anchored firmly in the Cross)*:

9 Receiving the end of your Faith, *even* the Salvation of *your* souls *(refers to the coming Resurrection, when we will then be Glorified)*.

10 Of which Salvation the Prophets have enquired and searched diligently *(Old Testament Prophets carefully and dili-*

gently sought the meaning of the things they were prophesying as it concerned Christ and what He would do to redeem humanity [Gen. 49:10; Isa., Chpt. 53]), who Prophesied of the Grace that should come unto you (this "Grace" was not for their day, but for the coming dispensation, all made possible by the Cross):

11 Searching what (these men diligently searched their own Prophecies, and the Prophecies of other Prophets, so that they might know that of which was spoken), or what manner of time (what kind of time would usher in this particular unique Salvation? the time of Grace alone, which means the Law would be no more) the Spirit of Christ which was in them did signify (whatever the Spirit of God did in Old Testament times, all pertained to Christ, without exception), when it testified beforehand the sufferings of Christ (refers to the Message of the Old Testament, all given by the Holy Spirit, and all pointing to the coming Redemption of man, which would be brought about by the Cross of Christ), and the Glory that should follow. (This proclaims all the wonderful things made possible by the "Sufferings of Christ.")

12 Unto whom it was revealed (refers to the Church), that not unto themselves, but unto us they did Minister the things (proclaims the entirety of the Old Testament),

which are now reported unto you by them who have Preached the Gospel unto you (refers to what Christ did at the Cross, which the Prophets predicted) with the Holy Spirit sent down from Heaven (the Holy Spirit verified what Christ did at the Cross by coming from Heaven in a new dimension, thereby abiding in the hearts and lives of Believers, and doing so permanently [Jn. 14:16-17]); which things the Angels desire to look into. (In other words, the Church is the University for Angels.)

HOLY LIVING

13 Wherefore gird up the loins of your mind (in view of what the Lord has done for us, we should have a hopeful spirit of optimism), be sober, and hope to the end for the Grace that is to be brought unto you (actually speaks of the Glorification of the Saints) at the Revelation of Jesus Christ (refers to the coming Rapture of the Church);

14 As obedient children, not fashioning yourselves according to the former lusts in your ignorance (don't be ruled by the sin nature which ruled you before coming to Christ):

15 But as He which has called you is Holy (God is Holy, so we are to be Holy as well), so be ye Holy in all manner of conversation (refers to lifestyle);

16 Because it is written *(Lev. 11:44)*, Be ye Holy; for I am Holy. *(All of this can only be done in one way. Placing our Faith exclusively in the Cross of Christ gives the Holy Spirit latitude to help us, and He Alone can develop Holiness within our lives. It cannot be done by self-will, or by rules, regulations, etc.)*

17 And if you call on the Father *(should have been translated, "since you call on the Father")*, Who without respect of persons *(says in the Greek, "does not receive face"; God does not receive anyone's face; He is impartial)* judges according to every man's work *(God Alone is our Judge, not man; man can be fooled; God cannot!)*, pass the time of your sojourning *here* in fear *(a fear of self-trust)*:

REDEMPTION

18 Forasmuch as you know that you were not redeemed with corruptible things, *as* silver and gold *(presents the fact that the most precious commodities [silver and gold] could not redeem fallen man)*, from your vain conversation *(vain lifestyle) received* by tradition from your fathers *(speaks of original sin that is passed on from father to child at conception)*;

THE CROSS

19 But with the Precious Blood of Christ *(presents the payment, which proclaims the poured out Life of Christ on behalf of sinners)*, as of a Lamb without blemish and without spot *(speaks of the lambs offered as substitutes in the Old Jewish economy; the Death of Christ was not an execution or assassination, but rather a Sacrifice; the Offering of Himself presented a Perfect Sacrifice, for He was Perfect in every respect [Ex. 12:5])*:

20 Who verily was foreordained before the foundation of the world *(refers to the fact that God, in His Omniscience, knew He would create man, man would Fall, and man would be redeemed by Christ going to the Cross; this was all done before the Universe was created; this means the Cross of Christ is the Foundation Doctrine of all Doctrine, referring to the fact that all Doctrine must be built upon that Foundation, or else it is specious)*, but was manifest in these last times for you *(refers to the invisible God Who, in the Person of the Son, was made visible to human eyesight by assuming a human body and human limitations)*,

21 Who by Him do believe in God *(it is only by Christ and what He did for us at the Cross that we are able to "Believe in God")*, Who raised Him *(Christ)* up from the dead *(His Resurrection was guaranteed insomuch as He Atoned for*

all sin [Rom. 6:23]), and gave Him Glory (refers to the exaltation of Christ); that your Faith and Hope might be in God. (This speaks of a heart Faith in God, Who saves sinners in answer to our Faith in the Resurrected Lord Jesus Who died for us.)

22 Seeing you have purified your souls (in effect says in the Greek, "having purified your souls") in obeying the Truth (the great system of Truth respecting the Redemption of the world, which refers to the Cross) through the Spirit (everything is done "through the Spirit") unto unfeigned love of the Brethren (refers to love which is not hypocritical), see that you love one another with a pure heart fervently (the God kind of love, which can only come about as the Believer anchors his Faith in the Cross, and does so exclusively):

23 Being born again, not of corruptible seed (refers to the fact that the Born-again experience is not at all by virtue of any descent from human parents), but of incorruptible (which is the Lord Jesus Christ), by the Word of God, which lives and abides forever. (The story of the Bible is the story of man's Redemption, which is the story of the Cross.)

24 For all flesh is as grass (the Apostle is contrasting that which is begotten of God with that which is begotten by man [Isa. 40:6-8]), and all the glory of man as the flower of grass (refers to a very temporary glory). The grass withers, and the flower thereof falls away (considering that, our hopes had better be in the things of God, and not the things of man):

25 But the Word of the Lord endures forever (by contrast to that of man, which perishes quickly). And this is the Word which by the Gospel is preached unto you. (Preach the Cross, which brings Eternal dividends [I Cor. 1:21, 23; 2:2].)

CHAPTER 2

HINDRANCES

WHEREFORE laying aside all malice, and all guile, and hypocrisies, and envies, and all evil speakings (these things can be laid aside only as much as the Cross of Christ is the object of our Faith; that being the case, the Holy Spirit will perform the work He Alone can do),

SPIRITUAL GROWTH

2 As newborn babes (those recently saved), desire the sincere milk of the Word (the Word of God in general is a life sustaining factor in the spiritual sense), that you may grow thereby (spiritual growth is predicated on a knowl-

edge of the Word):

3 If so be you have tasted *("since you have tasted")* that the Lord *is* Gracious. *(This points to the Cross, which is the means of Grace.)*

4 To Whom coming *(come exclusively to Jesus)*, as unto a Living Stone *(Christ is the Rock)*, disallowed indeed of men *(refers to the rejection of Christ by Israel)*, but chosen of God, *and* precious *(men disallowed One Whom God had chosen, i.e., Christ)*,

CHIEF CORNERSTONE

5 You also, as lively stones *(because of being "in Christ")*, are built up a spiritual house *(refers to the Church; not the institutional Church, but rather all who are Born-again, i.e., the Family of God)*, an Holy Priesthood *(all Born-again Believers are members of the "Holy Priesthood," but Christ Alone is the Great High Priest)*, to offer up spiritual Sacrifices *(the word "Sacrifices" refers to the Cross and to our Faith ever being in that Finished Work; if it is truly "spiritual," then it most truly must have the Cross as its object)*, acceptable to God by Jesus Christ. *(Faith in Christ and the Cross alone is acceptable to God. This means Faith having anything else as its object is unacceptable.)*

6 Wherefore also it is con-tained in the Scripture *(Isa. 28:16)*, Behold, I lay in Sion a Chief Cornerstone, elect, precious *(suggests that the Image of Jesus as the Chief Cornerstone is an important one for Faith, or for unbelief)*: and he who believes on Him shall not be confounded *(shall not be put to shame)*.

7 Unto you therefore which believe *He is* precious *(refers to the estimate of Christ by those of us who believe in contrast to the view taken of Him by the world)*: but unto them which be disobedient, the Stone which the builders disallowed, the same is made the Head of the corner *(despite the fact that Christ was rejected by Israel, it is to Him that the world will answer)*,

8 And a Stone of stumbling, and a Rock of offence *(because of the Cross [I Cor. 1:23])*, *even* to them which stumble at the Word, being disobedient *(refers to unbelief)*: whereunto also they were appointed. *(All who reject Christ are appointed to be lost.)*

9 But you *are* a chosen generation *(a chosen or a new race, made up of all who have accepted Christ)*, a Royal Priesthood *(Christ is King and High Priest; due to being "in Him," we as well are "Kings and Priests" [Rev. 1:6])*, an Holy Nation *(a multitude of people of the same nature)*, a Peculiar People *(each Saint is God's unique*

possession, just as if that Saint were the only human being in existence); that you should show forth the praises of Him Who has called you out of darkness into His marvellous light *(He saved us by virtue of what He did at the Cross, for which we should ever praise Him)*:

10 Which in time past *were* not a people *(without God, there is no standing in any capacity)*, but *are* now the people of God *(made possible by what Jesus did at the Cross)*: which had not obtained Mercy, but now have obtained Mercy. *(Mercy is a product of Grace, which is a product of the Cross.)*

BELIEVERS

11 Dearly beloved, I beseech you as strangers and pilgrims *(no one is really a pilgrim in the Biblical sense who has not first become a stranger to this world)*, abstain from fleshly lusts, which war against the soul *(tells us that the "sin nature" is still with us as Christians)*;

12 Having your conversation *(lifestyle)* honest among the Gentiles *(the word "Gentiles," as used here, does not refer to Gentiles as in contrast to Jews, but to the unsaved world, the world of people without Christ)*: that, whereas they speak against you as evildoers, they may by *your* good works *(separated from sin)*, which they

shall behold *(to view carefully as a personal witness)*, glorify God in the day of visitation *(refers to this Day of Grace)*.

RULERS

13 Submit yourselves to every Ordinance of man for the Lord's sake *(Peter is speaking here of Civil Government)*: whether it be to the king, as supreme *(providing the Ordinance does not violate the Word of God)*;

14 Or unto Governors, as unto them who are sent by him *(the local police)* for the punishment of evildoers *(covers all Civil Government)*, and for the praise of them who do well. *(Evil is to be punished and doing right is to be rewarded, which pertains to a stable society.)*

15 For so is the Will of God *(Civil Government is ordained by God)*, that with well doing you may put to silence the ignorance of foolish men *(presents the fact that true Christians are the greatest asset of any nation)*:

16 As free *(the freedom we have in Christ)*, and not using *your* liberty for a cloak of maliciousness, but as the servants of God. *(The liberty we have in Christ does not make us above the Law of the Land.)*

17 Honour all *men (if honor is due)*. Love the brotherhood *(refers to the Christian family of Be-*

lievers). Fear God. *(He who properly fears God will not dishonor any man, will love his Brethren, and will as well give due recognition to constituted Civil authority.)* Honour the king *(in effect, refers to honoring the Office).*

SERVANTS

18 Servants *(slaves),* be subject to *your* masters with all fear *(indicates that slaves, as a class, formed a large part of the early Christian community);* not only to the good and gentle, but also to the froward. *(Christian slaves were to conduct themselves Christlike, whether their master was good or not. This admonition covers the modern employer and employee in the same manner.)*

19 For this *is* thankworthy *(refers to an action beyond the ordinary course of what might be expected),* if a man for conscience toward God endure grief, suffering wrongfully. *(Even though treated badly, the believing slave is to continue to conduct himself Christlike, which will always be noted by God.)*

20 For what glory *is* it, if, when you be buffeted for your faults, you shall take it patiently? *(If, in fact, the slave has done wrong, he should accept his punishment without complaint.)* but if, when you do well, and suffer *for it,* you take

it patiently, this *is* acceptable with God. *(This means not accepting the wrong treatment with patience is not acceptable with God. This can only be done by the Holy Spirit helping such a one, which He definitely will do, providing the Faith of such an individual is ever anchored in the Cross.)*

CHRIST

21 For even hereunto were you called *(called to act Christlike, irrespective):* because Christ also suffered for us *(Peter reminds these slaves that Christ also suffered unjustly, for He the Just One died on behalf of unjust ones),* leaving us an example, that we should follow His steps *(we are to reproduce Christ in our lives, which we can only do by the help, guidance, leading, and power of the Holy Spirit [Jn. 16:7-16]):*

22 Who did no sin *(Christ was the only sinless human being Who ever lived),* neither was guile found in His mouth *(He never sinned by speaking hypocritically or falsely, not even one time):*

23 Who, when He was reviled, reviled not again *(He did not respond in kind);* when He suffered, He threatened not *(when He suffered unjustly, He did not call down wrath from Heaven, which He definitely could have done);* but committed *Himself* to Him Who

Judges Righteously (He committed His defense to God, which we as well should do):

24 Who His Own Self bear our sins in His Own Body on the tree (gave Himself in Sacrifice on the Cross, taking the full penalty for our sins, which was physical death; it was not Christ's suffering that redeemed us, although that definitely was a part of what happened, but rather the price He paid by the giving of Himself), that we, being dead to sins, should live unto Righteousness (we are "dead to sins" by virtue of us being "in Christ" when He died on the Cross, which is done by our exhibiting Faith in Christ [Rom. 6:3-5]; and we were raised with Him in "newness of life," which guarantees us a perfect, spotless Righteousness): by Whose stripes you were healed. (This refers to the healing of our souls, and the healing of our physical body as well. The Atonement included everything man lost in the Fall, but we only have the Firstfruits now, with the balance coming at the Resurrection [Rom. 8:23].)

25 For you were as sheep going astray (we were like a flock without a shepherd); but are now returned unto the Shepherd and Bishop of your souls (refers to the Lord Jesus Christ; He Alone is the true "Shepherd," and He Alone is the true "Bishop" of our souls; if we allow man to take His place, we spiritually wreck ourselves; man can only serve as an under-shepherd).

CHAPTER 3

WIVES AND HUSBANDS

LIKEWISE, you wives, be in subjection to your own husbands (Peter is now dealing with Christian wives who have unsaved husbands, telling them how to win them to the Lord; the wife is to be in subjection, up to the point of violating Scripture; the Word of God is to be obeyed first of all, and without fail); that, if any obey not the Word (unsaved husbands who will not hear the Word of God), they also may without the Word be won by the conversation (lifestyle) of the wives (proper Christian behavior);

2 While they behold your chaste conversation (a Godly behavior) coupled with fear (the word "fear" here means "reverence," for the Lord and her husband; at the same time, it could be reversed for an unsaved wife).

3 Whose adorning let it not be that outward adorning of plaiting the hair, and of wearing of gold, or of putting on of apparel (is not meant to condemn these things, but rather that the lady's Faith be in Christ and the Cross);

4 But let it be the hidden man of the heart (is in contrast to the

"outward man of the body"), in that which is not corruptible *(is said to be such in contradistinction to gold and apparel), even the* ornament of a meek and quiet spirit *(presents a heart free from passion, pride, envy, and irritability)*, which is in the sight of God of great price. *(This presents the fact that having such an inward character is valuable in the sight of God.)*

5 For after this manner in the old time *(Old Testament Times)* the Holy women also, who trusted in God *(does not refer to a special class of women, but rather ordinary women who trusted the Lord)*, adorned themselves, being in subjection unto their own husbands *(presents the Apostle using the Old Testament as a foundation for what he now proclaims)*:

6 Even as Sarah obeyed Abraham, calling him lord *(presents Sarah as being a beautiful example of the "Holy women" mentioned by Peter in the previous Verse)*: whose daughters you are *(in a sense, all Believers, whether Jews or Gentiles, are sons and daughters of Abraham)*, as long as you do well, and are not afraid with any amazement. *(This could be better translated, "Whose daughters you are, as long as you obey the Lord, which will remove all fear of failure.")*

7 Likewise, you husbands, dwell with *them* according to knowledge *(Peter is now speaking of Christian husbands, and not the unsaved husbands to whom he had been alluding in previous Verses; the Holy Spirit has given correct knowledge on the subject)*, giving honour unto the wife *(refers to that which is unique in Christianity, which is likewise a type of subjection)*, as unto the weaker vessel *(pertains to the physical and never to the moral or intellectual)*, and as being heirs together of the Grace of Life *(the husband is to pay due honor to the wife because she is a joint-heir with him of Eternal Life, the Gift of God)*; that your prayers be not hindered. *(In effect says prayers will be hindered if these admonitions to both husbands and wives are ignored. In fact, to ignore anything the Holy Spirit says is not wise, to say the least.)*

RELATIONSHIP

8 Finally, *be ye* all of one mind *(involves an agreement not only in Doctrine, but also in practical aims)*, having compassion one of another *(evincing regard for each other's welfare)*, love as Brethren *(carries the idea of "family")*, be pitiful *(tender-hearted)*, be courteous *(friendly-minded, kind)*:

9 Not rendering evil for evil, or railing for railing *(presents the very opposite of the system of the*

world): but *contrariwise* blessing *(we should reward "evil" and "railing" with "Blessing")*; knowing that you are thereunto called, that you should inherit a Blessing *(proclaims the key to being Blessed by God)*.

10 For he who will love life, and see good days *(the formula for Blessing continues [Ps. 34:12-16])*, let him refrain his tongue from evil, and his lips that they speak no guile *(this Command is Universal in its reference and, therefore, includes enemies as well as others)*:

11 Let him eschew evil *(turn aside from such)*, and do good *(as stated, do not render evil for evil, but rather good for evil)*; let him seek peace, and ensue it. *(This refers to doing things that favor peace, even as the Holy Spirit has given instructions here through Peter.)*

12 For the eyes of the Lord *are* over the Righteous *(means the Lord is looking intently at all Believers who are trusting Him)*, and His ears *are open* unto their prayers: but the Face of the Lord *is* against them who do evil. *(This is an expression denoting disapproval, and a determination to punish them.)*

13 And who *is* he who will harm you *(considering that God is protecting you, what harm can they do!)*, if you be followers of that which is good? *(This proclaims the* condition placed on this great Promise of God.)*

PERSECUTION

14 But and if you suffer for Righteousness' sake, happy *are you (such suffering is the result of Righteousness, and not the cause of Righteousness; we must not confuse the two)*: and be not afraid of their terror, neither be troubled *(Righteousness guarantees the protection of the Lord [Isa. 8:12-13])*;

15 But Sanctify the Lord God in your hearts *(should be translated, "set apart Christ as Lord in the heart")*: and *be* ready always to *give* an answer to every man who asks you a reason of the hope that is in you *(every Believer must know the Word of God)* with meekness and fear *(never from a Holier-than-thou stance)*:

16 Having a good conscience; that, whereas they speak evil of you, as of evildoers, they may be ashamed who falsely accuse your good conversation *(Godly lifestyle)* in Christ. *(Irrespective of what people may say, the Righteousness of Christ will ultimately prevail. In other words, those who falsely accuse will ultimately be proven wrong.)*

WILL OF GOD

17 For *it is* better, if the Will of God be so, that you suffer for well

doing *(at times, God does ask us to suffer for Righteousness' sake)*, than for evil doing *(refers to suffering chastisement, which the Holy Spirit knows we need and every true Christian experiences more or less; as should be obvious, this is different than suffering for "well doing")*.

18 For Christ also has once suffered for sins *(the suffering of Christ on the Cross was but for one purpose, and that was "for sins"; while we as Believers might suffer for sins as well, such is never in the realm of Atonement; the price has been fully paid, which means there is nothing left owing)*, the just for the unjust *(Christ was the Perfect Sacrifice, the One Who was born without original sin, and Who lived a Perfect Life, never failing even in one point; He Alone was the "Just")*, that He might bring us to God *(refers to the way being opened for sinful man to come into the very Presence of God)*, being put to death in the flesh *(refers to the fact that Jesus died physically in order to serve as a Sacrifice, which means He didn't die spiritually, as some claim!)*, but quickened by the Spirit *(raised from the dead by the Holy Spirit [Rom. 8:11])*:

SPIRITS

19 By which also He went *(between the time of His Death and Resurrection)* and preached *(announced something)* unto the spirits in prison *(does not refer to humans, but rather to fallen Angels; humans in the Bible are never referred to in this particular manner; these were probably the fallen Angels who tried to corrupt the human race by cohabiting with women [II Pet. 2:4; Jude, Vss. 6-7]; these fallen Angels are still locked up in this underworld prison)*;

20 Which sometime *(in times past)* were disobedient *(this was shortly before the Flood)*, when once the longsuffering of God waited in the days of Noah *(refers to this eruption of fallen Angels with women taking place at the time of Noah; this was probably a hundred or so years before the Flood)*, while the Ark was a preparing *(these fallen Angels were committing this particular sin while the Ark was being made ready, ever how long it took; the Scripture doesn't say!)*, wherein few, that is, eight souls were saved by water. *(This doesn't refer to being saved from sin. They were saved from drowning in the Flood by being in the Ark.)*

WATER BAPTISM

21 The like figure *(refers to Water Baptism as a symbol)* whereunto *even* baptism does also now save us *(speaks of the Baptism into Christ, which takes place at con-*

version; it is done by Faith, and has nothing to do with Water Baptism, although that *serves as a symbol* [Rom. 6:3-5]) (not the putting away of the filth of the flesh *(proclaims the fact that Water Baptism cannot cleanse the soul)*, but the answer of a good conscience toward God,) *(Refers to the fact that one engages in Water Baptism because one has already been made clean by Faith in the Lord Jesus, which in turn gives one a good conscience toward God.)* by the Resurrection of Jesus Christ *(which refers to the Cross, and the Believing sinner being raised with Christ in "newness of life" [Rom. 6:4-5]):*

CHRIST EXALTED

22 Who *(Jesus Christ)* is gone into Heaven *(His Mission is complete)*, and is on the Right Hand of God *(proclaims the fact that His Sacrifice was accepted)*; Angels and authorities and powers being made subject unto Him. *(This refers to all, whether Holy or unholy. The "Cross" is the means by which all of this was done [Col. 2:14-15.]*

CHAPTER 4

VICTORY OVER SIN

FOREASMUCH then as Christ has suffered for us in the flesh *(refers to the Cross, with "flesh" referring to the fact that He died physically, and not spiritually as some claim)*, arm yourselves likewise with the same mind *(doesn't mean we are to attempt to imitate Christ in suffering, but rather to make the fact He suffered our source of victory; He suffered in the flesh that we might have victory over the flesh)*: for he who has suffered in the flesh has ceased from sin *(refers to the struggle between the flesh and the Spirit; "suffering in the flesh" by the Believer refers to stopping any dependence on self-effort, and depending totally on the Holy Spirit, Who demands that our Faith be in the Sacrifice of Christ [Rom. 8:1-2]);*

2 That he no longer should live the rest of *his* time in the flesh to the lusts of men *(since being saved, the sin nature is no longer to rule over us)*, but to the Will of God. *(This refers to the Divine Nature ruling over us, which comes about as a result of our total dependence on Christ and the Cross. In fact, Christ and the Cross are never to be separated, which refers to the benefits of the Cross coming down to us even unto this hour [I Cor. 1:17].)*

3 For the time past of *our* life may suffice us to have wrought the will of the Gentiles *(refers to our life before coming to Christ)*, when we walked in lasciviousness,

lusts, excess of wine, revellings, banquetings, and abominable idolatries *(works of the flesh [Gal. 5:19-21])*:

4 Wherein they think it strange that you run not with *them* to the same excess of riot *(the unsaved do not understand the reasons why the Believer left the old life)*, speaking evil of *you (one of the great ways one knows that one is now living for God, as hurtful as it might be)*:

JUDGMENT

5 Who shall give account *(the coming Great White Throne Judgment, where all unbelievers will appear)* to Him *(refers to Christ)* Who is ready to judge the quick *(living)* and the dead. *(Now, He is the Saviour. Then, He will be the Judge.)*

6 For for this cause was the Gospel Preached also to them who are dead *(the dead spoken of here have to do with Believers who heard the Gospel while they were alive, and accepted it)*, that they might be judged according to men in the flesh *(doesn't matter how men may judge us, which is in contrast to the Judgment of God)*, but live according to God in the Spirit. *(This refers to every Saint of God who has lived and died, and who is now with the Lord.)*

7 But the end of all things is at hand *(paints everything in the light of Eternity; whatever our length of days on this Earth, it is nothing more or less by comparison to Eternity; we must always keep this end in view)*: be ye therefore sober, and watch unto prayer. *(Without prayer, there cannot be a proper relationship with the Lord.)*

8 And above all things have fervent charity *(love)* among yourselves: for charity *(love)* shall cover the multitude of sins. *(When one Christian truly loves his fellow Christian, he will not publish abroad his failings, but will cover them up from the sight of others.)*

9 Use hospitality one to another without grudging. *(Don't do such because it is commanded, but do it from love for God and man.)*

SPIRITUAL GIFTS

10 As every man has received the Gift *(everything good we have is a Gift from God)*, even so Minister the same one to another *(refers to being of service in anyway we can)*, as good stewards of the manifold Grace of God *(speaks of the great Gift all of us have been given; we should walk wisely in this Gift of Grace)*.

11 If any man speak, *let him speak* as the Oracles of God *(let him speak according to the Word of God)*; if any man Minister, *let him do it* as of the ability which

God gives *(refers to the giving of ourselves to the Work of God in any manner, but more specifically it refers to us giving of our financial resources for the Cause of Christ)*: that God in all things may be glorified through Jesus Christ *(refers to what Christ did at the Cross and through nothing else)*, to Whom be praise and dominion for ever and ever. Amen. *(He is due all praise because of His great Sacrifice, which took back dominion.)*

THE FIERY TRIAL

12 Beloved, think it not strange concerning the fiery trial which is to try you *(trials do not merely happen; they are designed by wisdom and operated by love; Job proved this)*, as though some strange thing happened unto you *(your trial, whatever it is, is not unique; many others are experiencing the same thing!)*:

13 But rejoice *(despite the trial)*, inasmuch as you are partakers of Christ's sufferings *(refers to suffering for Righteousness' sake)*; that, when His Glory shall be revealed *(refers to His Second Coming)*, you may be glad also with exceeding joy. *(There will be great joy in the heart of every Saint when we come back with the Lord at the Second Coming.)*

14 If you be reproached for the Name of Christ, happy *are you (should have been translated, "since you are reproached")*; for the Spirit of Glory and of God rests upon you *(refers to the Holy Spirit)*: on their part He is evil spoken of, but on your part He is glorified. *(This refers to the fact that the world, and even the apostate Church, reproaches this sacred influence of the Holy Spirit by their treatment of true Christians. But if we conduct ourselves correctly, the Lord is Glorified in our lives.)*

15 But let none of you suffer as a murderer, or *as* a thief, or *as* an evildoer, or as a busybody in other men's matters. *(This Scripture plainly tells us that if the Christian doesn't place His Faith entirely in the Cross, which guarantees the help of the Holy Spirit, these things Peter mentioned can definitely happen. That's why it is imperative every Believer knows and understands the Message of the Cross.)*

16 Yet if *any man suffer* as a Christian *(which sometimes happens for Righteousness' sake)*, let him not be ashamed *(such a one is not suffering because of lack of Faith, but rather because of his Faith)*; but let him glorify God on this behalf. *(If we truly suffer for Righteousness' sake, such suffering will always glorify the Lord. We should rejoice accordingly [Vs. 13].)*

JUDGMENT

17 For the time *is come* that judgment must begin at the House of God *(Judgment always begins with Believers, and pertains to their Faith, whether in the Cross or otherwise; the Cross alone is spared Judgment, for there Jesus was judged in our place)*: and if it first *begin* at us, what shall the end *be* of them who obey not the Gospel of God? *(If God will Judge His Own, how much more will He Judge the unredeemed? The Cross alone stays the Judgment of God. Let that ever be understood.)*

18 And if the Righteous scarcely be saved *(can be saved only by trusting Christ and the Cross, and nothing else)*, where shall the ungodly and the sinner appear? *(If the great Sacrifice of Christ is rejected and spurned, where does that leave those who do such a thing? There is no hope for their Salvation.)*

19 Wherefore let them who suffer according to the Will of God *(it really doesn't matter what we have to go through in order to live for God, the end result will be worth it a million times over)* commit the keeping of their souls *to* Him in well doing *(victory is assured if we continue to look to the Cross)*, as unto a Faithful Creator. *(This means God hasn't created an insufficient Salvation. He has cre-*ated a Way through the Death of Christ that guarantees victory, if we will only follow that Way.)*

CHAPTER 5

PASTORS

THE Elders *(Pastors)* which are among you I exhort *(pertains to Pastors of local Churches)*, who am also an Elder *(proclaims the fact that the great Apostle was a Pastor as well, Pastoring then at Babylon [Vs. 13])*, and a witness of the sufferings of Christ *(who was with Christ throughout our Lord's Ministry, even unto His Death)*, and also a partaker of the glory that shall be revealed *(if the Cross is accepted, the Glory is revealed)*:

2 Feed the flock of God which is among you *(Preach the Cross [I Cor. 1:21, 23; 2:2])*, taking the oversight *thereof*, not by constraint, but willingly *(privileged to do so, and not because we have no choice)*; not for filthy lucre *(money must not be our motive)*, but of a ready mind *(not swayed by money or anything else, only to do the Will of God)*;

3 Neither as being lords over God's heritage *(the Greek Text speaks of a high-handed autocratic rule over the flock, which is forbidden of a true Shepherd)*, but being examples to the flock *(presents instruction which the Apostle*

had lived in a most unique way).

4 And when the Chief Shepherd shall appear *(the Lord Jesus Christ, at the Rapture of the Church),* you shall receive a crown of glory that fades not away *(refers to the victory crown).*

COMMANDS

5 Likewise, you younger *(associate Pastors in the local Church),* submit yourselves unto the Elder *(senior Pastor).* Yes, all *of you* be subject one to another *(refers to mutual understanding),* and be clothed with humility *(refers to the virtue that must grace all other virtues, which can only come by Faith in the Cross)*: for God resists the proud *(He sets Himself in array against the proud person),* and gives grace to the humble. *(One who places his Faith exclusively in the Cross of Christ.)*

6 Humble yourselves therefore under the Mighty Hand of God *(the Cross alone and one's Faith in that Finished Work can make one humble),* that He may exalt you in due time *(proclaims the route to the Blessings of God)*:

7 Casting all your care upon Him *(refers here to a direct and once-for-all committal to God of all that would give us concern)*; for He cares for you *(translated literally, "for you are His concern").*

8 Be sober *(mentally self-con-*trolled)*, be vigilant *(awake and watchful)*; because your adversary the Devil, as a roaring lion, walks about, seeking whom he may devour *(we are faced with a very powerful adversary)*:

9 Whom *(the Devil)* resist stedfast in the Faith *("the Faith" always refers to what Jesus did at the Cross; our Faith must be ever anchored in that Finished Work),* knowing that the same afflictions are accomplished in your Brethren who are in the world. *(Every true Christian faces the onslaught of the Evil One.)*

BENEDICTION

10 But the God of all Grace *(refers to God as the Source of all Grace),* Who has called us *(a Divine summons)* unto His Eternal Glory by Christ Jesus *(through what Jesus did at the Cross),* after that you have suffered a while *(the transition from the "flesh" to the "Spirit," which is never easy, fast, or simple),* make you perfect *(knit together with the Spirit),* stablish, strengthen, settle *you (on a firm foundation which cannot be moved, as the Grace of God comes to us in an uninterrupted flow).*

11 To Him *(the Lord Jesus Christ)* be Glory and Dominion forever and ever. Amen. *(This is because of what He did at the Cross.)*

12 By Silas, a faithful Brother

unto you, as I suppose, I have written briefly, exhorting, and testifying that this is the true Grace of God wherein you stand. *(This proclaims the fact that this subject concerning living for God is so vast, but yet the Apostle attempted to address it in this short Epistle.)*

13 The *Church that is* at Babylon *(refers to the same city mentioned in the Old Testament, the Babylon on the River Euphrates; there is no proof that this statement is a synonym for Rome, as some claim),* elected together with *you,* salute you *(those who elect to trust Christ and the Cross are, at the same time, elected to experience the Grace of God);* and *so does* Mark my son *(refers to John Mark, who wrote the Gospel which bears his name; he was not the actual son of Peter, but a son in the Faith).*

14 Greet you one another with a kiss of charity *(the custom in those days).* Peace *be* with you all who are in Christ Jesus. Amen. *(This speaks of Sanctifying Peace, which comes through the Cross.)*

THE SECOND EPISTLE GENERAL OF
PETER

CHAPTER 1

INTRODUCTION

SIMON Peter, a servant and an Apostle of Jesus Christ *(the position of "servant" is placed first; if one cannot be a true servant for the Lord, then one cannot be an Apostle; the Lord guides the Church by the Office of the Apostle through the particular Message given to the individual, which will always co-incide directly with the Word of God; Apostles aren't elected, they are called of God)*, to them who have obtained like Precious Faith with us *(proclaims the Faith that Gentiles can now be saved exactly as Jews, in fact all coming the same way)* through the Righteousness of God and our Saviour Jesus Christ *(this Righteousness is obtained by the Believer exhibiting Faith in Christ and what He did at the Cross)*:

2 Grace and peace be multiplied unto you through the knowledge of God, and of Jesus our Lord *(this is both sanctifying grace and sanctifying peace, all made available by the Cross)*,

3 According as His Divine Power has given unto us all things *(the Lord with large-handed generosity has given us all things)* that *pertain* unto life and Godliness *(pertains to the fact that the Lord Jesus has given us everything we need regarding life and living)*, through the knowledge of Him Who has called us to Glory and Virtue *(the "knowledge" addressed here speaks of what Christ did at the Cross, which alone can provide "Glory and Virtue")*:

4 Whereby are given unto us exceeding great and Precious Promises *(pertains to the Word of God, which alone holds the answer to every life problem)*: that by these *(Promises)* you might be partakers of the Divine Nature *(the Divine Nature implanted in the inner being of the believing sinner becomes the source of our new life and actions; it comes to everyone at the moment of being "Born-again")*, having escaped the corruption that is in the world through lust. *(This presents the Salvation experience of the sinner, and the Sanctification experience of the Saint.)*

GROWING IN GRACE

5 And beside this *(Salvation)*,

giving all diligence *(refers to the responsibility we as Believers must show regarding the Christian life)*, add to your Faith Virtue *(this is Faith in the Cross, which will bring "Virtue"; the type of "Virtue" mentioned here is "energy" and "power")*; and to Virtue knowledge *(this is the type of knowledge which keeps expanding)*;

6 And to knowledge temperance *(self-control)*; and to temperance patience *(our conduct must honor God at all times, even in the midst of trials and testing)*; and to patience godliness *(being like God)*;

7 And to godliness brotherly kindness *(carries the idea of treating everyone as if they were our own flesh and blood "brother" or "sister")*; and to brotherly kindness charity *(love)*.

8 For if these things be in you, and abound *(continue to expand)*, they make *you that you shall* neither *be* barren nor unfruitful in the knowledge of our Lord Jesus Christ. *(Once again, this "knowledge" refers to what Christ did at the Cross, all on our behalf.)*

9 But he who lacks these things is blind, and cannot see afar off *(the reason one may lack these things is he is spiritually blind; in other words, such a one has made something other than the Cross the object of His Faith)*, and has forgotten that he was purged from his old sins. *(Such a Believer is once again being ruled by the "sin nature" exactly as he was before conversion, which is always the end result of ignoring the Cross.)*

10 Wherefore the rather, Brethren, give diligence to make your calling and election sure *(this is what Jesus was speaking of when He told us to deny ourselves and take up the Cross daily and follow Him [Lk. 9:23]; every day, the Believer must make certain his Faith is anchored in the Cross and the Cross alone; only then can we realize the tremendous benefits afforded by the Sacrifice of Christ)*: for if you do these things, you shall never fall *(presents the key to Eternal Security, but with the Promise being conditional)*:

11 For so an entrance shall be ministered unto you abundantly into the Everlasting Kingdom of our Lord and Saviour Jesus Christ. *(The entrance into the Kingdom is solely on the basis of Faith evidenced in Christ and the Cross [Eph. 2:13-18; Jn. 3:16].)*

GROUNDED IN TRUTH

12 Wherefore I will not be negligent to put you always in remembrance of these things *(as Peter, this is the reason I keep highlighting the Cross)*, though you know *them,* and be established in the present truth. *(The "Truth"*

is "Jesus Christ and Him Cruci-fied" [Jn. 8:32; I Cor. 2:2].)

13 Yes, I think it meet (neces-sary), as long as I am in this tab-ernacle (refers to the physical body), to stir you up by putting you in remembrance (by ever keeping Christ and the Cross before you);

14 Knowing that shortly I must put off this my tabernacle (Peter is saying that He knows he won't live much longer after writing this Epistle), even as our Lord Jesus Christ has shown me. (This pos-sibly refers to Christ's prediction given to the Apostle, recorded in John 21:18-19.)

15 Moreover I will endeavour that you may be able after my decease to have these things al-ways in remembrance. (This pre-sents the third time the Apostle makes reference to keeping in re-membrance the conditions of en-trance into Eternal Life [Vss. 12-13, 15]. He will use the word again in II Pet. 3:1.)

16 For we have not followed cunningly devised fables (refers to "heresies" taught by "false teach-ers"; in other words, anything that leads one away from Christ and the Cross), when we made known unto you the Power and Coming of our Lord Jesus Christ (what Christ could do in one's life, which the Cross made possible), but were eyewitnesses of His Majesty. (This pertains to the Transfigura-tion, which was an actual demon-stration of Christ coming in His Glory to Earth to set up His King-dom [Mat. 16:27-28; 17:1-8; 24:29-31; 25:31-46; Rev. 19:11-21].)

17 For He (Christ) received from God the Father Honour and Glory (pertains to the "Majesty" of the Son of God, which Peter mentioned in the previous Verse), when there came such a Voice to Him from the ex-cellent Glory (refers to the Voice of God), This is My beloved Son, in Whom I am well pleased. (God is well pleased with us only as long as we are "in Christ.")

18 And this voice which came from Heaven we heard, when we were with Him in the Holy Mount. (Peter was not relating something secondhand, but rather that which had happened to him personally.)

19 We have also a more sure Word of Prophecy (Peter is speak-ing here of the Old Testament, which is the Word of God, and even more sure than his personal expe-rience); whereunto you do well that you take heed, as unto a light that shines in a dark place (in ef-fect, states that the Word of God is the only True Light, which alone can dispel the spiritual darkness), until the day dawn, and the Day Star arise in your hearts (the "Day Star" is Christ; "arising in our hearts" pertains to the Rapture):

20 Knowing this first (harks back, as stated, to the Old Testa-

ment, which in effect was the Bible of Peter's day), that no Prophecy of the Scripture is of any private interpretation. *(This refers to the fact that the Word of God did not originate in the human mind.)*

21 For the Prophecy *(the word "Prophecy" is used here in a general sense, covering the entirety of the Word of God, which means it's not limited merely to predictions regarding the future)* came not in old time by the will of man *(did not originate with man)*: but Holy men of God spoke *as they were* moved by the Holy Spirit. *(This proclaims the manner in which the Word of God was written and thereby given unto us.)*

CHAPTER 2

FALSE PROPHETS

BUT there were false Prophets also among the people *(refers to the false prophets who plagued Israel of Old)*, even as there shall be false teachers among you *(the false teacher is one who presents a way of Salvation, or a way of Sanctification, other than the Cross)*, who privily shall bring in damnable heresies *(the idea is that these false teachers would teach some true Doctrine, and then cleverly include false teaching with it; it is the introduction of false teaching alongside the True that makes* it very subtle, and which abrogates the True), even denying the Lord Who bought them *(refers to denying the Cross)*, and bring upon themselves swift destruction *(upon themselves and upon those who follow them, which refers to the ultimate loss of the soul)*.

2 And many shall follow their pernicious ways *(actually most!)*; by reason of whom the way of Truth shall be evil spoken of *(proclaims the fact that not only is the Truth castigated, but the bearer of Truth as well! in short, it is a denigration of the Cross)*.

3 And through covetousness shall they with feigned words make merchandise of you *(the people are exploited instead of developed; the underlying cause is "money")*: whose judgment now of a long time lingers not, and their damnation slumbers not *(the Judgment seems to be delayed, but it definitely is not idle; sooner or later all who travel the path of "damnable heresies," which refers to any way other than the Cross, will ultimately face "utter ruin and destruction")*.

THE PENALTY

4 For if God spared not the Angels who sinned *(refers here to a specific type of sin, which was actually the sin of fallen Angels cohabiting with women that took*

place before the Flood, and then after the Flood [Gen. 6:1-4]), but cast *them* down to hell *(refers to "Tartarus," visited by Christ after His Death on the Cross and immediately before His Resurrection; in fact, He preached "unto the spirits in prison," which refers to these fallen Angels [I Pet. 3:19-20]),* and delivered *them* into chains of darkness *(where they have been imprisoned),* to be reserved unto Judgment *(refers to the coming "Great White Throne Judgment," when they will then be cast into the Lake of Fire [Rev. 20:10]);*

5 And spared not the old world *(the world before the Flood),* but saved Noah the eighth *person (there were eight people in the Ark),* a Preacher of Righteousness *(proclaims the fact that Noah preached to the Antediluvians for a number of years, but without success),* bringing in the Flood upon the world of the ungodly *(lends credence to the thought that God would have spared the old world had the Antediluvians heeded the Message Preached by Noah; Grace spurned is always Judgment pronounced);*

6 And turning the cities of Sodom and Gomorrha into ashes condemned *them* with an overthrow *(tells us in no uncertain terms what God thinks of Sodomy),* making *them* an example unto those who after should live ungodly *(Sodom and Gomorrha were* meant as a warning);

RIGHTEOUSNESS

7 And delivered just Lot *(refers to Lot and his two daughters; his wife perished [Gen. 19:15-26]; Lot was "just," meaning that his Faith was in Christ, even though his actions at times were not commendable),* vexed with the filthy conversation *(lifestyle)* of the wicked *(presents the attitude of this man with the behavior of the Sodomites):*

8 (For that Righteous man dwelling among them *(Lot did not become contaminated by the vices of Sodom),* in seeing and hearing, vexed *his* Righteous soul from day to day with *their* unlawful deeds;) *("Vexed" pertains to "torment or torture," meaning he was not only vexed with the sin of Sodom, but vexed at himself as well. In this word, we find a certain sense of personal culpability. The situation in which Lot now finds himself was ultimately due to his own selfish choice.)*

9 The Lord knows how to deliver the Godly out of temptations *(modern Believers are delivered "out of temptations" by placing their Faith exclusively in Christ and the Cross, which then gives the Holy Spirit latitude to help),* and to reserve the unjust unto the Day of Judgment to be punished *(in*

effect says that all who reject Jesus Christ and what He did at the Cross will definitely be judged):

FALSE TEACHERS

10 But chiefly them who walk after the flesh *(refers to false teachers who are advocating a way of victory other than the Cross [Rom. 8:1)* in the lust of uncleanness *(proclaims that which is guaranteed to happen as a result of "walking after the flesh")*, and despise Government. *(This refers to despising the Lordship of Christ, meaning to despise His Way, which is the Cross.)* Presumptuous *are they*, selfwilled *(refers to arrogance)*, they are not afraid to speak evil of dignities. *(When one speaks against the Cross, one is speaking against the Godhead.)*

11 Whereas Angels, which are greater in power and might *(greater than men)*, bring not railing accusation against them before the Lord. *(When reporting to the Lord concerning fallen Angels, etc., Righteous Angels merely report facts as they are without bitterness and railing.)*

12 But these *(false teachers)*, as natural brute beasts *(evidence no more common sense than an animal)*, made to be taken and destroyed *(proclaims what will happen to all false teachers)*, speak evil of the things that they un-

derstand not *(reduces their ridicule to their rejection of the Finished Work of Christ)*; and shall utterly perish in their own corruption *(presents the only conclusion for those who reject the Cross)*;

13 And shall receive the reward of unrighteousness *(ultimately the loss of one's soul)*, as they who count it pleasure to riot in the day time *(speaks of false teachers who live luxuriously off the money they get from those they have led astray by their false doctrine)*. Spots *they are* and blemishes *(a soiled unrighteousness because it is self-righteousness)*, sporting themselves with their own deceivings while they feast with you *(putting on a show of Righteousness, which is only deception)*;

14 Having eyes full of adultery *(spiritual adultery, which refers to ways other than the Cross [Rom. 8:1-4])*, and that cannot cease from sin *(if our Faith is in anything other than the Cross, we will find ourselves being unable to "cease from sin")*; beguiling unstable souls *(enticing with bait, which the modern Word of Faith Doctrine does)*: an heart they have exercised with covetous practices *(the love of money)*; cursed children *(children of cursing, referring to a curse placed on all who attempt to establish a way other than the Cross [Gal. 1:8-9])*:

15 Which have forsaken the

right way *(means they once knew the right way, but now they have forsaken it; the "right way" is the "Cross")*, and are gone astray, following the way of Balaam *the son* of Bosor *(that "way" is money)*, who loved the wages of unrighteousness *(this false prophet was willing to prostitute himself to secure gold)*;

16 But was rebuked for his iniquity *(Balaam was sinning)*: the dumb ass speaking with man's voice forbad the madness of the Prophet. *(A dumb animal rebuked the Prophet. Modern popular theology denies this, and so accuses the Holy Spirit of falsehood.)*

17 These are wells without water *(despite the claims, there is no water of life in the teaching of these false prophets)*, clouds that are carried with a tempest *(for dry and thirsty hearts, these "clouds" carry no water of life; the word "tempest" proclaims the fact that much is promised, but nothing is delivered)*: to whom the mist of darkness is reserved forever. *(It is either the Cross or Eternal darkness!)*

18 For when they speak great swelling *words* of vanity *(false doctrine is often presented in such a way as to impress the listener)*, they allure through the lusts of the flesh *(the allurement is the appeal of material things)*, through much wantonness *(particular types* of bait used to catch the hearers)*, those who were clean escaped from them who live in error. *(New converts or even Christians not well grounded in the Faith become easy marks for these "hucksters.")*

19 While they promise them Liberty *(they guarantee their way will lead to riches and happiness)*, they themselves are the servants of corruption *(while they are promising liberty, they are themselves in bondage, as is anyone who doesn't have the Cross as the object of his Faith)*: for of whom a man is overcome, of the same is he brought in bondage. *(If the false teaching is followed, which is the opposite of Grace, bondage will be the result [Gal. 5:1].)*

20 For if after they have escaped the pollutions of the world through the knowledge of the Lord and Saviour Jesus Christ *(they were saved by trusting Christ and the Cross)*, they are again entangled therein, and overcome *(proclaims the fact that if the Believer ceases to place his Faith and trust in what Jesus did at the Cross, that entanglement in the pollutions of the world will once again become a fact; it cannot be otherwise)*, the latter end is worse with them than the beginning. *(If Believers reject the Message of the Cross after it is plainly given, there is nothing left but destruction.)*

21 For it had been better for

them not to have known the way of Righteousness *(Peter is dealing with individuals who have had the privilege to hear the Gospel, accept Christ, and then for whatever reason cease to believe, and thereby lose their way)*, than, after they have known *it*, to turn from the Holy Commandment delivered unto them. *(It's bad enough to have never known the way. However, to have known it and then turn to another direction is unthinkable. Yet millions have done so. The far greater majority of the modern Church falls into this category. They have abandoned the Cross for other things.)*

22 But it is happened unto them according to the true Proverb *(Prov. 26:11)*, The dog is turned to his own vomit again; and the sow that was washed to her wallowing in the mire. *(This completely refutes the Unscriptural Doctrine of Unconditional Security, and gives the reason — a departure from Christ and the Cross.)*

CHAPTER 3

REMEMBER

THIS second Epistle, beloved, I now write unto you *(he had addressed his first Epistle to the same group of people)*; in *both* which I stir up your pure minds by way of remembrance *(by reminding* them of what is going to happen in the last of the last days)*:

2 That you may be mindful of the words which were spoken before by the Holy Prophets *(we are plainly told here that, as Believers, we must know and understand the Old Testament along with the New)*, and of the Commandment of us the Apostles of the Lord and Saviour *(refers to the New Testament, but at the same time the Verse says we cannot understand the New unless we first understand the Old)*:

SCOFFERS

3 Knowing this first, that there shall come in the last days scoffers *(speaks of the times in which we now live; they scoff at the Cross)*, walking after their own lusts *(which will happen when the Cross is rejected)*,

4 And saying, Where is the Promise of his coming? *(This refers to the Second Coming, not the Rapture. Endtime events as predicted in the Bible are met with scoffing.)* for since the fathers fell asleep, all things continue as *they were* from the beginning of the Creation. *(The two major themes of the Word of God are the Atonement and Endtime events. If we have a proper understanding of the Atonement, we will have, I think, a proper understanding of the latter.)*

5 For this they willingly are ignorant of *(their ignorance was a willful ignorance; in other words, the evidence was presented and then rejected)*, that by the Word of God the Heavens were of old, and the earth standing out of the water and in the water *(everything was created by the Word of God; this Verse points to Genesis 1:2; it speaks of the original Creation and the rebellion by Lucifer, which left the world in a convoluted state)*:

6 Whereby the world that then was *(speaks of the pre-Adamite Creation)*, being overflowed with water, perished *(doesn't refer to Noah's Flood, but rather the Flood of Genesis 1:2; this is when Lucifer led his revolution against God)*:

7 But the Heavens and the earth, which are now *(refers to the present Heavens and Earth as restored to a second perfect state in the days of Adam [Gen. 1:3; 2:25; Ex. 20:11])*, by the same Word are kept in store *(refers to the fact that all Creation is dependent solely on the Will of God)*, reserved unto fire against the Day of Judgment and Perdition of ungodly men. *(This refers to the coming "Great White Throne Judgment" [Rev. 20:11-15]. At this time, the Heavens and Earth will be renovated by fire.)*

8 But, beloved, be not ignorant of this one thing *(considering that we have the Word of God, there is no reason for the Believer to be ig-norant concerning spiritual things)*, that one day is with the Lord as a thousand years, and a thousand years as one day. *(A human promise may be weakened or destroyed by time. However, a Divine Promise is as certain of fulfillment in a thousand years as in one day.)*

9 The Lord is not slack concerning His Promise, as some men count slackness *(if it seems as though God delays the fulfillment of His Promises, it is for the purpose of getting more people into the Kingdom of God)*; but is long-suffering to us-ward *(God suffers long with man, attempting to bring him to a place of Repentance)*, not willing that any should perish, but that all should come to Repentance. *(The dispensation of the Cross has been the longest of all, and it is that because God keeps calling after sinners to be saved. He has made a way through the Cross for all to be saved. Most, however, refuse His Way.)*

FIRE

10 But the Day of the Lord will come as a thief in the night *(the conclusion of the Millennium; what will happen at that time will be unexpected, and for a variety of reasons)*; in the which the Heavens shall pass away with a great noise, and the elements shall melt with fervent heat, the earth

also and the works that are therein shall be burned up. *(This does not speak of Annihilation, but rather passing from one condition to another.)*

11 *Seeing* then *that* all these things shall be dissolved *(the present is temporal)*, what manner *of persons* ought you to be in *all* Holy conversation *(lifestyle)* and godliness *(pertains to the correct view of things)*,

12 Looking for and hasting unto the coming of the Day of God *(concerns the Coming eternal, perfect Earth, which will last in that condition forever and forever)*, wherein the Heavens being on fire shall be dissolved, and the elements shall melt with fervent heat? *("The Day of God" will be ushered in by the cataclysmic events of this Verse. There must be no sin left in the Universe.)*

13 Nevertheless we *(Believers)*, according to His Promise *(the Lord has promised that a new day is coming [Isa. 65:17])*, look for new Heavens *(this is the Promise!)* and a new earth, wherein dwells Righteousness. *(This proclaims the condition of the coming "New Heavens and New Earth" [Rev., Chpts. 21-22].)*

ADMONITIONS

14 Wherefore, beloved, seeing that you look for such things *(if one believes the Bible, one will believe its account of Endtime events)*, be diligent that you may be found of Him in Peace, without spot, and blameless *(which can be done only by the Believer ever making the Cross the Object of his Faith)*.

15 And account *that* the longsuffering of our Lord *is* Salvation *(His longsuffering, which refers to this Day of Grace that has now lasted longer than any other Dispensation, is in order to bring the unredeemed to Himself)*; even as our beloved Brother Paul also according to the wisdom given unto him has written unto you *(doesn't say which Epistle, but probably refers to Hebrews)*;

16 As also in all *his* Epistles, speaking in them of these things *(proclaims the fact that Paul's Epistles are inspired)*; in which are some things hard to be understood *(could refer to Prophecy, or to the great teaching Paul gave on the Cross)*, which they that are unlearned and unstable wrest, as *they do* also the other Scriptures, unto their own destruction. *(This presents the fact that some Christians purposely twist the Scriptures, attempting to make them mean something the Holy Spirit never intended.)*

17 You therefore, beloved, seeing you know *these things* before *(the Holy Spirit, through Peter, tells those to whom the Apostle was writing that they were not without un-*

derstanding *regarding what was being taught*), beware lest you also, being led away with the error of the wicked (*refers to being led away from the Cross*), fall from your own stedfastness (*refers here to the proper application of one's Faith; the Cross of Christ must always be the object of the Saint's Faith; if we shift our Faith to anything else, we "fall" [Gal. 5:4]*).

18 But grow in Grace (*presents the only way the Saint can grow*), and *in* the knowledge of our Lord and Saviour Jesus Christ. (*This "knowledge" refers not only to Who Christ is [the Lord of Glory], but as well what He did in order that we might be Redeemed, which points to the Cross.*) To Him be Glory both now and forever. Amen. (*This refers to such belonging to Him, because He is the One Who paid the price for man's Redemption.*)

THE FIRST EPISTLE GENERAL OF
JOHN

CHAPTER 1

INTRODUCTION

THAT which was from the beginning *(speaks of Jesus Christ; He is from everlasting)*, which we have heard *(John was personally with Christ for 3-1/2 years)*, which we have seen with our eyes *(John saw what Christ was as a Man)*, which we have looked upon *(what he saw was more than a passing glance; it was "gazing with a purpose")*, and our hands have handled *(refers to the fact that Christ was human)*, of the Word of Life *(says in the Greek, "The Word of The Life," referring to the fact that Christ is also God)*;

2 (For the life was manifested *(not hidden, but rather revealed)*, and we have seen it *(made visible to the human race through the humanity of our Lord)*, and bear witness *(we can testify to the fact)*, and show unto you that Eternal Life *(this "Life," which Christ is and has, is "Eternal")*, which was with the Father *(the Son is the same essence as the Father)*, and was manifested unto us;) *(This was made visible to us, and given to us as well.)*

FELLOWSHIP

3 That which we have seen and heard declare we unto you *(hence this Epistle)*, that you also may have fellowship with us *(something possessed in common by both, in this case Christ)*: and truly our fellowship *is* with the Father, and with His Son Jesus Christ. *(Fellowship with Christ guarantees fellowship with the Father.)*

4 And these things write we unto you, that your joy may be full. *(This should have been translated, "our joy may be full." John wanted others to know Christ as He knew Christ.)*

5 This then is the Message which we have heard of Him *(presents the true Message of the Cross in comparison with the false)*, and declare unto you, that God is Light *(as to His nature, essence, and character, God is Light)*, and in Him is no darkness at all. *(Spiritual darkness does not exist in Him, not even one bit.)*

6 If we say that we have fellowship with Him, and walk in darkness, we lie *(to claim Salvation while at the same time "walking in darkness" automatically dismisses our claims)*, and do not the

Truth (such a life is a "lie," and is not "true"):

7 But if we walk in the Light, as He is in the Light, we have fellowship one with another (if we claim fellowship with Him, we will at the same time walk in the Light, which is the sphere of His walk), and the Blood of Jesus Christ His Son cleanses us from all sin. (Our Faith being in the Cross, the shed Blood of Jesus Christ, constantly cleanses us from all sin.)

SIN

8 If we say that we have no sin (refers to "the sin nature"), we deceive ourselves (refers to self-deception), and the Truth is not in us. (This does not refer to all Truth as it regards Believers, but rather that the Truth of the indwelling sinful nature is not in us.)

9 If we confess our sins (pertains to acts of sin, whatever they might be; the sinner is to believe [Jn. 3:16]; the Saint is to confess), He (the Lord) is faithful and just to forgive us our sins (God will always be true to His Own Nature and Promises, keeping Faith with Himself and with man), and to cleanse us from all unrighteousness. ("All," not some. All sin was remitted, paid for, and put away on the basis of the satisfaction offered for the demands of God's Holy Law, which sinners broke, when the Lord Jesus died on the Cross.)

10 If we say that we have not sinned (here, John is denouncing the claims of sinless perfection; he is going back to Verse 8, speaking of Christians who claimed they had no sin nature), we make Him a liar (the person who makes such a claim makes God a liar, because the Word says the opposite), and His Word is not in us. (If we properly know the Word, we will properly know that perfection is not in us at present, and will not be until the Trump sounds.)

CHAPTER 2

THE ADVOCATE

MY little children, these things write I unto you, that you sin not. (This presents the fact that the Lord saves us from sin, not in sin. This Passage tells us that, as Believers, we don't have to sin. Victory over sin is found exclusively in the Cross.) And if any man sin, we have an Advocate with the Father, Jesus Christ the Righteous (Jesus is now seated at the Right Hand of the Father, signifying that His Mission is complete, and His very Presence guarantees intercession [Heb. 7:25-26; 9:24; 10:12]):

2 And He is the propitiation (satisfaction) for our sins: and not for ours only, but also for the sins of the whole world. (This per-

tains to the fact that the satisfaction is as wide as the sin. *If men do not experience its benefit, the fault is not in its efficacy, but in man himself.)*

EVIDENCE

3 And hereby we do know that we know Him *(refers to a "know so" Salvation)*, if we keep His Commandments. *(This can be done only as the Believer understands that the Cross is the solution for all things, and that it must ever be the object of our Faith. That being done, Christ will live through us by means of the person of the Holy Spirit, and the Commandments will be kept, referring to the entirety of the New Covenant [Gal. 2:20].)*

4 He who says, I know Him, and keeps not His Commandments *(if our claims do not correspond with His demands, then we really don't know Him)*, is a liar, and the Truth is not in him. *(If one's life is not changed by what is professed then one really doesn't have what is professed.)*

5 But whoso keeps His Word *(we are to abide by the Word of God, ever making it the rule of our lives, and we can do so if our Faith is solidly placed in the Cross)*, in him verily is the Love of God perfected *(refers to the "Fruit" of one who "keeps His Word")*: hereby know we that we are in Him *(refers to Romans 6:3-5)*.

6 He who says he abides in Him *(pertains to a claim being made)* ought himself also so to walk, even as He *(Christ)* walked *(pertains to the manner in which we order our behavior)*.

PROOF

7 Brethren, I write no new Commandment unto you *(to love the Brethren is not a new Commandment)*, but an old Commandment which you had from the beginning. *(To love the Brethren has been the foundation and the keynote of the Plan of God from the very beginning.)* The old Commandment is the Word which you have heard from the beginning. *(Since the old Commandment of Love has ever been before the Believer, there is no excuse to not walk after this direction.)*

8 Again, a new Commandment I write unto you *(the Commandment of Love is both old and new)*, which thing is true in Him *(Christ)* and in you *(if we are "in Him," then we should be like Him)*: because the darkness is past *(pertains to the time before Christ)*, and the true Light now shines. *(The "true Light" is Christ, which Light will shine forever, and pertains to the time since Christ has come.)*

9 He who says he is in the Light, and hates his brother, is in

darkness even until now. *(How can we claim to have love, and at the same time hate our Brother? Such a person isn't saved, despite his claims.)*

10 He who loves his Brother abides in the Light *(the type of love addressed here is the God kind of Love, which one cannot have unless one is truly saved)*, and there is none occasion of stumbling in him. *(To walk in the light is to be governed by love, which removes the stumbling blocks.)*

11 But he who hates his Brother is in darkness, and walks in darkness *(this is an individual who has once known the Lord, but is losing his way with God simply because of hatred in his heart for a fellow Christian; consequently, he walks in darkness)*, and knows not where he goes, because that darkness has blinded his eyes. *(The penalty of living in spiritual darkness is not merely that one does not see, but that one goes spiritually blind, which makes one an open target for false doctrine.)*

12 I write unto you, little children, because your sins are forgiven you for His Name's sake *(because of what He did for us at the Cross).*

13 I write unto you, fathers, because you have known Him *who is* from the beginning. *(This refers to those who are mature in the Christian life.)* I write unto you,

young men, because you have overcome the wicked one. *(This refers to Believers who have now come to the place where they are living in the Power of the Spirit, and their victory over Satan is a consistent one.)* I write unto you, little children, because you have known the Father. *(This refers to Believers who haven't been saved very long. The Greek word used here is "paidion," and refers to a child in training. It is the business of the "Fathers" and the "young men" to train the young converts in the ways of the Lord.)*

14 I have written unto you, fathers, because you have known Him *who is* from the beginning. *(John is repeating himself here in order that the "Fathers" may ever know and understand that God's prescribed order of victory has gotten them to this place [a place of overcoming strength], and they must not allow false doctrine to come in and destroy that.)* I have written unto you, young men, because you are strong, and the Word of God abides in you, and you have overcome the wicked one. *(Never forget how you have overcome, which is by Faith in the Cross of Christ [II Pet. 2:2].)*

15 Love not the world, neither the things *that are* in the world. *(The "world" spoken of here by John pertains to the ordered system of which Satan is the head.)* If any

man love the world, the love of the Father is not in him. *(God the Father will not share the love that must go exclusively to Him with the world.)*

16 For all that *is* in the world *(there is nothing in the system of this world that is of God)*, the lust of the flesh *(refers to evil cravings)*, and the lust of the eyes *(craves what it sees)*, and the pride of life *(that which trusts its own power and resources, and shamefully despises and violates Divine Laws and human rights)*, is not of the Father, but is of the world. *(These things have the system of the world as their source, not the Heavenly Father.)*

17 And the world passes away, and the lust thereof *(whatever the allurements of the world, they soon fade)*: but he who does the Will of God abides forever *(the one who keeps on habitually doing the Will of God)*.

FAITH

18 Little children, it is the last time *(all the period, from the First to the Second Advents may, in this sense, truly be called, "the last time")*: and as you have heard that Antichrist shall come *(the Apostle is speaking of the coming man of sin, who will make his debut after the Rapture of the Church)*, even now are there many Antichrists *(in the Greek is "Pseudochrists," and refers to one who claims to be of Christ)*; whereby we know that it is the last time. *(We know this is the last dispensation before the Second Coming of the Lord.)*

19 They went out from us, but they were not of us *(the crowd John speaks of claims to be of the True Church, but John says, "they were not of us")*: for if they had been of us, they would *no doubt* have continued with us *(had they been of the True Church, they would not have succumbed to false doctrine)*: but *they went out*, that they might be made manifest that they were not all of us. *("Them going out" means they turned their backs on the Christ of the Cross.)*

20 But you have an unction from the Holy One *(every True Believer has the "Anointing," of the Holy Spirit)*, and you know all things. *(This should have been translated, "you all know.")*

21 I have not written unto you because you know not the Truth *(what John is writing in this Epistle only reinforces what they have already known)*, but because you know it, and that no lie is of the Truth. *(The Truth will never produce a lie, and a lie can never produce the Truth.)*

22 Who is a liar but he who denies that Jesus is the Christ? *(Anyone who denies in any fashion Who Jesus is and What He has*

done to Redeem humanity is a "liar.") He is Antichrist, who denies the Father and the Son. *(He who denies the Trinity is Antichrist. God the Father and God the Son are represented here, and it is the Holy Spirit Who inspires the Text. So we have here the Trinity.)*

23 Whosoever denies the Son, the same has not the Father *(no matter the claims, if Jesus is denied, so is the Father)*: [but] he who acknowledges the Son has the Father also. *(If the Son is accepted, the Father is as well, for the Son is the only way to the Father [Jn. 10:30, 38].)*

24 Let that therefore abide in you, which you have heard from the beginning. *(We must not deviate from the True Gospel, which originally brought us to Christ.)* If that which you have heard from the beginning shall remain in you, you also shall continue in the Son, and in the Father. *(It is the responsibility of the Believer to nurture the stability and growth of correct Doctrines by a Holy life and a determination to cling to them and remain true to them.)*

25 And this is the Promise that He has promised us, *even* Eternal Life *(which we obtain by accepting Christ and what He did for us at the Cross).*

26 These *things* have I written unto you concerning them who seduce you. *(All false doctrine comes under the heading of "seducing spirits" in one way or the other, and is, therefore, labeled "Doctrines of Devils" [I Tim. 4:1].)*

27 But the Anointing which you have received of Him *(the Holy Spirit)* abides in you *(abides permanently to help us ascertain if what we are hearing is Scriptural or not)*, and you need not that any man teach you: but as the same Anointing teaches you of all things *(no Believer needs anything that's not already found written in the Word)*, and is Truth, and is no lie *(the Holy Spirit will guide us into all Truth [Jn. 16:13])*, and even as it *(the Anointing)* has taught you, you shall abide in Him *(refers to the fact that what we are taught by the Spirit, regarding the Word of God, helps us to abide in Christ).*

28 And now, little children, abide in Him *(presents the condition of fruit-bearing [Jn. 15:4, 7])*; that, when He shall appear *(the Rapture)*, we may have confidence *(speaks of the heart attitude of the Saint, who lives so close to the Lord Jesus that there is nothing between him and his Lord)*, and not be ashamed before Him at His Coming. *(This presents the fact that some certainly will be ashamed.)*

29 If you know that He is Righteous *(could be translated, "Since you know that He is Righteous")*, you know that every one who

does Righteousness is born of Him. *(All who are truly Born-again do "Righteousness.")*

CHAPTER 3

LOVE

BEHOLD, what manner of love the Father has bestowed upon us *(presents that which is foreign to this present world, and in fact comes from another world)*, that we should be called the sons of God *(we are "sons of God" by virtue of adoption into the Family of God, derived through the Born-again experience)*: therefore the world knows us not, because it knew Him not. *(The world does not recognize nor acknowledge Believers as sons of God, just as they did not recognize nor acknowledge Christ to be the Son of God.)*

2 Beloved, now are we the sons of God *(we are just as much a "son of God" now as we will be after the Resurrection)*, and it does not yet appear what we shall be *(our present state as a "son of God" is not at all like that we shall be in the coming Resurrection)*: but we know that, when He shall appear *(the Rapture)*, we shall be like Him *(speaks of being glorified)*; for we shall see Him as He is. *(Physical eyes in a mortal body could not look upon that glory, only eyes in glorified bodies.)*

RIGHTEOUSNESS

3 And every man who has this hope in Him *(the Resurrection)* purifies himself *(takes advantage of what Christ did for us at the Cross, which is the only way one can be pure)*, even as He *(Christ)* is pure *(places Christ as our example)*.

4 Whosoever commits sin transgresses also the Law *(the Greek Text says, "the sin," and refers to Believers placing their Faith in that other than the Cross; such constitutes rebellion against God's prescribed order and is labeled as "sin")*: for sin is the transgression of the Law. *(This refers to the moral Law — the Ten Commandments. Rebelling against God's order, which is the Cross, opens the door for works of the flesh [Gal. 5:19-21].)*

5 And you know that He was manifested to take away our sins *(He did so at the Cross; the Christian cannot practice what Christ came to take away and destroy)*; and in Him is no sin. *(This presents the fact that He was able to be the Perfect Sacrifice to take away the sin of the world, which completely destroys the erroneous doctrine that Jesus died spiritually, as some claim.)*

6 Whosoever abides in Him sins not *(does not practice sin)*: whosoever sins *(practices sin)* has not seen Him, neither known

Him. (As stated, Jesus saves from sin, not in sin. If we look to the Cross, "sin will not have dominion over us" [Rom. 6:14].)

7 Little children, let no man deceive you (the entirety of this Epistle is a warning against anti-nomianism, which teaches that sin doesn't matter because Grace covers it): he who does Righteousness is Righteous (truly being Righteous will truly do Righteousness, i.e., "live Righteously"), even as He is Righteous. (We have been granted the Righteousness of Christ, so we should live Righteous, which we can if our Faith Eternally abides in the Cross.)

8 He who commits sin (practices sin) is of the Devil (whoever is truly born of God does not live a life of habitual sinning); for the Devil sinneth from the beginning (from the beginning of his rebellion against God). For this purpose the Son of God was manifested, that He might destroy the works of the Devil. (This proclaims what was done at the Cross [Col. 2:14-15].)

9 Whosoever is born of God does not commit sin (does not practice sin); for his seed remains in him (refers to the Word of God): and he cannot sin (cannot continue to practice sin), because he is born of God. (This refers to the repugnancy of sin in the heart of the true Christian.)

10 In this the Children of God are manifest, and the children of the Devil (there is no comparison between the two): whosoever does not Righteousness is not of God, neither he who loves not his Brother. ("Righteousness" and "Love" are the two manifestations of the Child of God.)

LOVE

11 For this is the Message that you heard from the beginning, that we should love one another. (The first attribute made evident in the new Christian is "Love.")

12 Not as Cain, who was of that wicked one, and slew his Brother (presents the prototype of evil). And wherefore slew he him? (Cain was not a murderer because he killed his Brother, but killed his Brother because he was a murderer.) Because his own works were evil, and his Brother's Righteous (points directly to the Cross; the rejection of God's way [the Cross], which Cain did, is labeled by the Holy Spirit as "evil"; Abel accepted the Cross [Gen., Chpt. 4]).

13 Marvel not, my Brethren, if the world hate you (expect no better treatment from the world than Abel received from Cain).

14 We know that we have passed from death unto life, because we love the Brethren (love for the Brethren is the first sign of "spiri-

tual life"). He who loves not *his* Brother abides in death. *(Love for the Brethren must characterize the Salvation profession. Otherwise, our claims are false.)*

15 Whosoever hates his Brother is a murderer *(the absence of love proclaims the presence of hatred; where hatred is, there is murder)*: and you know that no murderer has Eternal Life abiding in him *(comes back to the absence of love)*.

16 Hereby perceive we the Love of God *(speaks of knowledge gained by experience)*, because He laid down His Life for us *(the highest proof of love is the Sacrifice of that which is most precious)*: and we ought to lay down *our* lives for the Brethren. *(This proclaims Christ as our example, and what the meaning of true love actually is.)*

17 But whoso has this world's good *(refers to the necessities of life)*, and sees his brother have need *(it is seeing a Christian in need of the necessities of life over a long period)*, and shuts up his bowels *of* compassion from him *(presents the individual who has the means to truly help, but refuses to do so)*, how dwells the Love of God in him? *(His actions proclaim the fact that despite his profession, there is actually no love of God in him.)*

18 My little children, let us not love in word, neither in tongue *(let us not merely talk love)*; but in deed and in truth. *(True love demands action.)*

19 And hereby we know that we are of the Truth *(the evidence of love is the guarantee of Truth)*, and shall assure our hearts before Him. *(Am I loving as I ought to be? Our hearts will tell us!)*

20 For if our heart condemn us *(our failures in duty and service rise up before us, and our heart condemns us)*, God is greater than our heart *(the worst in us is known to God, and still He cares for us and desires us; our discovery has been an open secret to Him all along)*, and knows all things *(presents God Alone knowing our hearts; this is the true test of a man)*.

21 Beloved, if our heart condemn us not *(does not claim sinless perfection, but represents the heart attitude of a Saint that, so far as he knows, has no unconfessed sin in his life)*, *then* have we confidence toward God *(implies no condemnation)*.

22 And whatsoever we ask, we receive of Him *(speaks of prayer, and that we must keep asking for that which is desired)*, because we keep His Commandments *(Christ has already kept all of the Commandments; our Faith in Him and the Cross gives us His Victory, and is guaranteed by the Holy Spirit [Rom. 8:1-2, 11])*, and do those things that are pleasing in His sight *(pertains to the fact that the Cross is ever the object of our Faith*

[Heb. 11:6]).

23 And this is His Commandment *(is given to us in the singular)*, That we should believe on the Name of His Son Jesus Christ *(stands for all the Son of God is in His wonderful Person, and above all what He did for us at the Cross)*, and love one another, as He gave us Commandment. *(Proper Faith guarantees proper love [Mat. 22:37-40].)*

24 And he who keeps His Commandments dwells in Him, and He in him. *(Faith in Jesus Christ and what He did for us at the Cross proclaims the fact that we are dwelling in Him, and He is dwelling in us [Jn. 14:20; Rom. 6:3-5].)* And hereby we know that He abides in us, by the Spirit which He has given us. *(The knowledge that God is abiding in the Saint comes from the Holy Spirit. He bears witness in connection with our human spirit, as energized by Him, that we are children born of God [Rom. 8:16].)*

CHAPTER 4

TEST THE SPIRITS

BELOVED, believe not every spirit *(behind every doctrine there is a "spirit"; if it's true Doctrine, the Holy Spirit; if it's false doctrine, evil spirits)*, but try the spirits whether they are of God *(the criteria is, "is it Scriptural?")*: because many false prophets are gone out into the world *(and they continue unto this hour)*.

2 Hereby know ye the Spirit of God *(as Believers, we are to know what the Spirit of God sanctions)*: Every spirit that confesses that Jesus Christ is come in the flesh is of God *(the Incarnation of Christ speaks of the Cross of Christ, the very reason for which He came; this means the Spirit of God will place his sanction on the Cross and the Cross alone; anything else is not of God)*:

3 And every spirit that confesses not that Jesus Christ is come in the flesh is not of God *(Christ came in the flesh to go to the Cross; this refutes the error of Gnosticism, which claims the flesh of Christ was evil, as much as all matter they claim is evil; also, anyone who denigrates or even minimizes the Cross in any way is not of God)*: and this is that *spirit* of Antichrist *(the spirit that denies the Cross is the spirit of the Antichrist)*, whereof you have heard that it should come; and even now already is it in the world. *(The Doctrine of the Cross is essential to the Christian system. He who does not hold it cannot be either regarded as a Christian or recognized as a Christian Teacher.)*

4 You are of God, little children, and have overcome them *(some of the Christians of John's*

day were tempted to believe the Doctrine that denigrated the Cross, but had overcome that temptation): because greater is He *(the Holy Spirit)* Who is in you, than he *(Satan)* who is in the world.

5 They are of the world *(refers to the false teachers of Verse 3)*: therefore speak they of the world *(refers to the fact that the source of their false doctrines is the world)*, and the world hears them *(because the false teachers are saying what the world wants to hear)*.

6 We are of God *(those who accept Christ and the Cross)*: he who knows God hears us; he who is not of God hears not us. *(Man's attitude toward the Message of the Incarnate Saviour ranks him on God's side or the world's.)* Hereby know we the Spirit of Truth, and the spirit of error. *(The "Spirit of Truth" is the Holy Spirit, who leads us into all Truth, which refers to "Jesus Christ and Him Crucified [I Cor. 1:23; 2:2]. The "spirit of error" refers to any doctrine that denigrates or ignores the Cross, which is fostered by Satan, who employs seducing spirits [I Tim. 4:1].)*

GOD IS LOVE

7 Beloved, let us love one another: for love is of God *(speaks of agape love, of which the world knows nothing, and in fact cannot have to any degree)*; and every one who loves is born of God, and knows God. *(This is the God kind of love, and cannot be faked. In fact, something will always happen to show what type of love the person possesses, whether it's the God kind or that of the world.)*

8 He who loves not knows not God; for God is love. *("As to His nature, God is love.")*

9 In this was manifested the Love of God toward us *(if we truly have the Love of God in our hearts, we will as well manifest such love toward our fellow man)*, because that God sent His only begotten Son into the world *(our Lord is the uniquely Begotten Son of God in the sense that He proceeds by eternal generation from God the Father, co-possessing eternally with God the Father and God the Spirit the essence of Deity)*, that we might live through Him. *(It is only through Christ and what He did at the Cross that we can find life, and as well live through Him as He lives through us [Gal. 2:20].)*

10 Herein is love *(the Greek says, "herein is the love")*, not that we loved God, but that He loved us *(the unconverted human race does not love God; nevertheless, He loved the human race)*, and sent His Son *to be* the propitiation for our sins. *("Propitiation" is the Sacrifice, which fully satisfied the demands of the broken Law and*

did so by our Lord's Death on Calvary's Cross. His Death eternally satisfied the Righteousness of God.)

11 Beloved, if God so loved us, we ought also to love one another. *(The Love of God is portrayed by the Cross more so than anything else. For us to understand His love, we have to first understand the Cross.)*

12 No man has seen God at any time. *(The idea is no one has ever yet seen Deity in all its essence.)* If we love one another, God dwells in us *(Saints having this agape love habitually for one another shows that this love, which God is in His nature, has accomplished its purpose in our lives)*, and His love is perfected in us. *(The words "His Love" do not refer to our love for Him, or even to His Love for us, but to the Love that is peculiarly His own, which answers to His nature.)*

13 Hereby know we that we dwell in Him, and He in us *("dwells" speaks of fellowship between two or more individuals; in this case, God and ourselves)*, because He has given us of His Spirit. *(The Holy Spirit has been caused to take up His permanent residence in us.)*

14 And we have seen and do testify *(John was an eye witness of Jesus Christ, both to Who He was and to What He did as well)* that the Father sent the Son *to be the* Saviour of the world. *(His Mis-*sion was to Redeem lost humanity, which He did at the Cross.)*

15 Whosoever shall confess that Jesus is the Son of God *(the confession John speaks of here is a lifetime confession, and represents the sustained attitude of the heart)*, God dwells in him, and he in God *(proclaims the union of the Father in the Believer and the Believer in the Father, all made possible by what Christ did at the Cross)*.

16 And we have known and believed the Love that God has to us. *(The love God has shown to us is manifested in Him giving His Son to die on the Cross.)* God is Love *(which is proven by His act of the giving of His only Son)*; and he who dwells in love dwells in God, and God in him. *(This is all made possible by the Cross, and only by the Cross.)*

17 Herein is our love made perfect *(our Love is brought to fruition, i.e., "made complete," by a continued confession of Jesus Christ as the Son of God, and what He did for us on the Cross)*, that we may have boldness in the Day of Judgment *(the Judgment addressed here is the coming "Judgment Seat of Christ")*: because as he is, so are we in this world. *(Christ is totally victorious, and due to the fact that we are in Him, we as well can be totally victorious in this world.)*

18 There is no fear in love *(the*

type of "fear" spoken of here is not a Godly fear or a filial reverence, but rather a slavish fear for a master or of a criminal before a Judge); but perfect love casts out fear (God has a perfect love for us, and if we have a perfect love for Him, which we surely can have, then we know He is going to sustain us, so there's nothing then to fear): because fear has torment. (It is guilt that makes men fear what is to come.) He who fears is not made perfect in love. (If we do not properly understand the Cross, then we are not made perfect in love.)

19 We love Him, because He first loved us. (The first initiation of Love was on the part of God, and not us, as was necessary.)

20 If a man say, I love God, and hates his Brother, he is a liar (as James said, "does a fountain send forth at the same place sweet water and bitter?" [James 3:11]): for he who loves not his brother whom he has seen, how can he love God whom he has not seen? (If a professed Christian does not love one who bears the Divine Image, Whom he sees and knows, how can he love God, Whose Image he bears, yet has not seen?)

21 And this Commandment have we from Him (the Holy Spirit, through John, proclaims all of this as a "Commandment"), That he who loves God love his Brother also. (True love for God will always bring forth the correct action.)

CHAPTER 5

THE NEW BIRTH

WHOSOEVER believes that Jesus is the Christ is born of God (the word "believeth" is not a mere intellectual assent to the fact of the Incarnation, but a heart acceptance of all that is implied in its purpose — the substitutionary death of the Incarnate One for sinners): and every one who loves Him Who begat loves him also who is begotten of Him. (This simply states that those who love God as their Father also love God's Children.)

2 By this we know that we love the Children of God (we know we love God if we love those who bear His Image), when we love God, and keep His Commandments. (Jesus said the same thing in John 14:15.)

3 For this is the Love of God, that we keep His Commandments: and His Commandments are not grievous. (This is easy to do, providing we look exclusively to the Cross. Otherwise it is impossible [Mat. 11:28-30].)

4 For whatsoever is born of God overcomes the world (if we follow God's prescribed order, we will overcome the world): and this is the victory that overcomes the

world, *even* our Faith. *(John is speaking here of Faith in Christ and the Cross, which then gives the Holy Spirit latitude to work within our lives.)*

5 Who is he who overcomes the world, but he who believes that Jesus is the Son of God? *(It is not he who "does," but who "believes.")*

LIFE

6 This is He Who came by water and blood, *even* Jesus Christ *(refers to the Living Word becoming flesh [Jn. 1:1, 4], which is symbolized by "water" and then as the Lamb of God Who took away the sin of the world, which was effected by the shedding of His Blood on the Cross of Calvary)*; not by water only, but by water and blood *(testifies to the fact that the Incarnation within itself, although absolutely necessary, was not enough; the phrase also testifies to the absolute necessity of the Atonement).* And it is the Spirit Who bears witness, because the Spirit is Truth. *(The Holy Spirit bore witness to the Divine Birth of Christ, and to the Divine Sacrifice of Christ [Mat. 1:18; Heb. 9:14].)*

7 For there are Three Who bear record in Heaven *(the Law has ever required the Testimony of two or three witnesses [Deut. 17:6; 19:15; Mat. 18:16; II Cor. 13:1]),* the Father, the Word *(Jesus Christ is the Word [Jn. 1:1]),* and the Holy Spirit: and these Three are One. *(The only sense three can be one is in essence and unity, as is clear in John 17:11, 21-23.)*

8 And there are Three who bear witness in earth *(as in Heaven, so on Earth)*, the Spirit, and the water, and the blood *(speaks of the Holy Spirit; the humanity of Christ, while never ceasing to be Deity, and the Atonement, i.e., "the Cross")*: and these Three agree in One. *(These Three agree that Christ is Very Man while at the same time being Very God, Who died on the Cross to Redeem fallen humanity.)*

9 If we receive the witness of men, the witness of God is greater *(if we receive witness of sinful men who can so easily deceive, we should gladly receive the witness of God, Who cannot possibly deceive)*: for this is the witness of God which He has testified of His Son *(centers on the Cross).*

10 He who believes on the Son of God has the witness in himself *(that Witness is the Holy Spirit [Rom. 8:16])*: He who believes not God has made Him a liar *(presents the problem of unbelief as the basic difficulty in the human race)*; because he believes not the record that God gave of His Son *(proclaims the fact that the proof is undeniable).*

11 And this is the record *(the*

"record" is the Word of God, which is the story of the Cross), that God has given to us Eternal Life (the Life of God flowing into and literally becoming a part of the Believer), and this life is in His Son. (Christ is the Source, while the Cross is the means.)

12 He who has the Son has Life (through the Cross); and he who has not the Son of God has not life. (This rules out all the fake luminaries of the world.)

PRAYER

13 These things have I written unto you who believe on the Name of the Son of God (all that John writes is to bring to the mind of His readers the fact that they have Life Eternal because they believe on the name of the Son of God); that you may know that you have Eternal Life (not a mere experimental knowledge, but an absolute knowledge), and that you may believe on the Name of the Son of God (keep believing).

14 And this is the confidence that we have in Him (proper believing gives us proper confidence, which is proper assurance), that, if we ask any thing according to His Will, He hears us (we should pray with the provision expressed or implied, "if it be Your Will"):

15 And if we know that He hears us, whatsoever we ask (pre-sents the fact that we are assured of this, even though we may not see an immediate answer to prayer), we know that we have the petitions that we desired of Him (providing it's His Will).

RESTORATION

16 If any man see his Brother sin a sin which is not unto death (refers to direction other than the Cross, done in ignorance), he shall ask, and He shall give him life for them who sin not unto death. (The Believer who understands God's prescribed order of victory, which is the Cross, should pray for those who are ignorantly going in a direction opposite of the Cross.) There is a sin unto death (speaks of unbelief; this group is not opposing the Cross because of ignorance, but rather because they simply do not believe in the Atoning work of Calvary): I do not say that he shall pray for it. (While it is pointless to pray that God would forgive such a person, it is proper to pray that the blindness of their unbelief will be removed.)

17 All unrighteousness is sin (refers to any deviation from the Word): and there is a sin not unto death. (This is a lack of trust in the Cross due to ignorance, not unbelief. While such sin will bring great disturbance upon the individual, it will not cause one to lose

their soul.)

VICTORY

18 We know that whosoever is born of God sins not *(does not practice sin)*; but he who is begotten of God keeps himself *(should have been translated, "but He [Christ] Who is Begotten of God keeps him")*, and that wicked one touches him not *(is the person who keeps his Faith in Christ and the Cross)*.

19 *And* we know that we are of God *(because of trusting in Christ and what He did for us at the Cross)*, and the whole world lies in wickedness *(refers to the world system)*.

ETERNAL LIFE

20 And we know that the Son of God is come *(presents that which is not simply a historic fact, but rather an abiding operation)*, and has given us an understanding, that we may know Him Who is true *(the real "One" as opposed to spurious gods)*, and we are in Him Who is true, *even* in his Son Jesus Christ *(by virtue of being "Baptized into His Death" [Rom. 6:3-5])*. This is the True God, and Eternal Life. *(Jesus Christ is truly God, and Faith in Him guarantees "Eternal Life.")*

21 Little children, keep yourselves from idols. Amen. *(This does not refer here to the heathen worship of idol gods, but of the heretical substitutes for the Christian conception of God, or anything that pulls us away from Christ and the Cross.)*

THE SECOND EPISTLE OF
JOHN

INTRODUCTION

THE Elder *(normally refers to "Pastor," however, this seems to be a title given to John, and for the obvious reasons; he was the last Apostle of the chosen Twelve to die)* unto the elect lady and her children *(it is believed that this woman was a devout Christian who lived near Ephesus; it also seems her home was the meeting-place of the local assembly)*, whom I love in the truth *(refers to the Love of God)*; and not I only, but also all they who have known the Truth *(the bond that had pulled this aged Apostle to this dear lady and her to him is "Truth")*;

2 For the truth's sake, which dwells *(love is a product of Truth)* in us, and shall be with us forever. *(Truth cannot change.)*

3 Grace be with you, Mercy, and Peace, from God the Father, and from the Lord Jesus Christ, the Son of the Father, in Truth and Love. *(The Cross makes all this possible.)*

LOVE

4 I rejoiced greatly that I found of your children walking in Truth *(her children were conducting themselves in the sphere of Truth as it is in Christ Jesus, doing so on a daily basis)*, as we have received a Commandment from the Father *(relates the fact that the Truth by which they were walking was not their own concoction, but rather was according to the Word of God)*.

5 And now I beseech you, lady, not as though I wrote a new Commandment unto you, but that which we had from the beginning, that we love one another *(the great hallmark of Christianity)*.

6 And this is love, that we walk after His Commandments *(presents the proper expression or evidence of love to God)*. This is the Commandment, That, as you have heard from the beginning, you should walk in it. *(This presents the Commandment by which the followers of the Lord are to be peculiarly characterized, and by which we are to be distinguished in the world.)*

DECEIVERS

7 For many deceivers are entered into the world *(a false teacher who leads others into heresies, i.e., "away from the Cross")*, who confess not that Jesus Christ is come

in the flesh *(a denial of the Incarnation)*. This is a deceiver and an Antichrist. *(All false doctrine begins with a misconception or misinterpretation of the "Person" of Christ.)*

8 Look to yourselves, that we lose not those things which we have wrought *(is the same as Paul's "examine yourselves" [II Cor. 13:5])*, but that we receive a full reward *(refers to the coming Judgment Seat of Christ, where and when every true Christian will give account)*.

9 Whosoever transgresses, and abides not in the Doctrine of Christ, has not God. *(The "Doctrine of Christ" is in brief "the Cross." If one leaves the Cross, one transgresses, and no longer has the Lord, which means that the soul will be lost if such direction is continued.)* He who abides in the Doctrine of Christ, he has Both the Father and the Son *(Gal. 5:1-6)*.

10 If there come any unto you, and bring not this Doctrine *(Jesus Christ and Him Crucified)*, receive him not into *your* house, neither bid him God speed *(to receive such shows acceptance)*:

11 For he who bids him God speed is partaker of his evil deeds. *(To help or finance false Apostles makes the person doing such a part of the false doctrine, which is serious indeed!)*

BENEDICTION

12 Having many things to write unto you, I would not *write* with paper and ink: but I trust to come unto you, and speak face to face, that our joy may be full. *(What he said in this short Epistle is evidently all the Holy Spirit wanted him to write at this time, at least to this particular lady.)*

13 The children of your elect sister greet you. Amen. *(John was speaking of the flesh and blood sister of the "elect lady" to whom he was writing. The simplicity of the great Apostle — the personal friend of the Risen Lord, the last of the great pillars of the Church — in transmitting this familiar Message makes a most instructive finish to what is throughout a beautiful picture.)*

THE THIRD EPISTLE OF
JOHN

INTRODUCTION

THE Elder *(John refers to himself by this title)* unto the well-beloved Gaius *(could well be the same one mentioned in Acts 19:29; 20:4; Rom. 16:23; I Cor. 1:14)*, whom I love in the truth. *(As the previous Letter was written to a wealthy woman telling her to shut her door against Preachers of a false gospel, so this Letter was written to a wealthy man to open his door to Preachers of the True Gospel.)*

2 Beloved, I wish above all things that you may prosper *(refers to financial prosperity, and should be the case for every Believer)* and be in health *(speaks of physical prosperity)*, even as your soul prospers *(speaks of Spiritual Prosperity; so we have here the whole Gospel for the whole man)*.

3 For I rejoiced greatly, when the Brethren came and testified of the truth that is in you *(Christian workers were always going out from Ephesus on preaching and teaching missions, and bringing reports from various Churches back to John)*, even as you walk in the Truth *(refers to the manner of one's behavior)*.

4 I have no greater joy than to hear that my children walk in Truth. *(Quite possibly Gaius was a convert of John.)*

FELLOWHELPERS

5 Beloved, you do faithfully whatsoever you do to the Brethren, and to strangers *(little did this man know that what he was doing would be heralded in the Word of God, and known all over the world for all time)*;

6 Which have borne witness of your charity *(love)* before the Church: whom if you bring forward on their journey after a Godly sort, you shall do well *(to "bring forward" as used here refers to standing good for the maintenance and expenses of visiting Preachers)*:

7 Because that for His Name's sake they went forth *(it was for the sake of the Name of Jesus that these Preachers went forth)*, taking nothing of the Gentiles. *(This refers to virgin territory regarding the Gospel, i.e., different places where they would plant Churches. In planting these Churches, they asked for no money from the new Gentile converts.)*

8 We therefore ought to receive such *(to be of help to such*

Preachers, both prayerfully and financially), that we might be fellowhelpers to the Truth. (Through John, the Holy Spirit here proclaims the fact that Believers should give of their financial resources to help take the Truth to others.)

DIOTREPHES

9 I wrote unto the Church (speaks of a local Church, but we aren't told its location): but Diotrephes, who loves to have the preeminence among them, receives us not. (If it is to be noticed, John calls the name of this individual and warns against him, even as he should have done. To be sure, anyone who was not of Truth would not receive John.)

10 Wherefore, if I come, I will remember his deeds which he does, prating against us with malicious words (there is no evidence whatsoever that this is said in a vindictive or vengeful spirit; and we must remember that the Holy Spirit is inspiring John to write these words; in other words, this man had to be exposed): and not content therewith, neither does he himself receive the Brethren, and forbids them who would, and casts them out of the Church. (The idea is that Diotrephes would cast those who would side with John out of the Church, or else seek to do so. Consequently, silence on John's part would have been wrong, just as it is wrong now for Preachers to be silent regarding false Apostles and false doctrine.)

TESTIMONY

11 Beloved, follow not that which is evil, but that which is good. (In effect, John is referring to Diotrephes as "evil." At the same time, he is boldly stating that what he [John] preaches is "good" and, therefore, "of God.") He who does good is of God: but he who does evil has not seen God. (The Holy Spirit, through John, very clearly draws the line. One cannot have it both ways.)

12 Demetrius has good report of all men (this man was probably the bearer of this Letter to Gaius; he was a stranger to the members of the local Church of which Gaius was a member, and needed a word of commendation from the Apostle), and of the Truth itself: yes, and we also bear record; and you know that our record is true. (There could be no higher recommendation, especially considering that the Holy Spirit sanctioned these words.)

BENEDICTION

13 I had many things to write, but I will not with ink and pen write unto you (John ends this Letter in much the same way he

ended his Second Epistle):

14 But I trust I shall shortly see you, and we shall speak face to face. *(Evidently, the Apostle planned to visit this particular Church shortly.)*

Peace *be* to you. *Our* friends salute you. Greet the friends by name. *(This was a small Church, but yet very important, even as the Holy Spirit here proclaims.)*

THE EPISTLE GENERAL OF
JUDE

INTRODUCTION

JUDE, the servant of Jesus Christ, and Brother of James (*Jude was the half-brother of the Lord Jesus Christ as well*), to them who are Sanctified by God the Father (*should have been translated, "to them who are loved by God the Father"*), and preserved in Jesus Christ (*in effect says, "God the Father is keeping the Saints guarded by Jesus Christ"*), and Called (*the idea, as presented here by the Holy Spirit through Jude, is that God does not want to lose the people He has Called to be His Own through false doctrine*).

2 Mercy unto you, and Peace, and Love, be multiplied (*all of this is made possible by the Cross, and the Cross alone*).

FALSE TEACHERS

3 Beloved, when I gave all diligence (*a compulsion generated by the Holy Spirit*) to write unto you of the common Salvation (*he had at first thought to write an Epistle similar to Romans, but the Holy Spirit, although the Author of the compulsion, did not lead in this direction*), it was needful for me to write unto you (*the implication is that whatever was to be written had to be written at once, and could not be prepared for at leisure*), and exhort *you* that you should earnestly contend for the Faith (*refers to the fact that the Saints must defend the Doctrines of Christianity with intense effort*) which was once delivered unto the Saints (*refers to the fact that no other Faith will be given; the idea is that God gave the Christian Doctrines to the Saints as a deposit of Truth to be guarded*).

4 For there are certain men crept in unawares (*false teachers had crept into the Church*), who were before of old ordained to this condemnation, ungodly men (*they came in by stealth and dishonesty; however, their methods were by no means new; they would assume an outward expression of light*), turning the Grace of our God into lasciviousness (*refers to the fact that "Grace" had been turned to license*), and denying the only Lord God, and our Lord Jesus Christ (*if we deny the Cross, which is God's Plan of Redemption, we are at the same time denying Both the Father and the Son*).

5 I will therefore put you in remembrance (*suggests something*

of anxiety and upbraiding, which may be compared to the tone of Paul in writing Galatians), though you once knew this, how that the Lord, having saved the people out of the Land of Egypt, afterward destroyed them who believed not *(unbelief destroyed the Israelites in the wilderness, and it will do the same presently).*

6 And the Angels which kept not their first estate, but left their own habitation *(these particular Angels did not maintain their original position in which they were created, but transgressed those limits to invade territory foreign to them, namely the human race; they left Heaven and came to Earth, seeking to cohabit with women, which they did [Gen. 6:4]),* He *(the Lord)* has reserved in everlasting chains under darkness unto the Judgment of the Great Day *(these Angels are now imprisoned [II Pet. 2:4], and will be judged at the Great White Throne Judgment, then placed in the "Lake of Fire" where they will remain forever and forever [Rev. 20:10]).*

7 Even as Sodom and Gomorrha, and the cities about them in like manner *(the Greek Text introduces a comparison showing a likeness between the Angels of Verse 6 and the cities of Sodom and Gomorrah; but the likeness between them lies deeper than the fact that both were guilty of committing sin;* it extends to the fact that both were guilty of the same identical sin), giving themselves over to fornication, and going after strange flesh *(the Angels cohabited with women; the sin of Sodom and Gomorrah, and the cities around them, was homosexuality [Rom. 1:27]),* are set forth for an example, suffering the vengeance of eternal fire *(those who engage in the sin of homosexuality and refuse to repent will suffer the vengeance of the Lake of Fire).*

8 Likewise also these *filthy dreamers defile the flesh (Jude likens these false teachers to "filthy dreamers," and refers to their doctrines as being the fruits of mere imagination and fancies),* despise dominion *(they refuse to live by the Word of God, but rather fabricate their own religion),* and speak evil of dignities *(refers to reviling the Word of God, and more particularly Christ and the Cross).*

9 Yet Michael the Archangel *(no other Angel bears the title of Archangel, as recorded; there are others who are Chief Angels, and Michael is only one of them [Dan. 10:13]),* when contending with the Devil he disputed about the body of Moses *(after the death of Moses, Satan demanded the body of the Lawgiver which was denied him by Michael, the Archangel),* did not bring against him *(against Satan)* a railing accusation, but said, The

Lord rebuke you (a "railing accusation" would have placed Michael on the same level with the Devil to which the great Archangel would not stoop, and rightly so!).

10 But these (false teachers) speak evil of those things which they know not (the adage here applies, "fools rush in where Angels fear to tread"): but what they know naturally, as brute beasts (Jude refers to these false teachers as being in the class of unreasoning animals), in those things they corrupt themselves (could have been translated, "by these things are being brought to ruin").

11 Woe unto them! (Concerning apostasy and apostates, the Holy Spirit says to them, "Woe!") for they have gone in the way of Cain (the type of a religious man who believes in God and "religion," but after his own will, and who rejects Redemption by blood), and ran greedily after the error of Balaam for reward (the error of Balaam was that he was blind to the higher morality of the Cross, through which God maintains and enforces the authority and awful sanctions of His Law, so that He can be Just and the Justifier of the believing sinner; he loved the wages of unrighteousness in coveting the gifts of Balak [Num. 22:7, 17, 37; 24:11; II Pet. 2:15]), and perished in the gainsaying of Core (the gainsaying of this man was his rebellion against Aaron as God's appointed Priest; this was, in principle, a denial of the High Priesthood of Christ [Num., Chpt. 16]).

12 These are spots (rocks) in your feasts of charity, when they feast with you (these false teachers participated in the Lord's Supper, thereby claiming to be Godly), feeding themselves without fear (furthering their own schemes and lusts instead of tending the flock of God): clouds they are without water (such disappoints the ground that needs rain; likewise, these false teachers look good outwardly, but inwardly there is no substance), carried about of winds (they seek Believers with itching ears; they have no true course of the Word of God); trees whose fruit withers, without fruit (there is no proper fruit, simply because good fruit cannot come from a bad tree), twice dead (they were dead in trespasses and sins before being saved, and now they have gone back on God and are dead again, i.e., "twice dead"), plucked up by the roots (they are not like the true tree planted by the waters);

13 Raging waves of the sea (refers to the destruction caused by false doctrine), foaming out their own shame (false doctrine is like the foam or scum at the sea shore); wandering stars (an unpredictable star which provides no guidance for navigation), to whom is reserved the blackness of darkness

forever *(refers to their eternal doom [II Pet. 2:4])*.

14 And Enoch also, the seventh from Adam *(the Old Testament person of that name, the man who "walked with God" [Gen. 5:18-24])*, Prophesied of these *(the translation should read, "Prophesied with respect to these false teachers of these last days")*, saying, Behold, the Lord comes with ten thousands of His Saints *(is actually, "His Holy ten thousands," which literally means "an unlimited number"; this quotation is taken from the Book of Enoch, which was lost for many centuries with the exception of a few fragments, but was found in its entirety in a copy of the Ethiopia Bible in 1773)*,

15 To execute Judgment upon all *(refers to Christ Judging the nations of the world, which will commence at the beginning of the Millennial Reign)*, and to convince all who are ungodly among them of all their ungodly deeds which they have ungodly committed *(the word "ungodly" is used four times in this Verse, telling us that the ungodliness is total; as well, "all" is used four times, which means that none will escape this Judgment)*, and of all their hard *speeches* which ungodly sinners have spoken against Him *(every ungodly statement against Christ will be addressed at that time)*.

16 These are murmurers, complainers, walking after their own lusts *(Jude has in mind men who cannot get enough to satisfy their lusts, and thus complain)*; and their mouth speaks great swelling *words*, having men's persons in admiration because of advantage *(refers to showing "respect of person"; they use flattery for the sake of profit)*.

EXHORTATIONS

17 But, beloved, remember ye the words which were spoken before of the Apostles of our Lord Jesus Christ *(actually refers to that given by Peter and others)*;

18 How that they told you there should be mockers in the last time *(refers to the last days, in fact the very time in which we now live)*, who should walk after their own ungodly lusts *(refers to charting a course which is not of God, but rather after the flesh; they have forsaken the Cross!)*.

19 These be they who separate themselves *(should be translated, "these be they who separate"; they have forsaken the Cross, purposely choosing another way)*, sensual *(refers to that which is not of the Spirit, but rather of the flesh)*, having not the Spirit *(refers to those who operate outside the Cross of Christ)*.

20 But you, Beloved *(contrasts the Saints with the false teachers)*, building up yourselves *(to build toward the finish of the structure*

for which the foundation has already been laid) on your most Holy Faith *(Jesus Christ and Him Crucified)*, praying in the Holy Spirit *(our praying must be exercised in the sphere of the Holy Spirit, motivated and empowered by Him)*,

21 Keep yourselves in the Love of God *(we are to see to it that we stay within the circle of His love, which can only be done by Faith constantly making the Cross its object)*, looking for the Mercy of our Lord Jesus Christ unto Eternal Life *(looking for the Rapture of the Church, with all of this made possible by what Jesus did on the Cross)*.

22 And of some have compassion, making a difference *(the false teachers should be addressed on a case by case situation, referring to the fact that some have to be handled differently than others; "some with compassion")*:

23 And others save with fear *(this particular group needs to be dealt with directly and vigorously)*, pulling them out of the fire *(the fire of destruction)*; hating even the garment spotted by the flesh *(presents works of the flesh, which always characterize those who follow a direction other than the Cross)*.

BENEDICTION

24 Now unto Him Who is able to keep you from falling *(as we've repeatedly stated, Christ is the Source of all things, but the Cross is the means)*, and to present *you* faultless before the Presence of His Glory with exceeding joy *(the Holy Spirit will, at the appointed time, present us to the Father, and will do so "with exceeding joy"; this refers to the Believer standing blameless before the Judgment Seat, all because of Christ and what He did at the Cross [Col. 1:22; I Thess. 3:13])*,

25 To the only wise God our Saviour *(speaks of the Cross)*, be Glory and Majesty, Dominion and Power, both now and ever. Amen *(every Believer will share in all of this, and do so forever; once again, all because of the Cross)*.

THE
REVELATION TO JOHN

CHAPTER 1

INTRODUCTION

THE Revelation of Jesus Christ, which God gave unto Him *(the Revelation given here is of Jesus Christ, not John, as many think; John was only the instrument used to write the account)*, to show unto His servants things which must shortly come to pass *(refers to the beginning of the events, which continue on unto this hour, and in fact will continue forever; it is the Church Age and beyond)*; and He sent and signified *it* by His Angel unto His servant John *(even though the Revelation came to Christ, it was delivered to John by "His Angel")*:

2 Who bear record of the Word of God *(regarded himself merely as a witness of what he had seen, and claimed only to make a fair and faithful record of it)*, and of the Testimony of Jesus Christ *(John was merely a witness of the Testimony that Christ had borne)*, and of all things that he saw *(refers to the visions and symbols given to John)*.

3 Blessed *is* he who reads, and they who hear the words of this Prophecy, and keep those things which are written therein *(all who obey these admonitions are promised a Blessing)*: for the time *is* at hand *(refers to the beginning of the fulfillment of these things which begins with the Church, as recorded in Revelation, Chapters 2 and 3, and continues forever)*.

SALUTATION

4 John to the seven Churches which are in Asia *(these particular Churches were selected by the Holy Spirit to portray the entirety of the Church Age)*: Grace be unto you, and Peace, from Him which is, and which was, and which is to come *(refers to Sanctifying Grace and Sanctifying Peace, all made possible by the Cross)*; and from the seven Spirits which are before His Throne *(is given to us in this manner to emphasize the sevenfold aspect of the operations of the Holy Spirit [Isa. 11:2])*;

5 And from Jesus Christ, *Who* is the faithful Witness *(earthly life of perfect obedience)*, and the first begotten of the dead *(refers to His Resurrection, which is the Firstfruits [Rom. 8:23])*, and the prince of the kings of the earth. *(This refers*

to His rulership of the world, which is a key theme of the Book of Revelation.) Unto Him Who loved us, and washed us from our sins in His Own Blood *(the Cross proves the fact of His Love in no uncertain terms)*,

6 And has made us kings and priests unto God and His Father *(made possible by what Christ did at the Cross, and only by what Christ did at the Cross)*; to Him be Glory and Dominion forever and ever. Amen. *(Christ is the Redeemer, so He deserves the "Glory and Dominion," which will be His forever and ever.)*

THE THEME

7 Behold, He comes with clouds *(the Second Coming of Christ is the chief theme of this Book; the word "clouds" represents great numbers of Saints)*; and every eye shall see Him *(refers to all who will be in the immediate vicinity of Jerusalem, and possibly even billions who may very well see Him by Television)*, and they also which pierced Him *(the Jews, and they will then know beyond the shadow of a doubt that Jesus is Messiah and Lord)*: and all kindreds of the earth shall wail because of Him. Even so, Amen. *(The "wailing" will take place because of the Judgment Christ will bring upon the world for its sin and shame.)*

8 I am Alpha and Omega, the beginning and the ending *(the First, the Last, the only God)*, saith the Lord, which is, and which was, and which is to come, the Almighty. *(The word "Almighty" guarantees He will be able to accomplish all that He says.)*

THE VISION

9 I John, who also am your Brother, and companion in tribulation *(John was a fellow-partaker in the tribulation which was then coming to all the Churches)*, and in the Kingdom and Patience of Jesus Christ *(Christ will ultimately establish His Kingdom on this Earth, but we must use patience in waiting for it)*, was in the Isle that is called Patmos *(an island about 37 miles west-southwest of Miletus in the Aegean Sea)*, for the Word of God, and for the Testimony of Jesus Christ. *(He was not in prison for crimes committed, for he had committed none, but because of his stand for our Lord.)*

10 I was in the Spirit *(he entered into a new kind of experience relative to the Spirit's control over him)* on the Lord's Day *(Sunday)*, and heard behind me a great Voice, as of a trumpet *(the Voice John heard is heard unto this hour all over the world, and in fact will ever be heard; it is the Voice of our Lord!)*,

11 Saying, I am Alpha and Omega, the First and the Last *(Christ is all in all)*: and, What you see, write in a Book *(constitutes what we now have and refer to as the "Book of Revelation")*, and send *it* unto the Seven Churches which are in Asia; unto Ephesus, and unto Smyrna, and unto Pergamos, and unto Thyatira, and unto Sardis, and unto Philadelphia, and unto Laodicea. *(This phrase presents these Churches that were all selected Personally by Christ.)*

12 And I turned to see the Voice that spoke with me. And being turned, I saw Seven Golden Candlesticks *(presents the symbolism for the seven Churches)*;

13 And in the midst of the Seven Candlesticks *One* like unto the Son of Man *(Jesus is Head of the Church, the Centerpiece of its activity)*, clothed with a garment down to the foot *(indicates His position as King-Priest)*, and girt about the paps with a Golden Girdle *(presents kingly apparel; Christ is the King-Priest)*.

14 His Head and *His* Hairs *were* white like wool, as white as snow *(Majesty and Authority)*; and His Eyes *were* as a flame of fire *(portrays penetrating scrutiny and fierce Judgment)*;

15 And His Feet like unto fine brass, as if they burned in a furnace *("brass" signifies His humanity, but superhuman)*; and His Voice as the sound of many waters *(the Voice of Power)*.

16 And He had in His Right Hand Seven Stars *(represents the Pastors of these seven Churches)*: and out of His Mouth went a sharp twoedged Sword *(represents the Word of God)*: and His Countenance *was* as the sun shines in His Strength *(represents His Glory)*.

17 And when I saw Him, I fell at His feet as dead *(the idea is that John thought he was going to die)*. And He laid His right hand upon me, saying unto me, Fear not *(in effect, Christ is telling John he will not die)*; I am the First and the Last *(He Alone is God, the Absolute Lord of history and the Creator)*:

18 *I am* He Who lives *(will never die again and has life in Himself; the Fountain and Source of Life to others; the One Who has immortality [Jn. 1:4; 14:6; 1 Tim. 6:16])*, and was dead *(represents the Living One entering into death, into our death, in His human nature so that as the great High Priest He might finish the Sacrifice for sins, which He did)*; and, behold, I am alive for evermore, Amen *(He will never die again, and death is totally defeated)*; and have the keys of hell and of death. *(He Alone determines who will enter death and hell, and who will not.)*

19 Write the things which you have seen *(this Verse is the key to the understanding of the Book of*

Revelation; it is broken up into three parts: the first concerns the Vision of Christ in the midst of the Candlesticks, Chapter 1), and the things which are *(the second concerns the Churches, Chapters 2-3)*, and the things which shall be hereafter *(the third concerns events after the Rapture of the Church, includes the Great Tribulation and Eternity ever-after, Chapters 4-22)*;

20 The mystery of the Seven Stars which you saw in My Right Hand *(portrays the fact that these Pastors belonged to Christ)*, and the Seven Golden Candlesticks. The Seven Stars are the Angels *(Pastors)* of the Seven Churches: and the Seven Candlesticks which you saw are the Seven Churches. *(This represents the entirety of the Church Age, even as we shall see.)*

CHAPTER 2

EPHESUS

U NTO the Angel *(pastor)* of the Church of Ephesus write *(the Ephesian Church represents the Apostolic time period, which closed out around A.D. 100)*; These things says He who holds the Seven Stars in His Right Hand *(all Pastors belong to the Lord, that is if they truly are of the Lord)*, Who walks in the midst of the Seven Golden Candlesticks *(Christ is the Head of the Church [Col. 1:18])*;

2 I know your works *(repeated to all Seven Churches; it implies Divine knowledge)*, and your labour, and your patience, and how you cannot bear them which are evil *(which have departed from true Doctrine)*: and you have tried them which say they are Apostles, and are not, and have found them liars *(presents the Doctrinal soundness of the Ephesian Believers)*:

3 And have borne *(they set a course, and did not deviate from that course)*, and have patience *(continued to believe when things were not going well)*, and for My Name's sake have laboured, and have not fainted. *(They were diligent in their efforts, and would not quit.)*

4 Nevertheless I have some-what against you *(something is wrong, despite their zeal)*, because you have left your first love *(not "lost" your first love, but rather "left" your first love; it refers to a departure from the Cross, and is so serious that it will lead the Church to ruin unless repentance is forth-coming)*.

5 Remember therefore from where you are fallen *(this means they fell from Grace, which means they had stopped depending on Christ and the Cross [Gal. 5:4])*, and re-pent, and do the first works *(go back to the Cross)*; or else I will come unto you quickly, and will remove your candlestick out of

his place, except you repent. *(Christ is the Source of the Light, but the Cross is the means. They are to come back to the Cross, or else the Light will be removed.)*

6 But this you have, that you hate the deeds of the Nicolaitanes, which I also hate. *(The word "Nicolaitanes" means "laity-conquerors." They are Preachers who exploit the people instead of spiritually developing them, which all false doctrine does. The Lord hates this, and so should we!)*

7 He who has an ear, let him hear what the Spirit says unto the Churches *(the Holy Spirit is saying that the Church must come back to the Cross)*; To him who overcomes will I give to eat of the tree of life, which is in the midst of the Paradise of God. *(The Christian can be an overcomer only by placing his Faith exclusively in Christ and the Cross, which gives the Holy Spirit latitude to work.)*

SMYRNA

8 And unto the Angel of the Church in Smyrna write *(refers to the Martyr Church, with the time span being approximately from A.D. 100 to about A.D. 300)*; These things says the First and the Last *(Christ is the Beginning of things referring to Creator, and the End of all things referring to His total and complete control)*, which was dead, and is alive *(refers to the Cross and the Resurrection)*;

9 I know your works, and tribulation, and poverty, (but you are rich) *(Smyrna was poverty stricken outwardly, but the Lord proclaimed them spiritually rich; the Church at Laodicea claimed to be rich, but the Lord said they were poor)* and *I know* the blasphemy of them which say they are Jews, and are not *(from this Verse we learn that God doesn't consider Jews who reject Christ as truly Jewish)*, but *are* the Synagogue of Satan. *(The worship of Christ-rejecting Jews is concluded by the Lord to be Satanic.)*

10 Fear none of those things which you shall suffer: behold, the Devil shall cast *some* of you into prison, that you may be tried; and you shall have tribulation ten days *(is believed to represent the ten major persecutions Rome hurled at the Church of that day, spanning about 200 years)*: be thou faithful unto death, and I will give you a Crown of life *(many paid with their lives)*.

11 He who has an ear, let him hear what the Spirit says unto the Churches *(the Spirit is saying that, at times, there may be suffering)*; He who overcomes shall not be hurt of the second death *(refers to the Lake of Fire [Rev. 21:8])*.

PERGAMOS

12 And to the Angel *(Pastor)* of the Church in Pergamos write *(referred to as the State Church, which laid the groundwork for the Catholic system; its time span was approximately A.D. 300 to A.D. 500)*; These things said He which has the sharp sword with two edges *(a symbol for the Word of God)*;

13 I know your works, and where you dwell *(dwell spiritually)*, even where Satan's seat *is (Satan had become part of this Church)*: and you hold fast My Name, and have not denied My Faith *(despite the terrible condition of this Church, some were holding fast to Christ and were continuing to look to the Cross)*, even in those days wherein Antipas *was* My faithful martyr, who was slain among you, where Satan dwells. *(This persecution came from within the Church.)*

14 But I have a few things against you, because you have there them who hold the doctrine of Balaam, who taught Balac to cast a stumblingblock before the Children of Israel, to eat things Sacrificed unto idols, and to commit fornication. *(This Church was committing spiritual adultery, meaning they had shifted their Faith from the Cross to other things, with money being the underlying cause, which refers to the State Church.)*

15 So have you also them who hold the doctrine of the Nicolaitanes, which thing I hate. *(At Ephesus, it was the "deeds of the Nicolaitanes," and now it's the "doctrine." This refers to unscriptural Church Government, which grossly exploited the people.)*

16 Repent *(come back to the Cross)*; or else I will come unto you quickly, and will fight against them with the sword of My mouth. *(This will bring to bear the Word of God, the part that speaks of Judgment.)*

17 He who has an ear, let him hear what the Spirit says unto the Churches *(the Spirit is saying that all Church Government must, without fail, be Scriptural)*; To him who overcomes will I give to eat of the hidden Manna, and will give him a white stone, and in the stone a new name written, which no man knows saving he who receives *it. (This refers to the fact that Believers shall receive a new name, in harmony with the perfect renewal of our being.)*

THYATIRA

18 And unto the Angel of the Church in Thyatira write *(called the "Papal Church," signifying the beginning of Catholicism; it began about A.D. 500 and continues unto this hour)*; These things saith the Son of God, Who has

His eyes like unto a flame of fire, and His feet *are* like fine brass *(presents Christ in the role of Judgment, as He must be concerning the Church going into idol worship)*;

19 I know your works, and charity, and service, and faith, and your patience *(some in this Church, as wrong as it was, continue to love the Lord; the Lord knew who they were)*, and your works; and the last *to be* more than the first. *("Works" are mentioned twice, with the last being in a negative sense, meaning they were depending on this instead of Christ and the Cross.)*

20 Notwithstanding I have a few things against you, because you suffer that woman Jezebel, which calls herself a Prophetess, to teach and to seduce My servants to commit fornication, and to eat things Sacrificed unto idols. *(The Lord is speaking here of spiritual fornication and adultery, which means they had forsaken Christ and the Cross for other things [Rom. 7:1-4].)*

21 And I gave her space to repent of her fornication; and she repented not. *(The Church did not heed the Message, and in fact continues in their "Salvation by works" unto this day, which of course is false.)*

22 Behold, I will cast her into a bed, and them who commit adultery with her into great tribulation, except they repent of their deeds. *(The "bed" refers to false teachers who taught Salvation by works, which was spiritual adultery. Again, there was a warning to repent.)*

23 And I will kill her children with death *(speaks of spiritual death)*; and all the Churches shall know that I am He which searches the reins and hearts *(a continuous, ongoing searching)*: and I will give unto every one of you according to your works. *(One can look at the works of an individual and ascertain exactly where their Faith is. True works proclaim the Fruit of the Spirit.)*

24 But unto you I say, and unto the rest in Thyatira, as many as have not this doctrine *(have not succumbed to the teaching of Jezebel)*, and which have not known the depths of Satan, as they speak *(the teaching of "Jezebel" was "spiritual adultery," which was a departure from the Cross and is labeled here as "the depths of Satan")*; I will put upon you none other burden *(meaning their total burden was the opposing of "Jezebel teaching," which was a tremendous responsibility within itself)*.

25 But that which you have *already* hold fast *(hold to the Cross, and don't allow your Faith to be moved to other things)* till I come *(the Rapture of the Church)*.

26 And he who overcomes, and keeps My works unto the end *(it*

is "His Works," and not "our works"; pure and simple, it is what Jesus did at the Cross on our behalf), to him will I give power over the nations (speaks of the coming Kingdom Age):

27 And he shall rule them with a rod of iron; as the vessels of a potter shall they be broken to shivers (refers to the fact that the Saints of God in the coming Kingdom Age under Christ will rule the nations, not allowing evil to prevail or even to take root): even as I received of My Father. (In the day of His Coming, we shall share in His Power and Glory of Victory.)

28 And I will give him the Morning Star. (The "Morning Star" is the bright planet [Venus], which is most beautiful and leads on the morning — the harbinger of the day. This says the coming Kingdom Age will be glorious beyond compare.)

29 He who has an ear, let him hear what the Spirit says unto the Churches. (The Spirit is saying that to leave Christ and the Cross is to commit spiritual adultery, which will result in spiritual death.)

CHAPTER 3

SARDIS

AND unto the Angel (Pastor) of the Church in Sardis write (the Sardis Church is referred to as the "Reformation Church," which began about A.D. 1500, and continues more or less unto this hour); These things saith He Who has the Seven Spirits of God (represents the Holy Spirit in all His fullness and capacity), and the Seven stars (refers to the Pastors of these Seven Churches); I know your works, that you have a name that you live, and are dead. (Our Lord begins with words of censure, i.e., "dead spiritually.")

2 Be watchful (this Church is exhorted to look into its real condition), and strengthen the things which remain, that are ready to die (they need to come back to the Cross, or they will lose their way completely): for I have not found your works perfect before God. (Their works were based on a dead Faith, which always produces bad works.)

3 Remember therefore how you have received and heard, and hold fast, and repent (go back to the Cross). If therefore you shall not watch, I will come on you as a thief, and you shall not know what hour I will come upon you. (Judgment will come, but Sardis will not see or hear due to spiritual deafness and spiritual blindness.)

4 You have a few names even in Sardis which have not defiled their garments (the Lord always has a few); and they shall walk with Me in white: for they are worthy. (We are made worthy only

by our Faith in Christ and the Cross.)

5 He who overcomes, the same shall be clothed in white raiment *(the Righteousness of Christ, gained only by Faith in Christ and the Cross)*; and I will not blot out his name out of the Book of Life *(proving that names can be blotted out)*, but I will confess his name before My Father, and before His Angels. *(The key to this great "confession" is Faith in Christ and His great Sacrifice.)*

6 He who has an ear, let him hear what the Spirit says unto the Churches. *(The Spirit is saying that Righteousness cannot be obtained without Faith in a spotless Sacrifice.)*

PHILADELPHIA

7 And to the Angel *(Pastor)* of the Church in Philadelphia write *(is referred to as the Missionary Church, and had its beginning in about the year 1800, and continues unto this hour)*; These things says He Who is Holy, He Who is true, He Who has the key of David, He Who opens, and no man shuts; and shuts, and no man opens *(refers to the fact that Christ has total authority)*;

8 I know your works: behold, I have set before you an open door, and no man can shut it *(this "open door" refers to the way being made for the Gospel to be sent to the entirety of the world)*: for you have a little strength, and have kept my Word, and have not denied My Name. *("Little strength" is not an indication of spiritual infirmity, but of few in number. However, these few [speaking of those who truly know the Lord] have touched the world with the Gospel of Jesus Christ.)*

9 Behold, I will make them of the Synagogue of Satan, which say they are Jews, and are not, but do lie *(proclaims the fact that God doesn't recognize the spiritual claims of national Israel)*; behold, I will make them to come and worship before your feet, and to know that I have loved you. *(This refers to the coming Kingdom Age, when Christ will rule Personally over the entirety of the Earth, with Israel restored. Israel will then bow at the feet of Christ, Whom the Gentiles accepted.)*

10 Because you have kept the Word of My patience, I also will keep you from the hour of temptation, which shall come upon all the world, to try them who dwell upon the earth. *(The Church will be Raptured out before the Great Tribulation.)*

11 Behold, I come quickly *(again refers to the Rapture)*: hold that fast which you have, that no man take your crown. *(The Devil will use religious men to try to move us away from our Faith in Christ and*

the Cross.)

12 Him who overcomes will I make a pillar in the Temple of my God *(the "overcomer" is the one who trusts explicitly in Christ and what He did for us at the Cross)*, and he shall go no more out *(refers to a constant position in the presence of God)*: and I will write upon him the Name of My God, and the Name of the city of My God, *which is* New Jerusalem, which comes down out of Heaven from My God: and *I will write upon him* My new Name. *(At the Cross, Christ identified with our sin by suffering its penalty. Now he identifies with our most excellent Blessing, as He is the Source of all.)*

13 He who has an ear, let him hear what the Spirit says unto the Churches. *(The Spirit is saying we must be ready for the Rapture, which can only be done by Faith constantly exhibited in Christ and His Finished Work.)*

LAODICEA

14 And unto the Angel *(Pastor)* of the Church of the Laodiceans write *(this is the "Apostate Church"; we do not know when it began, but we do know it has begun; it is the last Church addressed by Christ, so that means the Rapture will take place very shortly)*; These things says the Amen, the faithful and true witness *(by contrast to His Church, which is not faithful and true)*, the beginning of the Creation of God *(Jesus is the Creator of all things)*;

15 I know your works, that you are neither cold nor hot *(characterizes that which is prevalent at this present time)*: I would you were cold or hot *(half measures won't do)*.

16 So then because you are lukewarm, and neither cold nor hot *(if a person is lukewarm towards something, it means he hasn't rejected it, but at the same time he has by no means accepted it; in the Mind of God, a tepid response is equal to a negative response)*, I will spue you out of My mouth. *(There is no prospect of Repentance here on the part of this Church, or Restoration. In fact, there is Divine rejection.)*

17 Because you say, I am rich, and increased with goods, and have need of nothing *(they equated the increase in material goods with spiritual Blessings, which they were not)*; and knowest not that you are wretched, and miserable, and poor, and blind, and naked *(the tragedy lay in the fact that while this Church gloated over material wealth, she was unconscious of her spiritual poverty; again indicative of the modern Church!)*:

18 I counsel you to buy of Me gold tried in the fire, that you may be rich *(what they needed to "buy"*

could not be purchased with money, but only with the precious Blood of Christ, which price has already been paid; but the modern Church is not interested!); and white raiment, that you may be clothed, and that the shame of your nakedness do not appear *(refers to Righteousness which is exclusively of Christ, and is gained only by Faith in Christ and the Cross; this tells us that the Laodicean Church is extremely self-righteous; not having the Righteousness of Christ, they are "naked" to the Judgment of God)*; and anoint your eyes with eyesalve, that you may see. *(The modern Church is also spiritually blind.)*

19 As many as I love, I rebuke and chasten *(implies a remnant)*: be zealous therefore, and repent. *(The modern Church desperately needs to repent for its rebellion against God's Divine Order [Christ and the Cross] and following cunningly devised fables [II Pet. 1:16].)*

20 Behold, I stand at the door, and knock *(presents Christ outside the Church)*: if any man hear My voice *(so much religious racket is going on that it is difficult to "hear His Voice")*, and open the door *(Christ is the true Door, which means the Church has erected another door)*, I will come in to him, and will sup with him, and he with Me. *(Having been rejected by the Church, our Lord now appeals to* individuals, and He is still doing so presently.)*

21 To him who overcomes will I grant to sit with Me in My Throne *(the overcomer will gain the prize of the Throne, which can only be done by one ever making the Cross the object of his Faith)*, even as I also overcame, and am set down with My Father in His Throne. *(This presents Christ as our Substitute, going before us, and doing for us what we could not do for ourselves.)*

22 He who has an ear, let him hear what the Spirit says unto the Churches. *(In plain language, the Holy Spirit is saying, "come back to Christ and the Cross!")*

CHAPTER 4

THE THRONE

AFTER this I looked *(represents the time after the Churches, or in other words after the Rapture)*, and, behold, a door was opened in Heaven *(gives John the ability to see what is taking place there)*: and the first voice which I heard was as it were of a trumpet talking with me *(is actually the Voice of Jesus, harking back to Rev. 1:10)*; which said, Come up hither, and I will show you things which must be hereafter *(after the Rapture of the Church)*.

2 And immediately I was in

the Spirit *(John saw these things in a Vision)*: and, behold, a Throne was set in Heaven, and *One* sat on the Throne *(God the Father)*.

3 And He Who sat was to look upon like a jasper and a sardine stone: and *there was* a rainbow round about the Throne, in sight like unto an emerald. *(This proclaims the Glory of God, which is beyond comprehension.)*

4 And round about the Throne *were* four and twenty seats *(Thrones)*: and upon the seats I saw four and twenty Elders sitting *(these men represent the entirety of the Work of God as it pertains to Believers, with no doubt a mixture of Prophets and Apostles)*, clothed in white raiment *(represents the Righteousness of Christ)*; and they had on their heads crowns of gold *(signifying authority)*.

5 And out of the Throne proceeded lightnings and thunderings and voices *(whatever all of this is, it is constant)*: and *there were* seven lamps of fire burning before the Throne, which are the Seven Spirits of God. *(This represents the totality and universality of the Holy Spirit. The number "Seven" is God's number, denoting perfection.)*

LIVING CREATURES

6 And before the Throne *there was* a sea of glass like unto crystal *(presents that which is perfectly transparent)*: and in the midst of the Throne, and round about the Throne, *were* four Beasts *(living creatures)* full of eyes before and behind. *(This is introducing creatures we have no knowledge of and which are beyond comprehension, as so much in Heaven actually is.)*

7 And the first Beast *(living creature)* was like a lion, and the second Beast like a calf, and the third Beast had a face as a man, and the fourth Beast *was* like a flying eagle. *(These strange creatures are before the Throne constantly.)*

8 And the four Beasts *(living creatures)* had each of them six wings about *him;* and *they were* full of eyes within *(signifying the revealing of their innermost nature and being)*: and they rest not day and night *(proclaiming that these beings are "spirit" and not "flesh")*, saying, Holy, Holy, Holy, Lord God Almighty, which was, and is, and is to come. *(Using the threefold repetition calls attention to the infinite Holiness of God.)*

HEAVENLY WORSHIP

9 And when those Beasts *(living creatures)* give glory and honour and thanks to Him Who sat on the Throne, Who lives forever and ever *(if these creatures can constantly give God "Glory, and*

Honor, and Thanks," how can we who have known the glorious Redemption of our Lord do any less!),

10 The four and twenty Elders fall down before Him Who sat on the Throne, and worship Him Who lives forever and ever (the action of the 24 Elders, who represent the Church of the Living God in Heaven, proclaims what the Church on Earth ought to be), and cast their crowns before the Throne, saying (presents the acknowledgement of their royal estate; it all comes from God!),

11 You are worthy, O Lord, to receive Glory and Honour and Power (unless the Lord's worth is fully sensed by the worshiper, one's own unworthiness will never be realized): for You have created all things, and for Your pleasure they are and were created. (In effect, the praises of these 24 Elders tell us that the Creation, and that means every part of the Creation, is going to be completely restored, and all because of what Christ did at the Cross!)

CHAPTER 5

THE SEALED BOOK

AND I saw in the Right Hand (signifies power) of Him Who sat on the Throne a Book written within and on the backside, sealed with Seven Seals. (The "Seven Seals" signify that the "time of Jacob's trouble" is about to begin, which will rapidly bring to a conclusion that which must be done.)

2 And I saw a strong Angel proclaiming with a loud voice (this strong Angel is probably Gabriel, as evidenced by Gabriel's appearance to Daniel), Who is worthy to open the Book, and to loose the Seals thereof? (This implies moral fitness [Rom. 1:4].)

3 And no man in Heaven, nor in earth, neither under the earth, was able to open the Book, neither to look thereon. (We should look very carefully at the words "no man.")

4 And I wept much, because no man was found worthy to open and to read the Book, neither to look thereon. (This pertains to the fact that this Book is so very, very important. It contains not only the information regarding the coming Judgment upon this Earth, but as well the message that this Judgment, as tendered by God, will ultimately lead to the Redemption of the Earth.)

THE LION AND THE LAMB

5 And one of the Elders said unto me, Weep not (states that man's dilemma has been solved): behold, the Lion of the Tribe of Judah, the Root of David, has prevailed to open the Book, and to

loose the Seven Seals thereof (presents Jesus Christ).

6 And I beheld, and, lo, in the midst of the Throne and of the four Beasts, and in the midst of the Elders, stood a Lamb as it had been slain (the Crucifixion of Christ is represented here by the word "Lamb," which refers to the fact that it was the Cross which Redeemed mankind; the slain Lamb Alone has Redeemed all things), having seven horns (horns denote dominion, and "seven" denotes total dominion; all of this was done for you and me, meaning that we can have total dominion over the powers of darkness, and in every capacity; so there is no excuse for a lack of victory) and seven eyes (denotes total, perfect, pure, and complete illumination of all things spiritual, which is again made possible for you and me by the Cross; if the Believer makes the Cross the object of his Faith, he will never be drawn away by false doctrine), which are the Seven Spirits of God sent forth into all the Earth (signifying that the Holy Spirit, in all His perfection and universality, functions entirely within the parameters of the Finished Work of Christ; in other words, it is required that we ever make the Cross the object of our Faith, which gives the Holy Spirit latitude, and guarantees the "dominion," and the "illumination" [Isa. 11:2; Rom. 8:2]).

7 And He (the Lord Jesus Christ) came and took the Book out of the Right Hand of Him (God the Father) Who sat upon the Throne. (All of Heaven stands in awe as the Lamb steps forward to take the Book.)

WORSHIP

8 And when He (the Lord Jesus) had taken the Book, the four Beasts (living creatures) and four and twenty Elders (representatives of the Church) fell down before the Lamb (proclaims to us the Deity of Christ), having every one of them harps, and golden vials full of odours, which are the prayers of Saints. (In the Greek, this refers to the 24 Elders only. All the prayers that have ever come up before God for things to be rectified are about to be answered.)

9 And they sung a new song, saying (which only the Redeemed can sing), You are worthy to take the Book, and to open the Seals thereof (proclaims that by His Death He has acquired a right to approach where no other one could approach, and to do what no other one could do): for You were slain (refers to the Cross, which has made everything possible), and have redeemed us to God by Your Blood (proclaims the manner in which Redemption was purchased) out of every kindred, and tongue, and people, and nation (proclaims the fact that

Salvation secured by the Death of Christ universally applies to all classes and peoples of the Earth);

10 And have made us unto our God kings and priests *(the Scripture abundantly proclaims that whatever Jesus is because of the Cross, that's what we are also)*: and we shall reign on the earth *(refers to the coming Millennial Reign).*

11 And I beheld, and I heard the voice of many Angels round about the Throne and the Beasts and the Elders: and the number of them was ten thousand times ten thousand, and thousands of thousands *("ten thousand" is the greatest number expressed by the Greek vocabulary, and in itself may denote an unlimited number; but here we have a quadruple plural — ten thousands of ten thousands, and thousands of thousands — which in the Greek actually says "myriads of myriads," i.e., "an innumerable host");*

12 Saying with a loud voice *(considering the tremendous number, actually beyond comprehension, what a sound this must have been)*, Worthy is the Lamb that was slain to receive power, and riches, and wisdom, and strength, and honour, and glory, and blessing. *(Through and by the Cross, the sevenfold Blessing is given to Christ and is given to us as well. Let us say it again and again, "The Cross! The Cross! The Cross!")*

13 And every creature which is in Heaven, and on the earth, and under the earth, and such as are in the sea, and all that are in them, heard I saying *(the Death of Christ as Atonement is the ground or basis of the restoration of all things, and is implied in Philippians 2:8-11)*, Blessing, and honour, and glory, and power, *be* unto Him Who sits upon the Throne *(God the Father)*, and unto the Lamb forever and ever. *(What Jesus did at the Cross guaranteed the total defeat of Satan and all his minions of darkness, which will ultimately cleanse Heaven and Earth in totality and forever.)*

14 And the four Beasts *(living creatures)* said, Amen. *(The four "Living Ones" say "Amen" to the fourfold Blessing.)* And the four *and* twenty Elders fell down and worshipped Him Who lives forever and ever. *(This records the fact that not only is God eternal, but what Jesus did at the Cross will have eternal results as well.)*

CHAPTER 6

THE FIRST SEAL

AND I saw when the Lamb opened one of the Seals *(refers to the Crucified, risen Christ, and is proven by the use of the word "Lamb")*, and I heard, as it were the noise of thunder, one of the four Beasts *(living creatures)* saying, Come and see. *(This will follow the Rapture of the Church, but we aren't told exactly how long after the Rapture the Great Tribulation will come. "Come and see," says that it is destined and cannot be avoided.)*

2 And I saw, and behold a white horse *(symbolic; proclaims the Antichrist presenting himself to the world as a prince of peace)*: and he who sat on him had a bow *(mentions no arrows; he preaches peace, but is preparing for war, as symbolized by the "bow")*; and a crown was given unto him: and he went forth conquering, and to conquer. *(The "crown" represents the fact that he will conquer many countries. At first he does so by peace, but will quickly graduate to war.)*

THE SECOND SEAL

3 And when He *(Christ)* had opened the second Seal, I heard the second Beast *(Living Creature)* say, Come and see. *(As we see here, all the events on Earth are decided first of all in Heaven.)*

4 And there went out another horse *that was red (portrays another symbol, this time war)*: and *power* was given to him *(the Antichrist)* who sat thereon to take peace from the earth, and that they should kill one another: and there was given unto him a great

sword. *(This proclaims the fact that more people will be killed during the time of the Great Tribulation than at any other similar time frame in history.)*

THE THIRD SEAL

5 And when He had opened the third Seal, I heard the third Beast *(Living Creature)* say, Come and see *(is as the previous two, opened by Christ; the time frame for this will most probably be in the second year of the Great Tribulation)*. And I beheld, and lo a black horse *(represents famine, which always follows war)*; and he who sat on him had a pair of balances in his hand *(refers to the scarcity of food, and is meant to portray that fact)*.

6 And I heard a voice in the midst of the four Beasts say, A measure of wheat for a penny, and three measures of barley for a penny *(the world has rejected the Cross, and the world now faces Judgment)*; and *see* you hurt not the oil and the wine. *(The petition that the olive tree and grape vine are not to be hurt is that these particular plants need no cultivation. Hence, their ruthless destruction is forbidden.)*

THE FOURTH SEAL

7 And when He had opened

the fourth Seal, I heard the voice of the fourth Beast say, Come and see *(presents a horror of unprecedented proportions)*.

8 And I looked, and behold a pale horse *(symbolic of death)*: and his name that sat on him was Death, and Hell followed with him *(signifying that almost all who died went to Hell)*. And power was given unto them over the fourth part of the earth, to kill with sword, and with hunger, and with death, and with the beasts of the earth. *(This probably refers to the Middle East and its vicinity.)*

THE FIFTH SEAL

9 And when He *(Christ)* had opened the fifth Seal *(there is no announcement concerning the opening of this Seal, as it had been with the others)*, I saw under the Altar *(the Altar of Incense)* the souls of them who were slain *(does not refer to an intermediate state, for the Resurrection has already taken place, and all now in Heaven have Glorified Bodies; the word "soul" is merely used in the sense of identification and not as a state)* for the Word of God, and for the testimony which they held *(corresponds with Revelation 12:11)*:

10 And they *(the souls under the Altar)* cried with a loud voice, saying, How long, O Lord, Holy and True *(pertains to far more than a cry for vengeance; more than anything else, it is a cry for the entire episode of sin and shame to end; it is a culmination of the cry of the ages)*, do you not judge and avenge our blood on them who dwell on the earth? *(It is certain that the Lord will "Judge" and "Avenge" [Mat. 12:36].)*

11 And white robes were given unto every one of them *(symbolizes the Righteousness of the Saints [Rev. 19:8])*; and it was said unto them, that they should rest yet for a little season, until their fellowservants also and their Brethren, who should be killed as they *were*, should be fulfilled. *(They will have to wait until the conclusion of the Great Tribulation, probably about another five years.)*

THE SIXTH SEAL

12 And I beheld when He *(Christ)* had opened the sixth Seal, and, lo, there was a great earthquake *(the first of several)*; and the sun became black as sackcloth of hair *(probably caused by dust filling the air due to the earthquake)*, and the moon became as blood *(doesn't mean the moon was actually turned to blood, but that it "became as blood," again probably referring to the dust particles filling the air)*;

13 And the stars of Heaven fell unto the earth *(refers to meteorites or shooting stars)*, even as a fig tree casts her untimely figs, when she is shaken of a mighty wind. *(There will be a bombardment on the Earth of these meteorites, which will cause untold damage.)*

14 And the Heaven departed as a scroll when it is rolled together *(pertains to the shaking of the Heavens, which instigates the meteorites)*; and every mountain and island were moved out of their places. *(This proclaims power of unimagined proportions. The greater thrust will more than likely be in the Middle East.)*

15 And the kings of the earth, and the great men, and the rich men, and the chief captains, and the mighty men, and every bondman, and every free man, hid themselves in the dens and in the rocks of the mountains *(presents this as a wasted effort, for men cannot hide from God; as well, it takes in everyone from poverty to plenty)*;

16 And said to the mountains and rocks *(foolish man now prays to the rocks)*, Fall on us, and hide us from the face of Him Who sits on the Throne *(pertains to God the Father; let all understand, mankind, and that means everyone, is going to have to deal with the One Who sits on the Throne)*, and from the wrath of the Lamb *(the Lamb is the Saviour today; tomorrow the Lamb is the Judge)*:

17 For the great day of His wrath is come *(the "Great Day" is the coming Great Tribulation, which will last for seven years)*; and who shall be able to stand? *(This refers to the fact that man has set himself against God ever since the Fall. Now man will see exactly how powerful God actually is.)*

CHAPTER 7

144,000 JEWS

AND after these things *(the first parenthetical Passage, coming between the sixth and seventh Seals)* I saw four Angels standing on the four corners of the earth *(represents the universality of God's administration)*, holding the four winds of the earth *(actually refers to Judgment, which will be stopped for a short period of time)*, that the wind should not blow on the earth, nor on the sea, nor on any tree. *(The winds of Judgment strive to be turned loose, but they are held in abeyance by the omnipotence of Almighty God.)*

2 And I saw another Angel ascending from the east *(the advent of this Angel portrays the fact that this is the beginning of the restoration of Israel)*, having the Seal of the Living God *(pertains to the Seal of Salvation [II Tim.*

2:19]): and he cried with a loud voice to the four Angels, to whom it was given to hurt the earth and the sea *(the Judgments are to be held in check),*

3 Saying, Hurt not the earth, neither the sea, nor the trees, till we have sealed the servants of our God in their foreheads. *(This is not literal, but rather a token, as the sprinkled blood on the lentil protected the house from the destroying Angel at the first Passover.)*

4 And I heard the number of them which were sealed: *and there were* sealed an hundred *and* forty *and* four thousand of all the Tribes of the Children of Israel *(12,000 from each Tribe; these are the First-fruits of Israel which are included in the First Resurrection, with all of Israel coming to Christ at the Second Coming).*

5 Of the Tribe of Judah *were* sealed twelve thousand. Of the Tribe of Reuben *were* sealed twelve thousand. Of the Tribe of Gad *were* sealed twelve thousand.

6 Of the Tribe of Aser *were* sealed twelve thousand. Of the Tribe of Nephthalim *were* sealed twelve thousand. Of the Tribe of Manasses *were* sealed twelve thousand.

7 Of the Tribe of Simeon *were* sealed twelve thousand. Of the Tribe of Levi *were* sealed twelve thousand. Of the Tribe of Issachar *were* sealed twelve thousand.

8 Of the Tribe of Zabulon *were* sealed twelve thousand. Of the Tribe of Joseph *(Ephraim) were* sealed twelve thousand. Of the Tribe of Benjamin *were* sealed twelve thousand. *(The Tribe of Dan is omitted, and no reason is given.)*

TRIBULATION SAINTS

9 After this I beheld, and, lo, a great multitude *(pertains to martyrs who gave their lives for the Lord Jesus Christ in the Great Tribulation)*, which no man could number *(represents the many, possibly millions, who will be saved in the Great Tribulation)*, of all nations, and kindreds, and people, and tongues, stood before the Throne, and before the Lamb *(by use of the word "Lamb," we know and realize that their sin-stained garments have been washed in the Blood of the Lamb)*, clothed with white robes, and palms in their hands *(could be paraphrased, "dressed in richest wedding garments of purest, dazzling, white"; these are God's Blood-bought; the palms represent joy [Neh. 8:17])*;

10 And cried with a loud voice *(proclaims great joy)*, saying, Salvation to our God which sits upon the Throne, and unto the Lamb. *(Once again, we are told here how God has brought about Salvation.*

It is through what Jesus did at the Cross, and through that means alone.)

11 And all the Angels stood round about the Throne, and *about* the Elders and the four Beasts, and fell before the Throne on their faces, and worshipped God *(this tremendous volume of worship and praise has to do with what Jesus did at the Cross, in His Atoning for all sin by the giving of Himself in Sacrifice),*

12 Saying, Amen *(is the proclamation that God has provided Salvation to humanity through the work of the Lamb)*: Blessing, and Glory, and Wisdom, and Thanksgiving, and Honour, and Power, and Might, *be* unto our God forever and ever. Amen. *(As the praises to God the Father are sevenfold, they are also sevenfold to God the Son [Rev. 5:12]. This shows that both God and the Lamb are regarded in Heaven as entitled to equal praise.)*

13 And one of the Elders answered, saying unto me *(proclaims one of the 24 addressing questions that are in John's mind, but have not been asked)*, What are these which are arrayed in white robes? *(This would be better translated, "Who are these?")* and whence came they? *(Where do they come from?)*

14 And I said unto him, Sir, you know *(presents reverent regard, but definitely not worship)*. And he said to me, These are they which came out of great tribulation *(refers to a specific group)*, and have washed their robes, and made them white in the Blood of the Lamb. *(They were saved by trusting Christ and what He did at the Cross. In the Book of Revelation, the emphasis placed on the Cross is overwhelming.)*

15 Therefore are they before the Throne of God, and serve Him day and night in His Temple *(all of this particular group came out of the Great Tribulation)*: and He Who sits on the Throne shall dwell among them. *(The One Who sits on the Throne will cast His protecting Tabernacle over all the Saints of God, which in effect is His Presence.)*

16 They shall hunger no more, neither thirst any more; neither shall the sun light on them, nor any heat *(proclaims a perfect environment)*.

17 For the Lamb which is in the midst of the Throne shall feed them *(not only did the Lamb save them, but He as well "shall feed them"; not only does our Salvation come by and through what Jesus did at the Cross, but we "live" by what Jesus did for us at the Cross as well)*, and shall lead them unto living fountains of waters *(symbolic of the Holy Spirit [Jn. 7:37-39])*: and God shall wipe away all tears from their eyes. *(All*

things causing sorrow will be forever gone.)

CHAPTER 8

THE SEVENTH SEAL

AND when He had opened the seventh Seal *(this is the last Seal)*, there was silence in Heaven about the space of half an hour. *(This silence proclaims the intense expectancy of what is about to come upon the world. In other words, if it has been bad thus far, the intensity of the Judgment is about to increase many fold.)*

2 And I saw the seven Angels which stood before God *(the Greek Text says, "the seven Angels of the Presence of God")*; and to them were given seven Trumpets. *(We have had the Seven Seals of Judgment. Now the world will experience the Seven Trumpet Judgments.)*

3 And another Angel came and stood at the Altar, having a Golden Censer *(this is the "Altar of Incense" in Heaven)*; and there was given unto him much Incense *(represents the perfection, merit, and virtue of the Life of Christ; everything speaks of Christ, and more particularly of what He did at the Cross; incidentally, this Altar of Incense in Heaven is the Pattern for the Altar of Incense that stood in the Tabernacle on Earth imme-diately before the Veil during the time of the Law)*, that he should offer *it* with the prayers of all Saints upon the Golden Altar which was before the Throne. *(The prayers of all the Saints are very precious in the sight of God, yet at the same time imperfect. Added to our prayers must be the Incense, which is a type of the sweet savor of the merit of the life, death, and Resurrection of Christ.)*

4 And the smoke of the Incense *(even though we aren't given the information in this Verse, the Angel has taken coals of fire from the Brazen Altar and placed them in his Golden Censer)*, which came with the prayers of the Saints *(for our prayers to be effective in Heaven, they must always be mixed with the intercessory Work of Christ [Heb. 7:25-26])*, ascended up before God out of the Angel's hand. *(Knowing our prayers come "up before God," at least if we pray according to the Will of God, should inspire every Saint to a greater prayer life.)*

5 And the Angel took the Censer, and filled it with fire of the Altar *(this is the Brazen Altar in Heaven that typified the Death of our Lord, which was necessary in order that man might be Redeemed; as is obvious here, Heaven is filled with the portrayal of that Sacrificial, Atoning Death)*, and cast it into the earth *(with the Salvation of the Cross being rejected*

by the Earth, the Judgment of the Cross will now commence): and there were voices, and thunderings, and lightnings, and an earthquake. (All of this speaks of the fact that it is Judgment coming, and Judgment such as the world has never seen before [Mat. 24:21].)

6 And the Seven Angels which had the Seven Trumpets prepared themselves to sound. (As stated, if the Cross is rejected, Judgment must follow. These events will take place about two and one half years into the Great Tribulation.)

THE FIRST TRUMPET

7 The first Angel sounded (the first Trumpet Judgment), and there followed hail and fire mingled with blood, and they were cast upon the earth (this will be literal, and will be a fulfillment of the Prophecy of Joel [Joel 2:30-32]; this is similar to the seventh plague upon Egypt [Ex. 9:22]): and the third part of trees was burnt up, and all green grass was burnt up (probably refers to a third part of the Mediterranean area being affected; even though all of this will affect the entirety of the Earth, as would be obvious, the greatest concentration will be in the Middle East).

THE SECOND TRUMPET

8 And the second Angel sound-ed, and as it were a great mountain burning with fire was cast into the sea (more than likely, this will be a giant meteorite which will fall into the Mediterranean Sea): and the third part of the Sea became blood (similar to that which had taken place in Egypt so long ago [Ex. 7:20-21]);

9 And the third part of the creatures which were in the Sea, and had life, died; and the third part of the ships were destroyed (concerns the part affected by the meteorite, or by whatever manner God chooses to do this).

THE THIRD TRUMPET

10 And the third Angel sounded, and there fell a great star from Heaven, burning as it were a lamp (more than likely another meteorite), and it fell upon the third part of the rivers, and upon the fountains of waters (a third part of the land area; speaks of the Old Roman Empire area [Dan. 7:7-8]);

11 And the name of the star is called Wormwood (this huge meteorite, which will fall, will carry with it the properties of the bitter, nauseous plant known as "Wormwood" [Jer. 9:15]): and the third part of the waters became wormwood; and many men died of the waters, because they were made bitter. (Conceivably this could take the lives of hundreds of thousands,

if not millions.)

THE FOURTH TRUMPET

12 And the fourth Angel sounded, and the third part of the sun was smitten, and the third part of the moon, and the third part of the stars; so as the third part of them was darkened, and the day shone not for a third part of it, and the night likewise. *(Once again let us emphasize the fact that these Judgments aren't symbolic, they are literal! Jesus said this would happen [Lk. 21:25-26].)*

13 And I beheld, and heard an Angel flying through the midst of Heaven, saying with a loud voice *(it is possible this Angel will be visible to people on Earth, and could well be portrayed by Television)*, Woe, woe, woe, to the inhabiters of the earth by reason of the other voices of the Trumpet of the three Angels, which are yet to sound! *(The three "woes" are meant to correspond with the three remaining Trumpet Judgments.)*

CHAPTER 9

THE FIFTH TRUMPET

A ND the fifth Angel sounded *(presents the fifth Judgment, and as stated the first "woe")*, and I saw a star fall from Heaven unto the earth *(actually refers to Satan, as the next phrase proclaims [Lk. 10:18])*: and to him was given the key of the bottomless pit. *(Christ gives this "key" to Satan, although He may use an Angel to hand the key to the Evil One [Rev. 20:1].)*

2 And he *(Satan)* opened the bottomless pit; and there arose a smoke out of the pit, as the smoke of a great furnace; and the sun and the air were darkened by reason of the smoke of the pit. *(This will probably be concentrated in the old Roman Empire territory.)*

3 And there came out of the smoke locusts upon the earth *(these are demon locusts, even as the following Verses prove)*: and unto them was given power, as the scorpions of the earth have power *(refers to the sting in their tails, and the pain this will cause)*.

4 And it was commanded them that they should not hurt the grass of the earth, neither any green thing, neither any tree *(normal locusts destroy plant life; but these are not allowed to do so)*; but only those men which have not the Seal of God in their foreheads *(refers to the 144,000 Jews who have accepted Christ as their Saviour [Rev. 7:2-8])*.

5 And to them it was given that they should not kill them, but that they should be tormented five months *(this will be literal, yet these creatures will be invisible)*: and their torment *was* as the

torment of a scorpion, when he strikes a man *(pain and swelling)*.

6 And in those days shall men seek death, and shall not find it; and shall desire to die, and death shall flee from them. *(For pain to be so bad that people want to die is bad indeed! Evidently painkilling drugs will not work. It will be interesting how medical doctors diagnose all of this, to say the least.)*

7 And the shapes of the locusts *were* like unto horses prepared unto battle; and on their heads *were* as it were crowns like gold, and their faces *were* as the faces of men. *(These are demon spirits, but will be invisible. If they could be seen, this is what they would look like. We aren't told their origin in the Bible. We know they were not originally created in this manner, but evidently became this way in the revolution instigated by Lucifer against God [Isa. 14:12-20; Ezek. 28:11-19].)*

8 And they had hair as the hair of women, and their teeth were as *the teeth* of lions. *(They were, no doubt, originally created by God to perform a particular function of praise and worship, even as the "living creatures," but they have suffered this fate due to rebellion against God.)*

9 And they had breastplates, as it were breastplates of iron; and the sound of their wings *was* as the sound of chariots of many horses running to battle. *(We are given a glimpse here into the spirit world. This is the reason such foolish efforts as humanistic psychology are helpless against such foes. The only answer is Christ and the Cross.)*

10 And they had tails like unto scorpions, and there were stings in their tails: and their power *was* to hurt men five months. *(This Judgment is limited to five months, which tells us Satan can only do what God allows him to do.)*

11 And they had a king over them, *which is* the Angel of the bottomless pit *(gives us further insight into the spirit world of darkness)*, whose name in the Hebrew tongue *is* Abaddon, but in the Greek tongue has *his* name Apollyon. *(This is a powerful fallen Angel, who evidently threw in his lot with Lucifer in the great rebellion against God. Only four Angels are named in Scripture, "Gabriel, Michael, Lucifer, and Apollyon," the first two being Righteous.)*

12 One woe is past *(refers to the fifth Trumpet Judgment)*; and, behold, there come two woes more hereafter. *(The word "behold" calls attention to the fact that the two remaining "woes" will be exceedingly horrific.)*

THE SIXTH TRUMPET

13 And the sixth Angel sound-

ed *(this is the second "woe")*, and I heard a voice from the four horns of the Golden Altar which is before God *(this is the "Altar of Incense"; the "voice" is probably that of the same Angel who came and stood at the Altar, and had much Incense [6:9; 8:3])*,

14 Saying to the sixth Angel which had the Trumpet, Loose the four Angels which are bound in the great river Euphrates. *(These are evil Angels, hence previously "bound." The river "Euphrates" signals the area. It is where it all began, it is where it will all end, and it is being prepared even now.)*

15 And the four Angels were loosed, which were prepared for an hour, and a day, and a month, and a year, for to slay the third part of men. *(These four Angels are not to be confused with the four Angels of Revelation 7:1. Those are Righteous Angels, while these four are evil. They are executors of God's wrath. Once again, this Judgment will be mostly confined to the old Roman Empire territory.)*

16 And the number of the army of the horsemen *were* two hundred thousand thousand *(200 million)*: and I heard the number of them. *(This is not symbolic of a human army, but rather demon spirits, which as well will be invisible.)*

17 And thus I saw the horses in the vision *(demon horses)*, and them that sat on them, having breastplates of fire, and of jacinth, and brimstone: and the heads of the horses *were* as the heads of lions; and out of their mouths issued fire and smoke and brimstone. *(All of this presents demon spirits riding demon horses.)*

18 By these three was the third part of men killed, by the fire, and by the smoke, and by the brimstone, which issued out of their mouths. *(Quite possibly, over three hundred million people will die as a result of this particular plague. Whatever they think to be the cause, the actual cause will be what is described here.)*

19 For their power is in their mouth, and in their tails: for their tails *were* like unto serpents, and had heads, and with them they do hurt. *(Once again, we are here given a glimpse into the spirit world. That's the reason Paul said we "wrestle not against flesh and blood, but against principalities, against powers, against the rulers of the darkness of this world, against spiritual wickedness in high places" [Eph. 6:12]. As well, that is why all efforts to oppose such are fruitless, other than Christ and the Cross.)*

20 And the rest of the men which were not killed by these plagues *(once again, probably confined to the Middle East area)* yet repented not of the works of their

hands *(as is obvious here, men do not easily repent)*, that they should not worship devils, and idols of gold, and silver, and brass, and stone, and of wood: which neither can see, nor hear, nor walk *(all worship of God must be based strictly on the Sacrifice of Christ and the Name of Christ, else it is a "work of man's hands," which God can never accept [Eph. 2:13-18]):*

21 Neither repented they of their murders, nor of their sorceries, nor of their fornication, nor of their thefts. *(The Holy Spirit again emphasizes the fact that they will not repent. Repentance by the world must be in the realm of the sin of man creating another god. In the Church, Repentance must be in the realm of the sin of the creation of another Sacrifice.)*

CHAPTER 10

THE MIGHTY ANGEL

A ND I saw another mighty Angel come down from Heaven *(this is Christ [Rev. 1:16; Dan. 10:5-6])*, clothed with a cloud *(refers to the Glory of God upon Him, for He is God [Ex. 40:34-38]):* and a rainbow *was* upon His Head *(refers to Peace and Mercy)*, and His face *was* as it were the Sun *(concerns the degree of Glory)*, and His feet as pillars of fire *(speaks of Judgment; rejecting Mercy and Peace always brings Judgment):*

2 And He had in His Hand a little Book open *(proclaims the same Book of Revelation, Chapter 5, but here it is open; in fact, He is the One Who opened it [5:5; 6:1]):* and He set His right foot upon the sea, and His left foot on the earth *(proclaims dominion, meaning Righteousness will ultimately prevail on this Earth),*

3 And cried with a loud voice, as *when* a lion roars *(signals power and victory):* and when He had cried, seven thunders uttered their voices. *(We aren't told what these seven thunders stated, or what they meant.)*

4 And when the seven thunders had uttered their voices, I was about to write *(proclaims the fact that John wrote all of this down, which refers to the entirety of this Book of Revelation):* and I heard a voice from Heaven saying unto me, Seal up those things which the seven thunders uttered, and write them not. *(John knew what they were, but was forbidden to relate it in the Book. Therefore, speculation is useless.)*

5 And the Angel which I saw stand upon the Sea and upon the earth lifted up His Hand to Heaven *(presents most likely the right hand, with the Book held in the left hand; it concerns an oath),*

6 And swear by Him Who lives forever and ever, Who created Heaven, and the things that therein are, and the earth, and the things that therein are, and the sea, and the things which are therein *(proclaims the fact that the world belongs to God by virtue of Him being its Creator)*, that there should be time no longer *(could be translated, "that there should be delay no longer"; the prayer of Christ, "Thy Kingdom come, Thy will be done on Earth as it is in Heaven," is about to be answered)*:

7 But in the days of the voice of the seventh Angel, when he shall begin to sound *(proclaims the beginning of the last half of the Great Tribulation, which will be worse than ever)*, the Mystery of God should be finished *(this "Mystery" pertains to the reason God has allowed Satan to continue his reign over this Earth for these thousands of years [II Cor. 4:4])*, as He has declared to His servants the Prophets *(Isa. 14:12-20; Ezek. 28:11-19)*.

THE LITTLE BOOK

8 And the voice which I heard from Heaven spoke unto me again *(it is the same voice which told him to seal up those things the seven thunders uttered, and write them not)*, and said, Go *and* take the little Book which is open in the Hand of the Angel *(Christ)* which stands upon the Sea and upon the Earth. *(This presents the third time Christ is presented in His dominion role, which guarantees the certainty of such action.)*

9 And I went unto the Angel *(Christ)*, and said unto Him, Give me the little Book *(refers, as stated, to the same Book mentioned in Chapter 5)*. And He said unto me, Take it, and eat it up *(presents idiomatic language meaning to digest its contents)*; and it shall make your belly bitter, but it shall be in your mouth sweet as honey. *(The Word of God is always sweet. But in this case it speaks of Judgment, and will, therefore, be bitter in the belly, as all Judgment is bitter.)*

10 And I took the little Book out of the Angel's hand, and ate it up *(he digested its contents)*; and it was in my mouth sweet as honey: and as soon as I had eaten it, my belly was bitter. *(Signifying the further Judgment that was about to come. It pertained to the last half of the Great Tribulation, which will be the worst of all.)*

11 And He *(Christ)* said unto me, You must prophesy again before many peoples, and nations, and tongues, and kings. *(Jesus is telling John that the stand He has taken by putting one foot on the Sea and the other on the Earth does not prove His formal*

possession of the Earth at this time. This will not take place until about three and one half years later. Consequently, John must continue to prophesy, which in effect is the second half of the Book of Revelation.)

CHAPTER 11

THE TWO WITNESSES

AND there was given me a reed like unto a rod: and the Angel *(Christ)* stood, saying, Rise, and measure the Temple of God, and the Altar, and them who worship therein *(refers to the literal Temple which will be rebuilt in Jerusalem, with Israel once again instituting the Sacrifices; in fact, plans are being made at this moment for the rebuilding of this structure; as well, Daniel prophesied of this event some 500 years before Christ [Dan. 9:27]).*

2 But the Court which is without the Temple leave out, and measure it not; for it is given unto the Gentiles *(refers to the Court of the Gentiles, which was the furthest Court from the Temple; this "measurement" is for Judgment):* and the Holy City *(Jerusalem)* shall they tread under foot forty *and* two months. *(This refers to the period that will end the "times of the Gentiles" [Lk. 21:24]. At the mid-point of the Great Tribu-*

lation, the Antichrist will turn on Israel, actually attacking her and she will be temporarily defeated. He will occupy the Temple, making it his religious headquarters [II Thess. 2:4]. He will occupy it for three and one half years.)

3 And I will give *power* unto My two witnesses *(Enoch and Elijah, two men who have not yet died, actually being translated before they saw death [Gen. 5:21-24; Mal. 4:5-6]),* and they shall prophesy a thousand two hundred *and* threescore days, clothed in sackcloth. *(This refers to three and one half years, the last half of the Great Tribulation. The clothing and sackcloth suggests that the witnessing includes the Preaching of Repentance [Isa. 37:1-2; Dan. 9:3-5].)*

4 These are the two olive trees, and the two candlesticks standing before the God of the earth. *(Both represent the two witnesses, and refer to the vision given by the Lord to the Prophet Zechariah [Zech., Chpt. 4].)*

5 And if any man will hurt them, fire proceeds out of their mouth, and devours their enemies *(pertains to Judgment and not literal fire):* and if any man will hurt them, he must in this manner be killed. *(This proclaims the protection of the Lord, and in whatever manner it is needed. No doubt the Antichrist will seek to kill them in many ways.)*

6 These have power to shut Heaven, that it rain not in the days of their Prophecy (*doesn't mean that there will be no rain for three and one half years, but that they can shut up Heaven as often as they so desire; no doubt there will be months without rain*): and have power over waters to turn them to blood (*at that time, what this miracle will be ascribed to is anyone's guess*), and to smite the earth with all plagues, as often as they will (*refers to sicknesses and diseases of every nature, along with plagues of insects, such as flies, frogs, etc.*).

7 And when they shall have finished their testimony (*will be at the conclusion of the three and one half years of Great Tribulation; ironically, this is the same period of time of Christ's earthly Ministry*), the Beast that ascends out of the bottomless pit shall make war against them, and shall overcome them, and kill them. (*The Beast out of the Abyss is a Satanic Angel, not the human spirit of some dead man. It is the one described by John in Rev. 17:8. He is a fallen Angel who will be invisible, but will greatly help the Antichrist. And with the help of this fallen Angel, the Antichrist will kill the two witnesses, but not until their Ministry is completed*).

8 And their dead bodies *shall lie* in the street of the great city, which spiritually is called Sodom and Egypt, where also our Lord was Crucified. (*As is obvious, it is Jerusalem. Satan will turn this city into the capital of homosexuality [Sodom] and worldliness [Egypt]*.)

9 And they of the people and kindreds and tongues and nations shall see their dead bodies three days and a half (*no doubt by Television, which will be beamed all over the world*), and shall not suffer their dead bodies to be put in graves (*proclaims the spectacle lasting three and one half days*).

10 And they who dwell upon the earth shall rejoice over them, and make merry, and shall send gifts one to another (*proclaims a worldwide celebration because the two witnesses who have caused so many problems for the Antichrist have now been killed*); because these two Prophets tormented them who dwell on the earth. (*This proclaims that which true Prophets have a tendency to do.*)

11 And after three days and a half the Spirit of Life from God entered into them, and they stood upon their feet (*refers to these two men being raised from the dead; this will no doubt be Televised all over the world as well*); and great fear fell upon them which saw them. (*It will be a miracle, as is obvious, of astounding proportions.*)

12 And they heard a great voice

from Heaven saying unto them, Come up hither. *(These will be Raptured at the very conclusion of the Great Tribulation. They will be among the last of those included in the First Resurrection of Life.)* And they ascended up to Heaven in a cloud; and their enemies beheld them. *(As stated, Television will portray this miraculous scene, with it being observed all over the world.)*

13 And the same hour was there a great earthquake *(this is one of five times that earthquakes are mentioned; it is the last one that will take place and happens under the seventh Vial, which is at the very conclusion of the Great Tribulation)*, and the tenth part of the city fell *(refers to Jerusalem)*, and in the earthquake were slain of men seven thousand: and the remnant were affrighted, and gave Glory to the God of Heaven. *(There is some indication in the Greek Text that some of these people gave their hearts to Christ.)*

THE SEVENTH TRUMPET

14 The second woe is past *(this woe took place under the Sixth Trumpet Judgment [Rev. 9:12-21])*; and, behold, the third woe comes quickly. *(It is not the earthquake of Verse 13, but rather the casting out of Satan under the Seventh Trumpet [Rev. 12:12].)*

15 And the seventh Angel sounded *(marks the beginning of the last three and one half years of the Great Tribulation)*; and there were great voices in Heaven, saying, The kingdoms of this world are become *the Kingdoms* of our Lord, and of His Christ; and He shall reign forever and ever. *(This is said in anticipation, and will definitely come to pass at the conclusion of this three and one half year period at the Second Coming of the Lord.)*

16 And the four and twenty Elders, which sat before God on their seats *(throne)*, fell upon their faces, and worshipped God *(these Elders are human beings, possibly some of the Prophets and Apostles of the Bible, and represent the entirety of the Plan of God as it refers to Redemption)*,

17 Saying, We give You thanks, O Lord God Almighty, which are, and was, and are to come *(pronounces Him as "the Eternal One")*; because You have taken to Yourself Your great power, and have reigned. *(This once again speaks of anticipation, in other words what the Lord is going to do, and which He most definitely will do.)*

18 And the nations were angry, and Your wrath is come *(has to do with the coming battle of Armageddon [Ps., Chpt. 2])*, and the time of the dead, that they should be Judged, and that You should

give reward unto Your servants the Prophets, and to the Saints, and them who fear Your Name, small and great *(refers to the coming Judgment Seat of Christ, not the Great White Throne Judgment)*; and should destroy them which destroy the earth. *(Once again speaks of the Battle of Armageddon, in which Christ will engage at the Second Coming [Rev., Chpt. 19].)*

19 And the Temple of God was opened in Heaven *(in some way it might be similar to Solomon's Temple, for which the Heavenly Temple was the pattern)*, and there was seen in His temple the Ark of His Testament *(refers to the Ark of the Covenant, which again served as the pattern for the Ark of the Covenant in the Tabernacle and Temple on Earth during the time of the Law)*: and there were lightnings, and voices, and thunderings, and an earthquake, and great hail. *(This presents that which is symbolic of the awful Presence of God and His Majesty and Glory.)*

CHAPTER 12

THE SUN-CLAD WOMAN

AND there appeared a great wonder in Heaven *(should have been translated, "a great sign in Heaven")*; a woman clothed with the Sun *(speaks of National Israel with the "Sun" being a symbol of her Glory)*, and the moon under her feet *(speaks of dominion, hence the mention of her feet)*, and upon her head a crown of twelve stars *(speaks of dominion regained and Israel restored)*:

2 And she being with child cried *(pertains to the 144,000 Jews who will be saved in the first half of the Great Tribulation [Rev., Chpt. 7])*, travailing in birth, and pained to be delivered. *(This concerns spiritual pregnancy, with the agonies of childbirth typifying in the physical what will take place in the spiritual [Isa. 66:7-8].)*

GREAT RED DRAGON

3 And there appeared another wonder in Heaven *(should have been translated, "another sign")*; and behold a great red dragon *(denotes Satan and his murderous purpose, typified by the color of "red")*, having seven heads *(refers to Empires that persecuted Israel, even until John's day; those Empires were Egypt, Assyria, Babylon, Medo-Persia, Greece, and Rome)* and ten horns *(represents ten nations that will be ruled by the Antichrist in the last days, and will greatly persecute Israel; actually, the seventh head is those "ten horns"; Daniel tells us that these "ten horns" representing ten nations will be in the old Roman Empire*

territory, which refers to the Middle East and parts of Europe [Dan. 7:7]), and seven crowns upon his heads (represents the fact that Satan controlled these particular kingdoms).

MANCHILD

4 And his tail drew the third part of the stars of Heaven (this goes all the way back to the original rebellion of Lucifer against God; at that time, one-third of the Angels threw in their lot with him; we know these "stars" represent Angels, because Verse 9 tells us so), and did cast them to the earth (is given to us more clearly in Verses 7-9): and the dragon stood before the woman which was ready to be delivered (does not pertain to the birth of Christ as many claim, but rather the manchild which is the 144,000 Jews who will give their hearts to Christ [Chpt. 7]), for to devour her child as soon as it was born. (This pertains to the fact that the Antichrist will hate these Jews who have come to Christ. This will take place in the first half of the Great Tribulation, and may well be the primary reason the Antichrist will turn on Israel at that time.)

5 And she (Israel) brought forth a manchild (as stated, this is the 144,000 Jews who will come to Christ during the first half of the Great Tribulation [Chpt. 7];

we aren't told exactly how this will be done), who was to rule all nations with a rod of iron (Israel, under Christ, will definitely fill this role in the coming Millennial Reign): and her child was caught up unto God, and to His Throne. (This refers to the Rapture of the 144,000, which will take place at about the midpoint of the Great Tribulation.)

6 And the woman fled into the wilderness (the "woman" is National Israel; at the midpoint of the Great Tribulation, the Antichrist will turn on Israel and defeat her, with many thousands of Jews fleeing into the wilderness), where she has a place prepared of God (this place is actually ancient Petra, located in Jordan [Isa. 16:1-5]), that they should feed her there a thousand two hundred and threescore days. ("They" mentioned here refers oddly enough to the Arabs of Jordan. The 1,260 days constitute almost all of the last half of the Great Tribulation. Incidentally, Petra is now empty of people, awaiting the arrival of Israel.)

MICHAEL

7 And there was war in Heaven (pertains to the "Mystery of God" being finished [10:7]): Michael and his Angels fought against the dragon; and the dragon fought

and his Angels *(this pertains to Satan and all the Angels who followed him being cast out of Heaven, which will take place at the mid-point of the Great Tribulation; why the Lord has allowed Satan and his minions to remain in Heaven all of this time, we aren't told; it is a "Mystery," but it will now be finished)*,

8 And prevailed not *(Satan will then be defeated; incidentally, it is not Satan who instigates this war, but rather the Archangel Michael at the Command of God)*; neither was their place found any more in Heaven *(joins with the close of the Book of Revelation, where the Evil One has no more place on Earth as well, but rather the place of torment forever and ever [20:10])*.

9 And the great dragon was cast out, that old serpent, called the Devil, and Satan *(he is referred to as "the Great Dragon" because of his propensity to "steal, kill, and destroy" [Jn. 10:10]; he is the "old serpent" because in his first appearance in the Bible, he chose to work through a serpent; thereby he is what the curse caused the serpent to be, wryly subtle and treacherous)*, which deceives the whole world *(deception is his greatest weapon; he deceives, and is himself deceived)*: he was cast out into the earth, and his Angels were cast out with him *(pronounces the beginning of the end for this evil mon-ster)*.

OVERCOMERS

10 And I heard a loud voice saying in Heaven *(presents the white-robe wearers of Revelation 6:10-11)*, Now is come Salvation, and Strength, and the Kingdom of our God *(presents the triumph of Christ)*, and the power of His Christ *(refers to the fact that Christ will rule this world, not Satan)*: for the accuser of our Brethren is cast down, which accused them before our God day and night. *(This implies that either Satan or one of his fallen Angels is before the Throne of God, accusing the Brethren constantly [Job, Chpts. 1-2].)*

11 And they overcame him by the Blood of the Lamb *(the power to overcome and overwhelm the kingdom of Satan is found exclusively in the Blood of the Sacrifice of the Son of God, and our Faith in that Finished Work [Rom. 6:3-5, 11, 14])*, and by the word of their testimony *(the "testimony" must pertain to the fact that the object of our Faith is the Cross, and exclusively the Cross, which then gives the Holy Spirit latitude to work within our lives)*; and they loved not their lives unto the death. *(This refers to the fact that the Believer must not change his testimony regarding the Cross to*

something else, even if it means death.)

12 Therefore rejoice, *you* Heavens, and you who dwell in them. *(Heaven rejoices because Satan has no more access to those portals.)* Woe to the inhabitants of the earth and of the Sea! for the Devil is come down unto you, having great wrath *(the "woe" mentioned here is the third and final woe, and pertains to Satan being cast out of Heaven, down to this Earth; he will have great anger)*, because he knows that he has but a short time *(in order to carry out his plan; failing that he is doomed!)*.

PERSECUTION

13 And when the dragon saw that he was cast unto the earth, he persecuted the woman which brought forth the manchild. *(That's when, as stated, the Antichrist will break his seven year Covenant with Israel, attacking and defeating her [Dan. 9:27].)*

14 And to the woman were given two wings of a great eagle, that she might fly into the wilderness, into her place *(the Lord will help Israel at that time, and do so greatly; as stated, this refers to Petra, which is located in modern Jordan)*, where she is nourished for a time, and times, and half a time, from the face of the serpent *(refers to three and one half years, the last half of the Great Tribulation; the Antichrist will take his armies elsewhere, thinking to take care of this remnant a little later [Dan. 11:44])*.

15 And the serpent cast out of his mouth water as a flood after the woman *(refers to the army of the Antichrist, which has just defeated Israel and is now bent on completely destroying her)*, that he might cause her to be carried away of the flood. *(The man of sin fully intends to destroy Israel at this time, but the Lord will intervene to stop him, as the next Verse proclaims.)*

16 And the earth helped the woman *(probably refers to the Lord sending an earthquake)*, and the earth opened her mouth, and swallowed up the flood which the dragon cast out of his mouth. *(This proclaims the action that helps the woman [Israel] hurts the dragon. As stated, it will probably be an earthquake!)*

17 And the dragon was wroth with the woman *(Israel has escaped out of the clutches of Satan one more time)*, and went to make war with the remnant of her seed *(after the Rapture of the 144,000 Jews, with their Testimony still ringing out over Israel, no doubt many other Jews will accept Christ at that time and make up the "Remnant")*, which keep the Commandments of God, and have the Testimony of Jesus Christ. *(As*

stated, this refers to the fact that this Remnant of Jews, ever how many there will be, will have accepted Christ, hence greatly angering Satan.)

CHAPTER 13

ANTICHRIST

AND I stood upon the sand of the sea (not a body of water, but a sea of people), and saw a beast rise up out of the sea (pertains to the Antichrist, now empowered by Satan as no other man ever has been), having seven heads and ten horns (represents seven Empires that have greatly persecuted Israel in the past, with the "ten horns" actually being the seventh head; the "ten horns" representing ten nations are yet future), and upon his horns ten crowns (the horns now being crowned show that these ten nations have now come to power, and will use that power to help the Antichrist; they will be located in the Middle East and in parts of Europe and possibly North Africa, all being in the old Roman Empire territory [Dan. 7:7-8]), and upon his heads the name of blasphemy. (Satan controls these Empires, and will control the ten nations, therefore, the name "blasphemy.")

2 And the beast which I saw (represents the fallen Angel who will be let out of the bottomless pit to help the Antichrist [Rev. 11:7]; both the fallen Angel and the Antichrist are referred to as a "beast," but they are two different beings) was like unto a leopard (this fallen Angel will help the Antichrist to speedily conquer; Daniel describes this event as well [Dan. 7:6]), and his feet were as the feet of a bear (carries the characteristics of the ancient Medo-Persian Empire, which is ferociousness), and his mouth as the mouth of a lion (portrays the finesse, grandeur, and pomp of the Babylonian Empire): and the dragon (Satan) gave him (the Antichrist) his power, and his seat, and great authority. (So, the Antichrist will have Satan helping him as well as this powerful fallen Angel, and no doubt a host of other fallen Angels and demon spirits.)

3 And I saw one of his heads as it were wounded to death (doesn't refer to the Antichrist, but rather one of the Empires of the past, which greatly persecuted Israel; it pertains to the Grecian Empire under Alexander the Great, and in reality speaks of the same fallen Angel helping Alexander; when Alexander died, this fallen Angel who helped him to conquer so speedily was locked away in the bottomless pit [Dan. 7:6]); and his deadly wound was healed (refers to the fact that this fallen Angel will be released out of the bottom-

less pit to aid and abet the Anti-christ [Rec., Chpt. 17]; it is doubt-ful the Antichrist will know or realize the source of his power, tak-ing all the credit unto himself): and all the world wondered after the beast. (This refers to the part of the world he has conquered, but with the entirety of the world defi-nitely paying him homage as he now seems to exude superhuman ability.)

4 And they worshipped the dragon which gave power unto the beast (refers to the fact that men worship power): and they wor-shipped the beast, saying, Who is like unto the beast? who is able to make war with him? (This pro-claims the means by which power is worshiped.)

5 And there was given unto him a mouth speaking great things and blasphemies (power-ful claims will be made, with the Name of Jesus being ridiculed); and power was given unto him to con-tinue forty and two months (the last three and one half years of the Great Tribulation; despite his pow-er, the Lord still controls the time frames, and in fact, all events).

6 And he opened his mouth in blasphemy against God, to blaspheme His Name (he will use all the power of print, Radio, Tele-vision, and computers to demean the God of the Bible; it will be a regimen of blasphemy on a world-wide basis, such as the world has never known before), and His Tab-ernacle (refers to Heaven), and them who dwell in Heaven. (Even though it refers to all Believers in Heaven, pointedly it refers to the 144,000 Jews who have been Rap-tured and are now in Heaven. The insults will be thick and fast, in effect ridiculing Heaven.)

7 And it was given unto him to make war with the Saints, and to overcome them (this will in-clude all Believers all over the world; as well, the Text implies by the word "overcome" that the Lord will allow such to happen): and power was given him over all kindreds, and tongues, and na-tions. (This doesn't include the entirety of the world, but rather the area over which he has con-trol, which is basically the area of the old Roman Empire.)

8 And all who dwell upon the earth shall worship him (first of all, we're speaking here of wor-ship, not dominion of nations; as well, the word "all" doesn't refer to every single human being, but rather people from all nations of the world, however many that num-ber might be), whose names are not written in the Book of Life (refers to the fact that Believers will not worship the Antichrist) of the Lamb slain from the foundation of the world. (This tells us that the only way one's name can be plac-

ed in the Book of Life is by acceptance of Jesus Christ as one's Lord and Saviour, and what He did for us at the Cross. Also, the phrase "from the foundation of the world" proclaims the fact that the Doctrine of "Jesus Christ and Him Crucified" is the foundation Doctrine of all Doctrines. In other words, every Doctrine from the Bible must be built on the foundation of the Cross of Christ, otherwise it is bogus.)

9 If any man have an ear, let him hear (refers to the ability to hear spiritually, and to hear properly in this manner; Jesus used the term many times [Mat. 11:15; 13:9, 43; Mk. 4:9; etc.]).

10 He who leads into captivity shall go into captivity (could be translated, "He who is destined to captivity will go into captivity"; it refers to the fact that those who will not hear the Word of the Lord, but rather the Word of the Antichrist, are guaranteed the worst type of spiritual bondage): he who kills with the sword must be killed with the sword. (This pertains to the nations of the world that will follow the Antichrist in his quest for world domination and power. The Second Coming of the Lord will bring swift and sure Judgment upon them.) Here is the patience and the faith of the Saints. (This refers basically to Israel, and that her Redemption is very near, which will take place at the Second Coming.)

11 And I beheld another beast coming up out of the earth (refers to the false prophet; by the use of the word "Earth," the Holy Spirit is telling us that this man is not from above, but rather from the masses of people); and he had two horns like a lamb (he has a lamblike appearance which is intended to deceive), and he spoke as a dragon (refers to the fact that he will be greatly anointed by the Devil; in a sense, the Antichrist will claim to be Christ, while the false prophet will try to fill the role of the Holy Spirit).

12 And he exercised all the power of the first beast before him (the power or authority exercised by the false prophet will come directly from Satan, and not through the Antichrist), and causes the earth and them which dwell therein to worship the first beast (the false prophet is promoting Earth and not Heaven, meaning he will promise Heaven here on Earth; the promises he makes will be tied to the "worship" given to the Antichrist), whose deadly wound was healed (doesn't refer to an assassination attempt or even to the Antichrist being killed and raised from the dead as some teach, but rather that the powerful fallen Angel, who helped bring the Grecian Empire into power under Alex

ander the Great and has been locked up for many, many centuries, has now been loosed and is helping the Antichrist; this "deadly wound being healed" speaks of his release from the bottomless pit [Dan. 7:6; Rev. 11:7; 13:2]).

13 And he *(the false prophet)* does great wonders *(signs)*, so that he makes fire come down from Heaven on the earth in the sight of men *(will be literal, which means it's not a trick; he will do this through the power of Satan)*,

14 And deceives them who dwell on the earth by *the means of* those miracles which he had power to do in the sight of the beast *(refers to the efforts of the false prophet to elevate the Antichrist; the word "beast" is used interchangeably between the Antichrist, the false prophet, and the fallen Angel; whatever they call themselves, the Holy Spirit refers to them as "beasts")*; saying to them who dwell on the earth, that they should make an image to the beast *(it is an image for the purpose of worship, and will probably be set up in the Temple built by the Jews in Jerusalem)*, which had the wound by a sword, and did live *(refers to the Antichrist somehow being wounded, a wound incidentally which should have taken his life; that he lives is construed as a miracle, with credit probably going to the false prophet; this is not* the "wound" of Verse 3; that was on "one of his heads," which had to do with an Empire [actually the Grecian Empire], and not an individual; this wound of Verse 14 pertains to an individual, in this case the Antichrist).

15 And he *(the false prophet)* had power to give life unto the image of the beast *(should have been translated, "For he had power to give spirit unto the image of the beast"; that is the actual word used in the Greek; to give life is solely the prerogative of the Godhead)*, that the image of the beast should both speak, and cause that as many as would not worship the image of the beast should be killed *(by the powers of darkness, this image will be able to somehow speak, and will as well pronounce the sentence of death upon all who will not worship the image of the beast; this will probably be in Jerusalem!)*.

16 And he caused all, both small and great, rich and poor, free and bond, to receive a mark in their right hand, or in their foreheads *("all" represents only those in his domain, not the entirety of the world; this domain will include virtually the entirety of the area of the old Roman Empire, which includes North Africa, the Middle East, and most of modern Europe; this will be a literal mark)*:

17 And that no man might buy or sell, save he who had the mark *(we are told in Verses 11-13 that the seduction of the Antichrist will be religious; now we are told in Verses 16 and 17 it will be economic)*, or the name of the beast, or the number of his name. *(The thought is that either the "name" of the beast or his "number" will be required as a brand or mark upon all.)*

18 Here is wisdom *(this is the wisdom of God)*. Let him who has understanding count the number of the beast *(the idea is that it is the number of a man, not of God, which means he will give account to Jehovah, Whom he has repeatedly blasphemed)*: for it is the number of a man; and his number is Six hundred threescore and six. *(It is the number of a man, not a kingdom, not a religion, not a dispensation, but a man. The number will be 666.)*

CHAPTER 14

THE LAMB

AND I looked, and, lo, a Lamb stood on the Mount Sion *(is the same portrayal as Revelation 5:6; Christ being referred to here as a "Lamb" proclaims the fact that our Redemption was accomplished at the Cross; in fact, the title "Lamb" as it refers to Christ is used some 28 times in the Book of Revela-* tion, all denoting the Atoning Work of Christ on the Cross; incidentally, this is the Heavenly "Mount Sion")*, and with Him an hundred forty and four thousand, having His Father's Name written in their foreheads. *(This is the number of Jews who came to Christ in the first half of the Great Tribulation. Some of the early Manuscripts, which are probably correct, read, "Having His Name [the Name of the Lamb] and the Father's Name upon their foreheads." Considering that this was inspired by the Holy Spirit, in this one Verse we have the Doctrine of the Trinity.)*

2 And I heard a voice from Heaven, as the voice of many waters, and as the voice of a great thunder *(proclaims the type of praise and worship being offered; it sounds like a waterfall mixed with thunder; is this typical of the modern Church? it ought to be!)*: and I heard the voice of harpers harping with their harps *(portrays the musical accompaniment)*:

3 And they sung as it were a new song before the Throne, and before the four Beasts, and the Elders *(this song is for the 144,000 only; it could very well be Psalm 149; also, the "new song" mentioned here is not so much that the song itself is new, but that what it says can only be carried out by those represented by the 144,000, which is Redeemed Israel)*: and no man

could learn that song but the hundred *and* forty *and* four thousand, which were redeemed from the earth. *(They were Redeemed by trusting Christ and what He did at the Cross, which is the only way anyone can be Redeemed.)*

4 These are they which were not defiled with women; for they are virgins. *(It refers to the 144,000 who did not corrupt themselves with idolatry. Faith in anything other than Christ and the Cross constitutes spiritual adultery, which is idolatry. In fact, millions in the modern Church are guilty of this sin, due to not understanding the Cross.)* These are they which follow the Lamb whithersoever He goes. *(By use of the word "Lamb," they took up their Cross exactly as Jesus demands of all [Lk. 9:23-24].)* These were redeemed from among men, *being* the Firstfruits unto God and to the Lamb. *(By use of the word "Firstfruits," this tells us that the entire nation of Israel is coming to Christ, which in fact will happen at the Second Coming.)*

5 And in their mouth was found no guile *(no hypocrisy)*: for they are without fault before the Throne of God. *(This pertains to "Justification by Faith," which trust in Christ Alone can bring about.)*

THE ANGELS

6 And I saw another Angel fly in the midst of Heaven *(this is a different Angel from the one described in Rev. 8:13)*, having the everlasting Gospel to preach unto them who dwell on the earth, and to every nation, and kindred, and tongue, and people *(refers to the same Gospel of Grace preached by Paul and the Apostles [Heb. 13:20]; as well, the implication is that this Angel will be observed by inhabitants on Earth, who will as well hear him Preach; it is the first recorded instance of an Angel preaching; no doubt, Television cameras will record his appearance and his Ministry, projecting him and his Message into all the world)*,

7 Saying with a loud voice *(denotes significance and urgency; it is, in fact, a Command to all the nations of the world)*, Fear God, and give Glory to Him *(is in contrast to the message being preached by the false prophet)*; for the hour of His Judgment is come *(regards the seven Angels with the seven vials of plagues shortly to be poured out on the Earth)*: and worship Him Who made Heaven, and earth, and the sea, and the fountains of waters. *(Evidently the Antichrist is claiming the power of creation. The Angel counters by announcing to the entire world exactly Who the Creator actually is.)*

8 And there followed another Angel, saying *(this Angel replaces the one who had been preaching*

the Everlasting Gospel, and makes another announcement), Babylon is fallen, is fallen, that great city (Babylon, as here addressed, will be rebuilt; she will fall at the conclusion of the Great Tribulation), because she made all nations drink of the wine of the wrath of her fornication. (As Babylon was the site of Earth's first organized rebellion against God [Gen. 11:1-9], it will as well be the site of the last great organized rebellion. As it began, so shall it end.)

9 And the third Angel followed them, saying with a loud voice (presents the last of this Heavenly trio), If any man worship the beast and his image, and receive his mark in his forehead, or in his hand (proclaims a warning of unprecedented proportion; this is a declaration that every single individual is responsible),

10 The same shall drink of the wine of the Wrath of God, which is poured out without mixture (there will be no Mercy in this Judgment) into the cup of His indignation (when the cup gets full, the Judgment of God will commence; this "cup" is not only full, but is running over with evil); and he shall be tormented with fire and brimstone (refers to everyone who receives the mark of the beast, and speaks of Eternal Hell) in the Presence of the Holy Angels, and in the Presence of the Lamb (refers

to the Great White Throne Judgment [20:11-15]):

11 And the smoke of their torment ascendeth up forever and ever (refers to the fact that a conscious existence will be forever): and they have no rest day nor night (refers to an unbroken continuance of torment), who worship the beast and his image, and whosoever receives the mark of his name. (All who take the mark of the beast in the coming Great Tribulation will, in essence, be blaspheming the Holy Spirit, for which there is no forgiveness [Mk. 3:29].)

12 Here is the patience of the Saints (a Message to those on Earth who have come to Christ during the Great Tribulation; by use of the word "patience," we are told that this persecution is soon to come to an end): here are they who keep the Commandments of God, and the Faith of Jesus. (The only way the Commandments of God can be kept is by the Believer placing His Faith in Christ and the Cross. The Holy Spirit will then grandly help such an individual.)

13 And I heard a voice from Heaven saying unto me, Write (according to the balance of this Verse, it is the Holy Spirit Who is speaking to John), Blessed are the dead which die in the Lord from henceforth (this refers to the Great Tribulation period, when many will die for their Testimony rather

than serve the Antichrist): Yes, says the Spirit, that they may rest from their labours *(is the exact opposite of the beast worshippers who have no rest)*; and their works do follow them. *(The translation should read, "Their works follow with them.")*

ARMAGEDDON

14 And I looked, and behold a white cloud, and upon the cloud *One* sat like unto the Son of Man *(presents, as is obvious, the Lord Jesus Christ; "white" denotes purity; "cloud" denotes glory; "Son of Man" has reference to the humanity of Christ, which always points to the Cross)*, having on His Head a golden crown *(presents the victor's crown)*, and in His Hand a sharp sickle *(represents the reaping that's going to be done at the Battle of Armageddon, as the balance of this Chapter portrays)*.

15 And another Angel came out of the Temple, crying with a loud voice to Him Who sat on the cloud *(the first Angel preached the "Everlasting Gospel"; the second predicted the fall of Babylon; the third proclaims a warning concerning the taking of the mark of the beast; the fourth announces the Battle of Armageddon, even though it will be some three years yet in coming)*, Thrust in your sickle, and reap: for the time is come

for you to reap; for the harvest of the earth is ripe *(speaks of the Battle of Armageddon, which is soon to take place, and portrays the fact that the evil of the Antichrist will have reached a crescendo)*.

16 And He Who sat on the cloud thrust in His sickle on the earth *(refers to Christ, Who will orchestrate this momentous event)*; and the earth was reaped *(that which takes place on Earth, at least as it regards momentous events, are first of all orchestrated in Heaven)*.

17 And another Angel came out of the Temple which is in Heaven *(presents the fifth Angel of this Chapter)*, he also having a sharp sickle *(portrays the fact that Angels will have a great part to play in the coming Battle of Armageddon)*.

18 And another Angel came out from the Altar *(is the pattern Altar after which the Brazen Altar on Earth was fashioned)*, which had power over fire *(refers to the fire on the Altar)*; and cried with a loud cry to Him Who had the sharp sickle, saying, Thrust in your sharp sickle, and gather the clusters of the vine of the earth; for her grapes are fully ripe. *(The repetitiveness of these statements proclaims the absolute significance of what is about to happen, and that its outcome will affect the Earth greatly.)*

19 And the Angel thrust in his sickle into the earth, and gath-

ered the vine of the earth *(he gathers "the vine of the Earth" into a place called in the Hebrew tongue, "Armageddon")*, and cast *it* into the great winepress of the Wrath of God *(refers to the assembled nations that will gather in the Valley of Jehoshaphat)*.

20 And the winepress was trodden without the city *(refers to the actual Battle itself pressing in on Jerusalem, with the intent of completely destroying the city and slaughtering the Jews)*, and blood came out of the winepress, even unto the horse bridles, by the space of a thousand *and* six hundred furlongs *(1600 furlongs is a distance of about 175 miles; the blood no doubt will be mixed with water, and in some places will be approximately six feet deep; it is possible that millions will be killed in this Battle)*.

CHAPTER 15

SEVEN VIALS

AND I saw another sign in Heaven, great and marvellous, seven Angels having the seven last plagues *(proclaims the concluding Judgments upon the territory of the Antichrist, which will be the worst)*; for in them is filled up the Wrath of God *(should have been translated, "anger of God")*.

2 And I saw as it were a sea of glass mingled with fire *(is that which is immediately before the Throne of God and mentioned in Revelation 4:6)*: and them who had gotten the victory over the beast, and over his image, and over his mark, *and* over the number of his name *(this group was murdered by the Antichrist)*, stand on the sea of glass, having the harps of God *(presents a picture of peace and tranquility)*.

3 And they sing the song of Moses the servant of God *(is the song given to us in Deuteronomy 32:1-43; it is recorded that Moses wrote this song and taught it to the people [Deut. 31:22])*, and the song of the Lamb *(this is the second song, and begins with the Crucifixion, which was absolutely necessary if man was to be redeemed, and closes with Jesus Christ as "King of kings, Lord of lords")*, saying, Great and marvellous *are* your works, Lord God Almighty *(refers to Christ; while all His works are "great and marvelous," what He did at the Cross presents itself as the greatest work of all)*; just and true *are* Your ways, Thou King of Saints. *(Christ is our King by virtue of what He did at the Cross, and our Faith in that Finished Work.)*

4 Who shall not fear You, O Lord, and glorify Your Name? *(This leaps ahead to the Millennial Reign. At that time, every human being on the face of the Earth will*

fear the Lord, and will glorify His Name as well.) for You only are Holy (speaks of the origination of Holiness, and that this Holiness can be given to Believers by virtue of what Christ did at the Cross): for all nations shall come and worship before You (refers to the Millennial Reign); for Your Judgments are made manifest (refers to the fact that the Judgment of God will be poured out upon the Antichrist during the Battle of Armageddon, where he will be defeated along with the entirety of his Army).

THE TEMPLE

5 And after that I looked (refers to the Vials about to be poured out), and, behold, the Temple of the Tabernacle of the Testimony in Heaven was opened (has reference to the Holy of Holies, where the Ark of the Covenant was kept; this is a witness both to the Holiness of God's Character and the Justice of His Government):

6 And the seven Angels came out of the Temple, having the seven plagues (constitutes the Vial Judgments), clothed in pure and white linen (indicates the perfect Righteousness of the acts that are to be performed on Earth), and having their breasts girded with golden girdles (presents the same attire as that of our Lord [Rev. 1:13], signi-

fying that what they are about to do pertains solely to the Work of Christ; in other words, Christ is in charge of all the Judgments).

7 And one of the four Beasts ("Living Ones" described in 4:7-8) gave unto the seven Angels seven golden Vials full of the Wrath of God (proclaims the fact, as stated, that these Judgments on the Earth will be the worst of all), Who lives forever and ever (proclaims the fact that God is Eternal).

8 And the Temple was filled with smoke from the Glory of God, and from His power (presents itself as very similar to the dedication of Solomon's Temple, in which the latter Temple was a replica of the one in Heaven); and no man was able to enter into the Temple, till the seven plagues of the seven Angels were fulfilled. (Constitutes the last few months of the Great Tribulation. The idea of no man being able to enter the Temple during this period of time seems to be that no one would be permitted to enter to make intercession, to turn away God's wrath, to divert Him from His purpose.)

CHAPTER 16

THE FIRST VIAL

AND I heard a great voice out of the Temple saying to the seven Angels (this is the "great"

Chapter of the Bible, the word occurring 11 times), Go your ways, and pour out the Vials of the Wrath of God upon the earth. *(This refers to the kingdom of the Antichrist, and not to the entirety of the Earth. That kingdom will be comprised of North Africa, the Middle East, and much of Europe [Dan. 7:7].)*

2 And the first *(Angel)* went, and poured out his Vial upon the earth *(constitutes the first plague)*; and there fell a noisome and grievous sore upon the men which had the mark of the beast, and *upon* them which worshipped his image. *(This proves that these plagues will be poured out only on the kingdom of the beast.)*

THE SECOND VIAL

3 And the second Angel poured out his Vial upon the sea *(the Mediterranean)*; and it became as the blood of a dead *man (pertains to the entire Mediterranean Sea; the blood of a dead man is almost black, and is coagulated)*: and every living soul died in the sea *(should have been translated "living creatures"; therefore every person on ships in the Mediterranean will die, along with all fish)*.

THE THIRD VIAL

4 And the third Angel poured out his Vial upon the rivers and fountains of waters *(speaks of all underground rivers as well; in other words, all the water throughout the kingdom of the beast is poisoned)*; and they became as blood. *(This is not to be explained away as being merely symbolic. This will actually happen.)*

5 And I heard the Angel of the waters say *(in the Book of Revelation, we find that a great variety of Ministries are assigned to Angels; this Angel is the "Angel of the waters")*, You are Righteous, O Lord *(proclaims the fact that what the Lord is doing is Righteous; in fact, everything He does is Righteous!)*, which are, and was, and shall be *(refers to the fact that God doesn't change)*, because you have judged thus *(proclaims the fact that God would be unrighteous if He didn't Judge accordingly)*.

6 For they have shed the blood of Saints and Prophets *(refers to those who will be murdered by the Antichrist during the time of the Great Tribulation because of their allegiance to the Lord Jesus Christ)*, and you have given them blood to drink; for they are worthy. *(This proclaims the fact that the beast worshipers are getting their just desserts.)*

7 And I heard another out of the Altar say *(should have been translated, "and I heard the Altar say," referring to those who have*

been murdered by the Antichrist and are asking for vengeance [6:9-11]), Even so, Lord God Almighty, True and Righteous are your Judgments. (This proclaims the fact that the prayers of those at the Altar who cry for vengeance are about to be answered.)

THE FOURTH VIAL

8 And the fourth Angel poured out his Vial upon the sun (refers to that which is totally beyond the scope of man); and power was given unto him to scorch men with fire. (Adds to the "boils," and as well exacerbates the problem of the water shortage. Evidently, the sun at that time will pour out more heat on the Earth than ever before. As well, it seems this plague will also be confined to the generalized area of the Antichrist. If that is the case, the Lord will have to stop the heat from effecting other parts of the globe.)

9 And men were scorched with great heat (as the next Verse states, this is done only in the geographical area of the Antichrist), and blasphemed the Name of God, which has power over these plagues (those in the geographical area of the Antichrist will know that God is doing this, but yet will continue to blaspheme His Name): and they repented not to give Him Glory. (This tells us some-thing about the hearts of men. It is seldom that miracles bring men to Repentance. Repentance must come from the heart and stem from Faith, which must ever have Christ and the Cross as its object.)

THE FIFTH VIAL

10 And the fifth Angel poured out his Vial upon the seat of the beast (specifies that its coverage area is "the seat of the beast"; the core of this could refer to Jerusalem, which is now the religious headquarters of the Antichrist); and his kingdom was full of darkness (these plagues are possible to Faith, though not to reason); and they gnawed their tongues for pain (refers to the "boils" described in Verse 2),

11 And blasphemed the God of Heaven because of their pains and their sores (they blamed God for their situation, even though He plainly told them not to take the mark of the beast [14:10]), and repented not of their deeds. (This presents the fact that the heart of man is so incurably corrupt that even the fiercest Judgments fail to affect its attitude, spirit, or conduct.)

THE SIXTH VIAL

12 And the sixth Angel poured out his Vial upon the great river

Euphrates; and the water thereof was dried up *(refers to preparations for the coming Battle of Armageddon)*, that the way of the kings of the east might be prepared *(actually says in the Greek, "the kings of the sun-rising"; this will no doubt include the armies of China and Japan, plus others which will join the Antichrist in the coming Battle of Armageddon).*

THREE UNCLEAN SPIRITS

13 And I saw three unclean spirits like frogs *(while John saw these demon spirits in his vision, they will be invisible to all others; these invisible creatures are functioning presently on Earth, even as they have since the Fall, and there is only one power that affects them, and that is the Name of Jesus [Mk. 16:17])* come out of the mouth of the dragon, and out of the mouth of the beast, and out of the mouth of the false prophet. *(This concerns the fact that this ungodly trio connives to secure the help of other nations regarding the coming battle of Armageddon.)*

14 For they are the spirits of devils *(refers to a flood of demon spirits working in conjunction with the three unclean spirits)*, working miracles *(which will probably be done through the false prophet and others; proclaims the fact that*

all miracles are not necessarily from God)*, which* go forth unto the kings of the earth and of the whole world, to gather them to the battle of that Great Day of God Almighty. *(As is obvious here, there are nations the Antichrist doesn't control, whose help he will seek. But while he thinks all of this is his plan, "God Almighty" is actually orchestrating all events. The Antichrist will think to destroy Israel, but God will in fact destroy him.)*

15 Behold, I come as a thief *(refers to the fact that the Antichrist has been so successful with his propaganda that very few in the world of that time will actually be expecting Christ to return)*. Blessed is he who watches, and keeps his garments *(points to those on Earth who worship and serve the Lamb, and that they must be constantly vigilant lest their loyalty to Him be diverted through Satanic deception [Mat. 24:43; I Thess. 5:2-4])*, lest he walk naked, and they see his shame. *(This refers to being naked to the Judgment of God, and suffering the consequences at the Second Coming, or even before that event.)*

16 And He gathered them together *(the pronoun "He" refers to God)* into a place called in the Hebrew tongue Armageddon. *(This refers to a literal place where a literal battle will be fought. It*

is the Mount of Megiddo overlooking the plain of Megiddo west of the Mount, and apparently including the Plain of Esdraelon, i.e., Valley of Megiddo.)

THE SEVENTH VIAL

17 And the seventh Angel poured out his Vial into the air *(this is the last Judgment; it signifies an earthquake such as the world has not previously known, which will effect not only particular cities, but also entire nations)*; and there came a great voice out of the Temple of Heaven, from the Throne, saying, It is done. *(The mighty Voice that shouted "Finished" from the Cross will now shout "Finished" from the Throne.)*

18 And there were voices, and thunders, and lightnings *(the Divine purpose in Grace was finished at the Cross; here the Divine purpose in wrath is finished; this Vial Judgment could well take place simultaneously with the Second Coming)*; and there was a great earthquake, such as was not since men were upon the earth, so mighty an earthquake, *and so* great *(presents the last cataclysmic upheaval)*.

19 And the great city was divided into three parts *(refers to Jerusalem)*, and the cities of the nations fell *(refers to the Middle East, and possibly parts of Europe as well)*: and great Babylon came in remembrance before God, to give unto her the cup of the wine of the fierceness of His wrath. *(This earthquake, the greatest of them all, will center on Babylon and will completely destroy the city that is scheduled to be rebuilt at this present time [2003]. The first organized rebellion against God began at Babylon, and it will end at Babylon [Gen. 11:1-9].)*

20 And every island fled away, and the mountains were not found *(pertains to the colossal magnitude of this earthquake)*.

21 And there fell upon men a great hail out of Heaven, *every stone about the weight of a talent (about 100 pounds; one can well imagine the damage that such would cause)*: and men blasphemed God because of the plague of the hail; for the plague thereof was exceeding great. *(Once again, those in the kingdom of the beast will know that this plague is from God, but instead of repenting, they will continue to blaspheme Him.)*

CHAPTER 17

THE GREAT WHORE

AND there came one of the seven Angels which had the seven Vials, and talked with me *(probably is the seventh Angel; however,* we actually have no way of truly knowing), saying unto me, Come hither; I will show unto you the judgment of the great whore who sits upon many waters (the "great whore" refers to all the religions of the world that ever have been, which are devised by men as a substitute for "Jesus Christ and Him Crucified"; God's Way is Christ and Him Crucified Alone; as well, the "many waters" are a symbol for multitudes of people [Vs. 15]):

2 With whom (the great whore, i.e., all type of religions) the kings of the earth (from the very beginning, most nations have been ruled by some type of religion) have committed fornication (all religions devised by men, and even the parts of Christianity that have been corrupted, are labeled by the Lord as "spiritual fornication" [Rom. 7:1-4]), and the inhabitants of the earth have been made drunk with the wine of her fornication (proclaims the addiction of religion; the doing of religion is the most powerful narcotic there is).

3 So he (the Angel) carried me (John) away in the spirit (a vision) into the wilderness (every religious effort that attempts to take the place of the Cross is a spiritual wilderness): and I saw a woman sit upon a scarlet coloured beast (the woman is organized religion; by that we mean any religion or form of religion claiming to have a way of Sal-vation or victory other than the Cross; the "scarlet color" indicates blood and pertains to great persecution), full of names of blasphemy (refers to this "woman" opposing the Plan of God in every capacity), having seven heads and ten horns. (This pertains to the scarlet colored beast, not the woman. The "seven heads" represent seven Empires that persecuted Israel in the past, with the last one yet future. They are "Egypt, Assyria, Babylon, Medo-Persia, Greece, and Rome." The "ten horns" represent ten nations that will arise out of the old Roman Empire territory and persecute Israel, and is yet future. These ten nations make up the seventh head. The Roman Empire, which made up the sixth head, was the last of the Empires that persecuted Israel before her destruction as a nation in A.D. 70. When the ten-horned kingdom arises, which it will shortly, it will persecute Israel as well.)

4 And the woman was arrayed in purple and scarlet colour (all of this pertains to Israel, but with a carry over into the Church Age; the "purple" represents the dominion of these religions over nations, with the "scarlet color" representing the persecution of Israel), and decked with gold and precious stones and pearls (these religions have always been very rich; a case in point is Islam, which controls some 60% of the oil reserves of the

world), having a golden cup in her hand *(all of these religions have an allurement, symbolized by the cup being golden)* full of abominations and filthiness of her fornication *(proclaims what this cup holds, despite its outward attractiveness):*

5 And upon her forehead *was* a name written *(the "forehead" symbolizes the fact that all these religions are devised by man, and not by God),* MYSTERY, BABYLON THE GREAT *(the word "mystery" separates spiritual Babylon from literal Babylon; it is "great in the eyes of the world, but not in the eyes of God"),* THE MOTHER OF HARLOTS AND ABOMINATIONS OF THE EARTH. *(This proclaims the actual content of this "golden cup," even though it looks wonderful on the outside. If it's not "Jesus Christ and Him Crucified," then it is labeled by the Lord as "harlots and abominations." Regrettably that includes much of modern Christianity as well.)*

6 And I saw the woman drunken with the blood of the Saints *(refers to these Empires and their false religions, which persecuted Israel during Old Testament times, actually up to the time of Christ),* and with the blood of the martyrs of Jesus *(points to the millions in the Church Age who gave their lives for the Cause of Christ; the Roman Empire began these* persecutions of Christians, and was followed by the Catholic Church): and when I saw her, I wondered with great admiration *(John is amazed at seeing all of this).*

7 And the Angel said unto me, Wherefore did you marvel? *(The Angel knew John would marvel at the scene that unfolded before his eyes, and would need an explanation.)* I will tell you the mystery of the woman, and of the beast that carries her, which has the seven heads and ten horns.

8 The beast who you saw was *(represents a fallen Angel who helped the leaders of these Empires of the past in their efforts to destroy Israel),* and is not *(was not active during the time of John)*; and shall ascend out of the bottomless pit *(this powerful, fallen Angel was confined to the bottomless pit about 2,300 years ago and remains there still, but will be released soon to help the Antichrist),* and go into perdition *(means that after his escapade of helping the Antichrist on Earth, he will be consigned to the Lake of Fire [20:10]):* and they who dwell on the earth shall wonder, whose names were not written in the Book of Life from the foundation of the world*(presents the fact that all the unsaved people on Earth during the time of the Great Tribulation will be startled and amazed as they observe the Antichrist, who will do things no other man has*

ever done; this will be because this fallen Angel is helping him, but of which he is not aware), when they behold the beast who was, and is not *(was not functioning during John's day)*, and yet is *(will be released out of the bottomless pit to help the Antichrist)*.

9 And here *is* the mind which has wisdom *(is the mind that knows and believes the Word of God)*. The seven heads are seven mountains, on which the woman sits *(represents these seven Empires which were controlled by false religions, i.e., "demon spirits")*.

10 And there are seven kings *(actually refers to the "seven heads," speaking of the leaders of these Empires, whomever they may have been)*: five are fallen *(five of the Empires were fallen during John's day; they are Egypt, Assyria, Babylon, Medo-Persia, and Greece)*, and one is *(refers to the Roman Empire, which was in existence during John's day, and could, therefore, be spoken of in the present tense)*, *and* the other is not yet come *(refers to the ten nation confederation symbolized by the ten horns, which in John's day had not yet come, and in fact has not come even yet)*; and when he comes, he must continue a short space. *(The "ten horns" will be the seventh head, and refers to ten nations that will arise shortly and persecute Israel, which will probably take place in the first half*

of the Great Tribulation, a time span of about three and one half years.)

11 And the beast *(fallen Angel)* that was, and is not, even he is the eighth *(this fallen Angel will help the Antichrist, and will head up the eighth Empire to persecute Israel)*, and is of the seven *(refers to the fact that he helped all the Empires of the past, with the exception of Rome, in their efforts to persecute Israel; but this fallen Angel gave the greatest help to Alexander the Great, who headed up the Grecian Empire; we know this because John, in his Vision, said, "and the beast which I saw was like unto a leopard," with that animal being one of the symbols of ancient Greece [Rev. 13:2; Dan. 7:6])*, and goes into perdition *(refers to the fact that irrespective of his power and plans, Eternal Hell will be the due of this Satanic Prince; the same goes for Satan, the Antichrist, the False Prophet, every fallen Angel, every demon spirit, and in fact all the unredeemed who have ever lived)*.

12 And the ten horns which you saw are ten kings *(Dan. 7:7)*, which have received no kingdom as yet *(refers to John's day)*; but receive power as kings one hour with the beast. *(These ten nations will come to power before the Antichrist, making up the seventh head. Then they will be taken over by the Antichrist, who is referred*

to by Daniel as the "little horn" [Dan. 7:8]. The "one hour" refers to the "short space" this confederation of the ten kings and the Antichrist will hold together. It will last for approximately three and one half years, and will be destroyed by the Second Coming of Christ [Dan. 2:34-35].)

13 These have one mind (this ten nation confederation, making up the seventh head, will all be in agreement respecting their joining with the Antichrist because they don't have the power to successfully oppose him), and shall give their power and strength unto the beast (refers to the Antichrist now coming to full power, and making up the eighth kingdom as described in Verse 11).

14 These shall make war with the Lamb (has to do with the Antichrist attacking Israel as it regards the Battle of Armageddon; Satan hates Israel for many varied reasons, but above all because of Jesus; so, to attack Israel is to attack the Lamb), and the Lamb shall overcome them (speaks of the Second Coming, but also speaks to the fact that Jesus is worthy to administer Judgment and Justice because of what He did at the Cross): for He is Lord of lords, and King of kings (proclaims the fact that this "Lamb" is "King" of all and "Lord" of all, and all because of the Cross): and they who are with Him are called,

and chosen, and faithful. (Every Saint of God who has ever lived, both Jews and Gentiles, will come back with Christ at the Second Coming.)

15 And he (the Angel) said unto me (John), The waters which you saw (refers back to Verse 1, and presents the word "waters" being used as a symbolism), where the whore sits (if it's not Jesus Christ and Him Crucified [I Cor. 1:23; 2:2], then God refers to it as the "Great Whore"), are peoples, and multitudes, and nations, and tongues. (This covers the entirety of the world, and tells us that billions have died and gone to hell as a result of following false religions.)

16 And the ten horns which you saw upon the beast (pertains to the ten nation confederation, which will make up the seventh head), these shall hate the whore (at least some, if not all, of the ten nation confederation will come out of the Middle East; Islam rules this part of the world, and it is a rule which has all but destroyed these countries; the implication is the religion of Islam will be put down by this confederacy), and shall make her desolate and naked, and shall eat her flesh, and burn her with fire. (This proclaims the fact that the ten nations under the Antichrist will institute and carry out a campaign of elimination as it regards the religion of Islam, and in fact

any other religions in his domain. All of these religions will be replaced by "beast worship.")

17 For God has put in their hearts to fulfil His Will (while the ten nations have their own agenda, God will use it to bring about His Will), and to agree, and give their kingdom unto the beast (the ten leaders of these nations will give their authority to the beast, i.e., "the Antichrist"), until the Words of God shall be fulfilled. (This will last "until" the Great Tribulation has ended, which will be at the Battle of Armageddon in which these nations will be totally destroyed [Dan. 2:34-35].)

18 And the woman which you saw is that great city (refers to rebuilt Babylon portrayed in Revelation, Chapter 18), which reigns over the kings of the earth. (Rebuilt Babylon will not only be one of the commercial centers of the world, but as well the religious center. The Antichrist will have replaced Islam and other religions with himself as the one being worshiped. It all began at Babylon, and it will all end there [Gen. 11:1-9; Rev. 18:10].)

CHAPTER 18

BABYLON

A ND after these things I saw another Angel come down from Heaven (this Angel seems to be different from the Angels of Rev. 17:1), having great power (he is greater than any one of the Seven); and the earth was lightened with His Glory (represents the fact that this Angel, who immediately precedes the Coming of Christ, must of necessity be one of, if not the greatest Angel in the Creation of God, due to the magnificence of that Coming and especially of the One Who is Coming; it could be either Gabriel or Michael).

2 And he cried mightily with a strong voice, saying, Babylon the great is fallen, is fallen (he is speaking of literal Babylon, the city, and as well of Mystery Babylon, the religion), and is become the habitation of devils, and the hold of every foul spirit, and a cage of every unclean and hateful bird (proclaims the city in the last of the last days as an infestation of demon spirits of every sort; in other words, it will be the capital of evil in all the world; vultures and such like are used at times in the Word of God as symbols for demon spirits [Mat. 13:32]).

3 For all nations have drunk of the wine of the wrath of her fornication, and the kings of the earth have committed fornication with her (pertains to the time of the Antichrist, but as well to all that Babylon has represented from

the very beginning of time, i.e., "false religions"), and the merchants of the earth are waxed rich through the abundance of her delicacies. (*From his headquarters in Babylon, the Antichrist will make it possible for many to get rich during the time of the Great Tribulation, therefore, ingratiating himself to many nations of the world.*)

4 And I heard another voice from Heaven (*presents that which is different from the Angel of the first Verse*), saying, Come out of her, My people, that you be not partakers of her sins (*the short phrase, "My people," refers to all Believers all over the world for all time, but the primary thrust is to Israel; in fact, the entire Book of Revelation, even though broadly addressing itself to the entirety of mankind, is primarily for Israel; this is the time of Jacob's trouble [Jer. 30:7]), and is designed to bring Israel back to God*), and that you receive not of her plagues. (*If Believers fail to come out from among the world, i.e., "the world's system," we will experience Judgment the same as unbelievers.*)

5 For her sins have reached unto Heaven (*carries the idea of rebellion against God, which is the ruin of mankind*), and God has remembered her iniquities. (*The only way God will forget sins and iniquities is by man placing his Faith and Trust in Christ and what Christ has done for us at the Cross [Heb. 8:6,12].*)

6 Reward her even as she rewarded you (*Saints are not called to render vengeance, but rather the statement is made that God will do such; the idea is that every act of hurt by the world or the apostate Church against God's people will be answered in kind; but in this case, it pertains more so to the Jews than anything else [Gen. 12:3]*), and double unto her double according to her works (*in a sense pertains to the fact that the future rebuilt city of Babylon will suffer the Judgment of the ages; the effort by President Bush to change the Government in Iraq, which in fact was the right thing to do, is a part of the process which will enable Babylon to be rebuilt*): in the cup which she has filled fill to her double. (*God's answer to man's rebellion will be the destruction of Babylon, and in a cataclysmic way.*)

7 How much she has glorified herself (*pertains to the characteristics of religion*), and lived deliciously (*refers to the earthly rewards of religion; at its base, one will always find "money"*), so much torment and sorrow give her (*refers to the fact that Judgment has been laid up for this city of Babylon, symbolic of man's system, which is a system without God; we reap what

we sow [Gal. 6:7]): for she said in her heart, I sit a queen, and am no widow, and shall see no sorrow. *(She calls herself "a queen," while the Lord refers to her as "the great whore," which pronounces her doom.)*

8 Therefore shall her plagues come in one day, death, and mourning, and famine *(points to the great earthquake of Rev. 16:18);* and she shall be utterly burned with fire: for strong is the Lord God Who judges her. *(The idea is that Satan, through the Antichrist, will boast of his great strength, so the Lord will, in effect, show the Antichrist and the world what strength really is.)*

BABYLON'S FALL

9 And the kings of the earth, who have committed fornication *(speaks of "spiritual adultery"; the worship of anything other than God and trust placed in anything except Christ and Him Crucified is "spiritual adultery")* and lived deliciously with her, shall bewail her, and lament for her *(Babylon, and we speak of the system, is their god, so they lament for their god),* when they shall see the smoke of her burning *(signals far more than the destruction of one city; it is the end of a system, a way, a false way, a terrible way, and will be carried out at the very conclusion of the Great Tribulation, which will usher in the Second Coming),*

10 Standing afar off for the fear of her torment *(the destruction of this city will no doubt be Televised all over the world; as well, much of the world will fear the same Judgment is coming upon them, knowing that God has done this),* saying, Alas, alas, that great city Babylon, that mighty city! *(Proclaims the lament, knowing that her destruction signals the end of Satan's rule and reign.)* for in one hour is your judgment come. *(Ancient Babylon gradually decayed, but this Babylon will be totally destroyed "in one hour," proving that this city must be rebuilt.)*

11 And the merchants of the earth shall weep and mourn over her; for no man buys their merchandise any more *(those who have sold their souls to this system will now weep and mourn over her destruction):*

12 The merchandise of gold, and silver, and precious stones, and of pearls, and fine linen, and purple, and silk, and scarlet, and all thyine wood, and all manner vessels of ivory, and all manner vessels of most precious wood, and of brass, and iron, and marble,

13 And cinnamon, and odours, and ointments, and frankincense, and wine, and oil, and fine flour, and wheat, and beasts, and sheep,

and horses, and chariots, and slaves, and souls of men. (*The last phrase probably refers to the drug business.*)

14 And the fruits that your soul lusted after are departed from you, and all things which were dainty and goodly are departed from you, and you shall find them no more at all (*this proclaims the fallacy of investing in a system of this world instead of the things of God [Mat. 6:19-21]*).

15 The merchants of these things, which were made rich by her, shall stand afar off for the fear of her torment, weeping and wailing (*the idea is that the system of this world, symbolized by rebuilt Babylon, is about to end, with another system taking its place, which will be the Kingdom of our Lord*),

16 And saying, Alas, alas, that great city, that was clothed in fine linen, and purple, and scarlet, and decked with gold, and precious stones, and pearls! (*This points to a conclusion regarding the word "great," which is not shared by the Lord.*)

17 For in one hour so great riches is come to nought (*should serve as a warning to all who put their trust in such things*). And every shipmaster, and all the company in ships, and sailors, and as many as trade by sea, stood afar off (*God took out in one hour what men took many years to build*),

18 And cried when they saw the smoke of her burning, saying, What *city is* like unto this great city! (*They cried over their financial loss, but seemed to show no concern for their lost souls.*)

19 And they cast dust on their heads, and cried, weeping and wailing, saying, Alas, alas, that great city, wherein were made rich all who had ships in the sea by reason of her costliness! for in one hour is she made desolate. (*The casting of dust on their heads does not point to Repentance, but rather to the sorrow of their financial loss.*)

20 Rejoice over her, *you* Heaven, and *you Holy* Apostles and Prophets; for God has avenged you on her. (*While men cry over the destruction of Babylon, the Lord tells Believers to "rejoice."*)

21 And a mighty Angel took up a stone like a great millstone, and cast *it* into the sea (*is a fulfillment of Mat. 18:6*), saying, Thus with violence shall that great city Babylon be thrown down, and shall be found no more at all (*proclaims the manner in which the era of evil will end; it will be with "violence," which in effect speaks more so of the Second Coming of Christ than anything else*).

22 And the voice of harpers, and musicians, and of pipers, and trumpeters, shall be heard no

more at all in you *(the merriment has ended)*; and no craftsman, of whatsoever craft *he be,* shall be found any more in you *(refers to the way business is normally done; a few get filthy rich on the backs of the helpless poor)*; and the sound of a millstone shall be heard no more at all in you *(refers to grinding poverty, which characterizes much of the world; it is not that poverty will characterize Babylon, but that much of its riches will come from ill-gotten gains)*;

23 And the light of a candle shall shine no more at all in you *(Satan's false light will shine no more)*; and the voice of the bridegroom and of the bride shall be heard no more at all in you *(refers to a false foundation, exactly as the false light; in fact everything about the system of the world is false, built on a lie)*: for your merchants were the great men of the earth; for by your sorceries were all nations deceived. *(Witchcraft and the drug business, referred to by "sorceries," constitute the foundation of this commercial enterprise, which will be totally destroyed.)*

24 And in her was found the blood of Prophets, and of Saints, and of all who were slain upon the earth. *(The literal city of Babylon is symbolic of the Babylonian spirit, which has opposed the Work of God from the begin-*

ning until now.)

CHAPTER 19

PRAISE

AND after these things *(pertains to specifically Chapter 18, but also the entire Book of Revelation in a broader sense,)* I heard a great voice of much people in Heaven *(proclaims "praise," which is the exact opposite of what is happening on Earth)*, saying, Alleluia; Salvation, and Glory, and Honour, and Power, unto the Lord our God *(the song here, and it is a song, does not begin with ascribing "Salvation" to God, as the English version suggests; it rather affirms the fact; "The Salvation is God's; it is the echo of the ancient utterance — 'Salvation belongs unto God'")*:

2 For true and righteous *are* His Judgments *(neither man nor spirit beings, in all honesty, can fault God for what He has done regarding the system of this world)*: for He has Judged the great whore *(pertains to every false way of Salvation, irrespective of what it might be; no matter how beautiful it might look outwardly, the Lord refers to it as the "great whore")*, which did corrupt the earth with her fornication *(this refers to all the religions of the world, and for all time; however, it also refers to the fact that if the Preacher is not*

preaching "Jesus Christ and Him Crucified" as the answer to man's dilemma, then in some manner he is preaching and projecting a type of "spiritual fornication" [Rom. 7:1-4]), and has avenged the blood of His servants at her hand. (Almost all of the persecution against the true Saints of God in this world, and for all time, has come from apostate religion. It started with Cain [Gen., Chpt. 4].)

3 And again they said, Alleluia. (This "praise of the Lord" is because of the destruction of the literal city of Babylon. The "Alleluia" in Verse 1 was proclaimed concerning the destruction of Mystery Babylon.) And her smoke rose up for ever and ever (proclaims the fact that her Judgment is Eternal).

4 And the four and twenty Elders and the four Beasts (Living Ones) fell down and worshipped God Who sat on the Throne (the 24 Elders represent all the Redeemed of all the ages; they are in fact 24 men; the "four Living Ones" represent the Creation of God, and how that Creation can now serve its full purpose as originally intended), saying, Amen; Alleluia. (This "Alleluia" signals the end of all evil, and the beginning of all Righteousness.)

5 And a voice came out of the Throne (is silent regarding the identity), saying, Praise our God, all you His servants, and you who fear Him, both small and great. (Every true Believer will praise the Lord, and should do so continually.)

6 And I heard as it were the voice of a great multitude (this "great multitude" consists of every single Believer who has ever lived, all the way from Abel to the last one saved in the Great Tribulation), and as the voice of many waters, and as the voice of mighty thunderings (this is praise that expresses itself, and not merely the thoughts of a silent heart), saying, Alleluia: for the Lord God omnipotent reigns. (This "Alleluia" pertains to the Lord reigning as King, and doing so forever. Satan does not reign. The Lord God Omnipotent Reigns, and He is "All-powerful.")

7 Let us be glad and rejoice (all the Redeemed are about to be joined in Holy Matrimony to the Lamb Who has saved them), and give honour to Him (God has made it possible for mankind to be Redeemed, and did so through the Sacrifice of His Son, the Lord Jesus Christ): for the marriage of the Lamb is come, and his wife has made herself ready. (This presents a scene that will take place in Heaven immediately before the Second Coming. The "wife" is the Redeemed of all ages.)

8 And to her was granted that she should be arrayed in fine

linen, clean and white: for the fine linen is the Righteousness of Saints. *(The "fine linen" is symbolic of "Righteousness," which was afforded by what Christ did at the Cross.)*

9 And he said unto me, Write, Blessed *are* they which are called unto the Marriage Supper of the Lamb. *(The man speaking to John says this. The word "Lamb" is used, signifying that all of this is made possible because of what Jesus did at the Cross.)* And he said unto me, These are the true sayings of God. *(This refers again to the fact that all of this is made possible by what Jesus did regarding His Finished Work.)*

10 And I fell at his feet to worship him. And he said unto me, See *you do it* not: I am your fellowservant, and of your Brethren *(as is obvious here, this is a man; he looks so much like Jesus, because of his glorified form, that John thought it was Jesus; in a sense, this tells us what all Saints will look like in the coming Resurrection)* who have the Testimony of Jesus *(presents the fact that the Ministry of the Holy Spirit is to testify to Christ and of Christ)*: worship God *(tells us in these two words that we are not to worship Angels, Saints, or the Virgin Mary)*: for the Testimony of Jesus is the Spirit of Prophecy. *(This "Testimony" is His Atoning Work, i.e.,*

what He did at the Cross. Every "Prophecy" of the Old Testament points in some way to Christ and what He did at the Cross. As well, every proclamation presently uttered must in some way point to the Cross of Christ.)

THE SECOND COMING

11 And I saw Heaven opened *(records the final Prophetic hour regarding the Second Coming, without a doubt the greatest moment in human history)*, and behold a white horse *(in effect, proclaims a war horse [Zech. 14:3])*; and He Who sat upon him *was* called Faithful and True *(faithful to His Promises and True to His Judgments; He contrasts with the false Messiah of Rev. 6:2, who was neither faithful nor true)*, and in Righteousness He does Judge and make war *(refers to the manner of His Second Coming)*.

12 His eyes *were* as a flame of fire *(represents Judgment)*, and on His Head *were* many crowns *(represents the fact that He will not be Lord of just one realm; He will be Lord of all realms)*; and He had a Name written, that no man knew, but He Himself *(not meaning that it is unknown, but rather it is definitely unknowable; it will remain unreachable to man, meaning that its depths can never be fully plumbed)*.

13 And He *was* clothed with a vesture dipped in Blood *(speaks of the Cross where He shed His Life's Blood, which gives Him the right to Judge the world)*: and His Name is called The Word of God. *(His revealed Name is the Word of God, for He revealed God in His Grace and Power to make Him known, so the Believer can say, "I know Him.")*

14 And the armies *which were* in Heaven followed Him upon white horses *(these "armies" are the Saints of God, in fact all the Saints who have ever lived, meaning we will be with Him at the Second Coming)*, clothed in fine linen, white and clean. *(Harks back to Verse 8. It is the Righteousness of the Saints, all made possible by the Cross.)*

ARMAGEDDON

15 And out of His mouth goes a sharp sword *(represents Christ functioning totally and completely in the realm of the Word of God)*, that with it He should smite the nations *(refers to all the nations that will join the Antichrist in his efforts to destroy Israel; it is the Battle of Armageddon)*: and He shall rule them with a rod of iron *(refers to the fact that the Lord of Glory will not allow or tolerate in any shape, form, or fashion that which "steals, kills, and destroys")*:

and He treads the winepress of the fierceness and wrath of Almighty God *(refers to the Battle of Armageddon)*.

16 And He has on *His* vesture and on His thigh a name written, KING OF KINGS, AND LORD OF LORDS *(proclaims the fact that there will be no doubt as to Who He actually is)*.

17 And I saw an Angel standing in the sun *(proclaims the fact that Faith believes what is written, even if the mind cannot comprehend what is written)*; and he cried with a loud voice, saying to all the fowls who fly in the midst of Heaven *(denotes, as is obvious, supremacy over the Creation)*, Come and gather yourselves together unto the supper of the Great God *(this is symbolic, but it is spoken in this way to proclaim the magnitude of that coming time [Ezek. 39:2, 11-12])*;

18 That you may eat the flesh of kings, and the flesh of captains, and the flesh of mighty men, and the flesh of horses, and of them who sit on them, and the flesh of all *men, both* free and bond, both small and great. *(This proclaims the fact that the Power of Almighty God doesn't blink at those on this Earth who consider themselves to be "great." The Judgment will be identical for all [Ezek. 39:18-20].)*

19 And I saw the beast *(John saw the Antichrist leading this migh-*

ty army; *this is the "man of sin"
mentioned by Paul in II Thessalonians, Chapter 2*), and the kings
of the earth, and their armies (*refers to all the Antichrist could get
to join him; it includes the "kings
of the East" of Rev. 16:12*), gathered together to make war against
Him Who sat on the horse, and
against His army (*refers to Christ
and the great army of Heaven which
is with Him; as stated, this is the
Battle of Armageddon [Ezek., Chpts.
38-39]*).

20 And the beast was taken,
and with him the false prophet
who wrought miracles before
him (*refers to both of them falling in the Battle of Armageddon*),
with which he deceived them who
had received the mark of the
beast, and them who worshipped
his image (*pertains to Satan's chief
weapon, which is deception*). These
both were cast alive into a Lake
of Fire burning with brimstone
(*thus is the destiny of the Antichrist and the False Prophet, and
all who follow them*).

21 And the remnant were slain
with the sword of Him Who sat
upon the horse, which *sword* proceeded out of His mouth (*the Lord
Jesus will speak the word in the
Battle of Armageddon, and whatever He speaks will take place*): and
all the fowls were filled with their
flesh. (*This proclaims the end of
this conflict. The Antichrist and*

*his hoards will announce to the
world what they are going to do
regarding Israel, but the end result will be buzzards gorging on
their flesh.*)

CHAPTER 20

SATAN

A ND I saw an Angel come down
from Heaven (*continues with
the idea that Angels are very prominent in the Plan and Work of God*),
having the key of the bottomless
pit (*speaks of the same place recorded in Rev. 9:1; however, there
the key is given to Satan, but this
Angel of Rev. 20:1 "has the key,"
implying he has had it all along;
more than likely, God allows this
Angel to give the key to Satan in
Rev. 9:1*) and a great chain in his
hand (*should be taken literally*).

2 And he laid hold on the
dragon, that old serpent, which
is the Devil, and Satan (*as a "dragon," he shows his power; as a "serpent," he shows his cunning; as
the "Devil," he is the accuser; and
as "Satan," he is the adversary*),
and bound him a thousand years
(*refers to being bound by the great
chain carried by the Angel*),

3 And cast him into the bottomless pit, and shut him up, and
set a seal upon him (*speaks of the
abyss being sealed to keep him
there*), that he should deceive the

nations no more, till the thousand years should be fulfilled: and after that he must be loosed a little season. *(At the end of the thousand-year period, Satan will be loosed out of his prison. He will make another attempt to deceive the nations, in which he will not succeed. We aren't told how long this "little season" will be.)*

THE MILLENNIUM

4 And I saw Thrones, and they sat upon them, and judgment was given unto them *(refers to the 24 Elders who represent the entire Plan of God, which pertains to the Redeemed of all ages; we aren't told who these men are)*: and I saw the souls of them who were beheaded for the witness of Jesus, and for the Word of God, and which had not worshipped the Beast, neither his image, neither had received his mark upon their foreheads, or in their hands *(categorizes the Tribulation Saints who gave their lives for the cause of Christ; the idea is that these will be included in the first Resurrection of Life, and will enjoy all its privileges)*; and they lived and reigned with Christ a thousand years. *(This is the Kingdom Age.)*

5 But the rest of the dead lived not again until the thousand years were finished. *(This pertains to all the unsaved, in fact all those* who lived and died since the dawn of time. The souls and spirits of these people are now in Hell [Lk. 16:19-31].) This is the First Resurrection *(proclaims the fact that these two Resurrections, the Resurrection of the Just and the Resurrection of the Unjust, will be separated by 1,000 years).*

6 Blessed and Holy is he who has part in the First Resurrection *(this is the Resurrection of Life, which will include every Saint of God who has ever lived from Abel to the last Tribulation Saint; all will be given glorified bodies)*: on such the second death has no power *(the "second death" is to be cast into the Lake of Fire, and to be there forever and forever [Rev. 21:8]; all who are washed in the Blood of the Lamb need not fear the second death)*, but they shall be Priests of God and of Christ, and shall reign with Him a thousand years. *(All Believers who have part in the First Resurrection will at the same time serve as mediators, so to speak, between the population of the world and God and Christ. The "thousand years" portrays the Kingdom Age, when Christ will reign supreme over the entire Earth.)*

SATAN

7 And when the thousand years are expired *(should have*

been translated, *"finished"*), **Satan shall be loosed out of his prison** *(is not meant to infer a mere arbitrary act on the part of God; He has a very valid reason for doing this),*

8 **And shall go out to deceive the nations which are in the four quarters of the Earth, Gog and Magog** *(the main reason the Lord allows Satan this latitude is, it seems, to rid the Earth of all who oppose Christ; George Williams says: "The Creation Sabbath witnessed the first seduction, and the Millennial Sabbath will witness the last"; the "Gog and Magog" spoken of by John is a Hebrew term expressive of multitude and magnitude; here it embraces all nations, "the four quarters of the Earth"),* **to gather them together to battle: the number of whom** *is* **as the sand of the sea** *(proclaims the fact that virtually all of the population at that particular time, which did not accept Christ during the Kingdom Age, will throw in their lot with Satan).*

9 **And they went up on the breadth of the earth, and compassed the camp of the Saints about, and the beloved city** *(pictures Satan coming against Jerusalem with his army, which will be the last attack against that city):* **and fire came down from God out of Heaven, and devoured them.** *(Stipulates that the Lord*

will make short work of this insurrection. In fact, very little information is given regarding this event, as is obvious.)

10 **And the Devil who deceived them was cast into the Lake of Fire and brimstone** *(marks the end of Satan regarding his influence in the world, and in fact in any part of the Creation of God),* **where the Beast and the False Prophet** *are* *(proclaims the fact that these two were placed in "the Lake of Fire and brimstone" some one thousand years earlier [Rev. 19:20]),* **and shall be tormented day and night forever and ever.** *(This signifies the eternity of this place. It is a matter of interest to note that Satan's first act is recorded in Genesis, Chapter 3 [the Third Chapter from the beginning], whereas his last act on a worldwide scale is mentioned in Revelation, Chapter 20 [the Third Chapter from the end].)*

GREAT WHITE THRONE JUDGMENT

11 **And I saw a Great White Throne** *(proclaims the final Judgment of the unredeemed, which will take place at the end of the Kingdom Age),* **and Him Who sat on it** *(proclaims none other than God; however, we must understand that it is the Person of the Godhead, the Lord Jesus Christ [Mat. 25:31]; He is the Saviour today; He will*

be the Judge tomorrow), from Whose face the Earth and the Heaven fled away; and there was found no place for them. (This means a New Heaven and New Earth are in the offing.)

12 And I saw the dead, small and great, stand before God (pertains to the second Resurrection, the Resurrection of Damnation [I Cor., Chpt. 15; I Thess. 4:13-18; Jn. 5:29]); and the Books were opened: and another Book was opened, which is the Book of Life: and the dead were Judged out of those things which were written in the Books, according to their works (proclaims the manner of Judgment).

13 And the sea gave up the dead which were in it; and death and hell delivered up the dead which were in them (points to the fact that every unredeemed person who has ever lived will face the Great White Throne Judgment; none will be exempted): and they were Judged every man according to their works (records the fact that this Judgment is not arbitrary, but is based on absolute Justice).

14 And death and Hell were cast into the Lake of Fire (combined, includes the wicked of all ages). This is the second death (Eternal separation from God and the Lake of Fire).

15 And whosoever was not found written in the Book of Life (refers to the record of all the Redeemed) was cast into the Lake of Fire. (This includes every single individual who isn't Redeemed, beginning with Adam and Eve. That is, if they didn't come back to God.)

CHAPTER 21

NEW HEAVEN AND NEW EARTH

AND I saw a New Heaven and a New Earth ("New" in the Greek is "kainos," and means "freshness with respect to age"; when it is finished, it will be new, as is obvious, but the idea is it will remain new and fresh forever and forever because there is no more sin): for the first Heaven and the first Earth were passed away (refers to the original Creation, which was marred by sin; "passed away" in the Greek is "parerchomai," and means "to pass from one condition to another"; it never means annihilation); and there was no more sea (refers to the giant oceans, such as the Pacific and the Atlantic; however, there will continue to be lakes, bodies of water, rivers, streams, etc.).

2 And I John saw the Holy City, New Jerusalem (presents a New City for this New Earth), coming down from God out of Heaven (in effect, God will change His headquarters from Heaven to Earth),

prepared as a bride adorned for her husband (*proclaims the Eternal Home of the Redeemed as a dwelling place*).

3 And I heard a great Voice out of Heaven saying (*according to the best manuscripts, the Voice now heard was heard "out of the Throne"*), Behold, the Tabernacle of God is with men, and He will dwell with them, and they shall be His people, and God Himself shall be with them, *and be their* God. (*Finally proclaims that which God intended from the beginning.*)

4 And God shall wipe away all tears from their eyes (*actually says in the Greek, "every teardrop," and refers to tears of sorrow*); and there shall be no more death, neither sorrow, nor crying, neither shall there be any more pain (*addresses sin and all its results*): for the former things are passed away (*refers to the entire effect of the Fall*).

5 And He Who sat upon the Throne said (*presents, for the second time in this Book, God Himself as the Speaker*), Behold, I make all things new (*refers to the fact of changing from one condition to another*). And He said unto me, Write: for these words are true and faithful. (*All said is "true," and God will be "faithful" to bring it all to pass as well.*)

6 And He said unto me, It is done. I am Alpha and Omega, the beginning and the end. (*The mighty declaration "Finished" heard at the morning of Creation, at Calvary, and now repeated here for the last time, closes all Prophecy. What He began, He now finishes.*) I will give unto him who is athirst of the fountain of the Water of Life freely. (*This statement doesn't pertain to the coming Perfect Age, for all then will have the Water of Life, but rather to the present. This "fountain of the Water of Life" is tied directly to the Cross of Calvary in that it is free to all who will believe [Jn. 3:16].*)

7 He who overcomes shall inherit all things (*the only way one can overcome is to place one's Faith exclusively in the Cross of Christ, which gives the Holy Spirit latitude to work in one's life, bringing about the Fruit of the Spirit*); and I will be his God, and he shall be My son. (*The overcomer is adopted into the Family of God and God treats him as a son, exactly as He does His Son, the Lord Jesus Christ.*)

8 But the fearful, and unbelieving, and the abominable, and murderers, and whoremongers, and sorcerers, and idolaters, and all liars (*all of this corresponds with the "works of the flesh," as outlined in Galatians 5:19-21*), shall have their part in the lake which burns with fire and brimstone: which is the second death

(proclaims the Eternal destiny of Christ-rejecters).

NEW JERUSALEM

9 And there came unto me one of the seven Angels which had the seven Vials full of the seven last plagues, and talked with me, saying, Come hither, I will show you the bride, the Lamb's wife. *(By use of the word "Lamb," we are taken back to the Cross, which has made all of this possible.)*

10 And he carried me away in the Spirit to a great and high mountain *(the "Spirit" referred to here is the Holy Spirit)*, and showed me that great city, the Holy Jerusalem, descending out of Heaven from God *(John saw it "descending," meaning that it is coming down to Earth; this will be after the Lord has made the "New Heavens and New Earth," in fact when God changes His headquarters from Heaven to Earth)*,

11 Having the Glory of God *(this is what makes the city what it is)*: and her light *was* like unto a stone most precious, even like a jasper stone, clear as crystal *(presents the radiance of God's Glory)*;

THE HOLY CITY

12 And had a wall great and high *(this wall is 216 feet high,*

counting 18 inches to the cubit; it is decorative only), and had twelve gates *(signifies three gates on the North, three on the South, three on the East, and three on the West; the gates on each side will be about 375 miles apart from each other)*, and at the gates twelve Angels *(proclaims the Glory of the City, and as well the Glory of God's Government)*, and names written thereon, which are *the names* of the Twelve Tribes of the Children of Israel *(proclaims the fact that "the Lamb's wife" is made up of every single Believer, whether on this side or the other side of the Cross; every gate will have the name of one of the Twelve Tribes; as well, this tells us how precious Israel is to the Heart of God)*:

13 On the east three gates *(will probably have the names Joseph, Benjamin, and Dan)*; on the north three gates *(will probably have the names Reuben, Judah, and Levi)*; on the south three gates *(will probably have the names Simeon, Issachar, and Zebulun)*; and on the west three gates *(will probably have the names Gad, Asher, and Naphtali)*.

14 And the wall of the city had twelve foundations *(the way of Salvation was shown to the Jews, hence the gates and the names of the Twelve Tribes inscribed on those gates; however, the foundation of Salvation was not really given un-*

til after the Cross, because it could not be given until after the Cross), and in them the names of the twelve Apostles of the Lamb. (On each foundation is the name of one of the Twelve Apostles. The foundation of the Salvation Message is based 100% on Christ and the Cross, hence the word "Lamb" being used.)

15 And he who talked with me (this is not the Angel who talked with John in Verse 9; the one now speaking identifies himself as a Prophet [Rev. 22:9]) had a golden reed to measure the city, and the gates thereof, and the wall thereof. (The measuring is done for a reason. It reveals the perfection, fulfillment, and completion of all God's purposes for His Redeemed people.)

MEASUREMENTS

16 And the city lies foursquare, and the length is as large as the breadth: and he measured the city with the reed, twelve thousand furlongs (translates into about 1,500 miles per side). The length and the breadth and the height of it are equal. (This presents astounding dimensions. It is about half the size of the United States, regarding length and breadth. If that is not enough to take one's breath away, it will also be 1,500 miles tall. The mind cannot comprehend this, but Faith believes.)

17 And he measured the wall thereof, an hundred and forty and four cubits (translates into about 216 feet, that is if we are using 18 inches to the cubit; as stated, the wall is strictly for ornamentation), according to the measure of a man, that is, of the Angel. (The designation of "Angel" is sometimes given to men, God, and the Creatures we refer to as Angels. This man, as Revelation 22:9 proclaims, is a Prophet.)

18 And the building of the wall of it was of jasper (presents a precious stone of several colors): and the city was pure gold, like unto clear glass (takes us beyond the imagination, beyond comprehension! but yet, this is literal).

19 And the foundations of the wall of the city were garnished with all manner of precious stones (describes beauty upon beauty). The first foundation was jasper; the second, sapphire; the third, a chalcedony; the fourth, an emerald;

20 The fifth, sardonyx; the sixth, sardius; the seventh, chrysolyte; the eighth, beryl; the ninth, a topaz; the tenth, a chrysoprasus; the eleventh, a jacinth; the twelfth, an amethyst. (The flooding of color in that incomparable City is beyond imagination. All of these stones named here are exquisite in color.)

21 And the twelve gates were twelve pearls (probably means

each gate, which is about 216 feet tall, is made of untold thousands of pearls); every several gate was of one pearl (seems to indicate that this particular gate, which is probably every third or fourth one, is made out of one gigantic pearl): and the street of the city *was* pure gold, as it were transparent glass *(refers to the fact that not only are all the buildings of "pure gold," [Rev. 21:18], but even the streets are made of pure gold).*

THE LIGHT

22 And I saw no Temple therein *(refers to a Temple such as in Old Testament times; actually there is a literal Temple in the New Jerusalem, but it will not serve the same purpose as the Temple on Earth [Rev. 3:12; 7:15; 11:19; 14:15, 17; 15:1-8; 16:1, 17]):* for the Lord God Almighty and the Lamb are the Temple of it. *(Before the Cross, a Temple on Earth was necessary because God could not dwell with man at that time, at least directly. Since the Cross, the Holy Spirit can dwell within man, because the terrible sin debt has been paid [Jn. 14:17; I Cor. 3:16].)*

23 And the city had no need of the sun, neither of the moon, to shine in it *(proclaims the fact that the Creator is not in need of His Creation; God has need of nothing, but all have need of God):* for the Glory of God did lighten it, and the Lamb is the Light thereof. *(The word "Lamb" signifies that all of this is made possible for Believers as a result of what Christ did at the Cross.)*

24 And the nations of them who are Saved shall walk in the light of it *(should have been translated, "And the nations shall walk by means of its light"; the words "of them who are Saved" are not actually in the best manuscripts; in fact, there will be no one in the world in that day who isn't Saved):* and the kings of the Earth do bring their glory and honour into it. *(This refers to leaders of nations, whatever they might be called at that particular time. All will give Glory to God, and all will Honor the Lord, and do so forever.)*

25 And the gates of it shall not be shut at all by day *(in fact, they will never be shut):* for there shall be no night there. *(This speaks of the City only, for outside the City there will be day and night eternally [Gen. 1:14-18; 8:22; Ps. 89:2-3; Jer. 31:35-36].)*

26 And they shall bring the glory and honour of the nations into it *(proclaims a Righteous commerce, and in every capacity).*

27 And there shall in no wise enter into it any thing that defiles, neither *whatsoever* works abomination, or *makes* a lie *(this means that all sin is forever ban-*

ished, and will never return): but they which are written in the Lamb's Book of Life *(refers to the Book of the Redeemed; the word "Lamb" refers to the fact that all are saved by placing their Faith and Trust in Christ and what He did for us at the Cross).*

CHAPTER 22

THE NEW JERUSALEM

A ND he showed me a pure river of Water of Life, clear as crystal *(symbolic of the Holy Spirit [Jn. 7:37-39]),* proceeding out of the Throne of God and of the Lamb. *(This "Water of Life" is made possible by what Jesus did at the Cross, hence the word "Lamb.")*

2 In the midst of the street of it *(proclaims the fact that this "pure River of Water of Life, clear as crystal" flows in the middle of this street of pure gold),* and on either side of the river, *was* there the Tree of Life *(the fruit of this Tree of Life must be eaten every month, and we're speaking of the part of the population who don't have Glorified bodies),* which bear twelve *manner* of fruits, *and* yielded her fruit every month *(we have the number "12" again, which signifies the Government of God as it relates to the manner of Eternal Life; there are twelve different types of fruit, but we aren't told*

what they are): and the leaves of the tree *were* for the healing of the nations. *(This pertains to the stopping of any type of sickness before it even begins. As stated, the population on Earth, which will never die and will not have Glorified Bodies, will need these things. These are they who were Saved during the Kingdom Age, and thereafter.)*

RULERS

3 And there shall be no more curse *(a curse was placed on the Earth at the Fall; it is being said here that there will be no more curse because there will be no more sin):* but the Throne of God and of the Lamb shall be in it *(the authority of rulership will be as great with God the Son as it is with God the Father; in fact, by the use of the word "Lamb," we are made to realize that all of this is made possible because of what Jesus did at the Cross);* and His servants shall serve Him *(the idea is that every Believer in the Perfect Age will so love the Lord and the Lamb that they will gladly "serve Him"):*

4 And they shall see His face *(shows intimate relationship);* and His Name *shall be* in their foreheads *(refers to ownership; we were bought "with a price," and that price was the Blood of the Lamb).*

5 And there shall be no night there *(this speaks of the New Jerusalem only, for night and day will be in the balance of the Earth forever)*; and they need no candle, neither light of the sun; for the Lord God gives them light *(presents the Source of this Light)*: and they shall reign forever and ever. *(It has never been known for servants to "reign" like kings; however, these servants shall!)*

ALPHA AND OMEGA

6 And he said unto me, These sayings *are* faithful and true *(proclaimed in this fashion simply because many of the statements made are so absolutely astounding they defy description)*: and the Lord God of the Holy Prophets sent his Angel to show unto His servants *(the Greek word "Aggelos" is translated "Angel" here, but should have been translated "Messenger"; we know this man is not an Angel, nor is he Christ)* the things which must shortly be done *(is not speaking of John's day, but rather the setting of the Vision is a time frame which has not come about even yet; it will take place immediately after the Rapture of the Church; from that point forward, which is what is meant here, we have "the things which must shortly be done," referring to the Great Tribulation)*.

7 Behold, I come quickly *(has more to do with the manner of His Coming than anything else; when He does come, which will be at the height of the Battle of Armageddon, it will be sudden, even immediate)*: blessed *is* he who keeps the sayings of the Prophecy of this Book. *(This is the only Book in the world that gives a preview of the future. Consequently, every Believer ought to study the Book of Revelation as much as they do any other Book in the entire Bible.)*

8 And I John saw these things, and heard *them (presents an impeccable witness)*. And when I had heard and seen, I fell down to worship before the feet of the Angel which showed me these things. *(John, it seems, will make the same mistake twice.)*

9 Then says he unto me, See *you do it* not *(presents the same words used by the previous man when John did the same thing [Rev. 19:10]*: for I am your fellowservant, and of your Brethren the Prophets, and of them which keep the sayings of this Book *(he evidently is one of the Great Prophets of the Old Testament, who eagerly awaits the fulfillment of these Prophecies as well)*: worship God *(includes both God the Father and God the Son)*.

10 And he said unto me, Seal not the sayings of the Prophecy of this Book *(refers to the fact that the things given in this Book are*

meant to be known and under- stood; they are not hidden truths): for the time is at hand (speaks of the immediate fulfillment of the events, which were to happen in consecutive order from John's day to eternity; it began with the Church Age, which is now almost over; the Great Tribulation will follow, con- cluding with the Second Coming, which will usher in the Kingdom Age, followed by the Perfect Age).

11 He who is unjust, let him be unjust still: and he which is filthy, let him be filthy still (pro- claims the fact that men are build- ing up their destiny by the actions and habits of their lives): and he who is Righteous, let him be Righteous still: and he who is Holy, let him be Holy still. (Records that which the Spirit of God can bring about in a person's life, ir- respective that they have once been "unjust and morally filthy." This is all done through the Cross, and only through the Cross.)

12 And, behold, I come quickly (is not meant to portray the "time" of His Coming, but rather the sud- denness of His Coming; the idea is that whatever we are at His Com- ing, whenever that Coming takes place, is what we will be forever); and My reward is with Me (the word "reward" can either be posi- tive or negative), to give every man according as his work shall be. (Our Faith, however placed, will produce a certain type of works. Only Faith in the Cross is accepted.)

13 I am Alpha and Omega (pre- sents the first letter in the Greek Alphabet [Alpha], and the last let- ter in the Greek Alphabet [Omega]; it is another way of saying, "the first and the last," which includes all in-between), the beginning and the end, the first and the last. (This doesn't mean Christ as God had a beginning, for He didn't. It is speaking of whatever is in ques- tion. Christ is the beginning of all things, and the end of all things.)

BLESSED

14 Blessed are they (presents the seventh and last Beatitude in the Book of Revelation) who do His Commandments (should have been translated, "who washed their robes in the Blood of the Lamb"; the Greek Text used for the King James Version of the Bible was the Textus Receptus; it is the Text that Erasmus, the famous Renaissance scholar, published in A.D. 1516; it was the first New Testament Greek Text ever published; since 1516, the world of scholarship and Archaeology has discovered thou- sands of earlier Greek Texts; by comparing these thousands of Manuscripts, the scholars can eas- ily ascertain the original Text the Apostle wrote), that they may have the right to the Tree of Life (pro-

claims the fact that this "right" can be attained in only one way, "by washing our robes in the Blood of the Lamb"), and may enter in through the gates into the city (proclaims the Eternal abode of the Redeemed; we shall enter that city by means of His Grace, which is the Cross of Christ).

15 For without are dogs (homosexuals), and sorcerers (witchcraft), and whoremongers (pertains to all type of immorality), and murderers (pertains not only to killing in cold blood, but as well murdering one's reputation through gossip), and idolaters (pertains to placing anything above God, or on a par with God; religion is the greatest idolatry of all), and whosoever loves and makes a lie (refers to anything that's untrue).

16 I Jesus (this short phrase is found only here in Scripture, emphasizing its importance; Christ is closing out the Book of Revelation here, but most of all, He is testifying to the Truth of what has been given) have sent My Angel to testify unto you these things in the Churches. (The word "Angel" here means "Messenger," and actually refers to the Pastors of the respective Churches in question, and actually for all time.) I am the Root and the Offspring of David (is meant to project the Incarnation of Christ), and the Bright and Morning Star. (The "Morning Star"

speaks of a new beginning that any person can have, irrespective of their present situation, if they will only look to Christ.)

INVITATION

17 And the Spirit and the Bride say, Come. (This presents the cry of the Holy Spirit to a hurting, lost, and dying world. What the Holy Spirit says should also be said by all Believers.) And let him who hears say, Come. (It means if one can "hear," then one can "come.") And let him who is athirst come (speaks of spiritual thirst, the cry for God in the soul of man). And whosoever will, let him take the Water of Life freely (opens the door to every single individual in the world; Jesus died for all and, therefore, all can be saved, if they will only come).

18 For I testify unto every man who hears the words of the Prophecy of this Book (proclaims the inerrancy of the Book of Revelation; in other words, John testifies that it is the Word of God), If any man shall add unto these things, God shall add unto him the plagues that are written in this Book (proclaims the fact that changing the meaning of the Prophecies in this Book can bring upon one the Judgment of God):

19 And if any man shall take away from the words of the Book

of this Prophecy *(the idea is that the "words of the Prophecy" should not be changed in any manner, whether by addition or deletion),* God shall take away his part out of the Book of Life, and out of the Holy City, and *from* the things which are written in this Book. *(This is a warning given to Believers, and should be understood accordingly!)*

20 He which testifies these things *(proclaims the fact that the Office of the Messiah as Saviour is repeated again and again throughout the Prophecy; He is the Lamb Who was slain, and His Blood washes from sin, and Alone makes fit for entrance into the Eternal City)* says, Surely I come quickly *(leaves the Promise to come as the last Message from the Lord Jesus to the Believers' hearts; and on this sweet note, the* Prophecy ends*)*. Amen. Even so, come, Lord Jesus *(proclaims the answer of the True Church to the Promise of Christ regarding the Second Coming).*

21 The Grace of our Lord Jesus Christ *(presents John using the very words of Paul in his closing benediction; Christ is the Source, but the Cross is the means)* be with you all. Amen. *(This proclaims the fact that it is the same Message for all, and is available to all. The word "Amen" closes out the Book of Revelation, and in fact the entire Cannon of Scripture, which took about 1,600 years to bring forth in its entirety. It gives acclaim to the Finished Work of Christ. It is done. And thereby all of Heaven, along with all the Redeemed, must say: "Amen.")*

NOTES

NOTES

NOTES

NOTES

NOTES

NOTES

NOTES

NOTES

PRACTICAL SUGGESTIONS
FOR THE COUNSELOR

---

1. You need to cultivate God's love and concern for those in need.

2. You need to keep your heart in an attitude of prayer that the Holy Spirit may speak through you.

3. As you listen to a person talk, seek to understand the reason behind his problem.

4. People sometimes tend to hide the real problem and cover it up a bit. You should ask questions so that you can understand the person and his problem and be able to counsel him better.

5. Help him to clarify his problem. As he begins to understand the problem, he may also begin to see the solution.

6. Use the Bible as you are able. Keep your advice to a minimum.

7. Listen. Try not to talk too much. The person must ultimately find his own solution, but you can help that person to receive right insight into his problem.

8. Do not be controversial. Controversy often results in tension, and as you speak against what the troubled person is saying, he will probably try harder to defend his position.

9. The person needs to feel that you are sincerely concerned. People are sometimes told to accept their problems, but they really need to be able to share their burdens with someone who cares.

10. As the person is seeking help, often the emotional help and sense of support from a good attitude of sympathy, understanding, and love are more valuable than the answers or advice.

11. Lead the person to see and understand that he is not alone in his problem. He can be reminded that others have faced the same problem and have overcome.

"There hath no temptation taken you but such as is common to man: but God is faithful, who will not suffer you to be tempted above that ye are able; but will with the temptation also make a way to escape, that you may be able to bear it." (I Cor. 10:13)

12. Regarding all the problems which we have listed, plus all we haven't listed, you are to make the individual understand that the Cross of Christ is his only answer. What makes the Cross so wonderful is, it addresses every single problem. If the person needs Salvation, of course they are to be first of all led to Christ. The section on "How to Be Saved" will help you with this.

If you're dealing with a Christian who needs help in some particular area, irrespective as to what that need is, as already stated, his answer is the Cross of Christ, and the Cross alone. You are to point this out to him, using the short article on the Cross as your guide. It was at the Cross where every single victory was won, and our faith in that Finished Work guarantees to us all that Jesus there did.

SCRIPTURES FOR THE ALCOHOLIC

"Wait on the LORD: be of good courage, and he shall strengthen thine heart." (Ps. 27:14)

"This poor man cried, and the LORD heard him, and saved him out of all his troubles." (Ps. 34:6)

"I am poor and needy; yet the LORD thinketh upon me: thou art my help and my deliverer." (Ps. 40:17)

"God is our refuge and strength, a very present help in trouble."
(Ps. 46:1)

"He will regard the prayer of the destitute, and not despise their prayer."
(Ps. 102:17)

"Wine is a mocker, strong drink is raging: and whosoever is deceived thereby is not wise."
(Prov. 20:1)

"Who hath woe? who hath sorrow? who hath contentions? who hath babbling? who hath wounds without cause? who hath redness of eyes? They that tarry long at the wine; they that go to seek mixed wine. Look not thou upon the wine when it is red, when it giveth his color in the cup, when it moveth itself aright. At the last it biteth like a serpent, and stingeth like an adder."
(Prov. 23:29-32)

"It is not for kings, O Lemuel, it is not for kings to drink wine; nor for princes strong drink: Lest they drink, and forget the law, and pervert the judgment of any of the afflicted."
(Prov. 31:4-5)

"Woe unto them that rise up early in the morning, that they may follow strong drink; that continue until night, till wine inflame them!"
(Isa. 5:11)

"Thou wilt keep him in perfect peace, whose mind is stayed on thee."
(Isa. 26:3)

"They that wait upon the LORD shall renew their strength."
(Isa. 40:31)

"Fear thou not; for I am with thee: be not dismayed; for I am thy God: I will strengthen thee; yea, I will help thee; yea, I will uphold thee with the right hand of my righteousness."
(Isa. 41:10)

"Woe unto him that giveth his neighbor drink, that puttest thy bottle to him, and makest him drunken also, that thou mayest look on their nakedness!"
(Hab. 2:15)

"And all things, whatsoever ye shall ask in prayer, believing, ye shall receive."
(Mat. 21:22)

"It is good neither to eat flesh, nor to drink wine, nor any thing whereby thy brother stumbleth, or is offended, or is made weak."
(Rom. 14:21)

"And be not drunk with wine, wherein is excess; but be filled with the Spirit."
(Eph. 5:18)

"Forgetting those things which are behind, and reaching forth unto those things which are before, I press toward the mark for the prize of the high calling of God in Christ Jesus."
(Phil. 3:13-14)

SCRIPTURES ON BACKSLIDING

"Create in me a clean heart, O God; and renew a right spirit within me. Restore unto me the joy of thy salvation."(Ps. 51:10, 12) (Suggest to the backslider that he read this entire Psalm.)

"Come now, and let us reason together, saith the LORD: though your sins be as scarlet, they shall be as white as snow; though they be red like crimson, they shall be as wool."
(Isa. 1:18)

"Let him return unto the LORD, and he will have mercy upon him; and to our God, for he will abundantly pardon."
(Isa. 55:7)

"I will heal their backsliding, I will love them freely." (Hos. 14:4)

"Forgetting those things which are behind, and reaching forth unto those things which are before, I press toward the mark for the prize of the high calling of God in Christ Jesus."
(Phil. 3:13-14)

"Wherefore he is able also to save them to the uttermost that come unto God by him, seeing he ever liveth to make intercession for them."
(Heb. 7:25)

"If we confess our sins, he is faithful and just to forgive us our sins, and to cleanse us from all unrighteousness."
(I Jn. 1:9)

SCRIPTURES ON DISCOURAGEMENT

"As I was with Moses, so will be with thee: I will not fail thee, nor forsake thee. Be strong and of a good courage." (Josh. 1:5-6)

"Why art thou cast down, O my soul? and why art thou disquieted within me? hope thou in God." (Ps. 42:11)

"I called upon the LORD in distress: the LORD answered me, and set me in a large place." (Ps. 118:5)

"For we walk by faith, not by sight." (II Cor. 5:7)

"[Cast] down imaginations, and every high thing that exalteth itself against the knowledge of God, and [bring] into captivity every thought to the obedience of Christ." (II Cor. 10:5)

"Be careful for nothing; but in every thing by prayer and supplication with thanksgiving let your requests be made known unto God. And the peace of God, which passeth all understanding, shall keep your hearts and minds through Christ Jesus." (Phil. 4:6-7)

"Let us hold fast the profession of our faith without wavering; (for he is faithful that promised)." (Heb. 10:23)

"Cast not away therefore your confidence, which hath great recompence of reward. For ye have need of patience, that, after ye have done the will of God, ye might receive the promise." (Heb. 10:35-36)

"[Cast] all your care upon him; for he careth for you." (I Pet. 5:7)

SCRIPTURES ON FEAR

Overcome Fear By Seeking God

"I sought the Lord, and he heard me, and delivered me from all my fears." (Ps. 34:4)

"Whoso hearkeneth unto me shall dwell safely, and shall be quiet from fear of evil." (Prov. 1:33)

Overcome Fear With Positive Faith

"Have not I commanded thee? Be strong and of a good courage; be not afraid, neither be thou dismayed: for the Lord thy God is with thee whithersoever thou goest." (Josh. 1:9)

"Yea, though I walk through the valley of the shadow of death, I will fear no evil: for thou art with me; thy rod and thy staff they comfort me." (Ps. 23:4)

"Strengthen ye the weak hands, and confirm the feeble knees. Say to them that are of a fearful heart, Be strong, fear not: behold, your God will come with vengeance, even God with a recompence; he will come and save you." (Isa. 35:3-4)

Fear Is Not From God

"For God hath not given us the spirit of fear; but of power, and of love, and of a sound mind." (II Tim. 1:7)

Fear Brings Bondage

"The thing which I greatly feared is come upon me, and that which I was afraid of is come unto me." (Job 3:25)

"The fear of man bringeth a snare: but whoso putteth his trust in the Lord shall be safe." (Prov. 29:25)

God Delivers Us From Fear

"The Lord is my light and my salvation; whom shall I fear? the Lord is the strength of my life; of whom shall I be afraid?" (Ps. 27:1)

"He shall cover thee with his feathers, and under his wings shalt thou trust: his truth shall be thy shield and buckler. Thou shalt not be afraid for the terror by night; nor for the arrow that flieth by day." (Ps. 91:4-5)

"Fear not, little flock; for it is your Father's good pleasure to give you the kingdom." (Lk. 12:32)

We Are Commanded Not To Fear

"Fear thou not; for I am with thee: be not dismayed; for I am thy God: I will strengthen thee; yea, I will help thee; yea, I will uphold thee with the right hand of my righteousness." (Isa. 41:10)

"Hearken unto me, ye that know righteousness, the people in whose heart is my law; fear ye not the reproach of men, neither be ye afraid of their revilings." (Isa. 51:7)

SCRIPTURES CONCERNING FINANCIAL MATTERS

Do Not Ignore Instructions

"Poverty and shame shall be to him that refuseth instruction: but he that regardeth reproof shall be honored." (Prov. 13:18)

Be Industrious

"The sluggard will not plow by reason of the cold; therefore shall he beg in harvest, and have nothing." (Prov. 20:4)

"Love not sleep, lest thou come to poverty; open thine eyes, and thou shalt be satisfied with bread." (Prov. 20:13)

God Will Provide

"I have been young, and now am old; yet have I not seen the righteous forsaken, nor his seed begging bread."   (Ps. 37:25)

"My God shall supply all your need according to his riches in glory by Christ Jesus."   (Phil. 4:19)

Seek God And He Will Bless You

"Wait on the LORD, and keep his way, and he shall exalt thee to inherit the land."   (Ps. 37:34)

"Seek ye first the kingdom of God, and his righteousness; and all these things shall be added unto you."   (Mat. 6:33)

God Wants To Prosper Us

"This book of the law shall not depart out of thy mouth; but thou shalt meditate therein day and night, that thou mayest observe to do according to all that is written therein: for then thou shalt make thy way prosperous, and then thou shalt have good success."

    (Josh. 1:8)

"Believe in the LORD your God, so shall ye be established; believe his prophets, so shall ye prosper."   (II Chron. 20:20)

"If they obey and serve him, they shall spend their days in prosperity, and their years in pleasures."   (Job 36:11)

"He shall be like a tree planted by the rivers of water, that bringeth forth his fruit in his season; his leaf also shall not wither; and whatsoever he doeth shall prosper."   (Ps. 1:3)

"Let them shout for joy, and be glad, that favour my righteous cause: yea, let them say continually, Let the LORD be magnified, which hath pleasure in the prosperity of his servant."

    (Ps. 35:27)

"I, even I, have spoken; yea, I have called him: have brought him, and he shall make his way prosperous."   (Isa. 48:15)

"The thief cometh not, but for to steal, and to kill, and to destroy: I am come that they might have life, and that they might have it more abundantly." (Jn. 10:10)

"Beloved, I wish above all things that thou mayest prosper and be in health, even as thy soul prospereth." (III Jn. 1:2)

Give And It Shall Be Given Unto You

"There is that scattereth, and yet increaseth; and there is that withholdeth more than is meet, but it tendeth to poverty." (Prov. 11:24)

"He that hath pity upon the poor lendeth unto the Lord; and that which he hath given will he pay him again." (Prov. 19:17)

"He that giveth unto the poor shall not lack: but he that hideth his eyes shall have many a curse." (Prov. 28:27)

"Cast thy bread upon the waters: for thou shalt find it after many days." (Eccl. 11:1)

"Give, and it shall be given unto you; good measure, pressed down, and shaken together, and running over, shall men give into your bosom. For with the same measure that ye mete withal it shall be measured to you again." (Lk. 6:38)

"I have showed you all things, how that so laboring ye ought to support the weak, and to remember the words of the Lord Jesus, how he said, It is more blessed to give than to receive." (Acts 20:35)

"But this I say, He which soweth sparingly shall reap also sparingly; and he which soweth bountifully shall reap also bountifully. Every man according as he purposeth in his heart, so let him give; not grudgingly, or of necessity: for God loveth a cheerful giver. And God is able to make all grace abound toward you; that ye, always having all sufficiency in all things, may abound to every good work." (II Cor. 9:6-8)

SCRIPTURES ON FORGIVENESS

"If thou bring thy gift to the altar, and there rememberest that thy brother hath ought against thee; Leave there thy gift before the altar, and go thy way; first be reconciled to thy brother, and then come and offer thy gift. (Mat. 5:23-24)

"If ye forgive men their trespasses, your heavenly Father will also forgive you: But if ye forgive not men their trespasses, neither will your Father forgive your trespasses." (Mat. 6:14-15)

"Then came Peter to him, and said, Lord, how oft shall my brother sin against me, and I forgive him? till seven times? Jesus saith unto him, I say not unto thee, Until seven times: but, Until seventy times seven." (Mat. 18:21-22)

"Be ye kind one to another, tenderhearted, forgiving one another, even as God for Christ's sake hath forgiven you." (Eph. 4:32)

"You, being dead in your sins and the uncircumcision of your flesh, hath he quickened together with him, having forgiven you all trespasses." (Col. 2:13)

"Put on therefore, as the elect of God, holy and beloved, bowels of mercies, kindness, humbleness of mind, meekness, longsuffering; Forbearing one another, and forgiving one another, if any man have a quarrel against any: even as Christ forgave you, so also do ye." (Col. 3:12-13)

"This is the covenant that I will make with them after those days, saith the Lord, I will put my laws into their hearts, and in their minds will I write them; And their sins and iniquities will I remember no more." (Heb. 10:16-17)

SCRIPTURES ON GRIEF

"Be strong and of a good courage; be not afraid, neither be thou dismayed: for the LORD thy God is with thee whithersoever thou goest." (Josh. 1:9)

"Neither be ye sorry; for the joy of the LORD is your strength." (Neh. 8:10)

"Be glad in the LORD, and rejoice, ye righteous: and shout for joy, all ye that are upright in heart." (Ps. 32:11)

"The righteous is taken away from the evil to come." (Isa. 57:1)

"As one whom his mother comforteth, so will I comfort you." (Isa. 66:13)

"Let thy widows trust in me." (Jer. 49:11)

"Lo, I am with you always, even unto the end of the world." (Mat. 28:20)

"Let not your heart be troubled: ye believe in God, believe also in me. In my Father's house are many mansions: if it were not so, I would have told you. I go to prepare a place for you. And if I go and prepare a place for you, I will come again, and receive you unto myself; that where I am, there ye may be also." (Jn 14:1-3)

"Willing rather to be absent from the body, and to be present with the Lord." (II Cor. 5:8)

"As sorrowful, yet always rejoicing." (II Cor. 6:10)

"For to me to live is Christ, and to die is gain." (Phil. 1:21)

"Rejoice in the Lord always: and again I say, Rejoice." (Phil. 4:4)

"I would not have you to be ignorant, brethren, concerning them which are asleep, that ye sorrow not, even as others which have no hope. For if we believe that Jesus died and rose again, even so them also which sleep in Jesus will God bring with him. We which are alive and remain unto the coming of the Lord shall not prevent them which are asleep. For the Lord himself shall descend from heaven with a shout, with the voice of the archangel, and with the trump of God: and the dead in Christ shall rise first: Then we which are alive and remain shall be caught up together with them in the clouds, to meet the Lord in the air: and so shall we ever be with the Lord. Wherefore comfort one another with these words."

(I Thess. 4:13-18)

SCRIPTURES ON GUIDANCE

"The secret of the LORD is with them that fear him; and he will show them his covenant." (Ps. 25:14)

"Teach me thy way, O LORD, and lead me in a plain path, because of mine enemies." (Ps. 27:11)

"I will instruct thee and teach thee in the way which thou shalt go: I will guide thee with mine eye." (Ps. 32:8)

"Commit thy way unto the LORD; trust also in him; and he shall bring it to pass." (Ps. 37:5)

"The steps of a good man are ordered by the LORD." (Ps. 37:23)

"He led them on safely, so that they feared not." (Ps. 78:53)

"Trust in the LORD with all thine heart; and lean not unto thine own understanding. In all thy ways acknowledge him, and he shall direct thy paths." (Prov. 3:5-6)

"I will lead them in paths that they have not known: I will make darkness light before them, and crooked things straight."

(Isa. 42:16)

"Howbeit when he, the Spirit of truth, is come, he will guide you into all truth: for he shall not speak of himself; but whatsoever he shall hear, that shall he speak: and he will shew you things to come. He shall glorify me: for he shall receive of mine, and shall shew it unto you. All things that the Father hath are mine: therefore said I, that he shall take care of mine, and shall shew it unto you."

(Jn. 16:13-15)

SCRIPTURES ON GUILT

"As far as the east is from the west, so far hath he removed our transgressions from us." (Ps. 103:12)

"Come now, and let us reason together, saith the LORD: though your sins be as scarlet, they shall be as white as snow; though they be red like crimson, they shall be as wool." (Isa. 1:18)

"I will forgive their iniquity, and I will remember their sin no more." (Jer. 31:34)

"He that heareth my word, and believeth on him that sent me, hath everlasting life, and shall not come into condemnation; but is passed from death unto life." (Jn. 5:24)

"There is therefore now no condemnation to them which are in Christ Jesus, who walk not after the flesh, but after the Spirit." (Rom. 8:1)

"Forgetting those things which are behind, and reaching forth unto those things which are before, I press toward the mark for the prize of the high calling of God in Christ Jesus." (Phil. 3:13-14)

"Their sins and their iniquities will I remember no more." (Heb. 8:12)

"The blood of Jesus Christ his Son cleanseth us from all sin." (I Jn. 1:7)

"If we confess our sins, he is faithful and just to forgive us our sins, and to cleanse us from all unrighteousness." (I Jn. 1:9)

SCRIPTURES ON HEALING

"If thou wilt diligently hearken to the voice of the Lord thy God, and wilt do that which is right in his sight, and wilt give ear to his commandments, and keep all his statutes, I will put none of these diseases upon thee, which I have brought upon the Egyptians: for I am the Lord that healeth thee."   (Ex. 15:26)

"Ye shall serve the Lord your God, and he shall bless thy bread, and thy water; and I will take sickness away from the midst of thee."
(Ex. 23:25)

"Bless the Lord . . . who healeth all thy diseases."   (Ps. 103:2-3)

"He sent his word, and healed them, and delivered them from their destructions."   (Ps. 107:20)

"He was wounded for our transgressions, he was bruised for our iniquities: the chastisement of our peace was upon him; and with his stripes we are healed."   (Isa. 53:5)

"I will restore health unto thee, and I will heal thee of thy wounds, saith the Lord; because they called thee an Outcast, saying, This is Zion, whom no man seeketh after."   (Jer. 30:17)

"Behold, I will bring it health and cure, and I will cure them, and will reveal unto them the abundance of peace and truth."
(Jer. 33:6)

"Unto you that fear my name shall the Sun of righteousness arise with healing in his wings; and ye shall go forth, and grow up as calves of the stall."   (Mal. 4:2)

"When the even was come, they brought unto him many that were possessed with devils: and he cast out the spirits with his word, and healed all that were sick: That it might be fulfilled which was spoken by Isaiah the prophet, saying, Himself took our infirmities, and bare our sicknesses."   (Mat. 8:16-17)

"When he had called unto him his twelve disciples, he gave them power against unclean spirits, to cast them out, and to heal all manner of sickness and all manner of disease." (Mat. 10:1)

"Jesus went forth, and saw a great multitude, and was moved with compassion toward them, and he healed their sick."

(Mat. 14:14)

"They went out, and preached that men should repent. And they cast out many devils, and anointed with oil many that were sick, and healed them." (Mk. 6:12-13)

"They shall lay hands on the sick, and they shall recover."

(Mk. 16:18)

"There came also a multitude out of the cities round about unto Jerusalem, bringing sick folks, and them which were vexed with unclean spirits: and they were healed every one." (Acts 5:16)

"God anointed Jesus of Nazareth with the Holy Ghost and with power: who went about doing good, and healing all that were oppressed of the devil; for God was with him." (Acts 10:38)

"The word of God is quick, and powerful, and sharper than any twoedged sword, piercing even to the dividing asunder of soul and spirit, and of the joints and marrow, and is a discerner of the thoughts and intents of the heart." (Heb. 4:12)

"Is any sick among you? let him call for the elders of the church; and let them pray over him, anointing him with oil in the name of the Lord: And the prayer of faith shall save the sick, and the Lord shall raise him up; and if he have committed sins, they shall be forgiven him." (James 5:14-15)

"Who his own self bare our sins in his own body on the tree, that we, being dead to sins, should live unto righteousness: by whose stripes we were healed." (I Pet. 2:24)

"Beloved, I wish above all things that thou mayest prosper and be in health, even as thy soul prospereth." (III Jn. 1:2)

SCRIPTURES CONCERNING MARRIAGE PROBLEMS

"Wait on the LORD: be of good courage, and he shall strengthen thine heart: wait, I say, on the LORD." (Ps. 27:14)

"He healeth the broken in heart, and bindeth up their wounds." (Ps. 147:3)

"Wives, submit yourselves unto your own husbands, as unto the Lord. For the husband is the head of the wife, even as Christ is the head of the church." (Eph. 5:22-23)

"Husbands, love your wives, even as Christ also loved the church, and gave himself for it. So ought men to love their wives as their own bodies. He that loveth his wife loveth himself. For no man ever yet hated his own flesh; but nourisheth and cherisheth it, even as the Lord the church." (Eph. 5:25, 28-29)

"Nevertheless let every one of you in particular so love his wife even as himself; and the wife see that she reverence her husband." (Eph. 5:33)

"Likewise, ye husbands, dwell with them according to knowledge, giving honor unto the wife, as unto the weaker vessel, and as being heirs together of the grace of life; that you prayers be not hindered." (I Pet. 3:7)

SCRIPTURES FOR PERSONAL PROBLEMS

"The LORD is my light and my salvation; whom shall I fear? the LORD is the strength of my life; of whom shall I be afraid?" (Ps. 27:1)

"Many are the afflictions of the righteous: but the LORD delivereth him out of them all." (Ps. 34:19)

"Cast thy burden upon the LORD, and he shall sustain thee." (Ps. 55:22)

"The LORD is on my side; I will not fear: what can man do unto me?" (Ps. 118:6)

"The way of the LORD is strength to the upright." (Prov. 10:29)

"He giveth power to the faint; and to them that have no might he increaseth strength." (Isa. 40:29)

"I the LORD thy God will hold thy right hand, saying unto thee, Fear not; I will help thee." (Isa. 41:13)

"Call unto me, and I will answer thee, and show thee great and mighty things, which thou knowest not." (Jer. 33:3)

"The people that do know their God shall be strong, and do exploits." (Dan. 11:32)

"Let the weak say, I am strong." (Joel 3:10)

"The LORD God is my strength, and he will make my feet like hind's feet, and he will make me to walk upon mine high places." (Hab. 3:19)

"What things soever ye desire, when ye pray, believe that ye receive them, and ye shall have them." (Mk. 11:24)

"Behold, I give unto you power . . . over all the power of the enemy: and nothing shall by any means hurt you." (Lk. 10:19)

"If God be for us, who can be against us?" (Rom. 8:31)

"Who shall separate us from the love of Christ? shall tribulation, or distress, or persecution, or famine, or nakedness, or peril, or sword? As it is written . . . Nay, in all these things we are more than conquerors through him that loved us." (Rom. 8:35-37)

"There hath no temptation [problem] taken you but such as is common to man: but God is faithful, who will not suffer you to be tempted [tested] above that ye are able; but will with the temptation [problem] also make a way to escape, that ye may be able to bear it." (I Cor. 10:13)

"I can do all things through Christ which strengtheneth me." (Phil. 4:13)

"I will never leave thee, nor forsake thee. So that we may boldly say, The Lord is my helper, and I will not fear what man shall do unto me." (Heb. 13:5-6)

SCRIPTURES ON SALVATION

"Verily, verily, I say unto you, He that believeth on me hath everlasting life." (Jn. 6:47)

"Jesus saith unto him, I am the way, the truth, and the life: no man cometh unto the Father, but by me." (Jn. 14:6)

"Sirs, what must I do to be saved? And they said, Believe on the Lord Jesus Christ, and thou shalt be saved, and thy house." (Acts 16:30-31)

"But God commendeth his love toward us, in that, while we were yet sinners, Christ died for us." (Rom. 5:8)

"The wages of sin is death; but the gift of God is eternal life through Jesus Christ our Lord." (Rom. 6:23)

"By grace are ye saved through faith; and that not of yourselves: it is the gift of God: Not of works, lest any man should boast." (Eph. 2:8-9)

"The blood of Jesus Christ his Son cleanseth us from all sin."

(I Jn. 1:7)

"Behold, I stand at the door, and knock: if any man hear my voice, and open the door, I will come in to him, and will sup with him, and he with me."

(Rev. 3:20)

SINNER'S PRAYER

Dear God in Heaven, I come to You in the name of Jesus. I'm so sorry for my sins and for the life I have lived. I ask You for forgiveness and to cleanse me with Your blood from all unrighteousness. You said in Your Holy Word, Romans 10:9, if we confess the Lord our God and believe in our hearts that God raised Him from the dead, we shall be saved. Right now I confess Jesus Christ as the Lord of my soul. With my heart, I believe that God raised Him from the dead. This very moment I accept Jesus Christ as my own personal Savior and according to His Word, right now I am saved. Thank You, Jesus, for dying for me and giving me eternal life. Amen.

SCRIPTURES ON SMOKING

"Know ye not that ye are the temple of God, and that the Spirit of God dwelleth in you? If any man defile the temple of God, him shall God destroy; for the temple of God is holy, which temple ye are."

(I Cor. 3:16-17)

"Ye are bought with a price: therefore glorify God in your body, and in your spirit, which are God's."

(I Cor. 6:20)

"Having therefore these promises, dearly beloved, let us cleanse ourselves from all filthiness of the flesh and spirit, perfecting holiness in the fear of God."

(II Cor. 7:1)

SCRIPTURES FOR THOSE THREATENING SUICIDE

"God is our refuge and strength, a very present help in trouble."
(Ps. 46:1)

"Him that cometh to me I will in no wise cast out." (Jn. 6:37)

"I am come that they might have life, and that they might have it more abundantly." (Jn. 10:10)

"Whosoever shall call upon the name of the Lord shall be saved."
(Rom. 10:13)

"My God shall supply all your need according to his riches in glory by Christ Jesus." (Phil. 4:19)

"Wherefore he is able also to save them to the uttermost that come unto God by him, seeing he ever liveth to make intercession for them." (Heb. 7:25)

"Cast all your care upon him; for he careth for you." (I Pet. 5:7)

SCRIPTURES FOR TENSION

"My presence shall go with thee, and I will give thee rest."
(Ex. 33:14)

"The eternal God is thy refuge, and underneath are the everlasting arms." (Deut. 33:27)

"The Lord is my light and my salvation; whom shall I fear? The Lord is the strength of my life; of whom shall I be afraid?" (Ps. 27:1)

"I had fainted, unless I had believed to see the goodness of the Lord in the land of the living. Wait on the Lord: be of good courage, and he shall strengthen thine heart: wait, I say, on the LORD."

(Ps. 27:13-14)

"The LORD will give strength unto his people; the LORD will bless his people with peace." (Ps. 29:11)

"Fret not thyself . . . Trust in the LORD . . . Commit thy way unto the LORD . . . Rest in the LORD, and wait patiently for him: fret not thyself because of him who prospereth in his way, because of the man who bringeth wicked devices to pass." (Ps. 37:1-7)

"Behold, God is my salvation; I will trust, and not be afraid: for the LORD JEHOVAH is my strength and my song; he also is become my salvation." (Isa. 12:2)

"They that wait upon the LORD shall renew their strength; they shall mount up with wings as eagles; they shall run, and not be weary; and they shall walk, and not faint." (Isa. 40:31)

"Come unto me, all ye that labor and are heavy laden, and I will give you rest. Take my yoke upon you, and learn of me; for I am meek and lowly in heart: and ye shall find rest unto your souls." (Mat. 11:28-29)

"In him we live, and move, and have our being." (Acts 17:28)

"Be not conformed to this world: but be ye transformed by the renewing of your mind." (Rom. 12:2)

"Let this mind be in you, which was also in Christ Jesus." (Phil. 2:5)

"Be careful [anxious] for nothing; but in every thing by prayer and supplication with thanksgiving let your requests be made known unto God. And the peace of God, which passeth all understanding, shall keep your hearts and minds through Christ Jesus." (Phil. 4:6-7)

SCRIPTURES FOR UNSAVED LOVED ONES

"Train up a child in the way he should go: and when he is old, he will not depart from it." (Prov. 22:6)

"If two of you shall agree on earth as touching any thing that they shall ask, it shall be done for them of my Father, which is in heaven." (Mat. 18:19)

"With God nothing shall be impossible." (Lk. 1:37)

"Believe on the Lord Jesus Christ, and thou shalt be saved, and thy house." (Acts 16:31)

"Likewise, ye wives, be in subjection to your own husbands; that, if any obey not the word, they also may without the word be won by the conversation of the wives." (I Pet. 3:1)

THE HOLY SPIRIT BAPTISM

The following will help as it regards the Baptism with the Holy Spirit.

1. A person must accept Jesus Christ as Savior before he can experience the Baptism with the Holy Spirit. (Jn. 14:17)

2. The Baptism with the Holy Spirit is an experience separate and apart from the initial Salvation experience, and is always received after one is saved. After the individual is saved, he is to ask the Lord to baptize him with the Spirit. (Lk. 11:13)

3. We cannot merit or deserve the Baptism with the Holy Spirit. It

1107

is a gift. Peter spoke of receiving the Gift of the Holy Spirit (Acts 2:38). Jesus said: "If you then, being evil, know how to give good gifts unto your children: how much more shall your Heavenly Father give the Holy Spirit to them who ask Him?"

(Lk. 11:13)

4. All Believers are commanded by Christ to receive.

(Acts 1:4-5)

5. When one is Baptized with the Spirit, always and without exception, he will speak with other tongues as the Spirit of God gives the utterance. There are no exceptions to this. In fact, speaking with other tongues is the initial, physical evidence, that one has been Baptized with the Holy Spirit.

(Acts 2:4; 10:44-46; 11:15-17; 19:2, 6; I Cor. 14:39)

6. The recipient of the Holy Spirit will then find that worshiping and praying in tongues will become a part of his devotion to God, and will be greatly restful and refreshing.

(Isa. 28:12; I Cor. 14:4)

7. The Holy Spirit Baptism is for all. Anyone and everyone who is saved should be Baptized with the Spirit. There are no exceptions.

(Joel 2:28-29)

8. After you have been baptized with the Holy Spirit, you are to understand that the Spirit works within you according to your Faith in the Cross of Christ. In other words, what Jesus did at the Cross provides the parameters in which the Holy Spirit works; consequently, you as a Believer, are to register Faith in the Cross of Christ at all times, which gives the Holy Spirit latitude within your life.

(Rom. 8:1-2)

SCRIPTURES ON THE HOLY SPIRIT BAPTISM

"For with stammering lips and another tongue will he speak to this

1108

"people. To whom he said, This is the rest wherewith ye may cause the weary to rest; and this is the refreshing." (Isa. 28:11-12)

"I indeed baptize you with water unto repentance: but he that cometh after me is mightier than I, whose shoes I am not worthy to bear: he shall baptize you with the Holy Ghost, and with fire." (Mat. 3:11)

"For John truly baptized with water; but ye shall be baptized with the Holy Ghost not many days hence." (Acts 1:5)

"And they were all filled with the Holy Ghost, and began to speak with other tongues, as the Spirit gave them utterance." (Acts 2:4)

"Now when the apostles which were at Jerusalem heard that Samaria had received the word of God, they sent unto them Peter and John: Who, when they were come down, prayed for them, that they might receive the Holy Ghost: (For as yet he was fallen upon none of them: only they were baptized in the name of the Lord Jesus.) Then laid they their hands on them, and they received the Holy Ghost." (Acts 8:14-17)

"While Peter yet spake these words, the Holy Ghost fell on all them which heard the word. And they of the circumcision which believed were astonished, as many as came with Peter, because that on the Gentiles also was poured out the gift of the Holy Ghost. For they heard them speak with tongues, and magnify God." (Acts 10:44-46)

"And as I began to speak, the Holy Ghost fell on them, as on us at the beginning. Then remembered I the word of the Lord, how that he said, John indeed baptized with water; but ye shall be baptized with the Holy Ghost. Forasmuch then as God gave them the like gift as he did unto us, who believed on the Lord Jesus Christ; what was I, that I could withstand God?" (Acts 11:15-17)

"He said unto them, Have ye received the Holy Ghost since ye believed? And they said unto him, We have not so much as heard whether there be any Holy Ghost. And when Paul had laid his hands upon them, the Holy Ghost came on them; and they spake with tongues, and prophesied." (Acts 19:2, 6)

"Wherefore, brethren, covet to prophesy, and forbid not to speak with tongues." (I Cor. 14:39)

"But ye, beloved, building up yourselves on your most holy faith, praying in the Holy Ghost." (Jude vs. 20)

WHAT MUST I DO TO BE SAVED?

THE PLAN OF SALVATION

A long time ago, a Roman Jailer asked of the Apostle Paul the most important question that could ever be asked, *"What must I do to be saved?"*

Paul's answer was immediate, to the point, clear, and concise. He said:

"Believe on the Lord Jesus Christ, and thou shalt be saved, and thy house" (Acts 16:30-31.)

That's how simple that it actually is.

A man named Nicodemus pretty much asked Jesus the same question. Jesus answered him by saying, *"You must be born again"* (Jn. 3:1-8).

ALL ARE SINNERS

The Bible tells us in Romans 3:23 that *"All have sinned and come short of the Glory of God."*

That means that all are sinners, actually born that way, in desperate need of the Saviour, the Lord Jesus Christ. In fact, there are no exceptions to this. That means you and me, and all others for that matter.

Paul also said in Romans 6:23, *"The wages of sin is death!"*

So, that means that unless something is done about this terrible situation, that all will be eternally lost. However, God did not leave things there. He loves us, every one of us. It is His Desire that *"Not any should perish, but that all should come unto repentance"* (II Pet. 3:9).

WHAT DID GOD DO ABOUT THIS SITUATION?

The Scripture plainly says, *"And God so loved the world* (so loved sinners, and that means you) *that He gave His Only Begotten Son, that whosoever believes on Him shall not perish, but have ever-lasting life"* (Jn. 3:16).

What does that mean?

Man as a sinner could not save himself. In other words, such was and is impossible; consequently, God literally became man, came into this world born of the Virgin Mary, and then died on Calvary to pay the price for man's Redemption. As should be obvious, the price was high. But thank God, it was everlastingly paid by Jesus Christ, that *"WHOSOEVER WILL, MAY COME AND TAKE THE WATER OF LIFE FREELY"* (Rev. 22:17).

WHAT DOES IT MEAN TO BELIEVE ON THE LORD JESUS CHRIST?

Going back to the Scripture which we quoted in the Foreword of this booklet, Paul says:

"If you shall confess with your mouth the Lord Jesus, and shall believe in your heart that God has raised Him from the dead, you shall be saved. For with the heart man believes unto Righteousness; and

with the mouth, confession is made unto Salvation" (Rom. 10:9-10).

To believe on the Lord Jesus Christ is more than just giving mental assent that He is the Son of God. Millions do that and aren't saved.

When the Scripture speaks of one believing, it simply means that one accepts Who Jesus is, which is the Son of God, and what He has done, which refers to Him dying on Calvary, in effect taking our place, in order that we might be saved.

It means to accept Him, and Him Alone as your Saviour, resolving to make Him the Lord of your life, and to follow Him with all of your heart, mind, soul, and strength as long as you live.

SUBSTITUTION AND IDENTIFICATION

As we have already stated, man being eternally lost and helpless to save himself, God had to provide a means of Salvation whereby sinful man could be made righteous. He did that by providing His Own Son, Who gave His Life on Calvary, thereby paying the terrible price which we could not pay. That price was His Own Precious Shed Blood.

He became our Substitute.

What does that mean?

It means He did for us what we could not do for ourselves. There was a terrible sin debt owing due to man's fallen condition. As stated, that refers to every single human being, none excepted. With no way to save ourselves, God had to provide a Saviour, which He did. It was done simply because He loves us so much (Jn. 3:16).

Jesus being the Substitute, if we identify with Him, which means to accept what He did at Calvary's Cross on our behalf, we will be saved. It is that simple!

He became our Substitute, and upon our identification with Him, we are rewarded with Eternal Life (Rom. 6:23).

FAITH AND NOT WORKS

The only thing required to obtain this glorious and wonderful

Salvation is to simply believe on Christ, exactly as Paul said, which means to have Faith in Him.

What does that mean?

It is actually very simple. The Lord made it this way in order that all may have equal opportunity.

It simply means that you believe or have faith in what He did, and accept it for yourself on a personal basis. That's all that God requires. But of course, to believe and have faith, even as we have already said, means to accept the Lord as your Saviour and, as well, to make Him the Lord of your life.

First of all, man must understand that he is a sinner. That includes all (Rom. 3:23). As such, he needs a Saviour. There is only one Saviour, only One Who has paid the price for man's Redemption, and that Saviour is the Lord Jesus Christ. In other words, if one does not accept Christ, one cannot be saved.

Millions attempt to earn their Salvation in many and varied ways other than accepting Christ. Or else they attempt to become saved by accepting Christ as well as adding other things to Christ.

The Scripture says: *"FOR BY GRACE ARE YOU SAVED THROUGH FAITH; AND THAT NOT OF YOURSELVES: IT IS THE GIFT OF GOD: NOT OF WORKS, LEST ANY MAN SHOULD BOAST"* (Eph. 2:8-9).

That means the Church cannot save you, and neither can Water Baptism save you, or anything else for that matter, as important as those things may be in their own way. I have said this because millions think that they are saved by being baptized in water, or joining a Church, or performing good works, etc.

While those things may be important in their own right, they have absolutely nothing to do with one being saved. One is saved simply by trusting Jesus Christ, even as we have already said.

That means that one can be saved anywhere: in Church, on the street corner, watching a Christian Telecast, listening to a Christian Radio Program, or even reading this Booklet.

Where one is doesn't matter. It is what one believes that really counts.

The moment that one confesses the Lord with one's mouth, and believes in one's heart, and does so truly, at that moment, and wherever you may be, you are saved. As we have stated several times, it is just that simple.

Incidently, when the Jailer asked Paul the question, *"What must I do to be saved?"*, he was actually at that time in the jail with Paul and Silas. Every evidence is that he at that moment, in that jail, believed on the Lord Jesus Christ, and was instantly saved (Acts 16:27-34).

IT IS TIME NOW!

In fact, if you have not already given your heart and life to Jesus Christ, it is time that you do so, and actually it can be done this very moment.

I am going to ask you to read these words below, and actually say them out loud. As well, I am going to ask you to believe them with all of your heart, and if you will do so, you will be instantly saved. Please say them with me as you read:

"DEAR GOD IN HEAVEN, I COME TO YOU TODAY AS A LOST SINNER."

"I AM ASKING YOU THAT YOU SAVE MY SOUL AND CLEANSE ME FROM ALL SIN."

"I REALIZE IN MY HEART MY NEED OF SALVATION, WHICH CAN ONLY COME THROUGH JESUS CHRIST."

"I AM ACCEPTING CHRIST INTO MY HEART AND WHAT HE DID ON THE CROSS IN ORDER TO PURCHASE MY REDEMPTION."

"IN OBEDIENCE TO YOUR WORD, I CONFESS WITH MY MOUTH THE LORD JESUS, AND BELIEVE IN MY HEART THAT GOD HAS RAISED HIM FROM THE DEAD."

"YOU HAVE SAID IN YOUR WORD WHICH CANNOT LIE, 'FOR WHOSOEVER SHALL CALL UPON THE NAME OF THE LORD SHALL BE SAVED' (ROM. 10:13)."

"I HAVE CALLED UPON YOUR NAME EXACTLY AS YOU HAVE SAID, AND I BELIEVE THAT RIGHT NOW, I AM SAVED."

If you have sincerely prayed these words, which I have written out for you, and believed in your heart upon the Lord Jesus Christ, you are at this moment saved, and your name is written down in the Lamb's Book of Life.

Congratulations!

SOME THINGS YOU SHOULD NOW BEGIN TO DO

In the next few pages, I am going to give you some simple instructions that you should follow in order to live an overcoming, Christian Life. They are very important.

You are now a *"new creature in Christ Jesus"* (II Cor. 5:17). As such, you have the Divine nature within your heart, which is the Nature of God, which means that the Holy Spirit actually now resides within your heart and life.

The entirety of your life is now going to be different. You have been cleansed from all sin and have embarked upon the greatest journey that one could ever undertake. A whole new world is about to open up to you.

You now have something to live for, and something to which you can look forward. Living for Jesus is the most exciting life that one could ever live, the most fulfilling, the most rewarding, the most wonderful. There is absolutely nothing in the world that can compare with this which you have just received and which will never end.

But of course, Satan, the enemy of your soul, is not happy at all about you giving your heart to Christ Jesus; consequently, he will do everything he can to cause you problems, even attempting to get you to turn back. However, if you will heed carefully the following instructions that we will give, Satan will not be successful in pulling you back, and total victory will be yours.

DAILY BIBLE STUDY

We are directed by the Word of God to study the Bible. Jesus said, in John 5:39, to *"search the Scriptures. . . ."*

Paul, writing under the inspiration of the Holy Spirit in II Timothy, said, *"Study* (the Scriptures) *to show yourself approved unto God, a workman that needs not to be ashamed, rightly dividing the Word of Truth"* (II Tim. 2:15). The only way that one can intelligently divide the Word of Truth, in other words, to know and understand sound Doctrine, is to know the Word of God.

For you to know the Bible is the single most important thing you can ever do. Consequently, you ought to make it a part of your daily life.

Jesus said, *"Man shall not live by bread alone, but by every word that proceedeth out of the mouth of God"* (Mat. 4:4).

That means that as natural food is necessary for your physical well-being, likewise, the study and understanding of the Word of God is necessary for your spiritual well-being. In other words, as much attention as you give to your three meals a day, you ought to give that much attention to the Word of God, and on a daily basis. As your natural food is necessary, so must be your spiritual food.

Everything that one wants to know about God is found in the Bible. God has expended much time and energy over many years giving us His Word. He did it for our benefit, as should be obvious. However, He isn't going to inject that information into us. If we want to know God, to understand Him, and to live for Him, in other words, to live completely in harmony with Him, we must read the instruction book, actually to study it, which is the Word of God.

When you were born as a little baby, someone poured milk into your system, and if they had not done so, you would have weakened and soon died. Nothing flourishes and grows without nourishment. And today, as a newborn (spiritually speaking), you must have nourishment if you are to stay alive spiritually, and flourish, and eventually grow into a mature person of strength and power in the Lord.

The Holy Bible is that nourishment. It is wonderfully conceived to afford both milk to the newborn, and meat to the more advanced. God in His Infinite Wisdom designed one Book capable of astounding and delighting the newest convert, while absorbing and stimulating the most seasoned Believer in Christ. It is truly, of all things in this world, *"all things to all men."*

The Psalmist said, *"Thy Word is a Lamp unto my feet, and a Light unto my path"* (Ps. 119:105).

In fact, the Word of God is the only true Light and the only true Lamp that's in the world today.

You should start studying the Bible, beginning with Genesis and read it all the way through, exactly as you would read any other Book. Admittedly, there are some things difficult to understand, especially for one who has just given his heart to the Lord; however, if you will ask the Lord to help you understand His Word, He will surely do so. The Psalmist also said, *"I have not departed from Thy Judgments: for Thou hast taught me"* (Ps. 119:102).

As we've already stated, you now have the Holy Spirit living in your heart and life, and He will teach you how to understand the Word if you will only ask for His help.

SOME THINGS THAT WILL HELP YOU

I am going to encourage you to avail yourself of the opportunity of securing our *Commentaries* written on the Bible, which will help you understand the Word of God, and as well, to secure our Cassette Teaching Series, which are available on almost every subject in the Word of God.

If you will write for a catalog, we will send you one instantly, which will give you all the information you need respecting these various different Bible Study Helps.

YOUR PRAYER LIFE

From the moment you accepted Christ as your Saviour, your life has been changed. You have experienced a joy and peace which the cares of the world cannot take away. This *"blessed assurance"* was given to you as a free gift from God. Without doubt, you feel the compulsion to thank Him for what He has done for you. It is completely fitting that you should feel this way.

In order to properly thank Him, which we should do constantly, we must develop a daily prayer life — exactly as we develop a daily time of Bible Study.

Prayer is communication with God. It is for the following:

1. Praise: As stated, we should praise the Lord, which means to thank Him for what He has done for us. The more we live for the Lord, the more we will realize the worth of our Salvation, and the more we will want to thank Him for that.

2. Communion: Prayer is one of the greatest ways to communicate with God. What a blessing to be able to talk directly to your Heavenly Father. As well, during times of prayer, the Lord will also speak to your heart, giving you leading and direction.

3. Petition: We are admonished to ask the Lord for the things that we need. He, as our Heavenly Father, desires to do good things for us. However, we must remember that it is His Will which we seek, and not our personal will. Consequently, all the things we ask Him for, and we should readily ask Him for whatever it is we need, should always be done with the idea in mind, that we want His Will and not ours. Please read the following Scriptures carefully (Mat. 18:18-19; Mk. 11:24; Lk. 11:9-10; Jn. 14:13-14; 15:7).

THE BAPTISM WITH THE HOLY SPIRIT

Now that you are saved, you should ask the Lord to baptize you with the Holy Spirit (Acts 2:4).

While it is certainly true that the Holy Spirit came into your heart and life the moment of your Salvation, still, He now wishes to endue you with power from on high. Consequently, Jesus told all of His followers immediately before His Ascension, that they should *"wait for the Promise of the Father"* (Acts 1:4). He was speaking of being *"Baptized with the Holy Spirit"* (Acts 1:5).

You must understand that there is a great difference in being *"born of the Spirit"* than being *"Baptized with the Spirit."* They are two different works altogether.

To be *"born of the Spirit"* is that which took place at your conversion, as the Holy Spirit brought you to Christ and performed the work of regeneration within your heart and life. To be *"Baptized with the Spirit"* is in order that you may have Power with God (Acts 1:8). Every Believer should ask the Lord to fill them with the Holy Spirit, and expect to receive (Lk. 11:13).

THE SIGN OF BEING FILLED WITH THE SPIRIT

Once one is Baptized with the Holy Spirit, many things will transpire in our heart and life. In other words, there will be many telltale signs that we have been filled.

However, the initial physical evidence that one has been Baptized with the Holy Spirit, is that they will speak with other Tongues as the Spirit of God gives the utterance (Acts 2:4; 10:45-46; 19:1-7).

There is nothing in the Bible which suggests that this awesome indwelling power of the Holy Spirit has been declared unavailable in our day. We know there are literally millions of committed, fruitful, effective Christians, who give all the credit for their effectiveness to the experience of having been Baptized with the Holy Spirit, with the evidence of speaking with other Tongues. In fact, for you to be what you ought to be in Christ, the Baptism with the Holy Spirit is an absolute necessity.

Jesus died on Calvary that men may be saved. The great Salvation process includes the Holy Spirit taking up abode within our hearts and lives. Every Christian needs Him desperately. And to be sure, His full potential cannot be realized, unless we go on and be Baptized with the Holy Spirit, which as stated, will *always* be accompanied by the speaking with other Tongues as the Spirit of God gives the utterance (Acts 2:4).

He is our *"Helper,"* and as well, *"guides us into all Truth"* (Jn. 16:7-15).

WATER BAPTISM

What is the significance of Water Baptism? Haven't we, by confessing Christ with our mouths, done everything the Bible tells us to do to insure Salvation? Is there any reason we should go further in proving the fact of our conversion? In Truth, there are several reasons for Water Baptism.

First of all, Jesus set the example for us by being baptized in water. He did it to *"fulfill all Righteousness"* (Mat. 3:13-15).

Water Baptism signifies the Death, Burial, and Resurrection of the Lord Jesus Christ. Hence, when He was Baptized in water, this signified that which He would do in order to secure our Salvation.

We likewise are to be Baptized in water, as a public proclamation of our submission to God, and acceptance of the Lord Jesus Christ, as our Savior. Water Baptism does not save us, or contribute anything toward our Salvation, but is rather a sign that we have already been saved, which we wish to declare to the entirety of the world. In fact, Water Baptism is the great symbol that one has given his heart and life to Jesus Christ.

As well, it typifies our death to the old life, with all that was ugly and ungodly being buried, and us being Resurrected into a new life in Christ Jesus. That's the reason that Water Baptism is by emersion. It signifies the old man being buried, and the new man being raised in newness of life (Rom. 6:4).

THE WILL OF GOD
FOR YOUR LIFE

Now that you have become a Child of God, the Lord has a perfect Will for your life. In other words, you are very important in the Kingdom of God, and the Lord will treat you accordingly.

Inasmuch as you have given your heart and life to Him, He will now open up the Kingdom of God to you, and your place in that Kingdom (Jn. 3:3). In fact, one of the great works of the Holy Spirit in your heart and life, is to bring about *"the Will of God"* for you (Rom. 8:27).

In other words, the idea is that your will be swallowed up in the Will of God, which is the most wonderful, fulfilling life there could ever be.

If you will allow the Holy Spirit to have His Way within your life, He will bring about the Will of God, and help you to walk in that Will, doing what the Lord wants you to do.

Actually, the Lord has a perfect Will for every Believer and that means you. What He has for you, cannot be done by anyone else. So you are to seek the Will of God, and you will find beautifully and wondrously, the Holy Spirit making Jesus more and more real in your heart, and bringing you to the place in which God desires that you be.

Isn't that wonderful to have such help, and above all, to have such leading and guidance (Jn. 16:13-15).

FAITH IN THE CROSS
OF CHRIST

As a new Believer you were saved by putting your Faith in Christ and what He did by paying the price for your Redemption on the Cross (Jn. 3:16).

However, not only is Faith in the Cross necessary for Salvation, it is necessary, as well, that you continue to have Faith in the Cross even on a daily basis, which will guarantee you Victory in your everyday life. This is the answer for Victory over cigarettes, alcohol, drugs, uncontrollable temper, depression, gambling, jealousy, envy, greed, every type of immorality, and in fact, every problem that besets humanity (I Cor. 2:2).

As the Believer constantly exhibits Faith in the Cross and should do so forever, the Holy Spirit then provides all the help necessary, in order for Victory to be had in every capacity (Jn. 14:16-17). In fact, there is no reason why any Christian should be dominated by any type of sin whatsoever. If Faith in the Cross is exhibited, the Holy Spirit will always guarantee Victory for the Believer. The key is the Cross, because it is through the Cross that the Holy Spirit works (Gal. 6:14).

CHURCH ATTENDANCE

The Church is the Body of Christ, not a particular building by the side of the road. Actually you are now a part of that Body, and Jesus Christ is its Head. So, if at all possible, it is very important that you find a good Church to attend.

The following is what should be taught and preached in the Church:

1. Salvation through the Blood of Jesus Christ should be preached. Any Church teaching Salvation by any means other than the shed Blood of Jesus Christ, in other words, what the Lord did on Calvary's Cross, in order to redeem humanity, is promoting something contrary to the Word of God (Mat. 26:28; Acts 20:28; Col. 1:20; Heb. 9:22; I Pet. 1:18-19).

2. The Church should teach the Baptism with the Holy Spirit, with the evidence of speaking with other Tongues, which is available to all Believers, and is received after conversion (Isa. 28:11-12; Acts 2:4; 10:45-46; 19:6; I Cor. 14:4-5, 14-18).

3. A victorious, overcoming Christian life should be preached (Rom. 6:11; I Cor. 15:57-58; Eph. 6:10-13; James 1:22; I Jn. 5:4-5; Rev. 2:7). This means victory over sin in every capacity.

4. Divine Healing according to the Word of God should be preached (Ex. 15:26; 23:25; Isa. 53:5; Mk. 6:13; James 5:14-15; I Pet. 2:24).

We believe that the Bible teaches that Jesus Christ heals today, the same as He did in Bible days.

5. The Rapture of the Church should be taught and preached. This refers to the time when the Church shall be taken out of this world in order to be with the Lord. It could happen at any moment, with every single Believer whether dead or alive, being resurrected. In fact, the Resurrection and the Rapture are one and the same (I Cor. Chpt. 15; I Thess. 4:13-17).

6. The soon and eminent return of our Lord to Earth, to take up His rightful position as King of kings and Lord of lords should be preached. He will be accompanied at that time by every Saint of God who has ever lived. In other words, all who were taken up in the Rapture (Resurrection), will then come back with Him to this Earth, which will begin the Kingdom Age (Rev. Chpt. 19).

7. Whatever Church is attended, should be a Church filled with a group of people, whether the number is little or large, with the consuming desire to take the Gospel of Jesus Christ to the entirety of the world. The taking of the Gospel to all is priority with God, as should be obvious.

Someone brought you the Gospel, and you should love the

Lord enough, to desire strongly that everyone else have the opportunity to hear exactly as you did. Whether they except or not, is their privilege; however, that they have the opportunity is absolutely paramount.

To be frank, the greatest way we can thank the Lord for giving us His Great Salvation, is to tell this grand story to others in whatever way we can, and as well, to help support those who are taking the Gospel to the world. That must be our consuming desire in all things (Mk. 16:15-16).

"For God so loved the world that He gave His only begotten Son, that whosoever believeth in Him should not perish, but have everlasting life" (Jn. 3:16).

THE CROSS, YOUR FAITH, AND THE HOLY SPIRIT

As the Word of God bears it out throughout its entirety, God has provided only one solution for sinful, hurting humanity. That solution is *"Jesus Christ and Him Crucified"* (Jn. 3:16; I Cor. 1:18, 23; 2:2; Col. 2:14-15). The Cross is the means, and the only means, by which the sinner can be saved, and as well, the only means by which the Christian can walk in victory.

Most of the Church readily understands the Cross as it regards the initial Salvation experience, but has little knowledge whatsoever as it regards the part the Cross plays in the victory of the Saint.

For lack of space I will have to be brief; however, the following information will be helpful:

THE CROSS

In the preceding article, I have dealt with Salvation for the sinner, so I will devote this section entirely to the solution of problems which all Christians face at one time or the other.

Every Christian must understand, that every single problem that faces humanity, was addressed by Jesus at the Cross (Col. 2:14-

15). This means that for every problem, the Christian should be directed to the Cross. He must understand that the solution is found there, and found only there.

The Lord gave to the Apostle Paul the meaning of the New Covenant, which pertains to what Jesus did for us at the Cross. So in effect, the meaning of the New Covenant is the meaning of the Cross.

In Romans Chapter 6, we are told as it regards the crucifixion of Christ, Who incidentally suffered as our Substitute, that we actually died with Him in His Crucifixion, were buried with Him, and were raised with Him in *"newness of life"* (Rom. 6:3-5). Of course we were not there as is obvious; however, upon faith being evidenced in Christ when we were initially saved, in the Mind of God, this is actually what happened. We were literally *"baptized into His death"* (Rom. 6:3). No, this is not speaking of Water Baptism, which is actually a symbol of this of which we speak, but rather the actual Crucifixion of Christ.

After becoming a Christian, all the days of our lives, we are to continue to look to the Cross as the source of all victory. Actually, the very meaning of the crucifixion pertains to something that happened in the distant past, but which has continuing results, and in fact, results which will never be discontinued.

We are not speaking of putting Jesus back on a Cross, or us getting on a Cross either. In fact, Jesus is now seated by the Right Hand of the Father, and in spirit, we are actually seated with Him (Eph. 2:6; Heb. 1:3).

We are speaking of the Believer continuing to receive the benefits of the Cross, and to do so forever (Heb. 13:20).

So the Believer is to understand, that the Source of all that he needs, is found entirely in the Cross, and only in the Cross. Unfortunately, most Christians haven't been taught this, and they look elsewhere for help. Let the Reader understand, that when we think of Christ we are not to think of Him apart from the Cross. That's why Paul kept using the phrase *"in Christ,"* or one of its derivatives such as *"in Him,"* over and over. The phrase refers to what Jesus did at the Cross.

Unfortunately, many Christians are not actually serving the Jesus Christ of the Bible, but rather *"another Jesus."* This refers to the fact that they are looking to a Jesus other than the Cross. Hence Paul said: *"For if he that cometh preacheth another Jesus, Whom we have not preached, or if you receive another spirit, which ye have not received, or another gospel, which ye have not accepted, ye might well bear with him"* (II Cor. 11:4). Let the Reader understand, that if it's not Jesus and Him Crucified, then pure and simple it's *"another Jesus,"* who is projected by *"another spirit,"* which means it's not the Holy Spirit, which amounts to *"another gospel."*

The Gospel of Christ is *"Jesus Christ and Him Crucified"* (I Cor. 2:2).

That's why Paul also said: *"But God forbid that I should glory (boast), save in the Cross of our Lord Jesus Christ, by Whom the world is crucified unto me, and I unto the world"* (Gal. 6:14).

FAITH

Understanding what we've just said, the Cross of Christ must always and without exception, be the object of faith as it regards the Child of God. This is very, very important! Paul devoted the entirety of Chapters 4 and 5 of Romans to this principle. He said:

"Who (Christ) was delivered (the Crucifixion) for our offences . . . by Whom also we have access by faith into this Grace" (Rom. 4:25-5:2).

While it is Faith that God always honors, and every Christian understands that, even more particularly, it is Faith in the Cross. This is the only type of faith that God will honor.

The reasons that most Christians get into trouble in some way, is because they do not understand the Cross as the source of all their needs being met, and that they must ever have faith in this Finished Work of Christ. That's why Paul also said:

"For by grace are ye saved through faith; and that not of yourselves: it is the Gift of God: not of works, lest any man should boast" (Eph. 2:8-9).

As we were saved by faith, we are kept by faith; however, Paul is speaking of Faith in the Cross of Christ, and Faith in the Cross exclusively (Eph. 2:13).

THE HOLY SPIRIT

The Believer must understand, that the power of sin is so great, that no individual on earth, even the strongest Christian can over-come this monster within his own strength and ability. It simply cannot be done. In fact, sin is so bad, that Jesus had to go to the Cross to answer this dilemma.

So, in order to overcome sin, we have to have the power of the Holy Spirit.

While it is true that every single Believer has the Holy Spirit, and more particularly, all Believers should as well, be Baptized with the Holy Spirit, which gives even more power; still, the work of the Holy Spirit within our hearts and lives is not automatic. Let's first of all look at how He works.

The Spirit of God doesn't demand much of us, but He does demand that we have Faith in the Cross of Christ (Jn. 16:13-14). Listen to what Paul said:

"For the Law (this is a law by which the Spirit works) *of the Spirit* (Holy Spirit) *of Life* (the Holy Spirit guarantees all the life that comes from Christ as a result of the Cross) *in Christ Jesus* (what Jesus did at the Cross) *has made me free from the law of sin and death"* (Rom. 8:2).

The reason that the Christian is in trouble in the first place, is because he doesn't understand how the Spirit works. He needs the Spirit's help, and needs it greatly; however, if we evidence faith in anything else other than the Cross of Christ as it regards our vic-tory, the Holy Spirit simply will not help us. In fact, that is *"the law."*

If we function within this *"law,"* which is actually *"the Law of the Spirit of Life in Christ Jesus,"* which refers to what Christ did at the Cross, which means that the Cross must ever be the object of our Faith, then we will walk in victory.

In Romans Chapter 8 and elsewhere, Paul constantly mentions *"the flesh."* What is he talking about?

He is speaking of the Christian's ability and strength outside of the Holy Spirit. He is in effect saying, if we try to live this life by trusting in our own strength, i.e., *"the flesh,"* we will fail and fail every time. Actually that's what he means by *"walking after the flesh"* (Rom. 8:1). To make it simpler, walking after the flesh is trusting in anything other than the Cross of Christ.

"Walking after the Spirit," is placing our faith and trust in the Cross of Christ (Rom. 8:1-2).

VICTORY AND RESTORATION

If the Christian is having problems in any capacity as it regards the world, the flesh, and the Devil, he is to be pointed toward the Cross, making the Cross the object of his faith, which will insure the help of the Holy Spirit.

If the Christian has failed miserably, which requires restoration, he is to be told why he failed, which means that he placed his faith in something else other than the Cross, which then means he was attempting to live this Christian life only by his own efforts and strength, which are always woefully insufficient.

He is to then be told that everything he needs is in the Cross, and he must get his Faith back in the Cross, which will insure the help of the Holy Spirit. This is true, Biblical restoration (Gal. 6:1-2).

For a complete treatment of this all-important subject, please see our Commentaries on Romans, Galatians, Ephesians, Philippians, and Colossians.

"For sin shall not have dominion over you: for you are not under the Law, but under Grace" (Rom. 6:14).

SCRIPTURES FOR SALVATION

The following verses related to soul winning are tinted in color in the text for your convenience in locating them.

Luke 19:10	John 14:6	Ephesians 2:8-9
John 1:12	Acts 16:31	Hebrews 2:3
John 3:3	Romans 3:23-24	Hebrews 12:2
John 3:16	Romans 5:8	I John 1:9
John 8:32	Romans 6:23	I John 5:11-12
John 10:9-10	Romans 10:9-10	Revelation 3:20

NOTES

NOTES

NOTES

NOTES

NOTES

NOTES

NOTES

NOTES

NOTES

NOTES

NOTES

NOTES

NOTES

NOTES

NOTES

NOTES

NOTES

NOTES